PREFACE

We were very honored to host the 1st **International Conference on Supercomputing** in Athens, Greece, which took place June 8–12, 1987, at the Ledra Marriott Hotel. The conference was organized and sponsored by the Computer Technology Institute (C.T.I.) of Greece, with funding provided by the Ministry of Industry, Energy, and Technology, and the Ministry of Culture and Sciences of Greece. Support was also received from the SIGARCH of the ACM. Cooperating organizations included the Center for Supercomputing Research and Development of the University of Illinois, EATCS, IFIP WG 2.5 on Mathematical Software, the Purdue Center for Vector and Parallel Processing, and the SIAM SG on Supercomputing. The purpose of this conference was to bring together researchers from universities, industrial laboratories, and other research institutions with common interests in architectures and hardware technology, software, and applications for supercomputers.

The conference attracted more than 150 participants from around the world. Authors from 12 countries submitted 107 papers, from which 52 were accepted and presented at the conference. In addition, 15 distinguished researchers presented invited papers. The papers from these presentations make up the current proceedings volume. Based on the quality of the papers presented and the response and excitement of the participants, the Program Committee has decided to hold annual meetings on the subject of supercomputing which will be sponsored by ACM SIGARCH.

The organization of this conference was the result of tireless efforts by various individuals. Notable among them are the members of the Program Committee and the Local Arrangement Committee. Exceptionally helpful were Mr. C. Manolopoulos, Mrs. A. Cotronis, Mrs. R. Efstathiadou, Mrs. H. Gourdoupis and Mrs. M. Halakatevakis of the Local Arrangements Committee. The secretarial support of Connie Heer from Purdue University and administrative support of G. Stathakis and G. Voulgaris from C.T.I. is also very much appreciated. Finally we wish to thank the General Secretariat of Research and Technology, the ACM SIGARCH, and Olympic Airways, for their support.

Elias N. Houstis
Theodore S. Papatheodorou
Constantine D. Polychronopoulos

1987 INTERNATIONAL CONFERENCE ON SUPERCOMPUTING

CHAIRMAN	CO–CHAIRMAN
David J. Kuck,	Theodore S. Papatheodorou,
University of Illinois	*University of Patras*

PROGRAM COMMITTEE

Jack Dongarra, *Argonne Laboratory*
Iain Duff, *HARWELL*
Elias N. Houstis, *Purdue University*
Jacque Lenfant, *University of Rennes*
Demetrios Maritsas, *University of Patras*
George Paul, *IBM*
Constantine D. Polychronopoulos, *University of Illinois*
John R. Rice, *Purdue University*
Paul Spirakis, *University of Patras*

INVITED SPEAKERS

Tilak Agerwala, *IBM*
Steve Chen, *Cray Research*
Jack Dongarra, *Argonne Labs*
Geoffrey Fox, *Caltech*
Creg Mundie, *Alliant Computers*
David Kuck, *University of Illinois*
Yoichi Muraoka, *Waseda University*
Ulrich Trottenberg, *SUPRENUM*

Arvind, *MIT*
Doug DeGroot, *Texas Instr.*
Iain Duff, *HARWELL*
Dennis Gannon, *Indiana University*
Ken Kennedy, *Rice University*
Jacque Lenfant, *University of Rennes*
John Rice, *Purdue University*

TABLE OF CONTENTS

A Supercomputing Performance Evaluation Plan

By David J. Kuck and Ahmed H. Sameh
Center for Supercomputing Research and Development
University of Illinois
305 Talbot Laboratory
104 South Wright Street
Urbana, Illinois 61801–2932

Abstract

Evaluating the performance of parallel processors and supercomputers is difficult because so many factors contribute to speed. The architecture, compiler, and algorithms used are all important, as are their interactions. In the past, it has been common practice to attempt to characterize each machine's performance by just one number. The complexity of the situation indicates that more work is needed to discover how best to characterize machines. An approach for the future is sketched in this paper.

1. Introduction

As computer systems become more complex, it becomes increasingly more difficult to have them deliver performance that is near their theoretical peak speed. In fact, many modern supercomputers and parallel processors deliver only ten percent or less of their peak performance potential, when applied to a variety of applications. And yet, vector and parallel processing has sharply increased in popularity since 1980. Architectural ideas that were once used exclusively in the supercomputing domain are now applied to mini–supers, super–minis, personal workstations, and even chip sets. Thus an outsider might inquire, "If everything is so bad about performance, why does everything look so good about the use of these ideas?"

The answer has several facets. First of all, the semiconductor–based performance enhancements that have delivered an average performance increase of ten–fold every 7 years over the past forty years have been falling off recently, forcing designers to embrace parallel processing. Secondly, parallel processors can be used as multiprocessors (i.e., separate jobs can be run on separate processors). Finally, many customers are in fact willing to pay for potential performance in terms of peak speeds, although the delivery of that speed is hard to realize (some customers even view as a positive benefit the research required to enhance performance).

Nevertheless, the underlying fact is that we still do not know how to design well–balanced hardware and software systems that easily deliver high performance to ordinary users. The difficulty of solution lies in the fact that many architectural and software components must work together properly to achieve the desired results. The performance results obtained when one moves from application to application, or algorithm to algorithm or even from problem size to problem size for a given computation may best be described as unstable in that seemingly small perturbations can lead to major performance changes.

Analytical models of global performance are hopeless in this situation. Even logical attempts to deduce how to compile certain vector operations for a machine with a rich instruction set, can lead to completely wrong results. At present, empirical results are the only ones that can be relied upon to assess the performance of these computer systems. See also [SeSS83], [FHHJ83] and [GJMY87], as examples for instrumentation and performance measurement of three multiprocessors.

Traditionally there have been many attempts to use benchmark programs to evaluate supercomputers (as well as ordinary computers). For an overview and many references see [NaRC86]. There are three basic purposes for benchmarking existing machines:

P1) Selection of a new machine,

P2) Tuning of an already purchased system, and

P3) Discovery of strengths to incorporate and weaknesses to be avoided in new machine designs.

It is important to note that in new machine selection several other criteria are of major importance. Existing machines and software systems may lead directly to a particular manufacturer. Thus, if a computing center already owns *n* Cray machines, performance will be a minor issue in selecting machine *n+1*. Or, if most scientists in a particular field use CDC Cyber 205's, then to take advantage of the specialized code that has been written, a new colleague will also want a Cyber 205. Besides existing machines and software, economic and political considerations may override all others. For example, in Japan there are few U.S. supercomputers and in the U.S. there are few Japanese supercomputers. Of course, performance is used as a final criterion, even in these cases.

Benchmarks are also used by some computer designers in simulating proposed systems, and in the future this should become easier to do. For hardware or software system designers, much more detail is required than for the selection or even tuning of existing systems.

Three basic questions in all benchmark selection are:

Q1) "Which benchmarks should I use, what areas are represented, how much work is involved,"

Q2) "What should I measure and what kinds of questions can be addressed by running these benchmarks," and

Q3) "How much confidence should I put in the results."

The paper presents some well-known ideas organized as follows. Section 2 discusses various types and treatments of benchmarks. Section 3 presents several performance measures that can be made on a set of benchmark codes. Sections 4 and 5 propose the construction and use of a large public database of performance information.

2. Benchmarks

In this section we first address (in Section 2.1) those types of benchmarks that have been used in the past as well as some that might be used in the future. Once one has chosen a specific benchmark set, there remains the question of how the benchmark is dealt with in the sense of modifying it, the data used, etc. These issues are addressed in Section 2.2.

2.1. Types of Benchmarks

The most venerable supercomputer benchmark is the suite known variously as the "Livermore Loops," the "MFLOPS" benchmark or the "Livermore Fortran Kernels," [McMa86] which date back to 1970. Consisting of a (time-varying) number of about 20 simple Fortran loops, the Livermore Loops have been attacked for their simplicity, for their irrelevance, for the statistical naiveté of quoting the arithmetic mean of the measured megaflops on each loop, etc. Nevertheless, they have survived for over 15 years and they have indeed provided a useful single-number metric for comparing machines. The idea of these loops was to provide very simple representations for much more complex computations.

At another extreme is the use of a single algorithm benchmark, such as a fast Fourier transform, or the Argonne Linpack benchmark, which arose in the 1980s in an attempt to compare the numerical performance of machines ranging from personal computers to supercomputers. It seems clear that benchmarking should be applications driven to be useful for any of the purposes mentioned above. If only a single algorithm is used (e.g., Linpack or FFT), how can one be confident that it represents the desired workload? Clearly if the algorithm is not even used in the workload of a facility under consideration, any correlation between the measurements and reality is purely fortuitous.

If the benchmark is an extract from real applications, one can hope to have more confidence in the results. But one cannot put very much confidence in a few lines of code as a representation of tens of thousands of lines in a real application.

Our recommendation as an advance over these naive approaches is to attempt to characterize the workload of a given machine by a collection of applications codes. Each of these codes is represented by a set of algorithms that consume major amounts of time, relative to the whole application, e.g., see Figure 1. For computers with vector and/or parallel processing capabilities, these major time consumers are often well-known, because they tend to run serially.

Clearly such an approach requires an ongoing effort as the best algorithms and even the overall application code may change in major ways over time. Also, the applications run (or to be run) on a particular machine may change (or be unknown). In that case, given a table such as that shown in Figure 1, one can simply use the entire algorithm suite in an attempt to characterize the broadest application set available. Indeed, this would lead computer architects and designers to machine configurations that approach a general purpose nature. Perhaps the goal is unreachable with vector/parallel machines, but a systematic demonstration of what is possible is long overdue.

	1	2	3	4	5	6	7	8	9	10
Lattice–Gauge (QCD)	X	.	.	X	.	.	.	.	X	.
Quantum Chemistry	.	.	.	X	.	.	.	X	X	X
Weather Simulation	.	.	.	.	X	X	.	.	.	.
Computational Fluid Dynamics	X	.	X	.	X	X	X	.	.	.
Adjustment of Geodetic Networks	X	X	.	.	.	.	.	.	.	.
Inverse Problems	.	X	.	.	X	.	.	.	.	.
Structural Mechanics & Dynamics	X	.	X	X	.	.	.	.	.	.
Electronic Device Simulation	X	.	X	.	.	X	X	.	X	.
Circuit Simulation	X	.	X	.	.	.	.	X	.	.

Column Labels

1. Sparse Linear Systems Solvers
2. Algorithms for Linear Least Squares (direct and iterative)
3. Nonlinear Algebraic System Solvers
4. Sparse Eigenvalue Problem Solvers (standard and generalized)
5. FFT's
6. Rapid Elliptic Problem Solvers
7. Multigrid Schemes
8. Stiff O.D.E. Solvers
9. Monte Carlo Schemes
10. Integral Transforms

Table of Applications vs. Algorithms

Figure 1

Perhaps the ultimate approach is to develop a set of algorithms that covers 95 percent of the running time of most applications. This might be done by constructing an encyclopedic set of algorithms and then dropping a subset whose performance could be predicted by those remaining. Such a set could be considered a robust predictor of the performance of new approaches to applications, because it would contain all of the best known parallel/vector versions of algorithms.

It must be remembered that no existing machine is likely to get good performance across all algorithms. This approach thus has the characteristic that it will show certain weaknesses in all machines, but at the same time it will perhaps indicate alternate approaches to problem solution on particular machines.

For the special purpose of machine design or for testing the performance sensitivity of a given system, another approach could be followed. Consider a list of key architectural features, together with the key parameters of each feature as in Figure 2. A suite of simple benchmarks could be written to drive each such architectural feature into a failure mode. For example, a sequence of loops, using increasingly more array variables could be used to saturate the vector registers and thereby cause a performance collapse on any machine [KKLW84]. A machine could be automatically scored on each parameter (or combinations of certain parameters). Used judiciously, such a suite could be effective in designing and tuning computer systems.

2.2. Treatment of Benchmarks

The specific form of a particular application code can cause major performance variations. Thus one could consider the "original" code, code with minor changes and added assertions or directives to the compiler, code with major changes including new algorithms

Feature	Parameters
adder/multiplier	pipeline length, chaining, multiple units
vector registers	length, number
cache	capacity, line size, . . .

Architectural Features and Parameters

Figure 2

inserted, etc.

An interesting performance number for discussion purposes is the best possible performance attained for a given application. Its appeal in being a "best effort" result is somewhat undercut by the difficulty one may have in attaining it, and its appeal may be substantially undercut if it can only be achieved with a greater effort than most users are able to make (for lack of time or ability).

At the other extreme is the performance of an application on an "as is" basis. The main difficulty with this idea is that today, there is no such thing as "naive" Fortran code. Any serious application code has been written for some machine and therefore probably contains biases in the program structure and data structures toward some specific machine.

We can attempt to overcome the hidden difficulties in both the "as is" and "best effort" results, and also provide interesting intermediate results as follows. The background of each initial code should be described as to who wrote it and for what machine(s) it was written. Its performance on a new machine can then be documented at several points: First, as received, next after using the best compiler restructuring together with computer directives, assertions, and "minor" code changes. Then, if algorithms are substituted, sections of the code are rewritten, data structures are modified, etc., the performance improvements for each step should be briefly documented.

The idea is that such a "diary" by the people who work on the code could indicate to others the magnitude of the effort involved. The diary could include what was done, what percentage of the code was changed, how long it took, how much it improved the situation, etc. The database we suggest later should contain such information or have pointers to it.

The running times of all programs depend on the size of the data structures being operated on, and of course are very often super–linear. Additionally, the running time on a given machine may depend dramatically on vector length, the number of registers, or other machine parameters. Finally, the time depends in very important ways on the need to do I/O or not. Thus, if the data overflows physical memory and backup storage is exercised heavily (via paging or explicit I/O), major and often unpredictable performance variations are possible.

In characterizing programs one should be careful to choose problems of various sizes because of the running time variations mentioned above and because in some cases the applications software and algorithms may require specialization in the I/O and non–I/O cases.

When conducting experiments the running time may be data–sensitive in several regards. First, the time may depend on convergence criteria that are very sensitive to the numerical values of the arguments. Thus a linear–system solver depends on the condition number of a matrix, while a sorting program depends on how well-ordered the data is in advance. Also, the word length may affect the running time in that if, say, 32-bit precision suffices, faster arithmetic operators can be used on certain machines.

3. Performance Measures

In this section, we sketch several measures of performance and discuss their relative merits for various purposes.

3.1. The Single Number Hypothesis

It has long been common practice to reduce a given machine's performance to a convenient single number for comparison purposes. Examples of this number include the clock speed, the peak speed, the magaflops of some benchmark, etc. Having a single number per machine allows us easily to compare a number of different machines. The unspoken hypothesis often is that one number is enough, at least to rank order several machines.

Many people do not believe that this hypothesis is true, and there is much evidence to show that rank ordering of machines can vary depending on what measure is used. For example, machine X can beat machine Y on application 1 but Y can surpass X on application 2. This leads to the question: "Should we combine the two performance numbers to get a single number, or should we keep them separate?" Ultimately, computer performance evaluation results have a lot in common with sports statistics. "Is my team really better than yours" can be argued from many points of view, and even if your team beats mine once, I may insist on four games out of seven to concede defeat.

There is much evidence demonstrating that the single number hypothesis is a myth. Often there is an order of magnitude (or more) performance variation from the worst to the best benchmark programs in a given benchmark suite. This is true for such simple benchmarks as the Livermore Loops as shown in Figure 3. It is also true for more complex benchmarks as used in selecting a machine for purchase.

For example, consider the LLNL Loops [McMa86] run on the IBM 3090 and the NAS XL/60 as shown in Figure 3. Accepting the single number hypothesis yields an arithmetic mean for IBM of 14.95 and for NAS of 14.31, while the more well regarded harmonic mean yields 8.11 for IBM and 8.77 for NAS; neither measure produces a clear distinction. Yet there are substantial differences between the performances of the two machines.

Note that each machine is a clear winner (by more than 50 percent) in 9 cases. If one had chosen by chance only the programs that deliver high megaflops (e.g. kernels 1, 3, 4, 7, 8, 9, 18, 23, with top performance above the 20 megaflops line), one would conclude that the IBM 3090 is the better of the two machines (in 7 of 8 cases). If one picked the kernels of medium performance (e.g. kernels 2, 5, 6, 10, 12, 17, 19, 20, 21, 22, with top performance in

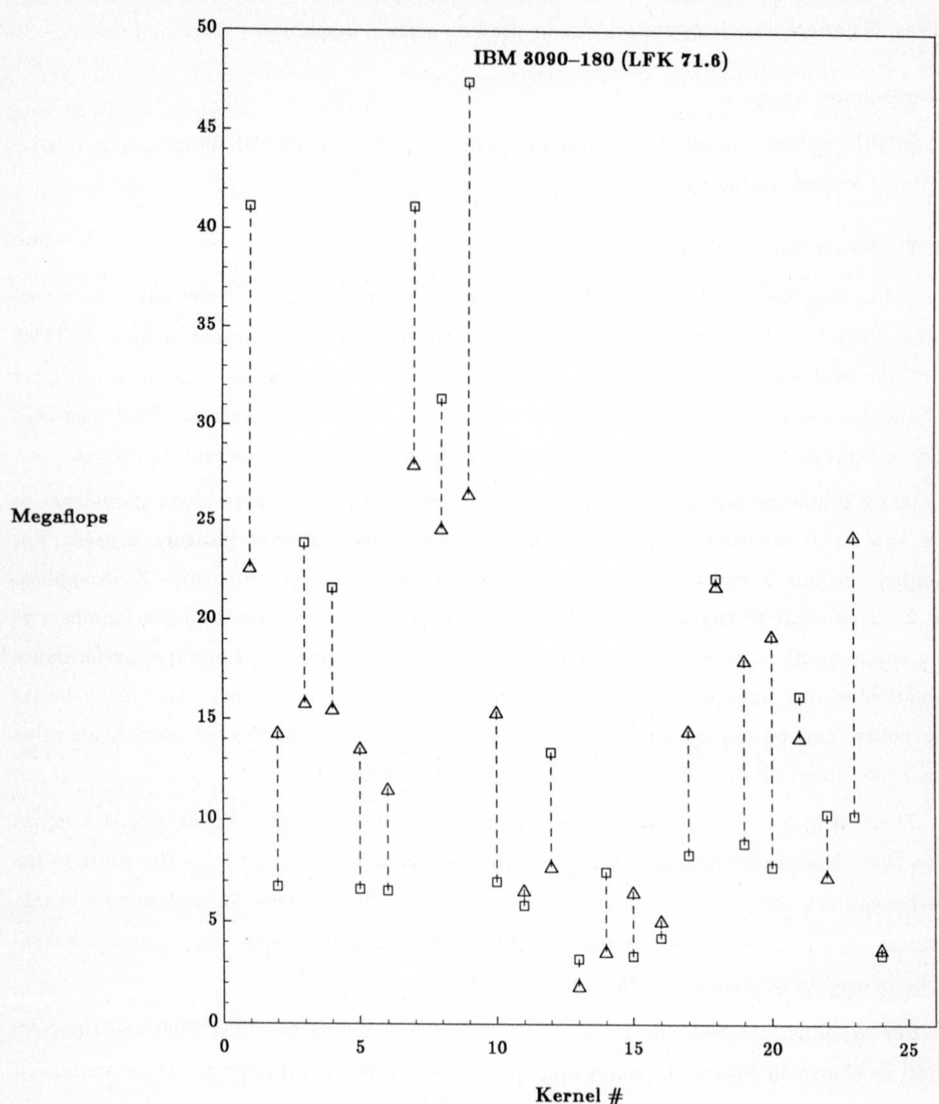

LLNL Ftn Kernels (DOspan=471)

Figure 3

the 8–20 megaflops range) one would conclude that in 7 of 10 cases the NAS XL/60 was best. Thus the conclusion depends on the choice of kernels, even if one looks at more than a single number. Notice also that the ratio of highest speed to lowest speed is 14.8 for IBM and 14.5 for NAS so a wide range of numbers is under consideration on each machine.

What is clearly indicated in a situation of this kind is first that consumers of the information should know of this fine structure in the data. Secondly, they should be provided with information about how the benchmarks for which each machine is very strong relate to real applications. Of course there may not be any "interesting" correlation for some users (in which case the single number hypothesis may be regarded as true) but for others the existence of a strong correlation may make a particular machine the clear choice.

Finally, system designers should be made well aware of the fine details of performance distinctions in situations where superficially similar machines show such strong performance differences. At the very least this should be an embarrassment to architects and system software people (as well as marketeers).

3.2. Peak Performance

These numbers are usually obtained by ignoring all data access delays and simply combining all of the arithmetic speed potential that a system has. When manufacturers cite such numbers they are guaranteeing that no user will ever get more performance than the quoted number. Real users must be cautioned that the performance goals to expect may be much lower. In fact, for each different type of job, users should have a corresponding degradation factor to use to obtain effective peak performance bounds when evaluating the performance of their codes.

The opening sentences of this paper may have some shock value to novices, but the following shows that for certain codes on particular machines even ten percent of the peak speed may be impossible to achieve. Assume a four processor system, with 32 bit as well as 64 bit arithmetic capabilities, and with chained multiply–add pipelines. If a given code requires 64-bit arithmetic (this halves the speed), cannot run in parallel (quartering the speed) and does no chained operations (halving the speed), the net effect is an immediate loss of a factor of 16 in performance. That code's peak performance potential is 6.25% of the manufacturer's listed peak speed.

By the time one accounts for data access delays, compiler weaknesses, the use of imperfect algorithms, etc., this user may obtain results closer to one percent than ten percent of the peak speed. The point here is that when pay raise time approaches, each user's boss should consider that user's peak performance potential (and not the number supplied by the computer manufacturer) in determining pay increases!

3.3. Unit Definitions

A commonly used unit is megaflops (millions of floating–point operations per second). This unit was introduced as an improvement over instructions per second or operations per second, because floating–point operations are closer to what engineering and scientific end users expect a machine to deliver. One problem with this unit is in the definition of a floating–point operation. Clearly, the four arithmetic operations should be counted, and comparisons seem reasonable to count. What about fetch and store? If the answer is "no," then what does one do about simple moves of floating–point arrays, e.g.,

$$X(I) = Y(I),$$

which may consume major amounts of time in real programs? Ultimately one must face the question of what to do about unary minus operations, which (by themselves) allow highly parallel bit serial machines to generate more megaflops than all others!

In spite of these difficulties there are software megaflops meters on a number of machines. It is important, obviously, to determine how such measurements were made, before comparing numbers for two machines. Two interesting statistics to gather across wide collections of machines would be megaflops measured over a typical hour of peak machine use and megaflops over a typical 24–hour period. The former would indicate what performance users were able to derive from a given machine, and comparison with other centers using the same machine type could indicate serious differences in the suitability of the machine to the collections of jobs run at various sites. Comparison of this number for different machines at sites running similar applications, would give an indication of the "delivered performance" of the different systems in the applications areas. Megaflops measured over a 24–hour period would in some cases indicate how well or poorly a system was actually used on a sustained basis.

3.4. Benchmark Set Turnaround Time

From the point of view of a computing center manager or machine owner, a key question is "How long does it take to run the entire workload." Elapsed time or turnaround time for a set of jobs is probably of less interest to managers than throughput, and turnaround time minimization can damage system throughput. However, we will discuss turnaround time because it is of much interest to end users (often more than throughput), as well as managers and owners.

In this context, given a set of jobs that are likely to consume comparable amounts of machine time, an important statistic is the speedup achieved by each job on a new machine as compared to a reference machine. If $T_p(i)$ represents the "parallel" time of job i when run on a vector/parallel system, and $T_r(i)$ represents the "reference" machine time, then speedup is defined as:

$$S_p(i) = T_r(i)/T_p(i) .$$

To characterize an entire workload, a useful approach is simply to compute the workload speedup:

$$S_p(w) = \frac{\Sigma T_r(i)}{\Sigma T_p(i)}$$

Thus, over the entire set of applications run on a given machine, the most important statistic is probably how poorly the worst running job performs. If one important job cannot take advantage of an advanced architecture, its running time (say $T_p(k)$) may completely dominate the overall time used on the system, and thus render the system ineffective, as was pointed out by Amdahl [Amda67]. On the other hand, this pessimistic view can be improved by observing that with today's parallel and vector algorithms, and restructuring compilers, most computations achieve some speedup at least on certain machines. Furthermore, as the number of different job types increases, there is a tendency for no single job to dominate the set.

4. Public Benchmark Database

We propose the development of a publicly accessible database of performance information. For a given application, the database should contain comparative information across various machines. For a given machine it should also contain comparative information across algorithms or computational approaches to a given application. Thus a user of the database could attempt to select a machine rationally for a given workload. Or, once one owned a machine, the user community could attempt to discover better ways to solve problems under consideration on that machine.

The database would be modeled after Figure 1, with a separate table for each machine as shown in Figure 4. Each point in this three dimensional array would contain performance information about the space requirements and timing, as shown in Figure 5.

In reality, each application and algorithm will split into several cases. Applications will split according to current approaches to modelling the real world. Algorithms will split according to various data structures and program structures used for a given algorithm type. Different versions of a given algorithm type may be used for different applications.

The traditional approaches to benchmarking can be observed in Figure 4. Solving a dense linear system of a certain size or computing a particular FFT at worst correspond to a particular row/column slice through the planes and at best correspond to several such slices. Kernels like the Livermore loops are simplified attempts to do this for a number of columns at once. The database we are proposing would contain much more complete information.

The proposed database could thus serve to allow different individuals to draw different conclusions. This would be a major improvement over the present sparsity of facts (e.g.,

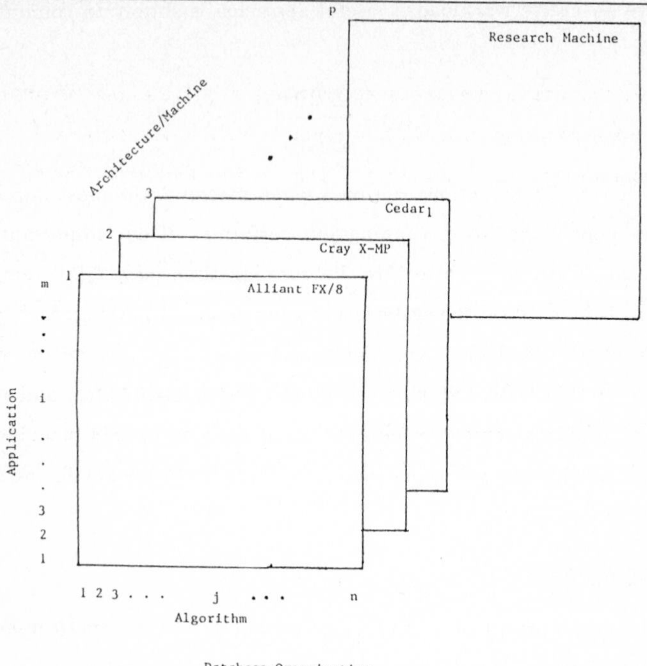

Database Organization

Figure 4

Space Allocation Effects	Timing Effects							
	Seconds or Megaflops				Memory Latency			
	Scalar	Vector	Parallel	Parallel Vector	Cache	Main Memory	...	Disk
Physical Memory Allotments (Code and Data), Page Size.	X X X							

Measurements to Make

Figure 5

one number per machine) in that a complex set of facts would be available to allow serious comparison and debate. In reference to our sports statistics analogy, this database would serve the role of a sports almanac. The alternative, which the single number hypothesis leaves us with, would in the world of college football reduce all teams over all years to a single rank–ordered list. Clearly, this is something that no two football fans could ever accept.

Figure 5 would show time, megaflops and speedup relative to earlier rows of the table for several sizes of physical main memory allocated. It would also show code and overall (or virtual) memory requirements and how they change as the program is modified. We show four entries for each of three cases. These cases are the initial code, (which almost certainly has a bias toward some particular architecture) a version with directives and simple changes of the code, and finally the best results which may be obtained by major changes, algorithm substitution, etc.

By "List Changes" we mean that one should give a sufficiently detailed representation so that someone could modify the code similarly for another machine. The fourth case concerns data access delays which may be hard to obtain, but which would be very useful to know. These are the delays caused by various memory levels.

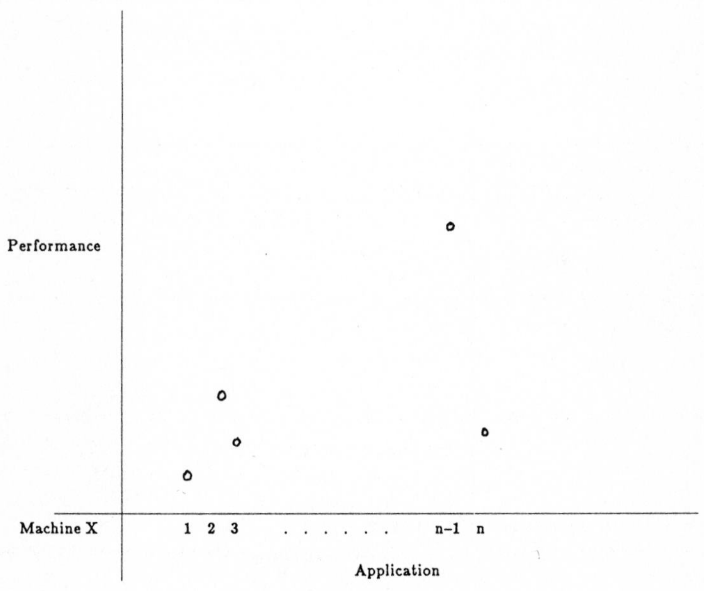

Performance Variation Across Applications

Figure 6

5. Uses of the Database

Assume that a large database exists. Let us first consider statistical ways of organizing and improving our use of the database. One goal would be the clustering of machines into equivalence classes of performance. Another goal would be, for each of these machine clusters, to discover small amounts of code that could be used to accurately predict the performance of large amounts of code.

5.1. Clustering of Machines

This type of correlation could be considered by using the kind of information shown in Figure 6. We could attempt to correlate the performance of various machines for particular applications, e.g., by considering inner products of the kind of data plotted in Figure 6 for two different machines. Machines with similar architectures and relative timing characteristics would be highly correlated with respect to performance on a range of applications and "clusters" of similar machines could be derived from large amounts of performance data.

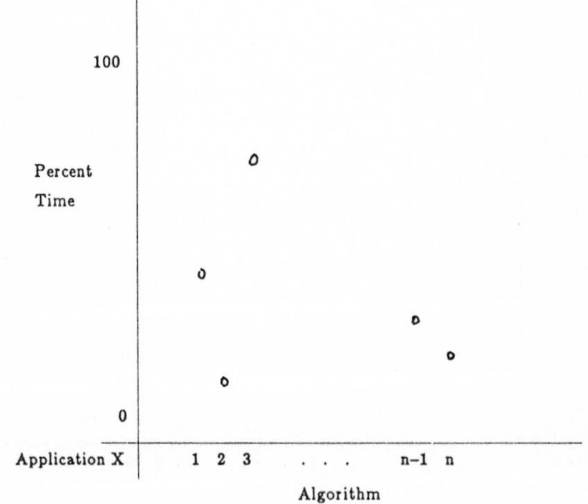

Algorithm Time consumption by an Application

Figure 7

5.2. Benchmark Size Reduction

Given a cluster of similar machines (or a single machine), how can we obtain a small amount of code that predicts the performance on these machines of a large amount of code? First, we could consider the correlation between applications, by algorithm type. The same approach as above could be applied between data of the type shown in Figure 7 for two or more applications. Thus, if several applications relied heavily on the same algorithms, this method would clarify how one application could be used to characterize an equivalence class of applications.

A second approach is to assume that the relatively small number of lines of code found in the key algorithms of a large application may accurately predict the performance of the large application. This could be determined as illustrated in Figure 8 by studying the correlation between the performance of each given application and the performance of a key algorithm (or the linear combination of several key algorithms). If a satisfactory correlation could be found over some class of machines, then the simple benchmark could be used to predict the performance of a whole application for a new machine with "similar architectural features."

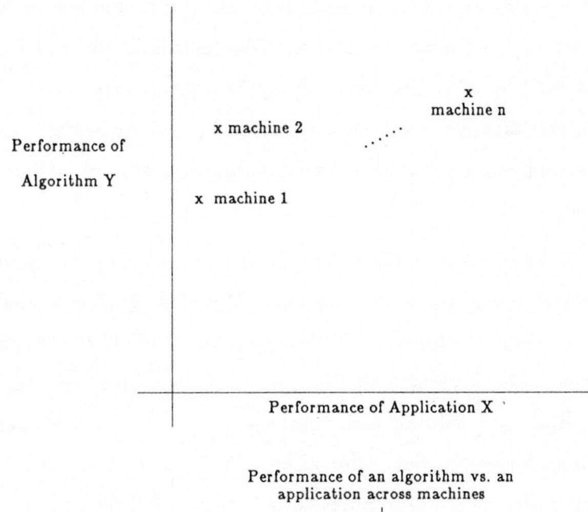

Performance of an algorithm vs. an application across machines

Figure 8

It might also be interesting to determine whether one application predicts the performance of another, in cases where algorithm use is quite similar. This could allow the detailed analysis of one application to predict the performance of other applications, without the need for execution of the other applications.

5.3. New System Designs

We have discussed above certain aspects of questions Q1 and Q2 of Section 1 and these could be applied for purposes P1 or P2, but the design of new hardware and software systems requires further insights. In several papers, the relations between data structures, program structures and machine structures have been discussed in qualitative terms [Kuck81], [Kuck82]. We propose that the qualitative terms of these earlier papers could in the future be quantified by such a database. This would require a further breaking down of the algorithms into their basic data structures (e.g., scalars, arrays with regular access patterns, etc.) and basic program structures, i.e., dependence graphs that are acyclic or cyclic.

If successful, this could lead to a user view of the database that was able to provide insight for purpose P3. The ultimate goal is to select algorithms and machines that work together effectively for a given set of applications.

6. Summary

In this paper we have collected a few well-known observations about the current state of performance evaluation for high-speed machines. Our conclusion is that too little is known at this time about performance, and the few facts that are available are too broadly applied. In some cases it is, of course, entirely appropriate to spend $1 M or even $20 M for a new computer system without much consideration of system performance. In other cases, reliance on a single number to compare two machines is absurd, when one is committing such a sum of money.

We propose the construction of a large database containing many details about a wide-ranging collection of applications programs. We also propose to make such a database publicly available via computer networks. Few people are likely to disagree with the technical merit of this idea. The difficulty lies in collecting benchmarks, making measurements, building, deploying and maintaining the database. This is an enormous undertaking, but one that we feel must urgently be undertaken. With a few colleagues, we have already begun to move in this direction. Our purpose in writing this paper is to enlist the thoughts and eventually the contributions of many people in joining the effort.

References

[Amda67] G. Amdahl. *The Validity of the Single Processor Approach to Achieving Large Scale Computing Capabilities.* **AFIPS Proc. SJCC**, Vol. 30, 1967.

[FHHJ83] H. Fromm, U. Hercksen, U. Herzog, K–H. John, R. Klar, and W. Kleinoder. *Experiences with Performance Measurement and Modeling of a Processor Array.* **IEEE Trans. on Computers,** Vol. C–32, No. 1, January, 1983.

[GJMY87] K. Gallivan, W. Jalby, A. Malony, and P–C. Yew. *Performance Analysis on the Cedar System.* **Center for Supercomputing Research and Development,** University of Illinois at Urbana–Champaign, Report No. 680, August 10, 1987, To appear as a chapter in the book **Performance Evaluation of Supercomputers**, edited by Dr. J.L. martin, to be published by North–Holland in January, 1988.

[KKLW84] David J. Kuck, Robert H. Kuhn, Bruce Leasure and Michael Wolfe, *The Structure of an Advanced Retargetable Vectorizer.* **The Proceedings of COMPSAC '80,** 1980, Reproduced in **Supercomputers: Design and Applications**, Kai Hwang, ed., IEEE Computer Society Press, 1986.

[Kuck81] D.J. Kuck, *Automatic Program Restructuring for High–Speed Computation.* **Proc of CONPAR 81, Conf. on Analysing Problem–Classes and Programming for Parallel Computing**, pp. 66–84, June, 1981.

[Kuck82] David J. Kuck. *High–Speed Machines and Their Compilers.* In: **Parallel Processing Systems**, D. J. Evans, ed. Cambridge University Press, pp. 193–214, 1982.

[McMa86] Frank H. McMahon, *The Livermore Fortran Kernels: A Computer Test of the Numerical Performance Range.* **Report UCRL – 537415**, Lawrence Livermore National Laboratory, 1986.

[NaRC86] Anon. *An Agenda for Improved Evaluation of Supercomputer Performance,* **National Research Council Report,** Washington, D.C., 1986.

[SeSS83] Z. Segall, A. Singh, R. Snodgrass, A. Jones and D. Siewiorek. *An Integrated Instrumentation Environment for Multiprocessors.* **IEEE Trans. on Computers,** Vol. C–32, No. 1, January, 1983.

A Perspective on Parallel Processing[1]

Tilak Agerwala
Stephen L. Harvey

IBM Corporation
P. O. Box 704
Yorktown Heights, NY 10598/USA

1. Background

Computing requirements in several application areas are unlikely to be satisfied solely by uniprocessors in the future. In addition to providing very high absolute computing performance, parallel processing offers the advantages of improved cost performance and upwardly scalable performance. To realize these benefits, researchers at IBM have been experimenting with parallel processing for several years. The initial focus was on highly parallel systems for specific design automation problems. Encouraged by successes in these projects and a growing conviction that parallel processing is very important, our research has expanded into more general application areas and systems approaches. We find it useful to discuss our work in two categories: specialized parallel processors and multipurpose parallel processors.

2. Specialized Parallel Processors

Specialized highly parallel processors are already being applied to the solution of important, computationally intensive problems. In these cases, the architecture, design, and programming are fine tuned to obtain very high performance on a well defined application. Sophisticated programming environments and general user support are not required and very good cost performance can be obtained. Moreover, it has been our experience that such processors can be prototyped by small teams at relatively low development cost. The Yorktown Simulation Engine (1), and the GF11 Supercomputer (2), described below, are examples of specialized parallel processors.

The Yorktown Simulation Engine (YSE) was motivated by a need to do gate level logic simulation for large VLSI designs at a much higher speed than was possible with conventional mainframes. The initial prototype consisted of 64 processors which were specialized for simulating binary logic. This prototype demonstrated the feasibility of cost effective high speed logic simulation and was subsequently extended, rede-

1 Supported in part by The Defense Advanced Research Projects Agency under Contract Number N00039-87-C-0122 (Multi-processor System Architecture).

signed, and replicated for internal use in several development laboratories. It is one of the earliest examples of a highly parallel processor system in production use.

The GF11 Supercomputer is an example of a highly parallel processor for an important scientific problem: Quantum Chromodynamics (QCD). Predicting the mass of the proton from QCD is expected to require approximately 3 X 10**17 operations. On a supercomputer that can sustain 100 MFLOPS, this computation would take 100 years. The GF11 has a peak performance of 11.5 GFLOPS and is expected to sustain 10 GFLOPS on the QCD problem. It should be able to complete the computations necessary to predict the mass of the proton in one year. This is a dramatic example of the use of parallel processing to bring an important but intractable scientific problem into the realm of feasibility. A block diagram of the GF11 is shown in Figure 1.

The GF11 has 576 processors in a modified Single Instruction Stream, Multiple Data Stream (SIMD) configuration. A powerful multi-stage permutation network can store 1024 preselected permutations (including broadcasts) and can switch between permutations every 200 ns at run time. Though the GF11 was designed for a specific problem, it appears suitable for a range of applications in engineering/scientific computing. In addition, the project is providing valuable experience on the architecture, design, and construction of highly parallel processors.

Specialized parallel processors that achieve hundreds of gigaflops or even a teraflop could be in limited use by the end of the decade. The availability of such computing power can have a significant impact on scientific investigations. Researchers at IBM are planning to exploit this potential for specific problems such as continuous speech recognition, analysis of communication networks, design automation, physics, and neural modelling.

3. Multipurpose Parallel Processing

Clearly, it is not practical to construct a specialized processor for every important application. We use the word "multipurpose" to refer to a processor that can be used effectively for a range of applications. The current state of the art indicates that a large set of applications is susceptible to parallelization and that machines of sufficient generality and performance can be built economically. Multipurpose parallel processing therefore has potential. However, several important technical issues remain to be resolved, examples of which are: the amount and granularity of parallelism in applications, whether the parallelism is specified by a user, detected by a compiler, or inherent in the language, the impact of communication latency and bandwidth on sustained performance, resource management techniques and their overhead, and the level of performance that can be sustained on an interesting set of applications.

Analysis and simulation are essential to start answering these questions. In some cases such as the GF11 they may be sufficient to justify the construction of a large scale prototype for solving a specific problem. For more general environments, analysis and simulation cannot resolve all important issues and it becomes necessary to construct nontrivial prototypes and to experiment with real applications and systems software. The Research Parallel Processor Prototype (RP3) **(3)** was conceived as an experimental facility capable of providing data on a full range of systems issues. Whereas GF11 will be a tool for physicists, RP3 will be a tool for computer scientists.

3.1 The Research Parallel Processor Prototype: Technical Plan

The RP3 project has two overall goals: to develop a multipurpose parallel processor and to provide an experimental facility for research in highly parallel processing. A key decision was made early in the project definition to use an existing microprocessor. The reason was to avoid the significant expense of developing a new processor architecture and associated compilers. A state-of-the-art 32-bit microprocessor, developed by IBM and readily available, was chosen. An overall performance of 1000 MIPS was considered sufficient to attract application developers. With a 2.5 MIPS microprocessor, a 512-way parallel processor would be required. With these basic assumptions, different architectural approaches were evaluated and the Ultracomputer **(4)** at NYU's Courant Institute was selected as a starting point. Several enhancements were subsequently made to the architecture and design. A block diagram of RP3 is shown in Figure 2.

The features that make RP3 a multipurpose parallel processor are summarized below:

1. The basic building block is a powerful, general purpose microprocessor.

2. RP3 is a Multiple Instruction Stream, Multiple Data Stream (MIMD) machine.

3. The interprocessor communication network is a self routing OMEGA network that provides very low latency, high bandwidth asynchronous communications. The high performance and flat structure of this network allows the machine to be used effectively without significant attention being paid to locality of communication.

4. RP3 has a global address space with very low overhead access to non-local memory, and combining network support for shared variable operations. The memory is arbitrarily partitionable between local and global at run time under software control. Both shared memory and message passing communication mechanisms are provided.

5. RP3 has a general I/O subsystem designed around a S/370 companion machine that handles remote terminal access and file management. An I/O and support processor provides the functions of diagnostics, initial program load and shutdown, measurements, and input/output.

Several important decisions that impact the suitability of RP3 as an experimental facility, are discussed below:

1. RP3 was to be a usable system not a laboratory curiosity. This placed requirements on practical aspects such as adequate I/O, reliability, diagnostics, and documentation for limited reproduction of the machine if desirable. The hardware implementation would be done with IBM components, both to insure some reliability standards and to have better control over the machine schedules.

2. It was felt that hardware and software facilities to monitor the behavior of the system at run time were critical for an experimental machine. Facilities to accurately measure opcode frequencies, cache hit ratios, frequencies and latency of local and global accesses, network latency, memory usage and access patterns, process communication and synchronizing behavior, and I/O activity, were planned for RP3.

3. UNIX[2] was chosen as the base for the operating system because of its widespread use in the academic community and also because a UNIX-based highly parallel operating system was being developed for the Ultracomputer at NYU. The Ultracomputer group accepted responsibility for developing a similar operating system, appropriately extended, for the RP3. For application development, the approach was to extend languages such as FORTRAN and C with constructs for expressing parallelism explicitly. This appeared to be the quickest way to provide some programming support in languages familiar to most users. Front end preprocessors would be written for an existing compiler which targets these languages to the chosen microprocessor. More advanced programming paradigms would be supported later. Thus, the approach to software was to provide a (relatively primitive) set of functions which would be sufficient to allow users to develop applications and which would enable further research on operating systems, languages, and compilers.

4. A small applications group was also formed to develop and analyze parallel applications and provide guidance to the systems and language design efforts. The areas of design automation, simulation, graphics, natural language processing, and vision were selected to serve as yardsticks to measure the adequacy of the architecture. It was clear from the start that experimentation with applications and development of advanced systems software would require significant participation from the scientific community external to IBM. The project was therefore to be run as an open project and plans were put in place to allow interactive remote access.

---

2 Unix is a registered trademark of AT&T.

3.2 The Research Parallel Processor Prototype: Current Status

Authorization to proceed with the design and construction of one segment (64 processors) of the RP3 was obtained in October, 1984. In mid-1987 much of the hardware work has been done. The power/mechanical systems are completed and working, and the processor memory element and I/O processor have been debugged and are running code. The floating point chip has not yet been incorporated and the performance monitoring chip remains to be designed. Initial multiprocessor configurations will be working soon and enough processors will be running architecture verification programs by mid-year to validate our systems approach and base architecture. We expect to complete the 64-way system by year-end 1987.

The complexity of the design was significantly greater than originally anticipated. Most of this complexity comes from two sources: 1) The logic required around the microprocessor to adapt it to a parallel processing system, and 2) the memory hierarchy. Excluding the floating point chip, the microprocessor, and arrays, the processor memory element consists of 155 thousand gates. Eleven unique part numbers, in three gate array technologies, were designed. These eleven chips, some of which are reused multiple times, contain 70 thousand gates. The interconnection switch, originally viewed as the most difficult part of the system, was done with a single chip part number replicated many times on a TCM (Thermal Conduction Module).

To handle the design complexity with limited resources, an advanced engineering design system was developed. This is one important by-product of the RP3 project. The design system has proven to be so successful that several development laboratories have installed it and are considering its use as their principal design tool. The overall RP3 design facility may also be used by other prototyping projects at IBM Research. The system is continuously enhanced as new needs arise.

The I/O subarchitecture and all call interfaces for the operating system have been defined. NYU has started the port of the UNIX 4.3[2] based parallel operating system from the Ultracomputer to RP3. NYU is also assisting us in a second experiment in which the MACH kernel **(5)** will be implemented on the RP3. An initial port to an early RP3 prototype is scheduled for late summer this year.

Preprocessors for parallel extensions to FORTRAN and C have been developed **(6,7,8)**. These preprocessors are used with VM/EPEX **(9,10)**, a second important by-product of the RP3 project. VM/EPEX emulates the RP3 on a S/370 by creating multiple virtual processes with local and shared memory. VM/EPEX, together with the preprocessors, allows development of parallel applications while the hardware is being constructed. This system has been installed at several IBM and external locations and is in use as an experimental vehicle for parallel programming. Numerous applications, source-level compatible with RP3, have been written and are being analyzed **(11,12,13,14)**. Most of this work has been on engineering/scientific problems because they are generally better understood.

A powerful set of performance tools has been developed. These tools allow one to gather parallel processor execution traces for subsequent "post mortem" analysis using various simulators **(15,16)**. This work is providing valuable insight into the performance of parallel systems **(17)**.

4. Related Work

In addition to GF11 and RP3, other architectures are also being studied. It is our view, for example, that dataflow offers the potential to exploit massive fine-grain parallelism. Recent work indicates that extensions to conventional architectures can be made incrementally to get much of the dataflow benefit **(18)**. Research on automatic extraction of parallelism from conventional languages such as FORTRAN **(19)** and APL **(20)** is also underway.

5. Summary/Conclusions

Parallel processing is one of the most important areas of computer science research. Experience with highly parallel processing is quite limited today and several architecture, systems, and software alternatives need to be investigated. In particular, much further work is required on software issues. Applications and software problems will be studied and resolved slowly as non-trivial hardware prototypes become available. Two such prototypes are currently being constructed at IBM Research. This paper has tried to place these efforts in proper perspective.

6. References

1. Pfister, G. F., "The IBM Yorktown Simulation Engine," *Proceedings of the IEEE*, June 1986, pp.850-860.
2. Beetam, J., Denneau, M., and Weingarten, D., "The GF11 Supercomputer," *Proceedings of the 12th Annual International Symposium on Computer Architecture*, Boston, MA, June 17-19, 1985, pp.108-113.
3. Pfister, G. F., Brantley, W. C., George, D. A., Harvey, S. L., Kleinfelder, W. J., McAuliffe, K. P., Melton, E. A., Norton, V. A., and Weiss, J., "The IBM Research Parallel Processor Prototype (RP3): Introduction and Architecture," *Proceedings of the 1985 International Conference on Parallel Processing*, August 1985, pp.764-771.

4. Gottleib, A., Grishman, R., Kruskal, C. P., McAuliffe, K. P., Rudolph, L., and Snir, M., "The NYU Ultracomputer - Designing an MIMD Shared-Memory Parallel Computer," *IEEE Transactions on Computers*, February 1983, pp.175-189.

5. Rashid, R. F., "Threads of a New System," *UNIX Review*, Vol. 4, Number 8, August 1986.

6. Stone, J. M., Darema-Rogers, F., Norton, V. A., and Pfister, G. F., "Introduction to the VM/EPEX Fortran Preprocessor," Research Report #11407, IBM T. J. Watson Research Center, Yorktown heights, NY, September 1985.

7. Darema, F., George, D. A., Norton, V. A., and Pfister, G. F., "A Single-Program-Multiple-Data Computational Model for EPEX/FORTRAN," *Parallel Computing*, to appear June 1987.

8. Chang, W. L. and Norton, V. A., "VM/EPEX C Preprocessor User's Manual," Research Report #12246, IBM T. J. Watson Research Center, Yorktown Heights, NY, October 1986.

9. Darema, F., "Applications Environment for the IBM Parallel Processor Prototype (RP3)," *Proceedings of the International Conference on Supercomputing*, Athens, Greece, June 8-12, 1987.

10. Darema-Rogers, F., George, D. A., Norton, V. A., and Pfister, G. F., "Environment and System Interface for VM/EPEX," Research Report #11381, IBM T. J. Watson Research Center, Yorktown Heights, NY, September 1985.

11. Darema, F., "Parallel Applications Development for Shared Memory Systems," Research Report # 12229, IBM T. J. Watson Research Center, Yorktown Heights, N.Y., August 1986.

12. Darema, F., Karp, A., and Teller, P., "Applications Survey Reports," Research Report # 12743, IBM T. J. Watson Research Center, Yorktown Heights, NY, August 1986.

13. Darema, F., Kirkpatrick, S., and Norton, V. A., "Simulated Annealing on Shared Memory Parallel Systems," *IBM Journal of Research and Development*, to appear June 1987.

14. Norton, V. A., "Parallelization of Quicksort using Fetch&Add," Research Report #11884, IBM T. J. Watson Research Center, Yorktown Heights, NY, May 1986.

15. So, K., Darema-Rogers, F., George, D. A., Norton, V. A., and Pfister, G. F., "PSIMUL - A System for Parallel Simulation of the Execution of Parallel Programs," Research Report #11674, IBM T. J. Watson Research Center, Yorktown Heights, NY, January 1986.

16. So, K., Bolmarcich, A. S., Darema, F., and Norton, V. A., " A Speedup Analyser for Parallel Programs," *Proceedings of the 1987 International Conference on Parallel Processing*, August 1987.

17. Darema, F., Pfister, G. F., and So, K., "Memory Access Patterns of Parallel Scientific Programs," *Proceedings of the 1987 ACM Sigmetrics Conference*, May 1987, pp.46-58.

18. Ekanadham, K. and Buehrer, R., "Dataflow Principles in Multiprocessor Systems," Research Report #12190, IBM T. J. Watson Research Center, Yorktown Heights, NY, September 29, 1986.

19. Allen, F., Burke, M., Charles, P., Cytron, R., and Ferrante, J., "An Overview of the PTRAN Analysis System for Multiprocessors," *Proceedings of the International Conference on Supercomputing*, Athens, Greece, June 8-12, 1987.

20. Chang, W. M., "Evon - An Extended von Neumann Model for Parallel Processors," *Proceedings of the Fall Joint Computer Conference* . Dallas, Texas, June 2-6, 1986, pp.362-371.

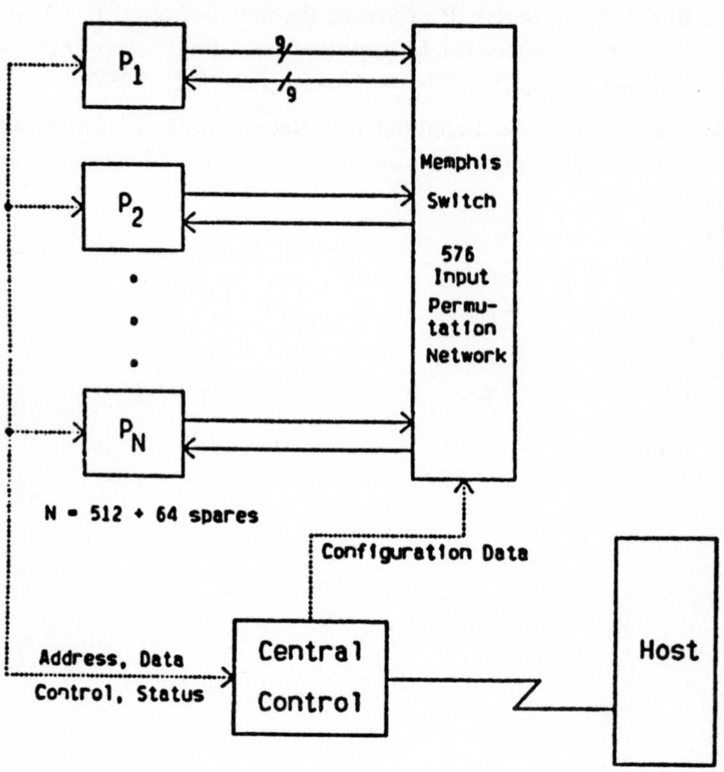

Figure 1. Block Diagram of GF11.

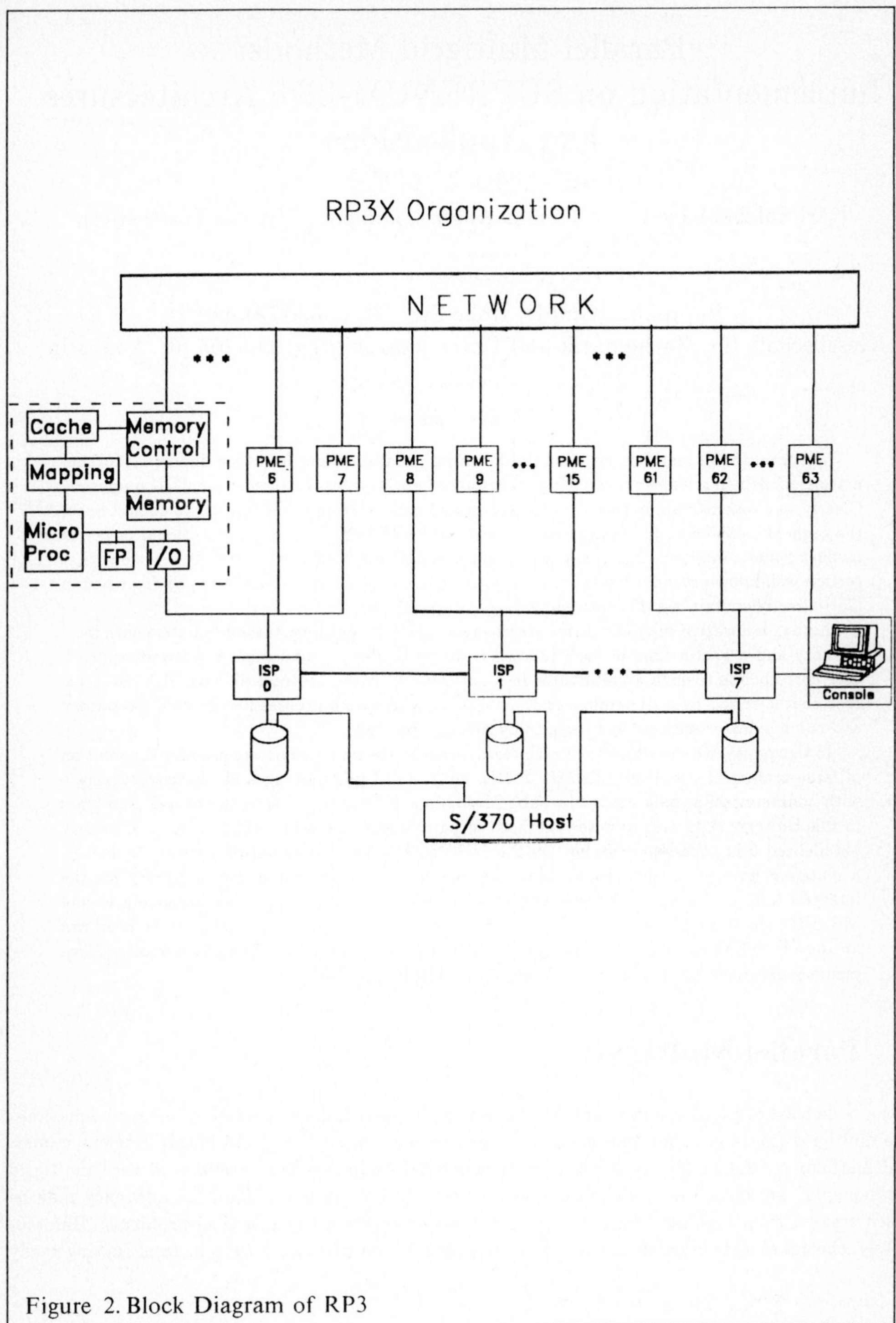

Figure 2. Block Diagram of RP3

Parallel Multigrid Methods: Implementation on SUPRENUM-Like Architectures and Applications

Karl Solchenbach Clemens-August Thole Ulrich Trottenberg

Suprenum GmbH, Hohe Str. 73, D-5300 Bonn
Gesellschaft für Mathematik und Datenverarbeitung, D-5205 St. Augustin

Abstract

Multigrid (MG) methods for partial differential equations (and for other important mathematical models in scientific computing) have turned out to be optimal on sequential computers. Clearly, one wants to apply them also on vector and parallel computers in order to exploit both, the high MG-efficiency (compared to classical methods) and the full computational power of modern supercomputers. For this purpose, parallel MG methods are needed. It turns out that certain well-known standard MG methods (with RB and zebra-type relaxation, as described in [25]) already contain a sufficiently high degree of parallelism.

Among innovative supercomputer architectures, MIMD multiprocessor computers with local memory and a vector unit in each processor are particularly promising. A software approch that corresponds to such architectures in a natural way is the abstract SUPRENUM concept. It is characterized by a dynamical process system, where each process has its own data space and communicates with other processes by message-passing.

In this paper, we show how such architectures and software concepts are used for the solution of large scale grid problems (discrete PDEs, etc.). Grid partitioning and blockstructuring – with communication only along the subgrid or block boundaries – are the natural approches in this context. Any grid oriented method, in particularly any MG method can be efficiently parallelized using these approaches. In the SUPRENUM project, powerful software tools (e.g. a mapping library for the process-processor mapping and a communication library for the intergrid data exchanges) are developed that make it very easy to implement single grid and MG methods on local memory multiprocessor systems. Parallel MG programs have been run on the SUPRENUM simulator [16], the SUPRENUM pre-prototype [22] and some other local memory machines like the Intel iPSC and the CalTech hypercube.

1 Parallel Multigrid

For a wide class of problems in scientific computing, in particular for partial differential equations, the multigrid (more general: the multi-level) principle has proved to yield highly efficient numerical methods [13,2,4,14,20]. However, the principle has to be applied carefully: if the "multigrid components" are not chosen adequately with respect to the given problem, the efficiency may be much smaller than possible. This has been demonstrated for many practical problems. Unfortunately, the general theories on multigrid convergence do not give much help in constructing really efficient multigrid algorithms. Although some progress has been made in bridging the gap between theory and practice during the last few years , there are still several theoretical approaches which are misleading rather than helpful with respect to the objective of real efficiency. The research in finding highly efficient algorithms for non-model applications therefore is still a sophisticated mixture of theoretical considerations, a transfer of experiences from model to real life problems and systematical experimental work. The emphasis of the practical research activity today lies – among others – in the following fields:

- finding efficient multigrid components for really complex problems, e.g. Navier-Stokes equations in general geometries
- combining the multigrid approach with advanced discretization techniques: using dynamic local multigrid refinements; adding artificial terms (viscosity, pressure, compressibility, etc.) in certain multigrid components; using "double" discretization, τ-extrapolation, defect correction in connection with multigrid to obtain higher accuracy; using coarse-grid continuation techniques etc. [2]
- constructing highly parallel multigrid algorithms

In this paper, we want to deal only with the last topic.

Multigrid (MG) methods are known to be "optimal", i.e. the number of arithmetic operations that have to be performed is proportional to the number of discrete unknowns which are to be calculated. This statement directly applies to standard sequential MG algorithms. With the availability of parallel computers, the question arises how MG methods are suited for parallel computing. Sometimes one can find the conjecture that MG is – in some sense – an essentially sequential principle, or the opinion that the full MG efficiency is obtained only on sequential computers and that there is always a loss of efficiency for MG on parallel architectures.

We do not intend to give a final answer to this question, but we want to contribute to a clarification of the situation.

First, one may distinguish the approaches where standard MG algorithms are discussed under the parallel aspect from those approaches where essentially new MG algorithms (or better: MG-like algorithms) are designed with respect to parallel computing. We will not discuss new algorithms of this latter type in this paper; we only want to make a few remarks about them.

The – in our opinion – most interesting proposal for such a variant has recently been made by Fredericson/McBryan [7]. Here on each level several coarse grid problems are solved simultaneously in order to improve the MG-convergence. This appraoch seems to be of considerable use particularly for massively parallel machines like the Connection Machine [18].

To the class of new MG-like algorithms belong also all those attempts where several levels are simultaneously employed. Such methods have been considered by Gannon/van Rosendale [8], Greenbaum [10], and others. A breakthrough has, however, not yet been achieved; for theoretical reasons, one may also doubt whether these approches can give a remarkable gain at all.

In this paper, we consider only standard MG methods under the parallel aspect. This means, in particular, that we regard the schedule according to which the different grid levels are passed through as essentially sequential. On each grid level, however, we perform each of the grid operations (the MG components: relaxation, computing of defects, interpolation, and restriction) as parallel as possible. It has been known for long that certain relaxation methods are parallel in a natural way, e.g.

- *Jacobi*-type relaxations

and

- *Gauss-Seidel*-type relaxations with *multi-color* (red-black, four color etc.) ordering of the grid points.

Clearly, also computing of defects, interpolation and restriction can be performed in parallel.

The first systematical papers on parallel MG were those of Grosch [11,12] and Brandt [3]. In [3] most of the essential phenomena with parallel MG are already discussed or at least mentioned. In particular, it is stated that the time complexity $T^*(N)$ (measured by the number of parallel arithmetic operations) of a suitable standard parallel full multigrid (FMG) solver for the 2D-Poisson model equation is $T^*(N) = O\left(log_2 N\right)^2$, where N = number of grid points.

In this paper, we consider two model problems in some detail:

Example 1: A parallel MG-solver for the 3D-Poisson equation on the unit cube $(0,1)^3$ with periodic boundary conditions. A V-cycle of this algorithm is characterized by the following components (for a more detailed description see [26]).

Discrete operator:	ordinary second order 7-point approximation Δ_h on a regular cubic grid with meshsize h and $N = h^{-3}$
Relaxation:	3D-red-black pointwise, all red (black) grid points are simultaneoulsy treated in the first (second) relaxation half step; $\nu_1, \nu_2 = 1$ relaxation steps.
Coarsening:	standard coarsening $h \longrightarrow 2h$
	ordinary 7-point operator Δ_{2h}
Grid transfers:	$h \longrightarrow 2h$: 3D full-weighting
	$2h \longrightarrow h$: trilinear interpolation
Cycle type:	V-cycle, correction scheme

The time complexity for a V-cycle of this algorithm is $T^*(N) = O(log_2 N)$.

Example 2: The 2D-Stokes equations

$$\begin{aligned} -\nabla^2 u + \frac{\delta p}{\delta x} &= f^1 \\ -\nabla^2 v + \frac{\delta p}{\delta y} &= f^2 \\ \frac{\delta u}{\delta x} + \frac{\delta v}{\delta y} &= f^3 \end{aligned}$$

defined on $\Omega = (0,1)^2$ with boundary conditions

$$\begin{aligned} u &= g^1 \\ v &= g^2 \end{aligned}$$

on $\partial\Omega$. In order to guarantee a unique solution the usual compatibilty condition is required additionally.

The Stokes equations are discretized in the usual way on a staggered quadratic grid (meshsize h). p is defined in cell centers, whereas u and v are defined on the centers of the cell faces.

A V-cycle of a parallel MG-solver for this discrete problem is characterized by the following components (see also [21] for details):

Relaxation:	One relaxation step consists of two parts: Firstly, the momentum equations are relaxed for u and v simultaneously using fixed values of p. Then a so-called distributive relaxation sweep [2] is performed which updates the unknowns u, v and p in order to fulfil the continuity equation. Both parts of the relaxation are performed in a red-black ordering. Altogether, $\nu_1 = 1$, $\nu_2 = 2$ of these relaxation steps are carried out on each level.
Coarsening:	standard coarsening $h \longrightarrow 2h$ on staggered grids (the coarse grid is no subset of the fine grid) ordinary 7-point operator Δ_{2h}
Grid transfers:	$h \longrightarrow 2h$: 2D half-weighting on staggered grids $2h \longrightarrow h$: bilinear interpolation
Cycle type:	V-cycle, correction scheme

The time complexity of this algorithm (V-cycle) is also $T^*(N) = O(log_2 N)$.

In the two algorithms above only *pointwise* relaxation is needed for smoothing, since the corresponding equations are isotropic. In [27] a systematical first study for the practically important case of anisotropic 3D-operators has been presented. Here line and/or plane relaxation have been used for smoothing, and corresponding parallel algorithms have been described.

2 Parallel supercomputers, the SUPRENUM prototype

For the last decade, a lot of programs for large-scale scientific computing have been developed and run on vector supercomputers of the CRAY-1 class with great success. Today, the evolution of single processor vector machines seems to be stagnating and most of the increasing computational power is achieved by using more than one processor in parallel. Examples for this development are the CRAY-X/MP, CRAY-2/3, ETA^{10}, and several smaller systems, all with a small number of processors.

On the other hand, certain highly parallel computers with a large number of processors are entering the supercomputer market (Intel's iPSC-VX, FPS-T-Series, AMETEK S14, NCUBE, Connection Machine). Typically, these multiprocessor computers do *not* necessarily provide a common (shared) memory for all single processors. In this paper, we will concentrate our conciderations on local memory multiprocessor computers.

The hardware architecture of these multiprocessor computers with local memory is characterized by P processor "nodes", each of which has (at least)

- *its own CPU*
- *a floating point arithmetic*
- *a private local memory unit*
- *a communication component*

The nodes are connected by an *interconnection network for communication.* This network typically consists of a subset of all possible node connections (tree, grid, ring, hypercube, ...). Also any other topology based on buses may be used. – Each floating-point unit may be based on a scalar or vector arithmetic processor. – Usually the multiprocessor computer is connected to a front end computer for control (initialization, termination), I/O, and user interaction.

Typical numbers of P for specific machines are

$P \leq$	128	Intel iPSC
$P \leq$	64	Intel iPSC-VX
$P \leq$	256	AMETEK S14
$P \leq$	16K	FPS-T-Series (theoretically)
$P \leq$	1K	NCUBE
$P =$	256	SUPRENUM prototype

(Also some architectures which do not fulfil the characteristic criteria may be used like multiprocessor computers of the type above. For example, the $P = 64K$ processors of the Connection Machine CM-1 may be clustered to functional units which can perform floating-point arithmetic.)

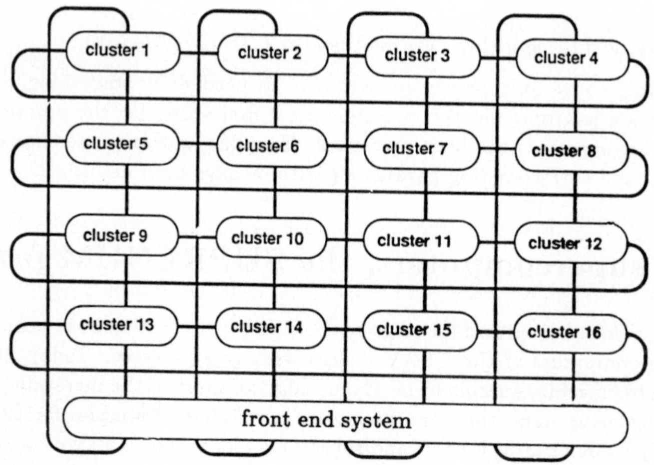

Figure 1: Structure of the SUPRENUM-prototype with 256 processors in 16 clusters

Figure 1 shows the overall structure of the SUPRENUM-prototype hardware as it was designed by Giloi [9]. In the SUPRENUM-prototype 256 nodes are connected via a two-level interconnection network of buses.

Each *node* consists of the MC68020 CPU, 8 Mbyte of private memory, a fast floating-point vector unit (8 Mflop/s peak performance, 16 Mflop/s with chaining) and dedicated communication hardware.

Up to 16 of these computing nodes are combined to a *cluster* using the *clusterbus* (256 Mbyte/s). Each cluster also contains a local disk (1 Gbyte), a disk controller node, a monitor node which supports performance measurements, a communication node for the connection to the second bus level (the SUPRENUMBUS), and a spare computing node for fault tolerance reasons.

As shown in Figure 1, 16 of these clusters are connected by a matrix of serial high-speed SUPRENUMBUSes (280 Mbit/s) and form the *high performance kernel.* The *SUPRENUM-prototype* is completed by a front end system which is used for operating and maintaining the high performance kernel as well as for software developement.

3 A software concept based on message-passing

For MIMD multiprocessor computers with local memory, a software concept has turned out to be suitable that is based on a *process* system and on a *message-passing communication* handling. The process concept for SUPRENUM (the so-called *abstract SUPRENUM architecture*) is a dynamic one which is characterized by the following elements:

- Processes are autonomous program units which run in parallel.
- Processes can terminate themselves and can create but not terminate other processes.
- Processes communicate only by exchange of messages, and no shared memory is available.
- Applications are started by one initial (or host) process typically running on the front end machine.
- In arithmetic expressions and communication instructions, array constructs are especially supported.
- The user defined process system is homogeneous and independent from the actual hardware configuration. The two-level architecture (cluster structure) is not reflected in the abstract SUPRENUM architecture and is completely transparent to the user. The processes are mapped to the clusters and nodes at run-time.

Figure 2 shows, that this abstract SUPRENUM architecture is the central model in the system software. The user should write his codes only in terms of processes.

The mapping of processes to nodes is supported by the *mapping-library.* It provides optimal mapping startegies for some standard process systems (like trees, rings, grids) and uses heuristical strategies for irregular process structures.

The SUPRENUM *operating sytem* consists of three components residing on the front end system, the cluster level and on the node level. The front end system is operated under UNIX V[1]. On the cluster level the operating system supports the local disk, the performance analysis and the connection between the two communication levels. In each node a small operating system (PEACE) is responsible for the process scheduling and the message handling.

The *programming language* for numerical computations is SUPRENUM-FORTRAN, an extended FORTRAN 77. The extensions include special process handling and message-passing constructs and an array syntax formulation according to the proposed FORTRAN-8X standard. Additionally Concurrent Modula-2 and a parallel version of C will be available.

[1]registered trademark of AT&T

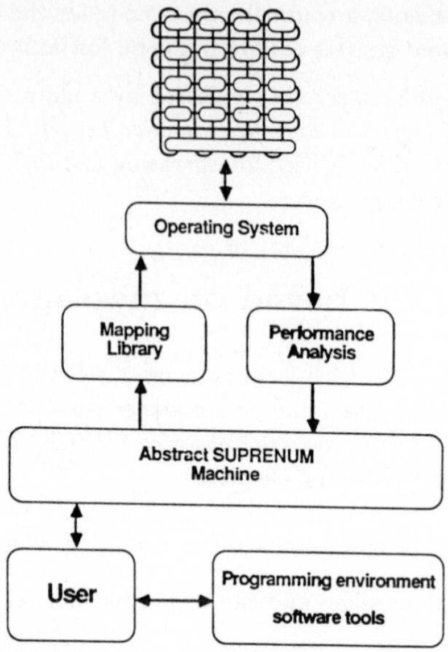

Figure 2: The SUPRENUM system software

Performance analysis tools will collect performance data from each cluster for graphical presentation. This enables the user to analyze the utilization of nodes and buses and to tune his parallel programs.

The SUPRENUM *programming environment* will provide a lot of tools which support the programmer in developing parallel software. Here, the syntax-directed editor, the communication library (see below), a SUPRENUM-simulator [16], an auto-vectorizer for SUPRENUM-FORTRAN and a visualization package for parallel program execution should be mentioned.

4 Grid partitioning

In Section 1 we have considered standard parallel MG algorithms which are highly parallel. However, if they are implemented on real vector or parallel computers, it usually is not possible to fully exploit their parallelism.

By the pipeline processors in vector computers for instance, only a low degree of parallelism can be achieved; and even highly parallel multiprocessor computers always have a certain limited number of simultaneoulsy working processing elements (say P). Nevertheless, the high degree of parallelism in the algorithms is useful or even necessary for several reasons. Firstly, it is preferable to construct algorithms which independently of P can be used on any parallel machine. Secondly, the full performance of vector units can usually be achieved the better the longer the occurring vectors are, i.e. the higher the degree of parallelism offered by the algorithm is. Finally, the recently designed high performance MIMD multiprocessor computers (like SUPRENUM) combine the – global – MIMD structure with – local – SIMD pipeline processing (vector floating point units) in each node. For such MIMD/SIMD systems, the MIMD and the SIMD degrees of parallelism are *multiplied* and have to be provided by the implemented algorithm.

We would like to emphasize that the communication problem in MIMD multiprocessor computers with local private memory has essential algorithmical implications. Since for such systems one has to make a decision about the interconnection structure of the nodes, this structure defines a "neighborhood" and by that, a topology of the nodes in a natural way. In the design of the algorithms this topology has to be taken into regard: Apart from the (sufficiently high degree of) parallelism that has to be provided by the algorithms, as a second important property "locality" of the algorithms of the algorithms with respect to the given topology is required. This means that the amount of data which have to be communicated, the number of communication packages, and the distances which have to be run through in the architecture become of essential significance.

If grid applications are to be implemented on MIMD multiprocessor computers, a straightforward approach is to use *grid partitioning* [26,19,23]. For all methods, single grid and MG, this means that the original domain is split into P parts (subdomains) in such a way that, with respect to the finest grid, each subdomain consists of (roughly) the same number of grid points (see Figure 3). Each subdomain is then assigned to one of the P processes of the parallel program. The partitioning generates certain artificial boundaries within the original domain.

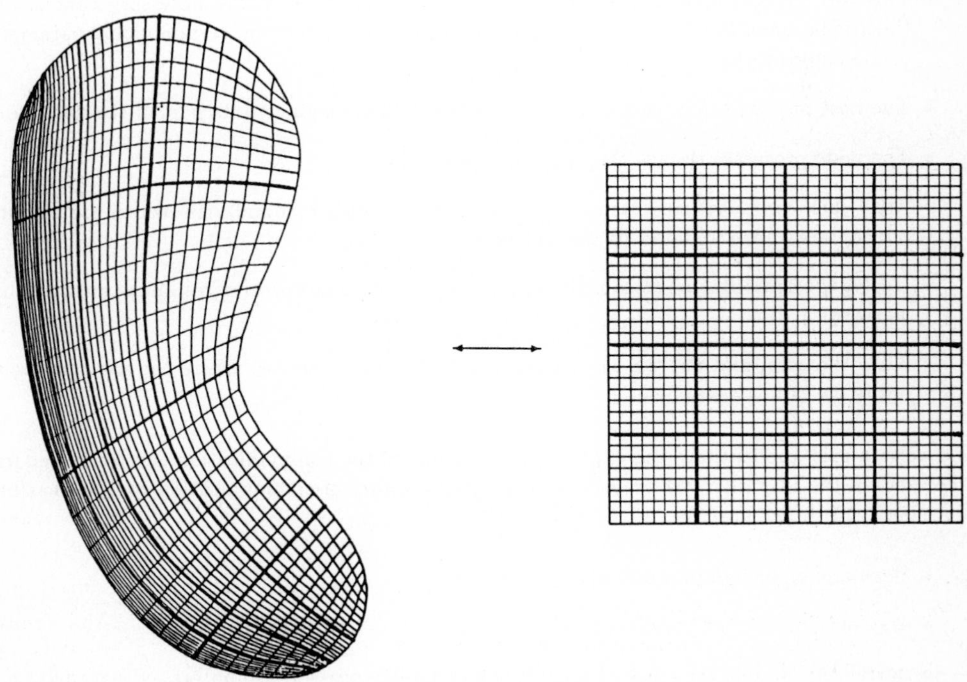

Figure 3: 2D-grid partitioned into 16 logically rectangular subdomains.

If we consider a typical component of a parallel grid algorithm, e.g. a parallel relaxation step, we see that on each subdomain this relaxation step can be carried out independently, provided all necessary data are available. Because of the only local dependencies of the grid points, each process needs foreign data only from boundary areas of neighboring subdomains. After the step is performed, again data have to be communicated (exchanged) along the artificial boundaries.

The extension of the single grid case to parallel MG is obvious: On the finest grid level, all communication is a strictly local one. Similarly, also on the coarser grids necessary communication is "local" relatively to the corresponding grid level (i.e. neighborhood is defined with respect to the grid level).

One should distinguish the grid partitioning approach as sketched above from the decomposition [5] or substructuring methods [1] which are often considered in connection with finite element discretizations on parallel computers. The decomposition and substructuring methods lead to algorithms which are numercially different from the undecomposed or sequential version. In contrast to that, parallel algorithms based on grid partitioning are algorithmically equivalent to their non-partitioned versions (running on sequential computers) as the results of the partitioned and the non-partitioned versions are identical.

For the simple grid partitioning approach only static features of the process concept (as described in the previous section) are needed.

Parallel programs on SUPRENUM and on similar machines typically have the following structure:

- The host process creates the set of processes and sends them the necessary control data (identification of their "neighbors", index range of the subdomain, certain global parameters of the algorithm).
- The host process sends each process the initial data belonging to its part of the domain.
- The node processes receive the initial information.
- After each computational step the points near the interior boundaries (which are stored in *overlap areas*) are updated by mutual exchange of data.
- During the computation certain globally needed results (like norms of residuals) are assembled treewise.
- After the computation, the results are sent to the host process, where the solution for the entire domain is assembled.

For certain grid applications, the explicit programming of the communication can be hidden from the user. In the SUPRENUM project, for example, a library of communication routines has been developed [15] which ensures

- clean and error-free programming,
- easy development of parallel codes,
- portability within the class of local memory multiprocessor computers. Programs can be ported to any of these machines as soon as the communication library has been implemented.

Good experiences have been made in porting programs from the Intel iPSC to the SUPRENUM simulation system and vice versa. A corresponding library for block-structured (see below) applications is currently under development. Most of the application software, which is written in the SUPRENUM project, will be based on these routines.

5 Some multigrid results

If a certain program is implemented on the multiprocessor architecture the central question is how much faster the calculations can be executed here than on a single processor.

This is measured by the *multiprocessor speed-up*

$$S(N,P) = \frac{T(N,1)}{T(N,P)}$$

($T(N,P)$ = execution time for the parallel algorithm for a problem of size N on P nodes).

As usual, we furthermore define the *multiprocessor (MP)-efficiency*

$$E(N,P) = \frac{S(N,P)}{P}$$

Usually E is essentially < 1. Reasons for MP-efficiency losses are:

- The algorithm may not be totally parallelizable.
- The amount of work given to each processor is not balanced.
- The algorithm requires communication. (Start-up time for the initialization of communication is needed as well as transfer time for each item of the message.)
- Additional overhead is necessary for organization (handling of loops, general decisions, etc.).

(Note that the quantity E gives *no* information about the quality of an algorithm – its efficiency in the common sense – at all. It only says something about its parallelizability. A numerically totally inefficient algorithm may be optimally "MP-efficient".)

Example 1:

The 3D-Poisson MG-solver has been implemented on the CalTech Mark II hypercube [26]. Multiprocessor efficieny rates are given in Table 1. Obviously, the problem with $N = 8^3$ grid points is too small for a system with $P = 32$ nodes. However, already medium-sized problems with $N = 32^3$ grid points achieve an MP-efficiency of more than 50%.

N	time	$S(N,32)$	$E(N,32)$
8^3	0.306	6.8	0.21
16^3	0.847	12.4	0.39
32^3	3.370	18.6	0.58

Table 1: Computing time, MP-speed-up and MP-efficiency for a multigrid method for the 3D-Poisson equation with periodic boundary conditions using V-cycle with $\nu_1 = 2, \nu_2 = 1$ relaxations.

Table 2 gives a comparison of the MG-solver with a standard relaxation solver and with a FFT solver. With respect to MG, one has to be aware that on (very) coarse grids the following phenomena occur:

- The number of processors exceeds the number of grid points in some dimension. Some of the subdomains contain no grid point on coarse levels.
- The volume/surface ratio is getting smaller as the grids get coarser. On message passing parallel systems the communication time may dominate the computing time thus leading to inefficient algorithms.
- Since the messages become shorter on coarser grids the "start-up" time which is necessary to initialize exchange of surfaces of subgrids becomes more important.

These are the reasons for the worse MP-efficiency of MG algorithms. There are, of course, ways to come around this difficulty. The parallel MG implemetation (but not necessarily the parallel MG algorithm) which runs on the finer grids may be modified when the computation proceeds to the very coarse grids. A possible coarse grid strategy is:

Collect all coarse grid points to fewer and fewer processes as the coarsening proceeds. Although the numerical work per process is increased and unbalanced, a lot of communication time can be saved. This *agglomeration* strategy is included in the communication library and causes no additional work for the user. Detailed investigations [24] show that – depending on the ratio of communciation versus calculation times – the correct coarse grid treatment may be crucial for the MP-efficiency.

method	time	$S(32^3, 32)$	$E(32^3, 32)$
relaxation	381.3	25.9	0.81
MG	3.4	18.6	0.58
FFT	22.0	29.8	0.93

Table 2: Computing time, MP-speed-up and MP-efficiency for different solvers applied to the 3D-Poisson equation with periodic boundary conditions and $N = 32^3$ grid points.

Although the MP-efficiency of the relaxation and the FFT solver is considerably better than for the MG-solver, the absolute computing time is essentially worse. So both, MP- *and* numerical efficiency are important in designing good algorithms for multiprocessor systems.

Example 2:

The 2D-Stokes MG solver (see Section 1) has been implemented on the Intel iPSC. Figure 4 shows the MP-efficiency rates in relation to the number of processors and the problem size. For a 64-hypercube, a problem size of $N = 256^2$ grid points is necessary in order to achieve an efficiency of more than 50%.

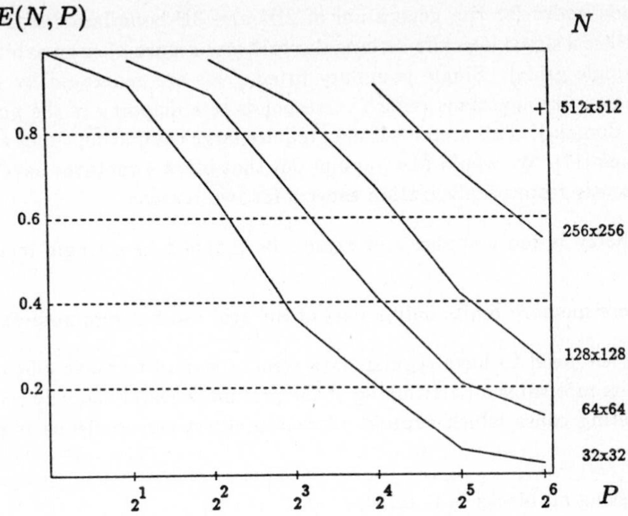

Figure 4: Parallel MG-code for the 2D-Stokes problem. Each curve shows the MP-efficiency for constant problem size N and increasing P.

6 Further applications in the SUPRENUM project

In the near future (up to 1988), the following CFD models will be implemented on the Suprenum computer.

- (Nonlinear) Potential equation for subsonic and transonic flow past airfoils. A Finite Volume (FV) discretization is used and a special relaxation is applied at grid points near the shock front (transonic case). This causes an inhomogeneous load distribution over the grid and special care has to be taken in order to avoid load unbalancing.
- Euler equations for 3D-computations employing advanced acceleration techniques. The system of equations is discretized by a FV scheme on a non-staggered grid. The stationary problem is solved by marching in pseudo time-steps (explicit Runge-Kutta method). The time marching can be viewed at as a Jacobi-type relaxation which is accelerated using coarser time-steps in a MG-like manner [28].
- Euler equations combined with boundary layer methods for the 2D- and 3D- simulation of flow past cars;
- Navier-Stokes equations (incompressible and compressible) for internal flows on general 2D- and 3D-domains. This is the most complex application imposing additional requirements on discretization, MG components and grid refinement strategies.
- Navier-Stokes (compressible) for the full simulation of the flow past cars (3D). This code allows also the simulation of large wake area which is impossible with Euler-/boundary layer methods.

- Grid generation codes for the generation of 2D- and 3D-boundary fitted grids. The grid structure is either a single logically rectangular grid (see Figure 3) or an arbitrary aggregation of blocks (=single grids). Single boundary fitted grids are generated by the solution of a system of Poisson-like equations (which corresponds to a mapping of the physical domain to a rectangular domain). This step itself may require large computing times and can be solved by MG methods [17]. We would like to point out that block structures have been introduced also independently from parallelization aspects for two reasons:

  - the geometry is too complex and cannot be mapped to a single rectangle (L-shaped domain)
  - due to core memory limits only a part of the grid can be computed at a time.

  In both cases the need to have regular data structures and to make efficient use of vector processing units motivates a partitioning of the grid into several logically rectangular blocks. Therefore existing codes which support block structures can easily be parallelized, in two steps:

  (1) by processing all blocks in parallel;

  (2) by parallelizing each block with respect to an overall balanced process size (load balancing).

In addition to the CFD codes, some selected simulation problems with huge computing time requirements will be implemented on Suprenum. These include particle simulation codes and nuclear reactor core simulations [6].

References

[1] Bjørstad, P.E., Widlund, O.B.: *Iterative methods for the solution of elliptic problems on regions partitioned into substructures.* SIAM J. Numer. Anal. 23, 6, 1986.

[2] Brandt, A.: *Multigrid techniques: 1984 guide with applications to fluid dynamics.* GMD-Studie No. 85, 1984.

[3] Brandt, A.: *Multigrid solvers on parallel computers.* In "Elliptic Problem solvers (M. Schultz, ed.)", Academic Press, New York, 1981.

[4] Braess, D., Hackbusch, W., Trottenberg, U. (eds.): *Advances in Multigrid methods.* Proceedings of the Conference Held in Oberwolfach, December, 8-13, 1984. Notes on Numerical Fluid Mechanics, Vol. 11, Vieweg, Braunschweig, 1984.

[5] Dihn, Q.V., Glowinski, R., Periaux, J.: *Solving elliptic problems by domain decomposition methods with applications.* In "Elliptic Problem Solvers II (G. Birkhoff and A. Schoenstadt, eds.)", Academic Press, New York, 1984, pp. 395-426.

[6] Finnemann H., Volkert, J.: *Parallel multigrid solvers for the neutron diffusion equation.* Proceedings of the International Topical Meeting on Advances in Reactor Physics, Mathematics and Computation, Paris, April, 27-30, 1987.

[7] Frederickson, P.O., McBryan, O.: *Parallel superconvergent multigrid.* Cornell Theory Center Technical Report CTC87TR12 7/87.

[8] Gannon, D.B., Rosendale, J,R. van: *Highly parallel multigrid solvers for elliptic PDEs: An experimental analysis.* Report 82-36, ICASE, NASA Langley Research Center, Hampton, VA, 1978.

[9] Giloi, W.K., Mühlenbein, H.: *Rationale and concepts for the Suprenum supercomputer architecture.* GMD, St. Augustin 1985.

[10] Greenbaum, A.: *A multigrid method for multiprocessors.* Appl. Math. Comp. 19, pp. 75–88, 1986.

[11] Grosch, C.E.: *Performance analysis of Poisson solvers on array computers.* Report TR 79-3, Old Domion University, Norfork, VA, 1979.

[12] Grosch, C.E.: *Poisson solvers on large array computer.* Proceedings 1978 LANL Workshop on vector and parallel processors (B.L. Buzbee and J.F. Morrison, eds.), 1978.

[13] Hackbusch, W., Trottenberg, U. (eds.): *Multigrid methods. Proceedings of the Conference held at Köln-Porz, November 23-27, 1981.* Lecture Notes in Mathematics Vol. 960, Springer, Berlin, 1982.

[14] Hackbusch, W., Trottenberg, U. (eds.): *Multigrid methods II. Proceedings of the 2nd Conference on Multigrid Methods, Cologne, Oct. 1-4, 1985.* Lecture Notes in Mathematics Vol. 1228, Springer, Berlin, 1986.

[15] Hempel, R., Schüller, A.: *Vereinheitlichung und Portabilität paralleler Anwendersoftware durch Verwendung einer Kommunikationsbibliothek.* Arbeitspapiere der GMD, Nr. 234, GMD, St. Augustin, 1986.

[16] Limburger, F., Scheidler, Ch., Tietz, Ch., Wessels, A.: *Benutzeranleitung des SUPRENUM-Simulationssystems SUSI.* GMD, St. Augustin, 1986.

[17] Linden, J., Stüben, K.: *Multigrid methods: An overview with emphasis on grid generation processes.* Arbeitspapiere der GMD Nr. 207, GMD, St. Augustin, 1986.

[18] McBryan, O.: *Numerical computation on massively parallel hypercubes.*, to appear.

[19] McBryan, O., Van de Velde, E.: *The multigrid method on parallel processors.* In [14].

[20] McCormick, S.F. (ed.): *Proceedings of the 2nd International Multigrid Conference, April 1985, Copper Mountain.* Appl. Math. Comp. Vol. 19, North Holland,1986.

[21] Niestegge, A., Stüben, K.: *A parallel multigrid method for the Stokes problem.* GMD-Arbeitspapier, GMD, St. Augustin , to appear.

[22] Peinze, K., Thole, C.A., Thomas, B., Werner, K.H.: *The SUPRENUM prototyping programme.* Suprenum-Report 5, SUPRENUM GmbH, Bonn, 1987.

[23] Rice, J.: *Parallel methods for PDEs.* Report CSD-TR-587, Purdue Univercity, West Lafayette, Indiana, 1986.

[24] Solchenbach, K.: *Parallel multigrid methods: Efficient coarse grid techniques.* Suprenum-Report, SUPRENUM GmbH, Bonn, to appear.

[25] Stüben, K., Trottenberg, U.: *Multigrid methods: Fundamental algorithms, model problem analysis and applications.* In [13]

[26] Thole, C.A.: *Experiments with multigrid methods on the CalTech-hypercube.* GMD-Studie Nr. 103, GMD, St. Augustin, 1985.

[27] Thole, C.A., Trottenberg, U.: *A short note on standard parallel multigrid algorithms for 3D-problems.* Suprenum-Report 3, SUPRENUM GmbH, Bonn, 1987.

[28] Wagner, B., Leicher, S., Schmidt, W.: *Applications of a multigrid finite volume method with Runge-Kutta time integration for solving the Euler and Navier-Stokes equations.* In GMD-Studie 110 (U. Trottenberg, W. Hackbusch, eds.), GMD, St. Augustin, 1986.

USING MEMORY IN THE CEDAR SYSTEM

Robert E. McGrath
Perry A. Emrath

Center for Supercomputing Research and Development
University of Illinois at Urbana-Champaign
104 South Wright Street
Urbana, Illinois 61801, USA

ABSTRACT

The design of the virtual memory system for the Cedar multiprocessor under construction at the University of Illinois is discussed. The Cedar architecture features a hierarchy of memory, some shared by all processors, and some shared by subsets of processors. The Xylem operating system is based on Alliant Computer Systems CONCENTRIX™ operating system, which is based on 4.2BSD UNIX™. Xylem supports multi-tasking and demand paging of parts of the memory hierarchy into a linear virtual address space. Memory may be private to a task or shared between all the tasks. The locality and attributes of a page may be modified during the execution of a program. Examples of how these mechanisms can be used are discussed.

1. Introduction

One of the problems faced by designers of shared-memory parallel processing computer systems is providing memory systems that are fast enough to satisfy the processors' request rate. One method of doing this is to use a hierarchy of memories. In fact, memory hierarchies have been utilized since the earliest days of electronic computing. In the past, this need has been dictated primarily by cost factors. One simply could not afford to build a large fast memory and had to settle for backing storage on magnetic drums or disks.

Today, cost is still a factor, but achieving the best possible speed at any cost is also coming into play. In a large parallel processor, the complexity of the connection network between processors and main memory, and the amount of memory needed by such a system, leads to a memory that is necessarily slower than can be achieved by a smaller non-shared memory. By using a hierarchy of memories, some local and fast, some global and slower, a parallel processor should be able to achieve better performance than one with just (slower) global memory. This, however, leads to the problem of how to program a parallel processor with a memory

This work was supported in part by the National Science Foundation under Grant Nos. US NSF DCR84-10110 and US NSF DCR84-06916, the U. S. Department of Energy under Grant No. US DOE-DE-FG02-85ER25001, and the IBM Donation.

hierarchy in order to achieve better performance [Kuck 1978, Hockney and Jesshope 1981, Hwang and Briggs 1984].

A parallel processor system, called Cedar, is being designed and implemented at the University of Illinois [Kuck et al. 1986]. One of the key architectural aspects of this system is the memory hierarchy and connection network. In addition to building a prototype, work is progressing on the development of an operating system, compilers, and applications.

This paper focuses on the operating system support for the Cedar memory system, as seen from the programmer's point of view. The next section provides an overview of the Cedar hardware, operating system, and programming model provided by the O/S. Section three defines the attributes of memory used by a program. The following section describes the structure of program object modules and executable files. The fifth section presents the dynamic (run-time) control of memory attributes and section six outlines two programming examples demonstrating the use and modification of memory attributes.

2. The Cedar System

The architecture of the Cedar system is based on a hierarchical main memory and the notion of processor clusters [Gajski et al. 1984]. Each cluster of processors has its own memory shared by all the processors in the cluster. In addition, every processor has access to the *global memory* via a packet-switched shuffle-exchange connection network [Lawrie 1975, Siegel 1985, Yew 1986, Zhu and Yew 1987]. Figure 1 illustrates the prototype Cedar memory hierarchy.

Each cluster, consisting of processors and cluster memory, is a modified version of the Alliant FX/8 multiprocessor[1] [Alliant 1986]. The interface to each processor, the interconnection network, and the global memory are being designed and built at the University of Illinois. The fact that disk drives are connected to cluster memories in the prototype is a result of using a single building block for the clusters. The global memory is the primary means of inter-cluster communication. Synchronization primitives have been designed into this memory to provide a variety of atomic operations [Zhu and Yew 1987].

The addressing mechanism is quite conventional. Address translations are performed by each processor using page tables stored in memory, where each page can effectively be marked invalid or protected (not writable). The physical address of a page determines whether a reference is to cluster memory or global memory. As a result, it is possible for every processor to be using a different page table, and any arbitrary page of a processor's virtual address

1. Alliant, FX/8, and Concentrix are trademarks of Alliant Computer Systems Corporation.

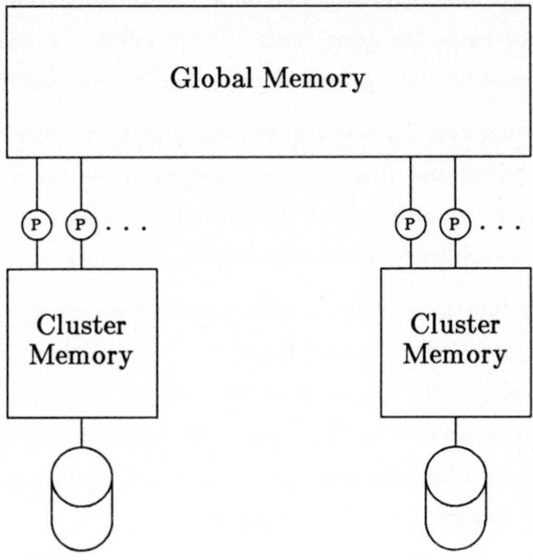

Figure 1. The Cedar memory hierarchy.

space can be mapped to global or cluster memory.

The operating system being developed for the Cedar system is called Xylem, and is based on Alliant's Concentrix operating system, which in turn is based on 4.2BSD Unix[2] [Emrath 1985]. Xylem supports all of Concentrix so that each cluster can operate as a stand alone FX/8, running Concentrix processes within the cluster. In addition, Xylem recognizes a different binary format for programs. When one of these programs is executed, a *Xylem process* is created and becomes known by all the clusters.

A Xylem process consists of one or more *cluster-tasks*. Each cluster-task (or just *task*) executes on one cluster, much like a Concentrix process. When a Xylem process is created, it starts as a single task. Each task may create and control other tasks within its process. There is no hierarchy between the tasks of a Xylem process, whereas Xylem processes are in the same kind of parent–child hierarchy as Unix or Concentrix processes.

Two levels of parallelism are available to a Xylem process. Each task of the process may execute in parallel on a cluster of processors, in the same way that Concentrix processes can execute in parallel as provided by Alliant. In addition, a process may have a task executing

2. Unix is a trademark of AT&T Bell Laboratories.

on each of several clusters. Ideally, all the tasks of a process execute concurrently on different clusters. However, the Xylem kernel (executing on all clusters) may find it necessary to assign multiple tasks from a process to the same cluster. Each physical cluster is time-sliced among all the Xylem tasks assigned to it along with any Concentrix processes in the cluster.

Xylem provides system calls for starting and stopping tasks, and waiting for other tasks to finish. System calls to set and clear *locks* are also available for coarse-grained inter-task synchronization. Any task can also request that an interrupt be sent to another task (in the same process) and have an arbitrary routine executed by that task.

One of the primary functions of Xylem is to provide convenient means for programmers (or compilers) to utilize the Cedar memory hierarchy. Each Xylem task has its own virtual address space, but part of this space may be shared with all the other tasks in the same process while other parts are private to the task. The remaining sections of this paper are devoted to describing the declaration and attributes of a program's address space, both the initial configuration and dynamic (run-time) changes.

3. Memory Attributes

Each cluster-task of a Xylem process has a linear virtual address space made up of fixed size pages.[3] Virtual addresses are 32 bits and point at bytes.[4] Each page of virtual memory is mapped into a page of physical memory by the memory management hardware and the Xylem operating system. Within a task, all the processors of the cluster share the same page tables, and hence the same address space. Each page has several attributes that indicate where and how the page can be accessed. The attributes are adjustable at the page level and the system makes no requirement that all pages with the same attributes be grouped together (i.e. have contiguous addresses). Pages with different attributes can be interspersed throughout the address space of a task.

One of these attributes, *locality*, specifies where in the Cedar memory hierarchy the page should be placed. Pages that are **global** are mapped into page frames of physical global memory. Pages that are **cluster** are mapped into cluster memory. The details of the physical addressing of memory are not visible to a user program. Though pages may be swapped out (to disk or between cluster and global memories), Xylem will always place a page according to its locality attribute when a user program references it.

---

3. In the current implementation, a page is 4096 bytes. This is system specific and may change.

4. Addressing is "left-to-right" in that a pointer to a multi-byte item (e.g. integer) points at the most significant byte of that item.

Another attribute of memory in a Xylem task is whether the page is **shared** or **private**. This attribute indicates how a task logically sees a page. A page that is **private** belongs to a single task within a process. When a task modifies a private page, the modification can be seen only by that task and no others. If another task has a private page at the same virtual address, it will be unchanged. Before a private page is modified, multiple tasks may share a physical copy, but when one task modifies it, a unique copy will be made for that task.

Figure 2 illustrates how **private** memory is mapped. The page at virtual address A has memory attributes **private cluster** (PC) for both tasks 1 and 2 (which belong to the same process). Each task has a distinct page in its local cluster memory. Virtual address B is **private global** (PG) memory, so each task has a unique page of data in the Cedar global memory, mapped at address B.

Pages that are not **private** are **shared**. A **shared** page is shared by *all* the tasks of a Xylem process. Furthermore, such a page must be at the same virtual address in all tasks. Xylem will never map a shared page to different virtual addresses in two tasks. If the page is also **global**, the contents of it can be seen by all tasks, and modifications by one task are immediately visible to the others. When multiple tasks cooperate using shared data,

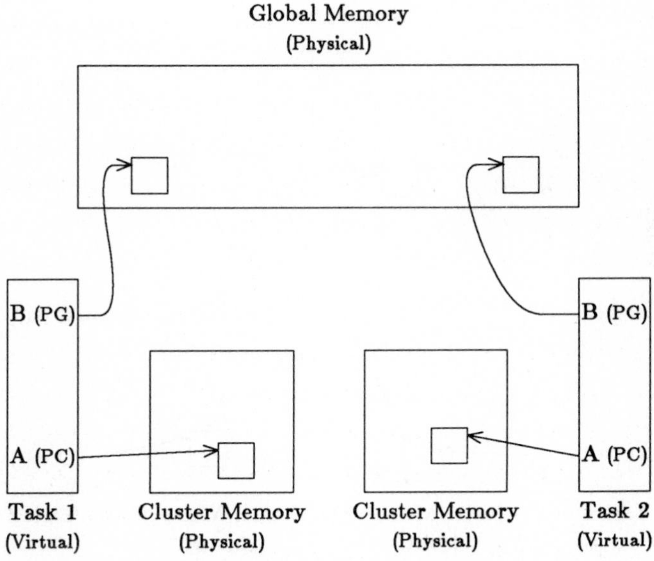

Figure 2. Xylem **private** memory mapping.

synchronization between them is the responsibility of the user program, by using either the hardware or operating system primitives.

Figure 3 illustrates how **shared** memory is mapped. The page at virtual address C has attributes **shared global** (SG), so all tasks in the process have that address mapped to the *same* page of Cedar global memory. The page at virtual address D is shown as **shared cluster**. This is a special case that requires explanation.

If a page is **shared**, the same copy should be seen by all the tasks in a process. A page that is **cluster** should be moved to cluster memory before a task can actually reference it. But two tasks will usually be executing on different clusters, leading to a conflict for **shared cluster** pages. Either the page should be moved back and forth between clusters as it is accessed by the tasks, or multiple copies are made, one in each cluster, and updates to any copy should be broadcast to all the other copies. It should be clear that both of these solutions can lead to inordinate amounts of overhead in the operating system. The overhead can be avoided by allowing the multiple cluster copies to simply become incoherent, but this would create a nightmare for user programs and such a feature would most likely be of little value.

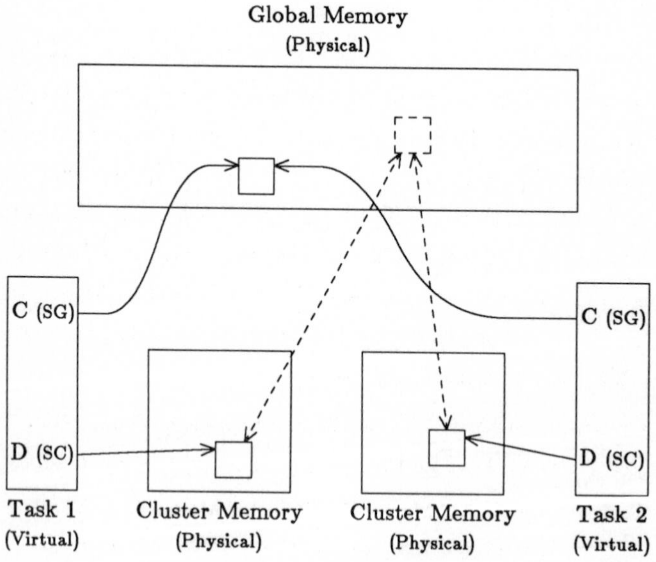

Figure 3. Xylem **shared** memory mapping.

The solution taken by Xylem is to treat **shared cluster** pages in one of two ways, depending on whether the page is writable or not. In either case, a backing page is kept in global memory. If the page is *not* writable, then a copy is brought into cluster memory when the page is referenced, and multiple copies are allowed. Incoherency is not a problem since the page cannot be modified. Normally, program code will fall into this category. If the page *is* writable, then access to the page is restricted to one task. When the first task references a **shared cluster** page that is writable, a copy of the page is brought into the cluster memory for that task, regardless of which task it is. If a second task references that same shared cluster page, the reference will not be allowed and a trap will occur. These traps can be caught by the task causing them if it has supplied Xylem with the address of a subroutine to be executed in such an event. Use of this feature will be demonstrated and discussed in section 5.

When a task starts, its memory map is initialized so that it has access to copies of all **private** pages that are declared in the program image. These private pages have initial contents specified by the program. The structure of program images will be described in the next section. When a task is started by another task, the **private** pages of the start*er* are *not* copied to or accessible by the start*ee*. In addition, the started task will have access to all of the **shared** pages in the process, since these are always accessible by all tasks in a process. Note that partially shared pages (i.e., pages accessible to multiple, but not all, tasks in a process) are not supported by Xylem.

Access to a page can be restricted through use of the *read*, *write*, and *execute* permission attributes.[5] Normally, these are used to protect program code from accidentally modifying itself or attempting to execute data. However, we will see later how these attributes may be used in other situations. If a task executing on a cluster attempts a memory access which is denied, a trap will occur. As with "shared cluster" traps, these can be caught by the task if it has supplied Xylem with a subroutine address. A **shared** page may have only one set of protection attributes. For example, it is not possible for one task to have read-only access to a **shared** page while another task has read-write access to the same page. Although supported by the hardware, Xylem imposes this restriction.

In summary, each cluster-task of a Xylem process has a virtual address space, some of which is fully shared with all the other tasks in its process, the rest being strictly private (or undefined). Each virtual page (shared or private) may be mapped to global memory or cluster memory, and may be protected against write, execute, or read (data) access.

5. The hardware does not support pages that are writable but not readable. This could be handled in kernel software, but there is currently no plan to have Xylem do so.

4. Program Construction

The binary image of a Xylem program consists of one or more *sections*. The Xylem assembler, *xas*, supports the definition of sections, the assignment of attributes to sections, and the placement of data in sections. The Xylem linker, *link*, constructs an executable version of a program, merging sections from separately compiled modules, resolving inter-module references, and assigning virtual addresses. The following text discusses Xylem *sections*, how *xas* defines them, and how *link* manipulates them. Most programmers will use a language translator, such as Cedar FORTRAN [CSRD 1986], and will not have to deal directly with the mechanisms described here. Many of the ideas and techniques used in our implementations are not new and variations can be found in many other systems [e.g. DEC 1984 and Cray 1986]. However, some aspects are specific to the Cedar Architecture and Unix compatibility.

4.1. Sections

A Xylem program object module describes the initial virtual address space for that module. This description involves partitioning the address space into *sections*. A *section* is a contiguous page-aligned area of virtual memory. Each section is given a name and attributes. In assembly language, this would be done by the programmer. For higher level languages, this would probably be handled by the compiler. The attributes of a section will determine whether the data in it is **shared** or **private**, whether the data is to be stored in **global** or **cluster** memory, and what access restrictions apply to the section. Each section may be wholly or partially initialized with data. Uninitialized memory will be filled with zeros.

The programmer (or compiler) assigns the attributes of a data item by placing it in a section with the desired attributes. Since the order of sections may be altered by the assembler and/or the linker, one cannot assume that two variables declared in adjacent sections in the program will be adjacent in the virtual address space. Similarly, two items declared in different sections may end up adjacent in the address space. If an item needs to be kept separate from others, or must be page aligned, it may be put in a separate section.

4.2. The Xylem assembler

Sections and their attributes may be defined using the Xylem assembler, *xas* [McDaniel 86]. Figure 4 summarizes the **.section** directive, which is used to define a section and assign its attributes. All *xas* instructions and data that occur after a **.section** directive (until the next one) are placed in the section of that name. The same section may be used in several places in the same source file and in several files that are later linked into a single program.

.section *name, attribute-list*

name is the identifier for the section. Code following this directive is appended to section *name.*

attribute-list specifies the attributes of the section, these being:

shared or **private**
global or **cluster**
read or **noread**
write or **nowrite**
noexecute or **execute**
append or **common**

Default attributes are those to the left.
Attributes must not conflict when re-entering a section.

Figure 4. Summary of the assembler **.section** directive.

All the data of a section in one source file is collected into a single, continous block by the assembler. *Xas* produces a "relocatable" file that may contain unresolved references and addresses defined relative to the beginning of sections.

Figure 5 gives an example of some assembler source code including **.section** directives, and shows the placement of this code in the object module. Section *s1* is used in two places in the source and the assembler combines these two pieces of code into one section. The order of data within a section is determined by the source, but the order of sections in the relocatable file is unspecified and is determined by the assembler.

4.3. The Xylem linker

The Xylem linker, *link*, constructs a single file in executable format from one or more relocatable files. If a section name appears in more than one of the relocatable files, it refers to the *same* section. The linker will consolidate all parts of a section into a single continuous area of virtual memory. Sections with the same name from each file are concatenated[6] to make a single larger section. All the relative references to the original sections are adjusted to account for their new position in the combined section. The consolidated sections are assigned

6. A section may be declared *common*, in which case sections with the same name from separate object modules will be overlaid.

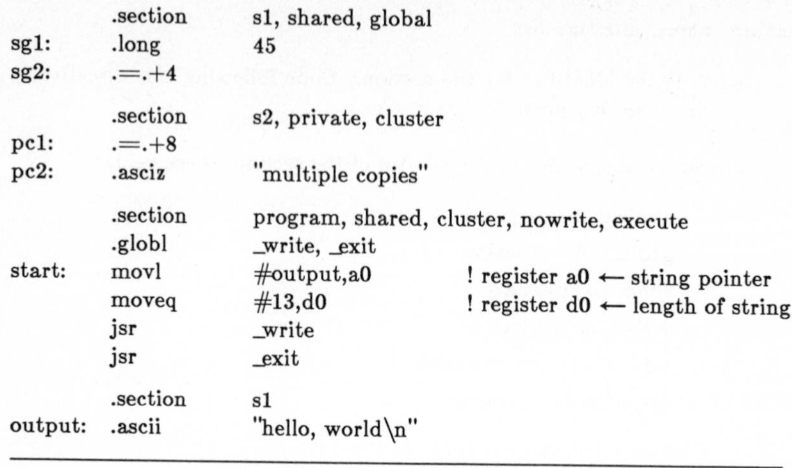

```
         .section    s1, shared, global
sg1:     .long       45
sg2:     .=.+4

         .section    s2, private, cluster
pc1:     .=.+8
pc2:     .asciz      "multiple copies"

         .section    program, shared, cluster, nowrite, execute
         .globl      _write, _exit
start:   movl        #output,a0        ! register a0 ← string pointer
         moveq       #13,d0            ! register d0 ← length of string
         jsr         _write
         jsr         _exit

         .section    s1
output:  .ascii      "hello, world\n"
```

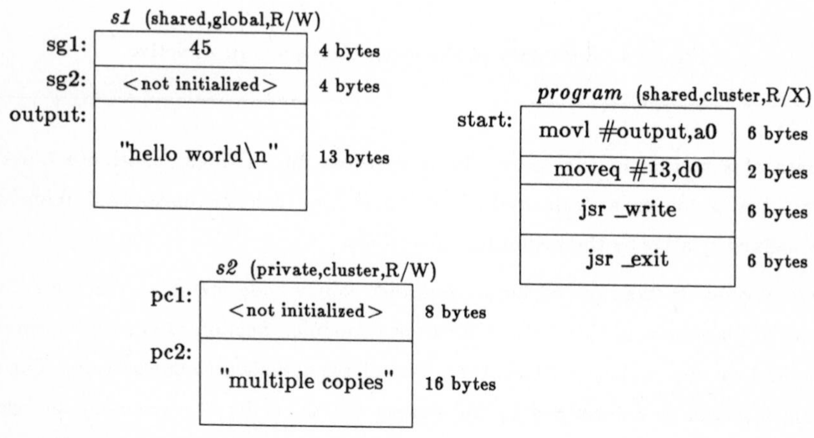

Figure 5. Example *xas* source code input and resulting sections.

absolute, page-aligned addresses and relative addresses are converted to absolute. The order of placement of sections in memory and their address assignments are determined by the linker and cannot be controlled by the user.

Figure 6 illustrates how the linker combines relocatable files. In the example, two relocatable files, **prog1.o** and **prog2.o**, are linked to create the executable file **program**. Figure 6(a) shows that **prog1.o** has four sections, named *prog, sub1, dataA*, and *dataB*. **Prog2.o** is shown as having four sections called *prog, sub2, dataB*, and *dataC*. Figure 6(b) shows the result of the command

link prog1.o prog2.o -o program

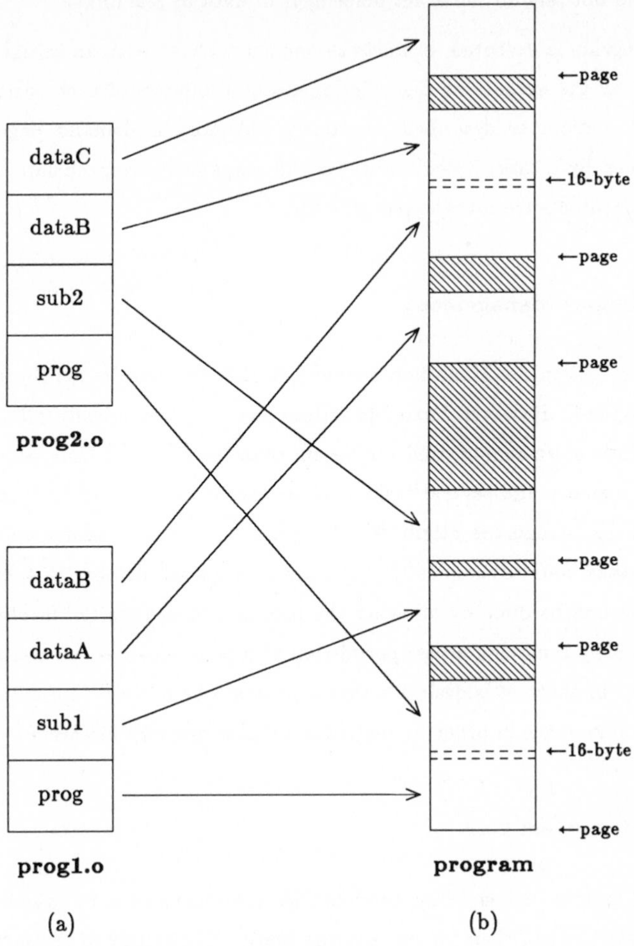

Figure 6. Linking object modules to form an executable program.

Sections named *prog* and *dataB* appear in both relocatable files, so the executable file contains one section called *prog* and one called *dataB*. In the executable file, *prog* contains the data from section *prog* in **prog1.o** followed by (on the next 16-byte boundary) the data from section *prog* in file **prog2.o**, and simlarly for section *dataB*.

After the sections are merged (or overlaid) each section is placed at an absolute virtual address, as illustrated in Figure 6(b). A section is guaranteed to start on a page boundary, and pieces of a combined section always start on a 16-byte boundary. In general, the precise order of the data in memory depends on the order of the files in the **link** command, but **link** may re-order the sections or the parts of sections combined from multiple input files. The programmer should not rely on the exact placement of data by the linker.

When the program is executed, it starts as one cluster task with an initial virtual address space as specified by the executable file. The memory attributes of each section apply to all the pages in that section, as described previously. Memory is demand paged, so when an address is referenced by a task, Xylem allocates and maps in the appropriate type of memory and initializes the contents from the executable file.

5. Run-time Memory Management

The preceding section described how memory is allocated and its attributes defined when a program is compiled. However, many programs need to dynamically allocate memory as they execute. This is more complicated for Xylem than for standard Unix, since there is more than one kind of memory and several tasks may be executing in parallel. It may also be useful for a program to change the attributes of a page in memory. Many applications would perform better if they could dynamically cache pages of global memory in cluster memory for faster access. This can be done by allowing the program to change the *locality* of pages as it executes. Temporarily removing access permission of a page may also be useful for debugging or error detection. In short, it is desirable that a program be allowed to manipulate attributes of the virtual memory space in order to control the Cedar memory hierarchy.

5.1. The Memctl System Call

The *memctl* system call is being provided as the mechanism by which programs may manipulate the attributes of their virtual address space. The syntax of the *memctl* call is:

```
memctl( request, address, length )
        int request;
        char *address;
        unsigned int length;
```

The arguments consist of a request code and a range of virtual addresses upon which to apply the requested service. The format of the request field is summarized in Figure 7. Bits 15-8 provide a function specifier while bits 7-0 are attribute values. Each of the currently defined functions will be described in detail. Since a page is the smallest unit of memory with which the operating system can deal, a request will affect those whole pages that include the range given, not just the range itself. Furthermore, the legality and result of the call may depend on the previous attributes of the page(s). This is discussed further below. It is the user

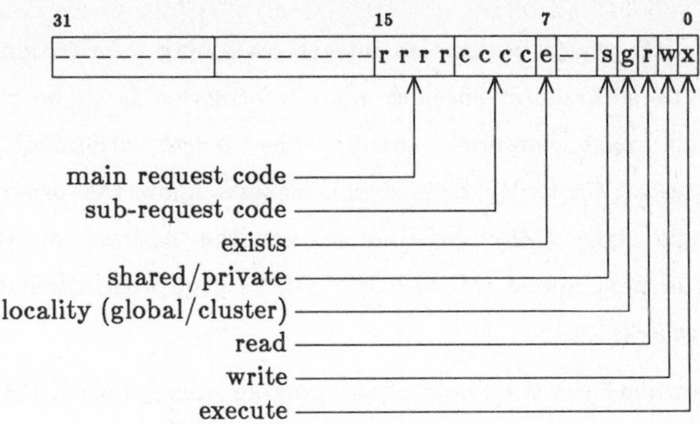

Figure 7. Format of *memctl* request code.

program's responsibility to know what is happening, capture and recover from non-fatal access errors, and to coordinate between multiple tasks.

5.2. Dynamic Allocation of Memory

Many programs wish to allocate memory as they execute. Standard Unix or Concentrix programs may use the *brk* system call to allocate memory at the "end" of the program static data space, growing upward much like a stack. However, Xylem has more than one kind of memory, so a single stack is inadequate and a more complicated mechanism is needed. This section describes the MEM_CREATE and MEM_DELETE requests.

Memory may be allocated using the MEM_CREATE request. This request will allocate pages that include virtual addresses *address* to *address* + *length* – *1*. The attributes of the memory allocated are determined by the value of the lowest byte in the request. If memory has already been allocated in the range, an error is returned. If the allocation succeeds, subsequent references to any of the addresses in the range will be to zero-filled pages of physical memory.

The MEM_DELETE request deallocates memory. Any physical memory mapped to virtual addresses *address* to *address* + *length* – *1* is released and any further access to those pages will result in an addressing error. This request is intended for the freeing of dynamically allocated memory, but in fact could be used to release any part of the program's static address space.

5.3. Manipulation of Memory Attributes

The MEM_INQUIRE request returns an integer containing information about the attributes of memory. The sub-request specifies what information is to be returned, and the *address* indicates the page inquired about. The *length* argument is ignored on MEM_INQUIRE requests. Currently defined sub-requests allow the program to fetch the attributes of a single page (MEM_MODE) or get the address of the next highest (MEM_NEXT_DIFF) or next lowest (MEM_PREV_DIFF) page with attributes different than those of the page at *address*.

Also, the program may get the limits of the program image (MEM_PROGRAM_LIMIT) or the reserved area for the system stacks (MEM_STACK_LIMIT). For these requests, the *address* argument is also ignored. Normally, programs are linked at the low end of the 32-bit address space, and the system places the machine stack near the high end of the address space. (Certain system defined items are placed above the stack.) When the program begins, it is guaranteed that no virtual memory exists between the program limit and the stack limit, so normally the user program should keep dynamic allocations between these limits.

Certain attributes of page(s) may be changed using the MEM_CHANGE request. These are the read, write, and execute permissions and the locality (global or cluster) of the page(s). The sub-request field is a mask of the attributes to be affected and the lowest 4 bits of the request code contain the new attribute values.

If the memory to be manipulated is shared by all tasks, not all attribute changes are allowed. Some changes would potentially result in the existence of multiple versions of the data in the page, an incoherent situation that is not allowed. For instance, enabling write permission of a **shared cluster** page is not allowed if any other task is using the page, that is, if another task currently has a cluster copy of the page. In many cases, these restrictions are made to avoid inter-cluster communications within the system.

5.4. Releasing Access to Shared Memory

The MEM_INVALIDATE request is provided to allow the program to release the local copy of a **shared cluster** page(s) or release access to **shared global** page(s). Cluster pages are written to their global backing copy before the memory is released. This call does not revoke access to the page(s) but merely invalidates the page table entries so that subsequent references are trapped. If an invalidated page is referenced again, it will be copied into cluster memory or the page table will be set to point at the global copy depending on the attributes of the page at the time of the reference. This scheme allows the program to make attribute changes that otherwise would not be allowed. In general, algorithms must synchronize when sharing data, so by using the MEM_INVALIDATE request before the synchronization point, a second synchronization is avoided in the system when the program intends to change the attributes.

6. Examples

Many programs need only one or two kinds of data. Shared data can always be placed in global memory and private data can always be put in cluster memory. But some programs would perform better by using cluster memory as a cache for global memory. Reference to a page of **shared cluster** memory will result in a copy of the data being pulled into the cluster and used there.

This is easy to do for read-only data, but if the data may be modified, coherence should be maintained between all the copies in cluster memories, and this would have to be done by software. The basic problem is to propagate any modifications to any and all cluster copies of the data, or alternatively, to discard all out-dated copies. If the operating system were to trap all writes to such data and flush all out of date copies, the overhead would be too great. Instead, a program can use *memctl* system calls to maintain efficient access to shared pages. Most of this burden can be contained in run-time library routines, providing the Cedar system a degree of flexibility.

This section presents two examples. The first is a program with distinct phases. A large shared data structure is used in quite different ways during each phase, with *memctl* calls being used to change its attributes. The result is a data structure that is "mostly shared", being brought into cluster memory when sharing is not needed and when the data is not being modified.

The second example illustrates a program with an intermittent, unpredictable need to share parts of a data structure. In this case, one task "owns" the data structure, but every once in a while another task needs to share part of it. Signals and *memctl* calls can be used to move a page from cluster memory into global memory where it can be safely shared. When the period of sharing is over, the page can be allowed to come back into cluster memory. The result is a data structure that is "mostly private".

6.1. "Mostly Shared" Data

Consider a program that has two (or more) tasks that execute in parallel on separate clusters. The tasks want to share a large array of data in a regular way. First the array is initialized. Each task computes using various parts of the array and then the array is updated as a whole. The computation and updating phases are synchronized and repeated until some condition is met. The tasks share array AR, but during the computation phase each task only reads various parts of the array. The precise elements used may depend on the data itself. Figure 8 sketches the pattern of accesses for this example.

This program might benefit by having the data be located in global memory during the initialization and update phases, but have the parts used in computation brought into cluster memory for faster access during the computation. This can be done by having the tasks use *memctl* to change the locality and writability attributes of the array AR from **global writable** to **cluster read-only** before entering the computation phase. The tasks synchronize at the end of the computation and use *memctl* to change the attributes back to **global writable** before doing any updating.

Under this plan, array AR is declared **shared global**. All tasks initially share a single copy in global memory, shown in Figure 9. The array may be initialized by a single task, or several tasks might cooperate to each initialize part of the array. After the array is initialized, it is made cacheable in cluster memory with the call

```
memctl( MEM_CHANGE(M_CLUSTER + M_NOWRITE), &AR, sizeof AR );
```

This changes the array from **shared global** to **shared cluster**. Subsequent references to AR will cause the operating system to copy pages into cluster memory. This is shown in Figure 10, where each task is using small parts of the array, and the parts used have been paged into

---

```
DIMENSION AR(1000)
SHARED GLOBAL AR

        Task 1:                                   Task 2:

initialize part of AR                    initialize part of AR

loop                                     loop
    synchronize                              synchronize

    read parts of AR                         read parts of AR
    during computation                       during computation

    synchronize                              synchronize

    update part of AR                        update part of AR
endloop                                  endloop
```

Figure 8. Two tasks (mostly) reading shared data

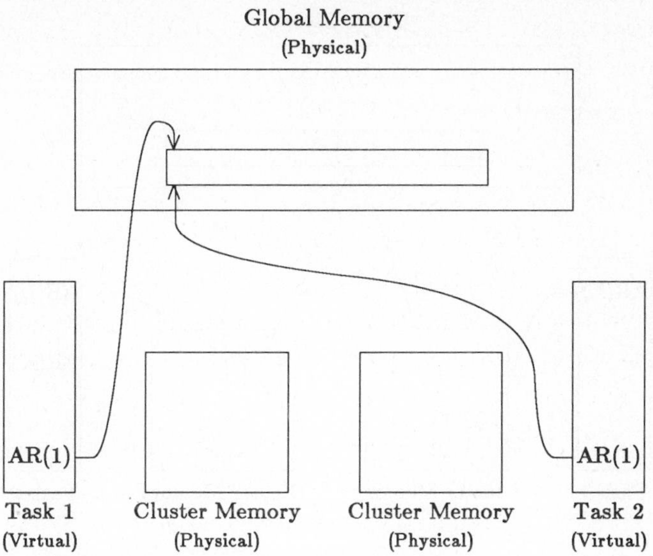

Figure 9. Memory mapping during initialization.

cluster memory by the kernel. There is no coherence problem because the memory is not writable.

After all tasks have finished the computation phase, the global copy of the array is to be updated. As each task completes its computation, it executes

memctl(MEM_INVALIDATE, &AR, sizeof AR);

to cause the pages that were copied into cluster memory to be released.

After all tasks have invalidated, the whole array AR can be made **global writable** again, allowing further modification of AR directly in global memory. This is done with the call

memctl(MEM_CHANGE(M_GLOBAL + M_WRITE), &AR, sizeof AR);

After this call, the array is accessed in global memory, as in Figure 9. The program may now proceed to update AR and re-iterate the sequence or terminate.

This example illustrates some key motivations for the *memctl* system calls. This program could easily run with array AR in global memory all the time. This is reasonable when the array is continuously being shared between all the tasks, but during periods when the array is only being read, better performance may be achieved by caching the array in cluster memory,

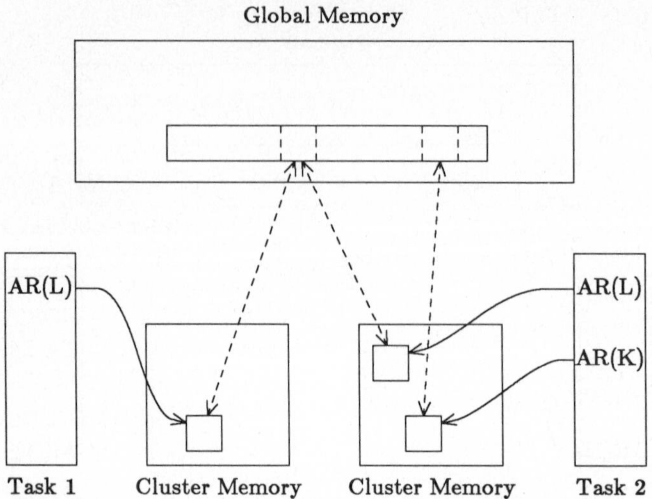

Figure 10. Memory mapping during computation phase.

depending on the actual access pattern.

It is also true that the program itself could copy the array into a buffer in each cluster memory before using it. This would be a waste if only localized parts of the array are actually accessed by any one task. If the parts needed by each task were known by the algorithm or could be determined by the compiler, it would be possible to copy only the part needed. In this example, however, we hypothesize that this is not possible as the exact parts of AR to be used are known only from the input data. Our solution is to change the attributes of the data structure and rely on the virtual memory system to pull just the referenced parts into the cluster.

6.2. "Mostly Private" Data

The second example is a program with two tasks that execute in parallel on two separate clusters. Each task reads and writes in separate areas of memory except for a short "update" period in which a small part of the data used by the other task must be read and written. Figure 11 shows a sketch of the pattern of data accesses by the two tasks. Since there are many reads and writes to the data arrays, it is highly desirable that they be in cluster memory for faster access. Yet, at some points in the program, the data must be accessible to another

```
DIMENSION A(100), B(100)
SHARED CLUSTER A,B

        Task 1:                              Task 2:

initialize A                         initialize B

loop                                 loop
    read and write A many times          read and write B many times

    if (condition) then                  if (condition) then
        read B(J)                            read A(M)
        write B(L)                           write A(N)
    endif                                endif
endloop                              endloop
```

Figure 11. Two tasks that occasionally share data.

task. However, we assume the data elements that will be shared and their frequency of access are determined by the input data.

Because the data in A and B are used by both tasks, they should be shared so that the writes by one task can be seen by the other. That is, when task 1 accesses B, it must see all modifications made by task 2 up to that time. We would like task 2 to be reading and writing B in cluster memory since most references to B are by task 2. When task 1 wants to access B(J), it may not be able to because the current contents of B(J) are in the cluster memory of the other cluster. Figure 12 shows this situation.

There are several possible approaches to this problem. If the "update" times can be determined at compile time, then the data can be kept in **private cluster** memory. The compiler could insert code in task 2 to copy the data to separate **shared global** variables for the update by task 1, synchronize, and then copy the results back to **private cluster** memory. This solution is good if the update times and the precise elements to be modified are known. However, in the case described here, the update of B by task 1 can happen at any time in the program, depending on the data. The update also affects only a small area of data, but the precise elements involved are determined by the data. There is no way for the compiler to know where to insert the code in task 2 to copy the data needed by task 1 into shared global memory.

For this problem, we again want cluster memory to act like a cache for global memory. What can be done by the operating system to provide this? The most conservative strategy would be to keep all copies of the data consistent at all times. This would mean that a master

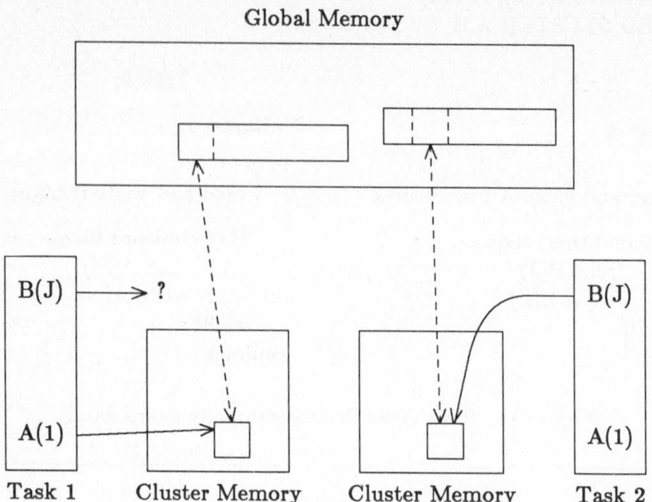

Figure 12. Memory mapping of **shared cluster** data.

copy of the shared cluster data would be maintained in global memory. When array A is modified, the change is made in both the cluster and global memory copies. Other copies are invalidated on all clusters. Unfortunately, this sort of "write-through" must be done by trapping to the operating system, which would have to do the work in software. Worse, the cross-cluster communication required to invalidate out-of-date pages is enormous. If the number of writes is more than miniscule, it would be more efficient to simply put the data in shared global memory.

Could a less conservative strategy be used? The operating system could let the global copy get out of date, and bring it up to date only during the updates when it is needed. Task 2 can read and write array B repeatedly in cluster memory. When task 1 wants to use B, it can be made consistent. The first access to B by task 1 would be trapped by the operating system, the data copied to global memory, and then to the cluster memory of task 1. Unfortunately, after that time both tasks are reading and writing B, so this solution degenerates to the previous. Every subsequent access must be trapped, as both tasks need valid copies.

The problem presented by this example is that there are only a few parts of the program where a few data items must be shared, but that neither the programmer nor the compiler can detect where this may happen. At the point when task 1 accesses array B, we should trap the access, have the data needed from B copied from task 2's cluster memory to global memory, and leave it there where both tasks can share it. Figure 13 shows this arrangement. Eventually, task 1 finishes with the update to B. At that time, ***and no sooner***, we would like to revert to the previous arrangement with B cached in task 2's cluster memory. The global copy of B may again become out of date, and a subsequent reference to B by task 1 would be trapped as before.

There are three critical features of the solution above. First, a page must be temporarily "locked" in global memory, "by-passing" cluster memory and allowing efficient sharing. Second, the page must be "unlocked" and allowed to be cached in cluster memory again. Third, the two actions must occur only at the proper time, the first being done on a memory access trap and the second only at the end of the sharing phase, which is most easily identified explicitly by the program. The *memctl* system call was designed to provide these capabilities.

The MEM_CHANGE request can be used to move page(s) from cluster to global memory. This call must be done by the task that is *using* the page, that is, the one that currently has a cluster copy. When a second task wants to share the data, it interrupts the first to tell it that a needed page should be moved to global memory. To accomplish this, the program is augmented by a trap handling routine and an interrupt handling routine, such as those outlined in Figure 14.

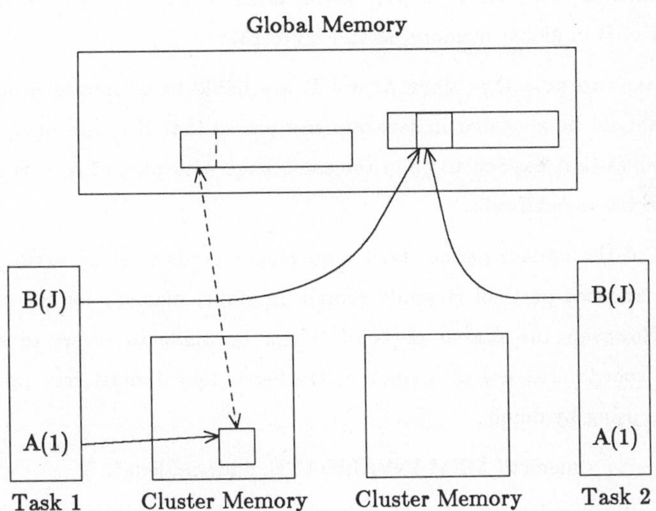

Figure 13. Memory mapping after a "cluster bypass"

```
sc_trap( address, owner ) {
        intr_ctask( owner, bypass, address )
        wait_intr()          /* wait for acknowledgement */
        return
}


bypass( sender, address ) {
        memctl( MEM_CHANGE(M_GLOBAL), address, 1 )
        intr_ctask( sender, NULL, 0 )           /* acknowledge */
        return
}
```

Figure 14. Routines to set up a "cluster bypass".

When task 1 attempts to use B, as in Figure 12, a trap occurs. This trap is caught and processed by the routine *sc_trap*. The kernel provides the trap handler with the address causing the trap and the task that currently "owns" the page. Task 1 then interrupts task 2 with a request to "bypass" cluster memory. Task 2 executes the *bypass* interrupt routine, calling *memctl* to make the page **global**. The system copies the data from cluster memory to global memory and discards the cluster copy. Both tasks 1 and 2 then proceed to use the "bypassed" part of B in global memory, as in Figure 13.

It is important to note that since A and B are liable to be moved around in memory, these variables should be allocated in separate sections so that they are page aligned. Otherwise, other variables that happen to be in the same page with part of A or B might be moved as a side effect of the *memctl* calls.

At the end of the update period, task 1 no longer needs to share array B. If no action were taken, the updated parts of B would remain in global memory for the rest of the life of the program. However, the shared parts of B can be made to revert to **shared cluster** memory by the coordinated use of *memctl* calls. First, task 1 must relinquish access to the parts of B it was using by doing

```
memctl( MEM_INVALIDATE, address, length );
```

where *address* and *length* specify the part of B that was made **global**. This call explicitly releases the page(s) that had actually been shared and makes them eligible to be copied back to task 2's cluster memory. Then task 2 can move the "bypassed" parts of B back to cluster memory by doing memctl(MEM_CHANGE(M_CLUSTER), address, length);

since it is the only remaining task using the page(s). This will cause the page(s) to be brought into cluster memory on the next access. If task 1 needs to share part of B again, then the entire "bypass" operation would be repeated.

The change from **global** back to **cluster** could be done at any time. However, if some other task is using a **global** page, that is, its page table is currently pointing at the global copy of the page, the *memctl* call to change it will leave the page **global** and return an error code. However, the kernel will loop over all the pages in the given range and change as many of them as it can. This avoids having the system communicate with every other cluster in order to invalidate page tables. If the program never invalidates shared pages, they will remain in global memory but the program will still function correctly. In general, the tasks of a program must synchronize anyway and by putting explicit MEM_INVALIDATE requests in the proper places, performance can be improved.

7. Conclusion

The Xylem virtual memory system provides access to the Cedar physical memory hierarchy in a natural and flexible manner. The structure of a Xylem executable file is very general, and is not tightly tied to a particular architecture. The definition of virtual memory to consist of sections which have attributes allows user programs to define and control the location of data items. The notion that some of the memory attributes may be changed during execution allows some sophisticated uses of the memory hierarchy.

Shared memory is easily expressed, facilitating many different models of inter-task communication. A user program may impose whatever structure it needs on its own sharing. For instance, monitors, semaphores, mail boxes, and message passing can be easily implemented using shared memory and Xylem or Cedar synchronization facilities. The Xylem operating system allows the programmer to place data in global memory for sharing or in cluster memory for speed. User programs may explicitly control the placement of data items, or optimizing compilers may seek to take advantage of the memory hierarchy.

The use of sections which have attributes leads naturally to the desire to change attributes during execution. It is not clear that changing between process-shared and task-private is meaningful, but changing the other attributes is reasonable or provides advantages in many cases. As the examples in section 6 indicate, there are applications which are difficult to implement well without allowing attributes of memory to be modified.

An important feature of using the virtual memory system to implement the moving of data between cluster and global memory (or the caching of data in cluster memory) is that the movement is done on a page by page basis rather than variable by variable. It is possible to have one page of an array cached in one cluster while another page of the same array is cached in a different cluster while a third page of the array is being accessed in global memory. The examples illustrate that this can be an advantage when a large data structure is shared by tasks on several clusters.

It should be emphasized that the binding of a page to global or cluster memory is always explicitly controlled by the user program. Furthermore, the kernel does no inter-task communication when changing the binding or access attributes of a page, other than interlocked access to the shared (software) page tables. It is clear that the tasks of a parallel user program must synchronize shared data accesses. By having each task of the user program explicitly invalidate its cluster memory before it synchronizes, as in the first example, the operating system can then change cluster pages to global without doing any inter-task communication. If the cluster invalidation mechanism were left to the kernel, it would have to communicate among all the tasks in order to invalidate cluster pages when changing them to global. Hence, forcing explicit control is potentially more efficient. In any case, inter-task communication costs are incurred at the direction of and only when the program wants them, as in the second example.

This paper has described memory management mechanisms provided by the Xylem operating system. It is important to note that most user programs will not use these mechanisms directly, but rather will use high level languages, such as FORTAN or LISP, and libraries of run time support routines. The mechanisms implemented by Xylem will be used primarily by libraries and compilers, which will provide convenient and appropriate interfaces and services for user programs.

REFERENCES

Alliant Computer Systems Corporation, *FX/Series Architecture Manual.* Part Number 300-00001-B. 1985.

Cray Research, Inc., *CAL Assembler Version 2 Reference Manual.* Doc. SR-2003. 1986.

Center for Supercomputing Research and Development, *Cedar Fortran Reference Manual.* Cedar Document No. 601. University of Illinois, Urbana, IL. 1987.

Digital Equipment Corporation, *VAX/VMS Linker Reference Manual.* Doc. AA-Z420A-TE. 1984.

Emrath, P. A., Xylem: An Operating System for the Cedar Multiprocessor. *IEEE Software*, Volume 2 (4), pp. 30-37. 1985.

Hockney, R. W. and Jesshope, C. R., *Parallel Computers.* Adam Hilger, Bristol. 1981.

Hwang, K. and F. A. Briggs, *Computer Architecture and Parallel Processing.* McGraw-Hill, New York. 1984.

Gajski, D., D. J. Kuck, D. H. Lawrie, and A. S. Sameh, CEDAR – A Large Scale Multiprocessor. *Proceedings of the 1983 International Conference on Parallel Processing.* Belaire, MI. 1983.

Kuck, D. J., *The Structure of Computers and Computations.* Wiley, New York. 1978.

Kuck, D. J., E. S. Davidson, D. H. Lawrie, and A. S. Sameh., Parallel Supercomputing Today and the Cedar Approach. *Science*, Volume 231, pp. 967-974. 1986.

Lawrie, D. H., Access and Alignment of Data in an Array Processor. *IEEE Transactions on Computers*, Volume C-24, pp. 1145-1155. 1975.

McDaniel, T., *Xas Reference Manual.* (Unpublished) Center for Supercomputing Research and Development, University of Illinois, Urbana, IL. 1986.

Siegel, H. J., *Interconnection Networks for Large Scale Parallel Processing.* D. C. Heath, Lexington, MA. 1985.

Yew, P. C., *Architecture of the Cedar Parallel Supercomputer.* CSRD Report 609. Center for Supercomputing Research and Development, University of Illinois, Urbana, Illinois. 1986.

Zhu, C. Q. and P. C. Yew, A Scheme to Enforce Data Dependence on Large Multiprocessor Systems. *IEEE Transactions on Software Engineering*, Vol. SE-13, No. 6, pp. 726-739. 1987.

Another Combining Scheme to Reduce Hot Spot Contention in Large Scale Shared Memory Parallel Computers

Gyungho Lee
The Center for Advanced Computer Studies
University of Southwestern Louisiana
P.O. Box 44330
Lafayette, LA. 70504

Abstract
Concurrent requests to a shared variable by many processors on a shared memory machine can create contention that will be serious enough to stall large machines. This idea has been formalized in the "hot spot" traffic [PfNo85], where a fixed fraction of memory requests is for a single shared variable. "Combining", in which several requests for the same variable can be combined into a single request, has been suggested as an effective method of alleviating the contention. Lee, Kruskal, and Kuck [LeKK86] introduced the idea of "k-way combining", which shows that the effectiveness of combining depends on k, the maximum possible number of requests combined into a single request at a switch. This paper introduces a scheme to remedy k-way combining in order to avoid the contention without incurring impractically large storages in switches of multistage interconnection networks.

1. Introduction

The popularity of shared memory parallel computers, in which processors and memory modules are interconnected through a multistage network, can be seen in several current projects, including the University of Illinois Cedar machine [GKLS83] [KDLS86], the NYU Ultracomputer [GGKM83] [EGKM85], and the IBM RP3 machine [PBGH85]. Sharing the memory in a parallel computer suggests the possibility of concurrent requests, i.e. many processors requesting the same memory location at the same time. We call this kind of shared memory contention due to concurrent requests "hot spot" contention, which intuitively becomes more serious as the *machine size* (i.e. number of processors) increases. In practice, there are many potential sources of hot spot contention, including synchronization to enforce data dependences in order to maintain the given semantics of a program, scheduling or shared queue accesses in operating systems, and programs based on machine models that allow concurrent memory accesses.

To reduce hot spot contention, when several requests directed at the same variable meet at a switch, they may be "combined" into a single request, which is forwarded toward the shared memory. This process will be explained in detail later. Combining has been suggested as an effective way of allowing concurrent requests to a common location. It can be found in the Columbia CHoPP [SuBK77], the NYU Ultracomputer, and most recently the IBM RP3 machine. The Cedar machine at the University of Illinois uses a limited version of combining, in which requests are combined only at the memory modules [ZhYe84].

Recently, Pfister and Norton [PfNo85] brought our attention to hot spot contention by demonstrating, through "hot spot traffic model", how disastrous it can be in large-scale machines. Also, Lee, Kruskal, and Kuck [LeKK86] observed that even with "pairwise combining" suggested for the NYU Ultracomputer and the IBM RP3 machine there is potentially serious contention due to hot spot traffic, and suggested the idea of "k-way ($k > 2$) combining" to remedy pairwise combining. This paper introduces a new combining scheme, called *balanced k-way combining,* to relieve the problem of large buffers and queues in switches with pairwise and k-way combining schemes.

This paper is organized as follows. Models for interconnection network and traffic are introduced in Section 2 and Section 3. The effects of hot spot contention is briefly discussed also in Section 3. In Section 4, some problems inherent in k-way combining, which includes pairwise combining, are discussed. The balanced k-way combining is introduced in Section 5, and its performance is presented in Section 6.

2. Multistage Interconnection Networks

We assume a machine that is built by interconnecting the processors and the memory modules via a buffered rectangular banyan network. Rectangular banyan networks [GoLi73] include Omega networks [Lawr75] and Delta networks [Pate81]. (For details and general characteristics of multistage interconnection networks, see, for example, [Feng81], [KrSn82], [Sieg85].)

A network is composed of n stages of 2×2 (crossbar) switches with FIFO queues (i.e. buffers) at each output port. We assume that the network is packet-switched and synchronous, so that packets can be sent only at times t_c, $2t_c$, $\cdots$, where t_c is the *network cycle time.* Without loss of generality, we assume $t_c = 1$. For the sake of definiteness, we make the following further assumptions:

- Each request is a single packet.
- Each queue can accept at each cycle up to two distinct requests, one from each input port. If at some cycle a queue has only one free location and two requests are directed to it, the queue randomly accepts one of the two (the other request remains on the queue of the previous stage).
- The enqueueing process of a request and the dequeueing process are overlapped, i.e. while the request in front of the queue (if there is one) is being removed, other requests can be inserted onto the queue.
- The service time of a request in a queue is the same as the cycle time. So, the delay of a request at a switch is the number of requests ahead of it in the queue.
- Each processor has an infinite queue for requests. If a request is blocked from entering the first stage it is placed on the queue, and the processor continues issuing requests.

We assume that the network is bidirectional; the *forward path* from processors to memory modules and the *return path* from memory modules to processors. Queues on the forward path will be called *forward queues.* On the return path, there are *return queues* exiting each switch to pass response from memory modules to processors.

A *multistage combining network* is a multistage interconnection network composed of "combining" switches. *Combining* works as follows: When several combinable requests conflict at a forward queue in a switch they are combined into a single request, which is forwarded towards the shared memory. A record of this is kept at the *wait buffer.* When the response from the memory returns, the switch satisfies all of the requests, one at a time (and the record is removed from the wait buffer).

The simplest requests to combine are reads and writes. Switches for the NYU Ultracomputer that combine "fetch-and-add" operations have been designed and partially implemented [DiKS86] [DKSS86]. Kruskal, Rudolph, and Snir [KrRS86] give a formal proof that combining networks work correctly, and discuss what type of memory requests can be combined.

One important parameter of combining schemes for good performance is the "degree" of combining — how many combinable requests can be combined into a single request at a switch. Lee, Kruskal, and Kuck [LeKK86] introduced the idea of "k-way combining": in *k-way combining* the degree is a finite integer k (> 2). *Pairwise combining*, which is the scheme suggested for the NYU Ultracomputer and the IBM RP3 machine, is a special case of k-way combining with $k = 2$. A combining of k (> 2) requests is represented as $k - 1$ pairwise combining, i.e. it uses $k - 1$ wait buffer locations. When the response returns from memory, all $k - 1$ locations are immediately freed and the k response messages are placed on the return queues to pass the messages toward processors. A combining scheme with $k = \infty$, i.e. any number of requests can be combined into a single request at a switch, is called *unbounded combining.*

3. Hot Spot Traffic Model

Pfister and Norton [PfNo85] suggested that the effect of hot spot contention could be studied with the *hot spot* traffic model: a fixed fraction of the total memory traffic is concurrent requests to a single shared variable. This captures the effect of all of the processors continually accessing a common synchronization variable. In the hot spot model, each request has a (finite) probability q of being headed to the same shared variable. The hot spot model is *nonuniform* in the sense that the requests are not uniformly distributed onto the memory modules. There are two types of request streams: the *noncombinables,* which are uniformly distributed to the memory modules as in the (usual) uniform model, and the *combinables,* which are headed to the same shared variable (and hence the same memory module).

A rectangular banyan network has a complete tree leading from the processors to each memory module (Figure 1). The tree will be called the *fan-in tree* or the *spread-out tree* depending on the direction in that requests traverse; it is called the fan-in tree when the requests traverse from processors to the hot spot, and the spread-out tree when the requests return to processors. In the hot spot traffic model, our concern is the tree leading from the processors to the hot spot.

For the results presented in this paper, we assume that at each cycle each processor issues a request with probability r, i.e. r is the rate of requests. Each request has probability q of being a combinable request. Let r_c be the rate of combinables (i.e. hot spot requests), and r_n be the rate of noncombinables. Then

$$r_c = qr \qquad \text{and} \qquad r_n = (1-q)r \ .$$

Let r^i be the rate of requests at stage i of the fan-in tree ($r^0 = r$). Let r_c^i and r_n^i be the rate of combinable requests and noncombinable requests, respectively, at stage i of the fan-in tree ($r_c^0 = r_c$ and $r_n^0 = r_n$; processors are at stage 0).

It is rather obvious that normal multistage networks without combining suffer serious contention under hot spot traffic. Since there is no combining, the rate of combinable requests keeps doubling at each stage approaching the root of the fan-in tree. In particular, the rate of requests at the ith stage will be, assuming infinite sized queues,

$$r_n + 2^i r_c \ .$$

For any finite value of r_c, after several stages, the requests will be arriving at each queue at a greater rate than the queue can forward them. Networks large enough to see this effect will not be stable [LeKK86].

With finite queues the situation is worse. Pfister and Norton [PfNo85] noticed a phenomenon they call *tree saturation.* When the queue at the root of the fan-in tree becomes full, the two queues feeding it can no longer send requests to it. They too will become full and stop the four queues feeding them from sending requests. Eventually the entire fan-in tree will consist of full queues. This will block the noncombinables even if they are not directed to the hot spot, and the throughput of the whole network will be reduced drastically.

Other studies confirm the results of Pfister and Norton [LeKK86] [LeeR86] [Wong86].

Kumar and Pfister [KuPf86] have observed that with finite queues even a relatively short period of hot spot contention will produce tree saturation. Furthermore, after the processors stop issuing hot spot requests, the network takes a long time for the machine to recover: when hot spot traffic begins all the processors "cooperate" to produce tree saturation, but only one memory module (the hot one) works to eliminate the tree saturation when the hot spot traffic ends. This suggests that for a fixed hot spot rate the effect will be even more pronounced for larger machines, which have more processors cooperating to produce the hot spot and still only one memory module working to eliminate a larger number of hot spot requests; this is confirmed by their simulations.

4. Problems with k-way Combining

To avoid the problem of the saturation effect, combining can be used. As the requests are combined through the stages of the network, one may expect that the hot spot contention can be relieved. It has been shown that with an idealized combining, i.e. combining with infinite degree and infinite sized wait buffers, the saturation effect can be avoided irrespective of machine sizes [LeeG87a] [LeKK86]. However, queues and buffers are of finite size in practice. Also the infinite degree of combining is difficult and costly to achieve in practice (the reason of which is explained later in this section). In this section, we consider how the finiteness of these factors — queue size, wait buffer size, and the degree of combining, affects the performance of multistage combining networks: which will expose our motivation for a new combining scheme.

4.1. The Degree of Combining

Multistage combining network with degree $k = 2$, i.e. pairwise combining, is unstable under the hot spot traffic. The reason is simple: Assume that at every stage of the fan-in tree every combinable request combines with another combinable request. Then in the fan-in tree at each input port of every switch the rate of combinables will be r_c and the rate of noncombinables will be r_n, and at the output port the rates will be the same. However, a combinable request will not always encounter another request to combine with because of its random arrival and the interference from noncombinables. Whenever a combinable request does not

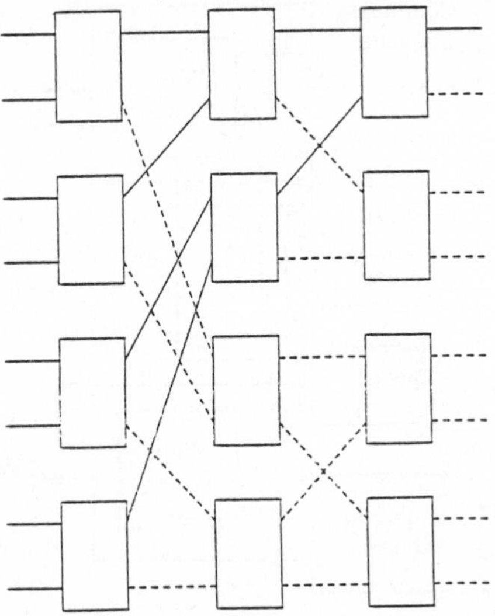

Figure 1. 3-Stage Rectangular Banyan Network of Degree 2

combine, it will be added to the traffic of the combinables coming out of the queue. Thus, the rate of combinables will necessarily increase toward the root of the fan-in tree. As the rate of combinables increases toward 1, the noncombinable traffic, which cannot be combined, starts to suffer from contention, and its interference to combinables becomes serious. Notice that combinables alone do not create contention because the two requests are combined into a single request whenever they conflict; with combinables alone, there is no contention even at the input rate of combinables $r_c = 1$, because the queueing system effectively changes to a single source system. Obviously, the effective arrival rate of combinables, i.e. the arrival rate considered after the requests are combined, will increase toward 1, and thus the effective arrival rate of requests will eventually reach $1 + r_n$, which is greater than the system can absorb. Experiments show that with pairwise combining, multistage networks quickly become unstable as the network size increases [LeKK86]: for example, with $r = 0.25$ and $q = 0.1$, the arrival rate of combinables alone at the ninth stage becomes greater than $1 - r_n$.

With finite queues and finite wait buffers, the network with unbounded combining actually can perform as bad as the one without combining. Although this seems rather strange, the reason is the variance in the number of requests to be combined into a single request. If there is an occasion that the large number of requests are combined into a single request (up to the size of the wait buffer), then the combining cannot happen until all those combined requests are removed from the wait buffer after some cycles. With small sized queues, this takes rather many cycles because the queues are also near full for most of the time at the later stages; the requests stored in the wait buffer cannot be removed until there are enough free cells in the queues to accommodate all those requests. Although the unbounded combining can make the network stable, it is very costly in practice to keep up with the high variance of the number of requests to be combined, which is proportional to machine size.

As the rate of combinables increases, the increased interference from the noncombinable traffic causes that a combinable request encounters more than one combinable request to combine with during its stay in the queue; which suggests $k > 2$ is needed to have a stable network. Lee, Kruskal, and Kuck [LeKK86] claims that with $k = 3$, the network will be stable, assuming infinite sized wait buffers. Experimental results support their claim: 3-way combining is almost as good as unbounded combining even when the request input rate $r = 1$.

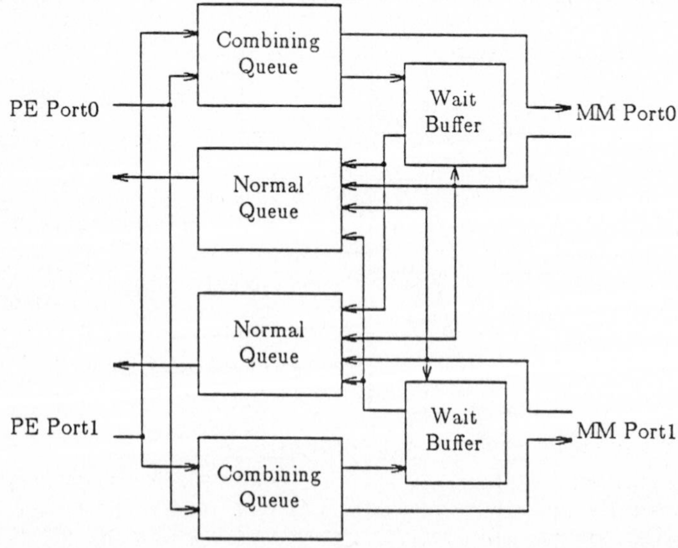

Figure 2. A Block Diagram of Combining Switch [DiKS86]

4.2. Return Queues

We have discussed the degree of combining based on the contention in the forward path, i.e. from the processors to the memory module. For the return trip, there must be two return queues exiting each switch to pass responses from the memory modules toward the processors. The performance of a network will be sensitive to the size of these return queues.

Although k-way ($k > 2$) combining avoids the contention on the fan-in tree, this is to some extent the result of exporting the contention to the return queues. With k-way combining, combinables are returning in bursts. Although the contention on the return queues due to the burst arrivals cannot be serious as with pairwise combining, this will increase the return queue size. Based on the experiments of nine stage networks [LeKK86], the size of return queues seems to need a considerable increase to keep 3-way combining effective: for example, with $r = 0.6$ and $q = 0.1$, the size of return queues needs to increase more than double the forward queues' to keep 3-way combining effective. Notice that inadequately sized return queues block the flow of requests from the wait buffers; which in turn makes 3-way combining ineffective.

4.3. Wait Buffers

The wait buffer size is an important factor for good performance because combining cannot happen if the buffer is full [LeKK86] [Wong86]. It is important to have adequate sized buffers to keep combining effective. Obviously, other schemes of combining cannot perform better than pairwise combining if the buffer size is limited to one.

Consider a switch at the ith stage of an n-stage network. At the wait buffer of the switch, assume combining happens with a request at some cycle. Then, those combined requests will remain in the buffer until a response from the memory arrives at the switch after some cycles. So, the average size of the buffer is determined by the average number of combining occurrences and the average number of cycles for the memory response. Let i_c be the average number of combining occurrences at the switch and t_i be the average time for the memory response for a combined request stored in the wait buffer. Then, we can say that the wait buffer is a queuing system with arrival rate i_c and service rate $1/t_i$. The arrival rate i_c is determined by traffic load and the depth of the switch position, i. The service rate is determined by the size of network n and the queuing delays at the stages greater than or equal to i. Given fixed traffic load and fixed network size, the average size of the wait buffer will be unbounded if there is severe contention creating long delays at later stages, or if the network size is large enough to make $i_c > 1/t_i$.

Wait buffer sizes become unbounded in the limit no matter whether the network is enhanced with any combining schemes considered; even with very small arrival rate at the buffer, the machine size can be large enough to make the traffic intensity at the buffer greater than 1. Multistage combining networks are unstable if the wait buffer size is finite. In practice, it may be interesting to know a "safe" range of the network sizes and an "adequate" size of the buffers for such safety. We suspect that such range is fairly limited irrespective of traffic rate. If the traffic rate is "light," combining becomes ineffective at earlier stages because combinables rarely have a chance to combine with. Irrespective of the traffic rate, as long as $r_c \neq 0$, the traffic quickly reaches the situation in which combining happens at a certain rate close to $1 - r_n$. If there are a few more stages after the traffic reaches the situation, the size of the wait buffers needs to be unbounded to keep the network stable.

5. Balanced Combining: A New Combining Scheme

Most of the problems of combining under the hot spot traffic comes from the fact that a concurrent request does not always encounter another request to combine with. If each concurrent request is combined with another request at every stage of the network, then the traffic load at the hot spot is the same as the first stage of the network, i.e. no contention on the paths to the shared variable and no burst of combinable traffic on the return paths to processors. If the distribution of combinings can be "balanced" through the stages of the network, then the size of wait buffers and queues does not become impractically large as long as the traffic load is moderate and the machine size is "well-limited".

Software combining tree suggested by Yew, Tzeng, and Lawrie [YeTL86] balances the traffic through the levels of combining tree to decrease the memory contention of hot spots. Assume a 10,000 processors want to access a shared variable. They communicate through a ten-ary tree of height three. The processors are partitioned into a thousand groups of ten processors each. Each group accesses a local variable at a leaf of the tree. When the last processor in each group finishes its access, it accesses the parent of the leaf. When the last of the ten processors accessing the parent finishes, it accesses the parent of the parent of the leaf. This will convert a hot spot with 10,000 accesses to 1111 mini hot spots with ten accesses each. Information from the shared variable can be broadcast to the processors by reversing the procedure, which doubles the time. The main advantage of their scheme is that they need no special combining hardware, which can be expensive. Furthermore, they can tune the performance by changing the fan-in. A disadvantage of their scheme is that it is slower than hardware combining, since it requires at least several shared memory accesses compared to just one. Another disadvantage is that the processors have to know ahead of time that they are cooperating in the access; otherwise, it will create severe artificial delays. We propose a new combining scheme, called "balanced k-way combining", which tries to dynamically distribute combinables waiting at the wait buffers through the stages of the network.

In k-way ($k > 2$) combining, the contention with pairwise combining is resolved by combining more than two requests into a single request at a switch. This creates contention on the spread-out tree, because a single response representing more than two requests causes burst of traffic when it returns from the memory. In *balanced k-way combining*, a combinable request is pulled back to stage $i - 1$ along the paths of the spread-out tree when it is combined with a request that was already combined with another request at stage i. So, if three requests are combined into a single request at stage i, then one request will remain in the queue to be forwarded to stage $i + 1$, and one of the other two requests will be at the wait buffer at stage i and the other will be pulled back to one of the wait buffers at stage $i - 1$. (See Figure 3 for a possible configuration of queues and wait buffers with pairwise, 3-way, and balanced 3-way combining.)

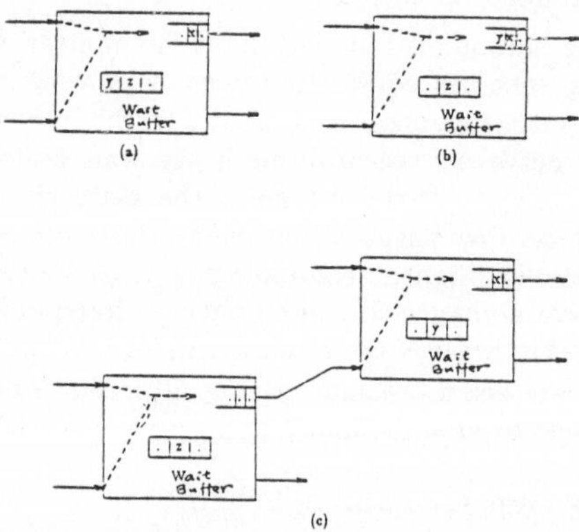

Figure 3. Three Combining Schemes:

when three requests are combined into a single request, shows possible contents of queues and wait buffers (a) for 3-way combining, (b) for pairwise combining, and (c) for balanced 3-way combining.

One may worry about that by pulling requests back to a previous stage, return traffic will increase, and the throughput of return paths will be reduced; which is not true. The requests waiting at a wait buffer will become a part of the return traffic when the response from memory arrives at the buffer. So, whether the requests are pulled back or not, the average load of the return traffic is always the same. By pulling requests back before the response arrives, the return traffic has a smaller variance of the traffic arrival; which in turn reduces the contention on the return paths.

To satisfy combinable requests pulled back when response from hot spot returns, it is important to pull requests back into "correct" wait buffers; otherwise, the requests pulled back never get responded. Since there are at least three requests combined when a request is pulled back, two or more requests are coming from the same port out of the two input ports at a switch. By selecting one of the requests from the same port to be pulled back, we can guarantee that the requests pulled back are always responded. Notice that not always the requests combined later are pulled back.

Concerning the implementation, we expect it to be not much more complicated than the current pairwise combining switch design [DiKS86] [DKSS86]. In the current pairwise combining switch, a request is marked if it combines with another request; which tells us when a request needs to be pulled back for balanced k-way combining. For pulling the requests back, a normal return path can be used, just like normal return traffic from the memory. A possible complication may occur due to the need of selecting the correct buffer at the previous stage; which we expected to be handled without much complication by using comparators in the current pairwise combining switch [LeeG87b].

Although one may wish to pull requests back to as many stages as possible for more even distribution of combinings through stages, it seems that it does not help much. One reason for this is that the possibility of having a common path for two requests through more than two stages is rare. Another reason is that combining of more than two requests mostly happens only at the bottleneck; before or after the stage at which the bottleneck occurs, pairwise combining is enough.

6. The Performance of Balanced Combining

To see the performance advantage of the balanced combining, we simulated nine stage networks with several combining schemes. Although one may consider various values of k in balanced k-way combining, we show the delays with balanced 3-way combining, i.e. $k = 3$, which is the minimum k enough to avoid contention in the fan-in tree. Remind that, as k increases, it becomes harder to provide enough wait buffer sizes in practice to keep up with a large variance in the number of requests combined.

We first simulated the network with infinite sized queues and wait buffers. In Figure 4, queueing delays on the fan-in tree are shown; obviously, balanced combining removes the hot spot contention in the fan-in tree because it is 3-way combining. In Figure 5, queueing delays on the spread-out tree are shown; the benefit of pulling requests back can be clearly seen. With balanced 3-way combining, the requests suffer faily uniform delays through the stages of the network when they return from the memory.

In Figures 6 and 7, the simulation results with finite sized queues and wait buffers are shown. (queue size = 6 and wait buffer size =10; the unit of size is one storage for holding a single request.) As can be expected, we can resolve the hot spot contention with paying less delays through the network and with less storage requirements in the switches by using balanced 3-way combining. The poor performance of 3-way combining is the result of small sized wait buffers; as noted earlier, 3-way combining effectively changes into pairwise combining with inadequate sized wait buffers. (By having adequate sized wait buffers, the performance of 3-way combining improves especially on the fan-in tree; see [LeKK86].)

Figure 8 shows the average length of wait buffers with various combining schemes.

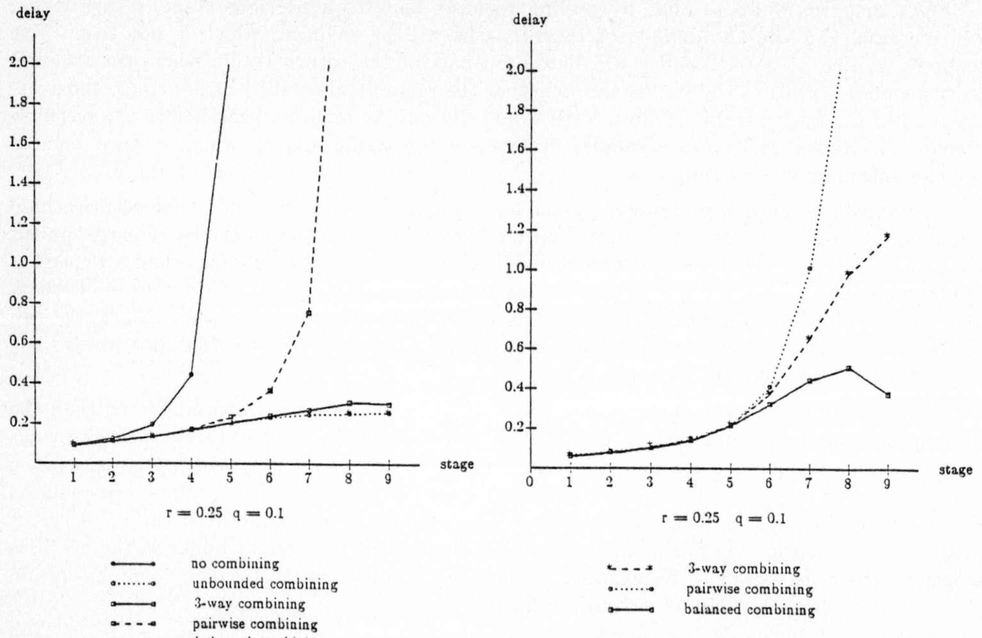

Figure 4. Queueing Delay on the Fan-in Tree – Processor to Hot Spot

Infinite Sized Queues and Wait Buffers

Figure 5. Queueing Delay on the Spread-out Tree – Hot Spot to Processors

Infinite Sized Queues and Wait Buffers

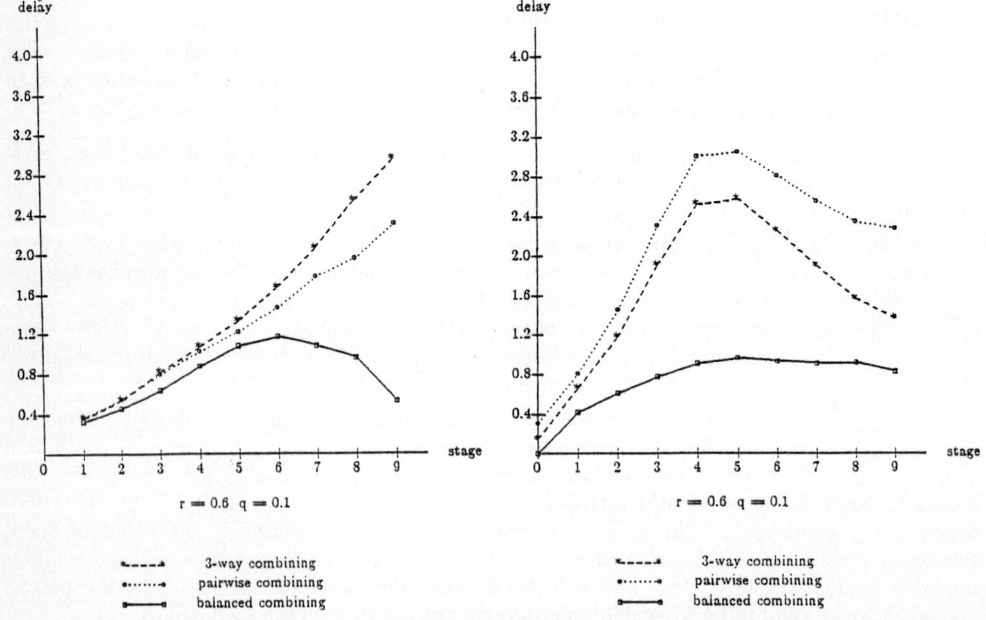

Figure 7. Queueing Delay on the Spread-out Tree – Finite Sized Queues

queue size =6; wait buffer size = 10

Figure 6. Queueing Delay on the Fan-in Tree – Finite Sized Queues

queue size = 6; wait buffer size = 10

Although the average length is reduced with balanced combining compared to other combining schemes, the average length is still considerable because it depends on the machine size; which is the result of the inherent property of shared memory machine — as the machine size increases, the distance between memory and processors becomes "longer." The "hump" on the curves for balanced and 3-way combining shows the effect of machine size on the average length of wait buffers.

Balanced k-way combining allows combining of more than two requests into a single request as k-way combining does; this avoids contention on the fan-in tree, and reduces the average length of wait buffers, compared to pairwise combining, because of reduced delays at later stages. Furthermore, by pulling a request back to one of the wait buffers at the previous stage, it achieves the effect that combining happens through two stages instead of a single stage; this reduces the bursts of combinable traffic on the spread-out tree and the average length of wait buffers. Remind that 3-way combining is enough to avoid hot spot contention on the fan-in tree, and that a combining of three requests is represented as two pairwise combining.

7. Conclusion

Considering the current efforts to develop supercomputers based on shared memory machine, it is important to understand the impact of hot spot contention on machine performance and to devise ways of resolving contention effectively. We believe that hot spot contention is one important factor limiting the "scalability" of shared memory machine, i.e. improving the performance by increasing the machine size. With pairwise combining, shared memory machine's scalability can be extended a little bit. With k-way combining ($k > 2$), the scalability can be extended further. We hope that with balanced k-way combining such extended scalability can be achieved with "small" sized wait buffers and queues in the switches of multistage interconnection network. Our experiments show that balanced k-way combining achieves what we hope for; little contention on both the fan-in tree and the spread-out tree, and the small average length of wait buffers.

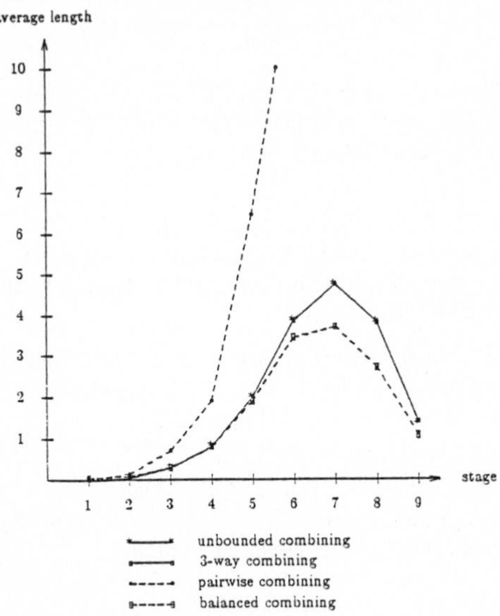

Figure 8. Average Length of Wait Buffers ($r = 0.25$ and $q = 0.1$)

Infinite Sized Queues and Wait Buffers

References

[DiKS86] S. Dickey, R. Kenner, and M. Snir, "An Implementation of a Combining Network for the NYU Ultracomputer" Ultracomputer Note #93, NYU, Jan. 1986.

[DKSS86] S. Dickey, R. Kenner, M. Snir, and J. Solworth, "A VLSI Combining Network for the NYU Ultracomputer" *IEEE Proc. of the Intl. Conf. on Computer Design,* pp. 110-113, Oct. 1986.

[EGKM85] J. Edler, A.Gottlieb, C. P. Kruskal, K. P. McAuliffe, L. Rudolph, M. Snir, P. J. Teller, and J. Willson "Issues Related to MIMD Shared-Memory Computers: The NYU Ultracomputer Approach", *The 12th Annual International Symp. on Computer Architecture,* June, 1985, pp.126-135

[Feng81] T. Y. Feng, "A Survey of Interconnection Networks", *IEEE Computer,* Vol.14 no.12 1981, pp. 12-27

[GKLS83] D. D. Gajski, D. J. Kuck, D. Lawrie, and A. Sameh, "Cedar — A Large Scale Multiprocessors", *Proc. of the 1983 International Conf. on Parallel Processing,* Aug. 1983, pp. 524-529

[GoLi73] G. R. Goke and G. J. Lipovski, "Banyan Networks for Partitioning Multiprocessor Systems", *The 1st Annual Symposium on Computer Architecture,* 1973, pp. 21-28

[GGKM83] A. Gottlieb, R. Grishman, C. P. Kruskal, K. M. McAuliffe, L. Rudolph, and M. Snir, "The NYU Ultracomputer - designing an MIMD shared memory parallel computer", *IEEE Trans. on Computers, Vol. C-32, No. 2, 1983*

[KrRS86] C. P. Kruskal, L. Rudolph, and M. Snir, "Efficient Synchronization on Multiprocessors with Shared Memory", *The 5th ACM SIGACT-SIGOPS Symp. on Principles of Distributed Computing,* Aug. 1986

[KrSn82] C. P. Kruskal and M. Snir, "Some Results on Multistage Interconnection Networks for Multiprocessors", NYU Ultracomputer note 41; also in *Proc. 1982 Conf. Informat. Sci. Syst.,* Princeton Univ., Princeton, NJ, Mar. 1982

[KrSn83] C. P. Kruskal and M. Snir, "The Performance of Multistage Interconnection Networks for Multiprocessors", *IEEE Trans. on Computers,* Vol. c-32, No. 12, Dec. 1983, pp.1091-1098

[KrSW86] C. P. Kruskal, M. Snir, and A. Weiss, "The Distribution of Waiting Times in Clocked Multistage Interconnection Networks", *Proc. of the 1986 International Conf. on Parallel Processing,* Aug. 1986, pp. 12-19

[KDLS86] D. J. Kuck, E. S. Davidson, D. H. Lawrie, and A. H. Sameh, "Parallel Supercomputing Today and the Cedar Approach", *Science,* Vol. 281, Feb. 28, 1986, pp. 967-974

[Lawr75] D. H. Lawrie, "Access and Alignment of Data in an Array Processor", *IEEE Trans. on Computers,* Vol. c-24, no.12 1975, pp.1145-1155

[LeKK86] G. Lee, C. P. Kruskal, and D. J. Kuck, "The Effectiveness of Combining in Shared Memory Parallel Computers in the Presence of 'Hot Spots'", *Proc. of the 1986 International Conf. on Parallel Processing,* Aug. 1986, pp.35-41

[LeeG87a] G. Lee, "A Performance Bound of Multistage Combining Networks", submitted for publication in *IEEE Trans. on Computers,* 1987

[LeeG87b] G. Lee, "A Balanced *k*-way Combining Switch", in preparation, 1987

[LeeR85] R. Lee, "On Hot Spot Contention", *ACM Computer Architecture News,* Vol.13 no.5 1985, pp.15-20

[Pate81] J. A. Patel, "Performance of Processor-Memory Interconnections for Multiprocessors", *IEEE Trans. on Computers,* Vol. c-30, 1981, pp. 771-780

[PBGH85] G. F. Pfister, W. C. Brantley, D. A. George, S. L. Harvey, W. J. Kleinfelder, K. P. McAuliffe, E. A. Melton, V. A. Norton, J. Weiss, "The IBM Research Parallel Processor Prototype (RP3): Introduction and Architecture", *Proc. of the 1985 International Conf. on Parallel Processing,* Aug. 1985, pp.764-771

[PfNo85] G. F. Pfister and V. A. Norton, "'Hot Spot' Contention and Combining in Multistage Interconnection Networks", *IEEE Trans. on Computers,* Vol. c-34, No.10, 1985, pp.943-948

[Sieg85] Howard Jay Siegel, *Interconnection Networks for Large-Scale Parallel Processing, Theory and Case Studies,* Lexington Books. 1985

[SuBK77] H. Sullivan, T. Bashkow, and D. Klappholtz, "A Large Scale Homogeneous Fully Distributed Parallel Machine", *Proc. of the Fourth Symp. on Computer Architecture,* 1977, pp. 105-124

[Wong86] M. C. Wong, "A Combining Omega Network: Performance vs Implementation" IBM Research Report, RC 11977 (#53952), June 1986.

[YeTL86] P. C. Yew, N. F. Tzeng, and D. H. Lawrie, "Distributing Hot-Spot Addressing in Large Scale Multiprocessor", *Proc. of the 1986 International Conf. on Parallel Processing,* Aug. 1986, pp.51-58

[ZhYe84] C. Q. Zhu and P. C. Yew, "A Synchronization Scheme and Its Applications for Larger Multiprocessor Systems", *Proc. 4th International Conf. Distributed Computing Systems,* May 1984, pp. 486-493

Applications Environment for the IBM Research Parallel Processor Prototype (RP3)

Frederica Darema

Computer Sciences Department
IBM T. J. Watson Research Center
Yorktown Heights, NY

The Research Parallel Processor Prototype (RP3) is an experimental highly parallel, high performance system designed at IBM Research for the purposes of research into hardware and software aspects of parallel processing. In this paper we provide an overview of the system hardware and discuss the programming environment requirements in terms of computational techniques, as we have implemented them in the EPEX emulation system, performance analysis tools and a summary of our experience with parallel applications.

1.0 Introduction

Currently a variety of MIMD architectures are being proposed and pursued as a means of providing increased computational power. The characterization of these architectures is that they employ multiple interconnected processors, executing independent instruction streams and cooperatively working to execute the same program. The *parallel architectures* have produced new domains of investigation, not only from the hardware point of view, but also in terms of the computational models employed to program such machines and the mapping of applications and algorithms on a given architecture. Actually, there exists a symbiotic relation between software and hardware, in that applications are *tuned* to the architecture for optimal performance and hardware designers are guided by the requirements of applications. The Research Parallel Processor Prototype (RP3) designed at IBM Research [1] is an attempt to investigate hardware and software aspects of highly parallel processing.

This Work Was Sponsored in part by Defense Advanced Research Projects Agency under contract # N00039-87-C-0122.

To gain experience in the requirements of programming of parallel systems we have developed an emulator system (EPEX) [2] that allows us to experiment with computational models and programming techniques for the RP3. We have used this system and performance tools that we have built upon it to gain experience with parallel applications and study their characteristics as well as investigate the performance of RP3 features.

In this paper we describe the characteristics of the RP3 machine and discuss the programming environments designed to employ the capabilities of the machine in terms of the computational models that we have implemented in the EPEX system. Finally we discuss our experience with parallel applications.

2.0 The RP3 Architecture

RP3 is being designed and built at IBM Research as an experimental system for research in both hardware and software aspects of highly parallel processing. In this section the most notable architectural features of RP3 are discussed; more detailed information is given in [1,3,4].

2.1 Features and Performance

RP3 is a highly-parallel MIMD system designed to accommodate 512 processing nodes, in its full configuration. The nodes are referred to as *Processor-Memory Elements*, or *PMEs*. Each PME has a 32-bit high-performance microprocessor [5], vector and scalar floating point co-processor, a 32K byte high-speed cache memory, and up to 8 Mbytes of main storage. The physical design of the 512-way system can be partitioned into eight identical *octants*, each a self-contained "mini-" RP3. Initially one of those octants is being constructed, with a functional system expected by year-end 1987.

Performance characteristics of a full-scale RP3 include the following:

- peak aggregate performance of 1300 MIPS
- up to 4 Gbytes of main storage
- 800 MFLOPS for single precision
- 200 Mbytes per second I/O rate
- 13 Gbytes per second inter-processor communication bandwidth.

The RP3 architecture supports the *fetch-and-add* instruction as the basic mechanism of synchronization. The fetch-and-add can provide the means of a non-blocking synchronization: when multiple processors issue a fetch-and-add to the same memory location the request could be satisfied in one memory cycle; other usual synchronization mechanisms, such as the test-and-set or the compare-and-swap, would require the usage of locks and result in serialization of multiple requests.

2.2 Memory Organization

The major difference of RP3 from other highly parallel systems is its memory organization. The entire aggregate of 4 Gbytes is distributed across all the processing nodes, (up to) 8MB per node. At one extreme, all the memory can be treated as shared (global) memory, available to all processors. In this configuration, RP3 appears as a pure shared memory parallel system like the NYU Ultracomputer [6]. At the other extreme, it can all be private (local) memory, accessed by the corresponding processing node without communication delays as then the requests bypass the network. In this case, inter-PME communication is accomplished by message passing and RP3 appears as a generalization of a hypercube [9] system. Applications designed, for example, to run on hypercube machines [9] would execute equally well on RP3. The message passing would be implemented either by copying data from one memory to another or by using a (small) portion of shared memory as mailboxes. Between those extremes, memory can be partitioned dynamically into local and global sections, as desired to meet the applications storage requirements for their private and shared data.

The flexibility of dynamic partitioning of the shared memory is an important capability: Requirements of some applications can be optimally matched by shared memory. Other applications can be partitioned in a manner such that they use only local memory, with minimal communication among the processors, and that would result in more efficient execution. In general though, access to large, complex data structures, is facilitated and the even distribution of irregular amounts of work (load balancing) is more easily achieved by using shared memory. The approach that results in optimal performance is application- and algorithm-dependent.

Two additional features in the memory organization of the RP3 are employed to improve performance. Each processing element has a high speed cache memory and the shared memory is interleaved. The cache on each PME can be used in the usual, *user transparent*, mode for the private data. Caheability of the shared data is possible but is not transparent; it is done under software control to maintain *cache coherence*. In a shared memory system when multiple processors are attempting to access the same memory module, contention in the network will most likely occur, resulting in degraded performance. To minimize such sources of contention, the RP3 shared memory is interleaved across the memory modules; in the current design consecutive double words of the applications' (shared) address space would reside in different memory modules.

2.3 Processor Interconnection

The processor interconnection system in the RP3 consists of two networks: a primary network which is a variant of an Omega network and provides high speed access to the global memory, and a second network that enables *combining* of memory references, as proposed in [6].

The primary network accommodates the major traffic of accesses to memory. To use the global memory effectively, the basic requirements for the interconnection network are high bandwidth and low latency. In the RP3 design, a memory reference to another processor's memory takes only 1.6 times as long as a local reference. The network is "flat," in the sense that all PMEs are equidistant from each other. This avoids forcing applications to match their (variable) structure to some fixed hierarchy.

The memory interleaving discussed earlier is designed to ease congestion in the network due to all processors attempting to access the same memory module. However there can still arise situations where multiple requests for the same piece of data (same memory location) happen to occur in a time interval sufficiently small, and memory and network contention results. The combining sub-network, provided in RP3, enables *combining* of specific memory references. In the RP3 architecture when data are referenced by special instructions (such as *fetch-and-add* [6], discussed earlier), the requests are automatically routed to the combining network. When multiple such requests to the same memory location occur close in time, they are combined by the network into single requests. The response to those requests is uncombined and passed back to the requesting processors.

Simulation and analysis [7,8], have shown that combining would be useful. It assists in avoiding the disastrous effects that inadvertent "hot spot" traffic patterns can have on network performance. In a 512 processor system, an imbalance in the network (memory) traffic that directs as little as 0.25% additional traffic to one location (the hot spot) can degrade network throughput by over 50%. In addition, such combinable synchronization primitives allow the creation of algorithms without serializing sections, a prerequisite for good performance in a highly parallel environment.

2.4 Software Support

The operating system support for RP3 will be a variant of the UNIX(tm) operating system. Standard features provided by the UNIX system will remain essentially unchanged, except of some additions to accommodate the use of RP3's special features, e.g., memory shared across processes. Internally, however, substantial modifications will be done to allow the system itself to operate as a highly parallel program and to make use of the special instructions such as the fetch-and-add provided in RP3. This work is being performed in conjunction with the New York University Courant Institute Ultracomputer Laboratory and Carnegie-Mellon University.

Language support will initially focus on FORTRAN, C, and possibly PASCAL. Initial work for these languages is being carried on within the RP3 group, based on the facilities described below in the EPEX system.

3.0 The EPEX System

The *Environment for Parallel EXecution (EPEX)* was developed for parallel execution on IBM/370's, to assist in the research of parallel systems' aspects before the RP3 hardware was complete. The system enables the development and testing of parallel programming techniques and of parallel applications. Applications parallelized under EPEX will be portable to RP3. Simulation tools built upon EPEX also enable the study of performance aspects of the applications and RP3.

EPEX provides several levels of support to the users. The lowest level creates a virtual multiprocessor with both shared and non-shared memory, as in the RP3. In addition, means are provided for the development of applications that can utilize the core features of RP3, particularly the private/shared memory and process coordination via *fetch-and-op* primitives. To facilitate application development higher level capabilities are also provided by EPEX at the level of language support and have been implemented for the FORTRAN and C languages.

EPEX operates on IBM System/370 systems under the VM/SP operating system [10]. A basic facility of VM/SP is the *virtual machine* that provides each user a virtual S/370. Multiple of these *virtual machines* are employed to emulate processors (or processes) in a multiprocessor system. To enable virtual machines to communicate with low overhead, and to mimic the shared memory organization of RP3, another VM/SP facility called *writeable shared segments* is used. These are designated sections of address space that can be read *and* modified by separate virtual machines. The process coordination is exposed in the application program level without further service requirements from the operating system.

Thus EPEX uses standard facilities of VM/SP to provide either real or simulated (*virtual*) highly parallel processing. When running on a real S/370 multiprocessor, such as the IBM 3081, 3084 or 3090, VM/SP will run the multiple virtual machines simultaneously, and real speedups can be obtained when running applications under EPEX. *Virtual* highly parallel processing is provided when a program under EPEX is executed using more virtual machines (processes) than there are processors. We have used up to 64 processes under EPEX. In this situation, real speedup proportional to the number of processes cannot, of course, be obtained. However, VM/SP provides a measurement called *virtual time*, which is the execution time each process would take if running stand-alone. This can be used to provide a usable indication of what the execution time would be if hardware with more parallelism were available. For more detailed information about EPEX, see [2,11].

While applications have been programmed under EPEX in five different programming languages, extensive high level support is available for two: FORTRAN and C. Both EPEX FORTRAN and EPEX C provide *preprocessor* support for the declaration of shared data, parallel loops, and lower-level primitives such as locks; however, they provide different models of computation. Both models and their implementation are targeted to be efficient for intermediate level parallelism, of the order of hundreds to thousands of instructions per independent computation. Our implementations, though, are suitable and extremely efficient for exploiting coarse grain parallelism, of the order of millions of instructions per independent task. In the next two sections we discuss the computational models that we have implemented under EPEX for FORTRAN and C languages.

4.0 The EPEX FORTRAN Model

4.1 Computational Model

EPEX FORTRAN implements a model where *all* processes begin executing the same program, though they can, and indeed generally must, take different paths through that program. We refer to this as Single-Program-Multiple-Data (SPMD) computational model [12]. It is similar to other models [13,14] that have appeared in the literature.

In the SPMD processing all processes participating in the parallel computation are created at the beginning of the execution and remain in existence until the end. However, during execution, at the same time different processes may be executing different instructions and act on different data. The default is that each line of code is executed by every process unless directives are inserted in the program that cause the processes to follow different paths. The tasks to be executed by each process are determined *dynamically* during execution, by the usage of synchronization directives that are imbedded in the program. As our SPMD model approach requires process initiation only once, at the start, obtaining work or waiting for work does not require any operating system calls. Thus the operating system interface to the parallel environment based on SPMD is simplified and the system overhead is minimized.

The following program structures are encountered in an SPMD model of computation: *parallel sections, serial sections* and *replicate sections.* Distribution of work to the various processes in *parallel sections*, such as parallel loops, is effected by having each process execute in-line synchronization directives. Since there exist sections in a program that need to be executed by one process only (*serial sections*), EPEX FORTRAN contains constructs that produce that effect. Predominantly there are serial sections and parallel sections in a program. Though in our model the default is replication of the computation by all processes, sections executed by every process (*replicate sections*) involve relatively small amounts of computation. Typically these are computations that could be executed by a single process. If, however, the serialization overhead is larger than the computation itself, then it is more efficient to let every process repeat the computation. Another case where replicate computation is desirable is to create computation parameters as private to each process.

EPEX FORTRAN has proven adequate for a large range of applications and is extremely efficient.

4.2 Expression of parallelism

EPEX FORTRAN provides to the user constructs and synchronization routines to be inserted in the program and to designate parallel execution. The constructs can be considered as extensions to the FORTRAN language to enable the user to explicitly declare parallelism. A *preprocessor* [15] is available to convert the constructs into the (FORTRAN) synchronization routines. These routines are also available to the user for direct invocation without the preprocessor. The preprocessed, or parallelized, FORTRAN program is compiled by the standard serial compiler. No tools are provided for automatic detection of parallelism (parallelizing compiler); the parallelization detection is the responsibility of the user.

Via the preprocessor constructs, FORTRAN is extended to support the computational model. Among the constructs provided are the following:

- @SHARED is used to designate shared data of the application and of the synchronization routines . The syntax is similar to the named COMMON statements in FORTRAN. All other data are by default private, including data specified in regular COMMON, which can also exist in the parallel program. This mechanism of declaring the shared data is quite convenient, as it is customary in FORTRAN programs to declare storage in common blocks.
- @DO and @ENDO designate and bound the scope of a parallel loop. Like the serial FORTRAN loop, the parallel loop has a loop index, with an initial and a final value and an (optional) step. Upon arrival at the beginning of the loop a process is dynamically assigned an iteration of the loop to execute, by performing a F&A to a shared variable. When the process finishes that iteration it returns to the beginning of the loop and requests more work. For increased efficiency more than one iterations can be assigned to a process at a time; this is specified by an (optional) parameter of the @DO construct, the CHUNK. When all the iterations of the loop have been assigned, processes (that have arrived in the loop) go to the end of the loop. There they either *wait* for all the iterations of the loop to finish, if the (default) WAIT option is in effect. If the NOWAIT option has been specified, then processes will continue execution of the subsequent section in the computation.
- @SERBEG and @SEREND constructs bound a section to be executed by one process only. As we endow each of the parallel processes with an *identity* (@MYNUM), the @SERBEG construct has an optional specification of the identity of the process to execute that section; else the section is executed on a first-come-executes basis. WAIT and NOWAIT options similar to the ones in the parallel loop apply here also.
- @WAITFOR designates that processes cannot go past this point until a condition specified in the argument of the construct is satisfied. The argument of the WAITFOR can be a logical condition of *wait-expresions.* The wait-expression can be a relational expression of FORTRAN variables or the label of a @DO-loop or @SERBEG, in which case it implies that the specified section should complete.

Thus this construct provides to user capabilities akin to a macro data flow environment.

- @BARRIER forces *all* processes participating in the execution to arrive at that point before subsequent execution proceeds.

The WAIT (default) option at the end of serial or parallel sections signifies that the execution of the section has to be completed before subsequent computation can proceed. The NOWAIT option signifies that when all the work in the section has been assigned then remaining processes can proceed to execute the subsequent section, thus it enables simultaneous execution of parts of the application program that are independent from each other. The NOWAIT and @WAITFOR options give flexibility in pipelining the computation of independent (serial or paralllel) sections.

4.3 Implementation features

Our implementation employs *work-based* synchronization instead of *process-based* synchronization. That is, process flow is determined by what work has been done and what still needs to be done, instead of which processes or how many processes have arrived at given points in the program. Processes, at most, wait for work in a given section to finish and not for every process executing the program to arrive at the synchronization point; that is, we eliminate process *join* except at *barrier* points. A slow process will not delay execution of the program (or sections of it) by other processes.

This is a flexible and efficient scheme. The synchronization methods provided allow repeated execution of parallel loops and serial sections without any blocking or explicit serialization. Computations involving sections that are mutually independent can be overlapped. With these techniques, correct execution of a program is independent of the number of processes (or processors) assigned to the program. If only one process is assigned to the program the result is consistent with the usual serial FORTRAN execution. If many processes are assigned to a program and it is run on a multiprocessor system, a speedup of the job execution time can be obtained.

The current implementation does not provide the capability of executing *parallel nesting*; that is, there is no automatic capability of nesting @DO's. This is not a restriction of the SPMD computational model. The user can implement the appropriate synchronization routines manually to achieve nested parallel execution and partition the shared data into hierarchies of sharing among groups of processes; the terms: serial, parallel and replicate section and data sharing will be within a certain hierarchy of groups of processes when parallel nesting is considered.

In the present implementation of one level parallelism, minimal modification of the program is required, the transition from uniprocessing to parallel processing is simplified. The resulting environment is flexible, easy to use and sufficient for many applications.

5.0 The EPEX C model

5.1 Computational Model

In EPEX C [16] a general fork-join model has been implemented. A given program is executed as a single thread of control by one process (designated usually as the *parent*) until a parallel section is encountered. Then multiple processes can enter the parallel section and cooperate in its execution. Upon completion of the parallel section, the execution continues by one process only until another parallel section is encountered. Efficiency in this environment is achieved because (high overhead operating system) processes are not created every time a parallel section is encountered. Instead, operating system prnocesses are created once in the beginning of the program execution. Then all processes, but one, are suspended from execution, except for occasional rescheduling by the operating system to interrogate program internal work queues.

5.2 Expression of the parallelism

In the C model, similarly to the FORTRAN model, there are extensions to the language to declare the storage classes and the control flow extensions. Again there are two classes of data, private and shared, declared by the reserved keywords:

- Private
- Shared

Since the C language provides dynamic storage allocation, the standard C routines "malloc( )" and "free( )" are used to allocate (private) storage have now analogous routines, "shalloc( )" and "shfree( )", to allocate and free shared storage.

For the regulation of the parallel flow of control the following parallel constructs are incorporated into the EPEX C:

- PARFOR() [join_option] designates a parallel loop. Its syntax conforms to the one of the serial FOR-loop, with optional arguments, such as the process join options discussed subsequently. Several processes can cooperate in the execution of the loop in a similar work-based scheduling manner as was discussed in the FORTRAN @DO-loop. The distinction between the FORTRAN implementation and the C implementation is that there can exist nested PARFOR's to accommodate the parallel execution of nested parallel loops.

  The synchronization options for the PARFOR are the following: JOIN, NOJOIN and ASYNCH. The JOIN and NOJOIN options are similar to their counterparts in the EPEX FORTRAN environment with the additional restriction that the parent spawning the processes for that section will participate in the execution of the parallel section and obey the same restrictions of WAIT/NOWAIT. The ASYNCH option has the effect that when the parent spawns the processes for that section will go on to execute in the subsequent section with the possibility of spawning and executing another parallel section.

- DOTOG is a construct that specifies independent statements within its scope that can be executed in parallel.
- REJOIN. This option at a point in the program has the effect that control past that point can proceed only after all the outstanding PARCALLs have been completed. It is like the @WAITFOR option in the EPEX FORTRAN, where the wait condition is for specific loops.
- BARRIER enforces synchronization of all the parallel processes that execute in that parallel section.
- PARSECT is a construct that allows sections of the program, containing more than one parallel loop and/or serial section, to be executed in the SPMD style discussed in the EPEX FORTRAN model.

5.3 Implementation Features

EPEX C provides low overhead and general fork/join support. As in the FORTRAN environment the synchronization is work based and dynamic allocation of work is the default. EPEX C provides capability of nesting, in principle to an arbitrary level, though in practice it is limited by the available resources. Execution of the parallel program is independent of the number of processes allocated by the operating system.

6.0 Characteristics of Parallel Applications

The EPEX system, the computational models and the language environments, have been used to parallelize and execute over 30 scientific application programs. These programs span diverse applications areas, such Fluid Dynamics, Molecular Dynamics, Solid State Physics, Seismic, Design Automation and Graphics that use techniques such as Finite Differences and Monte Carlo, and employ numerical algorithms such as FFT's, Linear Systems and Eigenvalue Solvers.

In this section we discuss the effectiveness of the programming environments we have developed, the parallelization characteristics of the applications and parallelization strategies that we have applied [17,18,19].

We find that the computational models discussed previously are suitable and sufficient for the expression of either intermediate or coarse grain parallelism. Process self-scheduling models enable simple interface to the operating system and imply low overhead, efficiency and load balancing. Few constructs are required, which has the nice implication that few language extensions are needed to enable existing (serial) languages to accommodate parallelism. For the EPEX FORTRAN model we have found, for example, that most parallelization directives involve the @DO, the @SERBEG and the @SHARED constructs. Concern has been expressed that in programming shared memory systems, in order to avoid race conditions, the imposition of hard barriers (declared by the @BARRIER construct) that force *all* processes to arrive at the barrier, would be frequent. In our parallel applications development we have found that this is not the case. Of the low level primitives provided by EPEX, the Fetch-and-Add [9] and the explicit capability to set locks appear to be the most useful.

We have observed certain common features in the parallelization characteristics of the applications. In general we have seen that the parallelism is exhibited in the form of many successive parallel loops. The degree of parallelism, e.g. the number of independent iterations (tasks) in a loop, is problem size dependent and in general is not fixed throughout the program. For the most part we have observed that the nature of the parallel loops inhibits combining of loops to produce larger chunks of work and reduce the parallelization overhead, or increase the degree of parallelism.

We have found that, in general, the size of the independent tasks can vary from hundreds to thousands and in some cases to millions of instructions. We have also found that the amount of serial execution is in general small, and that the parallelization overhead (with our synchronization mechanisms) is about 1% of the execution time or less.

In the rest of this section we present our experience with general techniques that can be applied to uncover parallelism in applications. These techniques surface either in coarse or intermediate -grain parallelism. Depending on the resulting granularity of the generated tasks the domain of applicability is intermediate or coarse grain systems.

The techniques can be divided into two categories: Those in the first category can be characterized as *mild* or *straightforward*; no modifications or minor modifications to the original serial algorithm or application program are made. The second category can be characterized as more *drastic* or *innovative*. In this category belong techniques that approach the problem in a different way, devise completely new (parallel) algorithms.

In the straightforward category we distinguish the following two techniques:

- Find the independent tasks. When a specific application (program) is at hand this translates into finding sections in the program independent from each other, and finding loops with independent iterations. Indeed the major targets of parallelization are DO-loops whose iterations are independent from each other.
- Reorganize the order of computation to create or increase size and number of the independent tasks. At the algorithm level, this might mean restructuring the sequence of operations. It can be as simple as interchanging loops in the application program, or as complex as modifying the method of the computation of given loops.

Techniques of this category can be implemented in parallelizing compilers.

The following basic techniques are emerging for the second category:

- Partition the problem into subproblems (subdomains); that is, apply domain decomposition. Partitioning can be either static or dynamic during execution time.

- Apply divide-and-conquer techniques to create independent tasks. That is, break the problem into subproblems each of which can be processed in parallel, then combine results and process the resulting (fewer) subproblems in parallel and so on.
- Increase the parallelism and the efficiency of the computation by imposing less synchronization among the parallel processes; that is, perform non-synchronized (chaotic) computation.
- Pipeline the execution of program sections that, except of some dependencies can be executed concurrently; for example, problems consisting of more than one phases.

We have observed that most application programs examined were straightforwardly parallelizable, that is, they used same algorithm and same program organization as the serial algorithm. This is of interest as it indicates that the existing serial algorithms lend themselves to parallelization.

A reason for that is that the underlying physical problems and their mathematical representation basically lend themselves to parallel execution. Many physical problems, to solve the equations governing the system, involve mapping the physical space and fields onto N-dimensional grids and the computations can be independent for the various grid points, or grid lines, or planes. Numerous applications involving either finite difference or finite elements methods, fall in this category. Other physical problems involve a system of particles and computations on each particle can be independent. Such problems include, for example, molecular dynamics or particle plasma simulations. Another type of problems are ones dealing with Hamiltonians of systems; again there the computations involving Hamiltonian matrix elements are independent from each other.

7.0 Applications Performance Analysis

Performance issues such as speedups, efficiencies, as well as detecting the sources of efficiency loss are important subjects in parallel processing. Based on the EPEX system we have developed two tools: The first, PSIMUL [17], enables instruction and address tracing of a parallel program and allows us to study memory access characteristics of the applications. The second, SPAN [21], is a tool that allows to estimate the speedup of an application for a range of number of processors and determine the optimal number of processors to be used for the problem. The variability in the degree of parallelism in the various sections of a program makes the decision of how many processors to apply in a problem non trivial, and SPAN can be used to obtain such information. In addition it provides information on section-by-section speedup and distribution of the computation versus overheads, that helps to pinpoint performance bottlenecks. Using these tools we have made performance measurements on a number of applications. Results of these studies are reported in [18,19], here we summarize some of these results.

An important issue in a shared memory system is the frequency of access to the shared data. This has implications in the expected traffic on the network. From the applications we have studied we find that, although the majority of the application data are shared, typically of the order of 80% or more, the average access frequency to the shared data ranges from 3 to 20% of all memory references. The reason the frequency is low, is that half of the memory references are instruction references, which are local. In addition, most statements in a parallel program, besides referencing the shared data, reference loop indices, temporary variables and constants that are also private. This finding is encouraging because frequent access to the shared memory implies longer delays and congestion of the network. However, even though average numbers are low, we observe temporary bursts of 80-100% shared memory accesses which indicate that some "rush hour" traffic will be observed transiently during execution on the RP3.

Another concern in a highly parallel shared memory system, is the creation of hot spots discussed earlier. There are two potential sources of hot spots: program constants accessed repeatedly in loops or loop bounds and synchronization points where processes when accessing task queues, for example obtaining independent iterations of a parallel loop. Compilers (or the users) can eliminate the first category of hot spot generators by creating private copies of such parameters. A feature of the RP3 is the combining switch discussed earlier, designed to avoid serialization and hot spots at synchronization points. Our performance measurements indicate that on major numeric application programs the potential for such bottlenecks is not significant. Non-numeric applications though, like the quicksort algorithm, find high fetch-and-add rates, and that its performance would benefit from combining [23]. In addition, it is expected that the operating system that uses fetch-and-add to manipulate its queues would also benefit from combining in the 512-way system.

8.0 Summary

The design goals of the RP3 are to provide a multi-purpose, highly parallel, shared memory system, to investigate the hardware design issues and the software requirements of highly parallel systems, in terms of the programming models needed, and the potential of the applications being efficiently run on such systems.

The computational models that we have implemented show that it is not difficult at all to program a machine like RP3. Many applications map naturally onto a parallel system, especially one providing shared memory, so we expect that a system like RP3 can effectively accommodate a large and diverse set of scientific and engineering applications.

9.0 Credits

The RP3 system, its software support and the applications environment discussed in this paper is the effort of several people. For the hardware design, the contribution of the following people is acknowledged: W. Brantley, D. George, S. Harvey, W. Kleinfelder, K. McAuliffe, E. Melton, V. A. Norton, G. Pfister and J. Weiss. The FORTRAN programming environment was developed by the author, A. Norton and J. Stone. The C environemt was developed by A. Norton and W-L. Chang. Parallel applications development primarily done by the author and A. Norton. The development ot the performance tools and measurements are collaborative work of the author with K. So, A. Bolmarcich and A. Norton.

10.0 References

[*1*] G. F. Pfister, W. C. Brantley, D. A. George, S. L. Harvey, W. J. Kleinfelder, K. P. McAuliffe, E. A. Melton, V. A. Norton, J. Weiss, *The IBM Research Parallel Processor Prototype (RP3): Introduction and Architecture* , *Proceedings of the 1985 International Conference on Parallel Processing* , Aug. 1985.

[*2*] F. Darema-Rogers, D. A. George, V. A. Norton, G. F. Pfister, **A VM Parallel Environment**, *IBM Research Report RC 11225* , 1/23/85.

[*3*] G. F. Pfister, W. C. Brantley, D. A. George, S. L. Harvey, W. J. Kleinfelder, K. P. McAuliffe, E. A. Melton, V. A. Norton, J. Weiss, *An Introduction to the IBM Research Parallel Processor Prototype (RP3)*, Jack Dongarra, editor, *Experimental Parallel Computing Architectures*, 1987.

[*4*] W. C. Brantley, K. P. McAuliffe and J. Weiss, *The RP3 Processor Memory Element*, *Proceedings of the 1985 International Conference on Parallel Processing* , Aug. 1985.

[*5*] IBM RT Personal Computer Technology, 1986. Form No. SA23-1057.

[*6*] A. Gottlieb, R. Grishman, C. P. Kruskal, K. P. McAuliffe, L. Rudolph and M. Snir, **The NYU Ultracomputer - Designing an MIMD Shared Memory Parallel Computer**. *IEEE Transactions on Computers*, pp.175-189, Feb. 1983.

[*7*] G. F. Pfister, V. A. Norton, **"Hot Spot" Contention and Multistage Interconnection Networks** , *Proc of the 1985 International Conference on Parallel Processing* , Aug. 1985.

[8] V. J. Kumar and G. F. Pfister, **The Onset of Hot Spot Contention** , *Proceedings of the 1985 International Conference on Parallel Processing* , Aug. 1986.

[9] C. L. Seitz, **The Cosmic Cube** , *Communications of the ACM*, 28(1):22-23, January 1985.

[10] IBM, VM/SP Introduction, 1986, Program Product GC19-6200.

[11] F. Darema, D. A. George, V. A. Norton, G. F. Pfister, **Environment and System Interface for VM/EPEX** IBM Research Report RC 11381 , 9/19/85.

[12] F. Darema-Rogers, D. A. George, V. A. Norton, G. F. Pfister, **A Single-Program-Multiple-Data Computational Model for EPEX/FORTRAN** . Accepted for publication in Parallel Computing

[13] H. F. Jordan, **Structuring Parallel Algoritms in an MIMD, Shared Memory Environment** , *Parallel Computing*, Vol. 3, May 1986, p. 93.

[14] Peiyi Tang, Pen-Chung Yew and Chuan-Qi Zhu, **Processor Self-Scheduling in Large Multiprocessor Systems** , *Proceedings of the 1986 International Conference on Parallel Processing* Aug. 19-22, 1986.

[15] J. M. Stone, F. Darema-Rogers, V. A. Norton, G. F. Pfister, **The VM/EPEX FORTRAN Preprocessor Reference** , *IBM Research Report RC 11407* , 9/30/85.

[16] Whei-Ling Chang and V. A. Norton, **The VM/EPEX C Preprocessor User's Manual, Version 1.0** , *IBM Research Report RC 12246* , 10/16/86.

[17] F. Darema, **Parallel Applications Development for Shared Memory Systems,** *IBM Research Report RC 12229* , 8/19/86.

[18] F. Darema, A. Karp, P. Teller, **Applications Survey Reports,** *IBM Research Report RC 12743* , 5/6/87.

[19] F. Darema, S. Kirkpartick, V. A. Norton, **Simulated Annealing on Shared Memory Parallel Systems,** *IBM Journal of Research and Development*, May 1987.

[20] K. So, F. Darema-Rogers, D. A. George, V. A. Norton, G. F. Pfister, **PSIMUL: A System for Parallel Simulation of Parallel Programs** IBM Research Report RC11674, 1/31/86.

[*21*] K. So, T. Bolmarcich, F. Darema and V. A. Norton, **A Speedup Analyser for Parallel Programs**. To appear in the Proceedings of the 1987 International Conference on Parallel Processing.

[*22*] F. Darema-Rogers, G. F. Pfister, K. So, **Memory Access Patterns of Parallel Scientific Programs**. SIGMETRICS Conference, May 1987.

[*23*] P. Heidelbeger, A. Norton and John Robinson, **Parallel Quicksort using Fetch-and-Add**. IBM Research Report RC12576, 3/11/87.

HIGH SPEED INTERCONNECTION USING THE CLOS NETWORK

William A. Payne III

AT&T Bell Laboratories
Naperville, IL 60566

Fillia Makedon

Illinois Institute of Technology[1]
Chicago, IL 60616

W. Robert Daasch

Illinois Institute of Technology[2]
Chicago, IL 60616

1. Introduction

The performance of supercomputers depends very much on the allowance of high speed communication between processors or clusters of processors. A high capacity interconnection network can be used to provide that communication. The class of networks described here are non-blocking, and as such provide the best network performance attainable. Algorithms are described here that allow the network to reconfigure very quickly, thus allowing its use for packet or statistical switching. These type switches can provide a mechanism for communication between processors in a vector processing array, dataflow machine, or telecommunication switch. This paper describes the use of the Clos networks for high capacity statistical or packet switching.

There are two primary concerns with the use of the Clos networks [1] for statistical switching. The high performance of these non-blocking networks is sometimes overshadowed by their difficult control algorithms and area complexity. This paper describes self-routing control algorithms for the Clos network when used for high speed statistical switching. The paper also describes an analysis of the area complexity of the Clos network.

An interconnection network is in a class of networks known as being self-routing if it has the capability of being set as a function of routing information specified to the network within the data path. Self-routing networks require distributed intelligence for path setup and no global busy/idle status for operation. The class of networks that includes the banyan, omega, and shuffle-exchange networks has been proven to be self-routing [2][3]. Crossbar networks are not normally considered to be self-routing but it has been shown that they too can be operated in this manner [4].

In order to set a path in the network, destination tags are appended to the information to be transferred. Each portion of the network, or stage of the network, etc., extracts the control information that is particularly targeted for itself and sets the path across its local switch. The Clos networks to be discussed here are assumed to be unbuffered. All storage of packets due to contention will be at the

---

1 F. Makedon is currently with the Department of Computer Science, University of Texas-Dallas, Richardson, TX, 75083-0688.

2 W. R. Daasch is currently with the Department of Electrical Engineering, Portland State University, Portland, OR 97207.

front-end of the network.

The Clos construction renders a strict sense non-blocking network with the least amount of crosspoints. Area complexity however is not only a function of crosspoints but also of the wiring interconnecting the crosspoints in the topology.

2. Clos Network Construction

The classical three staged Clos network is shown in Figure 1.

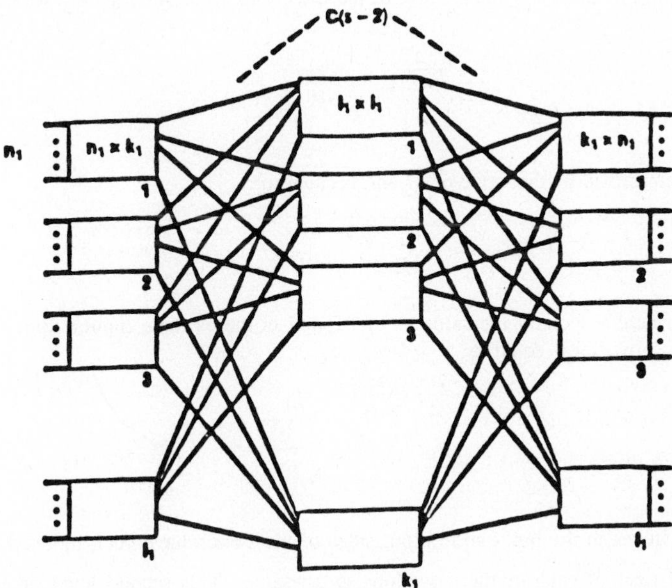

Figure 1. First Level of the Clos Network Construction

The input, middle, and output sections are all constructed of crossbar switches of varying size. The switch is strictly non-blocking if the number of middle stages $k \geq 2n-1$, where n in this case is equal to $N^{1/2}$ and N is the total number of inputs and outputs to the switch. Correspondingly the number of middle switches of size $N^{1/2}$ x $N^{1/2}$ must be $\geq 2N^{1/2}-1$.

We can now briefly describe the construction of the general s staged Clos network C(s) [1], [5], and [6]. The outer stages are defined by the first level of partitioning into sections of size n_1 x k_1. The partitioning parameter n_1 is defined as:

$$n_1 = N^{\frac{2}{s+1}} \tag{1}$$

The value of k_1 is such that the smallest number of crosspoints is required to maintain the condition of a strictly non-blocking network i.e.:

$$k_1 = 2n_1 - 1 \tag{2}$$

Thus there are $2n_1-1$ center sections in this initial three staged network. The number of input/output stages l_1 is simply:

$$l_1 = \frac{N}{N^{\frac{2}{s+1}}} = N^{1-\frac{2}{s+1}} \tag{3}$$

Each of the $2n_1-1$ center sections of size l_1 x l_1 is then constructed using the next smallest Clos network or C(s-2). The inner and outer sections of these networks comprising the center section would be partitioned according to C(s-2). Thus the size of these sections would be n_2 x k_2, where the value of n_2 is:

$$n_2 = N^{\frac{s-1}{s+1}\frac{2}{(s-2)+1}} = N^{\frac{2}{s+1}} = n_1 \tag{4}$$

The value of k_2 is determined by the value of n_2 and is equal to:

$$k_2 = 2n_2 - 1 = 2N^{\frac{2}{s+1}} - 1 = k_1 \tag{5}$$

We see that the size here is exactly the same as that found in the extreme input/output sections. The number of sections l_2 however is equal to:

$$l_2 = N^{(1-(\frac{2}{s+1})-(\frac{2}{s+1}))} = \frac{l_1}{N^{\frac{2}{s+1}}} \tag{6}$$

Thus the number switches in the input and output sides of the switch have been reduced by the factor $(\frac{2}{s+1})$ although the sizes of each of these sections is the same. This second level of partitioning is shown in Figure 2.

If we carried this to the next level of partitioning we would see again that n_4=n_3=n_2=n_1=n. The same would be true of the values of k, namely k_4=k_3=k_2=k_1=k. The value of l_i is however modified as the level of partitioning increases. These are the general rules for construction of the Clos network.

3. Self-Routing Algorithm

The following discussion introduces the concept of self-routing in the general s staged Clos. A Special Clos Network is also described for which the routing calculations and associated implementation is very simple.

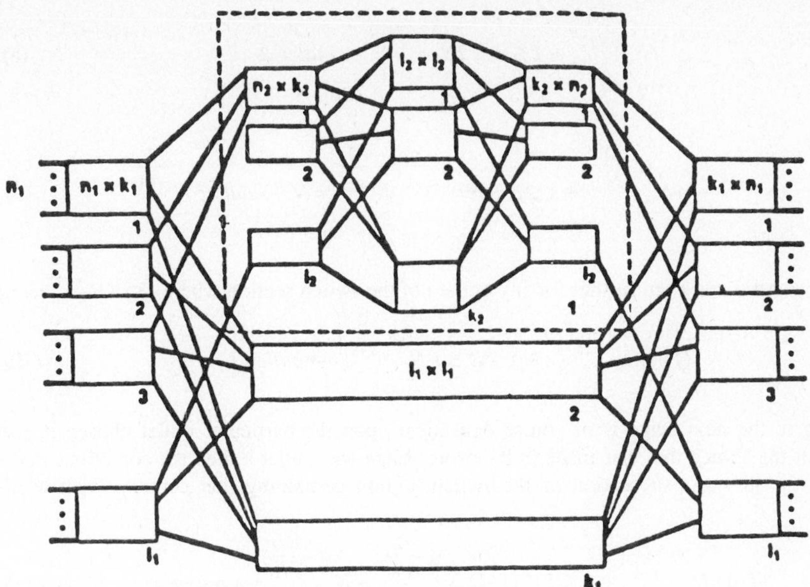

Figure 2. Second Level of the Clos Network Construction

3.1 General s Stage Clos Network C(s)

The general s staged Clos Network C(s) can be logically partitioned into two subnetworks. This partitioning is done due to the difference in routing operations performed in each half. In the first $\frac{s-1}{2}$ stages of the switch the routing algorithm requires that each switch section poll ALL idle links when a circuit request is received. This means that for each input, all possible paths are polled to the middle stage. In the last $\frac{s+1}{2}$ stages of the switch the destination routing begins. The routing decisions that must be made are based upon the particular stage observed. In the middle stage once an outlet is chosen then only $N^{(1-\frac{2}{s+1})}$ of the outputs can be addressed from that outlet. In the next stage once an outlet is chosen then only $N^{(1-\frac{2}{s+1}-\frac{2}{s+1})}$ of the outputs can be reached from that point. This process continues up to the last stage where the final choice is made ($N^{(1-\frac{2}{s+1}\cdot\frac{s+1}{2})} = 1$).

For the general s staged Clos network the routing in the middle stages and above have $N^{\frac{2}{s+1}}$ conditions that must be checked. The conditions for the middle stage are compared against the destination tag d as follows:

$$1 \le d \le N^{(1-\frac{2}{s+1})} \rightarrow outlet\ 1 \tag{7}$$

$$N^{(1-\frac{2}{s+1})}+1 \le d \le 2N^{(1-\frac{2}{s+1})} \rightarrow outlet\ 2 \tag{8}$$

. . .

$$(N^{\frac{2}{s+1}}-1)\cdot N^{(1-\frac{2}{s+1})}+1 \le d \le N^{(1-\frac{2}{s+1})}\cdot N^{\frac{2}{s+1}}=N \rightarrow outlet\ N^{\frac{2}{s+1}} \tag{9}$$

This can be generalized even further for any outlet j of the switch section where $1 \le j \le N^{\frac{2}{s+1}}$ namely:

$$(j-1)\cdot N^{(1-\frac{2}{s+1})}+1 \le d \le j\cdot N^{(1-\frac{2}{s+1})} \rightarrow outlet\ j \tag{10}$$

The routing in the next stage is of course dependent upon the particular outlet chosen in that stage. Suppose that the choice that was made in the center stage was outlet j, then the conditions that must be checked in the jth-most subsection of the switch section containing that center switch would be as follows:

$$(j-1)\cdot N^{(1-\frac{2}{s+1})}+1 \le d \le (j-1)\cdot N^{(1-\frac{2}{s+1})}+N^{(1-\frac{2(2)}{s+1})} \rightarrow outlet\ 1 \tag{11}$$

$$(j-1)\cdot N^{(1-\frac{2}{s+1})}+N^{(1-\frac{2(2)}{s+1})}+1 \le d \le (j-1)N^{(1-\frac{2}{s+1})}+2N^{(1-\frac{2(2)}{s+1})} \rightarrow outlet\ 2 \tag{12}$$

. . .

$$(j-1)\cdot N^{(1-\frac{2}{s+1})}+(N^{\frac{2}{s+1}}-1)\cdot N^{(1-\frac{2(2)}{s+1})}+1 \le d \le j\cdot N^{(1-\frac{2}{s+1})} \rightarrow outlet\ N^{\frac{2}{s+1}} \tag{13}$$

These routing decision comparisons would be very time consuming. In fact as the stage number increases, the routing calculations become more complex. This is because all of the comparisons are done on an absolute basis. One can remove this absolute addressing by subtracting out a bias from both the destination address tag and the comparison criteria. The equations above are very similar to the decisions to be made in the center stage except for the term $(j-1)\cdot N^{(1-\frac{2}{s+1})}$. This term can be thought of as a bias and provides an absolute address comparison for the destination tag. The bias can be subtracted out of the equations and the routing criteria in the next routing stage from the middle $(\frac{s+3}{2})$ become:

$$1 \le d \le N^{(1-\frac{2(2)}{s+1})} \rightarrow outlet\ 1 \tag{14}$$

$$N^{(1-\frac{2(2)}{s+1})}+1 \le d \le 2N^{(1-\frac{2(2)}{s+1})} \rightarrow outlet\ 2 \tag{15}$$

. . .

$$(N^{\frac{2}{s+1}}-1)\cdot N^{(1-\frac{2(2)}{s+1})}+1 \le d \le N^{(1-\frac{2}{s+1})} \rightarrow outlet\ N^{\frac{2}{s+1}} \tag{16}$$

The general routing comparison rule is directly determined from these equations. This is again generalized for any output j where $1 \le j \le N^{\frac{2}{s+1}}$ from this routing section namely:

$$(j-1)\cdot N^{(1-\frac{2(2)}{s+1})}+1 \le d \le j\cdot N^{(1-\frac{2(2)}{s+1})} \rightarrow outlet\ j \qquad (17)$$

One can readily see that the only difference between this routing rule and the one found in the middle stage is the difference in the exponent. If relative addressing can be achieved then all switch sections would be almost exactly alike. Relative addressing can be achieved by subtracting out the bias for the next stage once a given comparison has proven successful. The bias to be subtracted would be dependent upon both the output that was selected and the stage of the switch section. In general the bias has the value shown below:

$$(j-1)\cdot N^{(1-\frac{2(k-\frac{s-1}{2})}{s+1})} \qquad (18)$$

where k is the stage number of the switch section, and j is the outlet that the infomation is to be routed out on. Since destination routing is only done in the last half of the network, the value of k should be such that $\frac{s+1}{2} \le k \le s$.

Given that the routing bias is removed from the destination tag then a generalization can be made about the routing operations that should be performed in a given stage. This generalization is still dependent upon the stage k that a switch section is in and the outlet j that the information was routed out of in the previous section:

$$(j-1)\cdot N^{(1-\frac{2(k-\frac{s-1}{2})}{s+1})}+1 \le d \le j\cdot N^{(1-\frac{2(k-\frac{s-1}{2})}{s+1})} \rightarrow outlet\ j \qquad (19)$$

The value of k will be programmed into the switch section (via pin strapping) to indicate which stage the section is associated with. The bias value to be subtracted at each section output is determined by the particular outlet that is chosen due to a passed comparison. This outlet determines the value of j and along with the stage value k specifies the operation to be performed on the destination tag.

It is shown in [4] that the setup time algorithm for the Clos network is O(eln n).

3.2 Special Self-Routing Clos Network

A special case of the Clos Network is one for which the number of inputs/outputs are a power of two ($N = 2^t$). The number of inputs to a given switch section for an s staged network is then:

$$n = N^{\frac{2}{s+1}} = 2^{\frac{2t}{s+1}} \qquad (20)$$

Suppose that a relation is made between the value of t and the number of stages namely:

$$t = \frac{s+1}{2} \longrightarrow s = 2t - 1 \quad (21)$$

This means that the number of inputs to a given switch section is equal to 2. The minimum number of outputs that a switch must have in order to maintain the non-blocking quality is 2n-1 or in this case 3. In effect this network would be constructed of 2x3, 3x2, and 2x2 switches (switch nodes). The 2x3 switches would be used in the first half of the network while the 3x2 network would be used in the second half of the network. The 2x2 switches would be used in the center stage of the switch. Another interesting quality here is that these switch sizes are applicable no matter what size network is to be built. If we maintain the relation in Equation 21 then the switch section sizes would all be the same. When the number of inputs/outputs increases in a switch then extra stages must be added. A 4x4 and 8x8 version of this switch is shown in Figures 3 and 4.

The most important characteristic of this network is the ease by which self-routing can be performed. The destination tag d of course consist of a field of bits the lenght of which is $\log_2 N$. As has been shown in some of the other multistaged networks like the banyan, shuffle-exchange, omega, etc. the bits associated with the destination tag can be used to specify the path through the switch matrix. Here we are also making the assumption that the destination tag is specified such that $0 \leq d \leq (N-1)$.

The self-routing algorithm begins in the same manner as that for the general s-staged Clos Network. A circuit request arrival in one of the switch sections in the first half of the network generates circuit requests on all outputs that are currently not being used for information transfer. If requests occur simultaneously on the two inputs then one of them is deferred while the other is processed. Another way to handle the concurrency would be to partition the setup time such that each input has a specified setup period (assuming that this would be very small).

In the second half of the network we make the following rule. If the first bit in the destination tag is a 0, then the outlet to be chosen in the 2x2 and 3x2 switch nodes is the upper link. However if the destination bit is a 1, then the lower link should be chosen. We also make the rule that once a destination tag bit has been used then it is removed from the stream. If we assume that the outputs are ordered such that the uppermost one is output 0 and the lowermost one is output (N-1), then it can be readily seen that the above switching rule specifies a path to the destination. A destination can be reached from any input simply by the bits representing the destination tag.

Each of the switch nodes (2x3, 3x2, 2x2) can operate independently. Very simple logic and control would be required in order to implement them switches. In this routing scenario there is no need for subtraction, and there is no need to keep track of the outlet that was chosen in the previous stage. There is also no need to keep track of the stage that a switch node is in. All of these are taken care of by the removal of a destination bit once it has been used by a switch node. The removal of the bit effectively performs the necessary subtraction required in the general s staged Clos network.

The resultant is a non-blocking switch that is self-routing. The routing decisions are very simple and are based simply upon a bit in the destination address tag. There is no need to specify stage information as in the general case.

4. Area Complexity of the Clos Network

The area defined for the Clos network is defined to be the area within the smallest rectangle that can encapsulate it. The network has a parallelogram-like shape, due to the increasing length within the vertical dimension of the switch with each increase in stages towards the middle of the network. Each dimension of this shape will be bounded in order to get an idea on how much chip area will be required.

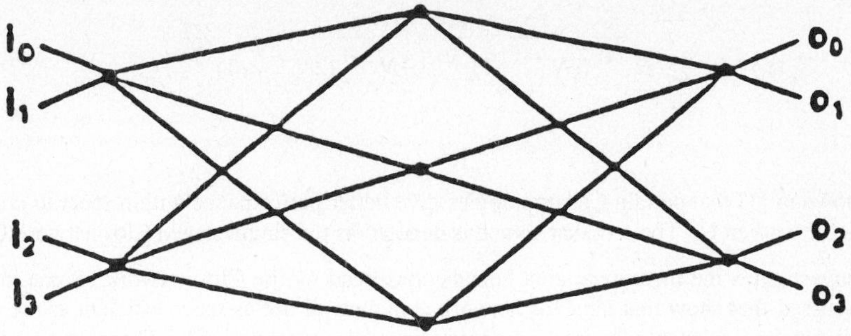

Figure 3. 4x4 Special Self-Routing Clos Network

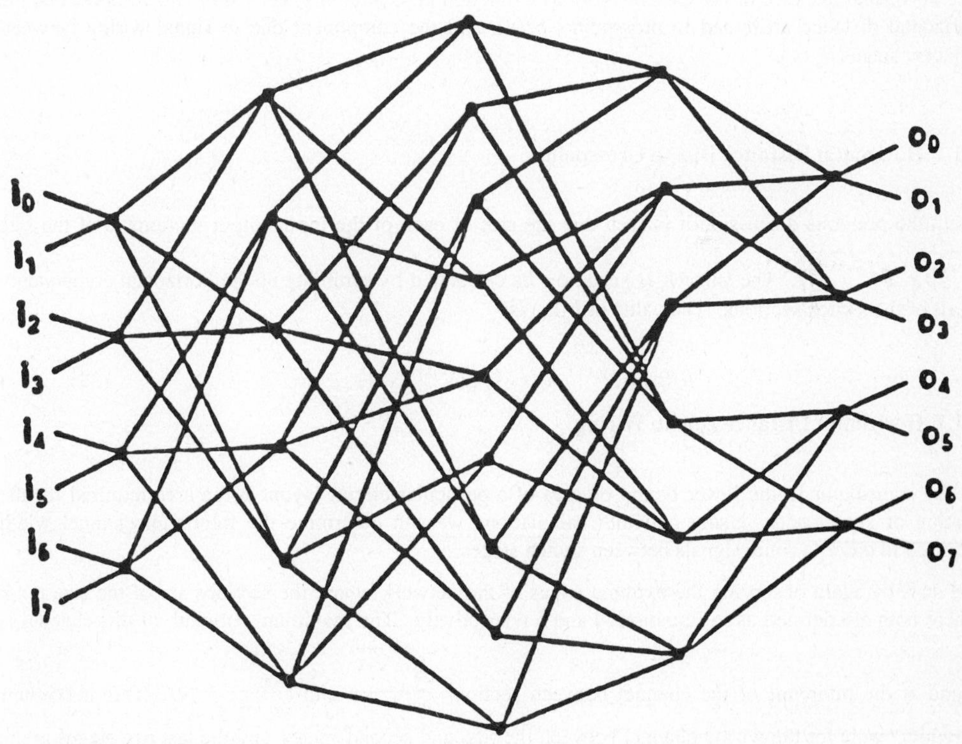

Figure 4. 8x8 Special Self-Routing Clos Network

The total number of crosspoints $X_c(s)$ for a Clos network of s stages (C(s)) is given by [1]:

$$X_c(s) = 2 \sum_{i=2}^{\frac{s+1}{2}} N^{\frac{2i}{s+1}} (2N^{\frac{2}{s+1}} - 1)^{\frac{s+3}{2} - i} + N^{\frac{4}{s+1}} (2N^{\frac{2}{s+1}} - 1)^{\frac{s-1}{2}} \qquad (22)$$

It has been shown in [1] that certain Clos topologies give better performance with respect to crosspoints than do others for a given N. The crossbar switch is denoted as the single staged Clos network C(1).

This section investigates the theoretical area bounds consumed by the Clos network. Some interesting results are discussed that show that the Clos network is in general not as space efficient as the crossbar, even though it requires substantially less crosspoints in some instances. The Thompson model [7] is used as the VLSI model for bounding the area. It will be extended somewhat here in order to get a tight bound on the area. Similar analysis has been performed for the shuffle-exchange network in [8], [9], [10], and [11]. The asymptotic limit found in these studies is compared to the results of the Clos network in one of the later sections. The crossbar network was compared to the banyan network [12] for VLSI area and speed performance in [13]. Although this was a very detailed design, the results were not extendable to other topologies because a relevant model was not developed.

4.1 Horizontal Distance Theoretical Bound

The horizontal distance of the Clos network as a function of s called h(s) consist of two components; the horizontal distance attributed to crosspoints $h_c(s)$, and the component due to signal wiring between adjacent stages $h_w(s)$.

4.1.1 Horizontal Distance Due to Crosspoints

From the previous discussion it is seen that the size of each of the input/output sections is of the size $N^{\frac{2}{s+1}} \times 2N^{\frac{2}{s+1}} - 1$. The value $h_c(s)$ can now be calculated by summing up the horizontal components of all of the switch sections. The value of $h_c(s)$ is:

$$h_c(s) = N^{\frac{2}{s+1}} + (s-1) \cdot (2N^{\frac{2}{s+1}} - 1) \qquad (23)$$

4.1.2 Horizontal Distance Due to Wiring

A key contributor to the lower bound on area of a particular circuit layout is the area required for the routing of signal nets. Using cutwidth calculations we can determine the minimum channel width required in order to route signals between switch stages.

We start by again observing the extreme edges of the network where the sections are of the size n x k where both are defined as in Equations 4 and 5 respectively. The maximum cutwidth of this channel is found at the midpoint of the channel between sections $\frac{N^{1-\frac{2}{s+1}}}{2}$ and $(\frac{N^{1-\frac{2}{s+1}}}{2})+1$. This maximum cutwidth cw(1) for the wiring channel between the first and second stages, and the last two stages in the switch is then equal to:

$$cw(1) = (2N^{\frac{2}{s+1}} - 1) \cdot N^{1-\frac{2}{s+1}} \tag{24}$$

In the center stages that are constructed using C(s-2) switches the number of sections for each switch is equal to l_2 and is defined in Equation 6. Since each of these switches is totally self-contained, there are no wires that interconnect any two of these switches between the second and third stage of switches. The resulting effect is that the maximum cutwidth of this channel is the maximum cutwidth found in any of the 2n-1 switches. The maximum cutwidth cw(2) in the second and $(s-2)^{th}$ wiring channel is equal to:

$$cw(2) = (2N^{\frac{2}{s+1}} - 1) \cdot N^{(1-(\frac{2}{s+1})-(\frac{2}{s+1}))} \tag{25}$$

In general we see that with each new stage addition that the number of sections in a given switch is reduced by the factor $N^{\frac{2}{s+1}}$. Thus for a given C(s) network the horizontal distance attributed strictly to wiring $h_w(s)$ is equal to:

$$h_w(s) = (2N^{\frac{2}{s+1}} - 1) \cdot 2 \sum_{j=1}^{\frac{s-1}{2}} N^{(1-\frac{2j}{s+1})} \tag{26}$$

The total horizontal distance h(s) as defined by Equation 27 is the sum of the component due to the crosspoints and that due to the interconnection wiring and is equal to:

$$h(s) = N^{\frac{2}{s+1}} + (2N^{\frac{2}{s+1}} - 1) \cdot [(s-1) + 2 \cdot \sum_{j=1}^{\frac{s-1}{2}} N^{1-\frac{2j}{s+1}}] \tag{28}$$

4.2 Vertical Distance Theoretical Bound

In the vertical direction we will bound the distance by determining the maximum length required to accomodate the center stage. The center sections consists of square switches of size $N^{\frac{2}{s+1}} \; x \; N^{\frac{2}{s+1}}$.

We again observe how the network grows from the input stage to the center in order to attain the vertical dimension at the center. In the first and last sections the number of outlets is equal to k or 2n-1. Each of these outlets connects to one of the 2n-1 C(s-2) switches comprising the middle of the network. As described earlier each of these C(s-2) switches also has outlets to each of the 2n-1 C(s-4) center switches. Thus the vertical dimension in the center stage of an s staged network v(s) is equal to:

$$v(s) = (2N^{\frac{2}{s+1}} - 1)^{\frac{s-1}{2}} \cdot N^{\frac{2}{s+1}} \tag{29}$$

A much more efficient value could be achieved by taking into account the varying number of switch sections in each stage of the network. This is not viewed to be practical since VLSI chips are normally square in dimension and designers would likely not be able to take full advantage of this unused area.

4.3 Total Area Theoretical Bound

The total area required to layout this circuit includes the area required for crosspoints and that required for interconnection wiring.

$$A(s) = A_c(s) + A_w(s) \tag{30}$$

The previous expressions can be used to calculate this area by regarding the following:

$$A(s) = h(s) \cdot v(s) = (h_c(s) + h_w(s)) \cdot v(s) \tag{31}$$

and is equal to:

$$A(s) = [(2N^{\frac{2}{s+1}} - 1) \cdot [(s-1) + (2 \sum_{j=1}^{\frac{s-1}{2}} N^{(1-\frac{2j}{s+1})})] + N^{\frac{2}{s+1}}] \cdot [(2N^{\frac{2}{s+1}} - 1)^{\frac{s-1}{2}} \cdot N^{\frac{2}{s+1}}] \tag{32}$$

This expression is plotted on logarithmic scales in Figure 5, for values of N ranging from 256 to 2^{14}, and the number of stages up to s=15 when applicable.

If one wants to get a more accurate idea of the area involved then the model must be extended somewhat. This area model assumes a one to one correspondence between the size of the processing element (crosspoint) and that of a strip of metal or polysilicon wire. A weighting factor γ is now introduced which takes into account the difference in magnitude between the two model elements (crosspoints and wiring). The expression for total area Equation 30 becomes:

$$A(s) = A_c(s) + \gamma \cdot A_w(s) \tag{33}$$

Expression 32 can now be written as:

$$A(s) = [(2N^{\frac{2}{s+1}} - 1) \cdot [(s-1) + (2\gamma \sum_{j=1}^{\frac{s-1}{2}} N^{(1-\frac{2j}{s+1})})] + N^{\frac{2}{s+1}}] \cdot [(2N^{\frac{2}{s+1}} - 1)^{\frac{s-1}{2}} \cdot N^{\frac{2}{s+1}}] \tag{34}$$

This expression is evaluated for a range of γ between 10^{-4} up to the VLSI model value of 1, on Figures 6 and 7. The switch sizes range from N=4 to $N=2^{20}$, while the number of switch stages ranged from s=3-15.

As one can see for the value of γ being small (on the order of < 0.10) that in many cases the multistaged Clos network renders a layout that requires less area than does the crossbar. In fact for values of γ that are greater than 0.125, the area required for the crossbar is always less than that required for the Clos. Thus the minimum γ is:

$$\gamma_{min} = 0.125 \tag{35}$$

For values of γ below γ_{min} a multistaged Clos network in some instances gives better VLSI area performance than does the crossbar. The crossbar network ALWAYS gives better area performance than the Clos network for values above γ_{min}.

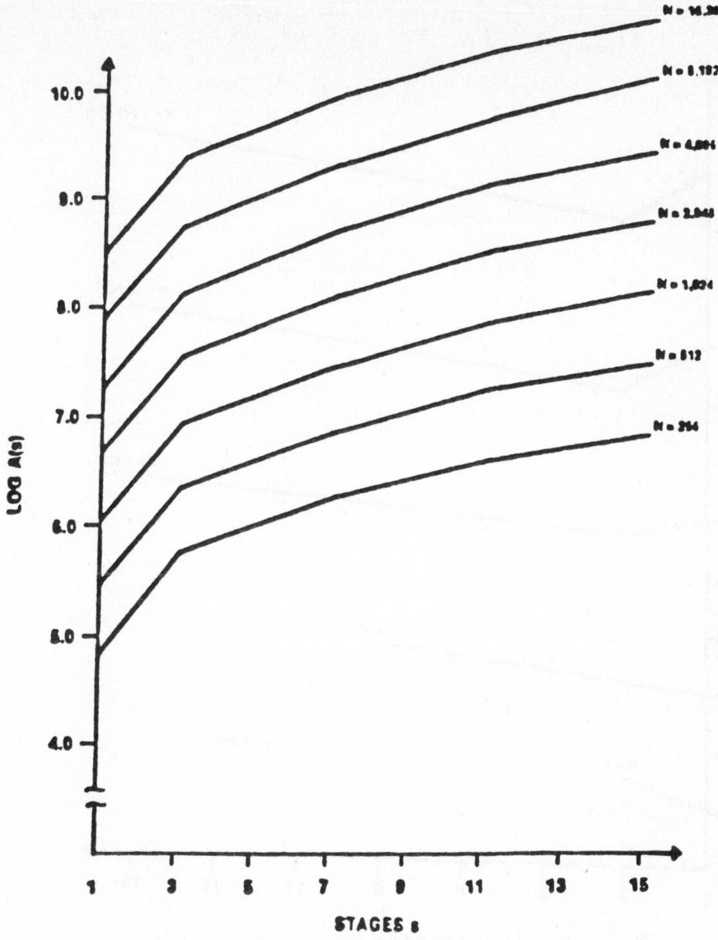

Figure 5. Area Required for the Clos Network

4.4 Layout Area Complexity

The upper bound on the area required for the layout can be calculated by using approximations. The value of s is usually small while that of N is relatively large. Thus we make the assumption that $N^{\frac{2}{s+1}} \gg 1$. Equation 34 can then be reduced to the following:

$$\hat{A}(s) = 2^{\frac{s+1}{2}} \cdot s \cdot N^{(1+\frac{2}{s+1})} + 2^{\frac{s+3}{2}} \cdot \gamma \cdot \left(N^2 - N^{(1+\frac{2}{s+1})}\right) + 2^{\frac{s+1}{2}} \cdot N^{(1+\frac{4}{s+1})} \tag{36}$$

The behavior of the equation can be better understood by observing it as a function of γ. When γ is very small the middle term is removed with the result that:

$$\hat{A}_{\gamma\, small} = 2^{\frac{s+1}{2}} \cdot s \cdot N^{(1+\frac{2}{s+1})} + 2^{\frac{s+1}{2}} \cdot N^{(1+\frac{4}{s+1})} \tag{37}$$

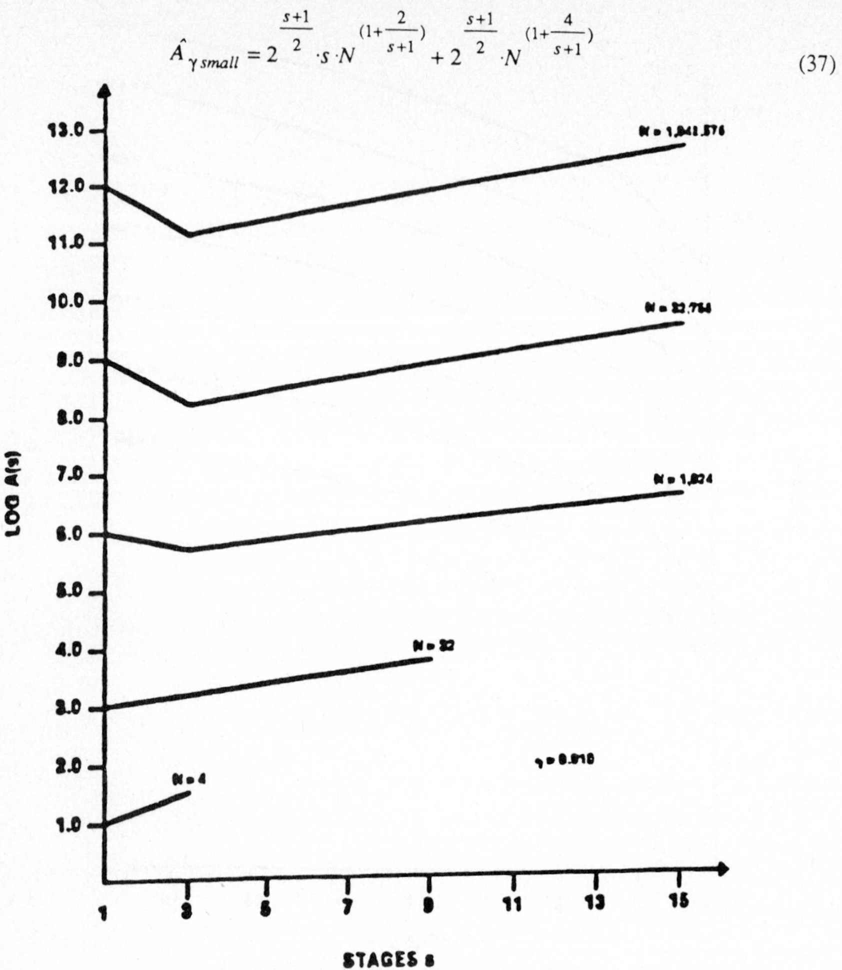

Figure 6. Area Required for γ=0.01

Since the value $2^{\frac{s+1}{2}} \leq 2^s$ the layout area for γ small is $O(s\, 2^s N^{(1+\frac{2}{s+1})})$.

When γ is large(≈1.0), the middle term is the dominant factor in Equation 36. In this case most of the layout area is due to interconnection wiring between switching stages:

$$\hat{A}_{\gamma\, large}(s) = 2^{\frac{s+3}{2}} \cdot \gamma \cdot (N^2 - N^{(1+\frac{2}{s+1})}) \tag{38}$$

The bound can be further refined by realizing that:

$$(N^2 - N^{(1+\frac{2}{s+1})}) \leq N^2 \tag{39}$$

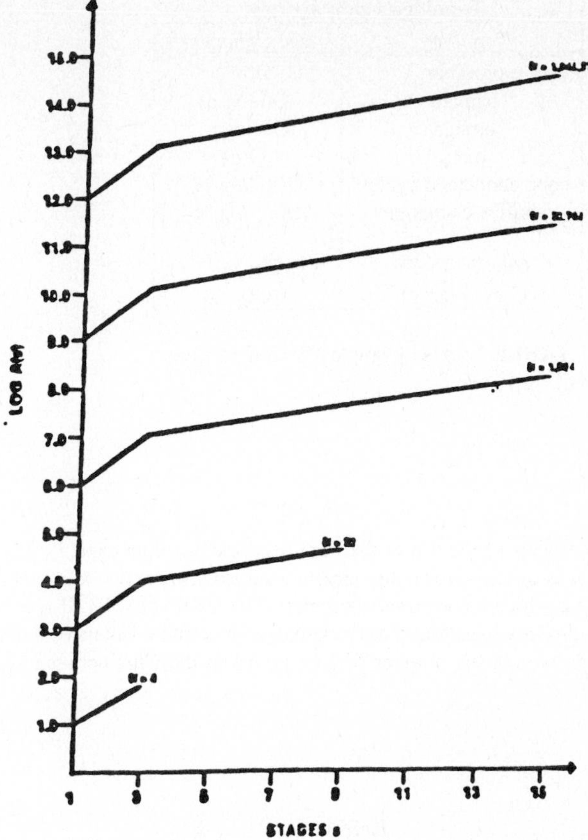

Figure 7. Area Required for γ=1.00

The function $\hat{A}_{\gamma\, large}(s)$ grows exponentially in s, due to the interconnection wiring. In practical designs the minimum sized layout is usually required. Since the above function is exponential in s, the minimal value is the only one of interest. For the structure to remain a Clos network the stage value s=3 is the minimum value of importance. Using the above condition, and the minimal s value it is seen that the function is bounded by:

$$\hat{A}_{\gamma large}(s) \approx 8N^2 \qquad (40)$$

Thus the function's complexity is O(N^2) for γ large.

These values are compared against other topologies in Table 1.

It is interesting to note the results. If the value of &gamma& is large, i.e. if the complexity of the crosspoints is small, then the area required to lay the Clos network out in VLSI is no better than that required for the crossbar. If however the complexity of the crosspoints is quite substantial, then the Clos network could provide a more area efficient layout than the crossbar.

Topology Comparisons	
Topology	*Area Complexity*
crossbar	$O(n^2)$
banyan	O(nlog n)
omega	O(nlog n)
trees	O(n)
cube connected cycles	$O(n^2/log^2 n)$
shuffle-exchange	$O(n^2/log^2 n)$
Clos (γ small)	$O(s\,2^s n^{(1+\frac{2}{s+1})})$
Clos (γ large)	$O(n^2)$

TABLE 1. Area Complexity Comparisons

5. Summary

This paper discussed two aspects of the use of the Clos networks for high capacity statistical switching. A self routing algorithm was described for the general s staged Clos network, as well as for a special case of the Clos network for which the routing is simpler. The topological VLSI area complexity of the Clos network was also studied and was found to be comparable in many instances to that of the crossbar network. This is true even though the number of crosspoints in the Clos network is usually less than that of the crossbar.

References

[1] C. Clos, "A Study of Non-Blocking Switching Networks," Bell System Technical Journal No. 32, pp. 406-424, 1953.

[2] D. Nassimi and S. Sahni,"A Self-Routing Benes Network and Parallel Permutation Algorithms," IEEE Trans. on Comp., Vol. C-30, No. 5, May 1981, pp. 332-340.

[3] K. E. Batcher, "Sorting Networks and Their Applications," Proc. AFIPS 1968 SJCC, Vol. 32, AFIPS Press, pp. 307-314.

[4] W. A. Payne, Complexity and Performance of Statistically Switched Interconnection Networks, PhD Dissertation, Dept. of Elec. Eng., Illinois Inst. of Tech., 1986.

[5] V. E. Benes, "Algebraic and Topological Properties of Connecting Networks," Bell System Technical Journal No. 41, 1962.

[6] V. E. Benes, Mathematical Theory of Connecting Networks and Telephone Traffic, Academic Press, 1965.

[7] C. D. Thompson, A Complexity Theory for VLSI, Phd Dissertation, Dept. of Comp. Sci., Carnegie-Mellon Univ., 1980.

[8] D. Hoey and C. E. Leiserson, "A Layout for the Shuffle-Exchange Network," Proc. of the 1980 IEEE Int. Conf. on Parallel Processing, August 1980.

[9] D. Kleitman, F. T. Leighton, M. Lepley, and G. L. Miller, "New Layouts for the Shuffle-Exchange Graph," Proc. 13th ACM Symp. on the Theory of Computing, May 1981.

[10] F. T. Leighton, "Optimal Layouts for Small Shuffle-Exchange Graphs," VLSI 81, edited by John P. Gray, Academic Press, London, August 1981.

[11] F. T. Leighton, Layouts for the Shuffle-Exchange Graph and Lower Bound Techniques for VLSI, PhD Dissertation, MIT, June 1982.

[12] L. R. Goke and G. J. Lipovski, "Banyan Networks for Partitioning Multiprocessor Systems," Proc. 1st Annual Computer Architecture Conference, Dec. 1973.

[13] M. Franklin, "VLSI Performance Comparison of Banyan and Crossbar Communications Networks," IEEE Trans. on Computers, April 1981.

Multipath Hierarchies in Interconnection Networks

Peter A. Franaszek and Christos J. Georgiou

Computer Sciences Department
IBM T. J. Watson Research Center
Yorktown Heights, NY 10598

The design of interconnection networks is a central problem in parallel computing. This is especially true for the case of shared-memory machines, where network latency is a limiting factor in system size. This paper discusses circuit and implementation issues which support one particular approach to network structure, a synergistic design comprised of a multiplicity of subnetworks.

1.0 Introduction

Consider a machine which has N processors, each with a cache and private memory, and N memory modules, which hold shared data. For simplicity, it will be assumed that a memory module is associated with each processor, so that an NxN network or switch is sufficient to connect a given processor with any other processor or memory module. The fact that data is shared may yield quite stringent performance requirements on the network, since a round trip may be required for every data reference. We will not further consider the issue of frequency of access or performance requirements, but simply note that in at least one instance [1], the performance requirements have led to a design where the network is implemented with a circuit technology considerably faster than that of the processors. This leads to the conclusion that the minimization of network latency is a significant problem.

The types of networks we consider are based on crossbars and/or multistage networks such as banyans [2]. By a crossbar, we mean a single-stage nonblocking circuit switch (implementable for example as an NxN array of crosspoints). The multistage networks are assumed to consist for a set of nodes each with a given number of inputs and outputs. Crossbars have a circuit complexity of $O(N^2)$, and multistage networks potentially O(NlogN), so it is sometimes argued that the latter are the ones of choice for large N. However, crossbars are fast, and for sufficiently small N, say N_0, may not be prohibitively expensive. On the other hand, for N large enough, say N_1, multistage networks may not have sufficiently high performance. With modern technology, it is not clear that $N_1 > N_0$ for the case of shared-memory computing. However, for some crossbar designs, both N_0 and N_1 may be too small, for a combination of performance and cost reasons. Here a favored approach may be one which employs a hierarchy of networks including both crossbars and possibly multistage networks to obtain a structure with sufficiently high performance [3]. This paper discusses a variety of circuit and implementation issues associated with this approach.

1.1 Overview of paper

The following is a synopsis of the paper. Section II briefly reviews reasons for a multinetwork structure. The emphasis here is somewhat different from that of [3], which concentrated on abstract network models. Section III examines the delays that are limiting factors to the performance of large multistage and crossbar networks. Section IV presents an example of a network with hierarchical multipath control and discusses its structure and operational details. Finally, section V offers complexity and performance estimates for such a network.

2.0 Performance Limitations and Design Strategies

This section considers the problem of how a fast network might be structured for the case of large N. The approach is straightforward: a listing of factors which constrain performance, and the inclusion of design features which minimize these constraints. Not surprisingly, no single network has all the desired features. Hence the suggestion of a design which includes multiple subnetworks.

It will be assumed that the network consists of a set of ***nodes*** (these may include the processors and memories as well as modules at intermediate stages in the network), and ***links*** which connect them. The functions associated with network operation are broadly of three kinds:

transport: the transmission of a message from node to node.

storage: messages need be held until their desired paths become available.

contention resolution: contention for a network resource must be resolved.

Contention can be either for paths or for access to network controllers. A given message may contend with (i) new messages, (ii) stored messages, and (iii) messages at succeeding nodes (because of possible buffer overflows). Storage delays are incurred where desired paths are not available, so that a nonblocking design is advantageous Transport delays include those associated with path selection, and are generally minimized by incorporating paths which are wide and have few chip crossings.

Consider the transmission of a message from D_i to M_j. Transport delays are inevitable. If path selection delays are lower than those avoided by a nonblocking design, then perhaps the best one can do in terms of raw speed is to use a crossbar with no contention resolution (it will be shown below that an appropriate design avoids speed compromises due to the possibility of collision), but with collision detection. Here the delays are those associated with setting the crosspoints and transmitting the data. If the $O(N^2)$ complexity associated with a crossbar is too great, there are still speed advantages to be gained from a design which incorporates nodes which are as simple as possible. This will generally mean no storage at intermediate nodes. Speed gains are then realized by reducing housekeeping functions such as checking for buffer overflows, and a design which minimizes the number of chip crossings by simplifying intermediate nodes.

Returning to the discussion of the crossbar, some means needs be included to handle the case where more than one D_i wishes to transmit to a given M_j at a particular time, that is, the case of a collision. Several alternatives present themselves:

Retransmission: This may be a worthwhile option, but carries risks associated with potential instabilities [4], as fanout restrictions imply that it is not feasible to have rapid dissemination of the traffic state.

Contention resolution before transmission: This solves the problem of potential collisions, but at the expense of slowing ***all*** messages. A design with wide data paths can yield collision rates of only a few percent.

Transmission or retransmission over an alternate path: The use of a separate network (or networks) to handle the case where there is contention. This network can be optimized for this case, and will generally not have to be exceedingly fast, as it will handle only a fraction of the traffic.

Alternative 3 is what we term a ***path hierarchy***. Its operation is analogous to that of a storage hierarchy, whose average performance in a good design is largely determined by the speed of the fastest component. The path hierarchies we will be considering here will have only two levels, but this need not be true in general. It should also be noted that path hierarchies are not necessarily limited to cases which include a crossbar.

Some interactions between system modules (processors and memories) include more than one transmission over the network (e.g. a line fetch, which requires a request and response). All messages may utilize the same network, but in some cases it may be advantageous to have return paths reserved by the initial message. Here this message is a request for a resource which includes return paths (over a separate data subnetwork). Delays associated with establishing these paths may be overlapped with delays such as memory fetches. Here the latency of the data subnetwork may approach that of a set of dedicated wires.

There are numerous issues associated with the design of the type of network outlined above. For example, how much speed and simplicity are gained by permitting a design which requires some sort of retransmission (i.e. one where messages can be lost in transit)? How much speed is sacrificed in a crossbar if collisions are permitted? These issues are discussed below, first from a general perspective, then via an example.

3.0 Multistage vs. crossbar network delays

In this section we will examine the performance implications of the implementation of the three essential network functions (i.e. transport, storage and contention resolution) in crossbar and multistage networks.

In its simplest form, a crossbar can be viewed as a grid of crosspoints C_{ij} , in which a single crosspoint must be activated to connect an input to an output. Because of the pin limitations of chip packages, however, large networks must be partitioned into smaller subnetworks. The partitions can be interconnected by means of buses [5], which would allow the interconnection of an input to an output to be done by the activation of a single partition. This implies that the transport delays of a large partitioned crossbar would be the same as those of a single stage network.

The number of crossbar partitions that can be interconnected by a single bus depends on the fan-out characteristics of the technology used for the partition implementation. For shared-memory multiprocessing applications with fairly large size N (e.g. N = 512), current VLSI technology allows the interconnection of the crossbar partitions by means of a single bus.

Multi-stage networks, on the other hand, are structured so that data transmissions must pass through $\log_k$ N sequential network stages. The network stages are connected by point-to-point interconnections -unlike the bus interconnections of crossbar networks- and, consequently, are not constrained by the fan-out characteristics of the technology. The performance of multistage networks, however, is limited by two other factors, namely data transfer delays between stages and contenion resolution delays at each stage.

Data transfer delays between stages can be significant, as the transmission speed of the off-chip data paths is considerably less than that of the on-chip paths (typically smaller by an order of magnitude). This is primarily due to transmission line capacitances and the simultaneous off-chip driver (OCD) switching limitations of chip packages [6]. The multistage networks are affected more severely by these delays because they have more stages. Fig. 1 illustrates this point.

The delays introduced at each stage of a multistage network by the need for contention resolution can magnify the in-between-stage transmission delays. In a typical multistage network, a message is routed from a stage to the next, first by the examination of one or more bits in the message header to identify the next stage, and then by a test of that stage to determine whether it is available to receive the message (i.e. not blocked). If the receiving stage resides on a separate chip than the sending stage,

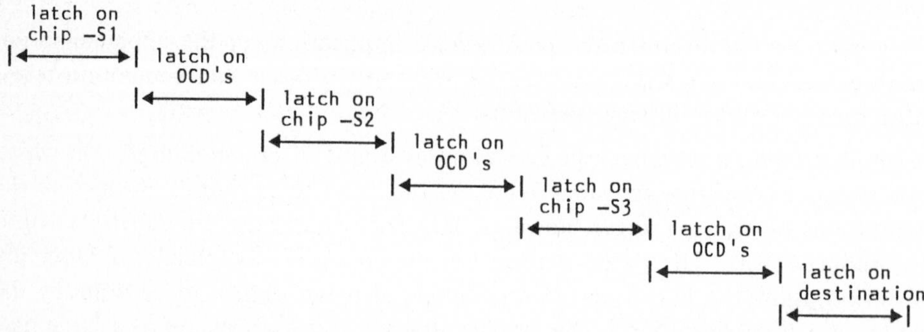

Figure 1. Crossbar vs. multistage network delays

the contention resolution test might require two-chip crossings, which of course, would add to the network transfer delay. The chip crossings could be minimized by integrating more than one stage on a single chip. The number of stages on a chip could vary, depending on the hardware complexity of a stage.

For multistage networks without store-and-forward capability [7] multiple stages could be integrated on a single chip, as allowed by the number of chip I/O pins and layout rules of the technology [8]. In such a network, if the next stage is blocked, the message is discarded and a signal is sent to the source to initiate retransmission. If, as is typically the case, the network is not a nonblocking design, retries may result in substantial local increases in apparent traffic, with significant performance degradation.

Multistage networks with buffering, on the other hand, decrease the overall network blocking factor [1], but at the expense of complexity which limits the number of stages per chip (and this increases the number of chip crossings). Additional delays are incurred for storage operations, as well as contention resolution, which is more complex than in the case without store-and-forward.

The above discussion suggests that there are significant speed advantages to be gained from a design which may require retransmission. However, such retransmission can result in additional contention which may yield unacceptable worst case performance. That is, neither class of networks may by itself provide adequate performance.

4.0 An example of a hierarchical network

4.1 Network organization

In this section we will illustrate the hierarchical network principles by means of a specific example, as shown in Fig. 2. For the purposes of this discussion, we assume that the network interconnects a shared-memory system with N processors and N memories, where N = 512. The network consists of five subnetworks, each one with 512 inputs/outputs. As previously discussed, basic characteristics of a network with hierarchical control are the separation of the control from the data flow and the transmission of control information via a hierarchy of physical paths. In our partic-

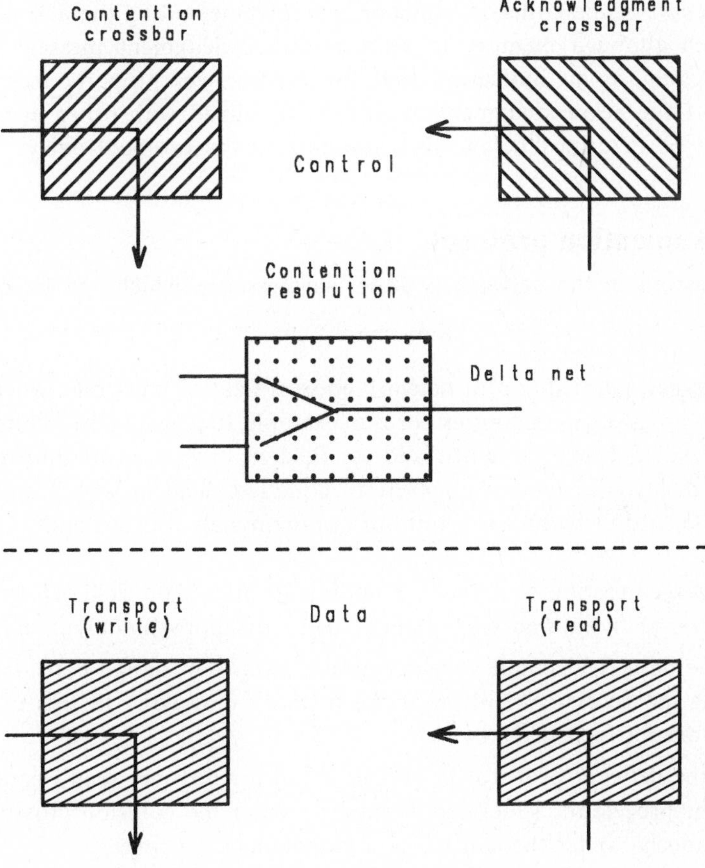

Figure 2. Hierarchical Network

ular example of Fig. 2, three subnetworks -collision crossbar, acknowledgment crossbar and Δ-net, as explained below- constitute the control portion of the network. The other two subnetworks -the transport crossbars- are used for the transfer of data in memory read or write operations.

The subnetworks used for the transfer of control information are partitioned into a two-level hierarchy of paths: a) a fast path, provided by the collision crossbar, which delivers requests reliably from a processor to a memory only in the absence of contention for that memory from other processors. The contention occurs when there are simultaneous requests directed to the same memory module from multiple processors. b) a slow path, provided by the Δ-net, which guarantees the delivery of messages to the memories under all traffic conditions. (We define as Δ-net a multistage network of $\log_k N$ stages with store-and-forward capability at each stage, such as that found in [1]). The function of the collision crossbar is complemented by the acknowledgment crossbar, which allows a memory to send an acknowledgment message to the requesting processor, as an indication that the request was properly received. The transmission of the acknowledgment message is pipelined with other memory operations, as will be described below, thus minimizing the protocol delays in the fast path.

4.2 Communication protocol

All communication in the network is done via messages, which can be one of two kinds:

a) request messages, consisting of a network address field of logN bits, where N is the number of processors/ memories (in our example that would be 9 bits), a cache line I.D. field (3 bytes), a return address field (9 bits), control information, for indicating the type of memory operation requested (read or write), and error detection code field (1 byte), for a total of approximately 8 bytes, and

b) data messages, consisting of a network address (9 bits), data field (16 bytes), cache line I.D. field (3 bytes) and CRC field (1 byte), or approximately 22 bytes.

The size of the data field could vary depending on system design considerations, or for minimizing the access contention at the memory modules. In this example, we chose a data transfer field of 16 bytes.

Fig. 3 shows the network protocol in greater detail for memory read operations. Requests from the processors, generated at time t_0, enter the collision crossbar subnetwork synchronously, under the control of a global clock (at time t_1).

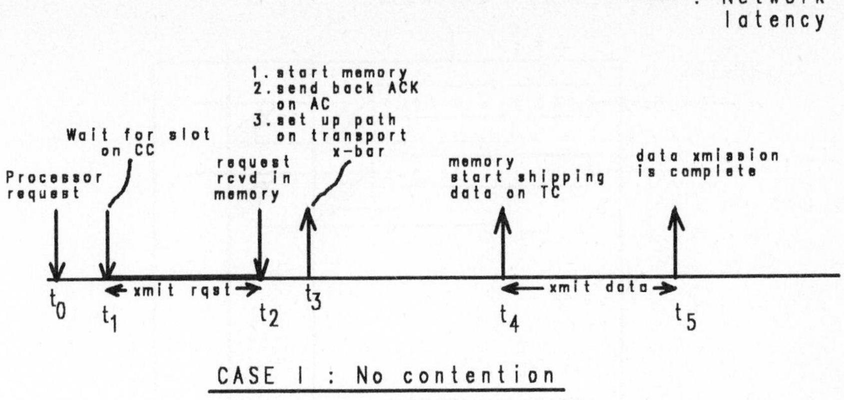

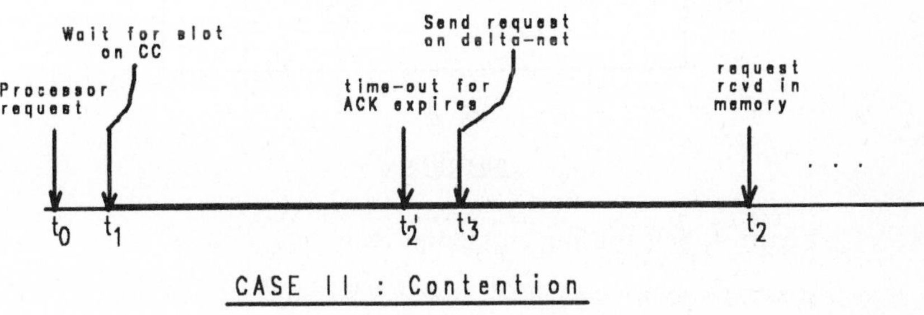

Figure 3. Hierarchical network data flow

In the case of ***non-contention,*** the request is received at the memory at t_2, at which time a determination is made as to whether a collision has occurred. The collision detection mechanism will be explained in the following sections. Upon arrival of the request in the memory, the following three concurrent operations are initiated at time t_3 : 1) the memory access cycle is started, 2) an acknowledgment message is sent back to the requesting processor, and 3) a path is set up on the transport crossbar for reads. When the data becomes available from the memory at t_4, it is shipped to the processor on the transport crossbar. The data transmission completes at time t_5.

In the case of ***contention***, the request is not received properly at the memory and, consequently, no acknowledgment message is sent to the requesting processor. The processor, upon expiration of a time interval T (at t_1') during which it expected to receive the acknowledgment, retransmits the request over the Δ-net (time t_1''). The request is received at the memory at time (t_2), and the same sequence of steps t_3 -t_5, as described in the "non-contention" case, is repeated.

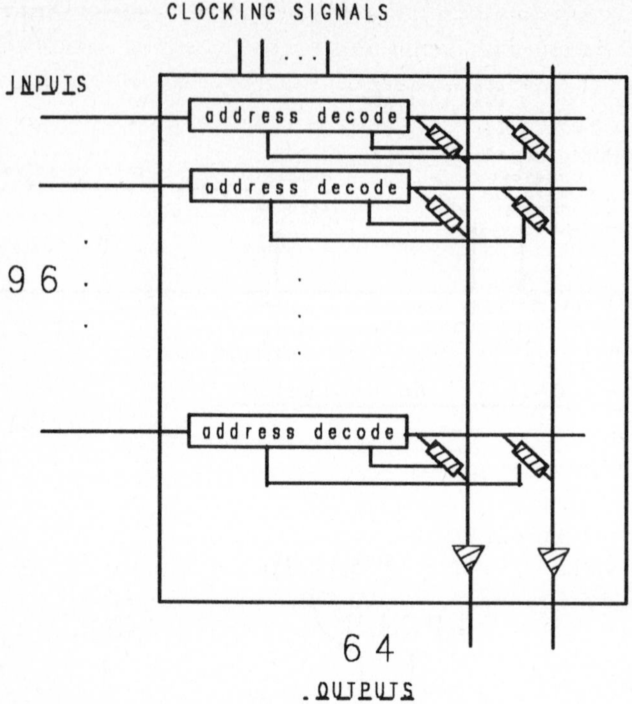

Figure 4. Self-routing crosspoint chip

4.3 Self-routing crosspoint chip

The basic building block of the collision, acknowledgment and transport crossbars is the self-routing crosspoint chip, shown in Fig. 4. The crosspoint chip is organized as a two-sided array of crosspoints C_{ij}. A message enters the chip serially from an input pin I_i and is directed to an address decoder circuitry A_i. The address bits of the message are then decoded to select an output O_j by activating a crosspoint C_{ij}. Once a path is thus established between an input and an output, the message, stripped of its destination address bits, starts flowing to the destination. The transfer of the message bits onto the chip, through the crosspoint and out to the destination forms a 3-stage pipeline, as illustrated in Fig. 1.

The bandwidth of the serial path is dependent on the technology used to implement the crosspoint chip. If the bandwidth provided by a single chip is insufficient, the required bandwidth can be obtained by using multiple chip planes in parallel. For example, if k chip planes are needed to achieve the required bandwidth, a frame of n address + m message bits will be divided into k frames of n address + m/k message bits. Each frame will then be sent via a separate crosspoint chip and all frames will be assembled at the destination, so that the original frame can be reconstructed.

Contention in the collision crossbar is detected at the message destination. If the output circuits of the crosspoint chips are designed to protect against current overload conditions, collisions could occur without damage to the network chips.

A variation of the above scheme could be provided by the introduction of a collision detection circuit at the outputs of each crosspoint chip. This circuit would monitor the status of each bus line and, if traffic or collisions are detected, will signal the source to abort the transmission and retransmit on the slow path.

5.0 Performance and complexity estimates

In order to demonstrate the validity of the hierarchical network approach, we embarked on a detailed feasibility study. Our basic objective was to show that with a currently available technology such as CMOS -a dense but low power dissipating technology- we could realize a network of size 512. The criteria for this evaluation were to achieve transfers of a 16-byte cache line from memory within 1.5 μsecs with reasonable hardware complexity (of the order of 2,000 chips).

5.1 Network delay

The message delay through the network depends on the delays incurred at the fast and slow paths. In the event of contention at the fast path (collision crossbar), the message is retransmitted over the slow path which, in our example, is provided by the Δ-net. We assume that in a typical application in a shared-memory system contention for the same memory module would be small and, therefore, contention for the network fast path would also be small. Performance simulation studies for such workloads done in [9] show the validity of this assumption.

The delays through the network can be derived more specifically as follows: The request is place into the contention crossbar at the beginning of a transmission synchronization period, provided by the network global clock. Since the synchronization clocks arrive every 8 clock cycles, we assume a 50% delay for the initiation of the transmission (Fig. 3), or 4 network cycles. The address header of a message (9-bits) requires 10 cycles to enter the collision crossbar, 3 cycles to traverse it, and 8 cycles for the 6 message bytes to be transmitted to the memory (over 6 switching planes). Thus, the request message takes 25 cycles to arrive at the memory.

We further assume that the memory access will require 18 cycles. This activity is overlapped with the transmission of the acknowledgment message to the processor via the acknowledgment crossbar and the set-up of the return path on the transport crossbar. Finally, the data message transfer on a 10-way parallel transport crossbar would require 3 cycles to traverse the network and 10 cycles for the message transfer, or 19 cycles. The total number of network cycles is, therefore, $25+18+19=62$. If we assume a cycle time of 20 nsecs, which is feasible with current CMOS technology, the total transfer delay would be 62x20 nsecs = 1,240 nsecs.

5.2 Complexity estimates

The basic building block of the network is a 96x64 crosspoint chip. Such a chip would require a 200-pin package, which is well within the capabilities of current technology [7]. A 512-port collision crossbar plane, therefore, could be constructed by a matrix of 6x8=48 chips. If we assume that 6 planes are needed to provide the desired bandwidth, the collision crossbar would require 288 chips. Likewise, the acknowledgment crossbar could be constructed with 96 chips (2 planes) and the transport crossbar with 960 chips (20 planes -- 10 for reads and 10 for writes). We assume that the Δ-net could be constructed with 384 chips, for a design such as that found in [1] but with a denser -and slower- technology. Thus, the hierarchical network, consisting of the above five subnetworks, could be built with a total number of 1,728 chips packaged on 24 printed-circuit boards. The network logic would occupy a volume of 3 cubic feet.

6.0 Conclusions

In this paper we presented a new approach to interconnection networks for high-performance multiprocessor systems. First, we examined the functions performed by interconnection networks, in general, and identified the delays that are limiting factors to the performance of conventional multistage networks. Then we proposed a network structure which optimizes the delays of each network function, by separating the control flow from the data flow and transmitting the control information through a hierarchy of physical paths with varying transfer speeds. We showed that the control hierarchy could be implemented by using fast networks provided by crossbars and slower networks provided by Δ-nets. Finally, we presented the results of a feasibility study, which showed that the hierarchical control networks are realizable with current VLSI technology.

References

[1] G.F. Pfister, W.C. Brantley, D.A. George, S.L. Harvey, W.J. Kleinfelder, K.P. McAuliffe, E.A. Melton, V.A. Norton, and J. Weiss, "The IBM Research Parallel Processor Prototype (RP3): Introduction and Architecture", *Proceedings of 1985 Int'l Conf. on Parallel Processing*, pp. 764-771

[2] L.R. Goke and G.J. Lipovski, "Banyan Networks for Partitioning Multiprocessor Systems", *Proceedings of 1st Annual Symposium in Computer Architecture,* Univ. of Florida, Gainsville, FL 1973, pp. 21-28

[3] P. Franaszek, "Path Hierarchies in Interconnection Networks", *IBM Journal of R&D,* Jan. 1987, pp. 120-131

[4] W.A. Roseukranz, "Some Theorems on the Instability of the Exponential Back-off Protocol", *Performance '84,* E. Gelembe (Editor), Elsevier Science Publishers B.V. (North-Holland), 1984

[5] C.J. Georgiou, "Fault-Tolerant Crosspoint Switching Networks", *Proceedings of 14th Int'l Conf. on Fault-Tolerant Computing,* FTCS-14, Kissimmee, FL, 1984, pp. 240-245

[6] E.E. Davidson, "Electrical Design of a High-Speed Computer Package", *IBM Journal of R&D,* vol. 26, No. 3, May 1982

[7] R. Grondalski, "A VLSI Chip Set for a Massively Parallel Architecture", *Proceedings of 1987 Int'l Solid-State Circuits Conf.,* ISSCC 87, New York City, pp. 198-199

[8] M.A. Franklin, "VLSI Performance Comparison of Banyan and Crossbar Communications Networks", *IEEE Transactions on Computers,* pp. 283-291, April 1981

[9] A. Tantawi, "Performance Modelling and Analysis of a Hierarchically Interconnected Multiprocessor", in preparation.

PERFORMANCE ANALYSIS OF MULTI-BUFFERED PACKET-SWITCHING NETWORKS IN MULTIPROCESSOR SYSTEMS

Hyunsoo Yoon, Kyungsook Y. Lee, and Ming T. Liu
Department of Computer and Information Science
The Ohio State University
2036 Neil Avenue Mall
Columbus, OH 43210

ABSTRACT: In this paper, we extend Jenq [1]'s performance analysis method of single-buffered banyan networks, to be applicable for the multi-buffered packet-switching interconnection networks in multiprocessor systems. Earlier analyses on the buffered interconnection network performances assumed either single or infinite buffers at each input (output) port of a switch. As far as the multi-buffered interconnection network is concerned, only some simulation results for the delta networks have been known [2].

We first model the performance of the single-buffered delta networks using the state transition diagram of a buffer. We then extend the model to account for the multiple buffers.

The results of the multi-buffered delta networks obtained through this analytic approach are compared with the known simulation results. We also show the state equations for the multi-buffered data manipulator networks to demonstrate the generality of the model.

1. Introduction

The packet-switching multistage interconnection networks (MINs) can be used for interconnecting a large number of processors and memory modules in multiprocessor systems, or for the resource arbitration and token distribution in the data flow computers [3]. They can also be used as a switching fabric of a packet switch for the high speed packet-switching computer communication [1, 4, 5]. Since the MINs play a critical role in the overall performance of such systems, extensive studies have been done on characterizing their performance behaviors.

The MINs can be categorized into two groups: the unbuffered MINs and buffered MINs, depending on whether there are buffer(s) at each switching node. In the unbuffered MINs, whenever a path conflict occurs at a switch among competing packets (requests), only one packet can take the resource and the others are discarded. With buffer(s) at each switch as in the buffered networks, the packets, which would be lost otherwise, can be stored as long as buffers are available when a conflict occurs.

A good body of performance analysis work exists both for the unbuffered [6, 7, 8, 9, 10, and references therein] and buffered MINs [2, 11, 1, 7]. For the performance analyses of the buffered networks, either a single buffer or infinite buffers at each input (or output) port of a switch have so far been considered. Dias and Jump [2, 11] analyzed the performance of the delta networks with single buffers and infinite buffers, based on the timed Petri-net model. Jenq [1] analyzed the performance of a packet switch based on the single-buffered banyan network, while the performance of banyan networks with infinite buffers was analyzed by Kruskal and Snir [7].

The performance of the multi-buffered MINs (multiple but not infinite buffers at each switch) has been known only through simulations [2, 11, 12]. In addition to the restriction in the number of buffers (either single or infinite), earlier performance analyses considered only the banyan (delta) networks, which provide a unique path for each input-output connection, constructed from (2×2) crossbar switches. Recently, the performance of the single-buffered delta networks constructed from switching elements (SEs) of arbitrary sizes, and of the single-buffered multiple-path networks (data manipulator type networks) have been analytically studied by us [13].

In this paper, we present a simple analytic model, which can be used to analyze the multi-buffered packet-switching MINs constructed from SEs of an arbitrary size and type (crossbar or bus).

Since the understanding of the effect of the buffer length to the performance, is very important in determining the most cost-effective MINs with an optimal performance, some simulation results already exist as mentioned before. In [2, 11], the authors give the following quoted conclusion, which is now a very well known and widely accepted result : "*Adding buffers to a packet switching networks can increase throughput. A word of warning - don't make them too large. For most application, the number of buffers should be limited to one, two, or three.*" As will be seen later, our analytic results agree with their simulation results.

This paper is organized as follows. In Section 2, the delta networks are briefly introduced. In Section 3, a new analytic model is used to analyze the performance of the single-buffered delta networks. The model is generalized for the multi-buffered delta networks in Section 4, and the analysis results are shown and compared with the known simulation results in Section 5. To demonstrate the generality of the model, the multi-buffered data manipulator type networks are analyzed in Section 6. The conclusions are given in Section 7.

2. The Delta Networks

An $(N\times N)$ delta network consists of n stages of N/a $(a\times a)$ crossbar switches, where $N=a^n$. A packet movement through the network can be controlled locally at each SE by a single base-a digit of the destination address of the packet. The delta network is chosen in this paper because it is very general, i.e., it is a subclass of the banyan network which encompasses all useful unique path MINs. It includes the cube, omega, indirect binary n-cube, shuffle exchange, and baseline network [6, 2]. An example of an (8×8) buffered delta network is given in Fig.1. For a detailed description of the delta network the reader is referred to [6, 2].

3. Performance Analysis of the Single-Buffered Delta Networks

In this section, we analyze the single-buffered delta network for its two important performance measures, throughput and delay. The *throughput* of a network is defined as the average number of packets passed by the network per unit time, and the *delay* is the average time required for a packet to pass through the network. We analyze the network under the uniform traffic model as in [6, 2, 11, 1, 7, 9, 10, 13], i.e., the followings are assumed.

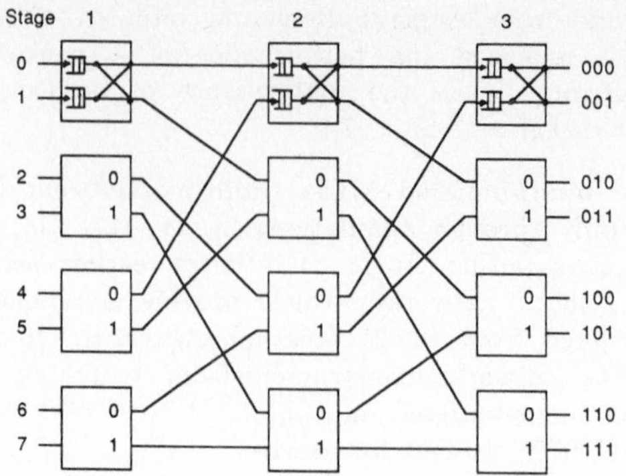

Figure 1: An (8×8) buffered delta network (n=3, a=2).

- The packet arrival rate at each network input port is identical.
- The packets are of fixed size and directed uniformly over all of the network outputs.
- The routing logic at each SE is *fair*, i.e., conflicts are randomly resolved.

These assumptions imply that, for each switching stage of the network, the pattern of packet distribution is identical and statistically independent for all SEs. Therefore, each switching stage can be characterized by a single SE, and this fact makes the analysis of the network very simple.

For the operation of the single-buffered network we assume the followings as in [2, 11, 1].

- Each input port of an SE has a single buffer to accommodate a single packet.
- The buffered network operates synchronously at a rate of τ (called *stage cycle*, and without loss of generality, it is assumed that τ=1.), which consists of two phases.
    - In the first phase, the availability of the buffer space at the subsequent stage along the path of a packet in current buffer is determined, i.e., the packet is informed whether it may go to the next stage or should stay in the current buffer.
    - In the second phase, packets may move forward one stage.
- A packet is able to move forward only if it is selected (among competing packets) by the routing logic of the current SE, *and* either the buffer of the SE it is destined to go at the next stage is empty *or* the packet in that buffer is able to move forward.

We first define the following variables, and derive a set of state equations relating these variables.

n = number of switching stages.

$p_0(k, t)$ = probability that a buffer of an SE at stage k is empty at the beginning of the t-th stage cycle.

$p_1(k, t)$ = $1 - p_0(k, t)$

$q(k, t)$ = probability that a packet is *ready to come* to a buffer of an SE at stage k during the t-th stage cycle.

$r(k, t) =$ probability that a packet in a buffer of an SE at stage k is *able to move forward* during the t-th stage cycle, *given that there is a packet in that buffer.*

$S =$ normalized throughput (throughput normalized with respect to the network size N.)

$d =$ normalized delay (delay normalized with respect to the number of switching stages, i.e., necessary stage cycles for a packet to pass a single stage.)

The probability that an SE at stage k has j packets in its buffers at the beginning of the t-th stage cycle is $\sum_{j=0}^{a}\binom{a}{j}p_1(k,t)^j p_0(k,t)^{a-j}$, and only $1-(1-1/a)^j$ fraction* of j packets will be ready to move forward, and the remaining packets will be blocked due to a switching conflict. Therefore,

$$q(k,t) = \sum_{j=0}^{a}\binom{a}{j}p_1(k-1,t)^j p_0(k-1,t)^{a-j}[1-(1-1/a)^j] = 1-[1-p_1(k-1,t)/a]^a .$$

Now, let $r'(k,t)$ be the probability that a packet in a buffer of an SE at stage k is *ready to move forward* during the t-th stage cycle, given that there is a packet in that buffer. Then, $r(k,t)$ and $r'(k,t)$ can be expressed as below.

$$r(k,t) = r'(k,t)[p_0(k+1,t)+p_1(k+1,t)r(k+1,t)]$$

$$r'(k,t) = \binom{a}{1}\sum_{j=0}^{a-1}\binom{a-1}{j}p_1(k,t)^j p_0(k,t)^{a-1-j}\,[1-(1-\frac{1}{a})^{j+1}]\,\frac{1}{j+1}$$

The $r'(k,t)$ results from the fact that there are $\binom{a}{1}$ different ways of choosing a particular buffer out of a buffers, and the other $a-1$ buffers may have j packets, $0 \le j \le a-1$, and the probability that the given packet will be chosen out of $j+1$ packets is $1/(j+1)$. Since $\binom{a}{1}\cdot\binom{a-1}{j}/(j+1) = \binom{a}{j+1}$, $r'(k,t)$ can be simplified to $q(k+1,t)/p_1(k,t)$ ** after some manipulations. In summary, the following set of state equations hold for the single-buffered delta network.

$$q(k,t) = 1-[1-p_1(k-1,t)/a]^a, \quad k = 2,3,\ldots,n \tag{1}$$

$$r(k,t) = [q(k+1,t)/p_1(k,t)][p_0(k+1,t)+p_1(k+1,t)r(k+1,t)], \quad k=1,2,\ldots,n-1 \tag{2}$$

$$r(n,t) = [1-\{1-p_1(n,t)/a\}^a]/p_1(n,t) \tag{3}$$

$$p_0(k,t+1) = [1-q(k,t)][p_0(k,t)+p_1(k,t)r(k,t)], \quad k = 1,2,\ldots,n \tag{4}$$

$$p_1(k,t+1) = 1-p_0(k,t+1) \tag{5}$$

For the above equations, we assume that as soon as the packets are available at the

---

*This equation was originally given by Patel 6].

**This equation can also be derived from the concept of conditional probability, $P(A|B) = P(A\cap B)/P(B)$.

network output, they are removed instantaneously, which results in Eq. (3). We also assume that at time t=0 the network is in the state with no packet in any buffer. Note also that q(1,t) is the load applied to the network, which is considered as an independent input parameter. With these initial conditions, the above set of equations can be solved iteratively to get the time-independent steady-state value. As an example, Table 1 shows the initial values of $p_1(k, t)$, $q(k, t)$, and $r(k, t)$, and how those variables change and converge to the steady-state values for the successive stage cycles, where n=4 and $q(1,t)$=1.0. Letting $x(k)$ be $x(k, t)$ in the steady-state, the normalized throughput (S) and the normalized mean delay (d) can be obtained by the following equations.

$$S = p_1(n)r(n) \tag{6}$$

$$d = \frac{1}{n}\sum_{k=1}^{n} \frac{1}{r(k)} \tag{7}$$

Equation (7) results from the fact that the stage delay encountered by a packet is the reciprocal of the probability that the packet is able to pass the stage. We note that Eqs.(1)-(7) reduce to Jenq's equation [1] when a = 2.

Before we generalize the above equations for the multi-buffered networks, we note that Eqs. (4) and (5) can be rewritten as below.

$$p_0(k, t+1) = p_0(k, t)\bar{q}(k, t)+p_1(k, t)\bar{q}(k, t)r(k, t) \tag{8}$$

$$p_1(k, t+1) = p_0(k, t)q(k, t)+p_1(k, t)[q(k, t)r(k, t)+\bar{r}(k, t)] \quad , \tag{9}$$

where (and throughout this paper) $\bar{z}(k, t)$ defined as $1.0 - z(k, t)$ for any variable z. Note that in the single-buffered networks a buffer has two possible states : the empty state (state 0) and full state (state 1). In the above equations, we interpret p_i as the probability that a buffer is in state i, and all other terms as transition probabilities of moving from one state to another. Therefore Eqs. (8) and (9) can be represented by the following state transition diagram of a single buffer in Fig. 2. With this interpretation, we can readily extend the analysis of the single-buffered networks to the multi-buffered networks, as will be presented in the next section.

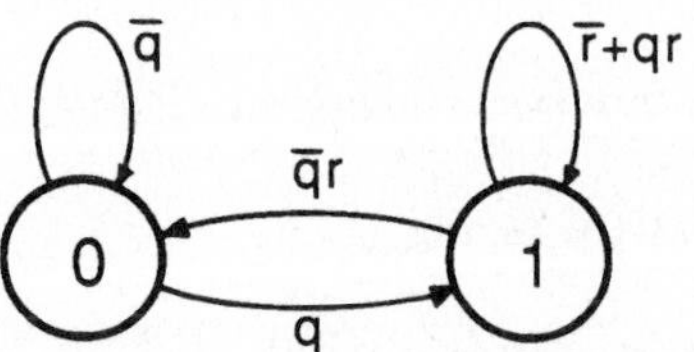

Figure 2: The state transition diagram of a single buffer representing Eqs. (8) and (9). The q and r denote q(k,t) and r(k,t), respectively.

4. Performance Analysis of the Multi-Buffered Delta Networks

In this section we assume that each input port of every SE has a finite queue of buffers so that multiple packets can be placed. (As before one buffer can accept a single packet). A packet is now able to move forward if either there is at least one empty buffer at the next stage, or a packet in the full queue at the next stage is able to move forward. We note that a packet in an infinite-buffered network is always able to move forward regardless of the status of the buffer at the next stage, rendering the analysis much simpler than for the finite-buffered network. In addition to the variables n, q, S, and d defined in the previous section, we define the following variables.

m = queue size (number of buffers at each input port of an SE).

$p_j(k, t)$ = probability that there are j packets in the queue of an SE at stage k at the beginning of the t-th stage cycle, j=0,1,...,m and $\sum_{j=0}^{m} p_j(k, t) = 1.0$. (e.g., p_0, $\bar{p}_0$, p_m, and $\bar{p}_m$ are the probabilities that the queue is empty, not empty, full, and not full, respectively.)

$r(k, t)$ = probability that a packet in the queue of an SE at stage k is able to move forward during the t-th stage cycle, given that there is at least one packet in the queue (i.e., queue is not empty).

With these variables, $q(k, t)$ and $r(k, t)$ can be expressed as below which is a generalized version of Eqs. (1) and (2).

$$q(k, t) = 1-[1-\bar{p}_0(k-1, t)/a]^a$$

$$r(k, t) = [q(k+1, t)/\bar{p}_0(k, t)][\bar{p}_m(k+1, t)+p_m(k+1, t)r(k+1, t)]$$

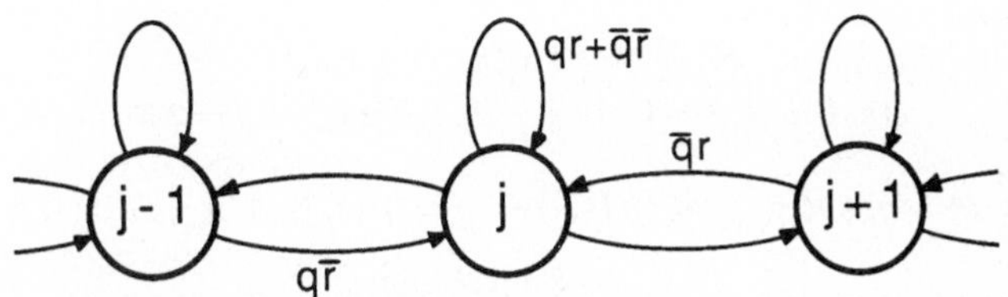

Figure 3: The transition diagram of a buffer in non-boundary state j, $1<j<m$, at stage k.

Now consider the probability $p_j(k, t)$. Since a single packet is transmitted per stage cycle, if a queue is in a non-boundary (neither full nor empty) state j, containing j packets at time t+1, the possible previous states of the queue at time t are j-1, j, or j+1 containing j-1, j, or j+1 packets. The probability $p_j(k, t+1)$ that a queue is in state j at time t+1 must be the sum of the (mutually exclusive) probabilities that the queue was in state j-1, j, or j+1 at time t, each multiplied by the probability of arriving at state j. We thus have

$$p_j(k, t+1) = p_{j-1}(k, t)q(k, t)\bar{r}(k, t) + p_j(k, t)[q(k, t)r(k, t)+\bar{q}(k, t)\bar{r}(k, t)] + p_{j+1}(k, t)\bar{q}(k, t)r(k, t).$$

The transition probabilities of moving from one state to another have been obtained by considering the ways in which one could move between the two states and the respective probabilities. For example, if the queue is to remain in state j, there could have been either one departure and one arrival (with the probability $q{\cdot}r$), or no departure and no arrival (with the probability $\bar{q}{\cdot}\bar{r}$). The state transition of a buffer in non-boundary states are shown in Fig.3, which is a pictorial description of the above equation.

The complete state transition diagram of a buffer of length m is given in Fig.4.

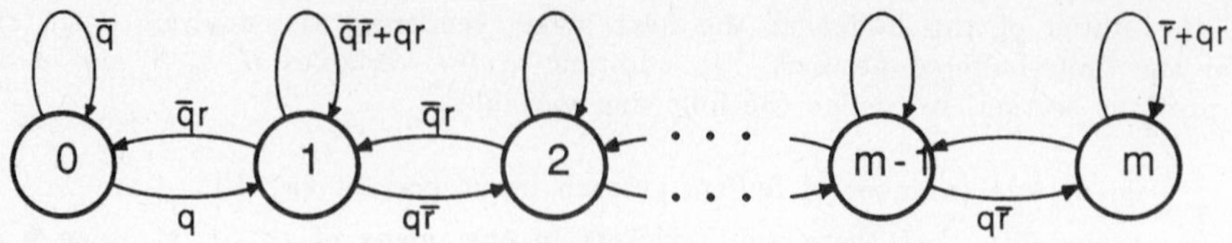

Figure 4: The complete state transition diagram of a buffer of length m, at stage k.

In summary, the following set of state equations hold for the m-buffered delta network, where m is the length of the buffer at each input port.

$$q(k,t) = 1-[1-\bar{p}_0(k-1,t)/a]^a, \quad k = 2,3,\ldots,n \tag{10}$$

$$r(k,t) = [q(k+1,t)/\bar{p}_0(k,t)][\bar{p}_m(k+1,t)+p_m(k+1,t)r(k+1,t)], \; k = 1,2,\ldots,n-1 \tag{11}$$

$$r(n,t) = q(n+1,t)/\bar{p}_0(n,t) \tag{12}$$

$$p_0(k,t+1) = \bar{q}(k,t)[p_0(k,t)+p_1(k,t)r(k,t)] \tag{13}$$

$$\begin{aligned} p_1(k,t+1) = {} & q(k,t)[p_0(k,t)+p_1(k,t)r(k,t)] + \\ & \bar{q}(k,t)[p_1(k,t)\bar{r}(k,t)+p_2(k,t)r(k,t)] \end{aligned} \tag{14}$$

$$\begin{aligned} p_j(k,t+1) = {} & q(k,t)[p_{j-1}(k,t)\bar{r}(k,t)+p_j(k,t)r(k,t)] + \\ & \bar{q}(k,t)[p_j(k,t)\bar{r}(k,t)+p_{j+1}(k,t)r(k,t)], \quad j = 2,3,\ldots,m-1 \end{aligned} \tag{15}$$

$$p_m(k,t+1) = q(k,t)[p_{m-1}(k,t)\bar{r}(k,t)+p_m(k,t)r(k,t)] + p_m(k,t)\bar{r}(k,t) \tag{16}$$

$$k = 1,2,\ldots,n$$

From Eqs. (13)-(16), it can be verified that $\sum_{j=0}^{m} p_j(k,t+1) = 1.0$. In the steady-state, a packet arrives at an output port of the network with probability $\bar{p}_0(n)r(n)$. Let $R(k)$ be the probability that a particular packet in the queue of an SE at stage k is able to move forward. Then we have

$$S = \bar{p}_0(n)r(n) \tag{17}$$

$$d = \frac{1}{n}\sum_{k=1}^{n} \frac{1}{R(k)}, \quad \text{where} \quad R(k) = r(k)\sum_{i=1}^{m} [p_i(k)/\bar{p}_0(k)]\frac{1}{i} \tag{18}$$

Note that Eqs. (10)-(18) reduce to Eqs. (1)-(7) when m=1.

5. Performance Analysis Results and Comparisons

Equations (10)-(18) derived in the previous section are very powerful, in that they can be used to determine the normalized throughput and delay of the buffered delta network with any set of values for the following four parameters:

1. a = SE size,
2. n = number of stages = log_aN (N=network size),
3. m = buffer size, i.e., number of buffers at each input port of an SE, and

4. $q(1)$ = input load applied to the network.

Among the many possible variations of the parameters, the most interesting cases are computed and plotted in Figs. 5-11. Figures 5 and 6 show the normalized throughput and delay against the network size and buffer size. It is seen that the normalized throughput decreases as the network size increases, and as the buffer size decreases. The normalized delay decreases as the network size increases, and as the buffer size decreases. Notice, however, that the normalized delay of the single-buffered delta network slightly increases as the network size increases. (For a detailed analysis result of the single-buffered network, see [2, 11, 1, 13].)

Figures 7 and 8 show the normalized throughput and delay versus the number of buffers and network size. Note that these figures obtained by our analytic model are in a good agreement with the simulation results of [2] (their Fig.13 and Fig.14).

Figure 9 shows the effect of the SE size on the performance of the multi-buffered (4096×4096) delta networks. It shows the normalized throughput versus the switch size and number of buffers. Notice that the throughput does not increase monotonically with the size of SE as in unbuffered networks. This phenomenon has also been observed in [12] by simulations.

Finally, the normalized throughput and delay for the (1024×1024) delta networks versus the input load and number of buffers are shown in Figs. 10 and 11, respectively.

6. Application to the Networks of a Different Type

In this section, we show briefly that the analysis of multi-buffered delta networks in the previous section can easily be applied to the multi-buffered networks of a different type. For this purpose, the multi-buffered data manipulator type networks are chosen.

The data manipulator type networks include the augmented data manipulator (ADM), the inverse ADM (IADM), and the gamma network, which are described in detail in [14, 15, 16, 17]. The $(N \times N)$ ADM consists of $(log_2 N)+1$ stages, and each stage contains (3×3) SEs except for the first and last stages. The first stage consists of (1×3) SEs, and the last stage (3×1) SEs. The (3×3) SE is not a crossbar but a multiplexer-demultiplexer pair (or a bus with three inputs/outputs), which accepts only one input at a time and directs it to one of three possible outputs. The IADM network is identical to the ADM except that the stages are traversed in reverse order, and the gamma network is identical to the IADM except that each bus switch is replaced by a (3×3) crossbar switch. An (8×8) IADM (or gamma) network is shown in Fig.12.

By noting the differences between the delta and data manipulator type networks in the type and size of an SE and the number of switching stages, the following set of state equations can be formulated for the multi-buffered data manipulator type networks.

$$q(1, t) = \bar{p}_0(0, t)/3 \tag{19}$$

$$q(k, t) = \begin{cases} 1-[1-\bar{p}_0(k-1, t)/3]^3 & : \text{Gamma type} \\ [1-p_0(k-1, t)^3]/3 & : \text{ADM type}, \quad k = 2,3,\ldots,n \end{cases} \tag{20}$$

$$r(0, t) = \bar{p}_m(1, t)+p_m(1, t)r(1, t) \tag{21}$$

$$r(k, t) = [q(k+1, t)/\bar{p}_0(k,t)][\bar{p}_m(k+1, t)+p_m(k+1, t)r(k+1, t)], \quad k = 1,2,\ldots,n-1 \tag{22}$$

$$r(n,t) = [1/3 - p_0(n,t)^3/3]/\bar{p}_0(n,t) \tag{23}$$

$$p_j(k,t+1) = \text{Eqs.}(13)\text{-}(16)\,, \quad j = 0,1,\ldots,m, \quad k = 0,1,\ldots,n \tag{24}$$

$$S = \bar{p}_0(0)r(0) \tag{25}$$

$$d = \frac{1}{n+1}\sum_{k=0}^{n} \frac{1}{R(k)}\,, \quad \text{where} \quad R(k) = r(k)\sum_{i=1}^{m} [p_i(k)/\bar{p}_0(k)]\frac{1}{i} \tag{26}$$

We note that when $m=1$ these equations reduce to those in [13].

7. Conclusions

By interpreting the earlier performance analysis work on the single-buffered interconnection network [1] from the view point of buffer state transitions, we were able to generalize the technique for the multi-buffered interconnection networks. Thus, we were able to analytically estimate the performance of the multi-buffered delta networks. We compared the results with the already known simulation results, and verified that they are in a good agreement with each other.

The performance behaviors of the multi-buffered interconnection networks have previously been known only by simulations, and only the boundary cases (either single or infinite-buffers which are special cases of multi-buffers) have previously been analyzed. Our approach is general enough to handle the interconnection networks with any number of buffers. Furthermore, earlier performance analyses on the single-buffered networks have considered (2×2) switches only. However, our approach can handle arbitrary switch sizes.

The model is simple yet powerful enough to be applicable to other types of networks as well. As an example, we showed the state equations for the multi-buffered data manipulator type networks which are multiple-path networks.

References

[1] Jenq, Y.C., "Performance Analysis of a Packet Switch Based on Single-Buffered Banyan Network", IEEE Journal on Selected Areas in Communications,Vol. SAC-30, No. 6, December 1983, pp. 1014-1021.

[2] Dias, D.M. and Jump, J.R., "Analysis and Simulation of Buffered Delta Networks", IEEE Transactions on Computers,Vol. C-30, No. 4, April 1981, pp. 273-282.

[3] Chin, C.Y. and Hwang, K., "Packet Switching Networks for Multiprocessors and Data Flow Computers", IEEE Transactions on Computers,Vol. C-33, No. 11, November 1984, pp. 991-1003.

[4] Turner, J.S., "Design of an Integrated Services Packet Network", IEEE Journal on Selected Areas in Communications,Vol. SAC-4, No. 8, November 1986, pp. 1373-1380.

[5] Turner, J.S., "Design of a Broadcast Packet Switching Network", Proc. of IEEE INFOCOM, April 1986, pp. 667-675.

[6] Patel, J.H., "Performance of Processor-Memory Interconnections for Multiprocessors", IEEE Transactions on Computers,Vol. C-30, No. 10, October 1981, pp. 771-780.

[7] Kruskal, C.P. and Snir, M., "The Performance of Multistage Interconnection Networks for Multiprocessors", IEEF Transactions on Computers,Vol. C-32, No. 12, December 1983, pp. 1091-1098

[8] Lee M. and Wu, C.L., "Performance Analysis of Circuit Switching Baseline Interconnection Networks", Proc. 11th Annu. Comput. Arch. Conf., 1984, pp. 82-90.

[9] Kumar, M. and Jump, J.R., "Performance of Unbuffered Shuffle-Exchange Networks", IEEE Transactions on Computers,Vol. C-35, No. 6, June 1986, pp. 573-578.

[10] Varma, A. and Raghavendra, C.S., "Performance Analysis of a Redundant-Path Interconnection Network", Proc. of 1985 Int. Conf. on Parallel Processing, 1985, pp. 474-479.

[11] Dias, D.M. and Jump, J.R., "Packet Switching Interconnection Networks for Module Systems", IEEE Computer,Vol. 14, No. 12, December 1981, pp. 43-53.

[12] Bubenik, R.G. and Turner, J.S., "Performance of a Broadcast Packet Switch", Tech. Report WUCS-86-10, Washington University, Computer Science Department, June 1986.

[13] Yoon, H., Lee, K.Y., and Liu, M.T., "Performance Analysis and Comparison of Packet Switching Interconnection Networks", Proc. of 1987 Int. Conf. on Parallel Processing, August 1987.

[14] Feng, T., "Data Manipulating Functions in Parallel Processors and their Implementations", IEEE Transactions on Computers,Vol. C-30, No. 3, March 1974, pp. 309-318.

[15] Siegel, H.J., "Interconnection Networks for SIMD Machines", IEEE Computer,Vol. 12, June 1979, pp. 57-65.

[16] Smith,S.D., Siegel,H.J., McMillen,R.J., and Adams III,G.B., "Use of the Augmented Data Manipulator Multistage Network for SIMD Machines", International Conference on Parallel Processing, August 1980, pp. 75-78.

[17] Parker, D.S. and Raghavendra, C.S., "The Gamma Network", IEEE Transactions on Computers,Vol. C-33, No. 4, April 1984, pp. 367-373.

Table 1:

	t=0	t=1	t=2	t=3	t=4	t=5	t=6	t=7	t>7
$p_1(1,t)$	0.00	1.00	1.00	1.00	1.00	1.00	1.00	1.00	1.00
$q(1,t)$	1.00	1.00	1.00	1.00	1.00	1.00	1.00	1.00	1.00
$r(1,t)$	0.00	0.75	0.65	0.59	0.56	0.54	0.54	0.53	0.53
$p_1(2,t)$	0.00	0.00	0.75	0.79	0.80	0.81	0.82	0.82	0.82
$q(2,t)$	0.00	0.75	0.75	0.75	0.75	0.75	0.75	0.75	0.75
$r(2,t)$	0.00	0.00	0.81	0.73	0.68	0.66	0.65	0.65	0.65
$p_1(3,t)$	0.00	0.00	0.00	0.61	0.67	0.70	0.71	0.71	0.72
$q(3,t)$	0.00	0.00	0.61	0.63	0.64	0.65	0.65	0.65	0.65
$r(3,t)$	0.00	0.00	0.00	0.85	0.78	0.76	0.75	0.74	0.74
$p_1(4,t)$	0.00	0.00	0.00	0.00	0.52	0.58	0.61	0.62	0.63
$q(4,t)$	0.00	0.00	0.00	0.52	0.56	0.57	0.58	0.59	0.59
$r(4,t)$	0.00	0.00	0.00	0.00	0.87	0.85	0.85	0.84	0.84

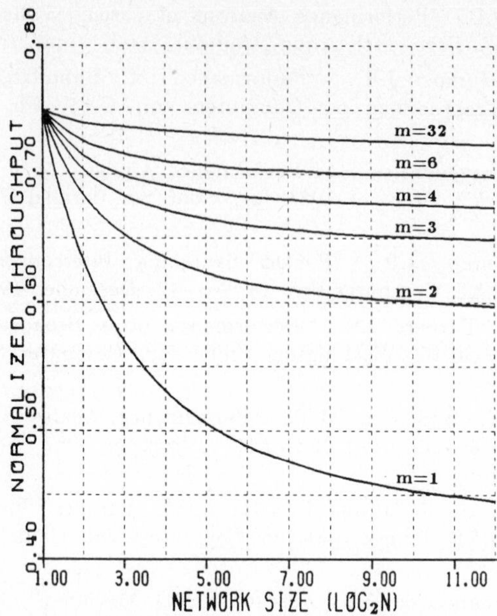

Figure 5: Normalized throughput versus network size of m-buffered ($N \times N$) delta networks ($a=2$, $q(1)=1.0$).

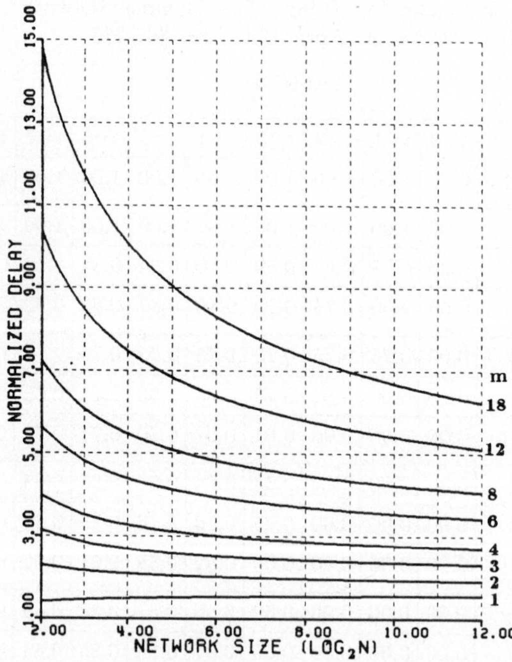

Figure 6: Normalized delay versus network size of m-buffered ($N \times N$) delta networks ($a=2$, $q(1)=1.0$).

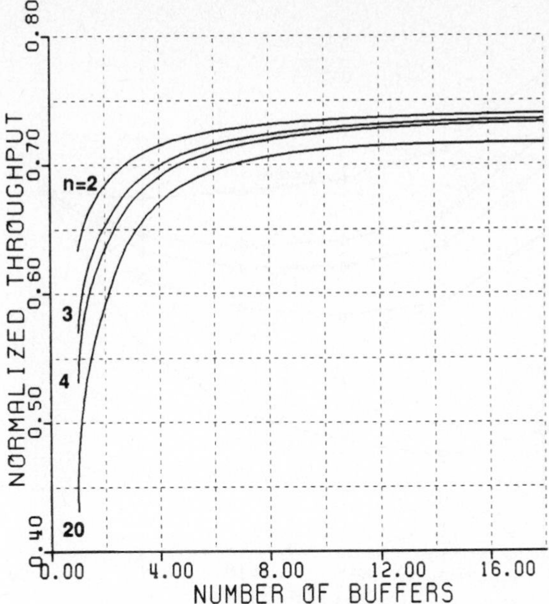

Figure 7: Normalized throughput versus the number of buffers of multi-buffered delta networks (a=2, $q(1)$=1.0).

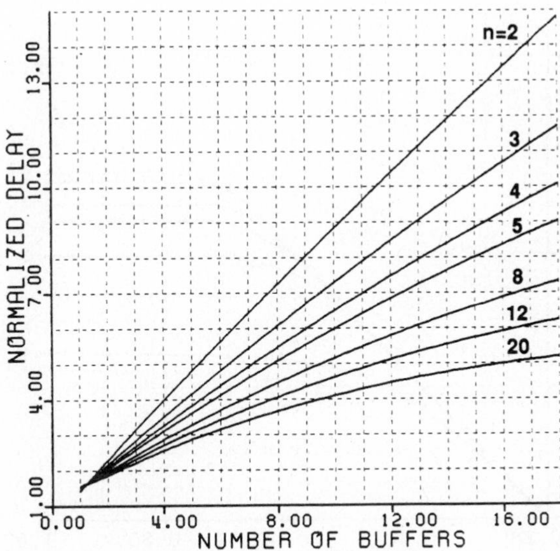

Figure 8: Normalized delay versus the number of buffers of multi-buffered delta networks (a=2, $q(1)$=1.0).

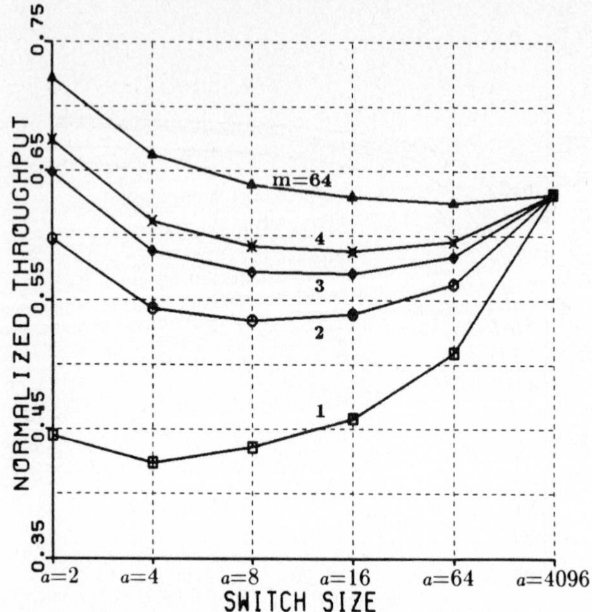

Figure 9: Normalized throughput versus the size of SEs of multi-buffered (4096×4096) networks ($q(1)$=1.0).

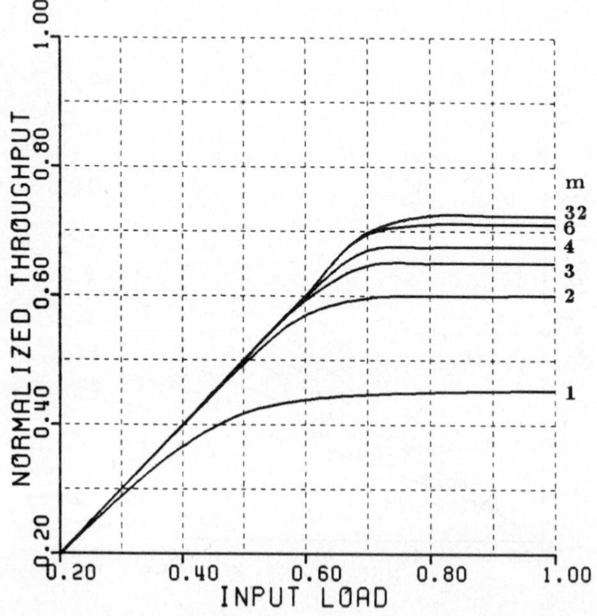

Figure 10: Normalized throughput versus input load ($q(1)$) of multi-buffered (1024×1024) delta networks (a=2).

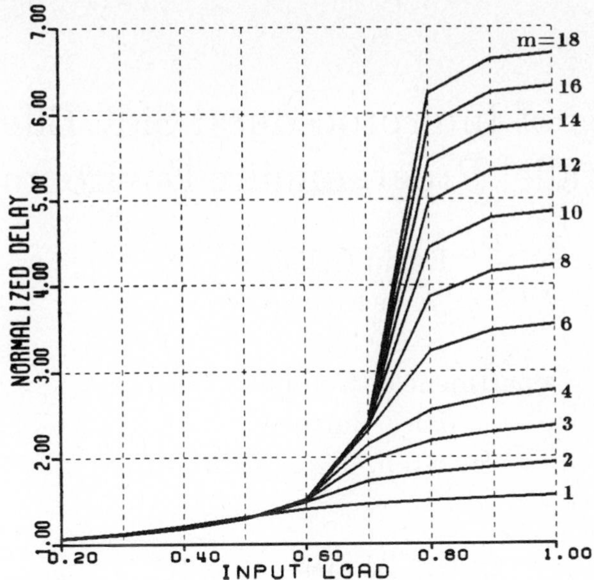

Figure 11: Normalized delay versus input load ($q(1)$) of multi-buffered (1024×1024) delta networks (a=2).

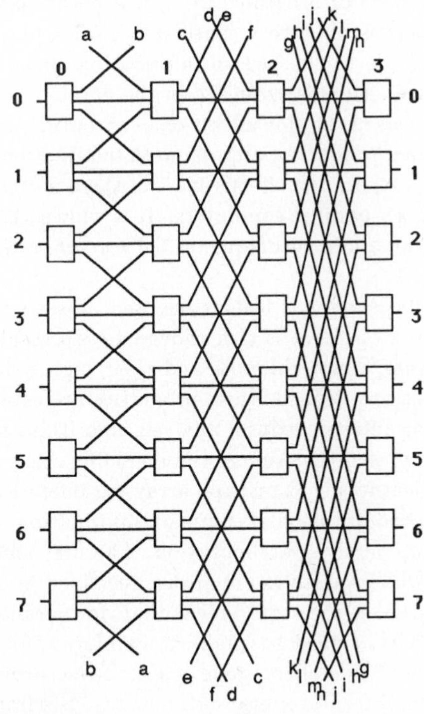

Figure 12: An (8×8) IADM (or gamma) network

Analysis of Interprocedural Side Effects in a Parallel Programming Environment

David Callahan
Ken Kennedy

Department of Computer Science
Rice University
Houston, Texas 77251

Abstract

This paper addresses the analysis of subroutine side effects in the **ParaScope** programming environment, an ambitious collection of tools for developing, understanding, and compiling parallel programs. In spite of significant progress in the optimization of programs for execution on parallel and vector computers, compilers must still be very conservative when optimizing the code surrounding a call site, due to the lack of information about the code in the subroutine being invoked. This has resulted in the development of algorithms for *interprocedural analysis* of the side effects of a subroutine, which summarize the body of a subroutine, producing approximate information to improve optimization. This paper reviews the effectiveness of these methods in preparing programs for execution on parallel computers. It is shown that existing techniques are insufficient and a new technique, called *regular section analysis,* will be described.

Regular section analysis extends the lattice used in previous interprocedural analysis methods to a one that is rich enough to represent common array access patterns: elements, rows, columns and their higher dimensional analogues. Regular sections are defined, their properties are established and the modifications to existing interprocedural analysis algorithms required to handle regular sections are presented. Among these modifications are methods for dealing with language features that reshape array parameters at call sites.

In addition to improved precision of summary information, we also examine two problems crucial to effective parallelization. The first addresses the need for information about which variables are always redefined as a side-effect of a call and the second addresses the requirement that, for parallel programming, information about side effects must be qualified by information about any critical regions in which those side effects take place. These problems are solved by extensions to existing interprocedural dataflow analysis frameworks.

1 Introduction

For the past several years, we have been concerned with the development of new tools that support parallel programming. This research has led to the implementation of PTOOL, a system that permits the user to determine whether the iterations of a given loop may safely be executed in parallel [ABKP86]. PTOOL is based upon a deep analysis of interstatement *dependence* in a Fortran program. Informally, one statement depends on another if it can use a value computed by that statement at run time; the implication is that the two statements cannot have their execution order reversed. Two regions in a program may be safely executed in parallel if neither contains a statement that depends on some statement in the other. PTOOL helps the programmer introduce parallelism by using dependence to determine when regions, particularly separate loop iterations, can be executed in parallel.

In order to support large-granularity parallelism, it was evident that a systematic analysis of *interprocedural* dependences was essential. This is achieved in PTOOL through a preliminary analysis of the side effects of procedure calls, which can be used to determine when a call should be one of the endpoints of a dependence.

Once the implementation was completed, experiments with PTOOL showed that the analysis was too coarse to support parallelization through data decomposition, an unacceptable inadequacy. The problem arose because, following the literature [Bar77, Ban78], our implementation treated arrays as units. That is, if any location in the array is modified the analysis reports that the whole array is modified. This granularity is not fine enough for parallelization because data decomposition involves computing with different parts of an array on different processors. To support this, our analysis must be able to determine the subarrays that are affected as a side effect of each procedure call.

This paper describes a new method for collecting interprocedural summary information that is significantly more precise in describing the accesses of subroutines to arrays, providing resolution fine enough to describe the common substructures of arrays: elements, rows columns and diagonals. We are in the process of implementing this new method in a parallel programming environment called **ParaScope** that is based in part on PTOOL. We begin with a discussion of that environment.

2 ParaScope

When completed, ParaScope will be an environment for developing, understanding, compiling and debugging large parallel scientific programs. It is the logical outgrowth of two major projects at Rice University. The $\mathbb{R}^n$ **Project** has produced the $\mathbb{R}^n$ **Programming Environment**, an integrated collection of tools that support the development of scientific programs written in Fortran [HK85]. A principle goal of this project was to develop methods for compiling and optimizing whole programs. Hence, support for interprocedural analysis and optimization was built in from the very beginning [CKT86]. The $\mathbb{R}^n$ project has pioneered mechanisms by which the tools of the environment can cooperate to provide the advantages of compiling the whole program at once while retaining the efficiency of separate compilation. However, it is designed to support only traditional scalar optimizations.

The **Supercomputer Software Project** has concerned itself with analysis and transformation tools to support the programming of parallel and vector computer architectures. It has produced two major systems: **PFC**, which automatically transform a program to parallel form, and **PTOOL**, an interactive advisor on parallel programming. Both systems are based on a deep analysis of data dependence and both employ interprocedural data flow analysis. In the next sections we describe these tools and the role that interprocedural analysis plays in them.

2.1 Automatic Detection of Parallelism

PFC [AK82, ACK87] is a system for automatically translating sequential Fortran programs into explicitly parallel form. Its principal mechanism is the conversion of sequential DO loops to parallel DO loops, the separate iterations of which may be executed concurrently. The test for the correctness of this conversion is based on *data dependence analysis* [Kuc78, Ken80, Wol82, All83].

The data dependence graph $G = (V, E)$, as used in PFC, is a directed multigraph. The nodes represent statements and the edges represent possible memory access overlaps. An edge from v to w exists if statement v may access some memory location M and, later, statement w may access the same location. When at least one of these statements modifies that location, the edge represents an execution order requirement: the source of the edge must be executed before the sink.

Dependences are classified by whether each statement modifies the memory accessed. If the first statement modifies M but the second statement does not, then the dependence is called a **true** dependence. If the second statement modifies M but not the first, the dependence is an **anti** dependence. If both statements modify M, then the dependence is called an **output** dependence [Kuc78].

If the statements v and w are contained in n common loops, we can refer to separate instances by using an **iteration vector**. An iteration vector is simply the values of the loop control variables of the loops containing the statements. The set of iteration vectors corresponding to all iterations of the loop nest is called the **iteration space**[1]. Using iteration vectors, we can define a **distance vector** for each dependence: if v accesses location M on iteration $\vec{i}_v$ and w accesses location M on iteration $\vec{i}_w$, the distance vector for this dependence is $\vec{i}_w - \vec{i}_v$. Under this definition, the kth component of the distance vector is equal to the number of iterations of the kth loop (numbered from outermost to innermost) between accesses to M.

The outermost loop corresponding to a non-zero element of the distance vector is said to **carry** the dependence and the index of that component is called the **level** of the dependence. The loop that carries a data dependence is the outermost loop such

[1]We assume here that loops are normalized to iterate from one to some upper bound in steps of 1.

that the source and sink of the dependence are in different iterations. A dependence that is not carried by any loop (*i.e.*, accesses occur on the same iteration), is called **loop independent**.

A primary use of data dependence analysis is the detection of parallel loops. This is based on the following theorem [AK85]:

Theorem 1 *If a loop does not carry a data dependence, then the separate iterations can be executed concurrently.*

The more aggressive transformations used by PFC to uncover additional parallelism are discussed elsewhere [ACK87].

The effectiveness of automatic detection of parallelism is dependent on the accuracy of the data dependence graph. Powerful tests have been developed to accurately test for data dependences between subscripted references to array variables. While these tests generally apply only when subscript expressions are affine functions of loop control variables, in practice, they are extremely precise for scientific programs. Precise handling of subscripted array references is critical to the success of PFC because it attempts to generate parallelism through data decomposition—that is, it tries to execute all iterations of a given loop concurrently, which is possible only if each iteration is working on a different subsection of the principle data arrays.

2.2 PTOOL

PTOOL [ABKP86] is an interactive adviser designed to assist in the prevention of errors arising from unintentional data sharing or unforeseen load-store orders for shared data in parallel programs. Similar in spirit to the DAVE system [FO76] and the ART system [AM85], PTOOL helps the user locate bugs in a program by using (static) data dependence analysis to detect anomalies in the data flow properties of the program.

PTOOL is composed of two principal components: PSERVE, a modified version of PFC that computes a database of dependence information, and PQUERY, a program browser that uses the dependence information to help the programmer understand the data-sharing errors that might arise in a parallel loop. In a typical PTOOL session, the user would first submit the whole Fortran program to PSERVE for analysis. Then he would enter the PQUERY browser and select a series of loops as candidates for parallelism. For each loop, PTOOL will either report no anomalies, in which case the loop can be run completely in parallel, or report the existence of anomalies in the form of loop carried data dependences. In the latter case, the user can then review each of the data dependences, to determine how to modify the program to eliminate them.

PTOOL also attempts to determine which variables used or defined in a selected loop must be shared by all parallel iterations and which may be private to a single iteration. It then displays only those dependences involving variables that are shared[2], significantly limiting the number of dependences presented to the user.

As with any program analysis tool designed to report anomalies, *false positives*—dependences that do not really exist but are inserted because of lack of precision in the dependence testing procedure—present a significant problem. To minimize these, PTOOL makes extensive use of interprocedural analysis to improve the accuracy of the data dependence database for loops that contain calls to external routines.

2.3 Critique of PTOOL

At an April 1987 workshop for PTOOL users from the Los Alamos and Livermore National Laboratories, IBM Palo Alto Scientific Center and the Cornell Theory Center, we isolated several important deficiencies in the interprocedural analysis performed by PTOOL. These deficiencies fall into three categories:

- the inability to deal with side effects to subarrays of the whole array,
- the inability to develop information about which variables are always redefined, or *killed*, as a side effect of a call and
- the inability to properly analyze the impact parallel language constructs such as critical regions.

Let us treat each of these deficiencies in more detail.

Subarray Analysis To see the importance of analyzing side effects to subarrays, consider the routine DGEFA from LINPACK [DBMS79], which implements Gaussian elimination with partial pivoting to perform an LU decomposition of a matrix. The principal candidate for parallelization is the elimination loop containing a call to DAXPY:

```
      DO 30 J = KP1, N
         T = A(L,J)
         IF (L .EQ. K) GO TO 20
            A(L,J) = A(K,J)
            A(K,J) = T
   20    CONTINUE
         CALL DAXPY(N-K,T,A(K+1,K),1,A(K+1,J),1)
   30 CONTINUE
```

The subroutine DAXPY performs a scaled vector addition. In this context, DAXPY looks like:

[2]The user can examine these variables by explicitly changing the status of a variable and informing PTOOL that it should be considered shared.

```
      SUBROUTINE DAXPY(N,DA,DX,INCX,DY,INCY)
      :
      DO 10 I = 1,N
10       DY(I) = DY(I) + DA*DX(I)
      :
      END
```

Interprocedural summary information reports that the second use of A in the parameter list of the call to DAXPY may be modified. This information alone is not sufficient to establish that the access to A is in fact contained in the jth column. Hence, PTOOL displays data dependences between that array reference and the other references to A in the loop.

Dramatic examples can be found in simulation codes that have a driving loop such as:

```
      DO 10 J = 1,NUMPTS
10       CALL MAINLOOP(J)
```

where the value of J is used to index into shared arrays. Again, information at the granularity of a *variable* is insufficient to detect parallelism.

Attendees at the PTOOL workshop recommended that we give the higest priority to the solution of this problem. In Section 3, we describe the method of *regular sections*, which addresses this deficiency.

Kill Analysis As we pointed out earlier, an important function of PTOOL is the determination of which variables used in a particular loop must be shared by all iterations if the loop is converted to a parallel DO. When the live range of a variable is contained in a single iteration of a DO loop, PTOOL assumes that that variable is local (or private). Since PTOOL only displays dependences that involve shared variables, accurate recognition of local variables is important to prevent the user from being deluged by false dependences associated with scalar variables.

PTOOL performs *flow-insensitive* interprocedural analysis, which determines the set of side effects that *may* occur on some control flow path—a design decision dictated by the computational intractability of flow-sensitive analysis [Mye81]. Unfortunately, *may* summary information is insufficient to accurately determine the live ranges of scalars in some situations, as the following loop fragment, taken from a Los Alamos code, illustrates.

```
      DO 10 I = 1,N
         CALL TRACK(X,Y,Z,...)
           :
10       CONTINUE
```

Assume that the subroutine TRACK initializes the scalars X,Y and Z. Standard interprocedural *may* information would indicate that each scalar may be modified, implying that it may not be. Hence, the scalars appear to be live immediately before the call to TRACK and will be treated as shared. As a result, all the dependences involving these scalars will be displayed to the user. In the example from which this loop was taken, PTOOL displayed over a thousand unnecessary dependences because of this problem[3].

Section 5 describes an extension to our framework for interprocedural constant propagation [CCKT86] that provides an approximate solution to the problem of kills.

Parallel Language Constructs Although PTOOL was originally designed to take sequential Fortran as input, in practice it is frequently presented program that have been parallelized by the insertion of compiler directives that identify parallel loops and critical regions [4].

Without modification, PTOOL is useful for analyzing parallel loops because dependences in parallel loops simply indicate the possibility of schedule-dependent results. However, PTOOL has no understanding of critical regions. In particular, the users at the workshop complained that PTOOL reported data dependences both of whose endpoints were in critical regions governed by the same lock variable. From one point of view, PTOOL *should* report these data dependences since they indicate *non-determinism* in the input program. On the other hand, a more pragmatic viewpoint would hold that, when a programmer uses a critical region, he is asserting that he is aware of the concurrent access *and that he is aware of the non-determinism.* The latter viewpoint was preferred by users at the workshop.

To support this point of view, PTOOL must recognize data dependences generated by accesses in the same critical region so that they can be suppressed unless explicitly requested. When both accesses that generate a carried data dependence are in the same subroutine as the loop under consideration, we can determine which data dependences should be suppressed by direct inspection of their endpoints. Unfortunately, to do this interprocedurally requires information not currently available from the standard summary analysis. Section 6 describes a modification to the interprocedural summary framework that allows suppression of the appropriate dependences.

3 Analysis of Subarray Side Effects

In this section we present an approach to providing a more precise analysis of side effects to arrays. We begin with a review of other proposals for the solution of this problem, indicating their deficiencies. We then introduce a new approach, called **regular section analysis**, which overcomes most of these deficiencies. A particular regular section lattice is then introduced and analyzed in detail.

[3]The program contained a single very large loop in which the call to TRACK initialized every scalar.

[4]These directives are usually implemented by calls to library routines.

3.1 Previous Approaches

A simple way to enhance the precision of interprocedural dependence testing is to expand the called subroutine inline [AC72], thereby making the subroutine body available for local analysis. This approach is the most precise but also the most expensive, not only because of the potential for an explosion in code space but also because most algorithms for optimization are not linear and increasing the size of loop nests through inline expansion will amplify this problem.

To gain some of the benefits of inline expansion without its drawbacks, an interprocedural dependence test can be used. To illustrate, we present the following code fragment.

```
CALL SOURCE (A)
:
CALL SINK (A)
```

Assume that A is a multidimensional array. We wish to determine whether there should be a dependence edge from the first CALL statement to the second, due to a definition of A within SOURCE and a use of A within SINK. The condition for the existence of such an edge can be simply stated: it should exist if the set of locations within A that are modified by SOURCE has a nonempty intersection with the set of locations in A that are used in SINK. More formally, suppose we can compute the following quantities:

- the set M^A_{SOURCE} of locations in A that may be modified by an invocation of SOURCE and
- the set U^A_{SINK} of locations in A that may be used in SINK.

Then there should be a dependence edge, based upon A, between the two calls if

$$M^A_{SOURCE} \cap U^A_{SINK} \neq \emptyset.$$

In terms of this definition, several issues must be considered in evaluating the performance of algorithms for interprocedural dependence testing.

- the complexity of representing the sets M^A_{SOURCE} and U^A_{SINK},
- the cost of merging the representations of accesses along two distinct control flow paths when those paths merge. merge (since many representation schemes form a lattice, we shall refer to this as the *meet* operation),
- the cost of determining whether the *intersection* of two representations is empty (dependence testing),
- the complexity of the algorithm for computing the representations, in terms of number of meets and number of intersections, and whether the algorithms can deal with recursion and

- the precision of the representations, since these can only approximate the true access sets.

We shall evaluate previously-proposed methods for analysis of side effects in terms of these criteria.

Classical Methods Methods to simply summarize the effects of subroutines can be used to approximate their bodies for the purpose of optimization around the call site The classical methods [Ban78, Bar77, CK85] compute, for each parameter and global variable, two bits of information which indicate that that variable *may* be modified and *may* be used. Because the representation is so simple, the meet and intersection are very efficient, consisting of single-bit logical operations. Furthermore, there exist algorithms that compute complete solutions on the call graph using a number of meets that is nearly linear in the number of procedures and call sites in the call graph, even when recursion is permitted[5] [CK85].

Unfortunately, our experience with PFC and PTOOL (as described above) indicates that the granularity of interprocedural summary information is too coarse to support a dependence test precise enough for effective detection of parallelism. The problem is that only access sets representable in this system are "the whole array" and "none of the array". It is not possible to accurately represent side effects to subarrays. This limitation is disastrous for parallelization of loops that contain call sites, because the most effective way to parallelize a loop is through data decomposition, in which each parallel iteration works on a different subsection of a given array.

Triolet Analysis Triolet has proposed an approach that would determine the convex hull of the set of array locations affected as a side effect of a procedure call [TIF86]. This method scores high in precision, but the representation is complex and the meet and intersection operations are extremely inefficient. Hence, this method is too expensive to use in a compiler [Ban86]. Furthermore, Triolet's approach does not handle recursion and, since it is not based on lattices, there seems to be no easy way to extend it to recursive programs.

Burke-Cytron Analysis A less expensive method, proposed by Burke and Cytron [BC86], summarizes the accesses made by specific array reference inside a loop by linearizing to a one-dimensional reference and retaining loop bounds information for the loops that enclose that reference. Two suggestions are made for implementing the meet operation; both involve retaining all the information of the individual accesses (at least when the references are non-identical). Although this yields a reasonably efficient meet, it makes the intersection operation hopelessly inefficient, since each individual modification access must be tested against each use access,

[5]If the call graph contains no cycles, these methods take linear time.

for every array. Furthermore, maintaining information about each array reference along all possible execution paths in the call graph is clearly not viable because of the space requirements.

Burke and Cytron suggest that less precise methods for combining information could be found, but it is not yet clear whether this approach will lead to a practical system. As with Triolet, their approach does not extend to recursive programs.

3.2 Regular Sections

The problem with the previous techniques is the generality of the information they maintain—they achieve high precision at the expense of analysis time. It is not even clear whether such high precision is necessary. Conceivably, a simpler and more efficient analysis might be precise enough to handle most of the important cases for parallelization.

Therefore, we seek a method that achieves the limited goal of recognizing important special cases of array side effects. For example, it would be extremely useful to recognize when the modification of an array made by a procedure call is limited to a single column or row of the array.

Fortunately, the approach currently used to solve interprocedural data flow analysis problems can be generalized to develop more precise information about side effects. Although it may not be immediately clear from perusing the papers, the published algorithms for interprocedural analysis (e.g. Cooper and Kennedy [CK85]), can be extended to work on vectors of lattice elements, where each lattice element represents a set of locations accessed within a single array. Consider the example lattice of reference patterns to the array A shown in Figure 1. Note that I, J, and K are arbitrary symbolic input parameters to the call.

The interprocedural analysis algorithms will work correctly, although more slowly, on vectors of lattice elements (instead of bit vectors) if all the lattices have the finite chain property—that is, there exist no descending chains of unbounded length. The running times of the algorithms for such lattices is directly proportional to maximum lattice depth and time to execute a single meet operation.

Hence, it is easy to see that we can perform interprocedural analysis for sections of arrays. We will call any section that can be precisely described in the chosen lattice a *regular section*. The only remaining problem is to choose a definition of regular section with the right blend of precision and efficiency. Our decision was based on the requirements that enough information be provided to parallelize loops in scientific programs and yet still retain a lattice structure.

3.3 A Regular Section Lattice

The regular section lattice that we have chosen does not attempt to represent all possible array accesses. Instead, it describes those array access that correspond to "decomposition" of data aggregates: elements, rows, columns, diagonals and higher dimensional analogues. The following definition captures this notion:

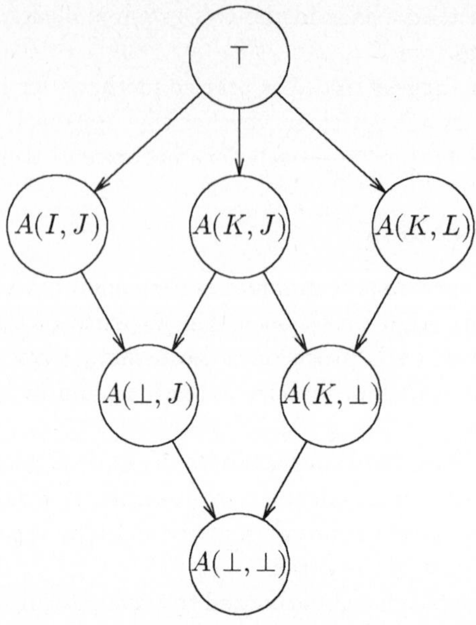

FIGURE 1: Lattice of Array Access Information

Defintion 1 *A* **Regular Section Descriptor (RSD)** *is a pair of the form* $\langle A; \vec{\theta} \rangle$ *where* A *is the name of an array variable and* $\vec{\theta}$ *is a vector of subscript positions such that each* θ_i *is either a constant (routine invariant) expression or is of the form* $\pm I_j + \alpha$ *where* α *is routine invariant.*

A **regular section** is a set of locations of an array. The regular section described by a **constant** RSD $R = \langle A, \vec{\theta} \rangle$, where each expression is an integer constant, is the set of all subscript vectors $\vec{b}$ such that there exists a vector of integers $\vec{i}$ such that:

$$b_j = \theta_j[\vec{i}]$$

where $\theta_j[\vec{i}]$ is the value of θ_j with each occurrence of I_k replaced with the constant i_k. This regular section will be denoted $A^{-1}(R)$. Note that i_k may be negative and that the array A is used as if any vector of integer values refers to a unique element of A. This interpretation reflects an assumption implicit to data dependence testing and related transformations: subscript ranges are respected and hence subscripts can be handled independently. Symbolic RSD's are interpreted as functions from assignments of values to program variables to regular sections. The variables I_j are a formal collection of names. Intuitively they represent iteration through as set of values and well be referred to as **induction variables.**

The access patterns that can be described with RSD's include: single elements, complete rows and columns, and diagonals as well as their higher-dimensional analogues. Two access patterns that cannot be described precisely are triangular regions and discontiguous portions of rows:

```
      DO 10 I = 1,N
         A(2*I) = ...
         DO 10 J = 1,I
            B(I,J) = ...
10    CONTINUE
```

Since the primary application of summary information is for detection of parallel DO loops, this loss of precision does not seem very significant.

A major component of a data flow framework [KU77] is a lattice of possible values for each node in the flow graph. For summary problems, the lattice elements typically are mappings from variables to values in a sublattice. The standard sublattice has two elements: $\top$ (top) indicating no access and $\perp$ (bottom) indicating that the variable *may* be accessed. We propose a new sublattice, the elements of which are regular sections represented by regular section descriptors.

The next section details the properties of this sublattice. In particular we will construct a meet operator, $\wedge$, which is reflexive, idempotent, and associative over the sublattice. Furthermore, the implementation of $\wedge$ guarantees that $R_1 \wedge R_2$ represents the "smallest" regular section that contains the union of the regular sections described by R_1 and R_2. The details of this analysis are fairly tedious, so the reader may wish to skip to Section 3.5, which discusses the efficiency of this meet operation.

3.4 Regular Section Properties

Much of this section establishes the relationship between syntactic representations for regular sections and the regular sections themselves. We begin by testing for equality by defining normal forms.

An equivalence relation between two RSD's is easy to define: since an induction variable I_j can assume any integer value, an expression $I_j + \alpha$ can also assume any integer value, so replacing all occurrences of I_j by $\pm I_j + \alpha$ preserves regular sections. Likewise, if I_k does not appear in an RSD R, replacing each occurrence in R of I_j by I_k preserves regular sections. Two RSD's are equivalent if a sequence of these replacements can transform one into the other. An RSD $R = \left\langle A, \vec{\theta} \right\rangle$ is in **normal form** when for each I_j that appears in R, $\theta_j = I_j$. It is clear that every RSD is equivalent to exactly one normal form RSD. Transforming an RSD into the equivalent normal form is called **normalizing** and the result of normalizing R will be denoted $\eta(R)$. Two RSD's that normalize to the same RSD are said to be **equivalent**, and the set of RSD's that normalize to a particular normal form is called an **equivalence class**. Note that every RSD in an equivalence class has the same number of distinct induction variables. This will be important in showing that the lattice of RSD's does not have infinite chains.

Defintion 2 *The* **rank** *of an RSD is the number of distinct induction variables that occur in the subscript expressions of that RSD. The rank of an RSD R will be denoted $\rho(R)$*

Observe that if k is the number of dimensions in the array associated with an RSD, that RSD has k-subscript positions and each of these can reference at most one induction variable. Therefore we have argued the following lemma:

Lemma 1 *If k is the number of dimensions of an array A, then $0 \leq \rho(R) \leq k$ for all regular section descriptors of regular sections of A.*

To impose a lattice structure on these RSD's we need to develop a notion of "approximation" suitable for regular section descriptors. We use the following definition based on regular sections:

Defintion 3 *An RSD R_1* **approximates** *an RSD R_2 if (under every assignment of values to program variables) the regular section described by R_1 contains the regular section described by R_2. This is denoted $R_1 \sqsubseteq R_2$.*

In general, the notion of approximation is undecidable because it assumes the ability to determine when two arithmetic expressions are equal under all assignments of values to variables. We assume that some mechanism is provided for testing of equality of two expressions and the precision of that mechanism will affect the precision with which we can test for equality of two regular sections. In practice, we do not expect this to be a problem.

The next theorem ties together the syntactic concepts of rank and equivalence with the geometric concept of containment.

Theorem 2 *If R_1 and R_2 are two RSD's, and $R_1 \sqsubseteq R_2$, then $\rho(R_1) \geq \rho(R_2)$ and if $\rho(R_1) = \rho(R_2)$, then R_1 and R_2 are equivalent.*

Proof: By contradiction: assume $\rho(R_1) < \rho(R_2)$, and let $\eta(R_1) = \left\langle A, \vec{\theta} \right\rangle$ and $\eta(R_2) = \left\langle A, \vec{\phi} \right\rangle$ be the normal forms of R_1 and R_2 respectively. Let I_j be an induction variable that appears in $\eta(R_2)$ but not in $\eta(R_1)$. If either R_1 or R_2 is symbolic, then assume every program variable is assigned a value of 0. There are two cases to consider:

1. $\phi_j = I_j$ and $\theta_j = \alpha$ where α is a constant.

2. $\phi_j = I_j$ and $\theta_j = \pm I_k + \alpha$ where α is a constant and $k < j$.

If $\theta_j = \alpha$, for some constant, then consider the array element obtained by setting each induction variable to 1 in $\eta(R_2)$ except for I_j which is set to $\alpha+1$. This defines a vector $\vec{b} \in A^{-1}(R_2)$ with $b_j = \alpha + 1$. The existence of this vector contradicts the assumption that the regular section described by $\eta(R_1)$ contains the regular section described by $\eta(R_2)$ (under the current variable assignment) since the regular section described by $\eta(R_1)$ contains only vectors $\vec{b}$ with $b_j = \alpha$.

If $\theta_j = I_k + \alpha$, where $k < j$, then again consider the array element obtained by setting each induction variable to 1 in $\eta(R_2)$ except for I_j which is set to α. This contradicts the assumption that the regular section described by $\eta(R_1)$ contains the regular section described by $\eta(R_2)$ (under the current variable assignment) since the regular section described by $\eta(R_1)$ contains only vectors $\vec{b}$ with $b_k - b_j = -\alpha$ and this vector has $b_k - b_j = 1 - \alpha$. If $\theta_j = \alpha - I_k$, this argument still holds, since the vectors of R_1 satisfy $b_k + b_j = \alpha$ but at least one in R_2 does not.

If $\rho(R_1) = \rho(R_2)$ and $\eta(R_1) \neq \eta(R_2)$, two cases hold. Either there exists I_j that appears in $\eta(R_2)$ and not in $\eta(R_1)$, in which case we apply a construction just like the above to show that the regular section described by R_2 is not contained in the regular section described by R_1 contradicting the hypothesis. Otherwise, there exists a subscript position j such that $\theta_j \neq \phi_j$ If these are both constants, then again the containment hypothesis is contradicted, and if θ_j is a constant and ϕ_j varies, say with I_k, a value can be selected for I_k so that $\phi_j[\vec{i}]$ differs from the $\theta_j[\vec{i}]$ and so containment is violated.

If θ_j varies with an induction variable, then, since $\eta(R_1)$ and $\eta(R_2)$ have the same rank, if $\theta_j = I_j$, I_j does not appear in $\eta(R_2)$ and there must exist some I_k that appears in $\eta(R_2)$ that does not appear in $\eta(R_1)$. Thus we reduce to a previous case.

If $\phi_j = I_j$ and θ_j is either constant or varies with some other induction variable, say I_k, we can select a value for I_j that is not equal to either θ_j , $I_k - \theta_j$, or $I_k + \theta_j$ and so violate the containment hypothesis.

The last case is $\phi_j = \pm I_k - \alpha$ and $\theta_j = \pm I_k - \beta$ where $k < j$, and either $\alpha \neq \beta$ or the signs of the induction variables are different. In any case, all vectors in the regular section described by R_1 satisfies either:

$$b_k - b_j = \beta$$

or:

$$b_k + b_j = -\beta$$

but there exist vectors in the regular section described by R_2 that do not. Hence the containment criterion is violated.
End of Proof.

Corollary 1 *$R_1 \sqsubseteq R_2$ and $R_2 \sqsubseteq R_1$ if and only if $\eta(R_1) = \eta(R_2)$.*

The next theorem provides a syntactic characterization of approximation which will provide the basis for an algorithm to merge two RSD's into a single RSD.

Defintion 4 *Let $R = \left\langle A; \vec{\theta} \right\rangle$ by an RSD, then a* **linear partition** *of R is a collection of sets $V_0, V_1, \ldots, V_{\rho(R)}$ where V_0 is the set of subscript positions of R that are constant (invariant expressions) and each V_i corresponds to a set of subscripts positions that vary with the same induction variable.*

Example: For RSD $\langle A; 3, I_2, I_3, I_2 \rangle$, a linear partition consists of $V_0 = \{1\}$, $V_1 = \{2,4\}$ and $V_2 = \{3\}$. When a set V_i other than V_0 has more than one element, that set represents a collection of subscripts that vary together – a diagonal. The set V_1 in this example is such a set.

Defintion 5 *Let $R_1 = \left\langle A; \vec{\theta} \right\rangle$ and $R_2 = \left\langle A; \vec{\phi} \right\rangle$ be two RSD's and let $V_0^1, \ldots, V_{\rho(R_1)}^1$ and $V_0^2, \ldots, V_{\rho(R_2)}^2$ be linear partitions of R_1 and R_2 respectively. Then R_1* **textually approximates** *R_2 (denoted $R_1 \preceq R_2$) if the following conditions are satisfied:*

(a) $V_0^1 \subset V_0^2$ and for all $j \in V_0^1$, $\theta_j = \phi_j$

(b) For all i such that $1 \leq i \leq \rho(R_1)$, there exists k, $0 \leq k \leq \rho(R_2)$ such that $V_i^1 \subset V_k^2$

(c) For all i, and $j, k \in V_i^1$, either $\theta_j - \theta_k = \phi_j - \phi_k$, where both sides are constants, or $\theta_j + \theta_k = \phi_j + \phi_k$, where both sides are constants.

Condition (a) indicates that the constant subscripts that appear in the "larger" RSD (R_1) must also appear in the "smaller" RSD (R_2). Condition (b) indicates that a diagonal constraint in the larger is contained in a diagonal constraint of the smaller. Condition (c) indicates that a diagonal constraint in R_1 is the same diagonal as in R_2 and not a parallel or orthogonal one. It is convenient to define a relation, $\equiv$, on subscript expressions that requires both sides to be invariants. Thus $\alpha \equiv \beta$ indicates that both α and β are invariant expression in addition to asserting their equality. We will not define equality for invariant expressions, leaving it unresolved what algebraic identities are used to prove equality of expressions that are not identical.

Theorem 3 *For any two RSD's R_1 and R_2, $R_1 \preceq R_2$ if and only if $R_1 \sqsubseteq R_2$.*

Proof: Assume $\vec{\theta}$,$\vec{\phi}$, and V_i^j are as in the last definition. Assume that $R_1 \sqsubseteq R_2$ but $R_1 \not\preceq R_2$, then there exists i and $j, k \in V_i^1$ such that one of the following four cases applies:

1. $i = 0$, $j \in V_0^1$ and $j \in V_0^2$ and $\theta_j \neq \sigma_j$. (violates condition (a) of Definition 5).

2. $i = 0$, $j \in V_0^1$ and $j \notin V_0^2$ (violates condition (a)).

3. $i \neq 0$, $j \in V_{l_1}^2$, $k \in V_{l_2}^2$ and $l_1 \neq l_2$ (violates condition (b)).

4. $i \neq 0$, $j, k \in V_l^2$, and $\theta_j - \theta_k \not\equiv \sigma_j - \sigma_k$ and $\theta_j + \theta_k \not\equiv \sigma_j + \sigma_k$ (violates condition (c)).

To show that each of these leads to a contradiction, we must select an assignment of values for program variables and construct an element, $\vec{b}$, in the regular section described by R_2 that is not in the regular section described by R_1 under this assignment. Unless otherwise specified, assume that every variable is assigned the value 0.

The first case is easy since every vector $\vec{b}$ in the regular section described by R_2 has $b_j = \alpha$ for some α and no vector $\vec{b}$ in the regular section described by R_1 has $b_j = \alpha$, the regular section described by R_2 is not contained in the regular section described by R_1, contradicting the hypothesis (example: Figure 2(a)).

The second case corresponds to the case in which $\theta_j = \alpha$ is a constant and $\phi_j = I_l + \beta$ for some l. The case where $\phi_j = -I_l + \beta$ is analogous. Define $\vec{i}$ by

$$i_k = \begin{cases} 0 & \text{if } k \neq l \\ \alpha - \beta + 1 & \text{otherwise} \end{cases}$$

and let $\vec{b} = \phi[\vec{i}]$. Note that $\vec{b} \in A^{-1}(R_2)$ by construction but $b_j = \alpha + 1 \neq \theta[\vec{i}\,']$ for all $\vec{i}\,'$ and therefore $\vec{b} \notin A^{-1}(R_1)$ contradicting the assumption that $R_1 \sqsubseteq R_2$ (example: Figure 2(b)).

The third case corresponds the case in which $\phi_j = \pm I_{l_1} + \alpha$ and $\phi_k = \pm I_{l_2} + \beta$ where $l_1 \neq l_2$. Let $\theta_j = \pm I_i + \delta$ and $\theta_k = \pm I_i + \gamma$. Again, assume that the sign of each loop induction variable is positive, all other case are analogous. Using the vector $\vec{i}$:

$$i_k = \begin{cases} 0 & \text{if } k \neq l_2 \\ \alpha - \beta + \delta - \gamma + 1 & \text{otherwise} \end{cases}$$

let $\vec{b} = \vec{\phi}[\vec{i}]$ so $\vec{b} \in A^{-1}(R_2)$ and $b_j = \alpha$ and $b_k = \alpha + \delta - \gamma + 1$, but all vectors $\vec{b} \in A^{-1}(R_1)$ must satisfy $b_k - b_j = \delta - \gamma$, hence $\vec{b}$ is not in $A^{-1}(R_1)$ contradicting the assumption that $R_1 \sqsubseteq R_2$ (example: Figure 2(c)).

The final case corresponds to ϕ_j and ϕ_k varying with the same loop, but the difference $\phi_j \pm \phi_k$ is not the same as $\theta_j \pm \theta_k$. Intuitively, orthogonal or parallel but distinct diagonals are being described. Let $\phi_j = \pm I_l + \alpha$ and $\phi_k = \pm I_l + \beta$ and θ_j and θ_k be as before. Again, consider the case where all induction variables have positive signs, the other cases being analogous. Using the vector $\vec{i}$:

$$i_k = \begin{cases} 0 & \text{if } k \neq l_2 \\ \alpha - \beta + \delta - \gamma + 1 & \text{otherwise} \end{cases}$$

construct $\vec{b} = \vec{\phi}[\vec{i}]$ so $\vec{b} \in A^{-1}(R_2)$ and $b_j = \alpha$ and $b_k = \alpha + \delta - \gamma + 1$. Again, all vectors $\vec{b} \in A^{-1}(R_1)$ must satisfy $b_k - b_j = \delta - \gamma$, hence $\vec{b}$ is not in $A^{-1}(R_1)$ contradicting the assumption that $R_1 \sqsubseteq R_2$ (example: Figure 2(d)).

To show that the converse holds, assume that $R_1 \preceq R_2$ holds. We want to show that $R_1 \sqsubseteq R_2$. This will be done by selecting an element b from the regular section described by R_2 and constructing a vector $\vec{i}\,'$ so $\vec{\theta}[\vec{i}\,'] = \vec{b}$ establishing that $\vec{b}$ is also in the regular section described by R_1. Let $\vec{b} \in A^{-1}(R_2)$ and let $\vec{i}$ be such that $\vec{b} = \vec{\phi}[\vec{i}]$. For each loop control variable I_k that appears in R_1 is contained in some

Case 1:	$R_1 = \langle A;2\rangle$	θ	$\vec{b} = \langle 3\rangle$
	$R_2 = \langle A;3\rangle$	ϕ	
	(a)		
Case 2:	$R_1 = \langle A;2\rangle$	θ	$\vec{b} = \langle 3\rangle$
	$R_2 = \langle A;I_1\rangle$	ϕ	
	(b)		
Case 3:	$R_1 = \langle A;I_1,I_1\rangle$	θ	$\vec{b} = \langle 0,1\rangle$
	$R_2 = \langle A;I_2,I_3\rangle$	ϕ	
	(c)		
Case 4:	$R_1 = \langle A;I_1,I_1+1\rangle$	θ	$\vec{b} = \langle 1,3\rangle$
	$R_2 = \langle A;I_1,I_1+2\rangle$	ϕ	
	(d)		

FIGURE 2: Examples for equivalence of $\sqsubseteq$ and $\preceq$: $\vec{b} \in A^{-1}(R_2), \vec{b} \notin A^{-1}(R_1)$

V_l^1. Select a subscript position j from that set. Setting $\theta_j[\vec{i}\,'] = \phi_j[\vec{i}]$ defines the value for i'_k. We claim now that $\vec{b} = \vec{\theta}[\vec{i}\,']$ which establishes that $A^{-1}(R_2) \subseteq A^{-1}(R_1)$ and hence $R_1 \sqsubseteq R_2$.

For each subscript position j, if θ_j is constant, then $j \in V_0^1 \subset V_0^2$ and $\theta_j = \phi_j$, therefore $\theta_j[\vec{i}\,'] = b_j$. Otherwise, assume $j \in V_l^1$, then by construction there exists $k \in V_l^1$ such that $\theta_k[\vec{i}\,'] = \phi_k[\vec{i}] = b_k$. By assumption we have:

$$\theta_j - \theta_k \equiv \phi_j - \phi_k$$

or:

$$\theta_j + \theta_k \equiv \phi_j + \phi_k$$

Assume the former, the case for the latter is analogous. The expressions on either side of these equations are constants and do not vary with $\vec{i}$. Thus:

$$\begin{aligned} \theta_j[\vec{i}\,'] &= \theta_k[\vec{i}\,'] + (\theta_j - \theta_k) \\ &= \theta_k[\vec{i}\,'] + (\phi_j - \phi_k) \\ &= \phi_k[\vec{i}] + (\phi_j - \phi_k) \\ &= \phi_j[\vec{i}] \\ &= b_j \end{aligned}$$

End of Proof.

This theorem provides a basis for an algorithm to combine two RSD's into a single RSD approximating them both. An important property of this algorithm is that it generates the "smallest" RSD that approximates both inputs. Otherwise more information is lost during the merge than is necessary to stay in the regular section framework. The approach used in the merge algorithm given below is to construct a partition of the result RSD that satisfies the conclusion of Theorem 3.

Algorithm 1 *RSD Merge*
Input. Two RSD's, $R_1 = \left\langle A; \vec{\theta} \right\rangle$ *and* $R_2 = \left\langle A; \vec{\phi} \right\rangle$.
Output. RSD R_3 *that approximates both* R_1 *and* R_2.
Method: Apply function Merge *shown in Figure 3*

The output of Algorithm 1 on inputs R_1 and R_2 will be denoted $R_1 \wedge R_2$.

The next theorems establish that the function *Merge* implements our need for a function to take two regular sections (specified by RSD's) and compute a new regular section (again specified by an RSD) that contains the union of the two input regular sections. Furthermore, the output is the smallest regular section that contains that union.

Theorem 4 $R_1 \wedge R_2 \sqsubseteq R_1$

Proof: By contradiction, assume $R_1 \wedge R_2 \not\sqsubseteq R_1$ which implies $R_1 \wedge R_2 \not\preceq R_1$. Let $R_1 = \left\langle A; \vec{\theta} \right\rangle$ and $R_1 \wedge R_2 = \langle A, \vec{\sigma} \rangle$ as in Figure 3. Let $V_0, \ldots, V_{\rho(R_1)}$ be a linear partition of R_1 and $W_0, \ldots, W_{\rho(R_1 \wedge R_2)}$ be a linear partition of $R_1 \wedge R_2$. By assumption and Defintion 5, there exists i and $j, k \in W_i$ such that one of the following conditions is true.

1. $i = 0$, $j \in W_0$ and $j \in V_0$ and $\theta_j \neq \sigma_j$.
2. $i = 0$, $j \in W_0$ and $j \notin V_0$
3. $i \neq 0$, $j \in V_{l_1}$, $k \in V_{l_2}$ and $l_1 \neq l_2$
4. $i \neq 0$, $j, k \in V_l$, and $\theta_j - \theta_k \not\equiv \sigma_j - \sigma_k$ and $\theta_j + \theta_k \not\equiv \sigma_j + \sigma_k$

Cases 1 and 2. These cases correspond to changing a constant and creating a constant subscript. The only way a subscript position in $R_1 \wedge R_2$ could be constant is if it were set by the assignment labeled 2 in Figure 3. But this proves that $\sigma_i \equiv \theta_i$, contradicting the assumption.

Cases 3 and 4. These cases correspond to creating a diagonal constraint or changing a diagonal constraint. Without loss of generality, assume $j < k$. By assumption, j and k are in the same set of the linear partition of $R_1 \wedge R_2$ and therefore the exists l such that Let $\sigma_j = I_l + \alpha$, $\sigma_k = I_l + \beta$. The cases where one or both of the induction variables is negated are completely analogous.

The only place that σ_k could be set to $I_l + \beta$ is the line labeled 3 in Figure 3 (line 4 if I_l is negated in σ_k). This indicates that $\sigma_k - \sigma_l \equiv \theta_k - \theta_l$. If $l \neq j$, then σ_j was also set at line 3 and so $\sigma_j - \sigma_l \equiv \theta_j - \theta_l$. This relationship trivially holds if $j = l$. Combining these equations we get:

$$\begin{aligned} \sigma_j - \sigma_k &\equiv \theta_j - \theta_l - (\theta_k - \theta_l) \\ &\equiv \theta_j - \theta_k \end{aligned}$$

function $Merge(R_1, R_2) : RSD$

/* Assume that $R_1 = \left\langle A, \vec{\theta} \right\rangle$ and that $R_2 = \left\langle A, \vec{\phi} \right\rangle$ are both */
/* normalized. */
/* */
/* Output will be $\langle A, \vec{\sigma} \rangle$ */
/* Let k be the number of dimensions of A */
/* Below, α represents a generic routine invariant */
/* expression */
/* The relation $\equiv$ indicates textual identity */
/* and that boths sides are invariant expressions (do not */
/* reference induction variables). */

  for i = 1 **to** k **do**
    if $\theta_i = I_i$ or $\phi_i = I_i$
1:       **then** $\sigma_i \leftarrow I_i$
    /* Check for identical constants */
    else $\theta_i \equiv \phi_i$
2:       **then** $\sigma_i \leftarrow \theta_i$
    else do
      /* See if current subscript is part of a */
      /* diagonal. */
      new $\leftarrow$ **True**
      for j = 1 **to** $i - 1$ **while** *new* **do**
        if $\sigma_j = I_j$ **then do**
          if $\theta_i - \theta_j \equiv \phi_i - \phi_j$ **then do**
            new $\leftarrow$ **False**
3:             $\sigma_i \leftarrow I_j + \theta_i - \theta_j$
          else if $\theta_i + \theta_j \equiv \phi_i + \phi_j$ **then do**
            new $\leftarrow$ **False**
4:             $\sigma_i \leftarrow -I_j + \theta_i + \theta_j$
5:       **if** *new* **then** $\sigma_i \leftarrow I_i$
  $Merge \leftarrow \langle A; \vec{\sigma} \rangle$

FIGURE 3: Algorithm to merge to RSD's: $R_1 \wedge R_2 = Merge(R_1, R_2)$

which established that j and k are in the same linear partition of R_1, contradicting the assumption of case 3. The equation also condtradicts that assumption of case 4.
End of Proof.

Theorem 5 *If $R_3 \sqsubseteq R_1$ and $R_3 \sqsubseteq R_2$, then $R_3 \sqsubseteq R_1 \wedge R_2$.*

Proof: By contradiction: let R_1, $W_0, \ldots, W_{\rho(R_1 \wedge R_2)}$, $\vec{\sigma}$, $\vec{\theta}$, $\vec{\phi}$ be as above. Assume R_3 is in normal form and is equal to $\langle A; \vec{\psi} \rangle$. Let $V_0^1, \ldots, V_{\rho(R_1)}^1$ and $V_0^2, \ldots, V_{\rho(R_2)}^2$ be linear partition for R_1 and R_2 and let $Z_0, \ldots, Z_{\rho(R_3)}$ be a linear partition of R_3. By assumption $R_3 \not\sqsubseteq R_1 \wedge R_2$ which implies $R_3 \not\preceq R_1 \wedge R_2$ and therefore there exists i and $j, k \in W_i$ such that one of the following conditions is true:

1. $i = 0$, $j \in Z_0$ and $j \in W_0$ and $\psi_j \neq \sigma_j$.

2. $i = 0$, $j \in Z_0$ and $j \notin W_0$

3. $i \neq 0$, $j \in W_{l_1}$, $k \in W_{l_2}$ and $l_1 \neq l_2$

4. $i \neq 0$, $j, k \in W_l$, and $\psi_j - \psi_k \not\equiv \sigma_j - \sigma_k$ and $\psi_j + \psi_k \not\equiv \sigma_j + \sigma_k$

Cases 1 and 2. By assumption, if subscript position j in R_3 is constant, then subscript position j in both R_1 and R_2 must be the same constant (Theorem 3) and so in function *Merge* for $i = j$, the condition at statement 2 is true and so $\sigma_j \equiv \theta_j \equiv \phi_j \equiv \psi_j$ and $j \in W_0$ contradicting the assumptions of cases 1 and 2.

Case 3. By assumption, there exists n_1 and n_2 such that $j, k \in V_{n_1}^1$ and $j, k \in V_{n_2}^2$. With out loss of generality, assume that $j < k$. Further assume that:

$$
\begin{aligned}
\theta_j &= I_p + \alpha_\theta & \phi_j &= I_q + \alpha_\phi & \psi_j &= I_r + \alpha_\psi \\
\theta_k &= I_p + \beta_\theta & \phi_k &= I_q + \beta_\phi & \psi_k &= I_r + \beta_\psi
\end{aligned}
$$

By the assumptions of cases 3 and 4 we have $\theta_j - \theta_k \equiv \phi_j - \phi_k \equiv \psi_j - \psi_k$. The cases for where any of I_p, I_q, or I_r is negated are analogous.

Assume that $\sigma_j = I_m + \gamma$ where $m < j$. For outerloop index `i` equal to k and inner loop index `j` equal to m, the condition guarding statement 3 are true. Therefore σ_k is not in the same set of the linear partition as σ_j only if there exists $n < m$ such that $\sigma_n = I_n$ and $\theta_k - \theta_n \equiv \phi_k - \phi_n$. However, $\sigma_j = I_m + \gamma$ implies that $\theta_j - \theta_n \not\equiv \phi_j - \phi_n$ which combines with the last equation to show that $\theta_j - \theta_k \not\equiv \phi_j - \phi_k$, contradicting the assumptions of cases 3 and 4. Hence, σ_k must be in the same set of the linear partition as σ_j, contradicting the assumptions of case 3. Furthermore, $\sigma_j - \sigma_k \equiv \theta_j - \theta_k \equiv \psi_j - \psi_k$ contradicts the assumptions of case 4.
End of Proof.

Theorem 6 $A^{-1}(R_1 \wedge R_2) \supseteq A^{-1}(R_1) \cup A^{-1}(R_2)$

Proof: Observe that the function *Merge* treats its parameters symmetrically and therefore $R_1 \wedge R_2 = R_2 \wedge R_1$. Therefore we have $R_1 \wedge R_2 \sqsubseteq R_1$ and $R_1 \wedge R_2 \sqsubseteq R_2$ and this theorem follows.
End of Proof.

Enough machinery has been developed to define a lattice based on regular sections and their descriptors. Let L be the set of normal form RSD's for some k-dimensional array variable A with the extra element $\top$. The element $\top$ corresponds to the empty set: no access is made to the array. The rank of $\top$ is defined to be -1 so that Theorem 2 extends to L. Define a partial ordering on L by $\sqsubseteq$. Define the meet operator $\wedge$ by:

$$R_1 \wedge R_2 = \begin{cases} R_2 & \text{If } R_1 = \top \\ R_1 & \text{If } R_2 = \top \\ merge(R_1, R_2) & \text{otherwise} \end{cases}$$

Under these definitions, the following theorems hold[6].

Theorem 7 *$\langle L, \wedge \rangle$ is a bounded lattice.*

Proof: We must show that $\wedge$ is idempotent, reflexive and associative (therefore $\langle L, \wedge \rangle$ is a lattice) and that there are no infinite chains.

For example, we will prove idempotency, proofs for refexivity and associativity are similar: since $R_1 \sqsubseteq R_1$, by Theorem 5 and Theorem 4, we have $R_1 \sqsubseteq R_1 \wedge R_1 \sqsubseteq R_1$ and therefore $R_1 = R_1 \wedge R_1$ by the corollary to Theorem 2.

If $R_1 \sqsubseteq R_2$ and R_1 is not equal to R_2, then $\rho(R_1) > \rho(R_2)$. Since the rank of a function is bounded(Lemma 1), the lattice L is also bounded.

End of Proof.

3.5 Complexity

Within the framework of classical algorithms extended to handle lattices, the worst case time complexity for interprocedural summary problems is proportional to the depth of the sublattice and the cost of a single merge operation. The depth of the sublattice $\langle L, \wedge \rangle$ is bounded by k, the largest number of dimensions of any variable in the program. This value also determines the time complexity of a single merge operation: the inner loop in Figure 3 executes at most k times and each such execution involves at most k constant time operations. Therefore the depth of the sublattice and the cost of a merge are $O(k)$ and $O(k^2)$ respectively. This indicates that cost of regular section analysis is $O(k^3)$ more than the cost of simple summary information. This estimate is misleading because the worst case information only applies when there are a significant number of diagonals. In general we expect RSD's to describe mostly rows and columns and so the inner loop of function *Merge* will be executed rarely. In practice, we expect the merge operation to be $O(k)$ rather than $O(k^2)$.

Intersection of regular section descriptors, the fundamental operation in dependence testing, is a restricted form of unification and, hence, can be done in $O(k)$ time.

---

[6] See Kam and Ullman [KU77] for appropriate definitions.

In summary, we have defined a lattice of regular section descriptors whose elements correspond to particular substructures of arrays. The cost of the meet and intersection operations for these descriptors is very low—in fact, they is proportional to the number of dimensions of the array being examined, except in a few infrequently-occurring cases.

There remains one problem to be solved if regular section analysis is to be sufficiently precise. At each call site, actual array parameters are bound to formal array parameters. This operation can be viewed as defining a collection of functions at each call site that model the effects of parameter binding. Such a function may map only part of a parameter array to the formal parameter. If we are to precisely translate regular sections of a formal parameter to regular sections of an actual parameter, we must detect this case. This is the subject of the next section.

4 Translation Functions.

Translation functions are associated with call sites map an RSD of the formal parameter, R_F, into an RSD of the actual parameter, R_A, in the following way: each subscript position of R_A is assigned either a constant expression or a subscript position of R_F. In the latter case, whatever expression appears in the subscript position of the R_F is copied over into the subscript position of the R_A. For example, at the call site:

```
REAL A(N,N,N),B(N,N),C(N,N)
CALL SUB1(A(1,1,J),B(1,1),C(I,J),N)
:
SUBROUTINE SUB1(X,Y,Z,N)
REAL X(N,N),Y(N,N),Z
:
END
```

For the first variable, an RSD for X of $\langle X;\alpha,\beta\rangle$ would translate to an RSD of A equal to $\langle A;\alpha,\beta,J\rangle$. An RSD for Y of $\langle Y;\alpha,\beta\rangle$ would translate to an RSD of B equal to $\langle B;\alpha,\beta\rangle$. An RSD for Z of $\langle Z;\rangle$ would translate to an RSD of B equal to $\langle C;I,J\rangle$.

Translation functions can be represented by simple templates that indicate for each subscript position, either a invariant expression or the index of the subscript of the formal parameter that will be mapped into that position.

The above examples are well structured. The rest of this section discusses translating array access information through call sites in Fortran which allows binding of formal arrays to actuals in less structured ways.

Languages such as Fortran and C allow programmers great freedom when passing arrays to subroutines. Only a pointer is passed and the programmer is free to base any shaped array on the location specified by that pointer. This generality of array parameter passing greatly complicates the translation of array summary information through a call site. Limiting information used in regular section descriptors allows a clean, bounded lattice to be developed. Not retaining certain information makes it difficult to translate information across call sites. Consider the following example:

```
REAL A(N,N)
CALL SUB1(A(I,I),N,N-I+1)
:
SUBROUTINE SUB1(V,INC,M)
REAL V(*)
J = 1
DO I = 1,M
   V(J) = ...
   J = J + INC
ENDDO
END
```

The fact that INC is bound to N, which is equal to the first bound of A, is needed to determine that the formal access is actually a row of the actual parameter. This fact is omitted from the RSD of V given by $\langle V; I_1 \rangle$.

A second example uses the same subroutine, but with the call site:

```
REAL A(N,N)
CALL SUB1(A(I,I),1,N-I+1)
```

The fact that only $N - I + 1$ elements of V are accessed is needed to determine that the formal access is actually a column of the actual parameter. Again, this information is omitted from the RSD.

The first of these problems can be handled by allowing RSD's to have coefficients associated with the loop induction variables. Minor modifications to the definition of normal form and textual approximation must be made. The merge operation adjusts coefficients so that containment is preserved. In general, the coefficient loop induction variable for a particular subscript position will either be the same as in the corresponding subscript position of the input RSD or it will be a divisor of that coefficient. This property preserves the finite chain property of the lattice. It is not clear whether this generality is necessary, since only a few coefficients are interesting: those that correspond to rows, diagonals and similar sections of the actual parameters. Thus it seems practical to perform some auxiliary analysis to determine how formal parameters relate to actual parameters.

The "coefficient" that is used as a stride in formal parameters and indicates how access patterns of the formal relate to access patterns of the actual can be derived from inspection of the direct accesses made to the formal parameter involved in the call site, and to the other formal parameters it is bound to indirectly: if $A(\theta)$ is an actual parameter bound to F, and we want to know if all accesses to A have coefficient c, then all accesses to F must have coefficient of c and θ must be one more than a multiple of c.

The "coefficient" of the most significant dimension that appears in accesses to the formal determines how the formal relates to the actual: if it is 1, then the formal is a column; if it N, the corresponding bound of the actual (as in the first example), then the access is a row; if it $N+1$, then the access is a diagonal. These are cases where the formal has one fewer dimension than the actual; there are analogues for the cases when the formal has even fewer dimensions.

The other piece of information is harder; the presence of gradually increasing upper bounds leads to a lattice that is unbounded. Consider the loop:

```
SUBROUTINE TEMP(A,N,M)
REAL A(*)
IF (N.LT.M) CALL TEMP (A,N+1)
A(N) = N
RETURN
END
```

In this case, we would need to merge N with $N+1$. If we took $N+1$ as the result and translated that though the call site to $N+2$ and merged again, we would get $N+2$. This cycle can not be terminated in a naive lattice with infinite chains.

However, from the point of view of translating information from a subroutine to a caller, there are only a finite number of "interesting" values for upper bounds. These values correspond to a limit where accesses contained in one subsection (row, column, or diagonal) would "overflow" into the next. In the second example, we are only interested in knowing whether the upper bound of accesses to V is either in the range $[1..M]$ or in the range $[M+1..\infty]$.

To determine how an RSD describing access to a formal parameter translates into an RSD for the actual parameter, we need to determine how the formal parameter's shape relates to that of the actual. The most common case is that they will be identical, but it will also be common for the formal parameter to have fewer dimensions then the actual. This is particularly true when the formal represents a subsection, like a row or column, of the actual. For simplicity, we will avoid the extreme cases where the shapes of the actual and the formal parameters are radically different. Worst case assumptions will be made for those situations. The cases we will consider more closely are those in which the formal parameter is a proper section of the actual:

Defintion 6 *A formal array parameter f with bounds $F_1, \ldots, F_k$ is a* **proper section** *of an actual array parameter a with bounds $A_1, \ldots, A_n$ and subscripts $\phi_1, \ldots, \phi_n$ if for all $j < k$:*

$$F_j = A_j$$
$$\phi_j = 1$$
$$\phi_k + F_k \leq A_k$$

The first example of this section illustrates a proper section.

When the coefficient indicates that the formal may be contained in a column (or higher dimensional analogue) we will need an upper bound for how much of the formal is accessed (as in the second example). Since the formal shape declaration need not provide this information, our goal is to find an expression for each formal array parameter which bounds the largest value used as an index in the most significant dimension of that array. These expressions can be combinations of integers and formal parameters or a special symbol representing an unknown upper bound. These expressions must satisfy two constraints. The first is that they must bound the direct accesses made to the formal array parameter by the routine it is declared in. This can be checked by inspection of the direct access to array variables when RSD information is collected as summary. The second constraint is that, at every call site where actual parameter $A(\theta)$ is bound to formal parameter F, if N_F is the bound for F and M is that bound after substituting the parameters of the call in for the formal parameters in N_F, then $M + \theta$ must be less than or equal to N_A, the bound for A[7].

No technique is known to construct these bounds precisely from the information in the access summary information and call site information. The problem of infinite ascending chains prevents use of the obvious iterative approach. The approach suggested below uses information about what solution is "interesting", and tries to construct a solution and prove it is a fixed point. It is an optimistic approach in the sense that Wegman-Zadeck constant propagation [WZ85] is optimistic, and is based on the observation that there are only a finite number of "interesting" solutions to the problem.

Initially, set the bound associated with each array to $\top$, indicating that no bound is needed. Where a formal parameter has a different shape than the actual it is bound to, and we need the bound on the formal to establish a particular relation between accesses to the formal and access to the actual, and the formal's bound is $\top$, construct an expression in the context of the formal parameter that establishes the relationship suggested by the coefficients. In the first example, no information is needed: the coefficient indicates row access and no upper bound is need. In the second example, the coefficient indicates a column access and we need to know if $N - I + 1$, which is M in the context of the formal parameter, is a valid bound. Thus M would be the initial bound for formal parameter V in the second example.

After this initial solution is constructed, we try to extend it to a fixed point by propagating bounds: where formal parameter F is passed as actual parameter and bound to another formal parameter G, any bound on F will imply a new bound on G. If G is not bound, then we make this new bound the bound for G. If G is already bound, then we see if the old bound implies the new bound. If not, we set the bound on F to $\perp$ to indicate an unknown upper bound. If the bound is set to bottom, and if some third formal H has been bound to F, then the bound on H

[7]This assumes that both F and A are one dimensional, if they are higher dimensional, then θ is the expression in the most significant subscript position of A.

will also be $\perp$. The bound $\perp$ can never imply any other bound. Propagation must terminate since every formal parameter is assigned a bound at most twice.

Where we fail to find a bound, and information is used from a call site involving a shape change, it may be that some other, larger bound can be used, and a new solution generated and tested. For example, for a call site with actual parameter $A(i, j, k)$, we may first try to show that the formal accesses only the column $A(I_1, j, k)$. If that fails, we may try to show that the formal accesses only the block $A(I_1, I_2, k)$. When second attempts are made, bounds set to $\perp$ are reset to $\top$. Note that each new bound we try is based on a larger (in rank) regular section for the actual. Therefore, at most k different bounds will be attempted.

Some amount of auxiliary work could be done to improve the ability to test whether one expression is bounded by another. In particular, during initial examination of a procedure, we could construct an expression for each scalar argument in a parameter list at a call site, in terms of formal parameters and integers, that bounds it. This auxiliary information may be as simple as recognizing that induction variables are bounded by loop upper bounds (which are likely to be easy to bound in terms of formal parameters) or a full blown technique to derive assertions about variables could be employed [Kar76, CH78]. This decision should wait until a (partial) implementation is available to determine the need for this auxiliary information.

A simpler approach to upper bound information might impose arbitrary structure on the lattice of upper bound information. An example would be to not use arithmetic properties to establish maxima. For example, when comparing N and $N + 1$, instead of selecting $N + 1$, consider these incomparable in the lattice and the result is $\perp$. A variant of this would be to keep k distinct bounds where k is some small constant (1 in previous case). For the case $k = 2$, $N \wedge N + 1$ would be $\{N, N + 1\}$ but $\{N, N + 1\} \wedge N + 2$ would be $\perp$.

In the ongoing implementation in PFC, we intend to tag each induction variable with range information to improve accuracy where that range information is available. We will experiment with various strategies for computing range information to determine the appropriate blend of cost and precision.

5 Approximating Kill Information

To accurately determine live ranges for variables as described in Section 2.3 we must know for each variables modified at a call not only that it *may* be modified but that it *must* be modified. Such information is sensitive to control flow within the external routine. Flow sensitive problems can be intractable [Mye81] in the presence of aliasing. In addition, we would expect that computation of a flow sensitive problem would be significantly more expensive the the flow insensitive problems currently being solved.

In addition to summary information, PFC also solves an interprocedural constant propagation problem [CCKT86]. The goal of this problem is to determine whether a parameter or global variable has the same value for all invocations of a routine. The basic algorithm constructs "jump functions" that map values of parameters upon entry to a routine to values of actual parameters at call sites in the routine.

In the absence of interprocedural summary information, it is not possible to propagate a constant value across a subroutine call. Such a limitation would severely degrade the effectiveness of constant propagation. The solution to this problem developed for PFC was to construct Jump functions without summary information but retain information indicating where the "value" was passed to a subroutine and may be altered by that subroutine. When summary information becomes available, this information is inspected and if the subroutine modifies the "value", the jump function must be altered to reflect this modification. The simplest approach is to change the jump function to $\perp$, the everywhere undefined function but a more aggressive approach that used the existing machinery was found: in addition to the jump functions described above, we also construct "return jump functions" which map the values of parameters upon entry to a routine to values of those parameters on exit of the routine.

In the absence of recursion, when we are adjusting jump functions and we encounter a reference to the output value of a subroutine, we simply expand the return jump function by replacing each occurrence of a formal parameter or global variable in the return jump function with the jump function associated with that variable and the current call site. Example:

```
I = 1
CALL INC(I)
CALL USE(I)
:
SUBROUTINE INC(J)
J = J + 1
END
```

The return jump function for J from INC is $R_{\mathtt{J}}^{\mathtt{INC}} = J + 1$ where the reference to J in the return jump function refers to the value of J upon entry to INC. The initial jump function associated with the variable I that is passed to subroutine USE points back to the reference to I in the call to INC and so when the update pass is made over the jump functions, the return jump function $R_{\mathtt{J}}^{\mathtt{INC}}$ is expanded by replacing the reference to J with the jump function associated with I at the call to INC. In this example, that jump function would be the constant 1. The resulting jump function for the occurrence of I in the call to USE would be 2.

The use of return jump functions improves the accuracy jump functions by tracking the modifications made by subroutines in a way that is nicely non-path specific. In the presence of recursion, any variable that is modified is assumed to be non-constant and so its return jump function is automatically set to $\perp$. In the presence of dynamic aliasing of reference formal parameters is what makes flow sensitive problems intractable [Mye81]. Our experience with Fortran is that aliasing is very rare and so we have taken a simple approach: jump functions also contain information indicating which parameters were involved in their construction. When alias information is available, a jump function is set to $\perp$ if it was built using a parameter that is aliased to a variable that is modified.

For kill information, the important observation is that if a scalar is not "used" during execution of a subroutine call and which has a jump function that is not $\perp$, then that scalar is dead immediately before the call to that subroutine. Hence, PFC already computes an approximation to kill information. Some tuning of this existing machinery should allow reasonably precise kill information.

The collection of return jump functions form a flat semi-lattice. These jump functions are represented by simple expression trees and any two distinct expression trees are considered different. The everywhere undefined function, $\perp$, approximates all of the other functions in this semi-lattice. This semi-lattice has not way of expressing that a scalar must be defined in a non-constant way: when two non-equal jump functions are merged, the result is $\perp$. Since most kills will not be constant, this is a major loss of information for the current approximation. Our solution is to add another layer to the semi-lattice of return jump functions.

This new semi-lattice is indicated in Figure 4. The top row of nodes, together with the node labeled $\perp$ and the nodes to the right of the node labeled *kill* are the basic flat, semi-lattice of return jump functions. The nodes to the right of *kill* represent unmodified values upon entry to a routine of formal parameters (f_1) and global variables (g_1). The new element *kill* approximates all of the jump functions that imply that the value has been modified but not those functions that imply a value upon entry that has not been modified. The *kill* node allows the fact that a parameter is killed by not assigned a simple value to be represented in that semi-lattice. The node labeled $\top$ (top) is approximated by all other elements in the lattice but has no interpretation as a function and is used only to make the semi-lattice a complete lattice.

In this lattice, if an actual parameter is modified at a call site and the return jump function of that parameter for the invoked subroutine is anything other than $\perp$, then that parameter is killed. In the absence of recursion, this new semi-lattice can be used exactly as the original was. In the presence of recursion we can still get reasonable information. Since return jump functions for parameters in one routine can refer to return jump functions in another, the set of all return jump functions in a program define a system of simultaneous equations over the semi-lattice of possible functions. In the absence of recursion, these equations can be solved by "back substitution". In the presence of recursion, we would like to find a maximal fixed point for the system of equation. The standard approach to finding such a fixed point is to select the top element of the lattice as an initial value for every "variable" and then iterate through the system of equations until a fixed point is found. This is the reason the element $\top$ was added to the semi-lattice: to provide a starting point from which to find a fixed point. The iteration process is exactly

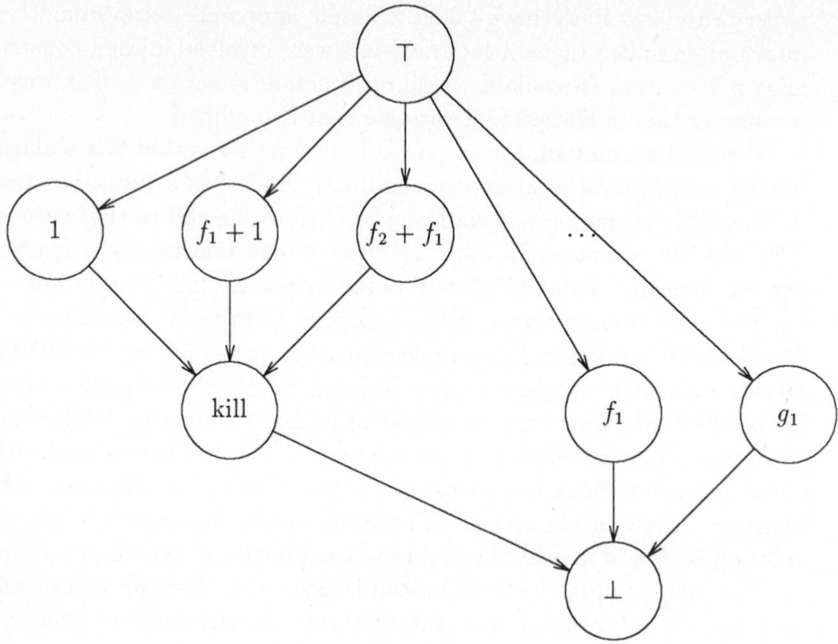

FIGURE 4: Lattice of for Return Jump Functions Augmented with Kill Information

the same as for constant propagation itself [WZ85, CCKT86].

We are in the process of modifying the implementation of interprocedural constant propagation in PFC to include this new lattice of return jump functions and to exploit the implied kill information it provides. Return jump functions represent an approximation to the general functions determined by the input program. In this light, we are exploring additional applications of return jump functions to the problems of flow sensitive USE [Coo83] and LIVE [Mye81] for both scalars and arrays.

6 Tracking Critical Regions

A critical region [Ben82] is a section of program that exactly one process will be allowed to execute at a time. A shared *resource*, r, is associated with each critical region:

```
region r begin
      ⋮
end
```

Exactly one process will be allowed to execute critical regions with the same associated resource. As discussed in Section 2.2, we want to suppress data dependences between memory references that are guarded by critical regions associated with the same resource.

Within a single procedure, it is straightforward to recognize when two memory references are contained in critical regions of the same resource. However, neither the current implementation of interprocedural summary analysis nor the regular section analysis described in section 3 provides information to solve this problem. We propose to modify a summary information lattice so that elements in the lattice are tagged with information indicating which critical regions guard that access. This solution here applies to either lattice.

Let $R = \{r_1, \ldots, r_n\}$be a finite collection resources. Let F_0 be the set of finite sequences of elements of R including the empty sequence. A sequence will be indicated by angle brackets: $\langle r_{i_1}, \ldots, r_{i_n} \rangle$. The empty sequence is denoted $\langle\rangle$. These are the possible *flavors* of memory references. If a memory reference is contained in a critical region associated with resource r_i, then it has flavor $\langle r_i \rangle$. If that critical region is nested inside a critical region associated with resource r_j, then the flavor would be $\langle r_j, r_i \rangle$ Let F be the finite subset of F_0 consisting of only sequences without repeated elements. It is an error for a process that is contained in a critical region associated with resource r_i to try to enter a critical region associated with that resource again. It is assumed that this will lead to deadlock. Thus F is the set of valid flavors for memory references. The element $\perp$ is added to F to indicate an error, specifically, nesting critical regions associated with the same resource. We define an operation $\|$ on F by

$$\langle a_1, \ldots, a_n \rangle \| \langle b_1, \ldots, b_m \rangle = \begin{cases} \perp & \text{if } \{a_1, \ldots, a_n\} \cap \{b_1, \ldots, b_m\} \neq \emptyset \\ \langle a_1, \ldots, a_n, b_1, \ldots, b_m \rangle & \text{otherwise} \end{cases}$$

Let L_S be the sublattice used in an interprocedural summary problem. It can be either the standard lattice or the regular section lattice described above. The primary lattice for interprocedural analysis consists of functions from program variables into the sublattice $(V \to L_S)$. We modify this to track critical regions by following combinations of flavors and variables: $(V \times F) \to L_S$. Translation functions in the standard interprocedural analysis problems map $V \to L_S$ into itself and represent the effects of parameter binding at a call site c. For example, if at call site c, the actual parameter w is passed to formal parameter v then a pair $\langle v, a \rangle$ is mapped to a pair $\langle w, b \rangle$ indicated by:

$$\textbf{backbind}_c(\langle v, a \rangle) = \langle w, b \rangle$$

Translation functions in the new framework will map from $(V \times F) \to L_S$ into itself and be of the form:

$$\textbf{backbind}_c(\langle v, f, a \rangle) = \langle w, g \| f, b \rangle$$

where v, a, w and b are the same as before. The flavor f ranges over possible flavors and g is the (static) flavor associated with the call site c.

The solution of these data flow problem provides for each entry and variable, a set of accesses to that variable of various flavors. Given two flavored references $\langle v, f_1, a_1\rangle$ and v, f_2, a_2 (where a_1 and a_2 are access patterns in L_S, $f_1 = \left\langle r^1_{i_1}, \ldots, r^1_{in}\right\rangle$, and $f_2 = \left\langle r^2_{i_1}, \ldots, r^2_{im}\right\rangle$), we should suppress data dependences generated accesses a_1 and a_2 to v if $\{r^1_{i_1}, \ldots, r^1_{i_n}\} \cap \{r^2_{i_1}, \ldots, r^2_{i_m}\} \neq \emptyset$.

In addition to suppressing data dependences, the flavors can be used to look for anomalies that might imply program bugs. One example would be the case where the flavors where $f_1 = \langle r, s\rangle$ and $f_2 = \langle s, r\rangle$ indicating the possibility of deadlock. Also, any instance of flavor $\perp$ computed via a backbind function indicates the possibility of attempting to dynamically nest critical regions associated with the same resource.

7 Summary

We have described an environment in which precise information about the side effects of array variables is necessary. To meet this need, a new lattice has been constructed that enhances the resolution of standard interprocedural summary analysis so that common substructures of arrays can be described. We have also discussed some of the difficulties in applying this method for Fortran arising due its very general array parameter binding rules.

These methods are being implemented in the current version of PFC and PTOOL and in the initial version of the ParaScope programming environment. When completed ParaScope will include several new tools:

- A special editor that incorporates the functions of PTOOL into the $\mathbb{R}^n$ editor, dynamically reconstructing the dependences in the editor itself. The editor will also provide advice on how the program could be transformed to achieve more parallelism.

- A system that examines the entire program attempting to enhance parallelism by rearranging procedure calls through inline substitution, linkage tailoring, and procedure cloning. This tool will plan its optimizations based on interprocedural analyses such as the one described in this paper.

- A debugging system that uses the results of static analyses such as those performed in PFC and PTOOL to help isolate schedule-dependent errors arising from inadvertently shared data.

Thus, the ParaScope system will extend the program preparation tools provided in the $\mathbb{R}^n$ environment to assist the programmer in understanding and enhancing the parallelism present in the program while developing and maintaining it.

References

[ABKP86] R. Allen, D. Baumgartner, K. Kennedy, and A. Porterfield.
Ptool: a semi-automatic parallel programming assistant.
In *Proceedings of the 1986 International Conference on Parallel Processing*, IEEE Computer Society Press, August 1986.

[AC72] F. E. Allen and J. Cocke.
A catalogue of optimizing transformations.
In *Design and Optimization of Compilers*, pages 1–30, Prentice-Hall, 1972.

[ACK87] Randy Allen, David Callahan, and Ken Kennedy.
Automatic decomposition of scientific programs for parallel execution.
In *Conference Record of the Fourteenth ACM Symposium on the Principles of Programming Languages*, Munich, West Germany, January 1987.

[AK82] Randy Allen and Ken Kennedy.
PFC: a program to convert Fortran to parallel form.
Technical Report MASC-TR 82-6, Dept. of Mathematical Sciences, Rice University, March 1982.

[AK85] Randy Allen and Ken Kennedy.
A parallel programming environment.
IEEE Software, 2(4):22–29, July 1985.

[All83] Randy Allen.
Dependence Analysis for Subscripted Variables and its Application to Program Transformation.
PhD thesis, Dept. of Mathematical Sciences, Rice University, April 1983.

[AM85] W. F. Applebe and C. E. McDowell.
Anomaly reporting — a tool for debugging and developing numerical algorithms.
In *First International Conference on Supercomputers*, Florida, December 1985.

[Ban78] J. Banning.
A Method for Determining the Side Effects of Procedure Calls.
PhD thesis, Stanford University, August 1978.

[Ban86] Uptal Banerjee.
A Direct Parallelization of Call Statements - A Review.
CSRD Rpt. 576, Center for Supercomputing Research and Development, University of Illinois at Urbana-Champaign, April 1986.

[Bar77] J. Barth.
An interprocedural data flow analysis algorithm.

In *Conference Record of the Fourth ACM Symposium on the Principles of Programming Languages*, Los Angeles, January 1977.

[BC86] M. Burke and R. Cytron.
Interprocedural dependence analysis and parallelization.
In *Proceedings of the SIGPLAN '86 Symposium on Compiler Construction*, pages 162–175, June 1986.

[Ben82] M. Ben-Ari.
Principles of Concurrent Programming.
Prentice-Hall, 1982.

[CCKT86] D. Callahan, K. Cooper, K. Kennedy, and L. Torczon.
Interprocedural constant propagation.
In *Proceedings of the SIGPLAN '86 Symposium on Compiler Construction*, June 1986.

[CH78] P. Cousot and N. Halbwachs.
Automatic discovery of linear restraints among variables of a program.
In *Conference Record of the Fifth ACM Symposium on the Principles of Programming Languages*, pages 84–96, 1978.

[CK85] K. Cooper and K. Kennedy.
Efficient computation of flow insensitive interprocedural summary information.
In *Proceedings of the SIGPLAN '84 Symposium on Compiler Construction*, July 1985.

[CKT86] K. Cooper, K. Kennedy, and L. Torczan.
The impact of interprocedural analysis and optimization in the $\mathbb{R}^n$programming environemnt.
ACM Transactions on Programming Languages and Systems, 8(4):419–523, October 1986.

[Coo83] Keith D. Cooper.
Interprocedural Data Flow Analysis in a Programming Environment.
PhD thesis, Dept. Of Computer Science, Rice University, April 1983.

[DBMS79] J. J. Dongarra, J. R. Bunch, C. B. Moler, and G. W. Stewart.
LINPACK User's Guide.
SIAM Publications, Philadelphia, 1979.

[FO76] Lloyd D. Fosdick and Leon J. Osterweil.
Data flow analysis in software reliability.
Computer Surveys, 8(3):305–330, September 1976.

[HK85] Robert T. Hood and Ken Kennedy.
A programming environment for fortran.
In *Proceedings of the eighteenth Hawaii International Conference on System Science*, pages 625–637, Western Periodicals, Noth Hollywood, CA, 1985.

[Kar76] M. Karr.
Affine relationships among variables of a program.
Acta Informatica, 6:133–151, 1976.

[Ken80] Ken Kennedy.
Automatic translation of Fortran programs to vector form.
Technical Report 476-029-4, Dept. of Mathematical Sciences, Rice University, October 1980.

[KU77] J. Kam and J. Ullman.
Montone data flow analysis frameworks.
Acta Informatica, 7, 1977.

[Kuc78] David J. Kuck.
The Structure of Computers and Computation.
Volume 1, John Wiley & Sons, New York, 1978.

[Mye81] E. Myers.
A precise interprocedural data flow algorithm.
In *Conference Record of the Eigth ACM Symposium on the Principles of Programming Languages*, January 1981.

[TIF86] R. Triolet, F. Irigion, and P. Feautrier.
Direct parallelization of call statements.
In *Proceedings of the SIGPLAN '86 Symposium on Compiler Construction*, pages 176–185, June 1986.

[Wol82] M. J. Wolfe.
Optimizing Supercompilers for Supercomputers.
PhD thesis, Dept. Of Computer Science, University of Illinois at Urbana-Champaign, October 1982.

[WZ85] M. Wegman and K. Zadeck.
Constant propagation with conditional branches.
In *Conference Record of the Twelfth ACM Symposium on the Principles of Programming Languages*, pages 291–299, January 1985.

Design and Rationale for MUPPET
A Programming Environment for Message Based Multiprocessors

H. Mühlenbein, O. Krämer, F. Limburger,
M. Mevenkamp, S. Streitz

Gesellschaft für Mathematik und Datenverarbeitung mbH
Postfach 1240, D-5205 Sankt Augustin 1

Abstract

MUPPET is a problem solving environment for scientific computing with message–based multiprocessors. It consists of four parts — concurrent languages, programming environments, application environments and man–machine interfaces. The programming paradigm of *MUPPET* is based on parallel abstract machines and transformations between them. This paradigm allows the development of programs which are portable among multiprocessors with different interconnection topologies.

In this paper we discuss the *MUPPET* programming paradigm. We give an introduction to the language *CONCURRENT MODULA-2* and the graphic specification system *GONZO* . The graphic specification system tries to introduce graphics as a tool for programming. It is also the basis for program generation and transformation.

Keywords: parallel algorithms, mutiprocessors, programming environments, parallel languages, mapping problem

1 Introduction

The new generation of scientific supercomputers depends more and more on parallel processing. Parallel computers can be divided into at least two groups:

- multiprocessors with shared memory
- multiprocessors with local memory

Multiprocessors with local memory operating asynchronously and routing messages within a network face problems encountered also in computer networks and distributed systems. In order to obtain a breakthrough an interdisciplinary approach is needed.

In our opinion there are at least three reasons to use parallel processing:

- performance
- fault tolerance
- simplicity

This research was funded by the German Ministry of Research and Technology under contract **ITR 8502 A 2** as part of the supercomputer project SUPRENUM.

Fault tolerance aspects are not discussed in this paper. Our major concern is performance and simplicity. Simplicity seems to be surprising because parallel processing is generally considered to be complicated. We believe instead that parallel processing needs a fresh start. This gives us insights into the structure of a problem and reveals an underlying unity and simplicity.

Our basic observation is as follows: Many systems in nature work in parallel. With the right application model and the right programming paradigm it should be easy to obtain a one-to-one mapping of the problem structure to the implementation structure. The right paradigm can be phrased "macro dataflow and object oriented".

In this paradigm we describe how the input and output of an entity relate, by expressing the associated input/output transformations and by connecting the input/output parts. Thus the system is described and constructed from a local point of view. Using a similar paradigm from the application to the programming layer makes the programming task significantly easier.

The connection between the layers is still deeper. A massively parallel computer is a complex application system by itself and should be discussed in the framework of complex systems [MGK87].

MUPPET (multiprocesor programming environment) is a long term effort to exploit this idea. *MUPPET* is part of the German supercomputer project SUPRENUM [BGM86], which is geared to build a supercomputer of more than one gigaflop. The first machine will be delivered in 1988.

MUPPET is embedded in a problem solving environment (PSE) for scientific computing. A PSE can be divided into at least four parts [Ford86]:

- (concurrent) programming languages
- programming environment: syntax editor, program templates, program library
- application environment: multigrid expert system, partial differential equations
- man machine interface: graphics, algorithm animation

Concurrent languages are necessary for driving multiprocessors efficiently. The programming environment tries to support the scientific programmer. Its goal is to make programming significantly easier, more reliable and cost effective by reusing previous code and programming experience to the greatest extent possible. The application environment supports the end user who does not want to do low level programming. Application environments should include knowledge about the application domain and application specific technical languages.

Most of the *MUPPET* tools run on a high-performance scientific workstation with a graphic oriented man-machine interface. The workstation is connected to the supercomputer through a local area network.

The standard tools of the programming and application environment (a language-based editor supporting programming in the small, a fragment library supporting incomplete specifications and an interpreter) are generated by the programming system generator PSG, which is described elsewhere [BaSn86]. This approach makes rapid prototyping of different language specific environments possible.

In this paper we give a general outline of *MUPPET* . The strength of *MUPPET* is the unifying principle on which all tools are based. Sometimes we had to omit scientific details .

In chapter two the *MUPPET* programming paradigm is introduced as a network of abstract machines. The problem of mapping processes to processors is discussed in chapters three and four. The language *CONCURRENT MODULA-2* is described in chapter five. Transformations between abstract machines are discussed in chapter six. We discuss different programming styles that can be applied using the *MUPPET* programming environment. In chapter seven we describe *GONZO* , the graphical specification tool. This tool incorporates all the experience we have gained so far in parallel programming.

2 Parallel programming paradigm and abstract machines

Programming is the conversion of an abstract (machine independent) algorithm into a program that can be run on a particular computer. A programming paradigm can be seen as a way of approaching a programming problem and thereby restricting the set of possible solutions.

The concept of abstract implementation – as opposed to concrete implementation in terms of a programming language – was coined in the software engineering community beginning with the early 70's. The purpose was to capture stepwise refinement by a series of implementation steps for "abstract machines". Each of these machines was to provide a more or less abstract level of software functionality. Abstract machines give the possibility to address **operational** aspects which is especially necessary for parallel and distributed programs. It is a widespread believe today that mathematical functions alone (the "input output behaviour") are inadequate for specification.

The above ideas have influenced the *MUPPET* programming paradigm. The interconnection structure of the multiprocessor is as far as possible hidden from the programming layer.

This approach has to be contrasted to other programming systems where the hardware interconnection structure is tied up with the programs. Because of this lack of abstraction many results in parallel algorithms are of limited use and cannot easily be transfered to different environments.

Following Browne [Brow86] we define a parallel computation as a graph where each node is the binding of an action to a data object and the edges are the dependancy relationships between the computations executed at the nodes. In this paper we use a higher abstraction to describe a parallel program on a parallel computer [Snyd84].

The model consists of

- a graph $G = (P, E)$ whose node set P represents processes and whose edge set E represents the communication scheme
- a similar graph $H = (N, L)$ representing the parallel computer (nodes N and links L)
- a funtion $\pi : P \rightarrow N$ mapping processes to processors.

The *MUPPET* programming paradigm can now be formulated as a parallel abstract machine. Basis is LAM — the local memory abstract machine. LAM provides the following operations for entities called processes:

(I) Processes in different abstract machines are disjoint (no shared variables)
(II) Processes can create other processes and can terminate
(III) Communication is done by asynchronous message passing between partners (processes which share some knowledge e.g. know each other)

Several research projects are now persuing this programming paradigm. In [FiFr84, p.344] it has been advocated also as a basis for coordinated computing. The LAM network allows arbitrary communication structures and a dynamic evolution of the process graph. The LAM programming paradigm is based on parallelism found in nature. It can be used to model the behaviour of nature in an easy way – that is multiple processes, giving birth to new processes, dying, exchanging information and working independently otherwise.

In applications with regular networks more specific abstract machines can be defined by adding additional constraints. This will be explained by RLAM – the ring local memory abstract machine. RLAM is defined informally by (I)–(III) and

(IV) In RLAM every process has exactly two communication partners, called the neighbors. Communication is restricted to neigbours only.

Similarly other topology oriented abstract machines can be defined like tree, lattice, hypercube and the direct interconnected abstract machines. These abstract machines have to be mapped onto real machines of a given connection scheme, e.g. lattice, hypercube, butterfly.

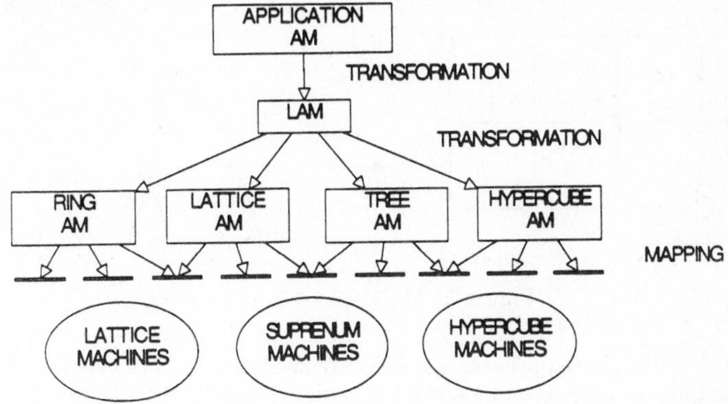

Figure 1: Abstract and implementation machines

The programming task can now be characterized as in Figure 1. The problem is formulated in an application oriented abstract machine, then it is transformed (manually and/or automatically) to a LAM implementation and may be to a more specific abstract machine implementation. This machine will then be mapped onto the topology of the real machine (automatically by the operationg system and/or by explicit mapping).

This layering defines clear interfaces, which can be used to create portable and efficient programs. The networks are chosen application dependent. If the given problem has naturally a regular communication scheme, e.g. a 2-D lattice structure, the programmer should use the 2-D lattice abstract machine directly without a transformation from LAM.

We conclude this chapter with a short survey. Several more or less similar abstractions have been proposed. Fox [FJLOS87] uses virtual machines, Segall implementation machines [SeRu85]. A NSF workshop report [SeSn86] defines informally "idealizied" machines for a broad spectrum of parallel architectures. The programming paradigm presented here comes close to the "multiphase, topology-oriented local memory machine".

3 The mapping problem

The LAM network allows communication between any pair of processes. Since it is technically too expensive to build large multiprocessors with direct connections between all processors, a tradeoff between the hardware architecture and the programming paradigm has to be made. The hardware architecture implements a topology with a limited number of neighbors for each processor and a message–passing system. Then, it is the task of the application program or the operating system to map the process structure to the processor structure. Now we will discuss this problem in more detail.

We divide process structures into three classes:
A process structure is called

- **static**, if its number of nodes and the communication structure is fixed,
- **multi–phased**, if different communication structures are used during different phases of the computation (see Figure 2),
- **dynamic**, if processes and communication links can be created during the runtime.

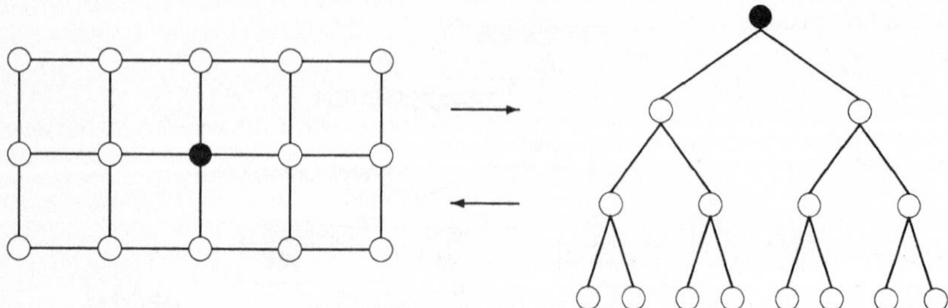

Figure 2: Multi–phase computation

Examples of multi–phased process networks are described in [SnSo86], [HoMü86] and [LeSt85]. The examples differ in what kind of synchronization is necessary to make the transition between the phases.

The general dynamic process network is difficult to deal with. Several researchers are therefore proposing dynamic networks with constraints. Most popular is the recursive spreading of processes within a 2-D lattice or a torus domain [Shap84]. It is interesting to note, that the problem, which kind of graphs can be defined by local evolution is an open research question (graphs that grow little by little [Uhr85]).

Most of the proposed hardware architectures can be described by a static processor structure. The strategies to solve the problem of mapping processes to processors can be divided into three methods:

- topology mapping
- mapping by optimizing a cost function
- adaptive mapping.

In the **topological mapping** method one looks for a mapping of the process graph $G = (P, E)$ on the machine graph H such that neighboring processes get assigned to processors with a distance of maximal 1 (neighboring processors). This problem is known to be equivalent to the graph isomorphism problem [Bokh81] and therefore is NP-complete. Many authors have examined this question for regular graphs on specific architectures, e.g. [Snyd84,SaSc85]. In fact, it has been the target of major research efforts.

Topological mapping can deal with homogeneous static process structures and to some extent with multi–phase networks. The target multiprocessor needs only to provide a small operating system without a routing function. A very interesting extension of the model is the application to fault–tolerant processor networks [MMW86].

If a solution for the topological mapping problem cannot be found, one has to look for sub-optimal solutions. In this case a cost function has to describe the communication behavior of the process system and has to define an optimization criterion. Heuristic methods can be used to find good approximations.

This approach of **optimizing a cost function** can solve a larger class of problems (non homogeneous networks, multi–phase networks) than topological mapping. The target multiprocessor has to provide an operating system with a rudimentary routing facility.

Adaptive mapping for machines with local memory is an open research question. It is necessary for evolving process graphs without information about the global process structure. Adaptive mapping can be implemented in a number of ways. In [NiSa86] a dynamic remapping stategy is analysed and in [ScJo85] user directives are used.

After this general survey we discuss the mapping problem in more detail. Intricate mapping strategies are very expensive. Therefore we investigate the relation between the cost for the mapping and the advantage gained by the mapping. We start with a simple cost function model.

Given a processor structure $H = (N, C)$

N set of processors
C matrix describing the cost per communication unit between two processors

and a process structure $G = (P, K)$

P set of processes
K matrix describing the amount of communication between two processes

find a mapping function

$$\pi : P \to N$$

such that

$$\Gamma_C = \min_{\pi} \sum_{r,s \in P} K_{r,s} C_{\pi(r),\pi(s)} \tag{1}$$

under the constraint, that the number of processes assigned to each processor are approximately equal.

This model defines a simple cost function for static process structures. We discuss the application of this model for a given machine, the SUPRENUM architecture (Figure 3, details see [BGM86]).

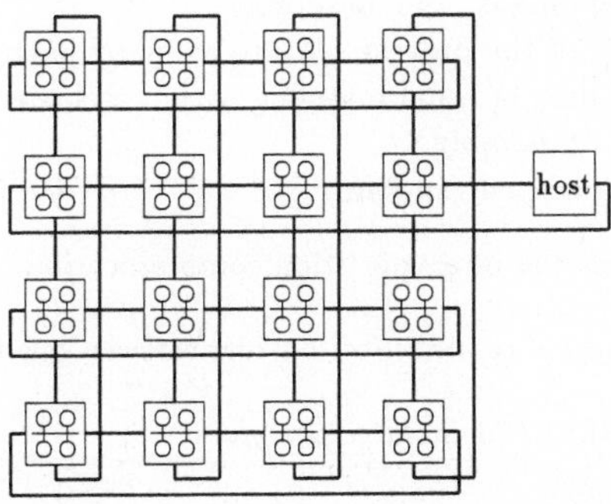

Figure 3: SUPRENUM architecture

The SUPRENUM architecture consists of $c_1 \times c_2$ clusters, where each cluster has p processors. The processors in a cluster are connected by a bus. The clusters are connected by row and column busses.

The estimation of the communication cost for this architecture is very complicated because the communication medium is shared. The communication cost is a function of several variables

— load of the communication medium, number of nodes and bus protocoll. We believe that such a complicated model is not necessary for our analysis. We will use a first order approximation taking three parameters into account.

We estimate the communication cost between processor i and processor k for a $(c \times c, p)$ configuration as follows:

$$C_{i,k} = \begin{cases} \varepsilon \approx 0 & i = k \\ p & i, k \text{ in the same cluster} \\ 2p + \alpha c & i, k \text{ in different clusters} \\ 2p + 2\alpha c & i, k \text{ in different rows/columns} \end{cases} \quad (2)$$

ε is the speed of the intraprocessor communication, α is the quotient of the speed of the intracluster bus and the intercluster ring.

The amount of communication K is application dependent. In this chapter we investigate regular, homogeneous communication structures (i.e. $K_{r,s} = K_{r',s'}$). We start our analysis with the following observation.

Lemma 1 *Any mapping strategy is optimal for* **any** *processor (process) structure if the process (processor) structure is completely connected.*

The lemma shows that mapping strategies are not important if the graphs are very densely connected.

We now make an **asymptotic sensitivity analysis** to investigate the performance gains by mapping. In this analysis we consider the tuple (process graph family, processor graph). A process graph family is a process graph with parameters, like a ring of length l, a torus of length $l \times l$, etc.

The SUPRENUM architecture is a processor graph family with the parameters $c \times c$ clusters and p processors within a cluster. The SUPRENUM architecture implements a general routing facility, therefore the following mapping strategies can be applied:

OPT	Optimal mapping
PART1	Optimal partition of the process set into as many partitions as processors are available; the mapping is done randomly
PARTS	Optimal partition of the process set into as many partitions as SUPRENUM clusters are available; optimal mapping within a cluster; the mapping of the partitions is done randomly
RANDOM	Every process is mapped randomly

Optimal partitioning minimizes the inter–partition communication.

Definition 1 *Let δ be the expected communication cost between two randomly selected processors.*

Lemma 2 *The* $(c \times c, p)$ SUPRENUM *architecture gives*

$$\delta = \frac{1}{c^2}((p-1) + 2(c-1)(2p+\alpha c) + (c-1)^2(2p+2\alpha c)) + \frac{\varepsilon}{c^2 p} \quad (3)$$

Proof : Two randomly selected processors are with probability $1/c^2p$ equal, with probability $(p-1)/c^2p$ within a cluster, with probability $2(c-1)/c^2$ within a row/column and with probability $(c-1)^2/c^2$ on different rows/columns. If we weight the probabilities with the communication cost (2), we obtain (3). □

With $p \to \infty$ or $c \to \infty$, we get $\delta \to \infty$. This shows the limited communication bandwidth of this architecture. In the SUPRENUM architecture we have $\alpha \approx 10$ if a dual intra–clusterbus is used, or $\alpha \approx 5$ otherwise. We now investigate the different mapping strategies for a ring of length l, a 2-D torus of size $l \times l$, a 3-D torus of length $l \times l \times l$ and a binary tree of depth l. Table 1 gives the results.

	Ring l	2-D Torus $l \times l$
OPT	$c^2p(p-1)+c^2(2p+\alpha c)$	$2cpl(\sqrt{p}-1)+2cl(2p+\alpha c)$
PART1	$c^2p\delta$	$2c\sqrt{p}l\delta$
PARTS	$c^2p(p-1)+c^2\delta$	$2cpl(\sqrt{p}-1)+2cl\delta$
RANDOM	$l\delta$	$2l^2\delta$

	3-D Torus $l \times l \times l$	Binary Tree 2^l
OPT	$p^2l^2+2cl^2(2p+\alpha c)$	$c^2p(p-1)+(c^2-1)(2p+\alpha c)$
PART1	$(p+2c)l^2\delta$	$(c^2p-1)\delta$
PARTS	$p^2l^2+2cl^2\delta$	$c^2p(p-1)+(c^2-1)\delta$
RANDOM	$3l^3\delta$	$(2^l-2)\delta$

Table 1: Total communication cost

The cost are normalized, such that

$$K_{r,s}C_{\pi(r),\pi(s)} = p,$$

if two communicating processes are on different processors in the same cluster. Details are given in [KrMü87]. In Figure 4 one of the many optimal mappings for the ring is shown.

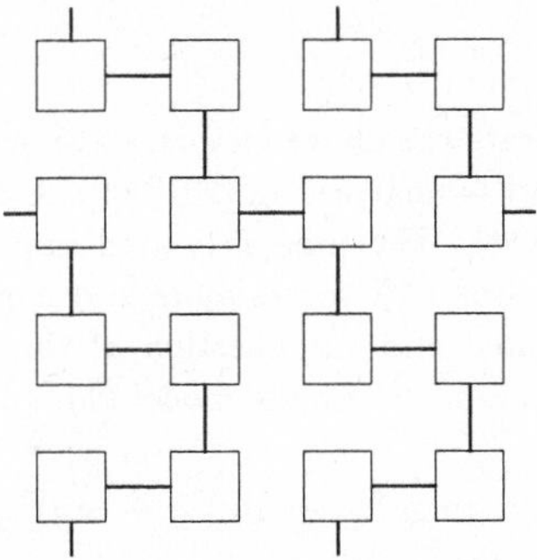

Figure 4: Optimal mapping of a ring

In all cases the cost for OPT and PARTS differ only by one term, the communication between two clusters $(2p+\alpha c)$ for OPT and δ for PARTS. The difference between these two functions increases with growing α and c (see Figure 5). It is quite small for the average SUPRENUM configuration $(p=16, c=4)$ and also acceptable for the largest configuration $(p=16, c=16)$. PART1 gives reasonable results whereas RANDOM gets worse with growing process network (l).

This rather simple qualitative analysis shows that optimal mapping is not necessary for the SUPRENUM architecture, but good partitioning is necessary and sufficient. The partitioning

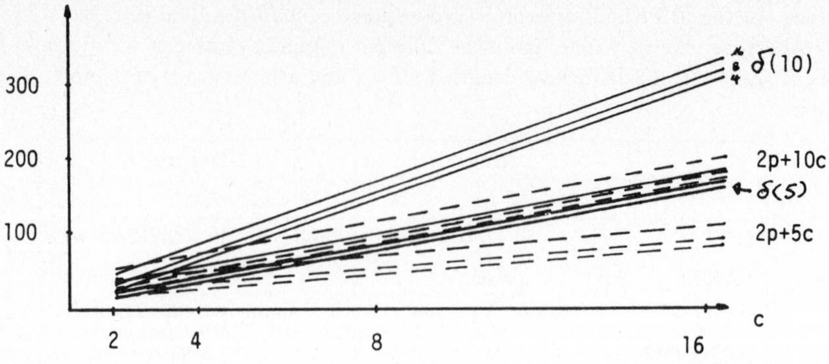

Figure 5: Communication cost δ (——) and $2p + \alpha c$ (- - -), for $\alpha = 5, 10$

problem can be solved rather easily. Graph partitioning is discussed in [KrMü87] in more detail, a new partitioning algorithm for static process structures with inhomogeneous communication is described in [MGK87].

The above analysis is based on process networks with point-to-point connections. The basic parameter is δ, the average point to point communication cost. Ullman [Ullm84b] proposed a generalization of δ for sorting applications, the "flux". The flux $f(p_i)$ of a network family is inversely proportional to the minimum time that it takes to get the data from any set of processors out of that set.

4 Complex models for the mapping problem

The cost function (1) is a very simple measure and does not take into account

- load balancing,
- communication delay.

Several models, which incorporate the above factors, have been proposed. A weighted sum of CPU-load and communication cost is analyzed in [EBP86]. A communication delay and a time constraint T is proposed in [HHR86]. The time T is used implicitely and limits the processing time on each processor. The reduction of T forces more and more processors to be used.

All these models are complicated and the question of the performance gain is difficult to answer. A straightforward extension of the simple model (1) is the following function:

$$\Gamma = \min_{\pi} \Gamma_C + \omega_L \Gamma_L + \omega_B \Gamma_B$$

with

Γ_C as defined in (1)
Γ_L penalty for unbalanced CPU-load
Γ_B penalty for network bottlenecks.

Γ_L can be defined as follows. Let T be the sequential execution time, T_r the execution time of process r, $|N|$ the number of processors, L_i the load of processor i, then

$$\Gamma_L = \frac{1}{|N|} \sum_{i \in N} (\overline{L} - L_i)^2 \tag{4}$$

with

$$\overline{L} = \frac{T}{|N|} \qquad L_i = \sum_{\substack{p \\ \pi(p)=i}} T_p$$

(4) can be called a mean value approximation. The same method can be applied to define Γ_B.

We believe, however, that these models are of limited practical value. They need many parameters, which are seldom known a priori. Heuristics to solve the optimization problem are difficult and the performance gains are uncertain.

Inhomogeneous process networks have to be mapped with a different strategy, which does not try to optimize globally, but only locally. We illustrate this statement with a very simple example. The inhomogeneous ring of Figure 6 is to be mapped onto a 2×2 torus.

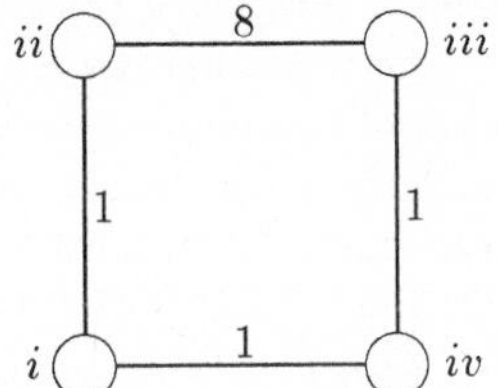

Figure 6: Inhomogeneous ring

We obtain an execution time $T = 8$ for a cycle if we assume that CPU and IO overlap. If we can split the communication between process *ii* and *iii* into two independent communication streams, we can get $T = 4$ by using two different communication links on the torus.

This idea can be generalized and leads to **adaptive routing**. Adaptive routing seems to be very promising in processor structures with a rich interconnection structure. A rich interconnection structure is characterized by many different routes between different processors and/or by almost equal communication cost between the processors.

Randomized routing is a simple implementation of adaptive routing. It has been proven for hypercubes that random routing gives a nearly optimal communication time for many interesting algorithms [Ullm84a].

Adaptive routing for the SUPRENUM architecture is very simple, because only the sending cluster has to decide, wether the row or column bus should be used. We conclude the discussion of the mapping problem with a summary.

- Topological mapping is optimal for regular, static and homogeneous process structures.
- Complex cost functions are difficult to obtain.
- Mapping with adaptive routing can be successfully applied in rich interconnection structures.

In [HMSCP86] it is correctly observed that random routing does not perform as well as topological mapping in many standard parallel processing tasks for hypercubes. We have shown the same result for the SUPRENUM architecture.

However, with a growing number of applications, a shift will occur from topology oriented mapping done a priori to more general adaptive mapping strategies implemented in hardware or operating system. It is outside the scope of this paper to describe the SUPRENUM operating system *PEACE* (see [Schr87]).

5 CONCURRENT MODULA-2

The *MUPPET* programming paradigm can be implemented by a new language or on top of existing languages. We chose Modula-2 [Wirt85] as the host language because it is well structured, offers a module concept for modular programming and separate compilation of modules.

A *CONCURRENT MODULA-2* program consists of a set of processes, communicating with acquainted processes by sending and receiving messages. In accordance to our programming paradigm we have introduced an abstraction mechanism for communicating processes. The language model is similar to the actor model of Hewitt [Hewi77].

Several modern programming languages [Cook80,Dann81,INMO83,FrHa83] have constructs to support inter–process communication. Some of the constructs are slightly higher–level than others, but most of them can be considered low–level, because they handle some primitive communication between two partners at a time.

A process in *CONCURRENT MODULA-2* can communicate with known processes addressing them by reference using process variables. Processes can be combined into sets. Sets can be used in SEND/RECEIVE statements. The usual operations on sets like union, exclusion, etc. support the creation and transformation of communication schemes. For incomming messages each process has its own mailbox in which the messages are collected. We chose the asynchronous message passing model because it is more fundamental, more efficient and increases parallelism.

The following description outlines the main features of *CONCURRENT MODULA-2* . A parallel program in *CONCURRENT MODULA-2* consists of a set of communication patterns and process modules that "import" some of these patterns. A special module, marked as the initial process module is created as the first process of the parallel application and typically behaves as a supervisor of the computation.

Processes in *CONCURRENT MODULA-2* may be created dynamically during the runtime with a create operation called NEWTASK. NEWTASK applied to a name of a process module creates and activates a new process and returns a reference to the active process, executing the corresponding process module. References to processes are values of type TASK or of a special process type denoted by the name of the process module. In the same way variables can be declared of type TASK or typed with the name of a process module.

Within a process module coroutines of Modula-2 may be used to structure the process and to get smaller entities of parallelism ("lightweight processes").

Processes terminate by executing an explicit termination statement. They cannot be killed by other processes, except by the initial supervisor process, controlling the computation.

Two processes can communicate successfully, if they know something common and use the same communication pattern. The use of patterns for the communication allows to check the message passing activity. Type checking is done during compile and link time, provided typed processes are used.

Patterns are similar to entry declarations in ADA [DoD80] and describe the structure of a message. The basic SEND operation is non-blocking.

```
SEND <pattern-name> <expression-list> TO <destination> ;
```

The destination can be a process reference, a process set, a name of a process module or ALL. In the first case the message is transmitted to the mailbox of the destination process, in the second case the message is sent to all processes of the set. The last two cases are obvious.

The blocking RECEIVE specifies the pattern and a formal message consisting of variables to bind to the message values. Optionally, the source process may be named.

```
RECEIVE <pattern-name> <variable-list> [FROM <source>] ;
```

The source can be a process variable, a process set or the name of a process module. If a process set is used the process waits for a message from an arbitrary process included in the set. To facilitate the programming of lock-step or server/client applications, *CONCURRENT MODULA-2* also supports synchronous communication by SEND ... WAIT and RECEIVE ... REPLY. Selective communication can be done by using the SELECT statement.

```
SELECT
    [ WHEN <boolean-expression>: ] <receive> <statements>
    { | [ WHEN <boolean-expression>: ] <receive> <statements> }
    [ ELSE <statements> ]
END ;
```

CONCURRENT MODULA-2 has been used to program different applications, ranging from partial differential equations to distributed problem solving.

We illustrate the flavor of the language by two examples — the bounded producer–consumer buffer and the sieve of Erasthostenes. In [FiFr84] the implementation of the bounded producer-consumer buffer in different languages is discussed. Our implementation has to be compared to the CSP implementation.

The bounded buffer program consists of the process modules for buffer, producer, consumer and supervisor. The task of the supervisor is to create buffer, producer and consumer processes and to install the communication. We are using SEND ... WAIT in the consumer process and anonymous RECEIVE ... REPLY in the buffer process (see Figure 7). In the CSP implementation the buffer has to know every consumer and producer [FiFr84].

The bounded producer–consumer buffer is a typical problem of distributed processing whereas the sieve is an example of parallel processing. Distributed processing is characterized by a small number of processes with different functions, parallel processing by a large number of processes of the same type.

The sieve of Erasthostenes is implemented flow oriented. The numbers are fed into a pipeline. Each pipeline process extracts multiples of its prime number. If a number reaches the end of the pipeline it is a new detected prime number.

The pipeline is created dynamically. In the algorithm is embedded an explicit mapping of the processes to the processors, numbered 1 to 32. This is done with the NEWTASK operation (see Figure 8).

6 Transformations between abstract machines

In this chapter we discuss how to find an abstract machine network for a problem and transformations between different abstract machines. We take as an example the matrix multiplication. The multiplication cannot easily be handled with our programming model. The explanation for this observation will be given at the end of the chapter.

The multiplication of two matrices A and B is defined by

$$c_{i,j} = \sum_k a_{i,k} \cdot b_{k,j} \tag{5}$$

In order to transform this problem to a network of abstract machines we have to make the following decisions:

- how to partition the problem domain
- how to distribute the partitions to processes

```
PARALLEL MODULE BoundedBuffer;
   DEFINE  Buffer, Consumer, Producer, supervisor;
   TYPE    BufferTask = TASK OF Buffer;
           supervisorTask = TASK OF supervisor;
   CONST   MaxSize=10; MaxData=100;
   PATTERN put(CARDINAL);
           get():(CARDINAL);
           InitProdCon(BufferTask,supervisorTask);
           terminate();

   MODULE Buffer;
      IMPORT get, put, terminate, MaxSize;
      VAR    in, out, n : CARDINAL;
             buf : ARRAY [0 .. MaxSize-1] OF CARDINAL;
      BEGIN
         n:=0; in:=0; out:=MaxSize-1;
         LOOP
            SELECT
               WHEN n < MaxSize:
                  RECEIVE put(buf[in]);
                  in:=(in+1) MOD MaxSize;
                  n:=n+1;
             | WHEN n > 0:
                  RECEIVE get DO
                     out:=(out+1) MOD MaxSize;
                     n:=n-1;
                  REPLY (buf[out]);
             | WHEN n = 0:
                  RECEIVE terminate;
                  TERMINATE;
            END; (* select *)
         END; (* loop *)
      END Buffer.

   MODULE Producer;
      IMPORT InitProdCon, put, terminate, BufferTask, supervisorTask, MaxData;
      VAR    BufferProcess : BufferTask;
             SupervisorProcess : supervisorTask;
             data : CARDINAL;
      BEGIN
         RECEIVE InitProdCon(BufferProcess,SupervisorProcess);
         FOR data:=1 TO MaxData DO
             SEND put(data) TO BufferProcess;
         END;
         SEND terminate TO SupervisorProcess;
      END Producer.

   MODULE Consumer;
      IMPORT InitProdCon, get, terminate, BufferTask, supervisorTask, MaxData;
      VAR    BufferProcess : BufferTask;
             SupervisorProcess : supervisorTask;
             data, i : CARDINAL;
      BEGIN
         RECEIVE InitProdCon(BufferProcess,SupervisorProcess);
         FOR i:=1 TO MaxData DO
             SEND get TO BufferProcess WAIT (data);
         END; (* for *)
         SEND terminate TO SupervisorProcess;
      END Consumer.

   MODULE supervisor;
      (* creating Producer Consumer and Buffer *)
      (* waiting on their termination messages *)
      END supervisor.

   INITIAL supervisor;
END BoundedBuffer.
```

Figure 7: Buffer processes

```
PARALLEL MODULE Sieve;
   DEFINE  PipelineProcess, Feeder;
   CONST   MAXCPU = 32;
   PATTERN init(INTEGER);
           primetest(INTEGER);
           isprime(INTEGER);

   MODULE PipelineProcess;
      USE    PipelineProcess;
      IMPORT primetest, init, isprime, MAXCPU;
      VAR    next : TASK OF PipelineProcess;
             pred : TASK;
             myPrime, cpu, no : INTEGER;
      BEGIN
         RECEIVE init(cpu);  pred := SENDER;
         RECEIVE primetest( myPrime );
         SEND    isprime( myPrime) TO pred;
         IF myPrime # 0 THEN
            cpu  := (cpu MOD MAXCPU) + 1;
            next := NEWTASK(PipelineProcess, cpu );
            SEND init( cpu ) TO next;
         ELSE TERMINATE;
         END; (* if *)
         LOOP
            SELECT
                RECEIVE primetest(no);
                   IF ( (no MOD myPrime) # 0 ) OR (no = 0) THEN
                      SEND primetest(no) TO next;
                   END;
              | RECEIVE isprime( no );
                   SEND isprime( no ) TO pred;
                   IF (no = 0) THEN TERMINATE; END ;
            END; (* select *)
         END; (* loop *)
      END PipelineProcess.

      MODULE Feeder;
         USE    PipelineProcess;
         IMPORT init, primetest, isprime;
         FROM   BFormatIO IMPORT WriteS, WriteInt, NewLine;
         VAR    PipeHead : TASK OF PipelineProcess;
                MaxNo, i : INTEGER;
                end : BOOLEAN;
         PROCEDURE  getPrimes(VAR noMore : BOOLEAN);
            VAR pr : INTEGER;
            BEGIN
               LOOP
                  SELECT
                     RECEIVE isprime( pr ) ;
                        WriteInt( pr, 3); WriteS( " is a prime "); NewLine();
                        noMore := (pr = 0);
                     ELSE EXIT;
                  END; (* select *);
               END; (* loop *);
            END getPrimes;

         BEGIN
            MaxNo:=500;
            PipeHead:=NEWTASK(PipelineProcess,1);
            SEND init(1) TO PipeHead;
            FOR i:=2 TO MaxNo DO
               SEND primetest(i) TO PipeHead;
               getPrimes( end );
            END; (* for *)
            SEND primetest(0) TO PipeHead;
            WHILE ( NOT end ) DO  getPrimes( end );  END;
         END Feeder.

      INITIAL Feeder;
  END Sieve.
```

Figure 8: Sieve of Erasthostenes implemented by pipeline process

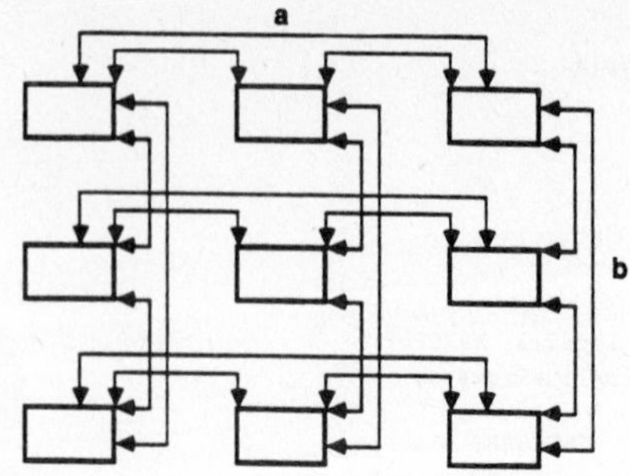

Figure 9: Network for matrix multiplication

The static distribution binds $a_{i,j}$,$b_{i,j}$ and $c_{i,j}$ to a process named $P_{i,j}$. The processes have to send their values to other processes and have to receive values from other processes. The communication matrix for N = 3 is shown in Figure 9. A straightforward implementation using the LAM network, is shown below:

```
FOR K := 1 TO N DO
  SEND ELEMENT(OWNA) TO P(I,K);
  SEND ELEMENT(OWNB) TO P(K,J);
  RECEIVE ELEMENT(A) FROM P(I,K);
  RECEIVE ELEMENT(B) FROM P(K,J);
  C = C+A*B;
END;
```

The dynamic communication behavior is shown in Figure 10. ! represents sending a message, ? receiving a message. The implementation produces a diagonal, starting in $P(1,1)$ and ending in $P(3,3)$. The history diagram shows that the communication is unbalanced, up to $2N$ messages can queue up for process $P(1,1)$. A qualitativ analysis gives

execution time $\sim 3N - 2$
efficiency $\sim N/(3N - 2)$

```
(1,1) | !!??▭!!??▭!!??▭
(1,2) | !!?________?▭!!??▭!!??▭
(1,3) | !!?________________?▭!!??▭
(2,1) | !!?________?▭!!??▭!!??▭
(2,2) | !!?______________? ▭!!??▭
(2,3) | !!?______________________?▭
(3,1) | !!?________________▭!!??
(3,2) | !!?______________________?▭
(3,3) | !!?________________________
```

Figure 10: History diagram

We look now for an implementation which uses a simpler network. Figure 11 shows a well known flow oriented implementation. In a flow oriented implementation the static binding between input data and processes is given up. The input data flows through the network. The node program can be written in *CONCURRENT MODULA-2* as follows:

```
FOR K := 1 TO N DO
  RECEIVE ELEMENT(A) FROM UP;
  RECEIVE ELEMENT(B) FROM LEFT;
  C = C+A*B;
  SEND ELEMENT(A) TO DOWN;
  SEND ELEMENT(B) TO RIGHT;
END;
```

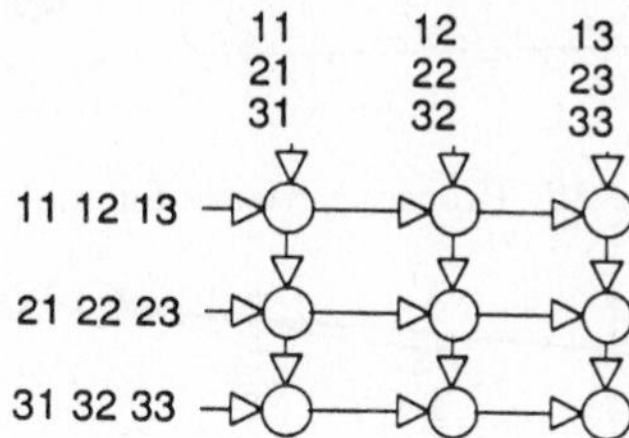

Figure 11: Flow oriented matrix multiplication

This implementation needs $2N$ input channels. The processes communicate only with their four neighbors. The analysis of the implementation gives:

execution time $\sim 3N - 2$
efficiency $\sim N/(3N - 2)$

So far we have considered only point–to–point connections. The SUPRENUM architecture supports multicast communication . A multicast implementation of the matrix multiplication is the following program:

```
FOR K := 1 TO N DO
  IF ( K # 1 ) THEN
     RECEIVE ELEMENT(B);
  END;
  IF ( I-J = 1-K ) OR (I-J = N-K+1) THEN
     SEND ELEMENT(A) TO ROW(I);
     C = C+A*B;
  ELSE
     RECEIVE ELEMENT(A);
     C = C+A*B;
  END;
  IF ( K < N ) THEN
     SEND ELEMENT(B) TO UP;
  END;
END;
```

The multicast implementation consists of N cycles. In one cycle the A elements of a diagonal are multicast in the rows. The products are computed and the B elements are shifted up in the columns. The shown implementation is not a true data flow implementation because the "firing" of A is not triggered by an external event but by global indices. The resulting network is shown in Figure 12.

$ROW(I)$ is just the set $\{P(I,J) : J = 1,..,N\}$. An implementation with active ROW processes is shown in Figure 13. $ROW(I)$ can now be used as a simple relay or as a line manager controlling the execution. The program is straightforward and omitted.

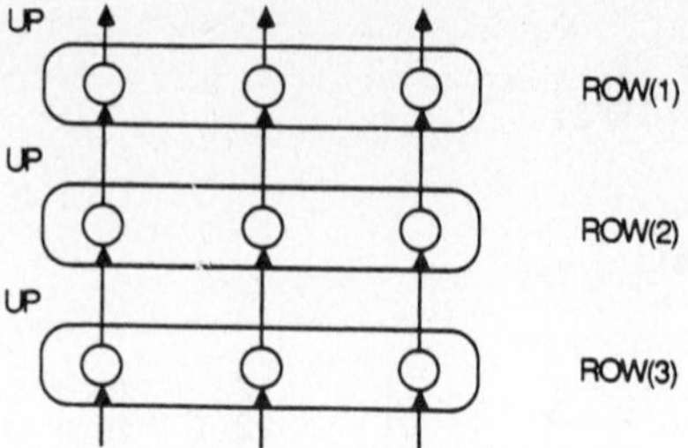

Figure 12: Process network for multicast

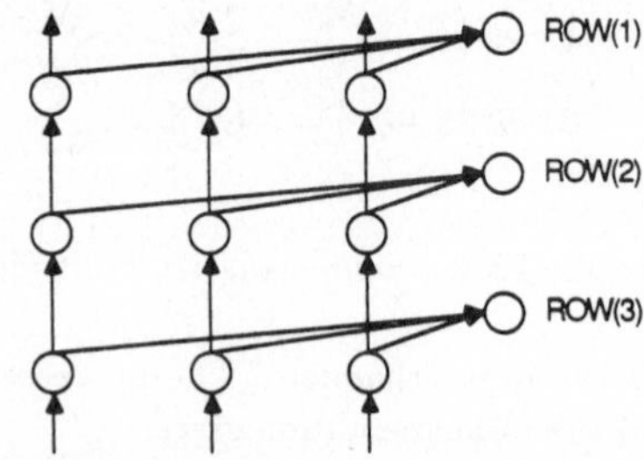

Figure 13: Network with active processes $ROW(I)$

This example demonstrates that different abstract machine networks can be used for an implementation. This leads to the problems

- estimation of the performance of an implementation,
- (automatic) transformation between different abstract machine networks.

The estimation is done in the *MUPPET* environment by a performance predictor derived from the mapping model of chapter 3, the second problem is ongoing research and will be discussed in a later paper. The transformation rules used are still rather informal. A solution needs a **mathematics for communication schemes.** First steps in this direction are the metric pattern theory [Gren85] and the automatic synthesis of systolic algorithms [Quin84].

We can now answer the question, why the matrix multiplication is that complicated to implement with the *MUPPET* programming paradigm. The reason is that the problem is staticly specified. The access sequence to the matrix elements is irrelevant to the specification, whereas in *MUPPET* each access pattern defines a new communication network.

In contrast, problems which are already specified flow oriented can easily be formulated in our programming paradigm. Examples are solving partial differential equations iteratively [HoMü86] and distributed problem solving. In [MGK87] a new parallel algorithm to solve the travelling salesman problem is described. This algorithm has been invented because of the *MUPPET* programming paradigm.

7 Graphical specification

The motivation to use graphics in the development of parallel programs is straightforward. Graph structures are usually drawn by the programmer as an aid in visualising the topology and communication scheme of the parallel algorithm. From here, the programmer traditionally describes this layout textually for interpretation by the computer. In doing so, he usually encodes the information inherent in his graph diagrams into some concurrent language. Even for non trivial applications this process can be complicated and error prone. Moreover, one may wonder if this process is necessary at all. Because of the regular, though involved, set of rules used in encrypting graph information for computer processing, this step is a natural target for automation.

The graphic environment of *MUPPET* — called *GONZO* — will contain the tools:

- The *GONZO -specificator* specifies the structure of a parallel program. The information given in the graphic specification eases also the task to visualize and animate parallel programs.
- The *GONZO -visualizer* shows graphically the execution of parallel programs, whose structure is specified by the specification tool. The *visualizer* represents graphically the message passing, ready and wait states of processes and the mailboxes.
- The *GONZO -animator* will display application dependent information.

So far, only a few systems use graphic for parallel program specification. A very successful system is the POKER parallel programming enviroment [Snyd84]. With the LAM programming paradigm in mind, it has the following limitations:

- It supports only static network structures.
- All connections have to be drawn manually
- Textual and graphic information have only limited semantic connections

Graphic support is also provided for the LGDF (Large Grain Data Flow) model (see [BaNu87]). The LGDF programming model consists of a network of nodes connected by a data path. A data path has a data area and a state which can be either empty or full. The empty/full state is changed explicitely by the programs ("firing rule").

The goals of the graphic tool *GONZO* are ambitious. *GONZO* has to support

- dynamic network structures,
- automatic generation of a textual program frame,
- semantic connection between graphic and textual information.

It is obvious that the graphic support of dynamic networks, which can be programmed in *CONCURRENT MODULA-2* , is complicated. Therefore, we use a more restricted programming model.

In *GONZO* a parallel computation is divided into different phases. A phase is characterized by the distribution of data across the processes, the processes themselves and the neighborhoods of the processes. Each phase consists of

- a set of process types,
- a set of incarnated processes,
- a set of ports for each process,
- a set of patterns for each port,
- a set of messages attributed by patterns for each port.

A process can be created only by an incarnation of a known process type. Incarnated processes are connected to their neighbors. This mechanism is called **replication**. Replication makes it possible to define large process structures with a few process types. Replication with automatic insertion of connections is a very powerful mechanism. It makes use of the automatic generation supplied for important regular graph objects (grid, tree, etc.). The user may include and connect previously saved graph structures. It is interesting to note, that the question, which graphs can be constructed by a replication algorithm with a bounded number of connections is an open research question ([Uhr85]).

The **port concept** defines the logical links to the neighbors. Neighbors are adressed symbolically by ports. For each port a set of patterns is specified.

This graphic information is used to generate a program frame in *CONCURRENT MODULA-2* . Process types have a natural correspondence, ports are translated to the process variables of the individual neighbors of each process. At runtime they are initialized by a (hidden) master process. In Figure 14 we show some of the features of the *GONZO-specificator* V1.

Currently, we are implementing the second version of the *GONZO-specificator*. Work has been started for the *visualizer*. *Animators* will be developed as far as new application areas are explored.

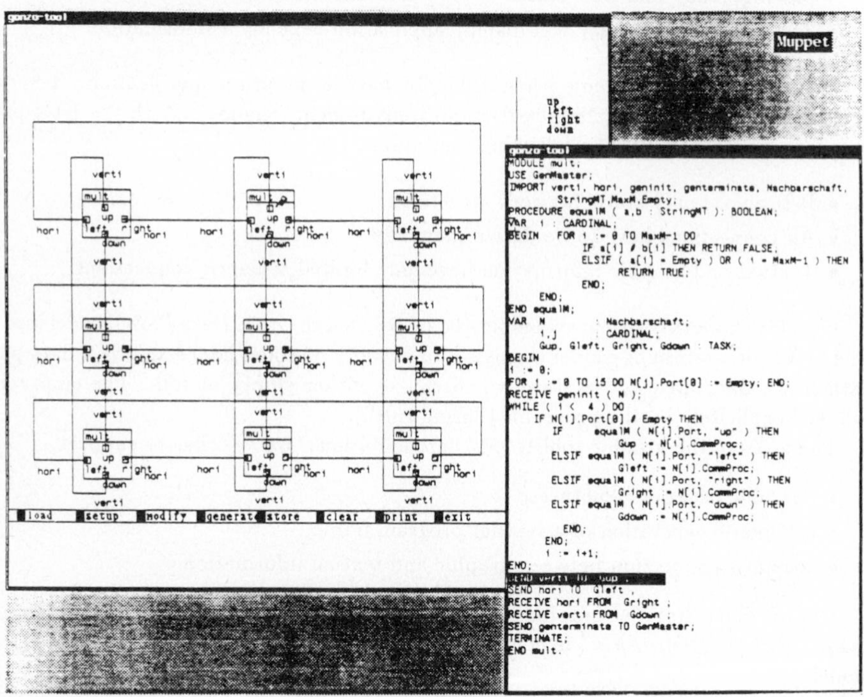

Figure 14: Screen image of *GONZO-specificator* V1

The picture has been created as follows. A process type *mult* has been defined with ports *up*, *down*, *left*, *right* and patterns *hori* and *verti*. Nine instances have been graphically connected. From this specification a program frame has been generated which is partially shown.

8 Experiences and conclusions

The *MUPPET* tools have been developed in connection with applications — numerical applications, combinatoric algorithms, distributed problem solving, connectionism models and parallel discrete event simulation. The basic tools — *CONCURRENT MODULA-2* and the simulation system *SUSI* (for some details see [MLSW86]) — are in use for a year.

We have found that many applications and parallel algorithms can be formulated either data–structure or data–flow oriented. The data–structure oriented approach emphasizes the global aspects of a system, whereas the data–flow approach concentrates upon the dynamic interaction of parallel processes by the flow of data. *MUPPET* supports the data–flow view. The data-flow approach leads to simple kernel programs, but new problems arise with the control part — initialization and termination of processes and the mapping of processes to processors.

We used at least two kinds of parallelism:

- algorithmic parallelism
- spatial parallelism

Algorithmic parallelism can be obtained by decomposing the algorithm into a number of simpler components with different functionality. Spatial parallelism can be explored in applications where it is possible to distribute the data between a number of processes. Algorithmic parallelism seems to be highly irregular whereas spatial parallelism is homogeneous and grows with the problem size.

The *MUPPET* environment can be used to obtain efficient and simple programs for spatial parallelism. We have developed new tools and integrated them into a coherent framework. These tools are based upon graph models supporting application specification, program specification, program implementation and program visualization at runtime.

More research has to be done to test the viability of the macro data flow approach. Of particular importance is the definition of relevant communication structures for a broad class of applications, the integration of these schemes into the programming language and the graphic specification system.

The next version of *MUPPET* will incorporate some of these ideas. We hope to end up with a new discipline — network programming. This new discipline is urgently needed for the new scientific paradigm arising in different fields of science, ranging from physics to cognitive psychology. The new scientific paradigm is in fact a very old one — seeing the world as a large collection of disparate entities with a dynamic connectivity and in continuous exchange (see [PrSt84]).

9 Acknowledgements

Many dedicated people have contributed to the first implementation of *MUPPET* . We thank D. Boles, E. Ehses, M. Gorges–Schleuter, T. Hennings, S. Warhaut and the numerous students. The work has been done in cooperation with the PIE project [SeRu85] of Carnegie Mellon University. The advice of Z. Segall has been very valuable.

References

[BaNu87] R. G. Babb II, D. C. Di Nucci: *Design and Implementation of Parallel Programs with Large–Grain Data Flow*, in: Characteristics of Parallel Algorithms; MIT Press, 1987.

[BaSn86] R. Bahlke, G. Snelting: *The PSG System: From Formal Language Definitions to Interactive Programming Environments*, ACM TOPLAS, Vol.8, No.4, Oct. 1986.

[BGM86] P. M. Behr, W. K. Giloi, H. Mühlenbein: *SUPRENUM: The German Supercomputer Project – Rationale and Concepts*, Proc. IEEE Int. Conf. on Parallel Processing, 1986.

[Bokh81] S. H. Bokhari: *On the Mapping Problem*, IEEE Transaction on Computers, C-30, No.3, 1981. pp 207–214

[Brow86] J. C. Brown: *Framework for Formulation and Analysis of Parallel Computation Structures*, Parallel Computing 3, 1986.

[Cook80] R. P. Cook: **MOD — A Language for Distributed Programming*, IEEE Transaction on SE, Vol.6, No.6, 1980. pp 563–571

[Dann81] R. B. Dannenberg: *AMPL — Design, Implementation and Evaluation of a Multiprocessing Language*, Tech. Report, Department of Computer Science, Carnegie Mellon University, 1981.

[DoD80] US DoD: *Reference Manual for the ADA Programming Language*, DoD–Report, July 1986.

[EBP86] A. K. Ezzat, R. D. Bergeron, J. L. Pokoski: *Task allocation heuristics for distributed computing systems*, Proc. IEEE Int. Conf. on Distributed Systems, 1986.

[Gren85] U. Grenander: *Pictures as Complex Systems*, in: Complexity, Language and Life: Mathematical approaches; J.L. Casti, A. Karlquist eds., Springer, Berlin, 1985.

[FiFr84] R. E. Filman, D. P. Friedmann: *Coordinated Computing*, McGraw-Hill, New York, 1984.

[FJLOS87] G. C. Fox, M. A. Johnson, G. A. Lyzenga, S.W. Otto, J.K. Salmon: *Solving Problems on Concurrent Processors Vol.I*, Caltech, to be published, 1987.

[Ford86] B. Ford: *The What and Why of Problem Solving Environments*, in: Problem Solving Environments for Scientific Computing; B. Ford ed., to be published, 1986.

[FrHa83] N. Francez, B. Hailpern: *A Communication Abstraction Mechanism*, ACM Operating System Review, Vol.19, No.2, 1985.

[Hewi77] C. Hewitt: *Viewing Control Structures as Patterns of Passing Messages*, Artificial Intelligence, Vol.8, 1977. pp 323–364

[HHR86] C. E. Houstis, E. N. Houstis, J. R. Rice: *Partitioning PDE Computations: Methods and Performance Evaluation*, Report Purdue University, available from authors, 1986.

[HMSCP86] J. P. Hages, T. Mudge, Q. F. Stow, S. Colley, J. Palmer: *A Microprocessor Based Hypercube Supercomputer*, IEEE Micro, Vol.6, No.5, 1986.

[HoMü86] H. C. Hoppe, H. Mühlenbein: *Parallel Adaptive Full–Multigrid–Methods on Mes/-sage/—Based Multiprocessors*, Parallel Computing 3, 1986. pp 269–287

[INMO83] INMOS ltd.: *Occam Programming Manual*, 1983.

[KrMü87] O. Krämer, H. Mühlenbein: *Mapping Strategies in Message–Based Multiprocessor Systems*, Proc. Conf. on Parallel Architectures and Languages Europe, Eindhoven, The Netherlands, June 15–19, 1987. pp 213–225

[LeSt85] D. P. O'Leary, G. W. Stewart: *Data-Flow Algorithms for Parallel Matrix Computations*, Comm. ACM, Vol.28, No.8, Aug. 1985.

[MGK87] H. Mühlenbein, M. Gorges–Schleuter, O. Krämer: *New Solutions to the Mapping Problem — The Evolution Approach*, Parallel Computing, to be published, 1987.

[MLSW86] H. Mühlenbein, F. Limburger, S. Streitz, S. Warhaut: *MUPPET, A Programming Environment for Message-Based Multiprocessors*, Proc. Fall Joint Computer Conference, Dallas, Nov. 1986.

[MMW86] E. Maehle, K. Moritzen, K. Wirl: *A Graph Model for Diagnosis and Reconfiguration and its Application to a Fault Tolerant Multiprocessor System*, Proc. IEEE Conf. on Fault Tolerant Computing, 1986. pp 292–297

[NiSa86] D. Nicol, J. Saltz: *Dynamic Remapping of Parallel Computations with Varying Resource Demands*, ICASE report 86–45, Nasa Langley, 1986.

[PrSt84] I. Prigogine, I. Stengers: *Order out of Chaos*, Bantam, New York, 1986.

[Quin84] P. Quinton: *Automatic Synthesis of Systolic Arrays from Uniform Recurrent Equations*, Proc. IEEE Int. Conf. on Parallel Processing, 1984. pp 208–214

[SaSc85] Y. Saad, M. H. Schultz: *Topological Properties of Hypercubes*, Yale University, Research Report RR–389, June 1985.

[Schr87] W. Schröder: *Concepts of a Distributed Process Execution and Communication Environment (PEACE)*, Technical Report, GMD FIRST, Berlin, 1987.

[ScJo85] K. Schwans, A. K. Jones: *Specifying Resource Allocation for Parallel Programs on the CM* Multiprocessor*, Ohio State University, OSU–CISRC–TR–85–10, 1985.

[SeSn86] Z. Segall, L. Snyder [ed.]: *Performance efficient parallel programming*, Proc. NSF Workshop at Carnegie Mellon University, 1986.

[SeRu85] Z. Segall, L. Rudolph: *PIE: A Programming and Instrumentation Environment for Parallel Processing*, IEEE Software, Nov. 1985. pp 22–37

[Shap84] E. Shapiro: *Systolic Programming: A Paradigm of Parallel Processing*, Proc. Int. Conf. on Fifth Generation Computer, Tokio, 1984.

[SnSo86] L. Snyder, D. Socha: *POKER on the COSMIC CUBE: The First Retargetable Parallel Programming Language and Environment*, Proc. IEEE Int. Conf. on Parallel Processing, 1986. pp 628–635

[Snyd82] L. Snyder: *Introduction to the Configurable, Highly Parallel Computer*, IEEE Computer, Feb. 1982. pp 47–56

[Snyd84] L. Snyder: *Parallel Programming and the POKER Programming Environment*, IEEE Computer, July 1984. pp 27–55

[Uhr85] L. Uhr: *Massively Parallel Multi-Computer Hardware – Software Structures for Learning*, in: Complex Systems – Operational Approaches; H. Haken ed., Springer, New York, 1985.

[Ullm84a] J. D. Ullmann: *Computational Aspects of VLSI*, Computer Science Press, 1984.

[Ullm84b] J. D. Ullmann: *Some Thoughts About Supercomputer Organization*, Proc. IEEE Compcon, San Francisco, 1984. pp 424–431

[Wirt85] N. Wirth: *Programming in Modula-2*, Third corrected Edition, Springer, Berlin, 1985.

An Overview of the PTRAN Analysis System for Multiprocessing

Fran Allen
Michael Burke
Philippe Charles
Ron Cytron
Jeanne Ferrante

Computer Science Department
IBM T. J. Watson Research Center
Yorktown Heights, New York 10598

PTRAN (Parallel TRANslator) is a system for automatically restructuring sequential FORTRAN programs for execution on parallel architectures. This paper describes PTRAN-A: the currently operational analysis phase of PTRAN. The analysis is both broad and deep, incorporating interprocedural information into dependence analysis. The system is organized around a persistent database of program and procedure information. PTRAN incorporates several new, fast algorithms in a pragmatic design.

1.0 Introduction

Since parallel architectures differ greatly in the number and power of processors, in connectivity, and in storage organization, our thesis [3] is that automatic or semi-automatic techniques are needed to effectively match programs to such systems and to achieve true portability. A compiling system exploiting parallelism must organize both code and data into potentially useful units of parallel work and provide dynamic selection and scheduling to account for execution-time parameters and system configurations. The Parallel Translator, PTRAN, under development at IBM's T. J. Watson Research Center, is a research system to develop technology for the automatic exploitation of parallelism. The specific target of our work is the translation of sequential FORTRAN programs to a variety of multiprocessing architectures.

Automatic formation of parallelism involves both functional and domain decomposition: the formation of code sequences into processes and the organization of data residences to match processes and hardware. Such a total reorganization of a "dusty-deck" FORTRAN program implies a translation system that understands data reference patterns across the entire program as completely as possible. Ideally, processes should be computationally independent and computational independence requires data independence. Therefore the primary task of a parallel translator is to find and create independent data items and, when this is not possible, to organize the storage and the computation so as to minimize synchronization and/or data copying. This requires determining as precisely as possible (and feasible) the data and storage relationships.

Consider the examples in Figure 1 and Figure 2 . Can regions R2 and R3 in Figure 1 be executed concurrently? How can the loops in Figure 2(a) be executed concurrently?

To make these determinations, PTRAN performs ***dependence analysis*** to establish the element-level reference patterns in a computation. In the example in Figure 1, dependence analysis determines that regions $R2$ and $R3$ can be executed in parallel because only the even elements of C are modified in $R2$ while only the odd elements are modified in $R3$. In the example in Figure 2, dependence analysis determines that there is no dependence between successive iterations of the i-loop but that an element produced in $A(j,*)$ on one iteration of the j-loop is used on the next iteration of the j-loop. Thus the outer loop can be transformed into multiple independent processes but the inner loop (the j-loop) would require synchronization.

```
R1:       create arrays A and B

R2:       do i=1, 100
             C(2*i) = A(i) + B(i)
          enddo

R3:       do i=1,100
             C(2*i+1)  = A(i) + B(i)
          enddo

R4:       use array C
```

Figure 1. Regions R2 and R3 in the program can be concurrent processes.

```
do  i=1,1000                              doall  np=1,1000
                                             (fork: i=process number)

   do  j                                     do j

      A(j,i)=A(j-1,i)+B(i)*C                   A(j,i)=A(j-1,i)+B(i)*C

   enddo                                     enddo
enddo                                     endall (join)

          (a)                                        (b)
```

Figure 2. The outer loop in (a) can be formed into the concurrent processes shown in (b).

Many code sequences of interest, particularly for coarse-grained parallelism, contain procedure calls. Dependence analysis must understand reference patterns in called routines as they affect particular call sites. Furthermore, the analyzed routine may reference external variables whose aliasing relationships and potential values are not visible in that routine.

Consider the example in Figure 3. How can the *k*-loop and/or the *i*-loop be formed into multiple processes? What, if anything, has to be done with the storage for the user's variables and for the compiler's temporaries?

```
sub P                                sub R (X,Y,L)
   common C(10)                         common C(10)
   dim A(10,10)                         dim X(L)

                                        do    i=1,L
   do  k =1,10                                 .
                                               .
      .                                     X(i)=Y+C(i)
      call R (A(1,k),B,10)                     .
      .                                        .
   enddo                                enddo
end                                  end
```

Figure 3. Interprocedural relationships

To provide accurate information for dependence analysis, PTRAN performs ***interprocedural analysis.*** Before dependence analysis is performed on routine *P* in the example in Figure 3, the interprocedural analyzer will have recorded that each call to *R* modifies elements of *A*, uses *B*, and uses *C*. Furthermore it has recorded whether or not *R* and anything called by *R* have history-keeping variables or produce other side effects. To deduce this information and to analyze *R* itself, the aliasing relationships involving the parameters and the common variables in *R* must be understood as precisely as possible. Interprocedural analysis makes that determination prior to the deep analysis of the routines.

The purpose of this paper is to describe the PTRAN analyzer: PTRAN-A. This system, currently nearing completion, extracts the data reference patterns in FORTRAN programs in preparation for the transformations performed by subsequent versions of PTRAN. The system does both broad (interprocedural) and deep analyses. The latter involves control flow, data flow and control dependence analysis, determination of constants and linear induction variables, and dependence analysis.

PTRAN-A features a persistent, structured database containing the translated routines and their inter- and intra-procedural relationships.

In developing the system, particular attention has been paid to creating a pragmatic system incorporating the most advanced techniques. Thus emphasis has been placed on compact encodings of the data, on using fast algorithms, and on decreasing code walks, I/O and other expensive activities.

Our work builds on the the pioneering work of Professor David Kuck at the University of Illinois [31, 40, 27, 29, 41, 21, 32], the work at Rice University [25, 6, 17, 20, 8], and elsewhere [30, 4, 36, 37]. Several new algorithms, while serving our concerns for a practical system, have led to a powerful and precise FORTRAN analyzer:

* The interprocedural analysis precisely characterizes those references relevant to parallelization at a call site with respect to:

    - the accessed regions of an array.
    - alias relationships among arrays.
    - interprocedurally relevant uses of variables. In particular, only those variables that are upwards-exposed with respect to procedure entries are of interest.

* Constant propagation efficiently finds constants inter- and intra-procedurally. For parallelization, such constants include loop and array bounds and the coefficients of subscript expressions. Other systems either arrest constant propagation at procedure boundaries or require multiple visits of program procedures.

* Control dependence analysis identifies essential control flow orderings and represents these through a control dependence graph [23]. Other systems represent such information through data dependences, which is inappropriate for multiprocessing. Because such conversions must be undone where vectorization is not possible, direct control dependence analysis forms a better basis for vectorization as well.

* Data dependence algorithms (Section 8.0) are improved in terms of efficiency, power, and precision by:

    - allowing early determination of independence, a uniform treatment of flow and anti-dependences, and incremental testing;
    - testing reshaped and interprocedurally aliased structures;
    - accurately testing subscripts that violate declared extents. This is accomplished through linearization, which also offers an inexpensive approach to precise multiple subscript analysis.

In the remainder of the paper we describe the PTRAN-A system, starting with an overview of the system in the next section. While the system is specifically targeted at FORTRAN, much of our work applies to other languages. The reader will therefore notice solutions to some problems not applicable to FORTRAN and terminology not usually used in a FORTRAN context. An example would be recognizing assignments to aliased formal parameters, prohibited by FORTRAN. An example of non-FORTRAN terminology is "global variables" instead of "common variables" when the method described applies to a general mechanism for sharing variables in procedures.

2.0 Overview of the PTRAN-A Structure

The PTRAN Analyzer performs three distinct tasks organized around the persistent interprocedural database that retains translated programs and relationships. These tasks are:

1. Translating a single routine and putting the result in the database. This translation involves the traditional syntactic and semantic analyses as well as recording information needed for basic interprocedural analysis. The ***translated routine*** includes the text, represented by a tree whose nodes correspond to source-level statements, a dictionary and other tables containing enough information to recreate (formatted) source as well as to compile it.
2. Constructing the static call graph of the system and using it to find the potential aliases at every procedure entry and for interprocedural constant propagation. The ***call graph*** consists of nodes representing routines and edges representing calls, with one edge for each call site. ***Forward analysis*** then propagates information down the call graph from calling to called procedures: ***Interprocedural constant propagation*** seeks to determine when a formal parameter will always have the same constant value upon entrance to its procedure; ***Alias analysis*** computes the set of potentially aliased variable-pairs for each procedure in the program. Visiting a call graph node in this phase does not require accessing its associated translated routine: the information required for forward analysis is extracted from the call graph and other tables already constructed for interprocedural analysis. Since not all referenced routines are available or translatable (for example, library routines written in assembly language), stubs describing the interprocedural effects of such routines must already exist in the database. The next section of the paper as well as [14] gives more details on the forward analysis.
3. Determining the dependence relationships in the program. Alias relations are known from the forward analysis; the precise context and reference patterns are now determined. This task, ***backward analysis***, involves three subtasks for each routine:
   a. Determining the effects of each call in the routine; i.e., determining the variables potentially modified by the call and those potentially used before being modified (such as history-keeping variables). This sophisticated interprocedural analysis [15] supports the determination of dependence relationships across call sites.
   b. Performing the deep analysis of each routine. This involves control and data flow analysis, constant propagation (including propagating those constants identified by the basic interprocedural analyzer), control dependence formation, linear induction variable detection, and dependence analysis. Each of these tasks is described in its corresponding section later in the paper.
   c. Determining summary information about the routine. This summary information is used to determine the effects of the calls to the routine (i.e., is used by task 3a). The prior deep analysis allows more precise summary information than would otherwise be possible.

Task 1, above, obviously involves examining the routine being translated. Task 2 can be done with data extracted during translation, with routines processed in call-graph order.[1] Task 3 involves reading each routine from the database and performing intraprocedural analyses. By examining these routines in reverse call-graph order, the determination of effects at call sites, task 3a, can be done just prior to this deep analysis of the routine containing the call sites. While the current implementation examines the routines only once after translation, the system has been designed to permit multiple traversals of the call graph to improve the results of the analysis.

After completing these three analysis tasks on a program, the database contains:

* for each program:
  - a call graph
  - a table of the common blocks
  - interprocedural aliases
  - interprocedural constants
  - interprocedural side-effects

---

(1) We assume in our exposition that call graphs are acyclic. Where recursion is not allowed, such as with FORTRAN programs, static cycles may nonetheless occur. An algorithm for transforming call graphs with cycles into acyclic graphs is presented in [15]. In the presence of graphs with dynamic cycles, the interprocedural algorithms presented here must be adjusted, with a resulting loss in either efficiency or precision [14].

* for each routine:

- its translated form (from which source can be reconstructed)
- its control and data flow graphs
- a table of definitions determined to be constant and their values
- dependence relationships and distance vectors

The analyses are now described in more detail, starting with a discussion of interprocedural analysis.

3.0 Computing Interprocedural Information

Our analysis is sharpened by the incorporation of information determined by interprocedural analysis. Our interprocedural analysis is of several kinds:

1. ***Interprocedural constant propagation*** seeks to determine when a formal parameter will always have the same constant value upon entrance to its procedure. This information sharpens the intraprocedural constant propagation analysis.

2. Two variables are said to be ***aliased*** at a point in a program if they refer to the same location in memory (or in the case of arrays, overlapping memory locations) at that point. A pair of variables is ***potentially aliased*** with respect to a procedure *P* if there is an invocation of *P* by which they are aliased. ***Alias analysis*** computes the set of potentially aliased variable-pairs for each procedure in the program. Where an array is involved in an alias, our analysis tries to determine the difference in starting address between the aliased variables (see Section 8.3). Aliases between variables impact the statement modification and use information that is the basis for data flow analysis.

   We assume a call-by-reference parameter passing mechanism that allows aliases to be interprocedurally generated and propagated. For example, if the same variable is passed by reference twice in the actual parameter list of a call site *s*, then the corresponding elements of the formal parameter list of the called procedure *P* are aliased in *P* when it is invoked at *s*. Also, if a "global" variable *X* is a reference parameter at *s* and is visible in *P*, then the corresponding formal parameter is aliased in *P* to the global when the call site is executed. In the absence of interprocedural aliasing information, unless assumptions can safely be made with respect to the programmer's use of interprocedurally aliased variables, the worst-case assumption must prevail that all possible aliases hold among distinct formal parameters and between formal parameters and globals. The worst-case assumption would result in extremely conservative data flow information.

3. The ***MOD*** set associated with a call site *s* consists of those variables possibly modified by execution of *s* that are either visible at *s* or ***global*** to the called procedure (as defined below). A variable is possibly modified by a procedure invocation iff it is modified along one of its execution paths. The ***MOD computation*** determines the *MOD* set for each call site in the program. Where possible, we associate array modifications with linear-access expressions over a linearized space. This allows precise information even where arrays are reshaped across procedure boundaries [15]. Producing *MOD* information yields much sharper information than the worst-case assumption that all actual parameters and global variables (along with the variables to which they are aliased) are possibly modified by the call.

4. The ***USE*** set associated with a call site *s* consists of those variables either visible at *s* or global to the called procedure that are used prior to redefinition along some execution path of *s*. Such variables are ***upwards-exposed*** with respect to *s*. The ***USE computation*** determines the *USE* set for each call site in the program. This set is to be distinguished from *REF*(*s*) [13], which includes all variables used along some execution path of *s* (regardless of definitions). Only the upwards-exposed uses of a variable with respect to a call site are relevant to transformations in the neighborhood of the call site. Thus *USE*(*s*) more precisely captures the relevant use information associated with a call site *s* than *REF*(*s*), and yields much sharper information than the worst-case assumption that every actual parameter and every common variable in the program is possibly used by the call. Where upwards-exposed use information is to be computed with respect to procedures in any case (see 4.0), the computation of *USE* is no more expensive than the computation of *REF*. As with array modifications, where possible we associate array uses with linear-access expressions over a linearized space.

With respect to global variables, we assume a block-structure model by which a variable is ***global*** to a procedure *P* if it is declared in a containing procedure (it is not necessarily visible to *P*). A language such as FORTRAN that disallows nested procedures conforms to our model as a special case. An ***external*** variable is declared at block level 0. The FORTRAN common block and PL/I external variable mechanisms allow for the declaration of external variables. In the context of automatic parallelization, upwards-exposed (static) local variables ("history-keeping" variables) must be treated as if they are global to the called procedure, although they are visible only within it [15].

We now discuss the *MOD* computation and its partitioning into subcomponents in our system. The modification effects of any statement, including a call site, can be determined independently of aliasing; factoring potential alias relations into these effects produces the modification set of the statement [13]. *SITEMOD*(*s*) consists of the relevant variables (see above) that are possibly modified by execution of *s* independently of alias relationships.

For efficiency and to provide a suitable basis for an incremental algorithm, the *SITEMOD* computation has itself been partitioned [18, 14]:

1. The computation of the ***immediate modifications*** (i.e., those that occur independently of procedure calls and aliasing) of formal parameters and global variables by each procedure.
2. The computation of the binding relationships among formal parameters and among global variables.

Note that the immediate modification information is intraprocedural: it has been recorded during the call-graph build phase. With respect to interprocedural analysis, then, *SITEMOD* has been reduced to computing binding relationships. We now consider this computation.

```
program MAIN
   dim A(500),D(500)
   common /V/ A

   call Q(D,5,D)

end MAIN

sub Q(X,M,Z)
   dim A(25,10),C(25,10)
   dim X(50,10),Z(50,10)
   common /V/ A,C

   do i = 1,50
      call R(M)
      call S(Z(i,1))
   enddo
end Q

sub R(N)
   dim A(50,10)
   common /V/ A

   do i=1,50
      do j=1,10
         A(i,j) = N
      enddo
   enddo
end R

sub S(X)

    X = ?
end S
```

Figure 4. Example

Where a formal parameter *A* is passed by reference to a formal parameter *B* and *B* is passed by reference to a formal parameter *C*, then *A* is "bound" to *B* and *C*, and *B* is "bound" to *C*. In general, a formal parameter *A* is ***bound*** to a formal parameter *B* iff there is a path in the call graph along which *A* is (directly or indirectly) passed by reference to *B*. The formal parameter binding relationships of a program can be represented by the matrix *FP__BOUND*, where *FP__BOUND(i,j)* is "one" iff formal parameter *i* is bound to formal parameter *j* along a path in the call graph. As the call graph is constructed, immediate formal parameter bindings are recorded in a bit matrix so that entry (*i,j*) of the matrix is set to "one" iff formal parameter *i* is passed to formal parameter *j* at a call site. Computing the transitive closure of this matrix yields *FP__BOUND*.

The global variables of the called procedure of a call site may be regarded as "passed" (to themselves) at the site. Global variable bindings are defined in a manner analogous to formal parameter bindings. Note that external variables are regarded as passed at all call sites: The transitive closure of the call graph captures all information about external variable binding patterns.

The example of Figure 4 illustrates interprocedural analysis. We adopt the notational convention of qualifying the name of a formal parameter by the name of the procedure to which it belongs. During the call graph construction, it is recorded that *Q.M* is passed to *R.N* and *Q.Z* to *S.X*. Forming the transitive closure of these bindings does not add new bindings, so *FP__BOUND* is determined as in Figure 5.

	Q.X	Q.M	Q.Z	R.N	S.X
Q.X	0	0	0	0	0
Q.M	0	0	0	1	0
Q.Z	0	0	0	0	1
R.N	0	0	0	0	0
S.X	0	0	0	0	0

Figure 5. FP__BOUND

In the next two sections we describe our forward and backward interprocedural analysis.

3.1 Forward Analysis: Aliasing and Interprocedural Constant Propagation

In the forward interprocedural analysis phase, the call graph is traversed in topological order as information is propagated from calling to called procedures. The information required for forward analysis is extracted from the call graph and other tables already constructed as discussed in Section 3.0.

The two interprocedural analyses performed during this phase are alias analysis and constant propagation to formal parameters.

In the example of Figure 4, alias analysis determines that *X* and *Z* are potentially aliased in *Q*. The constant 5 is associated with *Q.M* and *R.N* in a table that can later be accessed during intraprocedural constant propagation. In general, our forward analysis can recognize an actual parameter argument as a constant when:

1. It is an immediate constant, such as the constant 5 that is passed to *Q.M*.
2. It is a formal parameter already associated with a constant value and is not bound to any formal parameter that is immediately modified; e.g., *Q.M* in the call site that invokes *R*.

3.2 Backward Analysis: MOD and USE Computation

The topological traversal of the call graph is followed by a reverse topological traversal. The interprocedural analysis performed during this phase results in the computation of *MOD* and *USE* with respect to each call site. We now introduce terminology pertaining to the *USE* computation that is analogous to the terminology we developed with respect to the *MOD* computation. *SITEUSE*(*s*) is analogous to *SITEMOD*(*s*): aliasing is ignored. A variable is ***upwards-exposed*** with respect to a procedure *P* iff, along some path in *P*, it is used prior to redefinition (this includes use prior to redefinition at a call site in *P*). *UPEXUSE*(*P*) is the set of variables either visible in or global to *P* that are upwards-exposed with respect to *P*.

As a node is visited, the *SITEMOD* and *SITEUSE* sets for its call sites can be directly computed from ***summary information*** that has been computed with respect to the procedures that it calls. This summary information for a procedure includes the formal parameters and global variables that it possibly modifies, either immediately or by a call site, and *UPEXUSE*.

Consider the backward phase with respect to Figure 4. Prior to the backward (and forward) phase, it has been determined that *X* is immediately modified by *S* and *A* by *R*. From this summary information it is easily determined that the *SITEMOD* set of the call to *R* is {*A*,*C*} and the *SITEMOD* set of the call to *S* is {*Z*(*i*,1)}. Note the inclusion of range information for the array *Z*. Combining the *SITEMOD* information with the aliasing information that has already been determined, the *MOD* set for the call is {*X*(*i*,1),*Z*(*i*,1)} (aliasing information is factored in when data flow analysis is performed). Summary information for *Q* includes its modification of *A*, *C*, and the first column of *Z*. When the node for the main routine is visited, it is easily determined from this summary information that *SITEMOD* of the call to *Q* includes all of *A* and the first 50 elements of *D* (assuming column-major order). The computation of summary information for procedure *R* determines that *N* is in *UPEXUSE*(*R*). The call to *R* in *Q* thus contains *M* in its *SITEUSE* set.

Without interprocedural analysis, none of the call statements of the loop in subroutine *Q* can be concurrently executed, either within or across loop iterations. The analysis has determined that *Z*(*i*,1) and *X*(*i*,1) are in the *MOD* set of the call to *S*, that *A* and *C* are in the *MOD* set of the call to *R*, and that *M* is in the *USE* set of the call to *R*. There are no dependences between the calls to *R* and *S*, so the loop can be split into two loops that can be run concurrently with respect to each other: one executing the calls to *R* and the other the calls to *S*. Output dependences inhibit parallel execution of the iterations of the *R*-loop, but the iterations of the *S*-loop can be concurrently executed.

In the backward analysis phase, the translated routine for each node is accessed and analyzed. This intraprocedural analysis, traditional for optimizing compilers, has been improved in several respects, including the incorporation of interprocedural information. In the ensuing sections we describe the various phases of this analysis and our improvements.

4.0 Control and Data Flow Analysis

The control flow analysis builds the control flow graph [1] of the program, and determines the ***interval*** regions of this graph. The control flow graph is the basis for data flow analysis and for the construction of the control dependence graph. The nodes of the control flow graph correspond to nodes of the intermediate tree (and so to source-level statements). An interval [34] is a single-entry, strongly connected region in which every cycle includes the entry node.[2]

The loops of a procedure (do-loops, while-loops, loops formed from branch statements) are uniformly represented as intervals in the control flow graph. Our analysis of loops, then, does not require that loops be considered only in the form of do-loops. This requirement forces other automatic parallelization systems to convert some loops to this form and ignore others [7, 28]. The interval-partitioned control flow graph has been used as a space- and time-efficient basis for data flow analysis and program transformations, such as code motion, by ambitious and practical optimizing compliers [10, 24].

The primary purpose of data flow analysis is the construction of def-use chains [5]. The reaching definitions and live variables global data flow problems are solved by the interval analysis data flow technique. The *MOD* and *USE* information associated with call sites is incorporated into this analysis, which therefore includes definitions that reach the routine from below it in the call graph. Alias information is also incorporated into this analysis: If *X* and *Y* are potentially aliased in *P* and *X* is modified by a statement of *P*, then *Y* is possibly modified by the statement. Variables that are possibly modified by a statement (other examples include array elements and the members of mod at a call site) are associated with **preserving definitions:** i.e., they do not kill other definitions of the same variable.

Data flow analysis must also determine *UPEXUSE* for the routine. The variables that reach a routine from above in the call graph are transmitted at entry points via formal parameters, common variables, and static variables. For each entry point (including the main entry), a dummy definition is created for each formal parameter of that entry point, every common variable of a common block that is accessed by the routine, and the static variables of the routine that are defined by other than an initialization ("DATA") statement. These definitions represent values potentially transmitted by calling procedures, and are included in the reaching definition analysis and def-use construction. (As a result of interprocedural constant propagation, some of these definitions are associated with constants.) Where a dummy definition reaches a use in the routine, that use is upwards-exposed with respect to the routine. For procedure *P*, the summary information

2 For irreducible graphs, which contain at least one strongly connected region that is multi-entry, the identified region is the smallest single-entry region containing this one.

UPEXUSE(*P*) is easily computed, given that def-use chains have been built with respect to the dummy definitions.

5.0 Constant Propagation

Constant propagation is a well-known optimization [1] useful in many different contexts. In the PTRAN system, we determine the definitions which are integer constants to improve the subsequent phases of linear induction variable detection, data dependence analysis, and potential parallel process identification.

In order to accomplish this goal, our constant propagator uses interprocedurally determined constants.

```
   program MAIN

   call SAXPY2 (10,5,X,1,Y,1)

   end MAIN

      sub SAXPY2   (N,SA,SX,INCX,SY,INCY)
C
      real SX(1),SY(1),SA
      integer INCX,INCY,IX,IY,M,MP1,N,NBOUND
C
      if (N.LE.0) return
      if (SA .EQ. 0.0) return
C
      IX = 1
      IY = 1
      NBOUND = N * 10
      IF(INCX.LT.0)INCX = (N-10)*INCX + 1
      IF(INCY.LT.0)INCY = (N-10)*INCY + 1
      do 10 i = 1,NBOUND
        SY(IY) = SY(IY) + SA*SX(IX)
        IX = IX + INCX
        IY = IY + INCY
   10 continue
      return
      end
```

Figure 6. Subroutine SAXPY2

Consider the subroutine *SAXPY2* in Figure 6, adapted from *SAXPY*, an Eispack subroutine [35], and called as in program *MAIN*. Since there is only a single call to *SAXPY2* in the main routine, interprocedural constant propagation will determine that formal parameters *N*, *SA*, *INCX*, and *INCY* are all constants upon entry to the routine *SAXPY2*. Our analysis will then determine that *NBOUND*, *INCX*, and *INCY* are constants within procedure *SAXPY2*. Although there are definitions of *INCX* and *INCY within SAXPY2*, the constant propagator determines that all definitions of *INCX* and *INCY* reaching the definitions of *IX* and *IY* in the loop have the same constant value 1. It can be determined that *IX* and *IY* are linear induction variables independently of associating *INCX* and *INCY* with specific constant values. However, where *INCX* and *INCY* are not associated with constant values, they can be incorporated as symbolic constants into the subscript dependence test (Section 8.0) between the references to *SY*. For this example, the dependence equation can be divided by the symbolic constant, and independence can be shown in the the resulting dependence equation. The loop can therefore be parallelized.

The constant value of *NBOUND* will also be used by our parallel process identification phase as the maximum number of potential processes associated with the loop itself.

The algorithm now used for determining constant definitions is a variant of Reif and Lewis' constant propagation algorithm [33], which is a more efficient adaptation of [26]. Both algorithms would determine that *INCX* and *INCY* are constants in the example above. Our version propagates only through definitions, and produces a table of constants indexed by definition site. We plan to implement the Wegman-Zadeck constant propagation algorithm [38], which gets better results, since it can take advantage of which branch tests are constant. If procedure *SAXPY2* were called with $N = 20$, $INCX = 1$ and $INCY = 1$, then our present constant propagation routine would not determine that *INCX* and *INCY* are constants. However, using the Wegman-Zadeck propagation algorithm, since *INCX* and *INCY* are both greater than 0, the tests (*INCX.LT.*0) and (*INCY.LT.*0) both evaluate to false. This means the definitions of *INCX* and *INCY* inside the *if* statements are never executed, and thus only the initial values of 1 of *INCX* and *INCY* are ever used inside the procedure *SAXPY2*. Their algorithm would therefore determine that *INCX* and *INCY* are constants.

6.0 Control Dependence Analysis

During the execution of a sequential program, the results of some operations, such as branches, determine whether other statements will subsequently be executed. A control dependence graph [23] summarizes these conditions which may affect a statement's execution. Control dependences represent the necessary control flow relationships which must be respected by any execution of the program, whether parallel or sequential. By using control dependence, we can eliminate unnecessary sequencing, and thus expose potential parallelism.

```
S1:    if (A)
S2:       then  X = Y + Z
S3:       else  P = M - S
S4:               if (B)
S5:                  then W = Y - Z
S6:                  else Q = R * S
S7:               endif
S8:               S = M * N
S9:    endif
S10:   T = U * V
```

Figure 7. Control Dependence

Consider the example shown in Figure 7. S_2 is affected by the branch taken in statement S_1. However, S_{10} does not depend on which branch is taken by S_1 because both branches eventually cause S_{10} to execute. Therefore S_2 is control dependent on the test in S_1 but S_{10} has the same control dependences as S_1. This latter fact implies that S_1 and S_{10} could potentially be executed in parallel.

```
program MAIN

   call P1
   call P2
   call P3
   call P4

end MAIN
```

Figure 8. Control Dependences, continued

In the example shown in Figure 8, all of the procedure calls from the main procedure have the same control dependences. If our interprocedural data dependence analysis can determine there are no data dependences between them, then they too could all be executed in parallel.

Besides exposing potential parallelism in sequential programs, the notion of control dependence is useful in other contexts. In vectorization, it provides a more effective and efficient alternative in determining vectorization than guard expressions and allows better sequential code generation when vectorization fails. To the programmer attempting to parallelize sequential programs by hand, it represents necessary information to be provided, along with data dependence. It also provides a basis for improved data dependence analysis and code motion.

More formally, control dependence can be defined as follows from the control flow graph of a program. We assume there is a unique exit node *Exit* in the control flow graph.

Definition: Let G be a control flow graph, and let W and V be nodes in G. W is *post dominated* by V in G if every directed path from W to *Exit* contains V, and $V \neq W$ and $V \neq Exit$.

Definition: Let G be a control flow graph, and let X and Y be nodes in G. Y is *control dependent* on X iff

1. there exists a directed path P from X to Y with all Z in P (excluding X and Y) post-dominated by Y and
2. X is not post-dominated by Y.

In other words, from X, there is some edge that definitely causes Y to execute, and there is also some path that avoids executing Y.

Control dependences can be computed as a solution to a data flow problem defined directly from the definition above. However, a more efficient approach, using linear space for intermediate computations and less iterations, first constructs the post-dominator tree from the control flow graph, and in a single pass through the tree computes control dependences. This represents an improvement over [23], which uses quadratic space. This more efficient algorithm has been implemented in PTRAN.

7.0 Induction Variables

The identification of parallelism with respect to array references requires analysis of array subscripts. Independence of two subscripted references can be concluded only where subscripts are linear functions of linear induction variables from the intervals surrounding the subscripted references. Such variables cannot be discovered "by inspection" (on a statement-by-statement basis), because linear induction variables may not appear as the primary loop induction variable of an interval. Consider the example shown in Figure 9.

```
do i=1,N
   J = J + 1

   M = K - 3
   L = M + 17
   K = L + 5

   Q = 3 * M + 23

   G = 3 * F + 23
   F = G + 3

   if (R .eq. 0) then
      X = X + 1
      A(X) =
   endif

   B(X) =
enddo
```

Figure 9. Induction Variables

Although i and J are discovered as linear induction variables by inspection, deeper analysis is required to discover K, M, and L as linear induction variables. Most algorithms fail to find such mutually-defined linear induction variables. The fault lies in assuming that since M is defined in terms of K, and K has not yet been examined, that K is not an induction variable and so neither is M. In PTRAN, we find linear induction variables using a data flow technique, which assumes that all definitions are linear induction variables until a contradiction exists.

Note that Q is an induction variable (as a function of M). However, when evaluating F and G, the inductive sequence is not linear, and so neither F nor G is linearly inductive. Although the definitions of Q and G are similar, the PTRAN algorithm invalidates G after F has been visited.

Conditional branches affect the scope of an induction variable. The definition of *X* is inductive within the *if...endif* of the loop, but outside the *if*, *X* does not look like a linearly inductive sequence. For example, *X* describes unique values inside the *if*, so the definition of *A*() stores into distinct elements of *A*(). However, outside the *if*, *X* may pause at some value, causing duplicate stores into elements of *B*(). The assignments to *B*() would then require synchronization.

The linear induction variable algorithm in PTRAN finds mutually-defined linear induction variables (such as *K*, *L*, and *M* in the example of Figure 9) and also determines the scope of such variables for dependence analysis.

8.0 Data Dependence

The definitions-use chains discovered by data flow analysis (Section 4.0) may be overly conservative with respect to array references. For example, a def-use chain may relate a store into array *A* with a use of that array, but deeper analysis may show independence between the two references. Consider the example shown in Figure 10.

```
      do i=1,N
S1:      A(2*i)  =
S2:               = A(2*i + 1)
      enddo
```

Figure 10. Independent References

Statement *S*1 assigns only even elements of *A*, while the use of *A* references only odd elements of *A*. Thus, the two statements are actually independent.

PTRAN views data dependence analysis in three parts:

1. The formulation of a *dependence equation* between two storage references. Of interest are those statements that potentially reference the same storage locations.
2. The coupling of the dependence equation with a *context* in which the dependence should be tested.
3. The testing for *solutions* of the dependence equation in its associated context.

Each of these aspects in considered in the following sections.

8.1 Formulating a Dependence Equation

A dependence equation depicts the relationship between the access functions (subscripts) associated with "interesting" references, as identified by inter- and intra-procedural data flow analyses (Sections 3.0 and 4.0). For example, the references to *A* in Figure 11 are interesting.

```
do i=1,10
   A(3*i+5)  =
                = A(10*i-3)
enddo
```

Figure 11. Interesting References

In general, interesting references need not involve a single name. For example, data dependence must analyze references to aliased parameters, even though such parameters have distinct names.

The parallelization of the loop shown in Figure 11 would yield concurrently executing instances of the references to *A*. The dependence equation characterizes situations in which those references might coincide. The dependence equation must then contain two free variables: one for the value of *i* at the store of *A* and one for the value of *i* at the fetch of *A*. Let *x* and *y* represent the values of *i* at the store and fetch, respectively. The dependence equation that corresponds to the references is then:

$$3x - 10y = -8$$

where x and y are integer variables. In PTRAN, as in extant parallelization, subscript references are analyzable only to the extent they can be characterized by a linear diophantine equation.

Composing a multiple-subscript expression with the function that maps such expressions into underlying (single-dimensional) memory results in the ***linearized*** form of the expression. For multiple-subscript expressions, a dependence equation can be formulated for the linearized expressions or a separate dependence equation can be formulated with respect to each dimension [15, 16].

8.2 Establishing a Context for a Dependence Equation

Not every solution to a dependence equation is relevant to parallelization. A dependence equation must be viewed in a context that reflects conditions under which the dependence might hold:

1. Iteration variables assume only integer values, so a dependence exists only if some solution to the dependence equation assigns integer values to the free variables.
2. An iteration variable typically iterates over a fixed range. A solution to the dependence equation must assign values to the free variables that lie within the range of their associated iteration variables.
3. A *direction vector* (explained below) constrains the relationship between instances of iteration variables. A solution to the dependence equation must assign values to the iteration variable instances that respect a given direction vector.

Consider again the example of Figure 11. Although the dependence equation has infinite solutions, relevant solutions (considering points 1 and 2 above) assign x and y integer values in the range (1,2,...,10).

In fact the only solution of interest assigns $x = 4$ and $y = 2$. Thus, in iteration 4, the same location of A is written as is read in iteration 2. Since iteration 2 precedes iteration 4 when the loop executes sequentially, the fetch must precede the store. In general, consider two statements S_x and S_y.

A *flow dependence* exists from statement S_x to statement S_y if S_x computes and stores data that can subsequently be read by S_y.

An *anti-dependence* exists between S_x and S_y if S_x reads data from a location into which S_y can subsequently store.

An *output dependence* exists between S_x and S_y if S_x stores into a location into which S_y can subsequently store.

The dependence situation depicted in Figure 11 corresponds to an anti-dependence. Further, the dependence holds for the relationship between x and y: $x > y$. Following the notation of Wolfe, the nature of a dependence can be summarized by the direction vector Z. Each component of Z corresponds to one of the loops that surrounds the dependent references (i.e., nest level) [41]. Consider component z_k for interval k:

1. If z_k = "=", then the dependence holds within the same iteration of loop k.
2. If z_k = "<", then the dependence holds from some iteration of loop k to a subsequent iteration.
3. If z_k = ">", then the dependence holds from some iteration of loop k to an earlier iteration.

These relationships can be unioned in an intuitive way. A direction vector of "≤" implies "<" or "=". Let "*" imply the union of "<", "=", and ">". This direction vector asserts no relationship between x and y.

Consider the anti-dependence that holds from the fetch to the store in Figure 11. Using the above notation, the corresponding direction vector is "<", since $y < x$. This situation corresponds to a flow dependence that holds from the store to the fetch with direction vector ">" since $x > y$. The dependence algorithm in PTRAN utilizes this correspondence to avoid separate anti-dependence tests [15]. Def-use chains are tested for flow dependence, with the resulting direction vectors indicating whether the dependence is flow or anti-.

8.3 Solving a Dependence Equation

This section describes various methods of obtaining solutions to the formulated dependence equation in its specified context. Following the approach in Burke and Cytron [15], a decision algorithm will initially be invoked under the most general of relationships between instances of an iteration variable (direction vector of (*,*,...,*)), and then subsequently invoked on more refined direction vectors until either independence has been shown or dependence has been shown with respect to a specific direction vector. For example, if two loops surround a pair of references, then decision algorithms are first invoked on the root of the tree shown in Figure 12. Refinement proceeds toward the leaves of the tree. If independence can be shown at any node, then further refinement of that node is unnecessary.

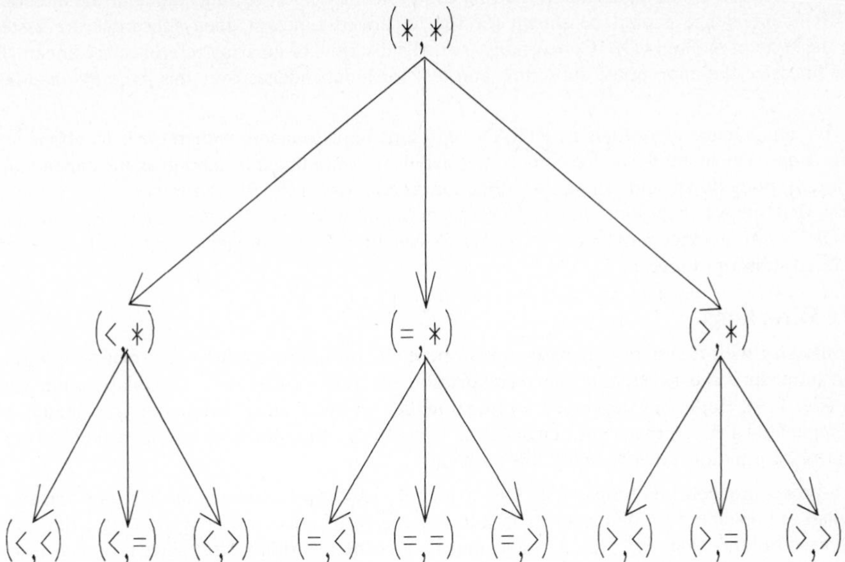

Figure 12. Direction Vector Tree for Two Loops

At each node of interest, the dependence equation must be evaluated in the specified context. The evaluation occurs through *dependence decision algorithms*, which vary with respect to speed and accuracy. The most expensive and precise test is an *exact* test. More practical are the inexact tests: *GCD* and *Banerjee-Wolfe* ([11, 12, 41]).

For the different dependence decision algorithms, Burke and Cytron discuss the tradeoffs between linearized and subscript-by-subscript dependence testing. With respect to power and precision, linearization is superior to subscript-by-subscript testing in the following respects:

1. Where relative starting address information has been determined for aliased arrays, linearization allows dependence testing between them, even where their shapes differ.
2. It allows dependences to be detected that are due to subscripts exceeding declared array ranges.
3. It can enforce simultaneity. Consider the example of Figure 13. Subscript-by-subscript testing cannot demonstrate independence in either dimension. However, the dependences that exist independently in each dimension cannot hold simultaneously, so no dependence exists. By linearizing the references to *A*, we couple the two equations into one, allowing us to determine independence.

```
do i=1,N
   A(2*i,2*i+1) =
                = A(i,i)
enddo
```

Figure 13. References Requiring Simultaneity

Linearization thus allows greater precision with respect to exact decision algorithms. It also allows greater precision with respect to inexact decision algorithms, if independence can be shown even where subscripts violate declared extents [15, 39].

PTRAN collects linear subscripts of a multiply-subscripted array into a single addressing function (linearization). Since the dependence tests require linear-form subscripts, and since linearization is only required for multiple subscripts, the linearization process itself is inexpensive. The linearized function is incorporated into the dependence algorithm as the first test performed upon visiting a node of the direction vector tree. If independence cannot be shown for the linearized function, then subscripts are tested separately (in the style of Wolfe [41]). Conceivably, not all subscripts of an array reference are linear. In such cases, we linearize the appropriate subscripts and test for independence over this *partially-linearized* function [9].

In summary, the dependence algorithms in PTRAN represent improvements with respect to efficiency, power, and precision. The hierarchical dependence test avoids recomputing information as the dependence algorithm proceeds both down and across the direction vector tree [15, 9]. References are cast in a linearized form that allows incorporation of interprocedural information. In particular, programming practices in FORTRAN are accommodated: reshapes of structures across procedure calls and subscripts exceeding declared subscript ranges.

9.0 Future Directions

A pragmatic difficulty with a system that bases transformations on interprocedural information is that a change to one procedure can necessitate the recompilation of many procedures. In collaboration with researchers at Rice [19], Burke has developed a general model for eliminating unnecessary recompilation. We plan to complement this approach with engineering techniques. In a practical system, a judicious use of interprocedural information would simplify this problem.

Inter- and intra-procedural constant propagation seek to identify important constants, such as loop and array bounds. We plan to implement the Wegman-Zadeck intraprocedural constant propagation algorithm [38], which finds more constants than our present algorithm: When the algorithm determines a branch test is constant during propagation, it eliminates the branch not taken and as a result finds more constants.

We also plan to generalize our interprocedural constant propagation analysis. Sometimes a formal parameter assumes a constant value c_1 along one path in the call graph and a constant value c_2 along another path. ***Path-specific*** interprocedural constant propagation seeks to associate paths in the call graph with constants and serves as a basis for path-specific dependence testing [15]. Path-specific interprocedural alias analysis can be performed and utilized in an analogous manner. Where a "constant" term in a dependence equation cannot be associated with a small set of constants, ***interprocedural range analysis*** [37] can delimit its range and provide the basis for dependence testing with symbolic constants that are associated with value ranges.

In general, enforcing simultaneity can require a single dependence test performed over multiple dependence equations [9]. By associating a separate dependence equation with each subscript, the equations are coupled by the induction variables common to the subscripts.

The analysis derived by PTRAN-A will serve as the foundation for many program transformations, targeted at increasing the efficiency of programs executed on multiprocessors. Such transformations will increase the locality of program references, stage the disposition of data in a storage hierarchy, and reorganize program storage. In another paper [2], we describe a multiprocessing environment capable of supporting the parallelism identified by PTRAN. This environment consists of two components: a process model and a storage model. The process model is flexible with respect to scheduling: Although potential processes are identified at compile-time, many factors concerning the benefits of multiprocessing a given section of code [22] are unavailable at compile-time. Our process model allows such factors to be considered at run-time, where they can contribute to process determination. The second aspect of our multiprocessing environment is a storage model that supports nested processes, requiring data to be shared or private with respect to selected processes.

Acknowledgements

In addition to the authors of this paper, Mary Mace was a member of the PTRAN project for several years. As an author in spirit of this paper, we thank Mary for her many contributions to our system as well as to the goals and directions of our work.

We have been fortunate to have many outstanding visitors. Andy Lowry, Todd Allen, and Sue Flynn contributed ideas and code; Remi Triolet, Karl Ottenstein, Joe Warren, and Narsingh Deo influenced our direction by suggesting new possibilities.

We are very grateful to Cathy McCarthy not only for her assistance in the preparation of this paper, but also for her untiring support of all our group's activities.

We thank IBM management for their encouragement and support of our work. Irving Wladowsky-Berger encouraged the formation of our project, and we thank him as well as Howard Brauer, Tilak Agerwala, and Abe Peled for their continual support.

Bibliography

1. A. V. Aho and J. D. Ullman. *Principles of Compiler Design.* Addison-Wesley, 1977.

2. Fran Allen, Michael Burke, and Ron Cytron. The PTRAN Multiprocessing Model, IBM Research, 1987. Report RC12552.

3. Frances E. Allen. Compiling for Parallelism. in G. Almasi, R. Hockney, and G. Paul, editor, *Proceedings of the IBM Institute Europe*, North-Holland Press, 1986.

4. F. E. Allen, J. L. Carter, J. Fabri, J. Ferrante, W. H. Harrison, P. G. Loewner, and L. H. Trevillyan. The Experimental Compiling System. *IBM Journal of Research and Development*, 24(6), November 1980.

5. Frances E. Allen and John Cocke. A Program Data Flow Analysis Procedure. *Communications of the ACM*, 19(3):137-146, March 1976.

6. John R. Allen. *Dependence Analysis for Subscript Variables and Its Application to Program Transformations*, PhD thesis, Rice University, Houston, Texas 1983.

7. J. R. Allen, Ken Kennedy, Carrie Porterfield, and Joe Warren. Conversion of Control Dependence to Data Dependence. *Conf. Rec. Tenth ACM Symposium on Principles of Programming Languages*, 1983.

8. Randy Allen, David Callahan, and Ken Kennedy. Automatic Decomposition of Scientific Programs for Parallel Execution. *Conference Record of the Fourteenth Annual ACM Symposium on Principles of Programming Languages*, pages 63-76, January 1987.

9. Todd Allen, Michael Burke, and Ron Cytron. A Practical and Powerful Algorithm for Subscript Dependence Testing, IBM, 1986. Internal Report.

10. M. Auslander and M. Hopkins. An Overview of the PL.8 Compiler. *Proceedings of the Sigplan '82 Symposium on Compiler Construction*, 17(6):22-31, June 1982.

11. Utpal Banerjee. *Speedup of Ordinary Programs*, PhD thesis, University of Illinois at Urbana-Champaign, Urbana, Illinois 1979.

12. Utpal Banerjee, Shyh-Ching Chen, David J. Kuck, and Ross A. Towle. Time and Parallel Processor Bounds for Fortran-Like Loops. *IEEE Transactions on Computers*, C-28(9):660-670, September 1979.

13. John Banning. An Efficient Way to Find the Side Effects of Procedure Calls and the Aliases of Variables. *Conf. Rec. Sixth ACM Symposium on Principles of Programming Languages*, 1979.

14. Michael Burke. An Interval Analysis Approach Toward Interprocedural Data Flow, IBM Research, 1984. Report RC11794.

15. Michael Burke and Ron Cytron. Interprocedural Dependence Analysis and Parallelization. *Proceedings of the Sigplan '86 Symposium on Compiler Construction*, 21(7):162-175, July 1986.

16. Michael Burke and Ron Cytron. Interprocedural Dependence Analysis and Parallelization (Extended Version), IBM Research, 1986. Report RC11794.

17. David Callahan, Keith D. Cooper, Ken Kennedy, and Linda Torczon. Interprocedural Constant Propagation. *Proceedings of the Sigplan '86 Symposium on Compiler Construction*, 21(7):152-161, July 1986.

18. Keith Cooper and Ken Kennedy. Efficient Computation of Flow Insensitive Interprocedural Summary Information. *Proceedings of the SIGPLAN 84 Symposium on Compiler Construction*, 1984.

19. Keith D. Cooper, Ken Kennedy, and Linda Torczon. Interprocedural Optimization: Eliminating Unnecessary Recompilation. *Proceedings of the Sigplan '86 Symposium on Compiler Construction*, 21(7):58-67, July 1986.

20. Keith D. Cooper, Ken Kennedy, and Linda Torczon. The Impact of Interprocedural Analysis and Optimization in the Rn Programming Environment. *ACM Transactions on Programming Languages and Systems*, 8(4):491-523, October 1986.

21. Ron Cytron. *Compile-time Scheduling and Optimization for Asynchronous Machines*, PhD thesis, University of Illinois at Urbana-Champaign, Urbana, Illinois 1984.

22. Ron Cytron. Useful Parallelism in a Multiprocessing Environment. *Proc. 1985 International Conference on Parallel Processing*, 1985.

23. J. Ferrante, K. Ottenstein, and J. Warren. The Program Dependence Graph and its Use in Optimization. *ACM Trans. on Programming Languages and Systems*, July 1987. To appear.

24. Stefan M. Freudenberger, Jacob T. Schwartz, and Micha Sharir. Experience with the SETL Optimizer. *ACM Transactions on Programming Languages and Systems*, 5(1):26-45, January 1983.

25. Ken Kennedy. Automatic Translation of FORTRAN Programs to Vector Form, Rice University, 1980. Report 476-029-4.

26. G. Kildall. A Unified Approach to Program Optimization. *Conference Record of First ACM Symposium on Principles of Programming Languages*, 1973.

27. David J. Kuck. *The Structure of Computers and Computations*. John Wiley and Sons, 1978.

28. D. J. Kuck, R. H. Kuhn, B. Leasure, and M. Wolfe. The Structure of an Advanced Vectorizer for Pipelined Processors. *Proceedings of CompSAC 80 (Fourth International Computer Software and Applications Conference)*, pages 709-715, October 1980.

29. D. J. Kuck, R. H. Kuhn, D. A. Padua, B. Leasure, and M. Wolfe. Dependence Graphs and Compiler Optimizations. *Conference Record of 8th ACM Symposium on Principles of Programming Languages*, 1981.

30. L. Lamport. The Parallel Execution of DO Loops. *Communications of the ACM*, pages 83-93, February 1974.

31. Bruce R. Leasure. Compiling Serial Languages for Parallel Machines, University of Illinois at Urbana-Champaign, 1976. M.S. Thesis.

32. David A. Padua and Michael J. Wolfe. Advanced Compiler Optimizations for Supercomputers. *Communications of the ACM*, 29(12):1184-1201, December 1986.

33. J. H. Reif and H. R. Lewis. Symbolic Evaluation and the Global Value Graph. *Conf. Rec. Fourth ACM Symposium on Principles of Programming Languages*, 1977.

34. J. T. Schwartz and M. Sharir. A Design for Optimizations of the Bitvectoring Class, New York University, September 1979. Courant Computer Science Report #17.

35. B. T. Smith, J. M. Boyle, J. J. Dongarra, B. S. Garbow, Y. Ikebe, V. C. Klema, and C. B. Moler. *Matrix Eigensystem Routines - Eispack Guide*. Springer-Verlag, Heidelberg, West Germany, 1976.

36. Remi Triolet. *Contribution a la Parellisation Automatique de Programmes Fortran Comportant des Appels de Procedure*, PhD thesis, L'Universite Pierre et Marie Curie (Paris VI), Paris, France 1984.

37. Remi Triolet, Francois Irigoin, and Paul Feautrier. Direct Parallelization of Call Statements. *Proceedings of the Sigplan '86 Symposium on Compiler Construction*, 21(7):176-185, July 1986.

38. Mark Wegman and Ken Zadeck. Constant Propagation with Conditional Branches. *Conf. Rec. Twelfth ACM Symposium on Principles of Programming Languages*, pages 291-299, January 1985.

39. Michael Wolfe. Personal Communication

40. Michael J. Wolfe. Techniques for Improving the Inherent Parallelism in Programs, University of Illinois at Urbana-Champaign, 1978. M.S. Thesis.

41. Michael J. Wolfe. *Optimizing Supercompilers for Supercomputers*, PhD thesis, University of Illinois at Urbana-Champaign, Urbana, Illinois 1982. Report No. UIUCDCS-R-82-1105.

TOOLS FOR PERFORMANCE EVALUATION OF PARALLEL MACHINES

A.P.W. Böhm *and* J.R. Gurd
Department of Computer Science
University of Manchester
Oxford Road, Manchester
M13 9PL, United Kingdom

ABSTRACT

There is widespread interest in the practical application of parallel computers to highly intensive computational problems. Since many diverse architectures have been proposed, it is important to be able to monitor them accurately and compare their performance in realistic application areas. To achieve this aim, better tools will be needed than those currently available, and appropriate models and measures need to be defined. This paper addresses these issues in the context of a project based on single-assignment programming with execution on a dataflow machine. Undoubtedly, the suggested techniques have wider applicability.

1 INTRODUCTION

1.1 Explicit and Implicit Parallel Programming

Few truly parallel computer systems have been applied to "real-world" problems, yet there are few who doubt that the future of high-performance computer architecture lies in the development of efficient highly parallel machines. Research papers have claimed for many years now that effective harnessing of MIMD hardware parallelism is the only long-term hope for greatly improved processing speeds. These claims are achieving some credibility now that high- and medium-performance system manufacturers, such as Cray, ETA, Alliant and Sequent are beginning to market products with a growing degree of MIMD parallelism [Johnson86]. However, exploitation of parallelism within a single application still seems to be a "black art", and many users of these new products eschew true multiprocessing and simply use their multiprocessor hardware to increase task-level throughput.

Designing a multiprocess version of a single applications program is a time-consuming and error-prone activity. This is in part due to the sequential nature of past computers and their programming languages. Commercial multiprocessor systems require use of *either* a modified sequential language, such as Fortran or C, *or* a completely new language with appropriate parallel constructs, such as Ada. Both options cause continuity problems for the user. However, the major cause of difficulty seems to be the inherent complexity of large concurrent programs, particularly those for which the programmer is entirely responsible for management of the concurrency (*explicit* parallelism). Novel tools are required to analyse and monitor program behaviour in order to assist the programmer in making the necessary decisions [Cohen86].

In the research community, the above difficulties have led to the development of *implicit* parallel systems, in which the programmer is relatively unconcerned with the existence of parallelism in the hardware. This can be achieved by "parallelisation" of existing sequential programs [Allen76, Kuck81], or by use of "declarative" programming languages [Ackerman82, Backus78, Glauert82, McGraw83, Pingali85]. In practice, even in implicit systems, there is a need for monitoring tools, if only to enable suitable compilers to be developed. Our experiences in developing a compiler to generate code for a dataflow machine from the declarative language SISAL have prompted us to think carefully about the general issues, discussed below, governing development of useful monitoring tools for parallel machines.

1.2 Levels of Abstraction

A common feature of current computer systems is the definition of several distinct levels of abstraction at which various modes of behaviour are of interest. At the "highest" level (i.e. that closest to the user), the programmer often thinks in terms of language features that have little relation to the machine-level implementation. For example, in modern "declarative" languages, the emphasis is often solely on mathematical relationships between objects defined in terms of the application concerned. At the lowest level, it is convenient to think in terms of machine behaviour, for example considering the execution of individual instructions and word-at-a-time transactions with memory. Nowadays the so-called "semantic gap" between these two levels has become so great that it is common to create one or more intermediate levels of abstraction at which interesting characteristics that are not readily accessible at the extremes can be described. Such levels are often referred to as "abstract machines". Where such intermediate levels are in use, it is important that information can be monitored at all levels.

1.3 An Experimental Parallel Processing Environment

The authors and their colleagues at the University of Manchester have been developing a dataflow computing system over the past decade. This work has so far involved two major components: Firstly, an operational dataflow computer has been constructed, and two simulator programs for it (one with timing, one without) have been written; Secondly, a code generator for the single-assignment language SISAL has been implemented (the front-end compiler being available from elsewhere). The remainder of the paper is based on our experiences of trying to implement realistic applications programs using these components. Consequently, an outline of the applications programming environment is necessary.

COMPILATION SYSTEM USER INTERACTION

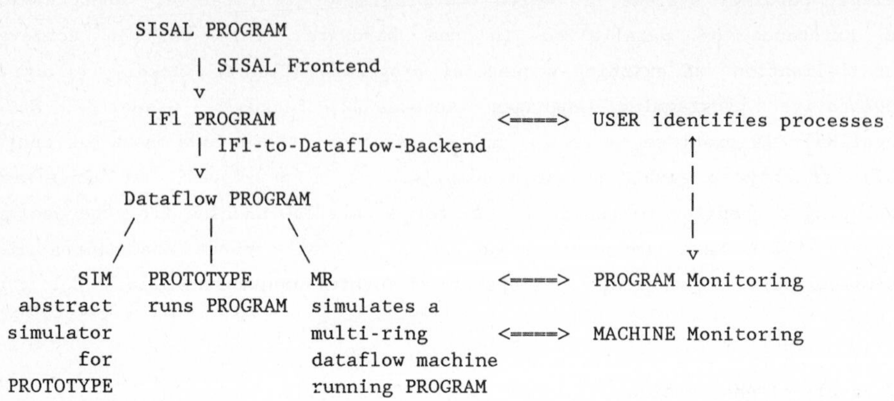

Figure 1. Levels of abstraction in the SISAL/dataflow system

Figure 1 shows the main parts of the SISAL/dataflow system. The primary compilation routes are shown on the left: A SISAL source program is converted to dataflow object code, in two stages, via an intermediate (machine-independent) language, IF1. The resulting code can be run on either the hardware or one of the simulator programs, SIM (abstract) or MR (complete, with timing). The intended points of interaction during the compilation process are indicated on the right hand side of the figure. These are described in more detail later.

2 THE PROGRAM LEVEL

2.1 SISAL - a High Level Parallel Programming Model

SISAL [McGraw83] is a general purpose single-assignment language designed for efficient execution on a variety of parallel computers. Because of its single-assignment property, the language lends itself naturally to parallel execution; sequencing will only occur where it is enforced by data dependencies. Apart from the usual scalar types, the data structures of SISAL include arrays, streams and records. Data objects of any type can be regarded as mathematical values. A SISAL program consists of a set of side-effect-free functions, one of which is the "main" program. The parameters and results of the main function are the input and output of the program. SISAL also has conditional expressions and two forms of FOR construct, one forming an iterative loop, the other a parallel "forall" expression.

The SISAL program shown in figure 2 calculates the number of ways a certain *amount* of money can be paid given a certain set of *coin values* using a straightforward divide-and-conquer method. Other ways of solving the same problem in SISAL are discussed in [Kindervater85].

```
define main

function count(amount, i: integer; values: array[integer] returns integer)
 let val := values[i] in
  if i <= 1 then if mod(amount, val) = 0 then 1 else 0 end if
  else for j in 0, amount/val
       c := count(amount-j*val, i-1, values)
       returns value of sum c
       end for
  end if
 end let
end function % count

function main(amount: integer returns integer)
 let values := array[1: 1,5,10,25,100];
     n_coins := array_limh(values)
 in
     count(amount, n_coins, values)
 end let
end function % main program
```

Figure 2. The SISAL program *COINS*

2.2 IF1 - an Abstract Program-Level Machine for SISAL

The single-assignment and functional properties of SISAL make it particularly suited to translation into data dependence graph format (DDGF). In essence, this is what is achieved in the front-end of the SISAL compiler. A machine-independent DDGF known as IF1 (Intermediate Format - version 1) has been defined specifically for this purpose [Skedzielewski85].

An IF1 program is a set of *graphs*, one for each SISAL function. Graphs consist of *nodes* and *edges*. Edges represent values travelling from node to node and are *typed* (the type descriptor being a tree of type records). Nodes represent operations and are of three main types. Firstly, there are *primitive nodes*, such as Plus, and Minus. Secondly, there are nodes that deal with *multiple values*, such as RGN (Range GeNerate), ASC (Array SCatter) and AGA (Array GAther). RGN yields a sequence of integers between a given lower and upper bound. ASC yields selected elements from an array, given a lower bound, an upper bound and an offset by which indices are to be shifted. AGA takes an integer lower bound together with a multiple value and creates the corresponding array. Finally, there are *compound nodes*, such as SELECT and FORALL, which recursively contain subgraphs. A SELECT node contains a TEST subgraph and two BRANCH subgraphs. The TEST subgraph yields a boolean that selects the appropriate BRANCH subgraph and is used to implement the SISAL conditional (**if** .. **then** .. **else** .. **end if**) construct. A FORALL node contains GENERATE, BODY and RETURNS subgraphs and is used to implement the SISAL **for all** construct.

The structure of the IF1 graph for function *count* in the SISAL program *COINS* (see figure 2) is sketched in figure 3. In order to keep the picture simple, detailed sub-graphs are represented textually and edges are omitted. Further details of IF1 graphs can be found elsewhere [Skedzielewski85, Gurd87a].

FUNCTION count

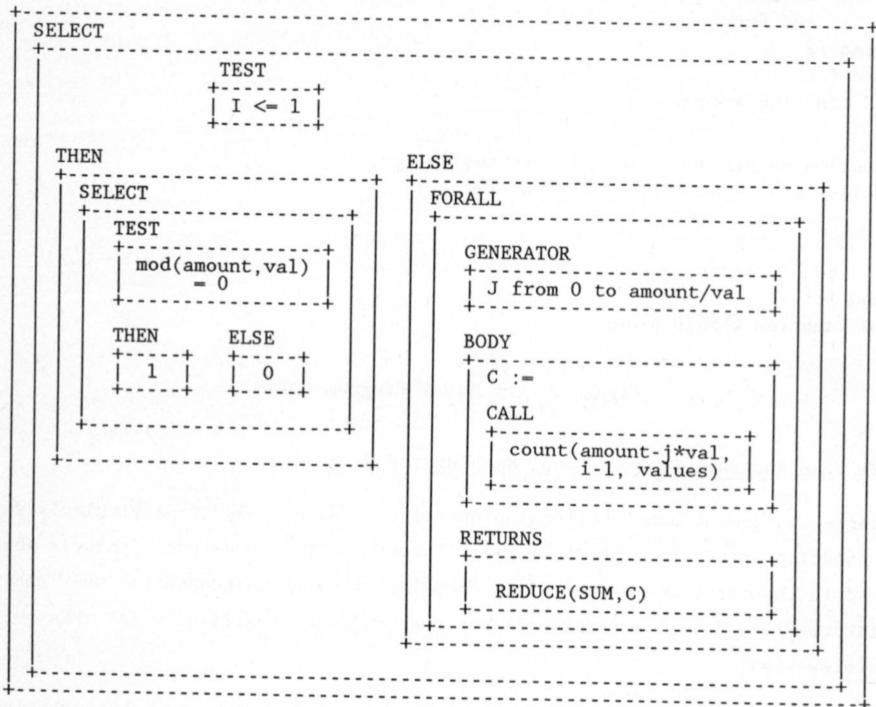

Figure 3. IF1 graph for function *count* in the SISAL program *COINS*

2.3 The *Call Graph*

In order to understand the run-time behaviour of a program, the programmer needs monitoring information at the level of the *abstract machine* of the programming language. For SISAL this means that the programmer thinks in terms of IF1 *processes*, which are of a much coarser grain than the instructions of, say, a dataflow machine. The *static call graph* of a program is a skeletal version of its IF1 representation, in which nodes represent only the function and loop bodies and there is an edge between node A and node B if A *activates* B. Figure 4 shows the static call graph for the program *COINS*.

During IF1-to-dataflow compilation, the programmer may interact with the compiler using the static call graph to provide helpful information. For example, he may wish to control the size of processes by *inlining* certain function calls (i.e. replacing them by their function bodies). He can specify the maximum size of function to be inlined, and the extent to which recursive functions are to be inlined [Böhm85].

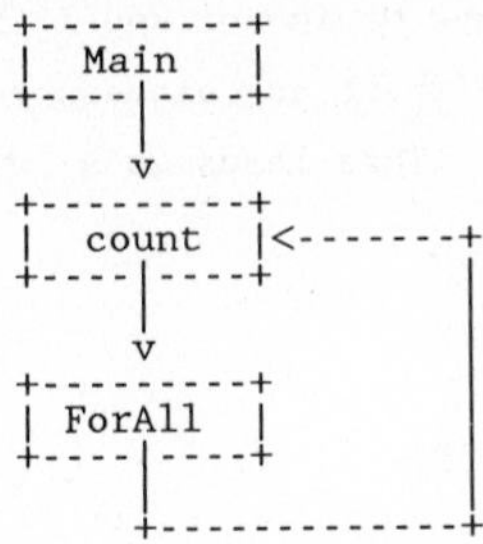

Figure 4. The *static call graph* for the *COINS* program

2.4 Observing Run-time Behaviour at the Program Level

In order to help the programmer understand the run-time behaviour of a program, its execution can be depicted as a *dynamic process tree*, i.e. an animated version of the static call graph. Nodes in this tree denote *activated* function or loop bodies, and edges represent actual function calls or loop activations. When a function or loop body terminates, the node representing it and the edge representing its activation disappear. In the SISAL/dataflow system, a graphics package running on a SUN/3 workstation monitors a dataflow program in execution and displays its process tree. By pointing at a node while the program is in execution, the user can get more detailed information, such as the access pattern or value of certain objects in the process.

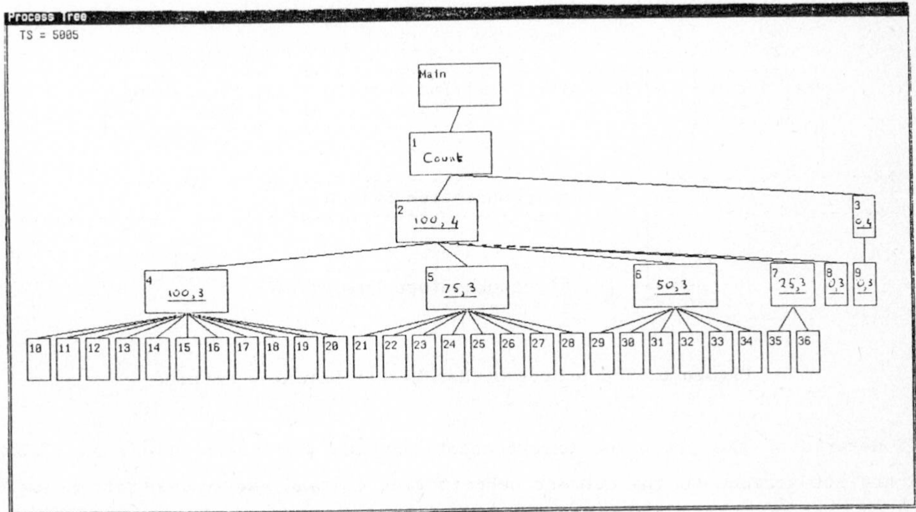

Figure 5. Dynamic process tree for unthrottled *COINS* program

Figure 5 shows how the dynamic process tree would be shown for the *COINS* program, with *amount* = 100, after 5005 timesteps on a dataflow machine with one processing element and one structure store (see section 3.2). The underlined numbers in the process boxes represent the values of *amount* and *i*, respectively. In this particular case, the program has been run without any process control, which means that maximum program parallelism is available. This leads to a "wide" process tree.

3 THE MACHINE LEVEL

3.1 The Manchester Dataflow Machine

A working prototype dataflow uniprocessor has been constructed over the past decade at the University of Manchester [Gurd85, Gurd87b]. The machine implements *tagged-token* dataflow, in which each token carries a *tag* distinguishing it from other tokens executing the same code, thus allowing for maximium parallelism. A tag (also called *colour*) contains an *activation name*, to distinguish various activations of the same function or loop body, and an *index*, to distinguish elements of a data structure. The prototype hardware comprises a processing element and a structure store unit, as shown in figure 6. The processing element is structured as a pipelined ring of four *modules*, namely the *token queue*, the *matching unit*, the *instruction store* and the *processing unit*. The processing unit contains up to twenty microcoded *function units* that are responsible for executing the instructions. Data structures are stored in a separate *structure store* that communicates with the processor via an interconnection *switch*. Multi-processor versions of the system can be constructed by replicating the uniprocessor "ring" and the structure store modulès, and expanding the interconnection switch. Such a system is known as a *multi-ring* dataflow machine.

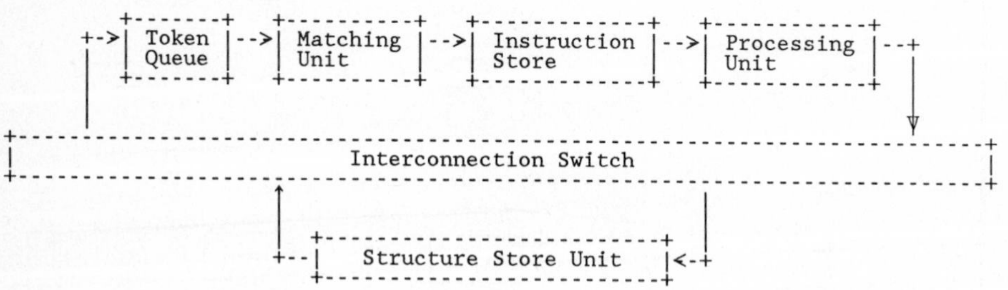

Figure 6. The prototype Manchester Dataflow Machine

Full details of the prototype uniprocessor hardware have been published elsewhere and are not germane to the current description. Instead, we concentrate below on a fully timed software simulator for a multi-processor version of the prototype.

3.2 MR - a Multi-Ring Dataflow Machine Simulator

The multi-ring dataflow machine simulator, MR, emulates a multiprocessor version of the Manchester Dataflow Machine and gathers *machine* and *program* statistics. MR is used to study time related machine phenomena such as *hot-* and *cold-spots*, *traffic* and *bottlenecks*, and *distribution* of *work* and *data* over the machine.

3.2.1 Bottom Level Structure

The MR machine is built out of *blocks* of the forn

```
             ------------
      0---->| module F |---->0
             ------------
     Buf1                   Buf2
```

where *Buf1* and *Buf2* are buffers that can hold a data *packet*. Packets have a *timestamp*, and there is a global *current time*, TS, representing the clockbeat of the machine. Function F is performed on packet P1 in *Buf1*, only if *Buf2* is empty AND timestamp(P1) is less than or equal to TS. If so, a packet P2 = F(P1) is put in Buf2 with a timestamp equal to TS plus the number of clockbeats to perform F(P1).

3.2.2 Top Level Structure

At the top level, a multi-ring machine consists of a number of *rings* interconnected by a *switch*. There are three types of ring, as shown in figure 7. There are NR *processing elements* (PEs), NS *structure stores* (SSs), and a *global allocator* (GA). Packets carry a *ring address* so that the switch knows where to send them.

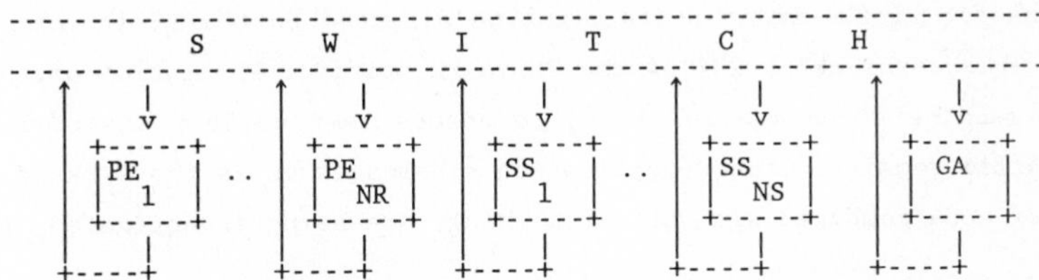

Figure 7. Overall structure of the simulated MR machine

Roughly speaking, a processing element executes dataflow instructions, a structure store manipulates data structures and the global allocator manages global resources such as large (interleaved) arrays and activation names. In principle, there could be more than one global allocator, but there are unsolved problems associated with distributing work among multiple allocators, and more research is needed before a complete scheme can be simulated. The simplified system introduces a potential bottleneck in that it imposes limits on NR and NS. Experiments to determine optimal values for NR and NS, given a single global allocator, are currently being performed.

3.2.3 The Switch

Previous simulation and emulation studies involved dataflow machines that consist of networks of (up to 128) PEs only [Barahona86, Foley86]. Simulation of this simple kind of machine has shown that it is possible to take advantage of the fine-grain dataflow parallelism by using a randomising *split function* to distribute work evenly over the PEs. It has been shown that, if the average parallelism of a program is about three times greater than the machine parallelism, then it will run on a multi-PE dataflow machine with at least 90% efficiency. The switch performance required by such a machine can be met using a buffered Banyan network topology, provided that the processing rate of individual switching elements is twice that of the rings.

For the more complex, heterogeous, extended machine, renewed investigation of the switch behaviour is needed. Amongst others, the following issues need to be addressed:

- The traffic to and from the SSs and the GA turns out to be significantly less than that to and from the PEs. As a consequence, the physical placement of the various kinds of ring on any particular kind of switch is of interest.

- The issue of *locality* must be faced. It is clearly possible to reduce switch traffic by arranging that tokens are, so far as is possible, directed to the ring in which they were created. However, any policy for achieving this is tantamount to turning the fine-grain dataflow model into a coarse-grain, process-orientated scheme, and can be expected to create the kind of distribution problems that coarse-grain, process-orientated machines have. As an example of such a policy, all tokens for single-input nodes might be directed to the PE in which they were created. This saves about 20% of the PE-to-PE traffic. Simulation of this kind of modified machine structure is needed to ensure that uniform distribution of PE-to-PE traffic remains. Other localisation schemes, such as those based on "smart" loading of code combined with better hashing, are being investigated.

- A dataflow machine with multiple global allocators and exploiting some form of locality may need a different switch topology. As in other dataflow architectures [Yuba85, Shimada86], some form of clustering may have to be considered.

The simulated MR switch is extremely simple. It consists of NR+NS+1 queues associated with the input to each ring. The output buffers of each ring are sampled every other time step, and token packets from full buffers are directed to the appropriate queue with timestamp equal to TS plus the delay through the switch, *SwDelay*. It therefore takes each token at least *SwDelay* time steps to cross the switch. The default value for *SwDelay* is **2*ceiling(log2(NR+NS+1))**.

3.2.4 A Processing Element

A processing element in the extended multi-ring dataflow machine simulates the behaviour of the prototype uniprocessor hardware [Gurd85]. One PE has the same computational power as the prototype (up to 2 MIPS). In order to decrease the amount of parallelism needed to saturate one PE, only half the buffers of the real machine are simulated. Furthermore the speed of the function units (FUs) in the processing unit can be increased so that fewer FUs yield the same processing rate. By this means, the internal parallelism in one PE is more than halved. Care has been taken that this does not change the computational power and internal speed-up characteristics of one PE. This makes it possible to perform multi-ring experiments on smaller programs, and also reflects the trend in recent dataflow machines to have as little internal parallelism as possible while keeping the same computational power [Shimada86]. The structure of a MR-simulated PE is shown in figure 8.

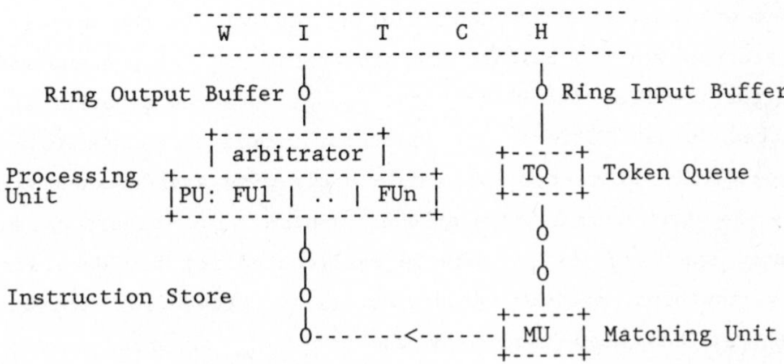

Figure 8. The structure of an MR-simulated processing element

The node store is simulated by a simple buffer. The dataflow program that would reside in the real machine's instruction store is a global data structure available to all PEs. Simulation of each time step goes "backwards": in trying to empty an output buffer of some $module_i$, it is first used as input buffer for $module_{i+1}$. Because the processing unit has internal parallelism, the FU result packets have to be sorted according to their time stamp. This is done in the arbitrator. When all result packets created by some FU have left the (internal) priority queue managed by the arbitrator, the FU is freed and can accept a subsequent executable packet.

3.2.5 A Structure Store

A structure store unit comprises an *allocator module* (AL), a *clearance module* (CLR) and *store control module* (STC). These three modules share a *memory module*, as shown in figure 9.

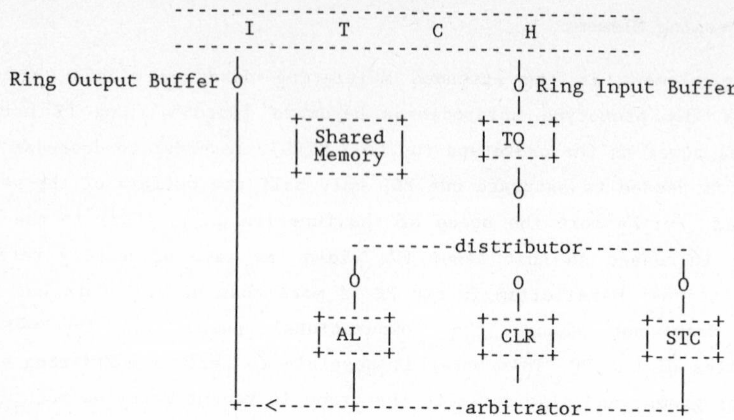

Figure 9. The structure of an MR-simulated structure store module

Processing elements send structure-manipulating requests to the various modules, and replies are returned via the switch. The arbitrator and token queue modules are the same as those for the PEs. The distributor module advances a packet at its input to one of its three output buffers. The allocator module is responsible for managing the storage space. The store control module deals with asynchronous accesses to the memory module in the normal data-driven fashion. The clearance module clears (resets) storage space so that it can be reallocated for new data structures. The shared memory contains *active structures* (i.e. those for which an explicit allocation request has been issued by the program), *deferred access chains*, and housekeeping information. The active structures live in an array of *cells* with the following format:

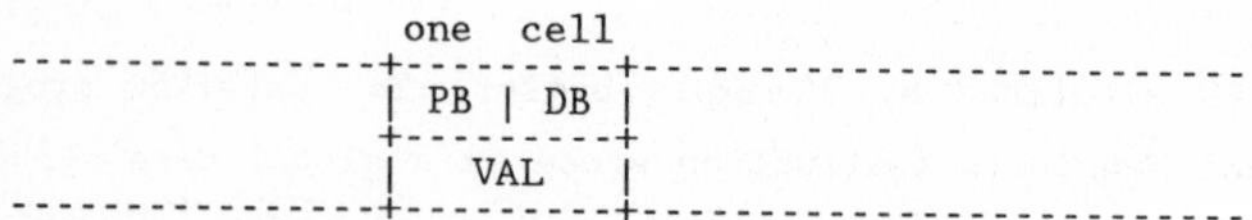

Every cell contains a *presence bit* (PB), a *defer bit* (DB), and a *value* field (VAL) which contains the data value stored without a tag. The presence bit indicates whether or not the value has yet been written. *Read accesses* fetch the data from the appropriate cell. Where the data has yet to be written (PB = FALSE), the read request is *deferred* until the data arrives. The first time this happens, the defer bit is set, and a *deferred access chain* of requests for this cell is created somewhere in the shared memory. The value field is used as pointer to the chain. *Write accesses* store data in the appropriate cell, setting the presence bit and releasing any deferred requests for that location at the same time. Overwriting (i.e. writing when PB is already true) causes a run-time error.

3.2.6 Structure Allocation and Clearance

A general allocation strategy is required to distribute the overall structure "address space" across the multiple structure store units. In the Manchester machine, the following heuristic is used [Sargeant86]. The storage space is occupied by *big* structures, such as arrays, and *small* structures, such as the nodes of trees. Big and small structures have different characteristics.

For big structures, the amount of work involved in accessing (writing and reading) the elements of the structure is far more than the work involved in allocating the storage. Consequently, the time taken to allocate storage is less critical than the time taken to access the elements. This leads naturally to an *interleaved allocation strategy* in which the big structures are allocated across all the structure stores whilst their administration is handled centrally in the global allocator. As mentioned earlier, this introduces a potential bottleneck, but the scheme extends naturally to a hierarchically managed (i.e. clustered) storage space.

On the other hand, there will be relatively many small structures for which the time to allocate storage is just as critical as the time to access their elements. A small structure is therefore allocated by a *local allocator*, residing inside the (single) structure store unit that holds the structure. Distribution of small structure allocations over the various structure store units is achieved by hashing.

The first location of each data structure is used as a reference count. Reference counting is done both on explicit request from the program, and as a side-effect of structure clearance. For the former, *increment/decrement reference count* instructions send a request to the appropriate store control unit. For the latter, clearing a pointer value in the structure store causes an *implicit decrement reference count* request to be transmitted. When a reference count goes to zero, the structure can be deallocated and its storage space reused. Before reuse, the storage space has to be *cleared*, i.e. all presence bits have to be reset. This is achieved by the CLR module. Small structures are cleared by a single CLR module, whereas big structures are cleared by all the CLR modules working in concert.

The above scheme seems the simplest possible for allocating structures in a dataflow machine with multiple structure store units. Although preliminary experiments show that it works reasonably well, more investigation and refinement is clearly needed.

3.2.7 Process Control

Executing a program such as *COINS* gives rise to a dynamic process tree of considerable depth and width, as shown in figure 5. In the prototype machine, the natural program execution order is *breadth-first*, even when this gives rise to amounts of parallelism that are too large to be exploited. Unfortunately, such highly parallel programs use excessive amounts of matching store and token queue. To avoid this, dataflow programs should be evaluated in *depth-first* order whenever there is excess parallelism available. The process of controlling software parallelism (so that it matches the available hardware parallelism) by scheduling the order of execution of instructions is known as *throttling* [Ruggiero87]. There exist certain software throttling mechanisms, such as loop serialisation [Böhm85], but these are usually crude, and they run the risk of destroying parallelism altogether. Instead, a mechanism that can respond dynamically to changes in the characteristics of an executing program is needed.

An IF1 *process*, as sketched in section 2, coincides on the machine level with all activity under a certain activation name. Such a process is activated by execution of a Generate Activation Name (GAN) instruction. Thus, process control can be achieved by suspending and unsuspending the execution of GANs according to the current status of the machine. In the extended dataflow machine a GAN instruction causes a PE to send a *GAN-request* to the global allocator. The global allocator uses the average length of the token queues in the PEs as a measure of the activity in the machine. Investigation of other measures of activity is in progress. The global allocator administers a *process* (activation name) *tree* and maintains a set of *suspended process queues* (SPQs), one for each level of the tree. When a GAN-request is received, it is administered in the process tree and suspended (if necessary) in the appropriate SPQ. At intervals the global allocator inspects the activity in the machine and decides whether to unsuspend the left-most, deepest-suspended process.

Figure 10 shows the effect of throttling on the *COINS* program. The program has executed roughly the same number of instructions (5010) as the unthrottled version shown in figure 5, but the throttle has significantly reduced the number of active processes. A black box with value *x* written in it represents *x* suspended processes.

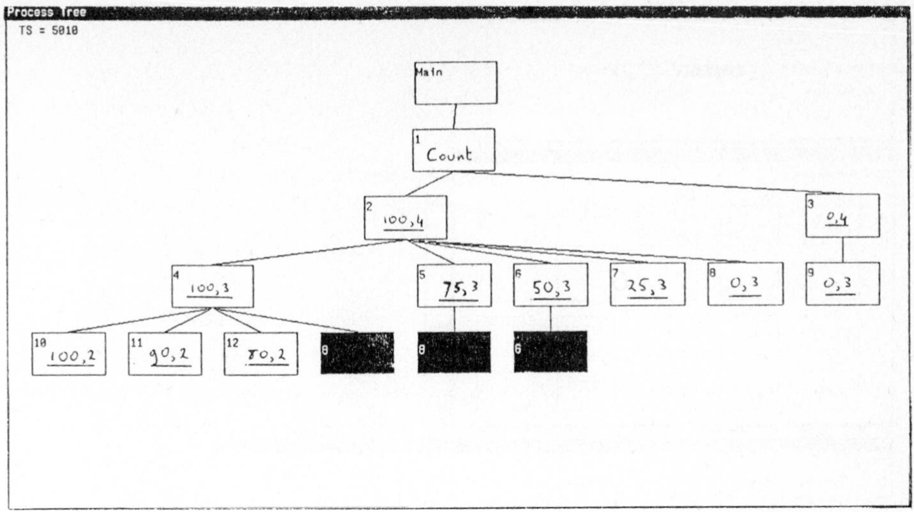

Figure 10. Dynamic process tree for throttled *COINS* program

3.3 Observing Run-time Behaviour at the Machine Level

MIMD machines are characteristically built using a large number of a small variety of *boxes*. This trend is being reinforced by the economics of VLSI systems. For each type of box, there are a number of characteristics to monitor. For the dataflow machine, the boxes are the processing elements (with characteristics such as token queue length, matching unit store occupancy and function unit utilisation), the structure stores (with characteristics such as token queue length, the number of store accesses, the number of allocations and the store occupancy), and the global allocator(s) (with characteristics such as the number of active and suspended processes and the number of big structures).

Information for each type of box can be displayed conveniently as a *matrix of meters*. Every row of the matrix represents one box and every column represents a characteristic (which may vary for fundamentally different types of box). For example, the authors are using a graphics package, *MatMet*, running on a SUN/3 workstation, to observe the behaviour of dataflow machine simulations. MR sends *MatMet* a description of the machine it simulates followed by measurements of the phenomena to be monitored. *Matmet* transforms this information into matrices of graphs and/or values, continuously displaying the state of the machine. The display can be played forward, stopped and played back.

An example display from *MatMet* is shown in figure 11. This depicts the run-time machine level behaviour of the throttled version of the *COINS* program, corresponding to the program level behaviour shown in figure 10. The machine simulated has 4 PEs, 1 SS and 1 GA.

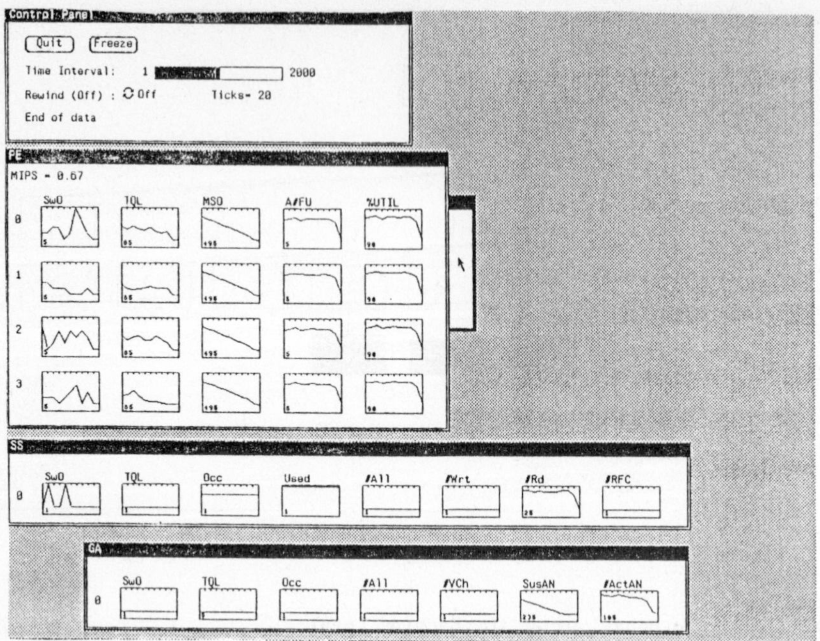

Figure 11. A sample screen while running *MatMet*.

Often the whole "history" of certain phenomena needs to be studied. This can be done using the *dump* facility in *MatMet*. Figures 12 and 13 are dumps showing the history of the token queue length (TQL), matching unit store occupancy (MSO) and function unit utilisation (%UTIL) for a single PE executing the program *COINS*, this time with input *amount* = 200. Figure 12 shows the graphs for unthrottled execution. Note the increasing numbers of tokens occupying the token queue (maximum 17800) and matching store (maximum 14400), due to too much program parallelism and lack of throttling.

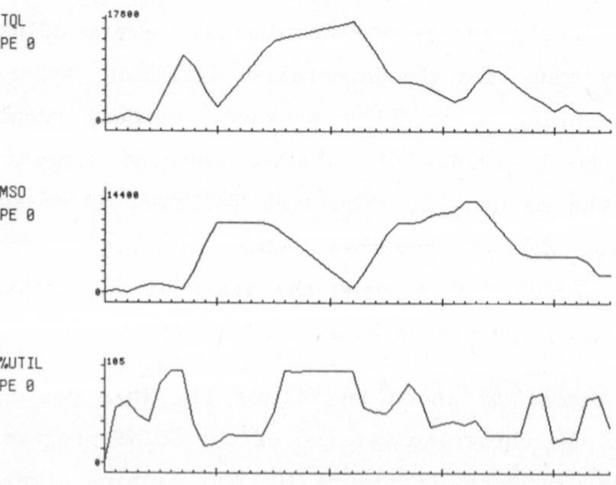

Figure 12. Execution histories for the "unthrottled" *COINS* program

Figure 13 illustrates the throttled version of the same program. Here, the numbers of stored tokens are kept well under control (maximum TQL < 400 and maximum MSO < 4100), *and* the function unit utilisation is considerably smoother.

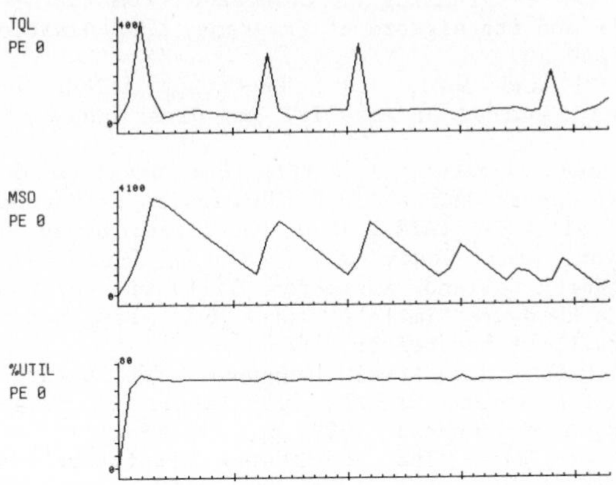

Figure 13. Execution histories for the "throttled" *COINS* program

4 CONCLUSIONS

We are convinced by our experience of implementing and using SISAL on the Manchester Dataflow Machine that deep understanding of even simple parallel computers is impossible without resort to sophisticated simulation and monitoring tools. The *MatMet* tool is already proving useful: it is no longer necessary for us to peer over fat listings for hours to locate problem spots. Furthermore, we see nothing that prevents the same techniques being applied to other multiprocessors. Indeed, we view it as essential that all parallel computers be equipped with tools of this kind. The more such tools have in common, the easier it will be for the end user to compare the merits of various systems under the range of conditions which apply to him.

Acknowledgements

The authors wish to acknowledge the considerable efforts of Heidi Tang in designing and implementing the graphical monitoring tools described above. The dataflow project at the University of Manchester has received support from the Science and Engineering Research Council of Great Britain, the UK Alvey Programme in advanced information technology, and Digital Equipment Company Limited. The SISAL language was designed by a joint research venture between Lawrence Livermore National Laboratory, Digital Equipment Corporation, Colorado State University and the University of Manchester.

REFERENCES

[Ackerman82] Ackerman, W.B., Dataflow Languages, *IEEE Computer* 15/2 (1982) pp. 1087-1095.

[Allen76] Allen, F.E. and Cocke, J., A Program Data Flow Analysis Procedure, *Communications of the ACM* 19/3 (1976) pp. 137-147.

[Backus78] Backus, J., Can Programming be Liberated from the von Neumann Style? A Functional Style and its Algebra of Programs, *Communications of the ACM* 21/8 (1978) pp. 613-640.

[Barahona86] Barahona, P. and Gurd, J.R., Processor Allocation in a Multi-ring Dataflow Machine, *Journal of Parallel and Distributed Computing* 3/3 (1986) pp.305-327.

[Böhm85] Böhm, A.P.W. and Sargeant, J., Efficient Dataflow Code Generation for SISAL, *Technical Report UMCS-85-10-2* (University of Manchester, 1985).

[Cohen86] Cohen, S. et al., The FAIM-1 User Interface: Human Engineering for the Fifth Generation, *in*: Woods J.V., (ed.), *Fifth Generation Computer Architectures* (North Holland, Amsterdam, 1986) pp. 257-273.

[Foley86] Foley, J.F., A Hardware Simulator for a Multi-ring Dataflow Machine, *Ph.D. Thesis*, (University of Manchester, 1986).

[Glauert82] Glauert, J.R.W., High-Level Languages for Dataflow Computers, *in*: Wallis, P., (ed.), *State of the Art Report on Programming Technology* (Pergamon-Infotech, Maidenhead, 1982) pp. 173-193.

[Gurd85] Gurd, J.R., *et al.*, The Manchester Prototype Dataflow Computer, *Communications of the ACM* 28/1 (1985) pp. 34-52.

[Gurd87a] Gurd, J.R. and Böhm, A.P.W., Implicit Parallel Programming: SISAL on the Manchester Dataflow Computer, *in*: Almasi, G., *et al.*, *Proceedings IBM Europe Institute on Parallel Processing* (North Holland, Amsterdam, 1987) pp. ?-?.

[Gurd87b] Gurd, J.R., *et al.*, The Manchester Dataflow Computing System, *in*: Dongarra, J.J., (ed.), *Experimental Parallel Computing Architectures* (North Holland, Amsterdam, 1987) pp. 177-219.

[Johnson86] Johnson, T. and Durham, T., *Parallel Processing: the challenge of new computer architectures* (Ovum Limited, London, 1986).

[Kindervater85] Kindervater, G.A.P. and Trienekens, H.W.J.M., Experiments with Parallel Algorithms for Combinatorial Problems, *Report OS-R8512* (CWI, Amsterdam, 1985).

[Kuck81] Kuck, D.J. *et al.*, Dependence Graphs and Compiler Optimisations, *Proceedings 8th Symposium on Principles of Programming Languages* (ACM, 1981) pp. 207-218.

[McGraw83] McGraw, J.R. *et al.*, SISAL - Streams and Iteration in a Single-Assignment Language, *Language Reference Manual* (Lawrence Livermore National Laboratory, Livermore CA, 1983).

[Pingali85] Pingali, K. and Arvind, Efficient Demand-Driven Evaluation, *ACM Transactions on Programming Languages and Systems* 7/2 (1985) pp. 311-333.

[Ruggiero87] Ruggiero, C.A. and Sargeant, J., Control of Parallelism in the Manchester Dataflow Computer, *Proceedings 3rd International Conference on Functional Programming Languages and Computer Architecture* (ACM, 1987) pp. ?-?.

[Sargeant86] Sargeant, J. and Kirkham, C.C., Stored Data Structures on the Manchester Dataflow Machine, *Proceedings 13th Annual Symposium on Computer Architecture* (ACM, 1986) pp. 235-242.

[Shimada86] Shimada, T. *et al.*, Evaluation of a Prototype Data Flow Processor of the SIGMA-1 for Scientific Computations, *Proceedings 13th Annual Symposium on Computer Architecture* (ACM, 1986) pp. 226-234.

[Skedzielewski85] Skedzielewski, S. and Glauert, J.R.W., IF1 - An Intermediate Form for Applicative Languages, *Reference Manual M-170* (Lawrence Livermore National Laboratory, Livermore CA, 1985).

[Yuba85] Yuba, T. *et al.*, SIGMA-1: A Dataflow Computer for Scientific Computations, *Computer Physics Communications* 37/1 (1985) pp. 141-148.

Strategies for Cache and Local Memory Management by Global Program Transformation

Dennis Gannon
Dept. of Computer Science, Indiana University and
CSRD Univ. of Illinois, Urbana-Champaign.

William Jalby
INRIA and CSRD Univ. of Illinois, Urbana-Champaign

Kyle Gallivan
CSRD Univ. of Illinois, Urbana-Champaign.

1. Introduction

Perhaps the most critical feature in the design of a shared memory parallel processor is the organization and the performance of the memory system. Generally, the shared memory is implemented as a set of independant modules which may be themselves interleaved and are connected to the processors via either a bus or a switch network. This organization exhibits several potential performance problems. First because of the long journey each memory reference must traverse in going to and from this shared resource the latency to access data may be very high. This effect can be very important especially in systems with a large number of processors connected to memory by a multistage network. In this case each globlal memory request must go through $\log_2(p)$ where p is number of processors. Furthermore, due to the contention both at the network level and the memory level (routing and memory banks conflicts), the practical bandwidth (and also the latency) can be severely degraded. A good example of such phenomenon is "hot spot" contention [PhNo85]. To overcome these problems, the key idea is to use a hierarchical memory system which is a technique already proven effective on sequential computers for speeding up memory access.

In a Hierarchial system the memory is organized in several levels which might be globally shared (each processor may access the whole level), partially shared (the processors "inside a cluster" share the access to a given level) or private (each processor has its own level, access to which is restricted to itself). The key principle is that local and private access do not suffer from the delays and contention encountered in going through the global communication medium. The transfers of data from one level to another is either entirely hardware managed (such as is done with caches memeory) or fully software managed (such as with registers where the user or, more preferably, the compiler generates code to move data between levels). For example, the ALLIANT FX/8 uses two levels of fully shared memory (trading size for speed): the main memory and a high bandwidth, shared cache. The memory is connected by a bus to the cache which is turn shared by the processors through a crossbar. Access to vector from the cache is 2 to 3 times faster than accessing from memory. Additionnaly, each processor has its own instruction cache and its own set of vector registers. On other machines only the main memory level is shared and each processor has a private data cache (for example, the Sequent Balance and Encore Multimax) or a local memory which might be physically distinct from the main memory (CRAY2) or just a portion of the shared memory as in the IBM RP3 and the BBN Butterfly. In these machines the difference between local and shared requests is that the local ones do not go through the network. Finally, the Cedar system has perharps one the most ambitious design of memory hierarchy. At the processor level there are instruction caches and vector registers, then the processors are grouped into clusters which share a local cluster memory, access of which is speeded up by a shared, cluster level cache and finally the clusters have accces to the globally shared memory through a multistage network. Additionnaly, each cluster has a prefetch unit controlled by software for prefetching data and therefore hiding the latency induced by the access to the global memory level.

However, the overall performance of all these hierarchical memory systems are highly dependant upon the address reference stream (more precisely its locality) of the program. Several studies ([CJST85] [GaJaM87] [GaJa87]) have shown how algorithm reorganization may result in a substantial performance improvement. It is crucial to notice that even in the case of hardware managed systems such as the ALLIANT FX/8, reorganizing the program in order to make references to the same variable closer in time (or reducing the size of the working set) will speedup sensibly program execution [GaJaM87] [GaJa87]. Similar phenomena have been observed in studies that considered the effect of program organization on paged memory behavior [KaMK69] and our approach can be considered following in the spirit of [AsKL81].

In this paper we consider the problem of automating the process of transforming programs to optimize the utilization of the memory hierarchy. For sake of simplicity, we will, at first, assume that the transfers between hierarchy levels are completely under software control. In this case, locality optimization is a 2-level process: first for a given program, solve the allocation problem (what data should be kept in cache and for how long), and, second, select an allocation strategy by restructuring minimizing the number of transfers. In fact, this basic strategy may still be applied to hardware managed levels, because reducing the number of transfers between levels is a problem that is the dual of maximizing the reuse of data (optimizing "hit ratio").

Our principle tool for solving the allocation problem is to consider it at a macroscopic level (loop level and section of arrays) rather at the microscopic level (instantiation of instruction and individual array elements). Using the fact that for scientific codes, most of the CPU time is spent in loop-like structure execution, we study the interaction between statements within a loop. By analyzing the sets of all the addresses referenced by each during the whole loop execution we derive an estimate of the effect these two statements have on the memory behavior. In fact, a similar analysis is already performed by vectorizers or parallelizers and is known as data dependence analysis. First we show that the theory of data dependences can be extended so that a more refined algebraic structure can be given to a class of data dependences associated with array index expressions that are common in scientific code. We call this class of dependences "uniformly generated". Next we associate a "reference window" with each data dependence. The reference window of a data dependence between 2 satements describes the set of elements (section of the array) that must be kept in the first level of memory so that if the first referece to the data is a not a local access, all following accesses will be local. In other words, for a given data dependence we try to determine the amount of space required to ensure that each data item referenced will be loaded into local memory or cache just once.

In sections 3 and 4 of the paper, we show that "uniformly generated" dependences have special properties that relate the structure of the data dependence graph to the lattice of reference windows and, given information about the loop bounds, we can estimate the size and "hit ratio" of the various windows. Now the problem is very similar to a classical bin packing problem: the size of the windows being the cost, and the "hit ratio" being the benefit associated with keeping a window. In fact, all the elements necessary to manage the data between the different levels can be done symbolically at compile time, while the final decision might only be taken at runtime by substituting values in the symbolic expressions.

In section 5 of the paper, it is shown that program transformations like loop interchange and blocking can have a substantial effect on the size of the windows and therefore on the demand for space in the fast level. While this is a well known fact to most programmers, it is shown that the data dependence modeling can be used a mechanism to predict when a loop interchange can improve performance. In section 6 we show how this mechanism can be used to decide which data should be moved from the global memory of a multiprocessor system to the local memory. We also briefly discuss the implications for multiprocessors with shared cache.

2. Definitions

In this paper we use the standard definitions for data dependences given in many places (for a recent overview see [PaWo86]). A flow dependence from a statement S_1 to a statement S_2 exists when a value computed in S_1 is stored in a location associated with some variable name x which is later referenced and used in S_2 and is denoted

$$\delta_x : S_1 \rightarrow S_2$$

An anti-dependence from S_1 to S_2 exists when a variable x referenced by S_1 must be used before it is overwritten by S_2 and is denoted

$$\bar{\delta}_x : S_1 \rightarrow S_2$$

An output dependence from S_1 to S_2 exists when both statements modify a common variable x and S_1 must complete before S_2 does. This is denoted by

$$\delta_x^o : S_1 \rightarrow S_2$$

In order to track memory references another dependence type , known as an input dependence, is used. Unlike the other three types of dependences, an input dependence does not impose a constraint on the potential parallel execution of the two statements, but we still use a notation similar to the others:

$$\delta_x^I : S_1 \rightarrow S_2$$

In the case of references to elements of structured variables such as vectors or arrays, most references occur within loops. In this paper we consider only simple "for loop" iterations though much of what we say applies to "while loops" and other tail recursive control structures. For each data dependence between two references nested within a loop, we extend the work of [Cytron85] and associate with the dependence a set of **distance vectors** which is defined as follows. Consider a nested sequence of k loops of the form shown below.

```
For i1 = L1 to U1
    For i2 = L2 to U2
        .....
            For ik = Lk to Uk
                ....
                S1
                ....
                S2
                ....
            endfor
        .....
    endfor
endfor
```

The module Z^k is called the **Extended Iteration Space** and the product $\prod_{i=1}^{k} D_i$ where D_i is the range of the ith induction variable $[L_i .. U_i]$, is called the **Bounded Iteration Space.** Both the extended and the bounded iteration spaces have a total order which is defined by the point in time at which the element is executed, i.e.

$$(v_1, v_2, ..., v_k) < (w_1, w_2, ..., w_k)$$

if there is a point s, $1 \leq s \leq k$, such that $v_i = w_i$ for $i < s$ and $v_s < w_s$. We will say a vector is **positive** if it is greater than zero in this order.

If a data dependence exists between a variable reference (which might be a component of a structured variable x) in S_1 at iteration

$$i_1 = i_1^0,\ i_2 = i_2^0,\ \cdots\ i_k = i_k^0$$

and the same variable (or component of x) in S_2 is referenced at iteration

$$i_1 = i_1^1,\ i_2 = i_2^1,\ \cdots\ i_k = i_k^1$$

Let

$$v_1 = i_1^1 - i_1^0,\ v_2 = i_2^1 - i_2^0,\ \cdots\ v_k = i_k^1 - i_k^0.$$

If this vector is positive in the total order of the iteration space, then we say the dependence exists and has a distance vector $\overline{V} = (v_1, v_2, ..., v_k)$ at time

$$\overline{I^0} = (i_1^0, i_2^0, ..., i_k^0).$$

In general there may be more than one distance vector at each point in time, because S_2 may reference the same component of x at several different points in the future. To make this more precise, let d be the dimension of the structure x and let k be the depth of loop nesting that we are considering. Let S_1 reference x by an indexing function $f: Z^k \rightarrow Z^d$ and S_2 reference x by the function $g: Z^k \rightarrow Z^d$. Then the dependence

$$\delta_x : S_1(...x[f(\overline{I^0})]...) \rightarrow S_2(...x[g(\overline{I^1})]...)$$

defines a family of distance vectors at iteration time $\overline{I}$ by the relation

$$V_{\delta,\overline{I}} = (\ v \in Z^k \mid v > 0 \text{ and } f(\overline{I}) = g(\overline{I} + v)\ ).$$

Note that we insist that the distance vectors point forward in time (which translates to the requirement that the leading non-zero component of the vector be positive.)

There are a number of important, very common special cases. We say the dependence is **Uniformly Generated** if there is a linear function $h: Z^k \rightarrow Z^d$ and two vectors C_f and C_g such that

$$f(\overline{I}) = h(\overline{I}) + C_f$$
$$g(\overline{I}) = h(\overline{I}) + C_g$$

In this case it is easy to see that

$$V_{\delta,\overline{I}} = (\ v \in R^k \mid v > 0,\ h(v) = C_f - C_g\ )$$

and that the right hand side is constant in time (independent of $\overline{I}$). Clearly if a non-negative member of $h^{-1}(C_f - C_g)$ does not exist the dependence does not exist. If $h^{-1}(C_f - C_g)$ is a single vector $(v_1, v_2, ..., v_k)$ then we say the dependence is **uniquely generated** and denote it by,

$$\delta_x(v_1, v_2, ..., v_k) : S_1 \rightarrow S_2$$

Another method of describing the set of distance vectors is to represent it as the sum of a uniquely defined positive vector plus the kernel of h. To do this let $v = (v_1, v_2, ..., v_k)$ be the smallest non-negative vector in $h^{-1}(C_f - C_g)$ then clearly

$$V_{\delta,\overline{I}} = (\ v + w \mid w \in Ker(h)\ )$$

where $Ker(h)$ is the kernel of the mapping, i.e. the set of all w such that $h(w) = 0$. The existence and uniqueness of v is because the time order is total and the function h is continuous.

To illustrate these ideas consider the loop

```
For i = 1 to n
        For j = 1 to n
S1              x[i,j] = 13.5
S2              y[i] = x[i-3,j+5] + 19.0
S3              z[j] = 1.4
S4              call f(3,z[j-7])
        endfor

endfor
```

This program has six dependences and we will look at three of them. On the variable x, there is a flow dependence for each (i,j) pair to iterates $(i+3,j-5)$ when $i<n-3$ and $j>5$. In this case $h(i,j) = (i,j)$ and $C_f = (0,0)$ and $C_g = (3,-5)$. Because the $Ker(h)$ is trivial we can write this as

$$\delta_x(3,-5) : S_1 \rightarrow S_2$$

For the variable y we note that for each j iteration $y[i]$ is modified. Thus for each j we have a family of output dependences one from each value of i to the next. In this case $h(i,j) = i$. This is a self dependence so we have $C_f = C_g$ and the set of distance vectors is just equal to $Ker(h)$ which is generated by the vector (0,1). This dependence vector is written as

$$\delta_y^o(1,0)^+ : S_2 \rightarrow S_2$$

Where the superscript "+" is used to denote that a full module of dependences are generated by this vector, i.e. we have $\delta_y(k,0)$ for all $k>1$ and $(k,0) = k(1,0)$. Such dependences are called **cyclic self-dependences** and are very important for cache management.

The third dependence involves the variable z. Here we have $h(i,j) = j$, $C_f = 0$ and $C_g = -7$. The kernel of h is generated by the vector (1,0) and $h(0,7) = C_f - C_g$. Hence the set of dependence vectors can be described as

$$\delta_z(\ (0,7) + (1,0)^+\ ) : S_3 \ \rightarrow \ S_4$$

where the vector summation is to denote the one parameter family of vectors

$$(0,7) \ + \ p*(1,0) \ = \ (p,7) \quad \text{for } all \quad p \in Z.$$

It is important to notice that for $p \geq 0$ this is a flow dependence, but for $p<0$ the direction in time is reversed and in fact we have described a set of antidependences

$$\hat{\delta}_z(-p,-7) : S_4 \ \rightarrow \ S_3 \quad all \quad p<0$$

Of course not all data dependences are uniformly generated. For example,

```
    For i = 1, n
S1      x[2*i+3] = 29.9
S2      y[i] = x[4*i+7] - 39.0
    endfor
```

has an anti-dependence from S_2 to S_1 which, at iteration i, has a distance vector

$$\hat{\delta}_x(i+2) : S_1 \rightarrow S_2 \quad 1 \leq i \leq (n-3)/2.$$

The vector is not uniformly generated because the vector is of the wrong form (it depends upon time) and the it is carried only by the even iterations. In this situation we use the classical "direction" vector notation. In the case above the distance is always positive, so we denote it as $\hat{\delta}_x(+)$. If, on the other hand the lower bound of the for loop was -3, the distances would have ranged from -1 to $(n-3)/2$ and we use the notation $\hat{\delta}_x(-/+)$. If the lower bound of the loop were -2, the vector would be $\hat{\delta}_x(0/+)$, etc.

3. The Cache Window for a Dependence Vector

For our purposes we are interested in the following question:

Let two references to a variable be linked by a data dependence. Under what conditions can we be assured that if the first reference to the variable brings the current value into cache, then the second reference will result in a cache hit?

In general this is a very hard problem whose answer depends on more than a single data dependence. One must know not only more global program information, but also a great deal about the way the cache replacement policy works. As described in section 1, we take the approach that the compiler can restructure the program and suggest a replacement schedule that will be reasonably good. The consequence of letting the compiler manage the cache is that we may focus attention on one variable at a time and estimate the effect of program restructuring on the demands that are made on cache resources by that variable.

If the compiler has complete control of the cache and it is to be managed much like a massive set of registers, the basic cache optimization problem can be stated as follows: when we read a scalar or an element of a structured variable, should we, or should we not, keep the element in cache. If we have complete knowledge of the data dependence structure of the program, a reasonable solution is to see of that reference was the source (tail) of a data dependence. This means the element will be referenced again, if so, and if there is room, we should keep the element. To make this idea more precise, we need the following.

DEFINITION. The **reference window,** $W(\delta_X)_t$ for a dependence $\delta_X : S_1 \rightarrow S_2$ on a variable X at time t is defined to be to be the set all elements of X that are referenced by S_1 before t that are also referenced (according to the dependence) after t by S_2.

For example, the loop

```
    for i = 1, n
S1    x[i] = 1.4
S2    x[i-3] = y[i]
    end;
```

has an output dependence $\delta_x^o(3)$. If we set a break point at the top of iteration i we see

$$W(\delta_x^o(3))_{t=i} = (x[i-3], x[i-2], x[i-1])$$

In this case, we see that to make sure every reference to x in statment S_2 (excluding those few not referenced at all by S_1) is a cache hit we must be sure that for all $t{=}i$ the past four elements referenced by S_1 are kept in cache.

A more complex example is given by

```
    for i = 1, m
S1    y[i] = x[i]
      for j = 1, m
S2          x[j] = 1.5
    end;
```

In this case there are three families of dependences. First there is an anti dependence

$$\bar{\delta}_x(0/+) \colon S_1 \rightarrow S_2$$

which describes the use of $x[i]$ prior to the reassignment in S_2 for all iterations in the future. It is not hard to see that

$$W(\bar{\delta}_x(0/+))_{t=i} = (x[1], x[2], \cdots x[i-1])$$

Second, from S_2 to itself, we have

$$\delta_x^o(1,0)^+: S_2 \rightarrow S_2$$

which again represents a family of dependences $\delta_x(k,0)$ generated by the distance vector (1,0). In each case, at the top of the loop all m elements of x have been referenced and will be referenced again. This implies

$$W(\delta_x^o(1,0))_t = (x[1], \cdots x[m])$$

At the top of loop i, all future references to $x[k]$ for $k > i$ in statement S_1 have been previously generated by assignments in S_2. Consequently,

$$\delta_x(+): S_2 \rightarrow S_1$$

has an associated window

$$W(\delta_x(+))_{t=i} = (x[i], x[i+1], \cdots x[m])$$

As the above example illustrates, different dependences generate different, but not necessarily disjoint, reference windows. In section 5 of this paper we will have need of a mechanism for picking families of dependence windows for cache management. Our problem here is to consider ways in which a "basis" of dependences can be chosen that somehow generates the entire family of reference windows for a given variable x so that we can measure the size of the total set of elements of x that must remain in cache. To do that we must first study a bit of the algebra relating the dependence graph to the family of reference windows.

DEFINITION. Suppose we have three dependences

$\delta_1 : S_1 \rightarrow S_2$

$\delta_2 : S_2 \rightarrow S_3$

$\delta_3 : S_1 \rightarrow S_3$

with the property that if $x[\bar{i}]$ is referenced by S_1 and later by S_3 then it is referenced some time in between by S_2. In this case we say that $\delta_3 = \delta_1 + \delta_2$.

The relationship between the reference windows for these three dependences is given by the following result.

Lemma 3.1. Let $\delta_3 = \delta_1 + \delta_2$ define a relation between references in statements S_1, S_2 and S_3.

$$\delta_1 : S_1 \rightarrow S_2, \quad \delta_2 : S_2 \rightarrow S_3$$

We then have

$$W(\delta_1)_t \cap W(\delta_2)_t \subset W(\delta_3)_t \subset W(\delta_1)_t \cup W(\delta_2)_t$$

Furthermore, if $W(\delta_1)_t \cap W(\delta_2)_t$ is not empty there is a cyclic self-reference

$$\delta_0 : S_2 \rightarrow S_2$$

and

$$W(\delta_1)_t \cap W(\delta_2)_t \subset W(\delta_0)_t .$$

Proof. Let $x[\bar{i}]$ be an element of $W(\delta_3)_t$. This means that it is referenced at, or before time t by S_1 and later by S_3. Either it has already been referenced by S_2 which means that it is in $W(\delta_2)_t$ or it has not which means that it is in $W(\delta_1)_t$. This prove the right hand inclusion. To prove the left hand inclusion notice that if $x[\bar{i}]$ is an element of both $W(\delta_1)_t$ and $W(\delta_2)_t$ then it has been referenced by both S_1 and S_2 and will be referenced by S_3 in the future. This last fact puts it in $W(\delta_3)_t$.

Assume that $W(\delta_1)_t \cap W(\delta_2)_t$ is not empty. Let $x[i]$ be in the intersection. Then by δ_1 $x[i]$ is referenced by S_2 after t and because of δ_2 it is referenced by S_2 at or before t. This implies the existence of δ_0 and $x[i]$ is a member of $W(\delta_0)_t$.

In general one would like to find a family of dependences that are mutually disjoint and generate the entire set of dependence windows. In other words we would like the intersection term in the above expression to be empty and the second inclusion to be a set equality. Unfortunately, this is not always true. For example,

```
        for i = 1 to m
S1          x[i] = 1.5
            for j = 1 to m
S2              y[i,j] = x[j]
            end;
S3          z[i] = x[j-4]
        end;
```

has 6 dependences. Among these, three dependences satisfy the addition formula ($\delta_3 = \delta_1 + \delta_2$) and we have

$$W_1(\delta_x{:}S_1 \rightarrow S_2)_{t=i} = (x[1], x[2], ..., x[i-1])$$

$$W_2(\delta_x{:}S_2 \rightarrow S_3)_{t=i} = (x[i-4], x[i-3], ..., x[m])$$

$$W_3(\delta_x{:}S_1 \rightarrow S_3)_{t=i} = (x[i-4], x[i-3], x[i-2], x[i-1])$$

which satisfies $W_3 = W_1 \cap W_2$ and not $W_3 = W_1 \cup W_2$. One of the reasons that this happens is that both the dependences $\delta_x{:}S_1 \rightarrow S_2$ and $\delta_x{:}S_2 \rightarrow S_2$ are not uniquely generated, i.e., they both have direction vectors (–/+). If we restrict our attention to uniformly generated dependences it is possible to state a stronger results. In particular, we have

Theorem 3.1. Let S_1 reference $x[h(i)+C_f]$, S_2 reference $x[h(i)+C_g]$ and S_3 reference $x[h(i)+C_k]$. Then if $h()$ is linear and the dependences

$$\delta_1{:}S_1 \rightarrow S_2 \quad \text{and} \quad \delta_2{:}S_2 \rightarrow S_3$$

both exist, then a dependence $\delta_3{:}S_1 \rightarrow S_3$ exists and, in the unbounded iteration space, we have

$$W(\delta_3)_t = W(\delta_1)_t \cup W(\delta_2)_t$$

Proof. Let $x[i]$ be in $W(\delta_1)_t$ and let $v_i \in V_{\delta_i}$ for i=1,2 be the smallest positive vectors in these sets. By definition $x[i]$ is referenced before t by S_1 and after t by S_2. Looking at the reference by S_2 we have $i = h(\bar{i})+C_g$ with $\bar{i} > t$. Pick $\bar{i}$ to be the smallest such vector that satisfies this condition. Because $h(v_2) = C_k - C_g$, we have $\bar{i} + v_2 > t$ and $i = h(\bar{i}+v_2)+C_k$. Hence, $x[i]$ is referenced by S_3 after t as long as $\bar{i}+v_2$ lies in the iteration space. This is always true in the unbounded space, but in the bounded space it may not always hold.

In the other direction, let $x[i]$ be in $W(\delta_2)$ be referenced by S_2 at $\bar{i} < t$. If we pick $\bar{i}$ to be as large as possible, then there exists $v \in V_{\delta_2}$ such that $\bar{i}+v > t$ where S_3 references $x[i]$. But $\bar{i}-v_1 < t$ defines a point where S_1 references $x[i]$, so $x[i]$ is in $W(\delta_3)$. But again, in the bounded iteration space this may not hold.

This proves that, in the unbounded iteration space, we have

$$W(\delta_1) \cup W(\delta_2) \subset W(\delta_3)$$

To prove the inequality the other way, we need only observe that if $x[i]$ is in $W(\delta_3)$ and is referenced by S_1 at i_1 before t and at i_3 by S_3 after t. Consider $i_2 = i_3 - v_2$. If $i_2 > t$ then $x[i]$ is in $W(\delta_1)$, otherwise it is in $W(\delta_2)$.

DEFINITION. We say that a window for a dependence **spans** a set of other windows if each is contained in the first.

Theorem 3.1 states that for any three references generated by the same function $h()$ that form a graph connected by dependences, there is a single dependence that has a window that spans the others. The next step is to show that this may be generalized to larger sets.

DEFINITION. $UG(x)$ is defined to be the subset of the atomic data dependence graph consisting of nodes that are references to variable x and edges that are uniformly generated dependences.

We say that a *source* for a directed graph is a node where all non-self cycle edges are outgoing and a *sink* is an edge where all non-self cycle edges are ingoing.

Theorem 3.2. Let $C \subset UG(x)$ be a connected component. Then C has a spanning dependence and following three statements are true.

1. **If p is a source then it is unique and there is a node q and a dependence $\delta{:}p \rightarrow q$ such that $W(\delta)$ spans C.**
2. **If q is a sink then it is unique and there is a node p and a dependence $\delta{:}p \rightarrow q$ such that $W(\delta)$ spans C.**
3. **If there are no sinks or sources in C then the references windows for dependences in C are all equal.**

Proof. We first show that C is complete in the sense that if x and y are nodes in C then there is a dependence between them. We use an induction based on Theorem 3.1. Let p and q be two nodes in C. Pick the shortest (undirected) path between p and q. If this path has length greater than 1 then let r be the node on the path connected to p and s be the node connected to r. Nodes p, r and s form a triangle with two sides that are dependences. As in the proof of Theorem 3.1 the existence of the third edge (between p and s) follows from the linearity of $h()$. Hence there is a shorter path between p and q which contradicts the assumption that the minimum was greater than 1. The fact that the source and sink are unique follow from this completeness.

We next prove that if there is a source or sink then there is a spans dependence edge connected to it. Let si be a sink for the graph and let $\delta_1{:}p \rightarrow q$ be an arbitrary edge not involving si. By the closure property there are two edges $\delta_2{:}p \rightarrow si$ and $\delta_3{:}q \rightarrow si$. By Theorem 3.1 δ_2 spans both. By the same argument all edges connected to si are totally ordered by the set inclusion of the corresponding reference windows, hence there is a maximal element that spans all other edges connected to si and hence all edges in C. If a source node exists then the same argument shows that there is an edge connected to the source that spans all others. If both a source and a sink exist then the spanning edge must be connected to both. If neither exist, then let q be any node. Then because q is not a source or sink there must be both an ingoing edge $\delta_1{:}x \rightarrow q$ and an outgoing edge $\delta_2{:}q \rightarrow y$. Again by Theorem 3.1 both δ_1 and δ_2 are spanned by an edge from x to y. This fact must be true for any outgoing and ingoing pair. This means that x can not be an end point to an edge to any maximal window that strictly spans any other, hence all the reference windows must be equal.

It should be noted that this result tells us how to pick a dependence that spans any connected component of a dependence graph in an unbounded iteration space. Unfortunately, in the bounded iteration space, Theorem 3.1 is no longer valid, and remain true only 'away from the boundary' of the iteration space.

Fortunately there is another mechanism that we can use to estimate window extents in a bounded iteration space. The key idea is that for each window in a bounded iteration space we can enclose the window in a moving "frame" of fixed size. Let D^k be the bounded iteration space and let x be a structured variable if dimension n. If we have a dependence

$$\delta_x: x[h(i) + C_1] \rightarrow x[h(i) + C_2]$$

we can define the following special subspaces of Q^k where Q is the field of rationals. Let e_i for $i = 1..k$ define the natural basis of Z^k that corresponds to the induction varibles $i_1, i_2, ..., i_k$. Define the subsets of Z^k,

$$V_j = span(e_j, e_{j+1}, ..., e_k)$$

where $span(u_1, ..., u_t)$ is defined as

$$[\ v \in Q^k \mid v = \sum_{r=1}^{t} \alpha_r u_r, \ with\ \alpha_r \in Q\ ]$$

We have

$$V_k \subset V_{k-1} \cdots \subset V_2 \subset V_1 = Q^k.$$

We can now characterize the window for δ_x as follows.

Theorem 3.3. Let r_1 be the largest integer such that $ker(h) \subset V_{r_1}$ and let $v \in h^{-1}(C_1 - C_2)$. Let r_2 be the index of the leading nonzero term in v and set $r = min(r_1, r_2)$. Define

$$X_v = \langle -s^*v + V_{r+1} \rangle \cap \overline{D}^k.$$

where $\overline{D}^k$ is the closure of the iteration space over the rationals and s is a rational in the range $[0, 1]$. We then have

$$W(\delta_x)_{t=(i_1,i_2,...,i_k)} \subset (\ x[I] \mid I \in h(i_1, ..., i_r, 0, 0, ...,0) + C_1 + h(X_v)\ )$$

Proof. Let $x[s_1] = x[s_2]$ be two references to the same element of x where $s_1 = h(t_1)+C_1$ and $s_2 = h(t_2)+C_2$ and $t_1 \leq t < t_2$. Because $s_1 = s_2$, we have

$$h(t_2 - t_1) = C_1 - C_2.$$

Letting $\bar{t} = t_2 - t_1$, we have $\bar{t} - v \in ker(h)$. Because $ker(h) \subset V_r$, we can let $h = \bar{t} - v$ which must take the form

$$h = (0, ..., 0, h_r, h_{r+1}, ..., h_k).$$

Now consider two case. First assume $t_1 > t - v$. We now have

$$t_1 \leq t < t_1 + v$$

Assume t_1 is of the form

$$t_1 = (\bar{i}_1, \bar{i}_2, ..., \bar{i}_k).$$

Because the first $r-1$ terms of v are zero we have

$$\bar{i}_j \leq i_j \leq \bar{i}_j + v_j$$

hence $\bar{i}_j = i_j$ for all $j < r$. Consequently, if we let

$$t_0 = (i_1, i_2 .... i_r, 0, 0, ..., 0)$$

then we can write

$$t_1 = t_0 - s^*v + w$$

where $s \leq 1$ is chosen to satisfy $\bar{i}_r = i_r - s^*v_r$ and w is of the form

$$(0, 0, 0, ..., w_{r+1}, w_{r+2}, \cdots w_k)$$

with $w_j = \bar{i}_j - i_j + s^*v_j$. Applying h() and adding C_1 we have

$$s1 = h(t_1) + C_1 = h(t_0) + C_1 + h(-s^*v+w)$$

which is of the correct form because $-s^*v+w \in X_v \cap \overline{D}^k$.

Now assume that $t_1 \leq t - v$. If $t_1+h < t-v$ we would have $t_2 = t_1+h+v < t$ which is wrong. Hence, $t_1 + h \geq t - v$. By applying an argument identical to the one above, we can pick a number $s \leq 1$ that gives us

$$t_1 + s^*h = t_0 - v + w$$

where $w_j = \bar{i}_j - i_j + s{*}h_j$ for $j > r$ and 0 otherwise. Again $-v+w$ is in X_v and because $h \in ker(h)$ we have

$$h(t_1) + C_1 = h(t_1 + s{*}h) + C_1$$

and the theorem is proved.

The advantage of the formulation in Theorem 3.3 is that the window has been enclosed in a moving frame. The term

$$h(\ i_1, i_2, ..., i_r, 0, 0, \cdots, 0\ )$$

describes how the frame moves in time. The term

$$C_1 + h(\ X_v)\ \ with\ \ X_v = <-s{*}v+V_{r+1},\ s\in[0,1]> \cap \bar{D}^k$$

is the time-independant "frame" for the window. Notice that $h(X_v)$ is independent of the choice of v because any other choice will differ from v by a member of $Ker(h)$. In the following section it will be shown that this formulation provides the necessary machinery to compute the size of cache windows.

4. Hit Ratios and Selecting Cache Windows.

Assume, for now, that we have a machine where the compiler can select which memory references to keep in cache. (For local memory this is always the case.) Clearly we would like to select those references belonging to reference windows associated with dependences that somehow generate a lot of cache hits. Our problem is twofold:

1. How do we compute the total size of a reference window and what is the cache hit ratio if we keep the entire window in cache?
2. How do we decide which windows to keep and which to disguard when the total is too big to fit in cache?

Another question that we would like to answer is if we have no control over the cache then can we estimate the hit ratios for hardware cache policies other than the one above? While the mechanisms described in this paper can be used to solve this problem, we will not consider it here.

Our basic cache scheduling algorithm will be as follows. First, at compile time, we select a set of dependence windows that we consider important. Our policy for cache replacement will be the following: we will read an element into the cache as soon as it enters the window and remove it from cache as soon as it leaves the window.

A simple way to estimate the total number of elements in cache for this policy is simply to sum the window sizes for each of the selected dependences. Unfortunately, as we have seen the relationship between cache window in a system of dependencies for a given variable can be rather complex. In particular, cache windows overlap and an element might be counted several times by this scheme. For example,

```
        for i = 1 to m
S1          x[i] = 1.5
            for j = 5 to 9
S2              y[i,j] = x[j]
            end
S3          z[i] = x[i-3]
        endfor
```

In this case there are 6 dependences listed below.

$$W_1(\delta_x(0/+):S_1 \rightarrow S_2)_{t=i} = (x[5], x[6], ..., x[min(i-1,9)])$$
$$W_2(\delta_x(+/-):S_2 \rightarrow S_3)_{t=(i,j)} = (x[max(5,i-3)], ..., x[9])$$
$$W_3(\delta_x(\ 3\ ):S_1 \rightarrow S_3)_{t=i} = ([x[i-3], x[i-2], x[i-1])$$
$$W_4(\delta_x(1,0)_*:S_2 \rightarrow S_2)_{t=(i,j)} = (x[5], ..., x[9])$$
$$W_5(\delta_x(0/+):S_3 \rightarrow S_2)_{t=i} = (x[5], ..., x[min(9,i-3)])$$
$$W_6(\delta_x(+/-):S_2 \rightarrow S_1)_{t=(i,j)} = (x[max(5,i)], ..., x[9])$$

Notice that, in fact, there are only two significant windows here. One is the window of size 3, W_3, and the other is the window of size 5, W_4. Each of these are based on uniquely generated dependences. The other windows are subsets of W_4. The correct cache policy for this program is to select W_3 and W_4 to be kept in cache. Also notice that W_3 sweeps over the entire x array while W_4 is constant in time (after $i = 1$). At some times they are disjoint, but at times they overlap and it is only during the period of overlap that the other dependences exist at all.

Because of the fact that these non-uniformly generated dependences have reference windows that tend to be either subsets of uniformly generated dependences or they have low hit ratios, we drop them from consideration for inclusion into the cache. (We will attempt to justify this restriction better in the next section.) For now our approach is based on the following strategy.

Let $UG(x)$ be the subgraph of the atomic data dependence graph consisting of those reference nodes involving the variable x and those edges corresponding to uniformly generated dependences. For each connected component $C \subset UG(x)$ we estimate the size and the "hit ratio" of the reference window for the spanning dominate dependence. If the total size is greater than the cache capacity, we attempt to restructure the program to reduce the size. If the program cannot be restructured but the cache can be managed by tagging the references that should be retained in cache, we attempt to solve the corresponding bin packing problem to select the reference windows that will give best performance.

Our nest task is to describe the machinery for the size and hit ratios of uniformly generated dependences. In some cases the task is easy.

For example, the loop

```
for i = 1 to n
          for j = 1 to m
S1          ... X[i,j] ..
S2          ... X[i-3, j+5] ...
          endfor
endfor
```

defines a dependence with distance vector $\delta_X(3,-5)$. At iteration (i_o, j_o) $X[i_o, j_o]$ is referenced. This element is not referenced again until iteration (i_o+3, j_o-5). Consequently, statement S_1 will have to access elements

```
                  X[i   ,j], X[i   ,j+1], ... , X[i   ,m],
X[i+1,1] ..       X[i+1,j], X[i+1,j+1], ... , X[i+1,m],
X[i+2,1] ..       X[i+2,j], X[i+2,j+1], ... , X[i+2,m],
X[i+3,1],..,X[i+3,j-5]
```

This set of elements defines the window $W(\delta_X)$ for this dependence at iteration $(i+3, j-5)$. Clearly any smaller set would not include reference $X[i,j]$ and would cause a cache miss for statement S_2.

In the more general case of a uniformly generated dependence δ from a term of the form

$x[h(I)+C]$ we need to consider the formulation from Theorem 3.3. Let $\bar{I} = (i_1, ..., i_k)$. Let $v \in V_\delta$ and r be chosen according to the conditions of the theorem. We have

$$W(\delta_x)_{t=\bar{I}} \subset h(i_1, ..., i_r, 0, 0, ..., 0) + C + h(X_v)$$

where

$$X_v = < -s^*v + span(e_{r+1}, ..., e_k) >$$

and e_j is the vector describing the extent of the jth induction variable. The problem is to compute the size of $h(X_v)$. There is a natural mapping to the quotient module

$$h: Z^k \rightarrow \frac{Z^k}{Ker(h)}$$

which identifies all point in iteration space that reference the same element of the variable x by mapping each index point i to its equivalence class $[i]$ mod h. If we let X be the set of all distinct elements of x, then there is an injection

$$In: \frac{Z^k}{Ker(h)} \rightarrow X$$

given by $In([i]) = h(i)+C$. For a point t in iteration space, let t_r be the projection on the first r components. Clearly we have another formulation of Theorem 3.3.

$$W(\delta_x)_t \subset h(t_r)+In(h(X_v))$$

so

$$|W(\delta_x)_t| \leq |h(X_v)|$$

To compute the size of $h(X_v)$ we use the following result. Let U be a convex subset of Z^k. The linear function $h()$ is composed of component functions of the form

$$h_i(v_1, \ldots, v_k) = \sum_{j=1}^{k} h_{i,j} v_j.$$

Lemma 4.1. Let $h_{i_1}, \cdots h_{i_r}$ be a linearly independent set of components of $h()$. Let VP be the set of vertecies of a bounded convex subset U of Z^k and let

$$p_i = gcd(\ h_{i,j} \ \ j=1..k\ )$$

and

$$s_i = max(1, \max_{v,w \in VP} (, |h_i(v) - h_i(w)|))$$

An upper bound on the size of the set $h(U)$ is given by

$$|h(U)| \leq \frac{s_{i_1}}{p_{i_1}} \frac{s_{i_2}}{p_{i_2}} \cdots \frac{s_{i_r}}{p_{i_r}}$$

The proof is by induction on r. When $r=1$ the image of h is a scalar in the bounded interval

$$[\ \min_{v \in U} h(v),\ \max_{w \in U} h(w)\ ].$$

Because U is convex and h is linear, the size of this range is bounded by s and the maximum occurs at the vertecies of U. But the image of h can assume values only every p points so the number of elements is bounded by $\frac{s}{p}$. In general, we observe that $\frac{s_{i_r}}{p_{i_r}}$ is the number of hyperplanes orthogonal to h_{i_r} that contain the image of U. Let V be one of the hyperplanes and consider the convex set $V \cap U$. By induction,

$$|h(V \cap U)| \leq \frac{s_{i_1}}{p_{i_1}} \frac{s_{i_2}}{p_{i_2}} \cdots \frac{s_{i_{r-1}}}{p_{i_{r-1}}}$$

and we have $|h(V)| \leq |h(V \cap U)| \frac{s_{i_r}}{p_{i_r}}$.

To apply this result observe that the determination of a maximal set of linearly independent elements is a standard linear algebra computation. The only messy part of the computation is the determination of of the index r and a vector in V_δ. The rest is given by

Lemma 4.2. Let δ be uniformly generated based at a reference of the form $h(I)+C$. Let $v \in V_\delta$ and let r be chosen as in Theorem 3.3. Assume the iteration space takes the form $D = \prod_{i=1}^{k} [0, d_i]$. We have

$$|W(\delta_x)| \leq |h(X_v)|$$

where the verticies of X_v in Lemma 4.1 may be taken to be

$$0, \ -v, \quad \text{and} \ (0, \ldots, 0, d_j, 0, \ldots, 0) \ \text{for} \ j \geq r+1$$

As an example consider the following matrix multiplication routine.

```
for i = 0 to n1-1
        for j = 0 to n2-1
                for k = 0 to n3-1
                        a[i,j] += b[i,k]*c[k,j];
                end;
        end;
end;
```

For each of the three variables the dependences are self cycles

$$\delta_a(0,0,1)^+, \ \delta_b(0,1,0)^+, \ \delta_c(1,0,0)^+$$

corresponding to the three functions

$$h^a(i,j,k) = (i,j) \quad r = 3$$

$$h^b(i,j,k) = (i,k) \quad r = 2$$

$$h^c(i,j,k) = (k,j). \quad r = 1$$

In each case the v may be taken to be zero because these are self cycles. The corresponding X sets are

$$X^a = ((0,0,0))$$

$$X^b = ((0,0,k) \mid 0 \leq k < n3)$$

$$X^c = ((0,j,k) \mid 0 \leq j < n2, 0 \leq k < n3).$$

In the first case we clearly have

$$|W(\delta_a)| = |([(0,0,0]) | = 1$$

where the square brackets denote equivalence classes mod $h()$. In the second case we invoke Lemma 4.1 and 4.2.

Notice that for the dependence $\delta_b(0,1,0)^+$, the verticies of X^b are

$$(0,0,0) \text{and} \ (0,0,n_3).$$

The components of $h_b()$ are

$$h_{b,1}(i,j,k) = i \qquad h_{b,2}(i,j,k) = k$$

and from Lemma 4.2,

$$p_1 = p_2 = 1, \quad s_1 = 1, \; s_2 = n_3.$$

We have,

$$|W(\delta_b)| \leq \frac{s_1}{p_1}\frac{s_2}{p_2} = n_3.$$

In the case of δ_c we have vertecies

$$(0,0,0), (0,n_2,0), (0,0,n_3).$$

Again p_i is always 1 and the component functions are

$$h_{b,1}(i,j,k) = j \quad h_{b,2}(i,j,k) = k$$

We get

$$s_1 = n_2, \quad s_2 = n_3$$

and this time,

$$|W(\delta_c)| \leq \frac{s_1}{p_1}\frac{s_2}{p_2} = n_2 n_3.$$

Notice that in the example above the function $h()$ was an injective map from X_v to $W(\delta)$. It is not hard to show when the dimension of the $Ker(h)$ is 1 then this is always true for a self-cycle.

In the case of loops that are not perfectly nested these formulas still may work. For example, in

```
For i = 1 to n
      For j = 1 to m
            x[i,j] = 15.4
      endfor
      for j = 1 to m
            y[i,j] = x[i-3, j+7]
      endfor
endfor
```

the "official" distance vector only reflects the level of "common" nesting, i.e. $\delta_z(3)$. The formula give a window size of 3. However, we may artificially extend the vector to $\delta_z(3,-7)$ and apply the formula to get the correct window size of $3m-7$. Consequently the formula is still valid here, but one must take extreme care in making the extension. An alternative approach is to recognize when a vector operation is carried by a dependence and scale the formula above by the size of the vector. For example,

```
For i = 1 to n

      x[i, 1:m ] = 15.4
      y[i, 1:m ] = x [ i-3, 7:m+7]
endfor
```

is equivalent to the example above, but the "vector scaled" formula would give us an upper bound of $3m$.

DEFINITION. The **hit ratio** $hr(W(\delta_z))$ of a dependence window which is selected to be in cache is defined to be the number of times elements of $W(\delta_z)$ are referenced while in cache divided by the total number of times they are referenced.

A uniquely generated dependence $\delta_x(v){:}S_1 \rightarrow S_2$, if kept in cache, will have a hit ratio of at least 1/2 because each element is referenced twice and the first reference is the read that loads the element in cache. If a dependence window is associated with a self-dependence $\delta_x(v)^+{:}S_1 \rightarrow S_1$ the ratio is much higher. In particular, we need to compute the number of times each element of the window is referenced. We introduce a new set which approximates $h^{-1}(W(\delta))$. Define the hull of a dependence δ at time t by

$$Hull(\delta)_{t=I} = (\, p \in D \mid I - v \leq p \leq I \text{ for } all\ v \in V_\delta \,).$$

The Hull is the set of all points p in iteration space that can reach to or beyond t by a vector from V_δ. Computing its size first involves computing its extent by finding the largest vector in V_δ that still lies in the iteration space. This vector spans a comvex domain that contains the Hull and we can use Lemma 4.1 to calculate the size.

For example,

```
for i = 0 to n-1
      for j = 0 to m-1
            y[i,j] = x[3*i - 2*j]
      end
end
```

has an dependence $\delta_x^I(2,3)^+$. Let $k = min(n/2, m/3)$. The hull of the dependence is the rectangle with lower left corner (0,0) and upper right corner $(2k, m)$. From Lemma 4.1 we have

$$|hull(\delta)| = min(mn, \frac{2m^2}{3}) \text{ and } |W(\delta)| \leq 2m + min(2m, 3n)$$

Because each element is read into the window once and the remaining references are hits we have

$$hr(W(\delta)) = \frac{|Hull(\delta)| - |W(\delta)|}{|Hull(\delta)|}$$

which for $2m >> 3n$ is approximately $\frac{n-2}{n}$.

In general, let $C \subset UG(x)$ be a connected component. Define

$$Hull(C)_{t=I} = (\, p \in D \mid I - v \leq p \leq \text{ for } all\ v \in V_\delta \text{ for } all\ \delta \in C \,)$$

Lemma 4.3. Let $C \subset UG(x)$ be a connected component with n nodes. If $h(X_v)$ elements are always kept in cache we will have a hit ratio of

$$hr(h(Hull(C)) \geq \frac{n\,|Hull(C)| - |h(Hull(C))|}{n\,|Hull(C)|}$$

Proof. Each of the n nodes represents a source of references for the variable. There will be at least n other references to each element of $Hull(C)$. The total number of distinct elements of the array x that are referenced is just $|h(Hull(C))|$.

Notice that, in general, $Hull(C) = Hull(\delta)$ where δ is a spanning dependence for C in the unbounded iteration space. Where this fails to be true is when C is not closed under transitivity in the bounded iteration space because there will be no corresponding dependence. For example in the loop

```
for i = 1 to 100
      x[i] = 1.0;
      y[i] = x[i-60];
      z[i] = x[i-140];
end;
```

In this case, there are only two dependences one of distance 60 from S1 to S2 and one of distance 80 from S2 to S3. In this case we form the transitive closure of C and work with the hull of the spanning dependence, even though the dependence may not exist in the bounded case. It is not hard to show that in this case $Hull(C) \subset Hull(\delta)$. From this point on, we assume that the iteration space is large enough to make sure C is closed.

Given these tools we may now formulate the basic cache management algorithm as follows. Let B be a block of code, most likely a subroutine. Assume, for now, that B has no subroutine or function calls that require a substantial amount of cache activity. Also assume that B is one large (possibly nested) loop. (If not, then apply the algorithm below to each subblock contained in a top-level loop in B).

```
initialize S = empty
for every variable x in B {
        let C_x^i for i = 1..n_x connected components of UG(x).
        let δ_x^i be the dominating dependence for C_x^i.
        let n_x^i be the number of nodes in C_x^i.

        for i = 1 to n_x do  S = S + {δ_x^i, n_x^i};
        }
set Cache = empty
set n = size-of-cache
while (n > 0){
        let (δ, n) be the pair in S with the maximum value of
                n |Hull(δ)| − |W(δ)|.
        if |W(δ)| ≤ n {
                Cache = Cache + W(δ)
                n = n - |W(δ)|
                }
        S = S - (δ, n)
        }
```

Elements are selected in order of decreasing value of the total number of hits generated by the component if it were kept in cache. It is easy to see that if you are given the choice of two windows to keep in cache, the one that generates the greatest total number of cache hits will yield the best overall memory access performance. Upon termination, *Cache* is the family of connected component that have the best memory reference performance.

The algorithm above is presented to give a simple selection method. It may be suboptimal. The complete solution of this selection problem is NP-complete, but good approximate algorithms do exist (see [SaSa75]).

5. Program Transformation That Improve Data Locality.

In the previous section it was shown that if we consider the union of all cache windows for uniformly generated dependences associated with variables in a program segment we can estimate the size and hit ratio of the elements in cache in terms of the loop bounds. Because the estimates are only based on uniformly generated dependences the hit ratio estimates will be lower bounds. Because windows belonging to different generating functions may overlap, our size estimates will tend to be upperbounds. If the union is too big to fit in cache, we have given an algorithm to select a reasonable subset to keep.

On the other hand, if the union of the cache window sizes are too big for cache, then another alternative is to try to restructure the program to reduce the size of the cache requirement. The basic set of transformations to do this are well known. In their study of paged memory management, Abu-Sufa, Kuck and Lawrie showed that a good strategy is to attempt to split loop and then remerge them together so that loops tend to use fewer different variables and if a variable is used more than once its uses tend to be clustered together.

In the case of cache management these same techniques apply and, in addition, several other transformations can be used. For example, consider the following program segment.

```
     for i = 1 to n
          for j = 1 to m
S2             x[i,j] = y[j];
S3             z[i,j] = y[j-3];
          end;
     end;
```

The uniformly generated dependence

$$\delta_y^I((0,3)+(1,0)^+): S_2 \rightarrow S_3$$

dominates the other two (self-cyclic) dependences. The window is

$$W(\delta_y^I) = (y[1], y[2], ..., y[m])$$

which has size m. By interchanging the loops (which does not change the meaning of the program) we have

```
     for j = 1 to m
          for i = 1 to n
S2             x[i,j] = y[j];
S3             z[i,j] = y[j-3];

          end;
     end;
```

and the dependence becomes

$$\delta_y^I((3,0)+(0,1)^+): S_2 \rightarrow S_3$$

which still dominates the other two (self-cyclic) dependences. The window is now

$$W(\delta_y^I)_{t=(i,j)} = (y[j-3], y[j-2], y[j-1])$$

which has size 3. If m was too big to let the window fit in cache then 3 will probably be small enough. In addition, this transformation did not change the cache hit ratio. In fact we have

Theorem 5.1. Any correctness preserving program transformation will leave the cache hit ratio of the reference windows of data dependences unchanged.

Proof. By definition, the reference window of a dependence $\delta_x : S_1 \rightarrow S_2$ at time t is the set of elements of x that have been referenced by S_1 in the past that will be referenced by S_2 in the future. This means that if the window is kept in cache there will be one initial load and the remainder of the references will be hits. A program transformation will not change the nature or total number of references. The ratio is the the total number of times an element of the window is referenced while in cache divided by the total number of times it is referenced. In these terms, both the numerator and denominator are invariant with respect to program transformation.

Unfortunately, loop interchange is not always powerful enought to reduce the size of the cache demand to do the job. There is, however, another technique known as loop blocking that can have a significant effect on the size of the cache requirements. Consider a nested sequence of k loops

```
for i_1 = 0 to n_1
        for i_2 = 0 to n_2
            ...
                for i_k = 0 to n_k
                        Body(i_1, i_2, ..i_k)
                end;
        end;
end;
```

We say the rth loop has been **blocked** if we apply the transformation which replaces the loop

```
for i_r = 0 to n_r
        ...
        ...
end;
```

with

$$\text{for } j_r = 0 \text{ to } \frac{n_r}{d_r}$$

```
        for i_r = d_r*j_r to d_r*(j_r+1)
                ...
                ...
        end;
end;
```

where the value d_r is called the blocking factor. This form of blocking is always legal in that it does not effect the order of execution of the statements nested within. Furthermore, by itself, it does nothing to reduce the size of the cache windows. Its power comes when it is used in combination with loop interchange.

For example consider the following simple code segment.

```
for i = 1 to n
        for j = 1 to m
                for k = 1 to n
                        a[i,k] += b[k]*c[j,k]
                end;
        end;
end;
```

In this case we have

$$|W(\delta_a)| = n$$

$$|W(\delta_b)| = n$$

$$|W(\delta_c)| = m*n.$$

Assume $n > m$ and mn is to big for the cache which is of size CS. We apply blocking to the "for k" loop and get

```
for i = 1 to n
        for j = 1 to m
                for r = 0 to n/d
                        for k = r*d to (r+1)*d
                                a[i,k] += b[k]*c[j,k]
                        end;
                end;
        end;
end;
```

Now, interchanging loops to bring the "for r" loop to the outer most position and normalizing the "for k" loop, we have

```
for r = 0 to n/d
        for i = 1 to n
                for j = 1 to m
                        for k = 1 to d
                                a[i,k+r*d] += b[k+r*d]*c[j,k+r*d];

                        end;
                end;
        end;
end;
```

The reference windows now have sizes

$$|W(\delta_a)| = d$$

$$|W(\delta_b)| = d$$

$$|W(\delta_c)| = m*d$$

Clearly, in this case we can choose d small enough so that the total window size $(m+2)*d < CS$ and every element will need to move only once from memory to cache and every other access will be a hit.

Unfortunately, it is not always possible to restructure so that we have a perfect memory reference behavior. For example, in the case of matrix multiply we can use blocking on three levels in the original algorithm shown below.

```
for i = 1,n
        for j = 1, n
                for k = 1,n
                        a[i,j] = a[i,j]+b[i,k]*c[k,j];
                end;
        end;
end;
```

The result takes the form shown on the next page and we have

$$|W(\delta_a)| = d1*d2$$

$$|W(\delta_b)| = d1*n$$

$$|W(\delta_c)| = n^2$$

```
for r = 0 to n/d1
      for s = 0 to n/d2
            for t = 0 to n/d3
                  for i = 1 to d1
                        for j = 1 to d2
                              for k = 1 to d3
                                    a[i+r*d1,j+s*d2] +=
                                          b[i+r*d1,k+t*d3]*c[k+t*d3,j+s*d2];
                              end
                        end
                  end;
            end;
      end;
end;
```

The reader will find it easy to verify that no matter how we block and reorder the loops there is always a window of size n^2. What this implies is that if n^2 is greater than CS we can not expect to get perfect cache performance. The question then becomes, how good can the cache hit ratio be made if we keep a subset of the full reference window?

To answer this question we observe that the computation of a reference window is also a function of the scope of the execution we are considering. In the case above, it is easy to see why the window for the variable c is so big. The entire (n^2 element) c array is accessed for each iteration of the outermost loop. If we restrict our view to the inner most 5 loops we see that

$$|W(\delta_c)| = d2*d3$$

which reflects the fact that for each r iteration of the outer loop, the five inner loops make $d1*n^2$ references to a sequence of sub-block of size $d2$ by $d3$ of the c array. Hence for each r iteration we reload each sub-block and the total hit ratio is

$$1 - \frac{1}{d1}.$$

As the value of r is incremented a different sub-block is loaded and the hit ratio is as above. Another way to say this is if

$$d1*d2 + n*d1 + d2*d3 \leq CS$$

then each element of a and b are accessed from memory only once and referenced from cache $n-1$ times, and each element of c is read from memory $\frac{n}{d1}$ times and referenced from cache $n - \frac{n}{d1}$ times.

In the program above we restricted the context of the program execution to derive a smaller cache window. In terms of the data dependences in the program, observe that the family of data dependence vectors V_δ for the variable c is

$$V_\delta = (p*v_r + q*v_i \mid p, q \in Z^+)$$

where the generating vectors v_r and v_i are

$$v^r = (1,0,0,0,0,0) \quad \text{and} \quad v_i = (0,0,0,1,0,0)$$

By restricting the context we have simply discarded the dependences related to the loop variable r and the dependence family is generated by v_i alone. The hull of the associated reference window contains the extreme points $(0,0,0,0,0,0)$ and $(0,0,0,d1,d2,d3)$. After applying Lemma 4.2 we have $|W(\delta_c(v_i))| = d2*d3$.

6. The Role of Concurrency.

In the case of programs executing on parallel processing systems most of the analysis above can be directly applied, but some care must be taken. There are two cases that are of interest to us. In the first case, we consider shared memory multiprocessors where each processor has either a local memory or cache for its own private use. Examples of this type of machine include the BBN Butterfly, the IBM RP3, the Encore Multimax and, at the level of processor clusters, the Illinois Cedar. The other case is where the processors share a cache. The prime example of this is the Alliant FX/8.

In these multiprocessor systems there are three basic forms of concurrency that are used in scientific computations. The two that are the most simple are parallelized loops and vectorization and the third is where the computation takes the form of a system user defined lightweight tasks.

Consider first the case of the multiprocessor with private local memory. In the light weight task model, tasks communicate through shared variables or message buffers. Because the code has already been partitioned into tasks, the analysis in the previous sections can be applied to optimize the performance of each separate processor. Because shared variables and shared message buffers can not be cached without potential coherency problems, there is little that can be done here.

A more interesting case is the parallelization of loops. Following Kennedy and Allen [Allen83] we give the following

Definition. Let a loop L_i be the ith loop in a nested sequence and let v_i be the vector $(0, 0, \cdots, 1, 0, ..., 0)$ with a 1 in the ith position and zero everywhere else. We say that the loop **carries no dependence** if v_i is orthogonal to V_δ for every flow, output, or anti-dependence δ between terms nested in L_i.

The basic theorem that permits the parallel execution of a loop is then stated as:

Theorem 6.1. A loop may be parallelized without the use of special synchronization if and only if the loop carries no dependence.

Proof: See [Allen83], [KKLPW81] or [Wolfe82].

The key point of this result is that all data dependences (except for input dependences) are resolved withing the body of the loop. Consequently each iteration can be executed on a separate processor. Any input dependences that may span the loop can be discarded, because the corresponding window would span two different caches or local memories. The resulting reference windows associated with the reduced graph tell us precisely the information we need to keep in the cache or local memory of each processor.

For example, consider the blocked loop in the previous section:

```
for r = 0 to n/d
    for i = 1 to n
        for j = 1 to m
            for k = 1 to d
                a[i,k+r*d] += b[k+r*d]*c[j,k+r*d]
            end;
        end;
    end;
end;
```

The outermost loop does not carry any dependences and hence, may be parallelized.

```
FORALL r = 0 to n/d
    for i = 1 to n
        for j = 1 to m
            for k = 1 to d
                a[i,k+r*d] += b[k+r*d]*c[j,k+r*d]
            end;
        end;
    end;
ENDFORALL;
```

The semantics of the FORALL is that each processor will take a single unique r iterate and execute it to completion and then take another until all iterations have been complete. For a fixed value of r, the three cache windows are (in terms of the local time for each processor as)

$$W(\delta_a)_{t=(i,j,k)} = a[i, 1+r*d \,..\, (r+1)*d]$$

$$W(\delta_b)_{t=(i,j,k)} = b[1+r*d \,..\, (r+1)*d]$$

$$W(\delta_c)_{t=(i,j,k)} = c[1..m, 1+r*d \,..\, (r+1)*d]$$

The way in which this information is used depends on the machine. For example, on the BBN Butterfly a local memory reference can be three times faster than a remote reference. (If a number of processors try to access the same element then this may be much worse.) Furthermore the microcode provides a block transfer mechanism that can copy a vector from global memory to a local are at very high speed. Hence for the Butterfly, we would be best to use this information to compile in special code that prefetches the cache window with block transfers as follows

```
blocal[1..d]       = block_transfer(b[1+r*d..(r+1)*d]);
clocal[1..m, 1..d] = block_transfer(c[1..m, 1+r*d..(r+1)*d]);
for i = 1 to n
    alocal[1..d] = block_transfer(a[i,.1+r*d..(r+1)*d]);
    for j = 1 to m
        for k = 1 to d
            alocal[k] += blocal[k]*clocal[j,k];
        end;
    end;
    a[i, 1+r*d..(r+1)*d] = block_transfer(alocal[1..d]);
end;
```

Notice that because the "for r" loop was perfectly parallelizable there was no need to be concerned about coherence problems. Also the form of the data dependences were enough to detect where the copies should be made and when an update was needed. Notice that there are only a few simple constraints that must be satisfied. First to parallelize the "for r" loop we would like to pick d small enough so the n/d is greater than or equal to the number of processors. Also, we need d small enough so that $(m+2)d \leq CS$ where CS is the local memory size on each processor. On the other hand the size of the task for each processor grows with d, and we would wish to pick d large enough so that the task size make the parallel loop overhead look small. Fortunately, on the Butterfly this overhead is relatively small.

In case a loop carries dependencies, we may still parallelize the program, but we must synchronize the processors so that the dependence constraint is satisfied. Such a loop schedule is often called a "do-across" schedule. For systems that have private local memories for each processor, it is not likely that we would chose to cache data that is involved in a data dependence constraint. This is because such a constraint requires that one processor write data to a shared location before another processor reads it, or it must read/write the data before another processor overwrites it. In any event, the dependencies associated with "synchronized" data must not be included in our computation of cache needs because it must be shared between processors. After excluding these dependencies, what we are left with are the dependencies associated with data that is not involved in a synchronization conflict. It is purely local and we can apply the theory above to estimate its size and hit ratios.

In the case of a system where the cache is shared by all processors, such as the Alliant FX/8, the situation is vastly different from the private memory case. In particular, in the private cache case, processors are best working on data that is completely disjoint form the other processors. On the other hand, if the cache is shared, processors will be best off when they share the data in cache.

6. Conclusions.

The ideas presented here represent only a first approximation to the problem of transforming programs to improve cache behavior. Many important refinements are needed. In particular, this paper only considers the special case of uniformly generated dependences. It is shown that, in this case, we may make a good approximation to the size of the cache windows if certain conditions are satisfied. The problems come in two places. First, the structure of the bounded iteration space can make it very hard to select a set of spanning dependences that really reflect the lifetime of a variable in cache. In particular, if we generate a spanning dependence by a transitive closure operation, the dependence will exist in the unbounded iteration space but it may not exist in the bounded case. If it does not exist in a given iteration space, but we use it to compute a cache window, we may overestimate the real cache demand. In general, this happens when the distance vectors are greater than the size of the iteration space.

The second shortcoming of the theory above is that if the dependences are not uniformly generated then the reference window for the dependence will, in general, not be of constant size. This can make it very hard to make a'priori choices of the best dependences to use for loading the cache. It should be possible to extend the theory so that we can detect upper bounds on reference windows for these non-uniformly generated dependences. These extensions should improve the range of programs where good estimates can be made.

Most of the theory in this paper assumes a cache that is completely under the control of the program. Even in the case of caches that are not completely managed by the user, the analysis developed in this paper may be usefull. It is easy to imagine a cache which is partially programmable by the user, namely one where cache loading is user programmed while the unloading is under control of the hardware. For example moving data from main memory can be performed by 2 kinds of instructions: fetch and store in the cache (the data is fetched from main memory and is stored in the processor registers as well as in the cache), fetch only (the data is fetched from main memory and stored in the processor registers but not kept in cache). The main advantage this policy is to avoid filling the cache (and therefore discarding usefull data) with useless data. The main difficulty lies in deciding at compile time by the restructurer what kind of move to perform. The key idea in managing such a cache is to force data that the analysis has decided should not be kept in cache to be fetched by fetch only instructions. The remaining problem is that we are not sure that the hardware unloading policy will follow our optimal programmed policy. However, if the hardware policy is based on an LRU scheme, it should be possible to analyze the behavior of the cache using our method because our static analysis generates a "worst case" stream of references and therefore we should be able to build a timetable indicating when the elements are touched. Using this information we will be able model the LRU policy and derive a good replacement scheme.

Currently, we are in the process of implementing the ideas described in this paper into a FORTRAN restructuring system being built at Indiana University and CSRD in Urbana. The objective is to show that an interactive program restructurer can take data provided by the program and the programmer and then make estimates about potential cache performance problems and also make suggestions about way that the programmer can restructure the code to avoid these problems. A detailed description of the software system and the results of experimental use will be given in a sequel to this paper.

7. References

[Allen83] J.R. Allen, "Dependence Analysis for Subscripted Variables and Its Application to Program Transformations," Ph.D. Thesis, Rice University, Houston, Texas, April 1983.

[AlKe84] J. Allen, and K. Kennedy, "A Parallel Programming Environment," technical report, Rice COMP TR84-3, July 1984.

[ASKL79] W. Abu-Sufah, D. Kuck and D. Lawrie, "Automatic Program Transformations for Virtual Memory Computers," Proc. of the 1979 Nat'l Computer Conf., June, 1979, 969-974.

[ASKL81] W. Abu-Sufah, D. Kuck and D. Lawrie, "On the Performance Enhancement of Paging Systems Through Program Analysis and Program Transformation," IEEE Trans. Comp. V. C30 no. 5, May, 1981, pages 341-356.

[BuCy86] M. Burke, R. Cytron, "Interprocedural Dependence Analysis and Parallelization," Proc. Sigplan 86 Symposium on Compiler Construction, 21(7):162-175, July 1986.

[CoMK69] Coffman, E., McKeller, "The organization of matricies and matrix operations in the paged multiprogramming environment," CACM V. 12 pp. 153-165. March 1969.

[CGST85] W. Crowther, J. Goodhue, E. Starr, R Thomas, W. Milliken, T. Blackadar, "Performance Measurements on a 128-node Butterfly Parallel Processor," Proceedings of 1985 International Conference on Parallel Processing, pp. 531-540, 1985.

[Cytron84] R. Cytron, "Compile-time Scheduling and Optimization for Asynchronous Machines," Ph.D. Thesis, University of Illinois, Urbana-Champaign Aug., 1984 Report No. UIUCDCS-R-84-1177).

[FeOt83] J. Ferante, K. Ottenstein, J. Warren, "The Program Dependence Graph and Its Uses in Optimization," IBM Technical Report RC 10208, Aug. 1983.

[GaJa87] Gannon, D., Jalby, W., "The Influence of Memory Heirarchy on Algorithm Organization: Programming FFTs on a Vector Multiprocessor," to appear in "The Characteristics of Parallel Algorithms," Gannon, Jamieson, Douglas, eds, MIT Press, 1987.

[Kenn80] K. Kennedy, "Automatic translation of Fortran programs to vector form," Rice Technical Report 476-029-4, Rice University, October 1980

[KKLW80] D. Kuck, R. Kuhn, B. Leasure and M. Wolfe, "The Structure of an Advanced Vectorizer for Pipelined Processors," IEEE Computer Society, proc. of the 4th Inter'l Computer Software and App. Conf., October, 1980, 709-715.

[KKLPW81]D. J. Kuck, R. H. Kuhn, B. Leasure, D. H. Padua and M. Wolfe, "Dependence graphs and compiler optimizations," Conference Record of Eighth Annual ACM Symposium on Principles of Programming Languages, Williamsburg, VA., January 1981.

[KuWM84] D. Kuck, M. Wolfe, and J. McGraw, "A Debate: Retire FORTRAN?," Physics Today, May, 1984, 67-75.

[Padua79] D. Padua, "Multiprocessors: Discussion of Some Theoretical and Practical Problems," Ph.D. Thesis, University of Illinois, Urbana-Champaign, Nov. 1979.

[PaKu80] D. Padua and D. Kuck, "High-Speed Multiprocessors and Compilation Techniques," IEEE Transactions on Computers, Vol. C-29, No. 9, September, 1980, 763-776.

[PaWo86] D. Padua and M. Wolfe, "Advanced Compiler Optimizations for Supercomputers," CACM, 29(12):1184-1201, Dec. 1986.

[PhNo85] G. Phister, A. Norton, "Hot Spot Contention and Combining in Multistage Interconnection Networks," Proceeding of the 1985 International Conference on Parallel Processing, 1985, 790-797.

[Poly86] C. Polychronopoulos, "On Program Restructuring, Scheduling, and Communication for Parallel Processor Systems," Ph.D. Thesis, University of Illinois Center for Supercomputer Research and Development. CSRD TR.595, Aug. 1986.

[SaSa75] Saraj, Sahni, "Approximate Algorithms for the 0,1 Knapsack Problem," JACM V. 22 no. 1 pp 115-124.

[KWDG87] Wang, K.-Y., Gannon, D., "Applying AI Techniques to Program Optimization for Parallel Computers," To appear in "AI Machines and Supercomputer Systems", Hwang, DeGroot, eds. McGraw Hill, 1987.

[Wolfe82] M. Wolfe, "Optimizing Supercompilers for Supercomputers," Ph.D. Thesis, Dept. of Computer Science, University of Illinois, Urbana-Chanpaign, 1982, Report no. UIUCDCS-R-82-1105.

ADVANCED LOOP OPTIMIZATIONS FOR PARALLEL COMPUTERS

Constantine D. Polychronopoulos

Center for Supercomputing Research and Development
and Department of Electrical and Computer Engineering
University of Illinois at Urbana–Champaign
104 South Wright Street
Urbana, Illinois 61801, USA

ABSTRACT

So far, most of the work on program dependence analysis has concentrated primarily on compile–time techniques, that are not always accurate and which are often conservative. By coupling the compiler's ability to perform elaborate program optimizations and the run–time system's more accurate knowledge of certain program characteristics, we can uncover and exploit even more parallelism in ordinary programs. By performing run–time dependence checking, certain types of loops that were previously treated as serial can be executed concurrently. This paper presents a run–time dependence checking scheme and a new compiler optimization aiming at parallelizing serial loops. In particular we present *cycle shrinking*, a compiler transformation that "shrinks" the dependence distances in serial loops, allowing parts of such loops to execute concurrently. Code reordering for minimizing communication and *Subscript blocking*, are also discussed briefly.

1. Introduction

Programming for serial computers is a well–understood process and a subject that has been studied extensively. The same cannot be said however for parallel machine programming. It is not an exaggeration to state that, for ordinary programming languages, there is a general consensus as to what characteristics a "good" language should possess. It would be unrealistic however to make the same statement for "parallel programming languages". In fact, there do not exist any truly parallel languages. So far the focus has been on extending existing languages with parallel constructs. Examples are the vector and parallel dialects of Fortran, Pascal etc. [Alli85], [ANSI86], [MeRo85], [MiUc84].

Parallel programming is a very complex task. Research in this area has only began, and we are far from understanding well the problem in its entirety. The complexity of parallel programming gives rise to a question about its future. Given that parallel programming is a very complex task, there are two possible solutions. Either programmers will need to become highly trained, or mechanisms and sophisticated tools will have to be deviced, that will make parallel programming a less complex and highly automated process.

This work was supported in part by the **National Science Foundation** under Grant No. NSF DCR84-10110 and NSF DCR84-06916, the **U. S. Department of Energy** under Grant No. DOE DE-FG02-85ER25001, and the **IBM** Donation.

It is our belief that the latter solution is more realistic and at the same time it does not preclude a sophisticated programmer from exercising total control over a particular parallel machine. Writing parallel programs will become a much easier process through the use of high level parallel languages and programming environments, which will be based on interactive restructuring compilers and debuggers. Program restructuring is a subject that has been studied for many years by a few researchers, and which has attracted great attention in recent years [AlCo72], [AlKe82], [Bane79], [Cytr84], [Kuck78], [Padu79], [PaWo86], [Poly86], [Poly87], [Wolf82]. Many vectorizing compilers have been developed in the past ten years [KKLW80], [Alli85], [Kenn80], [Brod81]. However, restructuring for parallel machines is still a relatively new subject. Some of the parallelizing compilers under development are the University of Illinois Parafrase II, the Rice PFC, and the IBM PTRAN.

In this paper we discuss some new techniques for transforming serial programs into a parallel form suitable for execution on parallel processor systems. These schemes can be implemented in a restructuring compiler with minimal effort, and for certain types of serial loops they can obtain significant improvement. More specifically, we discuss cycle shrinking, a compiler transformation that can partially parallelize certain types of serial loops. Two versions of this transformation (based on different uses of dependence distance information) are presented and compared. A more complete presentation of cycle shrinking is given in [Poly87]. The second major subject of this paper is run–time dependence analysis, through compiler–inserted bookkeeping and control statements. Loops with unstructured parallelism that cannot benefit from existing optimizations, can be parallelized through run–time dependence checking.

The rest of the material is organized as follows. Section 2 gives a short introduction to program dependences and defines the basic concepts. Section 3 discusses cycle shrinking; Section 3.1 covers singly nested loops, while Section 3.2 discusses the application of cycle shrinking to complex nested loops. Code reordering for reducing communication is discussed briefly in Section 4. Run–time dependence checking and the RDC transformation are presented in Section 5.1. Subscript blocking, another application of run–time dependence checking, is presented in Section 5.2. Concluding remarks are given in Section 6.

2. Data Dependences and Program Restructuring

The material presented in this paper requires some knowledge of data dependences and some associated concepts. Before we give a short introduction to data dependences however, we need to establish a basic notation.

A *program* is a list of $k \in N$ statements. S_i denotes the i-th statement in a program (counting in lexicographic order). I_j denotes a DO loop index, and i_j a particular value of I_j. N_j is the upper bound of a loop index I_j, and all loops are assumed to be normalized, i.e., the values of an index I_j range between 1 and N_j. The *stride* r_j of a loop index I_j is a positive constant by which I_j is incremented each time it is updated. We have two types of statements, *scalar* and *indexed* statements. An indexed statement is one that appears inside a loop, or whose execution is explicitly or implicitly controlled by an index (e.g., vector statements). All other statements are scalar. The *degree* of a program statement is the number of distinct loops surrounding it, or the number of dimensions of its operands. $S_i(I_1, I_2, \ldots, I_k)$ denotes a statement of degree k, where I_j is the index of the j-th loop or dimension. An indexed statement $S_i(I_1,\ldots, I_k)$ has $\prod_{j=1}^{k} N_j$ different *instances*, one for each value of each of I_j, $(j=1,\ldots, k)$. The first and last instance of a statement of degree k is $S_i(1, 1,\ldots, 1)$ and $S_i(N_1, N_2,\ldots, N_k)$ respectively. S_i will be used in place of $S_i(I_1,\ldots, I_k)$ whenever the set of indices is obvious. The *order of execution* is defined between pairs of statements instances S_i, S_j as follows. For (scalar) statements with degree 0 we say that S_i is executed before S_j and denoted by $S_i \underset{o}{\leq} S_j$ if $i \leq j$, i.e., if S_i lexically precedes S_j. For S_i, S_j with degree k (if they have different degrees then scalar order of execution applies as well), we have the following three cases. If S_i and S_j do not have common indices, then $S_i \underset{o}{\leq} S_j$ if $i \leq j$. If they have the same k indices, then $S_i(i_1, \ldots, i_k) \underset{o}{\leq} S_j(j_1,\ldots, j_k)$ if $i \leq j$ and there is an $1 \leq m \leq k$ such that $i_l = j_l$, $(l=1,\ldots,m)$, and $i_{m+1} < J_{m+1}$. If $i > j$, it is as above but with $m < k$. If S_i and S_j have $m < k$ common indices and $i_l = j_l$, $(l = 1,\ldots, m)$, then $S_i \underset{o}{\leq} S_j$ iff $i \leq j$. Otherwise the previous definition holds.

We also need to extend the definition of the IN(S) and OUT(S) sets (i.e., the sets of variables read and written by statement S respectively). We denote by $OUT(S_i(i_1,\ldots, i_k))$ the set of *variable instances* (not necessarily different) defined by statement instance $S_i(i_1,\ldots, i_k)$. Similarly, $IN(S_i(i_1,\ldots, i_k))$ is the set of variable instances used by the same statement instance.

Now we can proceed with the definition of data dependences. Two statements $S_i(I_1,\ldots, I_k)$ and $S_j(J_1,\ldots, J_k)$ are involved in a *flow* dependence $S_i\ \delta\ S_j$ if and only if there exist index

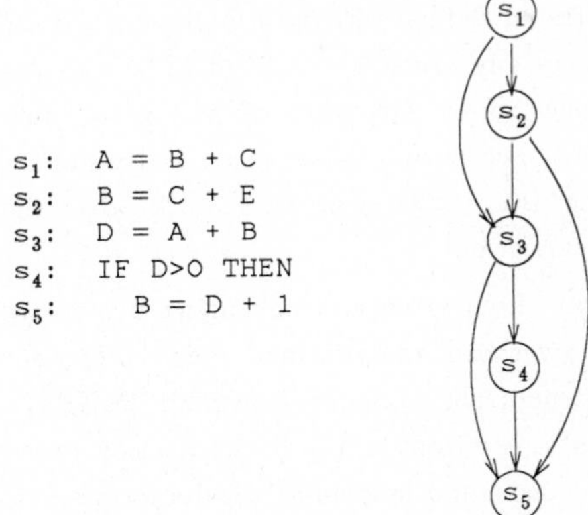

Figure 1. An example of data and control dependences.

values $(i_1, i_2,..., i_k)$ and $(j_1, j_2,..., j_k)$, such that $S_i(i_1,..., i_k) \underset{\circ}{\leq} S_j(j_1,..., j_k)$, and $OUT(S_i(i_1,..., i_k)) \cap IN(S_j(j_1,..., j_k)) \neq \emptyset$. An *antidependence* between S_i and S_j is defined as the flow dependence above, except for the last condition which now is $IN(S_i(i_1,..., i_k)) \cap OUT(S_j(j_1,..., j_k)) \neq \emptyset$. It is denoted by $S_i\ \bar{\delta}\ S_j$. An *output* dependence is again defined as above but with $OUT(S_i(i_1,..., i_k)) \cap OUT(S_j(j_1,..., j_k)) \neq \emptyset$, and it is denoted by $S_i\ \delta^o\ S_j$. In all three cases $S_i(i_1,..., i_k)$ is called the dependence *source* and $S_j(j_1,..., j_k)$ is called the dependence *sink*. Note that for a pair of statements S_i and S_j, $S_i\ \delta\ S_j$ denotes the *static dependence* and implies that a dependence exists at least between a pair of instances of the two statements. Clearly each static dependence may have several different *instances*.

For each data dependence involving statements $S_i(i_1,..., i_k)$ and $S_j(j_1,..., j_k)$ of degree k we define the r–th *distance* ϕ_r, or $\phi_r(\delta)$, to be $\phi_r = j_r - i_r$, $(1 \leq r \leq k)$. The k–tuple $<\phi_1, \phi_2,..., \phi_k>$ is called the dependence distance vector. The *true* distance or simply distance Φ_{ij} is defined as

$$\Phi_{ij} = \sum_{r=1}^{k} \phi_r \prod_{m=r+1}^{k} N_m \tag{1}$$

and gives the total number of iterations between the source and the sink of the dependence.

The program *data dependence graph* or DDG, is a directed graph $G(V,E)$ with a set of nodes $V = \{S_1, S_2,..., S_n\}$ corresponding to statements in a program, and a set of arcs $E = \{e_{ij} = (S_i, S_j) \mid S_i, S_j \in V\}$ representing data dependences between statements. Figure 1 shows the DDG of a set of scalar statements.

Several different transformations exist, that based on dependence information, can restructure serial programs into vector or parallel form, suitable for execution on SIMD and MIMD systems. In a restructured program, parallelism is usually explicitly specified via parallel constructs. In this paper the only type of parallel constructs used are various types of parallel loops. A DO loop denotes an ordinary Fortran loop, which is serial. A loop whose iterations can execute in parallel and in any order is called DOALL. The dependences in certain loops may allow only partially overlapped execution of successive iterations. These loops are called DOACROSS and are mentioned in only a few cases in this paper [Padu79], [Cytr84]. Of course, a loop is marked as being DO, DOALL, or DOACROSS after the necessary dependence analysis for that loop has been carrier out.

Loop parallelization, discovering and packaging unstructured parallelism, interprocedural analysis, compile–time overhead analysis, and many other complex tasks can be carrier out automatically by a restructuring compiler [PoKu87], [PoKP87]. In many cases user assertions can be useful or necessary. Automating the parallelization process makes parallel program writing possible for nonspecialists, and in general, results to more efficient code.

We plan to implement the transformations presented in this paper in Parafrase II, an interactive multi–language restructurer which is currently under development at the University of Illinois. Parafrase II will encompass most of the existing technology in the area, as well as new methods that have been developed recently. The compiler is designed to allow easy integration of new technology with minimal effort. In the remaining of this paper we discuss specific methods without reference to implementation details.

3. Cycle Shrinking

Some of the most important transformations are those that vectorize and parallelize serial loops. These transformations use the data dependence graph of a loop to determine whether the existing dependences allow the loop, or parts of it, to execute in parallel without violating the semantics. If no dependences exist this task is simple. In most cases however the dependence graph is complex, and appropriate tests are necessary to determine whether a pattern of dependences can allow vectorization or parallelization. Usually loops with dependence graphs that do not form strongly connected components can become fully or partially parallel. When the dependence graph forms a cycle node splitting can be used to break the cycle, assuming at least one of the dependences is an antidependence [KKLW80].

In many serial loops dependence cycles are impossible to break even after all known techniques are used. Dependence cycles that are impossible to break usually involve only flow dependences. In general, loops whose statements are involved in a dependence cycle are considered to be serial. In this section we present a transformation called *cycle shrinking* which can be used to extract any parallelism that may be (implicitly) present in a serial loop.

3.1. Simple Loops

Cycle shrinking is useful in cases where the dependence cycle of a loop involves dependences with distance greater than one. This scheme transforms a serial DO loop into two perfectly nested loops; an outermost serial and a parallel innermost loop. It is based on the observation that although there is a static flow dependence $S_1 \; \delta \; S_2$ between two statements S_1 and S_2 of a loop, there may be instances of S_1 and S_2 that are not involved in a dependence (since the dependence distance is greater than one). Cycle shrinking extracts these dependence-free instances of the statements inside a loop, and creates an inner parallel loop.

We can best describe cycle shrinking by considering initially dependence cycles where all dependences have the same distance $\lambda > 1$. In such cases cycle shrinking will speed up the loop by a factor of λ, called the *reduction factor*. First let us consider the case of singly nested serial loops with n statements $S_1, S_2, \ldots, S_n$ that are involved in a dependence cycle such that $S_1 \; \delta \; S_2 \; \delta \; \ldots \; S_n \; \delta \; S_1$. Furthermore assume that all n dependences have a constant distance $\lambda > 1$. For constant distance dependences, the array subscript expressions of elements that are involved in a dependence, must be of the form $I \pm a$, where $a \geq 0$ and I is the loop index. Then (assuming loops are always normalized without loss in generality) we have the following.

Lemma 1. The iteration space $[1 \ldots N]$ of a loop whose dependences are of constant distance λ, can be partitioned into subintervals or *groups* $V_0=[1 \ldots \lambda]$, $V_1=[\lambda+1 \ldots 2\lambda], \ldots, V_r=[r\lambda+1 \ldots N]$, so that the iterations of each group V_j are free of dependence sinks, assuming that groups $V_1, V_2, \ldots, V_{j-1}$, $(j=1, 2, \ldots, r)$ have been executed. (For simplicity assume that the first dependence starts from the first iteration of the loop.)

Lemma 1 indicates that serial loops with dependences that have equal (constant) distances can be partially parallelized. This can be done by transforming the serial loop into two

```
         DO I = 1, N
S1:        A(I+K) = B(I) - 1
S2:        B(I+K) = A(I) + C(I)
         ENDO
```

(a)

```
DO I = 1, N, K
   DOALL J = I, I+K-1
      A(J+K) = B(J) - 1
      B(J+K) = A(J) +C(J)
   ENDO
ENDO
```

(b)

Figure 2. (a) Example of loop with constant distance dependence cycle.
(b) The transformed loop of 2a.

perfectly nested loops. The innermost loop is a DOALL and at each time its index runs over the iterations of a group V_j, $(j=1,2,...,r)$, where $r = \lceil N/\lambda \rceil$. The outer loop is a serial DO loop whose index runs across groups V_j, $(j=1,2,...,r)$.

Consider for example the loop of Figure 2a. The dependence graph is shown next to it. Such loop would be treated as serial by the existing compilers. However, if cycle shrinking is applied the serial loop will be transformed to the loop of Figure 2b. The transformed loop can now be executed $\lambda = K$ times faster. The larger the distance λ, the greater the speedup. Values of λ=2 or 3 occur in numerical programs.

Let us consider now the case where the distance of each dependence (in the static dependence cycle) is constant, but distances between different static dependences are different. In this case we have a cycle $S_1 \; \delta_1 \; S_2 \; ... \; S_k \; \delta_k \; S_1$ where ϕ_i is the distance of the i-th dependence. Without loss in generality assume that $\phi_1 \geq \phi_2 \geq ... \geq \phi_n$. Then we have the following.

Corollary 1. If $\lambda = \min(\phi_1, \phi_2, ..., \phi_n) \equiv \phi_n$, then Lemma 1 holds true.

An example of a serial loop whose dependence cycle involves dependences with different distances is shown in Figure 3a. In this case ϕ_1=4 and ϕ_2=3. According to Corollary 1 the cycle can be reduced by a factor of λ=min(3,4)=3 resulting in the loop of Figure 3b.

The next case to be examined is when the distance of each static dependence is different for different instances of the dependence. In singly nested loops this happens when we have array subscripts of the form $aI \pm b$ where a is a nonzero integer. An example of such case is shown in Figure 4a. In this example the distance of each static flow dependence varies between

```
DO I = 1, N
   X(I)  = Y(I)  + Z(I)
   Y(I+3)  = X(I-4)  * W(I)
ENDO
```

(a)

```
DO J = 1, N, 3
   DOALL I = J, J+2
      X(I)  = Y(I)  + Z(I)
      Y(I+3)  = X(I-4)  * W(I)
   ENDOALL
ENDO
```

(b)

Figure 3. Another application of cycle shrinking.

```
DO I = 4, N
   A(4I-1)  = M * B(3I-1)
   B(4I-1)  = C(I)  + A(3I-1)
ENDO
```

(a)

```
DO J = 4, N, 2
   DOALL I = J, J+1
      A(4I-1)  = M * B(3I-1)
      B(4I-1)  = C(I)  + A(3I-1)
   ENDOALL
ENDO
```

(b)

Figure 4. Cycle shrinking with varying dependence distances.

different instances of the dependence. The minimum distance between all instances of both dependences in the example is $\lambda=2$. (Actually distances are monotonically increasing between successive iterations.) Corollary 1 can be applied in this case to transform the loop as in Figure 4b. Even though cycle shrinking extracts some parallelism from this loop, it is still a rather conservative solution, in the sense that it leaves some parallelism unexploited. A more general and powerful approach will be discussed in Section 5. Lemma 1 and Corollary 1 can be summarized in the following.

Corollary 2. A sufficient condition for a loop dependence cycle $S_1\ \delta_1\ S_2\ \delta_2 \ldots \delta_{n-1}\ S_n\ \delta_n\ S_1$ to be reduced by a factor of λ is

$$\lambda = \min_{1 \leq i \leq n} \{\phi(\delta_i)\}. \tag{2}$$

Theorem 1. Let `DO I = 1, N` be a `DO` loop with k statements that are all involved in a dependence cycle. If the reduction factor of the cycle is λ, then cycle shrinking increases the total parallelism in the loop by a factor of $\lambda * k$.

3.2. Complex Loops

In this section we discuss cycle shrinking for complex nested loops. There are three versions of cycle shrinking that can be used for nested loops. They differ in the way individual and true distances are used to compute the reduction factor, and they are discussed below.

Simple Shrinking: In this version the dependence cycle is considered separately for each individual loop in the nest. For a loop at nest–depth l only the l–th elements of the distance vector are considered. For each loop in the nest, cycle shrinking is applied as in the single loop case.

True Dependence Shrinking (or TD–Shrinking): In this version only true distances are used. Each dependence in the dependence cycle is labeled by its true distance computed by (1). Cycle shrinking is then applied as if the nested loop was a single loop. In this case a multidimensional iteration space is treated as a linear iteration space. It will be shown below that, as a result of this, loops are blocked by cycle shrinking in an "irregular" fashion.

Selective Shrinking: Here we consider each component of the distance vectors separately as in the case of simple cycle shrinking. In a loop nest of depth k we thus have k different dependence cycles, one for each individual loop. Each dependence in a cycle is labeled with the corresponding element of its distance vector. Next, selective shrinking computes the reduction factor λ_i, $(i=1, 2, \ldots, k)$ (using (2)) for each loop in the nest starting with the outermost loop. The process stops when for some $1 \leq j \leq k$, $\lambda_j \geq 1$. Then the j–th loop in the nest is blocked by a factor of λ_j. In addition, all loops nested inside the j–th loop are transformed to DOALLs.

It is clear that, by definition, selective shrinking is always better than simple shrinking. The conditions under which TD–shrinking is superior to selective shrinking are given in [Poly87]. Let us consider the application of the three versions of cycle shrinking to the loop of Figure 5a. Here the two statements are involved in a dependence cycle $S_1\ \delta\ S_2$ and $S_2\ \delta\ S_1$. The distance vectors for the two dependences are $<\phi_1^1, \phi_2^1> = <2,4>$, and $<\phi_1^2, \phi_2^2> = <3,5>$.

Simple shrinking considers the dependence graph with respect to indices `I` and `J` individually. For the loop of Figure 5a both graphs are cycles. Cycle shrinking can then be applied on each cycle separately. For the cycle corresponding to the outer loop the distances are 2 and

```
DO I = 3, N1
   DO J = 5, N2
      . . .
      A(I, J) = B(I-3, J-5)
      B(I, J) = A(I-2, J-4)
      . . .
   ENDO
ENDO
```

(a)

```
DO I1 = 3, N1, 2
   DO J1 = 5, N2, 4
      DOALL I = I1, I1 + 1
            DOALL J = J1, J1 + 3
                  . . .
                  A(I, J) = B(I-3, J-5)
                  B(I, J) = A(I-2, J-4)
                  . . .
            ENDOALL
      ENDOALL
   ENDO
ENDO
```

(b)

```
DO I1 = 3, N1, 2
   DOALL I = I1, I1 + 1
         DOALL J = 5, N2
               . . .
               A(I, J) = B(I-3, J-5)
               B(I, J) = A(I-2, J-4)
               . . .
         ENDOALL
   ENDOALL
ENDO
```

(c)

Figure 5. Simple and selective shrinking for multiply nested loops.

3. Cycle shrinking will shrink the outer loop by a factor of 2=min(2,3). Similarly the innerloop will be shrunk by a factor of 4=min(4,5). The resulting loop is shown in Figure 5b. The transformed loop can execute 8 iterations at a time in parallel, resulting in a speedup of 8.

The loop of Figure 5a will be transformed to that of Figure 5c if selective shrinking is used. Since the outermost loop has a reduction factor of 2, it is blocked as in Figure 5c and the inner loop becomes a DOALL. In this case $\lambda = 2N_2 - 8$.

Now let us compute the true distance for each dependence in the cycle and compare it to the individual distances. The true distances give us the *total* number of loop iterations (irrespectively of which loop) over which a dependence travels. Here we have

$$\Phi_{12} = \min(\Phi_{12}, \Phi_{21}) = 2N_2 - 4.$$

Thus the reduction factor $\lambda = 2N_2 - 4$ gives us the total number of loop iterations that can be executed in parallel during each step. For this example TD–shrinking works better than selective shrinking for any integer N_2.

Let us see now how the loop of Figure 5a can be transformed under TD–shrinking, assuming that the reduction factor λ is known (which is the case for our example). For our example let $N=N_1-3+1$ and $M=N_2-5+1$. The transformed loop is shown in Figure 6. The temporary variables T1 through T4 are used to mark the coordinates of the initial and the final points in the iteration space. The iteration space has a total of NM iterations. The transformed loop will sweep the iteration space by executing λ iterations in parallel at a time. $\lceil NM/\lambda \rceil$ barrier synchronizations are enforced by the outer loop which sees the iteration space as a linear space. If the index expressions in the loop body are to be preserved by cycle shrinking, the value of the outer serial loop must be decomposed into two coordinates, an I and a J coordinate.

```
DO K = 1, NM, λ

   T1 = (K DIV M) + 1
   T2 = ((K + λ) DIV M) + 1
   T3 = K MOD M
   T4 = M - ((K + λ) MOD M) + 1

   DOALL I = T1, T2
         IF I <> T1 THEN L1 = 5
         ELSE L1 = T3
         IF I <> T2 THEN L2 = N2
         DOALL J = L1, L2
               . . .
               A(I, J) = B(I-3, J-5)
               B(I, J) = A(I-2, J-4)
               . . .
         ENDOALL
   ENDOALL
ENDO
```

Figure 6. TD–cycle shrinking for the loop of Figure 5a.

Alternatively, we could linearize the corresponding arrays (i.e., A and B) in the loop body, and collapse the two DOALLs into a single DOALL with λ iterations. This would eliminate the extra statements inserted by TD–shrinking. Linearizing arrays is straightforward and we will not discuss it further [AhSU86].

The next case is non–perfectly nested loops. This case however is similar to the perfectly nested loop case, since only the common outer loop(s) is considered. The individual loops at the same nest–level in such a non–perfectly nested loop can be processed separately. Consider for example the loop of Figure 7a. Cycle shrinking can be applied to the two innerloops separately if necessary (not in this case of course since both loops are DOALLs). The outer loop

```
DO I = 3, N1
    DOALL J = 1, N2
        . . .
        A(I, J) = B(I-2, J)
        . . .
    ENDOALL

    DOALL K = 1, N3
        . . .
        B(I, J) = A(I-2, J-4)
        . . .
    ENDOALL
ENDO
```

(a)

```
DO L = 1, N, 2
    DOALL I = L, L+1
        DOALL J = 1, N2
            . . .
            A(I, J) = B(I-2, J)
            . . .
        ENDOALL

        DOALL K = 1, N3
            . . .
            B(I, K) = A(I-3, K)
            . . .
        ENDOALL
    ENDOALL
ENDO
```

(b)

Figure 7. Cycle shrinking for non–perfectly nested loops.

is serial because the two DOALLs are involved in a flow dependence cycle. Distances for the two dependences need only be computed with respect to index I. In this case the distances are 2, and 3, and thus $\lambda = 2$. After cycle shrinking the loop is transformed to that of Figure 9b.

Notice that according to Theorem 1 the improvement is not only a factor of $\lambda = 2$. In addition to executing every two iterations of the outer loop in parallel, the two innermost DOALLs can also execute in an overlapped fashion since they are completely independent. Therefore the available parallelism is increased by a factor of 4, assuming the inner loops are of equal size.

4. Code Reordering for Minimizing Communication

During the parallel execution of a program, interprocessor communication causes processor delays and interrupts that are reflected in the program's execution time. If the granularity of the program fragments that are scheduled to execute concurrently is not coarse, the overhead incurred by transmitting data between processors may outweight the benefits of parallel execution.

Communication per se, i.e., the number of data items that must be transmitted between two given tasks is constant. However, in multiprocessor systems the time it takes to transmit the same amount of data at two different instances may vary. In our case we want to measure the effect of communication on program speedup, that is, in terms of processor latencies, or execution time. Consider for example two tasks u and v, where v is data dependent on u. The number of data items that will be sent from u to v is constant for each such pair of tasks. In order to measure communication overhead precisely using a deterministic model, we must

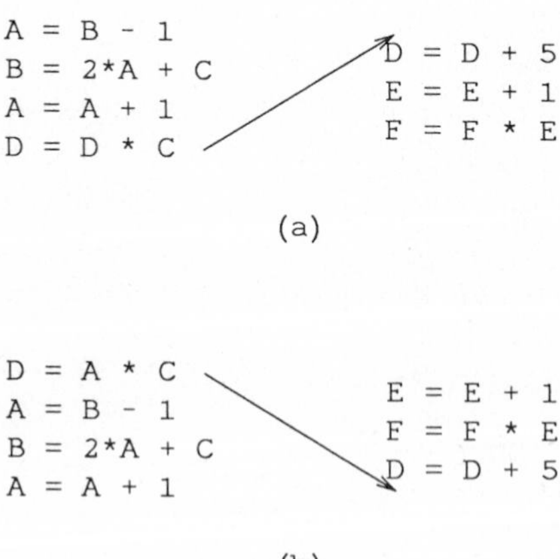

Figure 8. The impact of code reordering in the reduction of communication.

assume that the time it takes to transmit a unit of data between two processors is constant. Delays in processor initiation caused by communicating these data however vary and depend on several factors. One such factor is the relative position of the source of a dependence in the code of task u, and its sink in the code of task v.

Statement (or in general code) reordering can be used in several cases to improve or make possible the application of a certain optimization. For example reordering can be used to improve the effectiveness of DOACROSS loops [Cytr84]. Another application of code reordering is in the reduction of interprocessor communication in parallel computers [Poly86].

The compiler can be used to partition the program into data dependent or independent tasks. Different tasks of a program can execute on different processors, even when there are data dependences across tasks. Is such cases data computed by one or more processors must be communicated to other processors that need them. This communication takes place to satisfy the data dependences, and it affects the execution time of the corresponding tasks in the form of processor delays. In certain cases code reordering can be used to reduce or minimize potential communication delays.

Consider for example the two basic blocks of Figure 8a, where each basic block forms a task. The arc in Figure 8a indicates the intertask data dependence. If these two tasks were scheduled to execute simultaneously on two different processors, the processor executing the second task would have to wait until the first task finishes execution. If we assume that each assignment statement takes a unit of time to execute, then the execution time of the two tasks on two processors will be 7 units; the same as if the two tasks were executed on a single processor. If the statements are reordered as in Figure 8b however, the execution time on two processors would be 4 units of time; the second processor will receive the new value of D by the time it will need it. The problem of compiler optimizations for reducing potential interprocessor communication is a complex problem that remains unsolved.

5. Run–Time Dependence Testing

Most techniques that have been developed so far to analyze array subscripts and determine loop dependences, solve this problem at compile–time. This of course is desirable because there is no run–time overhead. Another alternative would be to determine data dependences dynamically at run–time. This approach has not been fully investigated yet. In this section we consider the problem of *run–time dependence checking* or RDC, and propose a hybrid solution.

```
DO I = 1, N
   A(2I-1) = B(I-1) + 1
   B(2I+1) = A(I+1) * C(I)
ENDO
```

Figure 9. A serial loop.

RDC is important for many reasons. The first and most obvious reason is that in many loops there exist array subscripts that are not amenable to compile–time analysis. In such cases subscript expressions are complex integer functions or even unknown functions about which the compiler cannot draw any conclusions. A particular example which is the subscripted subscript expressions, is treated more analytically later in this section. Another reason (which we consider even more important) for using RDC is the following. Even when the compiler can accurately determine loop dependences, not all instances of the statements may be involved in a dependence, or the distances of the same static dependence may vary between its different instances. This means that even when static dependences indicate that a particular loop is serial, we may still have several iterations of that loop that are dependence free and which could execute in parallel. RDC detects such cases, and it can exploit all parallelism in loops that would otherwise be considered serial. Only iterations that are involved in a dependence are executed in a restricted manner so as to satisfy dependences.

In the first part of this section we consider RDC for singly nested loops that contain array subscripts which cannot be analyzed with the existing compile–time techniques, or serial loops with varying dependence distances which can indeed have some parallelism. RDC can be extended for multiply nested loops following the same procedure.

5.1. The RDC transformation

The cycle shrinking transformation described in Section 3.1 can be used to partially parallelize serial loops when the dependence cycles involve dependences with constant distances. When the dependence distances vary between different iterations, cycle shrinking can still be applied as it was shown in Section 3.2. In such cases however cycle shrinking is rather conservative. RDC is a more appropriate approach since it sequentializes only those iterations that are involved in a true dependence. All remaining iterations can execute in parallel.

Consider for example the loop of Figure 9. The distance of the flow dependence $S_1 \; \delta \; S_2$ can take the values 1, 2, 3,.... If cycle shrinking is applied, a distance of 1 must be assumed. That amounts to a purely serial loop. In reality however the loop of Figure 9 is not totally serial. Figure 10 shows the unrolled version of this loop for the first 10 iterations, and the corresponding data dependences. It is clear that some of the iterations (e.g., iterations 1, 2, 3, 5, 7, 9) could be executed in parallel. RDC can detect such "unstructured" parallelism in statically serial loops.

The transformation which is carried out by the compiler has two phases. An *implicit* and an *explicit* phase. The implicit part involves computations performed by the compiler which are transparent to the user. The explicit phase transforms the loop itself.

The *scalar dependence graph* or SDG of a loop is a dependence graph which shows dependences based on the name of the variables involved and not on the subscripts. Many dependences in an SDG may be superfluous. The *name* of a dependence is the name of the variables involved in that dependence. Index expressions in array references are assumed to be 1–to–1 functions. Also loops are assumed to be normalized for simplicity in notation.

Let us describe the RDC transformation in more detail. The basic idea is to be able to determine at run–time whether a particular iteration of a loop depends on one or more previous

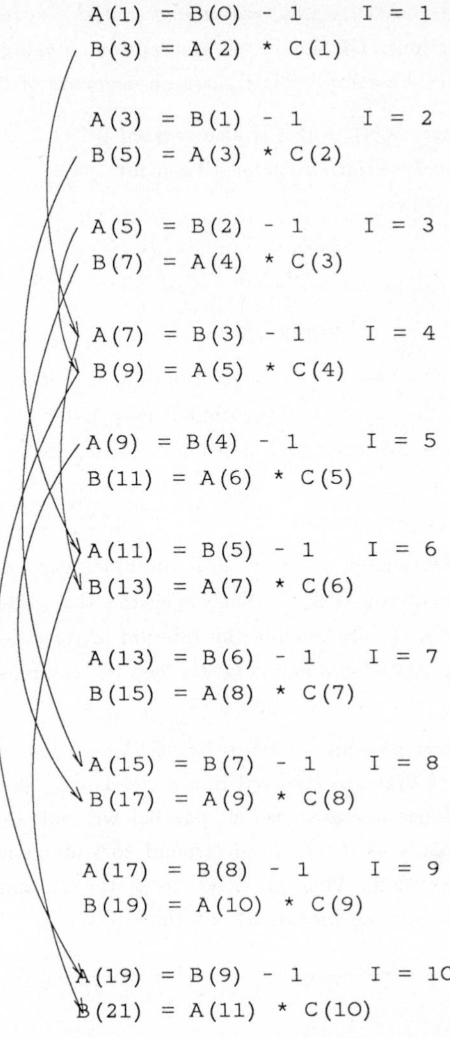

Figure 10. The unrolled version of the loop of Figure 9.

iterations. This requires some recording of relevant information from previous iterations. For a loop `DO I = 1, N` and for a dependence $S_j\ \delta_j\ S_{j+1}$ in that loop, we define the ***dependence source vector*** (or DSV) R_j to be a vector with N elements, where non–zero elements indicate the values of I for which S_j is a dependence source, and zero elements in R_j correspond to values of I for which S_j is not involved in a dependence.

The first step of the transformation is to create a DSV R_j for each flow dependence $S_j \; \delta \; S_{j+1}$ in a cycle. If $e_j(i)$ is the index expression of the left hand side of S_j, then DSV R_j has subscripts in the range $[e_j(1) \ldots e_j(N)]$, assuming index expressions are monotonically increasing/decreasing functions. (If the latter assumption is relaxed, the range is given by $[\min_{1 \le i \le N} e_j(i) \ \ldots \ \max_{1 \le i \le N} e_j(i)]$.) The compiler initializes all elements of S_j to zero. A bit–vector V_j with subscripts in the range $[e_j(1) \ldots e_j(N)]$ is also created for each S_j and is initialized to zero. Vector V_j is called the *synchronization vector*. Then for $I=1,2,\ldots,N$ the compiler initializes the elements of R_j and V_j as follows:

```
DOALL I = 1, N
    Rj(ej(I)) = I
    Vj(ej(I)) = 1
ENDOALL
```

This constitutes the implicit phase of the transformation. It creates a vector R_j for each dependence δ_j and stores in it the values of the original loop index I, for which we may have a potential dependence source. For each such dependence δ_j the explicit phase of RDC inserts the statement

$$\text{IF } (1 \le R_j(h_j(I)) < I) \text{ THEN WAIT ON } V_j(h_j(I))$$

at the beginning of the target loop, where $h_j(I)$ is the index expression of the dependence sink at the right hand side of statement S_{j+1}. When checking the value $R_j(h_j(I))$, we can have an out–of–bound condition if $h_j(I)$ lies outside the interval $[e_j(1) \ \ldots \ e_j(N)]$. In this case however, no dependence is possible. At the end of the target loop the compiler also inserts the statement

$$\text{CLEAR } V_j(e_j(I)) \ .$$

The effect of this is to detect possible unsatisfied dependences at run–time, and synchronize the execution of loop iterations that are involved in a dependence. Iterations which are not possibly involved in a dependence are executed in parallel without any constraints. The clear statement resets the elements of V which correspond to statements with dependence sources that have completed execution. This in effect frees the statements (iterations) with the corresponding dependence sinks, to execute at any time.

```
DOALL I = 1, N
    IF (1 ≤ R1(I+1) < I) WAIT ON V1(I+1)
    IF (1 ≤ R2(I-1) < I) WAIT ON V2(I-1)
    A(2I-1) = B(I-1) + 1
    B(2I+1) = A(I+1) * C(I)
    CLEAR V1(2I-1)
    CLEAR V2(2I+1)
ENDO
```

Figure 11. The loop of Figure 9 after the RDC transformation.

The transformed loop of Figure 9 is shown in Figure 11. The appropriate declarations of vectors R and V are omitted. When the transformed loop is executed as a DOALL, only those iterations that are involved in a dependence will be sequentialized. All other iterations will be executed in parallel. For example, if N=10 in Figure 11, iterations 1, 2, 3, 5, 7, and 9 will be free to execute in parallel immediately. Iterations 4, 6, and 8 must wait for iterations 3 and 5 to complete. Finally iteration 10 must wait for iteration 6 to complete. In a system with 6 processors the transformed loop will take only 3 steps to complete as opposed to 10 steps that would be required for the original serial loop.

5.2. Subscript Blocking

Subscript blocking is similar to RDC and can be used to parallelize loops with subscripted subscripts. The term *subscripted subscript* refers to a variable reference of the form A(f(I)) where A is the identifier of an array, and its subscript f(I) is itself a vector. Examples of loops with subscripted subscripts are shown in Figure 12. Usually the values of subscripted subscripts are unknown at compile-time. Therefore loops that write into array elements of the form A(f(I)) are usually treated as serial. There are two approaches in parallelizing such loops.

The first is by having the compiler generate appropriate code that will detect and exploit parallelism when it occurs at run-time. The second alternative would be to force the loop execute in parallel by synchronizing all its iterations. This however may involve high overhead since synchronization may be used even where it is not needed [ZhYL83].

In the case where the subscripts f(I) and g(J) are specified by a closed form expression a Diophantine equation can be formed. In many real cases however f(I) is simply a vector of integer values that is input to the program, or computed as part of the program. In such cases dependence analysis is impossible, and all loops of this type are serialized. None of the existing commercial or experimental optimizing compilers parallelize general loops with subscripted subscripts. Such loops are frequent in numerical programs that solve sparse systems, and in general manipulate sparse matrices, as well as in Fortran programs that implement combinatorial problems.

The subscript blocking transformation can be implemented in the compiler internally, or as a compiler transformation. It works by examining the values of the subscript vector, (f(I) in Figure 12 for example) and extracting the parallel iterations repeatedly. In general we distinguish two cases: 1) the subscript vector f(I) is known at compile-time, and 2) f(I) is computed at run-time. When f(I) is known at compile-time subscript blocking can be implicitly applied to transform the corresponding loop(s) into DOALL(s) with zero overhead. This is because the part of the transformation that checks the pattern of f(I) is done by the compiler and it is "charged" to compilation time. For the second case where f(I) is not known at compile-time the checking of f(I) must be done at run-time and that may introduce significant overhead. If the original loop is large enough, this overhead is amortized and is negligible compared to the benefits of the extracted parallelism.

Let us consider for example the case of Figure 12a which may involve output dependences. An output dependence may exist from A(f(i)) → A(f(j)) for i>j. If the loop involves only a

```
DO I = 1, N
   . . .
   A(f(I)) = ...
   . . .
ENDO
```

(a)

```
DO I = 1, N
   DO J = 1, N
      . . .
      A(f(I)) = ...
          ... = A(g(J))
      . . .
   ENDO
ENDO
```

(b)

Figure 12. Examples of loops with subscripted subscripts.

single statement, we may execute it automatically as a vector statement. If we assume that memory writes are always performed in the order they are issued, then the loop can be forced to execute as a vector statement without violating any dependences; only the most recent assignment for each element of A will be valid. The above assumption may be valid for SIMD systems but not necessarily for MIMD machines.

To parallelized loops of this type we apply subscript blocking which works as follows. Before we enter the loop where the vector subscript f(I) is used, we examine the values of f(I) and construct the "free-runs" or *source domains* at run-time. In other words we find subsets of successive iterations, none of which contains a statement which is a dependence sink. That is, the statements of a source domain are not involved in a dependence or they are sources of output dependences. To compute the source domains we use two auxiliary vectors V and R. V is a binary vector and R a vector with integer elements. Vector V is used to detect dependences as explained below and R holds the indices of the subscript-vector f(I) that correspond to loop iterations that are involved in a dependence.

Specifically after f(I) is generated, its elements are read and the corresponding elements of the bit-vector V are set to 1. Let m be the last index value inserted in vector R. If a conflict occurs at position x=f(i) of V and y=V(x), then the dependence is discarded if y<m. Otherwise the dependence is saved in vector R. In either case set V(f(I)) $\leftarrow$ I. Since this implies a

```
V(1:N) = 0;
R(1) = 1;
J = 1;

DO  I = 1, N
    IF V(f(I)) >= R(J-1) THEN
          R(J) = I;
          J = J+1;
    V(f(I)) = I;
ENDO

DO  K = 1, J
  DOALL  I = R(K), R(K+1)-1

           A(f(I)) = ...

  ENDOALL
ENDO
```

Figure 13. The subscript blocking transformation for the loop of Figure 12a.

dependence from some f(j) to f(i), j<i, index i is saved in R(k). All iterations up to R(k)-1 can therefore be executed in parallel. This procedure is performed by an extra loop that is created by the compiler before the source loop. The transformed loop of the example in Figure 12a is shown in Figure 13. Obviously the size of vectors f, V and R is equal to the size of array A. As shown in Figure 13 the original serial loop is transformed into a series of DOALL loops. If λ is the number of times a conflict was detected, then we have a total of $\lambda + 1$ DOALLs created out of the original loop.

6. Conclusions

Parallelism in algorithms and programs may implicitly exist, or may be specified at several different levels. When parallelism comes in fixed-size "quantums", it is rather easy to understand and exploit. The unstructured nature of parallelism makes its efficient exploitation and parallel programming to be very complex tasks. Devicing methods and tools that automatically perform these tasks is thus a very important research subject.

In this paper we discussed cycle shrinking and run-time dependence checking, two such compiler schemes that can be used to automatically transform serial loops to a parallel form. Cycle shrinking performs the loop parallelization at compile-time, and packages loop parallelism in "quantums". Run-time dependence checking however, prepares the loop for run-time parallelization. This is achieved by inserting extra code in a source program, which automatically performs dependence checking and bookkeeping during program execution. In this case parallelism is exploited at run–time in an unstructured fashion. Also, the extra code introduced by RDC may induce some run–time overhead. For loops with sparse dependences this overhead should be negligible compared to the resulting improvement.

Both cycle shrinking and RDC aim to parallelize the same type of serial loops in different ways. Given a loop with a dependence cycle, one or the other scheme will be more appropriate for that loop. Which method is more appropriate in each case should be the compiler's responsibility to discover with relatively little effort. We also discussed code reordering and subscript blocking. Code reordering for minimizing communication remains still an open problem, and one of great importance.

REFERENCES

[AhSU86] A.V. Aho, R. Sethi, and J.D. Ullman, *Compilers: Principles, Techniques, and Tools,* Addison-Wesley, Reading, Massachusetts, 1986.

[AlCo72] F.E. Allen and J. Cocke, "A Catalogue of Optimizing Transformations," *Design and Optimization of Compilers,* R. Rustin, Ed. Prentice-Hall, Englewood Cliffs, N.J., 1972, pp. 1-30.

[AlKe82] J.R. Allen and K. Kennedy, "PFC: A Program to Convert Fortran to Parallel Form," Techn. Rept. MASC-TR82-6, Rice University, Houston, Texas, March 1982.

[Alli85] Alliant Computer Systems Corp., "FX/Series Architecture Manual," Acton, Massachusetts, 1985

[ANSI86] American National Standards Institute, *American National Standard for Information Systems. Programming Language Fortran S8 (X3.9-198x).* Revision of X3.9-1978, Draft S8, Version 99, ANSI, New York, April 1986.

[Bane79] U. Banerjee, "Speedup of Ordinary Programs," Ph.D. Thesis, University of Illinois at Urbana-Champaign, DCS Report No. UIUCDCS-R-79-989, October 1979.

[Brod81] B. Brode, "Precompilation of Fortran Programs to Facilitate Array Processing," *Computer 14, 9,* September 1981, pp. 46-51.

[Chen83] S. Chen, "Large-scale and High-speed Multiprocessor System for Scientific Applications - Cray-X-MP-2 Series," *Proc. of NATO Advanced Research Workshop on High Speed Computing, Kawalik(Editor),* pp. 59-67, June 1983.

[Cytr84] R.G. Cytron, "Doacross: Beyond Vectorization for Multiprocessors (Extended Abstract)," *Proceedings of the 1986 International Conference on Parallel Processing,* St. Charles, IL, pp. 836-844, August, 1986.

[Beck81] J. R. Beckman Davies, "Parallel Loop Constructs for Multiprocessors," M.S. Thesis, University of Illinois at Urbana-Champaign, DCS Report No. UIUCDCS-

R–81–1070, May, 1981.

[Kenn80] K. Kennedy, "Automatic Vectorization of Fortran Programs to Vector Form," Technical Report, Rice University, Houston, TX, October, 1980.

[KKLW80] D.J. Kuck, R.H. Kuhn, B. Leasure, and M. Wolfe, "The Structure of an Advanced Vectorizer for Pipelined Processors," *Fourth International Computer Software and Applications Conference,* October, 1980.

[KKPL81] D.J. Kuck, R. Kuhn, D. Padua, B. Leasure, and M. Wolfe, "Dependence Graphs and Compiler Optimizations," *Proceedings of the 8–th ACM Symposium on Principles of Programming Languages,* pp. 207–218, January 1981.

[KDLS86] D. J. Kuck, E. S. Davidson, D. H. Lawrie, and A.H. Sameh, "Parallel Supercomputing Today and the Cedar Approach," *Science 231,* 4740 February 28, 1986, pp. 967–974.

[Kuck78] D.J. Kuck, *The Structure of Computers and Computations,* Volume 1, John Wiley and Sons, New York, 1978.

[MeRo85] P. Mehrotra and J. Van Rosendale, "The Blaze Language: A Parallel Language for Scientific Programming," Rep. 85–29, Institute for Computer Applications in Science and Engineering, NASA Langley Research Center, Hampton, Va., May 1985.

[MiUc84] K. Miura and K. Uchida, "Facom Vector Processor VP–100/VP–200," *High Speed Computation,* NATO ASI Series, Vol. F7, J.S. Kowalik Ed., Springer–Verlag, New York, 1984.

[NIOK84] S. Nagashima, Y. Inagami, T. Odaka, and S. Kawabe, "Design Consideration for a High–Speed Vector Processor: The Hitachi S–810," *Proceedings of the IEEE International Conference on Computer Design: VLSI in Computers,* ICCD 84, IEEE Press, New York, 1984.

[Padu79] D.A. Padua Haiek, "Multiprocessors: Discussions of Some Theoretical and Practical Problems," Ph.D. Thesis, University of Illinois at Urbana–Champaign, DCS Report No. UIUCDCS–R–79–990, November 1979.

[PaWo86] D.A. Padua, and M. Wolfe, "Advanced Compiler Optimizations for Supercomputers," *Communications of the ACM,* Vol. 29, No. 12, pp. 1184–1201, December 1986.

[PoKu87] C. D. Polychronopoulos and D. J. Kuck, "Guided Self-Scheduling: A Practical Scheduling Scheme for Parallel Supercomputers," to appear *IEEE Transactions on Computers,* **Special Issue on Supercomputing,** December, 1987.

[PoKP87] C. D. Polychronopoulos, D. J. Kuck, and D. A. Padua, "Utilizing Multidimensional Loop Parallelism on Large-Scale Parallel Processor Systems," accepted for publication, *IEEE Transactions on Computers,* September 1987.

[Poly86] C. D. Polychronopoulos, "On Program Restructuring, Scheduling, and Communication for Parallel Processor Systems," Ph.D. Thesis, CSRD No. 595, Center for Supercomputing Research and Development, University of Illinois, August, 1986.

[Poly87] C. D. Polychronopoulos, "More on Loop Optimizations," Technical Report, Center for Supercomputing Research and Development, University of Illinois, September, 1987.

[Wolf82] M. J. Wolfe, "Optimizing Supercompilers for Supercomputers," Ph.D. Thesis, University of Illinois at Urbana-Champaign, DCS Report No. UIUCCDCS-R-82-1105, 1982.

[ZhYe84] C. Q. Zhu and P. C. Yew, "A Synchronization Scheme and Its Applications for Large Multiprocessor Systems," *Proc. of the 1984 International Conference on Distributed Computing Systems,* pp. 486–493, May 1984.

MIMD-PARALLELIZATION FOR SUPRENUM

Michael Gerndt, Hans P.Zima*
Universität Bonn
Institut fuer Informatik III
Bertha-von-Suttner-Platz 6
D-5300 Bonn 1
Federal Republic of Germany

ABSTRACT

This paper describes the concept of an interactive software tool that is being developed in the SUPRENUM project for the MIMD-parallelization of Fortran 77 programs. The approach taken is oriented towards an important class of numerical programs operating on a large data domain. The starting point for the parallelization is the partitioning of the data domain; this forms the basis for an appropriate set of transformations yielding a parallel program that can utilize efficiently the massive parallelism of the SUPRENUM architecture.

Keywords: Multiprocessors, analysis of algorithms, program transformations

1 INTRODUCTION

The primary objective of the SUPRENUM project [Trott 86] is the development of a supercomputer system for large-scale scientific computing. Its architecture is characterized by a loosely-coupled hierarchical multiprocessing structure. The basic processing **node** is a single-board computer, consisting of a 32-bit microprocessor (MC 68020) connected to an 8 Mbyte dynamic memory, an 8 MFLOPS vector unit, and a dedicated communication processor. Each node has a local operating system which schedules its processes, supports the communication with other nodes, and manages the local resources. A **cluster** consists of up to 16 nodes which communicate via an ultra-fast parallel bus with

* The work described in this paper is being carried out as a part of the German Supercomputer project SUPRENUM and is being funded by the Federal Ministry for Research and Technology (BMFT), F.R. Germany, under the grant number ITR8502D0. The authors assume all responsibility for the contents of this paper.

a bandwidth of 256 Mbits per second. The structure of an overall system is characterized by a matrix of up to 16 clusters whose rows and columns are connected by ring busses. This will be called the **core system** in the following. A separate operating system machine manages the global resources, I/O, the distribution of the workload, and system recovery. Program execution on the core system is handled by the set of local node operating systems. A more detailed account of the SUPRENUM architecture is given in [BGM 86].

The main application envisaged for SUPRENUM is the numerical simulation of very large problems. Highly specialized algorithms are being developed for these problems, with a particular emphasis on the multigrid method [StuTr 82] which provides one of the fastest known disciplines for solving partial differential equations on general bounded domains. The differential equations are discretized on a grid with a fine mesh size; the solution process is a combination of standard relaxation methods and the computation of corrections on coarser grids. The computations at each grid point are usually local, a typical program will have from 10^6 to 10^9 grid points.

The language to be used in SUPRENUM for writing new numerical application programs is **MIMD Fortran**, an extension of Fortran 77. MIMD Fortran provides a new type of program unit which is called a **task**. A process comes into existence as a result of an activation. of a task. Tasks can be activated more than once; the resulting processes are distinct dynamic entities, with disjoint **local data segments**. Processes can directly access only their local data segment; communication with other processes may be established using asynchronous message passing facilities (SEND and RECEIVE) provided by the operating system. Different processes execute asynchronously as long as they are not restricted by explicit synchronization or communication.

Additional elements of the software environment include a very high-level specification language [WirRu 86], an interactive program development facility and a simulation system. An important criterion for the acceptance of the new machine by the user community is a software tool that supports the transformation of existing Fortran programs into parallel programs that can be efficiently executed on the SUPRENUM computer. Such a tool is the **SUPERB** system (SUprenum ParallelizER Bonn) that is currently being developed at the University of Bonn. An overview of its design has been presented in [ZBGH 86a]; a more detailed description of the system can be found in [ZBGH 86b]. This paper describes the approach to MIMD-parallelization in SUPERB.

The paper is organized as follows: Section 2 gives an overview of the parallelization system and establishes the context for the discussion of MIMD parallelization. The main steps of MIMD-parallelization are then discussed in sections 3 through 5. Concluding remarks are to be found in Section 6.

2 OVERVIEW OF THE PARALLELIZATION SYSTEM

SUPERB is an interactive source-to-source parallelizer: applied to a Fortran 77-program it produces a semantically equivalent parallel MIMD Fortran-program for the SUPRENUM machine. The overall parallelization process may be outlined as follows:

The **Front End** transforms a Fortran 77-program into an internal representation consisting of an attributed abstract tree, an associated symbol table, auxiliary control information such as the interprocedural call graph and intraprocedural program flow graphs, and initial data flow information [ASU 86, Hecht 77, Zima 82, Zima 83].

The central part of the system contains a set of services combined in the **Analysis Component** and the **Transformation Catalog.** The Analysis Component furnishes a collection of tools for data flow and dependence analysis. As is well known, the results of analysis play an important role for determining the applicability and effect of parallelization transformations. We are not discussing any details here but refer to the dependence concepts established by Kuck [Kuck 80], Allen, and Kennedy [AllKe 82, AllKe 83]. Corresponding to the machine architecture which, from a global point of view, is MIMD [Flynn 72], but, on the level of the basic processing node, contains a vector processing unit, parallelization is performed in two phases: First, an attempt is made to determine coarse-grained parallelism by distributing program execution over a set of processes (MIMD-parallelization); second, every process is analyzed for statements in loops that can be rewritten as vector operations (vectorization). While a large body of knowledge exists about automatic vectorization [Kuck 80, AllKe 82, Arno 82], MIMD parallelization has for practical purposes been carried out up to now almost exclusively manually [AdaVo 84, Holt 85].

The **Back End** uses the information contained in the transformed internal representation to produce a parallelized MIMD Fortran program. Directives are included to enhance the efficiency of a compiler creating object code for the SUPRENUM system.

We now turn to the proper subject of this paper, MIMD-parallelization. Due to the loosely-coupled architecture of SUPRENUM the problem of implementing MIMD-parallelization can be restated as the task of translating a sequential program into a parallel program with coarse grained parallelism and minimal communication and synchronization overhead. Early work begun in this field in the late 60's [Bern 66, Rama 69, Russ 69] has only very limited significance for our problem because loops - the only sources of massive parallelism - were not adequately taken into account. More recent proposals [Cytr 84] are not directly applicable to the highly specialized problem under discussion.

SUPERB is oriented towards the parallelization of an important class of numerical algorithms that can be characterized as follows: (1) The programs work on a mesh or mesh-like data domain, (2) the computations at the mesh points are local, i.e. depend only on the values of a small number of points in the neighborhood, and (3) the problems to be solved are very large. The approach to MIMD-parallelization taken in SUPERB is based on domain partitioning: the data domain of the sequential program is partitioned into sections in such a way that each section essentially defines the local data segment of a process. Thus the selected partition determines the process structure of the resulting parallelized program. Criteria for the choice of a partition include the size of the application, the number of processors available for an execution of the program, the ranges of DO-loops, and the structure of the dependences occurring between the statements of a loop.

MIMD- parallelization will be performed in three steps:

Step 1: Splitting the program

This step is necessary due to the requirement that all I/O operations and certain control functions such as the creation of processes must be executed on the operating system machine. As a consequence, the program is split into an **initial task** that includes all I/O and is executed on the operating system machine, and a **subtask** that describes the actual computation of the program. The activations of the subtask create the processes executing in the core system. Splitting is further discussed in Section 3.

Step 2: Partitioning the data domain

In this step, the arrays of the program's data domain are partitioned and associated with the local segments of processes. This will be discussed in Section 4.

Step 3: Transforming the subtask

The choice of a partition determines together with the process structure of the program a set of requirements for the transformation of the subtask. Statements in the subtask must in general be masked in order to guarantee that they are executed only in the processes they belong to, and communication statements must be inserted in order to satisfy any true dependences that exist between statements executed in different processes. Some aspects of this transformation relating to DO-loops will be discussed in Section 5.

In the current practice of application program development, MIMD-parallelization is performed manually. In contrast to this, SUPERB provides the user with analysis information and an elaborate set of tools to support the transformation. It must be made clear in this place, however, that due to the inherent incompleteness of analysis information, MIMD-parallelization cannot be done fully automatically. We assume a knowledgeable user to control and tune the parallelization process, possibly experimenting with different strategies and repeating some of the steps in difficult cases.

3 SPLITTING

A parallelized program consists of an **initial task** and a **subtask**. The operating system initiates the execution by starting the initial task, thus creating the initial process which executes on the operating system machine. All I/O-operations must be executed in this process. In addition, the initial process activates the subtask, creating processes that are executed in the core system. The initial task is activated only once for an application; it is terminated only after all subtask processes have terminated.

According to this organization which is closely related to the hardware architecture of SUPRENUM, the first step of MIMD-parallelization consists of the splitting of each program unit into code for the initial task and the subtask. Essentially, this means that all I/O-statements have to be collected in the initial task and the corresponding communication statements must be generated in the initial task and the subtask. We illustrate this by a simple example:

Example: Splitting of a main program

Original program:

```
   AMAX = 0.0
   DO 10 I = 1, 10000
    READ (5,1) A
    IF (ABS(A) - AMAX) 10, 10, 20
20  AMAX = ABS(A)
10 CONTINUE
   WRITE (6,1) AMAX
   STOP
1  FORMAT (F10.2)
   END
```

Result of transformation (abridged):

Initial Task

```
    .
    .
    .
    DO 10 I = 1, 10000
     READ (5,1) A
     SEND A
10  CONTINUE
    RECEIVE AMAX
    WRITE (6,1) AMAX
    .
    .
    .
 1  FORMAT (F10.2)
    END
```

Subtask

```
    .
    .
    AMAX = 0.0
    DO 10 I = 1, 10000
     RECEIVE A
     IF (ABS(A) - AMAX) 10, 10, 20
20   AMAX = ABS(A)
10  CONTINUE
    SEND AMAX
    .
    .
    .
```

This example highlights the basic idea of treating I/O-operations in the splitting process, but it is not realistic: due to a considerable start-up time for messages that dominates the time needed for communication of small messages, the 10000 SEND/RECEIVE operations to be executed in the loop would slow up the system to an intolerable degree. Standard techniques known from vectorization can be used to decisively improve the transformation: if scalar expansion [Kuck 80] is applied to A in the loop, the whole array can be transferred in a single message.

We finish the discussion in this section with a few additional remarks concerning some aspects of splitting not yet mentioned:

1. The initial task partially mimicks the control flow of the original program units. This has to be done for all parts of the program that contain I/O-statements.

2. The SUPRENUM communication mechanism does not guarantee that messages arrive in the order in which they were sent. As a consequence, the organization of message queues must be simulated in the application program. This is an implicit part of SEND and RECEIVE not shown in the example.

3. The initial process is terminated after a signal has been received from all subtask processes signifying the termination of their execution.

4 PARTITIONING THE DATA DOMAIN

The most important step in the MIMD-parallelization of a program is the selection of a partition for the data domain of the subtask.

The major part of the subtask's data domain consists of arrays. Partitioning of arrays is performed by subdividing them into sections that will be 1-1 associated with processes and allocated in their local data segment. The SUPRENUM architecture permits a process to directly access only its own local data segment: access to data of other processes can only be gained via message passing. Therefore, the sizes and shapes of array sections as determined by a given partition imply a certain communication overhead, and thus considerably influence the speed with which the final parallelized program can be executed. In general, partitioning cannot be done by the system alone: even with data flow and dependence analysis driven to their outmost theoretical and practical limits there is in general not sufficient information available to determine automatically an optimal partition for a given program. Instead, the parallelization system in this step relies heavily on the user who will have to make the strategic decisions, supported by analysis information provided by the system.

We now discuss the basic relationships underlying partitioning in more detail. Let:

N denote the number of processes created for the subtask,
$P = \{p_i \mid i = 1,...N\}$ the set of (subtask) processes, and
A an arbitrary arrray to be partitioned. A is interpreted as a set of subscripted variables.

Partitioning array A consists of two parts: specification of the **local segments** of A, and determination of an **overlap area** for each segment.

(1) Specification of the local segments

Specification of the local segments of A means the decomposition of A into N mutually disjoint subsets A_i of A (i = 1,...N) such that the following holds:

(a) $A = \bigcup_{i=1}^{N} A_i$

(b) A_i is to be associated with process p_i (i = 1,...N).
This means that all variables in A_i are to be allocated in the local data segment of process p_i, and all statements assigning a value to any such variable must be executed in p_i.

(c) For all i,j with 1 <= i,j <= N and $i \neq j$ A_i and A_j have no element in common.

(d) The function loc: ARRAYS x P --> SUBARRAYS
with loc(A,i) = A_i specifies for every array the partitioning with respect to each process.

(2) Determining the overlap areas

Assume that a process p_i $(i = 1,...N)$ needs read-access to a variable v not contained in its local data segment (i.e., v is not assigned to in p_i but in another process, say p_j). Then, the value of v must be sent from p_j to p_i using the communication mechanisms of the system, and p_i has to reserve space for v in its local data segment. All variables with these characteristics are collected in the overlap area of a process.

We define accordingly a function ovl: ARRAYS x P --> SUBARRAYS with ovl(A,p_i) = the overlap area for A with respect to process p_i.

We are now ready to discuss the composition of the local data segments of processes. In our approach not all arrays must be partitioned. Arrays with a small number of elements needed in many processes can be treated more efficiently if they are left unpartitioned: this means that these arrays are allocated in the local data segment of each process, and each process executes all assignments with respect to such arrays. Scalar variables are handled in the same way. As a consequence, unpartitioned arrays and scalar variables pose no problem with respect to communication.

The local data domain LOC(i) and the overlap area OVL(i) for each process p_i $(i = 1,...N)$ can now be defined as follows:

$$LOC(i) = \bigcup_{A \in ARRAYS} loc(A,p_i) \quad \{A \mid A \text{ is an unpartitioned array}\}$$

$$\{v \mid v \text{ is a scalar variable}\}$$

$$OVL(i) = \bigcup_{A \in ARRAYS} ovl(A,p_i).$$

The local data segment of process p_i is the union of LOC(i) and OVL(i).

<u>Example</u>:

Let A denote a two-dimensional array: A(100,100), and assume the computation to be characterized by the statement:

```
DO 10 J = 1, 100
 DO 20 I = 1, 100
  .
  .
  .
  A(I,J) = 0.25 * ( A(I,J+1) + A(I,J-1) + A(I-1,J) + A(I+1,J) )
  .
  .
  .
```

Now assume that N = 100, and the local segments of A are defined as "squares" with 10 elements in every dimension. Then each segment is of the form:

$$A(L_1:R_1,\ L_2:R_2)$$

with $L_1 = s*10 + 1$, $R_1 = t*10 + 1$ for some integer numbers s, t

with $0 <= s,t <= 9$, and $R_k = L_k + 9$ for $k = 1,2$.

The statement in the DO-loop shows that each inner local segment must be supplemented by an overlap area that includes exactly one element to the left and right in each dimension. Thus the segment specified above, together with its overlap area includes the following elements:

$$A(L_1-1:R_1+1,\ L_2-1:R_2+1)$$

As the example already indicated, the specification of the overlap area depends on the characteristics of the computations performed for the array. The choice of the partition, together with the dependence relationships determine the communication requirements of the program and the utilization profile of the vector units in the nodes.

The information provided by a partition can be used by the parallelizer to automatically generate the required data declarations and communication statements, and to modify the loops of the subtask by either masking the statements in their body or adjusting the loop range. This will be discussed in more detail in the following section.

5 TRANSFORMING THE SUBTASK

In this section we discuss transformations to be applied to the subtask in order to produce a correct and efficient parallel program. As loops are the only sources of massive parallelism, we restrict ourselves in the following to the discussion of DO-loops.

As mentioned above, a process that executes a specific iteration of a loop must have the required code and data items in its local data segment. MIMD-parallelization must distribute the loop iterations among the existing processes, as uniformly as possible and with a minimum of communication overhead. The ideal case occurs if the structure of the loops match perfectly the partitions for the arrays accessed in the loop, and there are but few dependences between statements executed in different processes. For a single loop the transformation can be sketched as follows:

Let B(I) denote a sequence of statements (the loop body), as a function of the loop induction variable I, and N the number of processes. Then:

```
    DO 10 I = 1, M
     B(I)
10  CONTINUE
```

will, if appropriate conditions are fulfilled, M = N*L, and B' is an adequately modified version of B, be transformed to:

```
    DOALL  K = 1, N
     DO 10 J = 1, L
      B'( (K-1)*L+J )
10   CONTINUE
    END DOALL
```

The DOALL notation signifies that the inner loops are executed in parallel by the N processes, with the degree of parallelism only restricted by the communication and synchronization required between different processes. We call each such inner loop a **process loop**. The meaning of the conventional dependence concept, when applied to process loops as primitives instead of statements, becomes different: loop-independent dependence [AllKe 83] does not exist, anti-dependence is resolved by the communication, and output dependence also cannot occur.

In the following we illustrate various aspects of the transformation by examples.

Example:

Let the arrays A, B, C be declared as A(0:1000), B(1:1000), C(1:1000). Assume that the partitions of A and C are characterized by local segments A(L:R) and C(L:R), respectively, where L and R are process-specific. The overlap area associated with A(L:R) contains A(L-1). The overlap area for the segments of C is empty. B is unpartitioned.

```
    DO 10 I=1,1000
S1:  A(I) = B(I) + A(I)
S2:  C(I) = A(I-1)
10  CONTINUE
```

The only dependence existing is a loop-carried true dependence [AllKe 83] from S1 to S2. Loop distribution is, therefore feasible. However, it requires the insertion of communication:

```
     DOALL (L,R,...)
      DO 20 I=L,R
       A(I) = B(I) + A(I)
20    CONTINUE
      SEND A(R)
      RECEIVE A(L-1)
      DO 30 I=L,R
       C(I) = A(I-1)
30    CONTINUE
     END DOALL
```

It can be easily seen that the attempt to parallelize this loop before distribution would have produced a synchronized DOALL-loop resulting in serial execution.

Example:

Assume that A, B, and C are defined and partitioned as in the previous example, with the only exception that the overlap area associated with A(L:R) consists of the variable A(R+1). We consider the following loop:

```
      DO 10 I=1,1000
 S1:   A(I) = B(I)
 S2:   C(I) = A(I+1) + A(I)
10    CONTINUE
```

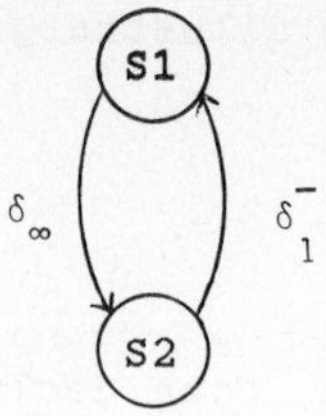

Here, the dependence graph is cyclic; vectorization therefore would not be feasible. However, considering the dependences that arise for process loops, we recognize that the loop-independent dependence and the anti-dependence both disappear. Parallel code can therefore be generated as follows:

```
      DOALL (L,R,...)
       SEND A(L)
       RECEIVE A(R+1)
       DO 10 I=L,R
        A(I) = B(I)
        C(I) = A(I+1) + A(I)
10     CONTINUE
      END DOALL
```

A final example shows that the insertion of communication statements must be performed judiciously in order to minimize the start-up overheads. A problem of a similar nature was already encountered in splitting (see Section 3).

Example:

Let the arrays A, B, C be declared as A(0:1000, 1:1000), B(1:1000, 1:1000), C(1:1000, 1:1000). Assume that the partitions of A, B and C are characterized by local segments with index ranges (L_1:R_1, L_2:R_2), and the associated overlap area of A contains exactly the elements {A(L_1-1,J) | L_2 <= J <= R_2}.

```
   DO 20 I = 1,1000
      DO 10 J = 1,1000
       A(I,J) = B(I,J)
                .
                .
                .
       C(I,J) = A(I-1,J)
10    CONTINUE
20 CONTINUE
```

can be transformed as follows:

```
DOALL (L1,R1, L2,R2,...)
   DO 20 I = MAX(L1,1), MIN(R1,1000)
     DO 10 J = MAX(L2,1), MIN(R2,1000)
      A(I,J) = B(I,J)
      IF (I=R1) THEN
         SEND A(I,J)
      ENDIF
              .
              .

      IF (I=L1) THEN
         RECEIVE A(I-1,J)
      ENDIF
      C(I,J) = A(I-1,J)
10    CONTINUE
20 CONTINUE
END DOALL
```

Parts of this loop can be executed in parallel; however the communication overhead is very high due to the large number of messages to be sent. An alternative approach consists of collecting all SEND and RECEIVE operations into a single statement:

```
DOALL (L1,R1, L2,R2,...)
   RECEIVE A(L1-1, L2:R2)
   DO 20 I = MAX(L1,1), MIN(R1,1000)
     DO 10 J = MAX(L2,1), MIN(R2,1000)
      A(I,J) = B(I,J)
              .
              .
              .
      C(I,J) = A(I-1,J)
10    CONTINUE
20 CONTINUE
   SEND A(R1, L2:R2)
END DOALL
```

In this approach, communication is much more efficient, however with a resulting loss of parallelism. It requires a conscientious examination of all relevant parameters - which in general are not completely known to the parallelizer - to provide the basis for a rational choice between the two alternatives.

The subtask processes obtained by MIMD parallelization can be subjected to vectorization. Its objective is the detection of statements in loops that can be rewritten as vector operations. The techniques for this transformation are well known [Kuck 80, AllKe 82, AllKe 83] and will not be further discussed here.

6 CONCLUSION

This paper discussed MIMD-parallelization as realized in the SUPRENUM parallelization system SUPERB. The loosely-coupled architecture of SUPRENUM causes difficulties that are not being encountered in systems with shared memory. These problems are met in two ways: First, it is acknowledged that not all necessary parameters for the transformation of a program into parallel form can be determined automatically. Therefore the approach to parallelization is inherently interactive, leaving strategic decisions that are beyond the capabilities of the system to the user. Second, the starting point of MIMD-parallelization is the choice of a partition for the program's data domain. This forms the basis for an appropriate set of transformations yielding a highly parallel program that can utilize the massive parallelism of the SUPRENUM architecture.

ACKNOWLEDGEMENT We would like to thank Barbara M.Chapman for her helpful comments on an earlier version of the paper.

REFERENCES

[AdaVo 84] Adams,L.M.,Voigt,R.G.: A Methodology for Exploiting Parallelism in the Finite Element Process
In: Kowalik,J.S.(Ed.): High-Speed Computation, NATO ASI Series, 373-392, Springer-Verlag (1984)

[ASU 86] Aho,A.V.,Sethi,R.,Ullman,J.D.: Compilers. Principles, Techniques, and Tools
Addison-Wesley (1986)

[AllKe 82] Allen,J.R.,Kennedy,K.: PFC: A Program to Convert Fortran to Parallel Form
Proc.IBM Conf.Parallel Comp. and Scientific Computations (1982)

[AllKe 83] Allen,J.R.: Dependence Analysis for Subscripted Variables and its Application to Program Transformations
Ph.D.Thesis, Rice University, Houston, Texas (1983)

[ANSI 86] American National Standards Institute X3J3: Fortran 8X Version 98 (Jan 1986)

[Arno 82] Arnold,C.N.: Performance Evaluation of Three Automatic Vectorization Packages
Proc.1979 Internat.Conf.Parallel Processing,235-242 (1982)

[Bern 66] Bernstein,A.J.: Analysis of Programs for Parallel Processing
IEEE Trans.Electronic Computers EC-15, 757-762 (Oct 1966)

[BGM 86] Behr,P.M.,Giloi,W.K.,Muehlenbein,H.: SUPRENUM: The German Supercomputer Architecture - Rationale and Concepts
Proc.1986 International Conference on Parallel Processing (1986)

[Cytr 84] Cytron,R.G.: Compile-Time Scheduling and Optimization for Asynchronous Machines
Ph.D. Dissertation,Dept. of Computer Science, University of Illinois at Urbana-Champaign (1984)

[Flynn 72] Flynn,M.J.: Some Computer Organizations and Their Effectiveness
IEEE Trans. Computers,C-21,No.9,948-960 (Sep 1972)

[Hecht 77] Hecht,M.S.: Flow Analysis of Computer Programs
North Holland (1977)

[Holt 85] Holter,W.H.: A Vectorized Multigrid Solver for the Three-Dimensional Poisson Equation
In:Emmen,A.H.L.(Ed.):Supercomputer Applications,Elsevier(1985)

[Kuck 80] Kuck,D.J.,Kuhn,R.H.,Leasure,B.,Wolfe,M.: The Structure of an Advanced Retargetable Vectorizer
Proc.COMPSAC '80 (1980)

[RamGo 69] Ramamoorthy,C.V., Gonzalez,M.J.: A Survey of Techniques for Recognizing Parallel Processable Streams in Computer Programs
In: Proc.AFIPS 1969 Fall Joint Comp.Conf., 1-15 (1969)

[Russ 69] Russell,E.C.: Automatic Program Analysis
Ph.D.Dissertation,Dept.of Electrical Engineering, University of California, Los Angeles, California (1969)

[StuTr 82] Stueben,K.,Trottenberg,U.: Multigrid Methods: Fundamental Algorithms, Model Problem Analysis and Applications
Proc.Conf.Multigrid Methods, Lecture Notes in Mathematics, Vol.960, Springer-Verlag (1982)

[Trott 86] Trottenberg,U.: SUPRENUM - an MIMD Multiprocessor System for Multi-Level Scientific Computing
Proc.CONPAR 86,48-52 (1986)

[WirRu 86] Wirtz,G.,Ruppelt,Th.: Entwurf einer Spezifikationssprache fuer SUPRENUM
Research Report SUPRENUM 861002, Bonn University (1986)

[ZBGH 86a] Zima,H.P.,Bast,H.-J.,Gerndt,M.,Hoppen,P.J.: Semi-Automatic Parallelization of Fortran Programs
Proc.CONPAR 86,287-294 (1986)

[ZBGH 86a] Zima,H.P.,Bast,H.-J.,Gerndt,M.,Hoppen,P.J.: SUPERB: The SUPRENUM Parallelizer Bonn

[Zima 82] Zima,H.P.: Compilerbau I: Analyse
Reihe Informatik Band 36, Bibliographisches Institut, Mannheim (1982)

[Zima 83] Zima,H.P.: Compilerbau II: Synthese und Optimierung
Reihe Informatik Band 37, Bibliographisches Institut, Mannheim (1983)

LOOP QUANTIZATION OR UNWINDING DONE RIGHT

Alexandru Nicolau[1]
Department of Computer Science
Cornell University
Ithaca, New York 14853

Abstract— Loop unwinding is a known technique for reducing loop overhead, exposing parallelism and increasing the efficiency of pipelining. Traditional loop unwinding is limited to the innermost loop in a group of nested loops and the amount of unwinding is either fixed or has to be specified by the user, on a case by case basis. In this paper we present a general technique for automatically unwinding multiply nested loops, explain its advantages over other transformation techniques and illustrate its practical effectiveness. Loop Quantization could be beneficial by itself, or coupled with other loop transformations (e.g., Do-across).

1. Introduction

Loop unwinding has been long known as an effective way to increase the efficient utilization of pipelined machines. More recently loop unwinding has emerged as a primary technique for exploiting fine-grained parallelism within loops, notably for Very Large Instruction Word machines, a form of very tightly coupled multiprocessors [9]. Loop unwinding helps exploit fine-grain parallelism by providing a large number of operations (the unwound loop body) which can then be scheduled by operation-level code transformations such as Trace Scheduling [10] or Percolation Scheduling [19]. The operations in the unwound loop body come from previously separate iterations and thus are freer of the order imposed by the original loop. Inside this (larger) loop-body, operations can be scheduled for parallel execution (by the compiler) subject only to data dependencies. Large amounts of parallelism which is too irregular to exploit by traditional methods (e.g., vectorization) can be found in this way.

The basic unwinding technique is very simple. The body of the loop together with the control code (i.e., counter and exit-test) is replicated a number of times. For example, figure 1b shows the effect of unwinding the loop in figure 1a three times. This form of unwinding is usually used for simple *for* loops, but other forms of iteration can be dealt with in similar fashion.

The unwound loop can sometimes be simplified by removing the intermediate tests and jumps introduced by the unwinding process. This may require static (i.e., compile-time) knowledge about the number of times the loop will be executed. For example, if the user knows that the loop will be executed a multiple of three times, the extra tests and jumps in figure 1b could be removed. Alternatively, if the pattern of memory references of the loop can be determined by static analysis (e.g., using disambiguation techniques [4], [18]), some extra memory locations can be allocated to allow extra iterations of the unwound loop to execute safely. For example, even if no information about the number of times the loop in figure 1a is executed is available at compile time, we may still safely remove the tests and jumps as before, if we add 2 extra elements to array A. Note that this increase is a function of the number of times the loop is unwound, not of the number of times the original loop body gets executed. More complex methods for the removal of tests and jumps from unwound loops exist, including testing at run-time the number of times a

[1]This work is supported in part by NSF grant DCR 8502884, ONR grant N00014-86-K-0215, and the Cornell NSF Supercomputing Center.

```
For i = x, y do                 For i = x, y, 3 Do
    A[i] := expr(i);                A[i] := expr(i);
End;                                If i>y Then Goto exit;
                                    A[i + 1] := expr(i + 1);
                                    If i + 1>y Then Goto exit;
                                    A[i + 2] := expr(i + 2);
                                End;
                              exit:
```

Figure 1: Simple Loop Unwinding: (a) Original Loop. (b) Loop Unwound 3 times.

loop is executed and then executing an appropriately unwound loop based on this information. While such methods can effectively deal with statically unpredictable loops and references, they introduce some overhead.

The above description surveys current uses of loop unwinding. But current techniques do not allow unwinding multiply nested loops. This is a major disadvantage, as it significantly limits the usefulness of loop unwinding, particularly for fine-grained parallelism architectures such as VLIW's [7], [11], ROPE [20], Microflow [22] and Alliant [3]. In this context, the parallelism may be distributed across several nested loops, so unwinding only one of the loops will not achieve the best results. This situation occurs frequently and is illustrated in section 3. In addition, the correctness criteria we apply for multiple loop unwinding would be useful in the context of Do-across [8], when limited resources (processors) are available and pipelining only the innermost loop doesn't achieve good speedups.

In the rest of this paper we present a technique, called Loop Quantization, that overcomes this problem by allowing correct multiple-loop unwinding for arbitrary nested loops. We will also describe how the decision on the bounds of Quantization can be automated. That is, we will show how to automatically determine the amount of unwinding needed to efficiently execute a loop on a particular machine. While the user may be able to make such decisions for single loop unwinding, dealing with multiple loop unwinding by hand requires significant effort and is extremely error prone. Loop quantization is being integrated in a parallelizing compiler under development at Cornell.

Quantization allows the extraction of parallelism that was previously believed to be detectable only at runtime [13]. Furthermore, quantization applies in cases where higher-level parallelism exploitation methods (like vectorization and loop interchange) do not apply, but where a significant amount of fine-grained parallelism is still present.

Loop Quantization can help achieve significant speedups in scientific code by allowing better pipelining and fine-grain parallelism exploitation. The main loop of weather code, for example, is naturally amenable to Quantization, as are the Livermore loops[16] in their nested context. Since Quantization rearranges the order of execution of the loop iterations less than other transformations, and since it can expose even irregular fine-grain parallelism, it can be applied to a large variety of code. Furthermore, quantized loops naturally map onto parallel architectures with hypercube or cube-connected-cycles topologies (e.g., Cosmic-cube[21], Microflow[22]).

2. Loop Quantization

Given enough processors, optimal speedups can be achieved if all nested loops were fully unwound. Since no artificial constraints would be introduced by the indexing order, the only limitation would be imposed by data dependencies.[2] Techniques such as Percolation Scheduling

[2] A data dependency is a relationship between two instructions that use a common register or memory location.

could then be applied to exploit the available parallelism. Unfortunately, such complete unwinding is not usually feasible because of processor and memory limitations[3] and because the loop bounds are not always known at compile time. Still, even if the amount of unwinding is limited, we need the ability to unwind all loops. Unwinding just the innermost loop is not satisfactory, since it exposes parallelism only in that loop, whereas the parallelism is often available between several of the outer loops.

The basic idea of Loop Quantization is to unwind a few iterations of all nested loops. The way we do the unwinding is constrained by three factors:

1. Correctness. Quantization should not alter the order in which data-dependent statements are executed.

2. Available parallelism. Unwind so as to maximize the parallelism exposed – i.e., minimize dependency chains.

3. Space considerations.

2.1 Formalization of Loop Quantization

We will now formalize the problem of Loop Quantization. This will enable us to derive formal conditions for when and how quantization can be applied. These conditions are introduced in section 2.2. The actual use of these conditions in the automatic quantizations of loops is described in section 2.3.

We will consider n nested loops, where loop n is the innermost and loop 1 is the outermost, as shown in figure 2. A *loop index* I_l is associated with each loop l. We will denote by i_l particular values of I_l. An *increment*, K_l, may also be specified for each loop l. We will denote particular values of K_l by k_l. Originally, the loops are assumed to be normalized to range from 1 to N_l with increments of 1 (our system can bring them into this normal form).

In the following discussion we assume that the n loops are the only ones affected by the quantization and that indirect references (i.e. references involving computed addresses) are linear functions of the iteration vectors.[4] We will also assume that two references to an array A, namely $A[i_1, i_2, ..., i_n]$ and $A[j_1, j_2, ..., j_n]$ are equal if and only if $i_1 = j_1, i_2 = j_2, ..., i_n = j_n$. That is, no ambiguous *equivalence* and *common* statements are used.

To unwind loop i k_i times, the loop-body is duplicated k_i times. In the first duplication of the original body the index I_i is unchanged; in the second, each occurrence of I_i is replaced with $I_i + 1$, and so on, all the way up to $I_i - k_i - 1$. For the next outermost loop, $(i - 1)$, the newly unwound body is itself replicated k_{i-1} times, with indexes I_{i-1} to $I_{i-1} + k_{i-1} - 1$ replacing I_{i-1}. This is essentially equivalent to unwinding all the nested loops fully, when their upper bounds are $k_1, .., k_n$ respectively. For this unwinding to be useful, it must preserve the semantics of the original loop. Informally, this means that each statement S executed for some original index-vector value $\bar{i} = (i_1, ..., i_n)$, will have available to it exactly the same data when the unwound loop is executed as it would have in the original loop. In particular, if the statement was accessing a value computed in an iteration preceding it (i.e., calculated by a statement with an index vector $\bar{j} \leq \bar{i}$, where "$\leq$" denotes lexicographic ordering[5]), it should be able to access this value in the unwound loop. Similarly, the statement S should not access values computed in later iterations of the original loop(s). Our goal is to find a set $\{k_1, ... k_n\}$ of loop increments (steps) such that

---

The second operation cannot begin until the first operation is finished using the register or memory.

[3]Mainly processor limitations—if we were to have enough processing power to execute the unwound loops in parallel, we could probably afford the memory.

[4]An iteration (or index) vector [15] consists of the setting of the induction variables that uniquely identify an iteration of the nested loops.

[5]That is, the relation is determined by the pairwise comparison from left to right of the elements of $\bar{i}$ and $\bar{j}$. The first pair of elements that are not equal determines the result of the comparison. This comparison can often be made (symbolically) even when the elements are expressions involving variables. For example the expression $2j + 3i + 4$ is greater than or equal to $i + 3$ for all positive values of i and j. Our system can automatically determine this. Note that this is *not* syntactic comparison, but symbolic evaluation akin to MACSYMA [5].

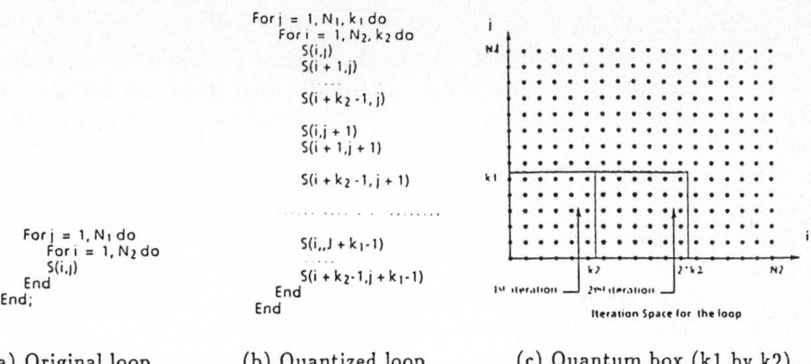

(a) Original loop (b) Quantized loop (c) Quantum box (k1 by k2)

Figure 2: Sample 2 dimensional loop quantization

the quantized loops preserve the semantics of the original ones (i.e., given the same input they both produce the same output).

If only the innermost loop is unwound no problems arise, as this preserves the execution order of the iterations. However, when other loops are also unwound, the looping consists of a *n-dimensional* box B with dimensions k_1 by k_2 by...k_n (see figure 2). All the statements in B are executed before the box is shifted (by a "quantum jump") along any of the dimensions. The movement along the n dimensions, while quantized, is still in the normal loop order (i.e., first along dimension n, then along dimension $n-1$, etc). This obviously alters the order of execution. A statement S_1 in the original iteration $(i_1+1, i_2, ..., i_n)$ may be included in this box (in fact it will be, if loop 1 is unwound at all) and thus may be executed before a statement S_2 in the original iteration $(i_1, ..., i_n + k_n)$ (which already falls outside the box), even though in the original execution the latter would precede the former. This will not present any problem if S_1 does not require the results of S_2, or if S_2 does not use information that is altered by S_1. If such dependencies exist, however, the particular quantization is illegal, although other quantizations may succeed. We will discuss the choice of a particular quantization in section 2.3. We need not worry about incorrect execution order when both dependent statements are inside the same box since the execution order of such statements is preserved by the quantization.[6]

To fix the dependency problem, we could increase the size of the box to include any dependent references. This would ensure correctness, since all dependent pairs of operations whose order would be reversed as a result of quantization would now be contained in the box and thus executed subject to their dependencies. Unfortunately, this process can be self replicating, and the unwinding might have to repeat until the bound of the array encompassing the problematic references is reached. Since in many applications one of the dimensions of the array is quite small, full unwinding on that dimension may be reasonable.

In cases where dimensions are large or full unwinding along some dimension cannot resolve the problem, the alternative is to only allow unwindings of loops which do not cause dependencies to be violated. For example, a quantization yielding a box B bounded by $(i_1, ..., i_n)$ and $(i_1 + k_1 - 1, ..., i_n + k_n - 1)$ must be disallowed if B contains references to a variable written in the original iteration $\bar{j} = (i_1, ..., i_{n-1} + k_{n-1} - 2, i_n + k_n)$, which occurs in a box executed after B. Limiting the amount of unwinding to avoid violating dependencies should not be much of a constraint as long as we are utilizing the (limited) resources fully. If utilization is too low we can unwind one of the loops further.

[6]Since Loop Quantization changes the order of the iterations less drastically than more global transformations (e.g., interchange), quantization can succeed even when global transformations would not apply.

2.2 Loop Quantization Conditions

2.2.1 Dependencies We will now formally define the dependencies and the conditions under which they may be violated by loop quantization. Assuming that useless writes to memory are eliminated by dead-code removal, two types of dependencies may be violated as a result of Loop Quantization:

Write-before-Read: A memory location is written in iteration $\bar{i}$, and in iteration $\bar{j} > \bar{i}$ the same memory location is read.

Write-after-Read: A memory location is read in iteration $\bar{i}$, and in iteration $\bar{j} > \bar{i}$ the same memory location is written.

The execution order of all statements connected by such dependencies must be preserved to ensure semantic correctness. The order of independent statements is irrelevant.

To determine whether a dependency exists between two statements and to establish the dependency type, reads in one statement are compared with writes in the other. Since scalar variable accesses are invariant with respect to the loops, they cannot affect the semantic correctness of the quantization. Furthermore dependencies between references in the same iteration are not affected by quantization. Thus, it is sufficient to only consider dependencies caused by indirect references occurring in different iterations.

Memory disambiguation techniques for determining (to the extent possible at compile time) whether two indirect references might access the same memory location can be found in [4], [18]. They involve the derivation of primitive expressions for the array indexes. These expressions contain compile-time constants, and variables whose values cannot be derived at compile-time. To determine whether two references conflict, the primitive index expressions are symbolically equated and the resulting diophantine equation is solved. If there are (integer) solutions to the equation, then the two references might access the same memory location, and a potential conflict (data-dependency) must be assumed. For simplicity of notation we will assume that index references are reduced to the primitive form $(a_1 i_1 + b_1, ..., a_n i_n + b_n)$, where $\bar{i}$ is the iteration vector, and the a_l's and b_l's are constants. The following discussion applies to arbitrary array indexes. Of course, the more complex the index expressions, the less likely they are to be disambiguated by the compiler increasing the number of dependencies that have to be assumed.

2.2.2 Quantization Conditions Given two conflicting indirect references $A[a'_1 i_1 + b'_1, ..., a'_n i_n + b'_n]$ and $A[a''_1 j_1 + b''_1, ..., a''_n j_n + b''_n]$, we can express the second iteration vector $\bar{j}$ as a function of the first iteration vector $\bar{i}$ by

$$\bar{j} = (a'_1 i_1 + (b'_1 - b''_1))/a''_1, ..., (a'_n i_n + (b'_n - b''_n))/a''_n) = (a_1 i_1 + b_1, ..., a_n i_n + b_n) = (j_1, ..., j_n)$$

for values of i_l's such that the j_l's are all integers (this must be possible, otherwise there would be no conflict).

Equating $\bar{i}$ and $\bar{j}$ elementwise from left to right, we may determine whether $\bar{i} < \bar{j}$, or $\bar{i} > \bar{j}$. For quantization to be legal, we need to ensure that the order of the conflicting references is preserved under quantization. Assuming that original iteration $\bar{i}$ occurs in a box with *lower bound*[7] $\bar{L} = (l_1, ..., l_n)$ and original iteration $\bar{j}$ occurs in a box with lower bound $\bar{L} = (l'_1, ..., l'_n)$, then one of the following conditions must hold:

$$\mathbf{1.\ if}\ \bar{i} > \bar{j}\ \mathbf{then}\ \bar{L} \geq \bar{L'}\ or \mathbf{2.\ if}\ \bar{i} < \bar{j}\ \mathbf{then}\ \bar{L} \leq \bar{L'}$$

Since the i_e's runs from 1 to N_e and the new indexes run from 1 to N_e by increments of k_e, we get:

$$\bar{L} = (\lfloor (i_1 - 1)/k_1 \rfloor k_1 + 1, ..., \lfloor (i_n - 1)/k_n \rfloor k_n + 1),\ \ and \bar{L'} = (\lfloor (j_1 - 1)/k_1 \rfloor k_1 + 1, ..., \lfloor (j_n - 1)/k_n \rfloor k_n + 1).$$

[7] The lower bound of a box B is the index vector of the quantized loop for which the original loop iteration with index vector $\bar{i}$ gets executed.

As with the original iterations, the lower bounds of the quantized boxes occur in lexicographic order. That is, the box associated with $\overline{L}$ will precede during execution the box associated with $\overline{L'}$ if and only if $\overline{L} < \overline{L'}$. Thus by element-wise (symbolic) comparison we can determine if either one of the two conditions above is satisfied.

2.3 The Use of Loop Quantization Conditions

The conditions presented above can be used in several ways. The simplest is to let the system perform a prespecified unwinding (i.e., use some fixed k_e's, possibly determined by range analysis of the bounds of arrays and loops). Dependent statements are checked against the conditions derived in the previous section, for all values of each I_e. If the conditions are satisfied then the unwinding is performed, otherwise k_e's are decreased and the process is repeated. While this could be extremely expensive, it provides a straightforward solution for cases where only a few nested loops with few dependent statements exist and the N_i's are known at compile time. A deficiency of this approach is that it does not provide any information about what k_e's may be appropriate or on how to unwind so as to best utilize the space we are willing to trade for speed.

A more reasonable approach, which we are incorporating in our percolation scheduling compiler, improves efficiency and applies even when the bounds of the loops are not known. We notice that $a > b$ implies $\lfloor a/k \rfloor \geq \lfloor b/k \rfloor$. Furthermore, $a - b \geq k$ implies $\lfloor a/k \rfloor > \lfloor b/k \rfloor$. These rules can be used to compare $\overline{L}$ and $\overline{L'}$ symbolically, without computing specific values for each iteration. This can also help in picking the right unwinding (i.e., pick $k_e \leq k$). Doing such symbolic comparison, we may determine that:

- $\overline{L} \geq \overline{L'}$. If this is the condition needed to ensure the legality of the transformation, the quantization can be performed, using arbitrary k_e's. Otherwise an attempt is made to change "$\geq$" to "$=$" to ensure correctness. This may require full unwinding on one (or more) dimensions.

- $\overline{L} \leq \overline{L'}$. If this is the condition needed to ensure the legality of the transformation the quantization can be performed using arbitrary k_e's. Otherwise an attempt is made to change $\leq$'s to $=$ to ensure correctness. This may require full unwinding on one (or more) dimensions.

- *Undetermined situation.* This will occur whenever we have no strict ordering (i.e., none of "$<$" or "$>$" or "$=$" hold) between $\overline{L}$ *and* $\overline{L'}$, and there are some "$\leq$'s" and "$\geq$'s" between various elements. For example, for $\overline{L} = (\lfloor (a+1)/k \rfloor, \lfloor b/k \rfloor)$ and $\overline{L'} = (\lfloor a/k \rfloor, \lfloor (b+1)/k \rfloor)$ we have $\lfloor (a+1)/k \rfloor \geq \lfloor a/k \rfloor$ and $\lfloor b/k \rfloor \leq \lfloor (b+1)/k \rfloor$. This is undetermined, since

$$\begin{aligned} &\overline{L} = \overline{L'} \text{ when } a = 1,\ k = 3,\ b = 1; \\ &\overline{L} > \overline{L'} \text{ when } a = 2,\ k = 3,\ b = 1; \\ &\overline{L} < \overline{L'} \text{ when } a = 1,\ k = 3,\ b = 2. \end{aligned}$$

  In such cases we may obtain the desired relation by changing $\leq$'s to $=$'s (or $\geq$'s to $=$'s) by using different k_e's, or if that fails, possibly by full unwinding on some dimensions.

In general, if $i_e = dk + c$, $j_e = d'b + c'$, and $i_e - j_e \geq k + (c - c')$, then it follows that $\lfloor i_e/k \rfloor > \lfloor j_e/k \rfloor$. This together with the other constraints on the various variables can be used with integer programming techniques to find a set of maximal k_e's satisfying the above conditions. The simpler alternative used in our compiler is to establish an upper limit on the unwinding, say K_x for loop x. Such a bound occurs naturally in practice, as a function of the size of resources (the number of processors) available. In this case, we can start with K_x and apply the legality tests for quantization. If the tests succeed, we're done, and if they fail we repeat the process, performing a binary search on the range of possible values $k_x \leq K_x$. In the worst case, we will have performed $log(K_x)$ attempts before finding a legal k_x.

When a conflict occurs, the system can compare $\overline{L}$ and $\overline{L'}$, and decide which dimension(s) (if any) could be fully unwound to satisfy the conditions. For example, if there is a value e such that for all i such that $i < e$ we have $l_i \geq l'_i$ and $l_e \leq l'_e$, then the safety of quantization is undetermined. If full unwinding on dimension e is feasible doing so will force $l_e = l'_e$ since for any original iterations i_e and j_e, we have $i_e \leq N_e$ and $j_e \leq N_e$. That is, for all i_e and j_e we have $l_e = l'_e$. Thus the conflict on the eth dimension will be eliminated, since all the potentially conflicting references will be in the same box.

While the above approach may already be practical, to date we have also developed efficient algorithms to analyzes the dependencies of the loops and produce a *maximal* quantization i.e., one with the largest possible degree of freedom in unwinding on all the nested loops. We have also identified an important subclass of quantizations (*strict quantizations*), in which no dependencies among the iterations in the same quantum box exist. For such quantizations we can find the *best* quantization (i.e., strictly superior to all others legal quantizations). Furthermore, strict quantizations have a natural, concise representation that makes the parallelism explicit—the size of the quantum box and the knowledge that the quantization is strict suffices. In arbitrary loops a *best* quantization may not even exist, and there may be several—incomparable—maximal quantizations. The algorithms are discussed in detail in [1].

As for space efficiency, intuitively, there is no point in unwinding on a dimension if dependencies exist on that dimension that prevent software pipelining or parallelization.[8] This indicates that there is no possible performance gain for the statements under consideration. To decide if the unwinding will achieve any speedup, all statements in the loop body must be considered. Even when no major overlap can occur, exit-tests might still be eliminated, and initialization and tests from several original iterations may be done in parallel. Whenever additional unwinding is not deemed to be worth the cost (a user or system settable parameter) unwinding stops.

This method may be hindered by the presence of arbitrary conditional jumps in the loop body that limit the ability to disambiguate dependencies at compile time and to accurately evaluate the real (run-time) speedup achieved by a given unwinding. This accuracy can be significantly improved by the use of conditional-jump probability information. Such information can be obtained by the system using test runs and/or analysis, or can be supplied by the user. We have found such information to be easily available in typical scientific code.

2.4 Enhancements for Loop Quantization

Box Slanting and *Dimension Reversal* are two transformations that can further enhance the applicability of loop quantization. Box Slanting consists of slanting the quantum box to become parallel to the dependencies that prevent the simple quantization, thereby enabling the safe quantization of the loop. An illustration is given in figure 3. The loop in this figure does not yield at all to simple quantization, but is arbitrarily quantizable with Box Slanting. It is interesting to note that the overhead involved in Box Slanting is very small (the loop is broken into a prolog loop, a main loop, and epilog loop). Of course, the transformation works only when the quantization-preventing dependencies have a fixed slope, that is, when the indices creating these dependencies are *afine* (i.e., of the form $i + constant$). However, this is not a major drawback, as a large fraction of the references encountered in scientific code are indeed afine.

Dimension Reversal simply consists of the reversal of the direction of a loop producing quantization-preventing dependencies—if this reversal would not violate any (other) dependencies. In figure 3 this transformation would also allow arbitrary quantization. Furthermore the two transformations could be combined for maximum flexibility (e.g., in figure 4) neither of the transformations would work on its own, but together they would allow arbitrary quantization of the loop. Further details on these transformations and an algorithm for Slanting are found in [1].

[8] See [15] for a rigorous definition of loop carried dependencies.

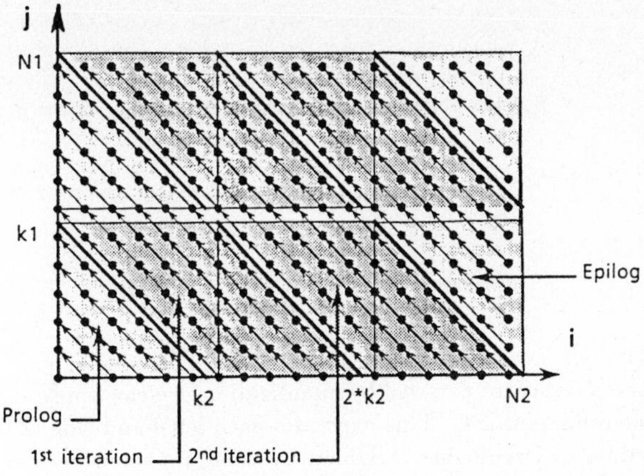

Iteration Space for the loop:

```
For j = 1,N1 by k1 do
    For i = 1,N2 by k2 do
        A[i,j]: = f(A[i + 1,j-1]);
```

Figure 3: Only Slanting or Reversal can allow quantization

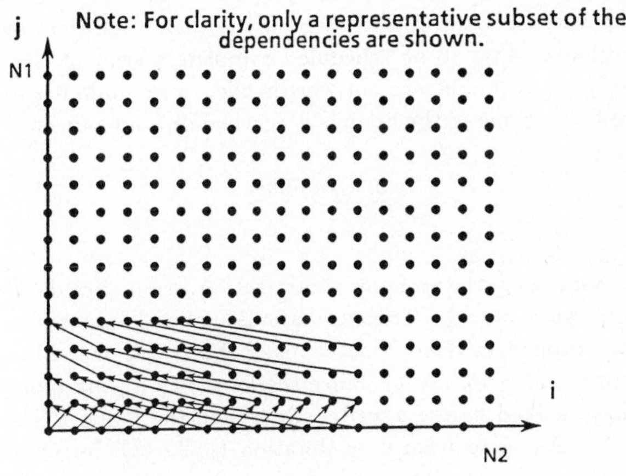

Iteration Space for the loop:

```
For j = 1,N1 by k1 do
    For i = 1,N2 by k2 do
        A[i,j]: = A[2i + 1,j-1] + A[i + 1,j + 1];
```

Figure 4: Both Reversal and Slanting are needed to allow quantization

```
   Do i=1,n
   Do j=1,n
(1)  T1=X[i+16,j];
(2)  T2=X[i+1,j];    /* Notice that statements (2 and 4) form a recurrence */
(3)  T1=T1+T2;
(4)  X[i+1,j+1]=T1;
   Od; Od;
```

Figure 5: Original Recurrence code

2.5 Folding and Balancing

To best exploit the parallelism exposed by quantization, we can apply another transformation similar to tree height reduction [14]. This expresses each left-hand-side (LHS) of an assignment in terms of initial values or irreducible variables, by using repeated back-substitution (and constant/variable folding [18]) on the quantized body of the loops. The highest tree is then balanced by using efficient algorithms that take advantage of commutativity, distribution, and associativity [17], [6]. Subtrees corresponding to other LHS—if any—are identified and reused (common subexpression elimination). The process is repeated for all independent statements in the loop and each operation is scheduled for execution subject to its dependencies (e.g., by Percolation Scheduling).

If the machine is "reasonably well utilized" by the final schedule (a system or user specified bound), or the code size is getting to be "large" (another user or system specified bound) quantization stops. Otherwise, we increase the unwinding (incrementally) and build a new overall schedule. If the new part of this schedule is isomorphic to the part added in the previous schedule and there is no overlap between them (i.e., a *no-gain situation*—the trees have exactly the same structure and the two halves have to be scheduled completely sequentially to ensure semantics preservation) then the last unwinding was not worthwhile, so we undo it and stop. Otherwise we repeat the process until either one of the bounds is reached or a no-gain situation is encountered.

3. Examples

3.1 Example 1

As an illustration, consider the way Loop Quantization techniques deal with recurrences. In figure 5 we have a simple piece of code. Transformations such as loop interchange or vectorization do not apply here. For example, in the original loops, $X[17,2]$ will be read in iteration $(i = 1, j = 2)$, and written in iteration $(i = 16, j = 1)$. Since the loop on j is innermost, $(1,2)$ occurs before $(16,1)$ and thus we have a read before a write. Reversing the loops will write into $X[17,2]$ in iteration $(j = 1, i = 16)$ and read from it in iteration (j=2,i=1); but since the loops are now reversed, the write will occur before the read, which is obviously not semantically equivalent to the original code. The interchange is therefore illegal. Vectorization is unfeasible, even if we use expansion and loop distribution (breaking); the first statement could be vectorized, but that would only reduce the execution from $4*n^2$ to $3*n^2+1$ steps, even assuming an array of processors of size n. This would be wasteful if n is large. A similar speedup ($3*n^2$ execution steps) could be achieved on a multiprocessor by running the first two statements in parallel. Even if more than two processors were available on a traditional multiprocessor, attempting to distribute the loop across the processors will incur very heavy communication costs due to the tight dependencies between the iterations.

Our techniques, on the other hand, can quantize the loop by unwinding on both i and j, which will expose enough fine-grain parallelism to keep the available processors busy (e.g., in a

VLIW machine, or any other type of tightly coupled multiprocessor). This quantizing is legal even though loop interchange is impossible. This is because quantization, unlike interchange, preserves the relative order of execution of the critical statements inside the "box". By comparing

$$(1)\ T1 := X[i+16, j]$$

and

$$(4)\ X[i'+1, j'+1] := T1;$$

our disambiguator system can determine that conflicts between iteration $\bar{i} = (i, j)$ and $\bar{j} = (i', j')$ can occur when $i' = i - 15$ and $j' = j + 1$. Since $i > i'$, it follows that $\bar{i} > \bar{j}$ and thus

$$\overline{L} = (\lfloor (i-1)/K_i \rfloor K_i + 1,\ \lfloor (j-1)/K_j \rfloor K_j + 1)$$

must be greater or equal to

$$\overline{L'} = (\lfloor (i-16)/K_i \rfloor K_i + 1,\ \lfloor j/K_j \rfloor K_j + 1)$$

if quantization is to be allowed. In general this is not the case, as

$$\lfloor (i-1)/K_i \rfloor \geq \lfloor (i-16)/K_i \rfloor$$

but

$$\lfloor (j-1)/K_j \rfloor \leq \lfloor j/K_j \rfloor$$

and thus there is no definite ordering for arbitrary K_i, K_j. However, since $i - i' = 15$, chosing $K_i = 15$ will ensure that

$$\lfloor (i-1)/15 \rfloor > \lfloor (i-16)/15 \rfloor$$

and therefore $\overline{L} > \overline{L'}$. K_j has no influence over this, and thus any value chosen for it will still preserve correctness. For this example we will assume that $K_j = 15$ as well. The other dependency that needs to be examined for the legality of loop quantization is between

$$(2)\ T2 := X[i+1, j]$$

and

$$(4)\ X[i'+1, j'+1] := T1;$$

where $\bar{i} = (i, j)$, $\bar{j} = (i' = i, j' = j - 1)$, and thus $\bar{i} > \bar{j}$. Since $i = i'$ and $j > j'$, it follows that $\overline{L} \geq \overline{L'}$ allowing semantically correct quantization. The resulting loop is shown in figure 6.

Our system will decide that the 15 unwindings along i (i to i+14) are independent of each other, and can be done in parallel. Applying folding and balancing (tree height reduction) techniques to each such group (for j to j+14), we can, resources permitting, execute each in 6 steps: 1 for loading, 4 for computing sums and storing, and 1 for storing the last results (see figure 7). To fully exploit this parallelism, we need 16 processors per unwinding on i, for a total of 15*16 processors[9]. The speedup achieved is from $4 * n^2$ steps to $6 * (n/k_1) * (n/k_2)$, (in our example, $k_1 = k_2 = 15$). If more resources were available, we could unwind more, getting even more dramatic speedups. In particular, if the loops were fully unwound the speedups would be optimal. Even when this is impossible, we will still get good performance given the available resources.

[9] By reducing the speedup slightly, from 6 to 8 time steps per unwinding of i, we could do with only 15*8 processors by adding 2 extra steps for initial and intermediate storage of results.

```
Do i=1,n,15
Do j=1,n,15
  T1=X[i+16,j];         /* j+0, i+0  */
  T2=X[i+1,j];
  T1=T1+T2;
  X[i+1,j+1]=T1;
  ................
  T29=X[i+2,j+15];    /* j+15,i+0  */
  T30=X[i+1,j+15];
  T29=T29+T30;
  X[i+1,j+16]=T29;

......................

  T1=X[i+31,j];         /* j+0, i+15 */
  T2=X[i+1,j];
  T1=T1+T2;
  X[i+16,j+1]=T1;
  ................
  T29=X[i+31,j+15];    /* j+15,i+15 */
  T30=X[i+16,j+15];
  T29=T29+T30;
  X[i+16,j+16]=T29;
Od; Od;
```

Figure 6: Same Recurrence with quantized unwinding

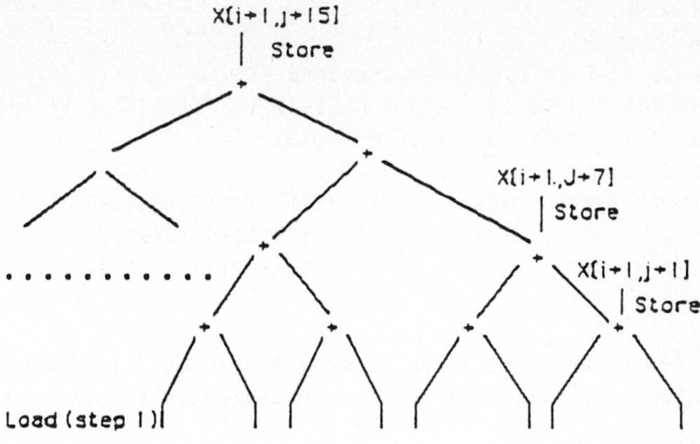

Figure 7: Balanced tree for i, j..j+14

```
      DO 100 I1 = 0, N
      DO 100 I2 = 0, N
      DO 100 I3 = 0, 9
S1:      A(I1,I2+1,I3] = B(I1,I2,I3+2) * C(I1,I2) + U(I1,I2) * V(I1,I2)
S2:      B(I1+1,I2,I3) = A(I1,I2,I3+6)* D(I1,I3)
100: CONTINUE
```

Figure 8: Sample Loop from [HeuLitt82]

3.2 Example 2

This example illustrates how Loop Quantization can expose parallelism previously observable only at runtime (e.g., [13]).

To simplify the discussion we will assume that intermediate exit-tests have been removed by any of the methods described. Consider the original loop in Heuft's and Little's example, shown in figure 8. As a result of the tests described in section 2.3, we can determine automatically that the loop can be quantized safely. The details of the quantization proper for this loop are similar to those for the previous example and are omitted. Based on symbolic analysis, the system can determine a correct and effective quantization subject to the data-dependencies present and the resources available. Assuming that we had enough processors[10] the quantization shown in figure 9 would yield optimal speedups for the given unwinding.

If the inner loop would not be limited to 9 iterations, but rather N, and more processors were available, we would like to automatically infer—by analyzing the dependency pattern (figure 9)—that unwinding more on the innermost loop would not lengthen the execution time, since it would not introduce any longer dependency-chains. While we can achieve this by explicitly unwinding and testing as described in the previous section, such symbolic inference would be more efficient. Furthermore, explicitly doing this could be a waste of time if we couldn't ascertain that the quantization is legal. In fact in the above example, simple quantization would be illegal if the inner loop would run to N and all the loops were unwound 9 times. However, the quantization

[10]Three hundred are required for this example, under the same assumptions as in [13]

```
      DO 100 I1 = 0, N, 9
      DO 100 I2 = 0, N, 9
      DO 100 I3 = 0, 9, 9 /* completely unwound */
S1:      A(I1,I2+1,I3] = B(I1,I2,I3+2) * C(I1,I2) + U(I1,I2) * V(I1,I2)
S2:      B(I1+1,I2,I3) = A(I1,I2,I3+6)* D(I1,I3)
      ............................................
S1:      A(I1+9,I2+10,I3+9] = B(I1+9,I2+9,I3+11) * C(I1+9,I2+9)
                            + U(I1+9,I2+9) * V(I1+9,I2+9)
S2:      B(I1+10,I2+9,I3+9) = A(I1+9,I2+9,I3+15)* D(I1+9,I3+9)
100: CONTINUE

S1 in iteration (i1,i2,i3) depends on S2 from iteration (i1-1,i2,i3+2)
S2 in iteration (i1,i2,i3) depends on S1 from iteration (i1,i2-1,i3+6)
```

Figure 9: Quantized Loop and Dependency Pattern

```
For X=0,1,...
Set A = {All instances of S1 for index values:
                  (I3=X,X+9; (I2=X,X+9; (I1=i)))
            All instances of S2 for index values:
                  (I3=X,X+9; (I2=X; (I1=X,X+9))) }

Set B = {All instances of S1 for index values:
                  (I3=X,X+9; (I2=X; (I1=X+1,X+9)))
            All instances of S2 for index values:
                  (I3=X,X+9; (I2=X+1,X+9; (I1=X;))) }
```

Figure 10: Compact representation of Quantized loop

could be made correct by using Box Slanting, and the algorinthms mentioned previously could be applied to determine a maximal or possibly best—if best exists for the loop—quantization.

Finally the actual code generation has to be done, to map the 3-d structure of the quantized loop body, onto the actual hardware. This can be achieved naturally (subject to the dependency constraints discovered by the system) for a machine with a cube-connected-cycles topology, such as Microflow [22]. Ideally, the system would always express this information implicitly in a compact symbolic representation—as it does for Strict-quantizations. Unfortunately, such a representation for arbitrary loops could be quite complex, as shown in figure 10. Of course, the quantized loop can always be expressed explicitly, by unwinding. The code derived from such a representation for execution on the Microflow architecture is shown in figure 11.

This is equivalent, given the number of processors used, to the bounds claimed by Heuft and Little.

```
0. X:=0;
1. Broadcast X;
2. Execute all members of Set A in parallel;
3. Execute all members of Set B in parallel;
4. Increment X and Repeat steps 1..4, unless Set B is empty.
```

Figure 11: Compact representation of Quantized loop

References

[1] A.Aiken and A.Nicolau. *Loop Quantization: An analysis and Algorithm.* Technical Report No.87-821, Department of Computer Science, Cornell University, March 1987.

[2] J.R.Allen and K.Kennedy. *Automatic Loop Interchange.* In the Proceedings of the Symposium on Compiler Construction, SIGPLAN Notices, Vol.19 No.6, 1984.

[3] Alliant. Product Summary. *Alliant Computer Systems Corporation.* Acton Mass. January 1985.

[4] U.Banerjee. *Speedup of Ordinary Programs.* University of Illinois Computer Science Technical Report UIUCDS-R-79-989, Oct. 1979.

[5] R.Bogen. *MACSYMA Reference Manual.* Symbolics Inc., Cambridge, Mass. December 1983.

[6] R.Brent. *The Parallel Evaluation of General Arithmetic Expressions.* Journal of the ACM 21, pp. 201-206, 1974.

[7] A.E.Charlesworth. *An approach to Scientific Array Processing: The Architectural Design of the AP-120b/FPS-164 Family.* IEEE Computer, Vol.14, No.3, pp.18-27, 1981.

[8] R.Cytron. *Doacross: beyond vectorization for multiprocessors.* Proceedings of the 1986 International Conference on Parallel Processing, pp.836-844, Aug.1986.

[9] J.A.Fisher, J.R.Ellis, J.C.Ruttenberg and A.Nicolau. *Parallel Processing: A Smart Compiler and a Dumb Machine.* Proc. of the ACM Symposium on Compiler Construction, 1984.

[10] J. A. Fisher. *The Optimization of Horizontal Microcode within and beyond Basic Blocks: an Application of Processor Scheduling with Resources.* New York University Ph. D. thesis, New York, 1979.

[11] J.A.Fisher *Very long instruction word architectures and the ELI-512.* Yale University Department of Computer Science, Technical report # 253, 1982.

[12] J. R. Goodman, J. Hsieh, K. Liou, A. R. Pleszkun, P. B. Schechter, H. C. Young. *PIPE: A VLSI Decoupled Architecture.* The 12th Annual International Symposium on Computer Architecture, June 17–19, 1985, Boston, MA, 20–27.

[13] R.W.Heuft and W.D.Little. *Improved Time and Parallel Processor Bounds for Fortran-like Loops.* IEEE Transactions on Computers Vol.31, No.1, 1982.

[14] D.J.Kuck. *Parallel Processing of Ordinary Programs.* In Advances in Computers, Vol. 15, pp. 119-179, 1976.

[15] R.H.Khun. *Optimization and Interconnection Complexity for: Parallel Processors, Single-Stage Networks and Decision Trees.* Ph.D. Thesis, University of Illinois at Urbana-Champaign, 1980.

[16] F. H. McMahon. *Lawrence Livermore National Laboratory FORTRAN Kernels: MFLOPS.* Livermore, CA. 1983.

[17] Y.Muraoka. *Parallelism Exposure and Exploitation in Programs.* University of Illinois, Urbana, Dept. of Computer Science, Tech. Rep. 71-424, 1971.

[18] A.Nicolau. *Parallelism, Memory Anti-Aliasing and Correctness for Trace Scheduling Compilers.* Yale University Ph.D. Thesis, June 1984.

[19] A.Nicolau. *Percolation Scheduling: A Parallel Compilation Technique.* Cornell University, Dept. of Computer Science Technical Report TR-85-678, May 1985.

[20] A. Nicolau and K. Karplus. ROPE: a Statically Scheduled Supercomputer Architecture. *First International Conference on Supercomputing Systems,* St. Petersburg, FL, December 1985.

[21] C.L.Seitz. *The Cosmic Cube.* Communications of the ACM, Vol.28, No.1 January 1985.

[22] J.Solworth and A.Nicolau. *Microflow: A fine-grain Parallel Processing Approach.* Cornell University, Dept. of Computer Science Technical Report TR-85-710

Vector Optimization vs. Vectorization

Michael Wolfe

Kuck and Associates, Inc.
1808 Woodfield Drive
Savoy, Illinois, 61874, USA

This paper differentiates between vectorization (and also concurrentization) and vector optimization (or concurrency optimization). Vectorization (concurrentization) is the process of translating serial DO (or FOR) loops into vector code for a vector computer (concurrent code for a multiprocessor computer). Vector optimization (concurrency optimization) uses vectorization (concurrentization) but adds some intelligence to decide which loop(s) to run in parallel. Loop interchanging and generation of multiple versions of a loop are discussed as vector optimization tools.

1.0 Introduction

Vectorization is the process of translating serial DO loops into vector code for execution on a computer with vector instructions, such as the Cray X-MP, Cyber 205, Convex C-1 and others. Concurrentization (also called parallelization) is the process of translating serial DO loops into concurrent code on a computer with multiple processors, such as the Sequent Balance 8000, Encore Multimax and others. Some computers, such as the Alliant FX/8, have multiple processors, each with vector instructions, so both vectorization and concurrentization are used by the compiler. The techniques for discovering when a loop can be vectorized or concurrentized are discussed elsewhere.

We distinguish between vectorization and vector optimization by defining the latter as the process of translating serial DO loops into the best or fastest code for execution on a vector computer. Several factors affect vector optimization. First, blind vectorization of a DO loop may not always be faster than serial execution of that loop; on machines with a large vector startup penalty, such as the Cyber 205, the time for a very short vector operation is dominated by the startup cost. Second, because of interleaved memories, "stride-one" array access may be much more efficient than other constant strides; if the inner loop has many non-stride-one array references, vectorizing an outer loop may be more efficient. Third, even when the proper loop is vectorized, there may be alternatives to executing different code segments (such as IFs). These and similar factors apply equally to concurrentization and multiprocessor computers. Rather than confuse the issue with a different name for concurrency optimization, we use "vector optimization" to mean both optimization of vectorization and concurrentization. With multi-vector computers, the problem of vector optimization is even harder, since there are several ways to execute a loop: concurrent, vector, concurrent/vector or scalar. To make life even more difficult, some of the criteria (such as loop limits or branch frequency) are not known until execution time.

We discuss how to approach the problems of vector optimization from a machine independent point of view. We have worked with the KAP preprocessor [6, 8] and have gained experience with these problems over the past several years. The most important tool available to the compiler in vector optimization is the ability to interchange loops. Generation of multiple versions of a loop can also solve certain problems.

2.0 Inspecting Loop Limits

The first and most obvious approach for vector optimization is to inspect the loop limits. If the loop limits are small constants (such as a loop that goes from 1 to 3) then the loop should probably not be executed in vector or concurrent mode. The crossover point between scalar and parallel execution will differ depending on the machine. On the Cray X-MP, very short vectors (as short as 2 or 3) are reported to be as fast or faster than scalar execution. On the Cyber 205, the crossover point depends on the operations inside the loop. If the loop contains a divide, vector execution is more likely to be faster since the vector divide unit is pipelined, while the scalar divide unit is not. Also, on the Cyber 205, if the loop contains non-stride-one array references, vectorization of the loop would require a separate gather operation [8]. The gather operation slows down the vector execution, making the crossover point at which vector performance exceeds scalar performance that much higher.

3.0 Loop Unrolling

Even if the compiler has decided that the loop limits are too small for parallel execution to be better, the loop can be optimized in several ways. For very small loop limits, the loop can be completely unrolled, as below:

```
        do I = 1,3
         A(I) = B(I) + C(I)
        enddo

    becomes

        A(1) = B(1) + C(1)
        A(2) = B(2) + C(2)
        A(3) = B(3) + C(3)
```

Unrolling has the advantage of removing the serial loop overhead. Also, if this little loop appears in the middle of a larger loop (perhaps with larger loop limits), the larger loop can then be vectorized or concurrentized. This is especially useful for compilers that only vectorize innermost loops (such as the CFT compiler for the Cray X-MP [5]); unrolling a small inner loop brings another loop into consideration for vectorization.

4.0 Loop Interchanging

Another optimization for loops with small loop limits is to interchange the small loop with an outer loop that has larger loop limits. Loop interchanging is often regarded as a method for discovering parallelism when the innermost loop is serial. However, it is a powerful vector optimization tool as well. For instance, interchanging the two loops below:

```
        do I = 1,1000
           do J = 1,3
              A(J,I) = B(J,I) + C(J,I)
           enddo
        enddo
```

will allow the I loop to be vectorized, leaving the J loop serial. For multiprocessors, the parallel loop should be interchanged outwards, to reduce the cost of starting up the concurrent processors.

Compilers can also use loop interchanging to reduce the number of non-stride-one operands. On a computer such as the Cyber 205 where a separate gather or scatter is required for each non-stride-one vector operand, vectorizing the inner loop below:

```
do I = 1,N
   do J = 1,N
      A(I,J) = B(I,J) + C(I,J)
   enddo
enddo
```

would require two vector gathers (for B and C) and a vector scatter (for A), just to compute the one vector add (assuming Fortran column-major storage order). By interchanging the two loops, the I loop could be vectorized, and no gathers or scatters would be needed. This is not quite so critical for vector register machines, such as the Cray X-MP, where a vector load is required for all operands regardless of the stride. Even there, however, certain strides (multiples of the number of memory banks, usually a power of two) have reduced performance due to repeated fetches or stores to the same memory bank. In cases where the stride is unknown or known to give poor performance, loop interchanging can be used to get a stride of one. Some results of the use of loop interchanging as a vector optimization are shown in Huson [8]. Loop interchanging is discussed in more detail by Wolfe [14, 13] and Allen [1].

5.0 Multiple Version Loops

Even when loop interchanging is available, the best execution time cannot be guaranteed since some of the parameters affecting the decision of which loops to vectorize or concurrentize may not be known until runtime. In cases such as this, generating two (or more) versions of the loop and deciding which version to execute at run time may help. For instance, the relative values of the loop limits below may not be known by the compiler:

```
do J = 1, M
   do I = 1, N
      A(I,J) = ...
      ...
   enddo
enddo
```

On a vector computer, if M is larger than N, then interchanging the loops and executing the J loop in vector mode may be better than executing the I loop in vector mode, especially when N is very small. However, the decision cannot be made at compile time. An interactive programming environment might request such information from the user. Instead, a compiler can try to guarantee the best performance by generating two versions of the loop, choosing between them by testing the relative values of the loop limits:

```
if ( N > M ) then
   do J = 1, M
      do I = 1, N
         A(I,J) = ...
         ...
      enddo
   enddo
else
   do I = 1, N
      do J = 1, M
         A(I,J) = ...
         ...
      enddo
   enddo
endif
```

The same method applies to multiprocessor computers, except that loop interchanging need not always be used, since a loop at any nest level can be executed in concurrent mode.

A deeply nested structure can give rise to many different loop orderings; obviously the compiler should not generate an explosion in the size of the compiled program. The compiler must be able to choose the best two or three versions of a loop that will result in good performance all the time, and the best possible performance most of the time.

The problem of code expansion increases in the case of a multi-vector computer, such as the Alliant FX/8. Here, there are many methods to execute a nested loop construct:

1. all serial loops,
2. vectorize any one loop,
3. concurrentize any one loop,
4. concurrentize an outer loop and vectorize an inner loop, and
5. run a single loop in concurrent-vector mode.

Depending on the loop limits or other characteristics of the loop, any one of these methods may be best. When loop interchanging is allowed, the potential combinatorial explosion in the size of the program is apparent. Again, the compiler must find the best two or three execution modes from which to choose at run time.

6.0 Other Multiple Version Constructs

Loop limits are not the only construct that can be tested to generate multiple versions of a code segment. Multiple versions of a loop can be used to satisfy data dependence relations or to test the increment of a vectorized loop [3] (when an increment of one would produce more efficient stride-one array references).

Within a loop, many vector computers have two or more ways to execute vector IF statements. One method, the standard model, is to generate a bit vector or mask vector from the IF condition, and to use this bit vector to control which vector results are computed or stored. The Cyber 205 can use a bit vector to control each vector operation, while the Cray X-MP uses its mask register to merge two vector registers (the results from the THEN and ELSE parts of the vector IF, perhaps).

Another method, which may be better when the density of the bit vector is sparse or when the number of operations to be performed under control of the bit vector is large, is to compress the vector operands, saving only those operands where the bit vector value is 1 (or 0 for the ELSE clause). The conditional vector operations can then be performed with a shorter vector length (equal to the number of 1 bits in the bit vector). So, another candidate for multiple versions is a conditional, where the density of the bit vector is used to decide whether to use controlled stores (masked operations) or compressed operands.

On the Cyber 205, vector operands can be compressed with a single vector operation. The cost of this extra vector operation must be taken into account when the density of the bit vector is tested [7]. If the number of compresses needed is greater than the number of conditional operations, then the controlled store method should always be used; the time to execute the vector compresses would exceed the time to complete the conditional operations using controlled stores.

Some models of the Cray X-MP have indexed gather and scatter instructions. These machines can generate an index vector from the mask vector, containing the indices of the 1 bits in the mask, and use this index vector to load only the elements of the vector operands that are needed in the conditional. Again, the cost of generating the index vector and the added cost of the indexed load vs. a simple vector load must be figured in with the density of the bit vector in deciding whether to use merges or indexed loads.

7.0 Modelling the Computer

When performing vector optimization as described here, either choosing one "best" version of a loop to generate or choosing which version out of several to execute at run time, a good model of the computer must be built into the compiler. A simple model will suffice for simpler computers; for instance, a preference for longer vectors and for stride-one array operands may be sufficient for a simple vector computer.

For more complex machines where the number of vector pipelines may differ (as with the Cyber 205) or the number of processors may change from site to site (as with the Alliant FX/8), the compiler must have a parameter driven model of the machine to tune the generated code to the particular configuration. Arnold [2] suggests a very detailed machine model for vector optimization for the Cyber 205. This model includes such parameters as the number of vector pipelines on the machine, the startup cost of the different vector operations, the relative speed of vector arithmetic and vector gathers and scatters, and of course the speed at which scalar operations execute. He found that his model could predict with fair accuracy the performance of vector code, but was much less precise on the performance of scalar code. It is also relatively costly to implement, since it did not give a formula by which to choose the vector vs. scalar execution; instead, the compiler would estimate the execution time of vector and scalar execution (actually several vector execution methods, allowing for loop interchanging and different ways to execute vector IFs), and choose the one that gave the smallest time. If the estimate was done symbolically (such as when the loop limits are not known), the resulting formulas could be used to choose the best execution method at run time.

8.0 Other Techniques

Other techniques also fit into the context of vector optimization. Strip mining [9] is used for vector computers to insure that the vector length does not exceed the hardware maximum. Even a computer like the Cyber 205 has a maximum vector length, although it is very large (65535). Strip mining combined with loop interchanging is also useful to reduce traffic between a vector register set and the main memory [14, 1, 10], between levels of a virtual memory [12], and between a cache memory and main memory [6].

Loop collapsing is used to combine nested loops in order to get a longer vector length and has long been used for the Cyber 205 [4]. It can also be used in a multiprocessor environment to execute nested loops in parallel [11]. Besides being useful to reduce overhead and increase efficiency, the use of loop collapsing also reduces the need for generating multiple versions of a loop. In particular, if two loops are collapsed and both run in parallel (vector or concurrent), then no decision need be made about which vector length is the greater and which loop should be left serial.

9.0 Summary

Loop vectorization and loop concurrentization are fairly well known techniques. In order to really optimize the performance of loops for vector and concurrent computers, compilers must be capable of making vector optimization decisions such as those described in this paper. Vectorization is no longer enough. Compilers and translators which perform high level vector optimizations, such as KAP, will prove superior to ordinary compilers for complex parallel and vector computers.

Bibliography

1. John R. Allen and Ken Kennedy. Automatic Loop Interchange. *SIGPLAN Notices*, 19(6):233-246, June 1984. Proc. of the ACM SIGPLAN '84 Symp. on Compiler Construction.

2. C. N. Arnold. Vector Optimization on the Cyber 205. in H. J. Siegel and Leah Siegel, editor, *Proc. of the Int'l Conf. for Parallel Pricessing*, pages 530-536, IEEE Computer Society Press, Aug. 23-26 1983.

3. Mark Byler, James Davies, Christopher Huson, Bruce Leasure, and Michael Wolfe. Multiple Version Loops. *Proceedings of the 1987 Int'l Conf. for Parallel Pricessing*, St. Charles, Illinois, Aug. 18-20 1987. To appear.

4. Control Data Corporation. Fortran 200 Reference Manual, Control Data Corporation, March 1984. Pub. No. 60480200, rev. D.

5. Cray Research, Inc. Fortran (CFT) Reference Manual, Cray Research, Inc., August 1981. Pub. No. SR-009, rev. H.

6. James Davies, Christopher Huson, Tom Macke, Bruce Leasure, and Michael Wolfe. The KAP/S-1: An Advanced Source-to-Source Vectorizer for the S-1 Mark IIa Supercomputer. *Proc. of the 1986 Int'l Conf. on Parallel Processing*, pages 833-835, IEEE Computer Press, St. Charles, Illinois, Aug. 19-22 1986.

7. A. Dickinson. Optimizing Numerical Weather Forcasting Models for the Cray-1 and Cyber 205 Computers. *Int'l Symp. on Vector Processing Algorithms*, Colorado State University, Boulder, Colorado, August 1982.

8. Christopher Huson, Tom Macke, James Davies, Michael Wolfe, and Bruce Leasure. The KAP/205: An Advanced Source-to-Source Vectorizer for the Cyber 205 Supercomputer. *Proc. of the 1986 Int'l Conf. on Parallel Processing*, pages 827-832, IEEE Computer Press, St. Charles, Illinois, Aug. 19-22 1986.

9. D. Loveman. Program Improvement by Source to Source Transformation. *Journal of the ACM*, 20(1):121-145, January 1977.

10. David A. Padua and Michael J. Wolfe. Advanced Compiler Optimizations for Supercomputers. *Communications of the ACM*, 29(12):1184-1201, December 1986.

11. Constantine D. Polychronopoulos. On Program Restructuring, Scheduling, and Communication for Parallel Processor Systems, U. of Il. Center for Supercomputing Res. & Dev., August 1986. CSRD Rpt. No.595.

12. W. A. Abu-Sufah, D. J. Kuck, and D. H. Lawrie. On the Performance Enhancement of Paging Systems Through Program Analysis and Transformations. *IEEE Trans. on Computer*, C-30(5):341-356, May 1981.

13. Michael Wolfe. Advanced Loop Interchanging. *Proc. of the 1986 Int'l Conf. on Parallel Processing*, pages 536-543, IEEE Computer Society Press, St. Charles, Illinois, Aug. 19-22 1986.

14. Michael J. Wolfe. *Optimizing Supercompilers for Supercomputers*, PhD thesis, University of Illinois at Urbana-Champaign, Urbana, Illinois 1982. Report No. UIUCDCS-R-82-1105.

The Performance of Software–managed Multiprocessor Caches on Parallel Numerical Programs.

Hoichi Cheong and Alexander V. Veidenbaum
Center for Supercomputing Research and Development
University of Illinois at Urbana–Champaign
Urbana, Illinois, 61801

1. Introduction

In recent years interest has grown in multiprocessor architectures that can have several hundred processors sharing memory and all working on solving a single problem ([GGKM83], [GKLS83], [Phis85], [Crow85]). Such multiprocessors are characterized by a long memory access time, which makes use of cache memories very important. However, the cache coherence problem makes the use of private caches difficult. The proposed solutions to the cache coherence problem ([FuHa78], [Good83], [YePD83], [Tang76]) are not suitable for a large–scale multiprocessor. We proposed a different solution that relies on a compiler to manage the caches during the execution of a parallel program [Veid86]. In this paper we discuss the performance evaluation of private cache memories for multiprocessors in general and present the results of performance improvement for parallel numerical programs using the caches managed with compiler assistance. The effect of cache organization and other system parameters such as cache block size, cache size, and the number of processors in the system on performance is shown.

2. System Model

The architecture we are interested in is a shared memory multiprocessor system with the general organization shown in Figure 1. The system has P processors. The processors are connected to an interleaved shared memory through an interconnection network. There is no direct communication channel between any pair of processors. The processors can only communicate with each other through shared memory. The reason for this restriction is that we assume P to be very large.

This work is supported in part by National Science Foundation under Grant No.US NSF DCR84–10110, the U.S. Department of Energy under Grant No. US DOE DE–FG02–85ER25001, and the IBM Donation, IBM Corporation.

2.1. Global Memory and Networks

We assume the networks to be of the shuffle–exchange type [Lawr75] to be able to interconnect a large number of processors. The network operation is packet–switched. A one word wide (unique) data path exists in the networks between any processor and any memory module. Memory access time in this system includes the network delays.

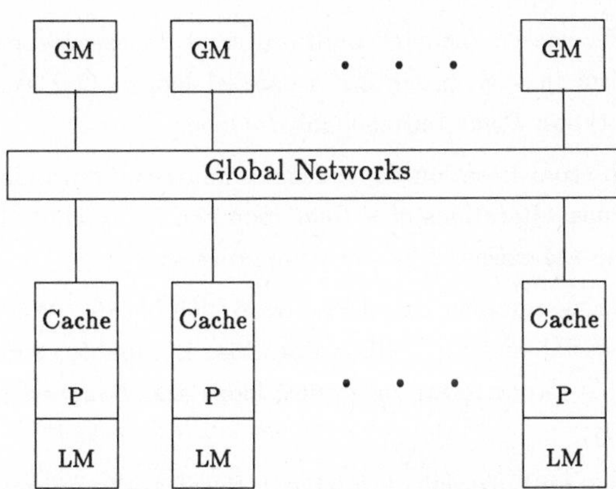

Figure 1: The System Architecture.

2.2. Processor Organization

Each processor has an integer unit, a floating–point unit, a private cache, and a local memory. We do not model the processor in detail except for cache access. We make several assumptions about the cache organization. (These assumptions are based on practical considerations of designing a multiprocessor cache.)

2.2.1. Cache Memory

Each processor has separate data and instruction cache memories. The use of the data cache memory can be turned on and off by software. This allows the cache to be by–passed.

Each cache has a block fetching unit that can fetch a block of words from the global memory (one word at a time with the networks used) when a read miss occurs.

The caches are direct–mapped, and the data cache is a *write–through* cache. Only the word written to memory is updated in the cache, i.e. there is no *miss–on–write.* (We use *write–through* policy because it makes cache management easier.) We also assume that there can be no coherence problems in instruction caches.

Each cache memory word has an address tag and a status tag. Status tag bits are *valid*, *reserved*, or *pending*. A cache memory word is tagged *pending* when a read miss occurred but has not been serviced yet. All words of a block being fetched on miss other than the word that caused the miss are marked *reserved*. The *reserved* tag bits are used to avoid multiple misses on the same block. The contents of the whole data cache can be invalidated by a *Flush* instruction.

3. Parallel Programs

We want to use the shared memory multiprocessor to execute parallel programs. The main source of parallelism in such programs is parallel loops. Our study focuses on parallel programs with two loop types: *Doall* [LuBa80] and *Do* loops.

A *Doall* loop has no cross–iteration dependences, i.e., results produced in one iteration are not used in other iterations. Iterations of a *Doall* loop can be executed by different processors. All iterations of a *Do* loop are executed by the same processor.

We used a restructuring compiler called Parafrase ([KKLW80], [Wolf82]) to generate parallel programs from their serial versions. While Parafrase is capable of detecting other types of parallel loops, such as first–order linear recurrence loops and *Doacross* loops [Padu79], we did not use those in this study.

We used the following optimizations available in Parafrase to improve data locality:

(1) Adjacent *Doall* loops are combined in a larger loop if possible. (The larger loop has better locality due to the way we enforce coherence.)

(2) Multiply nested *Doall* loops are collapsed into a singly–nested *Doall*, if possible. (This allows a better assignment of loop iterations to processors.)

4. Coherence Enforcement

To be able to use private caches on a multiprocessor, coherence has to be enforced. In [Veid86], we proposed an algorithm to enforce coherence by using the assistance of a restructuring compiler and showed its correctness. We are going to use this method to enforce coherence in our simulations. In this section we briefly describe the algorithm.

Coherence problems in parallel programs described above are due to dependences [Kuck78] between statements executed on different processors. The compiler can, by doing dependence analysis, detect when coherence can be violated and can insert a cache management instruction at such a point.

For example, suppose processor A has a copy of variable $X(i)$ in its cache before the start of a *Doall* loop L. Next, processor A and processor B execute different iterations of loop L. If processor B changes $X(i)$ in loop L, processor A's copy of $X(i)$ becomes invalid. Any subsequent use of $X(i)$ by A after loop L will cause an error.

4.1. Solution

For parallel programs with *Doalls* as the only type of parallel loops, coherence enforcement can be described as follows: each processor executing a *Doall* loop does a *Flush* at the entrance of the loop to ensure that it gets the most updated copies of variables from the global memory. The processor that continues the execution after the end of the *Doall* flushes its cache after the synchronization point so that variables produced in the loop and used after loop completion will be fetched from the global memory. Global memory always has the most recent copy due to the use of *write-through* policy. The cache is also flushed after *Call* statements because the parallelism of the called routine is assumed unknown. Each processor thus manages its own cache and requires no communication with other processors to do so.

For the example above, *X(i)* used by processor A will come directly from global memory after flushing the cache.

The following additional system support is assumed:

(1) The execution of *Doall* loops requires barrier synchronization at the beginning and the end of a loop.

(2) Words written to the global memory before synchronization point are guaranteed to reach the global memory before the synchronization instruction is issued.

Because the cache is flushed to enforce coherence, the *write-through* policy is a natural choice for the update policy. *Write-through* requires no extra bookkeeping for variables updated, nor explicit stores before flushing.

5. Evaluation of a Multiprocessor Cache Performance

Our goal is to investigate the cache performance. We simulate the execution of real programs on a multiprocessor system emulator using the cache and compare it to the simulated execution time of systems: 1) without any cache memory or 2) without the data cache. In this section, we discuss issues related to the evaluation of the multiprocessor cache performance.

5.1. Performance Evaluation Metrics

How does one measure the effect of using caches? For a uniprocessor system, the hit ratio is traditionally used as a measure of cache performance. Is the hit ratio a good performance metric for multiprocessor systems?

Cache speedup

Cache speedup, the ratio of execution time of a system without cache to execution time of the same system with cache, is the real performance improvement indicator. Given T_p^c, the execution time of a p-processor system with cache and T_p, the execution time a p-processor system without cache, cache speedup S_p^c is defined as $S_p^c = \dfrac{T_p}{T_p^c}$.

Hit ratio and speedup relationship

The execution time of a program on a P–processor system can be expressed as a sum of time periods τ_n, during which n processors are executing in parallel. For each τ_n, *alu* operations account for a portion of the time and memory accesses account for the rest. Let these quantities be T_n^{op} and T_n^M for a system without the cache. We have

$$T_P = \sum_{n=1}^{n=P} (T_n^{op} + T_n^M)$$

T_n^M can be expressed as $T_n^M = f_n \cdot t_m$, where t_m is the memory access time. It should be observed that T_n^M is not equal to the total time spent accessing memory by all n processors. Rather, it is the time spent by n processors accessing memory in parallel. T_n^{op} is the time spent by n processors doing *alu* operations in parallel.

When the cache is used, a part of f_n can be cache accesses. Let there be f_n^c such accesses. Then we can express S_p^c as follows:

$$S_p^c = \frac{\sum_{n=1}^{n=P} (T_n^{op} + f_n \cdot t_m)}{\sum_{n=1}^{n=P} (T_n^{op} + (f_n - f_n^c) \cdot t_m + f_n^c \cdot t_c)}$$

If we assume the memory access time to dominate, we have

$$S_p^c \approx \frac{\sum_{n=1}^{n=P} (f_n \cdot t_m)}{\sum_{n=1}^{n=P} ((f_n - f_n^c) \cdot t_m + f_n^c \cdot t_c)} = \left(1 - \left(1 - \frac{t_c}{t_m} \right) \cdot \frac{\sum_{n=1}^{n=P} f_n^c}{\sum_{n=1}^{n=P} f_n} \right)^{-1}$$

On a uniprocessor system the term $\left(\sum_{n=1}^{n=P} f_n^c \right) / \left(\sum_{n=1}^{n=P} f_n \right)$ becomes $\frac{f_1^c}{f_1}$, which is the hit ratio "h". And the speedup formula

$$S_1^c \approx \left(1 - \left(1 - \frac{t_c}{t_m} \right) \cdot \mathrm{h} \right)^{-1}$$

is a good approximation of the effect of the cache on memory access time.

Since the quantity $\left(\sum_{n=1}^{n=P} f_n^c \right) / \left(\sum_{n=1}^{n=P} f_n \right)$ relates to S_p^c in the same manner as the hit ratio "h" does to speedup in the uniprocessor case, we call this quantity multiprocessor cache hit ratio h_P.

Note that h_P is a function of P and is not measured the same way as the conventional uniprocessor hit ratio "h" is measured. "h" and h_P are the same when a program is either totally serial or totally parallel. When a program has both serial and parallel code the two measures become quite different.

We measure h_P in a P–processor system in our study. For the parallel programs we used, parallel execution occurs in *Doall* loops. Assuming all processors executing a *Doall* loop perform approximately the same amount of computation, we use the number of cache accesses and memory accesses of the processor (referred to as P_1) that was never idle during the entire program execution to represent $\sum_{n=1}^{n=P} f_n^c$ and $\sum_{n=1}^{n=P} f_n$, respectively.

h_P consists of two parts, h_P^S, the hit ratio in the portion of code executed by one processor, and h_P^p, the hit ratio in the portion of code executed by more than one processor. While h_P is a measure of the hit ratio of P_1 and thus approximately accounts for the hit ratio in the course of the execution of entire program, h_P^p is the hit ratio of a typical processor which executes only the DOALL loops. h_P is related to h_P^S and h_P^p in the following manner:

$$h_P = \gamma \times h_P^S + (1 - \gamma) \times h_P^p$$

where γ is the ratio of the number of memory references made by P_1 in the serial portion of code to all the memory references made by P_1. h_P is thus a weighted average of h_P^S and h_P^p. h_P asymptotically approaches h_P^S if γ is close to one and it approaches h_P^p if γ is close to zero. When γ is larger than one–half, we say that the program is serial code dominant and parallel code dominant when γ is less than one–half.

5.2. Benchmark Programs

We selected several widely used and very time consuming numerical application programs for our simulations. For each program, a subroutine which uses most of the execution time is identified and simulated. A list of these subroutines and their simple descriptions are given in Table 1.

6. Simulation

The following is a brief description of the simulation process we used for cache performance evaluation. The simulation consists of two parts: *trace generation* and *timing simulation*.

6.1. Trace Generation

The trace generator uses a Fortran subroutine restructured for multiprocessor execution as input [AbKw85]. It generates an intermediate language trace that contains the following information:

(1) Instruction fetches, data fetches and data stores for each instruction,

(2) Memory allocation for code and data,

(3) Processor allocation to parallel loops.

Program statements necessary for address computations and determining the flow of control are evaluated during tracing. The cache management instructions are actually inserted during tracing.

Subroutine	Program	No. of Instructions Traced (in Thousands)	Description
Newrz	SIMP2	80	New velocity computation and volume change in a Lagrangian hydrodynamics program
Step	ARC3D	900	Computational fluid dynamics
Cmslow	BARO	46	Nonlinear tendency computation in a barometer program
Implk	BLUNTFIN	1300	Implicit integration routine in a compressible Navier Stokes equation solver
Ffs99	SPEC77	16	FFT routine in weather prediction program
Ftrvmt	SHEAR3	4	FFT routine in a stress analysis program
Lblkerna		100	A kernel of experimental physics computation
Parmvr	PIC	400	Particle in cell program
Ux	VORTEX	1400	A PDE solver
Matmul1		1700	Matrix multiply by strip partition
Matmul2		1700	Matrix multiply by block partition

Table. 1: Benchmark Subroutines.

6.2. Timing Simulation

The timing simulator executes the statements of a subroutine contained in the trace emulating a multiprocessor system. It is an event-driven simulator.

The events simulated are instruction fetch, operand fetch, operand store, cache access, network/memory access, and block fetching. Only some of those are allowed to overlap, such as block fetching, execution, and network/memory access. The instruction execution in the processor is not pipelined.

6.3. Simulation Parameters

The basic parameters of the system model are described below:

1. *Local memory*

We assume that there is a sufficiently large amount of local memory for each processor to handle compiler-generated temporaries. This assumption frees us from the details of the register allocation problem which is outside of the scope of this paper.

2. *Cache response time*

Cache write and read cycle times are one clock. The *Flush* instruction takes one clock.

3. *ALU time*

We assume two clocks for all *ALU* operations.

4. *Global memory access time*

The global memory access time is 10 clocks (unless specificed otherwise) and it includes network delays.

5. *Block fetch timing*

We assume the block fetch unit can generate one read request per clock.

6. *Read miss time penalty*

A read miss costs four extra clocks in the case of block size larger than one and three extra clocks in the case of block size one (block fetch unit is bypassed) in addition to memory access time.

7. Results

In this section, we present the results of our simulations. We measured the cache speedup and the hit ratio due to different parameters in a multiprocessor system, such as the number of processors, the block size, and the global memory access time.

7.1. Cache speedups

We measured cache speedups for our benchmark set with and without the data cache for a 32–processor multiprocessor model. The results are presented in Table 2.

Since an instruction cache does not have a coherence problem, we simulated an architecture where each processor only has an instruction cache. The hit ratios for instructions are very high and the increase in cache block size does not have any effect on speedups. The latter is due to the structure of our benchmarks (and numerical programs in general) with most of the time spent executing DO loops.

The addition of the data cache gives an average speedup of between 1.18 and 1.45 over the I–cache alone for different block sizes. The increase in the block size has a pronounced effect on the speedup of most programs and is quite noticeable in the average and maximum speedups.

Several programs show speedup loss with the addition of the data cache. The reason for this is the cost of cache access in our model. The cache miss penalty is three (block size $= 1$) or four (block size > 1) clocks and cache access time is 1 clock. When the hit ratio is low the effective memory access time becomes longer than the memory access time in the no–cache case. Our random benchmark sample turned out to have three such programs. The reason for their low hit ratio lies in the program structure (see section 7.3). Note that higher miss cost for larger block size is compensated by higher hit ratios and increase in speedup.

Subr.	I cache only			I & D cache			I & D over I only		
	blk 1	blk 2	blk 4	blk 1	blk 2	blk 4	blk 1	blk 2	blk 4
parmvr	1.48	1.48	1.48	1.72	2.24	2.72	1.16	1.51	1.84
lblkern	1.69	1.70	1.70	1.44	1.59	1.72	0.85*	0.93*	1.01
ffs99	1.43	1.53	1.60	1.36	1.74	2.16	0.93*	1.13	1.35
cmslow	1.44	1.54	1.62	1.60	2.03	2.42	1.11	1.32	1.49
ftrvmts	1.50	1.57	1.61	1.43	1.58	1.79	0.95*	1.01	1.11
ux	2.35	2.35	2.36	3.07	3.09	3.11	1.31	1.31	1.32
implk	1.81	1.81	1.81	1.89	1.94	1.95	1.04	1.07	1.08
step	1.84	1.84	1.84	3.09	3.14	3.18	1.68	1.71	1.73
newrz	1.65	1.68	1.70	2.08	2.60	3.05	1.26	1.55	1.79
matmul1	1.82	1.82	1.82	1.94	2.28	2.64	1.07	1.25	1.45
matmul2	1.79	1.79	1.79	2.93	3.13	3.25	1.64	1.75	1.82
mean	1.71	1.74	1.76	2.05	2.31	2.54	1.18	1.32	1.45
σ	0.27	0.24	0.23	0.67	0.60	0.57	0.27	0.28	0.31

Table. 2: Cache speedup for 32 processors, 8K data and 8K instruction caches

7.2. Locality

Locality in the address stream has traditionally been divided into temporal and spatial [Smit82]. Let us look in more detail at each type of locality and relate it to the behavior of parallel numerical programs and the coherence enforcement algorithms.

Both the temporal and spatial locality can be subdivided into short–term and long–term locality with respect to time. A short–term temporal locality will refer to a reuse of a variable soon after a previous use. A long–term temporal locality then refers to a reuse taking place after a longer period of time. The short–term spatial locality will refer to a use of a variable soon after another variable with an address next to it was used. Exactly what short and long time means here is not very important. The partitioning is qualitative in nature.

The reason we introduce the above is to study the cache behavior during the execution of a parallel numerical program. There are several questions we want to answer for each type of locality:

1) Does it exist and in what quantity (in relation to other types),
2) How is it affected by parallel execution,
3) What is the effect of the cache organization.

Executing a program on multiple processors may affect the locality in different ways. First of all, parallel execution can result in some loss of locality since different portions of the program are executed by different processors. Second, coherence enforcement by flushing the cache also leads to locality loss. Finally, each processor now has it's own cache, therefore the total cache size usable by the program is much larger (referred to as combined cache effect).

In the case of multiply–nested parallel loops, the program structure changes as more processors are allocated to it. When the number of processors is small the inner parallel loops remain serial. If more processors are available such loops may be executed in parallel which will require additional flushing of the cache.

In terms of the program structure one can relate different types of locality to DO loops. In a singly–nested loop one can have both short–term temporal and short–term spatial locality. In a multiply–nested loop one can have long–term temporal and spatial locality between different instantiations of the inner loop. Long–term locality can also exist between different loops. Note that the coherence enforcement algorithm does not destroy locality in a loop unless it has parallel loops or subroutine calls nested inside, but will destroy locality between parallel and serial loops or between parallel loops in sequential order.

7.3. Hit ratios and locality

In this section we present the results of measuring the different types of hit ratios and discuss the effects of different types of program structure on locality. The values of h, the conventional hit ratio, h_1, the uniprocessor hit ratio, h_P, the multiprocessor hit ratio, h_P^S and h_P^P, the serial and parallel parts of the parallel hit ratio (as defined in Section 5) are shown in Tables 3 and 4 for 32 and 128 processors, respectively.

By comparing "h" to h_1 we can estimate the locality loss due to parallel execution of a program and flushing. The following discussion of locality loss is based on Table 3. The values in Table 3 are measured with finite size cache, and the advantage of a larger combined cache will favor the "h" values. Therefore, the locality loss may be even higher.

The subroutines in our benchmark set can be divided into three groups depending on their program structure:

(1) The Step and Ux routines have very little serial code, and almost the entire routine is enclosed by an outermost DOALL loop with large loop bounds. Inner DOALL loops are serialized, and thus no flushing is needed inside the loop. There is no locality of loss due to flushing, and the loss of locality due to parallel execution is small. h_1 and "h" values of these routines are not very different in the 32 processor case in Table 3. The Matmul1 and Matmul2 routines also have similar structure and have no locality loss due to flushing or parallel execution.

(2) Routines Parmvr, Ffs99, Cmslow, and Newrz have a mixture of serial and DOALL loops. They are all affected by locality loss due to flushing in the 32 processor case. The "h" values are lower than those of h_1. However, the increase in block size gains a large amount of spatial locality and results in smaller difference between "h" and h_1.

(3) Lblkern, Implk, and Ftrvmt have a serial loop enclosing most of the code in the routines and flushing is needed on every iteration of the serial loop (due to the enclosed DOALL loops and subroutine calls). Long–term locality suffers severely. The routines in this group have by far the lowest "h" values in Table 3 and two of them have largest and the second largest difference between "h" and h_1.

Subr.	h			h_1			h_P			h_P^S			h_P^p		
	blk 1	blk 2	blk 4	blk 1	blk 2	blk 4	blk 1	blk 2	blk 4	blk 1	blk 2	blk 4	blk 1	blk 2	blk 4
parmvr	82.3	90.6	94.5	88.8	93.9	96.4	51.0	75.3	87.3	44.2	71.9	85.7	89.0	93.9	96.1
lblkern	7.12	27.5	38.9	96.5	96.8	96.9	13.3	33.4	43.5	67.3	79.6	83.6	3.2	25.2	36.8
ffs99	44.9	65.4	79.6	88.8	93.7	96.5	29.1	57.9	75.3	3.3	50.7	74.7	45.1	64.1	78.3
cmslow	50.3	72.2	82.9	79.5	89.7	94.8	47.6	68.3	78.7	18.1	25.3	32.5	50.4	72.5	83.1
ftrvmts	41.5	44.2	46.2	93.2	96.0	97.8	30.7	42.5	53.9	29.4	49.9	62.4	42.8	43.6	44.4
ux	90.9	92.5	93.4	93.2†	93.4†	93.8†	90.9	92.5	93.4	0.00	0.00	0.00	90.9	92.5	93.4
implk	32.7	57.4	58.1	49.8	66.8	74.7	42.3	49.4	49.5	46.7	46.7	46.7	30.8	59.1	59.7
step	95.2	96.7	97.4	95.8†	97.0†	97.6†	95.2	96.7	97.4	20.0	40.0	60.0	95.2	96.7	97.4
newrz	59.1	78.7	88.9	81.6	90.5	95.1	58.7	78.4	88.6	33.3	33.3	66.7	58.8	78.6	88.8
matmul1	43.7	65.6	79.6	49.8*	63.8*	87.3*	43.7	65.6	79.6	0.0	0.0	0.0	43.7	65.6	79.6
matmul2	87.9	93.5	96.2	93.0*	95.4*	96.6*	87.9	93.5	96.2	0.0	0.0	0.0	87.9	93.5	96.2

Table. 3: Data hit ratios for 32 processors, 8 K data and 8 K instruction caches

Subr.	h			h_1			h_P			h_P^S			h_P^p		
	blk 1	blk 2	blk 4	blk 1	blk 2	blk 4	blk 1	blk 2	blk 4	blk 1	blk 2	blk 4	blk 1	blk 2	blk 4
ffs99	41.8	50.6	63.2	88.8	93.7	96.5	16.7	49.2	69.8	3.3	50.7	74.7	39.7	46.6	61.5
cmslow	40.2	61.4	70.6	79.5	89.7	94.8	36.0	54.5	63.3	18.1	25.3	32.5	40.2	61.5	70.7
ux	82.7	89.0	92.1	93.2†	93.4†	93.8†	82.7	89.0	92.1	0.0	0.0	0.0	82.7	89.0	92.1
step	93.0	95.6	96.9	95.8†	97.0†	97.6†	92.9	95.6	96.9	20.0	40.0	60.0	92.9	95.6	96.9
newrz	56.2	74.9	84.6	81.6	90.5	95.1	55.9	74.3	84.2	33.3	33.3	66.7	56.2	74.8	84.4
matmul1	25.0	37.5	68.7	49.8*	63.8*	87.3*	25.0	37.5	68.7	0.0	0.0	0.0	25.0	37.5	68.7
matmul2	93.8	96.6	97.8	93.0*	95.4*	96.6*	93.8	96.6	97.8	0.0	0.0	0.0	93.8	96.6	97.8

Table. 4: Data hit ratios for 128 processors, 8 K data and 8 K instruction caches

† Extrapolated from 4 processor simulation
* By estimation

We tried to evaluate the combined cache effect by running infinite cache simulations on 32 processors but the effect is non–existent.

7.4. The effect of cache size

In this section we show the results of varying the cache size on the hit ratios. Most of our experiments were performed assuming an 8K word cache (the size we consider realistic at this moment). As more processors become available to a program, one expects an increase in the size of problems people want to solve. A smaller cache size gives some indication of how the 8K word cache would perform if the problem size were increased. The data hit ratios for three different cache sizes are shown in Table 5. Note that only five subroutines from our benchmark set are shown here. For all other routines, the infinite cache and the 1K word cache behave the same as 8K cache.

For subroutines shown, the infinite cache gives very high data hit ratios for all but one of the routines (parmvr). The Ux, Step, Matmul1, and Matmul2 subroutines have an outermost parallel loop. Flushing, therefore, has no effect on these routines. The block size has a small effect for these routines. Since the hit ratio for block size of one is over 90%, these four programs have a lot of temporal locality, and it dominates the spatial locality. The parmvr subroutine consists of a series of singly–nested loops all of which, except the last one, are parallel. Therefore the subroutine has no long–term locality as the cache is flushed after every loop. It does have short–term temporal and spatial locality in each loop.

In the case of 8K cache Parmvr have the same hit ratios as with the infinite cache. Ux, Step, and Matmul2 show a small decrease, and Matmul1 has a large decrease in hit ratios. The largest drop is seen in the case of block size of one, i.e. the temporal locality is lost (especially true in the matrix multiply routines). The effect of block size is large here. With the block size of four we get almost the same hit ratios as on infinite cache. The reason is the spatial locality which was there before (on infinite cache) but was not as important. As temporal locality is lost, i.e. the data has to be fetched again, and again, the spatial locality produces a noticeable improvement in hit ratios.

Subr.	Infinite			8 K			1 K		
	blk 1	blk 2	blk 4	blk 1	blk 2	blk 4	blk 1	blk 2	blk 4
parmvr	51.3	75.6	87.7	51.0	75.3	87.3	45.4	50.4	52.7
ux	96.9	98.4	99.2	90.9	92.5	93.4	50.9	74.7	86.5
step	96.9	98.4	99.1	95.2	96.7	97.4	78.4	83.2	85.3
matmul1	93.5	96.8	98.4	43.7	65.6	79.6	43.7	65.4	79.3
matmul2	97.6	98.9	99.4	87.9	93.5	96.2	48.7	73.1	84.5

Table. 5: Data hit ratios for various cache sizes (for 32 processors)

The same trend, that is the loss of temporal locality but a gain in spatial locality, is seen again as we use a 1K word cache. In addition, Parmvr subroutine shows almost no increase in hit ratios as the block size is increased, due to the overwriting of data within a given iteration of loops. This somewhat decreases short–term temporal locality and almost completely wipes out short–term spatial locality.

The overwriting of cache blocks is partially due to the direct–mapped cache organization. The set–associative organization will help in such cases to a certain degree. The results in this section indicate that as problem size grows, even caches we consider large today will benefit from set–associative organization in the future.

7.5. The effect of the number of processors

We varied the number of processors in the system while the problem size (array dimensions and loop bounds) and cache organization remained fixed. This was done for the subroutines which show speedup S_p increase beyond 32 processors. (see Table 6). The same global memory access time of ten clocks was used in all simulations. While increasing the number of processors can add more network stages, using the same global memory access time will only make the cache speedups more conservative (see discussion in 7.6). The cache speedup (over the system without cache) and the values of combined hit ratio for instructions and data are plotted for individual routines as a function of the number of processors in Figures 2.a through 2.g. As more processors are allocated to a program, the three different effects on cache behavior we described earlier, namely locality loss due to parallel execution and flushing and locality increase due to larger total cache size, can be observed.

Subroutine	Number of Processors		
	32	128	∞
newrz	30.5	114.0	759.6
matmul2*	30.0	116.2	234.6†
matmul1*	30.0	104.8	179.5†
cmslow	27.6	76.8	157.0
ux††	27.1	108.4	1327.9
step††	21.2	84.2	435.3
ffs99	12.9	23.1	25.4
parmvr	7.1	8.3	8.8
implk	5.4	6.2	6.2
lblkernal	5.2	5.3	5.3
ftrvmt	4.1	4.1	4.1

Table. 6: Multiple processor speedup

* Execution time for 1 processor case is estimated

† Simulated for 256 processors instead

†† Execution time for 1 processor case is extrapolated from 4 processor case.

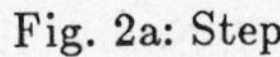
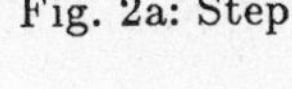

Fig. 2a: Step

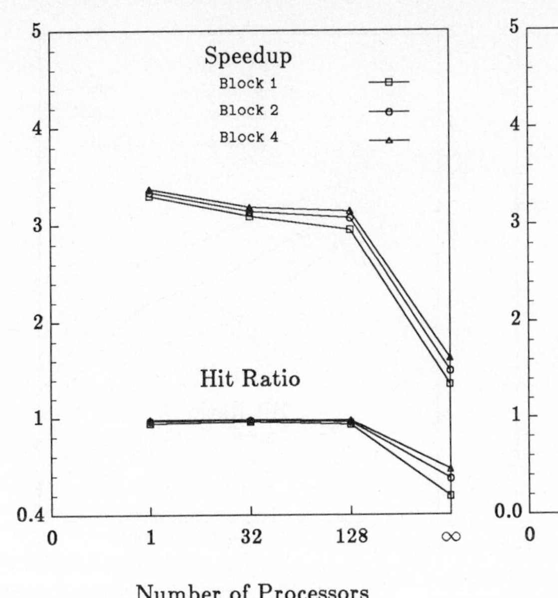

Fig. 2b: Cmslow (Baro)

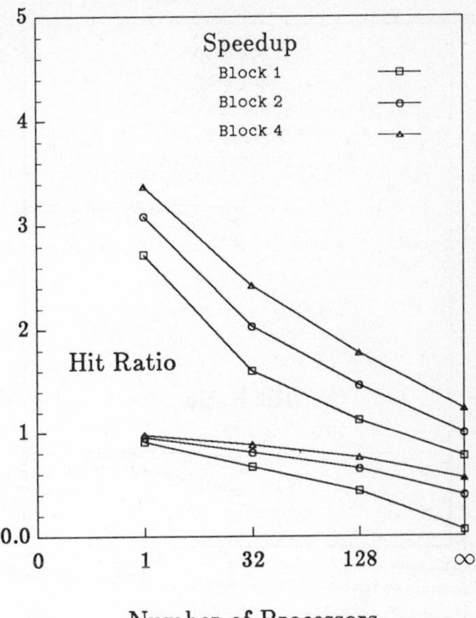

Fig. 2c: FFS99 (Weather)

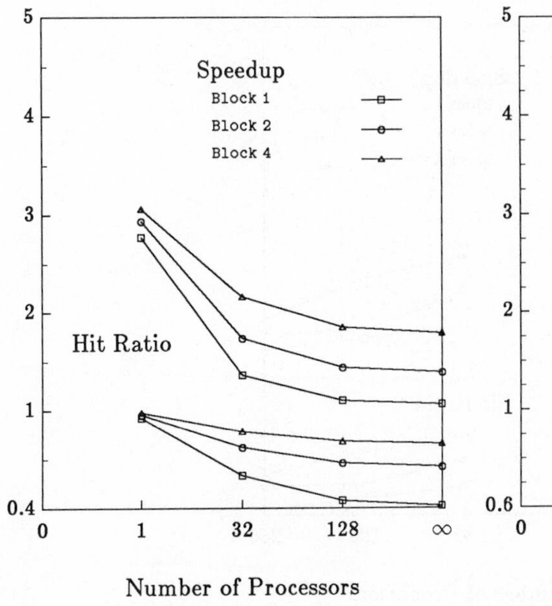

Fig. 2d: UX (Vortex)

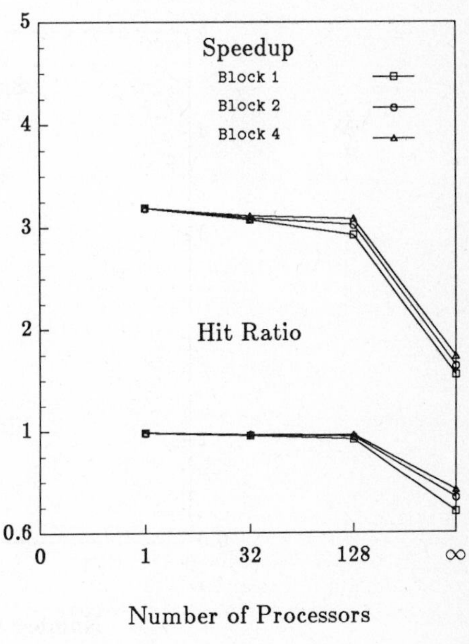

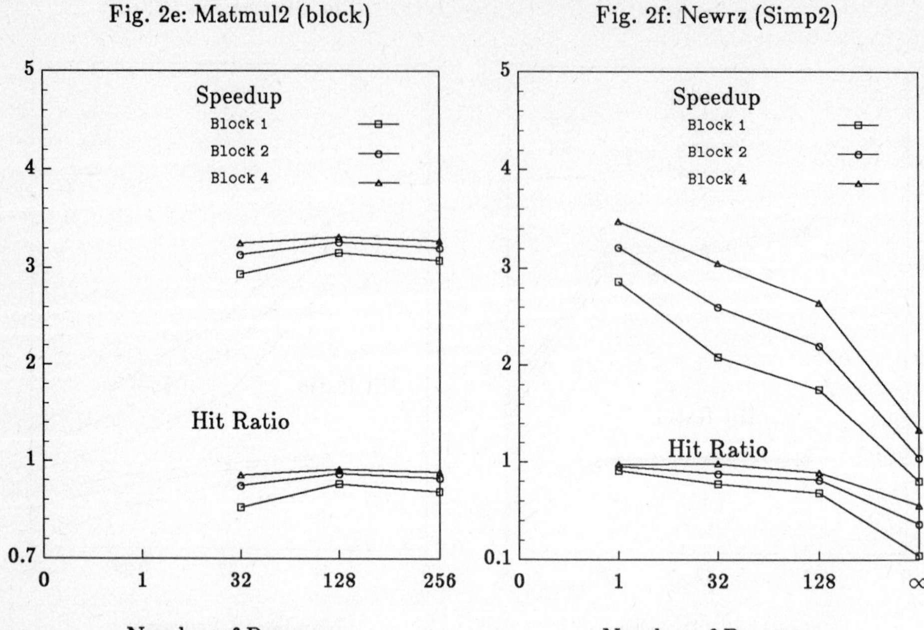
Fig. 2e: Matmul2 (block)
Speedup
Block 1
Block 2
Block 4
Hit Ratio
5
4
3
2
1
0.7
0
1
32
128
256
Number of Processors
Fig. 2f: Newrz (Simp2)
Speedup
Block 1
Block 2
Block 4
Hit Ratio
5
4
3
2
1
0.1
0
1
32
128
∞
Number of Processors

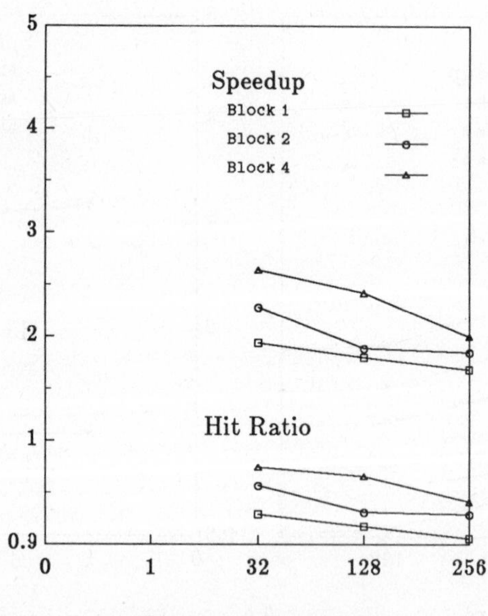
Fig. 2g: Matmul1 (Strip)
Speedup
Block 1
Block 2
Block 4
Hit Ratio
5
4
3
2
1
0.9
0
1
32
128
256
Number of Processors

The loss of locality due to parallel execution and flushing can be observed in the cache speedup and hit ratio decrease for all programs on 32 processors as compared to the uniprocessor execution. The subroutines Matmul1, Step, and Ux are parallel at the outermost DO loop level and have large enough loop bounds to show the same cache behavior on 32 and 128 processors. Subroutines Newrz, Cmslow, and FFs99 have show a decrease in speedup and hit ratio values from 32 processor case to 128 processor case due to the parallel execution of inner loops. Finally, a large drop in cache speedup and hit ratios in the unlimited processor case represents the fact that all parallel loops are now allocated the maximum number of processors. For all practical purposes the only loops left in a subroutine are the serial loops. Everything else becomes a straight–line code with a lot of Flush instructions. This leads to a large loss of locality for both data and instructions. (Note that Matmul1 and Matmul2 are simulated with 256 processors instead of unlimited number of processors.)

The Matmul2 subroutine demonstrates the speedup increase due to a larger combined cache size in the system (from 32 8K data caches to 128 8K data caches in our experiments) and the ability of the program structure to exploit it. Matmul2 performs a 256×256 matrix multiplication by partition. In the 32 processors case a partition each processor calculates plus the input data are too large for the processor's 8K cache. In the 128 processor case the partition each processor calculates becomes smaller and everything fits into the 8K cache. In both cases only the outermost loop is parallel, and the program structure each processor executes remains basically the same. Therefore, the algorithm used in Matmul2 preserves the long–term temporal locality better with a smaller partition in the 8K private cache and has the ability to exploit the larger combined cache size of the 128 processor system. Further reduction of partition size in the case of 256 processors does not help since everything a processor needs is already in the cache.

In general, depending on the program structure, both the benefit of the larger combined cache size and the loss due to increased amount of parallelism may be present as the number of processors is increased. These conflicting effects influence the cache speedup and hit ratio values in different directions. The overall trend is a drop in hit ratios if more than one processor is used, followed by either an increase or a decrease in the hit ratios as the number of processors is increased up to a certain point (depending on which of the effects dominates), and finally a drop as the combined cache becomes large enough. The only effect is the loss of locality due to parallel execution.

7.6. The Effect of Memory Access Time

We performed simulations for two different values of the global memory access time (10 and 15 clocks) on a 32–processor architecture. The results are shown in Table 7. While the hit ratios are the same in both cases, the cache speedups are higher for all subroutines with slower global memory. Seven programs achieve speedup values larger than 3 and three of them have values larger than 4 when the memory access time is 15 clocks and the block size is 4.

The effect of larger block size is also larger for slower memory. The increase in the average speedup is 12.2 percent going from block size of one to block size of two and 10.4 percent

Subr.	$t_m = 10$			$t_m = 15$		
	blk 1	blk 2	blk 4	blk 1	blk 2	blk 4
parmvr	1.72	2.24	2.72	2.03	2.80	3.55
lblkern	1.44	1.59	1.72	1.66	1.88	2.06
ffs99	1.36	1.74	2.16	1.55	2.09	2.70
cmslow	1.60	2.03	2.42	1.84	2.46	3.03
ftrvmts	1.43	1.58	1.79	1.65	1.86	2.15
ux	3.07	3.09	3.11	4.20	4.24	4.28
implk	1.89	1.94	1.95	2.26	2.35	2.35
step	3.09	3.14	3.18	4.22	4.33	4.40
newrz	2.08	2.60	3.05	2.51	3.29	4.02
matmul1	1.94	2.28	2.64	2.33	2.85	3.42
matmul2	2.93	3.13	3.25	3.90	4.25	4.47
mean	2.05	2.30	2.54	2.56	2.95	3.31
σ	0.67	0.60	0.57	1.04	0.95	0.91

Table. 7: Cache speedup for different global memory access time t_m
(32 processor, 8K data and 8K instruction cache)

from block size 2 to block size 4 (for ten clock memory). In the 15 clock case, the increase is 15.2 percent for block size one and 12.2 percent for block size 4.

7.7. Optimizations and algorithm restructuring

There are several things a compiler or a programmer can do to improve cache performance such as

(1) Assign array variables on block size boundaries.

(2) Assign consecutive iterations to a processor.

(3) Interchange loop for stride one access.

We used 2) and on one occassion (Matmul1) 3) in our experiments for increasing the cache performance.

The effect of optimizations and algorithm restructuring can be large as can be observed for the matrix multiply subroutine $C = A \times B$ (see also [JaMe86]). A text–book version of the algorithm was run through Parafrase and the outer two loops recognized as DOALLs. This algorithm results in about a 30% hit ratio (32 processors, 8K I cache and 8K D cache). In this case matrix B is accessed by column and matrix A by row. This results in low short–term spatial locality. Long–term temporal and spatial locality also suffer as the algorithm needs the whole second matrix to produce a row of the resulting matrix. Since the matrices are bigger than the cache size the long–term locality is non–existent.

Interchanging DOALLs for stride–1 access results in a 70% hit ratio, as now both matrices are accessed by column. In this scheme, a processor calculates an eight row strip of matrix C by columns.

$$column_j(C) = \sum_{i=1}^{i=N} B_{ij} \cdot column_i(A)$$

Each column of matrix A is used once for calculating a column of the C matrix strip and is re–used for every iteration of j (or N iterations of i). The columns of the A matrix strip can be re–used. However, the 8K cache is too small to keep all columns of A in the direct mapped cache since they are overwritten by other columns of A with a periodicity of every 32 columns. The long–term temporal locality still suffers.

The final algorithm multiplies matrices by partition. Each processor computes a 46×46 block of C and the matrices are intentionally stored in 257×257 arrays to reduce the effect of direct mapping. The C block is the inner product of a row of A blocks and a column of B blocks. Each processor multiplies one block of A and a block of B to produce a partial result of the C block. After the partial result is computed the A block and B block can be discarded. The partial result of C block is also calculated by columns as in the previous algorithm. The 8K cache can hold most of the A block and the algorithm preserves the long–term temporal locality (columns of A block re–used every 46 iterations of the innermost loop). The gain in long–term locality accounts for 44 percent increase in the hit ratio from the previous algorithm.

Since overwriting a part of the A matrix block still occurs with with 46×46 partition size, the solution is not optimal with respect to an 8K cache. Optimal results can be obtained if we have a large cache or we go to smaller partition sizes. Results in the 128 processor case have much higher hit ratios with partition size 23×23, and the gain in long–term temporal locality results in an increase of additional 5.9 percent (difference of "h" values at block size 1 in Tables 3 and 4).

8. Conclusion

In this paper we studied the effect of data caches on the performance of parallel numerical programs (and vice versa). The private data caches with coherence enforced by software worked quite well. The data hit ratios are lower than on a uniprocessor, but, except for pathological cases, are between 75 and 97% for a block size of four words. The reasons why data hit ratios are lower are explained and have to do with parallel execution and coherence enforcement. While low by uniprocessor standards, a 75% data hit ratio still gives a lot of performance improvement since the (shared) memory access time is much longer on a multiprocessor. There is enough spatial locality in numerical programs, and a larger cache block size improves the hit ratios and the performance noticeably. Cache performance decreases as the number of processors in the system is increased if care is not taken in designing or optimizing the programs. But as long as the program remains mostly parallel and the parallelism is not over–utilized, cache performance remains fairly constant. The performance will actually improve in this constant hit ratio region as the system size grows and the memory access time gets longer. With respect to cache size, we observed a considerable performance degradation when the cache size was decreased. In most cases this was due to the loss of temporal locality and can only be helped by better algorithm design. In some cases, however, direct mapping was the reason. While we do not expect caches to get smaller the problem sizes will grow with machine size and the effect will be the same. Therefore we think set–associative caches become a better choice as the machine size grows even if the cache is as large as 8K words unless, of course, cache size grows with the system size.

One final note about our results. The architecture we used in our simulations is very simple, without any pipelining and with large miss penalties. Can one extrapolate cache performance of a pipelined machine from these results? The answer is that on a pipelined machine the cost of a cache miss is even higher, and cache speedup therefore should be greater (see Appendix I for simplified analysis).

Acknowledgements

We would like to thank William Jalby, Pen Yew, Constantine Polychronopoulos, and Madhu Sharma of the Cedar project technical staff for many fruitful discussions.

Appendix A

We use simplified analysis to show that the cache speedup is greater in a system with pipelined processors than one in a system with non–pipelined processors.

Let S_π be the cache speedup in a system with pipelined processors and $S_{\bar{\pi}}$ be the one in a system with non–pipelined processors.

The following notation is used:

$\alpha =$ the fraction of instructions that have a memory reference ($0 < \alpha \leq 1$).

$N =$ number of *alu* operations in the program.

$T_{op} =$ *alu* operation time in a non–pipelined processor.

$t_{op} =$ time of a pipelined *alu* segment.

$t_m =$ average global memory access time (including network delay).

$t_c =$ cache memory access time.

$t_{\hat{m}} =$ cache miss time.

$h_P =$ multiprocessor hit ratio.

Let's assume that there is one *alu* operation per instruction. Then, we have:

$$S_{\bar{\pi}} = \frac{(T_{op} + t_m \cdot \alpha) \cdot N}{\Big((T_{op} + t_c \cdot \alpha) \cdot h_P + (T_{op} + t_{\hat{m}} \cdot \alpha)(1 - h_P) \Big) \cdot N}$$

$$= \frac{T_{op} + t_m \cdot \alpha}{T_{op} + \Big(h_P \cdot t_c + t_{\hat{m}} \cdot (1 - h_P) \Big) \cdot \alpha}$$

Let's substitute the term multiplied by α in the denominator by X and divide through by T_{op}. We have:

$$S_{\bar{\pi}} = \frac{1 + t_m \cdot \alpha \cdot (\, T_{op}\,)^{-1}}{1 + X \cdot \alpha \cdot (\, T_{op}\,)^{-1}}$$

For a pipelined processor, the average execution time of an instruction without global memory access is t_{op} and t_m with global memory access. Then,

$$S_{\pi} = \frac{(\, t_{op} \cdot (\, 1 - \alpha\,) + t_m \cdot \alpha\,) \cdot N}{\left(t_{op} \cdot (\, 1 - \alpha\,) + (\, h_p \cdot t_c + t_{\hat{m}} \cdot (\, 1 - h_p\,)\,) \cdot \alpha\right) \cdot N}$$

$$= \frac{1 + t_m \cdot \alpha \cdot (t_{op} \cdot (\, 1 - \alpha\,))^{-1}}{1 + X \cdot \alpha \cdot (\, t_{op} \cdot (\, 1 - \alpha\,))^{-1}}$$

Let $\beta = T_{op} \cdot (\, t_{op}\,)^{-1}$, $V = t_m \cdot \alpha \cdot (\, T_{op}\,)^{-1}$ and $W = X \cdot \alpha \cdot (\, T_{op}\,)^{-1}$, we have,

$$S_{\bar{\pi}} = \frac{1 + V}{1 + W}$$

and

$$S_{\pi} = \frac{1 + V \cdot \beta \cdot (\, 1 - \alpha\,)^{-1}}{1 + W \cdot \beta \cdot (\, 1 - \alpha\,)^{-1}} = \frac{1 + V \cdot \gamma}{1 + W \cdot \gamma}$$

The quantity γ is larger than 1. To satisfy $S_{\pi} \geq S_{\bar{\pi}}$, we need,

$$\frac{1 + V}{1 + W} \leq \frac{1 + V \cdot \gamma}{1 + W \cdot \gamma} \qquad => $$

$$(\, V - W\,) \cdot (\, \gamma - 1\,) \geq 0$$

It can be easily verified that V is larger than W if t_m and $t_{\hat{m}}$ are equal and h_p is larger than 0. When $t_{\hat{m}}$ is larger than t_m, V is larger than W if h_p satisfies the following:

$$h_p > \frac{t_{\hat{m}} - t_m}{t_m - t_c}.$$

Since γ is larger than one, cache speedup in a pipeline processor system is larger than the one in a non-pipelined system with the assumption that t_m is equal to $t_{\hat{m}}$ and h_p is positive.

References

[AbKw85] W. Abu-Sufah and A. Y. Kwok, "Performance Prediction Tools for Cedar: A Multiprocessor Supercomputer," *The 12th Annual International Symposium on Computer Architecture, pp. 406-413,* June, 1985.

[Crow85] W. Crowther et al, "Performance Measurements on 128-node Butterfly(TM) Parallel Processor," *Proceedings of the 1985 International Conference on Parallel Processing, pp. 531-540,* 1985.

[FuHa78] S.H. Fuller and S.P. Harbison, "The C.mmp Multiprocessor," Department of Computer Science, Carnegie-Mellon University, Technical Report, 1978.

[GGKM83] A. Gottlieb, R. Grishman, C.P. Kruskal, K.P. McAuliffe, L. Rudolph, and M. Snir, "The NYU Ultracomputer — Designing an MIMD Shared-Memory Parallel Machine," *IEEE Trans. on Computers,* Vol. C-32, No. 2, pp. 175-189, February 1983.

[GKLS83] Daniel Gajski, David Kuck, Duncan Lawrie, and Ahmed Sameh, "Cedar — a Large Scale Multiprocessor," *Proceedings of the 1983 International Conference on Parallel Processing, pp. 524-529,* August, 1983.

[Good83] J.R. Goodman, "Using Cache Memory to Reduce Processor-Memory Traffic," *Proceedings 10th International Symposium on Computer Architecture, pp.124-131,* June, 1983.

[JaMe86] W. Jalby, and U. Meier, "Optimizing Matrix Operations on a Parallel Multiprocessor with a Hierarchical Memory System" *Proceedings 1986 ICPP, pp.429-432,* August, 1986.

[Kuck78] David J. Kuck, "The Structure of Computers and Computations," Volume 1, John Wiley and Sons, New York, 1978.

[KKLW80] D.J. Kuck, R.H. Kuhn, B. Leasure, and M. Wolfe, "The Structure of an Advanced Vectorizer for Pipelined Processors," *Fourth International Computer Software and Applications Conference,* October, 1980.

[Lawr75] D. H. Lawrie, "Access and Alignment of Data in an Array Processor," *IEEE Transactions on Computers,* vol. C-24, no. 12, pp. 1145-1155, December, 1975.

[LuBa80] S. F. Lundstrom and G. H. Barnes, "Controllable MIMD Architecture," *Proceedings of the 1980 International Conference on Parallel Processing, pp. 19-27,* 1980.

[Padu79] D.A. Padua Haiek, "Multiprocessors: Discussions of Some Theoretical and Practical Problems," Ph.D. Thesis, University of Illinois at Urbana-Champaign, DCS Report No. UIUCDCS-R-79-990, November 1979.

[Phis85] G.F. Pfister et al, "The IBM Research Parallel Processor Prototype," *Proceedings of the 1985 International Conference on Parallel Processing, pp. 764-772,* 1985.

[Smit82] A. J. Smith, "Cache Memories," *Computing Surveys, Vol. 14, No.3, pp. 473-530,* September 1982.

[Tang76] C. K. Tang, "Cache System Design in the Tightly Coupled Multiprocessor System," *Proceedings AFIP National Computer Conference, vol.45, pp.749–753,* 1976.

[Wolf82] Michael J. Wolfe, "Optimizing Supercompilers for Supercomputers," Ph.D. Thesis, University of Illinois at Urbana–Champaign, 1982.

[Veid86] A. V. Veidenbaum, "A Compiler–Assisted Cache Coherence Solution for Multiprocessors," *Proceedings of the 1986 International Conference on Parallel Processing, pp. 1029–1036,* 1986.

[YePD83] W.C. Yen, J.H. Patel, E.S. Davidson. "Shared Cache for Multiple–Stream Computer Systems," *IEEE Trans. on Computers, Vol. C-34, No. 1, pp. 56–65,* January, 1983.

Realization of a Knowledge-Based Parallelization Tool in a Programming Environment *

Thomas Brandes, Manfred Sommer

Department of Mathematics / Computer Science, University of Marburg

D-3550 Marburg, Lahnberge

*This work was supported by Siemens AG, Munich, West-Germany

Abstract:

Achieving a high level of parallelism is necessary for software developed for current supercomputers. Therefore, modern programming environments that can also support the development of software for these computers should contain a parallelization tool. Such a software tool analyzes the parallelism of a given program part and suggests optimizing transformations.

A knowledge-based design of the tool makes the extension with new parallelization issues easy, the parallelization better understandable, and the adaption to arbitrary parallel hardware possible. This paper describes how to realize a parallelization tool in a knowledge-based way without becoming inefficient and how to formalize the parallelization process for this purpose.

Key Words: parallelization, programming environment, knowledge base, dependence.

1. Introduction

It is hard to write programs in high level languages which exploit effectively parallel hardware. Although autovectorizing and autoparallelizing compilers exist, the potential of parallelism is often too small to generate runtime-efficient code. Therefore, a parallelization tool supporting the development of software for supercomputers is needed. This tool should be realized in a programming environment [BrSo87].

As modern programming environments [Nagl85, Enge86, TeRe81, DHKL84, KSS86] are already equipped with optimization tools to realize e.g. data-flow analysis for 'dead code elimination' or control-flow analysis to identify loops [ASU86], the tools can be integrated. Additionally, interprocedural analysis can be done naturally and efficiently [KeHo86]. High level data structures used in programming environments are trees or graphs, which are suitable for deleting, inserting and replacing operations. They can also be used to implement transformations needed for parallelization. With unparsing the current state of parallelization can be displayed in a textual representation of the high level data structure.

A knowledge-based design of the parallelization tool is appropriate for the next generation of programming environments. If all information is represented in a high level data structure, transformations are very complicated as the information must always be consistent. For a knowledge-based design only such information will be represented whose determination is complex and difficult. All other information needed for the operations of the tool is determined by rules, which represent a kind of knowledge.

Knowledge bases are specially designed to change and to grow easily, the supplement with new parallelization issues is simple. The rules of the knowledge-bases could also be used to explain reasonings; the parallelization process becomes more understandable. Different levels of knowledge imply different performance of the tool: few knowledge for the most common cases makes the tool fast, whereas the tool is slow if much knowledge for a complex analysis is utilized. Furthermore, with strategies and heuristics the order and the quality of transformations can be specified to get a parallelization appropriate to the software and hardware.

Many techniques for automatic vectorization and parallelization have been developed during the last years: hyperplane method, coordinate method [Lamp74], solving linear recurrences [Kogg74], renaming, expansion, node splitting, forward substitution, loop distribution, loop fusion [KKPL81], loop interchanging, [KeAl84], loop alignment, code replication [AlKe85], strip mining and loop collapsing [PaWo86]. This paper shows how these techniques and others can be realized in a knowledge-based way for a parallelization tool.

After introducing an appropriate high level data structure (2) some definitions and notations are presented (3). Knowledge-based specification of the parallelization (4) is based on simple transformation rules that change execution orders (5), remove dependences, and rearrange computations (6). With heuristics and strategies about these simple rules more complex rules can be constructed(7). Finally, we make some notes about the user interface of the parallelization tool (8).

2. High Level Data Structure

The high level data structure is based on a signature (= sorts + operation symbols) which defines terms of the abstract syntax. The following is a common subset of abstract syntax which appears in high level languages such as Pascal, Modula-2, Ada (for textual representations Modula-2 is used in this paper).

```
ASSIGN$STMT   : var$access    expression                          -> stmt
FOR$STMT      : used$id       range          <stmt>               -> stmt
IF$STMT       : expression    <stmt>         <stmt>               -> stmt
PROC$CALL     : used$id       <expression>                        -> stmt
WHILE$STMT    : expression    <stmt>                              -> stmt
REPEAT$STMT   : expression    <stmt>                              -> stmt
EXIT$STMT     :                                                   -> stmt
CASE$STMT     : expression    <alternative>                       -> stmt

ALTERNATIVE   : <range>       <stmt>                              -> alternative

EXPR          : expression    opnd           expression           -> expression
EXPR1         : expression    opnd                                -> expression
FUNC$CALL     : used$id       <expression>                        -> expression
                selector                                          -> expression
                var$access                                        -> expression

RANGE         : expression    expression     expression           -> range

ORD$CONST     : integer                                           -> selector
REAL$CONST    : real                                              -> selector
                used$id                                           -> selector

DEREF         : var$access                                        -> var$access
SELECTED      : var$access    selector                            -> var$access
INDEXED       : var$access    <expression>                        -> var$access
                used$id                                           -> var$access

USED$ID       : ident                                             -> used$id

predefined sorts: ident, opnd, integer, real

<s> stands for a list of terms of the sort s
```

A program part is a term of the abstract syntax and is represented as a tree in the following way:

1.) Every node (except list nodes) stands for a term and represents a syntactical structure of the program. The nodes are labeled with the operation symbol which is used to build the term. Every node has an attribute list to store additional information (e.g. types, values, addresses)

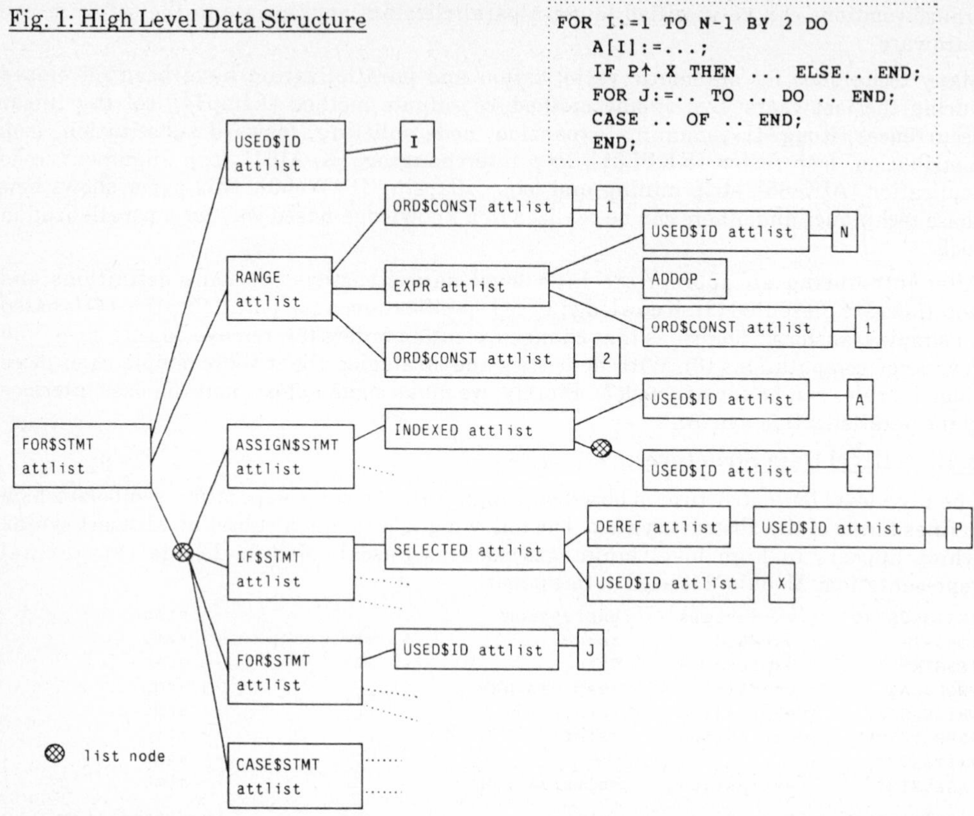

2.) To have as few nodes as possible and a low depth of the tree, list nodes are used and there are no additional nodes to make a 'var$access' or an 'used$id' to an 'expression'.
3.) Further information can be stored in additional edges, as it will be done with the labeled edges for dependences. Operations for these edges have to be implemented.
4.) Inserting, replacing and deleting of subtrees is necessary; a fast implementation is possible by pointers to father and brother nodes.

The following operations are examples for knowledge-based operations on the high level data structure:

- Get the list of (pointers to the) loops in which a syntactical structure appears
- Get the list of common loops for two syntactical structures
- Get all variable accesses in a subtree (e.g. in a statement)
- Get the name of a variable for a variable access
- Determine the access kind (read or write) for a given variable access
- Check whether a variable is changed in a loop or not
- Check whether a variable is unchanged between two accesses

Data dependences between variable accesses only are represented in the high level data structure. To determine data dependences between two arbitrary syntactical structures there are rules to build the union of dependence relations; there are also rules to determine control dependences (e.g. the statements in the then- and else-part are under the control of the condition in an if-statement, the left side in an assignment statement is under the control of the variable accesses in the right side).

3. Executions, Execution Orders and Dependences

Let v be a syntactical structure of a given program part p (p and v are nodes in the high level data structure, p is ancestor of v), and I_v the index set of all executions of v. I_v is a subset of Z^n ($I_v \subset Z^n = Z \times Z \times ... \times Z$, Z is the set of all integers, n is the number of loops in which v appears). The loops have not to be normalized (compare [KeAl84]). The jth execution of v is denoted by v(j).

Let $v_1,...,v_n$ be syntactical structures of a given program part p, $I_{v_1}, ... I_{v_n}$ the corresponding executions sets.

Definition: $v_1,...,v_n$, together with $I_{v_1}, ..., I_{v_n}$, are a partition of p, if all executions $v_i(j)$ together result in the execution of p.

Example 1: Partition

```
p ≡  FOR I:=2 TO N DO
         FOR K:=1 TO M-1 DO
             A[I,K]:=B[I,K]+C[I,K];
             B[I+1,K-1]:=A[I,K-1]+D[I];
         END;
     END;
```

```
v1 ≡ 2 TO N
v2 ≡ 1 TO M-1
v3 ≡ A[I,K]:=B[I,K]+C[I,K];
v4 ≡ B[I+1,K-1]:=A[I,K-1]+D[I];
Iv1 = {1}
Iv2 = {2,..,N}
Iv3 = Iv4 = {2,...,N} × {1,...,M-1}
```

All executions of v_1, v_2, v_3 and v_4 together result in the execution of the doubly nested loop.

By the given syntax of the program part p and by the semantic of the underlying programming language there is an order for every pair of syntactical structures, v_i and v_j:

$$O_{v_i<v_j} \subset I_{v_i} \times I_{v_j}, (x,y) \in O_{v_i<v_j} :\Leftrightarrow v_i(x) < v_j(y)$$

$v_i(x) < v_j(y)$ means that $v_i(x)$ is executed before $v_j(y)$ in the given execution order. If the number of common loops of v_i and v_j is n and these loops are sequential for-loops, then the execution order $O_{v_i<v_j}$ is given by:

$$O_{v_i<v_j} = \leqq_n \quad \text{if } v_i<v_j$$
$$O_{v_i<v_j} = <_n \quad \text{otherwise}$$

$v_i < v_j$ means that v_i is syntactically (textually) placed before v_j (attention: $v_j:=..v_i..$; here $v_i < v_j$). $<_n$ and $\leqq_n$ are the lexicographical order of Z^n and can be defined as follows (see also appendix):

$$x=(x_1, x_2, ..., x_n, ..., x_{n+a}) \in I_{v_i} \subset Z^{n+a} \qquad y=(y_1, y_2, ..., y_n, ..., y_{n+b}) \in I_{v_j} \subset Z^{n+b}$$
$$<_n \subset I_{v_i} \times I_{v_j} \subset Z^{n+a} \times Z^{n+b}, \ (x,y) \in <_n :\Leftrightarrow (x_1, x_2, ..., x_n) < (y_1, y_2, ..., y_n)$$
$$\leqq_n \subset I_{v_i} \times I_{v_j} \subset Z^{n+a} \times Z^{n+b}, \ (x,y) \in \leqq_n :\Leftrightarrow (x_1, x_2, ..., x_n) \leqq (y_1, y_2, ..., y_n)$$

Although the execution order has not to be the lexicographical order (if for e.g. the loops are FORALL-loops, see 5.3), the order can be exactly determined. It can be specified by rules how to get the order relation for two syntactical structures v_i and v_j.

A dependence between two different executions $v_i(x)$ and $v_j(y)$, denoted by $v_i(x) \rightarrow v_j(y)$, designates a situation where the order of executions must not be changed otherwise the semantic of the program part could be changed. The dependence relation $D_{v_i \rightarrow v_j}$ is a subset of the order relation $O_{v_i<v_j}$.

$$D_{v_i \rightarrow v_j} = \{ (x,y) \mid v_i(x) \rightarrow v_j(y) \} \subset O_{v_i<v_j} \subset I_{v_i} \times I_{v_j}$$

There are two different kinds of dependences: control dependences and data dependences.

A control dependence $v_i(x) \rightarrow_C v_j(y)$ arises if the control flow indicates that $v_i(x)$ has to be executed before $v_j(y)$, e.g. $v_i(x)$ produces a result that $v_j(y)$ needs, or only after the execution of $v_i(x)$ it can be told whether $v_j(y)$ is executed or not. Control dependences can be determined exactly by the syntax of the given program part.

A data dependence between two different executions arises if the same memory location is used at least once for an output. Three different kinds of data dependence are possible (see [KKPL81]):

$v_i(x) \rightarrow_T v_j(y)$: $v_j(y)$ uses the output of $v_i(x)$ as input; this is called true dependence or flow dependence

$v_i(x) \rightarrow_A v_j(y)$: $v_i(x)$ might wrongly use the output of $v_j(y)$ as input if they were reversed in order; this is called anti dependence

$v_i(x) \rightarrow_O v_j(y)$: $v_j(y)$ recomputes the output of $v_i(x)$; this is called output dependence

As the data dependences between two arbitrary syntactical structures is the union of all data dependences between their variable accesses, in the following only data dependences between variable accesses are examined.

Now v_i and v_j are two variable accesses to the same variable of which at least one is a write access ($I_{v_i} \subset \mathbf{Z}^{n+a}$, $I_{v_j} \subset \mathbf{Z}^{n+b}$, where n is the number of common loops). Every variable access can be regarded as a subscripted access (the dereferentiation of a pointer-variable is a subscripted access to the heap, the selection of a field component in a record can be considered as a subscripted access with a constant), so there are two subscript functions for the accesses:

$$f_i : I_{v_i} \rightarrow S, \quad f_j : I_{v_j} \rightarrow S \qquad \text{(S is the set of possible subscripts for the variable)}$$

The equality relation of the subscripts $f_i{=}f_j$ is defined as follows:

$$f_i{=}f_j \subset I_{v_i} \times I_{v_j}, \qquad (x,y) \in f_i{=}f_j \;:\Leftrightarrow\; f_i(x) = f_j(y).$$

With this equality relation the data dependence relation is given by:

$$D_{v_i \rightarrow v_j} = O_{v_i < v_j} \cap f_i{=}f_j, \qquad D_{v_j \rightarrow v_i} = O_{v_j < v_i} \cap f_i{=}f_j \qquad (\text{Note: } f_i{=}f_j = f_i{=}f_j^{-1})$$

A dependence is given if $f_i(x)$ is equal to $f_j(y)$ for two executions $v_i(x)$ and $v_j(y)$. In general, this equality cannot be determined exactly. With two relations $q_{<f_i=f_j}$ and $q_{>f_i=f_j}$ the equality relation is approximated in the following way:

$$q_{<f_i=f_j} \subset f_i{=}f_j \subset q_{>f_i=f_j} \subset I_{v_i} \times I_{v_j}$$

$q_{<f_i=f_j}$ gives information about real equality, $q_{>f_i=f_j}$ shows where equality has to be assumed. $q_{<f_i=f_j}$ should be as weak as possible and $q_{>f_i=f_j}$ as strong as possible. $q_{<f_i=f_j} = q_{>f_i=f_j}$ is the sharpest determination.

$q_{<f_i=f_j}$ and $q_{>f_i=f_j}$ can be used in the following way to get an approximation of the dependence relation:

Set: $p_{<v_i \rightarrow v_j} := O_{v_i < v_j} \cap q_{<f_i=f_j}$ $\qquad p_{>v_i \rightarrow v_j} := O_{v_i < v_j} \cap q_{>f_i=f_j}$

Then: $p_{<v_i \rightarrow v_j} \subset D_{v_i \rightarrow v_j} \subset p_{>v_i \rightarrow v_j} \subset O_{v_i < v_j} \subset I_{v_i} \times I_{v_j}$

The better the approximation of the equality relation is, the better is the approximation of the dependence relation. For a knowledge-based parallelization it is most important to describe as exactly as possible the dependence relation. Not only information about assumed dependences ($p_{>v_i \rightarrow v_j}$) is necessary, the information about real existing dependences ($p_{<v_i \rightarrow v_j}$) is also used to recognize the kind of computations, to specify some transformations (renaming, expansion, see 6.1) and to have information how good the dependence relation is determined.

To get the approximating sets $q_{<f_i=f_j}$ and $q_{>f_i=f_j}$ there exist many dependence tests (e.g. see [Lamp74], [Bane79], [Wolf82] and [KeAl84]). But these tests were inadequate to be used for a knowledge-based dependence determination. Hence, a new knowledge-based dependence test has been developed [Bran87]. The knowledge-based determination of the equality relation proves semantic properties for syntactical structures by deducting them from other properties and from the syntactical structure of the program part. With the rules nearly every property can be proved that is useful for the automatic determination of the equality relation (e.g. gcd-test, Banerjees inequality [Bane79], use of global knowledge).

Subsets of $I_{v_i} \times I_{v_j}$ are specified by a predicate; it is a mapping $p : I_{v_i} \times I_{v_j} \to \{\text{true, false}\}$. Such a predicate corresponds one to one to a subset of $I_{v_i} \times I_{v_j}$. A possible set of predicates with operations on them is presented in the appendix; the predicates are a generalization of direction vectors [Wolf82].

<u>Example 2: Predicates describing dependences between variable accesses</u>

```
FOR I:=1 TO N-1 DO
    A[I]:=B[I]+C[I];
    B[I]:=A[I+1]+F[I];
    END;
```

$v_1 \equiv$ B[I] (of 1.assignment)
$v_2 \equiv$ B[I] (of 2.assignment)
$v_3 \equiv$ A[I]
$v_4 \equiv$ A[I+1] $\quad I_{v_1} = I_{v_2} = I_{v_3} = I_{v_4} = \{1,\dots,N-1\}$

$f_1 : \{1,\dots,N-1\} \to Z,\ f_1(x)=x \qquad f_1{=}f_2 = ('0'),\ f_1(x)=f_2(y) \Leftrightarrow y-x=0$

$f_2 : \{1,\dots,N-1\} \to Z,\ f_2(y)=y \qquad f_2{=}f_1 = f_1{=}f_2^{-1} = ('0')$

$f_3 : \{1,\dots,N-1\} \to Z,\ f_3(x)=x \qquad f_3{=}f_4 = ('-1'),\ f_3(x)=f_4(y) \Leftrightarrow y-x=-1$

$f_4 : \{1,\dots,N-1\} \to Z,\ f_4(y)=y+1 \qquad f_4{=}f_3 = f_3{=}f_4^{-1} = ('1')$

$D_{v_1 \to v_2} = O_{v_1<v_2} \cap f_1{=}f_2 = [('0') \vee ('>')] \wedge ('0') = ('0')$

$D_{v_2 \to v_1} = O_{v_2<v_1} \cap f_2{=}f_1 = ('>') \wedge ('0') = \text{'false'}$

$D_{v_3 \to v_4} = O_{v_3<v_4} \cap f_3{=}f_4 = [('0') \vee ('>')] \wedge ('-1') = \text{'false'}$

$D_{v_4 \to v_3} = O_{v_4<v_3} \cap f_4{=}f_3 = ('>') \wedge ('1') = ('1')$

4. Knowledge-Based Specification of Parallelization

Kuck, Wolfe, Kennedy, Allen et al. [KKPL81, KeAl84, Wolf82, PaWo86] pursue optimization for the parallelization and vectorization by operations on the dependence graph or they make transformations based on information which is given by the dependence graph. Though transformations have now to be specified in a knowledge-based way, the dependence graph is used in a similar way.

a) Simple Transformation Rules

A simple transformation rule specifies a transformation for the given partition of a program part. With the predicates for the variable accesses and rules to determine dependences between arbitrary syntactical structures a dependence graph for the partition is built (outer loops are hold constant). This dependence graph is used to check the precondition for the transformation. If the transformation is safe, the transformation can be carried out in the specified way. Afterwards the predicates of dependence edges between variable accesses are updated. Hence, the description of the dependence relation is updated efficiently, a new expensive determination is not necessary.

b) Assessment Heuristics

If for a given situation more than one transformation rule can be applied or the same transformation rule can be applied in different ways, one has to decide which transformation leads to a better solution. So every possible transformation could be carried out and with assessment heuristics it will be decided which transformation is the most useful one. Many assessment heuristics might depend on the kind of parallel hardware that is used.

c) Strategies and Transformation heuristics

If for a given program part every transformation is tried out, parallelization becomes inefficient. With strategies and transformation heuristics it can be specified in which order and how often transformation rules are applied.

d) Complex transformation rules

A more complex transformation can be specified by a set of simpler transformations and by heuristics and strategies about them.

5. Changing Execution Orders

Many transformations (e.g. loop distribution, loop fusion, loop interchanging, coordinate method, hyperplane method) change the order of executions. Before representing these transformations as simple transformation rules it is formalized how the order can be changed and how to prove the precondition of a transformation.

5.1 Formalization of changing execution orders

Let p be a given program section and $v_1, ..., v_n$ with $I_{v_1}, I_{v_2}, ..., I_{v_n}$ a partition of p. The order of executions (denoted by $O_{v_i<v_j}$, see 3) is defined by:

i) the textual order $v_i<v_j$ (v_i is placed before v_j)
ii) the number of common loops for every pair $<v_i,v_j>$
iii) the lexicographical order of $\mathbf{Z}^n$, where n is the number of common loops

In the same way the order can be changed. As the lexicographical order of $\mathbf{Z}^n$ reflects the structure of loops, it has to be changed implicitly. This is done by defining bijective mappings $g_i: I_{v_i} \rightarrow I'_{v_i}$.

So changing the execution order can be defined by (see fig. 2):

a) bijective mappings $g_i: I_{v_i} \rightarrow I'_{v_i}$ for every i
b) $O'_{v_i<v_j} \subset I'_{v_i} \times I'_{v_j}$ for every pair $<i,j>$; $O'_{v_i<v_j}$ is given by textual order, number of common loops and kind of common loops

Fig. 2: Transformation Diagram:

$$\begin{array}{ccccc} D_{v_i\rightarrow v_j} & \subset & O_{v_i<v_j} & \subset & I_{v_i} \times I_{v_j} \\ \downarrow <g_i,g_j> & & & & \downarrow g_i \quad \downarrow g_j \\ D'_{v_i\rightarrow v_j} & \subset & O'_{v_i<v_j} & \subset & I'_{v_i} \times I'_{v_j} \\ & \uparrow & & & \\ & \text{Precondition} & & & \end{array}$$

It can be guaranteed that the semantic is not changed if the new order preserves the dependences; if one execution depends on another, the order between these executions must not be changed; so the following relation must hold (see fig. 2):

$$D'_{v_i\rightarrow v_j} \subset O'_{v_i<v_j}$$

where $D'_{v_i\rightarrow v_j} := <g_i,g_j>(D_{v_i\rightarrow v_j})$ is the image of $D_{v_i\rightarrow v_j}$ given by the following bijective mapping:

$$<g_i,g_j>: I_{v_i} \times I_{v_j} \rightarrow I'_{v_i} \times I'_{v_j}, \; <g_i,g_j>(x,y) := (g_i(x),g_j(y))$$

If this precondition is satisfied, the order can be changed by restructuring the tree in the high level data structure. The predicates for assumed dependences are used to prove the precondition:

Fig. 3: Extended Transformation Diagram:

$$\begin{array}{ccccccccc} p_{<v_i\to v_j} & \subset & D_{v_i\to v_j} & \subset & p_{>v_i\to v_j} & \subset & O_{v_i<v_j} & \subset & I_{v_i}\times I_{v_j} \\ \downarrow{\scriptstyle <g_i,g_j>} & & \downarrow{\scriptstyle <g_i,g_j>} & & \downarrow{\scriptstyle <g_i,g_j>} & & & & \downarrow{\scriptstyle g_i}\quad\downarrow{\scriptstyle g_j} \\ p'_{<v_i\to v_j} & \subset & D'_{v_i\to v_j} & \subset & p'_{>v_i\to v_j} & \subset & O'_{v_i<v_j} & \subset & I'_{v_i}\times I'_{v_j} \\ & & & & & \uparrow & & & \\ & & & & & \text{Precondition} & & & \end{array}$$

The extended transformation diagram shows also how the predicates of the dependence description are updated. A predicate p: $I_{v_i} \times I_{v_j} \to \{true,false\}$ that describes a dependence relation between variable accesses (and only such descriptions are stored in the high level data structure) is replaced by $<g_i,g_j>(p)$ where g_i and g_j are the corresponding mappings for the variable accesses. The operation "get $<g_i,g_j>(p)$ by p and g_i and g_j" is one of the most important operations on predicates.

Changing the order is always possible if the precondition is satisfied and the program transformation - carried out in the high level data structure - is specified. The predicates p between the variable accesses are replaced with $<g_i,g_j>(p)$. If an exact determination is not possible, $<g_i,g_j>(p)$ can be substituted by a weaker predicate for the assumed dependences or a stronger predicate for the real dependences.

In the following some transformations are examined. Every other transformation that change execution orders should be specified in this way.

5.2. Loop Vectorization

The simultaneous execution of a loop ($SIMFOR-Loop) means the execution of every iteration of the loop on an own processor and every execution is performed synchronously by the individual processors. This kind of loop is appropriate for SIMD-architectures [Lamp74].

Transforming a sequential loop into a loop that can be executed simultaneously is possible if there are no dependences between v_i and v_j unless v_i is textually placed before v_j.

```
FOR I:=a TO b BY c DO                 $SIMFOR I:=a TO b BY c DO
  v1 ........ vn          ----->        v1 ........ vn
END;                                  END;
```

Theorem 1: The transformation is valid if $D_{v_i<v_j} \neq \emptyset$ implies $v_i<v_j$.

Proof: see the following diagram.

$$\begin{array}{ccccc} D_{v_i\to v_j} & \subset & O_{v_i<v_j} & \subset & I_{v_i}\times I_{v_j} \\ \downarrow{\scriptstyle <id,id>} & & & & \downarrow{\scriptstyle id}\quad\downarrow{\scriptstyle id} \\ D_{v_i\to v_j} & \subset & O'_{v_i<v_j} & \subset & I_{v_i}\times I_{v_j} \end{array}$$

$$O_{v_i<v_j} = \begin{cases} \leqq_1 & \text{if } v_i<v_j \\ <_1 & \text{otherwise} \end{cases} \qquad O'_{v_i<v_j} = \begin{cases} I_{v_i}\times I_{v_j} & \text{if } v_i<v_j \\ \emptyset & \text{otherwise} \end{cases}$$

5.3. Loop Parallelization

The parallel execution of a loop ($FORALL-Loop) means the execution of every iteration of the loop on an own processor without any synchronization. This kind of loop is appropriate for MIMD-architectures [Lamp74].

Transforming a sequential loop into a parallel loop is possible if there are no loop carried dependences [ACK87]. This is the subject of the following theorem:

```
FOR I:=a TO b BY c DO                    $FORALL I:=a TO b BY c DO
  v1 ........ vn           ——→             v1 ........ vn
END;                                     END;
```

Theorem 2: The iterations of a sequential loop can be executed parallel without synchronization if for all v_i and v_j the relation $D_{v_i<v_j} \subset =_1$ holds.

Proof: see the following diagram.

$$\begin{array}{ccccc} D_{v_i \to v_j} & \subset & O_{v_i<v_j} & \subset & I_{v_i} \times I_{v_j} \\ \downarrow{\scriptstyle <id,id>} & & & & \downarrow{\scriptstyle id} \quad \downarrow{\scriptstyle id} \\ D_{v_i \to v_j} & \subset & O'_{v_i<v_j} & \subset & I_{v_i} \times I_{v_j} \end{array}$$

$$O_{v_i<v_j} = \begin{cases} \leqq_1 & \text{if } v_i<v_j \\ <_1 & \text{otherwise} \end{cases} \qquad O'_{v_i<v_j} = \begin{cases} =_1 & \text{if } v_i<v_j \\ \varnothing & \text{otherwise} \end{cases}$$

5.4. Loop Distribution and Loop Fusion

Loop distribution splits one loop into two loops, loop fusion is the inverse transformation (it is assumed that there are no data dependences for the loop header).

```
FOR I:=A TO B BY C DO                 FOR I:=A TO B BY C DO SL1 END;
  SL1; SL2                 ⇆
END;                                  FOR I:=A TO B BY C DO SL2 END;
```

Theorem 3: i) A loop distribution is possible if $D_{SL_2 \to SL_1} = \varnothing$.
ii) A loop fusion is possible if $D_{SL_1 \to SL_2} \subset \leq_1$.

Proof: see the following diagram.

$$\begin{array}{ccccc} D_{SL_i \to SL_j} & \subset & O_{SL_i<SL_j} & \subset & I_{SL_i} \times I_{SL_j} \\ \updownarrow{\scriptstyle <id,id>} & & & & \updownarrow{\scriptstyle id} \quad \updownarrow{\scriptstyle id} \\ D_{SL_i \to SL_j} & \subset & O'_{SL_i<SL_j} & \subset & I_{SL_i} \times I_{SL_j} \end{array}$$

$$O_{SL_i<SL_j} = \begin{cases} \leqq_1 & i=1, j=2 \\ <_1 & \text{otherwise} \end{cases} \qquad O'_{SL_i<SL_j} = \begin{cases} T & i=1, j=2 \\ \varnothing & i=2, j=1 \\ <_1 & i=j \end{cases}$$

Loop distribution and loop fusion of simultaneously executable loops is no problem; the following program parts are always equivalent.

```
$SIMFOR I:=A TO B BY C DO             $SIMFOR I:=A TO B BY C DO SL1 END;
  SL1; SL2                 ⇆
END;                                  $SIMFOR I:=A TO B BY C DO SL2 END;
```

The distribution of a parallel executable loop is also possible at every time. Loop fusion is not always possible (see also example 4 for loop alignment).

```
$FORALL I:=A TO B BY C DO                 $FORALL I:=A TO B BY C DO SL1 END;
   SL1; SL2                    ⇆
END;                                      $FORALL I:=A TO B BY C DO SL2 END;
```

Theorem 4: Loop fusion of parallel loops is possible if $D_{SL_1 \to SL_2} \subset =_1$

Proof: see the following diagram.

$$\begin{array}{ccccc} D_{SL_i \to SL_j} & \subset & O_{SL_i < SL_j} & \subset & I_{SL_i} \times I_{SL_j} \\ \downarrow <id,id> & & & & \downarrow id \quad \downarrow id \\ D_{SL_i \to SL_j} & \subset & O'_{SL_i < SL_j} & \subset & I_{SL_i} \times I_{SL_j} \end{array} \qquad O_{SL_i < SL_j} = \begin{cases} T & i=1, j=2 \\ \varnothing & \text{otherwise} \end{cases} \qquad O'_{SL_i < SL_j} = \begin{cases} =_1 & i=1, j=2 \\ \varnothing & \text{otherwise} \end{cases}$$

5.5. Statement Reordering

Changing execution orders is also possible by reordering of syntactical structures. Usually a sequence of statements, $S_1; ...; S_n$, is reordered.

Theorem 5: Let <' be a new reordering of a statement sequence $S_1; ...; S_n$; This reordering is allowed if $S_i \to S_j$ always implies $S_i <' S_j$ (means $D_{S_i \to S_j} = \{1\} \times \{1\}$ implies $O'_{S_i < S_j} = \{1\} \times \{1\}$).

Proof: see the following diagram.

$$\begin{array}{ccccc} D_{S_i \to S_j} & \subset & O_{S_i < S_j} & \subset & I_{S_i} \times I_{S_j} \\ \downarrow <id,id> & & & & \downarrow id \quad \downarrow id \\ D_{S_i \to S_j} & \subset & O'_{S_i < S_j} & \subset & I_{S_i} \times I_{S_j} \end{array} \qquad O_{S_i < S_j} = \begin{cases} \{1\} \times \{1\} & \text{if } S_i < S_j \\ \varnothing & \text{otherwise} \end{cases} \qquad O'_{S_i < S_j} = \begin{cases} \{1\} \times \{1\} & \text{if } S_i <' S_j \\ \varnothing & \text{otherwise} \end{cases}$$

5.6 Loop Interchanging, Hyperplane Method, Loop Alignment

Loop interchanging, hyperplane method and loop alignment are transformations that are applied to m directly nested loops.

```
FOR K1:=a1 TO b1 DO
  FOR K2:=a2 TO b2 DO
    ...
      FOR Km:=am TO bm DO Body
END ... END END;
```

=

This loop is shortly written as:

```
FOR (K1,...,Km) ∈ IBody DO
    Body;
END;

IBody = {a1,...,b1} × ... × {am,...,bm}
```

A new order is defined by a bijective mapping $g_{Body} : I_{Body} \to I'_{Body}$ for the innermost loop body (it is assumed that the ranges of the loops cause no data dependences).

Theorem 6: A transformation specified by a mapping $g_{Body}: I_{Body} \to I'_{Body}$ is allowed if $D'_{Body \to Body} \subset \leqq_m$, so if $<g_{Body}, g_{Body}>(D_{Body \to Body}) \subset \leqq_m$

Proof: see the following diagram.

$$\begin{array}{ccccc} D_{Body \to Body} & \subset & O_{Body < Body} & \subset & I_{Body} \times I_{Body} \\ \downarrow <g_{Body}, g_{Body}> & & & & \downarrow g_{Body} \quad \downarrow g_{Body} \\ D'_{Body \to Body} & \subset & O'_{Body < Body} & \subset & I'_{Body} \times I'_{Body} \end{array} \qquad O_{Body < Body} = \leqq_m \qquad O'_{Body < Body} = \leqq_m$$

After carrying out the transformation one of the following loops is given:

```
FOR (J1,...,Jm) ∈ g(IBody) DO            FOR (J1,...,Jm) ∈ H DO
    (K1,...,Km):=g^-1(J1,...,Jm);            (K1,...,Km):=g^-1(J1,...,Jm);
    Body;                                    IF (K1,...,Km) ∈ IBody THEN Body END;
END;                                     END;
```

If $g(I_{Body}) = \{c_1,...,d_1\} \times ... \times \{c_m,...,d_m\}$, it is easy to get the corresponding loop headers. Otherwise choose a set H with $H = \{c_1,...,d_1\} \times ... \times \{c_m,...,d_m\}$ and $g(I_{Body}) \subset H$.

If g_{Body} is a linear mapping, the transformation is the same as used in the hyperplane method [Lamp74]. A special case is loop interchanging, where g has the following form (π is a permutation of $\{1,...,m\}$):

Loop Interchanging: $g_{Body}: I_{Body} \rightarrow I'_{Body},\ g(j_1, j_2, ..., j_m) := (j_{\pi(1)}, j_{\pi(2)}, ..., j_{\pi(m)})$

There is a finite number of possibilities for loop interchanging, but an infinite number of linear mappings. So a transformation heuristic is needed to determine the mapping g_{Body} with the original predicates p as it is done by Lamport [Lamp74] for special cases.

Example 3: Loop Interchanging

```
FOR I:=1 TO N DO
   FOR K:=2 TO M DO
      A[I,K]:=A[I,K-1]+B[I,K];
   END;
END;
```

A[I,K]:=A[I,K-1]+B[I,K];

$D_{Body \rightarrow Body} = ('0','1')$

a) Loop Interchanging is possible as $D'_{Body \rightarrow Body} = ('1','0') \subset \leqq_2$.

```
FOR K:=2 TO M DO
   FOR I:=1 TO N DO
      A[I,K]:=A[I+1,K-1]+B[I,K];
   END;
END;
```

A[I,K]:=A[I+1,K-1]+B[I,K];

$D_{Body \rightarrow Body} = ('1','-1')$

b) Loop Interchanging is not possible as $D'_{Body \rightarrow Body} = ('-1','1') \not\subset \leqq_2$

Loop alignment is a transformation to make the fusion of two parallel loops possible [ACK87]. Here the following mapping is used:

$g_{Body}: I_{Body} \rightarrow I'_{Body},\ g(j_1, ..., j_m) = (j_1 + c_1, ..., j_m + c_m)$

Example 4: Loop Alignment

```
$FORALL I:=2 TO N DO A[I]:=B[I]+C[I]; END;
$FORALL I:=2 TO N DO D[I]:=A[I-1]; END;
```

$SL_1 \equiv$ A[I]:=B[I]+C[I]

('1')

$SL_2 \equiv$ D[I]:=A[I-1]

a) The fusion of the two loops (5.4) is not possible as $D_{SL_1 \rightarrow SL_2} \not\subseteq\ =_1$

```
$FORALL I:=2 TO N+1 DO IF I≥3 THEN A[I-1]:=B[I-1]+C[I-1] END{IF}; END;
$FORALL I:=2 TO N+1 DO IF I≤N THEN D[I]:=A[I-1] END{IF}; END;
```

b) Loop Alignment

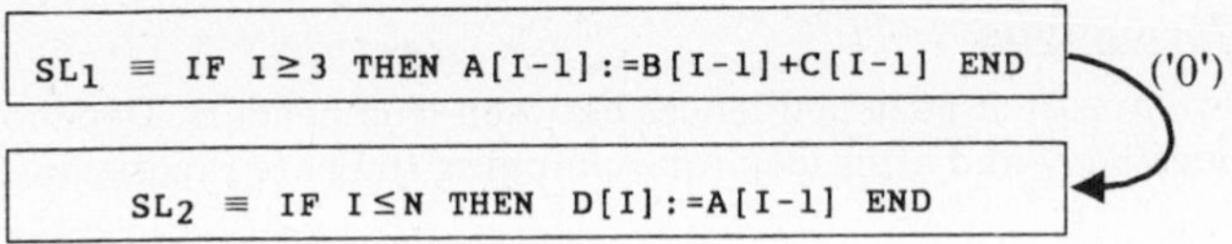

SL1 ≡ IF I≥3 THEN A[I-1]:=B[I-1]+C[I-1] END
('0')
SL2 ≡ IF I≤N THEN D[I]:=A[I-1] END

c) After alignment of the first loop the fusion of the two loops (5.4) is now possible as $D_{SL_1 \rightarrow SL_2}$ = '=' = 1'

5.7. Loop Collapsing, Strip Mining

Further transformations that change the execution order are [PaWo86]

- Strip mining: it is used for memory management. It transforms a singly nested loop into a doubly nested loop. Here we have the mapping : $g(j_1) := (j_1$ **div** c, j_1 **mod** $c)$
- Loop collapsing: two nested loops are transformed into a single loop. The mapping is defined by: $g(j_1 j_2) := c^* j_1 + j_2$

6. Removing and Repositioning of trouble-making Dependences

Changing the order as desired is often not possible because of the dependences. For many situations the dependences can be removed or repositioned to allow transformations and to increase the potential for parallelism.

6.1. Removing of Output Dependences

$v_i(x) \rightarrow_O v_j(y)$ means that $v_j(y)$ recomputes the output of $v_i(x)$ and therefore the order of these two executions must not be changed.

If $v_i(x)$ writes its output in an unused memory location, the output dependence does no longer exist. But we have to know which executions use the output of $v_i(x)$ as input before $v_j(y)$ recomputes the output. So we consider all executions between $v_i(x)$ and $v_j(y)$ and check whether they use the output of $v_i(x)$ as input or they do not. This means that the existence as well as the non-existence of a flow dependence has to be proved. Only if there is a flow dependence the new memory location has to be accessed.

With the dependence graph normally used it can only be proved that there is no flow dependence unless conditional statements are not allowed and only scalar variables are considered. In this case the predicates for assumed and real dependences are equal to the constant predicate 'true'. So Kuck et al. [KKPL81] presented algorithms based on this technique (called renaming and expansion) for scalar variables only.

But renaming and expansion are also possible for structured variables. If the edges are labeled with predicates for the real and assumed dependences, automatic renaming and expansion is possible for many additional cases.

Example 5: Renaming

```
FOR I:=2 TO N-1 DO                           FOR I:=2 TO N-1 DO
   A[I]:=B[I]+F[I];                             $NewA[I]:=B[I]+F[I];
   C[I]:=A[I]*2+A[I-1]+A[I+1];                  C[I]:=$NewA[I]*2+A[I-1]+A[I+1];
   A[I]:=D[I]+E[I];                ——→          A[I]:=D[I]+E[I];
   B[I+1]:=A[I]-F[I];                           B[I+1]:=A[I]-F[I];
   END;                                         END;
```

a) Old source

b) New source (A[I-1], A[I+1] are not renamed)

6.2. Other Kind of Transformations

For loop interchanging there must not be dependences between loop headers. Dependences can be positioned into the loop body and after loop interchanging they are repositioned into the loop header.

Example 6: Changing loop headers

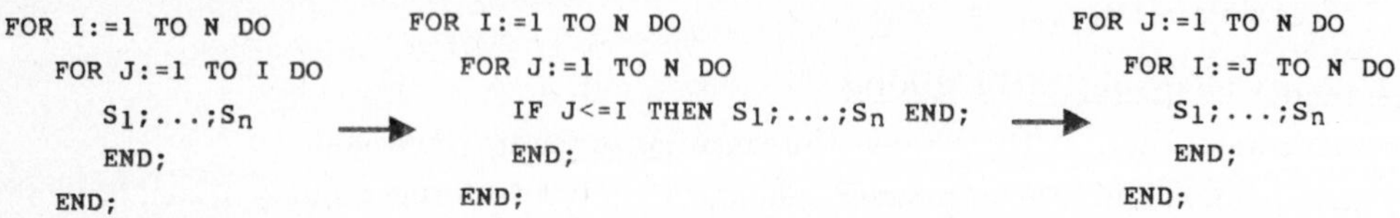

```
FOR I:=1 TO N DO                FOR I:=1 TO N DO                              FOR J:=1 TO N DO
  FOR J:=1 TO I DO                FOR J:=1 TO N DO                              FOR I:=J TO N DO
    S1;...;Sn        --->           IF J<=I THEN S1;...;Sn END;     --->          S1;...;Sn
    END;                            END;                                          END;
  END;                            END;                                          END;
```

Other kind of transformations are:

1) Node splitting [KKPL81] breaks a cycle by inserting a new assignment statement.
2) Code replication breaks an alignment conflict by evaluating some results twice (or more) in the body of a loop [ACK87].
3) Linear Recurrences [Kogg74] can be solved by rearranging the computation.

All these kinds of transformation are specified in the same way. The update of predicates is often very easy as dependence edges are only copied or moved.

7. Complex Transformation Rules

A complex transformation rule is specified by a set of simpler transformation rules and strategies and heuristics about them.

In the following it will be shown how to combine loop distribution (5.4), statement reordering (5.5) and loop vectorization (5.2) (perhaps with renaming and expansion) to a complex transformation rule used for automatic vectorization (as defined by Kuck et al. [KKPL81]).

```
FOR I:=a TO b DO        Vectorization        $SIMFOR I:=a TO b DO Si END;
  S1; ...; Sn        ------------------>     ...
  END;                                       FOR I:=a TO b DO Sj1; ... Sjmj END;
                                             $SIMFOR I:=a TO b DO Sk END;
```

Though loop distribution and loop vectorization can be applied as often as possible, loop distribution is sometimes only possible after statement reordering. Not every reordering of the statements should be tried out (n! possibilities). Therefore, the dependence graph for the statements S_1 ... S_n is built. The statements of every strongly connected component build one loop, the topological sorting of the strongly connected components shows how to reorder the statements. Every singulary node results in a simultaneously executable loop.

As not every statement reordering should be tried out, the above transformation strategy (build dependence graph, find strongly connected components, sort them toplogically) should be used. As the topological sorting is ambiguous, a further (assessment) heuristic is useful: Take the topological sorting with as few changes between vectorizible and non-vectorizible loops as possible. The last assessment heuristic should also be replaced by a transformation heuristic as there are sometimes too many possibilities of topological sorting.

Heuristics for other simple transformations are also necessary: how to find the best loop interchanging, how to find a good linear mapping for the hyperplane method. There are already many heuristics [Lamp74, ACK87]; these heuristics have to be made explicit for knowledge-based parallelization.

Complex transformation rules can be combined with corresponding heuristics to a more complex transformation rule. At last the whole parallelization is one complex transformation rule.

8. User Interface

The parallelization tool can be activated after the selection of a program section. A copy of the data structure is generated to prevent the original program from destruction. Additionally, an adaption of arbitrary high level data structures to an appropriate structure is possible. After the parallelization the old program section can be replaced with the new one.

After the activation all dependences between variable accesses are determined and stored in the high level data structure. The user can select the level of knowledge which is used for it. The determination of dependences must only be done once; but at any time the description of the dependence relation can be improved ($p_<$ weaker and $p_>$ stronger, see 3.), especially by assertions of the user. Based on the comparison of the predicates for real and assumed dependences the tool helps the user to make assertions where they are really needed.

During the parallelization process other optimization tools can be used, e.g. for dead code elimination. As an efficient incremental dependence analysis is not implemented yet, editing during the parallelization process should not be done otherwise the determination of dependences must be repeated.

The order of transformations can be specified (step by step) by the user or it can be chosen between different automatic modes. At least one mode should be a full automatic mode for those users which are not familiar with the parallelization process. The current state of parallelization can be displayed after transformations.

Dependence graphs can also be displayed; so the user can recognize dependence cycles which build a recurrence. Predicates are only for internal use, but they can be displayed and explained by the system if desired.

Example 7: User Interface

```
FOR I:=1 TO N-1 DO
   A[I]:=B[I]+C[I];
   B[I]:=A[I+1]+F[I];
   END;
```

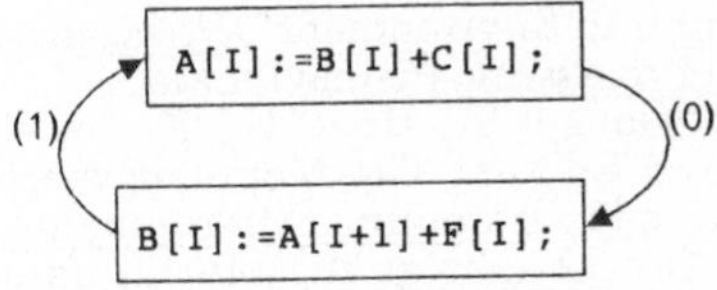

a) Original Source and its dependence graph: the system suggests node splitting

```
FOR I:=1 TO N-1 DO
   A[I]:=B[I]+C[I];
   $H[I]:=A[I+1]+F[I];
   B[I]:=$H[I];
   END;
```

b) After node splitting: the system suggests loop distribution

```
FOR I:=1 TO N-1 DO $H[I]:=A[I+1]+F[I] END;
FOR I:=1 TO N-1 DO A[I]:=B[I]+C[I] END;
FOR I:=1 TO N-1 DO B[I]:=$H[I] END;
```

c) After loop distribution: vectorization of every loop possible

9. Conclusions

It has been shown how to formalize the parallelization process for a knowledge-based parallelization tool. Though no formal models are presented how to specify transformation rules and heuristics about them, the quality of these rules and heuristics should be clear.

The techniques described in this paper have been implemented in a parallelization tool, which has been developed in cooperation with Siemens AG, Munich. Although it realizes at present a source to source transformation, the design is appropriate for a programming environment.

The tool is independent on the underlying programming language and on the underlying hardware architecture. Only language descriptions and rules have to be changed.

The tool is realized in an InterLisp environment. This turned out to be a very good choice. Not only the extension with new parallelization and vectorization issues is very easy, but also transformations are implemented simply.

During the development of the parallelization tool we have seen that automatic parallelization is a hard business. But the knowledge-based design and the corresponding formalization was really helpful and we hope that it will be helpful for many other people.

Acknowledgements

The authors would like to thank Gerd Völksen, Herbert Gasiorowski and Klaus Schmidt for their helpful comments about this paper.

References

[AlKe 85] Allen, J.R.; Kennedy, K.: „A Parallel Programming Environment", IEEE Software, July 1985

[ACK 87] Allen, R.; Callahan, D.; Kennedy, K.: „Automatic Decomposition of Scientific Programs for Parallel Execution", Proc. 14th ACM Symp. Principles Programming Lang., Munich, West-Germany, January 1987

[ASU 86] Aho, A.V.; Sethi, R; Ullman, J.D.: „Compilers: Principles, Techniques, and Tools", Addison-Wesley, Reading, Mass., 1986

[Bane 79] Banerjee, U.: „Speedup of ordinary programs", Ph. D. dissertation, Dep. Comp. Sci., University of Illinois, Urbana-Champaign, 1979

[Bran 86] Brandes, Th.: „Automatic Vectorization for High Level Languages based on an Expert System", Proceedings of CONPAR 86, Sept. 1986, Springer-Verlag

[Bran 87] Brandes, Th.: „Determination of Dependences in a Knowledge-Based Parallelization Tool", Dep. Math./Comp. Sci., University of Marburg, Germany, Technical Report MR87-2 (1987), 19 pp.

[BrSo 87] Brandes, Th., Sommer, M.: „A Knowledge-Based Parallelization Tool in a Programming Environment", Proceedings of 1987 International Conference on Parallel Processing, Pennsylvania

[DHKL 84] Donzeau-Gouge, V.; Huet, G.; Kahn, G.; Lang, B.: „Environments Based on Structured Editors: The Mentor Experience", in: Barstow, D.R. et al. (eds.): Interactive Programming Environments, McGraw-Hill

[Enge 86] Engels, G.: „Graphs as the central data structure in a software development environment", Dissertation, University of Osnabrück, Germany

[KeAl 84] Kennedy, K.; Allen, J.R.: „Automatic Translation of Fortran programs to Vector Form" (revised Jan. 86), Technical Report TR84-9, Dep. Comp. Sci., Rice University, Houston Texas

[KeHo 86] Kennedy, K.; Hood, R.T.: „Programming Language Support for Supercomputers", in Frontiers of Super Computing, University of California Press 1986

[Kogg 74] Kogge, P.M.: „Parallel Solution of Recurrence Problems", IBM J.Res. Development, March 1974

[KKPL 81] Kuck, D.J.; Kuhn, R.H.; Padua, D.A.; Leasure, B.; Wolfe, M.: „Dependence graph and compiler optimizations", Proc. 8th ACM Symp. Principles Programming Lang., Williamsburg, VA, Jan. 1981

[KSS 86] Kolb, D.; Sommer, M.; Stadel, M.: „Programming Environments", in Computer Physics Communications 41, Amsterdam, North-Holland

[Lamp 74] Lamport, L.: „The Parallel Execution of DO Loops", Comm. of the ACM: Vol. 17, No.2 (Feb., 74)

[Nagl 85] Nagl, M.: „An Incremental Programming Support Environment", in Computer Physics Communications 38, Amsterdam, North-Holland

[PaWo 86] Padua, D.A.; Wolfe, M.J.: „Advanced Compiler Optimizations for Supercomputers", Comm. of the ACM, Vol. 29, No. 12, (Dec., 86)

[TeRe 81] Teitelbaum, T.; Reps, Th.: „The Cornell Program Synthesizer: A Syntax Directed Programming Environment", Comm. of the ACM, Vol. 24, No. 9 (Sept., 81)

[Wolf 82] Wolfe, M.J.: „Optimizing super compilers for supercomputers", Ph. D. dissertation, Dep. Comp. Sci., Univ. Illinois, Urbana-Champaign, 1982

Appendix: Predicates and their Operations

A predicate p: $I_{v_1} \times I_{v_2} \rightarrow$ {true, false } is defined by a mapping p: $\mathbf{Z}^{n+x} \times \mathbf{Z}^{n+y} \rightarrow$ {true, false}; although every predicate can be used if the operations are defined in the right way, for the following predicates operations become very easy:

1. Predicates

An elementary predicate is a mapping p: $\mathbf{Z} \times \mathbf{Z} \rightarrow$ { true, false }; the following elementary predicates are used:

Elementary predicates

i) p='a', a $\in$ **Z** $p(n_1,n_2)$ = true :$\Leftrightarrow$ $n_2 - n_1 = a$

ii) p='<' $p(n_1,n_2)$ = true :$\Leftrightarrow$ $n_2 - n_1 < 0$

iii) p='>' $p(n_1,n_2)$ = true :$\Leftrightarrow$ $n_2 - n_1 > 0$

iv) p='true' $\forall n_1,n_2 \in Z$: $p(n_1,n_2)$ = true

v) p='false' $\forall n_1,n_2 \in Z$: $p(n_1,n_2)$ = false

Elementary predicates can be compounded to a predicate for $\mathbf{Z}^{n+x} \times \mathbf{Z}^{n+y}$ in the following way:

$(p_1,p_2,\ldots,p_n)$: $\mathbf{Z}^{n+x} \times \mathbf{Z}^{n+y} \rightarrow$ { true, false }

$i = (i_1,\ldots,i_n,\ldots)$, $j = (j_1,\ldots,j_n,\ldots)$: $(p_1,p_2,\ldots,p_n)(i,j)$:$\Leftrightarrow$ $p_1(i_1 j_1) \wedge \ldots \wedge p_k(i_n j_n)$

A predicate for $\mathbf{Z}^{n+x} \times \mathbf{Z}^{n+y}$ has always one of the following forms (this is possible because of the identities e) :

i) 'true' (constant predicate for $\mathbf{Z}^{n+x} \times \mathbf{Z}^{n+y}$)

ii) 'false' (constant predicate for $\mathbf{Z}^{n+x} \times \mathbf{Z}^{n+y}$)

iii) $(p_{11},p_{12},\ldots,p_{1n}) \vee (p_{21},p_{22},\ldots,p_{2n}) \vee \ldots \vee (p_{m1},p_{m2},\ldots,p_{mn})$ ($p_{ij} \in$ { 'a' | a $\in$ Z } $\cup$ { '<', '>', 'true' })

2. Operations on predicates

a) Conjunction

p_1, p_2: $Z^{n+x} \times Z^{n+y} \rightarrow$ { true, false }, $p_1 \wedge p_2$: $\mathbf{Z}^{n+y} \times \mathbf{Z}^{n+x} \rightarrow$ { true, false }

$(p_1 \wedge p_2)(i,j)$:$\Leftrightarrow$ $p_1(i,j) \wedge p_2(i,j)$

Rules for elementary predicates

i) $x \wedge y = y \wedge x$

ii) $x \wedge$ 'true' = x

iii) $x \wedge$ 'false' = 'false'

iv) $x \wedge x = x$

v) $a \neq b$: 'a' $\wedge$ 'b' = 'false'

vi) $a > 0$: 'a' $\wedge$ '>' = 'a'

vii) $a \leq 0$: 'a' $\wedge$ '>' = 'false'

viii) $a < 0$: 'a' $\wedge$ '<' = 'a'

ix) $a \geq 0$: 'a' $\wedge$ '<' = 'false'

x) '<' $\wedge$ '>' = 'false'

Rules for compounded predicates

i) $(p_1,p_2,\ldots,p_k) = (p_1,p_2,\ldots,p_k,$'true'$,\ldots,$'true'$)$

ii) $(p_1,p_2,\ldots,p_n) \wedge (q_1,q_2,\ldots,q_n) = (p_1 \wedge q_1, p_2 \wedge q_2,\ldots,p_n \wedge q_n)$

Rules for used predicates

i) $p \wedge q = q \wedge p$

ii) $p \wedge$ 'true' = p

iii) $p \wedge$ 'false' = 'false'

iv) $(p_1 \vee p_2 \vee \ldots \vee p_k) \wedge (q_1 \vee q_2 \vee \ldots \vee q_m) =$
$(p_1 \wedge q_1) \vee (p_1 \wedge q_2) \vee \ldots \vee (p_1 \wedge q_m) \vee (p_1 \wedge q_2) \vee \ldots \vee$
$(p_k \wedge q_1) \vee \ldots \vee (p_k \wedge q_m)$

v) (...,'false',...) = 'false'

b) Inversion

p: $Z^{n+x} \times Z^{n+y} \rightarrow \{ \text{true, false} \}$ $p^{-1}: \mathbf{Z}^{n+y} \times \mathbf{Z}^{n+x} \rightarrow \{ \text{true, false} \}$

$p^{-1}(j,i) :\Leftrightarrow p(i,j)$

Rules for elementary predicates

i) $a \in \mathbf{Z}$: $('a')^{-1} = '{-a}'$
ii) $('<')^{-1} = '>'$
iii) $('>')^{-1} = '<'$
iv) $'true'^{-1} = 'true'$
v) $'false'^{-1} = 'false'$

Rules for compounded predicates

i) $(p_1, p_2, \ldots, p_k)^{-1} = (p_1^{-1}, p_2^{-1}, \ldots, p_k^{-1})$

Rules for used predicates

i) $'true'^{-1} = 'true'$
ii) $'false'^{-1} = 'false'$
iii) $(p_1 \vee p_2 \vee \ldots \vee p_n)^{-1} = (p_1^{-1} \vee p_2^{-1} \vee \ldots \vee p_n^{-1})$

c) Predefined Predicates

$<_n := ('>','true',\ldots,'true') \vee ('0','>','true',\ldots,'true') \vee \ldots \vee ('0','0','>')$

$=_n := ('0',\ldots,'0')$

$\leq_n := <_n \vee =_n$

d) Stronger / Weaker Test

$p_1, p_2: \mathbf{Z}^{n+x} \times \mathbf{Z}^{n+y} \rightarrow \{ \text{true, false} \}$

$p_1 \subset p_2 :\Leftrightarrow \forall i,j: [p_1(i,j) \Rightarrow p_2(i,j)]$ (p_1 is stronger than p_2)

Rules for elementary predicates

i) $'false' \subset p$
ii) $p \subset 'true'$
iii) $'a' \subset 'a'$
iv) $a > 0$: $'a' \subset '>'$
v) $a < 0$: $'a' \subset '<'$

Rules for compounded predicates

i) $\forall i = 1,\ldots,n: x_i \subset y_i \Rightarrow (x_1, x_2, \ldots, x_n, x_{n+1}, \ldots, x_m) \subset (y_1, y_2, \ldots, y_n)$
ii) $\forall i = 1,\ldots,n: x_i \subset y_i \Rightarrow (x_1, x_2, \ldots, x_n) \subset (y_1, y_2, \ldots, y_n, \text{true}, \ldots, \text{true})$
iii) $m \leq n \Rightarrow (x_1, \ldots, x_m, \ldots, x_n) \subset (x_1, \ldots, x_m)$

Rules for used predicates

i) $'false' \subset p$
ii) $p \subset 'true'$
iii) $\forall i \in \{1,\ldots,n\}: \exists j \in \{1,\ldots,m\}: p_i \subset q_j$
$\Rightarrow (p_1 \vee p_2 \vee \ldots \vee p_k) \subset (q_1 \vee q_2 \vee \ldots \vee q_m)$

e) Identities

i) $p \vee 'true' = 'true'$
ii) $p \vee 'false' = p$
iii) $[p \subset q] \Rightarrow [p \vee q = q]$ Note: i) und ii) are special cases of iii)
iv) $(\ldots,'false',\ldots) = 'false'$
v) $(p_1,\ldots,p_n) = (p_1, \ldots, p_n, 'true', ,\ldots, 'true')$

Incremental Performance Contributions of Hardware Concurrency Extraction Techniques[1]

Augustus K. Uht
Dept. of Computer Science and Engineering, C-014
University of California, San Diego
La Jolla, California 92093 / U.S.A.

Abstract

Recently, new techniques for the hardware extraction of low-level concurrency from sequential instruction streams have been proposed in the form of the CONDEL machine models. The initial technique increased the concurrency extracted by using reduced (minimal) semantic dependencies arising from branches (procedural dependencies). Another scheme additionally implements reduced data dependencies. Also, a form of branch prediction is used to further improve performance. Although it has been demonstrated that all of these and other techniques improve performance, the relative degree of improvement for each new technique has not been shown; nor have the new set of procedural dependencies been enumerated. These issues are addressed in this paper.

Data dependencies are defined and discussed. A minimal set of procedural dependencies is presented and described, and examples are given. CONDEL and other hardware concurrent machine models are compared, in terms of degrees of concurrency realized. Specific performance data for the CONDEL machine models are obtained and analyzed. The experimental method, using simulations, is described. The simulation results of both a general purpose set and a scientific set of benchmarks are presented and analyzed, showing that the performance improvements for each concurrency extraction technique are orthogonal. Most of the concurrency extraction techniques demonstrate significant incremental performance contributions, with the exception of both the technique giving reduced data dependencies, and that having enhanced handling of special types of branches, such as calls and returns. It must be noted, though, that the reduced data dependency technique should still be used since it is a crucial part of the branch prediction technique, use of which does give a large performance improvement. In summary, all of the concurrency extraction techniques are useful in improving performance.

1. Introduction

Throughout the history of computers there has been a desire to improve uni-processor performance as much as possible. This is still a subject of some interest, both for old "dusty deck" applications, as well as to maximize scalar performance in general. Automatic and guaranteed parallelization of code at a high level has yet to be achieved, nor is it likely to be soon. In the mid-60s two new machines were introduced embodying the concept of *low-level concurrency extraction*, i.e., using hardware, in this case, to detect when nominally sequential instructions can be executed concurrently. One machine was the CDC 6600 [17]; it used an apparatus called the *scoreboard* to

---

[1]This work was supported by the Semiconductor Research Corporation under Agreement No. 82-11-007, by Carnegie Mellon University, by the University of California at San Diego, and by the author.

Most of the work described within was performed while the author was at Carnegie Mellon University, Pittsburgh, Pennsylvania, U.S.A.

Parts of this work appeared previously in [22, 23]; the repeated results consist of some of the specific simulation data, and the theorem descriptions. Most of this work is from the doctoral research presented in [21].

allow instructions to execute out of order in certain circumstances. The other machine, the IBM 360/91 [2], used the original version of the Tomasulo algorithm [20] to allow even more concurrency. (We will be specific about the dependencies that each machine enforced in Section 5.3.) Interest waned in both techniques shortly thereafter, due to the hardware costs involved and the limited performance improvements obtained (somewhat less than a factor of 2 for scientific code).

With the reduction in hardware costs in the last two decades, and the increasing demand for performance, there has been renewed interest in low-level concurrency extraction techniques using hardware. Most of the work has been along traditional lines of reducing data dependencies[2] only [1, 14, 24]. Other work has combined reduced data dependencies with branch prediction [11, 12]. Tjaden [18, 19] combined reduced data dependencies with reduced procedural dependencies[3] in a hardware algorithm using the *static instruction stream*[4] as the execution model. The machine was never implemented. Wedig [24] also developed advanced hardware structures to implement reduced data dependencies; the key structures are discussed in Section 2.

This author has also investigated hardware-based low-level concurrency extraction techniques, and has developed various machine models implementing many degrees of concurrency extraction [21, 22, 23]. Our work is built primarily on the results of Tjaden and Wedig. Our most advanced machine model, CONDEL-2 [21, 23], realizes minimal procedural and scalar-data dependencies, as well as a form of branch prediction requiring no state restoration or backtracking upon a prediction being discovered to be wrong; the static instruction stream model is used. The techniques described, while less costly than prior techniques, still require a significant amount of hardware. The marginal performance of a given technique may be such that it is not worth the hardware cost to implement it. From both this practical viewpoint, and as an academic interest, it is desirable to know what each concurrency enhancement technique contributes to overall performance improvement independently of other techniques (when possible). We call the contributed performance improvement of a given technique its *incremental performance contribution*. In this paper we derive incremental performance contributions of various concurrency extraction techniques from simulation data of the CONDEL machine models. The minimal set of procedural dependencies used is also presented. The dependency models are general. The concurrent machine models, and hence results, are applicable to low-level concurrency machines in general, and static instruction stream machines in particular, depending on the machine models considered.

The remainder of this paper is organized as follows. The basic machine model assumptions are given in Section 2. Section 3 contains a complete enumeration of all of the possible dependencies occurring in the execution of code; particular emphasis is on the enumeration of a minimal set of procedural dependencies, given here for the first time (as far as we know). The implications of the minimal set are also given. Section 4 contains examples of the effects of reduced procedural dependencies. In Section 5 other advanced concurrency enhancement techniques are described. The experimental methodology is described in Section 6. Section 7 contains the simulation results and analysis, including the incremental performance contribution derivations; other factors, including cost and cycle time are also considered. The conclusions are presented in Section 8, along with current and future research directions.

---

[2]These are conditions arising from the common use of variables in two or more instructions that require sequential execution of the component instructions; see Section 3.1.

[3]These are conditions requiring sequentiality which arise due to branches; see Section 3.2.

[4]This instruction stream uses the code in the order the code exists in memory, i.e., as it is written; see Section 2.1. The traditional instruction stream, i.e., the dynamic instruction stream, is the code in the order determined by the classic Program Counter.

2. Basic Machine Model Assumptions

The basic machine model used is called CONDEL (CONcurrent Directly Executed Language machine, with emphasis on the concurrent). Only the relevant elements of the CONDEL implementations are described here. Our basic assumptions are:

- The code input to the machine models is standard imperative machine code, consisting of pure assignment statements and branches (no single instruction may perform both an assignment and a branching function).
- The machine contains multiple processing elements or functional units. Externally, the machine appears to be SISD; internally, the operation is MIMD, such that the elements within an instruction or data stream are not necessarily related, except for being part of the same locality of execution.
- An instruction window is used (see Section 2.1).
- No code pre-processing or re-structuring is used. The compiler passes no information about the code to the hardware, other than the basic machine code itself.

2.1. Instruction Streams

There are two possible ways a CPU's execution unit can examine a program's instruction stream during the program's execution, dynamically or statically. The *dynamic instruction stream* is the code as seen in an order determined by the run-time control flow of the code, i.e., as indicated by the contents of a *program counter* (PC) in a traditional machine. The *static instruction stream* is the code ordered as it is stored in memory, which is normally just the source code order of the program. Tjaden's [19], Wedig's [24], and Uht's (CONDEL-1 and CONDEL-2) [21, 22, 23] schemes all examine the static instruction stream.

Executing the static representation of a program has two major advantages over executing its dynamic representation. The static order is basically independent of the control flow of the code, allowing reduced procedural dependencies; thus, multiple branches and other types of instructions can, in many cases, execute simultaneously, improving performance. In other words, both assignment and branch instructions occurring statically after a branch (B) may execute before B executes. THIS IS NOT BRANCH PREDICTION; THE INSTRUCTIONS ARE EXECUTED ABSOLUTELY. Additionally, if an entire loop fits in CPU storage, then memory accesses due to instruction fetches decrease dramatically, also improving performance. The static instruction stream is used in this work.

2.2. Primary Hardware

In this section the primary hardware components used in the CONDEL models are briefly reviewed. The hardware structures and logic for CONDEL-1, implementing reduced procedural dependencies, have been previously described in [21, 22]. CONDEL-2, additionally implementing both reduced data dependencies and a form of branch prediction, has been discussed in [21, 23]. More information on the models may be found in these references. The CONDEL structures are described to give the reader an idea of how low-level concurrency techniques may be implemented; other machine structures might be used to achieve some of the enhanced concurrency models, but are not considered here.

CONDEL employs an *Instruction Queue* [24] (see Figure 2-1) to hold a portion of the static instruction stream. Instructions enter at the bottom and are shifted up, into lower-numbered Instruction Queue rows, as the upper instructions finish executing. Any necessary decoding is performed *relatively statically* [21, 22], one instruction at a time, as an instruction enters the Queue. Each row of the Instruction Queue holds the code data corresponding to instruction i, including instruction i's opcode and operand identifiers, as well as a jump destination address if the instruction is a branch. The instructions in the Instruction Queue are accessed in parallel. The Instruction Queue is essentially a finite window of length n into the static instruction stream. The length n is a basic hardware restriction on code execution in CONDEL.

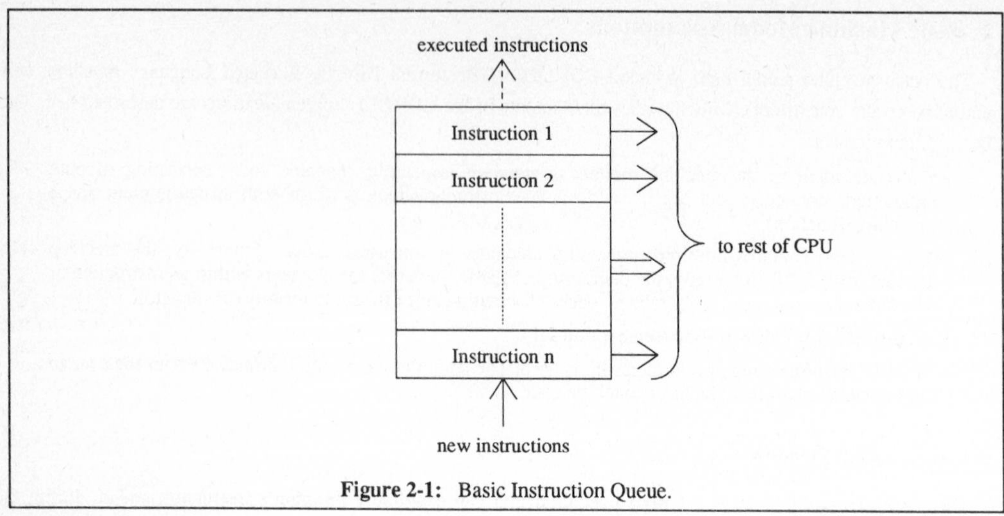

Figure 2-1: Basic Instruction Queue.

CONDEL also uses the *Advanced Execution (AE)* binary-valued matrix [24] to hold the dynamic instruction execution state. Each row of the matrix ($AE_{i,*}$) contains the execution state of instruction *i* for a subset of its total number of iterations. A row of the AE matrix corresponds to a unique element (instruction or row) in the Instruction Queue. The nominal execution order of the instructions corresponding to the Advanced Execution matrix rows is shown in Figure 2-2. This enforces the basic sequential bias of the input code when necessary (when dependencies are present). $AE_{i,j}$ is set either upon an actual execution of instruction *i* in iteration *j*, or upon execution of one or more branches in the Instruction Queue. The width of the AE matrix is *m*, implying that up to *m* iterations of an instruction are eligible for execution at any given time. *m* is an implementation parameter.

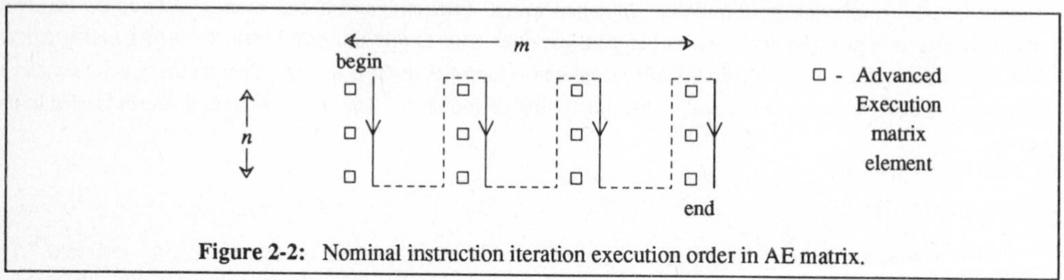

Figure 2-2: Nominal instruction iteration execution order in AE matrix.

There is also hardware [21, 22] to determine and use the semantic dependencies and branch domains[5]. The dependencies and domains are also computed relatively statically[6]. The dependency and domain information is stored in several $n \times n$ upper right triangular matrices. CONDEL-2 also has CPU storage to hold multiple copies of instruction sinks [24] and their addresses; the sink copies are required for reduced data dependencies, and both the sink copies and their addresses are required for a certain type of branch prediction. There is one copy of an instruction's sink per iteration, i.e., there is a one-to-one correspondence between sinks and AE elements. The storage does not appear in the instruction set architecture. CONDEL-2 contains unique logic to dynamically create links between instruction sinks and sources, creating a form of data flow code execution. There are also logic and structures used to decouple instruction execution from the storage of results to memory; this is primarily used for the branch prediction technique.

[5]These are the regions of influence of branches; see Section 3.2.1 for detailed definitions.

[6]The performance difference between this approach and a completely dynamic approach has not been completely investigated. The difference arises only when considering array accesses (see Section 6.3.1).

2.3. Basic Execution Algorithm

During execution cycles, the dependency information is combined with the dynamic execution state held in the Advanced Execution matrix to generate a set of instructions to be executed in the current cycle. These instructions are issued for execution. The set of executing instructions and the domain information is used to update the Advanced Execution matrix, whence the cycle repeats.

2.4. Instruction Set

The basic machine model assumes a three-address instruction set, in which an assignment instruction has one or two sources, and one sink. This allows for much concurrency at a reasonable cost. The assignment instructions primarily consist of the four basic arithmetic operations, logical operations, relational test operations, and array/indirect access operations. Array elements are specified with a base pointer and an offset. Indirect accesses are special cases of array accesses (the offset=0).

Branches consist of a jump address and one source; the source is tested to determine if the branch is to be taken. Only two types of branches are used: conditional forward, and conditional backward[7]. Assignment instructions and branches are orthogonal. Procedure calls and returns are taken to be special cases of branches whose jump addresses are outside of the Instruction Queue, i.e., *out-of-bounds* branches.

We assume that all instructions take one cycle to execute.

3. Dependency Types

Concurrency extraction starts with *dependency* detection. Two instructions are dependent if their execution must be ordered, due to either *semantic* or *resource* dependencies. In this section all possible semantic dependencies are enumerated, emphasizing the minimal procedural dependencies in Section 3.2.2.

A semantic dependency exists between two instructions if their execution must be serialized to ensure correct operation of the code. This type of dependency arises due to ordering relationships occurring in the code itself. There are two forms of semantic dependencies, *data* and *procedural.*

3.1. Data Dependencies

Data dependencies [4] arise due to instructions sharing source and sink names in certain combinations. Examples of data dependencies are shown in Figure 3-1. Referring to Relation 1, a data dependency (flow) exists between instructions 1 and 2 since instruction 1 modifies **A**, an input to (source of) instruction 2. Therefore instruction 2 must not execute in a given iteration until instruction 1 has executed in that iteration.

Under normal circumstances (when only one copy of a variable exists in the machine at any given time) any one of the relations existing implies that a data dependency exists between the two instructions. But, as demonstrated by Tomasulo [20], Tjaden [18], and Wedig [24], if multiple copies of a variable exist, then Relations 2 and 3 (collectively known as *shadow effects*) do not apply. As an example, consider the Relation 2 situation in Figure 3-1. Say two copies of **A** exist, then instruction 1 sources from the first copy and instruction 2 writes (sinks) into the second copy; therefore instructions 1 and 2 may execute concurrently.

In terms of scalar data dependencies, Torng's machine [1], and CONDEL-1 [22] enforce all three data

[7]Unconditional branches are special cases of the conditional branches.

```
                      Relation 1:      Relation 2:      Relation 3:
Hazard name:          Read-After-      Write-After-     Write-After-
                       Write (RAW)      Read (WAR)       Write (WAW)
Other name:           Flow dep.        Anti-dep.        Output dep.
                      -----------      -----------      -----------

                 1.   A = B + 1        C = A * 2        A = B + 1

                 2.   C = A * 2        A = B + 1        A = C * 2

                  (in all of the examples, the common use of
                  the variable A creates the data dependency)
```

Figure 3-1: Examples of the data dependency relations.

dependencies, while the IBM 360/91 [2], HPS [11, 12], and CONDEL-2 [23] enforce reduced data dependencies, i.e., only Relation 1 (flow) dependencies are observed, eliminating shadow effects. (See Table 5-1.)

3.2. Procedural Dependencies

Procedural dependencies arise as the result of the presence of branches in the input code. Any type of instruction may be procedurally dependent on one or more branches, but only on branches, and they must be previously-occurring branches, since procedural dependencies are unidirectional (not reflexive) [18, 21]. Most machines, including the IBM 360/91 [2], the CDC 6600 [17], HPS [11, 12], Torng's [1], Wedig's [24], etc., assume a *restrictive procedural dependency* model, in that all instructions are procedurally dependent on their most previous branch (in effect, this means that all instructions after a branch are dependent on the branch). Both Tjaden's [19] and Uht's [21, 22, 23] models, however, assume sets of reduced procedural dependencies (also see Table 5-1). Uht's set is somewhat less restrictive than Tjaden's, and is minimal for non-trivial sequential code; it is described below. As an example of a reduced procedural dependency condition, consider the following: an instruction which is between a forward branch and its target is procedurally dependent on the forward branch, since its execution is conditional upon how the branch executes, but an instruction after the target is not procedurally dependent on the forward branch, since it is guaranteed to execute regardless of how the branch executes, true or false [18].

After making some definitions, the minimal and hence complete set of procedural dependencies occurring in sequential code are enumerated and described below. Their necessity and sufficiency for non-trivial sequential code are proven in [21].

3.2.1. Definitions

The definitions given below serve both to formalize our use of familiar concepts, and to introduce some new terms needed in the enumeration section.

Iteration Types

Code that is being examined for execution will execute in 0 or more iterations. For example, code with no control flow (straight-line code) will execute in only one iteration. If a code section contains a loop, then multiple iterations may be executed.

In the theory, a distinction is made between those iterations (*present iterations*) already partially enabled (by a backward branch having previously executed true, or from the basic assumption that instructions execute one iteration [unless branched around]), and later (or *future*) iterations, that may be partially enabled in subsequent cycles (by a backward branch executing true later).

Definition 1: The *present* (or current) *iteration* of an instruction is an iteration under consideration for execution in the current cycle. No executed iterations of an instruction may be present iterations. If an instruction is fully executed, then its present iteration is considered to have executed.

Definition 2: A *future iteration* of an instruction is an iteration that may execute in some cycle after the cycle in which the current iteration of the instruction executes.

Current iterations of instructions are guaranteed to execute, unless skipped by a forward branch jumping past the instruction. All iteration types are either present or future.

Instruction Types

Definition 3: *ASsignment* instructions (AS) perform operations on source operands (inputs to the instructions, typically integers residing in memory locations) and store result(s) in one or more sink operands (outputs of the instructions, typically integers residing in memory locations). In CONDEL there is only one sink operand and two or fewer source operands per instruction. Note that assignment instructions have no direct effect on the control flow of the input code.

Definition 4: Syntactically, a *branch* consists of an opcode, a condition (C), and a *target address* (TA). Semantically, if C evaluates true, then control transfers to TA, i.e., the instruction at TA is the next instruction to be executed. This is a somewhat limiting definition, and has little meaning when considering the concurrent execution of a static instruction stream. An alternative semantic definition of branches, appropriate when concurrent execution is desired (as in this case), consists of two parts:

1. Forward Branch (FB): if C evaluates true, then all instructions between the FB and its TA, exclusive, are inhibited from executing in the FB's present iteration.
2. Backward Branch (BB): if C evaluates true, then the next iteration of the instructions from the BB to its TA, inclusive, are not inhibited by the BB. A future iteration of an instruction can only be enabled by a backward branch executing true, such that said instruction is between the BB and its TA, inclusive.

The condition C is a memory location. Typically C is set by relational instructions, e.g., $C \leftarrow A==B$ puts all ones into C if A=B, and puts zeroes into C if $A \neq B$. The evaluation of C may be as simple as testing it for equality to zero; other evaluations are possible; branch instructions may support multiple forms of condition evaluations.

Branch Domains

Definition 5: The *domain* of a branch consists of those instructions whose execution in a given iteration is directly dependent on the branch. Specifically:

The domain of a FB consists of all instructions between the FB and its TA, exclusive.

The domain of a BB consists of all instructions from the BB to its TA, inclusive.

Definition 6: The *super-domain* (SD) of a forward branch consists of the forward branch's domain in conjunction with the forward branch itself.

The *super-domain* of a backward branch is the same as its domain.

Summarizing the last two groups of definitions, we note that in other words, branches are seen as *enabling* or *disabling* the execution of instructions in their domains. (Also see [18].)

Branch Domain Characteristics

There are three types of domain interactions possible: *disjoint*, *nested*, and *overlapped*. See Figure 3-2 for examples of all three.

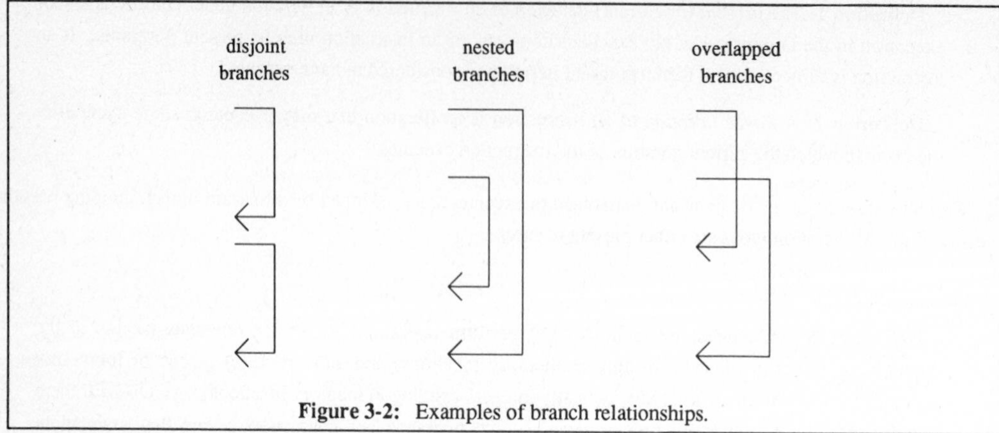

Figure 3-2: Examples of branch relationships.

Definition 7: Two branches, *i* and *j*, are *disjoint* iff their super-domains do not intersect.

Definition 8: Two branches, i and j, are *nested* iff one's super-domain is completely contained in the other's super-domain.

Definition 9: Two branches, i and j, are *overlapped* iff their super-domains intersect without either super-domain being a subset of the other. Note that by this definition, nested branches are **not** overlapped.

Sequential Code Types

All sequential code is considered to be either *unstructured* or *structured.*

Definition 10: *Unstructured* code is standard arbitrary sequential code; branches may jump to any instruction in the code.

Definition 11: *Structured* code is unstructured code under the constraint that the code contains no overlapped branches.

3.2.2. Minimal Procedural Dependencies: Enumeration and Implications

The minimal procedural dependencies are now enumerated and described[8]; theoretical implications of the minimal set are also given. In the remainder of the paper, specific procedural dependencies will be referred to by number, e.g., "PD 3" refers to item number 3 in the procedural dependency list below.

The following items enumerate the procedural dependencies of instruction i on instruction j for non-trivial sequentially-biased code. Note that statements 1-6 (labeled PD 1-6) are only concerned with a present iteration of instruction i. Statement 7 (labeled PD 7) is only concerned with future iterations of instruction i. The notation IQ_p indicates instruction p in the Instruction Queue. For the general case, take the Instruction Queue length to be infinite. These procedural dependencies hold for any section of static code. (As a reminder, recall that AS = assignment statement, FB = forward branch, and BB = backward branch.)

[8]These procedural dependencies are minimal with one minor exception: an outer loop forming backward branch is dependent on an inner loop forming backward branch, even in the case when there are no data dependencies between instructions in the inner loop and those just in the outer loop. This is an unlikely occurrence, as there will normally be such dependencies arising at the least from loop termination or counter reseting instructions. For example, the inner loop counter `I` appearing within the inner loop instruction: `I = I + 1`, is usually reset in the *outer* loop, creating the procedural dependency in any case.

1. IQ_i is an AS in the domain of FB IQ_j; see Figure 3-3.
2. IQ_i is a BB in the domain of FB IQ_j; see Figure 3-3.
3. IQ_i is a FB in the domain of FB IQ_j and the two FBs are overlapped; see Figure 3-4; this procedural dependency is only essential for unstructured code; note that non-overlapped FBs are completely procedurally independent.
4. IQ_i is a BB statically later in the code than BB IQ_j and the two BBs are either overlapped or nested; see Figure 3-5.
5. IQ_i is any type of instruction statically later in the code than BB IQ_j and IQ_i is data dependent on one or more instructions IQ_k in IQ_j's domain; see Figure 3-6.
6. IQ_i is any type of instruction statically later in the code than BB IQ_j and IQ_i is in the domain of an FB which is overlapped with IQ_j; see Figure 3-7; this procedural dependency is only relevant for unstructured code.
7. IQ_i is any type of instruction in BB IQ_j's super domain; i.e., future iterations of IQ_i are not enabled until one or more BBs whose domains contain IQ_i execute true; see Figure 3-8.

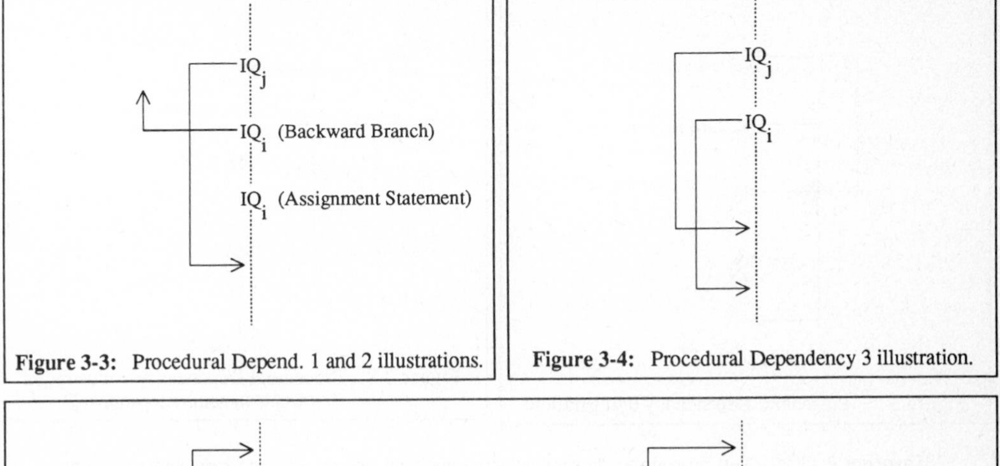

Figure 3-3: Procedural Depend. 1 and 2 illustrations.

Figure 3-4: Procedural Dependency 3 illustration.

Figure 3-5: Procedural Dependency 4 illustration.

In [21], the above listed procedural dependencies (PDs) are shown to be necessary and sufficient to describe all procedural dependencies in any code. Specifically, the following three theorems are proven[9]:

Theorem 1: Nested forward branches are not procedurally dependent on each other, i.e., they are *procedurally independent.*

[9] These theorems were presented, but not proven, in [22].

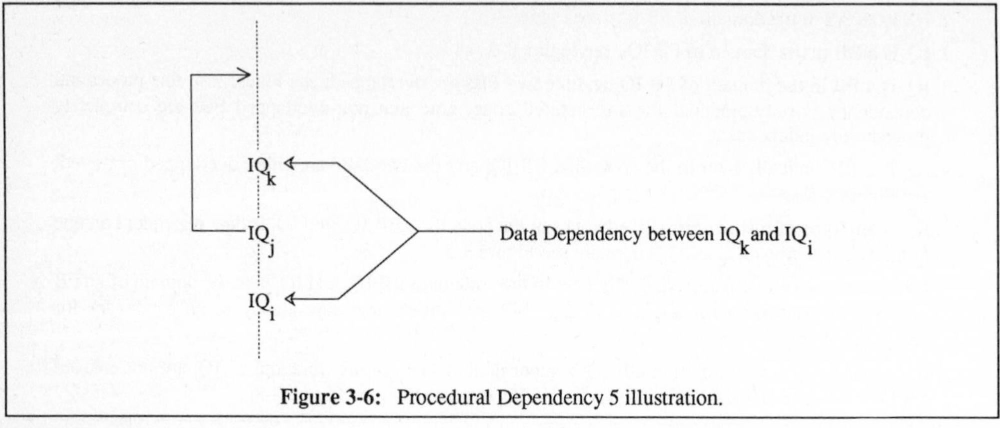

Figure 3-6: Procedural Dependency 5 illustration.

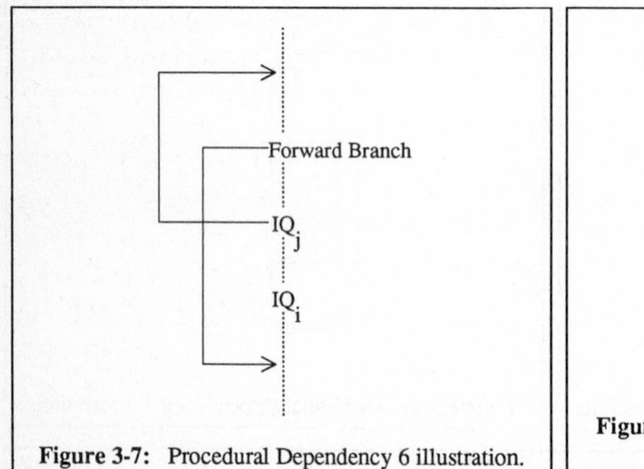

Figure 3-7: Procedural Dependency 6 illustration.

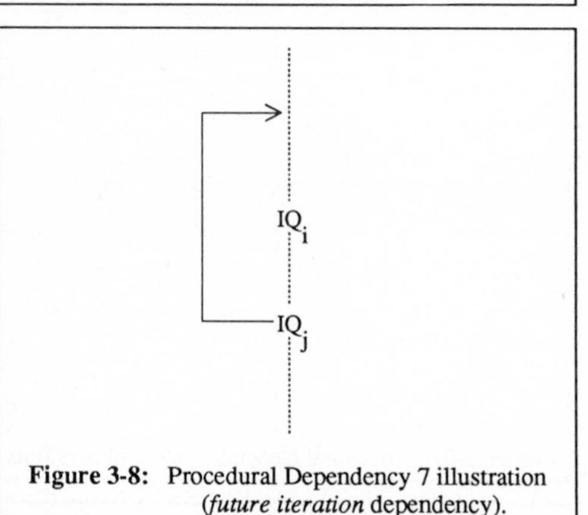

Figure 3-8: Procedural Dependency 7 illustration (*future iteration* dependency).

Theorem 2: The seven procedural dependencies enumerated above are necessary and sufficient to describe all procedural dependencies in any sequential code (i.e., unstructured code, in which all domain interactions are allowed).

Theorem 3: The set of procedural dependencies in structured code, i.e., code without overlapped branch domains, consists of PD's 1, 2, 4 (nested case only), 5, and 7. This is a subset of the dependencies determined to be necessary and sufficient for unstructured code in Theorem 2.

One of the implications of Theorem 3, which also follows from a union of Theorem 1 and a Tjaden [18] Lemma (stating that disjoint branches are procedurally independent), are the following corollaries:

Corollary 4: All forward branches in structured code are completely procedurally independent.

Corollary 5: All non-overlapped forward branches in unstructured code are procedurally independent with respect to themselves and with respect to backward branches not overlapped with the forward branches. (In effect, the forward branches are in a region of code which is at least locally structured.)

For emphasis, we re-iterate: the union of data and procedural dependencies in code forms the set of semantic dependencies existing in the code, and exists independently of any and all hardware the code might run on.

3.3. Resource Dependencies

Resource dependencies exist solely due to hardware restrictions of a particular machine's implementation. For example, if in a given cycle, three add instructions are eligible for execution, and only two adders are available, then a resource dependency exists. In this work, unless otherwise noted, no resource dependencies are assumed.

4. Examples of Reduced Procedural Dependencies

The first example is shown in Figure 4-1. The code shown can be thought of as being a realization of several disjoint or nested **IF-THEN** statements. Branches 3 and 5 execute before branch 2, and execute simultaneously. This is semantically possible due to the reduced procedural dependency model and theory of Section 3.2.2, Corollaries 4 and 5 in particular. It is also possible from a hardware implementation viewpoint due to the use of branch domain indicators and the AE matrix. In the example, branch 3 executing true causes instruction 3' to be *virtually executed*, i.e., for the iteration in question, the corresponding AE element is set without issuing instruction 3' for execution, thereby disabling 3' in that iteration. This in turn *resolves* the data dependency of instruction 6 on instruction 3' (arising from the common use of **X**). Since the data dependency of instruction 6 on 5' is resolved at the same time, instruction 6 is now free to execute in the next cycle (its inputs are now available, presumably having been written in other prior code, and it is procedurally independent). In general, if more than one forward branch is taken, all of the branches' domains are OR'd together to set AE elements.

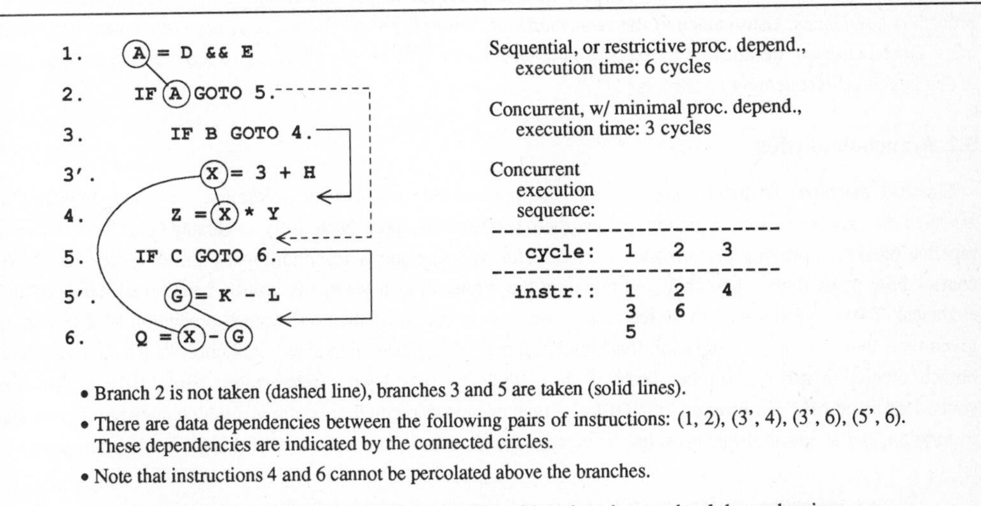

- Branch 2 is not taken (dashed line), branches 3 and 5 are taken (solid lines).
- There are data dependencies between the following pairs of instructions: (1, 2), (3', 4), (3', 6), (5', 6). These dependencies are indicated by the connected circles.
- Note that instructions 4 and 6 cannot be percolated above the branches.

Figure 4-1: Example of code execution with reduced procedural dependencies.

An example of a specific High-Level code realization is shown in Figure 4-2. Note that the realization consists of two disjoint branches; hence, the time to execute the conditional branch parts of the High-Level construct is a constant 1 cycle, regardless of whether either the **<thencode>** block or the **<elsecode>** block is to execute.

5. Other Advanced Concurrency Techniques

5.1. Very Reduced Procedural Dependencies

With a finite Instruction Queue, branch targets may not be contained in the Queue (branches with such targets are referred to as *out-of-bounds* branches), and thus require consideration beyond that of the basic minimal procedural dependency theory of Section 3.2.2. Normally, the execution of a procedure call or return, or an out-of-bounds

```
High-Level Code                          Symbolic Machine Code:

IF C THEN                                1.   IF ~C GOTO 3. --------
                                                                    |
        <thencode>                       2.        <thencode>       |
                                                                    |
    ENDTHEN                                                  <------
    ELSE                                 3.   IF C GOTO 5. ---------
                                                                    |
        <elsecode>                       4.        <elsecode>       |
                                                                    |
    ENDELSE                                                         |
ENDIF                                                        <------
<followingcode>                          5.   <followingcode>
```

- In the machine code both branches may execute simultaneously. Only one branch executes false, enabling a <*code> section.
- IF statement evaluation time: 1 cycle (constant).

Figure 4-2: High-Level code execution with reduced procedural dependencies.

branch, results in a flushing of the Instruction Queue. With very reduced procedural dependencies, however, calls and returns are executed when possible as they are about to be loaded into the Instruction Queue. Using an overlapped register scheme [15] with variably-sized register windows, this results in concurrency across many procedure boundaries. Using much of the same hardware, multiple out-of-bounds branches (which calls and returns are a special case of) are allowed to execute simultaneously. This in-turn gives high-speed execution of properly coded large CASE statement constructs [21].

5.2. Branch Prediction

Classical machines frequently seek to increase performance via *branch prediction*, in which branches are assumed to execute in one direction before their conditionals have been fully evaluated [13]. This decreases pipeline breaks, improving performance. Another similar technique is to conditionally execute code along both control flow paths from a branch [2], eliminating the wrong branch when the branch conditional has been fully evaluated. Two problems with these techniques are: rarely can more than one branch prediction be active at any given time, and some state restoration (backtracking) must take place upon a bad prediction[10]. To date, no known branch prediction scheme solving both of these problems has been implemented, particularly in low-level concurrent machines. In a form of CONDEL-2 a type of branch prediction is allowed which does not require state restoration, and allows multiple branches to execute ahead of time. The basic rule of this form of branch prediction is:

> *Instructions within an innermost loop assume that the Backward Branch comprising the loop will always execute true.*

Therefore iterations of instructions within an innermost loop are allowed to execute before they are enabled by the corresponding backward branch actually executing true; forward branches starting within such future loop iterations are also allowed to execute ahead of time. State restoration and backtracking is avoided by:

1. Using the multiple copies of sinks present in the reduced data dependency mechanism of CONDEL-2, along with a modified execution algorithm;
2. De-coupling instruction execution from instruction sink storage updating; only those sinks guaranteed to be modified are actually modified in main memory.

This form of branch prediction, as implemented in the static instruction stream environment of CONDEL, is called *Super Advanced Execution* (SAE).

---

[10] State restoration or backtracking, in the form of recovery code, is also needed in the software-based *trace scheduling* technique of Fisher [7, 8].

5.3. Comparison of Various Concurrency Techniques

A comparison of various hardware-based low-level concurrency extraction techniques in the literature with our models is shown in Table 5-1. Note that only the CONDEL-2 model achieves minimal semantic dependencies with branch prediction. (Also see footnote [10] vis-a-vis a software approach.)

Machine Model	Instruction Stream Model	Instruction Issue Type	Scalar Data Depend. Enforced	Procedural Depend. Model	Branch Prediction	Execution Algorithm Mode
CDC 6600 [17] (scoreboard)	dynamic	sequential	flow, anti-, output*	restrictive	no	parallel
IBM 360/91 [2, 20] (Tomasulo algorithm)	dynamic	sequential	flow	restrictive	no	parallel
Torng [1] (dependency counters)	dynamic	parallel	flow, anti-, output	restrictive	no	parallel
HPS [14] (modified Tomasulo algorithm)	dynamic	~parallel**	flow	restrictive	yes**	parallel
Tjaden [18, 19] (his most advanced model)	static	parallel	flow, output***	reduced***	no	sequential
Wedig [24] (his most advanced model)	static	parallel	flow	restrictive	no	sequential
CONDEL-1 [21, 22]	static	parallel	flow, anti-, output	reduced (minimal)	no	parallel
CONDEL-2 [21, 23] (dynamic source-sink linking)	static	parallel	flow	reduced (minimal)	yes	parallel

<u>Notes:</u> * When anti-dependencies are encountered in the CDC 6600, the dependent instruction is partially executed, blocking only on the final writing of the sink. Flow dependent instructions are also partially executed, but to a lesser extent.

** The HPS machine allows microinstructions to execute concurrently. Instructions are retired serially. The branch prediction technique proposed requires state restoration and backtracking, as do all known dynamic instruction stream prediction techniques.

*** Tjaden's models assumed that all of the semantic dependencies of the code to be executed are computed in software, and subsequently downloaded to the hardware.

Table 5-1: Comparison of hardware low-level concurrency techniques.

6. Experiment Methodology / Simulation Environment

Software simulations of the CONDEL machine models were performed to provide the data for subsequent analysis. The software simulation environment is shown in Figure 6-1. The CONDEL assembler is a stripped-down two-pass assembler, written in C, which converts CONDEL Assembly code to simulator-readable hex code. The remainder of the simulation environment and the experiment methodology are described below, including a section on how array accesses are treated.

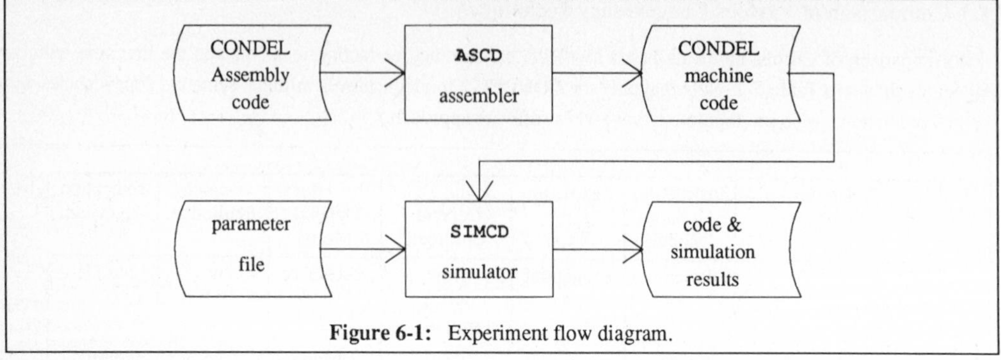

Figure 6-1: Experiment flow diagram.

6.1. The CONDEL Simulator

The simulator realizes all of the concurrency detection algorithms of the CONDEL models. This software, written in C, mimics the model hardwares' execution algorithms, executing the equivalent of machine code.

The simulator operates as follows. After initialization, including the storing of the input code into the model main memory, the simulator executes the major loop until the input program is fully executed. Each pass through the loop constitutes one of CONDEL's cycles. There are six or seven functions in the loop which, unless stated otherwise, execute in each pass. The functions are:

- if possible, load instructions into the Instruction Queue (IQ)
- determine the instructions to execute in the current cycle
- execute the branches
- update the Advanced Execution (AE) matrix
- execute the assignment instructions
- update memory (only for CONDEL-2)
- output simulation state for this cycle, if desired

Most of these steps would occur concurrently in real hardware.

Many parameters of the simulator are user-adjustable. They include the IQ length n, AE width m, various resource constraints, branch concurrency algorithm type, and data concurrency algorithm type. With the resultant flexibility of the simulator, it is possible to see the benefits of many different execution algorithm combinations under many different hardware implementation assumptions.

6.2. Benchmarks' Descriptions

Two sets of benchmarks were used, a General Purpose set and a Scientific set. The General Purpose benchmarks contain a relatively high degree of control flow complexity; the benchmarks perform a wide variety of tasks. The Scientific benchmarks exhibit a very low degree of control flow complexity, perhaps too low to be realistic; the benchmarks perform scientific application tasks. All of the benchmarks were hand-coded into an intermediate assembly code; unless noted otherwise, the coder acted as a typical compiler[11]; no advanced operations were assumed. Descriptions of all of the benchmarks follow.

[11]The following simple compiler features were assumed: mapping of assignment expressions to low-height binary execution trees, little re-use of registers, and HLL statement translation as given in [21].

6.2.1. General Purpose Benchmarks' Descriptions

The General Purpose benchmark set consists of ten programs. They are:

1. `ACM410` - ACM Algorithm 410 [6]; partially sorts a list of numbers
2. `ACM428` - ACM Algorithm 428 [26]; minimum redundancy alphabetic binary encoding; both ACM410 and ACM428 were used by Tjaden[12]
3. `BCDBin` - a BCD to binary conversion routine, written for an undergraduate final exam [21]
4. `Dhrystone` - a recently developed [25] systems programming benchmark; exhibits a variety of data and control flow; only one or two iterations of the component loops are executed (by the benchmark's design)
5. `GetBlk` - a modified frequently-called system function from Berkeley 4.1 UNIX[13]; finds a valid buffer block from a list
6. `HardShuffle` - mixes the contents of two arrays [10]
7. `MCF4` - the Military Computer Family Scale Vector Display test program [5]; scales a list of graphics vectors about a specified center
8. `MCF7` - the Military Computer Family Digital Communications Processing test program [5]; moves a message to a buffer
9. `Puzzle` - a reduced version of a test program [3] that solves a three-dimensional puzzle; uses much subroutine recursion
10. `ShellSort` - a version of the shell sort algorithm, from [9]

6.2.2. Scientific Benchmarks' Descriptions

The scientific set of benchmarks consists of the 14 standard Lawrence Livermore Loops [16], with the number of loop iterations of each loop reduced by about a factor of 10, to reduce simulation time. If anything, this makes the simulation results more conservative, since better performance of the models typically occurs as the number of loop iterations increases (reducing the effects of startup execution transients). Also, the library function call in loop 14 was removed, as the function's constituent code was unknown. Leaving the call in could have potentially altered the performance figures given, but not to a great extent.

6.3. Simulation Variables

The simulation dependent variable is the speedup S; S is defined as the number of cycles necessary to execute the given benchmark purely sequentially, divided by the number of cycles necessary to execute the benchmark concurrently. All instructions execute in one cycle. No penalty is assumed for instruction fetches and decodes in either the sequential or concurrent case.

There are two independent machine model variables, indicating the degree of either procedural or data concurrency allowed. Each variable has three possible values for a total of nine possible algorithmic models.

The first variable is procedural concurrency type *(pct)*. The procedural dependency models used by the simulator are indicated by the *pct* value, defined as:

- A - restrictive procedural dependencies; all instructions are procedurally dependent on their most previous branch, as in Wedig's model [24].
- B - minimal procedural dependencies as described in Section 3.2.2; only one out-of-bounds branch may execute in a cycle, and procedure instructions are unexpanded.
- C - very reduced procedural dependencies; same as B, but multiple out-of-bounds branches may

[12]The reader is cautioned against making a straight comparison to Tjaden's results, as it appears that Tjaden assumed that multi-operation high-level statements take one cycle to execute, whereas in this work such statements were de-composed into simple single-cycle operations.

[13]UNIX is a trademark of AT&T.

execute, and procedure instructions are conditionally expanded as described in Section 5.1; increases concurrency when a finite length Instruction Queue is used.

The second variable is data concurrency type *(dct)*. The data dependency and branch prediction models implemented in the simulator are indicated by the *dct* value, defined as:

- 1 - maximally restrictive data dependencies; all data dependency relations described in Section 3.1 hold; note that this model of data dependencies, as implemented in CONDEL-1, precludes the use of Super Advanced Execution (SAE), as there are only single copies of variables; no branch prediction is used.
- 2 - minimal (scalar) data dependencies; only flow dependencies hold for non-array accesses; no branch prediction (SAE) is used.
- 3 - same as 2, but the branch prediction technique of Section 5.2 (SAE) is used.

The CONDEL-1 model corresponds to *pct*=C and *dct*=1, while the CONDEL-2 model corresponds to *pct*=C and *dct*=3.

6.3.1. Array Access Dependencies

When *dct* equals 2 or 3, array accesses are not maximally restrictive. Data dependency Relation 3 (output) type related array accesses may be executed concurrently, due to the presence of multiple sink copies. However, since all array reads are made from memory, Relation 1 and 2 (flow and anti-) type related array accesses may not execute concurrently[14]. In other words, any two array accesses involving both an array read and an array write to the same array must be sequentialized; otherwise (with only array writes or only array reads taking place) the accesses may proceed concurrently.

When *dct*=1, however, no multiple sinks are present, so array writes to the same array are also sequentialized; i.e., array accesses are maximally restrictive. (Note: restrictive array accesses can be reduced or eliminated if non-conflicting accesses to the same array are given different names to the same array [at a level above the hardware].)

6.4. Review of the Major Assumptions

The major assumptions of the simulations are:

- Each instruction takes one cycle to execute. Instruction Queue loading is not considered[15].
- There is no pre-processing or restructuring of the input code.
- There are unlimited resources, except for n and m.

7. Simulation Results and Analysis

In all of the simulation summaries, the data points given are the arithmetic means of the constituent individual benchmarks, unless noted otherwise. Harmonic means are also computed for some data.

---

[14]This can be avoided if $O(n^2m^2)$ address comparators are provided to match array sources with array sinks, the addresses of which are not known until execute time; in this case the dependencies with previous array read instructions need not hold. The technique of CONDEL-2 uses much less hardware and is more practical; no comparators are used (for a similar execute-time function).

[15]It is believed that the likelihood of loading having a significantly negative effect on performance will be low; we are currently investigating this. The preliminary indications support the hypothesis.

7.1. Simulation Results

The simulation result data for the General Purpose set of benchmarks is summarized in Figure 7-1. The range of the individual benchmarks' speedups for *pct*=C and *dct*=3 is from 1.61 to 4.79, giving the displayed arithmetic mean value of 2.90, and a harmonic mean of 2.60. The performance of the various machine models did not improve appreciably with larger *n* or *m*.

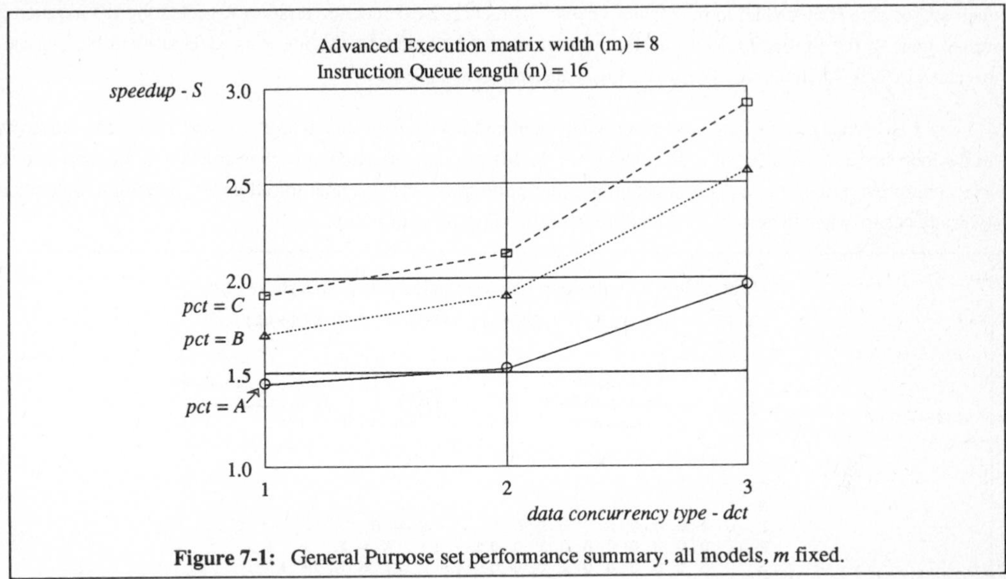

Figure 7-1: General Purpose set performance summary, all models, *m* fixed.

The simulation result data for the Scientific set of benchmarks is summarized in Table 7-1. In the table, two sets of data are presented: one includes all of the scientific benchmarks (all of the Livermore Loops), while the other set includes only those loops for which *loop-capture* occurred (each loop fit completely into the Instruction Queue), namely loops 1-6, 11, and 12. For both sets, the data is virtually the same regardless of the *pct* type, as the loops have a very simple control flow (it consists solely of a simple looping construct with no nested forward branches, etc.); therefore the *pct* type is not shown. The range of all of the individual benchmarks' speedups for *dct*=3 is from 1.66 to 11.69, giving the displayed arithmetic mean value of 4.72, and a harmonic mean of 3.48. The speedups for the loop-capture set did not improve appreciably with larger *n* or *m*. Preliminary indications of ongoing work indicate that the average performance improves further when *n* is increased to capture all of the loops.

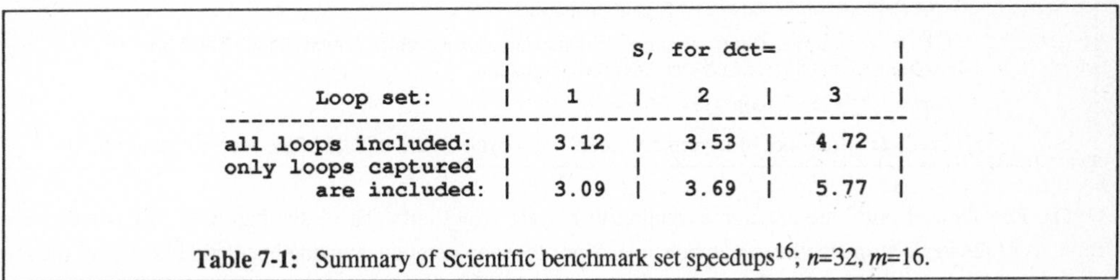

	S, for dct=		
Loop set:	1	2	3
all loops included:	3.12	3.53	4.72
only loops captured are included:	3.09	3.69	5.77

Table 7-1: Summary of Scientific benchmark set speedups[16]; *n*=32, *m*=16.

[16]The 5.77 figure was erroneously reported to be 6.46 (off by 12.5%) in [21, 23], due to an arithmetic error; the author extremely regrets the mistake. Fortunately, the conclusions of our work are not modified to a significant degree.

7.2. Simulation Snapshot

To illustrate the functioning of the CONDEL-2 model, the best-performing loop in the Scientific set (Loop 1) is examined. A snapshot of the Executably Independent (EI) matrix was taken during Loop 1's execution (about halfway through); it is shown in Figure 7-2. Each `1` in the EI matrix indicates that the corresponding instruction (row) is to execute in the corresponding iteration (column) in the current cycle. Instructions are executed as soon as their source data is available: in the previous cycle, instruction 2 executed in iteration 7, generating `K`'s iteration 7 value; thus, in the illustrated (next) cycle, instructions 3, 6, 10, and 14 (having `K` as an input) can be, and are, executed in their 7th iterations. Thus, data-flow execution is achieved.

Loop 1 is 14 instructions long, and the speedup exhibited for the case shown (*dct* = 3) was 11.69. The closeness of the loop size and the speedup is no coincidence. In this case, one iteration of each instruction in the loop is to be executed in the current cycle. This situation is called *saturation*, and is a goal for all codes' execution. Saturation typically occurs when there are limited inter-iteration dependencies in a loop.

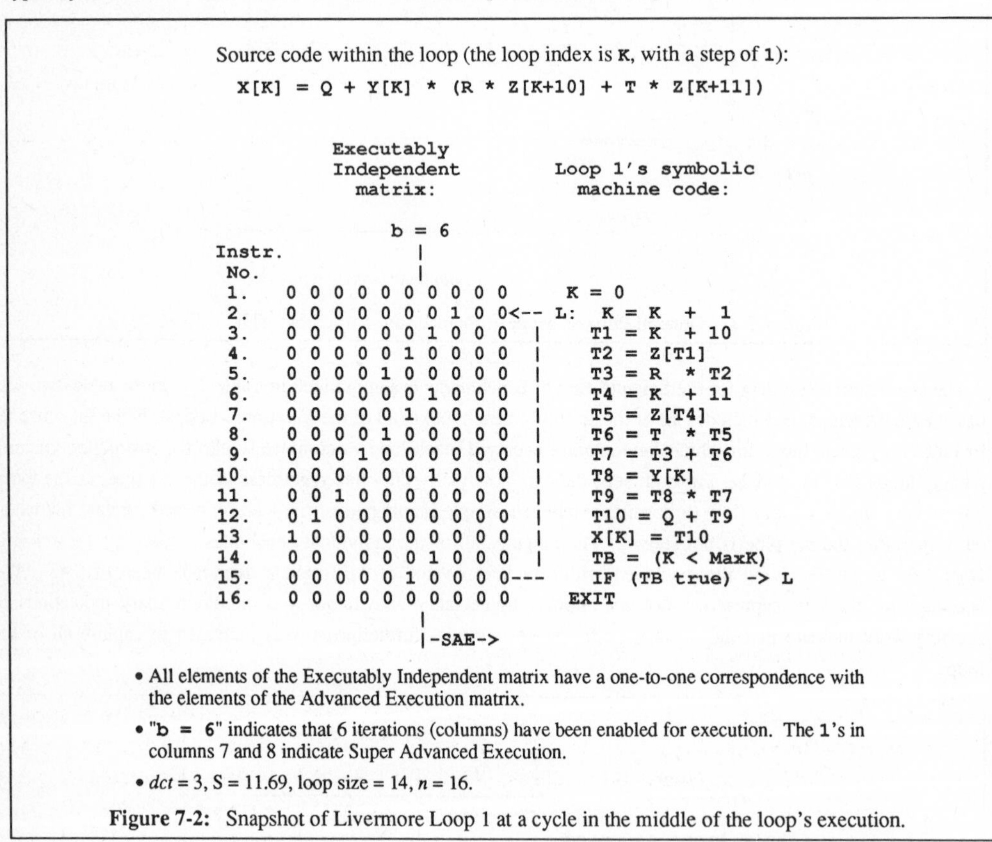

- All elements of the Executably Independent matrix have a one-to-one correspondence with the elements of the Advanced Execution matrix.
- "`b = 6`" indicates that 6 iterations (columns) have been enabled for execution. The `1`'s in columns 7 and 8 indicate Super Advanced Execution.
- *dct* = 3, S = 11.69, loop size = 14, *n* = 16.

Figure 7-2: Snapshot of Livermore Loop 1 at a cycle in the middle of the loop's execution.

The limitation of only one iteration executing in a cycle is not enforced by the hardware, but is rather a by-product of the models' instruction set architecture. Since the loop iteration counting instruction (`2.`) is of the form:

```
I = I + 1,
```

it is dependent on itself (in earlier iterations), and thus may only execute once a cycle. This in effect limits the other instructions in the loop to execute one iteration per cycle, since they directly or indirectly are dependent on `I` (for realistic code). The solution to this problem is architectural, in that an instruction generating multiple values per iteration is needed; i.e., something like the indexing component of a FORALL construct would be useful.

Other mechanisms which inhibited concurrency extraction in other benchmarks are described in [21]. Solutions to these inhibitors are also suggested (but not developed) in [21].

7.3. Performance Contribution Analysis

It is interesting to see to what degree each concurrency enhancement contributes to performance enhancement. To this end, the benchmark set data presented in Figure 7-1 and Table 7-1 are analyzed further. Let:

$S_{D\text{-}P}$ = speedup with *dct* of D, and *pct* of P

Then the average incremental speedup *SI* of the reduced data dependency technique with no SAE (*dct*=2) is:

$$SI_2 = [(S_{2\text{-}A}/S_{1\text{-}A}) + (S_{2\text{-}B}/S_{1\text{-}B}) + (S_{2\text{-}C}/S_{1\text{-}C})]/3$$

Note that this is actually three different values of SI_2 averaged over all procedural concurrency types. Other *SI* values are calculated similarly. The baseline case, for *basic concurrency extraction*, is for *pct*=A and *dct*=1; for the General Purpose benchmark set, $S_{1\text{-}A}$=1.44.

The *SI* figures for the General Purpose set data of Figure 7-1 are now presented. The numbers for the data concurrency techniques are shown in Table 7-2, while those for the procedural concurrency techniques are given in Table 7-3. The variances of all of the incremental contributions are small, indicating the basic orthogonality of the concurrency extraction techniques.

$S_{dct2\text{-}pct}/S_{dct1\text{-}pct}$, for

dct2	dct1	pct A	pct B	pct C	SI_{dct2}
2	1	1.06	1.10	1.12	1.09
3	2	1.29	1.34	1.36	1.33

Table 7-2: Data concurrency schemes' incremental performance contributions: General Purpose benchmarks.

$S_{pct2\text{-}dct}/S_{pct1\text{-}dct}$, for

pct2	pct1	dct 1	dct 2	dct 3	SI_{pct2}
B	A	1.19	1.25	1.30	1.25
C	B	1.11	1.13	1.14	1.13

Table 7-3: Procedural concurrency schemes' incremental performance contributions: Gen. Purpose benchmarks.

The net incremental contributions of each technique are summarized in Table 7-4. Note the close agreement between the calculated (from individual *SI*) and measured total speedups. The basic concurrency extraction algorithm gives the greatest incremental speedup, with SAE second. The least improvement comes from plain scalar shadow effects elimination; however, that technique is needed for the SAE algorithm. Since semantic dependencies are machine-independent, multiple sink copies are not specific to any one machine, and the speedups were not limited by the values of *n* and *m* used, the results are almost machine-independent; i.e., they are reasonably general (the main exception is that the Instruction Queue loading algorithm may vary from machine to machine and cause different results; we have used a good heuristic algorithm here).

The incremental performance contributions derived from the Scientific benchmark set results of Table 7-1 are shown in Table 7-5. Basic concurrency extraction overwhelmingly provides the greatest incremental performance contribution. The reduction of shadow effects alone provides little benefit, as was the case with the General Purpose set. SAE gives a significant performance contribution, particularly when combined with the shadow effects reduction contribution, whose hardware it uses. In [21] several performance inhibitors are identified as existing in

Concurrency extraction Type	Type designation	Speedup Contribution
Basic	1, A	1.44
Reduced data dep. (red. shadow effects)	2	1.09
Branch prediction (SAE)	3	1.33
Minimal procedural dependencies	B	1.25
Expanded CALLs and RETURNs, etc.	C	1.13
TOTAL Speedup (product of all speedups)		2.95
TOTAL Speedup (measured [3-C])		2.90

Table 7-4: Summary of incremental performance contributions of concurrency schemes for the General Purpose benchmark set.

the Livermore loops as coded. If they were to be removed, via software pre-processing, the effect on the above figures would likely be substantial. (For example, Livermore loop 2's speedup for *dct*=3 would go from 9.55 to 22.18, which alone would increase the speedup of the *dct*=3 model from 5.77 to 7.36, increasing the branch prediction incremental contribution from 1.56 to 1.99.)

Concurrency extraction Type	Type designation	Speedup Contribution (all loops)	(loops captured only)
Basic	1, A	3.12	3.09
Reduced data dep. (red. shadow effects)	2	1.13	1.19
Branch prediction (SAE)	3	1.33	1.56
Minimal procedural dependencies	B	1.00	1.00
Expanded CALLs and RETURNs, etc.	C	1.00	1.00
TOTAL Speedup (product of all speedups)		4.72	5.77

Table 7-5: Summary of incremental performance contributions of concurrency schemes for the Scientific benchmark set.

7.4. Other Considerations

7.4.1. Incremental Hardware Costs

The issue of hardware costs is now briefly discussed; for more information, see [21, 22, 23]. In the following discussion, note that only the costs of the algorithms' hardware is considered, i.e., the cost of processing elements, etc., is not included. The estimates given are rough. Also, the hardware architectures of the CONDEL concurrent execution algorithms are highly regular, potentially allowing a high density realization.

The incremental costs to go from model *pct*=B to C, and from model *dct*=2 to 3, are relatively small.

- The hardware cost of the *pct*=C concurrent execution algorithm (CONDEL-1) is less than 40Kgates more than a sequential processor, assuming a window length of 16; this is reasonable. The basic hardware cost is $O(Kn^2)$, where K is small.
- The incremental cost of the concurrency hardware for *dct*=3 over that of a sequential machine (or of CONDEL-2 over CONDEL-1) is estimated to be reasonable (about 250Kgates more are needed) for small n and m (n=16 and m=8), which are likely sufficient to obtain most of the concurrency from General Purpose applications. Scientific applications seem to require larger values of n and m to extract most of their inherent concurrency; thus, the cost figures are less attractive. The basic hardware cost is $O(Kn^2m^2)$, where K is small. This cost may be reduced in certain restricted implementations of CONDEL-2.

7.4.2. Performance with Reduced Resources

In the case of CONDEL-1, simulations show that 80% of the speedup is achieved with limited resources, including only 3 processing elements.

For CONDEL-2, the effects of reduced resources have not been determined, but the CONDEL-1 results are encouraging. Also, assuming a restricted number of processing elements, preliminary simulation and architecture studies indicate the possibility of a CONDEL-2 implementation exhibiting virtually no performance degradation over the unrestricted case.

7.4.3. Hardware Delays

Since both models contain few gate delays in their critical paths, and the execution algorithms are inherently parallel (by design), the performance improvements gained via concurrency exploitation are not negated by significantly longer cycle times.

8. Conclusions and Future Work

In this paper low-level concurrent execution of imperative instruction streams has been considered. We concentrated on hardware-based techniques; no software pre-processing or code re-structuring has been assumed.

A minimal set of procedural dependencies has been presented and described. Combining this set with minimal data dependencies (only flow dependencies) results in minimal semantic dependencies. These results are independent of the extraction technique applied, be it hardware- or software-based.

The analysis indicates that for non-trivial control flow, e.g., general purpose code, minimal procedural dependencies provide significant performance gains at reasonable cost. Reduced procedural dependency techniques (i.e., for finite Instruction Queue situations especially) beyond minimal procedural dependencies have relatively low performance pay-off *on average*, as is also the case for reduced data dependencies (without branch prediction). Branch prediction, which uses the hardware of the reduced data dependency technique, provides significant performance gains, as does basic concurrency extraction. The hardware cost for a CONDEL-2 machine with n=16 and m=8 is not excessive [21, 23]. At this time, the reduced data dependency and branch prediction techniques (*dct* = 2 or 3) are likely to be most cost-effective for general purpose machines.

Overall, most of the low-level hardware concurrency extraction techniques provide significant incremental performance gains. (The Livermore Loops are not good indicators of machines' performance on code containing significantly complex control flow.)

Clearly, from a research standpoint, a most important piece of future work is to combine the hardware approaches with software assists that readily remove concurrency inhibitors, and re-simulate the CONDEL machine models. Investigations of cost reduction, CONDEL implementation studies, Instruction Queue loading effects, and enhancements of branch prediction are also important, and are underway. It would also be of interest to apply CONDEL techniques to other levels of concurrency extraction, particularly at a higher global program level.

Acknowledgements

I am very grateful for the support given by the Semiconductor Research Corporation, Carnegie Mellon University, and the University of California at San Diego.

I am extremely indebted to Garold Tjaden and my advisor Bob Wedig for providing such fine starting points for my research. I am also grateful to Bob for much good advice during the course of my doctoral research.

The efforts of past and present members of the CONDEL project are also extremely appreciated. In particular, I would like to thank Ken Hughes, Al Ting, and Karen York at CMU, and Rick Ord, John Kolen, Harold Froehling, Kent Meyer, John Prohoroff, and Erika Karagouni at UCSD.

Lastly, but most importantly, innumerable thanks to my friend LD for sanity maintenance.

References

[1] Acosta, R. D., Kjelstrup, J., and Torng, H. C. An Instruction Issuing Approach to Enhancing Performance in Multiple Functional Unit Processors. *IEEE Transactions on Computers* C-35:815-828, September, 1986.

[2] Anderson, D. W., Sparacio, F. J. and Tomasulo, R. M. The IBM System/360 Model 91: Machine Philosophy and Instruction-Handling. *IBM Journal* :8-24, January, 1967.

[3] Baskett, Forest. The Puzzle Benchmark. This is an undocumented compute-bound program; obtained via Marc Rose of CMU and Scott Wakefield of Stanford University; fits a piece into a 3-D puzzle.

[4] Bernstein, A. J. Analysis of Programs for Parallel Processing. *IEEE Transactions on Electronic Computers* EC-15:757-763, October, 1966.

[5] Carnegie-Mellon University. MCF Test Programs and Data Specification. Benchmark programs in a generic language, and instructions for their coding and use.

[6] Chambers, J. M. Algorithm 410 - Partial Sorting. *Communications of the ACM* 14:357-358, May, 1971.

[7] Fisher, J. A. Trace Scheduling: A Technique for Global Microcode Compaction. *IEEE Transactions on Computers* C-30(7), July, 1981.

[8] Fisher, J. A. Very Long Instruction Word Architectures and the ELI-512. In *Proceedings of the 10th Annual International Symposium on Computer Architecture*, pages 140-150. ACM-SIGARCH and the IEEE Computer Society, June, 1983.

[9] Grogono, Peter. *Programming in PASCAL.* Addison-Wesley Publishing Company, Inc., Reading, Massachusetts, 1980.

[10] Hoevel, L. W. and Wakefield, S. The HardShuffle Program. Benchmark moving (shuffling) data between two arrays.

[11] Hwu, W., Melvin, S., Shebanow, M., Chen, C., Wei, J., and Patt, Y. An HPS Implementation of VAX; Initial Design and Analysis. In *Proceedings of the Nineteenth Annual Hawaii International Conference on System Sciences.* University of Hawaii, in cooperation with the ACM and the IEEE Computer Society, January, 1986.

[12] Hwu, W. and Patt, Y. HPSm, a High Performance Restricted Data Flow Architecture Having Minimal Functionality. In *Proceedings of the 13th Annual Symposium on Computer Architecture*, pages 297-306. ACM-IEEE, June, 1986.

[13] Lee, J. K. F. and Smith, A. J. Branch Prediction Strategies and Branch Target Buffer Design. *COMPUTER, IEEE Computer Society* 17(1):6-22, January, 1984.

[14] Patt, Y., Hwu, W., and Shebanow, M. HPS, a New Microarchitecture: Rationale and Introduction. In *Proceedings of MICRO-18*, pages 103-108. ACM, December, 1985.

[15] Patterson, D. A. and Sequin, C. H. A VLSI RISC. *COMPUTER, IEEE Computer Society* 15(9):8-21, September, 1982.

[16] Riganati, J. P. and Schneck, P. B. Supercomputing. *COMPUTER, IEEE Computer Society* 17(10):97-113, October, 1984.

[17] Thorton, J. E. Parallel Operation in the Control Data 6600. In *Proceedings of the Fall Joint Computer Conference*, pages 33-40. AFIPS, 1964.

[18] Tjaden, G. S. *Representation and Detection of Concurrency Using Ordering Matrices.* PhD thesis, The Johns Hopkins University, 1972.

[19] Tjaden, G. S. and Flynn, M. J. Representation of Concurrency with Ordering Matrices. *IEEE Transactions on Computers* C-22(8):752-761, August, 1973.

[20] Tomasulo, R. M. An Efficient Algorithm for Expoiting Multiple Arithmetic Units. *IBM Journal* :25-33, January, 1967.

[21] Uht, A. K. *Hardware Extraction of Low-Level Concurrency from Sequential Instruction Streams.* PhD thesis, Carnegie-Mellon University, December, 1985. Available from University Microfilms International, Ann Arbor, Michigan, U.S.A.

[22] Uht, A. K. An Efficient Hardware Algorithm to Extract Concurrency From General-Purpose Code. In *Proceedings of the Nineteenth Annual Hawaii International Conference on System Sciences.* University of Hawaii, in cooperation with the ACM and the IEEE Computer Society, January, 1986.

[23] Uht, A. K. and Wedig, R. G. Hardware Extraction of Low-level Concurrency from Serial Instruction Streams. In *Proceedings of the International Conference on Parallel Processing*, pages 729-736. IEEE Computer Society and the Association for Computing Machinery, August, 1986.

[24] Wedig, R. G. *Detection of Concurrency in Directly Executed Language Instruction Streams.* PhD thesis, Stanford University, June, 1982.

[25] Weicker, R. P. Dhrystone: A Synthetic Systems Programming Benchmark. *Communications of the ACM* 27(10):1013-1030, October, 1984.

[26] Yohe, J. M. Algorithm 428 - Hu-Tucker Minimum Redundancy Alphabetic Coding Method. *Communications of the ACM* 15:360-362, May, 1972.

ACCESS PATTERNS: A USEFULL CONCEPT IN VECTOR PROGRAMMING

Yvon JEGOU

IRISA / INRIA
Campus Universitaire de Beaulieu
35042 RENNES CEDEX
FRANCE

1 Introduction

In order to reach a high speed of computation, the data referenced in the instructions of a supercomputer must be shared by many memory banks. The accesses to these memory banks have to be either parallel as in array machines or interleaved as is usually the case on vector and pipeline architectures. The bandwith of the memory is tied to the bandwith of the addressing of the computer. To reach this goal, many supercomputers base their vector addressing on global vector or matrix descriptors. Usually, a vector is stored in memory at a sequence of locations whose addresses are in an arithmetical progression. Thus, it is described by few details : a base address and an address increment. This vector definition is consistent with the linear indexing expressions which are mostly used in Numerical Analysis.

The high level programming languages for supercomputers can be classified in the following way :

- classical sequential languages such as FORTRAN,
- SIMD languages such as ACTUS [Perrott 79] where the parallelism in the instructions and the access to the data is explicit,
- purely vector languages as APL, Hellena [Jégou 86], VECTRAN [Paul 75] and Fortran 8X [Wagener 84] which extend scalar operations to vectors and matrices.

Although a sequential language guarantees machine independancy of the programs, we think that it is not realistic to base the efficiency of the algorithms upon the automatic discovery of vector instructions by a vectorizer. It is more appropriate that a programmer must "think" vector when writing sequential programs in order to introduce good vectorization. On the other hand, the use of an SIMD language guarantees a good matching with the SIMD architecture. Vectors and matrices have to be explicitly mapped in some virtual parallel domain. However these languages do not abstract enough from the architecture in order to be used by non-specialists.

The third approach which consist in programming with vector languages allows efficient adaptation of a program to a class of vector, pipeline and array architectures. Such an approch has been used in Fortran 8X extensions for vector computation.

In the same way that the efficiency of a program run on a supercomputer depends heavily on the ratio of its vector to scalar instructions, the efficiency of a vector language is linked to the number of vectors that can be extracted from the data structures of the programs. We introduce the concept of an *access pattern* in a classical vector language in order to identify the maximum of vectors in the data structures of the programs. Then we prove that this concept allows the efficient compilation of these programs for many supercomputers. It is shown here that the access pattern concept is not only adapted to high speed computation but gives programmers many facilities for quite general array manipulations.

2 Vector computation

2.1 Vector languages

Vector languages allow global operations on vector and matrices. The efficiency of a vector language does not only depend on the predefined set of vector instructions but also on the data structures these instructions can be applied to. Among the most frequently accessed vectors in Numerical Analysis, one can find

- a row or a column of a matrix
- the main diagonal of a square matrix
- the half-row of a square matrix corresponding to the upper or lower triangle
- the vector formed by the odd or even elements of a vector.

Vectors are not the only data structures a vector language should manipulate. Global accesses to matrices are necessary for library subroutine calls for instance. The array notion must be general enough for efficient programming and a good vector langage shoud give access to various subarrays such as

- the transpose of a matrix
- a "plane" of a cube
- a matrix formed by the extraction of the odd elements of the odd rows from an existing matrix
- sub-matrices.

Some parameters such as the vector length may vary during program execution, for instance in linear system resolution. We introduce the *access pattern* concept to extend the usefulness of a classical vector language. Various vectors and subarrays are identified by applying access patterns to the data structures of the programs.

2.2 Supercomputers

Whether a supercomputer belongs to a vector, pipelined or array class of machines, its efficiency depends on the ratio of "vector instructions" executed. Asymptotic speed can only be reached by executing such instructions. Vector instructions refer to vector operands in main memory. In this paper, we consider the supercomputers for which a vector is stored at a sequence of addresses which form an arithmetic progression in memory. This is usually the case for vector or pipelined machines such as the CRAY-1 [Cray 77] and the VP200 [Miura 83]. Many array machines such as BSP [Burroughs 78] and OPSILA [Auguin 86] also consider such a linear vector mapping in memory. All these addressing facilities allow fast access to a great variety of vectors in the memory. High level langages should define general mechanismes to extract these vectors from the data structures in order to get efficient implementation of the algorithms on these machines.

3 The vector language Hellena

Hellena is a classical sequential programming language of the Pascal familly extended with vector manipulating facilities.

3.1 data types

In Hellena as in Ada or Pascal, all data are typed. A type defines a data structure and its set of possible values. The basic types `integer`, `real`, `boolean` and `ascii` are predefined. New types can be defined by the user, mainly array types is our concern.
The notation

```
array indices_domain of elements
```

defines an array data structure. `indices_domain` defines the dimension and the size of this array type. The elements of this array belong to the type `elements`.

A type declaration associates an identifier with a type definition. A variable declaration identifies a memory location where data of the corresponding type can be stored.

3.2 Operations

The Hellena language predefines the classical scalar operations on numerical data and then extends the application of these operations when the operands are arrays in the following way:

Let us consider an operator `O` defined on a scalar field `S` by

$$S \times S \Longrightarrow S$$

O:

$$s_1 \times s_2 \dashrightarrow s_3$$

this operator is implicitly extended to the following cases

$$S^n \times S^n \Longrightarrow S^n$$
$$ts_1 \times ts_2 \dashrightarrow ts_3$$

$$S^n \times S \Longrightarrow S^n$$
$$ts_1 \times s_2 \dashrightarrow ts_3$$

$$S \times S^n \Longrightarrow S^n$$
$$s_1 \times ts_2 \dashrightarrow ts_3$$

where ts_1, ts_2 and ts_3 are conformable arrays. Two data arrays are said to be conformable if their shapes are the same, that is, if they have the same number of dimensions and each dimension contains the same number of elements. These arrays need not have the same lower index bounds. A scalar is conformable with any array. These implicit extensions of the scalar operations avoid the introduction of specific operators on user defined array data types. For instance, the instruction

```
(1)      V1 := V2 + 2*V3 ;
```

has the following significance : The ith element of V2 is added to two times the ith element of V3 and the resulting value is assigned to the ith element of V1. The ith element of a vector V is the element identified by the indexing notation V(i - lower_bound_of_V + 1). If the vectors V1, V2 and V3 have the same index domain [1,n], instruction (1) is semantically equivalent to the sequential loop

```
for i := 1 to n
loop
    V1(i) := V2(i) + 2*V3(i) ;
end_loop  ;
```

3.3 Variables and objects

In Hellena, a variable name identifies a set of memory locations where a possible value of this variable can be stored. A variable declaration allocates a new set of locations identified by the variable identifier. A variable identification identifies already allocated memory location. For example, an indexing notation identifies the memory location where the accessed element is stored.

In Numerical Analysis, algorithms have to be applied on parts of data structures such as a row or a diagonal of a matrix. In sequential languages, only array elements can be identified by indexing. The notion of access pattern in Hellena allows identification of numerous sub-objects.

4 The access patterns

4.1 presentation

By applying an access pattern `P` to an existing object `A`, one can define a new object denoted `A.P` whose components are components of the object `A`. For instance, let us consider a 100 row, 100 column matrix `M` of type

```
array [1,100]*[1,100] of real
```

The notation `M.diagonal` defines a 100 element vector object where element `M.diagonal(i)` is the element `M(i,i)`, for all `i` in [1,100]. The relationship between the elements of the object `M` and the elements of the object `M.diagonal` is shown in figure 1 where the edges join the elements which share the same memory location. The new object `M.diagonal` has the same status as a declared variable of a program :

- it can be indexed
- it can be the parameter of any subprogram call where an object of this type is expected
- it can appear in any vector instruction
- it can be assigned
- an acces pattern can be applied to it

Figures 1 to 6 show frequently used access patterns in Numerical Analysis.

The object resulting from the application of an access pattern must have a well defined data type of Hellena. In figure 1, `diagonal` produces a vector (one dimensional array) ; `transpose` in figure 4 produces a matrix (two dimensional array) ; and `row` of figure 2 identifies a vector in which elements are vectors of same length.
In contrast, the length of the vectors resulting from the application of the pattern `upperrow(i)` in figure 6 depends on the parameter `i`. The short notation `M.upperrow` is not valid because the type of the resulting object would not be defined in Hellena.

4.2 Defining access patterns

Various access patterns such as `diagonal`, `row`, `column` and `transpose` are frequently used in Numerical Analysis programming and should be predefined in vector languages. In many cases, the introduction of a specific pattern in a program allows the extraction of new vectors from its objects and thus increases its ratio of vector instructions. We limit our demonstration to objects which are structured by arrays. In this case, defining an access pattern consists in giving the relationship between indexing functions of the original array and indexing functions of the resulting one. In Hellena, this relationship F is expressed by an indexing expression f of the original array depending on the indices of the result. A pattern declaration in Hellena has the following structure :

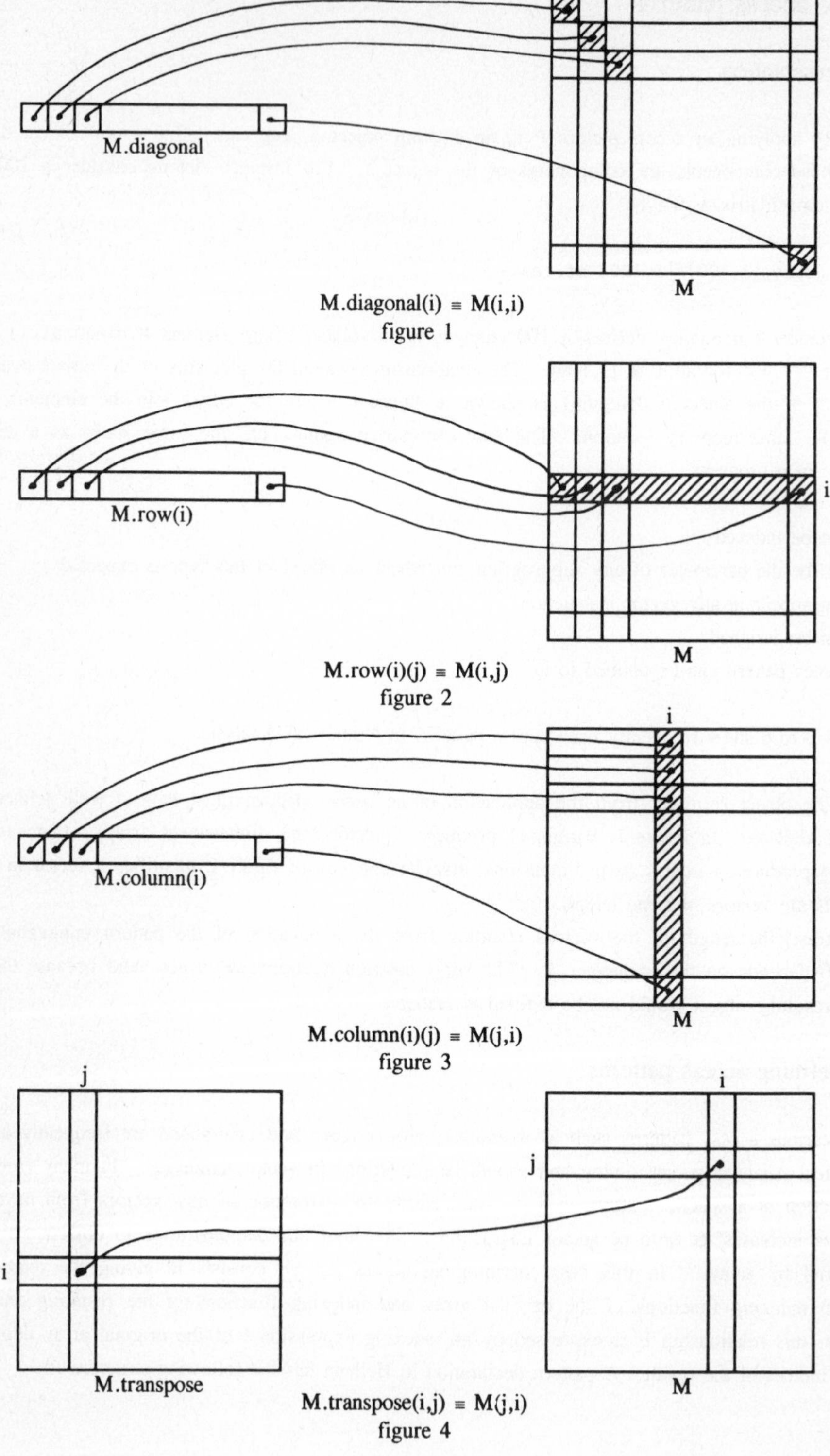

M.diagonal(i) ≡ M(i,i)
figure 1

M.row(i)(j) ≡ M(i,j)
figure 2

M.column(i)(j) ≡ M(j,i)
figure 3

M.transpose(i,j) ≡ M(j,i)
figure 4

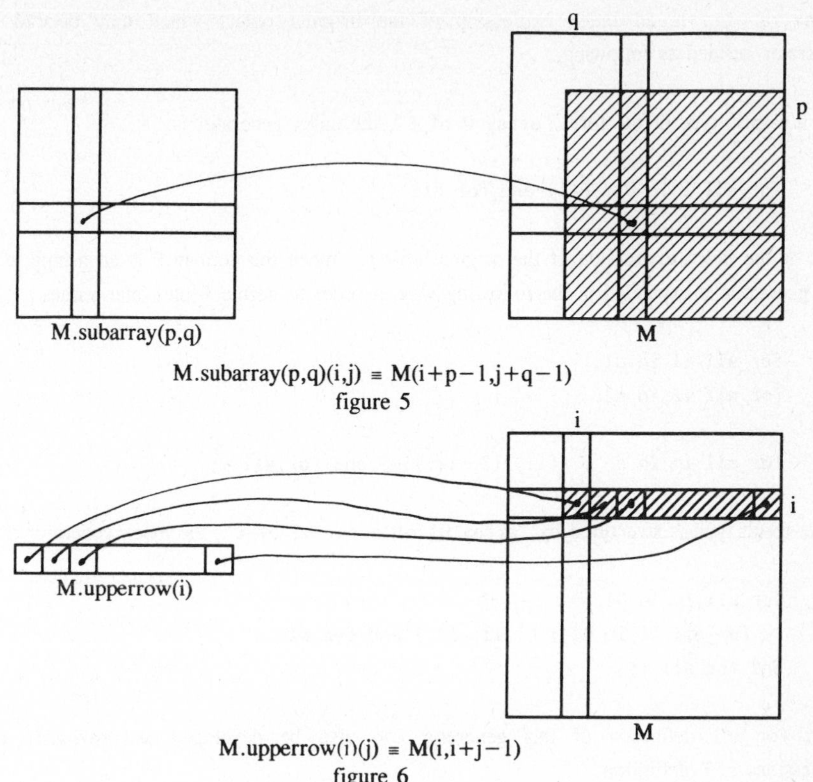

M.subarray(p,q)(i,j) ≡ M(i+p−1,j+q−1)
figure 5

M.upperrow(i)(j) ≡ M(i,i+j−1)
figure 6

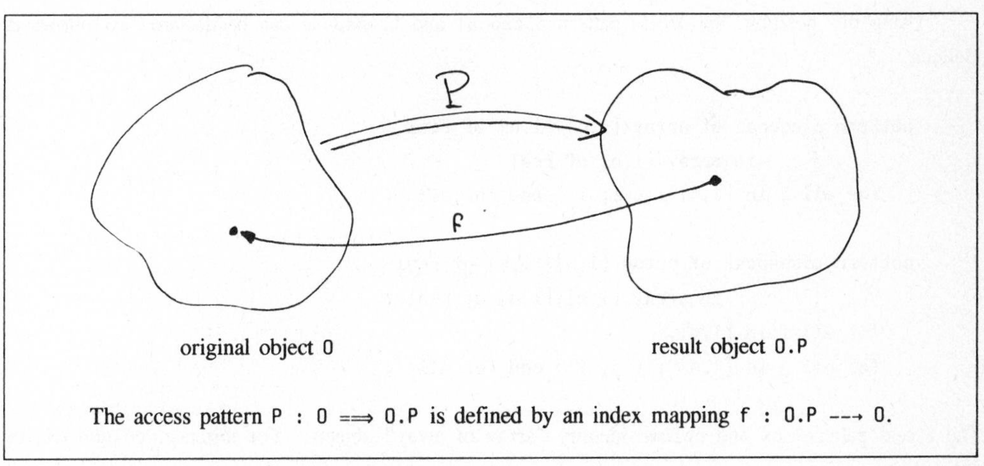

The access pattern `P : O ⟹ O.P` is defined by an index mapping `f : O.P --→ O`.

```
pattern identifier ( formal parameters )
      of entry_type
      in result_type : index_mapping
```

When applied to an object of `entry_type`, this pattern identifies an object of `result_type`.

`index_mapping` is an index expression of the original object which may depend on an index generator defined as following :

For a result_type of the form "**array** D **of** E", the index generator is

```
for_all I in D : F(I) end_for_all  ;
```

`F(I)` is the index expression of the original object. When the domain `D` is an n-tuple `d1*d2*...*dn`, this generator is expanded in the following way in order to define `F` on scalar values :

```
for_all i1 in d1,
for_all i2 in d2,
......
for_all in in dn : f(i1, i2, ...,in) end_for_all  ;
```

If the result type is structured by "**array** D1 **of array** D2 **of** E", the index generator is

```
for_all I1 in D1 :
   for_all I2 in D2 : F( I1, I2 ) end_for_all
end_for_all  ;
```

Each **for_all** definition of this generator can also be developed as previously to get scalar expressions in `F` definition.

Using this notation, the access pattern `diagonal` and `transpose` can be declared as follows in Hellena :

```
pattern diagonal of array [1,n]*[1,n] of real
              in array [1,n] of real :
   for_all i in [1,n] : ( i, i ) end_for_all  ;

pattern transpose of array [1,n]*[1,m] of real
               in array [1,m]*[1,n] of real :
   for_all i in [1,m],
   for_all j in [1,n] : ( j, i ) end_for_all  ;
```

The access pattern `row` and `column` identify "array of array" objects. For instance, `column` can be defined by

```
pattern column of array [1,n]*[1,m] of real
              in array [1,m] of array [1,n] of real :
   for_all j in [1,m] :
      for_all i in [1,n] : ( i, j ) end_for_all
   end_for_all  ;
```

When applied to an array M,

- M.column(k)(l) identifies the component M(l,k) of M,
- M.column(j) identifies the column j of M, which is a vector,
- M.column identifies an array of array which is mapped in the same memory space as M.

Note that, as the application of an access pattern produces a well formed object of Hellena, the two notation M.row(i) and M.transpose.column(i) identify the same vector.

In Numerical Analysis, accessing a run-time defined vector or matrix is frequent. This is, for example, the case in linear system resolution where the algorithm is applied to a sub-matrix whose number of rows and columns descreases at each iteration. Such sub-arrays can be identified by access patterns depending on parameters. The result type definition, the index generators and the index mapping function can depend on the parameters of the pattern. Let us consider the following declaration,

```
pattern submatrix ( value k : [1,n] ; )
     of array [1,n]*[1,n] of real
     in array [1,n-k+1]*[1,n-k+1] of real :
   for_all i in [1,n-k+1],
   for_all j in [1,n-k+1] : ( i+k-1, j+k-1 ) end_for_all ;
```

The notation M.submatrix(x) identifies the sub-matrix shaded in figure 7. In the following example, the size of the matrix on which the subprogram F is applied decreases at each iteration of the loop on i.

```
for i := 1 to n
loop
   F( M.submatrix(i) ) ;
end_loop  ;
```

The following access pattern lowerrow allows the identification of a row of the lower triangle of a matrix M as shown in figure 8.

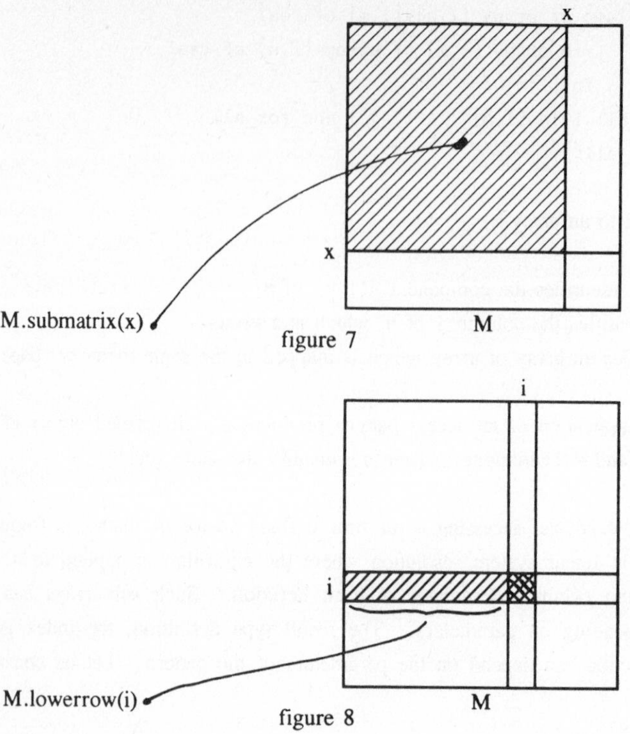

figure 7

figure 8

```
pattern lowerrow ( value i : [1,n] ; )
    of array [1,n]*[1,n] of real
    in array [1,i] of real :
  for_all j in [1,i] : ( i, j ) end_for_all  ;
```

4.3 Access pattern generalisation

In all the previous examples, the patterns were defined on completely specified object types. But, when writing library programs, the definition of access patterns should be as general as possible. For instance, the pattern `row` should be declared in such a way that it can be applied to two dimensional arrays independently of the exact definition of the index domains or the type of the elements. The language Hellena considers formal types wich impose minimal constraints on data structures. For example, the predefined formal type `discrete` includes all the scalar types allowed in the index domain specification of an array definition. All values of a program belong to the formal type `atype`. The minimal specifications of the access pattern `row` are

- the original type is a two dimensional array,
- the result type is a vector whose elements are vectors.

Using formal types, the pattern `row` can be specified as follow :

```
pattern row
    of array discrete*discrete of atype
    in array discrete of array discrete of atype :
     ... body of row ...
```

When such a pattern is invoked, the resulting type is computed from the effective entry type and from the body of the pattern specification. To do so, the programmer may refer to the entry type characteristics by the attribute notation `entity.attribute`.

Frequently used attributes of Hellena are

On an object `A` : `A.type_` is the type of the object `A`. If `A` is a formal parameter of a subprogram or an access pattern, `A.type_` identifies the type of the effective parameter at run time.

On a type `T` : the predefined attributes depend on the type constructor. If `T` is an array type, then `T.index` identifies the index domain of `T` and `T.elements` identifies the type of the elements of `T`. So, `T ≡ array T.index of T.elements`.
If `T` is a tuple, then the two attributes `left` and `right` are such that `T ≡ T.left * T.right` and the pair `(i,j)` belonging to `T` is such that `i` belongs to `T.left` and `j` belongs to `T.right`.
If `T` is a discrete type (every discrete type is ordered), then `T.lowbound` identifies the lowest value and `T.upbound` identifies the highest value belonging to `T` and `T ≡ [ T.lowbound, T.upbound ]`.
If `T` is a discrete type or a cartesian product of discrete types, then `T.cardinal` is the cardinal of `T`.

Inside the definition of an access pattern, the effective type of the object on which the pattern is applied is identified by the implicit name `operand_type`. Using this identifier and attribute notations, a quite general declaration of the pattern `row` can be written in Hellena as following :

```
pattern row
    of array discrete*discrete of atype
    in array discrete of array discrete of atype :
  for_all i in operand_type.index.left :
     for_all j in operand_type.index.right : ( i, j ) end_for_all
  end_for_all  ;
```

The precise rules are not described here and are used at compile time to determine the effective result type when such a pattern is invoked.

5 Compiling and implementing access patterns

5.1 Mapping arrays in memory

We consider a classical linear storage mapping scheme for arrays in the computer memory. The element $M(i_1,i_2,...,i_n)$ of an array M is then stored at the address

$$A + \Sigma_j (i_j - l_j) \times r_j$$

where

- l_j is the lower bound of the jth index,
- A is the base address, ie the address of the element $M(l_1,l_2,...,l_n)$,
- r_j is the address increment on dimension j.

The vector $r = (r_1,...,r_n)$ is such that, for all $i_1,...,i_n$,

$$r_j = \text{address of } M(i_1,...,i_{j-1},i_j+1,i_{j+1},...,i_n) - \text{address of } M(i_1,...,i_j,...,i_n)$$

This linear mapping of arrays in memory is frequently used by the compilers. For instance, an n rows m columns Fortran array is usually stored using the parameter values

$$r_1=1,\ r_2=n,\ l_1=1,\ l_2=1.$$

In Hellena, the value A and the increment vector $r = (r_1,...,r_n)$ define the mapping of the array in memory. The lower bound vector $(l_1,...,l_n)$ is associated with the array type.

This linear array mapping is conformal with addressing facilities of many supercomputers. Note that, when an object is an array of arrays, the base address and a first increment vector give access to the base address of an element which is itself described by a second increment vector.

5.2 Addresses computation

The linear mapping of an access pattern can be defined by the general notation

$$\forall j_1 \in [a_1, b_1],\ \forall j_2 \in [a_2, b_2], \ldots\ \forall j_h \in [a_h, b_h], \ldots\ \forall j_m \in [a_m, b_m],$$
$$(j_1, ..., j_h, ..., j_m) \rightarrow (\alpha_1 + \Sigma_i (j_i - a_i)\beta_{1,i}, ..., \alpha_k + \Sigma_i (j_i - a_i)\beta_{k,i}, ..., \alpha_n + \Sigma_i (j_i - a_i)\beta_{n,i})$$

When this pattern is applied to an array described by

base address A

increment vector $r=(r_1, ..., r_n)$

low bound vector $(l_1, ..., l_n)$

the resulting array is described by the base address AD and the offset vector $(R_1, ..., R_m)$

$$AD= A + \Sigma_k r_k(\alpha_k - l_k)$$

$R_k = \sum_k r_i \beta_{k,i}$

Let us consider an array M of type **array** [1,100]*[1,100] **of** real stored in Fortran mode and described by

$A = 1000$

$r_1 = 1,\ r_2 = 100$

$l_1 = 1,\ l_2 = 1$

The address of the element M(i,j) is 899 + i + 100*j

The pattern diagonal is described by

$a_1 = 1$

$\alpha_1 = 1,\ \alpha_2 = 1$

$\beta_{1,1} = 1,\ \beta_{1,2} = 1$

The object `M.diagonal` is then described by

$AD = 1000$

$R_1 = 101$

$Lb_1 = 1$

The pattern `upperrow` declared

```
pattern upperrow ( value i : [1,100] ; )
      of array [1,100]*[1,100] of real
      in array [1,99-i] of real :
    for_all j in [1,99-i] : ( i, i+j-1 ) end_for_all
```

is described by the parameters

$a_1 = 1$

$\alpha_1 = i,\ \alpha_2 = i-1$

$\beta_{1,1} = 0,\ \beta_{1,2} = 1$

The object `M.upperrow(x)` is then described by

$AD = 1000 + 101 * (x-1) = 899 + 101 * x$

$R_1 = 100$

$Lb_1 = 1$

6 Programming with access patterns

Access patterns can be directly applied to objects in the program instructions. This application costs no more than computing the base address of the resulting array and its increment vector. These data can directly feed the address generators of many supercomputers in vector mode. When memory allocation is static, the whole object descriptor is frequently computed at compile time.

A more general application of access pattern is variable identification. Let us consider the following sequence of Hellena declarations,

```
variable M : array [1,n]*[1,n] of real ;
variable D : M.diagonal ;
```

These declarations define two variables M and D. The memory space allocated for an array value of the first declaration is identified by M. Then a subset of this space is identified by D. Such an identification speeds up the address computation at run-time when frequent accesses to the same components are needed. The same identification process is also applied for parameter passing in subroutine calls. For instance, the subroutine NORM specified

```
subroutine NORM ( variable V : array discrete of real ;
                           R : real ; ) ;
```

can be called by the following instructions

```
NORM ( M.diagonal, X ) ;
NORM ( M.column(k), X ) ;
NORM ( M.upperrow(k), X ) ;
```

At run time, the descriptor (or its address) of the identified vector is passed (as well as the type descriptor if necessary) when calling this subroutine. Complementary parameters do not have to be added when a general use of a subroutine is expected, as is the case in normal programming languages.

7 Conclusion

Many programs written in Hellena have been run on a simulated array architecture as well as on OPSILA. The experiments show the adequacy of the access patterns in vector programming. By avoiding many unnecessary loops and indexing notations, the programs are more understandable and compact. The application domain of subroutines and functions is extended to numerous submatrices and, thus, allows an easier program structure and a more general library subroutine definition. The access pattern concept appears to be fundamental in programming methodology.

References

[Auguin 86]

Auguin M., Boery F., *The OPSILA Computer*, Colloque International Algorithmes et Architectures Parallèles, 14-18 Avril 1986, Luminy.

[Burroughs 78]

Burroughs Co., "BSP: Overview Perspective, and Architecture," document N°. 61391, Feb. 1978a.

[CRAY 77]

Cray Research, Inc., *CRAY-1 Computer System Hardware Reference Manual,* Bloomington, Minn., pub. N°. 2240004, 1977.

[Hwang 84]

Hwang K., Briggs F.A., Computer Architecture and Parallel Processing, McGraw-Hill, New York, 1984.

[Jégou 86]

Jégou, Y., *Le Language Vectoriel Hellena,* to be published in Rapports de recherche INRIA, France.

[Miura 83]

Miura, K., and Uchida, K., "FACOM Vector Processor VP-100/VP-200," *Proc. NATO Advanced Reasearch Worhshop on High-Speed Computing,* Julish, W. Germany, Springer-Verlag, June 20-22, 1983.

[Paul 75]

Paul, G., and Wilson, M.W., *The VECTRAN Language : An Experimental Language for Vector/Matrix Array Processing,* IBM Palo Alto Scientific Center Report 6320-3334, Aug.1975.

[Perrott 79]

Perrott, R.H., "A Language for Array and Vector Processors," *ACM Trans. on Programming Languages and Systems,* vol.1, N°.2, Oct.1979, pp.177-195.

[Wagener 84]

Wagener, J.L., SIGNUM Newslett. 19 (1984) 3 ; FORTEC Forum 3 ACM (1984) 2.

Scheduling Sequential Loops on Parallel Processors

Ashfaq A. Munshi*
Ridge Computers
4251 Mission College Blvd.
Santa Clara, Ca. 95054

Barbara Simons
IBM Almaden Research Center K53-802
650 Harry Rd.
San Jose, Ca. 95120-6099

Abstract. Automatic parallelization of code written in a sequential language such as FORTRAN is of great importance for compilers for parallel computers. We first discuss the problem of automatically parallelizing iterative loops on multiprocessors and then derive a scheduling problem that models a technique for the automatic parallelization. We present some polynomial time solutions for special cases of the scheduling problem along with an NP-completeness proof of a simple variant of the problem. We also analyze a naive heuristic for solving the general scheduling problem and prove that it gives a result that is at most a factor of three greater than optimal. Finally, we derive for the original compiler problem an approximation algorithm and present some test results. In the tests, which were run on a well known numerical analysis package, our technique always equalled and frequently surpassed the results obtained by the best known technique in the literature. Our approach is unique and represents one of the first attempts at understanding the complexity theoretic aspects of the problem of parallelizing sequential loops.

1. Introduction.

Fields such as mechanical engineering, electronic engineering, and manufacturing, to name but a few, are requiring computing speeds that a decade ago would have seemed unimaginable. To satisfy these computing demands, companies such as CRAY and CDC have built supercomputers. However, the demand for increased speed continues, while the relative improvement in computing speed is decreasing from one generation of supercomputers to the next. Thus, the search continues for alternatives.

The most promising of these alternatives is parallel computing. Using several relatively slow processors, parallel computers achieve average computing speeds that are a high percentage of the average computing speeds of supercomputers at a small percentage of the cost. To make these computers more attractive for the customer, the computer manufacturers provide compilers that run existing sequential programs efficiently on their parallel architecture. They do this because businesses are unlikely to discard large programs, simulators for instance, that have proved reliable for many years. Indeed, there are instances in which organizations dare not rewrite old, very large, and poorly documented code since they are unsure as to precisely what they do. Recognizing this need as well as the intellectual challenges posed by the problem of detecting parallelism in sequential code, researchers at the University of Illinois, under the direction of David Kuck, have studied this problem.

* This work was done while the author was at IBM A.R.C.

Much of their work has focused on the problem of detecting parallelism in loops, especially FORTRAN DO loops, since the majority of existing code is written in FORTRAN. One of the methods, known as DOACROSS [Cy84], assigns a unique processor to execute the loop for a unique value of the loop iteration variable. That is, if a loop is to be executed N times, and if there are at least N processors, then one processor is assigned to each iteration of the loop. Ideally, all N processors start at the same time and consequently finish at approximately the same time. Because of data dependences within the loop, however, this idealized version of DOACROSS usually is not possible. Data dependences may force certain processors to wait for results that must be computed by other processors before they can continue their local computations. In other words, processors may be forced to delay executing their local task due to data dependences.

More precisely, let K be the iteration variable of the loop, and suppose that a FORTRAN DO loop contains statements s_1, s_2, ... , s_n. Further, suppose that there is a dependence between statements s_i and s_j, with i>j, such that statement s_j requires in the Kth iteration a value computed by statement s_i in the $(K-1)^{st}$ iteration, i.e. s_j *depends* on s_i. This implies that processor K must wait until processor K−1 has computed s_i before K can compute s_j. Therefore, processor K must DELAY execution of its copy of the loop.

If instead of a dependence from s_i to s_j, the dependence had been from s_j to s_i, then, since s_j occurs before s_i, no delay is necessary. That is, by the time processor K reaches s_i, processor K-1 has already computed s_j, and hence processor K need not wait.

As the above discussion illustrates, dependences can cause processors to be delayed. A simple extension of the above argument shows that the amount of delay is precisely the length of the longest backward dependence [Cyt84]. A data dependence is *lexicographically backward* if $j-i < 0$; its length is defined to be $|j-i| + 1$.

If there are no backward dependences, the delay is zero; if there is a backward dependence from the last statement of the loop to the first, the delay is the length of the dependence, which in this case is the number of statements in the loop plus one. The notion of DELAY plays the central role in the DOACROSS schedules: a loop is parallel if it has zero delay and sequential if the delay is equal to the number of statements in the loop plus one*.

---

*Alliant Computer Corp. uses precisely the DOACROSS technique of [Cyt84] for running sequential FORTRAN programs on its eight processor machine, the FX/8.

A natural question is how to minimize the delay associated with a loop by re-arranging the code to make the loop more parallel. This question is of considerable practical importance, since its solution would allow a compiler to run sequential programs more efficiently on multiprocessor architectures.

The problem of minimizing the delay associated with a loop is modelled as a problem of scheduling jobs on intervals, where the optimization criterion is minimizing the maximum separation between adjacent jobs. Polynomial time solutions for some important special cases of this scheduling problem are presented, a simple variant of the original scheduling problem is shown to be NP-complete, an upper bound for a naive algorithm for the general case is analyzed, and an approximation algorithm for the original problem which uses some of the special case solutions is described. Empirical evaluations of our algorithms are also presented. Our approach is unique and represents one of the first attempts at understanding the complexity theoretic aspects of the delay problem. **2. Preliminaries and definitions.**

There are two types of dependences in a FORTRAN program: data dependence and control dependence. Control dependence is caused by conditional and unconditional branching. Allen [All] has shown that control dependence can be turned into data dependence via some simple transformations on the original program. The new program is semantically equivalent to the original one but possesses only data dependences. Given this fact, we can assume that such transformations have been performed and only data dependences need be considered.

Data dependence and the dependence graph are defined as follows.

Statement s_i is said to be *data dependent* on statement s_j when the following two conditions hold:

1. There exists a possible execution path such that statements s_j and s_i both reference the same memory location M and

2. the execution of s_j that references M occurs before the execution of s_i that references M [All].

Data dependence can be separated into two types: *loop independent* dependences and *loop carried* dependences. A loop independent dependence of s_i on s_j exists if s_i depends on s_j for the same fixed value of the loop iteration variable; otherwise, the dependence is said to be loop carried. Intuitively, a loop carried dependence requires the presence of the loop around the body of statements, whereas a loop independent dependence is present regardless of the loop. If two statements participate in a loop carried dependence, they can be permuted at will; statements in a loop independent dependence must occur in the given order.

Loops may be nested, or loop carried dependences might arise because of dependences on data computed several iterations prior to the current iteration. These potential complications are eliminated as follows. We first define *distance* to be the number of iterations one has to go back to find the source of the dependence. If the distance is greater than one, then the problem can be reduced to the case where the distance is one by *unwinding* the loop. That is, if the distance is k, then each successive set of k iterations of the loop is viewed as a single "large" loop. For nested loops the innermost loops are first processed as if they are isolated loops, that is as if they are not nested. Each innermost loop is then collapsed into a single statement, and the process is repeated on the new innermost loops until finally there is only one loop remaining.

The above simplifications allow us to assume that dependences occur only as a result of the previous iteration. We also assume that there are no nested loops. (For a further discussion see [Cyt] and [Mun]). Finally, we assume that the statements all have equal execution time.

Given a loop L, the *dependence graph,* $G_L(N,A)$, of L is a directed graph where the nodes of G_L represent statements (or jobs) and the arcs represent dependences. In particular $(s_j, s_i) \in G_L(A)$ iff s_i depends on s_j. (See figure 2).

As an example, consider the DO loop in figure 1. Note that s_4 depends on s_3 because s_4 references memory location A3(I) after s_3. Furthermore, the dependence is a loop independent dependence, for it occurs no matter what value I assumes. By contrast, statement s_2 is loop dependent on s_8 because s_2 and s_8 both reference memory location A8(I), but the reference is for different values of I. Applying the above definitions gives the dependence graph of figure 2. The delay optimization problem can now be phrased succinctly:

Given a loop L, find a permutation π of the dependence graph $G_L(N,A)$ such that the semantics of the loop are preserved and

$$\max_{(s_i,s_j) \in G_L(A)} \{\pi(s_i) - \pi(s_j)\} \text{ is minimized over all backward arcs.}$$

```
SUBROUTINE   SAMPLE
(A1,A2,A3,A4,A5,A6,A7,A8,A9,A10,A11,A12,A13,A14,A15,A16,A17,N)

REAL   A1(N),A2(N),A3(N),A4(N),A5(N),A6(N),A7(N),A8(N),A9(N),A10(N)
A11(N),A12(N),A13(N),A14(N),A15(N),A16(N),A17(N)


                  Loop independent              Loop carried

        DO 227 I=1,N
s1        A1(I) =  B(I)
s2        A2(I) =                                A8(I-1)
s3        A3(I) =                                A5(I-1)
s4        A4(I) =        A3(I)           +       A7(I-1)
s5        A5(I) =        A2(I)
s6        A6(I) =        A1(I)           +       A13(I-1)
s7        A7(I) =        A4(I)
s8        A8(I) =        A4(I) + A5(I)   +       A17(I-1)
s9        A9(I) =        A1(I)
s10       A10(I) =       A9(I)           +       A15(I-1)
s11       A11(I) =       A9(I)
s12       A12(I) =       A9(I)
s13       A13(I) =       A12(I)
s14       A14(I) =       A13(I)
s15       A15(I) =       A14(I)
s16       A16(I) =       A14(I)
s17       A17(I) =       A14(I)
227     CONTINUE
        RETURN
        END
```

Figure 1. A FORTRAN DO loop

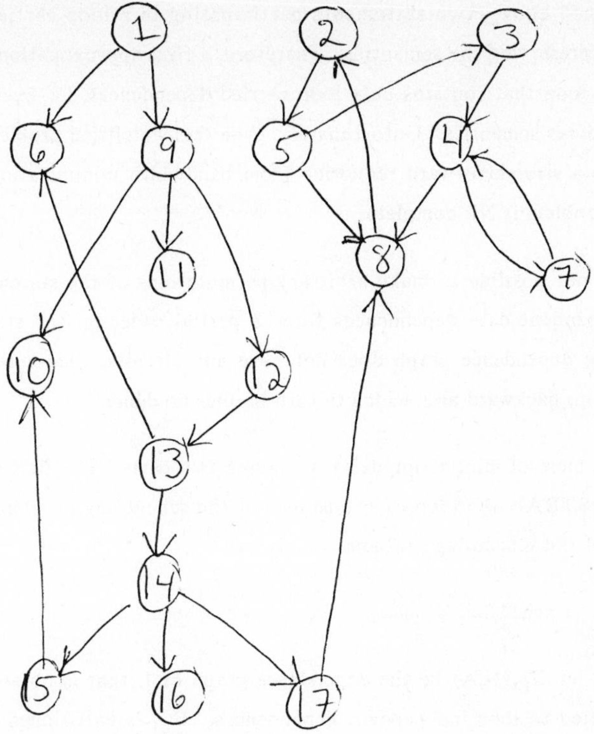

Figure 2. The dependence graph for figure 1

$\Sigma_1=\{1\}$, $\Sigma_2=\{9\}$, $\Sigma_3=\{12\}$, $\Sigma_4=\{2,3,13\}$, $\Sigma_5=\{4,5,14\}$, $\Sigma_6=\{6,7,8,10,11,16\}$, $\Sigma_7=\{15,17\}$

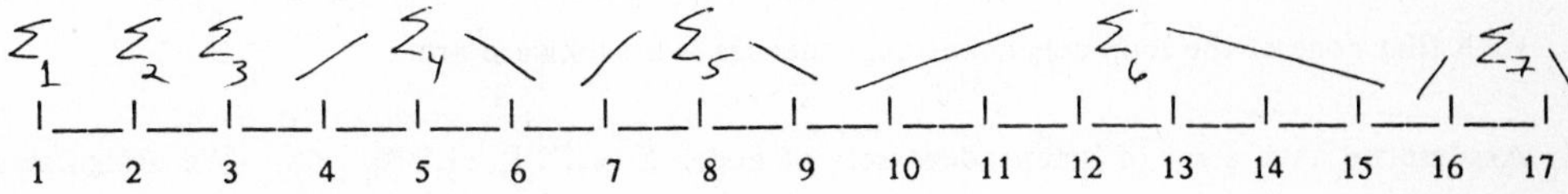

Figure 3. Independent sets and a partition of the number line for figure 1

As was mentioned above, two statements participating in a loop carried dependence can be permuted while preserving the semantics. Therefore, a first approximation to the delay problem is to consider a loop that contains only loop carried dependences, i.e. every permutation of the statements preserves semantics. Unfortunately, even this simplified problem is NP-hard [Cyt]; the reduction is a straightforward reduction from bandwidth minimization. Also, the decision version of the problem is NP-complete.

In general, it is not possible to make arbitrary permutations of the statements within the loop, since loop independent data dependences force a partial order on the statements of the loop. Note that if the dependence graph does not have any circuits, then a topological sort of the graph results in no backward arcs which in turn implies no delay.

We view the problem of minimizing delay as having two parts. The first part is the problem of mapping the FORTRAN DO loop to an instance of the scheduling problem, and the second part is the solution of the scheduling problem.

3. Constructing the scheduling problem.

Given a loop L, let $G_{LI}(N,A)$ be the dependence graph of L that is obtained when the dependences are restricted to loop independent dependences. G_{LI} is partitioned into *levels* as follows. All the nodes of G_{LI} that have no predecessors are at level 1. In general, all the nodes of G_{LI} that have predecessors only at level i-1 and possibly at levels below level i-1 are at level i. Note that if two nodes are at the same level, then they are independent with respect to G_{LI}. Therefore, G_{LI} can be partitioned into a set of independent sets $\Sigma = \{\Sigma_i\}$ by assigning all nodes at level i to the set Σ_i. We define the obvious total ordering $<$ on Σ: $\Sigma_i < \Sigma_{i+1}$.

Even though the nodes in Σ_i contain no loop independent dependences, they might contain some loop dependent dependences. If there are loop dependent dependences among the nodes in Σ_i, then Σ_i is partitioned into subsets until no loops dependent dependences remain among the nodes in each of the subsets. A total ordering is then applied to all the subsets such that the total ordering among the original sets in Σ is not violated.

An arc (s_i,s_j) with $s_i \in \Sigma_p$, $s_j \in \Sigma_q$ is *forward* if $p < q$ and *backward* otherwise. We note that if the loop dependent dependences of Σ_i do not form a loop in Σ_i, then the subsets of Σ_i can be ordered such that none of the loop dependent dependences is a backward arc.

Assume we have a set of independent sets of nodes $\Sigma = \{\Sigma_i\}$, with $\Sigma_{i-1} < \Sigma_i$. We assign sets of integers to the independent sets in Σ as follows. The integers from 1 to $|\Sigma_1|$ are assigned to Σ_1, the integers from $|\Sigma_1|+1$ to $|\Sigma_1| + |\Sigma_2|$ are assigned to Σ_2, and so on. The above construction partitions the integers 1...n, where n is the number of statements in the loop (as well as the number of nodes in G_L).

In addition to the partitioning of the first n integers, we construct a DAG that we call B(N,A), where $N(B) = N(G_L)$ and A(B) consists of all backwards arcs with endpoints in nodes in different independent sets. The scheduling problem consists of assigning an integer start time to all the nodes in N(B) such that:

1. each node is *scheduled,* that is assigned a start time, within the interval to which its set is assigned
2. no two nodes have the same start times and
3. the difference in start times of the endpoints of any arc in A(B) is minimized.

(See Figure 3 for an illustration of the construction). More formally:

Problem DP: Given an ordered set of disjoint intervals $I = I_1, \ldots, I_k$, a DAG B(N,A) of precedence constraints, and a mapping $f : N(B) \to I$ so that if $(i,j) \in A(B)$, then $f(i) < f(j)$, find a mapping $s : N(B) \to I^+$ such that for all $i,j \in N(B)$, $s(i) \in f(i)$, $|s(i)-s(j)| \geq 1$ for $i \neq j$, and $\max_{(i,j) \in A(B)}\{s(i)-s(j)\}$ is minimized.

To illustrate, consider again the dependence graph of figure 2. s_1 must precede s_9, which in turn must precede s_{12}, since these are loop independent dependences. Hence, the set containing s_1 must precede the set containing s_9, which must precede the set containing s_{12}. A set of independent sets and a total order of these sets is shown in figure 3. The independent sets are mapped into partitions of the interval [1,17]. Since the arc representing the loop carried dependence $s_{13} \to s_6$ is no longer a backward arc in the partition given in figure 3, the set of backward arcs involve only the statements s_2, s_3, s_4, s_5, s_7, s_8, s_{10}, s_{15}, and s_{17}. Consequently, B(N,A) contains only nodes corresponding to these statements and only those arcs which are backward arcs. The jobs corresponding to statements s_2 and s_3 must be scheduled in the interval [4,6], the jobs corresponding to s_4 and s_5 in [7,9], the jobs corresponding to s_7, s_8, and s_{10} in [10,15], and the jobs corresponding to s_{15} and s_{17} in [16,17].

This completes the mapping to the scheduling problem. The remainder of this paper is a study of the complexity of problem DP along with an NP-completeness result for a very closely related problem.

4. Scheduling chains.

A *chain* C = B(N,A) is a simple path where $B(N) = \{C_1, C_2, \ldots, C_n\}$ with $(C_i, C_{i+1}) \in A(B)$, $1 \leq i \leq n$, and $(C_i, C_j) \notin A(B)$ for $j<i$ or $j>i+1$.

Consider first an instance of problem DP where B(N,A) is a single chain.

Problem SCSI (single chain single interval): Let C = B(N,A) be a single chain with $f(C_i) = I_i$. Let the left and right endpoints of these intervals be l_i and r_i respectively with $r_i < l_{i+1} \leq r_{i+1}$ for $1 \leq i < n$, and r_i and l_i integers for $1 \leq i \leq n$.*
Find a mapping $s : N(B) \rightarrow I^+$ such that $s(C_i) \in I_i$ and $\max_{i<n}(s(C_{i+1}) - s(C_i))$ is minimized.

We model the SCSI problem as a scheduling problem, where a schedule is defined as follows.

A *schedule* is an assignment of start times, one for each job in the problem instance, where there is a 1-1 correspondence between jobs and the elements of N(B). A *feasible schedule* is a schedule in which each job is assigned a unique start time that falls within its assigned interval and in which the difference between any two start times is at least one. If the integer $c \in f(i)$, then c is called a *slot*. If no element of N(B) is mapped to c, then c is said to be *empty*.

An approach to solving problem SCSI is to initially schedule each job C_i at the right-most slot of its interval r_i. Then a left shift y_i is computed for each C_i so that the maximum separation between adjacent jobs is minimized.

Mathematically, this amounts to solving the following optimization problem:
$\min_{y_i} \max_i (r_{i+1} - y_{i+1}) - (r_i - y_i)$
subject to $0 \leq y_i \leq r_i - l_i$, r_i, l_i, and y_i integers.

This is equivalent to solving the integer linear program
min λ
subject to $(r_{i+1} - y_{i+1}) - (r_i - y_i) \leq \lambda$
and
$0 \leq y_i \leq r_i - l_i$, r_i, l_i, λ integers.

Observe that if the original FORTRAN loop is rearranged according to the schedule that is constructed, λ is equal to one less than the length of the longest backward arc. We first prove a lower bound for SCSI and then show that it is tight by giving an algorithm, algorithm SCSI below, which achieves the bound. Note that if the integer constraints are eliminated, then the trivial modification to algorithm SCSI that eliminates the ceiling from the definition of λ_{ij} produces an algorithm that is optimal with no increase in running time.

---

*We note that the algorithms for this and the MCSI problem work equally well if the endpoints are rationals. We use integer values throughout this paper because of the formulation of the original compiler problem.

If inequalities i through i+j are added together, we get $(r_{i+j}-y_{i+j}) - (r_i-y_i) \leq j\lambda$. Since $0 \leq y_{i+j} \leq r_{i+j}-l_{i+j}$ we have $y_{i+j}-y_i \leq r_{i+j}-l_{i+j}$. Adding this to the previous inequality gives

$$\lambda \geq \lceil ((l_{i+j} - r_i)/j) \rceil = \lambda_{ij} \; (\dagger)$$

This implies that $\lambda \geq \max_{i,j}\{\lambda_{ij}\}$, since i and j were chosen arbitrarily. We now show that this lower bound is tight.

Let $s(C_i)$ be the starting time of C_i, where C_i started at $s(C_i)$ executes in the interval $[s(C_i), s(C_i)+1)$. The algorithm for achieving the lower bound (†) is:

Algorithm SCSI(λ)

Set $s(C_1) = r_1$.
Set $s(C_i) = \min(s(C_{i-1})+\lambda, r_i)$, where $\lambda = \max_{ij}\{\lambda_{ij}\}$, for i=2, ..., n.

To prove that algorithm SCSI is correct, we assume for contradiction that for some job C_p, $s(C_p) < l_p$. Let $q=\max\{_{k<p}(s(C_k)=r_k)\}$. There must exist such a q since $s(C_1)= r_1$. Therefore, $r_q+(p-q)\lambda < l_p$, which implies $\lambda<(l_p-r_q)/(p-q)$, a contradiction. This proves the following theorem.

Theorem 1. Algorithm SCSI is an $O(n^2)$ time algorithm for optimally scheduling the jobs of a single chain, where n is the number of jobs.

Because the SCSI problem is symmetric the following algorithm also solves SCSI.

Algorithm REVERSE-SCSI(λ)

Set $s(C_n) = l_n$
Set $s(C_j) = \max(s(C_{j+1})-\lambda, l_j)$ for j=1, ... , n-1.

Yet another algorithm for the SCSI problem is obtained by performing binary search on λ and checking feasibility using algorithm SCSI with only the test value of λ. If $\lambda=O(2^n)$, the binary search approach gives an algorithm with running time no worse than $O(n^2)$. In summary,

Lemma 2. There exists an $O(n \log \lambda)$ algorithm for SCSI.

We next consider the problem of scheduling an arbitrary number of chains.

Let $C = \{C_1, C_2, ..., C_n\}$ be a set of chains, with C_i being the simple path $C_{i,1}, C_{i,2}, ..., C_{i,n_i}$, and let $I = \{I_1, I_2, ..., I_m\}$ be a set of intervals, with $r_i<l_{i+1}<r_{i+1}$ for $1 \leq i<m$ and r_i, l_i integers for $1 \leq i \leq m$. The *intervals associated with* C_i are the subset of I to which the nodes of C_i are

mapped by f. The *underlying* interval of a job is the interval into which the job is mapped by f. A λ-*feasible schedule* is a feasible schedule in which the difference between the start times of two adjacent jobs is no greater than λ.

Problem Multiple Chain Single Interval (MCSI): Given a set of intervals $I = I_1, \ldots, I_m$ with $l_i \le r_i < l_{i+1}$ for $1 \le i < m$ and a set of n chains $C_1, \ldots, C_n$, compute the minimum value of λ such that there exists a λ-feasible schedule for the problem instance. Algorithm MCSI(λ), presented below, constructs a feasible schedule if one exists for an instance of problem MCSI and a given value of λ. If no feasible schedule exists, it determines that there is none for the given value of λ.

The λ-*feasible intervals* for a chain C_i are the intervals obtained by applying algorithm SCSI(λ) and REVERSE-SCSI(λ) for a fixed value of λ to C_i together with the intervals associated with C_i. The left endpoint of the λ-feasible interval for $C_{i,j}$ is the start time assigned to $C_{i,j}$ by REVERSE-SCSI(λ) and the right endpoint is the start time assigned by SCSI(λ). The λ-feasible interval for $C_{i,j}$ is denoted by *λ-feas($C_{i,j}$)*, with the left endpoint (right endpoint) of λ-feas($C_{i,j}$) being denoted *left(λ-feas($C_{i,j}$))* (right(λ-feas($C_{i,j}$))). We will drop the use of λ when the meaning is obvious from the context. The left (right) endpoint of an interval I_k is denoted by *left(I_k)* *(right(I_k))*. Given a schedule for an instance of MCSI, a *conflicting set* is a set of jobs all of which have the same start time. The right-most conflicting set is the conflicting set with the latest start time.

Algorithm MCSI(λ)

1. Compute the λ-feasible intervals of each chain C_i separately. If any job has an empty feasible interval, then declare the problem instance infeasible and halt.

2. Schedule each job at the right-most slot of its feasible interval.

3. If each job is assigned a unique start time, then output the schedule and halt.

4. Let S be the right-most conflicting set and let $S' \subseteq S$ be the set of jobs in S that are scheduled at the left end point of their feasible interval. If $|S'| \ge 2$, then declare the problem instance infeasible and halt.

   4a) If there is a job $x \in S-S'$ such that x has no successor, shift x left one unit
   else
   4b) Let x be the job in $S-S'$ whose successor is scheduled earliest among all successors of jobs in $S-S'$. Shift x left 1 unit.

Go to step 3.

Example

$I = \{I_j : 1 \le j \le 6\}$, with $I_1 = [1..4]$, $I_2 = [5..7]$, $I_3 = [8..12]$, $I_4 = [13..15]$, $I_5 = [16..21]$, $I_6 = [22..24]$.

$C = \{A,B,C,D,E,F\}$, with $A = [I_1, I_3, I_4, I_5, I_6]$, $B = [I_1, I_3, I_5]$, $C = [I_1, I_2, I_4, I_5]$, $D = [I_1, I_2, I_3, I_5, I_6]$, $E = [I_2, I_3, I_5]$, $F = [I_3, I_4, I_5, I_6]$.

We first observe that $\lambda = 5$ is an infeasible value for the B chain, since $\lambda = 5$ implies that the third job in the B chain cannot start sufficiently late to reach I_5. However, for $\lambda = 6$, none of the chains is infeasible, and we get the following 6-feasible intervals:

A = [2,4], [8,10], [13,15], [16,21], [22,24]
B = [4,4], [10,10], [16,16]
C = [1,4], [7,7], [13,13], [16,19]
D = [1,4], [5,7], [10,12], [16,18]
E = [5,7], [10,12], [16,18], [22,24]
F = [8,12], [13,15], [16,21], [22,24]

The initial schedule in which all jobs are scheduled at the right-most slots of their feasible intervals is illustrated in figure 4; figure 5 shows the final 6-feasible schedule.

$I = \{I_j : 1 \le j \le 6\}$

$I_1 = [1..4]$, $I_2 = [5..7]$, $I_3 = [8..12]$, $I_4 = [13..15]$, $I_5 = [16..21]$, $I_6 = [22..24]$

$C = \{A,B,C,D,E,F\}$

$A = [I_1, I_3, I_4, I_5, I_6]$, $B = [I_1, I_3, I_5]$, $C = [I_1, I_2, I_4, I_5]$, $D = [I_1, I_2, I_3, I_5, I_6]$, $E = [I_2, I_3, I_5]$,
$F = [I_3, I_4, I_5, I_6]$

We first observe that $\lambda = 5$ is an infeasible value for the B chain, since $\lambda = 5$ implies that the third job in the B chain cannot start sufficiently late to reach I_5. However, for $\lambda = 6$, none of the chains is infeasible, and we get the following 6-feasible intervals:

A = [2,4], [8,10], [13,15], [16,21], [22,24]

B = [4,4], [10,10], [16,16]

C = [1,4], [7,7], [13,13], [16,19]

D = [1,4], [5,7], [10,12], [16,18]

E = [5,7], [10,12], [16,18], [22,24]

F = [8,12], [13,15], [16,21], [22,24]

Figure 4. An example of MCSI with λ-feasible intervals

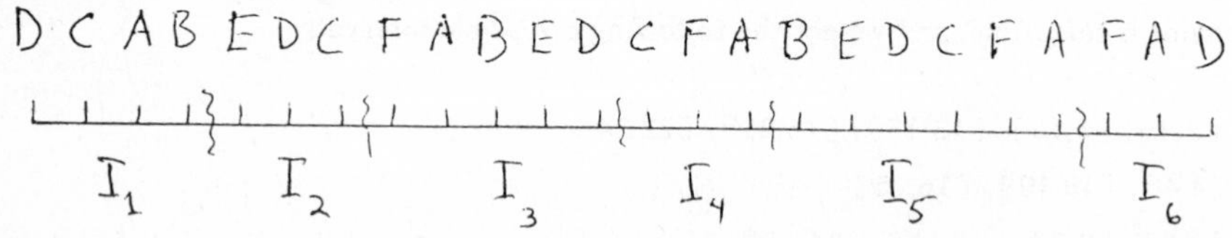

Figure 5. A 6-feasible schedule for the example of figure 4

Let SCH_k be the schedule constructed by algorithm MCSI after $k \geq 0$ left shifts.

Lemma 3. Suppose that for any $x,x' \in SCH_k$ such that x immediately precedes x′ we have $s(x')-s(x) \leq \lambda$. Then, in SCH_{k+1} $s(x') - s(x) \leq \lambda$.

Proof. The lemma clearly holds for all x,x′ such that x is not the job that is shifted left on the $k+1^{st}$ left shift. Suppose that x is the job that is shifted left on the $k+1^{st}$ left shift. If x is selected by step 4a, then the lemma follows trivially. So suppose x is selected by step 4b. Then if x is not the only job in S−S′, there exists a $y \in S-S'$ with immediate successor y′ such that $s(y') > s(x')$ in SCH_k. In SCH_{k+1} we have $s(y') - s(y) \leq \lambda$, $s(y') \geq s(x') + 1$, and $s(x) + 1 = s(y)$. Therefore, $s(x') - s(x) \leq \lambda$ in SCH_{k+1}. Finally, suppose that $S-S' = \{x\}$ in SCH_k. Then there exists some job $y \in S'$, which implies that $s(y) = \text{left}(\text{feas}(y))$ in SCH_k. Since both x and y are mapped to the same underlying interval, I_j, and since $\text{left}(\text{feas}(y)) > \text{left}(\text{feas}(x))$, y has an immediate successor y′. Suppose that $s(x') - s(x) = \lambda$ in SCH_k. By the induction assumption $s(y') - s(y) \leq \lambda$. Because $s(y) = \text{left}(\text{feas}(y))$, $s(y') - s(y) = \lambda$. But this implies that $s(y') = s(x')$ in SCH_k, a contradiction since S is the left-most conflicting set. Therefore, $s(x') - s(x) < \lambda$ in SCH_k; hence, $s(x') - s(x) \leq \lambda$ in SCH_{k+1}. □

Lemma 4. If Algorithm MCSI(λ) has performed k left shifts, then for all x, x′ such that x immediately precedes x′, $s(x')-s(x) \leq \lambda$ in SCH_k.

Proof. The basis follows trivially from the construction of feasible intervals together with step 2 of algorithm MCSI, and the induction step follows from lemma 3. □

Theorem 5. If algorithm MCSI(λ) halts at step 3, then it has constructed a λ-feasible schedule.

Proof. Because no job is ever shifted to the left of the endpoint of its underlying interval, every job is scheduled within its underlying interval. Since all conflicting sets are eliminated, no two jobs have the same start time. And lemma 4 guarantees that any pair of jobs that are adjacent in some chain are scheduled no more than λ apart. □

Lemma 6. At the beginning of an iteration of step 4, let S be the right-most conflicting set and let $x \in S$ be the job that is selected by the iteration of step 4 to be shifted left. Then $\text{left}(\text{feas}(x)) \leq \text{left}(\text{feas}(y))$ for all $y \in S$.

Proof. If x is shifted left by step 4a, then since x has no successors it follows from the definition of λ-feasible intervals that left(feas(x)) is also the left endpoint of the underlying interval. Hence the lemma holds.

Suppose that x is shifted left by step 4b. Let y be any other element of S. If $y \in S'$, then $\text{left}(\text{feas}(x)) \leq \text{left}(\text{feas}(y))$. So suppose that $y \notin S'$ and let x' and y' be the successors of x and y respectively. Note that both x' and y' must exist, since otherwise either x or y would have been shifted left by step 4a. Also, since S is the right-most conflicting set, $s(x') \neq s(y')$.

We use an induction argument based on the number of shifts.

Basis: x is the job shifted left by algorithm MCSI applied to SCH_0. Since x is shifted left, it follows that $s(x') < s(y')$. If x' and y' are in different underlying intervals, then the lemma clearly holds. If they are in the same underlying interval, then since no jobs have been shifted left prior to the shift of x, it follows from the definition of λ-feasible intervals that $s(x') = s(y')$, a contradiction.

Induction step: Assume the lemma holds for all previous shifts and let x be the job shifted left by algorithm MCSI applied to SCH_{k-1}. Again, if x' and y' are in different underlying intervals, the lemma holds. So suppose that x' and y' are in the same underlying interval. Because $s(x) = s(y)$, it follows from the definition of λ-feasible intervals that x' has already had at least $s(y') - s(x')$ left shifts applied to it. Since the algorithm always processes the right-most conflicting set, no new conflicting set is ever created to the right of the conflicting set that is currently being processed. Therefore, x' and y' had earlier been in the same conflicting set. By applying the induction assumption to x′ and y′, we get left(feas(x′)) ≤ left(feas(y′)), which implies left(feas(x)) ≤ left(feas(y)). □

Lemma 7. If algorithm MCSI declares a problem instance infeasible in step 4, then there is no λ-feasible schedule for the problem instance.

Proof. Assume that algorithm MCSI declares a problem instance infeasible in step 4, and let S_p be the conflicting set being processed when the infeasible condition is detected, with S_p being in the underlying interval I_v. Let S_0 be the right-most conflicting set in I_v in SCH_0.

By the definition of the right endpoint of a feasible interval, all jobs are started at the latest possible start time in S_0 subject to feasibility. Clearly if a λ-feasible schedule exists, then a λ-feasible schedule can be constructed by applying some set of left shifts to S_0. From lemma 6 it follows that if x is the first job in S_0 to be shifted left, then left(feas(x)) ≤ left(feas(y)) for all $y \in S_0$. By inductively applying lemma 6 we get that any other set of shifts applied to the conflicting sets of I_v would result in at least two jobs being assigned identical start times which are also the left endpoint of the feasible interval for each of the jobs. In other words, no matter what set of shifts is applied, there will be a pair of jobs assigned the same start time without the possibility of either being shifted left. Therefore, we can conclude that no λ-feasible schedule exists. In addition, we note that one can construct a minimal infeasible set of jobs in I_v such that the difference between the maximum right feasible endpoint and the minimum left feasible endpoint of the jobs in the set is less than the number of jobs in the set. Consequently, there is no λ-feasible schedule for the subproblem consisting of all the chains containing jobs in the minimal infeasible set. □

Theorem 8. If algorithm MCSI(λ) halts in steps 1 or 4, then there is no λ-feasible schedule for the problem instance.

Proof. Step 1 follows from the correctness proof for SCSI, and step 4 from lemma 7. □

The following theorem bounds the optimal value for λ.

Theorem 9. If there exists a feasible schedule for an instance of MCSI, with chains $C = \{C_1, \ldots, C_n\}$, then there exists a λ-feasible schedule with $\lambda_0 \le \lambda \le \lambda_0 + n-1$ where $\lambda_0 = \max_{1 \le i \le n} \lambda(C_i)$, and $\lambda(C_i)$ denotes the value of λ computed by algorithm SCSI for chain C_i.

Proof. The lower bound is obvious; the upper bound follows from algorithm UPPER, presented below.

Algorithm UPPER

If any interval has more jobs mapped into it than it has capacity, declare the problem instance infeasible and halt.

```
Schedule C_1 according to SCSI with λ = λ_0.
  For i=2 to n do
    Let {C_{i,1}, ... , C_{i,n_i}} be the jobs of C_i.
    Schedule C_{i,1} at the latest empty slot in f(C_{i,1})
    For j=2 to n_i do
      Let x = min(s(C_{i,j-1})+λ_0+i-1, right(f(C_{i,j}))).
      If x is an empty slot then set s(C_{i,j}) = x
      else do /* first test if jobs already schedule can be shifted right */
        if there exists t such that x < t ≤ right(f(C_{i,j})) and
        there does not exist C_{p,r} such that s(C_{p,r}) = t do
          let t_0 be the minimum such t
          increase the start times of all jobs with start times x, x+1, ..., t_0 by one (* shift
          right to create an empty slot *)
          Set s(C_{i,j}) = x
        od
      else let t_0 be the largest t such that left(C_{i,j}) ≤ t_0 < x /* if right shift failed, then
      schedule job as late as possible prior to x */
        and there does not exist C_{p,r} with s(C_{p,r}) = t.
        Set s(C_{i,j}) = x.
      od
    od
  od
end
```

The proof of the correctness of UPPER follows from the succeeding lemmas.

Lemma 10. The ith iteration of the outer loop in UPPER guarantees that $s^i(C_{i,j})+i-1 \geq s(C_{i,j})$, where $s^i(C_{i,j})$ denotes the start time assigned to $C_{i,j}$ by UPPER and $s(C_{i,j})$ denotes the start time assigned to $C_{i,j}$ by SCSI with $\lambda = \lambda_0$.

Proof. The proof is an induction on i. For i=1 we have that all jobs $C_{1,k}$ $1 \leq k \leq n_1$, satisfy the lemma since $s^1(C_{1,k}) = s(C_{1,k})$. Assume that all jobs scheduled in the first i-1 iterations satisfy the lemma.

$C_{i,1}$ is scheduled so that $s^i(C_{i,1})+i-1 \geq s(C_{i,1})$ because at most i-1 jobs can be scheduled to its right. Now assume that all jobs up to and including the $C_{i,k}$ satisfy the inequality. In particular, $s^i(C_{i,k})+i-1 \geq s(C_{i,k})$. This implies that $\min\{right(C_{i,k+1}), s^i(C_{i,k})+i-1+\lambda_0\} \geq \min\{right(C_{i,k+1}), s(C_{i,k})+\lambda_0\}$. Note that the right hand side of the inequality is the expression for $s(C_{i,k+1})$, while the left hand side is the value of x computed by UPPER. Hence, $x \geq s(C_{i,k+1})$.

There are three cases to consider. First, if UPPER schedules $C_{i,k+1}$ at x without shifting any jobs the lemma clearly holds for $C_{i,k+1}$. Second, if UPPER shifts some jobs right by one unit, the lemma still holds because by the induction hypothesis each such job satisfies $s^i(J)+i-2 \geq s(J)$ and shifting J by one unit to the right amounts to increasing $s^i(J)$ by one. Third, if UPPER schedules $C_{i,k+1}$ at some time $y < x$ then y cannot be more than i-1 units to the left of x because at most i-1 jobs could have been scheduled contiguously. Therefore, $y+i-1 \geq x$. Equivalently, $s^i(C_{i,k+1})+i-1 \geq x \geq s(C_{i,k+1})$. This proves the lemma. □

Theorem 11. Algorithm UPPER constructs a feasible schedule if one exists.

Proof. In order to prove this we need only prove that no job falls short of the left endpoint of its interval. Suppose there exists a job $C_{i,j}$ of C_i such that $s^i(C_{i,j}) < left(C_{i,j})$. From this it follows that $s^i(C_{i,j-1})+i-1+\lambda_0 < left(C_{i,j})$. By the previous lemma, $s(C_{i,j-1}) \leq s^i(C_{i,j-1})+i-1$. Hence, $s(C_{i,j-1}) + \lambda_0 < left(C_{i,j})$. This is a contradiction because it implies that λ_0 is not sufficiently large to construct a feasible schedule for C_i using SCSI.

UPPER fails only if it cannot shift and no empty slots exist to the left. This means that there is no room for the job to be scheduled. By a pigeon hole argument, this implies that the problem instance is infeasible. Furthermore, this condition would have been detected by the first statement of the algorithm. □

Lemma 12. There exists an instance of MCSI with chains $C_1, \ldots, C_n$ and intervals I_1, I_2 such that $\lambda = \lambda_0 + n - 1$.

Proof. For each C_i there are two jobs $C_{i,1}$ and $C_{i,2}$ with $f(C_{i,1}) = I_1$ and $f(C_{i,2}) = I_2$. For this instance $\lambda_0 = left(I_2) - right(I_1)$. Further, for any ordering of the jobs in the first interval, the ordering of the jobs in the second interval that minimizes λ is the same as that of first interval. This implies that $\lambda \geq \lambda_0 + n-1$ which in turn implies the lemma. □

Theorem 13. Given an instance of the MCSI problem, the running time required to determine the minimum value of λ for which a λ-feasible schedule exists is $O(m(n \log n)^2)$.

Proof. We note that by theorem 9 the optimum value of λ is bounded between λ_0 and λ_0+n-1. Therefore, the optimum value of λ can be determined in O(log n) iterations of algorithm MCSI. The running time of algorithm MCSI is dominated by the shifting of jobs in step 4. Since there are n chains, there can be no more than n jobs per interval. Therefore, the number of shifts per interval is bounded by $n(n-1)/2$. Since there can be no more than m intervals, the total number of shifts is $O(mn^2)$. Selecting the job to shift in step 4 can cost O(log n), thus giving a running time for a single iteration of algorithm MCSI of $O(mn^2 \log n)$. The bound follows from the first observation. □

We now turn our attention to a problem that is a simple variant of the original delay problem.

5. Scheduling chains on multiple intervals.

We now consider a variant of problem DP for an arbitrary number of chains.

Problem MCMI (multiple chains multiple intervals): Given a set of chains $C = \{C_1, \ldots, C_n\}$, a set of ordered disjoint intervals $I = I_1, \ldots, I_k$, a value λ, and a mapping $f : C_{i,j} \to \{I_{i,j_k}, 1 \leq k \leq 3\}$, find a mapping $s : C_{i,j} \to I^+$ such that $s(C_{i,j}) \in f(C_{i,j})$ and $\max_{i,j}\{s(C_{i,j+1}) - s(C_{i,j})\} \leq \lambda$.

Theorem 14. Determining if an instance of MCMI is feasible for any fixed λ is NP-complete.

Proof. The reduction is from 3-SAT. Let the instance of 3-SAT have n variables and m clauses. We construct an instance of MCMI with $\lambda = 4n+1$, containing a set of $4n(m+1)$ intervals, each of length one, and $2n+m$ chains. Assume the variables in the occurrence of 3-SAT are $x_1, \ldots, x_n$. For each variable x_i we construct a *variable chain,* VC_i and a *companion chain,* VC'_i, $0 \leq i \leq n-1$. In addition, for each of the m clauses in the instance of 3-SAT we construct a *clause chain,* CC_i, $0 \leq i \leq m-1$. Each variable chain and each companion chain contains $m+2$ nodes, each of which can be scheduled in one of two intervals. For the variable chains, these intervals correspond to setting the variables to either true or false. The companion chains are used to guarantee the consistency of the truth assignment. Each clause chain consists of a single node that checks the satisfiability of one of the clauses and which can be assigned to any of three intervals. (There is a simple modification that can be made to the reduction to restrict it to the case in which each node has only two intervals to which it can be assigned; for a discussion see [SS]).

For the variable and companion chains we have the following mappings to intervals.

$f(VC_{i,0}) = f(VC'_{i,0}) = \{2i, 2n+2i\}$.

$f(VC_{i,j}) = \{4jn+2i, 4jn+2n+2i\}$

$f(VC'_{i,j}) = \{4jn+2i+1, 4jn+2n+2i-1\}$

$f(VC_{i,m+1}) = f(VC'_{i,m+1}) = \{4(m+1)n+2i, 4(m+1)n+2n+2i\}$.

Each clause chain CC_i has a single node that is mapped into three intervals corresponding to the literals occurring in the clause as follows. If x_j occurs in CC_i in the positive form, then 4jn+2i is one of the intervals into which CC_i is mapped; if x_j occurs in the negative form, then 4jn+2n+2i is one of the intervals into which CC_i is mapped.

The following lemma demonstrates that we can obtain a unique assignment of values to the variables by encoding the scheduling of $VC_{i,j}$ to 4jn+2i as "false" and the scheduling of $VC_{i,j}$ to 4jn+2n+2i as "true".

Lemma 15. Suppose for some value of i, $s(VC_{i,0}) = 2i$. Then $s(VC_{i,j}) = 4jn+2i$ for $1 \leq j \leq m+1$. Similarly, if for some value of i, $s(VC'_{i,0}) = 2i$, then $s(VC'_{i,j}) = 4jn+2i+1$ for $1 \leq j \leq m$ and $s(VC'_{i,m+1}) = 4(m+1)n+2i$.

Proof. The proof follows immediately from the fact that $\lambda = 4n+1$. □

Note that lemma 15 implies that one can encode a consistent truth assignment to the variables of the instance of 3-SAT. We leave as an exercise for the reader that the clause chains can be scheduled if and only if there is a satisfying truth assignment for the variables. □

Having established the NP-completeness of the multiple intervals problem we turn our attention to problem DP with arbitrary precedence constraints. In the next section we prove an upper-bound on the performance of any algorithm that solves problem DP.

6. A general upper bound on the performance of a naive algorithm.

Consider an instance of problem DP with B(N,A) being the DAG of precedence constraints. Partition the elements of N(B) as follows.

N_p is the set of nodes in N(B) that have only predecessors;

N_s is the set of nodes in N(B) that have only successors;

N_{ps} is the set of nodes in N(B) that have both predecessors and successors;

N_0 is the set of nodes in N(B) that have neither predecessors nor successors.

Let A be any naive algorithm for solving DP with all of the following properties.

1. First A schedules the jobs in N_s, with each job going in the right-most empty slot in its interval;
2. Then A schedules the jobs in N_p, with each job going in the left-most empty slot in its interval;
3. Finally, A schedules the jobs of N_{ps} and N_0.

Let λ_A be the value that A computes for λ and λ_{opt} be the optimal value of λ for the problem instance. Then we have the following theorem.

Theorem 16. $\lambda_A \le 3\lambda_{opt}-2$.

Proof. First observe that a job in N_s cannot be scheduled by A further than $\lambda_{opt}-1$ from the right endpoint of its underlying interval, since otherwise some job in N_s would have its successor scheduled more than λ_{opt} away in any schedule. Similarly, any job in N_p cannot be scheduled by A further than $\lambda_{opt}-1$ from the left endpoint of its underlying interval.

Now, consider any arc $(y,z) \in A(B)$. Clearly, the length of this arc cannot be made larger than right(f(z)) - left(f(y)). We define $s_{opt}(x)$ to be the start time of some job x in some fixed optimal schedule.

Case 1. $y,z \in N_{ps}$. Let (x,y) and (z,w) be two neighboring arcs of (y,z). Clearly, right(f(z)) $\le$ left(f(w))-1 and right(f(x)) $\le$ left(f(y))-1. Adding these gives, right(f(z))$-$left(f(y)) $\le$ left(f(w)$-$right(f(x))-2. Now, left(f(w)) - right(f(x)) $\le s_{opt}(w)-s_{opt}(x) \le 3\lambda_{opt}$. Combining this with the previous inequality, we get left(f(z)) - right(f(y)) $\le 3\lambda_{opt}-2$.

Case 2. $y \in N_s$ and $z \in N_{ps}$. Let (z,w) be a neighboring arc of (y,z). From the observation made at the beginning we know that right(f(y))$-s_A(y) \le \lambda_{opt}-1$, where $s_A(y)$ denotes the start time assigned to y by algorithm A. Since $s_{opt}(w)-s_{opt}(y) \le 2\lambda_{opt}$, we have that $s_{opt}(w)-s_A(y) \le 3\lambda_{opt}-1$, and consequently, left(f(w))$-s_A(y) \le 3\lambda_{opt}-1$. Also, since right(f(z)) $\le$ left(f(w))-1, we get right(f(z))$-s_A(y) \le 3\lambda_{opt}-2$. Hence, the maximum length of arc (y,z) is bounded by $3\lambda_{opt}-2$.

The remaining cases are similar. □

7. An approximation algorithm.

The approximation algorithm builds on the results that have been established thus far. It is a critical path type algorithm which finds a set of "spanning" chains for the DAG B(N,A) and then uses algorithm MCSI for a starting solution. The arcs of B(N,A) that were not included in the spanning chains are then examined. If one of these arcs is larger than the λ generated by MCSI, a set of shifts is performed to decrease the length of this arc. If the shifting strategy fails, the value of λ is increased and MCSI is rerun on the spanning chains with the larger λ. If the shifting strategy succeeds, then another arc is examined. The process terminates when all arcs have length no greater than the current value of λ.

Algorithm APPROX

1. Call remove_triangles(B(N,A))

2. Call create_spanning_chains(B(N,A), $\{I_1, ..., I_k\}$)

3. Let $\{C_i\}$ be the set of spanning chains returned by step 2. Let S be the union of all singleton C_i's.

/* Now that the spanning chains have been computed and singleton jobs isolated, we can use MCSI to get an initial value of λ */

4. Using binary search to find the minimum feasible λ, call MCSI repeatedly on $\cup_i C_i - S$. Let λ be the computed minimum separation.

/* Now find two chains that have the property that a job in one chain has an arc in B(N,A) connecting it to the first job in the other chain. Find the right-most such pair that *exceeds* λ. Shift left the chain with the right-most such job keeping λ fixed if possible. */

5. Find the right-most pair of jobs i and k with the property that $i \in C_p$, $k \in C_q$, $(i,k) \in A(B)$, $p \neq q$, k is the first job of C_q, and $x = s(k)-s(i) > \lambda$.

If no such job exists goto 7.

Else do

    Call shift(λ,C_q)

    If (shift=true) do

        Call resolve_conflict

        Goto 5

    od

od

6. Let $\lambda = \lambda + 1$. Schedule ($\cup_i C_i - S$) using MCSI with the new value of λ. Goto 5.

/* Now schedule the "singleton chains". If these singleton chains had arcs attached to them, schedule them as close to the center between their predecessors and successors as possible. */

7. Schedule the jobs of S as follows. Let $m \in S$. If there exist p, q such that (p,m) and (m,q) $\in$ A(B), compute $x = (s(q)-s(p))/2$. Find $t \in f(m)$ such that $|t-x|$ is minimized and no job is scheduled at t. Let s(m) = t. If p does not exist, but there exist q as above, then find $t \in f(m)$ such that $|s(q)-t|$ is minimized and no job is scheduled at t. Let s(m) = t. Use a similar strategy if q does not exist and p does exist. If neither exists, then choose any starting point for m such that no other job is scheduled at that point.

Subroutine remove__triangles(B(N,A))

/* This subroutine removes arcs that are "subsumed" by larger arcs of B(N,A) and marks each remaining arc with a lower bound on the length of that arc */

1. If there exist three jobs J_1, J_2, J_3 such that (J_1,J_2), (J_2,J_3), and $(J_3,J_1) \in A(B)$, then delete the arcs (J_1,J_2) and (J_2,J_3). If J_2 becomes a singleton as a result, remove J_2 from N(B).

2. For all remaining arcs (i,j), label (i,j) with left(f(j))−right(f(i)).

3. Return.

Subroutine Create__spanning__chains

/* Using the labels attached by remove__triangles, construct in a greedy fashion a set of chains containing all jobs */

1. Declare all jobs available and let i=1.

2. Pick the left-most available job, k and add k to C_i. If k does not exist, goto 4. Otherwise, mark k unavailable.

3. Let $(k,m) \in A(B)$ such that m is available and the label of (k,m) is maximal (ties broken arbitrarily). Add m to C_i. Mark k unavailable. If m does not exist, let i=i+1 and goto 2.

Subroutine Shift(λ,C_q)

/* This routine shifts the chain C_q left if there is any "slack" in the chain. The slack hopefully propagates to the front of the chain, causing the first job to also shift left. */

1. Shift = false.

/* If there is a job scheduled at its left endpoint and its predecessor is λ away, the chain cannot be shifted */

2. If there exists a pair of jobs r,s in C_q with $(r,s) \in A(B)$ such that s(s) = left(f(s)) and s(s) − s(r) = λ, then return.

/* Find a job with "slack" */

3. Find the right-most job, m∈C>SUB/q/, such that $s(m+1)-s(m)<\lambda$, where $(m,m+1) \in A(B)$ and m can be shifted left by at most $\lambda-(s(m+1)-s(m))$ units without conflicts and without going past the left endpoint.

4. If m does not exist, let m be the last job of the chain if it can be shifted left without conflicts. Otherwise return.

5. Shift m as far to the left as possible without causing conflicts.

6. If m is the first job of C_q, left shift=true and return.

7. Goto 3.

This completes the description of the approximation algorithm for problem DP. It is worth noting that the approximation algorithm depends heavily on how the initial "spanning" chains are obtained. Perhaps there is a better method for choosing arcs than simply by examining the lower bound for the length of each arc. Indeed, there are simple examples to show that APPROX is not optimal because of the method of choosing these spanning chains.

8. Comparison with previous results.

In this section, results obtained by the algorithms presented here are compared with those of [Cyt84] on some routines of EISPACK.

The *percentage parallelism* of a loop with n statements and delay λ is $(n-\lambda)/n$ [Cyt84].

Figure 6 shows the percentage parallelism obtained by applying no optimizations, Cytron's algorithm CYT, and our algorithm APPROX. Note that significant improvements over [Cyt84] can be obtained using our algorithms, and that in several cases where algorithm CYT was not able to find any parallelism in the code, our algorithm did find some parallelism. Indeed, in some cases our results are better by a factor greater than three. This is because our technique for constructing independent sets also improves performance.

In summary, it has been shown that important special cases of the Delay Problem can be solved optimally in polynomial time. These solutions represent an improvement which is frequently considerably better than extant methods. Theoretical results have been established which show that, in fact, no algorithm can do worse than the performance of the method in the literature. Empirical evaluations show that in practice parallelism can be detected using our methods where none could be detected before.

Name	*Unopt*	*CYT*	*APPROX*
CINVIT	6.3	6.3	9.6
COMLR2	11.1	11.1	11.1
COMQR2	5.6	5.6	11.1
HQR2	0	0	3.0
HTRIB3	4.0	4.0	33.3
HTRIDI	18.8	25.0	37.5
HTRID3	3.1	3.1	14.2
INVIT	0.0	2.9	5.8
MINFIT	8.0	8.0	20.0
QZVEC	23.1	36.3	36.3
SVD	0	0	14.3
TQLRAT	0.0	0.0	7.7

Figure 6. Percentage parallelism obtained on EISPACK routines

9. Acknowledgements.

We would like to thank Ron Cytron for many helpful discussions and for figure 1 and Jeanne Ferrante and Nimrod Megiddo for valuable comments.

10. References.

[All] J. R. Allen, "Dependence Analysis for Subscripted Variables and its application to program transformations," Ph.D. Thesis, University of Texas at Austin.

[Cyt] R. G. Cytron, "Compile-time Scheduling and Optimization for Asynchronous machines," PhD Thesis, University of Illinois at Urbana-Champagne, 1984.

[Ken] N. W. Kennedy, "Automatic translation of Fortran programs to vector form," Rice Technical report 476-029-4, Oct. 1980.

[KKLW] D. J. Kuck, R. H. Kuhn, B. Leasure, M. Wolfe, "The structure of an advanced vectorizer for pipeline processors," 4th International computer software and applications conference, 1980.

[Lam] L. Lamport, "The parallel execution of DO loops," *Commun. ACM* 17, 1974, pp. 83-93.

[Mun] A. A. Munshi, unpublished manuscript.

[SS] B. B. Simons, M. Sipser, "On scheduling unit-length jobs with multiple release time/deadline intervals," *Operations Research,* Vol. 32, 1984, pp. 80-86.

Management of PDE-Software for Supercomputing

J.-Fr. Hake - W. Homberg
Zentralinstitut fuer Angewandte Mathematik (ZAM)
Kernforschungsanlage Juelich GmbH (KFA)
D-5170 Juelich, Fed. Rep. of Germany

Abstract

Many scientific processes can be modeled by a solution of partial differential equations. The increasing capabilities of modern computer systems strongly contribute to the computations of numerical solutions. Strategies for efficient problem solving in this field can be established with the concept of problem solving environments. A problem solving environment (pse) can be defined as a human interface to hardware and software to assist the user in the solution of a given class of problems.

The PDE pse developed at KFA Juelich/ZAM intends to support the user in the improvement and design of new components for the environment as well as in the accurate and efficient solution of partial differential equations. Predefined commands and several model problems lead to a more intensive concentration on the problem, because routine activities are reduced. The problem description becomes the central point of the work. Special emphasis is given to interactive pre- and postprocessing; i.e. syntactical check on the correctness of the formulated problems and support for the submission of jobs to the appropriate computer systems (IBM 3081 and CRAY X-MP). An interface to graphics software provides easy-to-use facilities for the representation of numerical results.

Keywords

mathematical software, problem solving environment, partial differential equations, numerical methods.

Introduction

Many scientific processes can be modeled by a solution of partial differential equations (pdes); this fact has led to the development of a large number of analytical and numerical techniques, where the latter class is implemented and distributed in form of software. For many algorithms, the solution of a pde on a computer can be divided into three steps:

- classification of the pde based on a theoretical analysis of the pde, and selection of a tool;
- discretization of pde, domain and boundary conditions, which is strongly based on the previous step, because theoretical insight leads to selection of appropriate tools and can significantly speed-up the computational process;
- solution of the discretized problem is achieved by solving large sets of linear resp. nonlinear equations depending on the pde and its boundary conditions.

The increasing capabilities of modern computer systems strongly contribute to an efficient performance of this process. Whereas the computers of the first generation just could deal with the solution of subtasks of a mathematical problem (e.g. small systems of linear equations), the Fifth Generation Computer

Systems (FGCS) are planned to provide complete solution strategies to very complex problems for a broad range of applications [10]. The support in problem solving given by the computer is intended to start at the initial level of problem specification; then, by knowledge-based analysis, the problem is processed towards its solution, which remains in many cases based on efficient numerical computing [11].

Although the existing computer systems do not completely achieve the objectives of the FGCS project, they already can contribute to the solution of scientific problems in several directions

- Powerful timesharing systems offer attractive features for the implementation of interactive dialogue managements to access the required tools.
- Results from the field of "Parallel Processing" indicate that numerical solutions to pde problems can be computed very fast.

Like most of the large research laboratories, KFA Juelich has a broad spectrum of research and development objectives implying a high demand for computing resources. Besides to an installation management for advanced systems, the computer center of the lab has to provide strategies to support the scientists in efficient and reliable problem solving. The next chapters describe the integration of high-level pde software originating from different sources into the high-speed computing environment at KFA Juelich and how this approach supports the solution of actual problems. Special emphasis is laid on the pre- and postprocessing part of the problem (computer algebra, graphics). For the user, the problem description becomes the central point of work.

Software for the Solution of PDEs

The existing software for the solution of pdes can be grouped into packages and libraries. Packages offer a unified view of a collection of methods or a simplified interface to a specific method to solve a class of problems; the problem must be formulated in terms of a preprocessor language which is supposed to be close to a certain area of applications. Subroutines from a library can be considered as modules for larger systems; this approach to pde software requires more experience in programming than the usage of packages.

Past software developments in the field of pdes have been surveyed by Machura-Sweet [17] and by Boisvert-Sweet [3]; they give an overview which is biased towards general-purpose software. The survey below emphasizes the importance of high-level mathematical software which accepts the pde as input and performs the discretization automatically. In particular, the software has to be part of public scientific domain and should be able to contribute to a problem solving environment in this field. The references point at the origins of the implemented algorithms, i.e. identical references for different products indicate the same root of the programs. A comparison focussing on the computational aspects of elliptic solvers for general two-dimensional regions is given by Chan and Saied [5].

- Libraries
  The Collected Algorithms from ACM[1] are distributed in form of Fortran subroutines [13], [14], [23], [25], [31]; [20], [21], [32], [33]. Portability is guaranteed with respect to the ACM algorithms policy.

  The Harwell Subroutine Library[1] is a collection of subroutines specialized in the field of numerical mathematics; like most of the other general purpose libraries in this field there are only a few programs for the solution of pde problems [1].

---

1 implemented at ZAM

The IMSL[1] [31] and NAG [6], [31] represent general purpose libraries in the field of numerical mathematics; distribution is on a commercial base.

- Packages

  ELLPACK[1] solves elliptic boundary value problems with variable coefficients for two resp. three dimensions [27]. The package is primarily directed to the solution of linear problems; it offers no explicit feature for the treatment of nonlinear problems.

  PDE/PROTRAN[1] solves a large class of two-dimensional elliptic, parabolic and eigenvalue pde problems with finite element techniques. Like its predecessor TWODEPEP, PDE/PROTRAN is distributed by IMSL on a commercial base [30].

  NASTRAN and PERMAS[1] represent two large-scale computer packages that solve a wide variety of engineering problems by the finite element method [4].

  Software developments for engineering problems in the field of boundary element techniques have been reviewed by Mackerle-Andersson [19].

This brief survey illustrates that the development of high-level pde software represents a very heterogeneous process leading to products which have nearly no interfaces to exchange information. Exept of ELLPACK, the packages do not allow great flexibility in the implementation on a multi-computer system.

KFA Multi-Computer System

With the increasing capabilities of computer networks (local and wide area) and the expanding spectrum of different computer architectures, it becomes important to consider how this situation can contribute to an efficient solution of pdes. The KFA multi-computer system serves as a base for the implementation of a prototype for the dialogue management of pde problems.

The present computer configuration consists of three IBM computers (1 IBM 4381, 2 IBM 3081) and one CRAY X-MP/22; another CRAY X-MP/48 has been installed in spring 1987. In addition, about 200 minicomputers and superminis are scattered throughout KFA to support distributed computing in several divisions, institutes and departments (processing of experimental data, monitoring of experiments).

The individual components of a multi-computer system can operate in different modes; therefore, one can expect more flexibility in the adaptation to a user-oriented problem solving. For the numerical treatment of pdes at KFA/ZAM this means

- Interactive Preprocessing under VM/CMS on IBM 3081, i.e.
  - selection of tool
  - formulation of problem
  - check for correctness
  - selection of appropriate computer architecture
- Processing under COS on CRAY X-MP or MVS on IBM 3081, i.e. access to
  - different computer architectures
  - algorithms, which have been optimized with resp. to the underlying architecture
- Interactive Postprocessing under VM/CMS, i.e.
  - generation of output
  - analysis of run-time messages
  - individual postprocessing.

The structure of the preprocessing step is more elaborate than shown by the above list; further details are given by Fig. 1. This step has to provide complete information to run a problem successfully; i.e. the problem description has to be correct (indicated by a faultless compile and go step for the problem with a coarse discretization). The subsequent processing step with realistic discretization parameters should only be initiated after a successful completion of the preprocessing step.

From the software point of view, the processing level can be considered as a reservoir of different methods in form of modules which are available for the solution of a particular class of problems. On a multi-computer system, every algorithm has to be implemented in a well adapted and highly optimized form to guarantee an efficient solution of the problem; this leads to at least one special version (program) of the algorithm for each computer architecture and therefore to differing results, i.e. results computed on one machine may not be exactly reproducible on another one.

Problem Solving Environments for PDEs

General Outline

The efficient use of computers for the solution of complex problems is strongly influenced by the existence of a clear, transparent and flexible interface; this becomes even more important for multi-computer systems where the contributions from the individual components have to be combined to achieve the final result. Thus, efficiency in problem solving can only be expected if interactive pre- and postprocessing are closely linked to high-speed number crunching. Strategies for efficient problem solving can be established with the concept of problem solving environments. They represent an attempt to focus user attention on the tools which might be relevant for the solution of a particular problem.

A problem solving environment (pse) can be defined as a human interface to hardware and software to assist the user in the solution of a given class of problems (e.g. pdes). A pse should be implemented as an integrated multi-tasking system of different functions which provides the user with appropriate i/o devices (e.g. graphical i/o) and also with high-speed computing facilities which can be represented as a hierarchy of computer architectures varying from mini- to supercomputers. Depending on the complexity of the user's problem, a pse should assist to access the different architectures.

Apart from a user-friendly link to the hardware, the software component of a pse should provide tools for problem analysis (e.g. knowledge base) and for programming (e.g. Fortran), including libraries, packages etc. which contribute to the scope of the pse. A pse can be an open or a closed system; i.e. the integration of new components is supported or not [9].

Within the last few years, much attention has been paid to the idea of a pse on pdes [12], [18]. The most advanced results for elliptic pdes have been contributed by the ELLPACK project [26]. But even for parabolic and hyperbolic problems, the idea of automatic code generation has already been discussed [8].

PDE Problem Solving Environment at KFA/ZAM

The PDE problem solving environment developed at KFA/ZAM provides a frame-work for the solution of pdes with software packages originating from different sources. Its implementation is based on the local computing facilities, but the principles are machine-independent and can be transferred to every multi-computer environment offering similar functions. PDE consists of tools, a dialogue management, a problem base, the Fortran programming environment of the computer systems and the KFA multi-computer system. A brief survey on the structure of PDE is given in Fig. 1; the connection of the components required for the preprocessing step is given in the dashed box. The capabilities of PDE are illustrated in more detail for the ELLPACK branch.

The user may enter the PDE pse by calling a CMS procedure PDE; the dialogue management of PDE responds with a survey menu on the tools available through this pse. After a certain selection has been achieved (ELLPACK), a procedure with identical name is executed and performs the necessary links to the components of the tool; esp. temporary storage is allocated which is used to keep the output from the various components of the tool (preprocessor, compiler etc.) and the computed results.

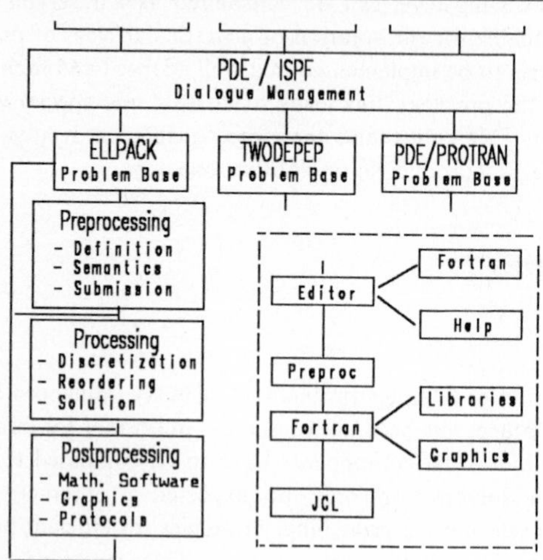

Fig. 1. PDE Problem Solving Environment

If the allocation of resources has been completed successfully, a list of the already existing ELLPACK problems is automatically presented (Fig. 2); this list serves as the central starting point for most of the activities where ELLPACK becomes involved. On top of the list, the user-owned datasets are given in alphabetical order; the lower part consists of a collection of examples which may serve both as an introduction to ELLPACK and as an illustration of the capabilities of the tool.

At this problem definition level the user has to provide resp. to create a dataset of type ELLPACK with a complete description of the problem to be solved; this can be done by modifying an existing dataset. In general, it consists of two parts; the first one represents a program written in terms of a preprocessor language, the second one consists of one or more Fortran subroutines containing additional information on the problem (variable coefficients of the equation etc.). At the end of the problem definition, the Fortran parts of the dataset should be free of syntax errors and the user can preprocess the dataset to generate a complete Fortran program, which is automatically compiled. This process may be iterated until a syntactically correct program exists.

After a successful completion of the syntax check, an appropriate computer architecture has to be selected in order to solve the problem numerically. Before starting the numerical solution of the real problem on a batch system, one can impose a semantical check on the correctness of the generated Fortran program by limiting the discretization process to a very coarse discretization; this leads to a few inexpensive operations which can be performed within the preprocessing level. In particular, the initial discretization can be visualized with the help of graphical output devices to assure a correct initial domain decomposition. If the user is working with a graphics terminal, this output is immediately available to him; otherwise, the information is stored for the postprocessing level. At run-time the generated program may require access to specific libraries (user-owned or system); PDE provides a feature where this information is directly passed to the job control language (jcl) generating module.

Now, the Fortran program is ready for execution and may be submitted to batch. The PDE pse supports this step by providing complete job control language for all linked components to run a successfully preprocessed problem without delay. All required information is generated automatically; the user has only to select the computer system where the processing step is intended to take place and must initiate the submission.

The first step of the postprocessing level consists in receiving the output of the processing level. All output from the batch computers is directed to the user's internal reader (if not specified otherwise during jcl generation), which is part of the CMS spool; the output is kept there temporarily for a few days depending on local CMS system conventions. The user may access the datasets belonging to his internal reader from the level where the list of problems is presented.

```
------- ELLPACK INPUT DATASETS - PAGE 1 -------

COMMAND ===>

        Filename   Filetype   Filemode   Date
        BURGERS    ELLPACK       A       05/16/86
        COLLATZ    ELLPACK       A       05/14/86
        PROB1      ELLPACK       D       03/19/86
        PROB2      ELLPACK       A       03/16/86
        PROB4      ELLPACK       F       02/04/86
        PROB6      ELLPACK       D       04/21/86

<PF1=HLP PF2=RFR PF3=QUIT PF4=CRAY PF5=FORTRAN >
<PF6=OUTPUT PF7=BACK PF8=FOR PF9=PREP PF10=MVS >
<   PF11=XEDIT  PF12=CMS  PF15=RETURN          >

------------------------------------------------
```

Fig. 2. Panel with List of Problem Descriptions

All packages and drivers of pde software provide line-printer output in form of tables to give access to the numerical values of the computed solution, which represents a base for further manipulations and graphical output. In contrast to the numerical results, which are always generated during the processing step, the production of a graphical representation of the solution can take place directly at the processing level or interactively in the postprocessing environment. The decision depends on the complexity of the given problem; PDE supports both approaches. Because most of the postprocessing depends very strongly on the individual user, it is important to connect this level closely to the complete graphics environment of the computer center.

Dialogue Management

The PDE dialogue management has to establish a link between the KFA multi-computer system and scientists intending to solve a pde problem. User-specific requirements are mapped onto the local resources by a hierarchically structured menu-driven dialogue. Input from the users is entered with help of panels which have to be filled in. Switching from one level to another is initiated by a set of predefined program function keys. During a dialogue, it is essential for the user that all his activities are processed in an open and transparent way to interrupt and modify the standard PDE scheme if necessary.

The full-screen oriented treatment of pdes with assistance from the PDE pse requires basic knowledge in working with the timesharing system which hosts the dialogue management, because the implemented dialogue has to reflect the structure and functions of the underlying computer system. In contrast to the interactive parts of PDE, only minor experiences with the batch computers are expected. In addition, the dialogue is based on the assumption that the user is familiar with the tool he selected; he has to know how to formulate the problem. At the problem definition level, flexibility and range of functions are mainly determined by the tool; PDE supports access to the various tools by an identical surface.

For PDE, user-friendliness is achieved by a simple, but powerful concept. At each level, the execution of the most relevant commands can be initiated by program function (PF) keys. The set of commands provided in conjunction with the PF keys has to be complete and consistent, i.e. the creation of complete jobs has to be easily achievable and commands, which are defined for more than one level, have to be located always on the same key. This approach reduces the input from the user for routine activities and results in more efficiency. At present, there exist two groups of PF keys:

- Processing Functions (PF1, ..., PF12)
- Auxiliary Functions (PF13, ..., PF24).

At each level, the bottom lines of the screen contain information on the commands to be executed by PF key. Moreover, each menu provides a command line to execute not predefined commands or to interrupt the actual work; in return the processing of the pde problem may be continued. This feature is based on the same mechanism used by other VM/CMS products; i.e. the users are supposed to be familiar with it.

```
-------            HELP PANEL (ELLPACK)            -------

COMMAND ===>

     Processing a problem requires:
     1. problem description (PF11)

            Filename ===> ......
            Filemode ===> .
     2. check for syntactical correctness (PF9)
        (preprocessor and FORTRAN compiler)
     3. submission of job to COS (PF4), MVS (PF10)
                                 CMS (PF12)
     4. access to results (PF6)
     A panel can be left with QUIT (PF3).

     <PF3=QUIT PF4=CRAY PF6=OUTPUT PF9=PREPOC>
            <PF10=MVS  PF11=XEDIT  PF12=CMS>
-----------------------------------------------------------
```

Fig. 3. HELP-Panel for ELLPACK

The PDE dialogue management offers HELP information to the user; this serves as an additional explanation for the commands which can be executed from the actual selected level. The following example illustrates the processing of a problem in more detail. Supposing a user has selected a tool and would like to work on a problem from the panel which provides the list of problem descriptions (Fig. 2). Pressing PF1 he can access the HELP information for this level, where the required job steps for the processing of a problem are listed. The HELP information itself is implemented as a panel

(Fig. 3); thus, the user may continue working on his problem directly from this panel having the relevant information on the screen.

In contrast to the mathematical software, which is mainly written in Fortran, the dialogue management has to be implemented in a language which is more suitable for the flexibility of dialogues. The dialogue management of PDE consists of a collection of REXX procedures which use the Interactive Systems Product Facility (ISPF). The REXX language is similar to PL/1 and procedures can easily be programmed at an appropriate high language level [15]. ISPF represents a tool to create menu-driven dialogues with a CMS full-screen support.

Graphics

Results for a specific problem can be accessed by PF key (PF6 in Fig. 2). For all problems, tabulated numerical results are generated during the processing step; these tables represent the base for the postprocessing level of the PDE pse. To keep the speedup gained from the efficient treatment of pdes during the processing step, it is very important to link the numerical results directly to the graphical functions of the postprocessing level, because in many cases the quality of the numerical data can only be judged by graphical representations. For existing software, the quality and range of graphical functions vary from ACM algorithms producing numerical data only to PDE/PROTRAN offering a set of functions. Thus, preference of a package is often based on its graphical components.

To offer identical graphical functions to the different packages the output modules have been modified to create the tables of output in a standardized form. This approach results in one pool of graphical functions for all packages. All KFA/ZAM graphics software is based on the Graphical Kernel System (GKS) [2].

The main goal of the graphical output level consists in offering a few but very user-friendly functions to process the numerical data in a standard way. At the moment, graphical output of each PDE tool is available in four forms:

- 3D-plots resp. 2D-plots
- Contour plots
- Sequences of 3D resp. contour plots for time-dependent problems
- Initial and final domain decomposition.

The user interface to the plot functions is implemented in form of panels (Fig. 4). For each plot, users have to fill in the information on the required plot function (3D20 means 3D-representation with respect to a rotation of 20° in the x-y plane), the column of the table representing the function to be plotted (u for the solution) and, for time-dependent problems, the number of the table identifying a specific time step. The information can be completed by a headline which simplifies the identification of the plots. As result the user receives a sequence of plots which can be individually modified afterwards. Again, the plot panel is supplemented by HELP information describing the options at this level.

Graphical output is device dependent. Therefore, the dialogue management provides a feature for the user to communicate the relevant information to the system. For each sequence of plots, it is possible to specify the device type, or, if the graphics equipment remains unchanged, the users can fix the information via PF key (PF5=GRDEVICE in Fig. 4); reset is performed in the same way.

Numerical Components and Expertise

On a multi-computer system, the numerical components strongly have to reflect the different computer architectures, because realistic pde problems are very resource consuming. In particular, they require the solution of very large linear resp. nonlinear systems. For the processing level, it is of great importance to provide fast solvers for this kernel task. A survey of recent results is given by Ortega and Voigt

[24]; they document the impact of vector and parallel computers to the numerical treatment of partial differential equations. For vector computers, one can observe that there exists software solving systems of linear equations at supervector speed which is achieved when vector instructions are used to reduce the number of instructions interpreted and functional unit execution is overlapped to execute more than one independent vector instruction concurrently [7].

```
----------- PLOT COMMAND INPUT --------------
COMMAND ===>

Distortion = 0/1 means: Plot distorted/undistorted
Skip = n means: Skip n output blocks before
                                 plotting the data
(Plot1,Plot2) defines the Plot-Vector

DIS-    SKIP (PLOT1,PLOT2)   <---- HEADLINE ---->
TORTION
 1        0   ( H  ,  U )  Burgers Equation at T=0
 1        9   (3D20,  U )  Burgers Equation   T=0.1
 1        9   ( *  ,  * )  Burgers Equation   T=0.1
              (    ,    )
              (    ,    )
 <PF1=HELP PF3=CANCEL PF5=GRDEVICE PF12=EXECUTE>
-----------------------------------------------
```

Fig. 4. Panel for Graphical Output Requests

The performance of a processor on a particular problem can roughly be characterized by its megaflop rate, i.e. the actual achieved number of million floating point operations per second; this number is bounded from above by the peak rate of the processor which can be determined from its physical structure (cycle time, maximum number of functional units operating in parallel). The following table illustrates the efficiency in the use of vector computers; the megaflop rates give a survey on recently published results [34]. They do not only depend on the Fortran code (e.g. the performance improving effect of loop unrolling), but also on the actual version of the operating system and compiler. The concept of the PDE pse intends to preserve this efficiency for the treatment of the complete problem starting from a problem description and finishing with graphical representations of the solution.

MFLOP Rate	CRAY -1	CRAY X-MP	CRAY -2	FUJITSU VP-200	HITACHI S-810/20
Peak Rate[2]	160	210	488	533	630
Innerproduct	15-33	77-96	62-64	178-331	216-259
LU-Decomposition	69-83	108-136		178	147
Cholesky-Decomp.	78-86	132		238-430	211
2D-Poisson Equation					
van der Vorst[35]	30-34	65-95		65	--
Meurant[22]	38-43	81-96		94	52
Saad[22]	49-54	113-144		303	140
PDE-Kernel[34]	55	96	10	90	49

2 For CRAY X-MP resp. CRAY-2 one processor only is considered.

First results from multitasking the conjugate gradient method for the CRAY X-MP show that for a two-processor version of the algorithm a speed-up of about 1.9 can be achieved. On a four-processor machine the actual observed speed-up is about 2.9; this loss of efficiency can be directly attributed to bank conflicts, i.e. the global memory cannot keep up with the arithmetic of four tasks [29]. For Fortran, the design of language constructs for multitasking is manufacturer dependent and still under development; at this stage one cannot expect the preprocessor packages to support research into this topic. The authors of ELLPACK consider the addition of new modules and modifications to the preprocessor language at installation site in principle, but they also issue a warning for the unexperienced user.

Incorporating numerical methods from different sources the concept of pses leads to a stronger unification; identical components become easily comparable. In most cases, only a population of methods can lead to more flexibility and powerful strategies in problem solving. Both ELLPACK and PDE/PROTRAN allow for discretizing a pde over two-dimensional regions with a Galerkin method. The table below illustrates the main differences.

	ELLPACK Spline Galerkin[3]	PDE/PROTRAN Quadratics, Cubics, Quartics[4]
1. Equation	$(au_x)_x + (bu_y)_y + fu - g = 0$ a,b,f,g are functions of x,y	$a_x(x,y,u,u_x,u_y) + b_y(x,y,u,u_x,u_y) + f(x,y,u,u_x,u_y) = 0$
2. Domain	rectangular	general
3. Boundary Cond.	Dirichlet	general
4. Finite Elements	rectangles	isoparametric triangles
5. Basis Functions	tensorproduct-B-splines	Lagrangian polynomials of degree 2,3,4

From the table one can conclude that, with respect to the type of equation, domain and boundary conditions, PDE/PROTRAN is capable to treat a broader class of problems, whereas ELLPACK offers more flexibility in selecting the basis functions. In contrast to PDE/PROTRAN, where one can only choose the degree of the basis functions, ELLPACK additionally allows to specify the order of differentiability for adjacent basis functions.

For nonlinear problems again, the packages supplement each other. PDE/PROTRAN treats nonlinear problems by a Newton-Raphson iteration which for linear problems reduces to one iteration giving the exact solution. ELLPACK is mainly directed to linear problems, but the ELLPACK modules can be regarded as kernels for a user-written fix-point iteration. This approach provides more flexibility, but requires more experience.

The concept of pses offers several ways to incorporate expertise. Algorithms representing the state-of-the-art in numerical treatment of pdes can be regarded as the base for an efficient processing of problems. Additional expertise can be introduced at the preprocessing level. A selection of model problems may serve as a starting point for newcomers. More advanced model problems may illustrate the capabilities and limits of a specific tool; in addition, sophisticated reformulations of a problem may extend the range of applicability for a tool. Problems suitable for more than one tool may document differences in the preprocessor languages as well as in the numerical components and establish connections between the tools. In particular, for linear elliptic problems of second order, there exists already a population of test problems [28]. The PDE pse provides access to a collection of model problems by a simple

---

3 Name of ELLPACK module.

4 Keywords for the selection of basis functions.

mechanism; the list of model problems existing for a specific tool is included in the list of input datasets which is automatically given to the user (Fig. 2).

Running several packages in one environment leads to increasing consideration of standards and interfaces. For the graphics interface, this topic has already been mentioned; but also for the mathematical software part, a standardization of parameter lists for the basic tasks could reduce the number of multiple subroutines for the same problem. The BLAS routines can be regarded as a starting point, but they also document the difficulties in establishing a standard [16].

Conclusions

The PDE problem solving environment developed at KFA offers unified and systematic access to hardware and software supporting the solution of pdes. Starting from a survey on the implemented tools, the numerical treatment of pdes is achieved from high-speed computer systems and state-of-the-art software. The processing of problems is simplified by a set of predefined commands such that the problem descriptions become the central point of work. This approach leads to a more comprehensive view on problem solving strategies and results in increased efficiency for the solution of the entire problem. In particular, the interfaces to graphics software and the modules for automatic generation of jcl for different computer systems contribute to this goal.

The structure of the PDE pse supports the addition of new tools; new components can easily be compared with already existing ones. The users gain more flexibility because a pool of methods is available. Several model problems establish connections between the tools and serve as a base for the efficient treatment of new problems.

Acknowledgements

The authors are indebted to Dr. P. Weidner for his substantial support. Several discussions with Dr. K.-U. Witt and W. Nagel are gratefully acknowledged.

References

[1] AERE Computer Science and Systems Division, Harwell Subroutine Library - A Catalogue of Subroutines, (AERE Harwell, UK, 1984).

[2] J. Bechlars - R. Buhtz, GKS in der Praxis (Springer–Verlag, Berlin - New York, 1986).

[3] R.F.Boisvert - R.A. Sweet, Mathematical Software for Elliptic Boundary Value Problems, in: W.R. Cowell, Ed., Sources and Development of Mathematical Software (Prentice-Hall, Englewood-Cliffs, 1984) 200-263.

[4] C.A. Brebbia, Ed., Finite Element Systems - A Handbook (Springer–Verlag, Berlin - New York, 1983).

[5] T.F. Chan - F. Saied, A Comparison of Elliptic Solvers for General Two-Dimensional Regions, SIAM J. Sci. Stat. Comput. 6 (1985) 742-760.

[6] P.M. Dew - J.E. Walsh, A Set of Library Routines for Solving Parabolic Equations in One Space Variable, ACM TOMS 7 (1981) 295-314.

[7] J.J. Dongarra - S.C. Eisenstat, Squeezing the Most out of an Algorithm in CRAY Fortran, ACM TOMS Vol. 10 (1984) 219-230.

[8] B. Engquist - T. Smedsaas, Automatic Computer Code Generation for Hyperbolic and Parabolic Differential Equations, SIAM J. Sci. Stat. Comput. 1 (1980) 249-259.

[9] B. Ford (Ed.), Problem Solving Environments for Scientific Computing, (North-Holland, Amsterdam, 1986).

[10] L.O. Hertzberger, The Architecture of Fifth Generation Inference Computers, FGCS 1 (1984) 9-21.

[11] F. Hoßfeld, Nonlinear Dynamics: A Challenge on High-Speed Computation, in: M. Feilmeier - J. Joubert - U. Schendel, Eds., Parallel Computing 83 (North-Holland, Amsterdam, 1984) 67-80.

[12] C.E. Houstis - E.N. Houstis - J.R. Rice, Partitioning and Allocation of PDE Computations in Distributed Systems, in: B. Engquist - T. Smedsaas, Eds., PDE Software, Modules, Interfaces and Systems (North-Holland, Amsterdam, 1984).

[13] E.N. Houstis - T.S. Papatheodorou, High-Order Fast Elliptic Equation Solver, ACM TOMS 5 (1979) 431-441.

[14] E.N. Houstis - W.F. Mitchell - J.R. Rice, Collocation Software for Second-Order Elliptical Partial Differential Equations, ACM TOMS 11 (1985) 379-412.

[15] IBM VM/SP System Product: System Product Interpreter Reference. SC24-5239.

[16] C.L. Lawson - R.J. Hanson - D.R. Kincaid - F.T. Krogh, Basic Linear Algebra Subprograms for Fortran Usage, ACM TOMS 5 (1979) 308-323.

[17] M. Machura - R.A. Sweet, A Survey of Software for Partial Differential Equations, ACM TOMS 6 (1980) 461-488.

[18] M. Machura, Problem Solving Environment for Partial Differential Equations: The User Perspective, in: B. Engquist - T. Smedsaas, Eds., PDE Software, Modules, Interfaces and Systems (North-Holland, Amsterdam, 1984).

[19] J. Mackerle - T. Andersson, Boundary Element Software in Engineering, Adv. Eng. Software 6 (1983) 66-102.

[20] N.K. Madsen - R.F. Sincovec, PDECOL, General Collocation Software for Partial Differential Equations, ACM TOMS 5 (1979) 326-351.

[21] D.K. Melgaard - R.F. Sincovec, General Software for Two-Dimensional Nonlinear Partial Differential Equations, ACM TOMS 7 (1981) 106-125.

[22] G. Meurant, The Conjugate Gradient Method on Supercomputers, Supercomputer Vol. 13 (1986) 9-17.

[23] D.P. O'Leary - O. Widlund, Solution of the Helmholtz Equation for the Dirichlet Problem on General Bounded Three-Dimensional Regions, ACM TOMS 7 (1981) 239-246.

[24] J.M. Ortega - R.G. Voigt, Solution of Partial Differential Equations on Vector and Parallel Computers, SIAM Review 27 (1985) 149-240.

[25] W. Proskurowski, Numerical Solution of Helmholtz's Equation by Implicit Capacitance Matrix Methods, ACM TOMS 5 (1979) 36-49.

[26] J.R. Rice, Software Parts for Elliptic PDE Software, in: B. Engquist - T. Smedsaas, Eds., PDE Software, Modules, Interfaces and Systems (North-Holland, Amsterdam, 1984).

[27] J.R. Rice - R.F. Boisvert, Elliptic Problem Solving with ELLPACK (Springer-Verlag, Berlin - New York, 1985).

[28] J.R. Rice - E.N. Houstis - W.R. Dyksen, A Population of Linear, Second Order Elliptic Partial Differential Equations on Rectangular Domains, Math. Comp. 36 (1981) 475-484.

[29] M.K. Seager, Parallelizing Conjugate Gradient for the CRAY X-MP, Parallel Computing Vol. 3 (1986) 35-47.

[30] G. Sewell, Analysis of a Finite Element Method. PDE/PROTRAN. (Springer-Verlag, Berlin - New York, 1985).

[31] R.F. Sincovec - N.K. Madsen, Software for Nonlinear Partial Differential Equations, ACM TOMS 1 (1975) 232-260.

[32] B.P. Sommeijer - P.J. van der Houwen, Software with Low Storage Requirements for Two-Dimensional Parabolic Differential Equations, ACM TOMS 10 (1984) 378-396.

[33] P.N. Swartztrauber - R.A. Sweet, Efficient FORTRAN Subprograms for the Solution of Separable Elliptic Partial Differential Equations, ACM TOMS 5 (1979) 352-364.

[34] A. van der Steen, Results on the Livermore Loops on some new Supercomputers, Supercomputer Vol. 12 (1986) 13-14.

[35] H.A. van der Vorst, The Performance of Fortran Implementations for Preconditioned Conjugate Gradients on Vector Computers, Parallel Computing Vol. 3 (1986) 49-58.

IMPLEMENTING CODES ON A SIMD / SPMD ARCHITECTURE
APPLICATION TO A SUBSET OF EISPACK *

Bernard PHILIPPE - Michèle RAPHALEN
IRISA / INRIA
Campus de Beaulieu
35042 Rennes Cedex FRANCE

0. Introduction.

The parallel computers are an efficient response to the needs of the scientific computation ; everyone may agree on this assertion but the discussion arises when it is time to select a parallel architecture.

At the lowest level, it seems that the desired computer must be able to process efficiently vector instructions. To reach this goal, the oldest idea was to build SIMD computers but, soon, pipelined processors were often prefered for their higher flexibility. Now, several pipelined processors can be interconnected asynchroneously ; hence they offer a two-level parallelism. Among the MIMD architectures, two classes can be defined :

- *architecture with shared memory* : the tightly-coupled processors can communicate through the global memory ; the communications are fast and they can be used efficiently to synchronize the different processes.

- *architecture with distibuted memory* : the processors are loosely-coupled and the communications, which are message-oriented, can be established directly from one of them to some others following some given topology of network ; a usual choice of network is a hypercube. There, an exchange has often a large start-up but also a large bandwidth. Hence, on these computers, it is very important to group the messages. For instance, global synchronizations highly deteriorate the performances.

The computers of the first class are efficient but often expensive ; those of the second class allow a larger degree of parallelism.

In this paper, our goal is not to respond on which computer to select, but to describe the possibilities of a third approach : the SIMD / SPMD architecture (Single Program Multiple Data stream) which is a SIMD architecture with the ability to break up into independent computers ; each of

* This work has been supported by the Centre Electronique de l'Armement (CELAR - French Ministry of Defense) under Grant n° 004 / 41 / 85.

them is made of a pair including a processor and its corresponding memory bank (there is already such a computer in France which is called OPSILA). Our object is to evaluate the efficiency of this architecture and how easy-to-use it is for numerical algorithms, namely in linear algebra. For this purpose, we selected some algorithms which seek for eigenvalues of a symmetric matrix and we adapted them to have a good efficiency on the architecture. The details of the implementation are given in [PhRa87].

After a description of the architecture and of the language which has been used (HELLENA), the algorithms and their implementation are shortly described. Different tests are reported on an emulator. Unfortunately, we cannot report experiments on OPSILA since they have just started. In the third section, we try to estimate the characteristics of the architecture for numerical computation.

1. Architecture and language.

1.1. The OPSILA architecture.

The OPSILA computer [AuBo86] is a vector / parallel computer which has been built at LASSY (Laboratoire Signaux et SYstèmes - Nice). The overall structure of the computer is given in figure 1.

The computer is made up of two main parts :

- the Scalar Control Unit (SCU)
- the Parallel Unit (PU)

The SCU is composed of a Scalar Processor (SP) and a Scalar Memory (SM). Scalar and vector instruction codes and scalar data are stored in the SM. The SP executes all scalar instructions. For every vector instruction, it initializes the instruction, ie. the descriptors of the involved vectors and of the vector instruction code, and sends this information to the PU.

In order that the SCU and PU run independently, they communicate via FIFO queues. The PU can use two processing modes :

- the SIMD (vector) mode
- the SPMD (parallel) mode

In SIMD mode, the NPROC PE's work under the control of the vector control unit and exchange data via the interconnection network (OMEGA network). The Instruction Processor (IP) fetches the descriptors of the vector instructions and their operands in the FIFO queues. A vector is a set of memory locations which addresses make an arithmetic sequence. An instruction processing vectors of length n is broken into $\lceil n / \mathrm{NPROC} \rceil$ sub-instructions processing vectors of length NPROC. The IP broadcasts the instructions to the PE's where they are executed.

In SPMD mode, the PE's run independently. The same code is duplicated in the NPROC memory banks and is decoded by the PE's. Each bank is associated with one PE. A PE can only process the data stored in its own bank. No data exchanges between the PE's are allowed in this mode.

Commuting between SIMD and SPMD modes corresponds to a FORK / JOIN mechanism.

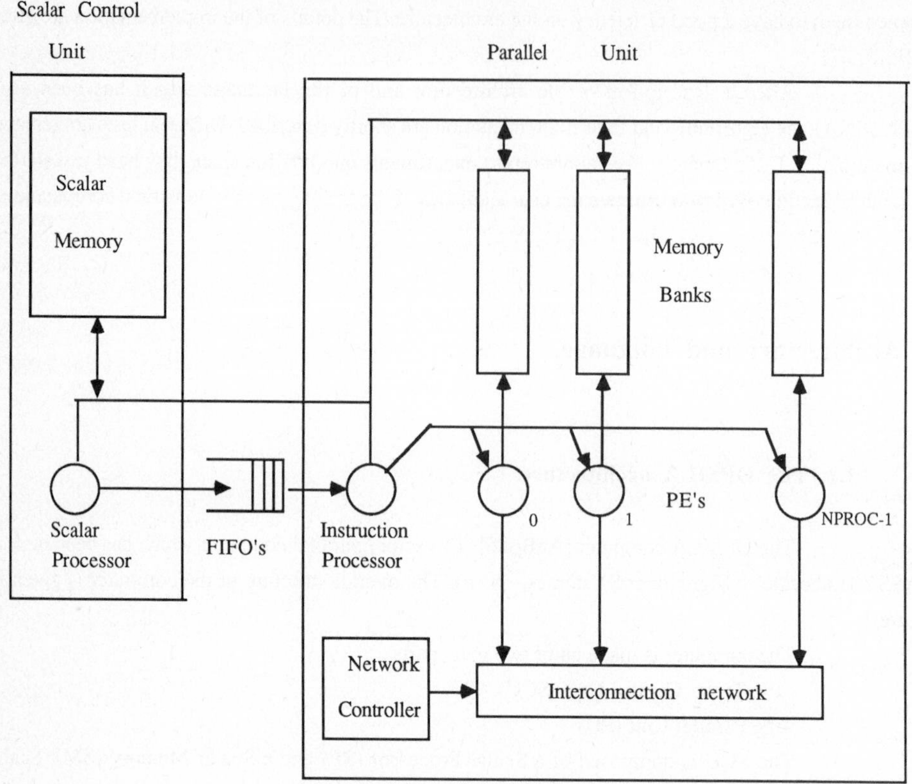

Figure 1-1 : Overview of the OPSILA architecture.

1.2. The language : HELLENA.

HELLENA [Je86] has been defined for writing applications on vector / parallel computers. It is based on the Pascal syntax with extensions for vector or SPMD instructions.

In HELLENA, the vector instructions arise from extending scalar operators to array operators. There are two ways for writing vector operations : either by referencing the vector itself, or by using the instruction **for_all** .

For example, let A, B, C be vectors of length n. One can write :

A:=B+C ;

or

```
for_all i in [1,n] :
 A(i):=B(i)+C(i) ;
end_for_all ;
```

The instruction **for_all** is the basic parallel instruction : its iterations are independent.

A special feature of the language is the *acces pattern.* . A pattern defines a subset of an array such as a row, a column, the diagonal of a matrix.
For instance the declaration :

```
pattern row of array [1,n]x[1,m] of real
            in array [1,n] of array [1,m] of real :
        for_all i in [1,n] :
          for_all j in [1,m] :
            (i,j)
          end_for_all ;
        end_for_all ;
```

defines the row acces pattern. Referencing row i of a two dimensional array A(n,m) will be done by : A.row(i).

The main interest for the patterns lies in their efficiency : the most part of index computing they involve is performed at compiling time.

A block of instructions to be run in SPMD mode is opened and closed by the instructions **spmd** and **end_spmd** which respectively correspond to the FORK and JOIN instructions.

Communications between the PE's are only allowed in SIMD mode. So, some variables have to be accessed in both modes. The declaration :

```
spmd
 variable x: real ;
end_spmd ;
```

creates NPROC reservations (one per bank). These locations form a vector of length NPROC which can be accessed in SIMD mode by : **in_spmd**'x.

The HELLENA compiler is made of three programs corresponding to the following steps :

- syntaxic analysis
- semantic analysis
- code production

The third step builds three files respectively containing the sequential, vector and SPMD codes.

The algorithms we shall now study are written in HELLENA. They have not been implemented on OPSILA, but on an emulator of this computer in order to measure the impact of the number of processors on the architecture [PhRa87].

2. Implemented algorithms.

We examine in this section the computation of the *eigensystem* of a *real symmetric dense matrix* A of order n.

Actually we restrict our paper to the methods leading to the computation of eigenvalues only. The algorithms we refer to are those defined by Wilkinson and Reinsch [WiRe71] and implemented in the EISPACK library [Ei76].

Which algorithm to select depends on the number of required eigenvalues.

If *all eigenvalues are required* , two methods are relevant :

- the Jacobi method : A sequence of Givens rotations is applied to the original matrix. The limit of the transformed matrices is a diagonal matrix where the diagonal entries are the eigenvalues of A. This method has been given up for a long time, but in parallel processing it presents a new interest, because one can choose to combine the rotations so that several elements are cancelled simultaneously in one step. However the complexity of the parallel algorithm remains the same ($O(n^3)$) for one sweep [BeSa86]. This makes the method competitive only for small matrices (order smaller than 100 for the Alliant FX / 8 [BeSa86]). When the order of A is high, the usual algorithm for finding all eigenvalues of A is the combination of

- Householder tridiagonalisation and QL algorithm : The algorithm is illustrated by the scheme :

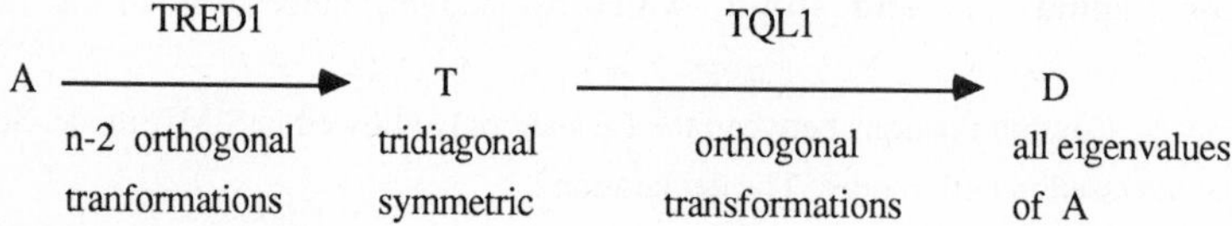

If *selected eigenvalues are required* a relevant method is the combination of

- Householder tridiagonalisation and bisection : The algorithm is illustrated by the scheme :

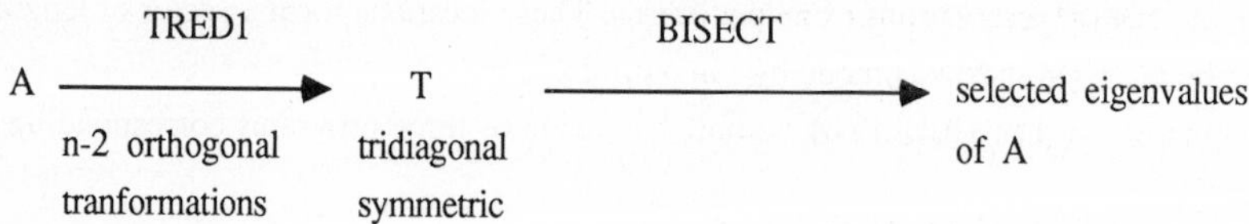

The border between the application domains of the last two methods is difficult to localize. However one can consider that when more than 40% of eigenvalues are required, the first scheme remains more efficient [Ei76].

We now examine the implentation of parallel versions of TRED1, TQL1 and BISECT on the OPSILA architecture.

2.1. Implementation of TRED1.

The original matrix is reduced to a symmetric tridiagonal matrix by a sequence of (n-2) orthogonal transformations. Each of these transformations is an orthogonal reflector on a hyperplane.

Since the whole algorithm can be expressed with vector operations, it is well suited to a SIMD architecture. But increasing the number of PE's does not consequently increase the speed-up in the same magnitude (Table 2-1). The loss of efficiency can be explained by :

- the length of involved vectors shrinks during the process. At the end, most of the PE's remain idle.

- furthermore, preparing a vector instruction is sequential. For short vectors, the time for initializing an instruction is large with respect to the computation time of the instruction.

	4 proc.	8 proc.	16 proc.
elapsed time	1.478	0.808	0.492
speed-up	1.0	1.8	3.0

(time unit : M cycle)

Table 2-1 : Speed-up of TRED1 on a matrix of order 64.

2.2. Implementation of TQL1.

The QL algorithm finds all the eigenvalues of a symmetric tridiagonal matrix

$T = [\, e_k \; d_k \; e_{k+1} \,] \in \mathbb{R}^{n \times n}$. It annihilates successively the sub-diagonal entries of T.

The s-th iteration is defined by :

$Q_s \,(T^{(s)} - k_s I) = L_s \;;\quad T^{(s+1)} = L_s \, Q_s^{\,t}$

where

- L_s is a lower triangular matrix.

- Q_s is an orthogonal matrix which is the product of (n-1) rotations.

- k_s is a shift which improves the rate of convergence.

The implemented algorithm is of SIMD type. It results of a study made by Sameh and Kuck [SaKu77]. A QL iteration consists in solving two linear recurrences (R1) and (R2). The vectors $d^{(s+1)}$ and $e^{(s+1)}$ of the diagonal and sub-diagonal entries of $T^{(s+1)}$ are functions of the solutions of the systems (R1) and (R2).

If we denote by A, B, C the following matrices

$$A=\begin{bmatrix} 0 & f_1^{(s)} & & 0 \\ & \ddots & \ddots & \\ & & & f_n^{(s)} \\ 0 & & & 0 \end{bmatrix} \quad B=\begin{bmatrix} 0 & 0 & e_2^{(s)2} & & 0 \\ & \ddots & \ddots & \ddots & \\ & & & & e_n^{(s)2} \\ & & & & 0 \\ 0 & & & & 0 \end{bmatrix} \quad C=\begin{bmatrix} 0 & e_1^{(s)2} & & 0 \\ & \ddots & \ddots & \\ & & & e_n^{(s)2} \\ 0 & & & 0 \end{bmatrix}$$

where $f_i^{(s)} = d_i - k_s$, we have to solve

$$(I - A + B) y = \boldsymbol{e}_{n+1} \quad \text{where } \boldsymbol{e}_{n+1} \text{ is the (n+1)-st unitary vector.} \qquad \text{(R1)}$$

$$(I - C) x = y^2 \qquad \text{(R2)}$$

Each of these two systems is solved in $\lceil \log_2(n+1) \rceil$ steps by the technic of recursive doubling [ChKu75]. The entries of $T^{(s+1)}$ are given by :

$$d_i^{(s+1)} = y_i \; y_{i+1} \; (r_i^{\,2} + e_i^{(s)\,2}) / x_i + s_i^{\,2} \; (d_{i-1}^{(s)} - k_s)$$

$$e_i^{(s+1)\,2} = s_i \; r_{i-1}$$

where

$$r_i^{\,2} = x_i / x_{i+1}$$

$$s_i = e_i^{(s+1)\,2} / r_i$$

The tests are done with the matrices L64=[-1,2,-1] of order 64 and W21+ of order 21 [Wi65].

Although the implemented QL algorithm involves a major part of vector computing, we observe that the saving in run time is not so good as expected when the number of PE's increases (Tables 2-2 and 2-3).

	4 proc.	8 proc.	16 proc.
elapsed time	2.213	1.128	0.738
speed-up	1.0	1.8	3.0

(time unit : M cycle)

Table 2-2 : Speed-up of TQL1 on the matrix L64.

We have seen (§ 2-1) that working on short vectors deteriorates the performances of an algorithm : in QL algorithm, the tridiagonal blocks become smaller and smaller when the work goes forward. Furthermore, the loop of the recursive doubling processes vectors which length is divided by two at each step.

	4 proc.	8 proc.	16 proc.
elapsed time	0.193	0.135	0.109
speed-up	1.0	1.4	1.8

(time unit : M cycle)

Table 2-3 : Speed-up of TQL1 on the matrix W21+.

Vectorizing a QL iteration by the technic of recursive doubling introduces additional computing. For that reason, when the number of PE's is small (<16), the use of a sequential version of TQL1 gives better results : for the matrix L64 and NPROC = 4, the sequential algorithm run twice faster than the vector algorithm.

2.3. TREPS : a parallel version of BISECT.

In EISPACK, the algorithm BISECT seeks for the eigenvalues of the tridiagonal matrix T which belong to a given interval I = [a, b]. This algorithm is based upon the Sturm sequence property. $p_n(\lambda)$ denoting the characteristic polynomial of T, the sequence of the principal minors of the matrix can be built using the following recursion [Wi65].

$$p_o(\lambda) = 1,$$

$$p_1(\lambda) = d_1 - \lambda, \qquad (2\text{-}1)$$

$$p_i(\lambda) = (d_i - \lambda)\, p_{i-1}(\lambda) - e_i^2\, p_{i-2}(\lambda), \quad i = 2, \ldots, n.$$

We assume that no subdiagonal element is zero, since if some e_i is equal to 0, the problem can be partitioned into two smaller problems. The sequence $\{ p_i(\lambda) \}$ is called the *Sturm sequence of* T *in* λ. The number of eigenvalues which are smaller than a given λ is equal to the number of sign variations in the Sturm sequence (2-1). Hence one can locate the eigenvalues by computing the Sturm sequences in selected points. Unfortunately, sometimes there arise under- or overflows in the computation of the recursion (2-1). To take care of this problem, the sequence $\{ p_i(\lambda) \}$ is replaced by the sequence $\{ q_i(\lambda) \}$ where

$$q_i(\lambda) = p_i(\lambda) / p_{i-1}(\lambda)\ ,\ i = 1, \ldots, n\ ;$$

hence, the recursion becomes

$$q_1(\lambda) = d_1 - \lambda, \tag{2-2}$$

$$q_i(\lambda) = d_i - \lambda - e_i^2 / q_{i-1}(\lambda), \quad i = 2, ..., n$$

and now, the number of negative terms are counted instead of the number of sign variations. Therefore, given an initial interval, we can find the eigenvalues lying in it by repeated bisection of the interval.

Since the computation of a Sturm sequence is highly sequential, the parallelism can be obtained by performing simultaneously the computation of several sequences. However, there are two ways for achieving this :

- performing bisection on several intervals,
- performing a partition of one interval into several intervals by a multisection which computes the Sturm sequences in several equally-spaced points of the interval.

It has been shown [LoPS87] that, in order to insure a good efficiency, the process can be split into two steps :

- isolation of the eigenvalues by repeated multisection,
- extraction of every eigenvalue from its interval.

For extracting an eigenvalue, we prefer to use the so-called algorithm *zeroin* [FoMM77] rather than bisection. That algorithm, which is based upon the sequent method, computes the zero of a function on a given interval ; here, it has been adapted to our problem to insure a better reliability : although the value $p_n(\lambda)$ is needed, the computation uses the recursion (2-2) and the algorithm can switch to bisection whenever $p_n(\lambda)$ is too small.

The whole algorithm is then

(i) look for zero entries e_i which allow to consider submatrices for the process ;

(ii) for every submatrix,

(ii-a) isolate the corresponding eigenvalues which lie in the interval I ;

(ii-b) extract the isolated eigenvalues from their interval ;

(ii-c) merge the sorted list of eigenvalues which corresponds to the submatrix with the general list.

Actually, the amount of computation which is involved in steps (i) and (ii-c) is negligeable with respect to the others steps. We focus now on the implementation of steps (ii-a) and (ii-b).

For the *isolating process*, every multisection computes NPROC Sturm sequences in parallel ; this computation is performed in SIMD mode but it has to take care of the special case (extremely rare) when a term of the sequence $\{ q_i(\lambda) \}$ vanishes ; this is done by the procedure MUSECT ; the HELLENA code is given in Table 2-4.

The *extraction of an eigenvalue* is an iterative process. Then for step (ii-b), we have to write an algorithm which can be expressed by a do-all loop since every extraction does not depend

```
MUSECT( value lb, ub : reel ; neval : integer ;
        variable S : array one_integer of integer ;) :
    ! This procedure computes the Sturm sequences in neval equally spaced points

    ! within the interval [lb, ub].

  variable

    U, V : array [1, nproc] of real ;
    h : real ;
    begin
        h := (ub - lb) / (neval + 1) ;

        for_all  k  in  [1, neval] :

            V(k) := lb + k * h ;
            U(k) := D(p) - V(k) ;
            S(k) := if  (U(k) < zero) then  1  else  0  end_if ;
        end_for_all ;
        for  i := p+1 increment to q
        loop
            if ( Union( U = zero) ) then

                for_all  k  in [1, neval] :
                    U(k) := D(i) - V(k) - (if U(k) = zero   then abs(E(i)) / macheps
                                                             else E2(i) / U(k) end_if ) ;
                    if (U(k) < zero) then S(k) := S(k) + 1 ; end_if ;

                end_for_all ;

                                   else

                for_all  k  in [1, neval] :
                    U(k) := D(i) - V(k) -  E2(i) / U(k) ;
                    if (U(k) < zero) then S(k) := S(k) + 1 ; end_if ;

                end_for_all ;
            end_if ;
        end_loop ;
    end ;
```

Table 2-4 : Example of SIMD code in HELLENA.

upon other extractions. This part of the algorithm is especially adapted to the SPMD mode : every processor can extract independently the list of eigenvalues corresponding to the intervals which are stored in its own memory banck ; the SPMD section of the code is given in Table 2-5.

```
spmd
        for j := 1 to nevbank
        loop
                EXTRACT( FSTEV(j), LB(j), RB(j) ) ;
        end_loop ;
end_spmd ;
```

Table 2-5 : Example of SPMD section of code in HELLENA.

To evaluate the efficiency of the code TREPS, all the eigenvalues of two different matrices have been sought. The matrix $L64 = [-1, 2, -1]$ is a good example of matrix with well-separated eigenvalues ; on it, TREPS concentrates most of its work during the extraction step. On the contrary, for the matrix $W21^+$ [Wi65], the eigenvalues are mainly computed during the isolation step since most of them are belonging to pairs of almost equal eigenvalues. These runs have been reported in Tables 2-6 and 2-7. The speed-ups which are exhibited seem to be fairly low even for L64; actually, the order of the matrices (and consequently the number of eigenvalues) is

	4 proc.	8 proc.	16 proc.
elapsed time	1.073	0.629	0.555
speed-up	1.0	1.7	2.1

(time unit : M cycle)

Table 2-6 : Speed-up of TREPS on the matrix L64.

	4 proc.	8 proc.	16 proc.
elapsed time	0.367	0.291	0.273
speed-up	1.0	1.3	1.3

(time unit : M cycle)

Table 2-7 : Speed-up of TREPS on the matrix $W21^+$.

small compared to the number of processors ; for L64 and 16 processors there are only 4 eigenvalues to be extracted for each processor and then these tasks can be not balanced. For W21+, the eigenvalues are computed by multisection and it is known [LoPS87] that it is not efficient to compute a small number of eigenvalues by large multisection, since it increases the number of Sturm sequence to compute. To evaluate the degree of parallelism with respect to the number of eigenvalues, we run TREPS on the matrix L32 seeking at every time a new number of eigenvalues ; runs were done for 4 and 8 processors in order to be consistent with the small size of the matrix. Results are reported in figure 2-8.

Taking these remarks into account, we can expect a good behaviour of the algorithm on a real computer for larger problems. There exists already efficient versions of TREPS for CRAY X-MP/48 and Alliant FX-8 but our goal here was to prove that the algorithm was well-adapted to a SIMD/SPMD architecture.

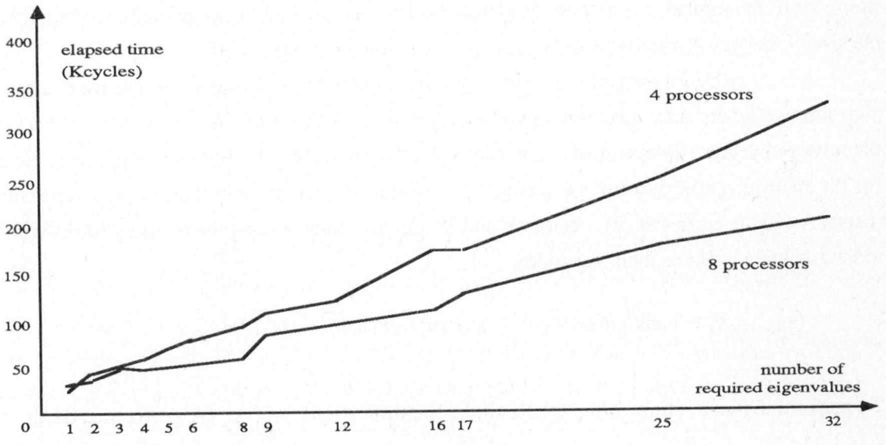

Figure 2-8 : Elapsed time with respect to the required number of eigenvalues (L32).

3. Advantages and disadvantages of a SIMD / SPMD architecture.

In this section, we want to describe the characteristics of the studied architecture and the algorithms which are well-suited to it.

First of all, vector computation is efficient on a SIMD computer . This is the lowest level of parallelism but not the less important ; for instance, the programs TRED1 and TQL1 are relevant to this class of algorithms.

SPMD mode allows do-all instructions. When in an algorithm all the iterations of a

number of processors	4	8	16
ratio SIMD / SPMD	3.9	3.9	3.1

Table 3-1 : Ratio of elapsed time between two versions of TREPS.

loop are independent they can be run in parallel in any order. By distributing them among the processors, they can be run in SPMD mode. For instance, in TREPS the extraction step was easy to express in this mode ; to evaluate its efficiency, this step has been also expressed in SIMD mode. The comparison with the original program is reported in Table 3-1 : the superiority of the original code is clear. In SPMD mode, the repartition of the iterations of a do-all loop is static (known at compiling time) but if the number of iterations is clearly higher than the number of processors then, on average, the size of the task is usually of the same magnitude for every processor.

SPMD mode allows some lack of regularity in the data. Sometimes, although the algorithm under consideration is made of vector instructions it cannot be considered of this kind since the involved vectors do not satisfy the definition of a vector (§ 1-1). For instance, this is the situation for the multiplication of a full vector by a sparse matrix : we assume that the non-zero entries of a matrix A and the entries of two vectors V and W are distributed among the memory banks with respect to their column index or their row index

$$(a_{ij}, x_j, y_j \in \text{bank}_k) \Longleftrightarrow (j \equiv k \mod \text{NPROC}).$$

To perform the instruction Y := A * X, all the multiplications $a_{ij} * x_j$ are performed during a SPMD step ; then these contributions are sent by circular permutations in SIMD mode to the bank which contains y_i.

Let us now look at the limits of the SPMD mode.

Broadcasting is frequent but efficient . Since there are no communications between processors in SPMD mode, it is usually necessary to duplicate the read-only data which are shared by all the iterations of the do-all loop before its execution. This was done in TREPS, with the tridiagonal matrix which is needed to compute the Sturm sequences. Hopefully, the network can broadcast efficiently these data.

Distributing the data among the banks is sometimes difficult. For instance in TREPS, the data structure corresponding to the list of intervals containing an eigenvalue is built during the isolation step (SIMD) while it is used during the extraction step (SPMD). In order to be able to access the same array in both modes, it is necessary to declare it in SPMD mode and then to identify it with a SIMD array. We can expect to have some pre-defined procedures to handle this problem at least for one-dimensional arrays.

There is no fine synchronization between tasks. The only way to synchronize the processes in SPMD mode is to turn back to the other mode ; consequently, the only synchronization on the architecture is of FORK-JOIN type. In this situation, it does not seem to be efficient to consider pipelined algorithm like do-across loops on this architecture. For the same argument, Divide-and-Conquer algorithms are not either well-suited for it ; moreover, data structure of these parallel algorithms would be hardly implementable.

4. Conclusion.

In this paper, we reported how a numerical library could be implemented on a SIMD / SPMD architecture. Some different kinds of procedures have been tested : they were selected to form a good sample. The tests were done on a simulator ; soonly, they should be done on the computer OPSILA. This implementation was also a way to evaluate how easy-to-use and how efficient can be this kind of architecture. Here are the outlines of what we feel after this experiment.

The best parallel architecture for our purpose is a MIMD computer with shared memory and vector processors. This fact does not seem to be questionable but it is an expensive choice and the extent of parallelism for these computers is usually limited except for hierarchical architectures as Cedar [KLSD84]. If we do not have at our disposal such a computer, we can project to use a multiprocessor with distributed memory like hypercubes. It is our feeling that a SIMD / SPMD architecture can be more efficient for most of the numerical algorithms. Hypercubes are profitable for pipelined algorithms like systolic algorithms for instance. In the contrary, the SIMD / SPMD architecture is profitable for vector computation and algorithms organized around do-all loops. For hypercubes, there is often a bottleneck with the high cost of the communications. This is specially true at the end of the process, when the partial results have to be brought back to the host. For the last class of parallel algorithms (Divide-and-Conquer algorithms), they can be implemented on hypercubes but not very easily, while it is hardly possible in SPMD mode.

In conclusion, let us say that the SPMD mode is not a universal response for multiprocessing in numerical computation but it can be a good compromise. Its field of application could include for instance image processing, finite element methods with domain decomposition or sorting algorithms.

REFERENCES

[AuBo86] AUGUIN M., BOERI F., *The OPSILA computer* , Proceedings of the International Workshop on Parallel algorithms &Architectures, Luminy, France, M. Cosnard and al. (editors), North-Holland, 1986, pp 143-153.

[BeSa86] BERRY M., SAMEH A., *Multiprocessor Jacobi algorithms for dense symmetric eigenvalue and singular value decomposition* , ICPP, Aug.19-22, 1986,pp 433-440.

[ChKu75] CHEN S.C., KUCK D., *Time and parallel processor bounds for linear recurrences systems* , IEEE Trans. Computers., Vol C24-7, 1975, pp 701-717.

[EI76] EISPACK GUIDE, *Matrix eigensystem routines* , Lecture notes in Computer Science n° 6, Springer-Verlag, 1976.

[FoMM77] FORSYTHE G.E., MALCOLM M.A., MOLER C.B., *Computer methods for mathematical computation* , Prentice Hall, 1977.

[KLSD84] KUCK D., LAWRIE D., SAMEH A., DAVIDSON E., *Construction of a large-scale multiprocessor* , Cedar document n° 45, University of Illinois at Urbana-Champaign, 1984.

[Je86] JEGOU Y., *HELLENA* , Rapport technique IRISA, 1986.

[LoPS87] LO S.S., PHILIPPE B., SAMEH A., *A multiprocessor algorithm for the symmetric tridiagonal eigenvalue problem* , SIAM Journal on Sc.and Stat. Comp., Vol. 8 n°2 - March 1987.

[PhRa87] PHILIPPE B., RAPHALEN M., *Recherche des éléments propres d'une matrice symétrique sur une architecture parallèle (SIMD / SPMD),* Rapport INRIA, to appear.

[SaKu77] SAMEH A., KUCK D., *A parallel QR algorithm for symmetric tridiagonal matrices* , IEEE Trans. Computers., Vol C 26, 1977, pp 147-153.

[Wi65] WILKINSON J.H., *The algebraic eigenvalue problem* , Oxford, 1965.

[WiRe71] WILKINSON J.H., REINSCH C., *Handbook for automatic computation* , Vol 2, Linear Algebra, Springer-Verlag, 1971.

SUPERCOMPUTING ABOUT PHYSICAL OBJECTS

John R. Rice*
Computer Science Department
Purdue University
West Lafayette, IN 47907
U.S.A.

Abstract

Scientific and technological advances in the next 5 to 10 years will make it feasible to create an integrated, interactive system for the design, manipulation and analysis of collections of physical objects. These advances will come in computing power through the mechanism of *parallel computation*, in *algorithms for geometry*, in *problem solving systems* to provide very high level user interfaces and in *graphics* to allow direct visualization of the behavior of the physical objects. In this paper we describe the project *Computing about Physical Objects* which is to explore the associated technical problems and to build prototypes of such systems. The focus here is upon the role of supercomputers in this area and, especially, their application to solving the partial differential equations that model many physical phenomena.

1. INTRODUCTION

Scientific and technological advances in the next 5 to 10 years will make it feasible to create an integrated, interactive system for the design, manipulation and analysis of collections of physical objects. These advances will come in *computing power* through the mechanism of parallel computation, in *algorithms for geometry* computations and manipulations, in *problem solving systems* to provide very high level user interfaces and in *graphics* to allow direct visualization of the behavior of the physical objects. In this paper we describe the project *Computing about Physical Objects* at Purdue University which is to explore the technical problems arising from creating these systems and to build prototypes of them. The focus is upon the role of supercomputers in this area and, especially, their application to solving the partial differential equations (PDEs) that model many physical phenomena.

The capabilities that are required for these systems fall into four categories:

Physical phenomena models. One must have accurate models and reliable methods to solve the resulting equations for things like heat flow, mechanics, combustion, structural analysis, fluid flow, etc.

Geometric designs and models. One must be create shapes easily and with great versatility. Most details of the creation must be automated and the results must be displayed in an informative, realistic fashion. Further, manipulation must be easy and allow for dynamic shape changes, motions, interactions, etc.

Software systems. Very high level, applications oriented user interfaces must be provided with the bulk of the problem solving automated. Large and diverse software systems must be integrated at a high level.

* Research supported in part by Strategic Defense Initiative grant ARO DAA929-83-K-0026.

Computing resources. The machines to support this system will require gigaflops of power, many megawords of memory with many gigawords of auxiliary storage and communication bandwidths of many megabytes/sec. to support 3D color movies.

2. COMPUTING ABOUT PHYSICAL OBJECTS

We are developing the tools for computing with models of physical objects. In the course of this work, we face problems of how to represent objects by suitable models, how to manipulate and edit these models, how to analyze and simulate the behavior of modeled objects. To see the varied nature of the work, and to gain a first impression the project consider designing a small water cooled piston engine diagramed in Figure 1.

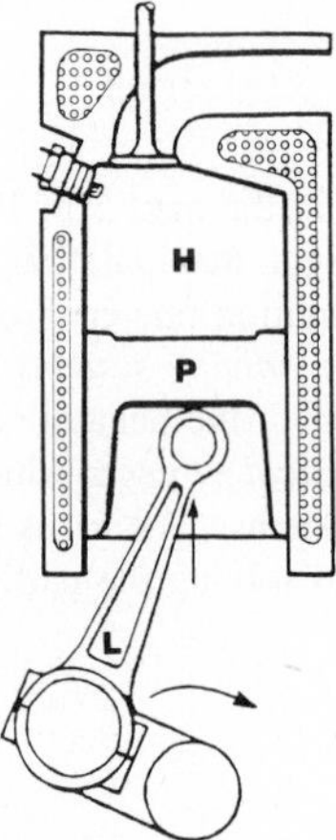

Figure 1. Cross section of a piston Engine. The source of heat and force is at H, the coolant within the block is shown with bubbles. The housing of the linkage L to the piston P is not shown.

Imagine we are at a point where the piston and its linkage to the crank shaft have been designed. Now we wish to design the block such that the engine is kept cool, strong, and light. So, the exterior geometry of the block must be designed, the shape and location of the water cooling lines must be determined, and a suitable material for the block must be selected.

Having chosen the shapes, assisted by a geometric modeling interface, the user must solve a system of partial differential equations (PDEs) to analyze the heat flow and stresses associated with this geometry and choice of block material. He may wish to simulate running the engine at different speeds which changes the strength of the heat source and the stresses on the moving parts. Systems of ordinary differential equations (ODEs) describe the acceleration and constraint forces on the piston linkage. With access to sufficient computing power, a user can quickly explore a wide range of shapes and materials preliminary to a refined, optimized final design.

What is involved in creating and simulating this scenario? First, complex object models must be created and coordinated. The geometric modeling subproject provides tools for this. The models are created through a user interface and require much automatic design support from the system. For example, the geometric design of piston and linkage requires a sophisticated solid modeling system. The ODEs describing the dynamic behavior of the piston linkage can then be derived automatically by the system for the geometry and material composition of the links. A subproject, called Project Newton, builds such a system. PDEs model the physical behavior such as heat flow, stresses and strains. They are identified and numerical methods are selected that are well suited to the problem's nature and the desired accuracy. A subproject, called Mathematical Software Systems, does this. The user should be allowed to specify a sacrifice some accuracy for the sake of speed or economy, the system can then allocate the computation among the available resources to achieve this objective - without detailed intervention by the user. The parallel processing subproject provides tools for this.

All aspects of this work require very high powered workstations and sophisticated graphics backed up by supercomputer power. Because of the scope of the effort, all projects use a very high level approach to software development and integration that must be backed up by powerful computing resources. The relationship of the principal subprojects is shown in Figure 2. We summarize each here.

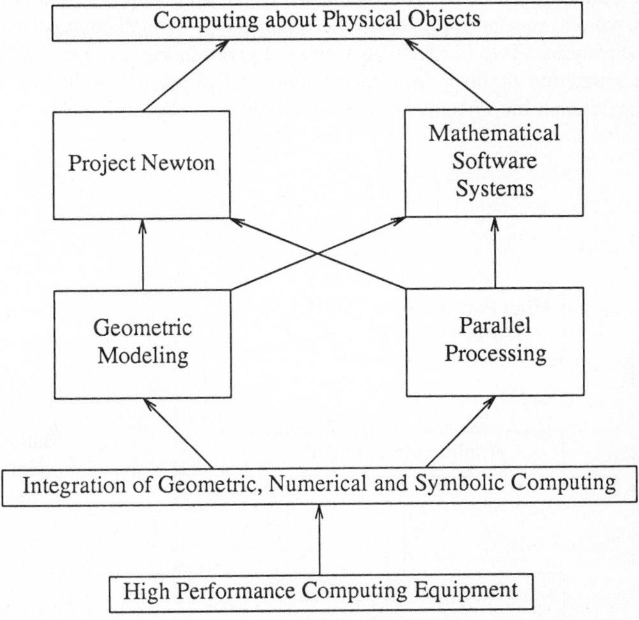

Figure 2. The relationship of the subprojects of Computing about Physical Objects.

Project Newton. The goal of this research is to develop a highly modularized and extensive system that duplicates the precise behavior of physical objects from their models. The work is part of a consortium effort involving groups both at Cornell and Purdue University.

Geometric Modeling. Geometric and solid modeling has reached a plateau that cannot be elevated unless a number of basic computational problems in mathematics are solved efficiently. This subproject focuses on these problems. Its results, as they mature, will impact the other projects significantly.

Mathematical Software Systems. A high level mathematical software system targeted toward elliptic partial differential equations is already operational. Its principal components are an interactive, mathematically based, graphically oriented interface and a broad range of problem solving modules. This 100,000+ lines of code system is built using various software tools so that it can readily evolve and be enhanced. It is an ideal vehicle to test approaches to future systems for computations about physical objects.

Parallel Processing. Computing with physical models requires enormous computing power which will come mostly from massive parallelism. Our work concentrates on three of the many aspects of this problem area. First, we will be heavily involved in the algorithmic infrastructure both for numeric and geometric computation. Second, we will study how to create an intelligent system for resource allocation without burdensome user input or intervention. We will consider both tightly coupled computing environments where algorithm specific, synchronous approaches seem to be most promising, and loosely coupled environments where we will concentrate on very general, heuristic approaches to resource allocation. Finally, we will monitor performance issues continually.

3. GEOMETRY BASED APPROACH

Our approach is based on the ELLPACK system described in [Rice and Borsvert, 1985] and [Rice, 1987]. The philosophy and many of the details of our approach is given there so instead of describing ELLPACK, we present our approach to the organization of mathematical software systems for partial differential equations. Two hierarchical views are given in Figures 3 and 4. Figure 3 shows five levels of software separating the user from the computing facility, levels that we believe will be present in most large scale scientific systems of the next decade.

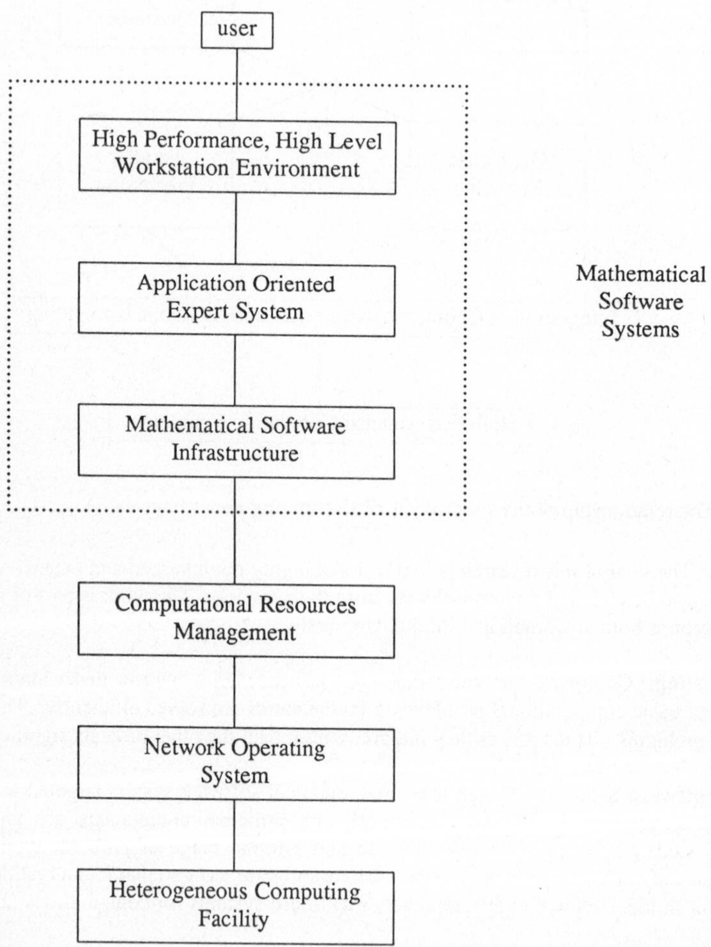

Figure 3. Schematic of the future organization of scientific computing. The mathematical software systems area is indicated by the dotted box.

Figure 4 shows the mathematical software system for this project. The workstation environment and application oriented expert system of Figure 3 is shown as the *user interface* here. It must communicate with the user in his own terms, thus if one is designing engine cylinders, then this interface must have a relevant vocabulary (e.g., piston, valve, block, ...) and operators (e.g., run engine, open valve, increase bore, ...). The mathematical software infrastructre of Figure 3 is decomposed into four layers in Figure 4. The top is the *physical objects system* which is application independent but which provides all the facilities to create, manipulate, simulate and analyze collection of physical objects.

The *physical objects* are self contained objects (in the sense of object oriented programming) that represent a specific physical object in the computational model. A physical object is partitioned into a collection of computational domains. Three reasons for this are: a) to separate physical phenomena. For example, the stresses and heat flows in a cylinder wall might be computed by unrelated software packages using completely different methods; b) iterative and time marching methods sometimes need two or three "copies" of the physical object; c) to divide the work. For example, if 100 processors

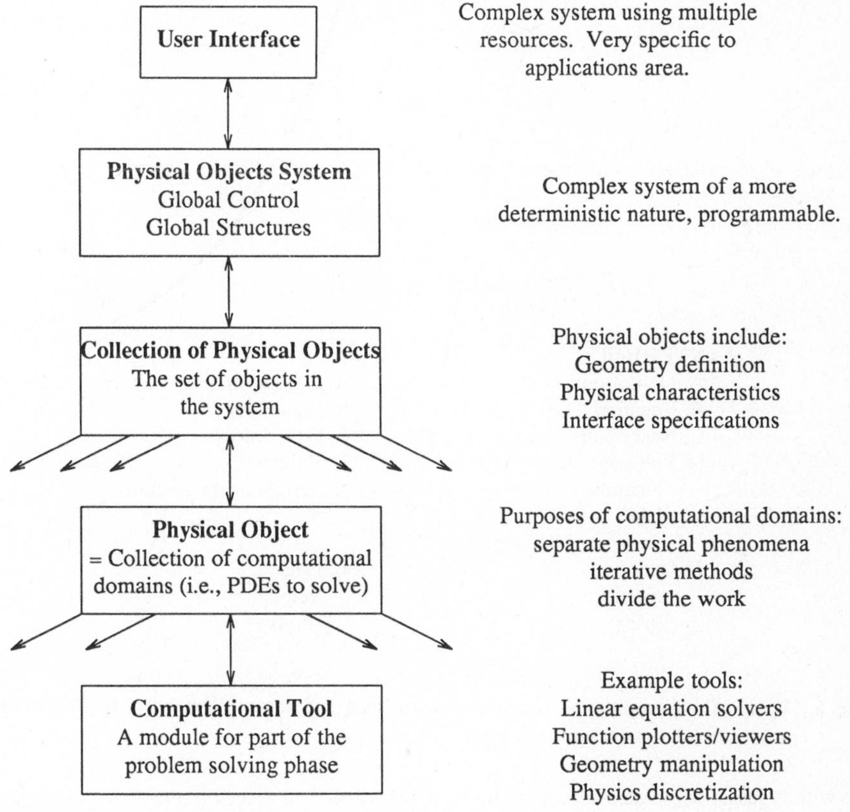

Figure 4. Hierarchical view of the mathematical software system to be used in the Computing about Physical Objects project.

were applied to computing the heat distribution in an engine block, then the block could be partitioned into 100 subdomains.

The *computational tools* in Figure 4 are the nuts and bolts of the software infrastructure. These include libraries of numerical methods, packages to display functions and shapes, procedures to move or modify basic geometric objects and so forth. There may well be a time where the computing facility contains hardware implementations of some of these tools. It will then be the task of the computational resources manager (see Figure 3) to access this hardware using the network operating system.

A key design concept in this project is to make the geometry the basic data structure. Equations, arrays, grids, properties, etc., are then attached to this data structure to create the full description (data structure) of the physical object. This is illustrated in Figure 5 where a computational domain is shown

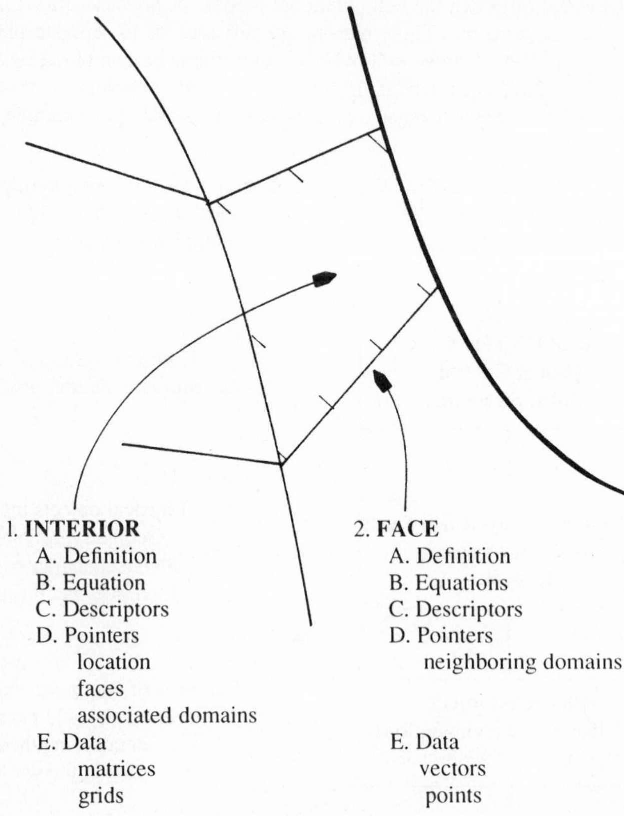

Figure 5. View of a Computation domain with interior and faces. The types of information in the associated data structures are listed.

along with types of associated information. Note that object interfaces (*faces*) have separate and complete data structures of the same nature as the domain's. A hypothetical example of the information about the two objects in Figure 5 follows.

1. Domain: **Lefthub -u**

   A. Faces (Top 1, Left 1, Left 2, Bot 2), Clockwise

   B. Variable = u

$$u_{xx} + \sigma(x,y,\mu) * u_{yy} - cos(x*v)*u = L(x,y,\tau)$$

   C. Solid brass, heat flow

D. Subframe (4,7)
Faces: Top 1, Left 1, Left 2, Bot 2
Copy: Lefthub -v
Map: Lefthub -u.mp.1, MAP.Lefthub-u.1 (x, y)

E. A(627,83), A.low(627,83), A.up(627,83)
x.grid(32), y.grid(21), grid.pts(32,21)

2. Face: **Top1 -u**

A. Parametrized, Ends (p, 2.2, 3.7)

B. B. u_x + *coeff* 4* (u – w) = coef 5(v)
Ends: (0.7, 8.2), (1.2, 9.6)
Copy: Top1 -v, Botleft -w
Domains: Lefthub -u
Map: Top1 -u.mp.1, MAP.Lefthub -u.1 (x, y)

C. Ellipse, continuous convection

D. Subframe (3,7)

E. xvals(12), yvals(12), params(12), type(12)
coeff5.vals(12), W.vals(12), BC.array(12,3)

4. ORGANIZATION OF THE COMPUTATIONAL SYSTEM

Figure 6 shows a high level block diagram of the computational system for Computing about Physical Objects. Note that the user appears twice, once at the top while the problem is being formulated and analyzed and at the bottom while the problem is being solved. The "expert" access to the system (appear right) is where information about the performance of software modules and machine is entered into the system. Due to space limitations, we do not discuss in detail most of this diagram, see the references for more information. We do discuss the parts most relevant to supercomputing: machine selection and problem partition.

Figure 7 shows the structure of the *machine selection* component of the system. We note at the top that a lot of information about the problem to be solved is collected by the user interface system. The

The computing facility to be used at Purdue initially includes common workstations, an Alliant FX/1 as a workstation, LISP machines, a Cyber 205 (2 pipe, 2 megawords), a FLEX/32 (7 processors) and an NCUBE (128 processors). There are also numerous mini-computers (VAX 11/780, 11/785, 8600) on the network.

If multiprocessors are available (as they will be for this project) then one must consider partitioning computations assigned to them. We envisage using precompiled libraries for problem solving so that any vectorization or parallelization is done independently of the specific problem to be solved. However, many numerical algorithms can be parametrized nicely in various ways and we plan to creat a software modules are to be analyzed in advance to obtain formulas to estimate computational requirements using this data. This allows concrete estimates to be made for the machines available and predicted performances are produced (they may well be reviewed by the user) which are the basis for the machine selection. At this point one can incorporate work load information about the available machines, we already have an experimental system for this. The selections are made on the basis of various values and these may be applied either statically (the computation is scheduled once and for all) or dynamically. Note a large and complex computation may be developed in this environment which has many different modules and phases. Thus we will systematically explore techniques to distribute different parts of the computation among different machines.

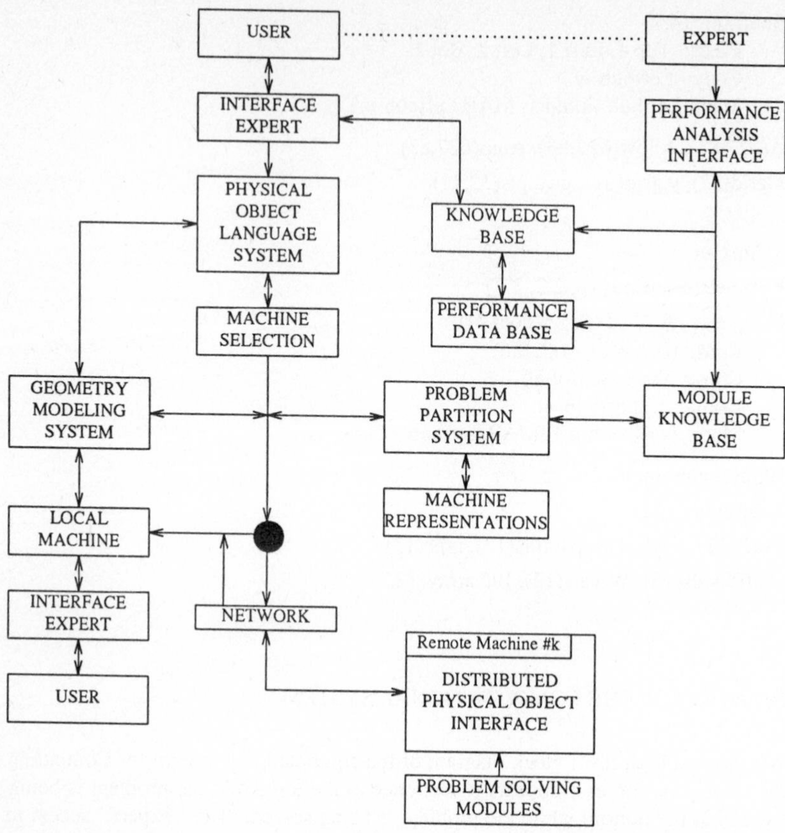

Figure 6. General high level block diagram of the computational system for the Computing about Physical Objects project.

partitioning environment where we can vary the amount of partitioning. For example, a ''small'' computation might be created by using 32 subdomains plus library modules with 32 as a parameter. A larger computation might use 256 subdomains on 256 processors plus the same library modules with 32 changed to 256. This approach is illustrated schematically in Figure 8 where the dotted line separates the advance software structure setup from the actual problem partition step.

5. THE PRINCIPAL TECHNICAL PROBLEMS AREAS

We now list the seven principal technical problem areas along with references to recent Purdue work in each area. One should also consult [Bajaj et. al., 1987] for an overview of the project. We see that the group at Purdue has already invested a large effort building up to this project, over 50 papers published in these seven areas and there are many unpublished technical reports. Thus we have a good start on the project but there is still an enormous amount of basic research, experimentation and development to be done to create these systems.

AREA 1: PDE Solvers. These software modules must be general, robust, efficient and parallelizable. The special emphasis at Purdue has been in collocation methods (using splines or piecewise polynomi-

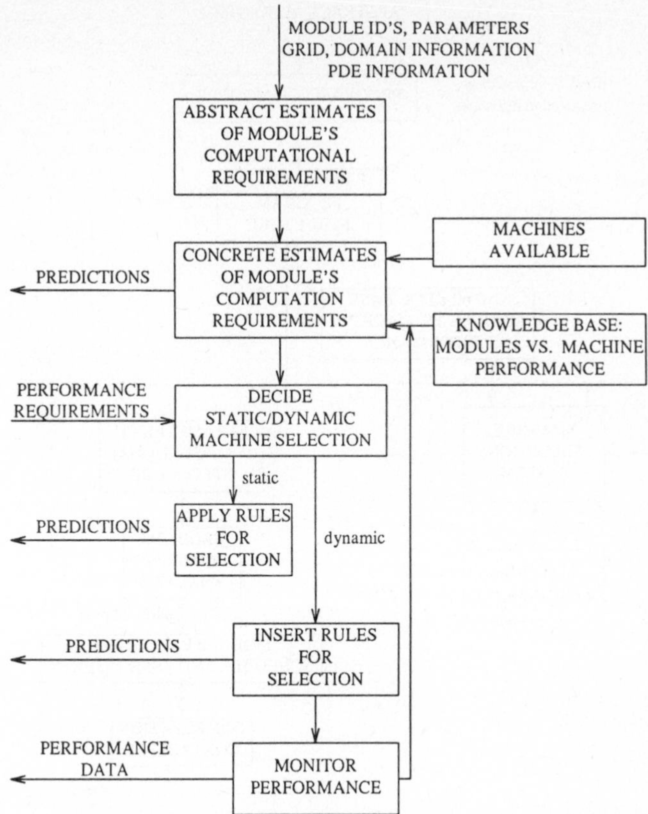

Figure 7. Schematic of the machine selection subsystem.

als), high order finite difference methods and adaptive methods. [Birkhoff and Lynch, 1985], [E. Houstis et. al., 1987], [E. Houstis et. al., 1988], [Lynch and Rice, 1978], [Rice, 1986a], [Rice, 1987a], [Rice, 1987c]

AREA 2: Partitioning of Parallel Computations. The partitioning (or program restructuring) can occur at compile time, load time or run time. It must be automatic but user controllable and be effective. [C. Houstis et. al., 1987a]

AREA 3: Actual Software System. It must be modular, hierarchically structured, efficient and machine adaptable. The Purdue group has built one PDE solving system with about 120,000 lines of Fortran code. [E. Houstis et. al., 1985a], [E. Houstis et. al., 1985b], [E. Houstis et. al., 1985c], [Rice, 1987b], [Rice and Boisvert, 1985], [Rice et. al., 1986]

AREA 4: Performance Analysis and Control. One must be able to predict with reasonable confidence both execution times and accuracy achieved. This involves benchmarking both hardware and software speeds, parametrizing software modules appropriately and, most difficult of all, assessing the actual accuracy of numerical methods. Extensive evaluation of PDE software performance has been done at Purdue. [Boisvert et. al., 1979], [Dyksen et. al., 1984], [C. Houstis et. al., 1987b], [Ribbens and Rice, 1986], [Rice, 1986b], [Rice, 1986c], [Rice et. al., 1981]

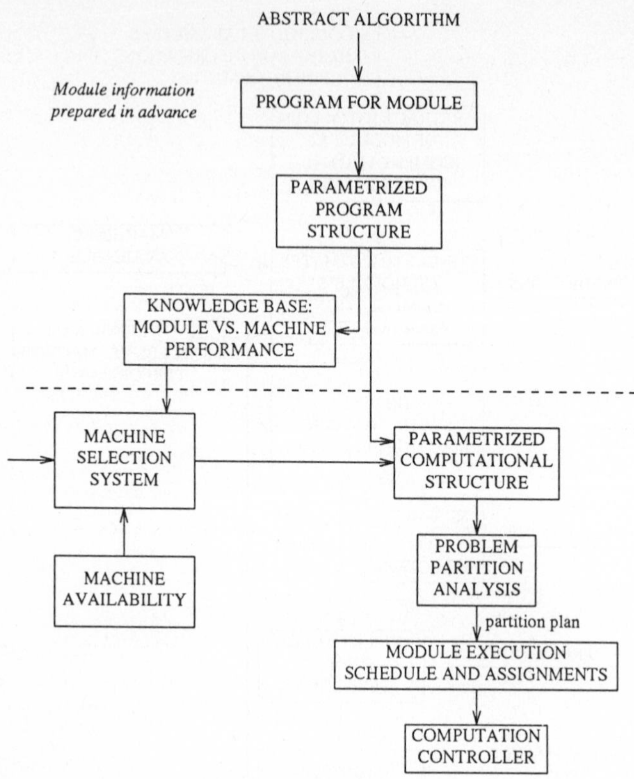

Figure 8. Schematic of the problem partition subsystem. The dotted line separates the advance software structure setup from the actual partition actions.

AREA 5: Computation Control. One must make reasonable resource use estimates in a distributed computation, synchronize the computations plus estimate accuracies and efficiencies being obtained. Purdue work is in the study of synchronous versus asynchronous approaches. [C. Houstis et. al., 1987a], [Marinescu and Rice, 1987a], [Marinescu and Rice, 1987b]

AREA 6: Geometric Computation. One must be able to create, modify, move and reshape collections of geometric domains. Multiple representations are probably required as well as basically new techniques. Purdue work here is in the areas of algebraic geometry algorithms, general 2D and 3D domain processing, domain mapping techniques and motion planning. [Ahbyankar, 1983], [Ahbyankar and Bajaj, 1987a], [Ahbyankar and Bajaj, 1987b], [Ahbyankar and Bajaj, 1987c], [Atallah and Bajaj, 1987], [Bajaj, 1985], [Bajaj, 1986], [Bajaj, 1987a], [Bajaj, 1987b], [Bajaj and Kim, 1987a], [Bajaj and Kim, 1987b], [Bajaj and Kim, 1987c], [Bajaj and Kim 1987d], [Bajaj and Kim 1987e], [Bajaj and Kim 1987f], [Bajaj and Moh 1987], [Bajaj, Hoffmann and Hopcroft 1987], [Bajaj, Liu and Wu 1987], [Hoffmann and Hopcroft, 1985], [Hoffmann and Hopcroft, 1986], [Hoffmann and Hopcroft, 1987a], [Hoffmann and Hopcroft, 1987b], [Hoffmann and Hopcroft, 1987], [Hoffmann et. al., 1986], [Ribbens, 1986], [Rice, 1984a], Rice, 1984b].

AREA 7: User Interface. It must natural, easy to use and highly graphics oriented. Purdue has built interactive, graphics, expert PDE systems interfaces. [Dyksen and Ribbens, 1987], [McFaddin and Rice, 1987], [Rice, 1985], [Rice, 1987d]

6. REFERENCES

Abhyankar, S. S., (1983), Desingularization of plane curves. In *Proc. Symp. in Pure Mathematics*, 40, 1-45.

Abhyankar, S. S., and C. Bajaj, (1987a), ''Automatic rational parameterization of curves and surfaces I: Conics and conicoids'', *Computer Aided Design*, 19,1, 11-14.

Abhyankar, S. S., and C. Bajaj, (1987b), ''Automatic rational parameterization of curves and surfaces II: Cubics and cubicoids'', *Computer Aided Design*, to appear.

Abhyankar, S. S., and C. Bajaj, (1987c), ''Automatic parameterization of rational curves and surfaces III: Algebraic plane curves'', CSD-TR-619, Computer Science, Purdue University.

Atallah, M., and C. Bajaj, (1987), ''Efficient algorithms for common transversals'', *Information Processing Letters*, 25, 2, 87-91.

Bajaj, C., (1985), ''The Algebraic complexity of shortest paths in polyhedral spaces''. In *Proc. 23rd Annual Allerton Conference on Communication, Control and Computing*, Univ. of Illinois, 510-517.

Bajaj, C., (1986), ''An efficient parallel solution for shortest paths in 3-dimensions''. In *Proc. 1986 IEEE International Conference on Robotics and Automation*, San Fransisco, 1897-1900.

Bajaj, C., (1987a), ''Exact and approximate shortest path planning''. In *Path Planning*, R. Franklin, ed., SIAM, to appear.

Bajaj, C., (1987b), ''On algorithmic implicitization of rational algebraic curves and surfaces'', CSD-TR-681, Computer Science, Purdue University.

Bajaj, C. and M. Kim, (1987a), ''Generation of configuration space obstacles I: The case of a moving sphere'', *IEEE J. of Robotics and Automation*, to appear.

Bajaj, C. and M. Kim, (1987b), ''Generation of configuration space obstacles II: The case of moving algebraic surfaces'', CSD-TR-586, Computer Science, Purdue University.

Bajaj, C. and M. Kim, (1987c), ''Generation of configuration space obstacles III: The case of moving algebraic curves'', *Algorithmica*, to appear.

Bajaj, C., and M. Kim, (1987d), ''Compliant motion planning with geometric models'', *Proc. of 3rd ACM Symposium on Computation Geometry*, 171-180.

Bajaj,C., and M. Kim, (1987e), ''Convex decomposition of objects bounded by algebraic curves'', CSD-TR-677, Computer Science, Purdue University.

Bajaj, C., and M. Kim, (1987f), '' Convex hull of objects bounded by algebraic curves'', CSD-TR-697, Computer Science, Purdue University.

Bajaj, C., C. Hoffmann and J. Hopcroft, (1987), ''Tracing algebraic curves: Plane curves'', CSD-TR-637, Computer Science, Purdue University.

Bajaj, C., C. Hoffmann, E. Houstis, J. Korb and J. Rice, (1987), ''Computing about physical objects'', CSD-TR-696, Computer Science, Purdue University.

Bajaj, C., C. Liu, and M. Wu, (1987), ''A face area evaluation algorithm for solids in CSG representation'', CSD-TR-682, Computer Science, Purdue University.

Bajaj, C., and T. Moh, (1987), ''Generalized unfoldings for shortest paths'', *Intl. J. of Robotics Research*, to appear.

Birkhoff, G. and R.E. Lynch, (1985), ''Numerical solutions of elliptic problems'', *SIAM Publications*, Philadelphia.

Boisvert, R.F., E.N. Houstis, and J.R. Rice, (1979), ''A system for performance evaluation of partial differential equations software''. *IEEE Trans. Software Engineering*, **5**, 418–425.

Dyksen, W.R., R.E. Lynch, J.R. Rice and E.N. Houstis, (1984), ''The performance of the collocation and Galerkin methods with Hermite bi-cubics,'' *SIAM J. Numer. Anal.*, **21**, 695–715.

Dyksen, W.R. and C.J. Ribbens, (1987), ''Interactive ELLPACK: An interactive problem solving environment for elliptic partial differential equations'', *ACM Trans. Math. Software*, **13**, to appear.

Hoffmann, C. and J. Hopcroft, (1985), ''Automatic surface generation in computer aided design'', *The Visual Computer*, **1**, 92-100.

Hoffmann, C. and J. Hopcroft, (1986), ''Quadratic blending surfaces'', *Comp. Aided Design*, 18, 301-306.

Hoffmann, C. and J. Hopcroft, (1987a), ''Geometric ambiguities in boundary representations'', *Comp. Aided Design*, 19, 141-147.

Hoffmann, C. and J. Hopcroft, (1987b), ''The potential method for blending surfaces and corners'', in *Geometric Modeling*, G. Farin, ed., SIAM, 347-366.

Hoffmann, C. and J. Hopcroft, (1987), ''Simulation of physical systems from geometric models'', special issue, *IEEE J. of Robotics and Automation*, (June).

Hoffmann, C., J. Hopcroft, and M. Karasick, (1986), ''Boolean operations on boundary representations of polyhedral objects'', in preparation.

Houstis, C.E., E.N. Houstis and J.R. Rice, (1984), ''Partitioning and allocation of PDE computations in distributed systems''. In *PDE Software: Modules, Interfaces and Systems*, (Engquist and Smedsaas, eds.), North-Holland, 67-85.

Houstis, C.E., E.N. Houstis and J.R. Rice, (1987), ''Partitioning PDE computations: Methods and performance evaluations'', *Journal Parallel Computing*, to appear.

Houstis, C.E., E.N. Houstis, J.R. Rice and M. Samartzis, ''Benchmarking of bus multiprocessor hardware for large scale scientific computing''. In *Advances in Computer Methods for Partial Differential Equations, VI*, (Stepleman and Vishnevetsky, eds), IMACS, 136-141.

Houstis, E.N., W.F. Mitchell, and J.R. Rice, (1985a), ''Collocation software for second order elliptic partial differential equations'', *ACM Trans. Math. Software*, **11**, 379–412.

Houstis, E.N., W.F. Mitchell, and J.R. Rice, (1986b), ''Algorithm 638 GENCOL: Collocation on general domains with bicubic Hermite polynomials'', *ACM Trans. Math. Software*, **11**, 416–418.

Houstis, E.N., W.F. Mitchell and J.R. Rice, (1985c), ''Algorithm 638, INTCOL and HERMCOL: Collocation on rectangular domains with bicubic Hermite polynomials'', *ACM Trans. Math. Software*, **11**, 416-418.

Houstis, E.N., M.A. Vavalis and J.R. Rice, (1987), ''Parallelization of a new class of cubic spline collocation methods''. In *Advances in Computer Methods for Partial Differential Equations, VI*, (Stepleman and Vishnevetsky, eds), IMACS, 167-174.

Houstis, E.N., E.A. Vavalis and J.R. Rice, (1988), ''Convergence of an $O(h^4)$ cubic spline collocation method for elliptic partial differential equations'', *SIAM J. Num. Anal.*, to appear.

Lynch, R.E. and Rice, J.R., (1978), ''High accuracy finite difference approximation to solutions of elliptic partial differential equations'', *Proc. Nat. Acad. Sci.*, **75**, 2541–2544.

Marinescu, D.C. and J.R. Rice, (1987a), ''Domain oriented analysis of PDE splitting algorithms'', *J. Info. Sci.*, **42**, to appear.

Marinescu, D.C. and J.R. Rice, (1987b), ''Analysis and modeling of Schwarz splitting algorithms for elliptic PDE's''. In *Advances in Computer Methods for Partial Differential Equations, VI* (Stepleman and Vishnevetsky, eds), IMACS, 1-6.

McFaddin, H.S. and J.R. Rice, (1987), ''Parallel and vector problems on the FLEX/32'', CSD-TR-661, Computer Science, Purdue University.

Ribbens, C., (1986), ''Domain mappings: A tool for the development of vector algorithms for numerical solutions of partial differential equations'', Ph.D. Thesis, Purdue University.

Ribbens, C.J. and J.R. Rice, (1986), ''Realistic PDE solutions for nonrectangular domains'', CSD-TR-639, Computer Science, Purdue University.

Rice, J.R., (1985), ''Problems to test parallel and vector languages'', CSD-TR-516, Computer Science, Purdue University.

Rice, J.R., (1986a), ''Parallelism in solving PDEs'', *Proc. Fall Joint Compiler Conf.*, IEEE, 540-546.

Rice, J.R., (1986b), ''Multi-FLEX machines: Preliminary report'', CSD-TR-612, Computer Science, Purdue University.

Rice, J.R., (1986c), ''Design of a tensor product population of PDE problems'', CSD-TR-628, Computer Science, Purdue University.

Rice, J., (1986), ''Adaptive tensor product grids for singular problems''. In *Algorithms for the Approximation of Functions and Data*, (J. Mason, ed.), Oxford University Press.

Rice, J.R., (1987b), ''ELLPACK: An evolving problem solving environment''. In *Problem Solving Environments for Scientific Computing* (B. Ford, ed.) North-Holland, to appear.

Rice, J.R., (1987c), ''Parallel methods for partial differential equations''. In *The Characteristics of Parallel Computations*, (Jamieson, Gannon, Douglass, eds), MIT Press, Chapter 8, 209-231.

Rice, J.R., (1987d), ''Using supercomputers today and tomorrow''. In *Proc. Fourth Army Conf. Appl. Math. Computing*, 1333-1343.

Rice, J.R., and R.F. Boisvert, (1985), ''Solving elliptic problems using ELLPACK'', Springer Verlag.

Rice, J.R., W.R. Dyksen, E.N. Houstis, and C.J. Ribbens, (1986), ''ELLPACK status report''. CSD-TR 579, Computer Science, Purdue University.

Rice, J.R., Houstis, E.N. and Dyksen, W.R., (1981), ''A population of linear, second order, elliptic partial differential equations on rectangular domains, Parts 1 and 2'', *Math. Comp*, **36**, 475–484.

Rice, J.R., (1984a), ''Numerical computation with general two dimensional domains''. *ACM Trans. Math. Software*, **10**, 443–452.

Rice, J.R., (1984b), ''Algorithm 624: A two dimensional domain processor''. *ACM Trans. Math. Software*, **10**, 453–562.

The LINPACK Benchmark: An Explanation*

Jack J. Dongarra

Mathematics and Computer Science Division
Argonne National Laboratory
Argonne, Illinois 60439-4844

1. Introduction

In this paper we will clear up some of the confusion and mystery surrounding the LINPACK Benchmark. We will examine what is measured and describe how to interpret the results of the programs. But first a bit of history.

The LINPACK Benchmark is, in some sense, an accident. It was originally designed to assist users of the LINPACK package [9] by providing information on execution times required to solve a system of linear equations. The first "LINPACK Benchmark" report appeared as an appendix in the LINPACK Users' Guide [9] in 1979. The appendix comprised data for one commonly used path in LINPACK for a matrix problem of size 100, on a collection of widely used computers (23 in all), so users could estimate the time required to solve their matrix problem.

Over the years other data was added, more as a hobby than anything else, and today the collection includes 200 different computer systems. In addition the scope of the benchmark has also expanded. The benchmark report describes the performance at three levels of problem size and optimization opportunity: 100×100 problem - inner loop optimization, 300×300 problem - two loop optimization, and 1000×1000 problem - three loop optimization (whole problem).

1. The LINPACK Package

The LINPACK package is a collection of Fortran subroutines for solving various systems of linear equations. The software in LINPACK is based on a *decompositional* approach to numerical linear algebra. The general idea is the following. Given a problem involving a matrix, A, one factors or decomposes A into a product of simple, well-structured matrices which can be easily manipulated to solve the original problem. The package has the capability

* Work supported in part by the Applied Mathematical Sciences subprogram of the Office of Energy Research, U. S. Department of Energy, under Contract W-31-109-Eng-38.

of handling many different matrix types and different data types, and provides a range of options.

The package itself is based on another package, called the Basic Linear Algebra Subroutines (BLAS)[25]. The BLAS address simple vector operations, such as adding a multiple of a vector to another vector (SAXPY) or forming an inner product (SDOT). Most of the floating-point work within the LINPACK algorithms is carried out by the BLAS, which makes it possible to take advantage of special computer hardware without having to modify the underlying algorithm. This approach thus achieves transportability and clarity of software without sacrificing reliability.

1. Selection of the Algorithm

Solving a system of equations requires $O(n^3)$ floating-point operations, more specifically, $2/3n^3 + 2n^2 + O(n)$ floating-point additions and multiplications. Thus, the time required to solve such problems on a given machine is simply

$$time_n = time_{100} \times \frac{n^3}{100^3}.$$

In the LINPACK Benchmark, a matrix of size 100 is used as the base since it represents a "large enough" problem. That is, the $O(n^2)$ term in the operation count does not have a major effect on the time for large n. Another reason for choosing the matrix size as 100 is that it requires only $O(100^2)$ floating-point elements and can be accommodated in most environments.

The algorithm used in the timings is based on LU decomposition with partial pivoting. The matrix type is real, general, and dense, with matrix elements randomly distributed in the range $(-1.0, 1.0)$. (The random number generator used in the benchmark is not sophisticated; rather its major attribute is its compactness. The generator produces pseudo-random elements and has a period that is rather short, 2^{14}. As a result, if one uses this generator for a matrix of order 800, the matrix will be singular to working precision.)

4. The LINPACK Benchmark

4.1 Operations

The LINPACK benchmark features two routines: SGEFA and SGESL (these are the single-precision versions of the routines; DGEFA and DGESL are the double-precision counterparts). SGEFA performs the decomposition with partial pivoting, and SGESL uses that decomposition to solve the given system of linear equations. Most of the time - $O(n^3)$ floating-point operations - is spent in SGEFA. Once the matrix has been decomposed, SGESL is used to find the solution; this requires $O(n^2)$ floating-point operations.

SGEFA and SGESL in turn call three BLAS routines: SAXPY, ISAMAX, and SSCAL. By far the major portion of time - over 90% at order 100 - is spent in SAXPY. SAXPY is used to multiply a scalar, α, times a vector, x, and add the results to another vector, y. It is called approximately $n^2/2$ times by SGEFA and $2n$ times by SGESL with vectors of varying length. The statement $y_i \leftarrow y_i + \alpha x_i$, which forms an element of the SAXPY operation, is executed approximately $\frac{n^3}{3} + n^2$ times, which gives rise to roughly $2/3n^3$ floating-point operations in the solution. Thus, the benchmark requires roughly 2/3 million floating-point operations.

The statement $y_i \leftarrow y_i + \alpha x_i$, besides the floating-point addition and floating-point multiplication, involves a few one-dimensional index operations and storage references. While the LINPACK routines SGEFA and SGESL involve two-dimensional arrays references, the BLAS refer to one-dimensional arrays. The LINPACK routines in general have been organized to access two-dimensional arrays by column. In SGEFA, the call to SAXPY passes an address into the two-dimensional array A, which is then treated as a one-dimensional reference within SAXPY. Since the indexing is *down* a column of the two-dimensional array, the references to the one-dimensional array are sequential with unit stride. This is a performance enhancement over, say, addressing across the column of a two-dimensional array. Since Fortran dictates that two-dimensional arrays be stored by column in memory, accesses to consecutive elements of a column lead to simple index calculations. References to consecutive elements differ by one word instead of by the leading dimension of the two-dimensional array.

4.2 Precision

In discussions of scientific computing, one normally assumes that floating-point computations will be carried out to 64-bit precision, that is, single precision on CDC or CRAY and double precision on IBM or UNIVAC. In the benchmark there are two sets of numbers reported, one for full precision and the other for half precision. Full precision refers to 64-bit arithmetic or the equivalent, and half precision is 32-bit floating-point arithmetic or the equivalent.

4.3 Timing Information

The results in the report reflect only one problem area: solving dense systems of equations using the LINPACK programs in a Fortran environment. In particular, since most of the time is spent in SAXPY, the benchmark is really measuring the performance of SAXPY. The average vector length for the algorithm used to compute LU decomposition with partial pivoting is $2/3n$ [15]. Thus in the benchmark with $n = 100$, the average vector length is 66.

5. Loop Unrolling

It is frequently observed that the bulk of the central processor time for a program is localized in 3% or less of the source code [27]. Often the critical code (from a timing perspective) consists of one or a few short inner loops typified, for instance, by the scalar product of two vectors. On scalar computers a simple technique for optimizing of such loops should then be most welcome. "Loop unrolling" (a generalization of "loop doubling") applied selectively to time-consuming loops is just such a technique[24, 17].

When a loop is unrolled, its contents are replicated one or more times, with appropriate adjustments to array indices and loop increments. Consider, for instance, the SAXPY sequence, which adds a multiple of one vector to a second vector:

```
      DO 10 i = 1,n
         y(i) = y(i) + alpha*x(i)
   10 CONTINUE
```

Unrolled to a depth of four, it would assume the following form:

```
      m = n - MOD(n,4)
      DO 10 i = 1,m,4
         y(i) = y(i) + alpha*x(i)
         y(i+1) = y(i+1) + alpha*x(i+1)
         y(i+2) = y(i+2) + alpha*x(i+2)
         y(i+3) = y(i+3) + alpha*x(i+3)
   10 CONTINUE
```

In this recoding, four terms are computed per loop iteration, with the loop increment modified to count by fours. Additional code has to be added to process the $MOD(N,4)$ elements remaining upon completion of the unrolled loop, should the vector length not be a multiple of the loop increment. The choice of four was for illustration, with the generalization to other orders obvious from the example. Actual choice of unrolling depth in a given instance would be guided by the contribution of the loop to total program execution time and by consideration of architectural constraints.

Why does unrolling enhance loop performance? First, there is the direct reduction in loop overhead -- the increment, test, and branch function -- which, for short loops, may actually dominate execution time per iteration. Unrolling simply divides the overhead by a factor equal to the unrolling depth, although additional code required to handle "leftovers" will reduce this gain somewhat. Clearly, savings should increase with increasing unrolling depth, but the marginal savings fall off rapidly after a few terms. The reduction in overhead is the primary source of improvement on "simple" computers.

Second, for advanced architectures employing segmented functional units, the greater density of non-overhead operations permits higher levels of concurrency within a particular segmented unit. Thus, in the SAXPY example, unrolling would allow more than one multiplication to be concurrently active on a segmented machine such as the CDC 7600 or IBM

370/195. Optimal unrolling depth on such machines might well be related to the degree of functional unit segmentation.

Third, and related to the above, unrolling often increases concurrency between independent functional units on computers so equipped. Thus, in our SAXPY example, a CDC 7600, with independent multiplier and adder units, could obtain concurrency between addition for one element and multiplication for the following element, besides the segmentation concurrency obtainable within each unit.

However, with vector computers and their compilers trying to detect vector operations, the unrolling technique had the opposite effect. The unrolling inhibited vectorization of the loop, the resulting vector code became scalar, and the performance suffered. As a result, the Fortran implementation of the BLAS when run on vector machines should not be unrolled. The LINPACK benchmark notes this by a reference in the table to rolled Fortran.

5. Performance

The performance of a computer is a complicated issue, a function of many interrelated quantities. These quantities include the application, the algorithm, the size of the problem, the high-level language, the implementation, the human level of effort used to optimize the program, the compiler's ability to optimize, the age of the compiler, the operating system, the architecture of the computer, and the hardware characteristics. The results presented for benchmark suites should not be extolled as measures of total system performance (unless enough analysis has been performed to indicate a reliable correlation of the benchmarks to the workload of interest) but, rather, as reference points for further evaluations.

Performance is often measured in terms of Megaflops, millions of floating point operations per second (MFLOPS). We usually include both additions and multiplications in the count of MFLOPS, and the reference to an operation is assumed to be on 64-bit operands.

The manufacturer usually refers to peak performance when describing a system. This peak performance is arrived at by counting the number of floating-point additions and multiplications that can be a period of time, usually the cycle time of the machine. As an example, the CRAY-1 has a cycle time of 12.5 nsec. During a cycle the results of both the adder and multiplier can be completed

$$\frac{2\ operations}{1\ cycle} * \frac{1\ cycle}{12.5 nsec} = 160 MFLOPS.$$

Table 1 displays the peak performance for a number of high-performance computers.

Table 1
Theoretical Peak Performance

Machine	Cycle time, nsec	Number of Processors,	Peak Performance, MFLOPS
Culler PSC	200	1	5
Multiflow TRACE 7/200	130	1	15
CONVEX C-1	100	1	20
SCS-40	45	1	44
FPS 264	38	1	54
Alliant FX/8	170	8	94
Amdahl 500	7.5	1	133
CRAY-1	12.5	1	160
CRAY X-MP-1	9.5	1	210
IBM 3090/VF-200	18.5	2	216
Amdahl 1100	7.5	1	267
NEC SX-1E	7	1	325
CDC CYBER 205	20	1	400
CRAY X-MP-2	9.5	2	420
IBM 3090/VF-400	18.5	4	432
Amdahl 1200	7.5	1	533
NEC SX-1	7	1	650
CRAY X-MP-4	9.5	4	840
Hitachi S-810/20	14	1	840
NEC SX-2	6	1	1300
CRAY-2	4.1	4	2000

By peak theoretical performance we mean only that the manufacturer guarantees that programs will not exceed these rates, sort of a *speed of light* for a given computer. At one time, a programmer had to go out of his way to code a matrix routine that would not run at nearly top efficiency on any system with an optimizing compiler. Owing to the proliferation of exotic computer architectures, this situation is no longer true.

The LINPACK Benchmark illustrates this point quite well. In practice, as Table 2 shows, there may be a significant difference between peak theoretical and actual performance [8]:

Table 2
LINPACK Benchmark
Solving a 100 x 100 Matrix Problem

Machine	Peak Performance, MFLOPS	Actual Performance, MFLOPS	System Efficiency
Culler PSC	5	2	.40
Multiflow TRACE 7/200	15	6	.40
CONVEX C-1	20	3.0	.15
SCS-40	44	8.0	.18
FPS 264	54	5.6	.10
Alliant FX/8	94	7.6 (8 proc)	.08
Amdahl 500	133	14	.11
CRAY-1	160	12	.075
CRAY X-MP-1	210	24	.11
IBM 3090/VF-200	216	12 (1 proc)	.11(.056)
Amdahl 1100	267	16	.060
NEC SX-1E	325	35	.11
CDC CYBER 205	400	17	.043
CRAY X-MP-2	420	24 (1 proc)	.11(.057)
IBM 3090/VF-400	432	12 (1 proc)	.11(.028)
Amdahl 1200	533	18	.034
NEC SX-1	650	39	.06
CRAY X-MP-4	840	24 (1 proc)	.11(.029)
Hitachi S-810/20	840	17	.020
NEC SX-2	1300	46	.035
CRAY-2	2000	15 (1 proc)	.030(.0075)

If we examine the algorithm used in LINPACK and look at how the data are referenced, we see that at each step of the factorization process there are vector operations that modify a full submatrix of data. This update causes a block of data to be read, updated, and written back to central memory. The number of floating-point operations is $\frac{2}{3}n^3$, and the number of data references, both loads and stores, is $\frac{2}{3}n^3$. Thus, for every *add/multiply* pair we must perform a load and store of the elements, unfortunately obtaining no reuse of data. Even though the operations are fully vectorized, there is a significant bottleneck in data movement, resulting in poor performance. On vector computers this translates into two vector operations and three vector-memory references, usually limiting the performance to well below peak rates. To achieve high-performance rates, this *operation-to-memory-reference rate* must be higher.

In some sense this is a problem with doing vector operations on a vector machine. The bottleneck is in moving data and the rate of execution are limited by these quantities. We can see this by examining the rate of data transfers and the peak performance.

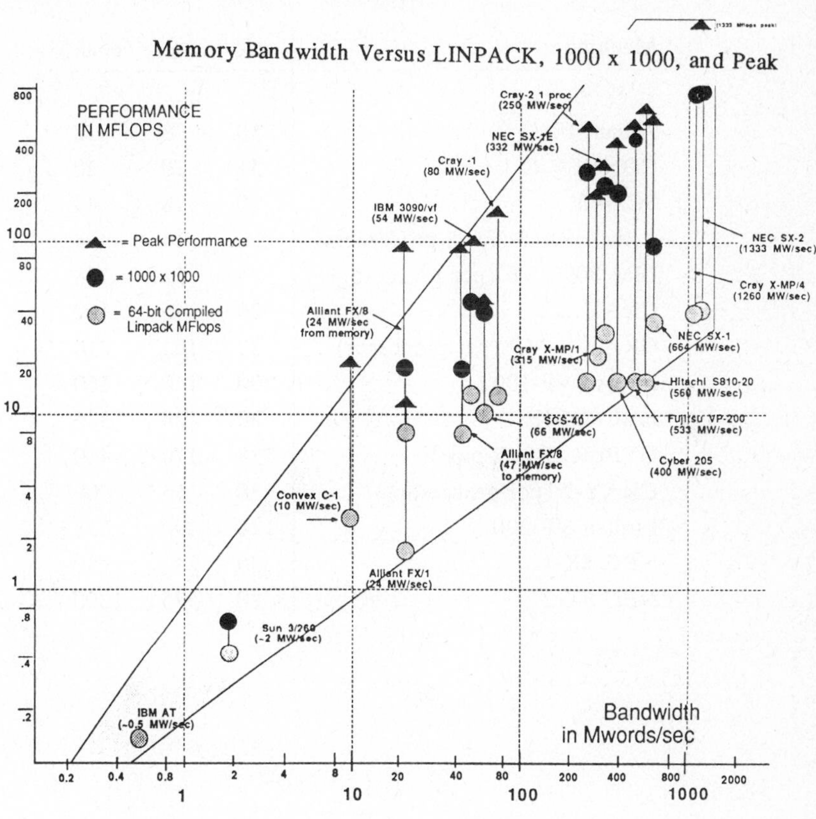

Figure 1

Memory Bandwidth and Peak Performance

To understand why the performance is so poor, considering the basic operation performed, a SAXPY. There are two parameters, $n_{1/2}$ and r_∞, that reflect the hardware performance of the idealized generic computer and give a first-order description of any real computer. These characteristic parameters are defined as follows:

$n_{1/2}$ - *the half-performance length* - the vector length required to achieve half the maximum performance;

r_∞ - *the maximum or asymptotic performance* - the maximum rate of computation in units of equivalent scalar operaitons performed per second (MFLOPS).[22].

SAXPY

Machine	$n_{1/2}$	r_∞	peak
Alliant FX/1	50	3	12
CONVEX C-1	31	10	20
SCS-40	20	18	44
Alliant FX/8 (for 8 processors)	150	14	94
IBM 3090/VF (per processor)	34	53	108
CRAY 1-S	20	45	160
CRAY X-MP (per processor)	37	101	210
Fujitsu VP-100	200	140	260
NEC SX-1E	20	120	325
CYBER 205 (2-pipe)	238	170	400
CRAY-2 (per processor)	30	55	500
Fujitsu VP-200	120	190	533
NEC SX-1	30	240	650
NEC SX-2	80	575	1300

SDOT

Machine	$n_{½}$	r_{∞}	peak
Alliant FX/1	150	3	12
CONVEX C-1	56	9	20
SCS-40	300	30	44
Alliant FX/8 (for 8 processors)	220	20	94
IBM 3090/VF (per processor)	41	52	108
CRAY 1-S	200	70	160
CRAY X-MP (per processor)	270	120	210
Fujitsu VP-100	200	180	260
NEC SX-1E	300	220	325
CYBER 205 (2-pipe)	135	90	400
CRAY-2 (per processor)	80	45	500
Fujitsu VP-200	320	350	533
NEC SX-1	390	350	650
NEC SX-2	480	575	1300

The information presented on SAXPY and SDOT was generated by running the following loops as in-line code and measuring the time to perform the operations.

SAXPY	SDOT
DO 10 i = 1,n y(i) = y(i) + alpha * x(i) 10 CONTINUE	DO 10 i = 1,n s = s + x(i) * y(i) 10 CONTINUE

The BLAS operate only on vectors. The algorithms as implemented tend to do more data movement than is necessary. As a result, the performance of the routines in LINPACK suffers on high-performance computers where data movement is as costly as floating-point operations.

In Figure 2 we display a graph comparing the price-performance of various computer systems based on the results from the first LINPACK benchmark (an example of applications programs where there are short vectors and many references to memory, both of which limit performance on today's high-performance computers). The performance data are taken from the first table in the benchmark report, solving a matrix of order 100 using the LINPACK software in full precision, in a Fortran environment. The price information is based on the best available information for the list price of a system. Since the graph is log-log, small changes will not affect the points greatly.

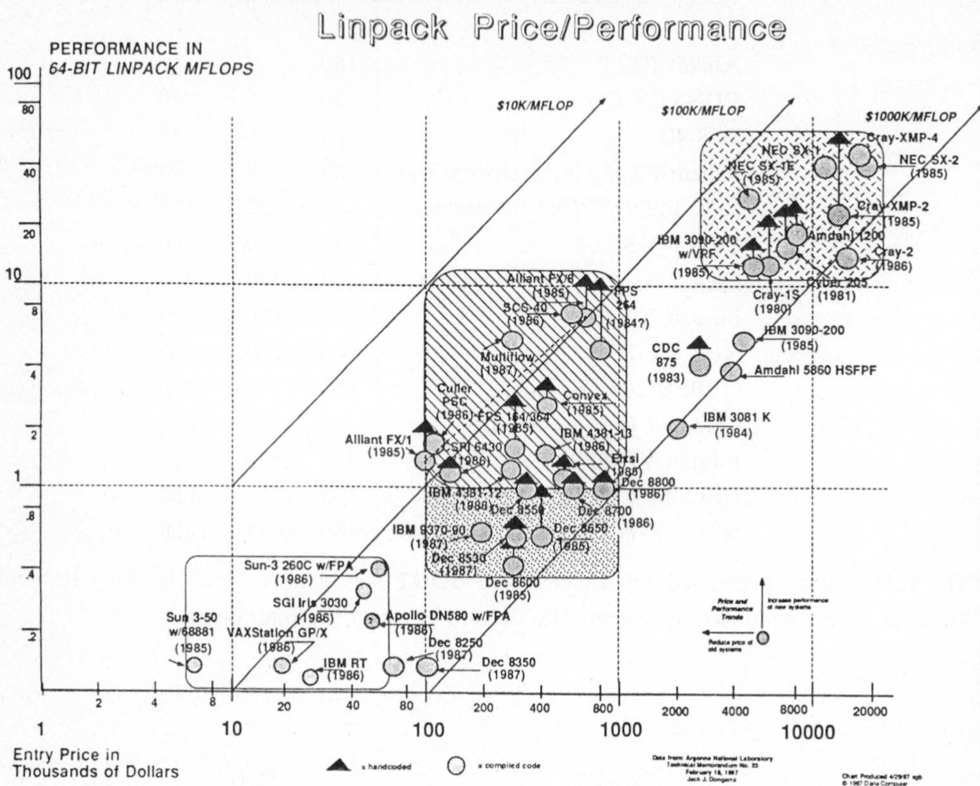

Figure 2
LINPACK Price Performance

The machines depicted in Figure 2 fall into four broad categories: supercomputer, mini-supercomputer, super-minicomputer, and workstation. The supercomputers cost between $1 million and $10 million and have a performance between 10 and 100 MFLOPS on the LINPACK benchmark. The mini-supercomputers cost between $100 thousand and $1 million and are in the range of 1 to 10 MFLOPS. The super-minis, like the mini-supercomputers, cost between $100 thousand and $1 million; however, their performance on this benchmark is an order of magnitude less (.1 to 1 MFLOPS). The workstations cost between $10 thousand and $100 thousand and are in the same range as the super-minis for performance.

As plotted, the best price-performance computers (for the LINPACK routines) will be those furthest to the left of the line that represents $100K/MFLOPS. In terms of these data, the best price-performance machines appear to be Sun-3 workstations, the Multiflow, and the Culler IPSC. Bear in mind that this price-performance benefit will be of little use to scientists who require the large memory or full power of a supercomputer. Nevertheless, it does raise an interesting question concerning the tradeoffs between having many users share the largest and most powerful machine available, and having the same number of users distributed among a larger number of less powerful systems.

7. Restructuring Algorithms

Advanced-architecture computers are usually based on memory hierarchies. By restructuring algorithms to exploit this hierarchical organization, one can gain high performance.

A hierarchical memory structure involves a sequence of computer memories ranging from a small, but very fast memory at the bottom to a large, but slow memory at the top. Since a particular memory in the hierarchy (call it M) is not as big as the memory at the next level (M'), only part of the information in M' will be contained in M. If a reference is made to information that is in M, then it is retrieved as usual. However, if the information is not in M, then it must be retrieved from M', with a loss of time. To avoid repeated retrieval, information is transferred from M' to M in blocks, the supposition being that if a program references an item in a particular block, the next reference is likely to be in the same block. Programs having this property are said to have *locality of reference*. Typically, there is a certain startup time associated with getting the first memory reference in a block. This startup is amortized over the block move.

Machines such as the CRAY-2, FPS 164/w MAX boards, Alliant FX/8, NAS AS/XL 60, Sperry 1100/90 w/ISP, Star Technology's ST-100, and IBM 3090/VF all have an additional level of memory between the main memory and the vector registers of the processor. (For a description of many advanced computer architectures see [13].) This memory, referred to as *cache*, or *local memory*, is relatively small (on the order of 16K words in some cases) and may not be under the control of the programmer. Nevertheless, the issue is the same: to come close to gaining peak performance, one must optimize the use of this level of memory (i.e., retain information as long as possible before the next access to main memory), obtaining as much reuse as possible.

7.1 Matrix-Vector Operations

One approach to restructuring algorithms to exploit hierarchical memory involves expressing the algorithms in terms of matrix-vector operations. These operations have the benefit that they can reuse data and achieve a higher rate of execution than the vector counterpart. In fact, the number of floating-point operations remains the same; only the data reference pattern is changed. This change results in a operation-to-memory-reference rate on vector computers of effectively 2 vector floating-point operations and 1 vector-memory reference.

Table 3 shows the results when the LINPACK algorithm for solving dense systems of linear equations was recast in terms of a matrix-vector multiplication. (The table labeled

"Matrix-Vector Operations" in the benchmark report gives a more complete list of the performance of the various computers when that software is run and the time measured.) This second benchmark involves a matrix of order 300; the larger matrix is intended to allow high-performance computers to reflect their potential performance. In this benchmark, the algorithm has been built on matrix-vector operations for Level 2 BLAS[14, 11, 12], which are currently being implemented by various computer vendors.

Table 3
Comparison with Matrix-Vector Operations
Solving a 100 x 100 Matrix Problem

Machine	Performance Before, MFLOPS	Performance After, MFLOPS	System Efficiency
CONVEX C-1	3.0	9.6	.48
SCS-40	8.0	13	.30
FPS 264	5.6	24	.44
Alliant FX/8	7.6 (8 procs)	11	.11
CRAY-1	12	38	.24
CRAY X-MP-1	24	48	.23
IBM 3090/VF-200	12	24(1 proc)	.22
Amdahl 1100	16	48	.18
NEC SX-1E	35	71	.22
CDC CYBER 205	17	24	.06
CRAY X-MP-2	24 (1 proc)	37 (2 procs)	.088
IBM 3090/VF-400	12	24(1 proc)	.22
Amdahl 1200	18	52	.098
NEC SX-1	39	74	.11
CRAY X-MP-4	24 (1 proc)	74 (4 procs)	.088
Hitachi S-810/20	17	48	.057
NEC SX-2	46	100	.076
CRAY-2	14	28 (1 proc)	.056

The Level 2 BLAS were proposed in order to support the development of software that would be both portable and efficient across a wide range of machine architectures, with emphasis on vector-processing machines. Many of the frequently used algorithms of numerical linear algebra can be coded so that the bulk of the computation is performed by calls to Level 2 BLAS routines; efficiency can then be obtained by utilizing tailored implementations of the Level 2 BLAS routines. On vector-processing machines one of the aims of such implementations is to keep the vector lengths as long as possible, and in most algorithms the results are computed one vector (row or column) at a time. In addition, on vector register machines performance is increased by reusing the results of a vector register, and not storing the vector back into memory.

Unfortunately, this approach to software construction is often not well suited to computers with a hierarchy of memory (such as global memory, cache or local memory, and vector registers) and true parallel-processing computers. For those architectures it is often preferable to partition the matrix or matrices into blocks and to perform the computation by matrix-matrix operations on the blocks. By organizing the computation in this fashion we provide for full reuse of data while the block is held in the cache or local memory. This approach avoids excessive movement of data to and from memory and gives a *surface-to-volume* effect for the ratio of operations to data movement. In addition, on architectures that provide for parallel processing, parallelism can be exploited in two ways: (1) operations on distinct blocks may be performed in parallel; and (2) within the operations on each block, scalar or vector operations may be performed in parallel.

7.2 Matrix-Matrix Operations

A set of Level 3 BLAS have been proposed; targeted at the matrix-matrix operations[10]. If the vectors and matrices involved are of order n, then the original BLAS include operations that are of order $O(n)$, the extended or Level 2 BLAS provide operations of order $O(n^2)$, and the current proposal provides operations of order $O(n^3)$; hence the use of the term Level 3 BLAS. Such implementations can, we believe, be portable across a wide variety of vector and parallel computers and also efficient (assuming that efficient implementations of the Level 3 BLAS are available). The question of portability has been much less studied but we hope, by having a standard set of building blocks, research into this area will be encourage.

In the case of matrix factorization, one must perform *matrix-matrix* operations rather than matrix-vector operations[18, 16]. There is a long history of block algorithms for such matrix problems. Both the NAG and the IMSL libraries, for example, include such algorithms (F01BTF and F01BXF in NAG; LEQIF and LEQOF in IMSL). Many of the early algorithms utilized a small main memory, with tape or disk as secondary storage[1, 6, 26, 19, 5, 7]. Similar techniques were later used to exploit common page-swapping algorithms in virtual-memory machines. Indeed, such techniques are applicable wherever there exists a hierarchy of data storage (in terms of access speed). Additionally, full blocks (and hence the multiplication of full matrices) might appear as a subproblem when handling large sparse systems of equations (for example, [20, 21, 7]).

More recently, several workers have demonstrated the effectiveness of block algorithms on a variety of modern computer architectures with vector-processing or parallel-processing capabilities, on which potentially high performance can easily be degraded by excessive transfer of data between different levels of memory (vector registers, cache, local memory, main memory, or solid-state disks) [16, 2, 23, 28, 3, 4, 29, 5, 18].

Our own efforts have been twofold: First, we are attempting to recast the algorithms from linear algebra in terms of the Level 3 BLAS (matrix-matrix operations). This involves modifying the algorithm to perform more than one step of the decomposition process at a given loop iteration.

Second, to facilitate the transport of algorithms to a wide variety of architectures and to achieve high performance, we are isolating the computationally intense parts in high-level modules. When the architecture changes, we deal with the modules separately, rewriting them in terms of machine-specific operations; however, the basic algorithm remains the same. By doing so we can achieve the goal of a high operation-to-memory-reference ratio.

Figure 3 shows the results for the third LINPACK benchmark, which solves a matrix of order 1000. (Table 6 in the benchmark report presents these results in greater detail.) For this case, manufacturers may implement any algorithm they wish to solve the linear equation. The only restrictions are that the results be correct and that the operation count used to report MFLOPS be $2/3n^3 + 2n^2$ independent of the actual number of operations or method used to computer the solution. Most of the implementations here are based on a version of LU decomposition using matrix-matrix operations.

The graph shows three sets of numbers for various computers: the LINPACK benchmark number, the best achieved performance using any algorithm to solve a 1000 by 1000 system of equations, and the theoretical peak performance of the system. From the graph, it is clear that the LINPACK numbers fall far short of peak performance; in general, they are an order of magnitude less than the peak. The second set of points provides a measure of the best performance attainable for this problem on the given systems (that is, what degree of the manufacturer's quoted peak performance has been achieved).

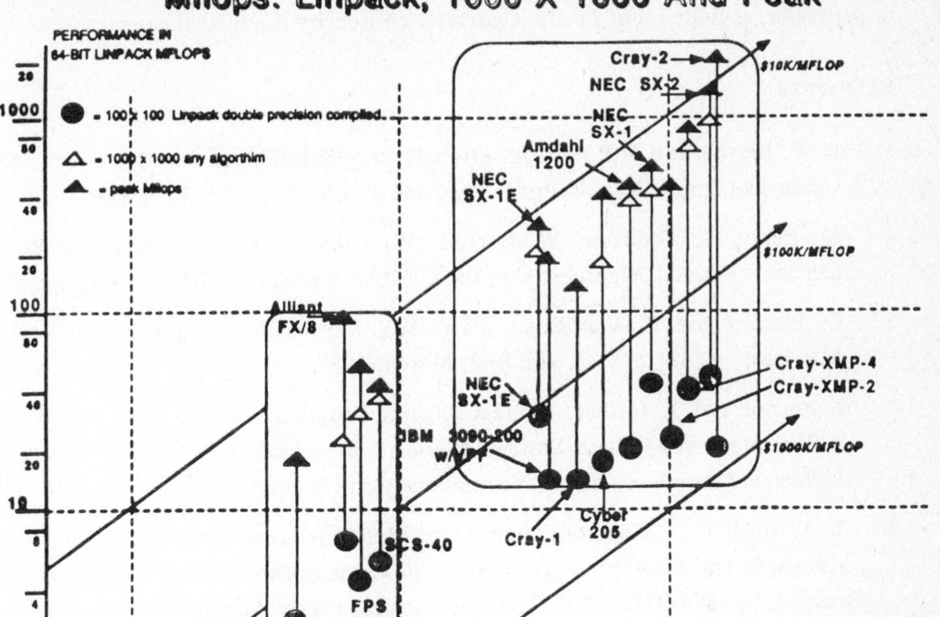

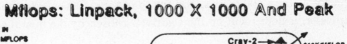

Figure 3
LINPACK / Best / Peak Performance

Concluding Remarks

Over the past several years, the LINPACK Benchmark has evolved from a simple listing for one matrix problem to an expanded benchmark describing the performance at three levels of problem size on several hundred computers. The benchmark today is used by scientists worldwide to evaluate computer performance, particularly for innovative advanced-architecture machines.

Nevertheless, a note of caution is needed. Benchmarking, whether with the LINPACK Benchmark or some other program, must not be used indiscriminately to to judge the overall performance of a computer system. Performance is a complex issue, dependent on a variety of diverse quantities including the algorithm, the problem size, and the implementation. The LINPACK Benchmark provides three separate benchmarks that can be used to evaluate computer performance on a dense system of linear equations: the first for 100 x 100 matrix, the second for a 300 x 300 matrix, and the third for a 1000 x 1000 matrix. The third benchmark, in particular, is dependent on the algorithm chosen by the manufacturer.

References

1. D.W. Barron and H.P.F. Swinnerton-Dyer, "Solution of Simultaneous Linear Equations Using a Magnetic-Tape Store," *Computer J.*, vol. 3, pp. 28-33, 1960.

2. M. Berry, K. Gallivan, W. Harrod, W. Jalby, S. Lo, U. Meier, B. Philippe, and A. Sameh, "Parallel Algorithms on the CEDAR System," *CSRD Report No. 581*, 1986.

3. C. Bischof and C. Van Loan, "The WY Representation for Products of Householder Matrices," *SIAM SISSC*, vol. 8, 2, March, 1987.

4. I. Bucher and T. Jordan, "Linear Algebra Programs for use on a Vector Computer with a Secondary Solid State Storage Device," in *Advances in Computer Methods for Partical Differential Equations*, ed. R. Vichnevetsky and R Stepleman, pp. 546-550, IMACS, 1984.

5. D.A. Calahan, "Block-Oriented Local-Memory-Based Linear Equation Solution on the CRAY-2: Uniprocessor Algorithms," *Proceedings International Conference on Parallel Processing*, pp. 375-378, IEEE Computer Society Press, August 1986.

6. B. Chartres, "Adaption of the Jacobi and Givens Methods for a Computer with Magnetic Tape Backup Store," *University of Sydney Technical Report No. 8*, 1960.

7. A.K. Dave and I.S. Duff, "Sparse Matrix Calculations on the CRAY-2," AERE Harwell Report CSS 197 (to appear Parallel Computing), 1986.

8. J.J. Dongarra, "Performance of Various Computers Using Standard Linear Equations Software in a Fortran Environment," Argonne National Laboratory MCS-TM-23, April, 1987.

9. J.J. Dongarra, J. Bunch, C. Moler, and G. Stewart, *LINPACK Users' Guide*, SIAM Pub., Philadelphia, 1976.

10. J.J. Dongarra, J. DuCroz, I. Duff, and S. Hammarling, "A Proposal for a Set of Level 3 Basic Linear Algebra Subprograms," Argonne National Laboratory Report, ANL-MCS-TM-88, April 1987.

11. J.J. Dongarra, J. DuCroz, S. Hammarling, and R. Hanson, "An Extended Set of Fortran Basic Linear Algebra Subprograms," Argonne National Laboratory Report, ANL-MCS-TM-41 (Revision 3), November 1986.

12. J.J. Dongarra, J. DuCroz, S. Hammarling, and R. Hanson, "An Extended Set of Basic Linear Algebra Subprograms: Model Implementation and Test Programs," Argonne National Laboratory Report, ANL-MCS-TM-81, November, 1986.

13. J.J. Dongarra and I.S. Duff, "Advanced Architecture Computers," Argonne National Laboratory Report, ANL-MCS-TM-57 (Revision 1), January, 1987.

14. J.J. Dongarra and S. C. Eisenstat, "Squeezing the Most out of an Algorithm in Cray Fortran," *ACM Trans. Math. Software*, vol. 10, 3, pp. 221-230, 1984.

15. J.J. Dongarra, F. Gustavson, and A. Karp, "Implementing Linear Algebra Algorithms for Dense Matrices on a Vector Pipeline Machine," *SIAM Review*, vol. 26, 1, pp. 91-112, Jan. 1984.

16. J.J. Dongarra and T. Hewitt, "Implementing Dense Linear Algebra Algorithms Using Multitasking on the CRAY X-MP-4," *SIAM J. Sci Stat. Comp.*, vol. 7, 1, pp. 347-350, January, 1986.

17. J.J. Dongarra and A. Hinds, "Unrolling Loops in Fortran," *Software-Practice and Experience*, vol. 9, pp. 219-226, 1979.

18. J.J. Dongarra and D.C. Sorensen, "Linear Algebra on High-Performance Computers," in *Proceedings Parallel Computing 85*, ed. U. Schendel, pp. 3-32, North Holland, 1986.

19. J. DuCroz, S. Nugent, J. Reid, and D. Taylor, "Solving Large Full Sets of Linear Equations in a Paged Virtual Store," *TOMS* , vol. 7,4, pp. 527-536, 1981.

20. I.S. Duff, "Full Matrix Techniques in Sparse Gaussian Elimination," *Numerical Analysis Proceedings, Dundee 1981, Lecture Notes in Mathematics 912*, pp. 71-84, Springer-Verlag, Berlin, 1981.

21. A. George and H. Rashwan, "Auxiliary Storage Methods for Solving Finite Element Systems," *SIAM SISSC*, vol. 6, pp. 882-910, 1985.

22. R.W. Hockney and C.R. Jesshope, *Parallel Computers*, p. Adam Hilger Ltd, Bristol, 1981.

23. IBM, "Engineering and Scientific Subroutine Library," *IBM*, vol. Program Number: 5668-863, 1986.

24. D. Knuth, "An Empirical Study of Fortran Programs," *Software-Practice and Experience*, vol. 1, pp. 105-133, 1971.

25. C. Lawson, R. Hanson, D. Kincaid, and F. Krogh, "Basic Linear Algebra Subprograms for Fortran Usage," *ACM Transactions on Mathematical Software*, vol. 5, pp. 308-323, 1979.

26. A.C. McKellar and E.G. Coffman Jr., "Organizing Matrices and Matrix Operations for Paged Memory Systems," *CACM*, vol. 12,3, pp. 153-165, 1969.

27. D. Pager, "Some Notes on Speeding Up Certain Loops by Software, Firmware, and Hardware Means," *IEEE Trans. on Comp.*, pp. 97-100, January 1972.

28. Y. Robert and P. Sguazzero, "The LU Decomposition Algorithm and Its Efficient Fortran Implementation on the IBM 3090 Vector Multiprocessor," IBM ECSEC Report ICE-0006, March 1987.

29. R. Schreiber, "Engineering and Scientific Subroutine Library, Module Design Specification," *SAXPY Computer Corporation, 255 San Geronimo Way, Sunnyvale, CA 94086*, vol. 1, 1986.

CLUSTER-PARTITIONING APPROACHES TO MAPPING PARALLEL PROGRAMS ONTO A HYPERCUBE

P. Sadayappan and Fikret Ercal

Department of Computer and Information Science
The Ohio State University
2036, Neil Avenue
Columbus, OH 43210, USA

ABSTRACT

The process-to-processor mapping problem is addressed in the context of a local-memory parallel computer with a hypercube interconnection topology. Two heuristic cluster-based mapping strategies are compared - 1) a **nearest-neighbor** approach and 2) a **recursive-clustering** scheme. The nearest-neighbor strategy is shown to be very effective with planar graphs and graphs with a high degree of locality while the recursive partitioning heuristic is better with highly irregular graphs.

1. INTRODUCTION

The effective exploitation of the potential power of parallel computers requires efficient solutions to the process-to-processor mapping problem. The problem is that of optimally allocating the processes(tasks) of a parallel program among the processors of the parallel computer in order to minimize execution time of the program. The optimal solution to the problem has been known to be NP-hard, except in a few specific contexts with very unrealistic constraints that typically do not hold in practice [1,2]. Hence the various approaches that have been proposed all seek to obtain satisfactory sub-optimal solutions in a reasonable amount of time [3-21]. This paper discusses two heuristic approaches based on cluster-partitioning - 1) a **nearest-neighbor** approach that was proposed in an earlier paper [10] and 2) a **recursive-clustering** approach that is developed in this paper. We compare and contrast the way in which these two approaches use heuristics to limit the configuration space of possible mappings that is (partially) searched to derive satisfactory mappings in polynomial time and we relate their relative effectiveness to the characteristics of the parallel program's task graph.

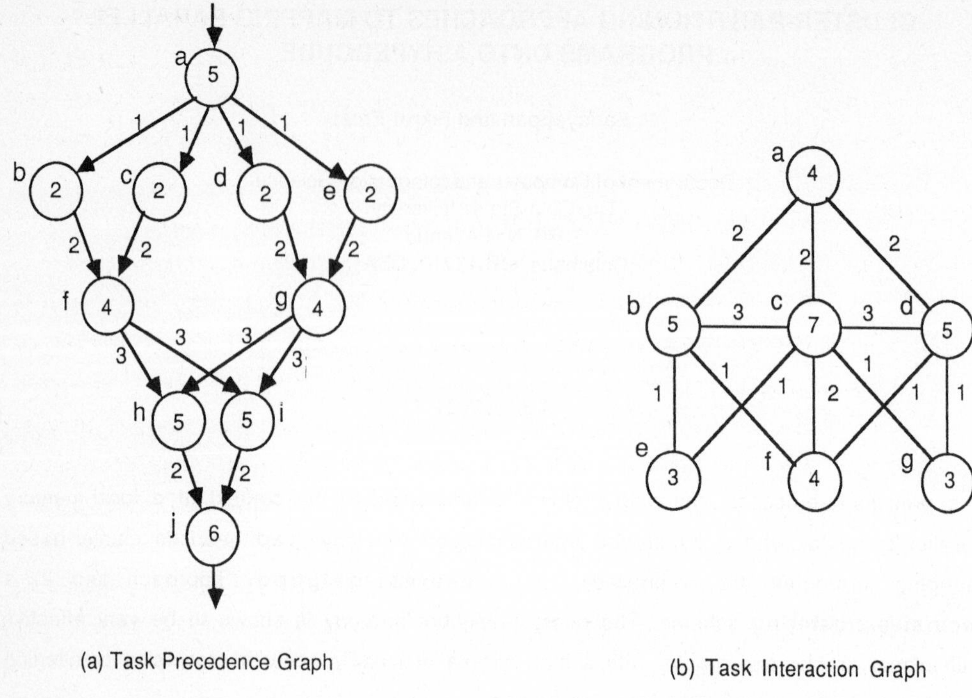

(a) Task Precedence Graph

(b) Task Interaction Graph

Figure 1. Two approaches to modeling parallel programs

The mapping problem has been investigated in two distinct settings that we refer to as the **Task Precedence Graph (TPG)** model and the **Task Interaction Graph (TIG)** model. In the TPG model, the parallel program is modeled as a collection of tasks with known (or estimated) computation times and explicit execution dependencies expressed in the form of precedence relationships. An example of this model is shown in Fig. 1a. The parallel program is represented as a graph whose vertices represent processes and the directed edges represent execution dependencies. In the example shown in Fig. 1a, process **h** can only commence execution after processes **f** and **g** have completed execution. The weight associated with a vertex represents the relative computation time required for its execution and the weight associated with an edge represents the relative amount of data that needs to be communicated between two tasks. Thus task **f** requires twice as much computation as **b** and the amount of data to be transferred between **f** and **h** is thrice as much as that between **a** and **b.** This model is very appropriate in the context of parallel programs that may essentially be represented as an acyclic task graph. It has been used, for example, in the context of mapping a robotics control computation onto a parallel processor system [13,14].

With the TIG model, the parallel program is also modeled as a graph where the vertices represent the parallel tasks and vertex-weights represent known or estimated computation costs of the tasks. In contrast to the TPG model, however, execution dependencies are not explicitly captured . The edges of a TIG represent communication requirements between tasks, with edge-weights reflecting the relative amounts of communication involved, but do not capture any execution dependencies. Thus in Fig. 1b, the relative amount of data communication required between tasks **a** and **b** is 2, but nothing is stated regarding the temporal dependencies between these two tasks resulting from the data transfer requirement. The TIG approach can be used to approximately model the behavior of complex parallel programs by lumping together all estimated communications between process pairs and ignoring the temporal execution dependencies. There is however a class of parallel programs, that we call **iterative parallel programs** [23], where the TIG model is quite accurate[10]. The characteristic of this class of programs is that execution proceeds as a sequence of sequential iterations, where at each iteration all parallel processes can execute independently, but each process then needs to communicate values computed during that iteration with processes it is connected to in the TIG, before it can commence its next iteration. Given a mapping of processes to processors, over a number of iterations, the slowest executing processor will clearly control program execution time. Thus minimizing iteration step completion time of the slowest processor (sum of computation time and inter-processor communication time for all inter-process communications that need to go across to other processors) will minimize execution time of the parallel program. Hence there is no need to explicitly model temporal dependencies and their satisfaction on a per-process basis, as the sequence of iterations of the iterative parallel program proceeds. This is the nature of the mapping problem addressed in this paper; an example of its use is presented in [10] in the context of parallelizing a finite element modeling program employing iterative techniques for the solution of systems of equations.

Given a parallel program that is characterized by a TIG, the mapping of the tasks to processors may either be performed statically (before program execution) or dynamically in an adaptive manner as the parallel program executes. The appropriate approach depends on the nature of the TIG - if the TIG that characterizes the parallel program is static, i.e. the vertex and edge weights can be accurately estimated a priori, then a static approach is more attractive, since the mapping computation only needs to be performed once. This is the case, for example, with iterative parallel programs. We only consider static mapping schemes in this paper.

If the physical communication costs of the parallel computer system can be quantitatively characterized, then by using it in conjunction with the parallel program's TIG, a cost function can be formulated to evaluate the effectiveness of any particular mapping of the tasks onto the processors. The mapping problem can thus be formulated as a problem of finding the particular mapping that minimizes this explicit mathematical cost function, and indeed many researchers have done so [2,3,10,15-18]. In some contexts, mapping schemes have been proposed that utilize intuition about the specific mapping context and do not use any explicit cost functions in the mapping procedure (for example, the Scattered Decomposition scheme proposed in [12] and heuristics proposed in [11]). Such schemes, which we call "domain-heuristic" schemes, are computationally very efficient. On the other hand, schemes that use explicit cost functions are often computationally time consuming, but are more generally applicable and potentially capable of obtaining better mappings. The primary problem with most of the approaches based on an explicit cost function is the exponentially large configuration space of possible mappings that needs to be selectively searched in order to determine a satisfactory sub-optimal mapping. Many proposed heuristics to do so have been shown to work relatively well on small task graphs (with a few tens of tasks), but have not been evaluated on large task graphs (with hundreds of nodes). The "flat" and unstructured viewpoint of the allocation as a mapping of each task onto a processor leads to the unmanageably large search space. If the task graph has N nodes and the parallel computer has P processors, the space of mappings to be searched has P^N possibilities.

We propose that hybrid approaches that combine characteristics of the domain-heuristic approach and the pure cost-function based approach are most attractive for the mapping problem. Instead of using "flat and unstructured" strategies aimed at minimizing a mathematically formulated cost function, domain-heuristics are used in conjunction with an explicit cost function to significantly reduce the search space of potentially good mappings. Some recently proposed approaches to mapping [19,20] may be viewed as such hybrid approaches.

Our approach to mapping is motivated by the following observations:

- Pairs of tasks that need to communicate a lot are better grouped together and mapped to the same processor in order to reduce communication costs. Thus the task-to-processor mapping problem may be viewed instead as a problem of forming clusters of tasks with high intra-cluster communication and low inter-cluster communication and allocating these clusters to processors in a way that results in low inter-processor communication costs. This view of mapping in terms of formation of clusters of closely coupled tasks helps reduce significantly the space of mappings that is selectively searched for a satisfactory solution.

- The clusters should be formed in such a way as to distribute the total computational load as uniformly as possible among the clusters. This requirement can often be in conflict with the requirement for minimal inter-cluster communication. We may hence identify computational load balancing and minimization of inter-processor communication as the two key objectives of the mapping. These two requirements can be identified with terms in typical cost functions used for mapping.

- Rather than use two explicit terms in the cost function, one representing load balancing and another representing communication costs, the search space can be reduced if only one of them is explicitly used during the traversal through the search space and the other is implicitly kept low through the use of a domain-heuristic incorporated into the search strategy. As explained later, the two schemes used in this paper represent two ways of doing so. The nearest-neighbor mapping scheme explicitly attempts load balancing among clusters, where as low communication costs are achieved implicitly through the use of a domain-heuristic. In contrast, the recursive-clustering approach explicitly attempts to minimize communication costs, while load balancing is achieved implicitly by the search strategy.

The paper is organized as follows. In section 2, we formalize the mapping problem that we address. In section 3, we discuss the nearest-neighbor approach to mapping and in section 4, we develop the recursive-clustering scheme. In section 5, we compare the effectiveness of the two schemes on a number of sample task graphs and summarize in section 6.

2. THE MAPPING PROBLEM

In this section, we formalize the mapping problem and develop the cost function that we attempt to minimize. The parallel program is characterized by a Task Interaction Graph G(T,E), whose vertices, $T = \{t_1, t_2, ..., t_N\}$, represent the tasks of a program, and edges E, correspond to the data communication dependencies between those tasks. The weight of a task t_i, denoted w_i, represents the computational load of the task. The weight of an edge e_{ij} between t_i and t_j, denoted

c_{ij}, represents the relative amount of communication required between the two tasks.

The parallel computer is represented as a graph $G(P,E_P)$. The vertices $P = \{p_0, p_1, ..., p_k\}$ represent the processors and the edges E_P represent the communication links. The system is assumed to be homogeneous with all processors being equally powerful and all communication links capable of the same rate of communication. Hence, unlike with the TIG, no weights are associated with the vertices or edges of the Processor Interaction Graph. The processors are assumed to either execute a computation or perform a communication at any given time but not simultaneously do both. The cost of a communication is assumed to be proportional to the size of the message and the distance between the sender and receiver. The distance $\mathbf{d_{qr}}$ between processors p_q and p_r is defined as the minimum number of links to be traversed to get from p_q to p_r, i.e. is the length of the shortest path from p_q and p_r.

The task-to-processor mapping is a function M: T--> P. $M(t_i)$ gives the processor onto which task t_i is mapped. The **Task Set (TS_q)** of a processor p_q is the set of tasks mapped onto it:

$$TS_q = \{ t_s \mid M(t_s) = p_q \} \qquad q = 0, 1, ..., k \qquad (1)$$

The **Work Load (WL_q)** of processor p_q is the total computational weight of all tasks mapped onto it:

$$WL_q = \Sigma \{w_j \mid M(t_j) = p_q \} \qquad q = 0, 1, ..., k \qquad (2)$$

The **Communication Set (CS_q)** of processor p_q is the set of TIG edges that go between it and some other processor under the mapping M:

$$CS_q = \{e_{ij} \mid M(t_i) = p_q \text{ and } M(t_j) \neq p_q \} \qquad q = 0, 1,..., k \qquad (3)$$

The **Communication Load (CL_q)** of processor p_q is the total weighted cost of the edges in its Communication Set, where each edge is weighted by the physical path length to be traversed under the mapping M:

$$CL_q = \Sigma^k{}_{r=0}\ \Sigma \{c_{ij}{}^* d_{qr} \mid M(t_i) = p_q \text{ and } M(t_j) = p_r\} \quad q = 0, 1, ..., k \quad (4)$$

An appropriate cost function to use in optimizing a mapping is the estimated parallel program completion time, which is the completion time of the processor that completes last. If we denote by $T_e(p)$, $T_c(p)$, $T_i(p)$ the computational execution time, the time spent for communication and the idle time respectively for processor p, then the total program completion time is given by:

$$T(p) = T_e(p) + T_c(p) + T_i(p) \qquad (5)$$

$T_e(p)$ can be accurately modeled using WL_p in (2). $T_c(p)$ is not easy to model accurately and in general $T_i(p)$ is the most difficult to model accurately because it is determined by synchronization delays during program execution that can effectively be determined only by simulating execution of the parallel program under the mapping. In certain situations (for example, see [10]), $T_c(p)$ can be modeled using CL_p in (4) and $T_i(p)$ ignored by taking the maximum among all processors, of the sum of $T_e(p)$ and $T_c(p)$ as the parallel program execution time:

$$T_M = MAX_p[T_e(p) + T_c(p)] = MAX_p[\, K_e{}^* \, WL_p + K_c{}^* \, CL_p \,] \qquad (6)$$

where weights K_e and K_c are used to allow for different relative time requirements for a unit computation and a unit communication step. The mapping problem now is one of finding the mapping M^* that minimizes the cost (6). Such a "minimax" criterion has been used in [10,18]. In general, however, it is not quite as appropriate to model $T_c(p)$ by CL_p since it essentially lumps all communication costs incurred in a multi-hop transmission of a message and associates it with the sender of the message, where as in practice all intermediate processors in the transmission will need to spend communication time in transmitting such a message.

An alternative approach to formulation of a cost function is to take a "summed cost" approach rather than a "minimax" approach. The "summed cost" approach may be motivated as follows. Ideally we would like that the total computational load be uniformly distributed among all processors and that no communication penalties be paid at all. In practice we cannot hope to attain this ideal but the merit of a mapping may be measured in terms of its deviation from the ideal. With respect to load distribution, this may be expressed as the sum among all processors of (the absolute values of) the deviation of the actually assigned load and the ideal average load. With respect to communication, since in the ideal case we would have no communication at all, the total communication load in the system serves as a good measure of the deviation from the ideal. A "total sum" cost function may thus be expressed as a sum of two terms: one representing the deviation from ideal of the load-balancing achieved, and another representing the deviation from the ideal of the total communication required by the mapping:

Cost = Penalty for computation inbalance + Penalty for communication

$$\text{Cost} = K_e * \sum^{k}_{i=0} | WL_i - \text{AVGload} | \quad + \quad K_c * \sum^{k}_{i=0} CL_i \qquad (7)$$

Variations of this "summed cost" approach to formulation of an appropriate cost function have been used by various researchers [15,16,21]. The mapping problem is now one of finding a mapping that minimizes (7). As explained in the previous section, the mapping schemes compared in this paper combine the use of domain-heuristics and the explicit minimization of a cost function. While the same cost function (7) is used to evaluate the mappings obtained with each of these schemes, in each case the use of a domain-heuristic results in one of the two terms in (7) being kept low implicitly by the search strategy so that only one of them is explicitly minimized. With the nearest-neighbor approach discussed in section 3, the communication cost is implicitly kept low while the load-deviation is explicitly minimized by the search procedure. The opposite is true of the recursive-clustering scheme presented in section 4, where load-balance is implicitly guaranteed by the algorithm and the total communication cost is explicitly minimized.

3. NEAREST-NEIGHBOR MAPPING

The nearest-neighbor mapping strategy was proposed in [10] as an effective approach to mapping finite element graphs onto processor meshes. Given a regular **m** x **n** rectangular mesh of processors $\{P_{ij}, i=1..m, j=1..n\}$, a *nearest-neighbor* of a processor P_{ij} is any processor P_{kl}, where k is either i-1,i or i+1, and l is either j-1,j or j+1. A nearest neighbor mapping is one where any pair of nodes that share an edge in the TIG are mapped onto nearest-neighbor processors. The essential idea behind the nearest-neighbor mapping approach is that if TIG nodes are grouped into clusters and assigned to processors in a nearest-neighbor fashion, then the total communication costs should be low due to the small communication distances required. Starting with an initial clustered nearest-neighbor mapping, successive incremental modification of the mapping is done to improve load-balancing among the processors while always maintaining the nearest-neighbor property. Thus the search strategy reduces the configuration space of possible mappings by incorporating a "cluster" viewpoint of the mapping as opposed to a "flat" individual-task-to-processor viewpoint. Moreover, the search space is further reduced by being explicitly concerned only with the load-balancing aspect of the mapping, while the implicit nearest-neighbor constraint in conjunction with the use of node clustering are depended upon to keep communication costs low. In this section we explain the approach through an example and refer the reader to [10] for algorithmic details.

The nearest-neighbor mapping algorithm proceeds in two phases:

1) An **initial mapping** is first generated by grouping nodes of the TIG into clusters and assigning clusters to processors in a manner that the nearest-neighbor property is satisfied.

2) The initial mapping is successively modified using a **boundary-refinement** procedure where nodes are reassigned among processors in a manner that improves load balancing but always maintains the nearest neighbor-property.

Allowing for the possibility that some of the processors do not get any nodes mapped onto them, a nearest-neighbor mapping of any TIG onto a processor mesh is clearly always possible. In the extreme case, all TIG nodes form a single cluster that is assigned to one of the processors, while all other processors are assigned no tasks at all. The initial mapping algorithm of course attempts to do considerably better than that extreme case. The initial-mapping procedure may be understood through the example in Fig. 2., requiring the mapping of a 40 node TIG onto a 2x4 mesh of 8 processors. Here the TIG is a "mesh graph", a graph that can be embedded onto some subset of a uniform 2-dimensional grid with a dilation of 1, i.e. the nodes of the TIG can be mapped onto the grid points of a uniform 2-dimensional grid in such a way that any two nodes of the TIG that share an edge are mapped onto adjacent (vertically or horizontally) grid points. We first use an example of a mesh graph to simplify the explanation of the initial mapping scheme and later point out how the scheme can be generalized for arbitrary graphs.

The basis for the initial mapping procedure is the 1-dimensional strip mapping scheme. Let us imagine that all processors in any row of the processor mesh are clumped together to create a "macro-processor". The 8-processor mesh in Fig. 2 can be so treated as a linear chain of 4 macro-processors, as seen if Fig. 2a. The essential idea behind the 1-D strip method is to partition the mesh graph into "strips", where each strip encompasses one or more contiguous

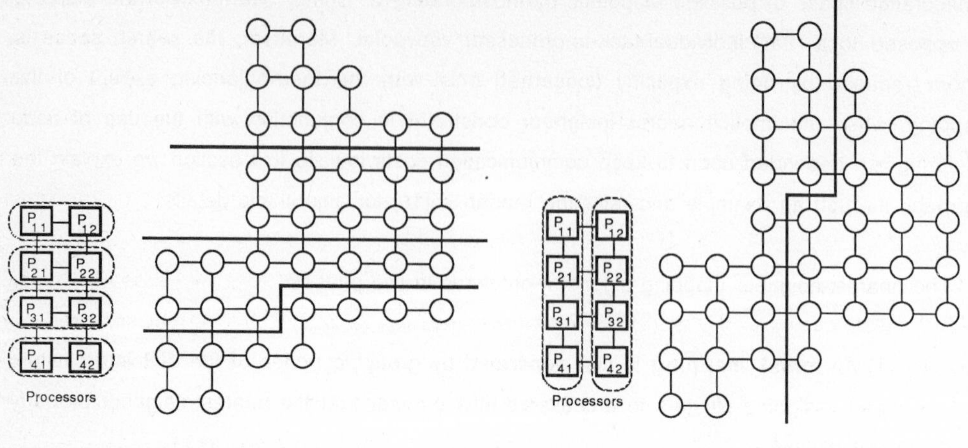

(a) Vertical strip-partitioning

(b) Horizontal strip-partitioning

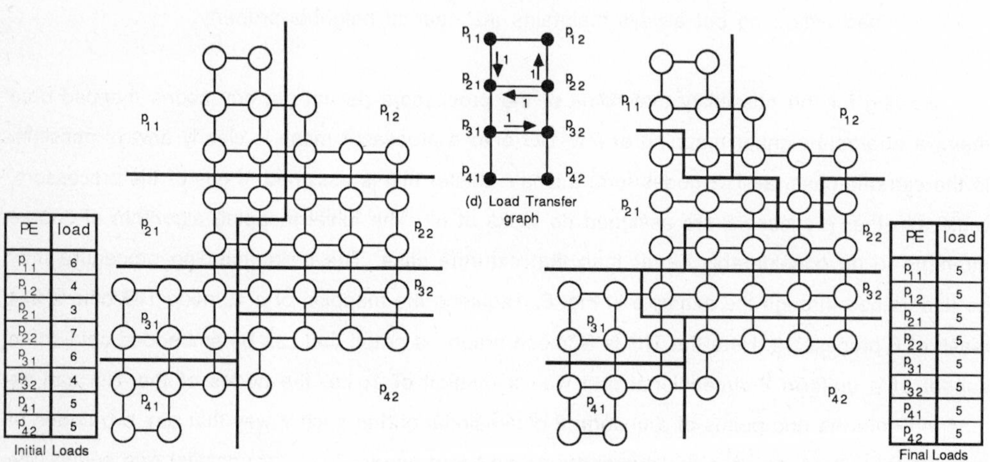

(c) Initial 2-D Nearest-Neighbor Mapping

(e) Final Mapping After Boundary Refinement

Figure 2. Illustration of the Nearest-Neighbor approach to mapping

rows (columns) of the graph. The mesh graph is covered by strips in such a way that each strip is adjacent to at most two other strips, one on either side of it. The number of strips used equals the number of processors (macro-processors) in the processor chain, and the strips can be made to each contain an equal number of mesh graph vertices (plus or minus one, if the number of graph vertices is not a perfect multiple of the number of strips created). Given a mesh with N nodes, to be mapped onto a linear chain of P processors, a load-balanced mapping needs to assign either ceil(N/P) or floor(N/P) nodes to each processor (the former number of nodes to (N modulo P) processors and the latter number to (P- (N modulo P)) processors). Starting with the leftmost node in the uppermost row of the mesh-graph, nodes are counted off and assigned to a processor by proceeding across the row of the mesh graph. If the first row is completely exhausted, then we begin at the left end of the next row and continue assigning nodes to the processor. When the required number of nodes has been assigned, we begin assigning the remaining nodes in that row to the next processor in the linear chain of processors. Proceeding in this manner, all nodes in the problem mesh get assigned to processors. Thus in Fig. 2a, the graph is partitioned into 4 strips containing 10 tasks each, to be assigned to each of the 4 macro-processors.

A similar procedure can be used to create a vertical 1-D strip partition of the same graph, as shown in Fig. 2b. Now we group all processors in a column together, to form a chain of two macro-processors. The TIG is partitioned into two vertical strips. By overlapping the two orthogonal strip-partitions generated, and forming the intersections, we can generate a number of regions, that equals the number of processors in the processor mesh, as shown in Fig. 2c. The nature of the construction guarantees that the generated partitions satisfy the nearest-neighbor property. Even though the two independent partitions of such a 2-D partition are each individually load balanced, the intersection partitions are generally not load-balanced, as can be seen from the table of assigned loads in Fig. 2c. This however serves as a good initial nearest-neighbor mapping that is then refined by the load balancing boundary refinement procedure.

One way of balancing the computational loads of the processors is to reassign some of the assigned nodes amongst the processors; for example, transfering one task from P_{22} to each of P_{12} and P_{21}, one task from P_{11} to P_{21} and one task from P_{31} to P_{32}, shown graphically in Fig. 2d as a load transfer graph. In general, given an initial mapping, it is possible to determine a set of load transfers that will balance the load, by setting up and solving a system of (generally) undetermined linear equations in integer variables. If this reassignment of tasks is done in such a way that the nearest-neighbor property is still maintained, then the final mapping will be a load-balanced, nearest-neighbor mapping. The reader is referred to [10] for the heuristic procedure that attempts the reassignment specified by the load transfer graph. The final mapping after application of the reassignment procedure is shown in Fig. 2e for the chosen example. The algorithm to perform this reassignment is named boundary-refinement due to the manner in which the reallocation is performed - by iteratively altering or refining the boundaries of the clusters formed by the initial partition. While its effectiveness depends on the initial partition generated, it has been found in practice that initial mappings where one or more processors get no assigned nodes have typically been load-balanced after boundary refinement.

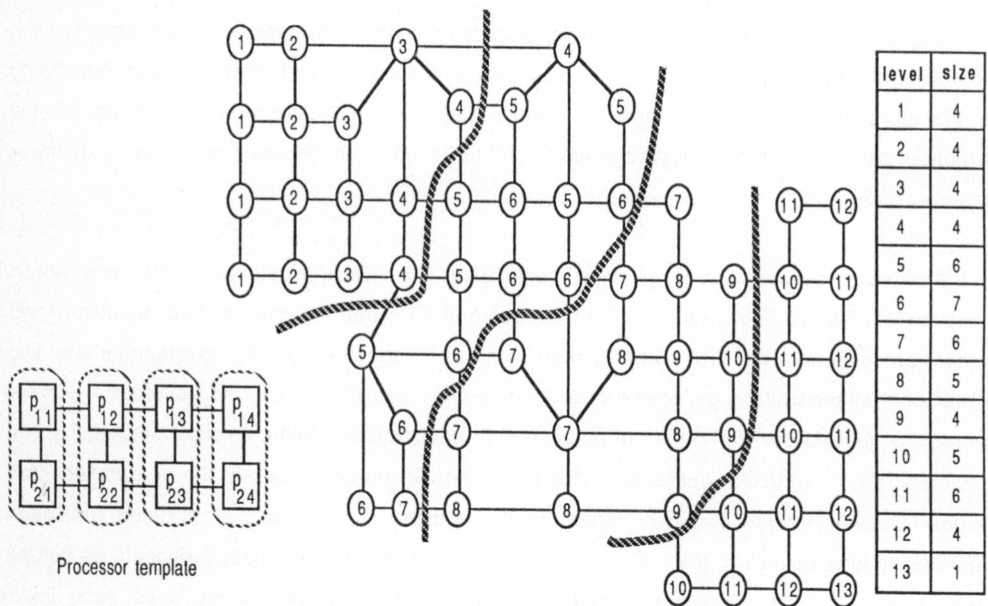

level	size
1	4
2	4
3	4
4	4
5	6
6	7
7	6
8	5
9	4
10	5
11	6
12	4
13	1

Total no. of nodes = 60 Av erage = 60/4 = 15 nodes/PE

Figure 3. Example of 1-D Strip-Partitioning of a Non-Mesh TIG

A generalization of the 1-dimensional strip method to non-mesh graphs is possible. This is illustrated through an example in figure 3. The essential idea again is to create strip-like regions to cover the graph, such that if a node is on a certain strip, all other nodes sharing an edge in the TIG with that node should lie either on the same strip or on an adjacent strip. In the case of mesh graphs, the process of generating strips was facilitated by the regularity of the mesh-graph and the natural grouping of nodes into columns and rows. This is not so for a general non-mesh TIG. Such a grouping is hence created by a *levelization* process that assigns a unique level to each node. Starting with a single randomly selected node, or if possible a peripheral node, or a set of connected peripheral nodes that are assigned to level 1, all nodes directly connected to these level 1 nodes, and that have not yet been assigned a level, are assigned a level number of 2. The same procedure is carried out with the nodes at level 2, and continued thus till all nodes are levelized. The nature of the levelization procedure ensures that a neighbor node of any node assigned level l will necessarily be at level $l-1$, l or $l+1$. Now, strip partitioning can be performed using the levels similar to using columns(rows) in the earlier described procedure for 1-dimensional strip partitioning for mesh-graphs, as seen in figure 3.

In the case of mesh graphs, mapping onto an mxn processor mesh was achieved by performing two independent 1-D partitions - one n-way and the other m-way; one in the horizontal direction and the other in the vertical direction. In the case of non-mesh graphs, the difficulty is in the generation of a second levelization that is orthogonal to the first one. This is because, unlike with mesh graphs, it is not meaningful to associate physical directions such as vertical and horizontal with the levels generated, as can be seen with many of the levels in figure 3. A heuristic is hence used to attempt the generation of a second levelization that is as orthogonal to the first one as possible. This is done by first identifying so called "corner" nodes of the TIG - these are peripheral nodes that form end-points of the maximum diameter(s) of the TIG, i.e. are nodes with maximum distance of separation in the TIG. Starting with an arbitrary corner node, one fourth of the peripheral nodes visited upon traversing the periphery in one direction are used as the nodes in level 1 of the first levelization; the same number of nodes visited upon traversing the periphery in the opposite direction are used for level 1 of the second levelization.

The nearest-neighbor approach can be expected to be quite effective in mapping TIGs that exhibit a great degree of locality, as is the case with parallel programs modeling physical systems using finite element methods, finite difference methods etc. When the TIG does not represent purely local interactions, but has "non-local" connectivity, the nearest-neighbor restriction becomes overly constraining and load balancing becomes extremely difficult. An alternate cluster-based mapping scheme is developed in the next section that is not so restrictive. Instead of using a search strategy that explicitly attempts load balancing while implicitly keeping communication costs low, as was the case with the nearest-neighbor scheme, the opposite view is used of explicitly attempting to minimize communication costs by using an explicit cost function while achieving load balancing implicitly through the nature of the developed algorithm.

4. MAPPING BY RECURSIVE CLUSTERING

A mapping scheme is developed in this section to map arbitrary TIGs onto a local-memory machine with a hypercube interconnection topology. The algorithm proceeds in two phases:

1) **Cluster Formation:** The TIG is first partitioned into as many clusters as the number of processors. Starting with the entire TIG as a single cluster, this is done recursively, by successively dividing a cluster into two equally weighted (as nearly as possible) partitions with minimal total weight of edges cut by the partition.

2) **Processor Allocation:** The clusters generated in the first phase are each allocated to some processor, one cluster per processor, in a manner that attempts to minimize the total inter-processor communication cost.

Both phases of the algorithm - the cluster-formation phase and the processor-allocation phase explicitly attempt minimization of communication costs through the use of an iterative improvement heuristic based on the Kernighan-Lin mincut algorithm [22] and load balancing is achieved implicitly in the first phase by the recursive partitioning algorithm.

The recursive partitioning algorithm uses a modified version of the Kernighan-Lin mincut algorithm to allow for variable vertex (node) weights. An initial two-way partition is created by assigning the nodes of the TIG, one by one, always to the partition with lesser total weight (randomly in case both are equal). This results in a load-balanced initial partition. After creating the initial load-balanced partition, node transfers from the partition with greater load to the partition with lesser load are tried with the iterative improvement heuristic. The iterative improvement heuristic is otherwise very similar to the Kernighan-Lin mincut heuristic, except for the use of node moves instead of node swaps. The use of node transfers in this fashion guarantees load-balance eventhough the individual vertex weights are variable. With a P processor system (where P is a power of 2), P clusters are created by this recursive partitioning procedure and numbered from 1 to P. The recursive partitioning procedure is illustrated using an example in Fig. 4a-c. The parallel processor system has 8 procesors and so the recursive partitioning procedure is applied upto depth $\log_2(8)=3$.

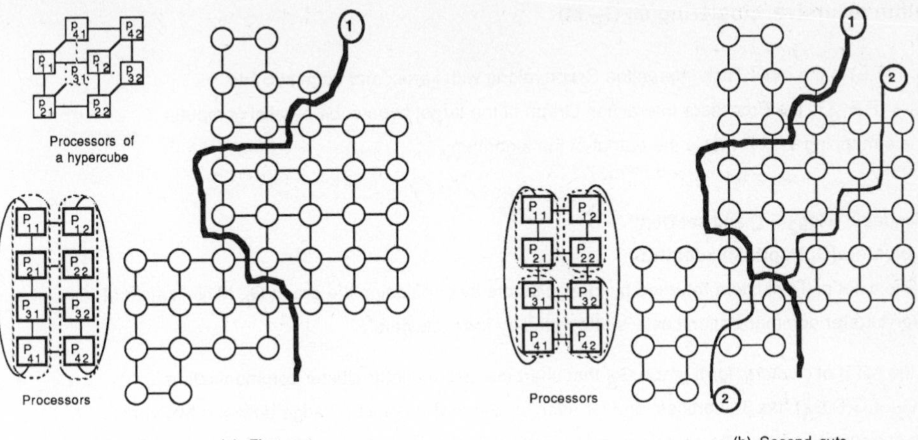

(a) First cut

(b) Second cuts

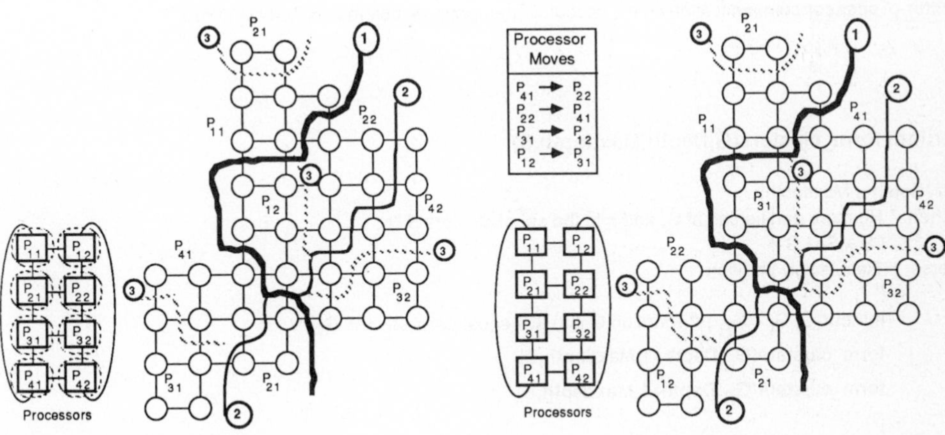

Total Inter-processor Communication Cost = 164

Total Inter-processor Communication Cost = 144

(c) Cluster Mapping Before Optimizing Inter-processor Communication Cost

(d) Cluster Mapping After Optimizing Inter-processor Communication Cost

Figure 4. Illustration of the Recursive-Clustering Algorithm

Algorithm recursive_clustering(G_I,G_P,M)

/* G_I = (T,E) is the input Task Interaction Graph, along with vertex and edge weights
G_P = (P,E_P) is the Processor Interaction Graph of the target hypercube parallel computer
M is a mapping V--> P that is the output of the algorithm
*/

- Set Maxdepth = $\log_2(|P|)$ and set Depth = 0
- **form_clusters(G_I,Depth,Maxdepth,S)**

/* S is a set of |P| clusters returned by form_clusters by partitioning the graph G_I. Minimization of **Inter-cluster** communication costs is attempted by form_clusters*/

- From the set S of clusters, form graph G_S that characterizes the inter-cluster communication

/* G_S = G(C,E_S) has |P| vertices, one for each cluster in S. G_S has an edge between two vertices if the corresponding clusters contain a vertex each of G_I that have an edge between them in G_I. The edges of G_S have weights that are the sum of weights of the relevant edges in G_I */

- **allocate_processors(G_S,G_P,M)**

/* The vertices of G_S are mapped to processors of G_P attempting to minimize total **Inter-processor** communication costs, accounting for physical communication distances */

Algorithm form_clusters(G,Depth,Maxdepth,S)

```
If (Depth = Maxdepth)
then /* No more partitioning of G; add it to the set of clusters S */
        { S = S U G }
else /* Recursively partition */
        {
        mincut(G, G_L , G_R ) /* Partition G into two equal parts G_L and G_R */
        form_clusters(G_L,Depth+1,Maxdepth,S)
        form_clusters(G_R,Depth+1,Maxdepth,S)
        }
```

Algorithm mincut(G_I,G_L,G_R)

- form an initial load-balanced partition of G_I = G(V,E), assigning its nodes into one of two clusters C_1 and C_2.
- mark all nodes as unlocked
- Associate a gain value g_v with each node and initialize g_v to zero

do{ - $\forall$ v ε V compute g_v = Total reduction in the cost of the cut when v is moved from its currently assigned cluster to the other cluster
- compute W_1 and W_2, the total vertex weights of nodes in C_1 and C_2 respectively.
- seqno <-- 0

do{
- seqno <-- seqno + 1
- Let C_i be the cluster with greater total weight and C_j the lesser total weight i.e. $W_i \geq W_j$, i,j ε {1,2},i≠j
- Identify $v^* \varepsilon P_i$ with maximal gain g_v^*
- If no such v^* exists, exit this loop
- Assume that v^* is moved to C_j , update the gain for all unlocked nodes and calculate new total weights W_1 and W_2 for C_1 and C_2
- Lock v^* and record the status of the movement and **gain**[seqno] <-- g_v^*

}while (there is at least one v to move)
- Choose k : $\mathcal{G}^*$ = $MAX_k(\Sigma^k_{i=1}$ gain[i])
- **If** { ($\mathcal{G}^*$ > 0) OR [($\mathcal{G}^*$ = 0) AND (better load balancing)] } **then** perform all moves from 1 to k

} while (($\mathcal{G}^*$ > 0) OR [($\mathcal{G}^*$ = 0) AND (better load balancing)])
- Form G_L and G_R from C_1 and C_2

Algorithm allocate_processors(G_S,G_P,M)

/* G_P = G(P,E_P) is a graph representing the interconnection of the hypercube
G_S = G(C,E_S) is a graph with |P| nodes, each node representing a cluster of nodes of original TIG
M is the mapping of clusters to processors returned */

- Start with initial mapping M that assigns cluster C_i to processor p_i
- Unlock all processor nodes

do{
- Calculate the gain for all processor pairs (p_i,p_j) assuming that the clusters currently assigned to p_i and p_j are swapped
- seqno <-- 0

do{
- seqno <-- seqno + 1
- Pick the unlocked processor pair (p_k,p_l) with maximum gain.
- If no such p exists, exit this loop.
- Assume that p_k and p_l are swapped, update gains for all unlocked processors
- Lock p_k and p_l

} while (there are unlocked processors)
- Choose k : $\mathcal{G}^*$ = $MAX_k(\Sigma^k_{i=1}$ gain[i])
- **If** ($\mathcal{G}^*$ > 0) **then** perform all moves from 1 to k by changing M

} while ($\mathcal{G}^*$ > 0)

The second phase attempts to minimize total inter-processor communication costs when the clusters generated in the first phase are allocated to processors, one cluster per processor. Where as the first phase formed clusters with minimal total inter-cluster communication costs, in the second phase, actual communication distances required with the cluster-to-processor mapping are taken into account in determining the mapping with minimal total inter-processor communication costs. An iterative improvement heuristic, again similar to the Kernighan-Lin heuristic is used here, as shown in algorithm **allocate_processors**. Pairs of clusters are considered for swapping that maximally decrease the total inter-processor comunication cost. This is illustrated in Fig. 4d, where it can be seen that the cluster initially assigned to P_{41} is finally assigned to P_{22} and vice versa, and the assignments to P_{31} and P_{12} are likewise exchanged. The total inter-processor communication cost decreases from 164 to 144 as a result of the second phase optimization.

5. COMPARISON OF EFFECTIVENESS OF MAPPING SCHEMES

In this section, we report on the results of evaluation of effectiveness of the two mapping approaches. Table 1 displays the results of evaluating the methods on six sample TIGs. The first two samples are mesh-graphs (taken from [12]) and are shown in Fig. 5a and 5b. These graphs exhibit a high degree of locality and are locally regular and uniform but very irregular at the outer periphery. These are representative of the kinds of graphs that result from exploiting parallelism from computations modeling physical systems by finite element and finite difference methods. Sample 3 (taken from [11]) and sample 4 (similar to those in [4]), shown in Fig. 5c and 5d, are non-mesh graphs. Unlike mesh graphs, these graphs are not uniform, but nevertheless exhibit considerable locality of interconnection. These are similar to those obtained with the use of multi-grid methods. The last two samples are completely random graphs, generated using a random generator. These graphs are hence very non-uniform and do not exhibit any locality of interconnection either.

The results are reported in Table 1. The cost function (7) was used to evaluate the mappings produced by the two methods. A value of 1 was used for K_c and K_e. With the recursive-clustering method, we report the costs before and after the second phase optimization for processor allocation of the clusters.

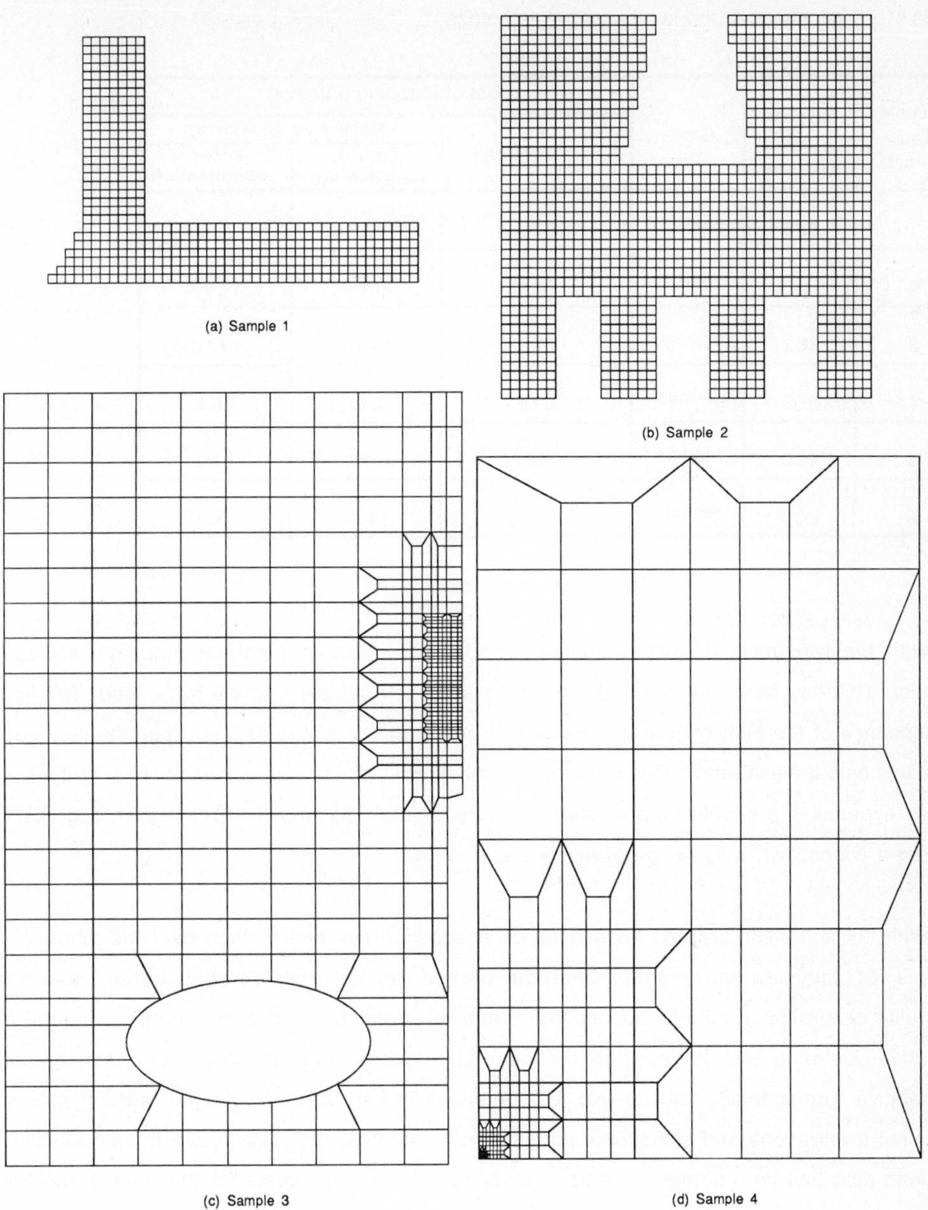

Figure 5. Sample problem graphs used for performance evaluation

Table 1 : Comparison of the two m apping schemes

Sample Task Graph	Number of vertices	Graph Type	Cost of Mapping obtained		
			Nearest-Neighbor	Recursive Clustering	
				before optimization	after optimization
1	505	mesh	570	822	738
2	1449	mesh	648	2086	1486
3	602	non-mesh	686	1458	1116
4	256	non-mesh	675	780	584
5	400	random	1532	718	644
6	800	random	3082	1474	1376

With the two mesh graphs (samples 1 and 2), the nearest-neighbor mapping is clearly superior. This has been the case with every mesh graph sample that we have tried. This is a consequence of the high degree of locality and planar nature of the TIG that permits very good mappings onto a mesh (and hence onto a hypercube). Eventhough only a mesh-subset of the links of the hypercube are utilized, the planar nature of the TIG implies that higher degrees of processor connectivity may not be of much use.

With the non-mesh graphs, there is no clear superiority of one method over the other. With sample 3, the nearest-neighbor method proved to be considerably better than the recursive-clustering method, but in the case of sample 4, the mapping obtained by recursive-clustering was better than the nearest-neighbor mapping. With non-mesh graphs, the relative "orthogonality" of the two 1-D partitions is very sensitive to the starting sets for the initial levelizations and sometimes produces quite inferior mappings. Even though sample 4 has less than half the number of vertices as sample 3, the final costs for the nearest-neighbor mapping were almost equal, where as with the recursive-clustering approach the final costs are in rough correspondence to the sizes of the graphs.

The recursive-clustering approach is consistently superior with random graphs, as can be seen from the costs with samples 5 and 6. The poor mappings obtained with the nearest-neighbor method can be attributed to the high degree of irregularity and lack of locality of interconnection with the random graphs. The recursive-clustering approach, however works quite as well as it did with the more regular graphs.

6. SUMMARY

In this paper, the process-to-processor mapping problem was addressed. Since the problem is NP-hard, efficient heuristics to obtain satisfactory sub-optimal solutions are required. An explicit cost function was formulated to evaluate the effectiveness of proposed mapping strategies. Two mapping strategies were described - the nearest-neighbor approach and the recursive-clustering approach. The former approach used a procedure that explicitly attempted to improve load balance and implicitly kept communication costs low. The latter method on the other hand explicitly attempted to minimize communication costs while load balance was implicitly guaranteed. The effectiveness of the mapping schemes was evaluated by using different sample Task Interaction Graphs. The nearest-neighbor approach was found to be superior with regular, locally conected graphs, while the recursive-clustering approach was found better with irregular non-local graphs.

REFERENCES

[1] H. Kasahara and S. Narita, "Practical Multiprocessor Scheduling Algorithms for Efficient Parallel Processing", *IEEE Transactions on Computers,* Vol. C-33, No.11, Nov. 1984, pp. 1023-1029 .

[2] H.S. Stone, "Multiprocessor Scheduling with the aid of Network Flow Algorithms", *IEEE Transactions on Software Engineering,* Vol. SE-3, 1, Jan. 1977, pp. 85-93 .

[3] K. Efe, "Heuristic Models of Task Assignment Scheduling in Distributed Systems", *Computer* Vol. 15, June 1982, pp. 50-56.

[4] M.J. Berger and S.H. Bokhari, "A Partitioning Strategy for Nonuniform Problems on Multiprocessors", *IEEE Transactions on Computers*, Vol. C-36, May 1987, pp. 570-580.

[5] S.H. Bokhari, "On the Mapping Problem", *IEEE Transactions on Computers*, Vol. C-30, March 1981, pp. 207-214.

[6] M. Ashraf Iqbal, J.H. Saltz, and S. Bokhari, "A Comparative Analysis of Static and Dynamic Load Balancing Strategies", in *Proc. 1986 International Conference on Parallel Processing*, 1986, pp. 1040-1047 .

[7] Virginia Lo and Jane W.S. Liu, "Task Assignment in Multiprocessor Systems", *Proc. 1981 International Conference on Parallel Processing*, 1981, pp. 358-360.

[8] J.W. Flower, S.W. Otto and M.C. Salama, "A Preprocessor for Irregular Finite Element Problems", Tech. report, Caltech Concurrent Cube Project, Report #292, June 1985.

[9] C. Aykanat, S.M. Doraivelu, F. Ercal, P. Sadayappan, K.Schwan, and B. Weide, " Parallel Computers for Finite Element Analysis", *1986 ASME International Conference on Computers in Engineering, Chicago*, ASME, Aug. 1986, pp. 43-50.

[10] P. Sadayappan and F. Ercal, "Nearest-Neighbor Mapping of Finite Element Graphs Onto Processor Meshes", *IEEE Transactions on Computers*, Vol. C-36, No. 12, December 1987.

[11] K. Schwan, W. Bo, N. Bauman, P. Sadayappan and F. Ercal, "Mapping Parallel Applications on a Hypercube", *Hypercube Multiprocessors 1987*, M. Heath editor, *SIAM*, Philadelphia, 1987.

[12] R. Morison and S. Otto, "The Scattered Decomposition for Finite Elements", Tech. report, Caltech Concurrent Cube Project, Report #286, May 1985.

[13] Y.L.C. Ling, "Layered Multiprocessor Architecture and Design in VLSI for Real-Time Robotic Control", Ph. D. thesis, The Ohio State University, Columbus, OH, Dec. 1986.

[14] Y.L.C. Ling, K.W. Olson, D.E. Orin, P. Sadayappan,"A Layered Restructurable VLSI Architecture For Robotic Control", *Proc. International Conference on Computer Design, October 1987.*

[15] O. Kramer and H. Muhlenbein, "Mapping Strategies in Message Based Multiprocessor Systems", *PARLE 87, Lecture Notes in Computer Science*, Springer-Verlag, 1987.

[16] Geoffrey C. Fox, "Load Balancing and Sparse Matrix Vector Multiplication on the Hypercube", Tech. report, Caltech Concurrent Cube Project, Report #327, July 1985.

[17] Virginia M. Lo, "Task Assignment to Minimize Completion Time", *Proc. of the 5th International Conference on Distributed Computing Systems*, May 1985, pp. 329-336.

[18] C. Shen and W. Tsai, "A Graph Matching Approach to Optimal Task Assignment in Distributed Computing Systems Using a Minimax Criterion", *IEEE Transactions on Computers*, Vol. C-34, March 1985, pp. 197-203.

[19] H. Muhlenbein, M. Gorges-Schleuter and O. Kramer, "New Solutions to the Mapping Problem of Parallel Systems: The Evolution Approach", *Parallel Computing*, Vol. 4, No. 3, June 1987.

[20] G. C. Fox and W. Furmanski, "Balancing the Hypercube on a Neural Network", Tech. report, Caltech Concurrent Cube Project, Report #363, Sept. 1986.

[21] J. Sheild, "Partitioning Concurrent VLSI Simulation Programs onto a Multiprocessor by Simulated Annealing", *IEE Proceedings Part-G,* Vol.134, No.1, January 1987, pp. 24-28 .

[22] B. W. Kernighan and S. Lin, "An efficient heuristic procedure for partitioning graphs", *Bell Systems Technical Journal*, Vol. 49, No. 2, 1970 , pp. 291-308.

[23] L. Adams, "Iterative Algorithms for Large Sparse Linear Systems on Parallel Computers", Ph. D. thesis, Univ. of Virginia (Oct. 1982). Also NASA Contractor Report 166027, NASA Langley Research Center.

A Parallel Graph Partitioning Algorithm for a Message-Passing Multiprocessor

John R. Gilbert and Earl Zmijewski
Department of Computer Science
Cornell University
Ithaca, New York 14853

1 Introduction

Many graph algorithms are based on finding a small set of vertices or edges whose removal divides the graph into two or more nearly equal parts. Examples include layout of circuits in a model of VLSI [15], efficient sparse Gaussian elimination [13,16], and solving various graph problems [17].

With the commercial availability of parallel machines, we are faced with the problem of developing efficient parallel algorithms for finding small separators of graphs. In this paper, we develop an algorithm for this problem that is based on a simple modification of the Kernighan-Lin algorithm [14] for finding edge separators on a single processor. We have designed our algorithm for a message-passing multiprocessor. One of the main advantages of our algorithm is that it can find separators of graphs that are too large to reside in the memory available to any single processor.

Our algorithm is designed for a class of message-passing multiprocessors typified by the currently available hypercube machines of Ametek, Intel, and NCUBE. These machines consist of several identical processors, each containing some local memory. They coordinate their activities by passing messages along a network of communication links. On these machines, the number of processors is typically quite a bit smaller than the size of the problem we want to solve, and communication is considerably slower than computation. Therefore we seek algorithms that do as much computation as possible locally, and use the least possible amount of communication. Our only assumption about the topology of the communication network is that any processor can communicate efficiently with any other processor. See Feng [6] for a survey of network topologies.

We have used our parallel separator algorithm in solving systems of linear equations of the form

$$Ax = b,$$

where A is a large sparse symmetric positive definite matrix. We can solve for x by computing the Cholesky factor L of A (i.e., the lower triangular matrix L such that $A = LL^T$) and then solving the systems $Ly = b$ and $L^T x = y$. The set of positions that are nonzero in L and zero in A is known as *fill*. To reduce the amount of fill, one generally solves the equivalent reordered system

$$(PAP^T)(Px) = Pb$$

for some permutation matrix P. Since A is positive definite, no pivoting is required to maintain numerical stability, and hence, we are free to choose P to make the factorization more efficient. We have developed a parallel ordering algorithm that uses our parallel separator algorithm. The algorithm attempts to find orderings that not only reduce fill, but also decrease the total volume of message passing and result in good processor utilization during the numeric factorization. We will consider only the ordering phase of sparse parallel Cholesky factorization. George, Gilbert, Heath, Liu, Ng, and Zmijewski [8,24,25,26] have examined symbolic and numeric factorization and triangular system solving. George, Liu, and Ng [11], in work done independently of ours, have used the elimination tree of a matrix to assign its columns to processors in a way that both reduces the communication and results in good processor utilization during the factorization.

Our paper is organized as follows. Section 2 reviews the Kernighan-Lin algorithm [14] for finding small edge separators of graphs. Section 3 contains a parallel version of this algorithm that is appropriate for message-passing multiprocessors. Section 4 provides some implementation details of the algorithm along with a discussion of its computational and communication complexity. Section 5 shows how the algorithm can be used to reorder the nonzeros of a sparse matrix in a way that reduces fill and communication during the factorization. Here, we assume the reader is familiar with the graph theoretic model of Cholesky factorization [10]. Section 6 contains some numerical results using both a hypercube simulator written by T. H. Dunigan of the Oak Ridge National Laboratory [4] and an Intel hypercube. Section 7 shows that the Kernighan-Lin algorithm will not necessarily find minimum edge separators for grid graphs. Section 8 contains remarks and conclusions.

2 The Kernighan-Lin Algorithm

In this section, we briefly review the Kernighan-Lin algorithm [14] for finding small edge separators on a single processor. We assume $G = (V, E)$ is an arbitrary graph with $2n$ vertices numbered from 1 to $2n$. Each edge (i,j) has a *cost* c_{ij}. Let $C = (c_{ij})$ be the cost matrix of G, where c_{ij} is the cost of (i,j) if it exists, and is 0 otherwise. We want to partition the vertices of G into two sets A and B of equal size, such that the total cost of all edges connecting vertices of A and B is minimized. In other words, we want to find a *minimum cost edge separator* that divides the vertices of G into two equal-sized sets. Note that if the costs are all one then a solution to this problem is an edge separator with the minimum number of edges. Although this problem is NP-complete, Kernighan and Lin have devised an iterative algorithm that works well in practice. In the remainder of this section, we will describe the central idea behind their algorithm.

Suppose the vertices of G are initially partitioned into two equal-sized sets, A and B, in some manner. Call an edge connecting a vertex of A to one of B an *external* edge. All other edges are *internal* edges. Let T be the total cost of all the external edges. Kernighan and Lin's algorithm reduces T by repeatedly swapping equal-sized subsets of A and B. It selects the subsets to guarantee that T decreases at each iteration of the algorithm. Hopefully, the algorithm will quickly converge to a solution near the optimum.

Before explaining how the subsets to be swapped are chosen, we will need some notation. Define the *external cost* E_a of a vertex $a \in A$ to be the total cost of its incident external edges,

$$E_a = \sum_{x \in B} c_{ax}.$$

Similarly, define the *internal cost*

$$I_a = \sum_{x \in A} c_{ax}.$$

Let $D_a = E_a - I_a$. Following Kernighan and Lin, we will refer to D_a as "the D value of vertex a." Define the corresponding quantities for the vertices of B.

If we swap $a \in A$ and $b \in B$ then we can update T by subtracting

$$g = D_a + D_b - 2c_{ab},$$

where g is called the *gain* in swapping a and b. Swapping a and b may alter the D values of other vertices incident on a and b. These D values can be recalculated as follows.

$$D'_x = D_x + 2c_{xa} - 2c_{xb}, \quad x \in A - \{a\} \tag{1}$$

$$D'_y = D_y + 2c_{yb} - 2c_{ya}, \quad y \in B - \{b\} \tag{2}$$

Using these definitions, we can state the Kernighan-Lin algorithm as follows. First, unmark all the vertices of G and compute their initial D values with respect to the current partition, A and B. Then locate two unmarked vertices, $a \in A$ and $b \in B$, that would produce the largest gain if swapped. Do not swap these vertices, but simply mark them and update the D values of the unmarked vertices using Equations 1 and 2. Repeat this process of marking vertices and updating D values until no unmarked vertices remain. The result is a sequence of pairs $(a_i, b_i) \in A \times B$ of vertices and their associated gains g_i, for $i = 1, \ldots, n$. Note that the gains g_i can be positive or negative and that $\sum_{i=1}^{n} g_i = 0$. Finally, determine which vertices of A and B to swap by finding the smallest k that maximizes $G = \sum_{i=1}^{k} g_i$. If $G > 0$, swap vertices $a_1, \ldots, a_k$ of A with $b_1, \ldots, b_k$ of B and repeat this entire process. Otherwise, stop. Since $G = 0$, no further improvements are possible using this approach.

One important feature of this algorithm is that it does not terminate upon encountering a negative gain. Hence, during a single iteration, it may consider the effect of swapping a pair of vertices that would increase T. The algorithm will only swap these two vertices if it can locate other pairs of vertices that can be swapped to produce an overall decrease in T. Thus, negative gains are tolerated provided they ultimately result in a better edge separator.

In a straightforward implementation, one iteration of this algorithm requires $O(n^3)$ time on a single processor. If C is stored as a dense matrix, the time to compute the initial D values is $O(n^2)$. Since there are $O(n^2)$ possible pairs of vertices, locating the pair with the maximum gain takes $O(n^2)$ time. Updating the remaining D values also takes at most $O(n)$ time. Since the process of locating pairs of vertices of maximum gain and updating D values is repeated n times, one iteration of the entire algorithm requires at most $O(n^3)$ time.

Kernighan and Lin implemented two faster methods for selecting pairs of vertices with large gains. In the first, not all vertices are considered, but rather some small number of the vertices with the largest D values. Using this idea, one iteration of the algorithm requires $O(n^2)$ time, but will not always select the pair of vertices with the largest possible gain at each step. Another approach sorts the D values of all the vertices before looking for the best pair. Employing this method, one iteration still requires $O(n^3)$ time in the worst case; however, for nonnegative edge costs, the actual running time will hopefully be $O(n^2 \log n)$, the time required for n sorts.

Both methods perform well in practice. Kernighan and Lin tested a variety of graphs with up to 360 vertices and various edge densities. In both implementations, they found that the algorithm almost always converges in 2 to 4 iterations and that the probability of a single iteration finding an optimal solution is approximately $2^{-n/30}$, where n is the number of vertices in the graph.

We conclude this section by noting that Kernighan and Lin proposed variants of their basic algorithm that can be used to partition the vertices of a graph into sets of different sizes or into more than two sets. In fact, the parallel algorithm in the next section is just a parallel version of one of their algorithms for partitioning the vertices of a graph into p sets, where p is a power of 2.

3 A Parallel Kernighan-Lin Algorithm

In this section, we assume that $G = (V, E)$ is an arbitrary graph whose vertices have been partitioned among $p \geq 2$ processors of a message-passing multiprocessor in some roughly even manner. We present a simple parallel version of the Kernighan-Lin algorithm for partitioning the vertices of G into p roughly equal-sized sets, each set residing on its own processor. Our goal is to produce a partition with few edges connecting vertices in different sets. Since we are primarily interested in large sparse graphs, we assume that G is stored as a collection of adjacency lists. A processor is assigned variable $v \in V$ if it has the list of vertices adjacent to v stored in its local memory. Finally, since we are interested in finding edge separators with the minimum number of edges, we assume that the edges all have cost one.

1. The processors divide themselves into two groups P_1 and P_2 with sizes different by at most one. If either group is empty, they stop. Otherwise, they select one processor in each group, say $l_1 \in P_1$ and $l_2 \in P_2$, as the leader of that group.
2. Each processor in $P_1 \cup P_2$ computes the D values of its vertices.
3. Each processor reports its D values to its leader. Each leader unmarks all of the vertices in its half of the partition.
4. Each leader l_i selects the vertex v_i with the largest D value.
5. The leaders request the adjacency lists of v_1 and v_2 from their assigned processors and update the D values of the unmarked vertices.
6. If at least one vertex in each half of the partition is unmarked, the processors repeat from step 4.
7. Using the list of vertex pairs and gains, the leaders decide which vertices to swap, and tell the other processors in their groups.
8. The processors carry out the swapping of vertices.
9. Beginning at step 2, the processors repeat until no further improvement is possible.
10. In parallel, P_1 and P_2 each apply the algorithm recursively, from step 1.

Algorithm 1: A parallel Kernighan-Lin algorithm.

Our algorithm begins by dividing the p processors into two sets P_1 and P_2 with sizes different by at most one. Sets P_1 and P_2 induce a roughly even division of the vertices. Our initial goal is to reduce the number of edges connecting vertices in P_1 to those in P_2. If $P_1 = \emptyset$ or $P_2 = \emptyset$ then there is nothing to do, so we stop. Otherwise, we perform the following procedure. First, we select one processor in each part, say $l_1 \in P_1$ and $l_2 \in P_2$, to be the *leader* of that part. If $s \in P_i$ then we will say that the leader of s is l_i. The leaders execute the simplified version of the Kernighan-Lin algorithm described below.

Each processor in $P_1 \cup P_2$ computes the D values of all its vertices, and reports these values to its leader. Each leader unmarks all of the vertices in its half of the partition. Next, each leader selects the unmarked vertex with the largest D value. The leaders mark these two vertices and save them on a list along with their gain. The leaders update the D values of the unmarked vertices using Equations 1 and 2. From these equations, we see that they need the adjacency lists of both selected vertices. The leaders request this information from the processors assigned the selected vertices and, upon receiving it, update the relevant D values. The leaders repeat this process of marking vertices and updating D values until all the vertices assigned to the processors in P_1 or P_2 have been marked.

The leaders now decide what vertices to swap using the same procedure as the Kernighan-Lin algorithm. They inform the processors of their decision, and the processors swap the selected adjacency lists. After swapping vertices, each processor still has the same number of vertices it had originally. The processors repeat this entire algorithm until the number of external edges between P_1 and P_2 cannot be decreased. Then, in parallel, P_1 and P_2 each apply this algorithm recursively. The entire procedure is outlined in Algorithm 1.

To reduce the number of messages passed between P_1 and P_2, we select vertices a and b to swap that maximize $D_a + D_b$; that is, we ignore a possible edge between a and b. Thus we may choose vertices whose actual gain is less than maximum by at most 2.

As it stands, the algorithm requires a lot of message passing; each processor repeatedly sends all of its adjacency lists to the current leader. Since we want to solve problems too large for a single processor, some of this message passing is unavoidable. However, we can reduce it by allowing a pair of leaders to stop marking vertices when further improvement seem unlikely. In our implementation, leaders stop marking vertices when the sum of all the gains computed so far becomes too negative or when they have encountered too many consecutive nonpositive gains. Since we are primarily interested in sparse graphs, once the sum of all the currently computed gains becomes very negative, it will likely remain negative. In addition, given a good initial assignment of vertices to processors, once a pair of leaders have seen several consecutive nonpositive gains, it is likely that no further improvement is possible using this approach. These modifications should improve the algorithm's running time without significantly affecting the sizes of the resulting edge separators. We will say more about the initial assignment of vertices to processors in Sections 7 and 8.

As the leaders execute the algorithm, the other processors are mostly idle. Although there is little parallelism at the beginning of this algorithm, more processors become engaged in active work as the algorithm proceeds, i.e., more processors become leaders.

4 An Implementation and Complexity Analysis

To analyze the computational and communication complexity of the parallel Kernighan and Lin algorithm, we will need some additional notation. Suppose G has n vertices, numbered from 1 to n, and m edges. Let p be the total number of available processors. To simplify the analysis, we assume that p is a power of two, n is a multiple of p, and $p \leq n \leq m$. We also assume that each processor initially has n/p vertices and knows the initial location of every vertex. Then each processor will have exactly n/p vertices throughout the computation. Let q be the maximum storage required by any processor for its vertices at any point during the computation. We call the execution of line 1 of Algorithm 1 a *level-k cut*, where k is the depth of the recursion. The first execution of line 1 is a level-0 cut. If $k \leq \log p$, there are 2^k level-k cuts, all of which can take place in parallel. After making a cut, the relevant processors try to generate a small separator by repeatedly executing lines 2–8 of Algorithm 1. We refer to a single execution as a level-k *iteration*, where k is the level of the cut. We will assume that the number of level-k iterations after any cut is bounded by some constant. Kernighan and Lin's experiments [14] support this assumption.

We begin by describing an implementation of the algorithm along with an analysis of its computational complexity. For now, we will ignore the message passing. Performing the initial level-0 cut takes $O(p)$ time. Then, in parallel, each processor in each half of the partition computes the D values of all of its assigned vertices in $O(q)$ time and reports them to its leader. Each leader constructs a heap out of the D values it receives. The heap is a balanced binary tree with the maximum D value stored at the root; see Aho, Hopcroft, and Ullman [1] for details of algorithms to construct and maintain a heap. A leader stores its heap as two n-vectors, one containing the D values and the other containing the vertices corresponding to these values. Each leader also maintains an n-vector of pointers from vertices of G to their D values in the heap. The leaders need these pointers to update D values efficiently as vertices are marked. Constructing the heap and the pointers into it takes $O(n)$ time.

A leader removes the vertex with largest D value from the heap (which corresponds to marking it) and remakes the heap, in $O(\log n)$ time. After receiving the adjacency lists of the current pair of marked vertices, a leader modifies the D values of their neighbors and adjusts the heap accordingly, using $O(\log n)$ time per modification. Since there are m edges in G, constructing the complete list of vertex pairs and gains for a level-0 iteration takes $O(m \log n)$ time. Determining the vertices to swap requires $O(n)$ time and (again ignoring message passing time) these vertices can be swapped in $O(m)$ time. Hence, the time for a single level-0 iteration is $O(m \log n)$, since $q \leq m$ and $p \leq n$. Since we have assumed that the number of iterations after any particular cut is bounded by some constant, the time required to find the level-0 edge separator is also $O(m \log n)$. At level $k > 0$, we find the 2^k edge separators in parallel. Thus, the entire algorithm takes

$$O(m \log n \log p)$$

time, ignoring the time for message passing.

To measure the communication complexity, we will count both the total number of messages and the total volume of message traffic, that is, the total number of integers passed in messages. We assume that each processor has an integer label which is known to every other processor. The processors use this labelling to partition processors and select leaders and, hence, require no message passing to perform a cut.

Now consider a single level-k iteration Let P' be the set of processors in one half of the current partition. In line 3 of Algorithm 1, each processor in P' reports its D values (and corresponding vertex labels) to the leader of P' in a *fan-in* fashion. The set P' contains $p/2^{k+1}$ processors, so this step requires $p/2^{k+1} - 1$ messages. The total number of integers passed is

$$\sum_{i=1}^{\log p'} \frac{p'}{2^i}(2^i \frac{n}{p}) = \frac{n}{2^{k+1}} \log \frac{p}{2^{k+1}},$$

where $p' = p/2^{k+1}$.

Each cut produces two leaders, both requiring a fan-in report of D values. For $0 \leq k \leq \log p$, there are 2^k level-k cuts, each requiring at most some constant number of iterations. Thus, execution of the entire algorithm produces

$$\sum_{k=1}^{\log p} O\big(2^{k+1}(\frac{p}{2^{k+1}} - 1)\big) = O(p \log p)$$

D value messages containing a total of

$$\sum_{k=1}^{\log p} O\big(2^{k+1}(\frac{n}{2^{k+1}} \log \frac{p}{2^{k+1}})\big) = O(n \log^2 p)$$

integers.

We could have implemented the reporting of D values by simply having each processor send a message containing its D values directly to its leader. In this approach, there would still be $O(p \log p)$ messages, but they would only contain a total of $O(n \log p)$ integers. We use the fan-in method because, on a hypercube, it can be implemented so that only adjacent processors need to communicate. The total number of integers sent over single links is the same —$O(n \log^2 p)$— in the fan-in and direct-to-leader methods; the total number of messages sent over single links is $O(p \log p)$ for fan-in and $O(p \log^2 p)$ for direct-to-leader. Since the machines we are interested in have a significant minimum cost per message, fan-in is more efficient. (Chamberlain and Powell [2,3] examine the fan-in approach to communication in the context of LU and QR factorization.)

To calculate the message traffic required for the remainder of the algorithm, first consider a single level-0 iteration. After constructing heaps of D values, the two leaders request adjacency lists from other processors, communicate vertices of maximum D value to each another, and tell processors what vertices to swap. The other processors send adjacency lists to leaders, and all of the processors carry out the swapping of vertices. All of this communication requires $O(n)$ messages containing a total of $O(m)$ integers. Hence, the entire algorithm requires $O(n \log p)$

messages containing a total of $O(m \log p)$ integers to carry out the communication not involving D values.

There is one subtle point concerning the swapping of vertices. At the start of the algorithm, each processor knows the location of each vertex. Thus, after the initial level-0 cut, the two leaders know what vertices are assigned to each processor. To tell each processor which of its vertices it must send to some other processor, the leaders send a total of $O(n) \leq O(m)$ integers in $O(p) \leq O(n)$ messages. After the swap, the leaders at the next level iteration will not necessarily know the location of each vertex. We can remedy this during the fan-in of D values by including the processor of origin with every D value. This will not change the complexity of fan-in. Therefore the entire parallel separator algorithm requires

$$O(n \log p)$$

messages containing a total of

$$O(\max(n \log^2 p, m \log p))$$

integers.

5 A Parallel Ordering Algorithm

As noted in Section 1, the first step in computing the Cholesky factorization of an $n \times n$ symmetric positive definite matrix $A = (a_{ij})$ is to find a permutation matrix P to reorder A. On single processor systems, one typically selects P solely to reduce fill. This is a good strategy since reducing fill, besides reducing the needed storage, also reduces the factorization time. On message-passing multiprocessors, defining a good ordering is more complicated. We want all of the processors to be busy throughout the factorization; that is, we want an ordering that allows for parallelism. Also, all hypercubes currently on the market require significantly more time to communicate a byte of data than to perform a floating point operation on that byte. Therefore, we also want to reduce the amount of communication needed during the factorization, perhaps even at the expense of more fill. Both the parallelism and communication in the computation depend not only on P but also on the placement of A on the processors. As we shall see below, it is possible to find a reordering of A and an assignment of its nonzeros to processors that results in good processor utilization during the factorization, while reducing both the fill and the communication.

George, Liu, and Ng [11] independently made similar observations and implemented an algorithm that sequentially orders the columns of a matrix on the host of a hypercube and then uses the elimination tree to assign the columns to processors. In what follows, we will use both narrow and wide vertex separators to order the columns of A. In a different setting, Liu [20] suggested both of these orderings and analyzed the parallelism that results during the outer product Cholesky factorization of grid graphs. We will discuss Cholesky factorization in terms of graphs [23] and will compute factorizations by columns. For a review of parallel sparse Cholesky factorization by columns see Gilbert and Zmijewski [24,25,26] and George, Heath, Liu, and Ng [8].

We can represent the structure of A by a graph $G = (V, E)$, where $V = \{v_1, \ldots, v_n\}$ and $(v_i, v_j) \in E$ if and only if $a_{ij} \neq 0$. An *elimination order* of G is an ordering of the vertices of G which we will write as a one-to-one function $\alpha : V \to 1, \ldots, n$. Finding an elimination order on G corresponds to finding a permutation matrix P for A. That is, column (row) i of A is column (row) $\alpha(i)$ of PAP^T. The *filled graph* G^*_α of G with respect to α is the graph with the same vertices as G, whose edges are all those edges (u, w) such that there is a path $u = v_1, v_2, \ldots, v_k = w$ in G with $\alpha(v_i) < \min(\alpha(u), \alpha(w))$ for $1 < i < k$. If L is the Cholesky factor of PAP^T, then $L + L^T$ is the adjacency matrix of G^*_α. Thus, finding P to reduce the amount of fill in L corresponds to finding an α to reduce the number of edges in G^*_α.

Nested dissection is an ordering heuristic that both reduces fill [10] and allows for parallelism [18,22]. Nested dissection begins by finding a set of vertices S contained in G whose removal would disconnect G into at least two components $C_1, \ldots, C_k$. The set S is a *vertex separator* of G. It orders the vertices of S after those in $C_1, \ldots, C_k$. Then no edge in G_α^* can connect two vertices in different C_i, since any path in G between two such vertices must go through S. Besides reducing fill, this property also allows us to eliminate vertices in different C_i in parallel [22]. To order the remaining vertices in V, we apply this procedure recursively to the subgraphs $C_1, \ldots, C_k$. Nested dissection orderings produce low fill if each separator is small and the components it divides its subgraph into are all roughly the same size. For example, planar graphs, two-dimensional finite element graphs, and graphs of bounded genus all have nested dissection orderings that produce at most $O(n \log n)$ fill [12,16].

We use our parallel edge separator algorithm to find nested dissection orderings. We assume the columns of A (i.e., the adjacency lists of G) have been distributed among the p processors of a message-passing multiprocessor in some roughly even manner and that the processors are numbered from 0 to $p - 1$. We further assume that the processor assigned column i of A is responsible for computing column $\alpha(i)$ of L, the Cholesky factor of PAP^T.

First, the processors run the parallel edge separator algorithm on G. We then use each edge separator to define a vertex separator as follows. Suppose some edge separator divides a subset of the processors into two groups, say P_1 and P_2. We can partition the vertices incident on the edge separator into two groups V_1 and V_2, depending on whether they reside in P_1 or P_2. Both V_1 and V_2 are vertex separators for a subgraph of G. We can select the smaller of the two sets, say V_1, as the vertex separator defined by this edge separator. We will call V_1 a *narrow separator*. Let V be the set of all vertices assigned to P_1 and P_2. If the vertices in V_1 are ordered after the vertices in $V - V_1$, no communication across the cut, i.e., between processors in P_1 and those in P_2, is required to eliminate the vertices in $V - V_1$. However, as the vertices in $V - V_1$ are eliminated, the corresponding columns of L will be sent to processors assigned vertices of V_1. Thus, no matter where the vertices of the narrow separator reside, communication across the cut will take place as the vertices that are not in the separator are eliminated.

Another possibility is to take all of $V_1 \cup V_2$ as the separator of the subgraph, since this guarantees that processors in P_1 and P_2 will not need to communicate until they begin eliminating vertices in $V_1 \cup V_2$. This is because no fill can occur between a vertex assigned to a processor P_1 and one assigned to a processor in P_2 until the first vertex in $V_1 \cup V_2$ is eliminated. We will refer to such vertex separators as *wide separators*. Since these separators are larger than narrow separators, they will give more fill. However, the number of columns of L that must be communicated across the cut is bounded by $|V_1 \cup V_2|$, the size of the wide separator. For narrow separators, the number of columns crossing the cut is bounded only by $|V|$, the number of columns assigned to processors in P_1 and P_2. Thus, for wide separators, one may hope that the increase in computation time will be more than offset by the decrease in communication time. Section 6 contains numerical factorization times using both narrow and wide separators to find orderings.

After defining vertex separators, each processor orders all of its vertices, beginning with those not contained in any separator. In our implementation, the processors use Sparspak's nested dissection routine [10] to order these vertices. Finally, the processors order the vertices contained in the vertex separators after all the other vertices, in such a way that vertices in level-k separators come after those in level-$(k+1)$ separators. The result is a nested dissection ordering whose first $\lceil \log p \rceil$ levels of vertex separators are based on the edge separators from the parallel Kernighan-Lin algorithm.

After all the vertices are numbered, those contained in the vertex separators are redistributed among the processors to balance the computational load during the factorization. In the case of a wide separator, we could *wrap* the vertices in V_1 onto the processors in P_1. That is, if $V_1 = \{v_1, \ldots, v_k\}$ and $P_1 = \{p_0, \ldots, p_{l-1}\}$, then we would reassign vertex v_i to processor p_j, where

Problem	Equations	Nonzeros	Density (%)
1	346	3226	2.69
2	512	3502	1.34
3	758	5994	1.04
4	878	7448	0.97
5	918	7384	0.88
6	1005	8621	0.85
7	1007	8575	0.85
8	1242	10426	0.68
9	1561	10681	0.44
10	1882	12904	0.38

Table 1: Test problems.

$j = (i-1) \bmod l$. Similarly, we could wrap the vertices in V_2 onto the processors in P_2. This redistribution of vertices would not change the edge separator between P_1 and P_2; however, it could increase the number of edges crossing higher numbered cuts and hence, increase the number of vertices incident on those edges. To avoid this problem, we reassign a vertex only if there is no increase the number of edges crossing other cuts. Whenever a given vertex cannot be reassigned, we note that its assigned processor has an extra vertex and skip this processor the next time around. More formally, if vertex v_i is assigned to processor p_j, we try to reassign it to processor p_k, where p_k is the first processor in the sequence $p_{(i-1) \bmod l}, p_{i \bmod l}, p_{(i+1) \bmod l}, \ldots$ that is assigned no more than $\lfloor i/l \rfloor$ vertices from the set $\{v_0, \ldots, v_{i-1}\}$.

In the case of a narrow separator, V_1 is wrapped onto all the processors in P_1 and P_2. Unlike wide separators, narrow separators are not designed to limit the number of columns communicated across cuts. Thus, we do not need to the take the same precautions in wrapping them that we did with wide separators.

Since vertex separators correspond to dense submatrices of L, and hence are more time consuming to eliminate, redistributing them evenly among all the processors should give better processor utilization. If we succeed in finding small separators, each processor will end up with roughly the same number of vertices. Since the separator vertices are wrapped, the load will be fairly well balanced. In our experiments, reassigning vertices required very little time and, in many cases, significantly reduced the running time of the remaining phases of the computation. Note that using either narrow or wide separators, at most $p/2^k$ processors need to communicate in order to eliminate the vertices in a level-k vertex separator. On a hypercube, this implies that the columns of L corresponding to level-k vertex separators can be computed in a dimension-k subcube. Not until the very end of the computation, when the columns of L associated with the level-0 vertex separator are being computed, do all the processors need to communicate.

6 Numerical Results

We have implemented the wide and narrow ordering algorithms of Section 5 that use the parallel Kernighan-Lin algorithm. We have added this code to Gilbert and Zmijewski's parallel elimination forest, symbolic factorization, and triangular system solver codes [24,25,26], and George, Heath, Liu, and Ng's parallel numeric factorization code [8,11]. The resulting collection of routines performs all phases of sparse Cholesky factorization in parallel. The code is written in Fortran and runs on both the Cornell Theory Center's Intel hypercube under Xenix with version 3.0 of the node operating system and, using the Oak Ridge National Laboratories' hypercube simulator [4], on a Vax 780 under Berkeley Unix. We have used the simulator to generate

Problem	Seq-wrap	Narrow	Wide
1	1.88	7.85	7.38
2	1.74	8.34	8.57
3	4.90	13.23	13.28
4	5.00	8.95	8.70
5	5.80	16.10	15.18
6	7.42	23.12	23.30
7	5.88	9.22	9.56
8	7.96	15.67	15.64
9	9.60	12.48	12.94
10	11.78	11.13	10.90

Table 2: Ordering times (seconds).

Problem	Seq-wrap	Narrow	Wide
1	3526 (2.13)	2402 (1.93)	1580 (1.74)
2	3166 (2.11)	1087 (1.57)	778 (1.39)
3	6689 (2.11)	2745 (1.84)	2070 (1.63)
4	8836 (2.13)	4558 (1.85)	3321 (1.64)
5	8849 (2.13)	4951 (1.95)	4230 (1.83)
6	10123 (2.13)	5694 (1.97)	4884 (1.83)
7	10438 (2.13)	4843 (1.83)	3318 (1.60)
8	12897 (2.13)	7534 (2.00)	6312 (1.82)
9	15825 (2.13)	7982 (1.97)	6334 (1.76)
10	18917 (2.13)	9537 (1.95)	7368 (1.75)

Table 3: Message traffic during numeric factorization.

Problem	Seq-wrap	Narrow	Wide
1	127294	110344	142954
2	36190	37197	45574
3	93408	112187	166011
4	192834	266103	500606
5	239274	277298	638908
6	458580	470572	897429
7	258793	315552	608565
8	558595	781817	1437048
9	629271	693393	1109808
10	841932	983679	1866030

Table 4: Flops during numeric factorization.

Problem	Seq-wrap	Narrow	Wide
1	5.06	4.39	3.88
2	3.13	2.22	2.33
3	6.81	5.99	6.53
4	9.91	7.43	10.13
5	10.51	9.18	14.30
6	14.29	17.72	23.46
7	11.25	7.99	12.17
8	17.99	19.51	28.73
9	19.81	16.65	23.40
10	25.45	22.02	34.66

Table 5: Numeric factorization times (seconds).

communication statistics and the Intel hypercube to measure running times.

We have compared three algorithms for ordering the columns of a matrix and assigning them to processors: the narrow and wide algorithms of Section 3, and a simple sequential strategy we will call *seq-wrap*. The seq-wrap method orders the matrix sequentially on the host using Sparspak's nested dissection routine and then distributes the columns to all the processors of the hypercube in a wrap fashion. Thus, this method orders the columns to reduce fill and distributes them in a way that should result in good processor utilization, but it ignores the issue of communication. We ran these three algorithms on the 10 finite element problems listed in Table 1. The first eight problems represent various physical structures and are described by Everstine [5]; the last two are derived from L-shaped triangular meshes and are described by George and Liu [9]. In running our experiments, we used all 16 processors of the Cornell Theory Center's Intel hypercube.

Table 2 lists the time required to perform the orderings. Under seq-wrap, we list the time the host uses to order the matrix, ignoring the time required to send the columns to the nodes of the hypercube. Under narrow and wide, we list the times for the parallel Kernighan-Lin algorithm. These include the time to swap columns amoung processors during the algorithm and the time needed to wrap the columns of the resulting separators. As with seq-wrap, we do not include the time to initially send the columns to the nodes. The initial orderings of problems 3, 5, 6, and 8 were very poor. Due to message-passing delays, narrow and wide both require more time then seq-wrap in all cases except the last. However, as we shall see below, narrow and wide orderings usually succeed in reducing the numeric factorization time. On single-processor machines, numeric factorization is the most time consuming step in solving sparse linear systems. For larger problems, we can expect narrow and wide to require less time than seq-wrap, provided the problem has a reasonable initial ordering. The parallel ordering algorithms also allow us to solve problems that are too large to reside in the memory of any one processor.

After ordering a matrix with one of the algorithms above and symbolically factoring it, we used George, Heath, Liu, and Ng's parallel numeric factorization code [8,11] (in an experimental version from February 1987) to compute the Cholesky factor. For each problem, Table 3 lists the total number of messages the processors pass during numeric factorizaton. Each message contains the nonzero values of a single column of the Cholesky factor, along with the positions of its nonzeros. Table 3 also lists, in parentheses after each total, the average distance travelled by the messages. Since we used a 4-dimensional cube, a message makes at most 4 hops. On the Intel hypercube, messages are broken up into packets of 1024 bytes, and the smallest message is 1024 bytes. Since almost all of the messages passed were smaller than 1024 bytes, we have listed only the total number of messages. Only the wide approach produced messages longer than 1024

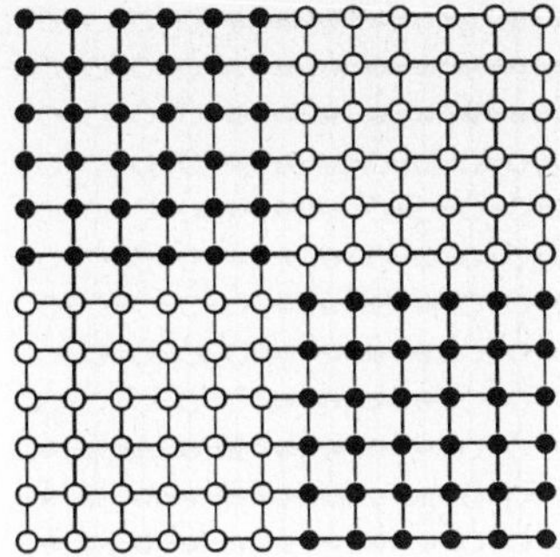

Figure 1: A partitioning of a 12×12 grid graph.

bytes and just for problems 8 and 10. In both of these cases, 1% of the messages were longer than 1024 bytes and all were less than 2048 bytes. As expected, the wide approach results in both the lowest total message traffic and lowest average distance travelled per message. For our test problems, narrow requires 32% to 66% fewer messages than seq-wrap, while wide requires 14% to 34% fewer messages than narrow.

Table 4 lists the total number of flops the processors perform during the numeric factorization. For most of the problems, the narrow method performs almost as well as Sparspak's nested dissection routine. Due to the large separators, the wide method requires about twice as many flops as the narrow method for the larger problems. For a fixed number of processors, the relative difference between the narrow and wide flop requirements will decrease as the sizes of the problems increase, since the percentage of the columns belonging to wide separators will decrease. Our test problems are all relatively small, and the percentage of columns belonging to wide separators range from 35%, for the largest problem, to 80%, for the smallest.

Table 5 lists the factorization times for the three methods. Even though the narrow approach requires somewhat more flops and the wide approach considerably more flops than seq-wrap, both methods frequently require less time. Factorization time depends not only on the number of flops, but also on the amount of communication and on how well the load is balanced. Narrow and wide require significantly less communication than seq-wrap, but may not do as well at balancing the load. For example, if the graph is irregular, interprocessor separators at the same level may be of very different sizes and, in fact, this happens with problems 6 and 8. As a result, seq-wrap produces the best factorization times for these problems. We plan on conducting further tests with larger matrices.

7 Remarks on the Kernighan-Lin Algorithm

We have seen that using either narrow or wide vertex separators to reorder large sparse symmetric positive definite matrices can decrease the factorization time by lowering the total volume of message traffic. Since both the amount of fill and message traffic depend on the size of these separators, our hope is that we can find small ones for certain types of graphs. In particular, we would like to know if the sequential version of the Kernighan and Lin algorithm presented in Section 2 will always find minimum edge separators for a particular class of graphs, regardless of the initial partition.

Let G be an $n \times n$ grid graph where n is even. Suppose it is initially partitioned as in Figure 1. The total number of external edges in G is $2n$, twice the minimum. (One minimum edge separator divides the first $n/2$ rows from the others.) The Kernighan-Lin algorithm will not necessarily find a partitioning with the minimum number of external edges. At each step of the algorithm, it

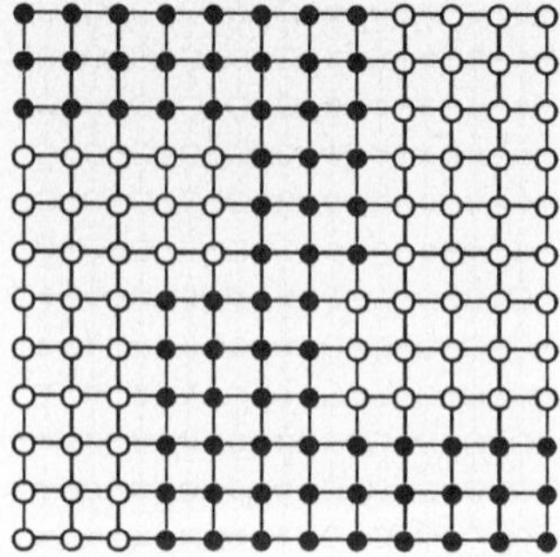

Figure 2: The partitioning after swapping the first 30 pairs of vertices.

must mark a pair of vertices that produces the maximum gain, and, due to the regularity of the graph, it usually has more than one choice. By carefully selecting the vertices to be marked at each step, we can force the algorithm to stop after one iteration without swapping a single pair of vertices.

To see this, think of actually swapping the vertex pairs as they are marked. In Figure 1, we can choose the sequence of pairs so that the black vertices in the upper left move to the right, trading places with the white vertices in the upper right. The black vertices in the lower right move to the left, trading places with the white vertices in the lower left. Figure 2 shows the partition after swapping the first 30 pairs of vertices. The black vertices in the lower half of Figure 2 resemble the letter L. As the swapping progresses from here, the vertical part of this L grows wider, while the horizontal part grows thinner. The upper black vertices behave similarly. The total number of external edges is never less than $2n$. Therefore the sum of gains is never positive, so the algorithm will not actually swap any vertices. Thus, the Kernighan-Lin algorithm does not necessarily find minimum edge separators even for grid graphs. It is important to note, however, that the algorithm can find a minimum edge separator for a grid graph partitioned as in Figure 1, if it chooses to mark the vertices in the proper order. We do not know if such an order exists for every initial partition of the graph.

8 Conclusion

Lipton, Rose, and Tarjan [16] have shown that random graphs do not contain good separators. However, many graphs one encounters in practice do have good separators, since most real-world problems have considerable structure. Therefore, finding good separators of graphs is important. Our experience with the Kernighan-Lin algorithm is that it always converges quickly, regardless of the initial partition, but that the quality of this partition affects the size of the resulting edge separator. We are currently examining ways to improve the Kernighan-Lin algorithm. One possiblity is to develop a parallel heuristic for finding good initial partitions, such as a technique for finding highly connected subgraphs of a graph. We could then use this partitioning as input to the algorithm. Another approach is to modify the Kernighan-Lin algorithm so that it uses global knowledge about the graph in breaking ties between the vertices of maximum gain. This could eliminate the problem with the grid graph in Section 7.

As we saw in our experiments, the parallel Kernighan-Lin algorithm can produce an assignment of columns to processors and an ordering that results in poor processor utilization during numeric factorization. This happens when separators at the same level are of very different sizes. One approach to this problem is to assign weights to the vertices and then partition them among the processors in a way that gives each processor roughly the same total weight. If we make the weight of a vertex proportional to the number of edges incident on it, this approach would allow denser parts of the graph to be distributed over more processors and may result in a more uniform distribution of the interprocessor separators. Kernighan and Lin have suggested a modification of their algorithm that will handle this case for positive integer weights. Namely, if a vertex has weight $k > 1$, it is replaced with a cluster of k vertices of weight 1, bound together by edges of appropriately high cost.

At the top level of the parallel Kernighan-Lin algorithm, the two leaders perform the entire computation, once the initial D values have been computed. Here, the only advantage of using more than two processors is that more memory is available for storing the graph, so bigger problems can be solved. Of course, as more processors become leaders, more processors become actively involved in the computation. Designing a more parallel algorithm for finding separators is an interesting problem.

In general, a parallel algorithm will perform better if it first decomposes the problem it is solving into parts that have high locality and require low communication overhead. Thus, finding good graph partitionings should be a useful first step for a wide variety of parallel problems. For example, in LU factorization with partial pivoting, if we use wide separators to partition the columns of the matrix, then our pivot searches will be confined to single groups of processors. We can also use wide separators in iterative methods, e.g., Jacobi and Gauss-Seidel splitting methods, to reduce the amount of communication.

The problem of finding a good ordering along with a good assignment of nonzeros to processors deserves further study. Peters examined aspects of this issue for shared memory multiprocessors [22] and message-passing multiprocessors [21]. Liu [19] suggested using tree rotations to create more evenly balanced elimination forests and thereby, better parallel orderings. Fox and Otto [7] describe a different approach to automatic partitioning and use it to solve various numerical problems on the Caltech hypercube.

Acknowledgements

We thank Laurie Hulbert for reading earlier drafts of this paper and for making suggestions that made it more readable. We also thank Alan George, Mike Heath, Joseph Liu, and Esmond Ng for allowing us to use their sparse parallel Cholesky factorization codes, and Mike Heath and Esmond Ng for providing us with the Oak Ridge National Laboratory hypercube simulator. Finally, we express our appreciation to Cornell University's Theory Center for the use of their Intel iPSC hypercube computer.

References

[1] Alfred V. Aho, John E. Hopcroft, and Jeffrey D. Ullman. *The Design and Analysis of Computer Algorithms.* Addison-Wesley Publishing Company, 1974.

[2] R. M. Chamberlain. *An algorithm for LU factorization with partial pivoting on the hypercube.* Technical Report CCS 86/11, Chr. Michelsen Institute, 1986.

[3] R. M. Chamberlain and M. J. D. Powell. *QR factorization for linear least squares problems on the hypercube.* Technical Report CCS 86/10, Chr. Michelsen Institute, 1986.

[4] T. H. Dunigan. *A message-passing multiprocessor simulator.* Technical Report ORNL/TM–9966, Oak Ridge National Laboratory, 1986.

[5] G. C. Everstine. A comparison of three resequencing algortihms for the reduction of matrix profile and wave front. *International Journal for Numerical Methods in Engineering*, 14:837–853, 1979.

[6] Tse-yun Feng. A survey of interconnection networks. *IEEE Computer*, 12:12–27, 1981.

[7] Geoffrey C. Fox and Steve W. Otto. *Concurrent computation and the theory of complex systems.* Technical Report CALT-68-1343, California Institute of Technology, 1986.

[8] Alan George, Michael T. Heath, Joseph Liu, and Esmond Ng. *Sparse Cholesky factorization on a local-memory multiprocessor.* Technical Report ORNL/TM-9962, Oak Ridge National Laboratory, 1986.

[9] Alan George and Joseph W. H. Liu. An automatic nested dissection algorithm for irregular finite element problems. *SIAM Journal on Numerical Analysis*, 15:1053–1069, 1978.

[10] Alan George and Joseph W. H. Liu. *Computer Solution of Large Sparse Positive Definite Systems.* Prentice-Hall, 1981.

[11] Alan George, Joseph W. H. Liu, and Esmond Ng. Communication results for parallel sparse Cholesky factorization on a hypercube. Submitted to *Parallel Computing*, 1987.

[12] John R. Gilbert and Robert Endre Tarjan. The analysis of a nested dissection algorithm. To appear in *Numerische Mathematik*, 1987.

[13] John Russell Gilbert. *Graph Separator Theorems and Sparse Gaussian Elimination.* Ph.D. thesis, Stanford University, 1980.

[14] B. W. Kernighan and S. Lin. An efficient heuristic procedure for partitioning graphs. *The Bell System Technical Journal*, 49:291–307, 1970.

[15] Charles E. Leiserson. Area-efficient graph layouts (for VLSI). In *Proceedings of the 21st Annual Symposium on Foundations of Computer Science*, pages 270–281, 1980.

[16] Richard J. Lipton, Donald J. Rose, and Robert Endre Tarjan. Generalized nested dissection. *SIAM Journal on Numerical Analysis*, 16:346–358, 1979.

[17] Richard J. Lipton and Robert Endre Tarjan. Applications of a planar separator theorem. *SIAM Journal on Computing*, 9:615–627, 1980.

[18] Joseph W. H. Liu. Computational models and task scheduling for parallel sparse Cholesky factorization. *Parallel Computing*, 3:327–342, 1986.

[19] Joseph W. H. Liu. *Equivalent sparse matrix reordering by elimination tree rotations.* Technical Report CS-86-12, York University, 1986.

[20] Joseph W. H. Liu. *The solution of mesh equations on a parallel computer.* Technical Report, University of Waterloo, 1974.

[21] Frans J. Peters. MIMD machines and sparse linear equations. In *Highly parallel computers for numerical and signal processing applications: Proceedings of a working conference of the International Federation for Information Processing Working Group 10.3*, North-Holland, 1986.

[22] Frans J. Peters. Parallel pivoting algorithms for sparse symmetric matrices. *Parallel Computing*, 1:99–110, 1984.

[23] Donald J. Rose, Robert Endre Tarjan, and George S. Leuker. Algorithmic aspects of vertex elimination on graphs. *SIAM Journal on Computing*, 5:266–283, 1976.

[24] Earl Zmijewski. *Sparse Cholesky Factorization on a Multiprocessor.* Ph.D. thesis, Cornell University, 1987.

[25] Earl Zmijewski and John R. Gilbert. *A parallel algorithm for large sparse symbolic and numeric Cholesky factorization on a multiprocessor.* Technical Report 86–733, Cornell University, 1986.

[26] Earl Zmijewski and John R. Gilbert. A parallel algorithm for sparse symbolic Cholesky factorization on a multiprocessor. To appear in *Parallel Computing.*

THE MAPPING OF APPLICATIONS TO MULTIPLE BUS AND BANYAN INTERCONNECTED MULTIPROCESSOR SYSTEMS: A CASE STUDY

Catherine E. Houstis *
Mokhtar Aboelaze
Electrical Engineering Department
Purdue University

Abstract

We study the mapping of a robot elbow manipulator application, to two different classes of multiprocessor systems the multiple bus and Banyan interconnected systems. A comparative performance analysis of the two systems is performed. The application is partitioned into communicating computational modules and three different partitions of it are approximated. Fast heuristic algorithms are used to produce assignments of modules to processors. A number of performance measures are also employed to evaluate the matching of application/architecture pairs.

1. INTRODUCTION

In previous work [HOUS83], [HOUS87a], we have outlined a mapping methodology which has been applied to the computations involved in the solution of partial differential equations. We continue this study here for a different application, a robot arm elbow manipulator and two different system architectures, multiple bus and banyan interconnected parallel multiprocessor systems.

The mapping problem arises when the number of computational modules required by the application exceeds the number of processors available or when the interconnection structure of the application's computational modules, differs from the interconnection structure of the parallel machine [BERM84]. In [BOKH81], the mapping problem is defined as the assignment of modules to processors and the problem of maximizing the number of pairs of communicating modules that fall on pairs of directly connected processors. It is also shown, that the mapping problem is equivalent to a graph isomorphism problem, or to a bandwidth reduction problem. In either case, an exact algorithm for the mapping problem is unlikely to be found. Research in this area has concentrated on efficient heuristics which give good solutions in most cases, [BERM85], [BOKH81], [JENN77], [ABRA86], [GILB87].

The application we consider here, is the solution of the Newton Euler equation for the motion of a six degree of freedom manipulator whose joints are all rotational, i.e., an elbow manipulator. The computations involved are modelled by a precedence graph, where each node in the graph represents a computational module's computation and memory requirements and each link represents communication requirements between modules. The decomposition of the applications computation is given in [KASA85], and it is broken down in such a way that parallelism is used to maximum advantage.

---

* This research was supported by NSF grant DMC-8508684A1.

The parallel multiprocessor system architectures, are composed of processors each having a local memory and shared memory modules and they are interconnected via multiple busses or a Banyan switch. The systems are homogeneous, i.e., they have identical processors and identical local or shared memories. The processors are assumed uniprogrammed. Communication is performed via message passing between the processors by using common access to shared memories and the interconnection network. The communication network of the multiprocessor system is represented by its performance characteristic which is the communication Queueing Delay vs its Utilization. This requires its performance analysis. We have used one of the multiples bus interconnection models presented in [MARS83], and performed a similar performance analysis. We have also performed a comparable analysis for the Banyan interconnection network.

The solution of the mapping problem, involves a number of steps which can be performed somewhat independently [HOUS87a]. (a) Schedule the computational modules into parallel clusters, (b) reduce the number of parallel clusters to the number of parallel processors in the machine then (c) imbed the application into the machine. We concentrate on a heuristic algorithm, that is used in step (a) and also in step (b) with a simple modification. Step (c) for the interconnection architectures used and homogeneous systems is trivial since there is a communication link between all processors, or processors can be considered equally distant. An arbitrary assignment of clusters obtained in step (b) to processors is sufficient. We have discussed this step (c) in [HOUS87c]. Thus we shall concentrate on steps (a), and (b).

In [HOUS83], [HOUS87a] only step (a) of this approach has been demonstrated for applications whose precedence graphs had no more than 50 communicating modules and a bus interconnected system architecture. In this work, a much larger graph is considered that has 105 nodes and two different system architectures are tested. The architectures are chosen so that the parallelism reduction, (step (b)), can be evaluated. We consider on one hand, a multiple bus architecture where the number of processors can be increased (or decreased) by one. In this case, the application's parallelism can be fully exploited since the number of processors can always be adjusted to equal the number of parallel clusters obtained in step (a). Then step (a) is a sufficient solution to the mapping problem. If the system has a fixed number of processors which are less than the clusters obtained, then the parallelism reduction step (b) is necessary. In a Banyan interconnected system, the number of processors can be increased (or decreased) only in powers of 2. Thus, if the number of clusters obtained is not a power of 2 then it is cost effective to use a system where the number of processors is the highest power of 2 and less than the number of clusters. In this case, the parallelism reduction, step (b), is unavoidable.

In a number of heuristic algorithms dealing with step (a) [CHU80] [EFE82], [JENN77], [STO78], [GYL76], [BERM87] an assignment of computational modules to processors is produced by minimizing the communication required among processors. We assign a cost to this communication which is the interconnection system's Queueing Delay. We claim that a different schedule is produced when the system's Queueing Delay is involved and that it is a more realistic schedule. We demonstrate this in Section 4.2. The use of Queueing Delay models simplifies the complexity of the mapping problem. A number of performance measures are also calculated which indicate how good *applications/architecture pairs* are *matched.*

In Section 2, the performance analysis of two interconnection networks is given. In Section 3, the application is presented and how different partitions of the application are obtained. In Section 4, step (a) of the mapping problem is summarized and the results obtained using the two systems and the considered application are given. In Section 5, the parallelism reduction, step (b), is performed and the resulting schedules are presented. A comparison of the performance of the two systems is also demonstrated. In Section 6, conclusions about this methodology, application and systems are discussed.

2. COMPARATIVE PERFORMANCE ANALYSIS OF INTERCONNECTION NETWORKS

In steps (a) and (b) of the mapping problem, the objective is to exploit the parallelism of the multiprocessor system and that of the application in order to obtain optimal speed ups for the application. For this, two conditions must be met. (1) The application's computations must be decomposed into smaller sub-computations that can run in parallel, and at the same time the amount of data transfer between these sub-computations must be kept at a minimum. We further discuss this problem in the next section. (2) The system overhead must also be kept at a minimum. Our work has concentrated on the second condition. The system overhead comes mainly from the communication conflicts of the processors at the different memory modules or at the interconnection network.

In the systems we consider, processors have approximately comparable capabilities. All processors share access to a common memory module, I/O channels, and peripheral devices. Most importantly, the entire system is controlled by a single integrated operating system providing interactions between processors and their programs at various levels. Besides the shared memories and I/O devices, each processor has its own local memory. Interprocessor communications can be done via the shared memories. In this mode of operation, each processor executes a program stored in its local memory, on a set of data stored in the same local memory. When processor i wants to communicate with another processor j, either requesting a set of data or providing to the other processor with some needed data, processor i forms a message and sends it to the common memory module of processor j, via the interconnection network.

There are many physical configurations for the interconnection network. The simplest form is the single bus, where a single bus is used by all the processors to access any memory module. The single bus is very inexpensive, but the bandwidth of such a network is usually low, since only one processor can use the bus at any time, and thus it is inadequate even for a small number of processors. At the other end of the spectrum is the crossbar switch. In a crossbar interconnection, any processor can access any memory module, given that no other processor is accessing the same memory module. Although the crossbar interconnection offers the highest possible bandwidth, it is very expensive, and considering todays technology, it is the most expensive part in the system. Moreover, it will be very hard to justify its use especially for large systems.

In this paper, we study two classes of interconnection networks. The multiple bus network and the multistage banyan network. Notice that the single bus and the crossbar network are both a special case of the multiple bus network.

2.1 Banyan network

The banyan networks have been proposed mainly for SIMD "Single Instruction Multiple Data" machines, where more than one processor executes the same instruction on a different set of data. However, they have been used successfully in MIMD "Multiple Instructions Multiple Data" machines. They can be divided into two main categories, Single stage and Multistage networks.

Single stage, also called recirculating networks, because data may have to circulate through more than one processor to reach their final destination. Fig. 1, shows the different configurations for the single stage cube network.

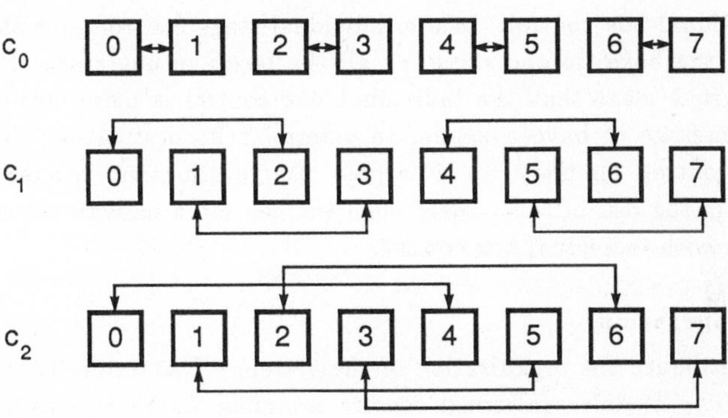

Fig. 1. Single Stage Cube Network.

Multi stage networks, connect k **processors, via log**k stages and allow communication between any two processors to take place in log$k$ steps. The multistage networks can be characterized by three parameters, [SIEG85], interchange box, topology and control structure.

Interchange box is a two input two output switch, used as the basic building block for the multistage interconnection network. Fig. 2, shows an interchange box with two inputs marked a_1 and a_2 and two outputs marked b_1 and b_2. There are four configurations for the interchange box (1) straight, where $a_1 \rightarrow b_1$, $a_2 \rightarrow b_2$; (2) exchange, where $a_1 \rightarrow b_2$, $a_2 \rightarrow b_1$; (3) upper broadcast, where $a_1 \rightarrow b_1$, $a_2 \rightarrow b_1$; and (4) lower broadcast, where $a_1 \rightarrow b_2$, $a_2 \rightarrow b_2$. A two function interchange box can only take the configuration of straight and exchange, while a four function interchange box can take any one of the four configurations [SIEG78].

Topology is the actual connection between the different interchange boxes in the different stages. One topology is the indirect binary k-cube, shown in Fig. 3, for k=8. The input to the first stage is numbered 0 through 7. Any interchange box in stage i is connected to two inputs that differ in the ith bit of their binary representation. Straight configuration for an interchange box will connect two numbers having the same i^{th} bit, while exchange configuration will connect two numbers that are different in their i^{th} bit. The indirect

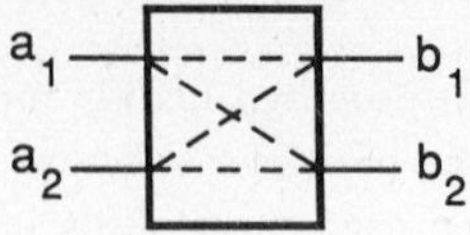

Fig. 2. Interchange box.

binary k cube network is used in the staran network [BATC76]. Another network is the Omega network, [LAWR75], shown in Fig. 4. The omega network is based on the perfect shuffle interconnection network, which routes data from position i whose binary representation is $i_{k-1} \cdots i_1 i_0$ to position $s(i)$ whose binary representation is $i_{k-2} \cdots i_1 i_0 i_{k-1}$.

Control structure. The control structure of the network can be either individual stage control or individual box control. In the individual stage control , the same control signal is used to set all the boxes in the stage, so all the boxes in one stage should have the same configuration. It is clear that the individual box control is more efficient, however, it will require every message to have a header to determine its destination. The individual boxes should have control circuitry to interpret the destination header and set its own configuration. In the rest of this paper, when we mention a banyan network we mean a multistage network with individual box control.

2.2 Modes of operation

We first introduce the organization of the system. The system is composed of k processors and k memory modules, (although we are assuming that the number of processors is the same as the number of memory modules, the same analysis can be applied when the number of processors is less than the number of the memory modules). Each processor has its own private memory module, where the program and the data are stored. If processor i wants to communicate with processor j, it prepares a message and sends it to the memory module number j where this memory can be accessed by processor j. We are assuming an asynchronous communication, so any processor can be in any one of three states.

1) The processor is executing a program in its local memory;
2) The processor is sending a message to another processor;
3) The processor is blocked waiting for the interconnection network to deliver a message to another processor.

Processors in the first stage are considered active processors, i.e., processors doing useful work not blocked or communicating with other processors. We do not account for the time taken by any processor to read a message sent by another processor to its memory module, since this is considered to be part of the program executed by the processor.

We are assuming that the time between the generation of messages is exponentially distributed random variable with mean $\frac{1}{\lambda}$, and the length of the message is an exponentially distributed random variable with mean $\frac{1}{\mu}$. We are also assuming that an access request from processor i is directed to memory module j with probability $p_{ij} = 1/m$ where m is the

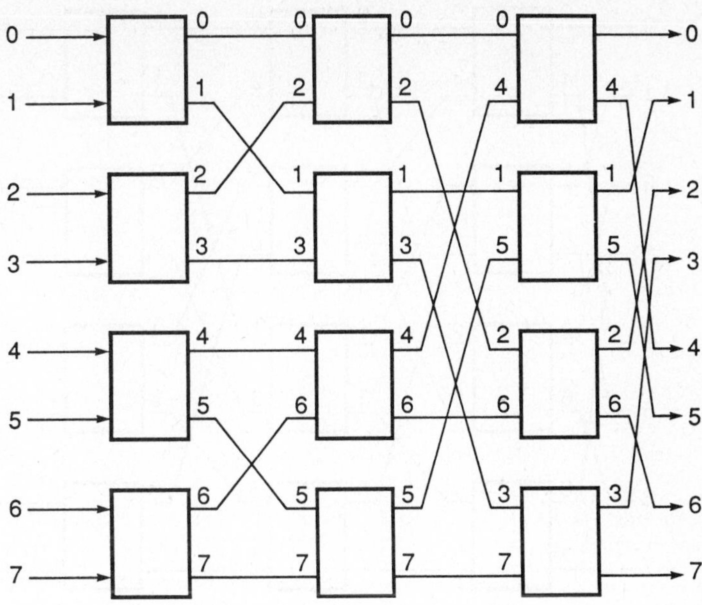

Fig. 3. Binary k-cube network ($k=8$).

number of memory modules ($m=k$). If any processor needs to send a message to another processor, it stops executing its program. Then, if the interconnection network can establish a path from the source processor to the destination module it will do so instantaneously with no delay and the sending processor will begin to send its message. When the message is completed the sending processor will return to its active state. If there is contention at the interconnection network or destination module the processor is put in queue, "blocked", waiting for the contention to be resolved and then transmits its message.

2.3 Performance Analysis of a Banyan Network

There have been some attempts to analyze the banyan network, [PATE79] [KRUS83]. However, in their analysis they considered the system to be synchronized. At the beginning of each cycle, every processor generates a message with a certain probability and they calculated the probability of message acceptance. In this paper, we assume the system to be asynchronous. The length of the message generated by any processor is an exponentially distributed random variable, and the time interval between the generation of two consecutive messages by the same processor is also an exponentially distributed random variable. We shall calculate the expected number of active processors, and the average delay encountered by an average message.

We are representing the system as an **M/M/c/K/K** queueing system "Machine repair model with K machines and c repairmen", [ALLE78]. This model, assumes a population of k identical devices (processors), each of which has an operating time of O time units between

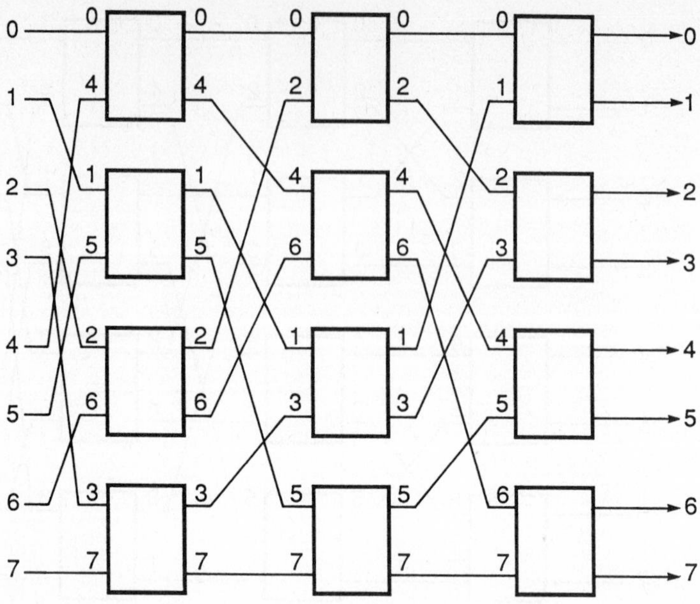

Fig. 4. Omega network.

breakdowns, O having a exponential distribution with average value of $\frac{1}{\lambda}$. The repairman (communicatioin network) repairs the machines with an average repair time of $\frac{1}{\mu}$ time units. Fig. 5, shows the state transition diagram for the **M/M/c/K/K** queueing system with a service rate c_i at state i. Notice that the service rate will depend upon how many customers (processors) are requesting service.

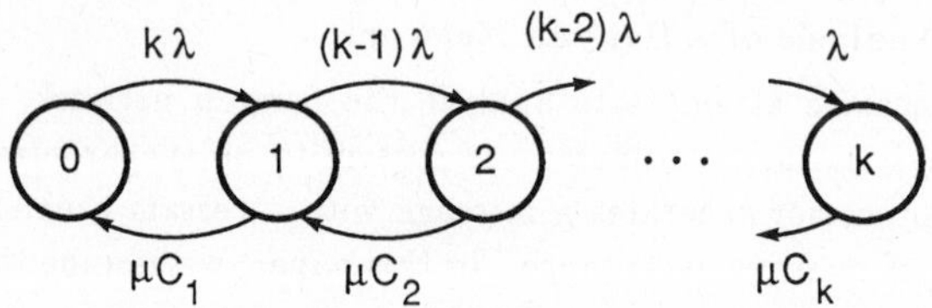

Fig. 5. State transition diagram for the **M/M/c/K/K** queueing system.

To calculate c_i, we have to know how many requests will go through the network if i processors request to send messages at the same time. Consider the first stage of the banyan network as shown in Fig. 3, or 4, where there are $\frac{k}{2}$ switches, each switch connected to 2 inputs. If one input is active, i.e., it is requesting to send a message and the other input is idle, then the average throughput of this switch is 1. If two inputs are active at the same time, then the average throughput of this switch is 1.5 [PATE79]. Thus, the expected number of messages to go through one stage of the banyan network given that there are i requests equals the expected number of switches with one active input $\times$ 1 + the expected number of switches with two active inputs $\times$ 1.5. The probability that any switch chosen at random has one active input is p_1, where

$$p_1 = \frac{2i(k-i)}{k(k-1))} .$$

The probability that any switch chosen at random has two active inputs is p_2, where

$$p_2 = \frac{i(i-1)}{k(k-1)} .$$

Since the number of switches in one stage is $k/2$, then the expected number of messages to go through one stage given i requests is $\phi(i)$, where

$$\phi(i) = (p_1+1.5p_2)\frac{k}{2} \qquad i \geq 1$$

$$\phi(1) = 1$$

In a banyan network with k inputs we have log$k$ stages. We can calculate the average number of messages to go through the network in a recursive manner. If *c(i)* is the *average* number of messages to go through the network given that there are i requests, then let $f_\ell(i)$ = expected number of messages that will go through the ℓ-th stage given that the input in the first stage will be i. Then,

$$f_\ell(i) = \phi(f_{\ell-1}(i))$$

$$\text{with } f_1(i) = \phi(i) = (p_1+1.5p_2)\frac{k}{2} = \frac{i(2k-0.5i-1.5)}{2(k-1)}$$

$$\text{and } c(i) = f_{\log k}(i)$$

After obtaining the service rate for the different states of the transition diagram in Fig. 5, the probability of being at state i is, P_i, where

$$P_i = P_0 \frac{k!}{(k-i)!} \left(\frac{\lambda}{\mu}\right)^k \prod_{j-1}^{i} \frac{1}{c(j)}$$

with P_0

$$P_0 = \left[\sum_{i=0}^{k} \frac{k!}{(k-i)!} \left(\frac{\lambda}{\mu}\right)^i \prod_{j=1}^{i} \frac{1}{c(j)}\right]^{-1}$$

The expected number of processors waiting in a queue is L_q, where

$$L_q = \sum_{i=1}^{k} u(i-c(i))P_i$$

and

$$u(x) = \begin{cases} x & x \geq 0 \\ 0 & x < 0 \end{cases}$$

The actual request rate is $\bar{\lambda}$, where

$$\lambda = \frac{k}{\frac{1}{\lambda}+W_q+\frac{1}{\mu}}$$

where W_q is the average time a processor spends in the queue. After applying Little's formula, we obtain

$$W_q = \frac{L_q}{\lambda} = (\frac{1}{\lambda}+W_q+\frac{1}{\mu})\frac{L_q}{k}$$

solving for W_q, we obtain

$$W_q = \frac{L_q(\frac{1}{\lambda}+\frac{1}{\mu})}{k-L_q}$$

By normalizing the time with respect to $\frac{1}{\mu}$ and noticing that the total delay is the sum of the waiting time and the service time, we obtain

$$D = \frac{k+L_q\rho}{k-L_q}, \quad where \quad \rho=\frac{\lambda}{\mu} .$$

D is the *average delay per message*. The *interconnection network utilization*, U is

$$U = 1 - P_0$$

and the number of Active Processors (AP) is

$$AP = \sum_{j=1}^{k} jP_j$$

2.4 Performance analysis of a multiple bus system

In a multiple bus system, we assume k processors and m memory modules connected through a b bus interconnection network, as shown in Fig. 6. When processor i needs to access memory module j, processor i will check to see if there is an available bus. If one is found and memory module j is free (no other processor is accessing it), then a path from processor i to memory module j is established immediately with zero delay. If there is no available bus or there is another processor accessing memory module j, then processor i is blocked in a queue waiting for a bus, or for memory module j, or for both. Marsan and Gerla, [MARS83], analyzed the Markov chain of such a system. They concluded that the exact Markov chain is not easy to handle, because the number of states will increase very rapidly with the system size. They introduced four approximations with moderate computational complexity. In this work, we use an approximation which is very similar to approximation C2 in their work, which gives a lower bound for the average number of active processors. We analyze the system using this approximate model, and we use P_i, where P_i is the probability of having i processors requesting access to the memory (either accessing a memory module or waiting in a queue). Using the machine repairman model with k servers, [ALLE78], the expected number of processors waiting in a queue is l_q, where

$$l_q = \sum_{i=0}^{k} u(i-c(i))P_i.$$

P_i is given in [MARS83] and is

$$P_i = \left[\frac{\lambda}{\mu}\right]^{k-i} \frac{k!}{i!} \prod_{j=0}^{k-i} \beta_j^{-1} P_k$$

and

$$P_k = \left[1 - \sum_{j=1}^{k-1} \left[(\frac{\lambda}{\mu})^{k-j} \frac{k!}{j!} \prod_{i=0}^{k-j} \beta_\ell^{-1}\right]\right]^{-1}$$

and $$\beta_\ell = \frac{\sum_{j=1}^{b-1} j p_j(\ell) + b \sum_{j=0}^{\ell-b} [p_b(j+b) p_{m-b}(\ell-2b-j+m)]}{\sum_{j=1}^{b-1} p_j(\ell) + \sum_{j=0}^{\ell-b} [p_b(j+b) p_{m-b}(\ell-2b-j+m)]}, \quad \ell \geq 0$$

where

$$p_j(\ell) = p_j(\ell-j) + p_{j-1}(\ell-j) + \ldots + p_1(\ell-j) + p_o(\ell-j)$$

with initial conditions

$$p_j(\ell) = 0 \quad \ell < j$$
$$p_0(\ell) = 0 \quad \ell > 0$$
$$p_j(\ell) = 1 \quad j \geq 0$$

In Fig. 7, 8 the performance of the two systems is plotted for 8 processor systems.

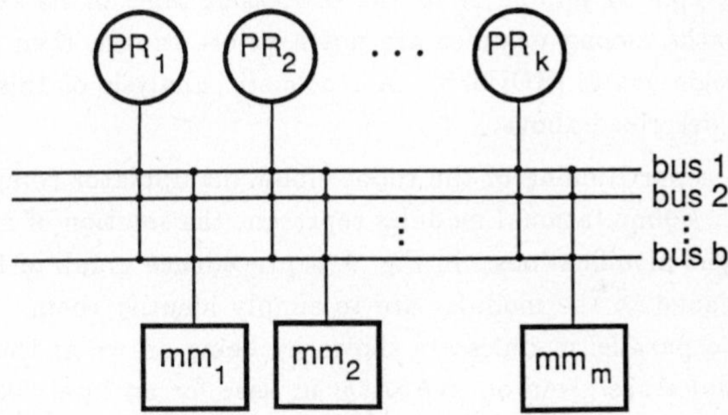

Fig. 6. A *kxmxb* multiple bus system.

3. A ROBOT ELBOW MANIPULATOR APPLICATION

The representation of an applications computations by a precedence graph requires a proper partitioning of the application into computational modules. Partitioning techniques via a system's compiler are presented in [SARK86]. There are applications which are amenable to mathematical decomposition techniques [OLEAR85], [BOKH81], [MARI87]. In the applications we have studied, [HOUS87a], knowledge of the application allow the use of mathematical decomposition to partition it and identify potential parallelism among modules. An integration of compiler techniques and decomposition techniques are needed for an appropriate partition.

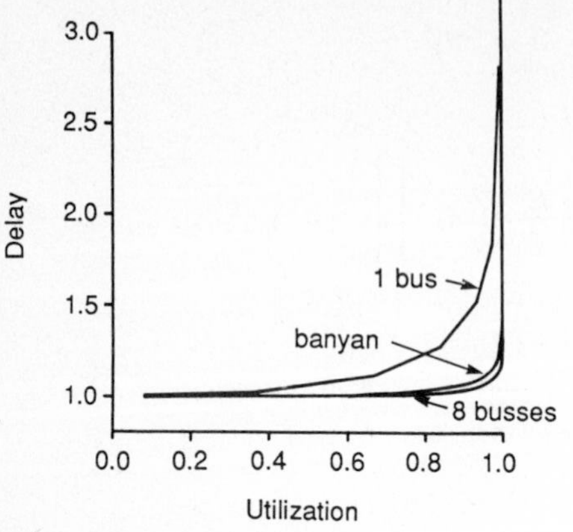

Fig. 7. Queueing delay vs. Utilization of interconnection networks.

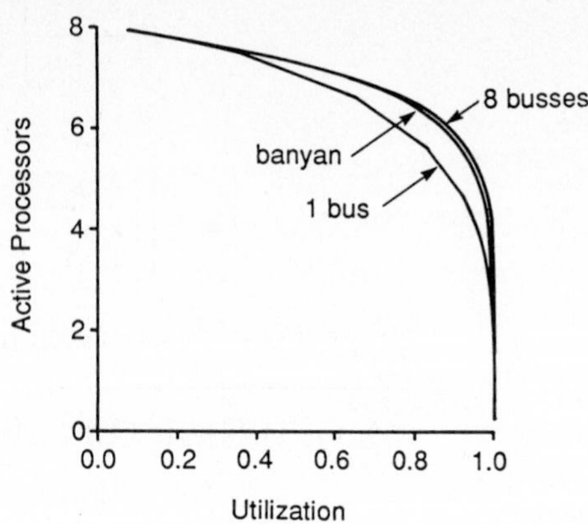

Fig. 8. Active Processors vs. Utilization of interconnection nets.

Once a partition is decided, the execution times of modules and communication times among modules have to be determined. In [HOUS87a] a parallel simulation language, SIMON, [FUJI85], was used to obtain these times along with the synchronization delay of each module. Since synchronization delay is an attribute of the application, it has been included in the graph by adding it to the processing time of its corresponding module. If communication paths among modules are not a priori known, then the partition is modeled by a stochastic logic graph [HOU87b]. A stochastic analysis of this graph results in a precedence graph as described above.

In [KASA85] a partitioning of the robot elbow manipulator computations is given at the equation level, i.e., computational modules represent the solution of an equation. We use this partition with slight modifications. In Fig. 9, a precedence graph of the application is shown. The numbers assigned to the modules are to simply identify them. Modules are grouped on different levels and parallel modules are shown by being drawn at the same level. The execution times of modules are given on [KASA85] in μsec for an Intel 8087 processor. The partition given in [KASA85] is such that very little communication is required among modules and it is considered negligible. We have modified this by assuming that the execution time, t_e, of a module, includes both processor's processing time and communication time. If t_x (μsec) is the processing time and t_y (μsec) is the communication time of a module, then $t_x+t_y=t_e$. We assume that synchronization delay is included in t_x. We assign t_y according to a uniform distribution to the outgoing links of its corresponding module. Thus, we have been able to investigate the effect of varying the ratio, r, between the amount of processing and communication of a module, where $r = t_x/t_y$. Three values of r have been used $r = 1, .1, 10$. We note at this point that by using r in this way, we only approximate what actually happens to a partition when the communication increases and processing decreases or vice versa. Usually, more communication is present when a partition is finer, i.e., module size (processing time) gets smaller but at the same time the number of modules is increased. By changing r, we

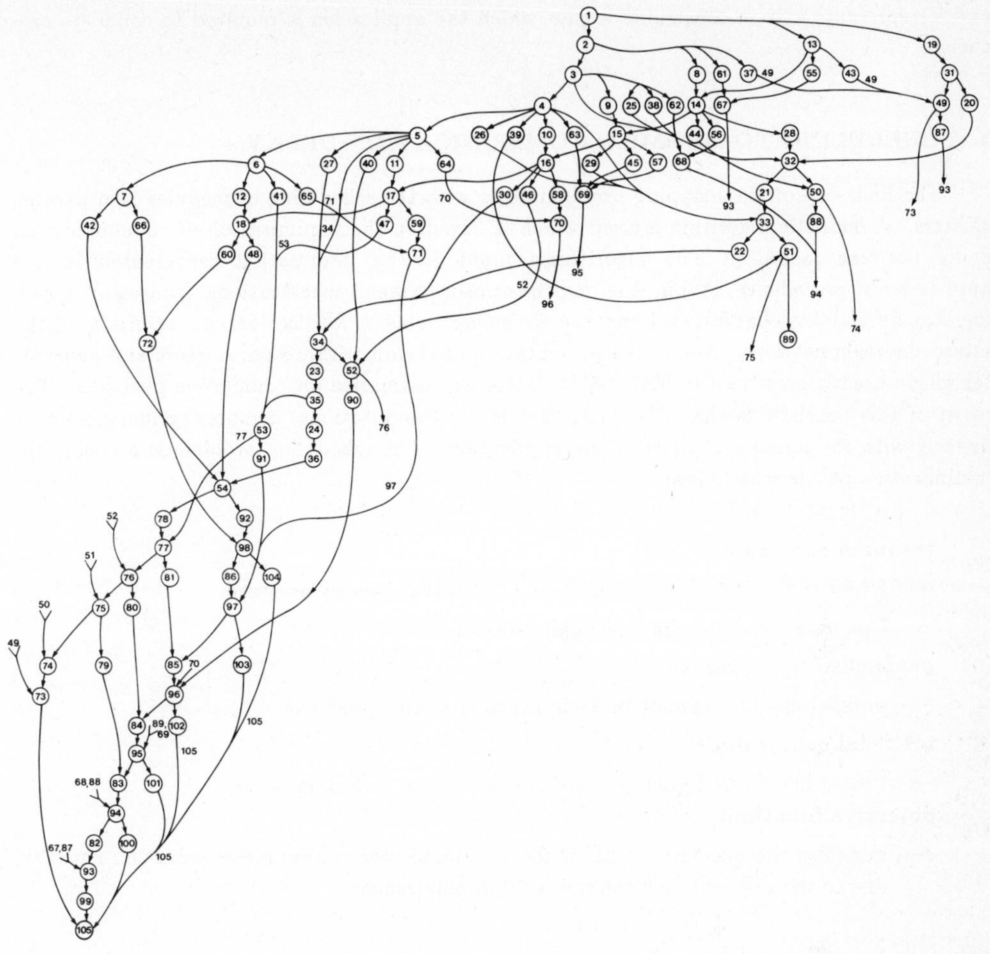

Fig. 9. The precedence graph of the robot elbow manipulator.

change the partition grain but without increasing or decreasing the number of modules.

From the communication requirements between a pair of modules, c_{ij}, we calculate the corresponding utilization of the interconnection network U, where

$$U = \frac{c_{ij}}{C \times T} .$$

where C is the capacity of the interconnection network and T is the time frame during which each parallel processor is running. This time frame will be described in the following section and it represents a time constraint within which the application is required to complete execution.

4. SCHEDULING TO MINIMIZE COMMUNICATION DELAY

The first step of the mapping problem deals with the scheduling of modules into parallel clusters. A heuristic algorithm is used which is based on the minimization of communication delay between modules. The algorithm's input is the information represented in the application's precedence graph, the multiprocessor system specifications (processor speed, memory availability, bandwidth) and the Queueing Delay vs Utilization characteristic of the interconnection network. A detailed presentation of the algorithm's parameters and heuristic technique used is presented in [HOUS87b]. Here we summarize for completion purposes. The merit of this heuristic is that it is fast, that is, its computational complexity increases only linearly with the number of links in the application. The scheduling problem is a constraint minimization problem as follows:

(i) **resource constraints:**

— Every computational module must fit into the memory assigned.

— Computations must have enough processor time.

(ii) **parallelism constraint:**

— parallel modules cannot be assigned to the same processor.

(iii) **artificial constraint**

— Processing time on each processor is limited to T (a parameter).

objective function:

— minimize the queueing delay of the multiprocessor system interconnection network, due to the application's communication requirements.

The *time frame T* is used to calculate the utilization of the interconnection network according to equation (1), for every c_{ij}. The corresponding queueing delay is then found from Fig. 7 depending on which interconnection network architecture is used. T is also used to calculate the processor's utilization every time a pair of candidate modules is merged, (see next section), and check if constraint (i) is satisfied. After the module assignment to processors is completed, the final processor utilizations are calculated using the final value of T.

4.1 The heuristic algorithm

For a specified *time frame* value of T

Start

Assign one processor per module.

Iteration

(a) make up a list of eligible pairs of modules which are ordered according to longest amount of required communication and thus queueing delay among them.

(b) If no constraints are violated merge the pair of modules which will result in the maximum reduction of the objective function. If there is more than one pair then merge the pair that results in the least processor loading; if there is still more than one, select a pair at random.

If we define by n_p the potential number of parallel modules in the application graph, and by c_p the number of parallel clusters obtained by the algorithm, then $c_p \geq n_p$. The initial value of T is large since the assignments of one module per processor represents the worst possible queueing delay in the systems. The value of T is decreased until $T = T_{PAR}$ where T_{PAR} is the shortest time for which the allocated processors can run the application in parallel. It turns out that T_{PAR} is a close *upper bound* of the elapsed time of the application when synchronization delay for each module is incorporated as part of the processing time of modules [HOUS87a]. T_{PAR} is the *optimal time frame*. Further reduction of T results in more and more processors to be used.

4.2 Results

The robot elbow manipulator application, shown in Fig. 9, was allocated to a kxmxb parallel multiple bus system architecture, where k is the number of processors, m is the number of common memory modules ($m{=}k$), and b is the number of common busses. In our application $n_p = 11$ and $c_p = 12$ or 13. A 13x13x1 and a 13x13x8 systems have been used. An 8 processor Banyan interconnected system was also used. In the case of a multiple bus architecture the number of parallel clusters obtained is equal to the number of processors in the system. Outputs of the heuristic algorithm for different values of the ratio r, (r = processing time/communication time per module), and the two multiple bus systems are shown in Figures 10a,b,c and Figures 11a,b,c. A schedule of assigned modules to each processor, its utilization and the optimal the frames T_{PAR} obtained are given. We are also showing the total processor utilization which includes the processing and communication delay required by all modules assigned cluster to a processor. A number of observations can be made by comparing Fig. 10 and Fig. 11.

First, we observe that optimal time frames are shorter in the case of an 8 bus system as compared to the 1 bus system, for $r = 1, 1/10$. This is expected, since the 8 bus system has higher bandwidth and thus less delay and there is enough communication between modules to affect the scheduling decision. Note that in both cases, different processor schedules have been obtained. In the case $r = 10/1$, communication delay does not play a significant role in scheduling (only total utilizations are slightly different when we compare the output of the 8 busses system, to the output of the 1 bus system). As a result identical schedules have also been obtained. From Fig. 7, one can see that unless communication between modules is such that it results in over 50% utilization of the interconnection network there is no significant difference in queueing delay between the 1 bus and the 8 busses system. We note that processor utilizations are low. This is due to the parallelism constraint of modules that limits their scheduling possibilities.

In Fig. 12, a schedule is shown which is based on minimizing the communication among modules without assigning a cost to it, namely, its corresponding queueing delay (no system is assumed). Note that the schedule produced is different as compared to the same case schedule in Fig. 10b (1 bus system). Thus, involving queueing delay in the scheduling decision instead of simply the amount of communication among modules produces different results. If we compare Fig. 12 to its corresponding case in Fig. 11b (8 busses system), then one observes that the same schedule has been obtained. This is due to the fact that a 13x13x8 system is practically a crossbar switch unless the communication between parallel modules is very high and thus resulting in interconnection utilization values greater than 80%, which is not the case in this application. One should not forget that if there are modules with high communication among them they are scheduled into the same processor unless they are parallel modules. This eliminates most of the high communication between modules.

system: 13×13×1, r = 1/1, T_{PAR} = 2206

Processor id	Total (%) utilization	Utilization (%)	Modules assigned
1	51.13	45.33	1 57 61 63 66 67 69 72 92 98 104
2	70.31	68.67	2 37 49 59 65 71 73 86 87 93 97 99 100 101 102 103 105
3	50.50	36.49	3 7 9 24 36 42 48 54 78
4	35.34	20.85	4 10 16 46
5	35.34	20.85	5 11 17 47
6	36.35	21.98	6 12 18 60
7	36.60	21.76	8 14 15 29
8	51.65	38.30	13 41 43 53 56 62 68 91
9	71.26	57.34	19 20 21 22 23 26 31 32 33 34 35
10	83.36	64.59	25 30 40 52 76 77 80 84 90 95
11	51.77	32.41	27 38 44 50 74 88
12	58.79	46.69	28 55 58 64 70 81 85 96
13	75.02	55.52	39 45 51 75 79 82 83 89 94

Fig. 10a. Schedule of module assignments of the robot elbow manipulator.

system: 13×13×1, r = 1/10, T_{PAR} = 4054

Processor id	Total (%) utilization	Utilization (%)	Modules assigned
1	10.88	3.05	1 27 28 61 66 67 72 92 98 104
2	18.94	4.26	2 7 24 36 37 42 48 49 54 78 87
3	14.82	4.62	3 9 58 64 70 81 85 96
4	15.86	2.06	4 10 16 46
5	15.86	2.06	5 11 17 47
6	15.86	2.17	6 12 18 60
7	16.29	2.15	8 14 15 29
8	10.16	2.24	13 25 43 57
9	18.93	5.67	19 20 21 22 23 26 31 32 34 35
10	18.93	5.40	30 39 45 51 55 75 79 83 89 94 100
11	9.80	5.76	38 44 50 73 74 82 88 93 99 102 105
12	19.29	7.80	40 41 52 53 76 77 80 84 90 91 95 101
13	15.31	5.25	56 59 62 65 68 71 86 97 103

Fig. 10b. Schedule of module assignments of the robot elbow manipulator.

system: 13×13×1, r = 10/1, T_{PAR} = 3304

Processor id	Total (%) utilization	Utilization (%)	Modules assigned
1	12.97	12.38	1 27 30 61 67
2	42.08	40.16	2 6 12 18 37 49 60 87
3	89.98	88.03	3 9 39 41 45 51 53 75 79 83 89 91 94 100
4	26.67	25.31	4 10 16 46
5	26.67	25.31	5 11 17 47
6	67.46	65.20	7 8 14 15 24 29 36 42 48 54 78
7	25.25	24.76	13 43 57 63 69
8	70.90	69.60	19 20 21 22 23 26 31 32 33 34 35
9	34.31	33.29	25 28 55 66 72 92 98 104
10	71.10	70.70	38 44 50 73 74 82 88 93 99 102 105
11	74.85	74.00	40 52 76 77 80 84 90 95 101
12	65.36	64.37	56 59 62 65 68 71 86 97 103
13	51.73	51.17	58 64 70 81 85 96

Fig. 10c. Schedule of module assignments of the robot elbow manipulator.

system: 13×13×8, r = 1/1, T_{PAR} = 2125

Processor id	Total (%) utilization	Utilization (%)	Modules assigned
1	58.87	58.35	1 61 66 67 72 73 87 92 93 98 99 100 101 102 103 104 105
2	44.27	30.12	2 27 37 41 49 53 91
3	81.15	62.35	3 9 39 45 51 75 79 82 83 89 94
4	32.92	21.65	4 10 16 46
5	32.92	21.65	5 11 17 47
6	34.00	22.82	6 12 18 60
7	74.58	55.76	7 8 14 15 24 29 36 42 48 54 78
8	61.06	52.24	13 43 56 59 62 65 68 71 86 97
9	70.36	59.53	19 20 21 22 23 26 31 32 33 34 35
10	27.30	22.12	25 57 63 69
11	57.89	48.47	28 55 58 64 70 81 85 96
12	76.96	64.71	30 40 52 76 77 80 84 90 95
13	44.00	31.29	38 44 50 74 88

Fig. 11a. Schedule of module assignments of the robot elbow manipulator.

system: 13×13×8, r = 1/10, T_{PAR} = 3881

Processor id	Total (%) utilization	Utilization (%)	Modules assigned
1	8.86	2.34	1 13 25 43 57 63 69
2	16.53	4.45	2 7 24 36 37 42 48 49 54 78 87
3	13.22	4.82	3 9 58 64 70 81 85 96
4	13.51	2.15	4 10 16 46
5	13.51	2.15	5 11 17 47
6	13.53	2.27	6 12 18 60
7	13.88	2.25	8 14 15 29
8	16.83	5.93	19 20 21 22 23 26 31 32 33 34 35
9	11.30	6.04	27 28 61 66 67 72 73 92 93 98 99 100 101 102 103 104 105
10	26.23	6.21	30 39 45 51 55 75 79 82 83 89 94
11	15.92	3.12	38 44 50 74 88
12	20.40	8.06	40 41 52 53 76 77 80 84 90 91 95
13	12.65	5.06	56 59 62 65 68 71 86 97

Fig. 11b. Schedule of module assignments of the robot elbow.

system: 13×13×8, r = 10/1, T_{PAR} = 3304

Processor id	Total (%) utilization	Utilization (%)	Modules assigned
1	12.96	12.38	1 27 30 61 67
2	42.02	40.16	2 6 12 18 37 49 60 87
3	89.93	88.03	3 9 39 41 45 51 53 75 79 83 89 91 94 100
4	26.63	25.31	4 10 16 46
5	26.63	25.31	5 11 17 47
6	67.40	65.20	7 8 14 15 24 29 36 42 48 54 78
7	25.24	24.76	13 43 57 63 69
8	70.87	69.60	19 20 21 22 23 26 31 32 33 34 35
9	34.28	33.29	25 28 55 66 72 92 98 104
10	71.08	70.70	38 44 50 73 74 82 88 93 102 105
11	74.82	74.00	40 52 76 77 80 84 90 95 101
12	65.33	64.37	56 59 62 65 68 71 86 97 103
13	51.72	51.17	58 64 70 81 85 96

Fig. 11c. Schedule of module assignments of the robot elbow manipulator.

system: no system, $r = 1/10$, $T_{PAR} = 3880$

Processor id	Total (%) utilization	Utilization (%)	Modules assigned
1	8.78	2.34	1 13 25 43 57 63 69
2	16.38	4.45	2 7 24 36 37 42 48 49 54 78 87
3	13.12	4.82	3 9 58 64 70 81 85 96
4	13.37	2.15	4 10 16 46
5	13.37	2.15	5 11 17 47
6	13.39	2.27	6 12 18 60
7	13.73	2.25	8 14 15 29
8	16.69	5.92	19 20 21 22 23 26 31 32 33 34 35
9	11.24	6.04	27 28 61 66 67 72 73 92 93 98 99 100 101 102 103 104 105
10	25.97	6.20	30 39 45 51 55 75 79 82 83 89 94
11	15.76	3.11	38 44 50 74 88
12	20.24	8.05	40 41 52 53 76 77 80 84 90 91 95
13	12.55	5.06	56 59 62 65 68 71 86 97

Fig. 12. Schedule of module assignments of the robot elbow manipulator.

From the available data, one can calculate performance measures such as speed up and efficiency [SIEG82], where

$$\text{speed up} = \frac{\text{elapsed time in uniprocessor system}}{\text{elapsed time in multiprocessor system}}$$

and if there are k processors in the multiprocessor system then

$$\text{efficiency} = \frac{\text{speed up}}{k}$$

On tables 1,2 speedups and efficiency measures are given for the different system architectures.

13×13×1 multiple bus system architecture		Speed up	Efficiency
	$r = 1$	5.308	.408
	$r = \frac{1}{10}$	.525	.040
	$r = \frac{10}{1}$	6.441	.495

Table 1: Speed up and efficiency data for the schedules of Fig. 10a,b,c.

13×13×8 multiple bus system architecture		Speed up	Efficiency
	$r = 1$	5.510	.423
	$r = \frac{1}{10}$	.548	.042
	$r = \frac{10}{1}$	6.443	.495

Table 2: Speed up and efficiency data for the schedule of Fig. 11a,b,c.

Step (a) was also applied when the parallel system has a Banyan interconnection network. The results are shown in Fig. 13a,b,c. 12 or 13 parallel clusters have been obtained. The number of clusters depends primarily on the parallelism of the application, (n_p), and the system involved in the scheduling decision. Our observation has been that for symmetric graphs or almost symmetric graphs, [HOUS87a], the number of clusters obtained is equal to the of parallelism of the graph. When the application graph does not possess any symmetry, like the one we used here, the numbers of clusters is greater or equal to the graph's parallelism. This is due to the mechanism of module merging which satisfies the parallelism and time frame constraint. It can be regarded as a limitation of our heuristic algorithm since it does not exhaust all possible schedules (NP complete).

system: 8 processor, Banyan Interconnection, $r = 1/1$, $T_{PAR} = 2212$

Processor id	Total (%) utilization	Utilization (%)	Modules assigned
1	49.54	45.20	1 57 61 63 66 67 69 72 92 98 104
2	74.22	72.99	2 37 49 59 65 71 73 82 86 87 93 97 99 102 103 105
3	40.67	26.44	3 6 9 12 18 60
4	31.62	20.79	4 10 16 46
5	31.62	20.79	5 11 17 47
6	71.65	53.56	7 8 14 15 24 29 36 42 48 54 78
7	28.82	22.60	13 30 43 56 62 68
8	67.58	57.18	19 20 21 22 23 26 31 32 33 34 35
9	60.56	52.20	25 39 45 51 75 79 83 89 94 100
10	46.79	32.32	27 38 44 50 74
11	55.60	46.55	28 55 58 64 70 81 85 96
12	87.66	78.64	40 41 52 53 76 77 80 84 90 91 95 101

Fig. 13a. Schedule of module assignments of the robot elbow manipulator.

system: 8 processor, Banyan Interconnection, $r = 1/10$, $T_{PAR} = 3883$

Processor id	Total (%) utilization	Utilization (%)	Modules assigned
1	8.79	2.34	1 13 25 43 57 63 69
2	16.39	4.45	2 7 24 36 37 42 48 49 54 78 87
3	13.38	2.15	4 10 16 46
4	13.38	2.15	4 10 16 46
5	13.38	2.15	5 11 17 47
6	13.40	2.27	6 12 18 60
7	13.75	2.25	8 14 15 29
8	16.71	5.92	19 20 21 22 23 26 31 32 33 34 35
9	11.24	6.20	30 39 45 51 55 75 79 82 83 89 94
10	26.00	6.20	30 39 45 51 55 75 79 82 83 89 94
11	15.77	3.11	38 44 50 74 88
12	20.26	8.05	40 41 52 53 76 77 80 90 91 95
13	12.56	5.06	56 59 62 65 68 71 86 97

Fig. 13b. Schedule of module assignments of the robot elbow manipulator.

system: 8 processors, Banyan Interconnection, $r = 10/1$, $T_{PAR} = 3306$

Processor id	Total (%) utilization	Utilization (%)	Modules assigned
1	12.95	12.37	1 27 30 61 67
2	42.00	40.14	2 6 12 18 37 49 60 87
3	89.88	87.99	3 9 39 41 45 51 53 75 79 83 89 91 94 100
4	26.62	25.30	4 10 16 46
5	26.61	25.30	5 11 17 47
6	67.36	65.17	7 8 14 15 24 29 36 42 48 54 78
7	25.23	24.75	13 43 57 63 69
8	70.83	69.57	19 20 21 22 23 26 31 32 33 34 35
9	34.27	33.27	25 28 55 66 72 92 98 104
10	71.05	70.67	38 44 50 73 74 82 88 93 99 102 105
11	74.79	73.96	40 52 76 77 80 84 90 95 101
12	65.30	64.34	56 59 62 65 68 71 86 97 103
13	51.69	51.14	58 64 70 81 85 96

Fig. 13c. Schedule of module assignments of the robot elbow manipulator.

5. REDUCTION OF PARALLELISM

In [HOUS87c] a number of heuristic algorithms have been discussed for the reduction of parallelism, step (b). Here we apply one of these heuristics and perform step (b).

Parallelism reduction in necessary when the number of parallel clusters obtained in step (a) is higher than the parallel processors in the system. In general, the number of clusters depends to a great extend on the parallelism of the application, and it is unlikely that it is equal to the number of available processors. There are multiprocessor system architectures where the number of processors can easily be adjusted to equal the number of clusters obtained. Multiple bus interconnection architectures present such feasibility as discussed in the previous section. In such case step (a) is sufficient.

In this work we are interested to test the performance of our method for a Banyan interconnected architecture. Since the number of parallel clusters obtain in Fig. 13a,b,c are 12 or 13 it is cost effective to assume that an 8 processor system is available and thus we need to reduce the number of clusters from 12 or 13, to 8. In the reduction of parallelism, step (b), we use the same heuristic algorithm as in step (a) with a simple modification, which is to eliminate the parallelism constraint. This is feasible since the input to the heuristic algorithm for the reduction step is the number of parallel clusters obtained in step (a). Each of these clusters is regarded as a single module and the communication between clusters forms the communication between modules. Thus, we start with a new graph which is the output of step (a). The communication cost is found as in step (a) by using the Queueing Delay vs Utilization of an 8 processor Banyan interconnected network as shown in Fig. 7. Since parallelism between the modules of the new graph is eliminated, it is always feasible to cluster the modules into a predetermined number of processors (in this case 8), by adjusting appropriately the time frame T constraint. The processor utilizations in step (a) are low and because of that, in order to get 8 clusters, we have to increase or decrease T until the desired number of clusters are obtained. The results in every case corresponding to step (a) are presented in Fig. 14a,b,c. Note that module 1 of Fig. 14 corresponds to cluster 1 of Fig. 13 and so on for the rest of the modules. We also note, that processor utilizations are much higher than in step (a) which results in a lower time frame in every case.

system: 8 processors, Banyan Interconnection, $r = 1/1$, $T_{PAR} = 2528$

Processor id	Total (%) utilization	Utilization (%)	Modules assigned		
1	43.34	39.54	1		
2	64.94	63.86	2		
3	82.49	59.51	3	4	5
4	62.68	46.86	6		
5	75.82	65.44	7	9	
6	59.12	50.02	8		
7	40.93	28.27	10		
8	62.66	54.76	12		

Fig. 14a. Parallelism reduction for the schedules shown in Fig. 13a.

system: 8 processor, Banyan Interconnection, $r = 1/10$, $T_{PAR} = 1083$

Processor id	Total (%) utilization	Utilization (%)	Modules assigned		
1	85.16	29.63	1	8	
2	81.49	48.77	2	9	11
3	89.81	25.01	3	4	
4	74.58	15.86	5	6	
5	50.97	8.06	7		
6	86.10	22.24	10		
7	74.40	28.88	12		
8	46.12	18.13	13		

Fig. 14b. Reduction parallelism for the schedules shown in Fig. 13b.

system: 8 processor, Banyan Interconnection, $r = 10/1$, $T_{PAR} = 3706$

Processor id	Total (%) utilization	Utilization (%)	Modules assigned		
1	74.25	73.10	1	8	
2	83.97	80.94	2	4	5
3	80.18	78.49	3		
4	89.75	87.81	6	9	
5	88.92	88.06	7	11	
6	63.38	63.04	10		
7	58.25	57.40	12		
8	46.11	45.62	13		

Fig. 14c. Reduction parallelism for the schedules shown in Fig. 13c.

system: 8×8×1, r = 1, T_{PAR} = 2421

Processor id	Total (%) utilization	Utilization (%)	Modules assigned		
1	82.02	78.66	1	13	
2	89.42	72.26	2	8	
3	71.30	54.71	3		
4	79.46	58.01	4	5	6
5	65.54	48.93	7		
6	61.79	52.23	9		
7	89.07	76.18	10	12	
8	50.84	42.53	11		

Fig. 15a. Reduction of parallelism for the schedule shown in Fig. 10a.

system: 8×8×1, r = 1/10, T_{PAR} = 1207

Processor id	Total (%) utilization	Utilization (%)	Modules assigned		
1	89.60	33.44	1	12	
2	56.68	14.31	2		
3	84.05	22.44	3	4	
4	70.06	14.23	5	6	
5	48.02	7.23	7		
6	57.31	19.05	8		
7	87.81	49.40	9	10	11
8	42.88	16.27	13		

Fig. 15b. Reduction of parallelism for the schedules shown in Fig. 10b.

system: 8×8×1, r = 1/10, T_{PAR} = 3804

Processor id	Total (%) utilization	Utilization (%)	Modules assigned		
1	72.34	71.22	1	8	
2	81.81	78.86	2	4	5
3	78.12	76.47	3		
4	87.44	85.56	6	9	
5	86.64	85.79	7	11	
6	61.75	61.42	10		
7	56.76	55.92	12		
8	44.93	44.45	13		

Fig. 15c. Reduction of parallelism for schedules shown in Fig. 10c.

system: 8×8×8, r = 1, T_{PAR} = 2421

Processor id	Total (%) utilization	Utilization (%)	Modules assigned		
1	82.00	78.66	1	13	
2	89.32	72.26	2	8	
3	71.20	54.71	3		
4	79.34	58.01	4	5	6
5	65.44	48.93	7		
6	61.73	52.23	9		
7	89.00	76.18	10	12	
8	50.79	42.53	11		

Fig. 16a. Reduction of parallelism for schedules shown in Fig. 11a.

system: 8x8x8, $r = 1/10$, $T_{PAR} = 1134$

Processor id	Total (%) utilization	Utilization (%)	Modules assigned		
1	80.11	28.30	1	8	
2	56.81	15.23	2		
3	84.99	24.21	3	7	
4	46.46	7.37	4		
5	69.94	15.15	5	6	
6	84.27	41.92	9	10	
7	54.74	10.66	11		
8	56.74	22.16	13		

Fig. 16b. Reduction of parallelism for schedules shown in Fig. 11b.

system: 8x8x8, $r = 10/1$, $T_{PAR} = 3804$

Processor id	Total (%) utilization	Utilization (%)	Modules assigned		
1	72.34	71.22	1	8	
2	81.81	78.86	2	4	5
3	78.12	76.47	3		
4	87.44	85.56	6	9	
5	86.64	85.79	7	11	
6	61.75	61.42	10		
7	56.76	55.92	12		
8	44.93	44.45	13		

Fig. 16c. Reduction of parallelism for schedules shown in Fig. 11c.

For comparison purposes we reduced the 13 cluster obtained in the case of the multiple bus architecture to 8 assuming an 8 processor system. The results are shown in Fig. 15 and Fig. 16. We compare the two architectures in Fig. 17 by showing time frames and average total processor utilizations u_p^t. Note that the *best match between the application* we studied *and the two systems* considered *depends on the ratio r*.

Banyan Interconnection	Multiple Bus Interconnection
(8 processor system) $r = 1/1$ $T_{PAR} = 2529$ $u_p^t = 67.07$	(8×8×1) $T_{PAR} = 2421$ $u_p^t = 73.68$ (8×8×8) $T_{PAR} = 2421$ $u_p^t = 73.70$
$r = 1/10$ $T_{PAR} = 1083$ $u_p^t = 74.83$	(8×8×1) $T_{PAR} = 1207$ $u_p^t = 1134$ (8×8×8) $T_{PAR} = 1134$ $u_p^t = 71.35$
$r = 10/1$ $T_{PAR} = 3706.3$ $u_p^t = 73.10$	(8×8×1) $T_{PAR} = 3804$ $u_p^t = 71.22$ (8×8×8) $T_{PAR} = 3804$ $u_p^t = 71.22$

Fig. 17. Performance comparison of multibus and Banyan architecture for the robot elbow manipulator application.

The smallest time frame and the highest processor utilization were obtained for $r = 1/10$, and a Banyan interconnection system. The 8x8x8 multiple bus system has a higher bandwidth than the Banyan network, and yet the schedule produced when a Banyan system was considered results in best performance. From this we conclude the usefulness of the mapping methodology in matching application to architectures. Speed ups and efficiency factors for the 8 processor systems are presented in Fig. 18.

	Speed up		Efficiency	
(8 processor systems)				
	Banyan	Multiple bus	Banyan	Multiple bus
$r = 1/1$	4.630	(1 bus) 4.836 (8 busses) 4.836	.578	(1 bus) .604 (8 busses) .604
$r = 1/10$	1.965	(1 bus) 1.763 (8 busses) 1.877	.245	(1 bus) .220 (8 busses) .234
$r = 10/1$	5.744	(1 bus) 5.596 (8 busses) 5.596	.718	(1 bus) .699 (8 busses) .699

Fig. 18. Comparison of speedups and efficiency for 8 processor Banyan and multiple bus interconnected systems.

7. CONCLUSIONS

The mapping of applications to multiprocessor systems provides a very good indication of how well the application is matched to the system. We have examined a robot elbow manipulator application which was partitioned into communicating modules at the equation level. A precedence graph representation was used. We have approximated different partitions of the same application by changing the ratio of processing to communication on a per module basis. Two classes of multiprocessor systems have been examined, the multiple bus systems and the Banyan multistage networks. They have been represented by their specification and their Queueing Delay vs. Utilization of their interconnection networks. A fast heuristic algorithm was used for the two different steps of the mapping method. In the first step, schedules of modules for every processors were produced. A full advantage of the application's parallelism was taken and the available system could match that. In the second step, a reduction of parallelism of the application was used to reduce the number of clusters to the number of available processors. For this step, new schedules were also produced. In the third step, the layout of the clusters to the processors is required. For the multiprocessor systems we have used it is a simple assignment of clusters to processors, since all processors are equally distant.

Our results indicated that the best match between an application and a system depends on the partition used, i.e., depends on r. The highest speed up was obtained when r was the highest and the parallelism of the application was fully exploited. This was possible only in the case of the multiple bus architecture systems. The processor utilization obtained were low. Thus, *for the particular application studied* best speed ups were obtained at the expense of underutilizing the system.

When the parallelism reduction step was applied (one less constraint) then the speed ups were lower but the processor utilizations were higher. After the application of this step it was possible to compare the match of the two different classes of systems to the application. Our results indicated again a dependence or r. For $r{=}1$ the multiple bus system produced the best speed up and at the same time highest average processor utilization while for $r{=}.1$,

10 the Banyan network produced best speed ups and the highest average processor utilizations.

Our results indicate the usefulness of the applied methodology to the solution of the mapping problem. It provides performance measures which closely agree with our initiation and at the same time it provides the assignments of modules to processors which are not at all obvious.

8. REFERENCES

[ABRA86] Abraham, S. G., Davidson, E. S., "Task assignment using Network flow methods for minimizing communication in n-processor systems," Technical Report, CSRD Rpt. No. 598, Center of Supercomputing Research and Development, National Center of Supercomputing Applications, University of Illinois at Urbana-Champaign, September 1986.

[ALLE78] Allen, A. O., *Probability Statistics and Queueing Theory,* Academic Press, 1978.

[BATC76] Batcher, K. E., "The Flip Network in STARAN," *1976 Int'l. Conf. on Parallel Processing,* Aug. 1976, pp. 65-71.

[BERM84] Berman, F. Snyder, L., "On mapping parallel algorithms in parallel architectures," *Proceedings of the International Conference on Parallel Processing,* 1984, pp. 307-309.

[BERM85] Berman, F., Goodrich, M., Koelbel, C., Robinson, III, W. J. Showell, K., "Prep-p: A mapping preprocessor for chip computers," *Proceedings of the International Conference on Parallel Processing,* 1985, pp. 731-733.

[BERM87] Berman, F., Haden, P., "A compartive study of mapping algorithms for an automated parallel programming environment," Computer Science Technical Report Number CS-088, University of California, San Diego, La Jolla, CA 92093.

[BOKH81] Bokhari, Shamid, H., "On the Mapping Problem," *IEEE Transactioins on Computers,* Vol. C-30, No. 3, 1981, pp. 207-214.

[CHU80] W. W. Chu, L. J. Holloway, M. T. Lan, K. Efe, "Task Allocation in Distributed Data Processing," *Computer,* November 1980, pp. 57-69.

[EFE82] K. Efe, "Heuristic Models of Task Assignment Scheduling in Distributed Systems," *Computer,* Vol. 15, No. 6, June 1982, pp. 50-56.

[FUJI85] Fujimoto, R. M., "The SIMON simulation and development system," *Summer Computer Simulation Conference,* 1985 (Univ. of Utah).

[GILB87] Gilbert, J. R., Zmijewski, E., "A parallel graph Partitioning Algorithm for a Message-Passing Multiprocessor," Technical Report, TR 87-803, Department of Computer Science, Cornell University, Ithaca, N.Y., January 1987.

[GYL76] V. B. Gylys, J. A. Edwards, "Optimal Partitioning of Workload for Distributed Systems," *Proceeding Compcon,* Fall 1976, pp. 353-357.

[HOUS83] Houstis, C. E., Houstis, E. N., Rice, J., "Partitioning and Allocation of PDE Computation to Distributed Systems," *PDE Software: Modules Interfaces and Systems,* Edited by B. Enguist and T. Smedsass, North Holland, 1983.

[HOUS87a] Houstis, C. E., Houstis, E. N., Rice, J. J., "Partitioning PDE Computation: Methods and Performance Evaluation," invited paper, *Journal of Parallel Computing,* No. 4, 1987.

[HOUS87b] Houstis, Catherine, "Allocation of Real-Time Applications to Distributed Systems," accepted for presentation in the *1987 International Conference on Parallel Processing,* August 1987.

[HOUS87c] Houstis, C. E., "Distributed Processing Performance Evaluation," accepted for presentation to the *Third International Conference on Data Communication Systems and Their Performance,* Rio di Janeiro, Brazil, June 22-25, 1987.

[JENN77] Jenny, C. J., "Process Partitioning on Distributed Systems," Digest of paper *National Telecommunications Conference,* 1977, pp. 31:1-31:10.

[KASA85] Kasahara, H., Narita, S., "Parallel Processing of Robot-Arm Control Computation on a Multiprocessor System," *IEEE Journal of Robotics and Automation,* Vol. RA-1, No. 2, June 1985, pp. 104-113.

[KLEI85] Kleinrock, Leonard, "Distributed Systems," *Communications of ACM,* Vol. 28, Number 11, 1985, pp. 1200-1213.

[KRUS83] Kruskal, C., Snir, M., "The performance of multistage Interconnection Nets for multiprocessing," *IEEE Transactions on Computers,* Vol. C-32, No. 12, 1983, pp. 1091-198.

[LAWR75] Lawrie, D., "Access and Alignment of Data in an Array Processor," *IEEE Transactions on Computers,* Vol. C-24, No. 12, Dec. 1975, pp. 1145-1155.

[MARS83] Marsan, M. A., Gerla, M., "Markov models for Multiple Bus Multiprocessor Systems," *IEEE Transactions on Computers,* Vol. C-32, No. 3, 1983, pp. 239-248.

[O'LEA85] O'Leary, D. P. and G. W. Stewart, "Data-flow algorithms for parallel matrix computations," *Communication of ACM,* Vol. 28, 1985, pp. 840-853.

[PATE79] Patel, J. H., "Processors-Memory Interconnections for Multiprocessors," in *Proc. 6th Ann. Symp. Computer Arch.,* pp. 168-177, Apr. 1979.

[MARI87] Marinescu, D., Rice, J., "Domain oriented analysis of DOE splitting algorithms," to appear in the *Journal of Information Science,* July 1987.

[SARK86] Sarkov, V., Hennessy, J., "Compile-time Partitioning and Scheduling of Parallel Programs," *Proceedings of the SIGPLAN 1986 Symposium on Compiler Instructions,* June 1986, pp. 17-36.

[SIEG78] Siegel, H. J. and Smith, H. D., "Study of Multistage SIMD Interconnection Networks," *5th Annual Symposium on Computer Architecture,* Apr. 1978, pp. 223-229.

[SIEG78] Siegel, H. J., McMillen, R. J., and Mueller, P. T., Jr., "A Survey of Interconnection methods for Reconfigurable Parallel Processing Systems," *1978 Int'l Conf. on Parallel Processing,* Aug. 1978, pp. 9-17.

[SIEG82] Siegel, L., Siegel, H. J., Swain, P. H., "Performance Measures for evaluating algorithms for SIMD machines," *IEEE Transaction on Software Engineering,* Vol. SE-8, No. 4, July 1984, pp. 319-331.

[SIEG85] Siegel, H., *Interconnection Networks for Large-Scale Parallel Processing,* Heath and Company, 1985.

[STO78] Stone, H. S., Bokhari, S. H., "Control of Distributed Processes," *Computer,* Vol. 11, No. 7, July 1978, pp. 97-106.

COMMUNICATION AND CONTROL COSTS OF DOMAIN DECOMPOSITION ON LOOSELY COUPLED MULTIPROCESSORS

Luigi Brochard

Ecole Nationale des Ponts et Chaussées
La Courtine, BP 105
93194 Noisy le Grand Cedex , France

Abstract
Communication and synchronization costs are a key problem in parallel computing. Studying an iterative method which requires only neighbor to neighbor communication, domain decomposition , we give different evaluations of speed-up depending on computation, communication and control costs. The effect of three different control costs for an iterative algorithm termination detection is studied. A linear control formulation is compared to experimental results on a loosely coupled array of eight processors. From the derived parameters, results for massively parallel systems are extrapolated.

Keywords
Communication, control, domain decomposition, iterative method, loosely coupled multiprocessor, parallel computing, speed-up.

Domain Decomposition

Domain decomposition methods are used to solve partial differential equations arising in physics (fluid dynamics, structural analysis ...), where instead of solving the original problem on the global domain, the problem is splitted into p smaller problems and solved on each subdomain.
Of course, those two formulations are not equivalent, and different methods [7,9,12] have been proposed to couple the subdomains with or without subdomain overlapping.
These methods, first introduced by Schwarz as alternate methods [11] for solving problems on irregular domains, has recently received a lot of attention in relation to parallel computation mainly because of its coarsest granularity level and its good adaptation to loosely coupled multiprocessors with its neighbor to neighbor type of communication and the small amount of data transfer induced if we assume each processor solves a subproblem storing the subdomain in its local memory.
In the following, we will consider iterative domain decomposistion methods where the coupling is done at every iteration through the exchange of boundary values between adjacent subdomains.
Assuming an equally balanced load between processors, let V be the total number of grid points of the global domain, $V^{(p)}$ the number of grid points of each subdomain,and $S^{(p)}$ the number of grid points of the exchange region. We first give an evaluation of $V^{(p)}$ and $S^{(p)}$, depending on the following parameters: let n be the physical space dimension, d the domain decomposition dimension, N the number of grid points in every direction of the domain, k the number of processors per decomposition direction and p the total number of processors given by :

$$p = k^d \quad k = 2,3,4... \tag{1}$$

For example, with n =2, k =4 and d =1 we have a slice decomposition , with d =2 we have a square decomposition and with n =3, d=3 we have a cube decomposition.

Under these assumptions for p processors , we have :

$$V^{(p)} = \frac{N^n}{k^d} \tag{2}$$

$$S^{(p)} = \frac{2.d.N^{n-1}}{k^{d-1}} \tag{3}$$

and

$$\frac{V^{(p)}}{S^{(p)}} = \frac{N}{2.d.k} \tag{4}$$

Assuming the number of processors per domain decomposition direction k can not be greater than the number of grid points per physical direction, the maximum number of processors p^* that can be geometrically assigned to the parallel computation and the corresponding V^* and S^* are given by:

$$p^* = N^d \tag{5}$$

$$V^* = N^{n-d} \tag{6}$$

and

$$S^* = 2.d.V^* \tag{7}$$

Speed-up formulation

Let $T_{elp}^{(p)}$, $T_{cpu}^{(p)}$, $T_{io}^{(p)}$, $T_{ctr}^{(p)}$ be the elapsed, computation, communication and control times of the process using p processors and $Sp^{(p)}$ the speed-up of the parallel process defined by:

$$Sp^{(p)} = \frac{T_{elp}^{(1)}}{T_{elp}^{(p)}} \tag{8}$$

where $T_{elp}^{(p)}$ and $T_{elp}^{(1)}$ are :

$$T_{elp}^{(p)} = T_{cpu}^{(p)} + T_{io}^{(p)} + T_{ctr}^{(p)} \tag{9}$$

$$T_{elp}^{(1)} = T_{cpu}^{(1)} \tag{10}$$

assuming there is neither communication nor control cost in a sequential process.
Considering that the number of iterations is independent of the number of processors and that computation, communication and control costs are constant throughout the iterative process, we will now evaluate the different components of the total elapsed time independently of the number of iterations.

Computation Cost

We suppose the computation time $T_{cpu}^{(p)}$ is given by:

$$T_{cpu}^{(p)} = t_{cpu} + cpu \ . \ cost\_cpu(V^{(p)}) \tag{11}$$

where t_{cpu} is the start-up time of the arithmetic processor, cpu the elemental time to perform one arithmetic operation, and where cost_cpu is the numerical algorithm complexity.
The t_{cpu} and cpu times depend only on the hardware features, while the cost_cpu function, depending on the algorithm, can be a linear function of V for O(N) algorithms, or a nonlinear function for $O(N^2)$ and O(Nlog(N))

algorithms where N, in this case, represents the problem size. In the following, we restrict our study to only linear algorithms such as multicolor relaxation methods which have shown a constant rate of convergence, independently of the number of processors [3].
Neglecting also the start-up time t_{cpu}, we have then the formulation:

$$T_{cpu}^{(p)} = cpu \,.\, V^{(p)} \tag{12}$$

where cpu will be the time to compute one grid point, taking into account the constant of the algorithm complexity.

Communication Cost
As we have seen previously, we suppose at every iteration each processor exchanges with its nearest neighbors the boundary values of the subdomain. As data is sent to only 2.d neighbors and as we do not assume communication overlapping [10], the communication time $T_{io}^{(p)}$ can therefore be written :

$$T_{io}^{(p)} = 2.d.t_{io} + io \,.\, cost\_io(S^{(p)}) \tag{13}$$

where t_{io} is the start-up time of communication, io the elemental time to send or receive one word between two processors, and where cost_io is an evaluation of the communication degradation depending on the number of words to transmit and on the topological properties of the network. In the following, as each processor communicates with its immediate neighbors, we suppose there is no communication degradation, leading to the formulation :

$$T_{io}^{(p)} = 2.d.t_{io} + io \,.\, S^{(p)} \tag{14}$$

Control Cost
The control cost includes two different kinds of overhead. One is the overhead due to the tasks activation and termination, namely the fork and join, which is done once and for all. The other is the overhead due to the algorithm synchronization and termination detection. Studying an iterative and synchronous method, this control is done at every iteration and therefore is the only one we will consider in the following.
The algorithm termination detection of an iterative algorithm is related to a convergence criterion evaluation. This convergence criterion can be a local or global one. If local, each process decides by itself its own termination, leading to an overhead independent of the number of processors. If global, each process has to send one word to a specific one or to all the others depending on the algorithm used.
Therefore, we will suppose the control cost is given by :

$$T_{ctr}^{(p)} = ctr \,.\, cost\_ctr(p) \tag{15}$$

where ctr is the elemental control time, and cost_ctr a function giving the control algorithm complexity depending on the number of processors. In the following, we will study the effect of constant, linear and logarithmic control costs on speed-up.

A speed-up evaluation without control cost

In this case, we assume there is no control cost or that control is negligeable compared to computation and we have then:

$$T_{elp}^{(p)} = T_{cpu}^{(p)} + T_{io}^{(p)} \tag{16}$$

Under our hypotheses and using (12)&(14), speed-up is now given by:

$$Sp(p) = \frac{p}{1 + a(p)} \tag{17}$$

where

$$a(p) = \frac{t_{io}}{cpu} \cdot \frac{2.d.p}{N^n} + \frac{io}{cpu} \cdot \frac{2.d.k}{N} \tag{18}$$

This function a(p) which caracterizes the communication overhead has two components. The first related to the start-up time has a linear dependency in p and decreases as N^{-n} with the problem size. The second related to the communication throughput has a linear dependency in k instead of p and decreases only as N^{-1} with the problem size, which is due to the perimeter effect coming from the ratio $S^{(p)}/V^{(p)}$ in (4).
If we have a slice decomposition the function a(p) is a linear function of p and we have :

$$a(p) = a \cdot p \tag{19}$$

where a is a constant independent of p, usually less than 1.
With square and cube decompositions, the throughput term is proportional to the square and respectively cubic root of p.
With such a formulation, speed-up is a monotonic function of p, asymptotic to 1/a or lim 1/a(p) depending on the decomposition dimension.
The speed-up function is however truncated by the maximum number of processors p^* in (5) which defines the maximum geometrical speed-up Sp^* by:

$$Sp^* = \frac{1}{a^* + 1/p^*} \tag{20}$$

with

$$a^* = \frac{t_{io}}{cpu} \cdot \frac{2.d}{N^n} + \frac{io}{cpu} \cdot \frac{2.d}{N^d} \tag{21}$$

Therefore, with usually large problems, the main cause of communication overhead should be the throughput term.
Both components of a(p) are proportional to the arithmetic processor speed cpu^{-1} and to the domain decomposition dimension d and the influence of the communication overhead increases with the arithmetic processor speed unless the parameters t_{io} and io are decreased in the same proportion.
For a fixed number of processors p and a given problem size N the optimal domain decomposition will depend on the predominant term of the communication overhead.
If the communication is start-up bound the domain decomposition dimension should be choosen to its minimum value 1, leading to a slice decomposition while if the communication is throughput bound, it should be choosen to its maximum value leading to a square decomposition for a 2D problem and to a cube decomposition for a 3D problem. But as the number of processors increases for a given problem size, the start-up time term, which is linear in p, leads to a more and more start-up bound problem.
So depending on the start-up parameter of the system compared to its throughput, and depending also on its vector performance, if each processor is a pipeline processor the vectors treated will be shorter with a square or cube decomposition than with a slice decomposition, one type of decomposition will be preferred to another.

Speed-up evaluations with control cost

We will now introduce the control time $T_{ctr}(p)$ in the speed-up evaluation and study the effect of linear and logarithmic control costs.

Linear control

We first suppose the control time is a linear function of the number of processors and is given by :

$$T_{ctr}(p) = ctr \, . \, p \qquad (22)$$

where ctr is the elemental control time. Under those assumptions, the speed-up is now given by :

$$Sp(p) = \frac{p}{1 + a(p) + b.p^2} \qquad (23)$$

where

$$b = \frac{ctr.}{cpu} \cdot \frac{1}{V} \qquad (24)$$

and where a is the communication parameter given by (18). The parameter b, which caracterises the control overhead is proportional to the cpu speed cpu^{-1} and to the elemental control time ctr. So, as we have seen already with communication, the control overhead increases with the arithmetic processor speed unless the parameter ctr is decreased in the same proportion. The parameter b , which has only one component, can be compared to the start-up term of the communication and decreases as N^{-n} with the problem size. It should be usually less than 1 and close to 0 for large problems.

Speed-up is now a nonmonotonic function of p asymptotic to 0, with a maximum speed-up and a critical number of processor over which speed-up decreases.

For example with a slice decomposition we have:

$$Sp^{max} = \frac{1}{a + 2.\sqrt{b}} \quad \text{and} \quad p_c = \frac{1}{\sqrt{b}} \qquad (25)$$

Logarithmic control

We suppose now the control time is a logarithmic function of the number of processors and is given by :

$$T_{ctr}(p) = ctr \, . \, \log(p) \qquad (26)$$

where ctr is the elemental control time. Under those assumptions, the speed-up is now given by :

$$Sp(p) = \frac{p}{1 + a(p) + b.p.\log(p)} \qquad (27)$$

where a is the communication parameter in (18) and b is the control parameter in (24).

As for the linear control, speed-up is a nonmonotonic function of p, where for a slice decomposition the maximum is defined by:

$$Sp^{max} = \frac{1}{a + b.(1-\log(b))} \quad \text{and} \quad p_c = \frac{1}{b} \qquad (28)$$

As b is usually less than 1, those values are greater than the linear control ones, leading to a much better efficiency. For example, if a = b =

10^{-2}, with a linear control the maximum speed-up 4.8 is reached for 10 processors while with a logarithmic control the maximum speed-up 11.5 is reached for 100 processors.

Experimental results

The experiments have been done with a multicolor SLOR domain decomposition method to solve a second order nonlinear partial differential equation on a rectangular domain [3]. In this case, the convergence criterion is a global one and a logical variable conv can be defined such as:

$$\text{conv} = \max_{i=1..p} | \text{err}_i | < \text{eps}$$

where err_i is the local error on each subdomain and eps the precision of the iterative method.
This algorithm can be implemented in two different control ways :

- in a master-slave way, where the master performs the sequential tasks if any and assumes a central control while the slaves perform the only parallel routine.
- in a parent-child way, where the parent only performs the sequential routines while control is performed by the children.

A third way can also implemented where the first or last available child executes each sequential task [4,5,8], leading to a hostless system.
Several experiments have been done on the 1CAP1 system of Departement 48B at IBM-Kingston. This system is a loosely coupled array of 10 attached processors FPS-164, hosted by an IBM 3081. Three different links exist to communicate data among the different processors. The first is through the standard IBM channels and connects the APs through the IBM host, while the second is done through several shared memories and connects directly the different APs. The third, which we did not use in the experiments, is a ring bus connecting the differents APs.

In our experiments, we implemented both master-slave and parent-child ways. In the first one, every slave process sends its local error to the master-host process which evaluates the maximum error and stops the slave processes if the global convergence criterion is satisfied. This kind of algorithm has been implemeted using the host chanels and is referred as "host-AP channel". In the second one, every child process broadcasts its local error among all others and evaluates the maximum error, controlling locally the global convergence criterion. This kind of algorithm has been implemented using the shared memeory in a message passing technique and is referred as "shared memory-child control". Different distributed solutions to this control problem can be found [1], whose efficiency depends on the network topology.
Figs. 1 and 2 present a comparaison of the experimental and of the linear cost speed-up evaluation with the "host-AP channel" algorithm for 32*42 and 64*84 grids. Figs. 3 and 4 present the same comparaison for the "shared memory-child control" algorithm.
In both simulations, the cpu value has been explicitly mesured on the system and represents the time to perform one grid point and not only one arithmetic operation, while the io parameters were taken from experimental measurements done in IBM-Kingston. On the contrary, the ctr value has been adjusted to fit experimentation and simulation. In both cases, the communication overhead is start-up bound and for both grids the adjustement between simulation and experimentation is quite good.
Using the "shared memory-child control" algorithm and the corresponding parameters, an extrapolation of speed-up on various finer grids is presented in Fig. 5.

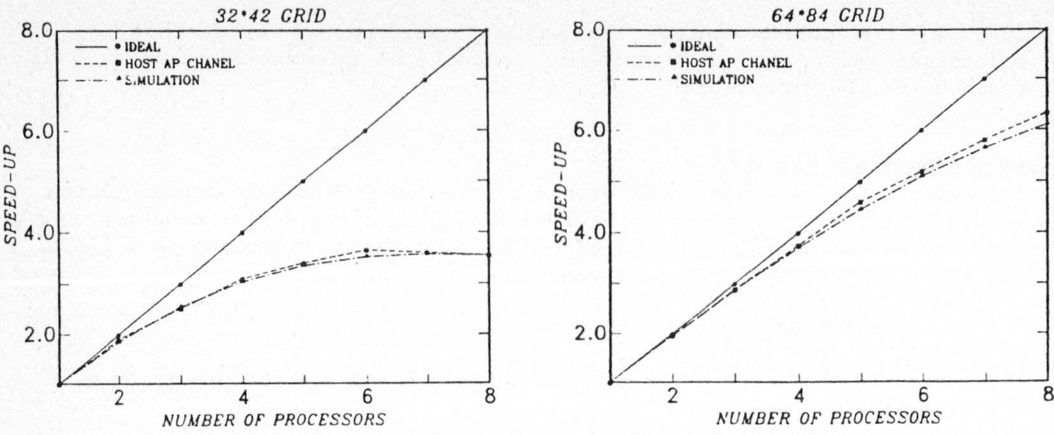

Figures 1 & 2
Experimental and simulated speed-up for centralised algorithm

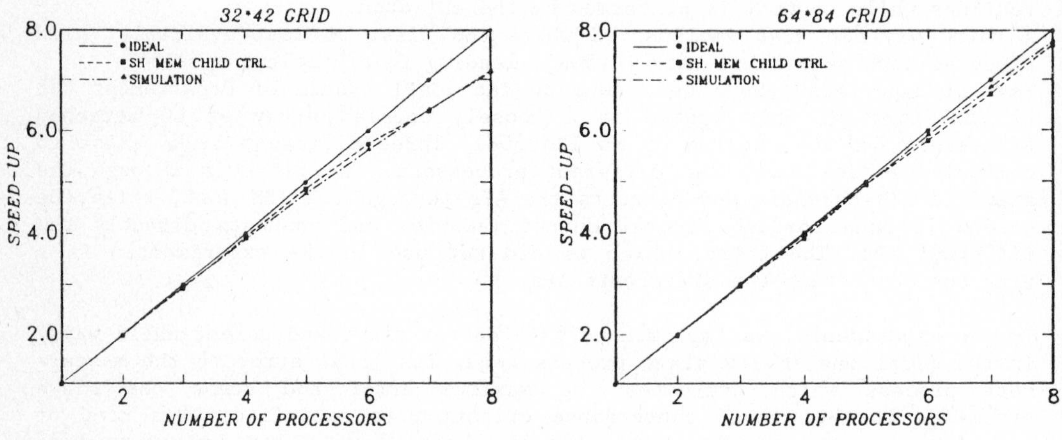

Figures 3 & 4
Experimental and simulated speed-up for distributed algorithm

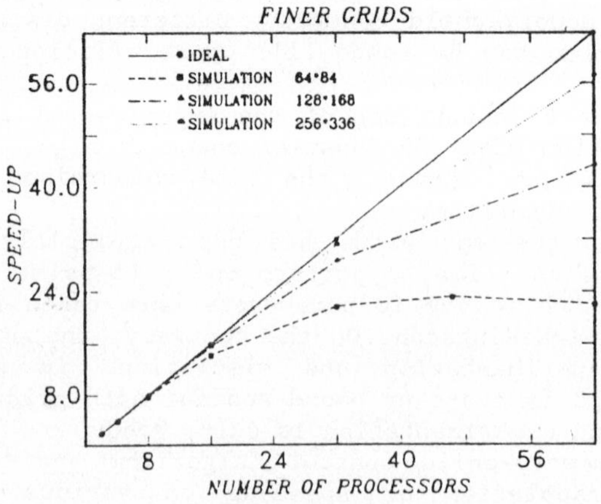

Figure 5
Speed-up extrapolation to finer grids

Conclusion

We have seen the different effects of computation, communication and control costs on the parallel speed-up of an iterative method where each processor exchanges data with its nearest neighbors. Under those hypotheses, we have studied the different components of the communication overhead and have observed that the only "local" communication cost, which is of course the main overhead for usual problems, cannot by itself be responsible for a slow-down of the parallel efficiency. This effect is induced by the control term whose "global" characteristic is badly suited to a loosely coupled multiprocessors architecture. Therefore distributed control algorithms, adapted to the architecture, and maybe control buses with very small start-up time, should be used to minimise this overhead. Thinking of massive parallel systems, this study shows clearly that a negligible effect for large problems and few processors can be of growing importance with larger systems, leading to a maximum number of processors which should be evaluated for every problem.

Acknowledgement

I would like to thank Dr. Enrico Clementi who gave me the opportunity to work on the 1CAP1 system of Department 48B at IBM-Kingston and make these experiments possible.

References

[1] Andre F., Herman D., Verjus J.P. Synchronization of parallel programs, The MIT Press, 1985.

[2] Axelrod T.S. Effects of synchronization bariers on multiprocessor performance. Parallel Computing , Vol 2, No 3, North-Holland, 1986, pp. 129-140.

[3] Brochard L. Domain decomposition and relaxation methods, Parallel Algorithms and Architectures, M. Cosnard Ed., Elsevier Science Publishers B.V., North-Holland, 1986, pp. 61-72.

[4] Brochard L. A shared memory MIMD computer: the Ultracomputer. La Recherche Aerospatiale, Paris, to appear.

[5] Darema F. Applications environment for the IBM research parallel project (RP3). Proceedings of International Conference on Surpecomputing, Athens 1987, Lecture Notes in Computer Science, Springer-Verlag, New York, to appear.

[6] Gannon D., Rosendale J.V. On the impact of communication complexity on the design of parallel numerical algorithms. ICASE Report 84-41 , NASA Langsley, 1984.

[7] Glowinski R., Dinh Q.V., Periaux J. Domain decomposition for elliptic problems, Finite Elements in Fluids, Vol 5. Gallagher Ed. Wiley & Sons, 1984, pp. 45-105.

[8] Gottlieb A., Lubachevsky B.D., Rudolf L. Basic techniques for the efficient coordination of very large number of cooperating sequential processors. ACM Trans. on Prog. Lang. and Syst., Vol 5, No 2, 1983, pp. 164-189.

[9] Rodrigue G., Sailor P. Inner/outer iterative methods and numerical Schwarz algorithms. Proc. of I.B.M. Conf. on Vector. and Parallel. Comput. for Scient. Comput.,Rome, 1985.

[10] Saad Y. Data communication in hypercubes. Research Report Yale Univ. DCS/RR-428, 1985.

[11] Schwarz H. Gesammelte Mathematische Adhandlungen, Vol. 2, Berlin, Springer, 1890, pp. 133-134.

[12] Widlund O. B. Iterative methods for elliptic problems on regions partitioned into substructures and the biharmonic Dirichlet problem. Proc. of Sixth Int. Symp. on Comp. Math. in Appl. Sci. and Eng., Glowinski and Lions Ed., 1984, pp. 33-45.

Half-Dynamic Scheduling with Data-flow Control

Hideki Sunahara
Mario Tokoro
Department of Electrical Engineering
Keio University
Yokohama 223 JAPAN

Abstract

The main problem of parallel processing concerns how to utilize the multiple processors. Much effort has been put into increasing the utilization of the processors. This paper proposes scheduling algorithms for multiple processors combining static scheduling and dynamic scheduling with data-flow control. Evaluation is made in terms of feasibility, efficiency, and performance, through computer simulations.

1 Introduction

Parallelism is one of the most interesting problems for obtaining high speed computer systems. How to utilize the multiple processors is the main problem in parallel processing. Scheduling algorithms for instructions are classified into two kinds: *static* and *dynamic*.

Static scheduling has no execution overhead. However, it can only be applied to special problems. For example, Coffman-Graham's algorithm[Coffman 76] can only be applied to a problem which is non-preemptive and has a **constant time** task execution on **two** processors. Hu's algorithm[Coffman 76] can be applied to a problem which is non-preemptive and a **tree** structured task system. *Static scheduling* is difficult to apply to problems which have a dynamic structure, such as loops and recursive calls.

Dynamic scheduling can apply to such problems, but it has execution overhead. A data-flow architecture is an example of an architecture which realizes *dynamic scheduling.* In recent years, various data-flow architectures have been proposed[Treleaven 82]. Data-flow architectures have advantages over conventional and other parallel computing architectures because they have capabilities for automatic detection and utilization of maximum parallelism in a program at execution time. However, they have some disadvantages in execution with a finite number of resources (e.g., execution units and memories). A data-flow program cannot always utilize the finite resources efficiently. This is because a non-deterministic selection among many ready instructions may choose other than the most critical ones. Data-flow architectures also have overhead at execution time, such as in searching for a token pair.

Thus, our concern is to develop a scheme to efficiently utilize a finite number of resources and decrease overhead at execution time. As an answer to this requirement, the authors introduced the working set concept for data-flow machines, proposing a data-flow architecture with hierarchical instruction memories [Tokoro 83] [Sunahara 84] [Sunahara 86]. The working set concept for a data-flow machine is based on the **simultaneity of execution** of a program. Several policies were proposed for working set management. Proposed policies were shown to be effective for programs which have a static structure through computer simulations [Tokoro 83] [Sunahara 84] [Sunahara 86]. However, the results for programs which have dynamic structure such as loops and recursive calls were not satisfactory. In this paper, a static pre-scheduling algorithm is proposed. Evaluation is made through computer simulations.

2 The Working Set Concept

A data-flow machine has multiple execution units. A data-flow program is represented as directed graph, where a node indicates an operation and a directed arc indicates the data dependency between the two nodes connected by it. Since every instruction which has all of its input data available can be executed in parallel, the execution of a program proceeds like a wave front on a graph.

In programs which do not include loops and function calls, the principle of locality does not apply as it does in conventional machines because in such programs each instruction is executed only once. Instead, we can establish a working set based on the **simultaneity of execution** of a program.

Two quantities called the **earliest execution level** (E-level) and the **latest execution level** (L-level) can be associated with each node of a graph providing the basis for **simultaneity.** Assuming the machine incorporates an infinite number of execution units, the E-level refers to the level (or timing) at which all of the input for each instruction becomes available. The L-level refers to the latest possible execution time without increasing the execution time. An instruction whose E-level is equal to its L-level is called the **critical node**. This leveling scheme can be regarded as an example of simple static scheduling.

The E-level and L-level for programs which include loops and function calls are associated with hierarchical leveling. Hierarchical leveling is a method which gives levels to nodes dynamically. The E-level and L-level for each data-flow graph for loop bodies and functions are computed individually as shown figure 1 (a). When a function call (or loop body) node is executed, the instructions for this function body are activated. Eventually, each instruction has a hierarchical level $(E_1.E_2.\cdots.E_i, L_1.L_2.\cdots.L_i)$ as shown in figure 1 (b), where i is the level of nesting.

3 Working Set Policies

3.1 A Model of the Data-flow Machine

Figure 2 shows our model for data-flow machines. The **EU** indicates multiple execution units which can execute instructions in parallel. The **PIM** is the Primary Instruction Memory which contains active instructions. An instruction can take in input data only when it is placed in this memory. In order to speed up the update of operand data (or ready tags) this memory is content addressable. The **SIM** is the Secondary Instruction Memory which contains dormant instructions. This memory is much larger than the PIM and has the capability of reading a page of memory cells at a reasonably high speed (but of course much slower than PIM). The **RM** is the Result Memory which temporarily stores result data from the EU until they are taken in by all the instructions that use them.

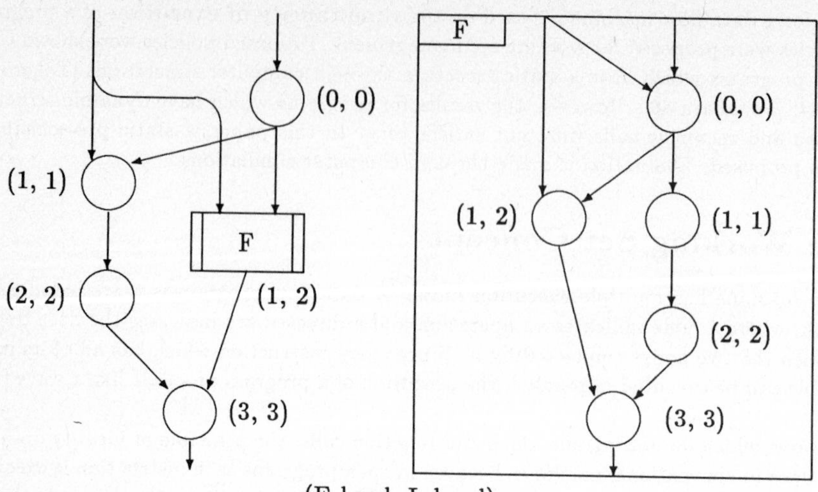

(E-level, L-level)

(a) levels are given to each node before execution.

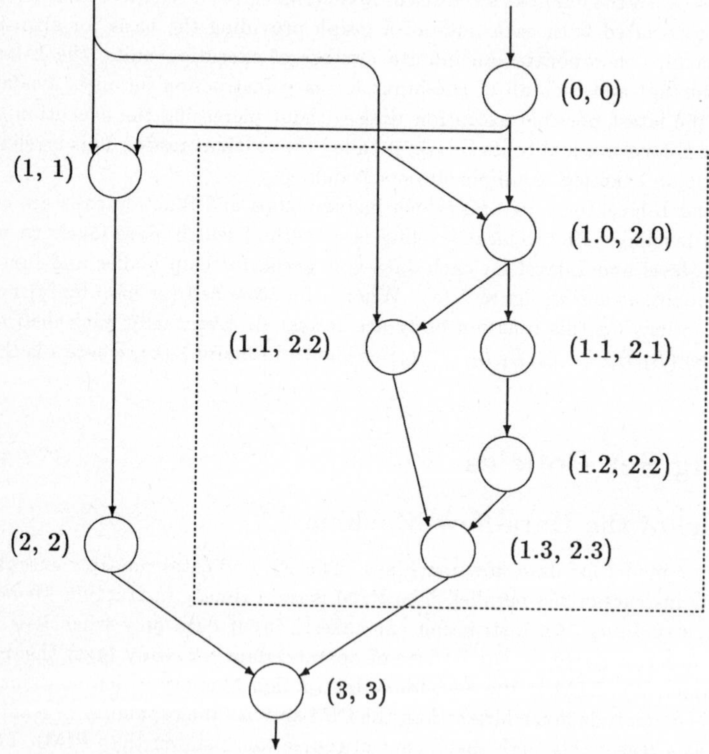

(b) levels are treated as hierarchical levels in execution.

Figure 1: E- and L-level

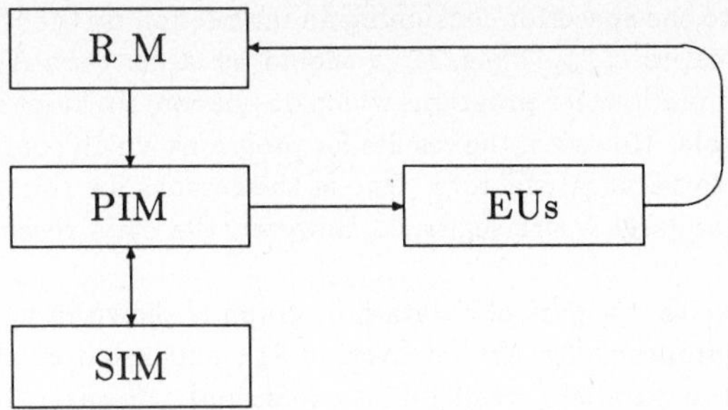

Figure 2: A model of a data-flow machine

3.2 Basic Policies

We have proposed four kinds of basic policies for our data-flow machine model: instruction segmentation policies, fetch policies, removal/replacement policies[Tokoro 83], and branch management policies[Sunahara 84]. The **instruction segmentation policies** define the size of a segment which is transferred between the PIM and the SIM. The **instruction fetch policies** refer to deciding when and which segments to transfer from the SIM to fill up the free memory cells in the PIM. In order to realize the pre-fetch mechanism, levels of each node are used in these policies. The **instruction removal/replacement policies** refer to deciding which segments are to be removed from the PIM so that new segments can be transferred from the SIM. The **branch management policies** provide the mechanism for removing never-executed instructions.

3.3 The Result of Previous Evaluation

Evaluation of the basic policies was made through computer simulation in previous papers [Sunahara 84] [Sunahara 86]. We made the following assumptions in the simulations:

1. the execution time of each instruction is constant and is one unit of time,

2. the time to transfer one page between the PIM and the SIM is one unit of time, and

3. all the other consumed time, such as the memory access time, is almost zero.

According to the simulations, segmentation by loop bodies or functions with the fetch policy based on E-levels or L-levels not needing for replacement policies, and with the management policy that fetches an alternative segment worked efficiently.

The page size for transferring pages between the PIM and the SIM is given by the following equation:

$$N_{EU} \times v_{exec} \leq P_{swap} \times v_{swap}$$

where N_{EU} is the number of EUs, v_{exec} is the average execution speed of the EU (the number of instructions per one unit of time), P_{swap} is the size of one physical page, and v_{swap} is the transfer speed between the PIM and the SIM (the number of pages per one unit of time). This equation holds because the speed for producing an instruction by transferring instructions must be faster than or equal to the speed for consuming an instruction by the EUs. Under the current assumptions, v_{exec} is equal to v_{swap}. Thus, P_{swap} should be larger than N_{EU}.

The results of the simulations for programs which do not contain loops and function calls were shown to be very favorable. However, the results for programs which contain loops and function calls were often shown to be unsatisfactory. One of the reasons for this was the fragmentation of the PIM caused by too large a size segment. However, the main reason was the hierarchical leveling.

For example, suppose that a part of a data-flow graph is shown in figure 3. In the dynamic data-flow architecture proposed by Arvind [Arvind 81], expansion of the function f and the function g is performed in parallel (breadth-first expansion). However, by using our execution mechanism, expansion of the function g is performed after expansion of the function f (depth-first), since the level of the node of the function f happens to be smaller than the level of the node of the function g. In such a case, since the parallelism of programs cannot be utilized maximally, the execution time of the programs increases. Thus, we need to consider an efficient mechanism for the expansion of the functions.

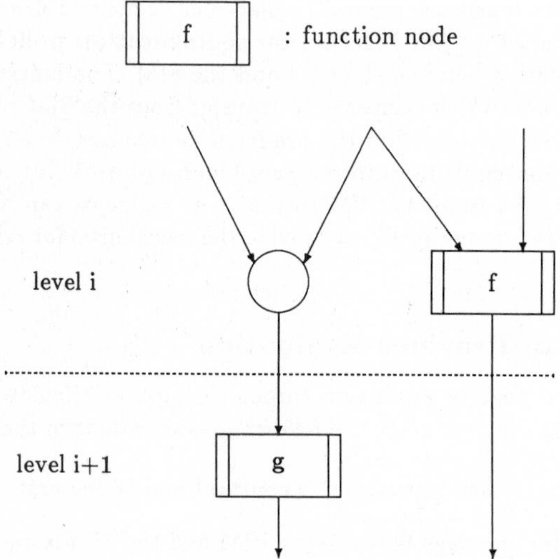

Figure 3: A problem in hierarchical levelling

4 Shading

In order to expand functions which have different levels in parallel, as soon as a function is invoked, its function node should be removed from the graph which calls this function. The segments of invoked functions are fetched by the round-robin scheme. However, if function nodes are removed from a graph, the instructions which receive the results of the called function are fetched before the instructions of the called function. This may cause a dead-lock.

To avoid this, the nodes of a graph should be divided into two groups: the group of instructions which should be executed before the function call and the group of instructions which

Table 1: Test programs

program name	characteristic			simulation parameters	
	number of instructions	average parallelism	maximum parallelism	number of EUs	size of one page
qsort(20)	7721	7.3	35	16	16
nqueens(4)	4045	17.7	58	16	16
nqueens(5)	15589	43.3	131	32	32

qsort(20): This is a program which sorts a list of 20 random integers by the quick-sort technique.

nqueens(4): This program is for the 4 queens problem.

nqueens(5): This program is for the 5 queens problem. The program code is the same as *nqueens(4)*.

should be executed after the function call. The graphs of the practical programs include several function nodes. Thus, the groups of instructions become more complex. Figure 4 shows the groups for a graph which includes four functions. These groups are called *shades*, and grouping instructions in *shades*is called *shading* in this paper. In figure 4, *"shade 0"* is a group of instructions which should be executed before all function calls. *"Shade 1"* is a group of instructions which should be executed after function *B* is finished. *"Shade 2"* is a group of instructions which should be executed after function *A* and *B* are finished. *"Shade 3"* is a group for function *D*. *"Shade 4"* is a group for function *C* and function *D*. Each shade will be fetched when required results are returned. For example, *"shade 1"* should be fetched when function *B* is complete.

Shades of each instruction can be obtained from data-flow analysis of the graph. The basic idea of this method is based on the concept of demand-driven mechanisms. Instructions in each shade are executed with a data-flow mechanism, and they are controlled according to their levels. Control of shades is performed with a demand-driven mechanism. Leveling and shading are simple static scheduling. Data-flow and demand-driven mechanisms are used to manage that part of the scheduling which cannot be decided before execution.

5 Evaluation of Shading

Computer simulations have been done to evaluate the efficiency of the *shading* proposed in the previous section. The assumptions in this simulation are the same as those described in section 3.2.

Test programs for this simulation is shown table 1. These programs are written in **VALID**†[1].

Figure 5 ~ figure 7 show some simulation results. A square mark in the graph shows the execution time for ideal scheduling on dynamic data-flow architecture with the same number of execution units. A size of the PIM for ideal scheduling indicates the required size of the instruction memory (or a matching memory).

The execution speed for *nqueens(4)* and *nqueens(5)* is improved by using shades, and it

[1]**VALID** is a functional programming language for a data-flow machine developed by the NTT Musashino Electrical Communication Laboratory[Amamiya 82]. "**VALID**" is an abbreviation for **VAL**ue **ID**entification language. The basic design philosophy is that the **VALID** semantics support programming based on a functional concept with Algol like syntax.

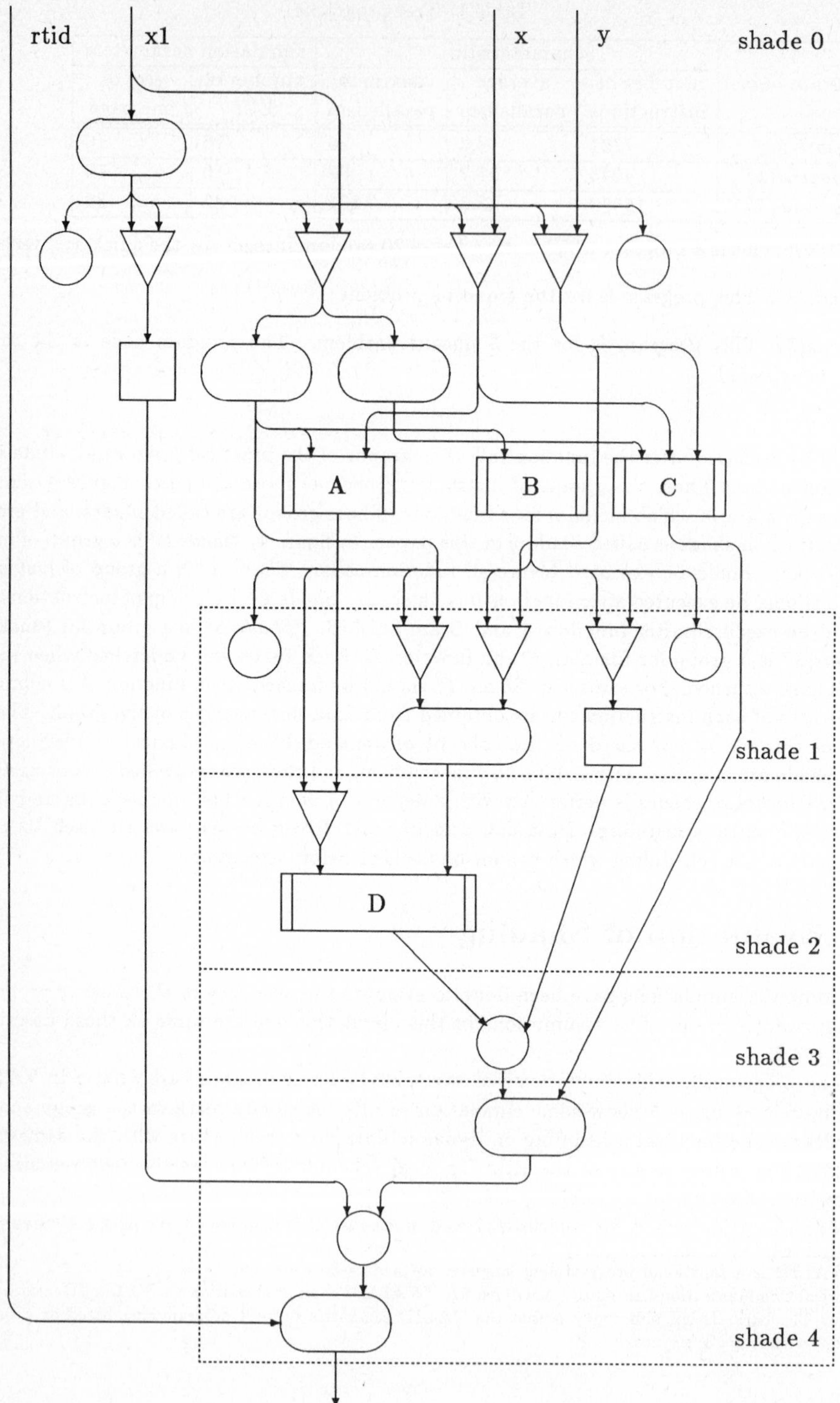

Figure 4: Shades

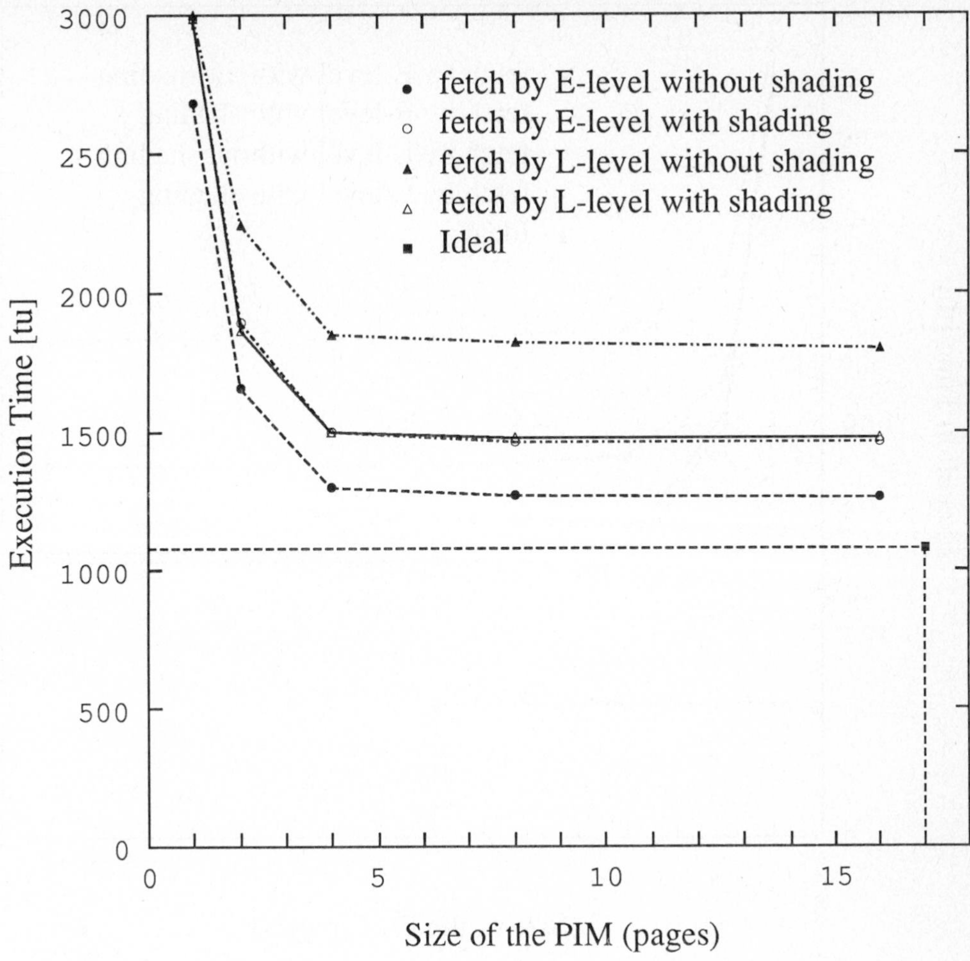

Figure 5: Simulation Result for qsort(20)

becomes closer to the ideal than the previous results. However, the execution speed for *qsort(20)* becomes slower when using shades, but it is already close the ideal execution speed in the previous results. The reason of this is the fragmentation caused by shading. Since instructions which have different shades should be stored in different segments, fragmentation occurs, and the fragmentation causes an increase in the number of segments transferred to the PIM. If the parallelism of executed program is large, transferring segments to the PIM overlaps with the execution of instructions. However, the average parallelism of *qsort(20)* is small. Thus, transferring segments to the PIM becomes a bottle-neck. In order to improve execution speed for the programs whose parallelism is small, the bandwidth between the PIM and the SIM should become larger.

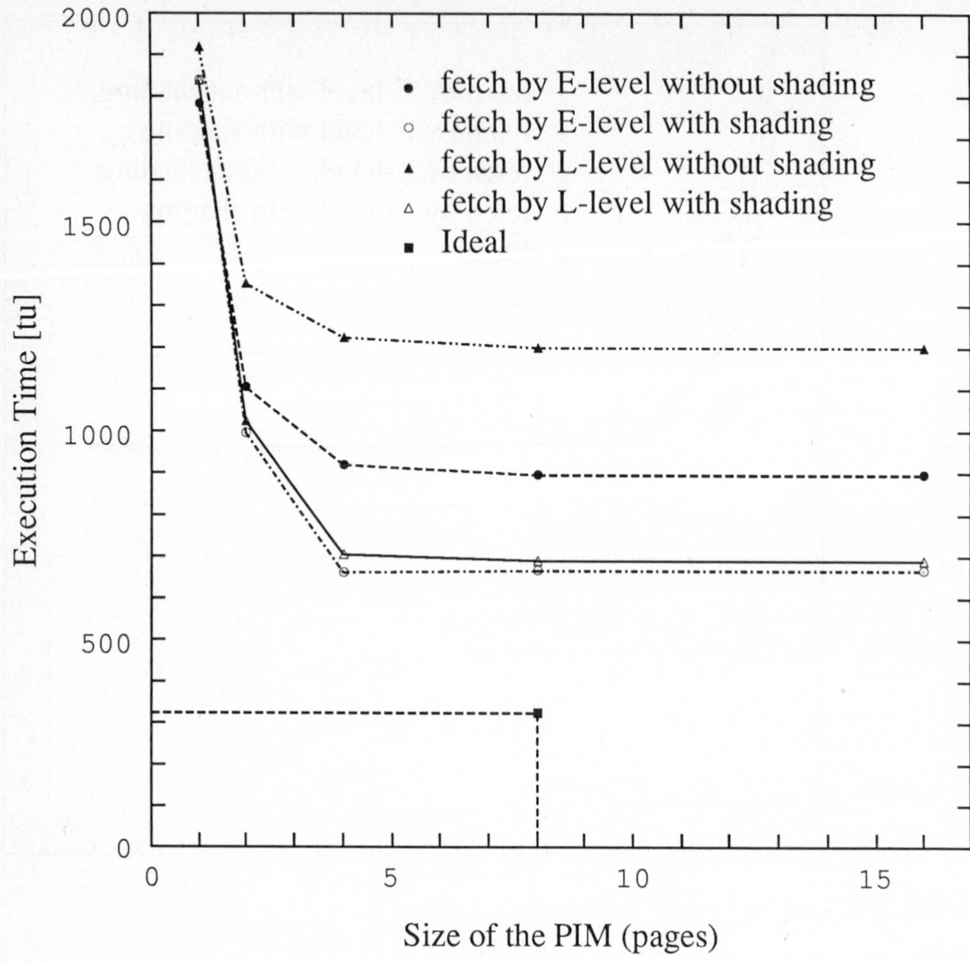

Figure 6: Simulation Result for nqueens(4)

6 Conclusion

This paper has proposed the shading method to manage hierarchically defined graphs, and evaluated its efficiency. Leveling and shading can be regarded as the simple static scheduling of data-flow graphs, and data-flow control is used to manage that part of the scheduling which cannot be decided before execution (dynamic scheduling).

The shading method worked efficiently for the programs whose parallelism is large. However, execution speed for the programs whose parallelism is small becomes slow since transferring segments to the PIM becomes a bottle-neck. Thus, the bandwidth between the PIM and the SIM should become larger for programs with small parallelism.

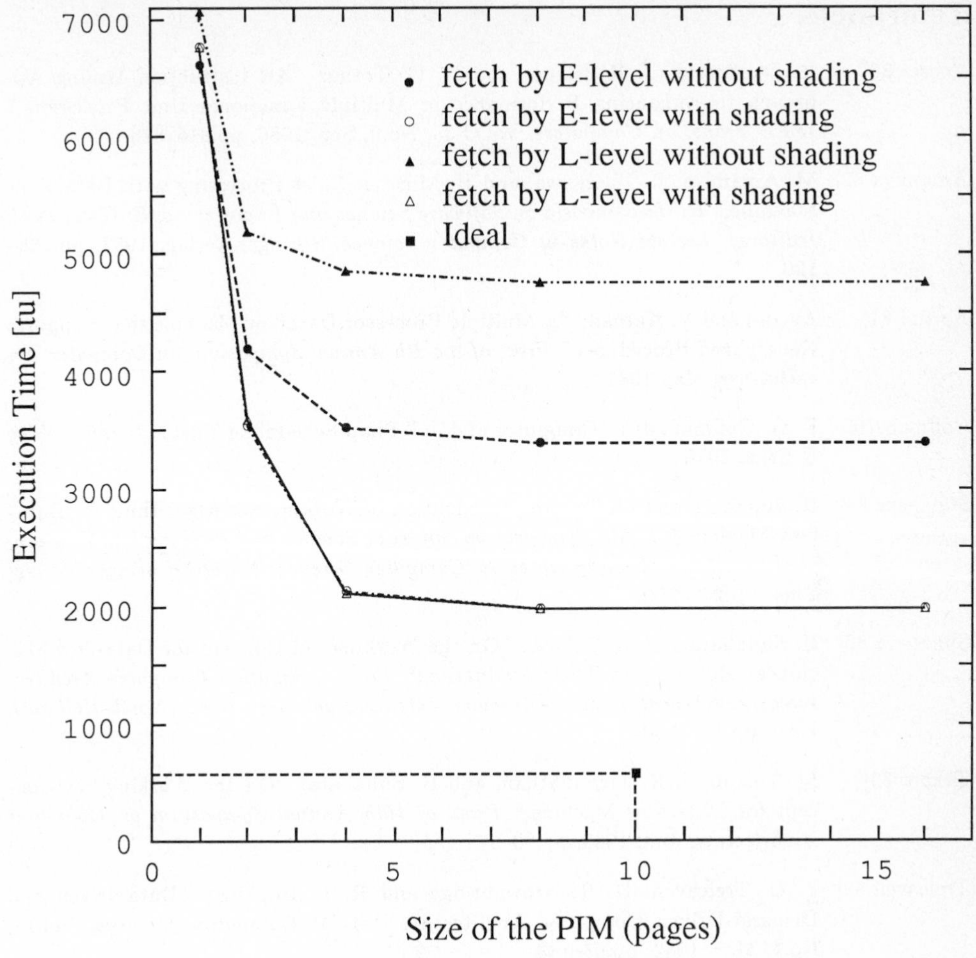

Figure 7: Simulation Result for nqueens(5)

We believe that the proposed method can apply to other parallel architectures, when the PIM is replaced by an instruction window with special hardware like the dispatch stack proposed in [Acosta 86].

Acknowledgment

The authors are grateful to Dr. Makoto Amamiya and Dr. Ryuzo Hasegawa of NTT Musashino Electrical Communication Laboratory for giving us permission to use the VALID interpreter system. The authors are thankful to Mr. Tatsuo Nagamatsu of Keio University for his help in the preparation of this paper.

References

[Acosta 86] R. D. Acosta, J. Kjelstrup, and H. C. Torng: "An Instruction Issuing Approach to Enhancing Performance in Multiple Functional Unit Processors," *IEEE Trans. on Computers*, Vol.C-35, No.9, Sep. 1986, pp.815–828.

[Amamiya 82] M. Amamiya, R. Hasegawa, and H. Mikami: "List Processing with Data Flow Machine," *RIMS Symposia on Software Science and Engineering, E. Goto, at.el. (editors), Lecture Notes in Computer Science*, Springer-Verlag, 1982, pp.165–190.

[Arvind 81] Arvind and V. Kathail: "A Multiple Processor Dataflow Machine that Supports Generalized Procedures," *Proc. of the 8th Annual Symposium on Computer Architecture*, May 1981.

[Coffman 76] E. G. Coffman, Jr.: "Computer and Job-Shop Scheduling Theory," *John Wiley & Sons*, 1976.

[Sunahara 84] H. Sunahara and M. Tokoro: "Evaluation of Working Set Algorithms for Dataflow Machine," *RIMS Symposia on Software Science and Engineering, E. Goto, at.el. (editors), Lecture Notes in Computer Science*, No.220, Springer-Verlag, 1984, pp.233–260.

[Sunahara 86] H. Sunahara and M. Tokoro: "On the Working Set Concept for Data-flow Machines: Policies and Their Evaluation," *Fifth Generation Computer Architectures, J.V. Woods (editor), Elsevier Science Publishers B.V. (North-Holland)*, 1986, pp.147–160.

[Tokoro 83] M. Tokoro, J. R. Jagannathan, and H. Sunahara: "On the Working Set Concept for Data-flow Machine," *Proc. of 10th Annual Symposium on Computer Architecture*, Jun. 1983, pp.90–97.

[Treleaven 82] P. C. Treleaven, D. R. Brownbridge and R. P. Hopkins: "Data-driven and Demand-Driven Computer Architecture," *ACM Computing Surveys*, Vol.14, No.1, Mar. 1982, pp.93–143.

A parallel block cyclic reduction algorithm for the fast solution of elliptic equations

E. Gallopoulos and Y. Saad
Center for Supercomputing Research and Development
University of Illinois at Urbana Champaign
Urbana, Illinois 61801
U.S.A.

Abstract. This paper presents an adaptation of the Block Cyclic Reduction (BCR) algorithm for a multi–vector processor. The main bottleneck of BCR lies in the solution of linear systems whose coefficient matrix is the product of tridiagonal matrices. This bottleneck is handled by expressing the rational function corresponding to the inverse of this product as a sum of elementary fractions. As a result the solution of this system leads to parallel solutions of tridiagonal systems. Numerical experiments performed on an Alliant FX/8 are reported.

1. Introduction

The numerical solution of linear elliptic partial differential equations is a problem of major importance in many fields of science and engineering. Aside from the traditional iterative methods, there exist several techniques that can solve many of the separable elliptic problems much faster [Hock70], [BuGN70], [Swar84]. The most widely used of these methods, which usually come under the general name *Rapid Elliptic Solvers* (RES), are based on either using the Fast Fourier Transform (FFT) to decouple the block tridiagonal systems into multiple scalar ones, or on using general *Block Cyclic Reduction* (BCR) as described in [Swee77], or finally, a combination of the above approaches as is the case in the FACR algorithm [Swar77], [Temp80]. For example, the solution of Poisson's equation on a rectangle discretized with an $n \times n$ grid, entails an asymptotic operation count of $O(n^3 \log n)$ and $O(n^2 \log^2 n)$ for the (iterative) SOR and ADI methods respectively, but only $O(n^2 \log n)$ for the cyclic reduction and FFT based methods.

With the advent of vector and parallel architectures, researchers have concentrated their efforts on making the best use of the computational resources in order to increase the

This work was supported by the National Science Foundation under Grants No. US NSF DCR84–10110 and US NSF DCR85–09970, the US Department of Energy under Grant No. DOE DE–FG02–85ER25001, by the US Air Force under Contract AFSOR–85–0211, and the IBM donation.

performance of these solvers [SaCK76], [OrVo85]. The FFT based methods are very suitable for such a task because of the amenability of the FFT to parallel computation and because of the immediate decoupling of the equations into multiple scalar tridiagonal systems. Thus, the development of highly efficient algorithms for the parallel/vector solution of multiple tridiagonal systems as well as for the FFT were instrumental in the acceptance of this approach. On the other hand, and despite some important advantages, the BCR methods didn't fare as well and little can be found in the literature concerning the implementation of BCR based elliptic problem solvers on the new generation supercomputers. The main reason for this is that as the BCR algorithm progresses, it appears that one must solve a steadily decreasing number of tridiagonal systems, the coefficient matrix of each being a matrix polynomial. The difficulty in the standard implementation is that one must solve in sequence a tridiagonal system per polynomial factor.

In this paper we describe a new method which is used to overcome this sequential bottleneck and in turn introduce parallelism at each step of the computation. Our approach can be used with success on most of the new supercomputers. An important advantage of the method is that it allows the efficient parallelization/vectorization of NCAR's FISHPACK (see [SwSw75]) which is entirely based on BCR for two-dimensional problems. Moreover, the technique can be easily applied to parallelize the Approximate Cyclic Reduction method, recently proposed by Swarztrauber in [Swar87].

The structure of the paper is as follows: Section 2 describes BCR and the computational bottleneck for a parallel system, sections 3 and 5 describe the new algorithm, and section 4 discusses implementation issues. In section 6 we present some numerical experiments and in section 7 we propose a few tentative concluding remarks.

2. Background: the main bottleneck in Buneman's algorithm

Consider a block tridiagonal system of the form

$$\begin{pmatrix} A & -I & & & \\ -I & A & -I & & \\ & \cdot & \cdot & \cdot & \\ & & -I & A & -I \\ & & & -I & A \end{pmatrix} \begin{pmatrix} v_1 \\ v_2 \\ \cdot \\ \cdot \\ v_n \end{pmatrix} = \begin{pmatrix} f_1 \\ f_2 \\ \cdot \\ \cdot \\ f_n \end{pmatrix} \tag{2.1}$$

where each block is an $m \times m$ tridiagonal matrix and the sub-vectors v_i and f_i are all of size m. Such systems frequently arise when discretizing an elliptic partial differential equation of the form

$$a(x)\frac{\partial^2 u}{\partial x^2} + b(x)\frac{\partial u}{\partial x} + c(x)u + \frac{\partial^2 u}{\partial y^2} = f(x,y)$$

with Dirichlet boundary conditions over, for example, a rectangular region.

For simplicity we assume at first that the block-size n of the system (2.1) is of the form $n = 2^{\mu}-1$. For a detailed description of the algorithm in the general case the reader is referred to [Swee77]. At the the $r-th$ step of BCR we have a system of the form:

$$\begin{pmatrix} A^{(r)} & -I & & & \\ -I & A^{(r)} & -I & & \\ & \cdot & \cdot & \cdot & \\ & & -I & A^{(r)} & -I \\ & & & -I & A^{(r)} \end{pmatrix} \begin{pmatrix} v_h \\ v_{2h} \\ \cdot \\ \cdot \\ v_{n,h} \end{pmatrix} = \begin{pmatrix} f_h \\ f_{2h} \\ \cdot \\ \cdot \\ f_{n,h} \end{pmatrix} \tag{2.2}$$

where $h = 2^r$, and each component of the right hand-side is put in the form

$$f_{jh} = A^{(r)} p_{jh}^{(r)} + q_{jh}^{(r)}. \tag{2.3}$$

Initially ($r = 0$) the vectors $p_i^{(0)}$ are zero while $q_i^{(0)} = f_j$. Equations whose block index j is odd are eliminated by multiplying each equation numbered $2jh$ by $A^{(r)}$ and adding to it equations $(2j-1)h$ and $(2j+1)h$. This yields a system of half the size involving only equations whose indices are even multiples of h. Specifically, the general equation becomes

$$-v_{(2j-2)h} + ((A^{(r)})^2-2I)v_{2jh}-v_{(2j+2)h} =$$
$$(A^{(r)})^2 p_{2jh}^{(r)} + A^{(r)}(q_{2jh}^{(r)} + p_{(2j-1)h}^{(r)} + p_{(2j+1)h}^{(r)}) + q_{2j-1)h}^{(r)} + q_{(2j+1)h}^{(r)}.$$

The above equation is then rewritten such that the new right-hand-sides will have a form similar to (2.3) in step $r+1$. This is achieved by defining

$$A^{(r+1)} = (A^{(r)})^2-2I \tag{2.4}$$

$$p_{2jh}^{(r+1)} = p_{2jh}^{(r)} + (A^{(r)})^{-1}(q_{2jh}^{(r)} + p_{(2j-1)h}^{(r)}+p_{(2j-1)h}^{(r)}) \tag{2.5}$$

$$q_{2jh}^{(r+1)} = 2p_{2jh}^{(r+1)}+q_{(2j-1)h}^{(r)} + q_{(2j-1)h}^{(r)}\ . \tag{2.6}$$

After $\mu-1$ steps of these transformations system (2.2) reduces to a system with a single block which can be solved directly. Then the back-substitution phase will consist of computing v_{jh}, for the odd values of j, using the fact that for even values of j, the v_{jh} have been computed in the previous step. Using (2.3), we see that we must compute, for j odd and $jh \leq n$:

for the odd values of j, using the fact that for even values of j, the v_{jh} have been computed in the previous step. Using (2.3), we see that we must compute, for j odd and $jh \leq n$:

$$v_{jh} = p_{jh}^{(r)} + (A^{(r)})^{-1}(q_{jh}^{(r)} + v_{(j-1)h} + v_{(j+1)h}) \,. \tag{2.7}$$

The above backward substitution steps are performed for $h=2^r$ decreasing from 2^μ to $2^0=1$. In summary, Buneman's variant of BCR takes the following form:

Algorithm 1

1. *Initialize:* $p_i^{(0)}=0$, $q_j^{(0)}=f_j$, $j=1,\ldots,n$ and $h=1$,

2. *Forward solution:*
   a. Form the matrix Y_r with columns $q_{2jh}^{(r)} + p_{(2j-1)h}^{(r)} + p_{(2j-1)h}^{(r)}$, $j = 1,\ldots,n_r/2$
   b. Solve the (multi)– linear system $A^{(r)}X_r = Y_r$
   c. Update the vectors p and q according to (2.5) and (2.6).
   d. If $h<n$ then $h = 2h$; go to a.

3. *Solve* for u, $A^{(r)}u = q_1^{(r)}$ and set $v_h = p_h + u$.

4. *Backward substitution:* while $h \geq 1$ do
   a. $h = h/2$
   b. Form the matrix Y_r with column vectors $q_{jh}^{(r)} + v_{(j-1)h} + v_{(j+1)h}$, $j=1,3,5\ldots,n/h$.
   c. Solve for U_r, $A^{(r)}U_r = Y_r$
   d. Update the solution vectors v_{jh}, $j=1$, 3 , .. according to (2.7).

The most time–consuming part of the above algorithm lies in the solution of the linear system in the forward and backward phases, i.e., in 2.b and 4.c. Clearly, the matrix $A^{(r)}$ is never formed explicitly. In fact the way in which 2.a and 4.c are usually performed is by first observing that the matrix $A^{(r)}$ is a known polynomial in A, specifically [Swee77]

$$A^{(r)} = 2T_{2^r}\left(\frac{A}{2}\right) \equiv \prod_{i=1}^{2^r} (A - \lambda_i I)$$

where T_k denotes the Chebyshev polynomial of the first kind of degree k and therefore

$$\lambda_i = 2\cos\frac{(2i-1)\pi}{2^{r+1}}, \; i = 1, 2, \ldots, 2^r.$$

When implemented on a serial computer, the linear systems corresponding to each of the factors and each of the right–hand–sides are solved in succession. Moreover, Gaussian elimination is used to solve these tridiagonal systems. On vector and parallel machines, these facts result in less efficient utilization of the available computational resources. An obvious but partial remedy is to still use Gaussian elimination but solve for all the right–hand–sides simultaneously. This will achieve good performance at the beginning of the forward sweep and at the end of the backward sweep since there are many such right–hand–sides. However, looking at the forward solution step only, the number of right–hand–sides decreases exponentially ($(n-1)/2$ then $(n-1)/4$, ..., 1), while the number of factors increases in the reverse order. This means that this high performance can only be enjoyed at the very first few steps. A similar situation occurs in the backward solution phase where the number of right–hand sides starts at one and then doubles at every step to reach the maximum number $(n+1)/2$ at the end of step 4.

Another way of introducing parallelism is to use (scalar) cyclic reduction for the tridiagonal systems. However, the cost of cyclic reduction in terms of operation count is high and its use may lead to disappointing speed–ups. This was in particular pointed out in [Saad87] in the context of Alternating Direction Implicit (ADI) methods.

3. The new algorithm

In this section, we continue with the assumption that we are solving a problem with Dirichlet conditions on the boundary and with a rectangular grid of dimension $n \times m$ with $n=2^{\mu}-1$. The basic problem to be solved at each step of BCR is of the form

$$\prod_{i=1}^{i=k} (A-\lambda_i I)X=Y \tag{3.1}$$

in which X and Y are matrices of dimension $m \times \nu$. The usual way of solving (3.1) is by means of the following algorithm:

Algorithm 2

1. Set $X_0=Y$
2. Do i=1,...,k
   a. Set $Y_i=X_{i-1}$
   b. Solve $(A-\lambda_i I)X_i=Y_{i-1}$
3. $X=X_k$

As was pointed out earlier when ν is large enough, the amount of vectorization and parallelization that is available in each of the inner loops of the above algorithm with the standard Gaussian elimination may be sufficient to deliver reasonable performance. The vector length with this simple approach is ν so that when ν is small, the delivered speed may become inadequate.

To introduce the alternative we propose, we start by observing that we are seeking the matrix $[g_k(A)]^{-1}Y \equiv s_k(A)Y$ where s_k is the rational function

$$s_k(t) \equiv \frac{1}{g_k(t)} \equiv \frac{1}{\prod_{i=1}^{k}(t-\lambda_i)} \tag{3.2}$$

We will need the following well–known elementary result:

Lemma 1

Every rational function

$$f(t)=\frac{u_l(t)}{g_k(t)}=\frac{u_l(t)}{\prod_{i=1}^{k}(t-\lambda_i)},$$

where the degree l *of* u_l *is less than* k *and where the poles* λ_i *are all distinct, can be expanded in terms of elementary fractions as follows*

$$f(t)=\sum_{i=1}^{k}\frac{\alpha_i}{t-\lambda_i}$$

where the scalars α_i *are given by*

$$\alpha_i=\frac{u_l(\lambda_i)}{g_k{}'(\lambda_i)}$$

In the context of BCR the polynomials involved are Chebyshev polynomials of the first and second kind, so that the partial fraction coefficients can be easily calculated (cf. section 5). For example, in the case we are describing, f is given by (3.2) with $g_k(t)=2T_k(t/2)$ and a little calculation shows that

$$\alpha_i=\frac{(-1)^{i-1}}{2^r}\cdot\sin\frac{(2i-1)\pi}{2^{r+1}}$$

As a result we can decompose the solution X as

$$X=\sum_{i=1}^{k}\alpha_i(A-\lambda_i I)^{-1}Y$$

where α_i are given by (3.5). This leads to the following rival for Algorithm 2:

Algorithm 3

1. Do for i=1,2,...,k
   Solve $(A-\lambda_i I)X_i=Y$
2. Compute $X=\sum_{i=1}^{k}\alpha_i X_i$

The clear advantage of Algorithm 3 over Algorithm 2 is that the tridiagonal systems involving the matrix $(A-\lambda_i I)$ are now decoupled and can be solved in parallel. In essence we have replaced a problem involving sequential solutions of tridiagonal linear systems by one which involves the simultaneous solution of independent tridiagonal linear systems and the linear combination of the partial results.

Two important questions might be asked at this point. First there is the danger of instability: the algorithm is not acceptable if it produces wrong answers. A simple analysis based on the exact expressions of the α_i*'s* shows that the process is extremely stable. This fact is also confirmed by the experiments. The second question concerns cost. The summation in step 2 of the algorithm involves an additional $2k\times m\times\nu\approx m\times n$ operations to be added to the usual $5\times m\times n+5\times k\times m$ associated with the traditional algorithm 2. Thus the additional operation count is not negligible: approximately 20% for small k and 10% for large k. The above are approximate operation counts obtained by dropping the less significant terms. Note however that this additional work is perfectly amenable to parallelization and high performance can be achieved.

4. Implementation issues

The most difficult issue that one faces when implementing the approach outlined in Section 3 is the fact that in the course of BCR, the two parameters k, the degree of the polynomial, and ν the number of right–hand sides, vary widely from one outer step to the other. In fact the relation $k\times(\nu+1)=\left\lfloor\frac{n+1}{2}\right\rfloor$ holds for the case when n is of the form $2^{\mu}-1$ which means that the two numbers k and $\nu+1$ will change exponentially and in inverse proportion of each other. As a result one must employ different strategies for the various cases: k large but ν small, ν large and k small, etc.

First we discuss one way of implementing the algorithm for a multi–vector processor architecture. The model architecture is that of an Alliant FX/8 which consists of 8 Computational Elements (CE's) each being a vector processor. From the above discussion we must distinguish two cases.

Case 1: ν is large. Here one can vectorize the operations with respect to the ν right–hand sides. Moreover if k is large enough (larger than the number of CE's) it is important to run concurrently the outer loop of step 1 in Algorithm 3. However, this becomes ineffective as k goes below the number of CE's since then fewer CE's would be active. In this particular case it is preferable to run the outer loop sequentially and perform the vector operations within the subroutine in a vector concurrent mode.

Case 2: k is large. The situation is the opposite of the previous one: vectorization of the operations should now be performed along the variables corresponding to the outer loop of Algorithm 3. Again the outer loop of step 1 in Algorithm 3 should be performed concurrently unless ν the number of right–hand sides is smaller than the number of CE's in which case it should be executed sequentially, with the vector loops run in a vector–concurrent mode.

Next we should say a few words on how Algorithm 3 can be implemented on a vector computer. Neither of the two approaches outlined above for the two different cases is likely to be effective because the vector lengths will decrease very quickly. An approach that seems best suited for a vector machine is to exploit the observation that at every step we have in fact a large number, namely $k\times\nu$, of tridiagonal systems to solve simultaneously. This leads to a process which is vectorizable with vector length equal to

$$k\nu = \left\lfloor \frac{n+1}{2} \right\rfloor - k \geq \left\lfloor \frac{n+1}{4} \right\rfloor$$

which will be satisfactory for reasonable size problems. These $k\nu$ simultaneous tridiagonal systems are obtained by simply reproducing the tridiagonal matrix $(A-\lambda_i I)$ involved in the (multi) linear system $(A-\lambda_i I)x=b_i$, $i=1,2,\ldots,\nu$ for each different right–hand–side. Step 1 of Algorithm 3, is therefore expanded into the simultaneous solution of exactly $k\times\nu$ independent tridiagonal systems each with a single right–hand–side. Although good performance can be achieved when n is large, this approach has a drawback which needs to be evaluated more carefully. Indeed, in order to achieve computations with vector lengths of $k\nu$, we must actually reproduce the computed data corresponding to forward solution in the tridiagonal solve ν times. For example, in the first step we can compute in vector mode all the divisions $1/(a_{11}-\lambda_i)$, $i=1,2,\ldots,k$ then create a copy of the result for each of the ν right hand sides. Although this involves no arithmetic, the price to pay may be far from negligible.

5. The general case

Sweet generalized the Buneman variant of BCR for general n and showed how it can be applied for any boundary conditions [Swee77]. We describe here the coefficients of the expansions necessary for the application of our method for general n as well as Dirichlet or Neumann boundary conditions. We postpone the description of the detailed, generalized algorithms to a forthcoming paper. As before, the key to the success of the method is the ability to express the matrix blocks at each step of BCR as a rational or polynomial matrix form. In fact, whereas before all the diagonal blocks in (2.2) involved the matrix polynomial $A^{(r)}$, in the general case the last diagonal block in (2.2) will be of the form $B^{(r)-1}C^{(r)}$ which can be shown to be a rational function in A. In particular $B^{(r)}$ and $C^{(r)}$ are matrix polynomials in A of degree k_r and l_r respectively, with $k_r = l_r + 2^r$. Depending on the boundary conditions and dimensions, these will be Chebyshev polynomials of the first or the second kind. Specifically, following the notation in [Swee77], the systems that must be solved at each step of the Buneman variant of BCR have one of the following five forms:

$$2\, T_{2^r}(\frac{1}{2}A)\, X = Y \tag{4.1}$$

$$U_{k_r}(\frac{1}{2}A)\, X = U_{l_r}(\frac{1}{2}A)\, Y \tag{4.2}$$

$$U_{k_r}(\frac{1}{2}A)\, X = 2\, U_{l_r}(\frac{1}{2}A)\, T_{2^r}(\frac{1}{2}A)\, Y \tag{4.3}$$

$$T_{k_r}(\frac{1}{2}A)\, X = T_{l_r}(\frac{1}{2}A)\, Y \tag{4.4}$$

and

$$T_{k_r}\,(\frac{1}{2}A)\;X = 2\;T_{l_r}\,(\frac{1}{2}A)\;T_{2^r}(\frac{1}{2}A)\;Y \tag{4.5}$$

where T_k and U_k denote, respectively, the Chebyshev polynomials of the first kind

$$T_k(\cos\theta) = \cos(k\theta),$$

and of the second kind

$$U_k(\cos\theta) = \frac{\sin((k+1)\theta)}{\sin\theta}\,.$$

Note in particular that (4.1) arises when $n = 2^{\mu}-1$ described in the previous section, (4.2) and (4.3) when $n \neq 2^{\mu}-1$ and with Dirichlet boundary conditions. (4.1), (4.4) and (4.5) arise in the corresponding circumstances but for Neumann boundary conditions.

In product representation

$$T_k(t) = \frac{1}{2}\cdot\prod_{i=1}^{k}\,(2t - \rho_k(i))$$

and

$$U_k(t) = \prod_{i=1}^{k}\,(2t - \sigma_k(i))$$

where

$$\rho_k(i) = 2\,\cos\frac{(2i-1)\pi}{2k}$$

and

$$\sigma_k(i) = 2\,\cos\frac{i\pi}{k+1}$$

From Lemma 1 it follows that we need to calculate:

i) for (4.1)

$$\alpha_i = \left[\frac{d}{dt}\left(2T_{2^r}\,(t/2)\right)\right]^{-1}$$

at $t = \rho_{2^r}(i)$ $(i = 1, \ldots, 2^r)$;

ii) for (4.2)

$$\beta_i = U_{l_r}\,(t/2)\,.\left[\frac{d}{dt}\,U_{k_r}\,(t/2)\right]^{-1}$$

at $t = \sigma_{k_r}(i)$ $(i = 1, \ldots, k_r)$;

iii) for (4.3)

$$\gamma_i = 2\, U_{l_r}(t/2)\,.\,T_{2^r}(t/2)\,.\left[\frac{d}{dt}\left(U_{k_r}(t/2)\right)\right]^{-1}$$

at $t = \sigma_{k_r}(i)$ $(i = 1, \ldots, k_r)$;

iv) for (4.4)

$$\delta_i = T_{l_r}(t/2)\,.\left[\frac{d}{dt}T_{k_r}(t/2)\right]^{-1}$$

at $t = \rho_{k_r}(i)$ $(i = 1, \ldots, k_r)$;

v) for (4.5)

$$\varsigma_i = 2\, T_{l_r}(t/2)\,.\,T_{2^r}(t/2)\,.\left[\frac{d}{dt}\left(T_{k_r}(t/2)\right)\right]^{-1}$$

at $t = \rho_{2^r}(i)$ $(i = 1, \ldots, k_r)$.

We note that in some cases, the degrees of the matrix polynomials in the numerator and denominator of the rational forms may be equal, in which case a simple modification is required in the application of Lemma 1. The next lemma follows after some algebraic manipulations and by using the relation $k_r = 2^r + l_r$.

Lemma 2

$$\alpha_i = \frac{(-1)^{i-1}}{2^r}\,.\,\sin\frac{(2i-1)\pi}{2^{r+1}}$$

$$\beta_i = \frac{2}{k_r+1}\,.\,\sin\frac{2^r i\pi}{k_r+1}\,.\,\sin\frac{i\pi}{k_r+1}$$

$$\gamma_i = \frac{2}{k_r+1}\,.\,\sin\frac{2^{r+1} i\pi}{k_r+1}\,.\,\sin\frac{i\pi}{k_r+1}$$

$$\delta_i = \frac{2}{k_r}\,.\,\sin\frac{2^{r-1}(2i-1)\pi}{k_r}\,.\,\sin\frac{(2i-1)\pi}{2k_r}$$

and

$$\varsigma_i = \frac{2}{k_r}\,.\,\sin\frac{2^r(2i-1)\pi}{k_r}\,.\,\sin\frac{(2i-1)\pi}{2k_r}$$

6. Numerical Experiments

We have applied our method to Poisson's equation

$$u_{xx} + u_{yy} = f(x,y),$$

on the unit square with Dirichlet boundary conditions. The right hand side f and the Dirichlet boundary conditions are defined so that the true solution is

$$u(x,y) = \sin\left[\frac{\pi.(x-y+2)^5}{(1+(x-y+2)^4)}\right]$$

This is identical with problem 11 of [RiHD81].

The resolution was chosen so that the number of points in each direction is $n = 2^{\mu}-1$, with μ ranging from 6 to 9. The resulting matrix has block dimension $n \times n$ with each block being of size $n \times n$.

Table 1 shows the timings and discretization errors for the original and modified versions of the NCAR package running on the CSRD Alliant FX/8 system using version 3 of the Concentrix operating system. All of the experiments were performed in double precision arithmetic. We note that the experiments were not done in single–user mode. Hence in order to reduce the effect of other user jobs on the timings, the main program solved the problem 4 times and the total runtime was then averaged. Supporting our previous comments regarding the error accumulation of the new algorithms, we found that the maximum difference between the true and the computed solutions was the same for both methods.

We should point out that the times reported are the total times and do not reflect the gains made in the steps which have been optimized namely the steps corresponding to solving the linear systems. If these were to be timed separately these gains could be substantially better especially for the smaller grid–size problems. For example it is estimated that for the 255×255 grid, the time not attributed to the solution of linear systems takes up to 0.5 sec.

Observe that as the grid–sizes increase the gains in total time appreciate steadily. This is to be expected from the very sequential nature of the original FISHPACK. For small grids the total gain in the linear systems is somewhat masked by the time spent in the parts of the algorithm that are not related to solving linear systems. Moreover, the benefits of vectorization and parallelization become visible only after a minimal vector length is available. Typically, on the Alliant FX/8, vector processing on each CE becomes more effective than scalar processing after the vector length exceeds 4.

Finally, the times on one CE do not show a speed–up when the grid–size is below n=255. Our algorithm has been optimized for the case where the number of CE's is 8 and does attempt to reduce the overhead when the number of processors is much smaller. Here it would have been better to use the alternative proposed for vector processors as discussed in Section 4.

7. Concluding remarks

Our preliminary results indicate that the method described in this paper is a promising alternative to FFT–based RES. Its reliance on a simple partial fraction expansion, makes it possible to apply the same idea to problems with Neumann or periodic boundary conditions,

Dimension	CE's	Original times (sec)	New Times (sec)
63	1	0.41	0.67
63	4	0.32	0.22
63	8	0.31	0.16
127	1	1.93	2.03
127	4	1.49	0.64
127	8	1.43	0.44
255	1	8.86	5.60
255	4	6.82	1.79
255	8	6.52	1.28
511	8	29.70	5.55

Table 1: Runtimes of the original and modified FISHPACK on Alliant FX/8

to problems involving other coordinate systems, as well as to the more general separable elliptic problems. Because of the simplicity of the technique, great care must be taken in choosing the parallel tridiagonal solvers to be used. The proper choice depends on many factors, particularly the exact set of computational resources available and the proper balance between parallelism and vectorization at each step of the computation. Moreover, it is important to note that using a square grid, as in the experiments, is a "worst case" situation. For any other rectangular grid, the improvement in speed with the new method will be even better. This is so, because of the strategy to vectorize and parallelize across systems, instead of seeking the vectorization within the tridiagonal system solver (e.g. using scalar cyclic reduction). A systematic description of the method for each case of boundary conditions, values of $n \neq 2^{\mu}-1$, its stability properties, as well as comparisons with other methods will be given in a forthcoming paper.

Acknowledgement. We would like to thank Kyle Gallivan for his helpful comments on the manuscript.

Bibliography

[BuGN70]

B. Buzbee, G. Golub, and C. Nielson, "On direct methods for solving Poisson's equation" *SIAM J. Numer. Anal*, vol. 7, pp. 627–656, (December 1970).

[Hock70]

R. Hockney, "The Potential Calculation and Some Applications", in *Methods Comput. Phys.*, v. 9, pp. 135–211, Academic Press, (1970).

[OrVo85]

J. Ortega and R. Voigt, "Partial differential equations on vector and parallel computers",

SIAM Review, pp. 213–240, (June 1985).

[RiHD81]
J. Rice, E. Houstis and W. Dyksen, "A population of linear, second order elliptic partial differential equations on rectangular domains. Part 1", *Math. Comp.*, v. 36, pp. 479–484, (1981).

[Saad87]
Y. Saad, "On the design of parallel numerical methods in message passing and shared-memory environments", Proc. International Seminar on Scientific Supercomputer, Paris, (2–6 February 1987).

[SaCK76]
A. H. Sameh, S. C. Chen, D. J. Kuck, "Parallel Poisson and biharmonic solvers", *Computing*, vol. 17, pp. 219–230 (1976).

[Swar77]
P. N. Swarztrauber, "The methods of cyclic reduction, Fourier analysis and the FACR algorithm for the discrete solution of Poisson's equation on a rectangle", *SIAM Review*, v. 19, pp. 490–501, (July 1977).

[Swar84]
P. N. Swarztrauber, "Fast Poisson solvers", in *Studies in Numerical Analysis*, G. H. Golub ed., pp. 319–369, Mathematical Association of America, (1984).

[Swar87]
P. N. Swarztrauber, "Approximate cyclic reduction for solving Poisson's equation", *SIAM J. Sci. Stat. Comput., v. 8, pp. 199–209, (May 1987).*

[SwSw75]
P. Swarztrauber and R. Sweet, "Efficient Fortran subprograms for the solution of elliptic partial differential equations", NCAR Technical Note IA–109, Boulder, (July 1975).

[Swee77]
R. A. Sweet, "A cyclic reduction algorithm for solving block tridiagonal systems of arbitrary dimension", *SIAM J. Numer. Anal.*, vol. 14, pp. 707–720, (September 1977).

[Temp80]
C. Temperton, "On the FACR(l) algorithm for the discrete Poisson equation", *J. of Comp. Physics*, v. 34, pp. 314–329, (1980).

Parallel LU–Factorization Algorithms for Dense Matrices

Thomas C. Oppe
David R. Kincaid

Center for Numerical Analysis
The University of Texas at Austin
Austin, Texas 78712-1067 USA

Abstract: Several serial and parallel algorithms for computing the LU–factorization of a dense matrix are investigated. Numerical experiments and programming considerations to reduce bank conflicts on the Cray X-MP4 parallel computer are presented. Speedup factors are given for the parallel algorithms.

1 Introduction

The solution by direct methods of the linear system $Ax = b$ where matrix A is a general nonsingular dense matrix proceeds in two steps:

- find a factorization (decomposition) of $A = LU$ where L is a lower triangular matrix and U is an upper triangular matrix, and
- solve $Ly = b$ by a forward substitution, followed by a solution of $Ux = y$ by back substitution.

The factors L and U are not uniquely determined by the equation $A = LU$, and it is common to force either L or U to have a unit diagonal. If matrix A is symmetric and positive definite, it is possible to find a Cholesky factorization ($A = LL^T$) or root-free Cholesky factorization ($A = LDL^T$) of the matrix, which has lower storage requirements. In this paper, it will be assumed that A is a general nonsingular dense matrix and that L is unit lower triangular.

To achieve numerical stability, partial or full pivoting is usually necessary in the factorization process. In the case of partial pivoting, rows are permuted and the system $PLUx = Pb$ is solved, where matrix P is a permutation matrix chosen during the factorization process. In the case of full pivoting, both rows and columns are permuted and the system $(P_1LUP_2)(P_2^Tx) = P_1b$ is solved, where P_1 and P_2 are permutation matrices. For the sake of clarity, pivoting will be ignored in the algorithms considered in this paper.

Several authors have considered the problem of LU–factorization on computers with advanced architectures. Jordan [10] gives timing formulas and performance data for a factorization algorithm for several early supercomputers such as the CDC STAR-100, CDC 7600, CRI Cray-1, TI ASC, Burroughs BSP, ICL DAP, and FPS AP-120. An earlier survey was done by Calahan, Joy, and Orbits [2]. Fong and Jordan [9] made the observation that the Cray-1's single data path between main memory and the vector registers necessitated the use of assembly language programming to achieve "supervector" speed on that architecture. Fong and Jordan [9] and Dongarra, Gustavson, and Karp [6], considered different reorderings of the three nested loops in the factorization algorithm from the standpoint of number of memory references and chaining ability on the architectures of Cray computers. Chen, Dongarra, and Hsiung [3], introduced an algorithm for computing L and U in parallel for a two-processor Cray X-MP. Dongarra and Hewitt [7], modified this algorithm to use four processors and compared it to another algorithm judged to be "best" for the Cray X-MP architecture. This latter algorithm used rank four updates to the remaining submatrix. Calahan [1] simulated a block LU–factorization algorithm on an n-processor Cray X-MP. Dongarra and Hiromoto [8] investigated parallel factorization schemes for the Denelcor HEP.

In Section 2, several serial algorithms for LU–decomposition are studied. Section 2.1 contains descriptions of the six algorithms resulting from reorderings of the three loops in a generic decomposition algorithm. Section 2.2 contains a description and derivation of an algorithm which is a hybrid of two of the generic algorithms. Section 2.3 describes an algorithm which uses rank two updates to the matrix. In Section 3, parallel versions of the serial algorithms described in Section 2 are presented. Section 3.1 describes a parallel version of one of the six generic algorithms described in Section 2.1. Section 3.2 describes a parallel version of the algorithm using rank two updates. Section 3.3 contains a parallel version of the hybrid algorithm presented in Section 2.2.

2 Serial Algorithms

In this section, several serial algorithms are presented for full matrix LU–decomposition. As in Dongarra, Gustavson, and Karp [6], it will be shown that considerations of chaining ability and memory access patterns lead to the preference of some algorithms over others for machines with a Cray-like architecture.

2.1 Serial Generic Gaussian Elimination Algorithms

Dongarra, Gustavson, and Karp [6] described six different versions of Gaussian elimination (GE) based on reorderings of the three loops in a generic Gaussian elimination algorithm:

Generic GE Algorithm

```
for ______
   for ______
      for ______
         A_{i,j} = A_{i,j} - (A_{i,k} * A_{k,j})/A_{k,k}
      end
   end
end
```

In the Generic Algorithm, the L and U factors overwrite the A array, and L is assumed to have a unit diagonal. Thus, the Generic Algorithm produces the Doolittle factorization [15]. As in [6], the six variants will be called the IJK, IKJ, JIK, JKI, KIJ, and KJI Algorithms according to the ordering of the loops. The ranges of the loops depend on the ordering of the indices.

In Algorithm KIJ, multiples of the pivot row k are subtracted from all succeeding rows to zero out elements below the diagonal.

Algorithm KIJ (SAXPYs on rows)

for $k = 1, n-1$
  $A_{k+1:n,k} = (-1./A_{k,k}) * A_{k+1:n,k}$
  for $i = k+1, n$
    $A_{i,k+1:n} = A_{i,k+1:n} + A_{i,k} * A_{k,k+1:n}$
  end
end

Thus, this algorithm can be called the "SAXPYs on rows" algorithm. SAXPY denotes a BLAS [12] routine which has the form $y \leftarrow y + \alpha x$ for vectors x and y and scalar α. The notation $A_{i:j,k}$ denotes column k of the matrix from row i to row j. Similarly, the notation $A_{k,i:j}$ denotes row k of the matrix from column i to column j. The multipliers are stored in L and the upper triangular reduced system is stored in U, both of which overwrite the array A. Since memory access is by rows and two-dimensional arrays are stored by columns in Fortran, this algorithm is not desirable for virtual memory machines or vector computers which require vector operations on elements which are contiguous in memory (e.g., the Cyber 205). On Cray computers, loops which access memory with a constant stride can vectorize, but the possibility of excessive bank conflicts exists if the leading dimension of matrix A has a factor which is a high power of two.

Algorithm KJI is the column-oriented version of Algorithm KIJ:

Algorithm KJI (SAXPYs on columns)

for $k = 1, n-1$
  $A_{k+1:n,k} = (-1./A_{k,k}) * A_{k+1:n,k}$
  for $j = k+1, n$
    $A_{k+1:n,j} = A_{k+1:n,j} + A_{k+1:n,k} * A_{k,j}$
  end
end

This algorithm was described by Moler [13] as preferable to the previous algorithm on a virtual memory machine. Also, since memory accesses are to sequential locations in memory, the possibility of bank conflicts on a Cray machine is eliminated. It may be considered the "SAXPYs on columns" algorithm. This version of Gaussian elimination is used in the LINPACK [4] package. Since each SAXPY is applied to a different column, there is no opportunity to keep an accumulation vector in a vector register on a Cray machine. For this reason, Fong and Jordan [9] concluded that this algorithm is I/O bound and can only perform at "vector" speed on a Cray computer and not at "supervector" speed (peak performance).

Both the KIJ and KJI Algorithms can be viewed as performing a sequence of rank one updates to the remaining submatrix, $A \leftarrow A + uv^T$:

for $k = 1, n-1$
  $A_{k+1:n,k} = (-1./A_{k,k}) * A_{k+1:n,k}$
  $A_{k+1:n,k+1:n} = A_{k+1:n,k+1:n} + A_{k+1:n,k} * A_{k,k+1:n}$
end

To reduce memory traffic and allow "supervector" speed on Cray computers, Fong and Jordan [9] proposed the JKI Algorithm:

Algorithm JKI (GAXPYs on columns)

for $j = 1, n$
  for $k = 1, j-1$
    $A_{k+1:n,j} = A_{k+1:n,j} + A_{k+1:n,k} * A_{k,j}$
  end
  $A_{j+1:n,j} = (-1./A_{j,j}) * A_{j+1:n,j}$
end

Note that in this algorithm, the j-th column of matrix A acts as an accumulation vector in the innermost loop. It can reside in a vector register until the k loop is complete. Unfortunately, the vector lengths are decreasing by one with each increment of the k loop, and a Cray computer does vector operations starting with the first element of vector registers. Fong and Jordan [9] suggested loading into a vector register the j-th column in reverse order. Dongarra, Gustavson, and Karp [6] call this algorithm the "GAXPYs on columns" algorithm. A GAXPY (for generalized SAXPY) indicates an operation of the form $y \leftarrow y + Mx$ where M is a matrix. In the above algorithm, M is a lower triangular matrix of dimension $n-1$ by $j-1$.

There is also a "GAXPYs on rows" algorithm:

Algorithm IKJ (GAXPYs on rows)

for $i = 2, n$
  for $k = 1, i - 1$
    $A_{i,k} = (-1./A_{k,k}) * A_{i,k}$
    $A_{i,k+1:n} = A_{i,k+1:n} + A_{i,k} * A_{k,k+1:n}$
  end
end

This algorithm has the disadvantages that memory accesses are not contiguous and that the operation of scaling the L elements is not vectorized. The GAXPY operation in this algorithm takes the form $y^T \leftarrow y^T + x^T M$ where M is a matrix. In this case, M is an upper triangular matrix of dimension $i - 1$ by $n - 1$.

The final two variants of Gaussian elimination are dot product formulations:

Algorithm JIK (SDOTs on columns)

for $j = 2, n$
  $A_{j:n,j-1} = (-1./A_{j-1,j-1}) * A_{j:n,j-1}$
  for $i = 2, j - 1$
    $A_{i,j} = A_{i,j} + \langle A_{i,1:i-1}, A_{1:i-1,j} \rangle$
  end
  for $i = j, n$
    $A_{i,j} = A_{i,j} + \langle A_{i,1:j-1}, A_{1:j-1,j} \rangle$
  end
end

Algorithm IJK (SDOTs on rows)

for $i = 1, n$
  for $j = 2, i$
    $A_{i,j-1} = (-1./A_{j-1,j-1}) * A_{i,j-1}$
    $A_{i,j} = A_{i,j} + \langle A_{i,1:j-1}, A_{1:j-1,j} \rangle$
  end
  for $j = i + 1, n$
    $A_{i,j} = A_{i,j} + \langle A_{i,1:i-1}, A_{1:i-1,j} \rangle$
  end
end

SDOT refers to the BLAS routine for computing the dot product of two vectors x and y, denoted $\langle x, y \rangle$. Each of these two algorithms compute dot products of row vectors with column vectors. Hence memory access patterns are not necessarily contiguous. Also, the dot product operation on a Cray computer is not as efficient as the SAXPY operation. For these reasons, the dot product formulations are not as popular on Cray machines. However, they may be preferable on a machine allowing dot products with extra precision accumulation.

For each of these six Generic Algorithms, the number of additions and multiplications is $\frac{2}{3}n^3 - \frac{1}{2}n^2 - \frac{1}{6}n$ and the number of reciprocals is $n-1$, except for Algorithms IJK and IKJ which compute $\frac{1}{2}(n-1)(n)$ reciprocals.

Table 1 gives timings in seconds for the six Generic Factorization Algorithms on a Cray X-MP computer run in uniprocessor mode. The runs reported in Table 1, as well as in all succeeding tables, were made in a dedicated machine environment to reduce the number of bank conflicts due to competing jobs. The real time clock timer IRTC was used. The sizes of the matrices used ranged from $N = 100$ to $N = 700$ in steps of 100. The leading dimensions of the matrices were set to $N+1$ in the program to eliminate the possibility of bank conflicts due to N having a high power of two as a factor. The matrix entries were generated randomly, and no pivoting was done. Using the operation counts listed above, megaflop rates for each of the runs were computed and are given in parentheses below the timings.

From Table 1, it can be seen that Algorithms KJI (SAXPYs on columns) and JKI (GAXPYs on columns) perform best, with both performing equally well. Algorithm KIJ (SAXPYs on rows) performs almost as well as Algorithm KJI. In general, KJI is to be preferred to KIJ since the possibility of memory bank conflicts does not exist. Algorithm IKJ (GAXPYs on rows) does not do as well as Algorithm JKI, probably due to the fact that the scaling of the L elements is not vectorized and that the operation count is higher. As expected, the two dot product formulations (Algorithms JIK and IJK) exhibited poorer performance than the other four formulations.

2.2 Serial Composite Algorithm

We now derive an algorithm for the LU–decomposition which allows the parallel computation of L and U. Suppose that the $n \times n$ nonsingular matrix $A = (A_{i,j})$ can be factored so that

$$A = LU$$

where $L = (L_{i,j})$ is unit lower triangular and $U = (U_{i,j})$ is upper triangular. In the factorization, we will be computing the matrix of multipliers whose elements are the negatives of the corresponding elements in L. Thus, we will assume a factorization of the form

$$A = (I - L)U = U - LU$$

where L is strictly lower triangular. From the formula for matrix multiplication, we have

$$A_{i,j} = U_{i,j} - \sum_{k=1}^{min(i-1,j)} L_{i,k}U_{k,j} \qquad (1)$$

since $L_{i,k} = 0$ for $k \geq i$ and $U_{k,j} = 0$ for $k > j$. Each step in the algorithm proceeds by determining a row of U and the corresponding column of L. The parallel version of the algorithm will compute the row and column simultaneously. Assume that we are at the beginning of the i-th step in the algorithm with rows $1, 2, \ldots, i-1$ of U and columns $1, 2, \ldots, i-1$ of L having been determined. Then for $j \geq i$, we have by Equation (1) that

$$U_{i,j} = A_{i,j} + \sum_{k=1}^{i-1} L_{i,k} U_{k,j} \tag{2}$$

Reversing the roles of i and j in Equation (1) we get

$$A_{j,i} = U_{j,i} - \sum_{k=1}^{min(j-1,i)} L_{j,k} U_{k,i} \tag{3}$$

Then for $j > i$, we have by Equation (3) that

$$\begin{aligned} A_{j,i} &= -\sum_{k=1}^{i} L_{j,k} U_{k,i} \\ &= -\sum_{k=1}^{i-1} L_{j,k} U_{k,i} - L_{j,i} U_{i,i} \end{aligned}$$

so

$$L_{j,i} = \left(A_{j,i} + \sum_{k=1}^{i-1} L_{j,k} U_{k,i} \right) \left(\frac{-1}{U_{i,i}} \right) \tag{4}$$

Equations (2) and (4) can be used to compute the i-th step of the algorithm with the computation of the i-th row of U and the i-th column of L.

The algorithm just established can be written as follows:

for $i = 1, 2, \ldots, n$

$$U_{i,i:n} = A_{i,i:n} + \sum_{k=1}^{i-1} L_{i,k} U_{k,i:n}$$

$$L_{i+1:n,i} = \left(A_{i+1:n,i} + \sum_{k=1}^{i-1} L_{i+1:n,k} U_{k,i} \right) \left(\frac{-1}{U_{i,i}} \right)$$

end

Note that $U_{i,i}$, which is calculated in the first loop, is needed for the scaling of the i-th column of L in the second loop. Thus, some modification of the algorithm will be necessary to make the computation parallel. Also note that the elements of L and U can overwrite the elements of A.

We now show that the two loops describe matrix-vector products. The first summation can be written as

$$\begin{aligned} \sum_{k=1}^{i-1} L_{i,k} U_{k,i:n} &= \begin{bmatrix} L_{i,1} & L_{i,2} & \cdots & L_{i,i-1} \end{bmatrix} \begin{bmatrix} U_{1,i:n} \\ U_{2,i:n} \\ \vdots \\ U_{i-1,i:n} \end{bmatrix} \\ &= L_{i,1:i-1} M_U \end{aligned}$$

where M_U is the matrix of $i-1$ row vectors $U_{k,i:n}$. Hence, the computation of a row of U can be seen as the computation of a row vector plus a row vector times a matrix:

$$U_{i,i:n} = A_{i,i:n} + L_{i,1:i-1} M_U$$

The subroutine SXMPY found in Dongarra and Eisenstat [5] computes a row vector times a matrix plus a row vector, i.e., $y^T \leftarrow y^T + x^T M$, and it can be used for this computation. The second summation can be written as

$$\sum_{k=1}^{i-1} L_{i+1:n,k} U_{k,i} = \left[L_{i+1:n,1} \quad L_{i+1:n,2} \quad \cdots \quad L_{i+1:n,i-1} \right] \begin{bmatrix} U_{1,i} \\ U_{2,i} \\ \vdots \\ U_{i-1,i} \end{bmatrix}$$

$$= M_L U_{1:i-1,i}$$

where M_L is the matrix of $i-1$ column vectors $L_{i+1:n,k}$. Hence, the computation of a column of L can be seen as the computation of a vector plus a matrix times a vector:

$$L_{i+1:n,i} = (A_{i+1:n,i} + M_L U_{1:i-1,i}) \left(\frac{-1}{U_{i,i}} \right)$$

The subroutine SMXPY from Dongarra and Eisenstat [5] computes a matrix times a vector plus a vector, i.e., $y \leftarrow y + Mx$, and it can be used for this computation.

The algorithm can be written as follows using only the single array A by storing the results back into A and adding loops for the summation:

Composite Algorithm

for $i = 1, n$
  for $k = 1, i-1$
    $A_{i,i:n} = A_{i,i:n} + A_{i,k} * A_{k,i:n}$
  end
  for $k = 1, i-1$
    $A_{i+1:n,i} = A_{i+1:n,i} + A_{i+1:n,k} * A_{k,i}$
  end
  $A_{i+1:n,i} = (-1./A_{i,i}) * A_{i+1:n,i}$
end

This variant of Gaussian elimination uses the JKI Algorithm (GAXPYs on columns) for L and the IKJ Algorithm (GAXPYs on rows) for U. It will be called the "Composite Algorithm" in this paper. This algorithm has an advantage over the JKI and IKJ Algorithms in that the vector lengths of the inner loops are independent of k. Hence the GAXPYs have the form $y \leftarrow y + Mx$ and $y^T \leftarrow y^T + x^T M$ where M is a full matrix. Thus, it is relatively simple in Fortran to force the accumulation vector y to reside in a vector register by unrolling the k loop. The CAL implementation of these full-matrix GAXPYs is also relatively simple. The operation count of the Composite Algorithm is the same as that of the six Generic Algorithms, $\frac{2}{3}n^3 - \frac{1}{2}n^2 - \frac{1}{6}n$ total additions/multiplies and $n-1$ reciprocals. As a disadvantage over the JKI and IKJ Algorithms, the vector lengths involved are shorter since L and U are computed separately.

Table 2 gives timings in seconds for three versions of the Composite Algorithm. The first version uses standard Fortran with the k loops rolled. Thus no attempt was made to keep vector operands in vector registers. The second version used Fortran versions of the GAXPYs (called SMXPY and SXMPY in [5]) in which the k loop was unrolled to a depth of 16. The third version used CAL-coded versions of SMXPY and SXMPY. Megaflop rates for each of the runs were computed and are given in parentheses below the timings.

From Table 2, it can be seen that the Composite Algorithm gives poorer performance than the KJI or JKI Algorithms unless the GAXPY operations are optimized. This is probably due to the shorter vector lengths of the computations. However, if the GAXPY operations are optimized with either unrolled outer Fortran loops or the use of CAL assembly code, the Composite Algorithm performs much better than any of the six variations as given in Table 1. The gain in performance is especially marked for small problem sizes. The improvement in going from unrolled Fortran loops to a CAL routine is significant (a factor of two improvement) for small problem sizes but is less significant for larger problem sizes. Note that the CAL version performs at almost the peak uniprocessor speed of the machine (235 megaflops) for the largest problem sizes. This is due to the fact that almost all multiplication, addition, and memory fetching operations are chained, thus keeping both arithmetic pipes busy.

2.3 Serial Rank Two Update Algorithm

Another uniprocessor algorithm tested was a variation of the rank one update Algorithms KIJ and KJI. This algorithm does a rank two update of the A matrix, $A \leftarrow A + u_1 v_1^T + u_2 v_2^T$:

Rank Two Update Algorithm

for $k = 1, n, 2$
$A_{k+1:n,k} = (-1./A_{k,k}) * A_{k+1:n,k}$
$A_{k+1:n,k+1} = A_{k+1:n,k+1} + A_{k,k+1} * A_{k+1:n,k}$
$A_{k+2:n,k+1} = (-1./A_{k+1,k+1}) * A_{k+2:n,k+1}$
$A_{k+1,k+2:n} = A_{k+1,k+2:n} + A_{k,k+2:n} * A_{k+1,k}$
$A_{k+2:n,k+2:n} = A_{k+2:n,k+2:n} + A_{k,k+2:n} * A_{k+2:n,k} + A_{k+1,k+2:n} * A_{k+2:n,k+1}$
end

This algorithm has the advantage that vector lengths are longer than for the Composite Algorithm and it can be made less memory intensive than the rank one update algorithms. The code for this latter algorithm was supplied by Tom Hewitt and Steve Grassl of Cray Research, Inc.

Table 3 gives timings in seconds for two versions of the Rank Two Update Algorithm. In the first version, almost all coding was done using standard Fortran. No attempt was made to keep vector operands in vector registers. The second version used a CAL implementation of the rank two update operation. For both versions, the last 64 by 64 submatrix was factored using an optimized CAL kernel. Megaflop rates for each of the runs were computed and are given in parentheses below the timings.

From Table 3, it can be seen that the Rank Two Update Algorithm (Fortran version) performs much better than the six Generic Algorithms and the Composite Algorithm (Fortran versions) of

Tables 1 and 2, respectively. This is probably due to the fact that a subroutine specially coded in CAL was used to factor the last 64 by 64 submatrix and that the rank two update loop requires fewer memory references. The version of the Rank Two Update Algorithm which uses a CAL implementation of the rank two update loop performs extremely well, even for small problem sizes. For the large size problems, the code is performing at 218 megaflops which is almost the peak speed of one processor (235 megaflops). The speedup in going from the Fortran version to the CAL version ranges from 1.7 for small problems to 1.35 for large problems.

3 Parallel Algorithms

The parallel algorithms studied in this paper for the LU–factorization are adaptations of the serial algorithms.

3.1 Parallel Generic Gaussian Elimination Algorithm

Of the six Generic Algorithms derived from reordering of loops, the KJI Algorithm (SAXPYs on columns) seems most suitable for multiprocessing. For this algorithm, each SAXPY corresponds to a different independent column (the j index), and it can be computed by a different processor. Also, the vector length is independent of j, which allows a balanced workload for each processor. Distinct array elements are modified for each value of j, so there is no need for protection against simultaneous modification of data. Unfortunately, a SAXPY is a memory intensive operation, and the speedup on a four-processor Cray X-MP will be limited by the memory's bank refresh time of four clock cycles. The parallel KJI Algorithm is:

Parallel KIJ Algorithm

for $k = 1, n-1$
`CMIC$ PROCESS`
  $A_{k+1:n,k} = (-1./A_{k,k}) * A_{k+1:n,k}$
`CMIC$ END PROCESS`
`CMIC$ DO GLOBAL`
  for $j = k+1, n$
    $A_{k+1:n,j} = A_{k+1:n,j} + A_{k+1:n,k} * A_{k,j}$
  end
end

The code was parallelized using the Cray microtasking directives. The `DO GLOBAL` directive causes the j loop to become a *fray*, or a section of code at which parallel processing can occur. Each incidence of the j index represent a unit of work, in this case a SAXPY, which is performed by the next available processor. The work between the `PROCESS` and `END PROCESS` directives is done by only one processor, and it must be completed before the fray. Thus, there is a synchronization before the fray and after it.

Table 4 gives timings in seconds for the microtasked version of the KJI Algorithm for 1,2,3, and 4 processors. As in Table 1, a wall clock timer was used to time the code, and the jobs were run in dedicated mode. Megaflop rates for each of the runs were computed and are given in parentheses below the timings. The speedup factor over one processor is given in parentheses under the megaflop rate. It can be seen that the speedup factor using four processors (and to a lesser extent, three processors) is less than expected. We believe this is due to excessive bank conflicts and the fact that the algorithm was not completely parallelized (e.g., the scaling of L).

3.2 Parallel Rank Two Update Algorithm

Another serial algorithm that was converted to a parallel algorithm was the Rank Two Update Algorithm. It was parallelized for p processors by assigning roughly $1/p$ of the columns in the rank two update operation to each processor:

Parallel Rank Two Update Algorithm

for $k = 1, n, 2$
`CMIC$ PROCESS`
$A_{k+1:n,k} = (-1./A_{k,k}) * A_{k+1:n,k}$
$A_{k+1:n,k+1} = A_{k+1:n,k+1} + A_{k,k+1} * A_{k+1:n,k}$
$A_{k+2:n,k+1} = (-1./A_{k+1,k+1}) * A_{k+2:n,k+1}$
$A_{k+1,k+2:n} = A_{k+1,k+2:n} + A_{k,k+2:n} * A_{k+1,k}$
`CMIC$ END PROCESS`
`CMIC$ DO GLOBAL`
for $iproc = 1, p$
$j1 = \lfloor (iproc - 1) * (n - k - 1)/p \rfloor + k + 2$
$j2 = \lfloor iproc * (n - k - 1)/p \rfloor + k + 1$
$A_{k+2:n,j1:j2} = A_{k+2:n,j1:j2} + A_{k,j1:j2} * A_{k+2:n,k} + A_{k+1,j1:j2} * A_{k+2:n,k+1}$
end
end

Table 5 gives timings in seconds for the microtasked version of the Rank Two Update Algorithm for 1,2,3, and 4 processors. Megaflop rates for each of the runs were computed and are given in parentheses below the timings. The speedup factor over one processor is given in parentheses under the megaflop rate. It can be seen that this algorithm behaves quite well under parallel execution with a maximum speedup of 3.74 for four processors. This excellent performance may be due to the fact that the rank two update kernel was coded in CAL, allowing memory references to be reduced by the use of vector registers to hold intermediate results. Also, the final 64 by 64 submatrix was factored by a special CAL kernel assuming short vector lengths. The maximum speed observed was 817 megaflops from a computer theoretically capable of a peak performance of 940 megaflops for four processors.

3.3 Parallel Composite Algorithm

The Composite LU–factorization Algorithm was also converted to a parallel algorithm. Since L and U elements are calculated in separate `DO` loops, it is natural to parallelize the algorithm for two processors by having one processor compute the U elements and the other processor calculate the L elements. This algorithm was investigated by Chen, Dongarra, and Hsiung [3] for the Cray X-MP2. A variant of this algorithm is discussed by Kincaid and Oppe [11]. It was adapted for the four processors of a Cray X-MP4 by Dongarra and Hewitt [7].

In adapting the Composite Algorithm for two processors, it was necessary to completely disassociate the computations for L from those for U. It can be seen from the original algorithm that scaling the L elements requires $A_{i,i}$, which is not known until the computations associated with U are complete. Thus the algorithm has been modified for two processors as follows:

Composite Algorithm For Two Processors

for $i = 2, n-1$
CMIC$ PROCESS
  $A_{i,i-1} = (-1./A_{i-1,i-1}) * A_{i,i-1}$
  for $k = 1, i-1$
    $A_{i,i:n} = A_{i,i:n} + A_{i,k} * A_{k,i:n}$
  end
CMIC$ ALSO PROCESS
  $A_{i+1:n,i-1} = (-1./A_{i-1,i-1}) * A_{i+1:n,i-1}$
  for $k = 1, i-1$
    $A_{i+1:n,i} = A_{i+1:n,i} + A_{i+1:n,k} * A_{k,i}$
  end
CMIC$ END PROCESS
end
CMIC$ PROCESS
$A_{n,n-1} = (-1./A_{n-1,n-1}) * A_{n,n-1}$
$A_{n,n} = An, n + \langle A_{n,1:n-1}, A_{1:n-1,n} \rangle$
CMIC$ END PROCESS

Note that the Cray microtasking directives `PROCESS` and `ALSO PROCESS` are used to demark processes which can be done in parallel. Thus, the scaling for the i-th column of L which was done in the serial algorithm at the end of the L computations is delayed until needed for the $(i+1)$-st column on the next iteration. The U computation needs only the scaled $A_{i,i-1}$ element, which is not needed by the L computation. Finally, for $i = n$, a single processor scales $A_{n,n-1}$ and computes $A_{n,n}$. Note that this algorithm is not exactly load-balanced since the L processor does more work than the U processor.

To adapt the Composite Algorithm for four processors, two processors each were used for L and U computations. Thus the vector lengths used in the GAXPYs were half of what they were for the two processor version. This approach can be generalized for an even number of processors.

Composite Algorithm For Four Processors

for $i = 2, n-1$
CMIC$ PROCESS
$A_{i,i-1} = (-1./A_{i-1,i-1}) * A_{i,i-1}$
CMIC$ END PROCESS
CMIC$ PROCESS
$jend = \lfloor (i+n)/2 \rfloor$
for $k = 1, i-1$
$A_{i,i:jend} = A_{i,i:jend} + A_{i,k} * A_{k,i:jend}$
end
CMIC$ ALSO PROCESS
$jbgn = \lfloor (i+n)/2 \rfloor + 1$
for $k = 1, i-1$
$A_{i,jbgn:n} = A_{i,jbgn:n} + A_{i,k} * A_{k,jbgn:n}$
end
CMIC$ ALSO PROCESS
$iend = \lfloor (i+n+1)/2 \rfloor$
$A_{i+1:iend,i-1} = (-1./A_{i-1,i-1}) * A_{i+1:iend,i-1}$
for $k = 1, i-1$
$A_{i+1:iend,i} = A_{i+1:iend,i} + A_{i+1:iend,k} * A_{k,i}$
end
CMIC$ ALSO PROCESS
$ibgn = \lfloor (i+n+1)/2 \rfloor + 1$
$A_{ibgn:n,i-1} = (-1./A_{i-1,i-1}) * A_{ibgn:n,i-1}$
for $k = 1, i-1$
$A_{ibgn:n,i} = A_{ibgn:n,i} + A_{ibgn:n,k} * A_{k,i}$
end
CMIC$ END PROCESS
end
CMIC$ PROCESS
$A_{n,n-1} = (-1./A_{n-1,n-1}) * A_{n,n-1}$
$A_{n,n} = An, n + \langle A_{n,1:n-1}, A_{1:n-1,n} \rangle$
CMIC$ END PROCESS

Table 6 gives timings in seconds for the microtasked version of the Composite Algorithm for 1,2, and 4 processors. Megaflop rates for each of the runs were computed and are given in parentheses below the timings. The speedup factor over one processor is given in parentheses under the megaflop rate. It can be seen from Table 6 that this algorithm achieves a good speedup for two processors but less so for four processors. This program uses all CAL versions of the GAXPYs but does not seem to be as fast as the Rank Two Update Algorithm with CAL kernels. Also, it was noted that this algorithm seemed to be more sensitive to timing variations from run to run, whereas the Rank Two Update Algorithm was more consistent in this regard.

4 Conclusions

Of the algorithms investigated in this paper, the Composite Algorithm and the Rank Two Update Algorithm seem to be best for the architecture of the Cray computer in both the uniprocessor and multiprocessor modes. These two algorithms have one thing in common—kernels in which certain vectors are accumulation vectors. Hence, it it possible to use the vector registers as memory caches to hold intermediate results, thus freeing the arithmetic pipes from interruptions due to the unavailability of vector operands. Dongarra, Gustavson, and Karp [6] remarked that the arithmetic for *LU*–factorization and other dense matrix operations comes for free on the Cray computer; that is, designing an efficient algorithm on the Cray machine is a problem of memory management.

It can also be concluded that there is not much room for improvement in the area of full matrix *LU*–factorization for full matrices on the present generation of Cray computers. The two best algorithms investigated in this paper perform at essentially the top speed of the machine; any further improvement would have to come from efforts to more delicately balance the processors.

Acknowledgements: We would like to thank Cray Research, Inc., for access to the Cray X-MP4 at Mendota Heights, MN. Also, the Cray X-MP2 of The University of Texas System was used and we wish to acknowledge its Center for High Performance Computing for assistance. This work was supported in part by the National Science Foundation under Grant MCS-8214731 and by the Department of Energy under Grant DE-AS05-81ER10954 with The University of Texas at Austin. Thomas C. Oppe's participation was supported by the Control Data Corporation through its PACER Fellowship Program.

N	KJI	JKI	IJK	IKJ	JIK	KIJ
100	0.01013 (65.3)	0.01010 (65.5)	0.04410 (15.1)	0.01219 (54.7)	0.04238 (15.6)	0.01039 (63.7)
200	0.05462 (97.3)	0.05477 (97.0)	0.19312 (27.6)	0.06396 (83.4)	0.18388 (28.9)	0.05646 (94.1)
300	0.15582 (115.2)	0.15575 (115.3)	0.48168 (37.4)	0.17776 (101.3)	0.46396 (38.7)	0.16096 (111.6)
400	0.33696 (126.4)	0.33576 (126.8)	0.89395 (47.7)	0.36924 (115.6)	0.85844 (49.6)	0.33885 (125.7)
500	0.61757 (134.7)	0.61790 (134.7)	1.58915 (52.4)	0.70916 (117.5)	1.53255 (54.3)	0.66236 (125.6)
600	1.02283 (140.6)	1.02288 (140.6)	2.34250 (61.5)	1.12141 (128.4)	2.27894 (63.1)	1.05264 (136.6)
700	1.56454 (146.0)	1.57077 (145.4)	3.46834 (65.9)	1.71638 (133.2)	3.37658 (67.6)	1.62171 (140.9)

Table 1: Six Generic Algorithms: Uniprocessor

N	Rolled GAXPYs	Unrolled GAXPYs	All CAL GAXPYs
100	0.01678 (39.4)	0.00747 (88.6)	0.00423 (156.4)
200	0.08231 (64.6)	0.03899 (136.3)	0.02757 (192.7)
300	0.21848 (82.2)	0.11412 (157.3)	0.08844 (203.0)
400	0.44427 (95.9)	0.25270 (168.5)	0.20603 (206.7)
500	0.80718 (103.1)	0.47269 (176.0)	0.39640 (209.9)
600	1.28083 (112.3)	0.79788 (180.3)	0.68097 (211.2)
700	1.92554 (118.6)	1.23949 (184.3)	1.07445 (212.6)

Table 2: Composite Algorithm: Uniprocessor

N	Fortran Loops	CAL Loops
100	0.00614 (107.8)	0.00364 (181.8)
200	0.04238 (125.4)	0.02540 (209.2)
300	0.13027 (137.8)	0.08365 (214.6)
400	0.28921 (147.3)	0.19748 (215.7)
500	0.53861 (154.5)	0.38258 (217.5)
600	0.91415 (157.3)	0.65971 (218.0)
700	1.41867 (161.0)	1.04488 (218.6)

Table 3: Rank Two Update Algorithm: Uniprocessor

N	Number of Processors			
	$p = 1$	$p = 2$	$p = 3$	$p = 4$
100	0.01187 (55.7) (1.000)	0.00678 (97.6) (1.752)	0.00528 (125.3) (2.250)	0.00440 (150.4) (2.695)
200	0.06387 (83.2) (1.000)	0.03336 (159.3) (1.914)	0.02376 (223.6) (2.688)	0.01870 (284.1) (3.415)
300	0.17575 (102.2) (1.000)	0.09117 (196.9) (1.928)	0.06492 (276.6) (2.707)	0.05173 (347.1) (3.398)
400	0.37530 (113.5) (1.000)	0.19718 (216.0) (1.903)	0.13921 (305.9) (2.696)	0.11297 (377.0) (3.322)
500	0.68045 (122.3) (1.000)	0.35192 (236.4) (1.934)	0.25045 (332.2) (2.717)	0.20647 (403.0) (3.296)
600	1.12069 (128.3) (1.000)	0.58435 (246.1) (1.918)	0.41549 (346.1) (2.697)	0.34599 (415.7) (3.239)
700	1.71196 (133.4) (1.000)	0.88657 (257.6) (1.931)	0.63488 (359.8) (2.697)	0.52578 (434.4) (3.256)

Table 4: KJI Algorithm: Multiprocessor

N	Number of Processors			
	$p=1$	$p=2$	$p=3$	$p=4$
100	0.00377 (175.5) (1.000)	0.00295 (224.3) (1.277)	0.00260 (254.5) (1.451)	0.00242 (273.5) (1.554)
200	0.02595 (204.8) (1.000)	0.01504 (353.3) (1.725)	0.01125 (472.3) (2.307)	0.00929 (572.0) (2.792)
300	0.08507 (211.1) (1.000)	0.04521 (397.2) (1.882)	0.03224 (556.9) (2.638)	0.02629 (683.0) (3.236)
400	0.19842 (214.6) (1.000)	0.10355 (411.3) (1.916)	0.07183 (592.9) (2.762)	0.05661 (752.3) (3.505)
500	0.38367 (216.9) (1.000)	0.19702 (422.3) (1.947)	0.13601 (611.8) (2.821)	0.10550 (788.7) (3.637)
600	0.66096 (217.6) (1.000)	0.33690 (426.9) (1.962)	0.23095 (622.7) (2.862)	0.18022 (798.0) (3.668)
700	1.04637 (218.3) (1.000)	0.53092 (430.2) (1.971)	0.36217 (630.7) (2.889)	0.27963 (816.9) (3.742)

Table 5: Rank Two Update Algorithm: Multiprocessor

N	Number of Processors		
	$p = 1$	$p = 2$	$p = 4$
100	0.00460 (143.9) (1.000)	0.00276 (239.8) (1.667)	0.00273 (242.4) (1.685)
200	0.02829 (187.8) (1.000)	0.01515 (350.7) (1.867)	0.01153 (460.8) (2.454)
300	0.08989 (199.7) (1.000)	0.04649 (386.2) (1.934)	0.02839 (632.4) (3.166)
400	0.20668 (206.1) (1.000)	0.10534 (404.3) (1.962)	0.06079 (700.6) (3.400)
500	0.39851 (208.8) (1.000)	0.20316 (409.6) (1.962)	0.11771 (706.9) (3.386)
600	0.68247 (210.7) (1.000)	0.34656 (415.0) (1.969)	0.19400 (741.3) (3.518)
700	1.07803 (211.9) (1.000)	0.54826 (416.6) (1.966)	0.29831 (765.7) (3.614)

Table 6: Composite Algorithm: Multiprocessor

References

[1] D.A. Calahan. "Task Granularity Studies on a Many-Processor Cray X-MP." *Parallel Computing*, Vol. 2, 1985, pp. 109-118.

[2] D.A. Calahan, W.N. Joy, and D.A. Orbits, "Preliminary Report on Results of Matrix Benchmarks on Vector Processors." U. of Michigan report SEL 94, May 1976.

[3] Steven S. Chen, Jack J. Dongarra, and Christopher C. Hsiung. "Multiprocessing Linear Algebra Algorithms on the Cray X-MP2: Experiences with Small Granularity." *Journal of Parallel and Distributed Computing*, Vol. 1, No. 1, August 1984.

[4] J.J. Dongarra, J.R. Bunch, C.B. Moler, and G.W. Stewart. LINPACK *User's Guide*, Society for Industrial and Applied Mathematics, Philadelphia, 1979.

[5] J.J. Dongarra and S.C. Eisenstat. "Squeezing the most out of an algorithm in CRAY Fortran." *ACM Transactions on Mathematical Software*, Vol. 10, No. 3, September 1984, pp. 219-230.

[6] J.J. Dongarra, F.G. Gustavson, and A. Karp. "Implementing Linear Algebra Algorithms for Dense Matrices on a Vector Pipeline Machine." *SIAM Review*, Vol. 26, No. 1, January 1984, pp. 91-112.

[7] Jack J. Dongarra and Tom Hewitt. "Implementing Dense Linear Algebra Algorithms Using Multitasking on the Cray X-MP4 (or Approaching the Gigaflop)." *SIAM Journal of Scientific and Statistical Computing*, Vol. 7, No. 1, January 1986, pp. 347-350.

[8] Jack J. Dongarra and Robert Hiromoto. "A Collection of Parallel Linear Equations Routines for the Denelcor HEP." *Parallel Computing*, Vol. 1, No. 2, 1984.

[9] K.W. Fong and T.L. Jordan. "Some Linear Algebraic Algorithms and Their Performance on CRAY-1." Los Alamos National Laboratory report LA-6774, June 1977.

[10] T.L. Jordan. "A Performance Evaluation of Linear Algebra Software in Parallel Architectures." Los Alamos National Laboratory report LA-8078-MS, October 1979.

[11] David R. Kincaid and Thomas C. Oppe. "A Parallel Algorithm for the General *LU*–Factorization." Center for Numerical Analysis report CNA-208, The University of Texas at Austin, April 1987.

[12] C.L. Lawson, R.J. Hanson, D.R. Kincaid, and F.T. Krogh. "Basic Linear Algebra Subprograms for Fortran Usage." *ACM Transactions on Mathematical Software*, Vol. 5, No. 3, September 1979, pp. 308-323.

[13] Cleve B. Moler. "Matrix Computations with Fortran and Paging." *Communications of the ACM*, Vol. 15, April 1972, pp. 268-270.

[14] *Multitasking User Guide*. Cray Computer Systems Technical Note. Publication SN-0222, Revision B, March 1986.

[15] G.W. Stewart. *Introduction to Matrix Computation*, Academic Press, New York, 1973.

A GROUP EXPLICIT SOLUTION SCHEME FOR NON-LINEAR PARABOLIC PDES ON MIMD PARALLEL SYSTEMS

M.P. Bekakos* & D.J. Evans†
Department of Computer Studies
Loughborough University of Technology
Loughborough, Leicestershire,
U.K.

0. ABSTRACT

The explicit methods although very suitable for parallel processing always deny us reasonable accuracy and some stability; on the other hand, the implicit schemes offer stability, but the exploitation of these methods for parallel processing may be difficult and possibly inefficient.

The class of Group Explicit (GE) methods, introduced herein, is the sort of semi-explicit schemes which enable us with a trade-off between stability and the possibility of them being suitable for implementation of parallel systems. Furthermore, it is possible to express the semi-explicit schemes in terms of pure explicit formulae to enable their efficient implementation.

1. INTRODUCTION

The experimental vehicle to investigate the effectiveness of the new method will be the one-dimensional non-linear parabolic p.d.e.

$$\frac{\partial u}{\partial t} = G(x,t,u,\frac{\partial u}{\partial x}, \frac{\partial^2 u}{\partial x^2}), \text{ for } 0\leq x\leq 1,\ t\geq 0; \tag{1.1}$$

to be more specific, we seek to solve Burgers' equation

$$\frac{\partial u}{\partial t} = \varepsilon \frac{\partial^2 u}{\partial x^2} - u\frac{\partial u}{\partial x}, \text{ for } \varepsilon>0\ , \tag{1.2}$$

which has been discussed by Burgers [BURG48] as a mathematical model of turbulence, and by Cole et al [COLE51] for the approximate theory for weak non-stationary shock waves in a real fluid. This equation can also be considered as a simplified form of the Navier-Stokes [AMES65] equation.

The new method combines stable asymmetric approximations to the partial differential equations which when coupled in groups of 2 adjacent points on the grid result in implicit equations which can be easily converted to explicit form.

In the following section we shall first discuss briefly the Standard Explicit scheme for the equation (1.2), against which the GE method will be compared, with

---

* Work completed under auspices of NATO and Greek Ministry of National Economy.
Now, Director at the Directorate for Informatics Development, Ministry of the Presidency of Government, Greece.

† Professor of Computer Science, Loughborough University of Technology, U.K.

the initial conditions, $u(x,0) = f(x),\ 0 \leq x \leq 1,$ (1.3)

and boundary conditions:

$$\left.\begin{array}{l} u(0,t) = g_1(t) \\ u(1,t) = g_2(t) \end{array}\right\},\ t>0 . \tag{1.4}$$

2. FORMULATION OF THE STANDARD EXPLICIT AND THE GE METHODS

With the increasing availability of parallel computers and their greater throughput, the explicit methods of solution not only offer simplicity, but also the capability that the solution can be obtained at every point concurrently.

In particular, for the Standard Explicit scheme, by taking the central-difference approximations for $\partial u/\partial x$ and $\partial^2 u/\partial x^2$ and a forward-difference approximation for $\partial u/\partial t$, the resulting finite-difference approximation is of the form [BEKA87],

$$U_{i,j+1} = \varepsilon r(U_{i+1,j} - 2U_{i,j} + U_{i-1,j}) + [1 - \frac{r\Delta x}{2}(U_{i+1,j} - U_{i-1,j})]U_{i,j}\ , \tag{2.1}$$

where,

$$U_{i,j} = U(i\Delta x, j\Delta t)\ ,$$
$$x = i\Delta x,\ i=0,1,2,\ldots,m$$
$$t = j\Delta t,\ j=0,1,2,\ldots$$
$$\Delta x = 1/m$$

and

$$r = \Delta t/\Delta x^2\ .$$

Note that, $U_{i,j+1}$ is a non-linear function in known terms $U_{i-1,j}$, $U_{i,j}$, and $U_{i+1,j}$, and therefore it can be computed directly without involving an iteration process.

The computational simplicity of the method, however, is contradicted from the very restrictive stability condition that the value of r should be $\leq 1/2$ in order to retain reasonable accuracy.

The principal idea behind the GE class of methods was to apply Saul'yev's asymmetric equations, the ladder-step formulae of which are given by

$$-raU_{i+1,j+1} + (1+ra)U_{i,j+1} = (1-rb)U_{i,j} + rbU_{i-1,j} \tag{2.2}$$

and

$$-rbU_{i-1,j+1} + (1+rb)U_{i,j+1} = (1-ra)U_{i,j} + raU_{i+1,j} \tag{2.3}$$

where,

$$\left.\begin{array}{l} a = \varepsilon - \frac{\Delta x}{4}(U_{i,j+1} + U_{i,j}) \\ b = \varepsilon + \frac{\Delta x}{4}(U_{i,j+1} + U_{i,j})\ , \end{array}\right. \tag{2.4}$$

not solely along the x lines in the (Right-to-Left) RL- and (Left-to-Right) LR-directions, but to groups of two points successively along every line.

The utilization of these semi-explicit formulae above offers a trade-off between some reasonable stability (denied by the explicit methods) and the possibility for their parallel exploitation (which is a very difficult task with the implicit schemes).

To formulate the GE equations we shall assume, without loss of generality, that the line segment $0\leq x\leq 1$ is divided into an even number m of equal sub-intervals; this implies that at every time-level the number of internal points is odd, i.e., $\underline{(m-1)}$. The coupled use of Saul'yev's asymmetric equations at the points (i,j+1) and (i+1, j+1) results, in fact, in a (2x2)-set of implicit finite-difference equations which can be easily converted to explicit form, as is presented in the following.

Consider any group of two points, i.e., (i,j+1/2) and (i+1,j+1/2), and use equations (2.2), (2.3) at these points, correspondingly; when grouped together they give the (2×2) system of equations

$$\begin{bmatrix} 1+a_1^{(n)}r & -a_1^{(n)}r \\ -b_2^{(n)}r & 1+b_2^{(n)}r \end{bmatrix} \begin{bmatrix} U_{i,j+1}^{(n+1)} \\ U_{i+1,j+1}^{(n+1)} \end{bmatrix} = \begin{bmatrix} 1-b_1^{(n)}r & 0 \\ 0 & 1-a_2^{(n)}r \end{bmatrix} \begin{bmatrix} U_{i,j} \\ U_{i+1,j} \end{bmatrix} + \begin{bmatrix} b_1^{(n)}rU_{i-1,j} \\ a_2^{(n)}rU_{i+2,j} \end{bmatrix} \tag{2.5}$$

with,

$$a_1^{(n)} = \varepsilon - \frac{\Delta x}{4}(U_{i,j+1}^{(n)}+U_{i,j}) \; ; \quad a_2^{(n)} = \varepsilon - \frac{\Delta x}{4}(U_{i+1,j+1}^{(n)}+U_{i+1,j})$$

$$b_1^{(n)} = \varepsilon + \frac{\Delta x}{4}(U_{i,j+1}^{(n)}+U_{i,j}) \; ; \quad b_2^{(n)} = \varepsilon + \frac{\Delta x}{4}(U_{i+1,j+1}^{(n)}+U_{i+1,j}) . \tag{2.6}$$

The explicit form of the above can be defined as

$$\begin{bmatrix} U_{i,j+1}^{(n+1)} \\ U_{i+1,j+1}^{(n+1)} \end{bmatrix} = \frac{1}{\Delta}\left\{ \begin{bmatrix} (1+b_2^{(n)}r-b_1^{(n)}r-b_1^{(n)}b_2^{(n)}r^2) & (1-a_2^{(n)}r)a_1^{(n)}r \\ b_2^{(n)}r(1-b_1^{(n)}r) & (1+a_1^{(n)}r-a_2^{(n)}r-a_1^{(n)}a_2^{(n)}r^2) \end{bmatrix} \begin{bmatrix} U_{i,j} \\ U_{i+1,j} \end{bmatrix} + \begin{bmatrix} (1+b_2^{(n)}r)b_1^{(n)}rU_{i-1,j}+a_1^{(n)}a_2^{(n)}r^2U_{i+2,j} \\ b_1^{(n)}b_2^{(n)}r^2U_{i-1,j}+(1+a_1^{(n)}r)a_2^{(n)}rU_{i+2,j} \end{bmatrix} \right\} \tag{2.7}$$

where the inverse of the coefficient matrix for $U_{i,j+1}$, $U_{i+1,j+1}$ has been estimated through the use of its adjoint matrix and the determinant,

$$\Delta = 1+a_1^{(n)}r+b_2^{(n)}r. \tag{2.8}$$

Note that, the superscript n refers to the nth iterative number.

3. THE G.E.U. (GROUP EXPLICIT WITH UNGROUPED ENDS) METHOD

In this paper the line segment $0\leq x\leq 1$ is divided into an odd number m of equal sub-intervals, which results in slightly different schemes if the number m was to be an even number (see Bekakos [BEKA86]); however, the concept of the GE class of methods can be similarly implemented and in fact the resulting schemes are much more balanced and computationally preferable for MIMD complexes of processors. Hence, at every time-level, the number of internal points is even, i.e. (m-1). This gives, at every time-level, either (m-1)/2 complete groups of two points, or (m-3)/2 groups of two points and one ungrouped point adjacent to each boundary.

The first GE scheme for this particular case, examined herein, is obtained by using, at every time-level, either of equations

$$U_{i,j+1}^{(n+1)} = \frac{1}{a_2^{(n)}}\{G_2(U_{i,j},U_{i+1,j})-b_2^{(n)}U_{i-1,j+1}^{(n+1)}\}\ , \tag{3.1}$$

$$U_{1,j+1}^{(n+1)} = \frac{1}{(1+rb^{(n)})}\quad\{rb^{(n)}U_{0,j+1}^{(n+1)}+(1-ra^{(n)})U_{1,j}+ra^{(n)}U_{2,j}\} \tag{3.2}$$

at the left ungrouped point, (m-3)/2 times either of the systems of equations

$$\begin{bmatrix} U_{i,j+1}^{(n+1)} \\ U_{i+1,j+1}^{(n+1)} \end{bmatrix} = \frac{1}{\Delta_1}\begin{bmatrix} a_2^{(n)} & -b_1^{(n)} \\ -b_2^{(n)} & a_1^{(n)} \end{bmatrix}\begin{bmatrix} G_1(U_{i,j},U_{i-1,j}) \\ G_2(U_{i+1,j},U_{i+2,j}) \end{bmatrix} \tag{3.3}$$

and

$$\begin{bmatrix} U_{i,j+1}^{(n+1)} \\ U_{i+1,j+1}^{(n+1)} \end{bmatrix} = \frac{1}{\Delta_2}\left\{\begin{bmatrix} (1+\hat{b}_2^{(n)}r-\hat{b}_1^{(n)}r-\hat{b}_1^{(n)}\hat{b}_2^{(n)}r^2) & (1-\hat{a}_2^{(n)}r)\hat{a}_1^{(n)}r \\ \hat{b}_2^{(n)}r(1-\hat{b}_1^{(n)}r) & (1+\hat{a}_1^{(n)}r-\hat{a}_2^{(n)}r-\hat{a}_1^{(n)}\hat{a}_2^{(n)}r^2) \end{bmatrix}\begin{bmatrix} U_{i,j} \\ U_{i+1,j} \end{bmatrix} + \begin{bmatrix} (1+\hat{b}_2^{(n)}r)\hat{b}_1^{(n)}rU_{i-1,j}+\hat{a}_1^{(n)}\hat{a}_2^{(n)}r^2U_{i+2,j} \\ \hat{b}_1^{(n)}\hat{b}_2^{(n)}r^2U_{i-1,j}+(1+\hat{a}_1^{(n)}r)\hat{a}_2^{(n)}rU_{i+2,j} \end{bmatrix}\right\} \tag{3.4}$$

with $\Delta_1 = a_1^{(n)}a_2^{(n)}-b_1^{(n)}b_2^{(n)}$ and $\Delta_2 = 1+\hat{a}_1^{(n)}r+\hat{b}_2^{(n)}r$,
from the second internal point to the $(m-2)^{th}$ point and either of equations,

$$U_{i,j+1}^{(n+1)} = \frac{1}{a_1^{(n)}}\{G_1(U_{i,j},U_{i-1,j})-b_1^{(n)}U_{i+1,j+1}^{(n+1)}\}\ , \tag{3.5}$$

$$U_{m-1,j+1}^{(n+1)} = \frac{1}{(1+ra^{(n)})}\{ra^{(n)}U_{m,j+1}^{(n+1)}+(1-rb^{(n)})U_{m-1,j}+rb^{(n)}U_{m-2,j}\} \tag{3.6}$$

at the last $(m-1)^{th}$ point which is left ungrouped at the far right of the line, adjacent to the boundary.

This scheme in implicit matrix form, for the particular case of Burgers' equation,

$$\frac{\partial u}{\partial t} = \varepsilon\frac{\partial^2 u}{\partial x^2} - u\frac{\partial u}{\partial x}\ ,\ \text{for}\ \ \varepsilon>0\ , \tag{3.7}$$

similarly as for the even number of equal sub-intervals case, is given by

$$(I+r\hat{G}_{1,j})\underline{U}_{j+1} = (I-r\hat{G}_{2,j})\underline{U}_j + \underline{b}_3$$

where,

$$\underline{b}_3^T = [\hat{b}_2^{(n)}rU_{0,j+1},0,\ldots,0,\hat{a}_1^{(n)}rU_{m,j+1}]\ ,$$

and

$$\hat{G}_{1,j} = \begin{bmatrix} \hat{b}_2^{(n)} & & & & & & \\ & G^{(1)} & & & & & \\ & & G^{(2)} & & & & \\ & & & \ddots & & & \\ & & & & G^{\frac{1}{2}(m-3)-1} & & \\ & & & & & G^{\frac{1}{2}(m-3)} & \\ & & & & & & \hat{a}_1^{(n)} \end{bmatrix}$$

$$\hat{G}_{2,j} = \begin{bmatrix} \dot{G}^{(1)} & & & & \\ & \dot{G}^{(2)} & & & \\ & & \ddots & & \\ & & & \dot{G}^{\frac{1}{2}(m-2)} & \\ & & & & \dot{G}^{\frac{1}{2}(m-1)} \end{bmatrix}$$

with

$$G^{(k)} = \begin{bmatrix} \hat{a}_1^{(n)} & -\hat{a}_1^{(n)} \\ -\hat{b}_2^{(n)} & \hat{b}_2^{(n)} \end{bmatrix} \quad \text{for } k=1,2,\ldots,1/2(m-3)$$

$$\text{and } j=0,1,2,\ldots, \tag{3.8}$$

$$\dot{G}^{(i)} = \begin{bmatrix} \hat{a}_2^{(n)} & -\hat{a}_2^{(n)} \\ -\hat{b}_1^{(n)} & \hat{b}_1^{(n)} \end{bmatrix} \quad \text{for } i=1,2,\ldots,1/2(m-1)$$

This scheme diagrammatically is described by the "brick" diagram in Figure 1.

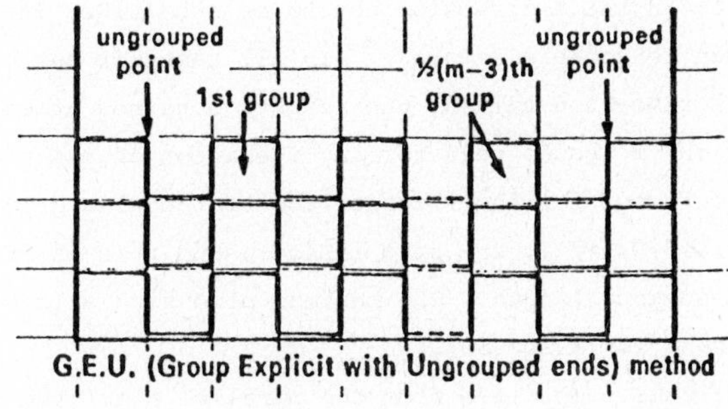

FIGURE 1: The representative diagram of this scheme.

From the aspect of the inherent parallelism of the implementation and in terms of the most efficient utilization of system's hardware and software potential, the explicit nature of the implementation, as well as the method itself, offers a plethora of alternating ways to exploit the parallelism concerning the task sizes that the total number of boundary and internal points can be divided into, to be allocated to the cooperating processors. After an extensive range of experiments we reached the conclusion that the implementation's granularity factor has to be made to be equal to the number of cooperating processors, in terms of the subset sizes of the boundary and internal points. Again, without any loss of generality and for a 'balanced' implementation, the considered total number of time-steps (ISTEP) and the number of internal grid points (NPOINT) have been chosen to be even and exactly divisible by any number of cooperating processors. To generate and terminate the NPROC paths each time, the $DOPAR/$PAREND construct is utilized, which is the most efficient and economical way to introduce parallelism in a program for the NEPTUNE prototype system*.

4. EXPERIMENTAL RESULTS

For the numerical experimentation with Burgers' equation the following exact solution has been chosen (see Madsen and Sincovec [MADS76]),

$$u(x,t) = \frac{0.1e^{-A}+0.5e^{-B}+e^{-C}}{e^{-A}+e^{-B}+e^{-C}} , \quad 0 \leq x \leq 1, \; t \geq 0 , \tag{4.1}$$

where,

$$\left.\begin{aligned} A &= \frac{0.05}{\varepsilon}(x-0.5+4.95t) \\ B &= \frac{0.25}{\varepsilon}(x-0.5+0.75t) \\ C &= \frac{0.5}{\varepsilon}(x-0.375) \end{aligned}\right\} . \tag{4.2}$$

This problem in practice would have a very small value of ε and this implies that the interval [0,1] in the x-direction has to be subdivided into a very fine grid in order to obtain reasonable accuracy. In all cases of our experimental work, despite the very small time-step values, the results obtained at each time-level were so accurate that there was no need for any iteration of the non-linear problem.

The deterministic factor for the sizes of the rectangular grids considered in the open rectangle $[0,1]\times[0,+\infty)$ is the grid ratio r, and this in order to maintain the same overall time-advance length. The maximum grid size allowed by the Multi-processor testbed in hand is (1920×480).

The experimental results obtained from the parallel algorithm for the Standard Explicit and the GEU methods are presented in Tables 1,2, along with the values of other parameters of the performance model estimated statically. The concepts of the parameters appearing in these Tables are as they were presented in [BEKA86],[BEKA87].

*A Multiple-Instruction stream, Multiple-Data stream (MIMD) type of system.

$N_{I.P.}$	N_{PROCS}	r	$M_{P.E}$	$M_{A.E.}$	$Tc^{(e)}$ (secs)	C_p	S_p	E_p	$F_p.T_8^{(e)}$	$M_{P.E.}$	$M_{A.E.}$	$Tc^{(e)}$ (secs)	C_p	S_p	E_p	$F_p.T_8^{(e)}$
240	Ø	0.5	.195053183E-01	.149965286E-03	195.383	195.383	1	1	1	.355070271E-01	.260531902E-03	385.738	385.738	1	1	1
	Ø,1				100.790	201.580	1.939	0.969	1.879			198.583	397.166	1.942	0.971	1.887
	Ø,1,2				69.720	209.160	2.802	0.934	2.618			137.003	411.009	2.816	0.939	2.642
	Ø,1,2,3				52.993	211.972	3.687	0.922	3.398			104.363	417.452	3.696	0.924	3.415
480	Ø	0.5	.106825903E-01	.106275082E-03	382.918	382.918	1	1	1	.200394355E-01	.199377537E-03	755.790	755.790	1	1	1
	Ø,1				197.950	395.900	1.934	0.967	1.871			392.053	784.106	1.928	0.964	1.858
	Ø,1,2				135.710	407.130	2.822	0.941	2.654			267.298	801.894	2.828	0.943	2.665
	Ø,1,2,3				102.730	410.920	3.727	0.932	3.473			202.205	808.820	3.738	0.934	3.493
960	Ø	0.5	.111256465E-01	.106096268E-03	759.735	759.735	1	1	1	.208908506E-01	.204622746E-03	1498.070	1498.070	1	1	1
	Ø,1				393.510	787.020	1.931	0.965	1.864			776.815	1553.630	1.928	0.964	1.860
	Ø,1,2				268.718	806.154	2.827	0.942	2.664			530.485	1591.455	2.824	0.941	2.658
	Ø,1,2,3				203.228	812.912	3.738	0.935	3.494			401.073	1604.292	3.735	0.934	3.488
1920	Ø	0.5	.115095451E-01	.103712082E-03	1513.813	1513.813	1	1	1	.227458738E-01	.204980373E-03	2987.858	2987.858	1	1	1
	Ø,1				786.073	1572.146	1.926	0.963	1.854			1548.110	3096.220	1.930	0.965	1.862
	Ø,1,2				535.260	1605.780	2.828	0.943	2.666			1054.413	3163.239	2.834	0.945	2.677
	Ø,1,2,3				404.855	1619.420	3.739	0.935	3.495			798.165	3192.660	3.743	0.936	3.503
TIME-STEPS:			120							240						

TABLE 1 : Experimental Results and Performance Measurements of the Parallel Algorithm for the Standard Explicit Method on the *'NEPTUNE'* Prototype System.

$N_{I.P.}$	N_{PROCS}	r	$M_{P.E.}$	$M_{A.E.}$	$Tc^{(e)}$ (secs)	C_p	S_p	E_p	$F_p.T_s^{(e)}$
240	Ø	0.5	.67063316E-01	.502884388E-03	766.268	766.268	1	1	1
	Ø,1				394.895	789.790	1.940	0.970	1.883
	Ø,1,2				271.700	815.100	2.820	0.940	2.651
	Ø,1,2,3				207.075	828.300	3.700	0.925	3.423
480	Ø	0.5	.364964530E-01	.363171101E-03	1500.133	1500.133	1	1	1
	Ø,1				775.268	1550.536	1.935	0.967	1.872
	Ø,1,2				532.595	1597.785	2.817	0.939	2.645
	Ø,1,2,3				402.493	1609.972	3.727	0.932	3.473
960	Ø	0.5	.407953449E-01	.399649143E-03	2974.615	2974.615	1	1	1
	Ø,1				1541.228	3082.456	1.930	0.965	1.863
	Ø,1,2				1053.690	3161.070	2.823	0.941	2.657
	Ø,1,2,3				797.498	3189.992	3.730	0.932	3.478
1920	Ø	0.5	.447628200E-01	.403463840E-03	5934.120	5934.120	1	1	1
	Ø,1				3072.303	6144.606	1.931	0.966	1.865
	Ø,1,2				2096.200	6288.600	2.831	0.944	2.671
	Ø,1,2,3				1588.353	6353.412	3.736	0.934	3.489
TIME-STEPS:			480						

TABLE 1*(cont.d.)*: Experimental Results and Performance Measurements of the Parallel Algorithm for the Standard Explicit Method on the *'NEPTUNE'* Prototype System.

$N_{I.P.}$	N_{PROCS}	r	$M_{P.E.}$	$M_{A.E.}$	$Tc^{(e)}$ (secs)	C_p	S_p	R_{S_p}	E_p	$F_p.T_s^{(e)}$	$M_{P.E.}$	$M_{A.E.}$	$Tc^{(e)}$ (secs)	C_p	S_p	R_{S_p}	E_p	$F_p.T_s^{(e)}$
240	Ø	1.0	.152023882E-01	.110328197E-03	182.435	182.435	1	1.071	1	1	.300644040E-01	.220596790E-03	361.038	361.038	1	1.068	1	1
	Ø,1				93.405	186.810	1.953	2.092	0.977	1.907			184.615	369.230	1.956	2.089	0.978	1.912
	Ø,1,2				63.180	189.540	2.888	3.092	0.963	2.779			124.425	373.275	2.902	3.100	0.967	2.807
	Ø,1,2,3				47.935	191.740	3.806	4.076	0.951	3.621			94.075	376.300	3.838	4.100	0.959	3.682
480	Ø	1.0	.592584908E-02	.592470169E-04	363.390	363.390	1	1.054	1	1	.109970570E-01	.109970570E-03	716.290	716.290	1	1.055	1	1
	Ø,1				186.390	372.780	1.950	2.054	0.975	1.901			367.170	734.340	1.951	2.058	0.975	1.903
	Ø,1,2				124.660	373.980	2.915	3.072	0.972	2.833			246.360	739.080	2.907	3.068	0.969	2.818
	Ø,1,2,3				93.990	375.960	3.866	4.074	0.967	3.737			185.750	743.000	3.856	4.069	0.964	3.718
960	Ø	1.0	.658917427E-02	.657439232E-04	724.058	724.058	1	1.049	1	1	.130981430E-01	.130712986E-03	1424.425	1424.425	1	1.052	1	1
	Ø,1				369.803	739.606	1.958	2.054	0.979	1.917			725.733	1451.466	1.963	2.064	0.981	1.926
	Ø,1,2				248.258	744.774	2.917	3.060	0.972	2.835			488.213	1464.639	2.918	3.068	0.973	2.838
	Ø,1,2,3				186.598	746.392	3.880	4.072	0.970	3.764			368.608	1474.432	3.864	4.064	0.966	3.733
1920	Ø	1.0	.690134242E-02	.689625740E-04	1449.140	1449.140	1	1.045	1	1	.127051361E-01	.126957893E-03	2856.785	2856.785	1	1.046	1	1
	Ø,1				735.848	1471.696	1.969	2.057	0.985	1.939			1453.493	2906.986	1.965	2.056	0.983	1.932
	Ø,1,2				495.085	1485.255	2.927	3.058	0.976	2.856			974.453	2923.359	2.932	3.066	0.977	2.865
	Ø,1,2,3				372.115	1488.460	3.894	4.068	0.974	3.791			733.708	2934.832	3.894	4.072	0.973	3.790
TIME-STEPS:			60								120							

TABLE 2 : Experimental Results and Performance Measurements of the Parallel Algorithm for the *G.E.U.* Method on the *'NEPTUNE'* Prototype System.

$N_{I.P.}$	N_{PROCS}	r	$M_{P.E.}$	$M_{A.E.}$	$Tc^{(e)}$ (secs)	C_p	S_p	R_{S_p}	E_p	$F_p \cdot T_s^{(e)}$
240	Ø	1.0	.56841306 4E-01	.42623281 5E-03	715.018	715.018	1	1.072	1	1
	Ø,1				367.410	734.820	1.946	2.086	0.973	1.894
	Ø,1,2				248.180	744.540	2.881	3.088	0.960	2.767
	Ø,1,2,3				187.918	751.672	3.805	4.078	0.951	3.619
480	Ø	1.0	.23186896 0E-01	.23072958 0E-03	1416.660	1416.660	1	1.059	1	1
	Ø,1				726.310	1452.620	1.950	2.065	0.975	1.902
	Ø,1,2				487.400	1462.200	2.907	3.078	0.969	2.816
	Ø,1,2,3				368.120	1472.480	3.848	4.075	0.962	3.702
960	Ø	1.0	.26171959 9E-01	.26118755 3E-03	2827.950	2827.950	1	1.052	1	1
	Ø,1				1448.135	2896.270	1.953	2.054	0.976	1.907
	Ø,1,2				969.343	2908.029	2.917	3.069	0.972	2.837
	Ø,1,2,3				730.743	2922.972	3.870	4.071	0.967	3.744
1920	Ø	1.0	.24241123 3E-01	.24223327 6E-03	5667.958	5667.958	1	1.047	1	1
	Ø,1				2876.640	5753.280	1.970	2.063	0.985	1.941
	Ø,1,2				1932.828	5798.484	2.932	3.070	0.977	2.866
	Ø,1,2,3				1454.243	5816.972	3.898	4.081	0.974	3.798
TIME-STEPS:			240							

TABLE 2 *(cont.d.)*: Experimental Results and Performance Measurements of the Parallel Algorithm for the *G.E.U.* Method on the *'NEPTUNE'* Prototype System.

The experimented grid sizes, when the grid ratio r=1, have been accordingly set to correspond to the grid sizes chosen for the Standard Explicit method, where $r=\frac{1}{2}$, for a direct comparison.

Some conclusions that can be apparently drawn from the examination of Table 2 are that, in terms of the S_p and E_p, they exhibit values very close to the optimum theoretical ones, i.e. $\lesssim p$ and $\lesssim 1$, respectively, whilst $F_p.T_s^{(e)}$ also exhibits optimum results of $\mathcal{O}(p)$.

In comparison with the parallel algorithm for the Standard Explicit method (hereafter being called the standard algorithm) all these parameters produce considerably better figures for the present algorithm; however, the extraordinary thing to be noted is that these better results have been obtained with smaller running time-complexities, for every number of cooperating processors, a fact which agrees with the implementor's should be real goal to minimize execution time and not simply to maximise Speed-up. In fact, the Relative Speed-up (R_{S_p}) parameter very clearly shows that the $\mathcal{O}(p)$ speed-up limit has been well surpassed and is being established to $>\mathcal{O}(r.p)$.

The same observation, with that for the standard algorithm, can be made concerning the real Cost (C_p) of the present algorithm which naturally increases, when increasing the number of cooperating processors, along with the S_p, while E_p decreases. In particular with the obtained Speed-up values, which are linear to the number of cooperating processors each time, they produce slightly better peaks when the grid size is (1920×240), for every specified combination of processors, while, as the number of internal points increases, the Speed-ups achieved with the stated combination of 3 and 4 cooperating processors analogously and smoothly increase, compared with the fluctuating figures of the standard algorithm. In consequence, for the same instances, the Efficiency and the $F_p.T_s^{(e)}$ parameters of the performance model similarly exhibit a continuous increase. The latter factor examined alone indicates the optimum, allowed by the system, grid size in terms of the acceleration in computation.

Finally, and in terms of the convergence of the solution achieved through the GEU method, the best accuracy obtained and consequently the optimum grid size was for (480×60).

5. A DETERMINISTIC APPROACH TO PERFORMANCE ANALYSIS

The deterministic performance analysis approach which is followed (see Bekakos and Evans [BEKA87]) views performance as the interaction of resources demanded by programs and provided by the multiprocessor system, in both system dependent and independent manner; it also matches algorithm to machine trying to avoid the danger of rejecting an algorithm because it performs badly on one particular parallel processor complex.

Although for all parallel systems the potential parallelism, the demands for shared data and the demands for synchronization have to be taken into account by the parallel algorithm, it is the last factor that is the determining feature for such asynchronous systems as the NEPTUNE parallel machine. For the present case, both algorithms are designed to minimize the amount of synchronization required without, however, limiting the parallelism up to four processors.

With respect to the performance analyses of the parallel algorithms investigated herein, for a grid of size (240×480), the program dependent Tables 3,5 summarize, in this sequence, the following parameters: Grid Size (G_S), program's PHase number (P_H), the Algebraic-complexities ($Ac_{(i,j)}$)/theoretical) Time-complexities ($Tc^{(t)}_{(i,j)}$) per point (or group of two points), the Implementation cycles (I_{cl}), the Algebraic-complexities (Ac_p)/(theoretical) Time-complexities ($Tc^{(t)}_p$) per parallel path of the algorithms, the Number of parallel paths allocated per processor ($N_{p(p)}$), the Loops of parallelism ($L_{o(//)}$), the processing-to-access to shared data ratio ($R_{a(s)}$) and the percentage overhead ($O^{(t)}_{st(s)}$), the processing-to-access to the parallel path scheduler ratio ($R_{a(//)}$) and the respective overhead ($O^{(t)}_{st(//)}$), the limits to performance in terms of a theoretical upper bound on the number of cooperating processors in connection with, their average "excess" access time ($S_{d(r)}$) and average access time ($S'_{d(r)}$) to the Shared data resource, and the cycle time of the parallel path Scheduling resource ($S_{h(r)}$), the percentage of the average Idle time ($Id^{(t)}_t$) (theoretically) and the Wasted time statically (W_{st}).

While these results are manually obtained from the program itself predicting somehow the experimental performance, Tables 4,6 are system dependent and present the "real" performance measures obtained when 'running' the algorithms on the system. The estimation of most of the above figures is not simply straightforward and the reader should refer to [BEKA87]. The additional parameters utilized in the latter Tables, in the sequence of their appearance, are: The uniprocessor (experimental) Time-complexity ($T^{(e)}_s$) when generating the load modules using the XPFCL command, the achieved Speed-ups (S_p), the total number of waiting cycles because no parallel path is available ($\sum_{i=1}^{p} c_{y_i}$), the processors cycle time (t_{cy}), the average time wasted dynamically ($Id^{(e)}_t$)(experimental), the 'blocked' time (t_b), the processors static ($O^{(e)}_{st(//)}$) and contention ($O^{(e)}_{cn(//)}$) (experimental) percentage Overheads when accessing the parallel path scheduling resource, the uniprocessor (experimental) Time-complexity ($T^{(e)}_s$) when generating the load modules using the XPFCLN command, the percentage of the total Overhead due to the control of the parallel mechanisms ($O^{(e)}_{tl(//)}$), the uniprocessor (experimental) Time-complexity ($T^{(e)}_s$) when generating the load modules using the XPFCLS command, the percentage of the total Overhead due to the shared data "loading" in the shared memory module, and the Wasted time dynamically (W_{dc}).

With respect to the complementary information required for the estimation of

G_S	P_H	PROCESSORS (p)		$Ac_{(i,j)}$	$Tc^{(t)}_{(i,j)}$ (secs)	I_{cl}	Ac_p	$Tc^{(t)}_p$ (secs)	$N_{p(p)}$	$I_{\alpha(//)}$	SHARED DATA		PARALLEL PATH		LIMITS TO PERFORMANCE			$Id^{(t)}_t$	W_{st} (secs)
		N_t	S_p								$R_{a(s)}$	$O^{(t)}_{st(s)}$	$R_{a(//)}$	$O^{(t)}_{st(//)}$	$S_{d(r)}$	$S'_{d(r)}$	$S_{h(r)}$		
240×480	3	$p \le 2N_{B.P.}$ $[p \mid N_{B.P.}]$	$O(p)$	60 flops	0.023	$\frac{960}{p}$	$\frac{57.6 \times 10^3}{p}$ flops	$\frac{22.176}{p}$	1	1	1:60 flops	0.003%	$1:\frac{57.6 \times 10^3}{p}$ flops	0.005p%	m_p=30,596	m_p=24,509	$m_p=\frac{18,480}{p}$		0.006
	4	$p \le N_{I.P.}$ $[p \mid N_{I.P.}]$	$O(p)$	56 flops	0.022	$\frac{240}{p}$	$\frac{13.44 \times 10^3}{p}$ flops	$\frac{5.174}{p}$	1	1	1:56 flops	0.004%	$1:\frac{13.44 \times 10^3}{p}$ flops	0.023p%	m_p=28,556	m_p=22,875	$m_p=\frac{4,312}{p}$	~1.5%	0.005
	5	$p \le N_{I.P.}$ $[p \mid N_{I.P.}]$	$O(p)$	14 flops	0.005	$\frac{240}{p}$	$\frac{3.36 \times 10^3}{p}$ flops	$\frac{1.294}{p}$	1	480	1:2 flops	0.098%	$1:\frac{3.36 \times 10^3}{p}$ flops	0.093p%	m_p=1,019	m_p=816	$m_p=\frac{1,078}{p}$		2.913

TABLE 3: A Program Dependent Performance Analysis of the Parallel Algorithm for the Standard Explicit Method.

G_S	$T^{(e)}_s$ (secs)	S_p			$\sum_{i=1}^{p} c_{y_i}$	t_{cy} (μsecs)	$Id^{(e)}_t$	t_b (μsecs)	PARALLEL PATH		$T^{(e)}_s$ (secs)	PARALLEL CONTROL	$T^{(e)}_s$ (secs)	SHARED DATA	W_{dc} (secs)
	[XPFCL]	Ø,1	Ø,1,2	Ø,1,2,3					$O^{(e)}_{st(//)}$	$O^{(e)}_{cn(//)}$	[XPFCLN]	$O^{(e)}_{tl(//)}$	[XPFCLS]	$O^{(e)}_{tl(s)}$	
240×480	766.268	1.940	2.820	3.700	5106	~10,800	~6.7%	~686	0.28%	0.42%	765.356	0.12%	764.558	0.1%	55.145

TABLE 4 : A System Dependent Performance Analysis of the Parallel Algorithm for the Standard Explicit Method.

G_S	P_H	PROCESSORS (p)		$Ac_{(i,j)}$	$Tc^{(t)}_{(i,j)}$ (secs)	I_{cl}	Ac_p	$Tc^{(t)}_p$ (secs)	$N_{p(p)}$	$I_{t(//)}$	SHARED DATA		PARALLEL PATH		LIMITS TO PERFORMANCE			$Id^{(t)}_t$	W_{st} (secs)
		N_t	S_p								$R_{a(s)}$	$O^{(t)}_{st(s)}$	$R_{a(//)}$	$O^{(t)}_{st(//)}$	$S_{d(r)}$	$S'_{d(r)}$	$S_{h(r)}$		
240×240	3	$p\leq 2N_{B.P.}$ $[p\vert N_{B.P.}]$	$O(p)$	60 flops	0.023	$\frac{480}{p}$	$\frac{28.8\times10^3}{p}$ flops	$\frac{11.088}{p}$	1	1	1:60 flops	0.003%	$1:\frac{28.8\times10^3}{p}$ flops	0.011p%	m_p=30,596	m_p=24,509	$m_p=\frac{9,240}{p}$		0.005
	4	$p\leq N_{I.P.}$ $[p\vert N_{I.P.}]$	$O(p)$	56 flops	0.022	$\frac{240}{p}$	$\frac{13.44\times10^3}{p}$ flops	$\frac{5.174}{p}$	1	1	1:56 flops	0.004%	$1:\frac{13.44\times10^3}{p}$ flops	0.023p%	m_p=28,556	m_p=22,875	$m_p=\frac{4,312}{p}$	~1.4%	0.005
	5	$p\leq N_{I.P.}$ $[p\vert N_{I.P.}]$	$O(p)$	49 flops	0.019	$\frac{120}{p}$	$\frac{5.88\times10^3}{p}$ flops	$\frac{2.264}{p}$	1	240	1:4 flops	0.049%	$1:\frac{5.88\times10^3}{p}$ flops	0.053p%	m_p=2,039	m_p=1,633	$m_p=\frac{1,886}{p}$		1.413

TABLE 5 : A Program Dependent Performance Analysis of the Parallel Algorithm for the *G.E.U.* Method.

G_S	$T^{(e)}_s$ (secs)	S_p			$\sum_{i=1}^{p} c_{y_i}$	t_{cy} (μsecs)	$Id^{(e)}_t$	t_b (μsecs)	PARALLEL PATH		$T^{(e)}_s$ (secs)	PARALLEL CONTROL	$T^{(e)}_s$ (secs)	SHARED DATA	W_{dc} (secs)
	[*XPFCL*]	∅,1	∅,1,2	∅,1,2,3					$O^{(e)}_{st(//)}$	$O^{(e)}_{cn(//)}$	[*XPFCLN*]	$O^{(e)}_{tl(//)}$	[*XPFCLS*]	$O^{(e)}_{tl(s)}$	
240×240	715.018	1.946	2.881	3.805	2712	~10,800	~3.9%	~686	0.16%	0.25%	714.163	0.12%	713.693	0.07%	29.290

TABLE 6 : A System Dependent Performance Analysis of the Parallel Algorithm for the *G.E.U.* Method.

the experiment dependent parameters appearing in the previous Tables, obtained from the shared array ITIME (see Bekakos and Evans [BEKA85]) in a maximum system utilization, was as follows:

i) The smallest run-time $T_p^{(e)}$ was ~187.908 secs;

ii) the total number of wait cycles was ~2712, which implied an average number of wait cycles per processor of ~678;

iii) the average experimental timing of all cooperating processors was ~187.912 secs.; and,

iv) the number of parallel paths run by each processor, considering the average of all cooperating processors but P_0, was 243.

Finally, the time the system was not used productively (W) being estimated by using the average experimental timing in iii), was ~36.630 secs.; a good approximation to this total wasted time can be obtained from the sum of the wasted times statically and dynamically given in the performance analysis Tables.

6. CONCLUSIVE REMARKS

With respect to the existing implicit schemes a major disadvantage of them, from parallel computational aspects, is the fact that the unknowns are usually related through an expression and little or no independencies exist to be exploitable by parallel architectures. With the increasing availability of parallel computers and their greater throughput, the explicit methods of solution not only offer simplicity, but also the capability that the solution can be obtained at every point concurrently. This important factor reinforces the need for improved explicit procedures for utilization on parallel computers.

The merit of the approach herein results in more accurate solutions because of truncation error cancellations. A clear advantage of this method is the independency of the points within a single time-level, which makes it naturally suitable for SIMD type architectures.

Finally, despite the small time-step values Δt the results at each time-level were so accurate that there was no need for any iteration of the non-linear problem.

7. REFERENCES

1. [ABDU83], Abdullah, A.R.B., "The Study of Some Numerical Methods for Solving Parabolic Partial Differential Equations", Ph.D. Thesis, L.U.T., 1983.

2. [AMES65], Ames, W.F., "Non-Linear Partial Differential Equations in Engineering", Academic Press, Inc., London, 1965, U.K.

3. [BEKA85], Bekakos, M.P. and Evans, D.J., "The Numerical Solution of Non-Linear Parabolic Equations on MIMD Parallel Computers", 1st European Workshop on Parallel Processing Techniques for Simulation, Oct. 28-29, 1985, Manchester, U.K.

4. [BEKA86], Bekakos, M.P., "A Study of Algorithms for Parallel Computers and VLSI Systolic Processor Arrays", Ph.D. Thesis, L.U.T., 1986.

5. [BEKA86a], Bekakos, M.P., and Evans, D.J., "Group Explicit Complete Method vs. Standard Explicit Method on MIMD Parallel Systems", CS-300, L.U.T., August, 1986.

6. [BEKA87], Bekakos, M.P., and Evans, D.J., "An Alternative Solution Method for Non-Linear Parabolic Equations on MIMD Parallel Computers", Intern. J.Comp.Maths., Vol. 23, No. 1, 1987.

7. [BEKA87a], Bekakos, M.P. and Evans, D.J., "A Model for the Deterministic Performance Analysis of MIMD Parallel Computer Systems", to appear.

8. [BURG48], Burgers, J.M., Adv.Appl.Mech., Vol. 1, 1948, pp.171.

9. [COLE51], Cole, J.D., et al, "On Quasi-Linear Parabolic Equations Occurring in Aerodynamics", A.Appl.Maths., Vol. 9, 1951, pp.225-236.

10. [EVAN83], Evans, D.J., and Abdullah, A.R.B., "The Group Explicit Method for the Solution of Burgers' Equation", CS-179, L.U.T., March, 1983.

11. [LARK64], Larkin, B.K., "Some Stable Explicit Difference Approximations to the Diffusion Equation", Math.Comp., Vol. 18, 1964, pp.196-202.

12. [MADS76], Madsen, N.K., and Sincovec, R.F., "General Software for Partial Differential Equations", in Numerical Methods for Differential Systems, eds. Lapidus, L., and Schiesser, W.E., Academic Press, 1976, pp.229-242.

GAUSSIAN ELIMINATION ON MESSAGE PASSING ARCHITECTURE

M. COSNARD, B. TOURANCHEAU[1] and G. VILLARD
Algorithmique Parallèle et Calcul Formel
CNRS, Laboratoire TIM3
Institut National Polytechnique de Grenoble
38031 GRENOBLE Cedex

1 Introduction

Networks of processors are now commercially available (especially with a hypercube topology). In models of such architectures each processor has a local memory and a few connected neighbours. The communication protocol is based on message passing: each processor receives data on the communication channels, executes some computations, sends results via the channels. In this case the execution time of an algorithm depends on the position of the processor in the network. Sequential algorithm leads to many parallel versions on such a model.

In this paper we study the parallel implementation of Gaussian elimination on a networks of processors. We follow previous works done by Saad [Saa86], Geist [Gei] and Geist and Heath [GH]. In these papers broadcast algorithms are introduced. We present a new way to implement the Gauss algorithm by considering local pivot rows. We show that the Local Pivot Row and Local Pivot Modified algorithms performs better on a ring of processors than the Broadcast algorithm on a complete network. This surprising result is balanced by a loss of stability. We show that pairwise pivoting or local partial pivoting can be incorporated to these algorithms. However global pivoting needs an election procedure and a global synchronisation which contradicts the local character of the algorithms.

2 The model

The target architecture is assumed to be a network composed of processors and connections between neighbours. The global behaviour is of MIMD type and hence no global synchronization mechanism is necessary. Moreover each processor holds a private

---

[1]This work is supported by the "Programme de Recherches Coordonnées C3" of the French National Center of Scientific Research (CNRS)

memory and no shared storage is available so that communicating is done by message passing [HB].

The first hypothesis on the model is that arithmetics and communications do not overlap, in oder to simplify the computation of the execution time of the algorithms. Remark that overlapping could not only lead to a gain of a factor at most two as pointed in [Saa85]. In fact, in asynchronous algorithms the synchronisation delays and the resulting idle time of the processors are no longer negligible.

Concerning communications, we assume that each processor is connected to every neighbour by one channel which can be used either for sending informations to the neighbour (output channel) or for receiving information from the neighbour (input channel). All the output channels can be used to send the same data to all the neighbours (broadcast facility) without any extra cost for duplication. An input channel and an output channel can be used simultaneously only for receiving and sending independent data (to different processors).

The time needed for transmitting (send or receive) n consecutive data to a neighbour processor is defined [Saa85] as :

$$\beta + n\tau$$

where β is a start-up time and t the inverse of the bandwith of the channel. It is clear that β and τ depens heavily on the architecture and in particular on the number of channels for each processor. Hence for a given value of p, the corresponding values for a complete network are greater than those for an hypercube, witch in turn are greater than the values for a ring of processors. Numerical values for real computers are the following (one byte on one channel):

Hypercubes	β (ms)	t (ms)
FPS T20	10	1.5
Ipsc	650	2.0

Control cost is not the aim of the present paper but we can remark that it would be an important part of the total execution time. As it was shown for iterative methods in [Bro] a non-constant control cost, for example linear in p, can lead to an optimum number of processors to increase the speed-up of parallel decomposition problems.

In this paper, the control consists for each processor in selecting the data which will be transmitted or processed. Moreover an extra cost comes from the need for each processor to determine the end of the algorithm. This overhead is difficult to modelize and will not be taken into account in this algorithmic study. Remark however that no control cost is due to synchronization since the algorithms are globally asynchronous. Local synchronisation corresponds to the communications between neighbours processors and hence can be

P_j are neighbours and P_j is ready to receive the message.

We assume that each processor possesses a vector unit with an adder/substracter divided in e_+ stages and a multiplier/divider divided in e_x stages. These two arithmetic units can be chained so that executing a SAXPY on two vectors of size n will take a time equal to :

$$(e_+ + e_x + (n-1))t$$

where t is the cycle time, i. e. the time to cross a stage.

Let A be the matrix to be decomposed. In the remaining the basic operations of each processor will be to eliminate some elements of the rows of A using a pivot row. Assuming that the processor possesses q rows of length m (numbered 2 to q+1) plus the pivot row (numbered 1), introducing a zero in each row can be done in the following way :

```
for i=2 to q+1 do
    a_i1:=a_i1/a_11
endfor

for i=2 to q+1 do
    for j=2 to m do
        a_ij:=a_ij-a_i1*a_1j
    endfor
endfor
```

The time needed for executing such an algorithm is :

$$(e_x+(q-1))t + (e_+ + e_x + (m-1)q-1)t = (e+mq)t$$

where $e=2e_x+e_+-2$

3 Broadcast row algorithm

As noted in [Saa86], the simplest way to implement Gaussian Elimination in parallel is to subdivide A into p blocks of n/p rows and to assign one block to each processor. We do not consider in this section the problem of implementing a pivoting strategy. The algorithm is based on two macro-operations : broadcast and eliminate. We denote P(i) the processor which possesses the ith row of A.

BR Algorithm :

```
processor Pi
seq
  for k=1 to n-1 do
    if row k is inside Pi then broadcast pivot row k to
                                  P1,...,Pi-1,Pi+1,...,Pp
    else receive the broadcast pivot row k
    endif
    perform the eliminations using pivot row k
  endfor
endseq
```

Seq, Alt and **Par** are the CSP/OCCAM operators [Hoa] [Row] which describe the SEQuential, ALTernative or PARallel behavior of the processes.

All the algorithms that will be presented in this paper are row oriented. Column oriented algorithms could also be defined in similar ways. However the LU row scheme factorization seems to be more efficient than the column factorization [ISS] for the solution of the associated triangular system.

Three strategies for subdividing A are described in [Saa86] and [Gei]. The first one consists in assigning consecutive rows to a given processor. In this case, at step n*i/p+1, i processors will be definitely idle, resulting in a decrease of efficiency. The second strategy consists in assigning the rows with the same number modulo p to a given processor. In this case, broadcasting is more expensive than in the previous strategy since at each step we must broadcast the pivot row to all the processors. However the elimination time will be smaller since the processors will be always active. The third mapping assumes that P_{i-1} and P_{i+1} are neighbours of P_i and assigns rows (2kp+1-number of the processor) to the even numbered processors and (2kp+number of the processor) to the odd ones (k=0,1,...). This reflection method causes comparable execution times than the preceding, but seems to produce a best overall balance. In order to simplify the presentation we choose the second strategy.

The total time depends heavily on the broadcasting facility. Let us assume that no special hardware is provided for this operation. Saad describes in [Saa85] various algorithms which divide the data to be transmitted into blocks of equal length (see further use of this idea in the LP algorithms). Using these algorithms and the second strategy for subdividing A, we obtain the following execution times for three different networks: a complete network, a hypercube and a ring of processors. Note that in this case the computation time is independant of the topology. The differences in the communication times come from the broadcasting facilities of each network. Remark that communication time includes delais introduced by synchronisation of the message passing protocol, i. e. communication time is the difference between total execution time and execution time.

Computation time :

$$T^{br}_{comp} = \sum_{k=1}^{n-1}\left(e+(n-k+1)\left\lceil \frac{n-k}{p} \right\rceil \right) t$$

$$T^{br}_{comp} = (n-1)\,e\,t + \left(\frac{n^3}{3p} + \frac{(p-1)}{4p} n^2 + \left(\frac{9p-p^2-12}{12p} \right) n \right) t$$

Communication time :

-ring

$$T^{r}_{comm} = \gamma^{r}_{n,p}\left[\frac{(n+2)(n-1)}{2}\,\tau_r + \left(n-\frac{p}{4}\right)\left(\frac{p}{2}-1\right)\beta_r \right] \qquad 1\leq\gamma^{r}_{n,p}\leq 2$$

-hypercube

$$T^{h}_{comm} = \gamma^{h}_{n,p}\left[\frac{(n+2)(n-1)}{2}\,\tau_h + \left(\left(n-\frac{p}{2}\right)(\log_2 p-1) + \log_2\left(\left(\frac{p}{2}-1\right)!\right) + \alpha'_{n,p}\left(\frac{p}{2}-1\right) \right)\beta_h \right]$$

$0\leq\alpha'_{n,p}\leq 1/2$, $1\leq\gamma^{h}_{n,p}\leq 2$

-complete network

$$T^{c}_{comm} = \frac{(n+2)(n-1)}{2}\,\tau_c + (n-1)\beta_c$$

The preceding formula lead to the following conclusions. The communication time of the complete network algorithm is less than the hypercube algorithm which is less than the ring algorithm as could be easily seen from the communicating facilities of each network. However the coefficients of the inverse of the bandwith (τ) are only within a factor of two. Since the bandwith of a complete network is presumably less than those of a hypercube or a ring, we deduce that the order could be reversed. With respect to the start up times the differences are much bigger: $np\beta_r$, $n\log_2 p\beta_h$ and $n\beta_c$. Note however that for fixed p and large n these terms are of order less than the t terms.

It appears hence that contrarily to the intuition the complete network does not present a much better performance than the ring network.

In the following paragraphs we shall propose various algorithms that compare favorably with the broacast algorithm. They are based on a ring topology but could clearly be implemented on a network with a ring as subgraph.

4 Pipelined Ring Algorithm

Broadcasting is an expensive and difficult operation. We shall show that we can avoid it using only nearest neighbour communications. Assume that the processor network (hypercube, complete,..) is arranged in a ring fashion and number the processors so that $P_{i-1\,(mod\ p)}$ and $P_{i+1\,(mod\ p)}$ are the neighbours of P_i (see figure 1).

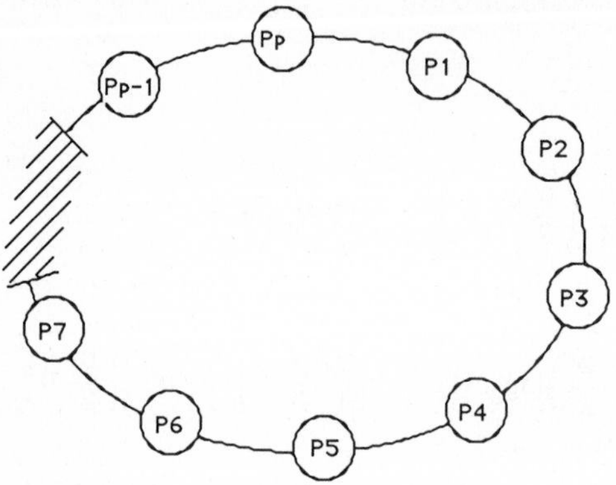

Figure 1: ring of processors

The PR algorithm introduced in [Saa86] is an asynchronous parallel algorithm such that each processor receives the pivot row, sends it to the next processor and then performs the eliminations on its own rows.

PR Algorithm (as noted in [Saa86]):

```
processor Pi
seq
  for k=1 to n-1 do
    seq
      if i=k mod p then send the kth row to Pi+1
                  else
                     seq
                     receive the kth row from Pi-1
                        if i≠k-1 then send the kth row to Pi+1 endif
                     endseq
      endif
      perform eliminations for all rows m>k with pivot row k
    endseq
  endfor
endseq
```

Remark that, for machines based on a large network of interconnections with no shared-memory, the algorithms often take the form :

Loop
data communication via network
arithmetics operations in parallel
endloop

But although all parallel algorithms can be put in this form, it is not necessary the optimal form ([GVR]).

The execution time can be computed as follows. Assuming that the rows are distributed using the second strategy described in the preceding paragraph, the processor which contains row n is P_p and it will end the process. The delays are introduced by the communication protocol and it will be easy to include them into the communication time. Hence we define the communication time as the total execution time when the computation time has a zero cost. A delay appears either when a processor is idle waiting for receiving the pivot row or when a processor is idle waiting for sending a pivot row to a processor which is still in its computation phase.
The computing time is obtained as in [Saa86] and with our vectorial architecture we get

$$T^{pr}_{comp} = (n-1)\, e\, t + \left(\frac{n^3}{3p} + \frac{(p-1)}{4p} n^2 + \left(\frac{9p-p^2-12}{12p} \right) n \right) t$$

For the communication time we assume that a send and a receive acting on rows of the same size take the same time and we divide the process in three parts. First the start-up of the pipeline will take (p-1) sends of the first pivot row (length n) to arrive in P_p. The execution of the eliminations will be decomposed in (n-p) steps of three sends (=receive), two for real communications and one for synchronisation in message passing (as it is shown in the figure 2 by the rectangular schemes). The third part of the process for the pth processor will take (p-3) steps composed of one receive and one waiting time of length (n-number of pivot row) and the last receive of length two.

$$T^{pr}_{comm} = (p-1)(n\tau+\beta) + \sum_{j=1}^{n-p} 3((n-j)\tau+\beta) + \sum_{j=n-p+1}^{n-3} 2((n-j)\tau+\beta) + 2\tau + \beta$$

$$T^{pr}_{comm} = \left(\frac{3n^2}{2} + np - \frac{5n}{2} - \frac{p^2}{2} + \frac{p}{2} - 4 \right) \tau + (3n+6)\,\beta$$

Notice that the formula given in [Saa86] is not exact, since the delays were not taken into account.

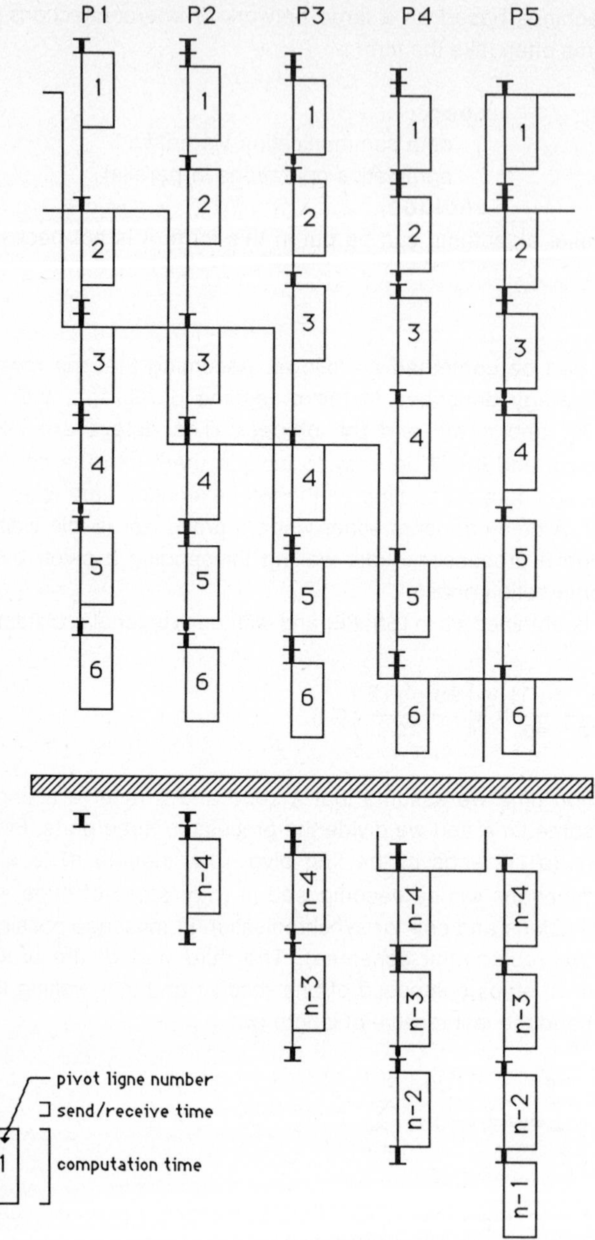

Figure 2 : time decomposition of the process using the PR algorithm

5 Local Pivots Ring Algorithm

Let us analyse the PR algorithm in order to reduce the delays due to communications. One major loss of communication time comes from the pipelining of the pivot rows. Indeed, the basic operation of each processor is to combine two rows with the same number of non-zero elements in order to introduce a new zero. Note that, contrarily to Given's eliminations algorithms [CDT], one of the two rows is not modified. So this row can be any row of the matrix A with a good configuration (i.e. the good number of zeros before the first non-zero element).

$$\begin{pmatrix} 1 & 0 \\ -\frac{a_{j1}}{a_{i1}} & 1 \end{pmatrix} \begin{pmatrix} a_{i1} & a_{i2} & \cdots & a_{in} \\ a_{j1} & a_{j2} & \cdots & a_{jn} \end{pmatrix} = \begin{pmatrix} a_{i1} & a_{i2} & \cdots & a_{in} \\ 0 & \alpha_{j2} & \cdots & \alpha_{jn} \end{pmatrix}$$

Figure 3: Elimination of a_{j1}

Each processor sends one row to its right neighbour (we assume that at the kth step of the elimination process, this row has a good configuration, i.e. the (k-1)th first elements are zeros and the kth is non-zero). It simultaneously receives one row from its left neighbour. Then it performs the corresponding elimination using this row as the pivot row. Clearly at step k of the elimination process, the processor which contains the kth row does not need to receive a pivot row from its left neighbour since it can use its kth row. Note that the important fact is that the kth row has not to be modified because it has its final configuration. So we can use the pivot row coming from the left neighbour but do not perform any elimination with the kth row. To be clear we describe first the sequential form of the algorithm.

LP sequential algorithm :

```
for k=1 to n-1 do
   for i=n to k+1 do
      eliminate a_ik using rows i and (i-k) (mod p)+k-1
   endfor
endfor
```

Row	Proc												
1	1	*											
2	2	1	*										
3	3	2	2	*									
4	4	3	3	3	*								
5	1	4	4	4	4	*							
6	2	1	5	5	5	5	*						
7	3	2	2	6	6	6	6	*					
8	4	3	3	3	7	7	7	7	*				
9	1	4	4	4	4	8	8	8	8	*			
10	2	1	5	5	5	5	9	9	9	9	*		
11	3	2	2	6	6	6	6	10	10	10	10	*	
12	4	3	3	3	7	7	7	7	11	11	11	11	*

figure 4: number r is in position (i,k) if a_{ik} is eliminated using rows i and r at the kth step of the LPR algorithm (p=4, n=12).

LPR Algorithm :

```
Processor P_i
seq
  for k=1 to n-1 do
    seq
      par
        receive a local pivot row from P_i-1 mod p
        send a local pivot row to P_i+1 mod p
      endpar
      compute eliminations on each row m > k
    endseq
  endfor
endseq
```

Remark that the send and receive operations can be performed in parallel since they act on different rows. A good way to implement the non-parallel communication scheme is that the even numbered processors execute a send (receive) while the odd execute a receive (send). It will just take two steps of communication.

Contrarily to the PR algorithm, the LPR algorithm can be executed in a synchronous manner, since the synchronisation is obtained from the send/receive protocol. The execution of the algorithm is described in the next figure .

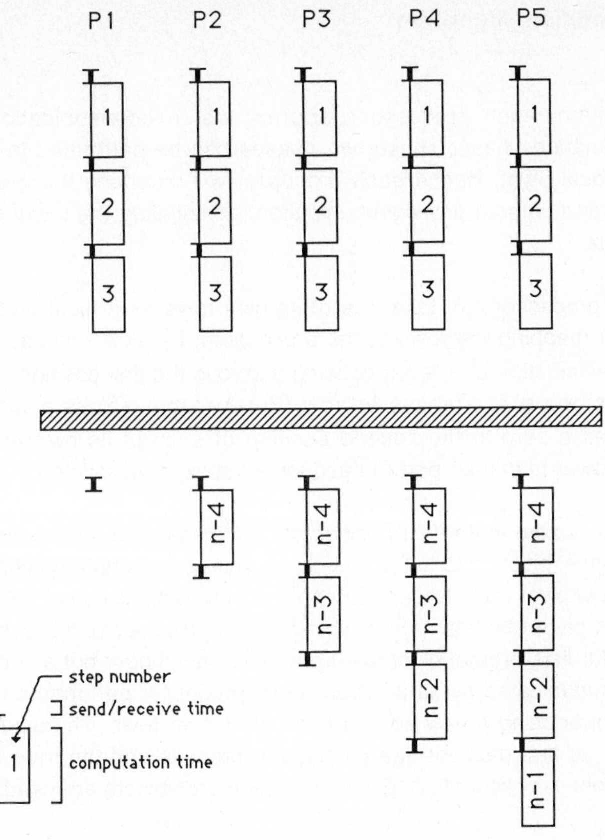

Figure 5: time decomposition of the process using LPR algorithm

The execution time can be computed as follows. The last processor executes n-2 steps which consist of a communication time (send/receive of length n-step+1) and a computation time (rows of length n-step). The last step consists of only one receive and a computation time. The computation time is equal to the computation time of the BR algorithm since the idle time of synchronisation is included in the communication time.

$$T^{lpr}_{comm} = \sum_{j=1}^{n-1}((n-j+1)\,\tau + \beta) = \left(\frac{n^2}{2}+\frac{n}{2}-1\right)\tau + (n-1)\,\beta$$

6 Local Pivot Modified Algorithm

In the LPR algorithm, each processor performs first a communication phase before executing the elimination phase. These two phases can be performed in a reverse order, using an internal local pivot. Hence each processor will introduce the greatest number of zeroes in its own rows without any communication, annihilating the lower triangular part of its n/p times n matrix.

At step one, each processor can take one of its own rows as a local pivot. Assuming the second strategy for mapping the rows to the processors, P_i takes row i as a local pivot and then executes the elimination phase (introducing a zero in the first position of each of its own rows). Then it uses one of the processed row (P_i takes row i+p) as another internal local pivot and introduces a zero in the second position of each of its own rows. This can be repeated until the lower triangular part of each local matrix is annihilated.

In order to introduce a zero in the first position of its first row, the processor receives a copy of the first internal local pivot of its left neighbour (sending to its right neighbour a copy of its own first internal local pivot row). Notice that the first processor does not need to perform this elimination since its pivot row has its final configuration. Hence the first processor does not receive a copy of the first internal pivot row from its left neighbour but a copy of the second. Using the data communicated by its neigbour each processor performs an elimination step which consists in introducing a new zero in each of its own rows. The algorithm goes on in the same way. Let us first describe the elimination process and the rows used in order to annihilate the element in position (i,k), assuming that p processors are used.

Elimination process in the LPM algorithm :

```
for k=1 to n-1 do
   for i=n to k+1 do
      eliminate a_ik using rows i and f(i,k,p)
   endfor
endfor
```

where f(i,k,p)=

```
if i≤p then f:=i-1
else if k≤⌈(i-p)/p⌉ then f:=i mod' p + (k-1)p
      else if k>i-p then if i mod p=1 then f:=i+p-1
                                       else f:=i-1
            else f:=i-p
```

and r mod's= if r=as then s
else r mod s

Row	Proc												
1	1	*											
2	2	1	*										
3	3	2	2	*									
4	4	3	3	3	*								
5	1	1	8	8	8	*							
6	2	2	2	5	5	5	*						
7	3	3	3	3	6	6	6	*					
8	4	4	4	4	4	7	7	7	*				
9	1	1	5	5	5	5	12	12	12	*			
10	2	2	6	6	6	6	6	9	9	9	*		
11	3	3	7	7	7	7	7	7	10	10	10	*	
12	4	4	8	8	8	8	8	8	8	11	11	11	*

Figure 6: number r is in position (i,k) if a_{ik} is eliminated using rows i and r in the LPM algorithm (p=4, n=12).

LPM Algorithm :

```
Processor P_i
seq
  for k=1 to n-1 do
    seq
      lpr_i:=i+È((k-i)/p)˘p
      while lpr_i<n do
        if rows m_1,m_2,...>lpr_i inside P_i have the same number of
        zeros in their first places
        then
          P_i executes eliminations on rows m_1,m_2,.. using row lpr_i
        endif
        lpr_i:=lpr_i+ p
      endwhile
      send/receive the good rows (using function f (i,k,p))
    endseq
  endfor
endseq
```

The execution of the algorithm is described in figure 8.

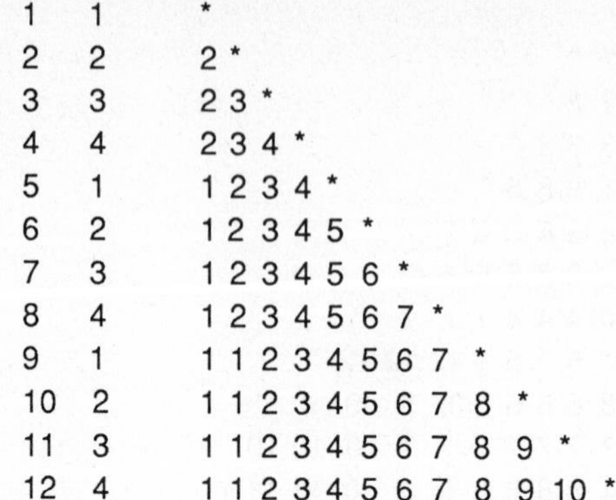

Row	Proc	
1	1	*
2	2	2 *
3	3	2 3 *
4	4	2 3 4 *
5	1	1 2 3 4 *
6	2	1 2 3 4 5 *
7	3	1 2 3 4 5 6 *
8	4	1 2 3 4 5 6 7 *
9	1	1 1 2 3 4 5 6 7 *
10	2	1 1 2 3 4 5 6 7 8 *
11	3	1 1 2 3 4 5 6 7 8 9 *
12	4	1 1 2 3 4 5 6 7 8 9 10 *

Figure 7: number r is in position (i,k) if a_{ik} is eliminated at the rth step of the LPM algorithm (p=4, n=12).

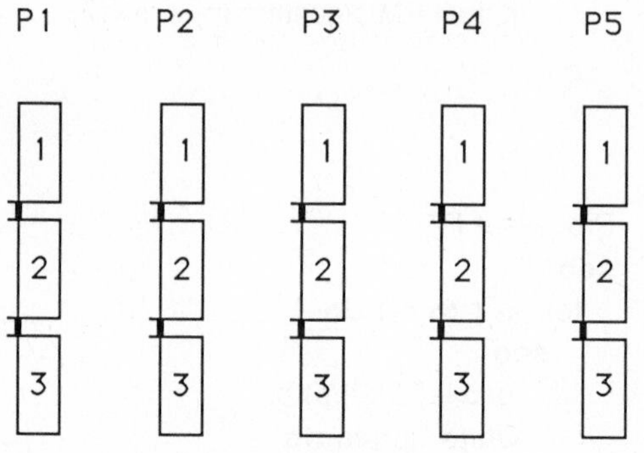

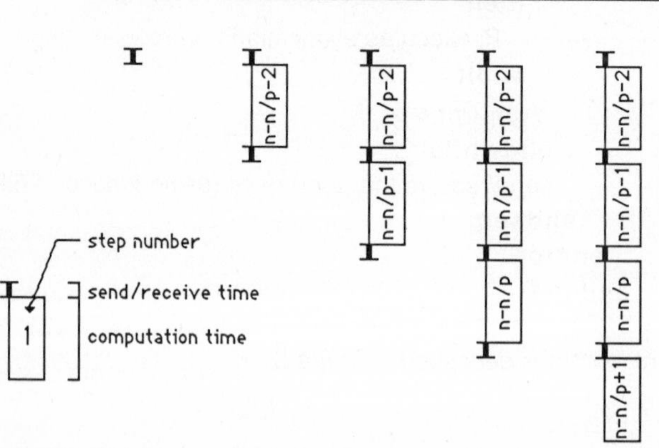

Figure 8: time decomposition of the process using LPM algorithm

The computation time is the same as in the previous algorithms. The communication time for the last processor is reduce to n-n/p-1 steps of a send/receive transmission and one step with just one receive transmission. There is a gain in transmission when the pivot row is inside the processor. We obtain:

$$T^{lpm}_{comm} = \sum_{j=1}^{n-1}((n-j+1)\,\tau + \beta) - \sum_{q=1}^{\frac{n}{p}-1}((n-qp+1)\,\tau + \beta)$$

$$T^{lpm}_{comm} = \left(\left(\frac{n^2}{2}+n\right)\left(1-\frac{1}{p}\right)\right)\tau + \left(n\left(1-\frac{1}{p}\right)\right)\beta$$

The number of β can be reduced by increasing the length of the messages i.e. if each processor sends several rows to his neighbour. The internal control may be more complicated because of the choice of the good rows to send. It could lead to p steps of communication, containing one β, with message of length n/p.

7 Comparison of the various algorithms

Let us recall the execution times of the BR, PR, LPR and LPM algorithms. They are listed in the following array under the hypothesis that p<<n.

$$T_{comp} = \frac{n^3}{3p}\,t + O(n^2)$$

$$T^{r}_{comm} = \frac{\gamma^{r}_{n,p}}{2}(n^2\tau_r + np\beta_r) + O(n) \qquad 1 \le \gamma^{r}_{n,p} \le 2$$

$$T^{h}_{comm} = \frac{\gamma^{h}_{n,p}}{2}(n^2\tau_h + 2n\log_2 p\,\beta_h) + O(n) \qquad 1 \le \gamma^{h}_{n,p} \le 2$$

$$T^{c}_{comm} = \frac{n^2}{2}\tau_c + (n-1)\,\beta_c + O(n\tau_c)$$

$$T^{pr}_{comm} = \frac{3}{2}n^2\tau + 3n\beta + O(n\tau) + O(\beta)$$

$$T^{lpr}_{comm} = \frac{1}{2}n^2\tau + n\beta + O(n\tau) + O(\beta)$$

$$T^{lpm}_{comm} = \left(1-\frac{1}{p}\right)\frac{n^2}{2}\tau + \left(1-\frac{1}{p}\right)n\beta + O(n\tau) + O(\beta)$$

We deduce that all the algorithms have the same computation times. With respect to the communication times, the complete or the hypercube networks do not present any advantage over the ring topology. From an algorithmic point of view the local pivot modified algorithm seems the most efficient.

8 Incorporating pivoting strategies

It is well known [GVL] that in order to obtain a precise solution Gaussian elimination must include a pivoting strategy. In general for numerical problems the following procedure (partial pivoting) is used: at the kth step take as the pivot row the one whose kth element has the greatest absolute value [GVL]. Recently it has been shown that pairwise pivoting is sufficient [Sor].

However for algebraic computations in finite fields matrices with of a great number of zeros are frequent. When we consider for example matrices over GF(p), p a prime number, the probability for an element to be zero is 1/p. In this case pivoting is different from partial pivoting since the first non zero element is convenient. We could be lead to search for this element not only in the kth column but also in the kth row. This is a variant to the global pivoting strategy where the search is extended to both row and column but is interrupted as soon as a non zero element is encountered.

Let us look how we can incorporate these strategies in the preceding algorithms. Recall first that the rows of the matrices are distributed equally among the p processors. Hence local strategies will always be better than global ones.

Partial or pairwise pivoting restricted to the rows of each processor can be introduced without any difficulty. In the BR and PR algorithms the processor which holds the kth row searches among its rows for a good one, permutes the kth row and the pivot row and sends it to all the processors. In the LPR and LPM algorithms each processor executes the preceding procedure for searching a pivot row before executing each step of elimination.

Let us now study how we can incorporate global strategies. Assume that we would like to introduce a complete partial pivoting (search over the whole kth column). In this case the LPR and LPM are no longer suitable since they are based on local pivots. Hence we shall only restrict ourselves to the BR and PR algorithms.

We consider first the case where we are searching a non zero element in the kth column. This is done using an election procedure. At the kth step of the BR algorithm, each processor begins a search for a row with a non zero element in its kth position. When a processor finds such a row it sends it to the processor P(k) (the processor which holds the kth row). As soon as P(k) receives a candidate, it incorporates the pivot row in its own rows (this is not necessary if there is such a row in P(k)), permutes it with the kth row and sends the pivot row to all the processors with a flag in order to show that it is the good one! Various procedures can be incorporated to this election procedure in order to disminish the number of messages in the network. The pivoting time is bounded by the time to search a non zero element over n-k+1 elements plus the time to broadcast a row.

A simple way to avoid the latter broadcast is the following. At the step k, P(k) searches among its rows for a convenient one and then executes the permutation between the two rows. If all the elements in position k are zeroes, P(k) searches for a non zero element in the kth row and executes a column permutation. Together with the pivot row it sends to the other processors the number of the corresponding column. Before executing an elimination step each processor will execute the column transposition. The pivoting time is bounded by the time to search a non zero element over 2(n-k+1) elements plus the time to execute two transpositions.

For the PR algorithm, the election procedure is no longer useful. At the kth step of the algorithm, each processor begins a search for a row with a non zero element in its kth position (good row). If P(k) finds such a row, then it sends it to its right neigbour and executes the corresponding eliminations. When a processor receives a good row from its left neighbour, it only transmits this row before executing the eliminations. If P(k) cannot find a row with a non zero kth element, it sends one of its rows and goes to the next step (since no eliminations are necessary). When a processor receives a bad row from its left neighbour and possesses a good one, it only transmits this good row and executes the eliminations. If it does not possess any good row, it sends one of its rows and goes to the next step. Hence this implies only a very minor modification in the original algorithm.

References

[Bro] L. BROCHARD, Communication and control costs on loosely coupled multiprocessors, Preprint, Ecole Nationale des Ponts et Chaussées, 1986.

[CDT] M. COSNARD, M. DAOUDI, B. TOURANCHEAU, Communication dans les Reseaux de Processeurs et Complexité d'Algorithmes, RR 636, IMAG Grenoble, 1986

[CMRT] M. COSNARD, M. MARRAKCHI, Y. ROBERT, D. TRYSTRAM, Parallel Gaussian elimination on an MIMD Computer, to appear in Parallel Computing

[GVR] D. GANNON, J. VAN ROSENDALE, On the impact of communication in the design of parallel algorithms, IEEE T.C. 33, 12 (1984) 1180-1194

[Gei] G.A. GEIST, Efficient parallel LU factorisation with pivoting on a hypercube multiprocessor, ORNL Preprint 6211 (1985)

[GH] G.A. GEIST, M.T. HEATH, Parallel Cholesky factorisation on a hypercube multiprocessor, ORNL Preprint 6190 (1985)

[Gen] W.M. GENTLEMAN, Some complexity results for matrix computations on parallel processors, JACM 25, 1 (1978), 112-115

[GVL] G.H. GOLUB, C.F. VAN LOAN, Matrix Computations, The John Hopkins Univ. Press, 1983

[Hoa] C.A.R. HOARE, Communicating Sequential Processes, Prentice Hall, Series in Computer Science (1985)

[HB] K. HWANG, F. BRIGGS, Parallel Processing and Computer Architecture, Mc Graw Hill 1984

[ISS] I.C.F. IPSEN, Y. SAAD, M.H. SCHULTZ, Complexity of dense linear system solution on a multiprocessor ring, Lin. Alg. Appl. (1986).

[LKK] R.E. LORD, J.S. KOWALIK, S.P. KUMAR, Solving linear algebraic equations on an MIMD computer, J. ACM 30 (1), 1983, p 103-117

[Row] D. ROWETH, Design and performance analysis of transputer arrays, J. Syst. Softw. 1,2 (1986) 21-22

[Saa85] Y. SAAD, Communication complexity of the Gaussian elimination algorithm on multiprocessors, Research report 348, Computer Science Dpt., Yale University (1985)

[Saa86] Y. SAAD, Gaussian elimination on hypercubes, in Parallel Algorithms and Architectures, Eds. M. Cosnard et all., North-Holland (1986) 5-18

[SS] Y. SAAD, M.H. SCHULTZ, Topological properties of hypercubes, Research Report 389, Computer Science Dpt., Yale University (1985)

[Sor] D.C. SORENSEN, Analysis of pairwise pivoting in Gaussian elimination, Tech. Rep., MCS-TM-26, Argonne National Laboratory, 1984

BASIC LINEAR ALGEBRA COMPUTATIONS ON THE SPERRY ISP

J.J. Du Croz
N.A.G. Ltd, 256 Banbury Road, Oxford OX2 7DE, England

J. Wasniewski
UNI-C, DTH, Bygning 305, DK-2800 Lyngby, Denmark

1. INTRODUCTION

This paper describes the results of running some tests to time basic linear algebraic computations on the Sperry 1100/90 series computer with ISP (Integrated Scientific Processor). The tests were undertaken in order to investigate how best to implement linear algebra subroutines from the NAG Library on the Sperry ISP.

2. THE SPERRY ISP

The ISP is tightly coupled to a Sperry 1100/90 mainframe system. It performs high-speed floating-point scalar and vector operations, using a pipelined machine organization. It has: 16 vector registers, containing either 64 single-precision numbers or 32 double-precision numbers, a high-speed random access cache memory of 4k words, primarily for storing the most frequently used scalar variables; and a high-performance storage unit (HPSU) of 4,194,304 words, partitioned into 8 banks of 524,288 words each. The theoretical peak performance is 133 megaflops (millions of floating-point operations per second) in single precision, and 67 megaflops in double precision.

The UFTN Fortran 77 compiler performs a considerable amount of automatic vectorisation, as well as providing array-processing extensions such as are proposed for Fortran 8x. In our tests we did not use these extensions; the compiler succeeded in vectorising all the loops that we wished it to.

The tests described below confirm that the ISP has similar performance-characteristics to other machines whose architecture is based on vector-registers, such as the Cray machines. This means that much of the work that has been done to implement NAG routines efficiently on other vector-register machines can be applied directly to the ISP. Some authors (e.g. Dongarra and Eisenstat [4]) distinguish between "vector speeds" and "supervector speeds" achievable on such machines. "Supervector speeds" are achieved when a sequence of vector operations is performed and the ratio of memory references to floating-point operations is reduced, as in the matrix-vector operations described in Section 5.

3. THE TIMING TESTS

The tests included timings of:

simple vector operations, each involving $O(n)$ scalar operations;

matrix-vector operations, each involving $O(n^2)$ scalar operations;

matrix operations, each involving $O(n^3)$ scalar operations.

For the results of similar tests on other high performance computers, see Daly and Du Croz [1].

The timing programs were coded in standard Fortran 77, and were compiled with the UFTN compiler, version 2R1, and run with Language Support System version 4R1. The programs were run in both single and double precision, but in this paper we concentrate on the single precision results. The pattern of the double precision results was very similar, although the speeds were slower. Some timings were also obtained for routines in the Extended Math Library (EML). Timings were measured using the library routine CLKCHC. Different timing runs of the same operation showed variations of up to 10%; the results presented were obtained in single runs: no attempt has been made to average the results of several runs.

4. VECTOR OPERATIONS

Two simple vector operations were studied: DOT (i.e an inner product) and AXPY (i.e. the addition of a multiple of one vector to another). The names are taken from the BLAS of Lawson, Hanson, Kincaid and Krogh [5]. These operations account for much of the computation in many fundamental algorithms of numerical linear algebra.

Figure 1 shows the speed of these operations when the vectors involved are contiguous (stride = 1). They show that a DOT operation is asymptotically twice as fast as AXPY. Also that in-line Fortran code is faster than EML library routines for both operations except for long vector-lengths.

The speeds of DOT and AXPY are affected by the way the vectors are stored in memory. DOT operations may be slowed down by a factor of 5, and AXPY operations by a factor of 4 when the stride between vector elements is unfavourable. These effects are typical symptoms of memory bank conflicts.

Corresponding results were obtained for DOT and AXPY operation on complex vectors. The pattern of results is the same, but the speeds are faster: this is typical of machines with vector registers - complex arithmetic involves a higher ratio of floating-point operations to memory references.

The timings for vector operations might suggest that the most efficient way to implement higher-level linear algebra computations on the ISP would be by means of inner-product operations. This is not so, however, as is seen when we look at matrix-vector operations.

5. MATRIX-VECTOR OPERATIONS

Four matrix-vector operations were studied: $c := c + Ab$; $c := c + A^T b$; $b := Lb$; $b := L^T b$. Here a, b and c are vectors, A is a square matrix, and L is a lower triangular matrix (stored in the lower triangle of a 2-dimensional array). Many computations in linear algebra can be organised in terms of matrix-vector operations of this kind - see Dongarra, Du Croz, Hammarling and Hanson [3]: the above operations correspond to the routines SGEMV and STRMV of that paper.

Each of the four operations can be coded either as a sequence of DOT operations or as a sequence of AXPY operations; the corresponding speeds for the operation $c := c + Ab$ are shown in Figure 2. (These results all refer to in-line Fortran code.) The third graph on the figure (labelled "unrolled") shows the speeds obtained when four successive AXPY operations are combined by the technique of "unrolling" vector loops (Dongarra and Eisenstat [4]). The fourth graph, labelled "coded MV routine", shows the speeds obtained by machine-language coding.

Figure 3 shows the effect of the unrolling technique in more detail: i.e. how the speed of the operation $c := c + Ab$ varies with the "depth" of unrolling (i.e the number of AXPY operations combined together); a depth of 4 gives a reasonable compromise between increased efficiency and greater complexity of code.

All the timings may of course be improved on with newer versions of the Fortran compiler or the EML Library. Figure 4 shows the very dramatic improvements observed in the performance of the unrolled code since we first began testing.

Note that figures 2, 3 and 4 show evidence of discontinuities in the graphs when n is a multiple of 64: this is the effect of the fixed length of the vector registers.

Table 1 summarizes the timings obtained for all four matrix-vector operations for $n = 320$ (n is the order of the matrix). The results of Section 4 show that at this value of n the speeds have not all reached their asymptotic rates, but this is a reasonably large value of n for dense linear algebra computations. The speeds for the operation $c := c + Ab$ may be compared with the speeds of other machines in Table 1 of Daly and Du Croz [1]. Most of the speeds given in these tables - and those shown in Figures 2, 3 and 4 - were obtained when the matrices A and L were stored in a 2-dimensional array with leading dimension 330 (with the aim of minimizing the presumed effects of memory-bank conflicts); the operations were also timed with the leading dimension set to 320: in some cases the speeds were significantly slower and they are given in parentheses in Table 1.

Table 1: speeds of matrix-vector operations (single precision)

Operation	DOT	AXPY	Unrolled
$c := c + Ab$	32 (17)	57	91 megaflops
$c := c + A^T b$	52	38 (18)	53 (20)
$b := Lb$	24 (14)	35	51
$b := L^T b$	31	30 (16)	40 (18)

In the operation $c := c + Ab$ the AXPY form works with contiguous vectors (stride = 1) while in the DOT form one of the vectors is a row of the matrix, hence has stride equal to the leading dimension of the array. In the operation $c := c + A^T b$, the DOT form works with contiguous vectors while in the AXPY form one of the vectors is a row of the matrix. The operations $b := Lb$ and $b := L^T b$ behave similarly, but here the vectors vary in length from n to 1 (the average length is $n/2$) so it is only to be expected that they will be slower.

6. MATRIX OPERATIONS

As examples of matrix computations we have timed preliminary implementations of selected routines from the Mark 11 NAG Library. The routines have been implemented as described by Daly and Du Croz [1] with the bulk of the computation occurring in 'kernel' routines each of which performs a matrix-vector operation similar to those studied in section 5.

Table 2 shows times in milliseconds (not speeds) for n = 50, 100, or 200. Each entry contains three timings in the following order:

Sperry ISP (single precision)
Sperry ISP (double precision)
Cray-1S (single precision)

Of course the times may be improved upon after further investigations and developments to the Fortran compiler. Note that at Mark 12 the NAG Library routines rely on the Level 2 BLAS of Dongarra, Du Croz, Hammarling and Hanson [3], rather than on the kernel routines used at Mark 11, so their performance will then be determined by the efficiency of available implementations of the Level 2 BLAS.

Table 2: time taken by selected NAG routines on ISP and Cray-1S

Routine	Function	n=50	n=100	n=200
F01CKF	Matrix multiplication	6	32	215
		9	56	372
		5	34	244
F03AFF	LU-factorization (for solving	15	56	239
	systems of linear equations)	17	69	318
		5	22	120
F01AXF	QR-factorization (for solving	11	52	291
	linear least-squares problems)	14	69	425
		9	49	297
F01AGF	Reduction of symmetric matrix to	18	75	366
	tridiagonal form (for computing	21	95	511
	eigenvalues and eigenvectors)	9	46	274
F01AKF	Reduction of unsymmetric matrix	14	56	281
	to Hessenberg form (for computing	17	76	386
	eigenvalues and eigenvectors)	5	25	150

Other figures for the performance of the ISP in solving systems of linear equations have been published by Dongarra [2].

7. CONCLUSION

The Sperry ISP appears to be an attractive machine for implementing standard linear algebraic algorithms. It has similar characteristics to other vector-processing machines with an architecture based on vector-registers. Good performance of standard algorithms can be obtained via efficient implementations of matrix-vector operations, and we strongly recommend that these are added to the EML Library.

REFERENCES

[1] C. Daly and J.J. Du Croz, Performance of subroutine library on vector-processing machines, Computer Physics Comm. 37, 181-186, 1985.

[2] J.J. Dongarra, Performance of various computers using standard linear equations software in a Fortran environment, Argonne National Laboratory report MCS/TM23, 1986.

[3] J.J. Dongarra, J.J. Du Croz, S.J. Hammarling and R.J. Hanson, An extended set of Fortran basic linear algebra subprograms, NAG technical report TR3/87, 1987, and Argonne National Laboratory report MCS/TM41 (revision 3), 1986.

[4] J.J. Dongarra and S. C. Eisenstat, Squeezing the most out of an algorithm in Cray Fortran, ACM Trans. Math. Software 10, 221-230, 1984.

[5] C.L. Lawson, R.J. Hanson, D. R. Kincaid and F. T. Krogh, Basic linear algebra subprograms for Fortran usage, ACM Trans. Math. Software 5, 308-323, 1979.

ACKNOWLEDGMENTS

We thank T. Kridle (Sperry) and E. Kofod (UNI-C) for enabling one of the authors (J.W) to visit the Sperry Corporation Test and Development Center in Roseville, Minnesota, and to have access to an ISP there. We also thank CILEA in Italy for access to their ISP.

Figure 1:

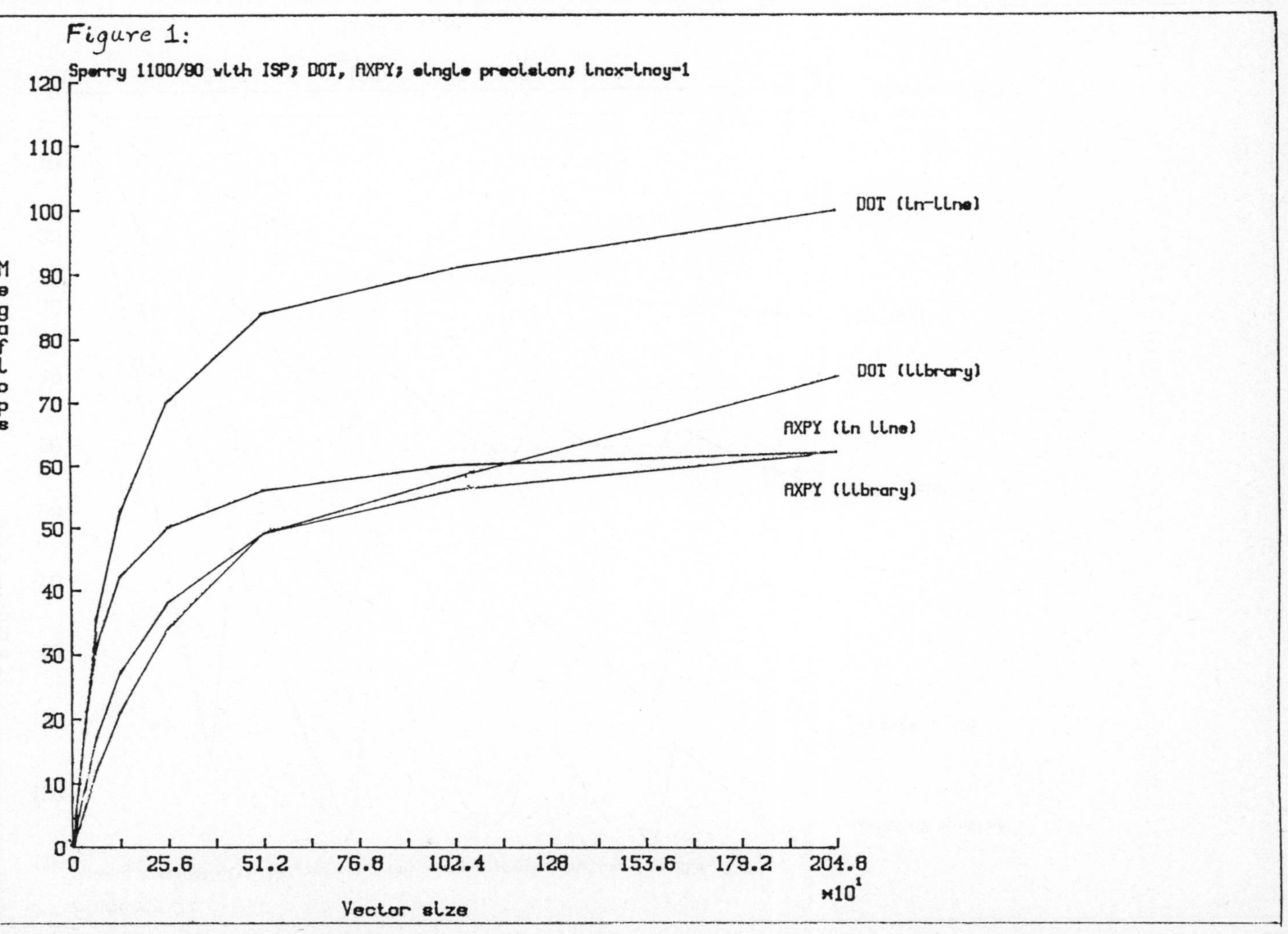
Sperry 1100/90 with ISP; DOT, AXPY; single precision; incx=incy=1
DOT (in-line)
DOT (library)
AXPY (in line)
AXPY (library)
Megaflops
120
110
100
90
80
70
60
50
40
30
20
10
0
0
25.6
51.2
76.8
102.4
128
153.6
179.2
204.8
x10^1
Vector size

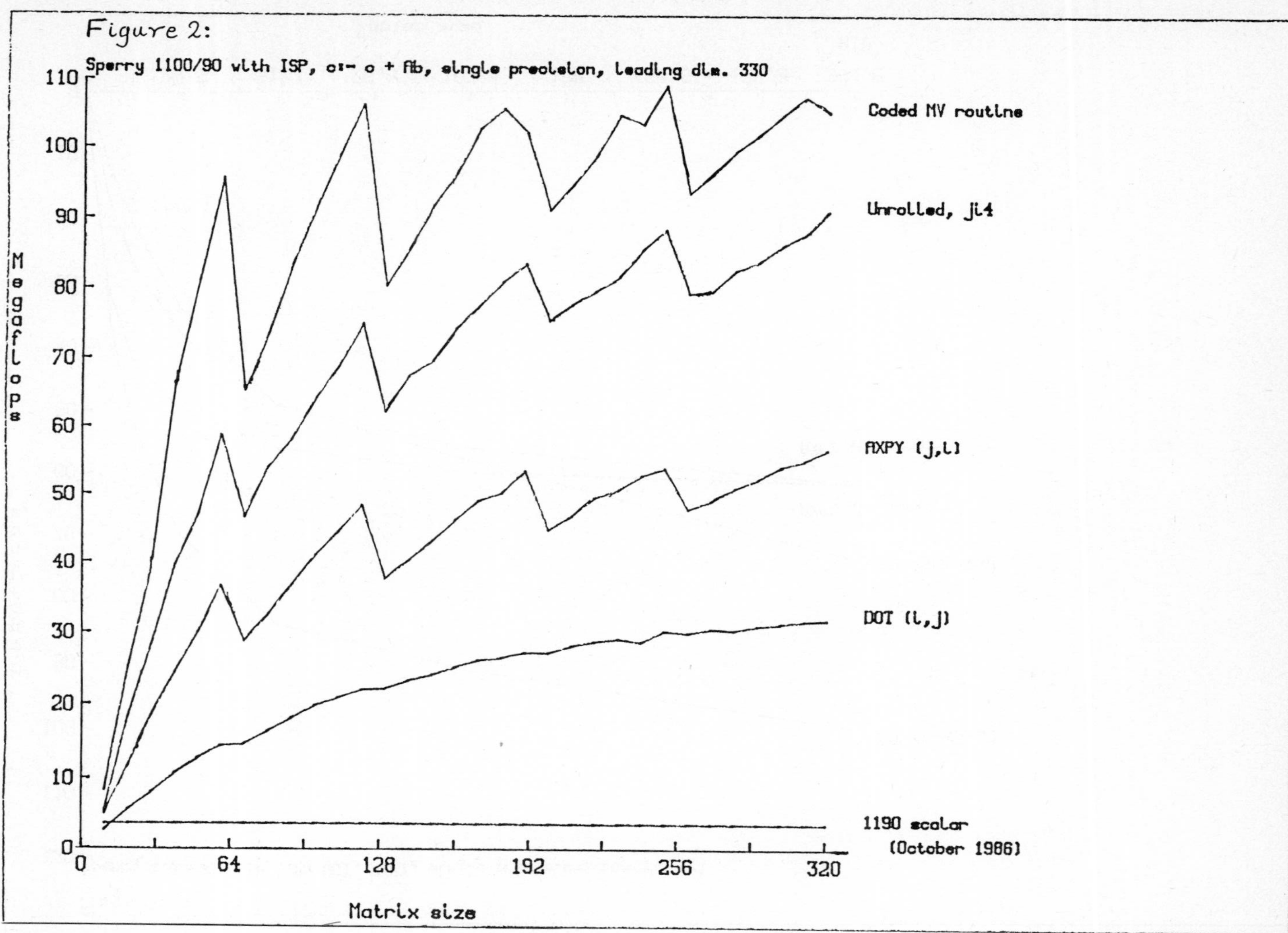

Figure 2:
Sperry 1100/90 with ISP, a:= a + Ab, single precision, leading dim. 330
Coded MV routine
Unrolled, j:4
AXPY (j,i)
DOT (i,j)
1190 scalar
(October 1986)
Megaflops
110
100
90
80
70
60
50
40
30
20
10
0
0
64
128
192
256
320
Matrix size

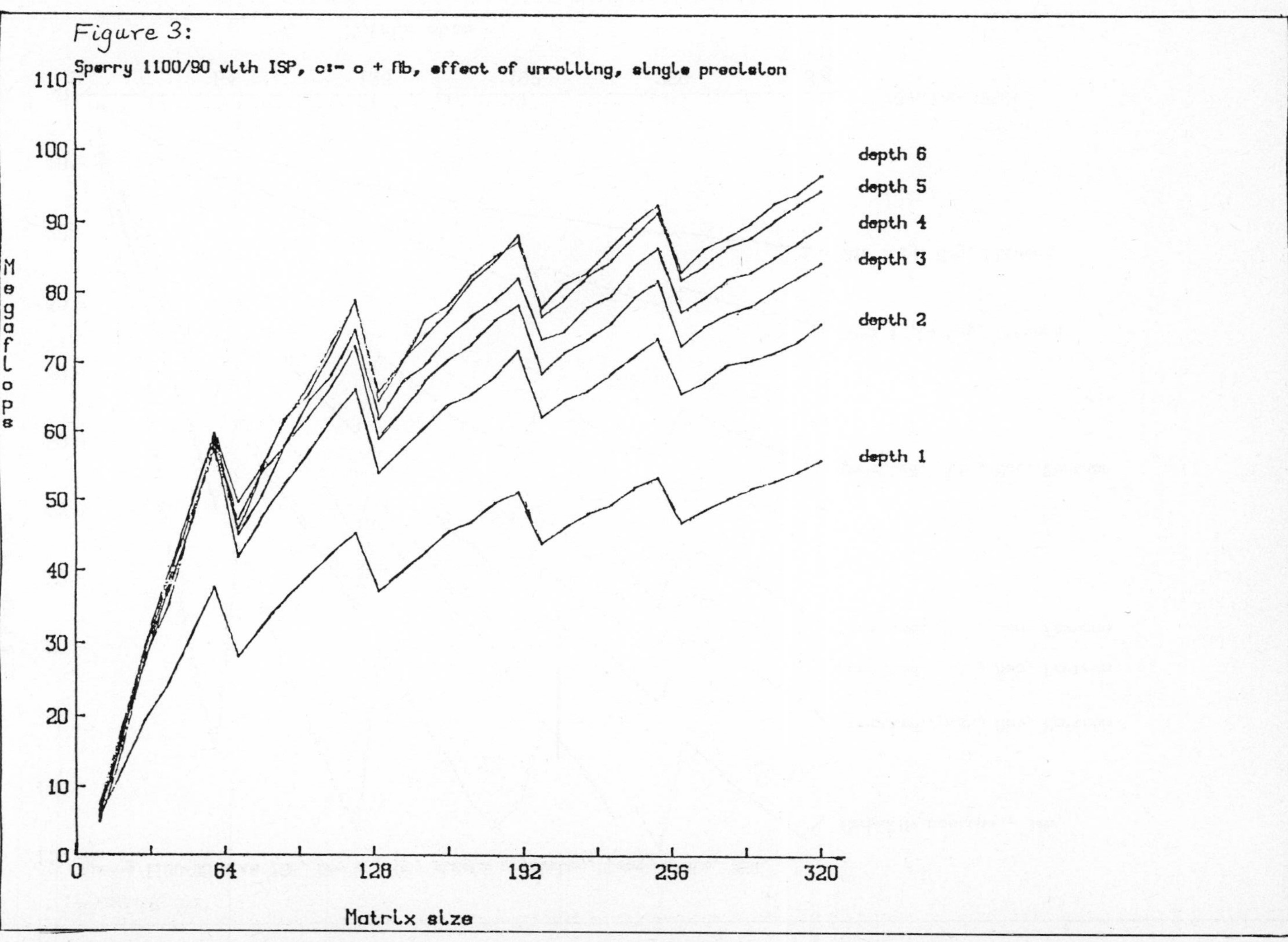
Sperry 1100/90 with ISP, c:= c + fb, effect of unrolling, single precision
Megaflops
110
100
90
80
70
60
50
40
30
20
10
0
0
64
128
192
256
320
Matrix size
depth 6
depth 5
depth 4
depth 3
depth 2
depth 1

Figure 3:

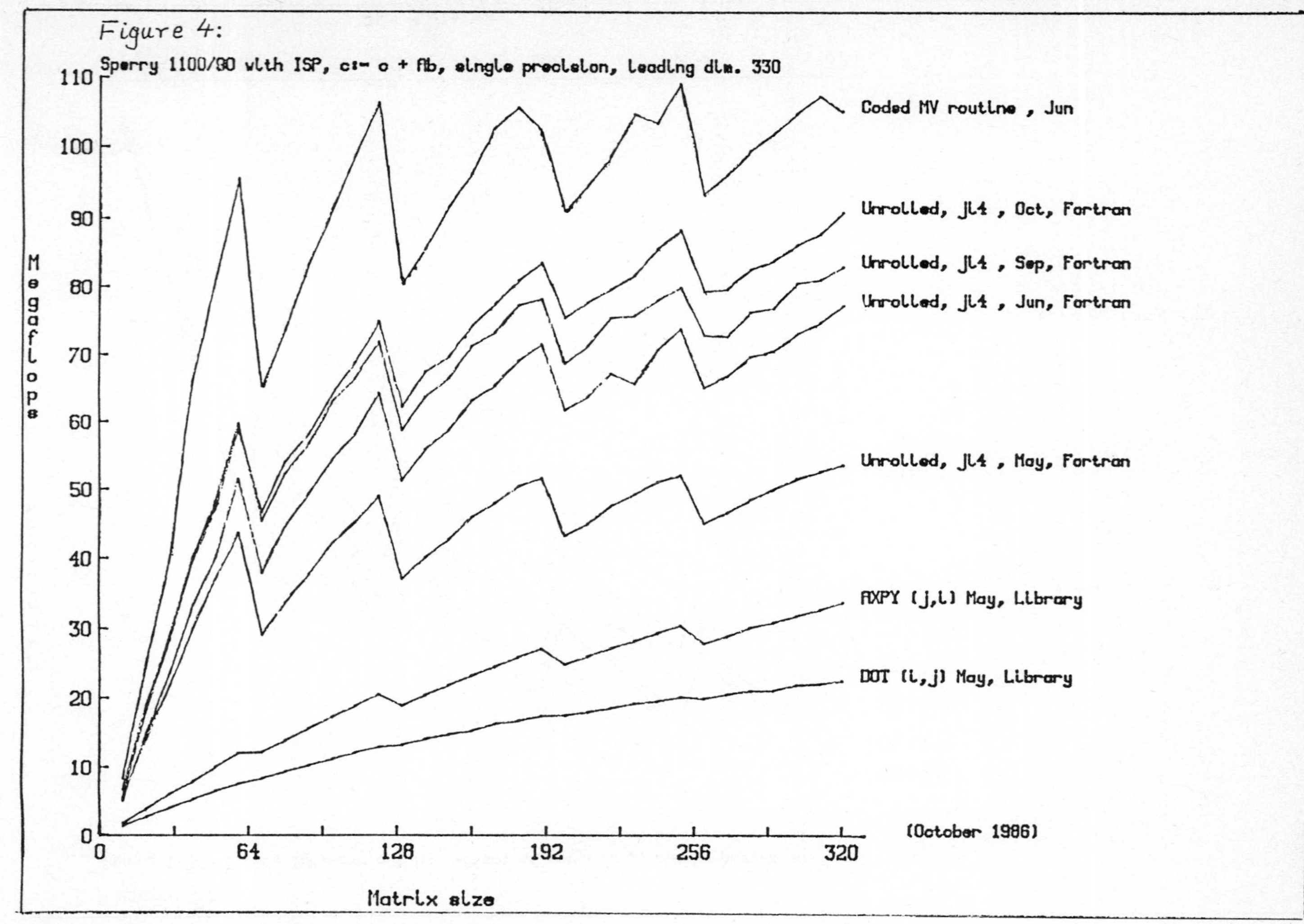
Sperry 1100/90 with ISP, c:= c + Ab, single precision, Leading dim. 330
Megaflops
110
100
90
80
70
60
50
40
30
20
10
0
0
64
128
192
256
320
Matrix size
Coded MV routine , Jun
Unrolled, jl4 , Oct, Fortran
Unrolled, jl4 , Sep, Fortran
Unrolled, jl4 , Jun, Fortran
Unrolled, jl4 , May, Fortran
AXPY (j,i) May, Library
DOT (i,j) May, Library
(October 1986)

Figure 4:

Future Scientific Programming on Parallel Machines

Arvind
Laboratory for Computer Science
Massachusetts Institute of Technology
Cambridge, Massachusetts

Kattamuri Ekanadham
IBM T.J.Watson Research Center
Yorktown Heights, New York

June 3, 1987

Abstract

A language for large scientific applications should facilitate both the encoding and debugging of programs at the highest level possible, and the generation of efficient code for parallel machines. Often these two requirements cannot coexist, and trade-offs must be made. Functional and other declarative languages offer relief on both counts. The use of higher-order functions, especially in curried forms, can raise the level of programming dramatically. In addition, such languages often have straightforward operational semantics which admits tremendous opportunities for parallel execution. Programs in declarative languages thus eliminate the problem of "detecting parallelism". This paper illustrates programming in one such language, Id Nouveau, and contrasts it with programming in Fortran. Using an excerpt from an application known as SIMPLE, it is shown how a program can be composed in Id Nouveau from small functions that directly relate to the mathematical and physical concepts of the problem. The difficulty of expressing these concepts in Fortran is discussed. Finally, it is shown that by performing simple transformations, such as in-line substitution of functions, the resulting Id Nouveau code becomes as efficient as an equivalent Fortran program written to run efficiently on a parallel machine.

1. Introduction

The world's fastest computers have traditionally been used first in scientific computing. Yet, the level of programming, as represented in typical commercial scientific packages or in the large codes written in national laboratories, is remarkably low. The usual excuse for this situation is that high performance is the name of the game in scientific computing, and the programmer must exercise fine-grain control over the execution environment to tailor his program on a given machine. Since all important programs need to be modified, the program during its lifetime (often spanning more than a decade) gets so complicated that the original algorithm is obscured and the efficiency of the program becomes more a question of faith than reason.

These observations would be easy to ignore if the development of new codes employed modern computer science techniques. In fact, the advent of parallel high-speed computing seems to be causing a regression in programming. Further, the users are being told that these new software problems are a natural consequence of the need to develop new algorithms for parallel machines. There can be no argument that in due course more suitable algorithms will emerge for parallel computers. However, this does not imply that algorithms already in use are necessarily inappropriate for parallel machines. We believe it is the use of Fortran to implement these algorithms which is at the root of the problem.

Two interrelated techniques for the development of software for purported general-purpose parallel machines are identifiable in the present commercial environment. Both are geared to "dusty decks" of Fortran, though they can be applied to new

Fortran programs as well. One requires the programmer to *annotate* the program to indicate the opportunities for parallel execution, and the other requires the compiler to *detect* the program fragments that can be executed in parallel [14]. A typical annotation is "Do-all" to execute all iterations of a Do-loop in parallel. Similar annotations are usually available for concurrently executing the statements of a block. Parallel execution requires synchronization which often has to be coded explicitly, too. Machine-specific concerns often require classification of variables as local or global, cacheable or non-cacheable, ultimately making the program more and more obscure. Since annotations interact with the storage model of the language, the meaning of programs changes in subtle ways. Annotations are rarely robust. For example, nested "Do-all's" may not be permitted because Fortran does not have dynamic storage allocation. Worst of all, wrong annotations invariably make the behavior of the program *non-deterministic*, that is, time- and machine configuration-dependent, thereby creating a nightmare during debugging.

Detection of parallelism by a compiler is much more desirable from the user's point of view [14]. However, even the most sophisticated techniques to detect parallelism trip on trivial impediments such as conditionals, function calls, input/output statements, etc., and fail to unravel most of the parallelism present in the original algorithm. Some parallelizing compilers provide feedback to the user regarding where the compiler had difficulty in deciding about parallel execution (see discussion of the Fujitsu Fortran compiler in [11]). Based on these suggestions a programmer can often restructure the source code to be more suitable for parallel execution. In principle, there is no reason why such a compiler cannot also accept annotations to improve the quality of generated code. Useful as this methodology is for dealing with "dusty decks", it only confirms the lack of expressivity of the source language.

Perhaps one reason why languages like Fortran still dominate the scene is the control placed in the hands of the programmer, which is used for extracting the last ounce of perceived efficiency from a system. Despite the pain attached to its use, Fortran use is likely to continue until a viable alternative demonstrates comparable performance.

Functional and declarative languages are said to offer many advantages in this context [5,17]. Their declarative nature eliminates the overspecification of the order of evaluation. Their operational semantics when expressed in terms of rewrite rules automatically exposes the parallelism present in a program. Functional languages with higher-order functions elevate the level of programming so that abstractions can be built closer to the concepts in the problem domain. Functional programs are easier to reason about because their output is determinate, that is, independent of the order of evaluation. However, functional languages traditionally have lacked good facilities for manipulating arrays and matrices; simulating such structures using traditional functional data structures often results in excessive storage demand or unnecessarily sequential code [3]. A declarative language called *Id Nouveau* [12,4] has been proposed as a solution to some of these problems. It is a functional language augmented with a novel array-like data structure called *I-structures*. This language is being used to program the M.I.T. Tagged-Token Dataflow machine. In addition to the requirement of generating good code, *Id Nouveau* is also supposed to embody the advantages of declarative programming, that is, clear and concise code that is easy to understand and reason about. The objective of this paper is to show, by a realistic example, the expressive power of this language as well as its ability to bring out the parallelism in a specification automatically.

In Section 2, we describe the example which has been excerpted from a hydrodynamics simulation program known as the SIMPLE code [6]. In Sections 3.2 and 3.3, we describe some matrix abstractions which are useful for writing the SIMPLE code and, we believe, many other codes. In order to make the paper self-contained for readers unfamiliar with functional programming, basic notions of functions and *I-structures* are introduced in Section 3.1 using the *Id Nouveau* syntax. The reader is referred to [12,3] for a more detailed treatment of *Id Nouveau* and *I-structures*. Section

3.4 presents the *Id Nouveau* solution to the main example.[1] In Section 4, we point out the difficulties in imitating the declarative style of programming in Fortran. In Section 5, we show that with "in-line substitution" of functions, the performance of the *Id Nouveau* program of Section 3.4 becomes comparable to that of an equivalent Fortran program. Section 6 discusses some storage efficiency issues. Finally, Section 7 presents our conclusions.

2. An example: Problem description

Our example problem is an excerpt from a hydrodynamics and heat conduction simulation program known as the SIMPLE code [6]. The document [6], along with the associated Fortran program, was developed as a benchmark to evaluate various high performance machines and compilers. The problem is to simulate the behavior of a fluid in a sphere, using a Lagrangian formulation of equations. To simplify the problem, only a semi-circular cross-sectional area is considered for simulation, as shown in Figure 1. The area is divided into parcels by radial and axial lines as shown. Each parcel is delimited by four corners as illustrated in Figure 1. The corners are called *nodes*. The regions enclosed by 4 nodes are called *zones* (illustrated by the shaded area in Figure 1). In the Lagrangian formulation, the nodes are identified by mapping them onto a 2-dimensional logical grid, in which the grid points have coordinates (k, l) for some $kmin \leq k \leq kmax$, $lmin \leq l \leq lmax$. The product, $kmax * lmax$, is often referred to as the *grid size* of the problem. The following quantities are considered in the simulation.

---

1 A complete *Id Nouveau* program for SIMPLE has been developed by the authors and is reported in [8].

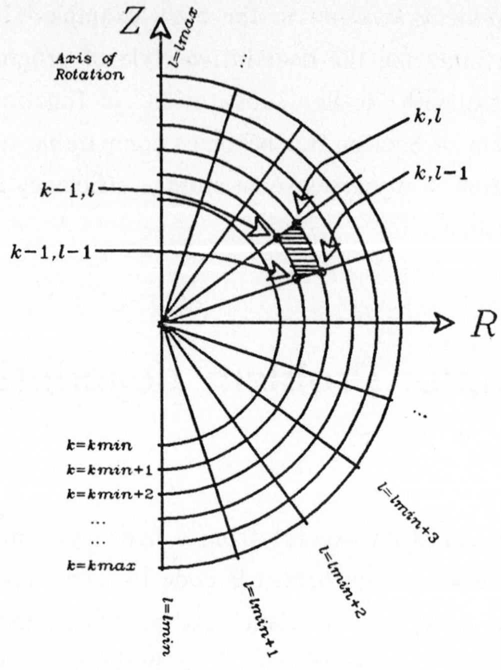

Figure 1: Fluid parcels in a 2-dimensional cross-section

1. $\vec{v}$: velocity components, u,w, of node (k,l) in the R-Z plane.
2. $\vec{x}$: coordinates, r,z, of node (k,l) in the R-Z plane.
3. α : Area of zone (k,l).
4. s : Volume of revolution per radian of zone (k,l).
5. ρ : Density of zone (k,l).
6. p : Pressure of zone (k,l).
7. q : Artificial Viscosity of zone (k,l).
8. ε : Energy within zone (k,l).
9. θ : Temperature of zone (k,l).

Each of these quantities is stored as a matrix of values, indexed by the indices of a node. The new values of these quantities are computed from the old after a time period of δt. Note that the first two quantities are associated with nodes and the remaining are associated with zones.

In order to incorporate appropriate boundary conditions, a fictitious layer of zones, called *ghost zones*, is added to the cross section, as depicted by the shaded area in Figure 2. Rows *kmin-1* and *kmax+1* and columns *lmin-1* and *lmax+1* contain the boundary nodes. Behavior of ghost zones is governed by the desired boundary conditions. Each quantity is associated permanently with a criterion to determine its boundary value. At each time step new boundary values for a quantity are computed according to the associated criterion.

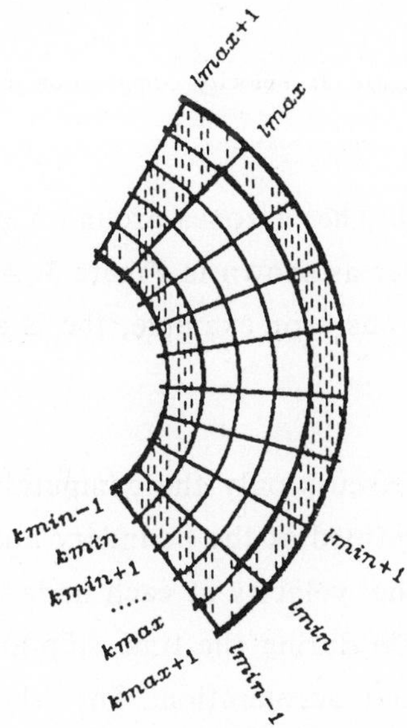

Figure 2: Ghost zones added for boundary conditions

For convenience, the following nomenclature is adopted to refer to the neighboring nodes and zones of a node. The neighboring nodes are named *north, south, east, west*. For example, in Figure 3 the north neighbor of node *(k,l)* is *(k-1,l)* and the west

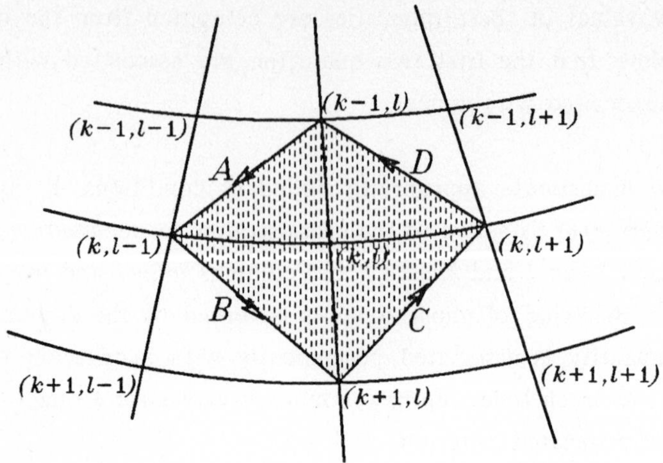

Figure 3: Velocity computation at a node

neighbor is the node *(k,l-1)*. The 4 zones around a node *(k,l)* are named *A, B, C, D* in a counterclockwise manner as shown in Figure 3. A zone is identified by specifying its *southeast* corner node. Thus, for example, the B zone of node *(k,l)* is referred by indices *(k+1,l)*.

In this paper, we will discuss only the computation of the new velocity at each node. The velocity is not defined at the boundary nodes and hence our example deals with only interior nodes. The velocity at each node is determined by first computing the acceleration at that node during the time step and incrementing the old velocity by the product of time and acceleration. The acceleration is obtained from the equation for conservation of momentum. After some simplifying algebra, the acceleration is given by

$$\frac{d\vec{v}}{dt} = \left[\frac{-\oint p\,dz - \oint q\,dz}{nodal\_mass}, \frac{\oint p\,dr + \oint q\,dr}{nodal\_mass} \right] \qquad \text{(A)}$$

In the numerator, the line integrals are to be taken over the boundary line of the shaded region around the node *(k,l)* shown in Figure 3. The line has four segments, one in each of the neighboring zones. While integrating, it is assumed that each zone quantity is constant along the line segment within that zone. Thus, for example, suppose we are integrating p with respect to z, along the line in zone A in Figure 3. Its value is given by the product of p in zone A and the difference of z between the two end points of line segment A, that is $p[k,l] * (z[k,l-1] - z[k-1,l])$. The denominator, *nodal_mass*, is the mass of the shaded area around the node *(k,l)* in Figure 3. This is approximated as one half of the total mass of the 4 zones meeting at node *(k,l)*. The mass of a *zone* is the product of its density and area.

3. Programming in a Declarative language

In this section, we discuss how some basic abstractions to manipulate matrices are programmed in *Id Nouveau* (simply *Id* from now on). We build these abstractions gradually, by way of examples, while introducing *Id*. Introduction to *Id* is informal and written with the purpose of helping the reader understand the main example to be presented later. However, care is taken to explain how the operational semantics of the language allows automatic unravelling of loops and concurrency in data structure operations.

3.1. Functions, I-structures and Parallel Execution

Functions: A function to add two numbers may be written in *Id* as follows:

$$add\ (i, j) = i+j; \qquad (1)$$

This function can be used to add, say *2* and *3*, by writing *add (2,3)*. In a declarative language such as *Id*, the operational meaning of a program can be explained in terms of *rewrite rules* because every definition can be read as a rewrite rule. A function application is rewritten as or *reduced* to the right hand side of its definition by substituting for the parameters. For example, *add (2,3)* is reduced to *2+3* by substituting *2* for *i* and *3* for *j* in the right-hand-side of the definition of *add*. This process of reduction is repeated until we arrive at a form that cannot be reduced any more; this is deemed the result of the computation. Assuming natural rewrite rules for primitive functions, such as +, we can reduce *2+3* to *5*. We could have also written the function to add two numbers as follows:

$$c\_add \;\; i \;\; j = i+j; \tag{2}$$

and applied it by writing *c_add 2 3*. It is customary in functional languages to write a function application as *f a* rather than *f(a)*. Further, to reduce the number of parentheses in expressions, function application is considered to be "left associative" by convention. Thus, the following expressions are equivalent:

$$f \;\; a \;\; b \qquad\qquad (f \;\; a) \;\; b \qquad\qquad ((f \;\; a) \;\; b) \qquad\qquad f \;\; (a) \;\; b$$

and none of them is equal to *f (a,b)*.

The difference between *add* and *c_add* is subtle and important. The *add* function takes one argument which must be a *Two-tuple*. (A tuple is a data structure, as will be explained shortly.) The rewrite rule for *c_add*, on the other hand, can be applied only when *c_add* is followed by two arguments. In functional language parlance, *c_add* has an *arity* of two, while *add* has *arity* one. The significance of this difference becomes apparent when we consider the following definition or *binding*:[2]

$$successor = c\_add\ \ 1; \qquad (3)$$

Successor or equivalently *(c_add 1)* is a function that adds one to a number, that is, *(successor n)* will behave like *(c_add 1 n)*. Expressions such as *(c_add 1)* are called *partial applications* because *c_add* is being applied to fewer arguments than are needed to "fire" the corresponding rewrite rule. Thus, partial applications remain irreducible until a sufficient number of arguments is supplied. Such expressions represent higher-order functions, which are essential for writing abstract programs. Notice, it will make no sense to write *(add 1)* because *add* expects a tuple as an argument. In functional languages, *c_add* is called the "curried" version of *add* after the famous logician Haskell B. Curry.

Tuple structures: Tuples are data structures and are formed in *Id* using commas. Thus, *((1,n),(1,n))* is a 2-tuple of two 2-tuples. We may represent the bounds of an array as a 2-tuple of integers and the bounds of a matrix as a 2-tuple of 2-tuples. Thus, *grid* in

$$grid\ \ n = ((1, n), (1, n)); \qquad (4)$$

is a function that takes a number n as an argument and returns a value that may be used to express the bounds for an $n \times n$ matrix. Functions that return multiple values can be simulated easily using tuples, as illustrated below.[3]

---

2 A binding is simply an association of a name with an expression. In contrast with a function definition, there are no arguments for the name on the left-hand side of a binding.

3 This is only in a manner of speaking - every function returns one value; A 2-tuple is considered to be one value, not two.

$$north\ (i, j) = (i\text{-}1, j);\qquad (5)$$
$$west\ (i, j) = (i, j\text{-}1);$$

Function *north* takes the indices of an element in a matrix and returns the indices of its north neighbor. Similarly, the function *west* returns the neighbor on the west side. As we shall see later, such abstractions are useful when calculations have to be performed for each node of a grid using values at neighboring nodes. For example, using these abstractions we can write *(north node)* where *node* is *(i,j)*, instead of the subscript expression *(i-1,j)*. Such abstractions significantly reduce the likelihood of errors in programming.

Blocks: A *block* expression in *Id* is a set of bindings followed by the key word "***in***" and a return expression. It provides a convenient way to share the computation of common subexpressions, as is shown in the following definition containing a block.

```
acceleration node =                                                        (6)
  {   d = nodal_mass node;
      n1 = – (line_integral p z node) – (line_integral q z node);
      n2 =   (line_integral p r node) + (line_integral q r node);
  in  n1 / d,  n2 / d};
```

For now, we will assume that *line_integral* and *nodal_mass* are some known functions and *p, q, r, z* are some known constants. This block contains three bindings, one each for *d, n1* and *n2*, and returns a 2-tuple. The use of identifier *d* in the return expression allows the computation of the subexpression *(nodal_mass node)* to be shared. *Id* uses "lexical scoping" rules. Thus, a name that is bound in a block *(e.g., n1)* is invisible outside the block. Similarly, a name used in a block, but is not defined in that block *(e.g., p)* imports the value from a binding to that name in the nearest enclosing block.

We explain the execution of block expressions in terms of rewrite rules.[4] In the following, we use the notation *e* => *e'* ‖ *form1* ‖ *form2* ... to show that *e'* is obtained by rewriting some subexpressions in *e*, while the computations in *form1*, *form2*, ... are started concurrently. In the following, let *node* denote some *value* such as *(2,3)*. Then the function application *acceleration node* can be reduced by substituting the body of the function:

```
acceleration node

    => {  d = nodal_mass node;
          n1 = - (line_integral p z node) - (line_integral q z node);
          n2 =   (line_integral p r node) + (line_integral q r node);
       in n1 / d, n2 / d }
```

A block is reduced to its return expression and the computations in all the bindings of the block are initiated concurrently as shown below.

```
    =>     n1 / d, n2 / d
        ‖ d = nodal_mass node
        ‖ n1 = - (line_integral p z node) - (line_integral q z node)
        ‖ n2 =   (line_integral p r node) + (line_integral q r node)
```

Note that the order in which bindings appear in the original expression is immaterial. Assuming the arities of *nodal_mass* and *line_integral* are satisfied, we may rewrite all the 5 function calls.

4 A precise operational semantics for *Id*, using dataflow graphs, is given in [16].

$$
\begin{aligned}
\Rightarrow \quad & n1 / d, \;\; n2 / d \\
\| \;\; & d = (\ldots\textit{body of nodal\_mass}\ldots) \\
\| \;\; & n1 = -\,(\ldots\textit{body with } p\ z \textit{ etc.}\ldots) - (\ldots\textit{body with } q\ z \textit{ etc.}\ldots) \\
\| \;\; & n2 = \;\; (\ldots\textit{body with } p\ r \textit{ etc.}\ldots) + (\ldots\textit{body with } q\ r \textit{ etc.}\ldots)
\end{aligned}
$$

We cannot predict the order in which the 5 function calls get reduced. As an example, suppose we rewrite expressions in the body of *nodal_mass* until it reduces to a value, designated by *v*. In *Id*, substitution for an identifier is performed only when the right-hand side of the corresponding binding reduces to a *value*, that is, a number, boolean, tuple or partial application [4].[5] The binding may be ignored after it has been substituted everywhere. In the sequel, we will use names such as *v, v1, ... etc.* to designate *values*. In the case of tuples, we will rely on the reader's intuition to figure out when a tuple represents a value as opposed to an unevaluated tuple. Substituting the *value* *v* for *d*, we get

$$
\begin{aligned}
\Rightarrow \quad & n1 / v, \;\; n2 / v \\
\| \;\; & n1 = -\,(\ldots\textit{body with } p\ z \textit{ etc.}\ldots) - (\ldots\textit{body with } q\ z \textit{ etc.}\ldots) \\
\| \;\; & n2 = \;\; (\ldots\textit{body with } p\ r \textit{ etc.}\ldots) + (\ldots\textit{body with } q\ r \textit{ etc.}\ldots)
\end{aligned}
$$

Similarly, the four *line_integrals* may be reduced to *v1, v2, v3* and *v4*, respectively, to produce

---

5 The subtlety here is that we do not wish to substitute arbitrary expressions for identifiers as it may result in recomputing the expression at each place of substitution. Since a *value* is irreducible, we can perform the substitution when the right hand side of a binding yields a *value*. For the same reason, when we replace a function application with its body, each parameter is replaced by a new name in the body and a definition is added to bind the new name with the corresponding argument expression. This ensures that each argument is evaluated only once, although it may be referred to many times in the body.

$$
\begin{array}{llllll}
\Rightarrow & n1\,/\,v,\;\; n2\,/\,v & \Rightarrow & n1\,/\,v,\;\; n2\,/\,v & \Rightarrow v5\,/\,v,\;\; v6\,/\,v & \Rightarrow v7,\;\; v8 \\
 & \| \;\; n1 = -\,v1 - v2 & & \| \;\; n1 = v5 & & \\
 & \| \;\; n2 = v3 + v4 & & \| \;\; n2 = v6 & &
\end{array}
$$

where *v5* through *v8* have obvious meanings.

At this stage, the expression cannot be reduced any further and we say that the answer has been found. It is worth noting that at several steps of this reduction sequence, we had a choice of subexpressions to reduce. Such a choice represents opportunity for parallel execution. The most wonderful property of *Id* (and other functional languages) is that the order in which we reduce reducible expressions has no effect on the final answer. This property, known as the *Church-Rosser property*, guarantees the *determinacy* of computation. When Fortran programs are parallelized by annotations, determinacy is not guaranteed by the language. It is the responsibility of the programmer to make sure that the annotated synchronizations preserve determinacy of the computation. It is the indeterminacy due to erroneous annotations that creates nightmares while getting a parallelized Fortran program to work.

Very frequently, curried functions are defined implicitly. For example, suppose definition (6) appears in a block where *p, q, r, z* are defined. The values of these variables can be supplied for computing the *acceleration*, by including them as additional arguments in the definition of *acceleration*. The use of such implicit arguments is permitted in *Id* for programming convenience; the compiler automatically transforms the programs (using a technique known as λ-*lifting* [9]) into equivalent programs, where all arguments are explicit. For example, the compiler will transform definition (6) as follows, where *acceleration′* is a new function of arity 5 and *acceleration* is its curried form.

```
acceleration' p q r z  node =
    {   d = nodal_mass  node;
        n1 = – (line_integral p z node) – (line_integral q z node);
        n2 =   (line_integral p r node) + (line_integral q r node);
    in  n1 / d,  n2 / d};

acceleration = acceleration' p q r z;
```

I-structures: Now we introduce *I-structures*, a novel data structuring facility which has been designed primarily to facilitate parallel programming. One can think of an *I-structure* as a special kind of array which is allocated at run time and whose elements can be written (that is, defined) no more than once. It is allocated by the expression ***array*** *(l,u)*, which allocates and retuns an "empty" array with index bounds *l* and *u*. We will show the execution of this primitive by the following rewrite rule:

array *(l, u)* => < *al, al + 1, ..., au* >

where each *ai* represents a memory location and <*al,al* + 1, ..., *au*> represents an *I-structure value.*[6] *I-structure* elements can contain any thing including other *I-structures*. Thus, one can define a matrix as an array of array. However, for the sake of efficiency we also provide matrix as a primitive data structure which may be allocated using the expression ***matrix*** *((l1,u1),(l2,u2))*. A component of an *I-structure A* may be assigned (written) no more than once using a "constraint statement": *A* [*i*] = *v*; It is a run-time error to write more than once into an *I-structure* location - the entire program is considered to be in error. The *i-th* component of an *I-structure A* is selected

---

6 We would like to point out that this rewrite rule takes us out of the scope of functional languages, because variables appearing on the right-hand-side are not taken from the variables on the left-hand-side. However, such rules are common and necessary for defining the operational semantics of logic languages.

by writing the expression $A[i]$. If A is the structure $\langle a1, \ldots au \rangle$, then the selection $A[i]$ first computes the index of the array. This is indicated by the reduction of $A[i]$ to the name ai. Then the location is read. The reading is indicated by the reduction of ai to a value. Thus, the expression $A[i]$ returns a value only after the location has been assigned a value. It is important to realize that no test for the "emptiness" of an element is provided for the programmer. This restriction is necessary to preserve the determinacy of the language.

The operational view of *I-structures* given above can also be described in terms of rewrite rules, as shown with the help of the following example. First, we reduce the block expression:

$$
\begin{array}{lll}
\{ & A = \textbf{array}\ (1, 10); & \Rightarrow \quad A[5] \\
 & A[5] = A[1] + 4; & \quad \| \ A = \textbf{array}\ (1, 10) \\
 & A[1] = 3; & \quad \| \ A[5] = A[1] + 4 \\
\textbf{in} & A[5]\ \} & \quad \| \ A[1] = 3
\end{array}
$$

After the storage allocation for the array is done, A becomes a value of the form $\langle a1, a2, \ldots, a10 \rangle$, and, hence, it can be substituted:

$$
\begin{array}{ll}
\Rightarrow & \langle a1, a2, \ldots, a10 \rangle [5] \\
 & \| \ \langle a1, a2, \ldots, a10 \rangle [5] = \langle a1, a2, \ldots, a10 \rangle [1] + 4 \\
 & \| \ \langle a1, a2, \ldots, a10 \rangle [1] = 3
\end{array}
$$

$$
\begin{array}{ll}
\Rightarrow & a5 \\
 & \| \ a5 = a1 + 4 \\
 & \| \ a1 = 3
\end{array}
$$

At this stage only $a1$ can be substituted because $a5$ has not yet become a *value*.

```
=> a5                  =>     a5             => 7
     ‖ a5 = 3 + 4             ‖ a5 = 7
```

The crucial point in understanding these rewrite rules is that one is allowed to substitute for an identifier only after the right-hand side of the equation associated with the identifier has been reduced to a value. If the right-hand side never becomes a value (that is, is never defined), then no substitution for the identifier is ever done and the "read" operation will take forever!

Loops: A *for-loop* expression in *Id* is a set of bindings to be executed repeatedly for a specified number of times. All iterations execute concurrently. The following example illustrates a for-loop.

```
{    A = array 1, 10 ;                                        (7)
     { for i from 1 to 10 do
          A [ i ] = i * i }
in   A }
```

First, the block expression is reduced. Then the loop is reduced to a set of parallel iterations, one for each value of the control variable. Each iteration is a copy of the body of the loop in which the corresponding value is substituted for the control variable, as shown below:

```
=>     A                               =>     A
     ‖ A = array 1, 10                      ‖ A = array 1, 10
     ‖ { for i from 1 to 10 do              ‖ A [ 1 ] = 1 * 1
            A [ i ] = i * i }               ‖ ...
                                            ‖ A [ 10 ] = 10 * 10
```

Suppose the storage allocation for the array is completed first. The name *A* is then replaced by its value $<a1, a2, ..., a10>$. Since A is the result expression, the answer (*i.e.*, an array descriptor) becomes available and other computations may use the array, even though the values of the array elements are still being computed. Each of the index selections is replaced by the corresponding names as discussed earlier. Finally, the individual values are stored into the corresponding elements.

```
=>      <a1, a2, ..., a10>                      =>      <a1, a2, ..., a10>
      ‖ <a1, a2, ..., a10> [ 1 ] = 1 * 1              ‖ a1 = 1
      ‖ ...                                           ‖ ...
      ‖ <a1, a2, ..., a10> [ 10 ] = 10 * 10           ‖ a10 = 100
```

It should be noted that the iterations are executed concurrently regardless of the nature of the computation. For example, in the following loop, although the multiplications proceed concurrently, the additions and the store operations take place sequentially as dictated by data dependencies.

```
{    A = array 0, 10 ;                  => ...   =>     <a1, a2, ..., a10>
     A [ 0 ] = 0;                                     ‖ a0 = 0
     { for i from 1 to 10 do                          ‖ a1 = a0 + 1 * 1
          A [ i ] = A [ i-1 ] + i * i }               ‖ ...
in   A }                                              ‖ a10 = a9 + 10 * 10
```

As another variation consider the following example, in which the additions and store operations take place in the reverse order. This shows that the loop specification is declarative in the sense that ***for** i **from** 1 **to** 10* specifies the *set* of indices and not the order of their traversal. The order, if any, is governed by data dependences.

```
{  A = array 1, 11 ;              => ...  =>    <a1, a2, ..., a10>
   A [ 11 ] = 0;                              ‖ a11 = 0
   { for i from 1 to 10 do                    ‖ a1 = a2 + 1 * 1
        A [ i ] = A [ i+1 ] + i * i }         ‖ ...
in A }                                        ‖ a10 = a11 + 10*10
```

Loops may also return a value. The set of bindings in such a loop is followed by the keyword "*finally*" and a return expression. All the iterations and the return expression are initiated concurrently. The following example illustrates the reduction of a set of elements to their sum.

```
{  s = 0 ;                        => ...  =>    s_10
in { for i from 1 to 10 do                    ‖ s = 0
        next s = s + i * i                    ‖ s_1 = s + 1 * 1
     finally  s } }                           ‖ s_2 = s_1 + 2 * 2
                                              ‖ ...
                                              ‖ s_10 = s_9 + 10 * 10
```

The key word ***next*** indicates that the value computed in the *i-th* iteration for the right hand side of the binding is bound to the name *s* in the i+1-*st* iteration. For clear exposition of this, the name *s* used in iteration *i* is renamed as s_i and the following rewrite rules show how the recurrence is computed sequentially. The key word ***finally*** indicates that *s* assigned in the last iteration is the value returned by the loop expression.

3.2. Abstractions to manipulate arrays/matrices

The array *A* in definition (7) can be thought of as an efficient representation for the function *square i = i * i* over the finite domain *(1,10)*. Instead of computing *square i* each time it is invoked, the values for all *i* in the domain are computed and stored in memory. Thus, *A* acts like a "cache" for the function *square*.[7] The following abstractions emphasize this viewpoint.

```
make_array (l, u) generate =                                    (8)
    {  A = array (l, u);
       {for i from l to u do
            A [ i ] = generate  i }
    in  A};

make_matrix ((l1, u1), (l2, u2)) generate =                     (9)
    {   A = matrix ((l1, u1), (l2, u2));
       {for i from l1 to u1 do
          {for j from l2 to u2 do
             A [ i, j ] = generate  (i, j) }}
    in  A};

A = make_array (1, 50) successor                                (10)
B = make_matrix (grid 50) add                                   (11)
```

In the two definitions (8) and (9), *generate* is the function that generates the elements of the corresponding structure and its finite domain is the set of all indices within the dimensions of the structure. For example, definition (10) builds a 50-element array in which the *i-th* element has value $i+1$. Similarly, definition (11) builds a 50 x 50 matrix, (using the *grid* function defined in (4)), in which the value of each element is the sum of the corresponding indices.

---

7 It would be nice if a language permitted the use of structures and functions interchangeably. However, this might introduce implementation inefficiencies and *Id* does not permit this for now.

An abstraction should enable us to model the essence of a concept so that it can be used in different circumstances. The robustness of an abstraction depends upon the flexibility with which the abstraction lends itself to a variety of uses. We will illustrate the robustness of the *make_array* and *make_matrix* abstractions defined above. We will show that these abstractions do not depend upon the type of the generating function, and that they expose all the parallelism present, irrespective of whether the computations of different elements are independent of each other or not.

Arbitrary generating functions: In definition (8), *make_array* expects a *generator* function whose type is

$$\textit{integer} \rightarrow \textit{anytype}$$

where *anytype* represents the type of array elements. Similarly, a *generator* for *make_matrix* must have the type

$$\textit{integer} \times \textit{integer} \rightarrow \textit{anytype}$$

Thus, the *make_matrix* abstraction works equally well with generator *add* (see definition (11)) which returns an integer, and generator *velocity* (given below) which returns a 2-tuple.

```
velocity  node =                                            (12)
      {  au, aw = acceleration  node;
         u, w = Old_V [ node ] ;
      in  u + au * time,   w + aw * time };

V = make_matrix  (grid 50)  velocity;                       (13)
```

As an aside, we point out that the function *velocity* computes the velocity components in the two dimensions at a point specified by *node*. *Acceleration* is the function defined in (6), which gives the component accelerations in the two dimensions at a given *node*. *Old_V* is the old velocity matrix. The new velocity is obtained by incrementing the old velocity by the product of time and acceleration.

Another dimension of flexibility is that the generator function itself be computed at runtime. We can illustrate this using function *c_add* (definition (2)) whose type is:

$$integer \rightarrow (integer \rightarrow integer)$$

If *c_add* is applied to *n* then the result would be a function with type

$$integer \rightarrow integer$$

Thus, it makes sense to use *(c_add n)* as a generator for the make-array abstraction as shown below:

make_array (1, 50) (c_add n)

This creates a 50-element array of integers, in which the value of each element is *n* plus its index. We leave it to the reader to figure out the elements (and their types) of the following array.

make_array (1, 50) c_add

Parallelism is dictated by data dependencies: Note that for both the abstractions (8) and (9), the structure (*i.e.*, its storage descriptor) is returned as soon as the storage is allocated; the binding of the elements takes place in parallel. The implementation must guarantee that any premature accesses are synchronized.[8] Furthermore, all the iterations execute concurrently, unless constrained by data dependences. For instance,

---

8 The I-structure implementation in the MIT Tagged-Token Dataflow Architecture uses tagged storage and deferred read lists for this purpose. For details see [2].

in definitions (10) and (11) all the iterations are independent and hence will execute in parallel. On the other hand, consider the following example in which the velocity is defined as constant 55.5 at the north and west boundaries of the matrix and it is propagated along a wavefront - so that the velocity at a node is the sum of the velocities of its north and west neighbors:

```
rec_velocity V (i, j) =                                          (14)
    if i==1 or j==1 then 55.5
    else V[ north (i, j) ] + V[ west (i, j) ]

V = make_matrix (grid 10) (rec_velocity V);                      (15)
```

where "==" is the relational operator for equality, to avoid overloading of the symbol "=". Definition (15) is recursive, as the name *V* is used in its own definition. However, the abstraction still works because the matrix is returned as soon as the storage is allocated. We show a partial reduction sequence to illustrate this point. For the sake of clarity, we name the curried form as *h* and evaluate the following block expression with mutually recursive bindings. The block expression is rewritten as before and the name *h* is substituted by its value (which is the partial application).

```
{   h = rec_velocity V;
    V = make_matrix (grid 50) h
in  V}

=>      V
    ‖ V = {  A = matrix ((1, 50), (1, 50));
             {for i from 1 to 50 do
                {for j from 1 to 50 do
                   A [ i, j ] = rec_velocity V (i, j)}}
          in  A};
```

Now replacing array A by its value $<a_{1,1}, ...a_{50,50}>$ and substituting for the application of the function *rec_velocity* we get

$$=> \quad <a_{1,1}, ...a_{50,50}>$$

```
‖ {for i from 1 to 50 do
     {for j from 1 to 50 do
        <a_{1,1}, ...a_{50,50}> [ i, j ] =if  i==1  or  j==1  then  55.5
        else  <a_{1,1}, ... a_{50,50}> [ north (i, j) ] + <a_{1,1}, ... a_{50,50}> [ west (i, j) ] }}
```

Now, one can see how the wavefront parallelism is unfolded as the velocities along each diagonal will be computed in parallel. The fact that the *make_matrix* abstraction is defined without regard to all these nuances of the function *generate* and that it automatically unravels all the parallelism present, no matter how the function *generate* is structured, shows that programming with such abstractions is highly desirable. Later, we will show how Fortran programmers go through all sorts of contortions to bring out this wavefront parallelism.

3.3. Some More Matrix Abstractions

We would like to introduce some more matrix-related abstractions which lead to not only clear programming style but also increased efficiency in execution.

Make_2_matrices: Given a generating function that produces a 2-tuple, the following function defines a pair of matrices, instead of a matrix of pairs:

```
make_2_matrices ((l1, u1), (l2, u2)) generate =                    (16)
    {   A = matrix ((l1, u1), (l2, u2));
        B = matrix ((l1, u1), (l2, u2));
        {for i from l1 to u1 do
           {for j from l2 to u2 do
              A [ i, j ], B [ i, j ] = generate (i, j) }}
    in  A, B};
```

For example, *velocity* of definition (12) is a function that returns a pair of values and (13) creates a matrix of pairs. The following creates a pair of matrices:

```
U, W = make_2_matrices (grid 50) velocity;
```

Sometimes it is convenient to maintain two matrices because there may be separate computations dealing with each velocity component. If a matrix of pairs were used, the components would have to be selected each time, thus causing some structure-accessing overheads. The pair of matrices could also be created using the *make_matrix* abstraction two times. For example, we could have defined:

```
velocity_u node =                                                  (17)
    {   au, aw = acceleration node;
        u, w = Old_V[ node ];
    in  u + au * time };
U = make_matrix (grid 50) velocity_u;

velocity_w node =                                                  (18)
    {   au, aw = acceleration node;
        u, w = Old_V[ node ];
    in  w + aw * time };
W = make_matrix (grid 50) velocity_w;
```

However, unlike *make_2_matrices*, the above definitions will unnecessarily compute the *acceleration* twice. In general, the behavior of *make_2_matrices* cannot be imitated by *make_matrix* without loss of efficiency.

In the hydrodynamics application, velocity is indeed represented as a pair of matrices, *U* and *W*, one for each component. However, since the velocity is recomputed in each iteration, both old and new velocities should be pairs of matrices. If *Old_U* and *Old_W* represent the component matrices for the old velocity, then we can define the new velocity matrices as shown below, computing the *acceleration* only once for each component:

```
velocity_uw  node =                                              (19)
      {    au, aw = acceleration  node;
           u = Old_U [ node ] ;
           w = Old_W [ node ] ;
      in   u + au * time,   w + aw * time };
```

```
U, W = make_2_matrices  (grid 50)  velocity_uw;                  (20)
```

Make_matrix_k_ranges: The generator *rec_velocity* (definition (15)) which is associated with matrix V of definition (14) can be viewed as a composite of the following two generators:

```
boundary_velocity  node = 55.5;
interior_velocity  V  node = add  (V [ north  node ],  V [ west  node ] );
```

On the north and west boundaries of the matrix, the generator is *boundary_velocity*, and for the remaining matrix the generator is *interior_velocity*. Since the two generating functions are to be applied for "well-defined" patterns of indices *(i,j)*, the evaluation of the conditional for the selection of the appropriate generator function seems to be wasteful. One way to eliminate the condition evaluation is to partition the set of indices into disjoint sets, so that a separate loop with appropriate generator can be used for each set. For example, we can define the following grids:

north_boundary = ((*1, 1*), (*1, 50*));
west_boundary = ((*2, 50*), (*1, 1*));
interior_nodes = ((*2, 50*), (*2, 50*));

which taken together cover the whole matrix. Now, all we need to do is to "fill" the matrix using the appropriate generator for each section. For this purpose define a *fill* abstraction as follows:

```
fill_matrix A ((l1, u1), (l2, u2)) f =                    (21)
    {for i from l1 to u1 do
       {for j from l2 to u2 do
          A [i, j] = f (i, j) }} ;
```

Definition (21) does not return any value and thus is non-functional. However, the single assignment restriction on the structures guarantees the determinacy of the final result. An I-structure behaves like a variable in logic programming in that its value is initially undefined but keeps getting more and more defined as the computation progresses. However, any values "read" from an I-structure always correspond to the final value of the structure. Alternatively, we can think of *A* as in *A* = ***matrix bounds***, as denoting a value which is the set of all matrices with those bounds. Each invocation of *fill_matrix* on matrix *A* is a constraint on the values the variable *A* can assume. Attempt to fill an element more than once amounts to imposing inconsistent constraints, and hence would result in an error.

Now we can define the matrix abstraction which uses 3 generating functions for 3 ranges of indices:

```
make_matrix_3_ranges dimensions ( (r1, f1), (r2, f2), (r3, f3) ) =          (22)
    {   A = matrix dimensions ;
        call fill_matrix A r1 f1 ;
        call fill_matrix A r2 f2 ;
        call fill_matrix A r3 f3 ;
    in  A };
```

```
V = make_matrix_3_ranges (grid 50)                                           (23)
  ( (north_boundary, boundary_velocity),
    (west_boundary,  boundary_velocity),
    (interior_nodes, (interior_velocity V)) );
```

Thus, definition (23) creates the same matrix as definition (15), but avoids the evaluation of the conditional for each element. Once again, all elements will be assigned concurrently. One can generalize the *make_2_matrices* and *make_matrix_3_ranges* and define more general abstractions, such as *make_n_matrices_k_ranges*, for various values of n and k. We leave this as an exercise for the reader.

3.4. Program for Velocity Computation

We will now illustrate how the velocity computation problem of Section 2 can be coded in *Id*. The velocity is stored in two matrices, U and W, one for each velocity component. Since the velocity is computed only for interior nodes, their dimensions should correspond to the interior nodes. The dimensions and the matrix abstraction can be defined as:

$$interior\_nodes = ((kmin,\ kmax),\ (lmin,\ lmax)) \tag{24}$$

$$new\_U,\ new\_W = make\_2\_matrices\ \ interior\_nodes\ \ velocity; \tag{25}$$

The velocity is obtained by incrementing the old velocity, *(U,W)*, by the product of time and acceleration. Note that the constant δt and the old velocity components *U* and *W* will be taken from the context (λ-*lifted* as discussed earlier).

```
velocity node =                                                      (26)
    {    u_dot, w_dot = acceleration node;
    in   U[node] + δt * u_dot,  W[node] + δt * w_dot};
```

Equation (A) (in Section 2) gives the acceleration at a node. Hence, we define:

```
acceleration node =                                                  (27)
    {    d = nodal_mass node;
         n1 = -(line_integral p z node)-(line_integral q z node);
         n2 =  (line_integral p r node) + (line_integral q r node);
    in   (n1 / d,  n2 / d)};
```

In order to define the line integrals and nodal mass, we need to have the notion of neighbor nodes and zones. Hence we define the following functions that reflect nomenclature used in the problem description to refer to the neighboring nodes and zones.

```
                                                                     (28)
north (i,j) = (i-1,j);            zone_a (k,l) = (k,l);
south (i,j) = (i+1,j);            zone_b (k,l) = (k+1,l);
east (i,j) = (i,j+1);             zone_c (k,l) = (k+1,l+1);
west (i,j) = (i,j-1);             zone_d (k,l) = (k,l+1);
```

The line integrals described in Section 2 take two quantities, for example p and z. Given a node, they integrate the first quantity with respect to the second along a line around the node. This is expressed by the following line integral function:

$$\begin{aligned} &line\_integral\ f\ g\ node = \\ &\quad f[zone\_a\ node] * (g[west\ node] - g[north\ node]) + \\ &\quad f[zone\_b\ node] * (g[south\ node] - g[west\ node]) + \\ &\quad f[zone\_c\ node] * (g[east\ node] - g[south\ node]) + \\ &\quad f[zone\_d\ node] * (g[north\ node] - g[east\ node]); \end{aligned} \tag{29}$$

Nodal_mass is the average of the masses of the four zones around a node. This is approximated as one half of the total mass of the 4 zones meeting at node *(k,l)*. The mass of a *zone* is the product of its density and area: $\rho[node] * \alpha[node]$. We can define the following function for mass around a node:

$$\begin{aligned} &nodal\_mass\ node = \\ &\quad 0.5 * (\rho[zone\_a\ node] * \alpha[zone\_a\ node] + \\ &\qquad \rho[zone\_b\ node] * \alpha[zone\_b\ node] + \\ &\qquad \rho[zone\_c\ node] * \alpha[zone\_c\ node] + \\ &\qquad \rho[zone\_d\ node] * \alpha[zone\_d\ node]); \end{aligned} \tag{30}$$

We believe that definitions (24) through (30) that define the velocity reflect the notions in the problem description of Section 2 very closely. They map the notions of *line_integral*, *acceleration*, neighborhood notions of *nodes* and *zones*, etc., directly into the program. Thus, if changes are to be made to the algorithm, it should be easy to relate to the problem description and change the abstractions as desired.

4. Matrix Abstractions in Fortran

The preceding section illustrates how the *Id Nouveau* style of programming not only helps in building higher-level abstractions, but also automatically unravels the parallelism to the maximum possible extent. Looking at the examples in the preceding section, a casual reader might get the impression that the style is purely syntactic in nature and that such abstractions could be easily built in an imperative language as well. In this section, first, we will show that Fortran lacks certain basic features, such as dynamic storage allocation, which are essential for writing robust abstractions. We will then show that annotations for parallelism in Fortran cannot easily capture the inherent parallelism in the problem specification. Finally, we will comment on the complexity of the annotated programs.

Basic Abstractions: The *make_matrix* abstraction may be expressed as follows in Fortran:

```
      subroutine make_matrix (A, r1, r2, c1, c2, f)
      integer r1, r2, c1, c2
      dimension A (r2, c2)
      do 10 i = r1, r2
      do 10 j = c1, c2
10    A (i, j) = f (i, j)
      return
      end
```

We would like to show why this program does not capture the subtleties of the make-matrix abstraction of (9). First, notice that without the dynamic allocation of storage, we cannot create a new matrix in this subroutine; we can only "fill" a matrix that has been supplied as an argument. Thus, it makes this subroutine the *fill* abstraction of definition (21) rather than the matrix abstraction of (9). Second, in Fortran, functions are restricted to return one value which must be a scalar. Hence, the above abstraction cannot be used to define a matrix of 2-tuples, such as the velocity matrix of definition (13). In fact, since the type of a matrix in Fortran has to be declared in advance, separate abstractions have to be defined for making integer and floating-point matrices. The idiosyncrasies of Fortran, such as restricting the lower bounds of arrays to one, etc., further restrict the generality of the abstraction. Note, we have passed *f*, a function, as an argument to this subroutine. The facility to pass function and subroutine names as arguments to other subroutines is not supported in all Fortrans.

The lack of higher-order functions and currying creates a further problem that shows up as an argument-passing problem in Fortran. Suppose we call *make_matrix* with function *g* as the last argument and that *g*, in turn, needs *x* as an argument. In the *Id* version, we would have passed *(g x)*, the curried form of *g*, as an argument to *make_matrix*. However, in Fortran, we will essentially have to write a new version of *make_matrix*, which will take *x* as an additional argument and pass it as an extra argument to *f*. Given all the restrictions on argument passing, it should be easy for the reader to see that there is no way of using the Fortran version of *make_matrix* to define a matrix recursively, as in (14) and (15). Problems only get worse when we try to define *make_2_matrices* in Fortran. One possible candidate for *make_2_matrices* is the following program.

```
      subroutine make_2_matrices (A, B, r1, r2, c1, c2, f)
      dimension A (r2, c2), B (r2, c2)
      do 10 i = r1, r2
      do 10 j = c1, c2
   10 call f (i, j, A (i, j), B (i, j))
      return
      end
```

Notice, the argument f must be a subroutine with 4 parameters. The first two arguments are the indices i and j. The last two arguments are values returned and, hence, are bound to the respective elements of the matrix. Such distinction of arguments and return values in a parameter list is inevitable when functions are only allowed to return one scalar value. Given all these problems, the style of programming we have shown in this paper is difficult to copy in the Fortran world. Most of the weaknesses we have pointed out in Fortran so far are not present in sequential languages that support dynamic allocation of storage. A good example of such a language is Common Lisp [15] or its semantically cleaner dialect Scheme [1]. Both of these languages will have some difficulty with the examples involving currying because of "applicative order evaluation".

Parallelization: Now we will examine the parallel execution of Fortran programs. There are many systems that parallelize Fortran. For a recent survey on this subject see [10]. This is usually done by annotating the Fortran program to indicate parallel segments and synchronizations. Different systems use different notations for parallelization of sequential codes. For example, in the subroutine make-matrix, the two loops will be executed in parallel by an annotation of the form ***doall*** replacing the "do" in the program. The ***doall*** annotation is specified (by the programmer or by the compiler) after performing subscript analysis of expressions in the loop body.[9] To the best of our knowledge, no parallelization scheme will be able to parallelize the make-matrix subroutine because the body invokes some arbitrary function f, which can potentially have side-effects that can render the iterations to be dependent and, hence, must be executed sequentially. Complex inter-procedural analysis can sometimes detect that the loops in make-matrix may be parallelized when it is invoked with a

---

9 Although subscript analysis might determine that both of the loops in the nesting can be parallelized, many of the present systems do not have the necessary support for dynamic instantiations and hence restrict that atmost one loop can be parallelized within a nesting. Ofcourse, this situation may change in the future.

particular generating function *f*. For example, if *f* is the *add* function as in (11) then the loops can be parallelized. But if *f* is the *interior_velocity* function of (23) to create a wavefront matrix, then the iterations cannot be parallelized. Thus, we need different versions of make-matrix for different generating functions, which implies that make-matrix is no more a general abstraction for building matrices.

In general, it is very hard to extract any parallelism from programs that have some form of recurrence. For example, the wavefront matrix of (23) does have some parallelism along the wavefronts. But in order to make this explicit in Fortran, the programmer must restructure the control substantially. To illustrate this point, first consider the following sequential version of an equivalent program. First the top row and left column are initialized with the constant. Then the recurrence relation is computed scanning from left to right and top to bottom.

```
      subroutine sequential_version (A, n)
      dimension A (n, n)
      do 10 j = 1, n
      A (1, j) = 55.5
10    A (j, 1) = 55.5
      do 40 i = 2, n
      do 40 j = 2, n
40    A (i, j) = A (i - 1, j) + A (i, j - 1)
```

One strategy to parallelize this is shown below. After initialization, we must traverse diagonally from the top left corner to the bottom right corner. Index *m* is used to count the diagonals, starting with $m=2$ for the top left corner and $m=n+n$ for the bottom right corner, so that a node (i,j) is on diagonal $m=i+j$. Since the top row and left column are initialized with 1, we need to traverse only diagonals $m=4$ through $m=n+n$. The diagonals are split into 2 groups, $m=4, n+1$ and $m=n+2,n+n$, so that in the first group we eliminate the top row and left column and choose rows 2 though the limit and in the second group we choose rows from the limit through n. The ***doall*** annotation is used to indicate that all the iterations of a loop should be executed in parallel. The ***barrier*** annotation is used to indicate that all processors must synchronize here before proceeding further.

```
      subroutine wavefront_matrix (A, n)
      dimension A (n, n)
      doall 10 j = 1, n
10    A (1, j) = 55.5
      doall 20 i = 2, n
20    A (i, 1) = 55.5
      barrier
      do 45 m = 4, n + 1
      doall 40 i = 2, m - 2
40    A (i, m - i) = A (i - 1, m - i) + A (i, m - i - 1)
45    barrier
      do 55 m = n + 2, n + n
      doall 50 i = m - n, n
50    A (i, m - i) = A (i - 1, m - i) + A (i, m - i - 1)
55    barrier
```

Complexity due to annotations: In order to encode and verify a program, it is important that the final form of the program must be such that one can relate to the algorithm and make inferences about portions of the program that perform different functions from the algorithm. In the above example of the wavefront matrix, although the parallelism is detected, the annotated program obscures the abstraction so much that we cannot relate the program easily to its description in the physical domain. Verifying the program becomes that much harder. As another example to show the advantages of *Id* over Fortran, we develop a parallel version of a program to sum up all the elements of an array. This program is discussed in some detail in [10]. The idea is that given some p, we want to divide the array into p bins and compute the partial sums in parallel. Finally all the partial sums are added up. The following *Id Nouveau* program accomplishes this: (In *Id Nouveau*, the text between a percentage sign (%) and the end of line is treated as a comment.)

```
cume_segment A (l, u) =
     {   cume = 0;
     in  {for i from l to u do
               next cume = cume + A [ i ] ;
         finally cume } };

% n is the size of the array and p is the number of processors
p_way_accumulate_array A n p =
     {   bin_size = fix ((n + p - 1) /p);    % fix gives the ceiling of n/p

         % define a function to the compute index bounds for bin j
         bin_bounds j = (j - 1) * bin_size + 1,   (min n (j * bin_size));

         % define a function to accumulate elements of bin j
         cume_bin j = cume_segment A (bin_bounds j);

         B = make_array (1, p) cume_bin;
     in  cume_segment B (1, p) } ;
```

We invite the reader to compare this program with the annotated FORTRAN version in [10] for clarity, parallelism and efficiency.

5. Optimizing the Velocity Program

Programming at a high level involves defining many functions, sometimes very simple functions such as *north, south, etc.* in this example. In any implementation, each function call introduces computational and other resource overheads. Programs targeted for maximum efficiency tend to eliminate such overheads by encoding the program at such a low level that the program often does not reflect the problem at all. This point is illustrated by the following equivalent Fortran program taken from a running version of SIMPLE.

```
C    COMPUTE ACCELERATION AND NEW VELOCITIES
      DO 100 L=LMN,LMX
        DO 110 K=KMN,KMX
          AU= (P(K,L)+Q(K,L))       *(Z(K,L-1)-Z(K-1,L)) +
     1      (P(K+1,L)+Q(K+1,L))     *(Z(K+1,L)-Z(K,L-1)) +
     2      (P(K,L+1)+Q(K,L+1))     *(Z(K-1,L)-Z(K,L+1)) +
     3      (P(K+1,L+1)+Q(K+1,L+1))*(Z(K,L+1)-Z(K+1,L))
          AW= (P(K,L)+Q(K,L))       * (R(K,L-1)-R(K-1,L)) +
     1      (P(K+1,L)+Q(K+1,L))     * (R(K+1,L)-R(K,L-1)) +
     2      (P(K,L+1)+Q(K,L+1))     * (R(K-1,L)-R(K,L+1)) +
     3      (P(K+1,L+1)+Q(K+1,L+1))* (R(K,L+1)-R(K+1,L))
          AUW = RHO(K,L)*AJ(K,L)  +RHO(K+1,L)*AJ(K+1,L)+
     1        RHO(K,L+1)*AJ(K,L+1)+RHO(K+1,L+1)*AJ(K+1,L+1)
          AUW = 2./AUW
          AU = -AU*AUW
          AW = AW*AUW
          U(K,L) = U(K,L)+DTN*AU
          W(K,L) = W(K,L)+DTN*AW
  110   CONTINUE
  100 CONTINUE
```

A good FORTRAN compiler can analyze all the expressions in the above program and deduce that all the iterations in the two nested loops can be executed concurrently. The analysis has to be fairly sophisticated, as it must deduce that *P, Q, R, Z, RHO, AJ* are all constant matrices (as far as the loop is concerned), that no side-effects are caused by any calls, and that the elements of *U* and *W* are computed pointwise from their old values without forming any recurrences. Any slight change to the program affecting the above decisions could make the compiler decision much harder. Alternatively, the programmer (who figures out all these facts) can annotate the program by specifying ***doall*** in place of ***do*** in the two loops. To a large extent, the programmer had already done a number of optimizations, such as the use of actual indices (as opposed to functions like *north*), and grouping and factoring of expressions in order to minimize the number of operations, memory references, etc. In addition, FORTRAN compilers usually produce very efficient code for programs like this, because the programs are highly "expression oriented" and therefore they are amenable to optimizations such as common subexpression elimination, strength reduction, moving out constant expressions from loop bodies etc. But it is extremely hard to decipher the algorithm of the problem description from the above program. And this is what makes it hard to modify the above program (for some minor change in the algorithm) and verify it. One can imagine the complexity added if this task is to be done with multiple processors in mind.

We have already shown that we can code this algorithm in *Id* without obscuring its structure. The reader can verify by applying the rewrite rules given in Section 3.1, that the inherent parallelism of the algorithm will be exposed during execution. Finally, we show that the efficiency of the Id program matches that of the FORTRAN program, when in-line substitutions for functions are made. Starting from (25) we performed in-line substitutions for all the functions (24) through (30). And then we performed a simple automatic renaming transformation to eliminate nested block definitions. Finally, standard common subexpression elimination transformations were performed to get the following program:

```
new_U, new_W =                                                        (31)
    {A = matrix  ((kmin, kmax), (lmin, lmax));
    B = matrix  ((kmin, kmax), (lmin, lmax));
    {for i from kmin to kmax do
      {for j from lmin to lmax do
        d = 0.5 * (ρ [ i, j ] * α [ i, j ] +
          ρ [ i + 1, j ] * α [ i + 1, j ] +
          ρ [ i + 1, j + 1 ] * α [ i + 1, j + 1 ] +
          ρ [ i, j + 1 ] * α [ i, j + 1 ]);
        z1 = z [ i, j - 1 ] - z [ i - 1, j ];
        z2 = z [ i + 1, j ] - z [ i, j - 1 ];
        z3 = z [ i, j + 1 ] - z [ i + 1, j ];
        z4 = z [ i - 1, j ] - z [ i, j + 1 ];
        r1 = r [ i, j - 1 ] - r [ i - 1, j ];
        r2 = r [ i + 1, j ] - r [ i, j - 1 ];
        r3 = r [ i, j + 1 ] - r [ i + 1, j ];
        r4 = r [ i - 1, j ] - r [ i, j + 1 ];
        pq1 = p [ i, j ] + q [ i, j ] ;
        pq2 = p [ i + 1, j ] + q [ i + 1, j ] ;
        pq3 = p [ i + 1, j + 1 ] + q [ i + 1, j + 1 ] ;
        pq4 = p [ i, j + 1 ] + q [ i, j + 1 ] ;
        n1 = - (pq1 * z1 + pq2 * z2 + pq3 * z3 + pq4 * z4);
        n2 = pq1 * r1 + pq2 * r2 + pq3 * r3 + pq4 * r4;
        u_dot, w_dot = n1 / d,  n2 / d;
        A [ i, j ],  B [ i, j ] = U [ i, j ] + δt * u_dot,  W [ i, j ] + δt * w_dot
    in A, B}
```

The reader can verify that the above program does the same number of *arithmetic, load, store* operations as the FORTRAN version given earlier.

6. Storage Requirements

It is often said that the "single assignment" rule in (*Id* and other) functional languages causes too much copying of structures and poor utilization of storage. This is true in general, but I-structures change the picture. They provide for producer-consumer parallelism at a very elementary level, without loss of determinacy. It should be emphasized that the use of additional storage in this model is mostly caused to facilitate as many parallel operations to proceed as possible. In the FORTRAN environment, often a programmer designs the memory structures and the program control in such a manner that the same memory area can be reused by many subcomputations. But invariably, this is based on the order of evaluation of the subcomputations. When subcomputations can potentially execute concurrently, such memory sharing is neither desirable nor possible. When FORTRAN programs are parallelized, additional storage in terms of private copies of variables is indeed provided when subcomputations are known to run in parallel. We will illustrate this more concretely through the following example of LU decomposition, whose parallelization is discussed extensively in [10].

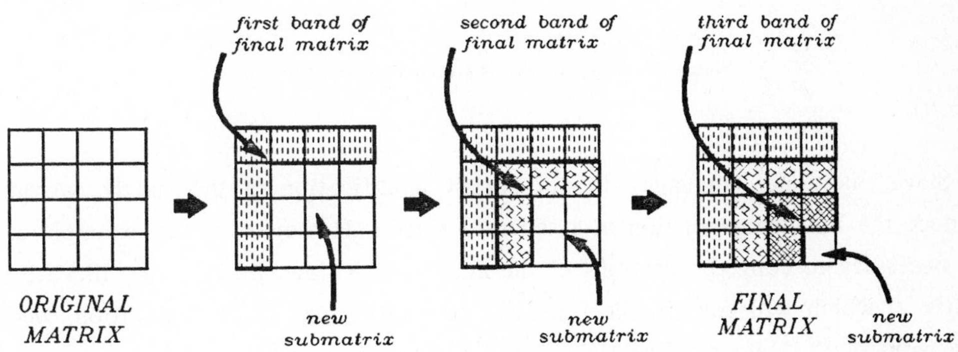

Figure 4: Computation of successive bands of the final matrix yielding LU decomposition

The problem of LU decomposition is to decompose an $n \times n$ matrix into lower and upper triangular matrices by Gaussian elimination method. In the FORTRAN program discussed in [10], the decomposed matrix is produced by successively modifying it as shown in Figure 4. In each iteration, a band of the final matrix is produced and the remaining submatrix is completely modified. Thus, iteration k modifies only the right submatrix bounded by the *k-th* row and *k-th* column. The steps executed in each iteration are shown in Figure 5. First the pivot is determined by finding the maximum element in the first column of the submatrix. Then the pivot row and top row are interchanged. Next the elements of the first column (other than the pivot) are multiplied by a multiplier. The top row and left column of the submatrix created in this manner forms the next band of the final matrix. Finally, the new submatrix is computed by incrementing each element with the product of corresponding elements in the band created above.

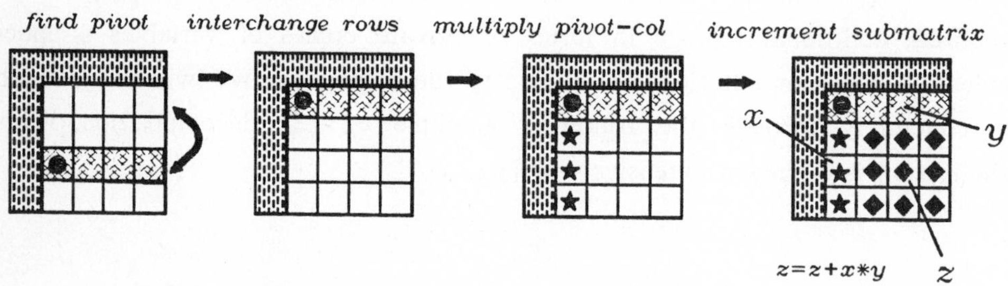

Figure 5: Steps in pivoting each diagonal element

Since functional languages do not permit modification of the matrix, we must produce the LU decomposition in a separate matrix. However, in this example, it is not necessary to copy the portions of the matrix each time. Initially we allocate the matrix D which will contain the final LU decomposition. In each iteration, we fill in a band of D. Instead of modifying the submatrix in each iteration, we create a new submatrix each time. The submatrices in successive iterations have smaller and smaller dimensions. Similarly, instead of interchanging the rows of a submatrix, we will select the elements of the appropriate row. The array P gives the indices which keep track of the order of interchanges needed for pivoting. The following *Id Nouveau* program performs these operations.

```
% finds the largest element in first column and returns that row number
find_pivot A =                                                          (32)
    {   ((l1, u1), (l2, u2)) = bounds A;
        m = l1;
    in  {for i from l1 + 1 to u1 do
            next m = if A [ i, l2 ] > A [ m, l2 ]  then i else m;
        finally m } };


decompose A n =                                                         (33)
  { D = matrix ((1, n), (1, n));
    P = array (1, n);
      B = { for k from 1 to n − 1 do
        r = find_pivot A;  % get number of pivot row
        P [ k ] = r;   % record the row interchange

        % fill the row of the new band with elements from pivot-row
        call fill_matrix D ((k, k), (k, n)) row_fill;
        row_fill (i, j) = A [ r, j ] ;

        % multiply pivot-col elements with multiplier t
        call fill_matrix D ((k + 1, n), (k, k)) col_fill;
        col_fill (i, j) = A [ i, k ] * t ;
        t = −1.0 / A [ r, k ];  % compute multiplier
```

```
        % compute elements of new sub-matrix
        % new-element = old-element + product of corresponding band elements
        % Because of interchange, pivot-row should be interpreted as the top row
        new_element (i, j) = D [ i, k ] * D [ k, j ] + A [ (if i==r then k else i), j ];
        next A = make_matrix ((k + 1, n), (k + 1, n)) new_element };
      finally A };
    D [ n, n ] = B [ n, n ];
  in  D, P };
```

In the parallel FORTRAN versions of this program [10], the elements of the sub-matrix are computed in parallel and are stored back in the same storage area of the matrix *A*. However, in order to guarantee determinacy, barrier synchronization must be used to prevent the next iteration to commence before all the elements of the sub-matrix are computed. In (33) the sub-matrices are created in separate memory areas, but the iterations can overlap. For instance, finding the pivot for iteration *k+1* can commence as soon as the first column of the sub-matrix **next** *A* is computed in iteration *k*. Thus, the *Id Nouveau* program uses additional storage to expose all possible parallelism. It is possible to constrain the execution of the loop in (33) so that the iterations execute sequentially. Then the storage for the matrix *A* can be reclaimed as soon as the iteration is completed. Thus, in functional programs also, it is possible to save storage at the expense of constraining some parallelism. Similarly, when subcomputations are known to run sequentially, one can use clever memory management schemes which can take directives so that copying can be avoided in certain cases. The *Id World* environment [13], provides facilities to experiment with such trade-offs between use of additional memory and execution of operations in parallel. In general, management of memory and processor resources in a parallel environment is an open problem and is a subject for further study [7].

7. Conclusion

Ideally, a high-level language should provide a way of writing abstractions which are as close to the problem domain as possible, as well as facilitate efficient implementations of these abstractions lest a user try to "get underneath" the abstractions. With the advent of parallel machines, a language such as FORTRAN fails on both counts. It was never very good for expressing high-level abstractions and, because it forces the user to specify a sequential order of evaluation, it also makes it very difficult to compile good code for a parallel machine. In the latter deficiency, Fortran is not alone; all high-level languages in widespread use today force the user to over-specify the algorithm. *Functional* and other *declarative* languages offer relief on both counts. In this paper, using the *make_array* and *make_matrix* abstractions, we have shown that the use of higher-order functions in *Id Nouveau* raises the level of programming without loss of parallelism or efficiency.

We have also discussed our attempts to write the *make__matrix* and other abstractions in FORTRAN. The primary difficulty in expressing these abstractions in FORTRAN has to do with the lack of dynamic storage allocation. In FORTRAN, one cannot allocate an array in a function or subroutine, and return it as a result. This restriction allows a user (with the help of the FORTRAN compiler) to make very efficient use of storage but often results in quite inelegant programs. The other major shortcoming of FORTRAN and most other imperative languages is the lack of support for curried higher-order functions. Without currying, there is no elegent way of dealing with functions with variable number of arguments. We think, without changing the language in a fundamental way, neither of these weaknesses is easy to fix.

Annotations in FORTRAN for parallel execution make a bad situation much worse. Incorporation of parallel-loop constructs and synchronization primitives permits the user to write programs whose behavior may inadvertently be time-dependent or configuration-dependent. This adds a new and treacherous dimension to debugging programs. In contrast, programs in *declarative* languages are determinate. Such languages eliminate the problem of "detecting parallelism"; however, the problem of managing resources for parallel execution remains. In our opinion it is still not fully appreciated that parallel execution of FORTRAN programs requires at least a limited notion of dynamic storage allocation, and invariably takes more storage than sequential execution. It may be best to adopt new and progressive ways at this stage rather than beat a three-legged horse!

Acknowledgements: We wish to thank Olaf Lubeck, Rishiyur Nikhil, Richard Soley, Natalie Tarbet and Ken Traub for their helpful comments on earlier drafts of this paper.

8. Bibliography

[1] Abelson,H. and G.J.Sussman, "Structure and Interpretation of Computer Programs", The MIT Press, Cambridge, Mass. (1985).

[2] Arvind and R.S.Nikhil, "Executing a Program on the MIT Tagged-token Dataflow Architecture", Proceedings of PARLE conference, Eindhoven, The Netherlands (June 1987).

[3] Arvind, R.S.Nikhil, K.K.Pingali, "*I-structures*: Data structures for Parallel Computing", To appear in Proceedings of Workshop on Graph Reduction, Santa Fe, New Mexico (Sept28-Oct1, 1986).

[4] Arvind, R.S.Nikhil and K.K.Pingali, "Id Nouveau reference Manual, Part II: Operational Semantics", CSG Memo , MIT Laboratory for Computer Science,Cambridge, Mass. (April 17, 1987).

[5] Backus,J., "Can programming be liberated from the von Neumann style? A functional style and algebra of programs", Communications of the ACM, vol 21, No 8. (Aug 1978).

[6] Crowley,W.P., C.P.Hendrickson and T.E.Rudy, "The SIMPLE code", UCID 17715, Lawrence Livermore Laboratory (Feb 1978).

[7] Culler,D.E., "Effective Dataflow Execution of Scientific Applications", Ph.D. Thesis, MIT Laboratory for Computer Science, Cambridge, Mass. (expected Dec 1987).

[8] Ekanadham, K. and Arvind, "SIMPLE: Part I - An Exercise in future scientific programming, RC 12686, IBM T.J.Watson Research Laboratory, Hawthorne, New York (April 29, 1987). bebitem.

[9] Johnsson,T., "Lambda lifting: transforming programs to recursive equations, Springer Verlag LNCS 201 (Proc. Functional Prog. lang. and Computer Arch., Nancy, France. (Sept. 1985).

[10] Karp, A.H., "Programming for Parallelism", Computer, vol 20, No 5, pp.43-57 (May 1987).

[11] Lubeck, O., J.Moore and R.Mendez, "A benchmark comparison of 3 supercomputers: Fujitsu VP-200, Hitachi S810,20 and Cray X-MP/2"/ Computer, vol 18, No 12, pp.10-24 (Dec 1985).

[12] Nikhil,R.S., "Id Nouveau reference Manual, Part I: Syntax", CSG Memo , MIT Laboratory for Computer Science,Cambridge, Mass. (April 17, 1987).

[13] Nikhil,R.S., "Id World reference Manual", CSG Memo , MIT Laboratory for Computer Science,Cambridge, Mass. (April 17, 1987).

[14] Padua, D.A. and M.J.Wolfe, "Advanced compiler optimizations for supercomputers, CACM Vol 29, No 12, pp.1184-1201 (Dec 1986).

[15] Steele, G.L., "Common Lisp: The Language", Digital Press, 30 North Ave., Burlington, Mass. (1984).

[16] Traub, K.R., "A Compiler for the MIT Tagged-token Dataflow Architecture", Master's Thesis, TR-370, MIT Laboratory for Computer Science, Cambridge, Mass. (Aug 1986).

[17] Turner, D.A., "The Semantic elegance of applicative languages", Proc. of ACM conf. on Functional programming languages and Computer architecture, Portsmouth, New Hampshire (Oct 1981).

DESIGN AND SCHEDULING OF MESH ARRAY OF HARDWARE UNIFIERS FOR LARGE-SCALE UNIFICATION

Yifong Shih and Keki B. Irani
Computing Research Laboratory
Department of Electrical Engineering and Computer Science
The University of Michigan
Ann Arbor, MI 48109

Abstract

We propose a hardware unification array consisting of $k \times n$ four-connected unification units to be used to speed up the process of finding suitable bindings for common variables among the predicates in a logic program. Four different algorithms (SIMPLEX, PCC, PwFLP and CP) to perform unification in the array are presented and their performances compared. The final level of unification in scheduling multiple arrays is found to be the most expensive, deserving the highest degree of hardware support.

Introduction

Recently there has been wide-spread interest in designing machines that are capable of performing parallel inference [1] based on logic programming languages such as Prolog [2]. Two types of parallelism [3] inherent in every Prolog program are the *OR parallelism*, which involves the parallel search of alternate and independent paths in the search graph, and the *AND parallelism*, which involves the parallel processing of consistent unification. While both types may involve simple unification [4] of variables, AND parallelism further requires validation of unifications of common variables among two or more predicates (hereafter referred to as *binding check*, or *binding*.) For instance, when the rule $P_1(x) \leftarrow P_2(x,y), P_3(y,z)$ is triggered, P_2 not only needs to bind its variable x to the variable x in P_1, but predicates P_2 and P_3 must also share the same value for their common variable y. Suppose there are k such predicates and for each predicate there exist in the program n clauses that are unifiable to it, then the complexity of binding all k predicates is $O(n^k)$. Unification is known to consume up to 60% of the execution time in a logic program. To overcome its huge cost, research in this area has concentrated on string matching hardware [5], uniprocessor Prolog machines [6,7], special unification chip [8] and linear pipeline of unification elements [9]. With the single exception of [9], which advocates binding predicates by passing bidirectional tokens along a unification pipeline, none has effectively dealt with implementing AND parallelism. In this paper we propose a unification array consisting of a rectangular grid of unification elements that is potentially faster than a pipeline array. The unification array executes AND-parallelism by first producing the collection of sets of clauses where each set contains every clause in the program that is unifiable to one predicate. Next, the array proceeds to locate all instances of bindings that satisfy all predicates by moving tokens from column to column until the result tokens appear at the output port of the array.

Although binding check is inherently tree-structured, we have chosen to map it into a rectangular mesh array in order to insure structural uniformity and good fault tolerance. A tree unification processor, although uniform in its structure, would be inappropriate because of heavy traffic congestion near its root and poor fault tolerance in general. (The entire subtree below a node is disabled if the node becomes inoperative.) Other structures such as hypercubes might be more efficient in some respects (for example, smaller network diameter) than an array, but a rectangular grid is by far the easiest to implement on a chip using VLSI design methodology. For these reasons it would appear that a mesh array is a good compromise. Later in this paper, performance evaluation will show that the unification array does achieve excellent speedup.

Terminology

We now briefly describe the operation and terminology of Prolog. For more detailed explanations readers should refer to [2].

Definition 1

A logic program written in Prolog consists of two types of statements, or *clauses*:

(1) Implication Rule:

$$P_0(w_1, w_2, \ldots, w_{n_1}) \leftarrow P_1(u_1, u_2, \ldots, u_{n_2}),$$

$$P_2(x_1, x_2, \ldots, x_{n_3}), \ \ldots, \ P_\delta(y_1, y_2, \ldots, y_{n_\delta}).$$

(2) Assertion (or Fact):

$$P_0(v_1, v_2, \ldots, v_m).$$

The P_i's represent predicate symbols and the lower case letters with subscripts are terms. An implication rule consists of two parts: the left of the arrow is known as the *clause head*, and the conjunction on the right is known as the *clause body*. A predicate in the conjunction is called a *sibling predicate*. The entire set of sibling predicates in a rule is referred to as an *AND group*. For brevity, we will assume the original goal always consists of a single predicate. The purpose of executing a logic program is to determine whether a predicate, representing the original goal, can eventually be unified to some facts in the program. A goal is said to be *solved* when it is successfully matched to some facts. The search for solutions proceeds by trying to pattern match the original goal and subsequent subgoals (obtained from the AND group of a rule when the rule is applied to a goal or subgoal) with clauses in the program. This pattern matching process in a logic program is referred to as *unification*. While unification is rather straightforward in OR parallelism (matching a subgoal agains different clauses), it is more complicated for AND parallelism because the siblings may share common variables. If every sibling in an AND group is to be unified without causing contradictions, all the instances of a shared variable must be bound to the same constant, variable or structure when the sibilings are unified. When a subgoal f_i is independently matched to a complete set of clauses ub_i (known as the *unification block* of subgoal f_i) that exists in a logic program without regard to the consistency of the values of the common variables shared by f_i is said to have undergone the *pattern matching phase* of the overall unification process. The second phase of the unification process becomes the problem of finding a complete set A in which every member is a δ-tuple $<c_1, c_2, \ldots, c_\delta>$, where c_i is a member of ub_i and δ is the number of predicates to be unified. The shared bound variables is every δ-tuple should be consistent. This phase of unification is called the *binding check phase*.

The Functional Overview of the Unification Array

The Architecture

The unification array is designed to function as a coprocessor for executing large-scale unifications where the number of siblings in a clause body and the size of the logic program are both large. When the host machine for the coprocessor encounters a unification task with large number of predicates, it turns the task over to the array. The host may then turn its attention to some other parts of the search graph when the array is busy. The unification array can be made to function either as a stand-alone coprocessor or as one of many such units working in tandem. In the worst case, where every predicate has at least one common variable, the array is required to check the validity of $\prod_{i=1}^{\delta} |ub_i|$ δ-tuples where $|ub_i|$ is the number of clauses in the unification block of the ith predicate. The array is constructed from a collection of small and simple unification units (UUs) connected in a mesh fashion (see Figure 1a).

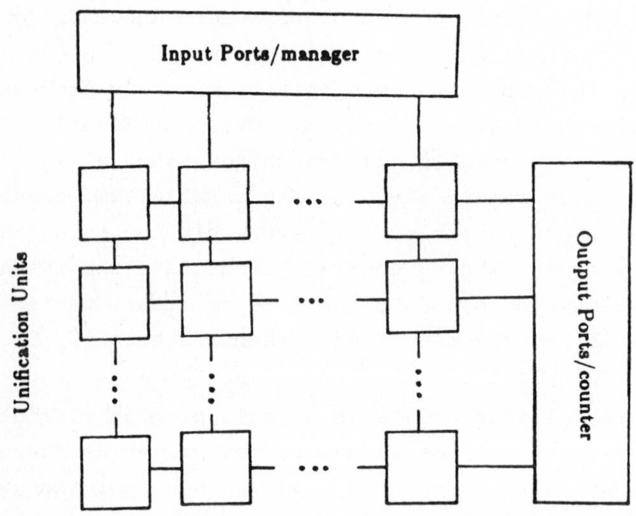

Figure 1a. A Unification Array

Each UU (Figure 1b) consists of a simple CPU, called the *unifier*, that is capable of executing both phases of unification, and two buffer memories, the *Resident Memory* (RM) and the *New Token Memory* (NTM), to store partial tuples in the form of tokens (Figure 2). The arbiter/multiplexer selects incoming tokens from one of the four lines connected to

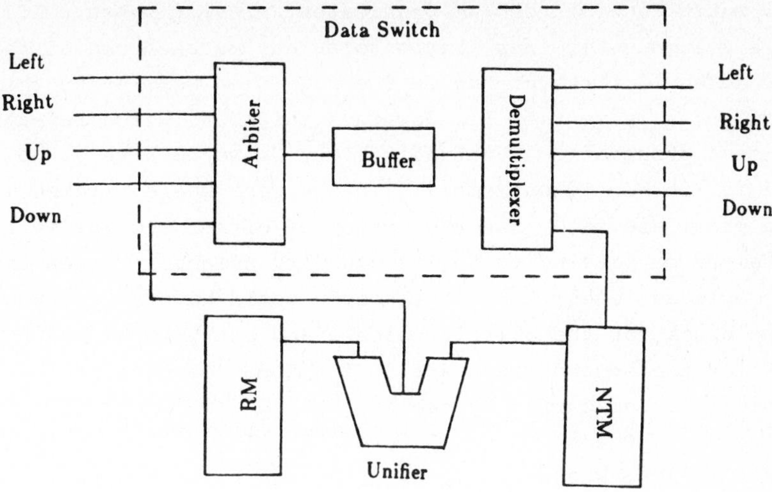

Figure 1b. A Unification Unit

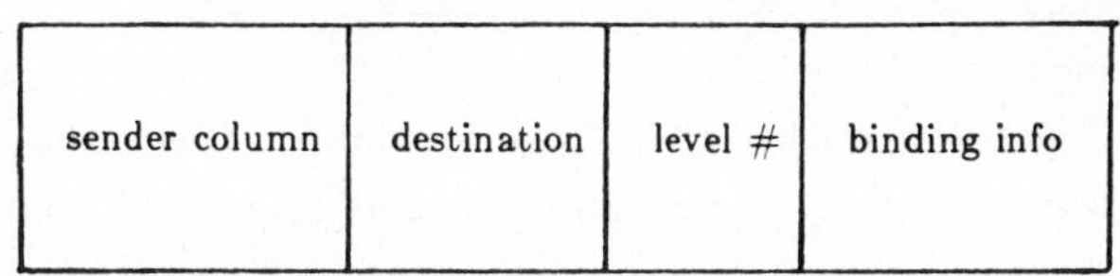

sender column	destination	level #	binding info

Figure 2. A Token Format

four UUs (left, right, up, down) and the output line of the unifier, and outputs it to any combination of the five lines (left, right, up, down and NTM.) The initial pattern matching phase is managed by the input port/manager while the output port/counter keeps track of the number of result tokens departing the output lines of the rightmost column.

The two phases of unification in a unification array proceed as follows:

(1) Pattern Matching Phase

Given δ subgoals to be unified (where δ is assumed to be equal to or smaller than twice the width of a unification array), the input manager first assigns a distinct pair of distinct subgoals to every column of UUs. Thus for a group of eight predicates, four columns of UUs are required. The manager then feeds all the clauses in the program, in the form of tokens, into every column. Every UU will then attempt to match each of the two predicates to every token. If the top UU of a column determines that a token has matched one of the subgoals, the token is first stored in the New Token Memory and then a copy of the token is sent to its downward neighbor, which repeats the store-and-send procedure. Eventually every UU would have a copy of this token in its New Token Memory. In the case where a token matches the second predicate, a UU has the option of either storing it in its Resident Memory or passing it to its downward neighbor. When this phase is completed, every UU in the column would have stored the entire unification block for the first predicate and partitioned the unification block for the second predicate. If a token matches neither predicate, then it is discarded by the top UU.

(2) Binding Check Phase

The Binding Check Phase will be discussed in more details later. Generally, binding checking is processed in levels. At each level columns in an array are grouped together as sender and receiver columns. The partial tuples produced at level-i by a sender column, called a *token pool* of level i, are sent to a receiver column for binding at level $i+1$. A *binding algorithm* determines the sender-receiver pairs at every level. When all the checking is done, the output port/counter terminates the phase after it has determined that all result tuples have gone through the output ports. The unification array is now ready for another task.

Token Movements

While a binding algorithm decides where a token is to be sent, the *data switch* takes a token and physically switches it onto the path toward the destination column described in the destination field of the token. The arbiter in the data switch has the responsibility of granting tokens access to the demultiplexer. The movement of tokens traversing through an input/output line combination in the horizontal direction is called the *horizontal movement*, while the movement of tokens traversing in the up and down directions is called the *vertical movement*. An example of the horizontal movement is a token going from the left input line to the right output line of a UU; an example of vertical movement is the movement through the UP/DOWN line pair.

A token travelling anywhere in the unification array, prior to exiting through the output ports, is a partial k-tuple that contains the binding information of some k distinct predicates. The tokens in the initial unification blocks are 1-tuple tokens; binding an m-tuple token with an n-tuple would produce an $(m+n)$-tuple. We define every member of a unification block as a level-0 token, and every column as a level-0 receiver column. Level-1 binding will take place between two level-0 pools of tokens to produce a new pool of level-1 tokens. In general, a level-$(i+1)$ binding operation between two pools of level-(i) tokens will produce a pool of level-$(i+1)$ tokens. Level-$(i+1)$ sender columns will then transmit these level-$(i+1)$ tokens to a level-$(i+1)$ receiver columns where level-$(i+2)$ binding will take place. Level-$(i+1)$ binding will only take place in the level-(i) receiver column when both pools of level-(i) tokens are available. If a UU does not contain any level-(i) tokens in either the RM or NTM, then it can not begin level-$(i+1)$ binding until each of two buffer memories has obtained at least one level-$(i+1)$.

While the exact details of the relationship between the sender-receiver columns and the buffer memories will be given later, it is important to note that in a receiver column every token of one level-i pool is partitioned among the RMs. It is the replication of the first pool that necessitates the creation of vertical tokens in the receiver column. For every token in the pool that has travelled to the receiver column, the token is first stored in NTM of the receiving UU. Then two vertical tokens identical to the original token are made; one is sent to the immediate neighboring UU above the destination UU and one to the immediate neighboring UU below. A UU in the receiver column that receives the replicated token through the UP or DOWN links would store the token first in its NTM and pass a replicate to the DOWN or UP links, respectively. The only exceptions to this passing scheme are the top and bottom UUs in the receiver column. In the case of the top UU, a horizontal token that is received is stored in the NTM with a replicate sent to the immediate downward neighbor; a vertical token received through its DOWN link is stored in the NTM with no replicates made. Similarly, for the bottom UU, a horizontal token that is received would be first stored in the NTM with a replicate sent to its immediate neighbor above, while a verticle token received through its UP link would be stored with no replicates made.

To illustrate the token movements, suppose a unification array has five rows and k columns. The UUs in every column are numbered from top to bottom consecutively from 1 to 5. Further, we suppose each unification unit UU_i in column r has a level-j token in its RM. A level-j horizontal token t_0 enters UU_3 of column r from some sender column s. UU_3 would first be instructed to store t_0 in its NTM, and to pass replicated t_0's to both UU_2 and UU_4. Upon receiving t_0, UU_2 and UU_4

would first store t_0 into their respective NTM's and then pass a replicate to UU_1 and UU_5, respectively. The vertical movements of t_0 stop when it has reached UU_1 and UU_5, where the token is again stored in the NTM's. When level-$(j+1)$ bindings between t_0 and other tokens in the resident memories are completed, and if the level-$(j+1)$ receiver column is different from column r, then a horizontal token (t_0, t_i), $1 \leq i \leq 5$, representing the result token from the binding of t_0 and t_i, would be sent to the new level-$(j+1)$ receiver columns. If column r is the level-$(j+1)$ receiver column, then the result token (t_0, t_i) for all i is simply stored in the resident memory of UU_i, and no horizontal tokens would be created.

The unifier inside every UU is a special hardware unit for running Robinson's Unification Algorithm by selecting the appropriate tokens from the RM and the NTM. After decoding the tokens to see if both are of the same level, unification proceeds as discussed before. The result of the unification is stored as variable and predicate binding information in the new token. The level number and receiver column of the new token are appropriately updated.

The array architecture we have presented works asynchronously in the sense that at any given time bindings may occur at different levels inside an array. The array is asynchronous because the different sizes of clauses cause varying amounts of information to be contained in the tokens, which in turn consume different processing times during unification.

It is likely that the results of some of the binding checking will produce invalid or inconsistent bindings for shared variables. When this occurs, a dummy token is created and sent to the receiver column. A dummy token may be distinguished from a normal token by the distinct dummy bit pattern contained in its binding information field. When a dummy token arraives at a receiver column through a horizontal link, corresponding up and down tokens are created but no token is stored in the New Token Memory. Instead, the new dummy tokens are immediately transferred to the up and down links, and to the receiver column at the next level. A UU receiving a vertical dummy token should pass it along the same direction it is travelling and, at the same time, send a replicate to the receiver column at the next level. A termination is signalled by the output port/counter when the number of exiting tokens, including the dummies, equals the product of the numbers of clauses in all unification blocks. This scheme might be inefficient if most partial tuples are dummies. We are currently examining another scheme in which a UU that has just produced a dummy token signals the output counter, which will then deduct an appropriate number from the final count of result tokens. A dummy token will never be formed in this situation.

Binding Algorithms

Binding algorithms control the movement of tokens to ensure that all necessary bindings take place inside an array. A binding algorithm is executed by a UU to determine the receiver column of a token that has just been formed based on the resulting partial tuple of a binding check between a token in the RM and another in the NTM. There are four binding algorithms, namely SIMPLEX, PCC, PwFLP, and CP, to be presented in this paper, in which SIMPLEX serves not as a practical algorithm but as a reference standard for later performance comparison of all binding algorithms. Each of the remaining three algorithms, namely PCC, PwFLP, and CP, is a successive refinement of the preceding algorithm.

The SIMPLEX Algorithm

SIMPLEX simply sweeps the array, one column at a time, from left to right starting with column 1, until all tuples have exited at the output ports. The level number in SIMPLEX equals the column number to which a token has travelled. The algorithm utilizes only one column of UUs per level. Level-1 bindings between the unification blocks produce one of the pools needed for binding in every column in every subsequent level. Except for column 1, which sends its level-1 tokens to the NTMs of column 2 for level-2 binding, every other column is instructed to store its level-1 results in its RM to wait for the arrival of the other pool in its NTM.

The Pairwise Column Comparison (PCC) Algorithm

The Pairwise Column Comparison algorithm is a much more efficient binding algorithm than SIMPLEX because it utilizes far more available columns. PCC does binding by pairing up columns and by executing all active column pairs in parallel. Starting with level 2, the entire array of k columns is grouped into $\frac{k}{2}$ sender-receiver pairs. The number of active pairs are halved in every successive level (an example with k=8 is given in Figure 3.) In PCC, every column that is assigned

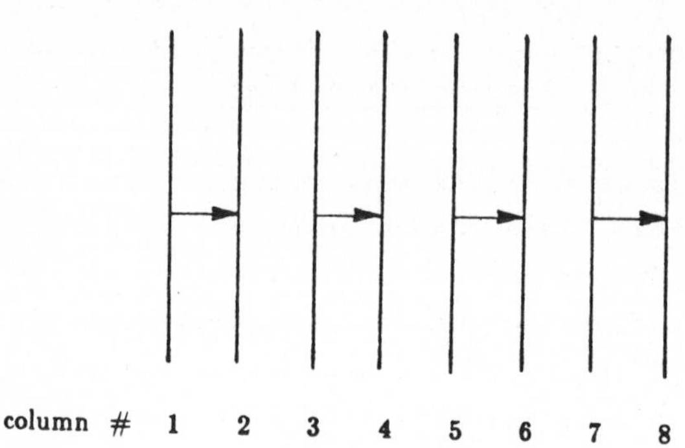

Level 2

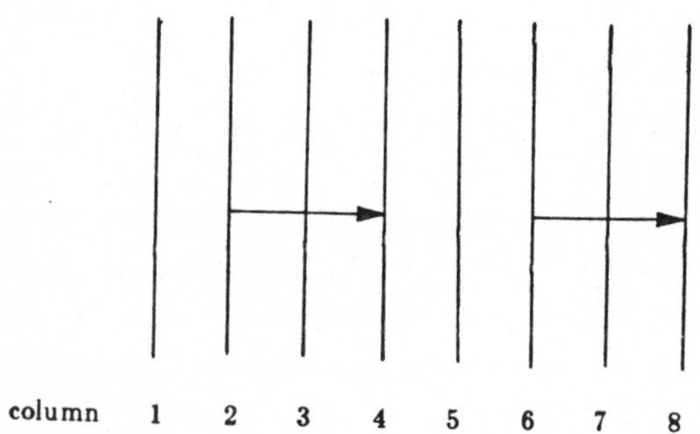

Level 3

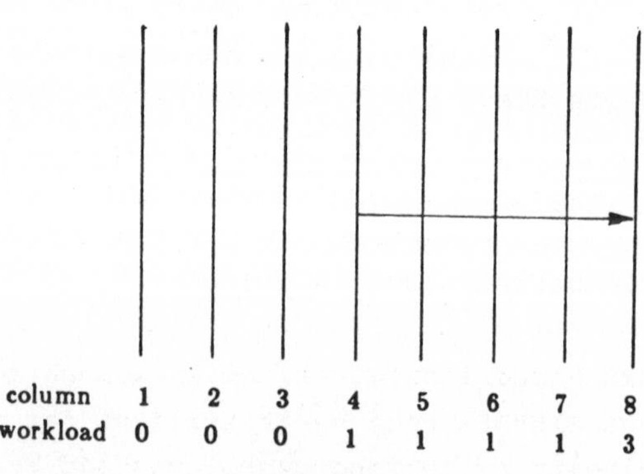

Level 4

Figure 3. Twofold Transit Method (k=8)

as a level-i sender column is instructed to send every token that it has acquired from the last level's binding to the NTMs of its level-i receiver column. If a column is designated as a level-i destination column, then it should store in its RM all the tokens it has itself produced from binding at the $(i\text{-}1)^{st}$ level. The destination column now awaits the arrival of the other pool in its NTMs for level-$(i+1)$ binding.

Algorithm PCC

```
(1)  Execute level-1 bindings; all level-1 receivers store the results
     in their RMs and all level-1 senders send results to the NTMs of
     the receivers;
(2)  REPEAT FOREVER
     IF there exist tokens at the same level in both the NTM and the
     RM of a column
     THEN
     begin
     Bind them to produce a new token;
     Set token level number to current token level +1;
     Look up TRANSIT_TABLE to find the destination column for the new
     token;
     Update the token's destination field;
     IF the destination column = current column number
     THEN
     Store the token into RM
     ELSE
     Request transfer to the NTMs of destination column
     end;
```

Let the total number of columns (the width) be k and the total number of rows (the length) be n. Then the algorithm PCC utilizes $\frac{k}{2^{i-1}}$ columns at level i, whereas SIMPLEX uses exactly one column per level.

TRANSIT_TABLE is a table containing all the sender-receiver pairs for every level. It decides the *transit method* for the algorithm PCC. Although various methods are possible, to minimize transit delay between columns, we must select one that can (1) evenly distribute the tokens so as not to cause excessive idle time for a token to be switched, and (2) always cause movement in the direction of the output ports (i.e., the right direction). Figure 3 shows a transit method called the *Twofold Transit Method* (TFTM) that satisfies our dual requirement.

At level i the TFTM allows columns $2^{j-1}i + 2^{j-2}$ to transmit tokens to their destination columns $2^{j-1}i + 2^{j-1}$, where $i=0,1,\ldots,\frac{k}{2^{j-1}}-1$. On every subsequent level, the number of sender-destination columns is reduced to half of that on the previous level while the distance between a pair of sender and receiver is doubled. Therefore, at the final level, column $\frac{k}{2}$ would be the sender and k would be the receiver.

Pairwise with the Final Level Partitioned (PwFLP) Algorithm

While the number of columns used by PCC decreases by a factor of two as the level number increases, the number of tokens produced at every level i increases exponentially as n^{2^i}, assuming the sizes of all initial unification blocks are n. Therefore, the problem of array under-utilization becomes most severe at the final level when only one column is used. One possible approach for solving this under-utilization problem is to simply collect each of the two pools of input tokens bound for the final level and divide them uniformly among the RMs in all the columns in the array, without creating any vertical tokens in the process (the interval in which this division takes place will be referred to as the *distribution phase* of the final level.) If we assume the algorithm PCC is used from level 1 to level log k (the level preceding the final level), then during the distribution phase each pool is uniformly divided into $\frac{k}{2}$ subsets and each subset is then transferred to a distinct column in the same half of the array (see Figure 4 (a)). Immediately after the distribution phase, the transit phase begins. The transit phase of the final level is divided into several passes. In

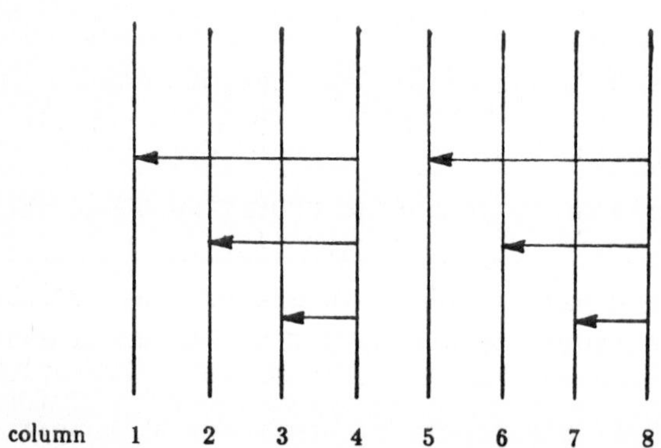

Figure 4 a. PwFLP Final Level-Distribution Phase

every pass each subblock of tokens residing in the RM of a column is bound with the subblocks of two other columns in the other half of the array. For an array with k columns, there are $\frac{k}{4}$ such passes. During the transit phase, one copy of every token in the RM of the sender column is sent to the NTM of the destination column in the other half of the array for the final-level binding (see Figure 4 (b)). This algo-

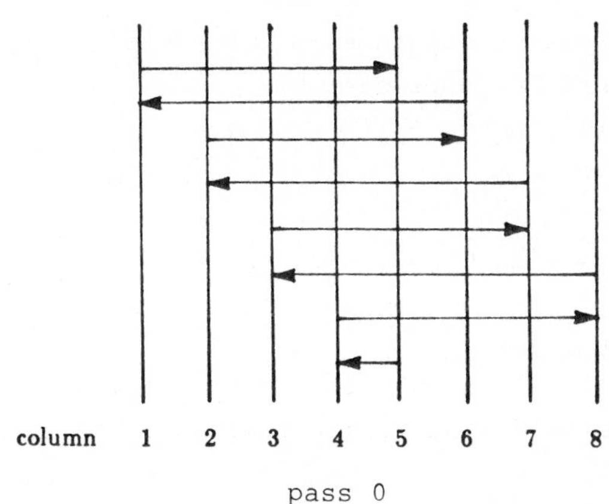

pass 0

Figure 4 b. PwFLP Final Level-Transit Phase

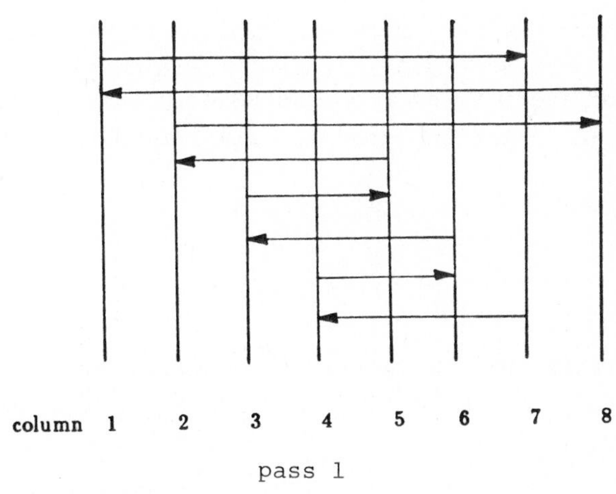

pass 1

rithm, called Pairwise with the Final Level Partitioned (PwFLP), is given below. The variable j, $0 \leq j \leq \frac{k}{4} - 1$, is the pass number in the final level transit phase and i is the column number of the column executing the algorithm.

Algorithm PwFLP

(1) IF the level number $\neq 1 + \log k$ THEN run PCC

(2) ELSE

begin

/* Distribution phase, final level */

Evenly distribute the input tokens of the final level produced at column $\frac{k}{2}$ to the RMs of columns 1 through $\frac{k}{2}$ without vertical duplications, and the tokens at column k to the RMs of columns $\frac{k}{2}$ + 1 through k without vertical duplications;

/* Transit phase, final level */

FOR j = 0 TO $\frac{k}{4}$ - 1 DO

begin

IF $\frac{k}{2} + 1 \leq i + 2j + \frac{k}{2} + 1 \leq k$

THEN

Send a copy of every level log k token from the RM of column i to the NTM of column $i+2j+\frac{k}{2}$ and from the RM of column $i+2j+\frac{k}{2}+1$ to the NTM of column i; bind and send final results to the output ports

ELSE

begin

Send a copy of every token from the RM of column $\frac{k}{2} + (i+2j+\frac{k}{2}+1)$ *mod* k to the NTM of column i; bind and send the final result to the output ports

IF $i+ \frac{k}{2} +2j>k$

THEN

Send a copy of every token from the RM of column i to the NTM of column $i + \frac{k}{2} +2j$; bind and send the final results to the output ports

end

end

end.

The final algorithm in this paper, the Complete Partition (CP) algorithm, duplicates the last level in PCC for all its levels.

Complete Partition (CP) Algorithm

This algorithm attempts to utilize all the resources 100% of the time by partitioning the input tokens, in a way similar to the final level of

PwFLP, for every level among as many columns as possible to get the optimal performance. At level i, $i \geq 2$, the columns of an array is divided into $\frac{k}{2^{i-1}}$ groups of 2^{i-1} adjacent columns per group. At level 2 there are $\frac{k}{2}$ groups, each group having two adjacent columns. One of the two columns in a group sends a copy of half of its tokens to the other column in the same group for level-2 binding. At the same time the other column also sends a copy of all its tokens to the first column for level-2 binding. At every other level i, $i>2$, each group of 2^{i-1} columns is further divided into two subgroups of 2^{i-2} columns each. At every level i there is a total of $\lceil 2^{i-3} \rceil$ passes. During a pass, a copy of all the tokens in one column in a subgroup is sent to a column in the other subgroup for binding; at the same time, a copy of the tokens in the later-mentioned column is sent to another column different from the first-mentioned column, but in the same subgroup as the first-mentioned column. The details are described in algorithm CP and an example for k=8 is given in Figure 5. We can observe that during a pass, exactly two distinct

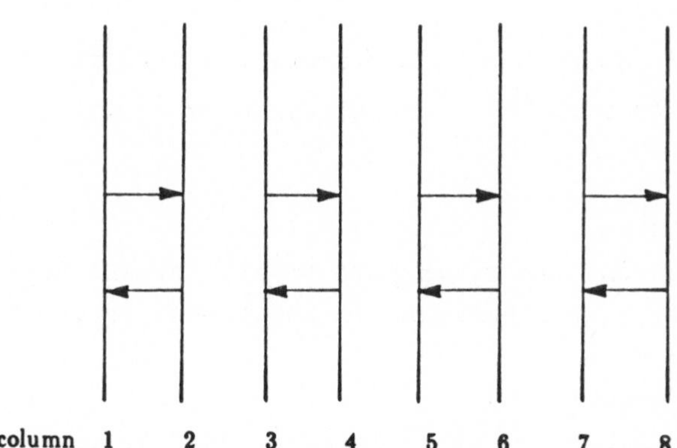

Figure 5a. CP Level 2 (one pass only)

blocks of tokens from the one subgroup is bound with the tokens from a column of the adjacent subgroup in the same group.

Figure 5 shows the horizontal movements during different passes at levels 2 and 3 for an eight-column array under algorithm CP. Level 4, which is not shown in the figure, is identical to Figure 4.(b).

In the following description of algorithm CP, l is the level number, i is the column number and j is the pass number.

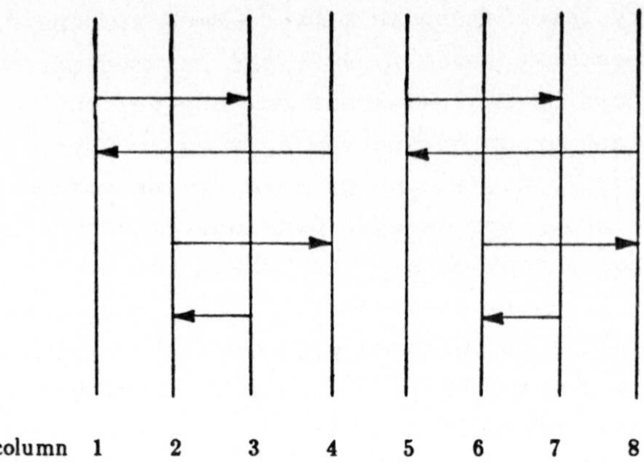

Figure 5b. CP Level 3 (one pass only)

Algorithm CP

```
(1)  IF l=1
     THEN
     Bind the unification blocks and store the results in the RMs
(2)  ELSE IF l=2
     THEN
     begin
     IF i is odd THEN
     Transfer a copy of the first half of all level-1 tokens to the NTM
     of column i+1; bind them with all the tokens in the RM and store
     result in the RM
     ELSE IF i is even
     THEN Transfer a copy of every level-1 token to the NTM of column i-
     1; bind them with the second half of the tokens in column i-1 and
     store results in the RM
     end
     ELSE
     begin
     FOR l=3 TO 1+log k DO
     FOR j=0 TO 2^(i-3)-1 DO
     begin
     IF 2^(l-2)+1 ≤ i+2j+2^(l-2)+1 ≤ 2^(l-1)
     THEN
     Send a copy of each level (l-1) token from the RM of column i to
```

the NTM of column $i+2j+2^{l-2}$ and from the RM of column $i+2j+2^{l-2}+1$ to the NTM of column i; bind and store results in the RM

ELSE

begin

Send a copy of each token from the RM of column $2^{l-2}+(i+2j+2^{l-2}+1)$ mod 2^{l-1} to the NTM of column i; bind and store in the RM

IF $i+2^{l-2}+2j>2^{l-1}$

THEN

Send a copy of every token from the RM of column i to the NTM of column $2^{l-2}+(i+2^{l-2}+2j)$ mod 2^{l-1}; bind and store in the RM

ELSE

Send a copy of every token from the RM of column i to the NTM of column $(i+2^{l-2}+2j)$; bind and store in the RM

end

end

all columns send final results toward the output ports;

end.

Performance Evaluation

There are two primary delays that may occur in the binding check phase, namely, (1) the binding delay caused by an unifier physically performing binding on two tokens, and (2) the transit delay incurred when tokens are moved from column to column. Often these two delays actually overlap each other because a unification array operates asynchronously. However, since any increase in either delay will definitively produce a proportional increase in the overall delay, the binding and transit delays, computed separately, are still indicative of the overall delays that can reasonably be expected in a unification array. Due to the lack of space, we will omit the analysis for transit delays. For the purpose of comparison we will use Prolog's backtracking algorithm as the sequential counterpart to the four parallel binding algorithms. A δ-tuple is obtained when backtracking proceeds all the way from the leftmost subgoal to the rightmost subgoal without finding any binding inconsistency. To find the next δ-tuple, the algorithm repeats the process all over again starting with the next unifiable clause for the leftmost subgoal. For the following analysis we assume that dummy tokens are never produced during binding. Let the unit binding time Δt_b to bind two tuples be the same throughout, then the total binding delay for the backtracking algorithm is:

$$TB_{BACK} = \Delta t_b \sum_{i=2}^{2k} n^i$$

$$= \Delta t_b \left(n^2 + n^3 + \cdots + n^{2k} \right)$$

Let $k = \frac{\delta}{2}$. At the first level of the SIMPLEX algorithm, unification takes place within each column. Thus at the beginning of level 2, every column possess n^2 tokens waiting to be bound by n number of UUs. Then

$$TB_{SIMPLEX} = \Delta t_b \sum_{i=1}^{k} n^{2i-1}$$

$$= \Delta t_b \left(n + n^3 + n^5 + \ldots + n^{2k-1} \right)$$

The binding delay of PCC is also easily computed as:

$$TB_{PCC} = \Delta t_b \sum_{i=1}^{1+\log k} n^{2^i-1}$$

$$= \Delta t_b \left(n + n^3 + n^7 + \ldots + n^{2k-1} \right)$$

Algorithm CP partitions the input level i into 2^{i-2} tokens, $i \geq 3$, except for level 2 where $\frac{n^2}{2}$ tokens are transferred to the other column to unify against n^2 resident tokens.

$$TB_{CP} = \Delta t_b \sum_{i=1}^{1+\log k} \frac{n^{2^i-1}}{2^{i-1}}$$

$$= \Delta t_b \left(n + \frac{n^3}{2} + \frac{n^7}{4} + \ldots + \frac{n^{2k-1}}{k} \right)$$

Since PwFLP is identical to PCC except for the last level, which is CP, its binding delay is a combination of both.

$$TB_{PwFLP} = \Delta t_b \left(\frac{n^{2k-1}}{k} + \sum_{i=1}^{\log k} n^{2^i - 1} \right)$$

$$= \Delta t_b \left(n + n^3 + n^7 + \ldots + n^{k-1} + \frac{n^{2k-1}}{k} \right)$$

Results

(k,n)	Backtrack	SIMPLEX	PCC	PwFLP	CP
(4,4)	86352	17476	16452	4164	4132
(4,8)	1.92×10^7	2.13×10^6	2.13×10^6	524808	524552
(8,4)	5.73×10^9	1.15×10^9	1.07×10^9	1.34×10^8	1.34×10^8

Table 1 Relative Binding Delays (in Δt_b)

(k, n)	SIMPLEX	PCC	PwFLP	CP
(4,4)	2184	115	264	168
(4,8)	66576	869	2064	1296
(8,4)	7.16×10^7	23052	73896	61608

Table 2 Relative Transit Delays (in Δt_t)

The n-times speedup of SIMPLEX over Backtracking is a little misleading because we have assumed that all columns work in parallel at the first level of every binding algorithm. When this assumption is taken away the speedup of SIMPLEX is exactly n. Table 1 confirms the expectation that the speedup of PCC should be less than kxn because not all the UUs are being used at any given level. The last two algorithms, PwFLP and CP, present the most interesting speedups in that their speedups are actually greater than the total number of UUs available. This result is explained by the fact that even without the support of a unification array, the level approach in binding algorithms is inherently faster than Backtracking. Coupled with the fact that PwFLP and CP utilize almost all and all, respectively, of kxn units, their speedups are therefore greater than $k \times n$. Table 1 shows that by going from $k=4$ to $k=8$ the ratio $\frac{speedup}{k \times n}$ goes up from 1.30 to 1.34. If the value of k is kept constant, an increase from $n=4$ to $n=8$ reduces the ratio from 1.30 to 1.14. As a consequence, the speedup using array unification is higher for an array that is designed with a larger width to unify clauses having a larger number of predicates and smaller unification blocks than for an array designed for smaller AND groups with large unification blocks.

Table 2, obtained from the analysis in [10], shows that the algorithm PCC exhibits the smallest transit delays of all four algorithms while algorithm CP comes in a close second. Therefore, it is reasonable to conclude that algorithm CP is an algorithm of choice in array unification.

Multiple Array Scheduling

As we cannot predict the overhead involved in the binding of common variables because their number varies, we also cannot predict the maximum width required for a unification array to run logic programs that could contain clauses with an arbitrary number of siblings. Therefore, having multiple arrays serves the purpose of resolving the problem of unifying more subgoals than what a single array can handle. Moreover, when more than one such unification task is requested by the PEs, they may proceed in parallel without incurring idle time waiting for a single array to become free. However, multiple arrays also bring an additional problem of efficient array scheduling. This is the problem that we shall examine for the remainder of this paper. We will present two scheduling algorithms, the PU and the SFLU, and compare their performances.

Let there be ψ unification arrays. Each array has n rows and k columns. We would like to unify more than δ subgoals, where $\delta > 2k$. We first define a *partition level* as a level on which every output partial tuple it produces has the same number of bound subgoals. For example, suppose we have 2 arrays of 3 columns each. We wish to unify 12 subgoals simultaneously. We will have to accomplish this task in several partition levels. The first partition level takes in 12 unification blocks using both arrays, and produces two output blocks, which are then bound inside one array at partition level 2. The output tokens from partition level 2 are the results of the unification.

Since we have only a limited number of unification arrays, a partition level may need to make more than one pass through the collection of arrays. We denote the number of input blocks and output blocks on partition level i as $IP(i)$ and $OP(i)$, respectively. $IP(1)$ is the number of initial unification blocks (i.e., the number of subgoals to be unified) discussed earlier in this paper. The number of tokens in an input block for level i is denoted by η_i. Since a unification array loads $2k$ blocks for every unification task, at partition level i, it would require $2k\eta_i$ input tokens and would produce a maximum of η_i^{2k} valid output tokens, which in turn become the input tokens for partition level i+1. Let $T_l(i)$ and $T_b(i)$ be the times needed for an array to load and bind $2k$ input blocks during one pass at partition level i, respectively. We will assume that $T_b(i)$ equals only the total binding delay within an array, not including the transit delay. Similarly, Δt_l and Δt_b are the unit times required to load a token and to bind two partial tuples, respectively.

To perform partition unification we assume that there exists a *token distribution unit* (TDU) that functions as the task supervisor whose main responsibility is the routing of the tokens produced by an array to another for further binding. If no arrays are currently available, tokens would be stored in the *temporary buffer memory* until the TDU finds a free array. Performance measures are given for partition unification on the basis of two first-come-first-serve array assignment schemes.

Partition Unification

Let there be δ initial unification blocks (i.e., $IP(1)=\delta$). When $\delta>k$ the initial blocks are distributed among $\lceil \frac{\delta}{2k} \rceil$ arrays of unification at the first partition level. The output blocks from the first partition level are then fed into idel arrays, if there are any, for unification at the second partition level. Sometimes when $IP(i)>2k\psi$ holds for a level i, the partition unification at level i will have to be done in $\lceil \frac{IP(i)}{2k\psi} \rceil$ number of passes. The process repeats until unification has reached the final level where the $IP(final)\leq 2k$. The scheduling of arrays in partition unification is described in the following algorithm *PU*:

Algorithm PU

/* PU schedules idle arrays for unification */

```
begin
FOR i:=1 to ⌈log_2k δ⌉ DO /* level by level */
begin
/* assign idle arrays and load blocks */
FOR j:=1 to ⌈IP(i)/2k⌉ DO
begin
locate an idle array;
load i^th-level blocks number, IP((J-1)*2k) to number IP(2kj-1),
into the array;
end
end
end PU;
```

When an algorithm PU is executed by the TDU, tokens would be routed to an idle array directly from another array, or if no arrays were previously available, from the temporary buffer memory.

Total Elapsed Time

To be able to compute the total elapsed time and speedup of the unification arrays under a first-come-first serve scheduling algorithm, we must first define the total elapsed time and show how it relates to the speedup of multiple arrays over a single array.

Definition 2

The *total elapsed time* (TT) of a set of unification arrays is the time interval between loading the first input token into the first assigned array at the first partition level, and the acquisition of the last result token on the final partition level (level $\lceil \log_{2k}\delta \rceil$). TT can be expressed as the sum of its binding and loading components.

$$TT = TT_b + TT_l \ ,$$

The total elapsed time can also be split into its level components.

$$TT = \sum_{i=1}^{\lceil \log_{2k}\delta \rceil} TT(i),$$

where $TT(i)$ is the interval between the moment the last token for the final pass on level i-1 is loaded, and the moment the same event occurs on the final pass at level i.

Let the arrays be numbered consecutively from 1 to ψ. Assume that the TDU schedules unifications sequentially starting with array 1, and that the time taken to load all input tokens and obtain the binding results at a given partition level are the same for all arrays. Therefore, array i will also finish its task before array i+1. An easy way to estimate the total elapsed time is to look at the time spent by the TDU. Assume that the delay to access tokens in the temporary buffer memory is included in Δt_l. There are then only two types of events that may cause the TDU to be idle:

(1) Wrap-around assignment idle (WAA).
Denote by I_{wa}. Let m be the array assigned on pass j, level i. The wraparound idle time is the idle time incurred by the TDU in waiting for the array m to finish bindings assigned to it, so it may be rescheduled for a unification task for the next pass, or for the first pass of level i+1 if pass j is the final pass of level i.

(2) Insufficient partition idle (ISP).
Unless IP(i) is smaller than $2k$, an array in general needs $2k$ input blocks available before it can proceed. The resultant delay caused by the unavailability of input blocks due to the consecutive array assignments is called an *ISP idle*.

There are two ways we may handle the ISP idle: either postpone all loading until every block is available, or start loading a block as soon as it becomes available. The later obviously incurs less delay than the first and will thus be the method of our choice.

Latency Theorems

The following theorems are helpful for building the relationships between loading and binding times relative to the values of n, k, δ, ψ, Δt_b and Δt_l. These theorems will form the foundation of assumptions for multiple-array scheduling on which the estimation for the total time elapsed will be based. Because of the lack of space, we will omit all proofs (interested readers please refer to [10]). In our analysis we assume that binding algorithm PwFLP is used for all arrays and for all levels. Since the binding at the final level in PwFLP dominates all the previous levels, we will ignore all but the final level in our computation. Thus,

$$T_b(i) = \frac{\eta_i^{2k}}{nk} \Delta t_b$$

for all i.

Theorem 1

If $T_b(i) > (\psi-1)T_l(i)$, then the wraparound idle is nonzero and is given by

$$I_{wa} = T_b(i) - (\psi-1)T_l(i)$$

Theorem 2

If $k \leq \frac{\eta_{i-1}^{2k-1}}{2}$ then $\frac{T_l(i)}{2k} \geq T_l(i-1)$, where η_{i-1} is the number of tokens in the input block for level i-1.

Theorem 3

If $\Delta t_l \leq \Delta t_b$ and $\psi < \frac{\eta_i^{2k-1}}{2nk^2}$, then $T_b(i) > \psi T_l(i)$, where a pass is a complete assignment of all ψ arrays.

In the above theorem $\psi T_l(i)$ corresponds to the time required to load all the arrays in one pass.

Theorem 4

If $\Delta t_l \geq \frac{\Delta t_b}{nk}$ then $\frac{T_l(i)}{2k} \geq T_b(i-1)$.

Theorem 5

The completion of unification in array j precedes the completion of unification in array j+1 by an interval of $T_l(i)$ if one of the following holds:

(a) Both arrays j and j+1 are executing on the same pass of level i, or

(b) Array j is the last array executing on the final pass of level i and array j+1 is the first array executing at the first pass of level i+1.

Theorem 6

If n, $k \geq 2$ then the following holds:

$$T_b(i) > \sum_{j=1}^{i-1} T_b(j).$$

Scheduling Assumptions

We now discuss the assumptions necessary for evaluating the execution time of partition unification. In the analysis the assumptions of uniform datum size and uniform number of shared variables in every subgoal are retained to simplify calculation. In addition, all the conditions that make Theorems 1 - 5 true are assumed. The assumptions are as follows:

(1) $T_l(i)$ and $T_b(i)$ are assumed to be the same for every array on every partition level. The array assignment thus proceeds consecutively starting the array #1 and continues in the sequence #2,3,4,.... When array #δ has been assigned, the scheduling repeats itself with array #1 again.

(2) $k < \frac{n_i^{2k-1}}{2}$ for all i.

(3) $\psi < \frac{n_i^{2k-1}}{2nk^2}$ for all i.

(4) $\frac{\Delta t_b}{nk} \leq \Delta t_l \leq \Delta t_b$.

(5) The condition of Theorem 5 holds.

(6) Transit algorithm PwFLP is used in internal binding. We ignore all transit delays, and all binding delays except those of the final internal level.

Depending on the value of IP(i), a level may or may not require more than a full pass to accomplish complete unification. Since the data are all uniform in size, the binding and loading delays for all arrays on the same partition level would also be identical. We may conclude that if assumption (1) holds, then all the remaining array assignment in every pass on every level would follow the consecutive patter in that only array j would be assigned immediately after array j-1 has been assigned and loaded. This regular assignment pattern will simplify our analysis enormously. The results will help us determine a suitable strategy for partitioned unification. This analysis, however, is not intended for estimating the exact amounts of loading and binding delays.

Splitting the Final Partition Level

An important conclusion to be drawn from Theorem 6 is that the final partition level should have the most hardware support because it binds a disproportionally large number of tokens. Unfortunately, this is not the case with algorithm PU as it attempts to unify the final partition level using only one array. To alleviate this problem we would propose a new algorithm *Split-Final-Level Unification* (SFLU) that assigns to every array in the array set work on the final partition level.

Let the number of blocks for the final level be γ. For every array algorithm SFLU loads γ-1 blocks plus a subblock, which is a subset of the remaining block, that is distinct for every array and contains exactly $\frac{1}{\psi}$ as many tokens as the remaining block. The collection of output tokens for all ψ arrays on the final partition level is the set of result tokens.

If we assume that Theorem 4 still applies to the final level in the sense that any column loading time, including the load time for the $\frac{1}{\psi}$ subblock, is larger than $T_b(final-1)$, then there would be no ISP idle between level *final*-1 and the final partition level. The idle time for the final level in SFLU is then

$$I_{id}^{final} = I_{wa}^{final} + \psi T_l(final)\left(\frac{2k-1}{2k} + \frac{1}{2k\psi}\right)$$

Where I_{id}^{final} and I_{wa}^{final} are the interlevel idle time and its wraparound component, respectively, at the final level in algorithm PU.

A Scheduling Example

This section shows an example for a 2-level 4-array scheduling for the above analysis. Assume we have four unification arrays, each having two rows and two columns. There are initially 16 unification blocks and each block has four tokens. Thus η_1=4. On partition level 1 the elapsed time of SFLU and PU on level 1 are identical. Therefore,

$$TT^{SFLU}(1) = TT^{PU}(1) = TT(1) = \psi T_l(1) = \delta k \eta_1 \Delta t_l = 64\Delta_l,$$

$$T_b(1) = \frac{\eta_1^{2k}}{nk}\Delta t_b = 64\Delta t_b,$$

and

$$\eta_2 = \eta_1^{2k} = 256.$$

On level two we have

$$T_l^{SFLU}(2) = \eta_2 \left(2k-1 + \frac{1}{\psi} \right) \Delta t_l = 832\Delta t_l$$

$$T_l^{PU}(2) = 2k\eta_2 = 1024\Delta t_l$$

$$T_b^{SFLU}(2) = \frac{1}{nk} \left(\frac{\eta_2^{2k}}{\psi} \right) \Delta t_b = 268435456\Delta t_b$$

$$T_b^{PU}(2) = \frac{\eta_2^{2k}}{nk} \Delta t_b = 1073741824\Delta t_b$$

Therefore, the inter-level idle time is given by

$$I_{wa}(2) = T_b(1) - \left[\psi-1 \right] T_l(1) = 64\Delta t_b - 192\Delta t_l$$

From the above we may compute the elapsed times on the second level.

$$TT^{SFLU}(2) = I_{wa}(2) + \psi T_l(2) + T_b^{SFLU}(2) = 3136\Delta t_l + 268435520\Delta t_b,$$

and

$$TT^{PU}(2) = I_{wa}(2) + T_l(2) + T_b^{PU}(2) = 832\Delta t_l + 1073741888\Delta t_b.$$

The total elapsed times for SFLU and PU are

$$TT^{SFLU} = TT(1) + TT^{SFLU}(2) = 3200\Delta t_l + 268435520\Delta t_b$$

$$TT^{PU} = TT(1) + TT^{PU}(2) = 896\Delta t_l + 1073741888\Delta t_b.$$

What are the total elapsed time using a single array to unify 16 unification blocks? It would require 4 passes for level 1 and one pass for level 2.

$$TT^{single} = 4T_l^{single}(1) + 4T_b^{single}(1) + T_l(2)^{single} + T_b^{single}(2)$$

where

$$T_l(1)^{single} = 2k\eta_1\Delta t_l = 16\Delta t_l$$

$$T_b(1)^{single} = \frac{\eta_1^{2k}}{nk} = 64\Delta t_b$$

$$T_l(2)^{single} = 2k\eta_2\Delta t_l = 1024\Delta t_l$$

$$T_b(2)^{single} = \frac{\eta_2^{2k}}{nk} \Delta t_b = 1073741824\Delta t_b.$$

Thus

$$TT^{single} = 1088\Delta t_l + 1073742080\Delta t_b.$$

Conclusion

We have described an array consisting of kxn four-connected unification units. It can be readily implemented in VLSI, and shows encouraging unification speedups of greater than kxn over the performance of Backtracking when algorithms CP and PwFLP are used. These two algorithms are also close in overall transit delays.

The example for the multiple array scheduling demonstrates that, like the situation in internal binding with an array, without utilizing the entire array set at our disposal for unification at the final partition level, the gains obtained from multiple arrays for loading and binding are minuscule at best. However, when the final partition level is split evenly among all the arrays the speedup in binding is almost exactly ψ. Although there is some increase in loading time, it is negligible insofar as the total elapsed time is concerned as long as Δt_l is of the same order of magnitude as Δt_b.

References

1. T. Moto-oka and H. Stone, "Fifth-Generation Computer Systems: a Japanese Project", IEEE Computer, (March 1984), pp. 6-13.

2. W.F. Clocksin and C.S. Mellish, Programming in Prolog, (1981), Springer-Verlag.

3. J.S. Conery and D.F. Kibler, "Parallel Interpretation of Logic Programs", Proceedings of 1981 Conference on Functional Programming Languages and Computer Architectures, (1981), pp. 163-170.

4. J.A. Robinson, "A Machine-Oriented Logic Based on the Resolution Principle, JACM, 12(1), pp. 23-41.

5. Y. Shobatake and H. Aiso, "A Unification Processor Based on Uniformly Structured Cellular Hardware", 13th Annual International Symposium on Computer Architecture, pp. 140-148.

6. T.P. Dobry, et. al., "Performance Studies of Prolog Machine Architectures", 12th International Symposium on Computer Architecture, pp. 180-190.

7. R. Nakazaki, et. al., "Design of a High Speed Prolog Machine (HPM)", 12th International Symposium on Computer Architecture, pp. 191-197.

8. P. Robinson, "The SUM: an AI Coprocessor", BYTE, (June, 1985), pp. 169-180.

9. H. Nakagawa, "AND Parallel Prolog with Divided Assertion Set", 1984 Symposium on Logic Programming, pp. 22-28.

10. Y.F. Shih, Parallel Processing of Production Systems: An Integrated Software and Hardware Approach, Ph.D. Dissertation, The University of Michigan, 1987.

A SYSTOLIC ARRAY STRUCTURE FOR MATRIX MULTIPLICATION IN THE RESIDUE NUMBER SYSTEM

Christos A. Papachristou and Suntae Hwang

Computer Engineering and Science Department
Center for Automation and Intelligent Systems
Case Western Reserve University
Cleveland, Ohio 44106, U.S.A.

ABSTRACT

This paper describes a new scheme for matrix multiplication in the residue number system (RNS) by a VLSI systolic structure. The basic goal is to accelerate matrix multiplication by exploiting the "double parallelism" involved in the systolic structure and in the RNS. The scheme consists of a $N \times N$ rhombus-like array of residue-based processors for RNS $N \times N$ matrix multiplication. Each processor operates in parallel, pipeline or hybrid modes using an arrangement of q moduli adders and multipliers, $q > 1$. The operations of residue addition and multiplication are performed by associative table lookup processing, which has been shown to be particularly efficient for fast residue arithmetic implementations in VLSI technology.

The time performance of this method was shown experimentally to be very good for large matrix multiplications. Thus, the proposed scheme could be very attractive in special purpose signal processing computers that require a lot of fast linear operations.

1. INTRODUCTION

Although the use of the residue number system (RNS) in computing has been studied for many years [Garn 64] as an alternative to binary arithmetic, there have actually been few applications. Due to the growing need for parallel scientific computations and the strong impact of VLSI technology, residue arithmetic has received renewed attention. Some research results have been reported recently on the impact of VLSI to RNS [Tayl 82] and on the use of the other promising technology such as optical memories [Gues 80, Papa 87].

The prime advantage of residue arithmetic is that the calculations associated with each modulus are performed independently, i.e., there is no carry propagation between the digits as in ordinary arithmetic. Due to this reason, the speed of RNS arithmetic processing can be extremely fast especially for large computations. Thus it may be attractive to design special purpose, residue-based, processors especially in applications that require many and fast consecutive additions and multiplications such as signal processors, digital filters, radar control and space shuttles.

The question of whether the residue number system can be successfully applied to general purpose computers is still open one, but again the application to special purpose computers is considered practical and feasible, especially systems that require a lot of linear operations.

An essential ingredient of several signal processing algorithms is matrix multiplication. The important problem of parallelization of this operation has received a lot of attention and several parallel algorithms have been suggested from the viewpoint of general-purpose multiprocessing. A very effective solution of this problem is by means of VLSI systolic arrays [Kung 80]. The purpose of this work is to propose a new systolic structure which is particularly useful for matrix multiplication in the RNS. The basic goal is to accelerate matrix multiplication by exploiting the "double parallelism" involved in systolic structure and in the RNS.

The proposed RNS systolic structure consists of a $N \times N$ rhombus-like array of residue-based processors for RNS $N \times N$ matrix multiplication. Each residue processor performs a recursive multiply-and-add operation and several internal and external transfers within a 2-phase clock cycle. There are three functional schemes of the processors, i.e., parallel, pipeline and hybrid processing. In the parallel case the residues of the input operands are processed simultaneously whereas in the pipeline case they are processed one by one; the hybrid scheme combines the other two. In all schemes the residue processor uses an arrangement of q moduli adders and multipliers, $q > 1$. The operations of residue addition and multiplication are performed by associative table lookup processing. The latter was introduced in [Gues 80, 84 and Papa 87] and it is particularly efficient for fast residue arithmetic implementation in VLSI technology. It should be noted that not only associative but any other table lookup or ROM-based processing is applicable within the context of the systolic structure.

An experiment was organized to evaluate the method and the results have been very encouraging. Several parameters were analyzed such as the relation of the number of processor I/O terminals (pins) versus the size of the moduli set, the selection of the moduli and the time complexity required for $N \times N$ matrix multiplication. In the latter we considered the processing time and the communication time requirements in the RNS systolic structure.

2. RESIDUE TABLE LOOKUP PROCESSOR

We now describe the basic structure of a Residue Table Lookup Processor, RTLP, for an RNS computer. The basic purpose of the RTLP is to form a fundamental cell in a regular systolic structure for RNS matrix multiplications. We shall first describe the overall functions of an RTLP and then show an implementation approach using associative table lookup processing. Other important details of an RTLP will follow.

Operation and Structure of RTLP. As shown in Fig. 2-1, each RTLP has hexagonal shape consisting of three (or four) input ports A_{in}, B_{in}, C_{in} (B'_{in}) and three output ports A_{out}, B_{out}, C_{out}. There are six registers each for each port, i.e., RA_{in}, RB_{in}, RC_{in}, RA_{out}, RB_{out} and RC_{out}, and also one more register, R_m, for masking operations. Furthermore, an RTLP contains a residue adder and a residue multiplier implemented by associative table lookup processing (details of lookup processing come later).

Basically, an RTLP communicates with the adjacent ones while it performs its internal computation. In other words, communication and computation can be performed simultaneously in an RTLP systolic structure to save time. More on this will be discussed in section 3. The RTLP can perform the following recursive computations in RNS within one time cycle.

$$RA_{out} := RA_{in} \quad (1)$$

$$RB_{out} := RB_{in} \quad (2)$$

$$RC_{in} := RC_{in} + (RA_{in} * RB_{in}) \quad (3)$$

$$RC_{out} := RC_{in} \quad (4)$$

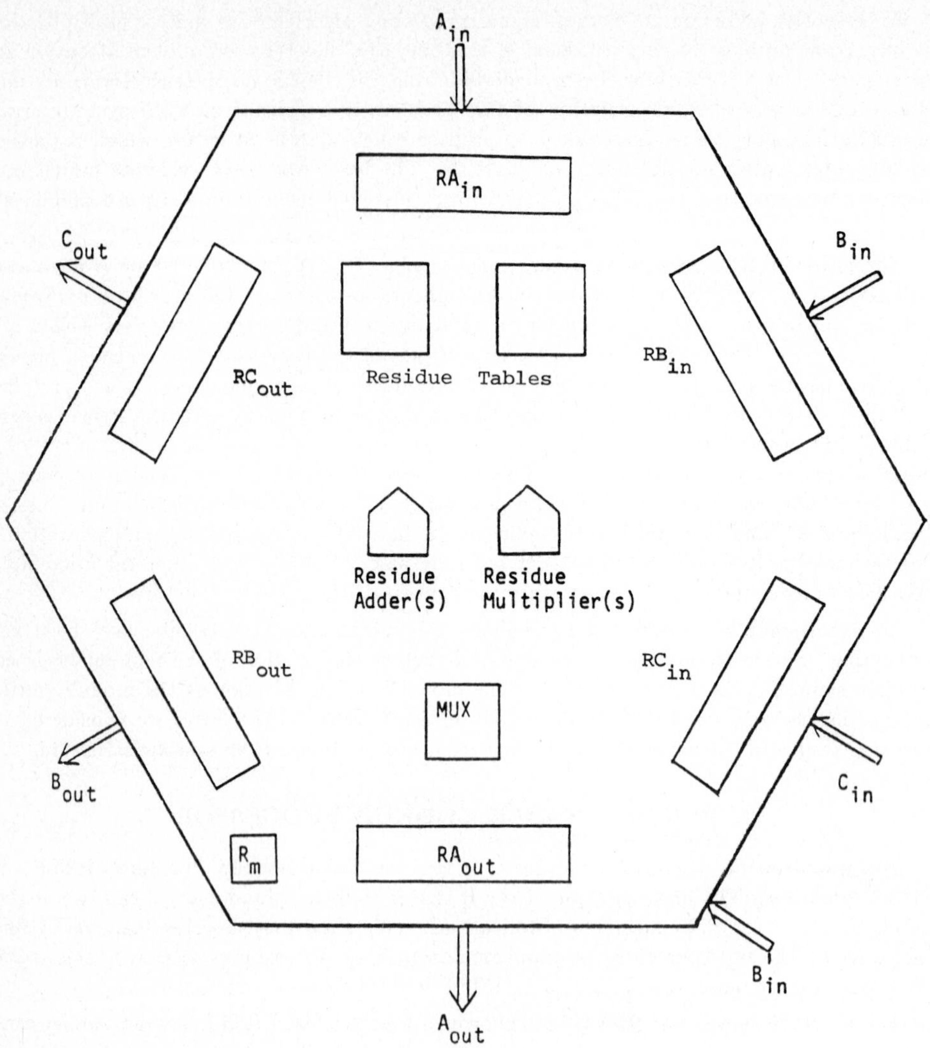

Figure 2-1. General RTLP Structure

In principle, each register stores a number expressed in residue form. We assume that there are q > 1 residue moduli, which are relatively prime, such that $M_1 < M_2 < ... < M_q$. To perform the above recursions in the RNS, we introduce two processing schemes: One by parallel processing and the other by pipeline processing.

Parallel Processing. Each register is partitioned into q subregisters corresponding to the q moduli. Thus a number X is stored in binary form in each subregister of a port as follows:

$$X \bmod M_1, X \bmod M_2, ..., X \bmod M_q .$$

In this scheme, the above recursive equations are performed in parallel for each modulus. This requires an arrangement of q residue adders and multipliers in RTLP that operate simultaneously.

Pipeline Processing. All registers are distinct and have sufficient length to store each residue of X in separate. These residues are pipelined through each port, one at a time for each modulus. In like manner, the recursive equations above are performed one at a time for each modulus using q residue adders and multipliers. However, only one arrangement of adder-multiplier is active at a time.

The trade off between the parallel and pipeline schemes is faster execution speed for simpler interconnection structure in terms of input/output RTLP connections. The latter is important because our main intention is to connect RTLPs in regular systolic structures for the purpose of RNS matrix multiplications. This will be described in section 3.

We should mention here the possibility of a hybrid processing scheme which combines the parallel and pipeline cases. In this scheme we form two or more groups of moduli with the aim to compute the above recursions *in parallel* for the moduli of each group. Then, pipelining of the results is performed group by group. This scheme requires q_1 subregisters at each RTLP port and q_1 arrangements of adder-multipliers, where $q_1 < q$ is the number of groups. In the hybrid scheme, the throughput is better than that of the pipeline case, whereas the I/O complexity is smaller than that of the parallel scheme.

In what follows, we describe how the residue addition and multiplication are performed in an RTLP by table lookup processing and then give more details about the implementation.

Table Lookup Residue Processing in RTLP. Due to advances in VLSI technology it is now feasible to implement residue operations by table lookup techniques using Read-only Memories (ROMs) [Jull 78]. This essentially requires storage of the entire truth tables associated with each addition and multiplication table modulo M_i, where $1 \leq i \leq q$. More specifically, it requires a memory size $2^{(\#I)} * (\#O)$, where (#I) and (#O) are the number of input and output bits, respectively. This disadvantage can be avoided by employing associative storage techniques [Koho 80] to store the residue addition and multiplication tables mod M_i, where i = 1, 2, ..., q. This scheme is described in detail in [Papa 87]. It should be noted that the main reason for using associative lookup tables is that it results in considerable storage saving with regard to conventional memory techniques [Papa 87]. Specifically, residue arithmetic has recently been shown to be potentially very efficient when applied to content addressable memory type lookup processors [Gues 84].

It should be understood that by associative table lookup processing we do not mean to use the type of content addressable memories (CAMs) referred to in the literature [Koho 80]. Although these memories, CAMs, are useful in several database type of operations (information retrieval), they are expensive and less cost-effective in terms of chip area in comparison to ordinary memories. However, our lookup tables require only *READ-type* of associative operations, not the other CAM operations and, hence, they are much simpler than CAMs.

Such associative tables can be efficiently implemented in VLSI technology by VLSI array structures such as PLAs. It appears that future technologies such as electrooptics [Gues84] may be even more efficient for implementing associative table lookup processing.

Fig. 2-2 illustrates a 2-operand RNS cell which implements by associative table lookup processing a distinct addition (or multiplication) table mod M_i i = 1, ..., q. This structure contains an array of associative memory modules such that each of the output bits corresponds to a distinct module. The basic implementation of 2-operand residue arithmetic by table lookup processing is illustrated in Fig. 2-3. Two n-bit inputs are used for arithmetic processing and an n-bit output is produced for the above case. The scheme employs q moduli and requires q addition and multiplication RNS cells mod M_i i = 1, 2, ..., q. The details of this scheme shown in Figs. 2-2 and 2-3 are in [Papa 87].

Moduli Selection and I/O Ports and Pins. The selection of moduli is an important issue in the design of RNS machines. Many system parameters should be considered, and conflicting requirements must be reviewed carefully in terms of technology, cost and performance. In the following we will consider two performance parameters, i.e., execution speed and system complexity as they apply to RTLPs. From the viewpoint of execution speed, a small number of large moduli is preferred in table lookup RNS machines, at least in case of moduli pipelining. However, it appears that a large number of small moduli may be advantageous with regard to hardware complexity at the expense of execution time [Gues 84]. The hardware complexity of an RTLP depends on: 1) the lookup storage requirements and, 2) the number of I/O pins at the RTLP ports. It was shown in [Gues 84 and Papa 87] that the required associative storage is reduced if we select a large number of small moduli, within approximately the same dynamic range*. The question is how this selection affects the total number of I/O pins of an RTLP. This matter will be settled in section 4 which provides extensive experimentation in support of this selection. This issue is important if RTLPs are to be implemented in single chip VLSI technology and then interconnected in systolic structures to perform matrix multiplication (section 3). It is useful to express the number of pins quantitatively using the following formulation.

In what follows, some rules are drawn in terms of the number of pins to make better moduli selection. It is desirable to have as few pins in each port as possible in expressing the same range of numbers. For the pipeline and hybrid cases, only the largest modulus has an effect on the number of pins, so the best choice is to select moduli that are very close to each other.

Let us now define the number of bits required to represent modulus M_k as n_k, hence $n_k = \lceil \log_2 M_k \rceil$, where k = 1, ..., q. We assume that each RTLP has N_p ports and there are q moduli, such that $M_1 < M_2 < \dots < M_q$ and they are relatively prime with each other. Note each RTLP has 6 or 7 ports (section 3). Then the number of total pins in an RTLP for each case is:

$N_p \times (\sum_{k=1}^{q} n_k)$ for the parallel case

$N_p \times n_q$ for the pipeline case

$N_p \times (n_q + n_{\lceil \frac{q-1}{2} \rceil})$ for the hybrid case

where for the last formula two parallel inputs for each port are assumed.

The number of bits of each register is n_q for RA_{in}, RA_{out}, RB_{in}, RB_{out}, and $\sum_{k=1}^{q} n_k$

* By dynamic range we mean the product of the moduli used minus one.

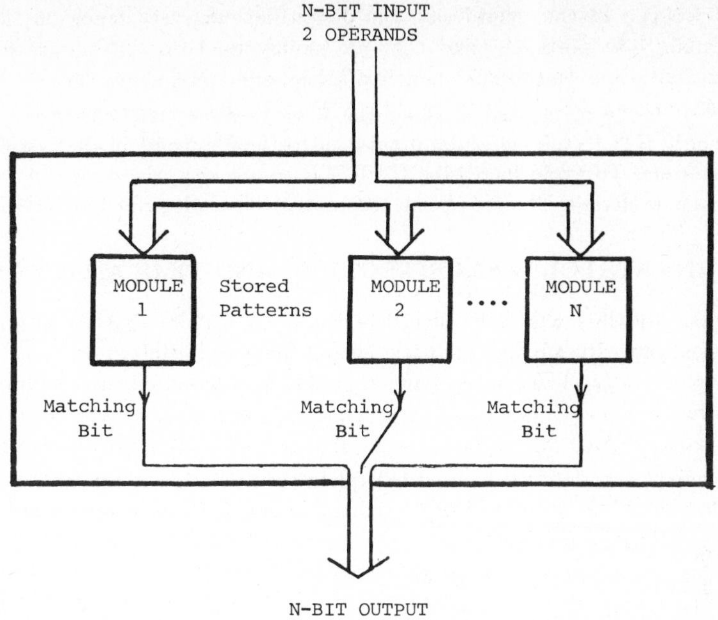

Figure 2-2. Residue Arithmetic Operation by Associative Table Lookup Scheme

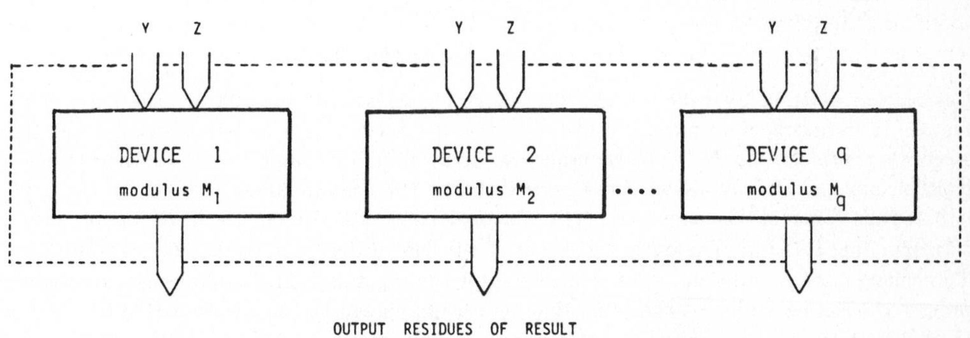

Figure 2-3. The Parallel Scheme of Residue Arithmetic Operation Using q Moduli

for RC_{in} and RC_{out}. In the hybrid case the design depends very much on the sizes and number of moduli. The ports C_{in} and C_{out} are mainly used for shifting the final outputs when all the computations on the same matrix diagonal are done (section 3).

A final point to be mentioned is about the RNS to binary and vice versa converters. Only the boundary RTLPs having initial inputs and/or final outputs in the systolic structure need such converters. To avoid increasing the RTLP complexity, the design of converters as separate devices is preferred. The conversion techniques will be described in the next section.

3. RNS SYSTOLIC ARCHITECTURE AND TIME ANALYSIS

This section describes a systolic structure based on RTLPs that is suitable for RNS matrix multiplications. Recall that the basic idea of matrix multiplication $C = A \times B$ in an RTLP, where $C = (c_{ik})$, $A = (a_{ij})$ and $B = (b_{jk})$, is based on the computation of the following recurrency:

$$c_{ik} := c_{ik} + (a_{ij} * b_{jk}) \tag{5}$$

The following vector notation will be used to explain the operation of the RNS systolic array. Let $X \ mod \ M_k = X \ @ \ M_k$. Then two numbers, a and b, can be represented in RNS as vectors of their residues as follows:

$$a = a \ @ \ M_1, \ a \ @ \ M_2, \ldots, \ a \ @ \ M_q \tag{6}$$

$$b = b \ @ \ M_1, \ b \ @ \ M_2, \ldots, \ b \ @ \ M_q \tag{7}$$

For the product $a * b$, noting the linear nature of the @ operation, we have

$$\begin{aligned} a * b &= (a \ @ \ M_1)*(b \ @ \ M_1), \ldots, (a \ @ \ M_q)*(b \ @ \ M_q) \\ &= (a * b) \ @ \ M_1, \ldots, (a * b) \ @ \ M_q \end{aligned} \tag{8}$$

Consider now two matrices $A = (a_{ij})$ and $B = (b_{jk})$. If we represent every element of A and B in RNS, then for the matrix product $C = A * B$ we have

$$\begin{aligned} c_{ik} &= \sum(a_{ij})(b_{jk}) \\ &= \sum(a_{ij} b_{jk}) \ @ \ M_1, \ldots, \sum(a_{ij} b_{jk}) \ @ \ M_q \\ &= \sum(a_{ij} \ @ \ M_1)(b_{jk} \ @ \ M_1), \ldots, \sum(a_{ij} \ @ \ M_q)(b_{jk} \ @ \ M_q) \end{aligned} \tag{9}$$

Description of RNS Systolic Array. The above equations, (8) and (9), are the basis of the systolic RNS matrix multiplier, illustrated in Fig. 3-1 for a 3×3 matrix multiplication. The structure consists of an $N \times N$ rhombus-like array of RTLPs and it includes the options of parallel, pipeline and hybrid schemes, provided that the corresponding RTLPs are used. The two inputs come at the top and right diagonal sides via the A_{in} and B_{in} ports of the corresponding RTLPs. The output goes out of the left vertical side via the C_{out} RTLP ports. To achieve more parallelism, data elements enter the top side RTLPs simultaneously and are processed together while, at the same time, are being passed to the adjacent RTLPs. The k-th RTLP at the top side is fed the k-th row and k-th column of matrices A and B, respectively, element by element, k=1,...,N. Specifically, the matrix elements are converted to RNS and then the q residues of each pair of elements, a_{kj}, b_{jk}, are processed by means of the recursive computations embedded in the RTLPs (section 2). The residue adders and multipliers are implemented by the fast-access content addressable lookup memories discussed in section 2.

Beginning with the top side diagonal, the computations are performed in synchronism at the RTLPs of each diagonal, and proceed step by step to the last diagonal side of the

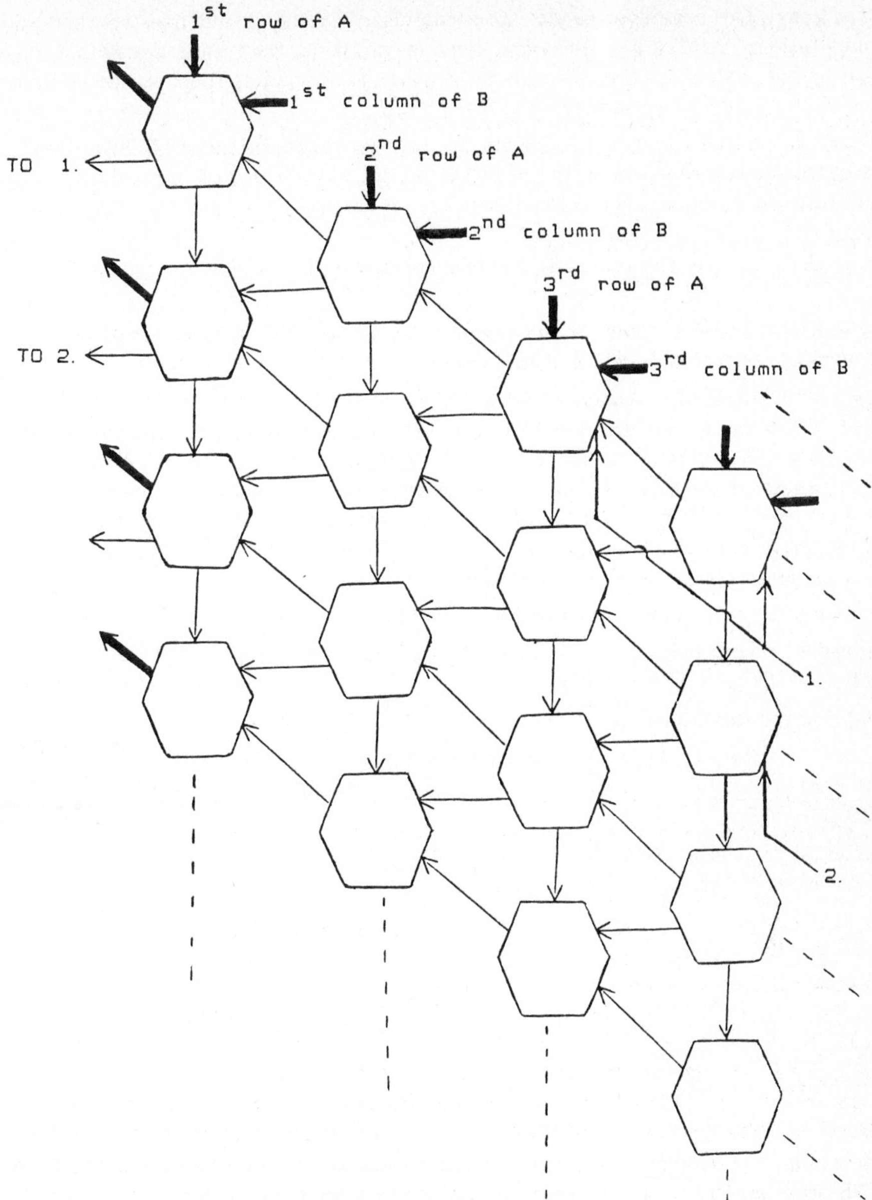

Figure 3-1. Systolic Array Architecture

rhombus array. The computed results are accumulated in the output registers, and when all the computations in RTLPs on the same diagonal are done, the results are shifted along the diagonal to the output of array through the pipeline (at the same time, the other RTLPs on another diagonal may be processing or also shifting).

Note, the product matrix coefficients are not generated in the RTLPs in their proper matrix order. However, assuming the resultant matrix is to be stored in memory, the following addressing formula could be used to store c_{ij} properly.

$$X_{i,j} \rightarrow C_{j,(((i+j+N-2) \bmod N)+1)} \qquad (10)$$

where in $X_{i,j}$, i is the order of the diagonal and j is the column order of the RTLP array.

In Fig. 3-2, the snap shots of the computation of the RNS systolic array are illustrated for the example of 3×3 matrix multiplication.

Timing and Complexity Analysis. To analyze the time performance of the RNS systolic array we will derive a time schedule of the RTLP operations. Without loss of generality, we will construct this schedule for the 3×3 matrix multiplication. There are two basic functions performed by each RTLP: internal processing and external communication. Thus the system time cycle consists of two phases: ϕ_1 (execution timing) and ϕ_2 (communication timing). Further, there are three directions of communication between RTLPs: 1) *horizontal* transfer; 2) *vertical* transfer; 3) *diagonal* transfer.

There are seven types of operations within each RTLP as follows:

1. Internal processing;
   $RC_{in} \leftarrow RC_{in} + (RA_{in} * RB_{in})$
2. Internal vertical transfer;
   $RA_{out} \leftarrow RA_{in}$
3. Internal horizontal transfer;
   $RB_{out} \leftarrow RB_{in}$
4. External vertical transfer;
   $RA(vert)_{in} \leftarrow RA_{out}$
5. External horizontal transfer;
   $RB(hori)_{in} \leftarrow RB_{out}$
6. Internal diagonal transfer;
   $RC_{out} \leftarrow RC_{in}$
7. External diagonal transfer;
   $RC(diag)_{in} \leftarrow RC_{out}$

On the basis of the above considerations the time scheduling table is shown in Fig. 3-3.

Generally, the time cycles required for processing the $N \times N$ matrix multiplication by the RNS array are $2N - 1$. However, N extra cycles are required for shifting the final outputs. Thus, $(2N - 1) + N = 3N - 1$ time cycles are required in total without considering the reordering of matrix output.

We will now derive a more precise estimate of the time complexity of the N $\times$ N matrix multiplication by the RNS array. The derivation is done for both cases, parallel and pipeline processing and it ignores the I/O RNS to/from binary conversions. Experimental results regarding the complexity are in section 4. The basic point is that all RTLPs on the same diagonal use the same cycle for execution and also the same cycle for communication. We define the following time units:

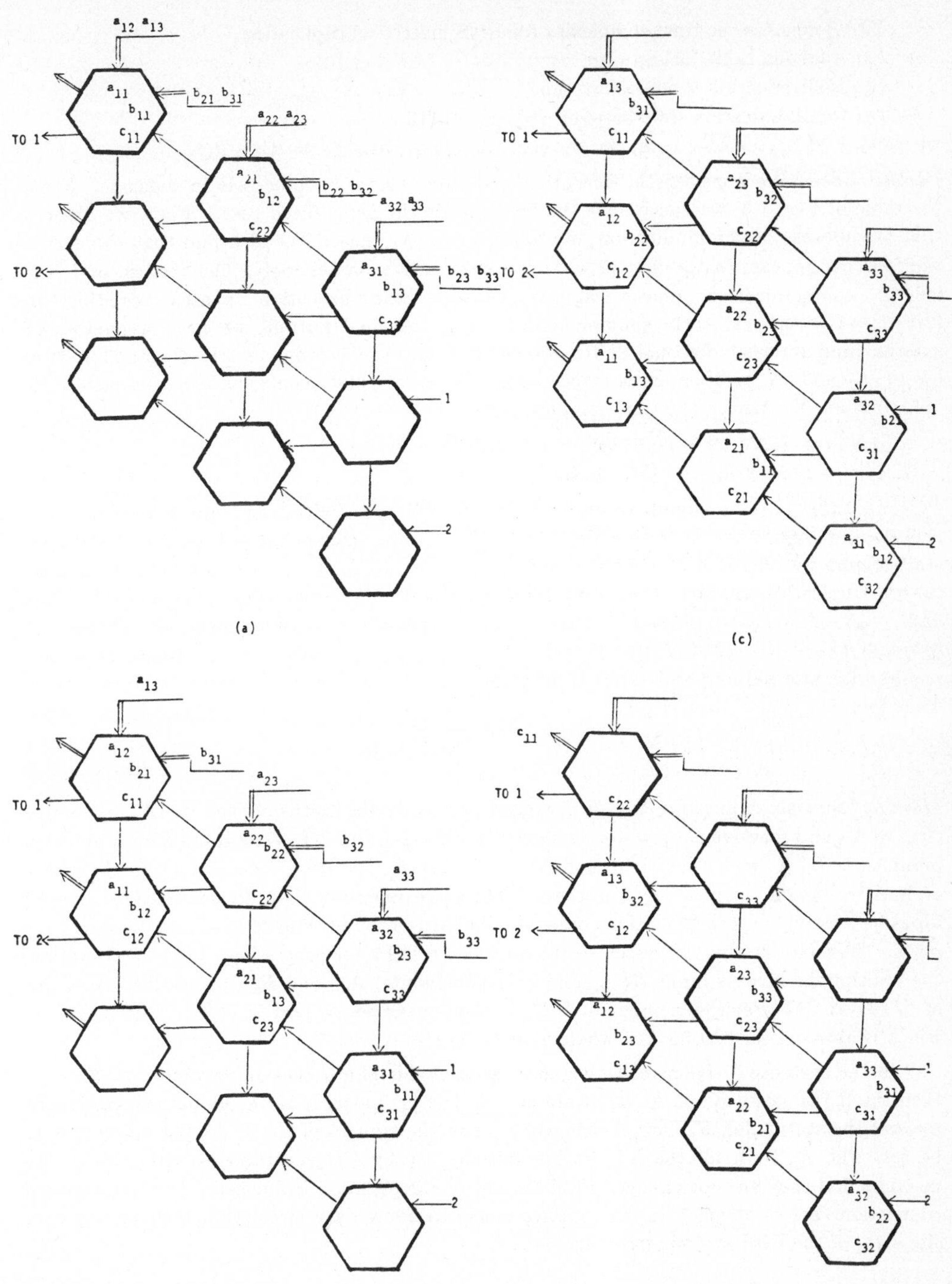

Figure 3-2. Snap-Shot

$T(N)$ denotes the time complexity for RNS matrix multiplication.

t_A : Addition table lookup time

t_M : Multiplication table lookup time

t_C : Communication time between adjacent RTLPs

where t_A and t_M together comprise the execution time, i.e., $t_P = t_A + t_M$.

Parallel Case: We consider the execution and communication processes in separate. From the table of Fig. 3-3, we can induce the formula for the generalized case. First, we observe that the process of communication appears in every ϕ_2 phase. We also find that the execution process appears in the first $(2N-1)$ ϕ_1's consecutive phases, only. The vertical and horizontal communication phases appear between the execution phases resulting in $(2N-1) - 1 = (2N-2)$ such communications. For the final output, we need a number of external and internal diagonal shifts which at worst, the bottom matrix diagonal, require $(N+1)\ t_C$ and $N\ t_P$ time units, respectively. The above statements can be easily proven by induction on N. Hence, the time complexity is

$$T(N) = ((2N-2) + N + 1)\ t_C + ((2N-1) + N)\ t_P$$
$$= (3N-1)\ t_C + (3N-1)\ t_P \qquad (11)$$

Pipeline case: Here, assuming q moduli, the results are derived and accumulated in the RTLPs, one by one for each modulus. As in the parallel scheme, we will construct the general formula by reference to the time scheduling table of Fig. 3-4. The vertical and horizontal communication appears in every ϕ_2 phase whereas the execution takes place in each of the first $(qN+N-1)\ \phi_1$ phases. Thus, the number of communication phases is $(qN+N-1) - 1 = (qN+N-2)$. Furthermore, $(N+1)\ t_C$ and $N\ t_P$ time units are required for internal and and external diagonal shifts, respectively, to derive the final output. Therefore, the time complexity is

$$T(N) = (qN+N-1+N)\ t_P + (qN+N-2+N+1)\ t_C$$
$$= (qN+2N-1)\ t_P + (qN+2N-1)\ t_C \qquad (12)$$

Masking Scheme: A masking flag, R_m, is used to specify the status of each RTLP, i.e., active ($R_m = 1$), and inactive ($R_m = 0$). As shown in Figs. 2-1 and 3-1, some RTLPs need an extra input port, B'_{in} and a multiplexer to choose either B_{in} or B'_{in} depending on the active or inactive status, respectively. If these RTLPs are inactive, they do not perform normal input processing but they receive data via the wrap-around connections into their B'_{in} ports. This data is directly passed to the adjacent RTLPs for processing. In the active state, the multiplexer ignores input B'_{in} and only two inputs, A_{in} and B_{in}, are active. Note out of N by N RTLPs, the number of RTLPs needing an extra port is $(1/2)\ (N-2) \times (N-1)$ which is always less than 50% of whole active RTLPs.

In the system CU (Control Unit), there is an N-bit global masking register. If $N = K$ then the RTLPs of a $K \times K$ array are active. The bit patterns in the global masking register and the status flag R_m are exchangeable upon the control of the CU when masking is to be set. The R_m's in all the RTLPs are initially set by CU according to the sizes of the matrices and they are not changed until the entire computation is finished. The wrap-around connections are established in the inactive states to allow data circulation between the oposite sides of the RNS systolic structure.

Time	Types of Operations in Each Diagonal		
Phase	1st *Diag.*	2nd *Diag.*	3rd *Diag.*
$T_1(\phi_1)$	1, 2, 3		
$T_1(\phi_2)$	4, 5		
$T_2(\phi_1)$	1, 2, 3	1, 2, 3	
$T_2(\phi_2)$	4, 5	4, 5	
$T_3(\phi_1)$	1, 2, 3	1, 2, 3	1
$T_3(\phi_2)$	4, 5	4, 5	
$T_4(\phi_1)$	6	1, 2, 3	1
$T_4(\phi_2)$	7	4, 5	
$T_5(\phi_1)$	6	6	1
$T_5(\phi_2)$	7	7	
$T_6(\phi_1)$	6	6	6
$T_6(\phi_2)$	7	7	7
$T_7(\phi_1)$		6	6
$T_7(\phi_2)$		7	7
$T_8(\phi_1)$			6
$T_8(\phi_2)$			7

Figure 3-3: Time Scheduling Table
(Parallel Case)

Time	Types of Operations in Each Diagonal		
Phase	1st *Diag.*	2nd *Diag.*	3rd *Diag.*
$T_1(\phi_1)$	1, 2, 3		
$T_1(\phi_2)$	4, 5		
$T_2(\phi_1)$	1, 2, 3	1, 2, 3	
$T_2(\phi_2)$	4, 5	4, 5	
$T_3(\phi_1)$	1, 2, 3	1, 2, 3	1
$T_3(\phi_2)$	4, 5	4, 5	
$T_4(\phi_1)$	1, 2, 3	1, 2, 3	1
$T_4(\phi_2)$	4, 5	4, 5	
$T_5(\phi_1)$	1, 2, 3	1, 2, 3	1
$T_5(\phi_2)$	4, 5	4, 5	
$T_6(\phi_1)$	1, 2, 3	1, 2, 3	1
$T_6(\phi_2)$	4, 5	4, 5	
$T_7(\phi_1)$	6	1, 2, 3	1
$T_7(\phi_2)$	7	4, 5	
$T_8(\phi_1)$	6	6	1
....	...	...	...

Figure 3-4: Time Scheduling Table
(Pipeline Case)

4. RESULTS AND CONCLUSIONS

An experiment was organized to evaluate various aspects of the proposed method for RNS matrix multiplication. From the derived results we can draw some useful conclusions: One is about the relationship of the number of RTLP pins versus the number of moduli, and the other is about the computation time required for RNS matrix multiplication. Figs. 4-1 and 4-2 summarize the results.

From Fig. 4-1, we can derive the following points: for the parallel case the number of moduli, q, does not have an effect on the time complexity at all, but in the pipeline case, it is one of the major factors which influence the time complexity. However, the more moduli are used in the pipeline scheme, the more time is required.

A potentially useful result we derived is that for several practical moduli sets and within a large dynamic range, a 1000 $\times$ 1000 matrix multiplication can be executed in the order of microseconds by associative table lookup processing using the RNS systolic structure. This may be very significant in several important practical applications.

From Fig. 4-2, we can find several interesting results in terms of the number of moduli and and the number of pins of the RTLPs. We conclude that, within approximately the same dynamic range, a small number of large moduli is better than many small moduli, for the parallel case, in terms of the number of RTLP pins. But for the hybrid and pipeline cases, it is better to have many small moduli rather than a small number of large moduli, at the expense of more time required for the execution.

The last thing to be mentioned is that if the moduli are as close as possible to each other, then we can reduce the number of pins required.

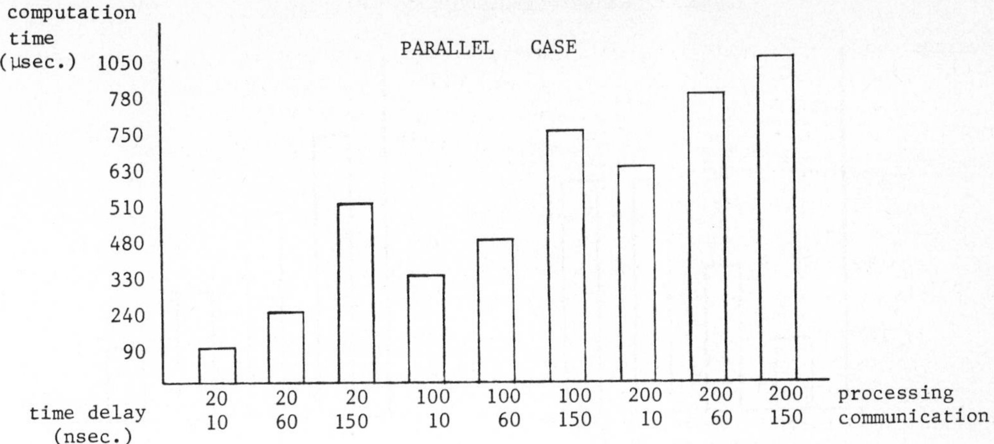

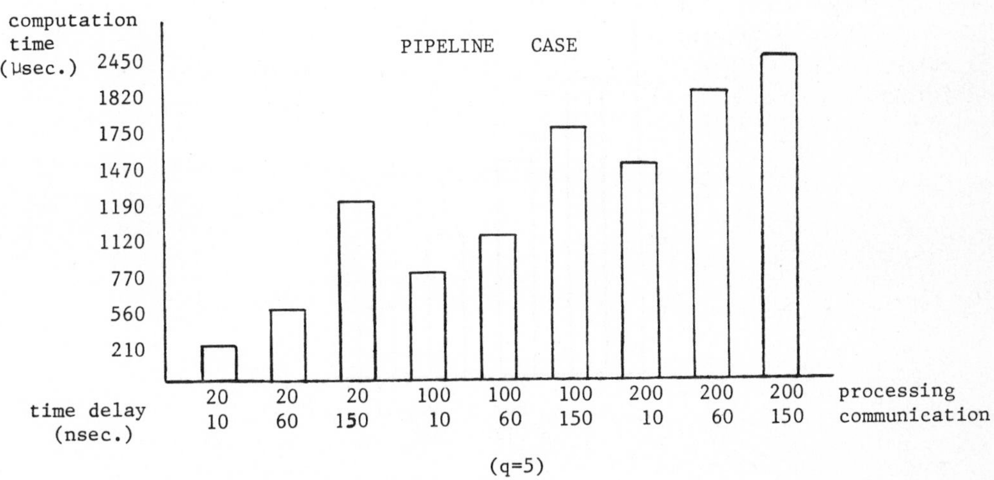

Figure 4-1. A Sample of Results Regarding The Computation Time for 1000 X 1000 Matrix Multiplication by The RNS Systolic Structure. The Horizontal Axis Provides Several Pairs of Values for The Processing And Communication Time Delay of An RTLP.

(Dynamic Range = 150,000)

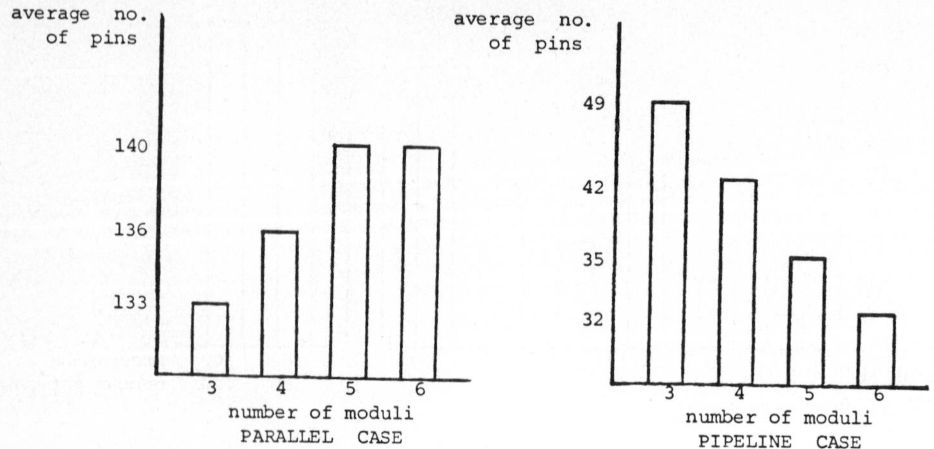

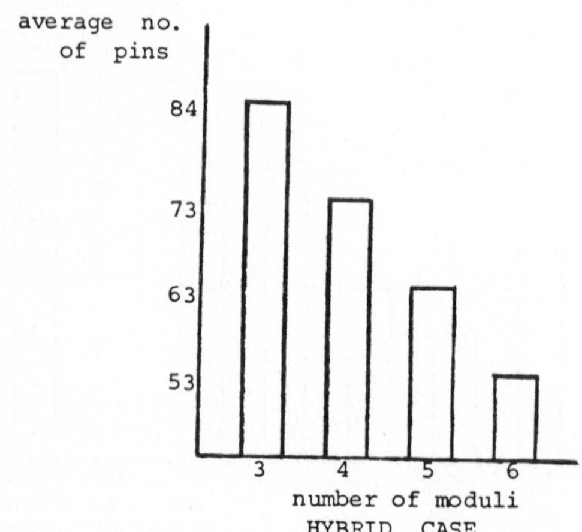

Figure 4-2. A Relationship of The Required Number of RTLP I/O Pins Versus The Number of Moduli within Approximately The Same Dynamic Range

REFERENCES

[Bren 82] Richard P. Brent, and H.T.Kung: A Regular Layout for Parallel Adders. IEEE Transactions on Computers, Vol. C-31, No. 3, 260-264, Mar. (1982)

[Bren 81] Richard P. Brent, and H.T.Kung: The Area-Time Complexity of Binary Multiplication. Journal of The Association for Computing Machinery, Vol. 28, No. 3, 521-534, July (1981)

[Brom 81] K. Bromley, J.J.Symanski, J.M.Speiser, and H.J.Whitehouse: "Systolic Array Processor Developments" in VLSI Systems and Computations. H.T.Kung, R.F.Sproull, and G.L.Steele(eds.): Carnegie-Mellon University, Computer Science Press, 273-284, Oct. (1981)

[Garn 65] H.L.Garner: "Number Systems and Arithmetic" in Advances in Computers, 6, 131-194, (1965)

[Garn 61] H.L.Garner et al.: Residue Number Systems for Computers. ASD TR 61-483, Information Systems Laboratory, Univ. of Michigan, Ann Arbor, Mich., Oct. (1961)

[Gues 84] C.C.Guest, M.M.Mirsalehi, and T.K.Gaylord: Residue Number System Truth-Table Look-Up Processing - Moduli Selection and Logical Minimization. IEEE Trans. on Computers, Vol. C-33, No. 10, 927-931, Oct. (1984)

[Gues 80] C.C.Guest, and T.K.Gaylord: Truth-Table Look-Up Optical Processing Utilizing Binary and Residue Arithmetic. Applied Optics, Vol. 19, No. 7, 1201-1207, Apr. (1980)

[Haye 78] John P. Hayes: Computer Architecture and Organization. McGraw-Hill, (1978)

[Hayn 82] Leonard S. Haynes, Richard L. Lau, Daniel P. Siewiorek, and David W. Mizell: A Survey of Highly Parallel Computing. Computer, Vol. 15, No. 1, 9-24, Jan. (1982)

[Huan 83] C.H.Huang: A Fully Parallel Mixed-Radix Conversion Algorithm for Residue Number Applications. IEEE Trans. on Computers, Vol. C-32, No. 4, 398-402, April (1983)

[Hwan 84] Kai Hwang, and Faye A. Briggs: Computer Architecture and Parallel Processing. McGraw-Hill, (1984)

[Jenk 77] W. Kenneth Jenkins, and Benjamin J. Leon: The Use of Residue Number Systems in The Design of Finite Impulse Response Digital Filters. IEEE Trans. on Circuits and Systems, Vol. CAS-24, No. 4, 191-201, April (1977)

[Jull 78] G.A.Jullien: Residue Number Scaling and Other Operations Using ROM Arrays. IEEE Trans. on Computers, Vol. C-27, No. 4, 325-336, April (1978)

[Knut 81] Donald E. Knuth: The Art of Computer Programming - Seminumerical Algorithms. Addison-Wesley, Vol. 2, 268-276, (1981)

[Koho 80] T. Kohonen: Content - Addressable Memories. Springer-Verlag, (1980)

[Kung 82] H.T.Kung: Why Systolic Architectures?. Computer, Vol. 15, No. 1, 37-46, Jan. (1982)

[Kung 81] H.T.Kung, L,M,Ruane, and D.W.L.Yen: "A Two-Level Pipelined Systolic Array for Convolutions" in VLSI Systems and Computations. H.T.Kung, R.F.Sproull, and G.L.Steele(eds.): Carnegie-Mellon Univ., Computer Science Press, 255-264, Oct, (1981)

[Kung 80] H.T.Kung and C.E.Leiseron: "Algorithms for VLSI processor arrays", Chapter 8 in Introduction to VLSI Systems. C.Mead and L.Conway: McGraw-Hill, (1980)

[Mead 80] Carver Mead, and Lynn Conway: Introduction to VLSI Systems. Addison-Wesley, (1980)

[Merr 64] Roy D. Merrill, Jr: Improving Digital Computer Performance Using Residue Number Theory. IEEE Trans. on Electronic Computers, Vol. EC-13, 93-101, Apr. (1964)

[Papa 87] C.A.Papachristou: Table Lookup Processing for Multi-Operand Residue Arithmetic. Journal of The Association for Computing Machinery, Vol. 34, No. 2, April (1987)

[Papa 83] C.A.Papachristou: Direct Implementation of Discrete and Residue-Based Functions via Optimal Encoding: A Programmable Array Logic Approach. IEEE Trans. on Computers, Vol. C-32, 961-968, Oct. (1983)

[Rca. 64] RCA, Aerospace Systems Division: Modular Arithmetic Computer Research. AL TDR 64-86, Burlington, Mass., April (1964)

[Szab 67] Nicholas S. Szabo, and Richard I. Tanaka: Residue Arithmetic and Its Applications to Computer Technology. McGraw-Hill, (1967)

[Tayl 82] Fred J. Taylor: A VLSI Residue Arithmetic Multiplier. IEEE Trans. on Computers, Vol. C-31, No. 6, 540-546, June (1982)

VLSI Arrays with Reconfigurable Buses*

Dionisios Reisis and V. K. Prasanna Kumar
Department of Electrical Engineering-Systems
University of Southern California
Los Angeles, CA 90089-0781
U. S. A.

Abstract : In this paper we consider mesh connected computers with reconfigurable buses. The architecture consists of $N^{1/2} \times N^{1/2}$ PEs, with PEs in each row and column connected to a shared bus. The buses are partitionable using $N^{1/2}-1$ switches embedded on each bus. This provides efficient global communication patterns for a variety of partitions of the mesh connected computer. We illustrate the suitability of the architecture by demonstrating efficient parallel solution to several graph problems and low level vision problems which have low interprocessor communication requirements. Compared to known reconfigurable architectures and other parallel architectures such as mesh of trees and pyramids, the proposed organization has low area requirement and simple switch control while providing fast parallel solutions to several problems.

1. Introduction

VLSI technology offers an environment for constructing parallel processing systems which consist of thousands of processors. Among many processor interconnection schemes that have been proposed, the mesh connected computer (MCC), seems to be a very attractive architecture with respect to simplicity, regularity, modularity and low cost of PE interconnections. Indeed, a large number of parallel algorithms have been designed and implemented on this organization [KUNG 77, NASS 80, NASS 81, MILL 84b].

A 2-dimensional mesh connected computer (2-MCC) of size $N^{1/2} \times N^{1/2}$ has $O(N^{1/2})$ diameter. Thus, solution to any problem involving all the N data items must take $O(N^{1/2})$ time. In the past, several researchers have studied related organizations which alleviate this problem while still keeping the total chip area to be "small". These organizations include: the pyramid computer [DYER 81, TANI 83, UHR 84], mesh of trees [LGHT 82, NATH 83], meshes with broadcasting [STOU 83], mesh with global bus [BOKH 84], array processors with multiple broadcasting [PRAS 85], mesh with a global mesh [CARL 85], etc. In this paper, we derive a VLSI implementable organization which can efficiently simulate the above organizations. Moreover, several parallel techniques developed on the CRCW P-RAM (Concurrent Read Concurrent Write Parallel Random Access Machine) model, can be implemented on this organization, leading to improved time bounds compared to implementations on mesh of trees and pyramids. We also illustrate the array performance by showing efficient parallel solutions to many graph based problems on the proposed array.

The proposed organization is based on a two dimensional MCC of size $N^{1/2} \times N^{1/2}$. In addition, the PEs in each row (and column) are connected to a broadcast bus as in [PRAS 85]. However, each broadcast bus can be divided into subbuses, so that distinct blocks can use the bus to broadcast data items in their local area. Thus, on a partitioned mesh blocks of various sizes can operate as smaller size reconfigurable meshes. The reconfiguration of the array is achieved by switches embedded in the broadcast bus. Each switch is located on the broadcast bus between two adjacent PEs, which control the switch in a distributed fashion. While this switch control mechanism reduces the overhead in partitioning the mesh, it also leads to efficient parallel solutions to many problems.

Reconfiguration is also addressed in the CHiP project [SNYD 82]. From an architectural perspective, the CHiP computer consists of a collection of homogeneous elements (PEs) placed at grid points in the plane with programmable switches interposed between the PEs. The PEs are computers with local

* This research was supported in part by USC Faculty Research and Innovation Fund and by DARPA under contract F 33615-84-K-1404 monitored by the Air Force Wright Aeronautical Laboratory.

storage for program and data. The key component in such a system is the switches which are used to provide desired interconnection patterns. Switches have local memory to store interconnection patterns and are controlled by the user program. Thus, various interconnections between PEs are accomplished by using different stored patterns. Programming such a system, mapping parallel solutions and related issues can be found in [BERM 83, BERM 84, CUNY 84, HEDL 82].

The reconfigurable array proposed in this paper differs significantly from the CHiP organization. As in the CHiP computer the PEs are placed at grid points in the plane with standard 2-MCC connections. In addition, the PEs in each row and column are connected to a shared row and column bus. The bus can be partitioned and configured using switches embedded in the bus. The switches are simple transistors without any local storage. Unlike the centralized control of the switches in the CHiP computer, the switches in the proposed array are controlled in a distributed fashion by the PEs adjacent to the switches. Thus, PE(i,j) and PE(i,j') which would take $|j'-j|$ steps to communicate in the 2-MCC, can communicate in one step on the proposed array. In fact, by suitable partitioning of the bus, several PEs in non overlapping segments can communicate in constant time.

A major advantage of the proposed organization is in efficient sparse data movement as well as in efficient operations on data. For example, logical operations such as AND/OR operation can be performed in $O(1)$ time, which is the same as the time taken on a CRCW P-RAM model. These operations take $O(N^{1/6})$ time on a 2-MCC with multiple broadcasting [PRAS 85], $O(logN)$ time on the mesh of trees [LGHT 82] or the pyramid computer [MILL 87]. Also several data movement operations can be performed in time which depends on the amount of data to be moved. For example, if there are k records to be moved, then this data movement can be performed in $O(k^{1/2})$ time. These data movement operations lead to efficient parallel solutions to problems with low interprocessor communication requirements, such as graph problems and problems related to digitized images.

We illustrate the suitability of the proposed array by implementing several parallel techniques using the reconfiguration feature of the array. The figures in a $N^{1/2} \times N^{1/2}$ digitized image can be labeled in $O(\log^2 N)$ time. This problem can be solved in $O(N^{1/4})$ time on the pyramid and in $O(\log^3 N)$ time [PRAS 86] on the mesh of trees. As another illustration we consider graphs with unordered edges as input. Using sparse data movement techniques we derive a $O(V^{1/2})$ time graph connectivity algorithm which compares favorably with the $O(logN + V^{1/2}[1+\log(N/V)]^{1/2})$ time pyramid algorithm [MILL 87] and is significantly faster compared to $O(N^{1/2}logN)$ [GOPA 85] 2-MCC algorithm.

The rest of the paper is organized as follows: In section II we describe the architectural features of the reconfigurable mesh. Section III illustrates the use of reconfigurable buses in efficient sparse data movement. In section IV we present some efficient parallel implementations of solutions to graph problems. Section V concludes with a discussion of the major results and a comparison of the proposed array with other related organizations.

2. A reconfigurable VLSI array

The PEs of the proposed architecture are organized as a two dimensional array of size $N^{1/2} \times N^{1/2}$. In addition, a broadcast bus is assigned to each row(column) which is shared by all the PEs in the row(column). PE(i,j) can access the broadcast buses of row i and column j. Each broadcast bus can be divided into $N^{1/2}$ elementary segments by $N^{1/2}-1$ switches embedded in the bus. A switch is placed between two adjacent PEs in a row(column). Let RS(i,j) denote the row switch which resides between PE(i,j) and PE($i,j+1$). Similarly, let CS(i,j) denote the column switch between PE(i,j) and PE($i+1,j$). There are $N^{1/2}-1$ switches on each bus and thus, they form two arrays of $N^{1/2} \times (N^{1/2}-1)$ switches. The array organization is shown in figure 2a.

A switch consists of transistors which control the data propagation along the bus. Let an elementary row bus segment be the part of the bus between RS(i,j) and RS($i,j+1$). A row bus segment between PE(i,j) and PE($i,j+k$) can be obtained, if PE(i,j) resets (sets to OFF) RS($i,j-1$) and PE($i,j+k$) resets RS($i,j+k$), $1 \leq j, j+k < N^{1/2}-2$. This row bus segment is a combination of $k+1$ elementary row bus segments. Combinations of the elementary bus segments can be used by a set of consecutive PEs in a row(column), as an isolated broadcast bus dedicated for communication among the PEs belonging to this set. Notice however, at most one PE can broadcast on a bus segment. i.e., if during a computation a segment of a bus is shared by k PEs, then at most one PE among the k PEs connected to the segment can use the segment to broadcast; thus, the algorithms must be designed to avoid conflicts on the bus.

Other than the buses and switches the array is similar to the standard 2-MCC. The array operates in SIMD mode. The PEs have constant number of $O(logN)$ bit registers. All the data paths are $O(logN)$ bits wide. Under the standard VLSI word model [ULLM 84], the layout area of the reconfigurable array is $O(N)$.

The switches can be controlled either in the centralized mode or the distributed mode. In the centralized control mode, the switches are controlled by the instruction to be executed. Notice that in the centralized switch control mode, all switches in a row(column) are controlled by a single bit. Each instruction has $\sqrt{N}-1$ bits to specify the switch setting. In many applications such a switch control using $\sqrt{N}-1$ bits is not needed. For example, in simulating organizations such as trees, pyramids, butterfly networks only few connection patterns are needed. Thus, it is possible to design an instruction set with $O(logN)$ bits to specify the bus partition; such design issues will not be addressed in this paper. The centralized mode provides a simple mechanism for configuring the buses.

In the distributed mode, row switch RS(i,j), $0 \le i \le N^{1/2}-1$ and $0 \le j \le N^{1/2}-2$, on a row bus is controlled by PE(i,j) and PE$(i,j+1)$. For this, each PE(i,j) has two one bit switch flags, $RSFL(i,j)$ and $RSFR(i,j)$ (Row Switch Flags Left and Right) which control its adjacent row switches. Similarly PE(i,j) has two column switch flags ($CSFU(i,j)$ and $CSFB(i,j)$). These flags are set/reset according to the outcome of computations within PE(i,j). The switch $RS(i,j)$ on the row bus operates based on the logical OR of the $RSFR$ flag of PE(i,j) and the $RSFL$ flag of PE$(i,j+1)$.

Reconfigurable architectures such as CHiP [SNYD 82], have switches between adjacent processors and each switch has a local switch memory. The switch memory stores interconnecting patterns. In our scheme the switch control is simple. Indeed in section 4 we show how the reconfiguration property can be efficiently utilized to yield fast parallel algorithms.

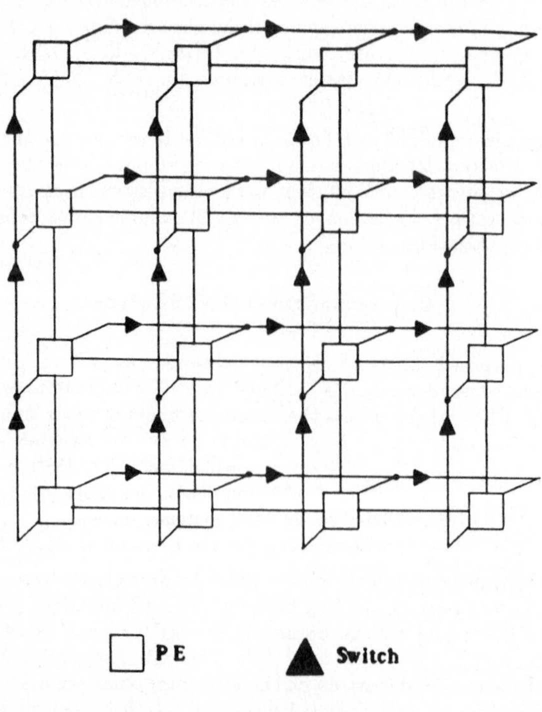

Figure 2a

3. Speeding up data movement using buses

The proposed array can provide efficient communication when the amount of data to be communicated is sparse. In this section we consider several such data operations and illustrate the techniques for efficient sparse data movement. First we begin with some elementary operations on data.

3.1 Basic operations on data

Suppose each PE in the array has a data item. Associative binary operations (such as finding minimum, maximum, sum etc.) can be efficiently performed using the partitionable buses. For example, grouping PEs into blocks of size 2^b , $1 \leq b \leq \log_2\sqrt{N}$ and using the leftmost PE within each block to store the result of the operation inside each block, it is easy to show:

Lemma 1: An associative binary operation on $N^{1/2}$ data items in each row can be performed in $O(logN)$ time for all rows in parallel.

The ability of the PEs to control the effective length of the bus can be exploited to implement some basic techniques used on the CRCW P-RAM model of computation. Suppose we want to compute the logical OR of the data stored in the i th row of the array and store the result of the operation in PE(i,0). In the CRCW P-RAM model each PE(i,j) with a 1 would write its 1 to PE(i,0). On the reconfigurable mesh a PE(i,j) can write to PE(i,0) in $O(1)$ time by broadcasting on its row bus. Notice that a straight forward technique in which, a PE of the i th row broadcasts if it has a 1, can result in conflicts on the bus. This can be alleviated by using the bus splitting mechanism. Each PE(i,j)having a 1 divides the bus into 2 parts by setting the bus control switch to its right to the low state. Thus, the i th row bus is partitioned into segments with at most one PE in each segment having a 1. Each PE with a 1 broadcasts its value on the bus. PE(i,0) will read a 1 from the leftmost segment, if it exists. Otherwise PE(i,0) assumes the result of the operation to be "false".

As another illustration of the reconfigurable buses, consider computing the maximum (or minimum) of $\sqrt{N}$ values in a row of the array. Assume that PE(0,j), $0 \leq j \leq \sqrt{N}-1$ has a value x_j and we want to store the maximum of all x_j's in PE(0,0). By a column broadcast followed by a row broadcast each PE(i,j) obtains the inputs x_i and x_j. The PEs in column j check whether the value x_j is the maximum. PE(i,j) compares x_i and x_j. PE(0,j) checks if there is a PE(i,j) with $x_i > x_j$ by performing a logical OR on the values generated by the comparison in the PEs in column j. There will be at least one PE(0,k) which will have as a result of the OR operation a "false", i.e. $x_k \geq x_j$, $0 \leq j \leq N^{1/2}-1$. Each PE(0,k) with a "false" as the result of the above operation, resets the switch $RS(0,k)$ and broadcasts the value x_k. So, PE(0,0) will read from the bus a value x_k, where $x_k \geq x_j$ for all j. Thus,

Lemma 2: On a $N^{1/2} \times N^{1/2}$ reconfigurable array,

a.Logical OR/AND operation on the data of each row (or column) can be performed simultaneously for all rows (or columns) in $O(1)$ time.

b. Maximum or minimum of $N^{1/2}$ data values in a row (column) can be computed in $O(1)$ time.

Notice that the above technique does not apply to problems such as computing the exclusive OR of $N^{1/2}$ values. Using the results on the size of the circuit to compute the exclusive OR function [FURS 81] we have: Suppose each PE in a row has a bit. Then the exclusive OR of these bits cannot be computed in constant time.

3.2 Sparse data movement

Two well known data movement operations on SIMD computers are random access read (RAR) and random access write (RAW). In RAR, each PE in a set of PEs (designated destination PEs) is to read a record from a PE in a set of PEs (designated source PEs). Each destination PE has a register which specifies the address of the PE from which the record is to be read. A PE can be a source as well as a destination PE.

Similarly in RAW each source PE is to write its record into the PE specified by its address register. The addresses held by the source PEs are distinct. On a $N^{1/2} \times N^{1/2}$ MCC these operations can be performed in $O(N^{1/2})$ time [NASS 81]. Notice that, since the diameter of a $N^{1/2} \times N^{1/2}$ MCC is $O(N^{1/2})$, the RAR and RAW operations require $O(N^{1/2})$ time independent of the amount of data to be moved. In the reconfigurable array, the data movement can be performed in time depending on the amount of data to be moved.

Theorem 1: Assume that the amount of data items to be moved (in RAR or RAW) is k, where $k \leq N$. Then on the reconfigurable mesh, RAR and RAW can be performed in $O(k^{1/2})$ time. Further this time is optimal.

The basic idea of the above data movement is to collect all the relevant data into a block of size $k^{1/2} \times k^{1/2}$ (say, the upper left) and then distribute the data items to the destination PEs. Consider for example, performing the RAW operation with k records to be moved. The records are divided into sets of $k^{1/2}$ items each and each such set is stored into a row of the block of size $k^{1/2} \times k^{1/2}$. In this block the records are sorted according to their destination and they are moved by using the broadcast buses.

An important step of the above method is the movement of the data from their initial location to a block of size $k^{1/2} \times k^{1/2}$. The reconfigurable buses play a crucial role in this. This step can be accomplished by distributing the data such that, the rows of the array are partitioned into $k^{1/2}$ sets with each set having at least $k^{1/2}$ data items and at most $2k^{1/2}$. Once such a partition of the rows is accomplished, the data in each row can be moved into the upper left block of size $k^{1/2} \times k^{1/2}$ in constant time. Thus, all the data to be moved can be collected in this block in $O(k^{1/2})$ time. Details of this algorithm are shown in [PRAS 87].

The optimality follows, since in the worst case all the active PEs can be located in a block of size $k^{1/2} \times k^{1/2}$, while the PEs which are to read the records lie outside the block. The time needed to move the k records out of this block is $\Omega(k^{1/2})$.

A similar data movement operation can be performed on the pyramid computer (using a different technique) in $O(k^{1/2}\sqrt{\log(N/k)})$ time [MILL 87].

3.3 Data compression

An interesting and useful data movement operation is to compress the data having the same key during the data movement. Assume that each PE has at most one record having a *key* field and a *data* field. Without loss of generality let the keys be in $\{1,2,...,k\}$ where $k \leq N$. Data compression will compress the data by performing an associative binary operation on the data of the records having the same key. For example, we may want to count the number of the records having the same key, for all the keys in parallel. On a $N^{1/2} \times N^{1/2}$ 2-MCC such data compression can be done in $O(N^{1/2})$ time using a sort on the keys. Note that this time is optimal on the 2-MCC. However, on the reconfigurable array this can be done in $O(k^{1/2})$ time, where k is the *number of distinct keys*.

Lemma 3: Data compression operation can be performed on k keys in $O(k^{1/2})$ time.

The basic idea of the above data movement is to compress keys within blocks of size $k^{1/2} \times k^{1/2}$ and then recursively merge blocks, so that data will be compressed over the entire array. Compression of data within a block of size $k^{1/2} \times k^{1/2}$ can be accomplished in $O(k^{1/2})$ time by sorting the records according to their key. There may be some keys absent from a block. For these keys a record is generated with a *null* data field. An important step is to merge four adjacent blocks of size $b \times b$, $k^{1/2} \leq b \leq N^{1/2}$, to result in compressed data in a block of size $2b \times 2b$. Note that, as the block size increases there are more buses available for merging the blocks. In order to efficiently use these buses, the compressed data within each block of size $b \times b$ are placed in the leftmost k/b columns within the block

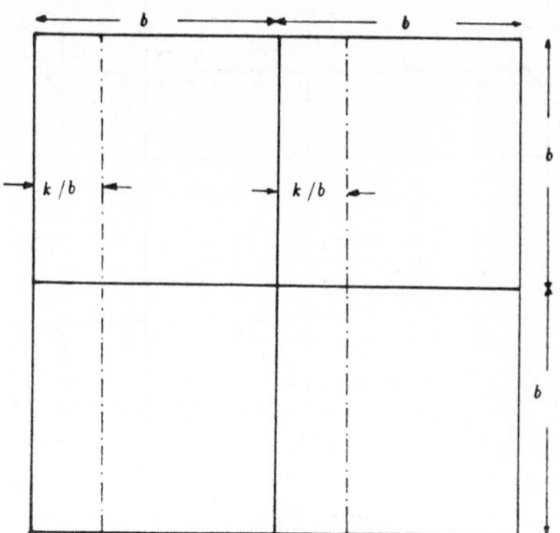

Figure 3.3a

in column major order on the keys as shown in figure 3.3a. The four blocks are merged by using two row and one column broadcast buses for each quadruple of records having the same key as shown in figure 3.3b. There are k/b records on each row of a block of size $b \times b$ so that the entire operation takes $O(k/b)$ time. After 4 blocks of size $b \times b$ are merged the compressed data can be redistributed into the leftmost $k/2b$ columns in the block in $O(k/2b)$ time. Thus, the entire data compression operation takes $O(k^{1/2})$ time. Details of the algorithm can be found in [PRAS 87].

4. Applications

In this section we illustrate the proposed organization for parallel solutions to several problems. The proposed array can provide efficient sparse communication between PEs. For example, the PEs separated by $O(N^{1/2})$ distance can communicate in constant time. The ability of the proposed array to support such sparse global information exchange leads to efficient parallel solutions which are superior to known solutions on the mesh connected computer, the mesh of trees organization and the pyramid computer.

4.1 Implementing graph algorithms

Many parallel graph algorithms involve sparse global communication during the computation. Such computations can be speed up on the proposed array. In this section we illustrate these features by considering the connected components problem under unordered edge input format. For these problems we use the techniques of the previous section for sparse data operations.

The input is a graph on V vertices, $N^{1/2} \leq V \leq N$. Initially each PE(p,q) has an edge (i,j). At the end of the algorithm the PE having the edge (i,j) has the labels of the component(s) to which vertices i and j belong. As usual we will designate the label of a component to be the least numbered vertex in the component.

The basic idea of the algorithm is similar to [HIRS 79]. We will only illustrate how the sparse data movement techniques of the previous section can be used to implement the basic steps of the algo-

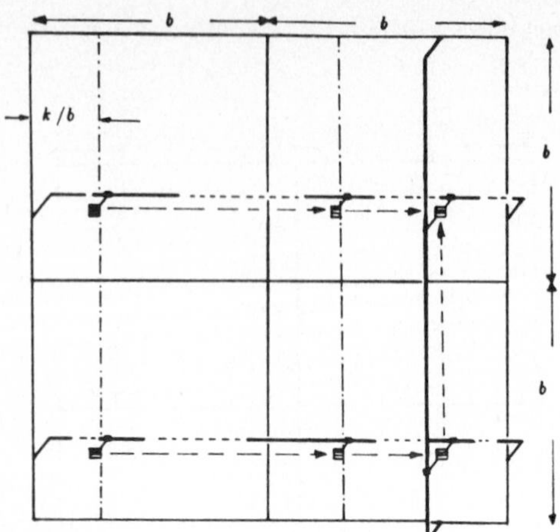

Figure 3.3b

rithm. Initially the label of vertex u is u. As the algorithm proceeds vertices are merged based on the adjacency information in the given graph. A collection of vertices which have been merged together is denoted a supervertex. Each step consists of two basic operations: During the first one, each supervertex chooses the least numbered supervertex (including itself) to which it is connected. The second operation updates the labels of vertices based on the edges chosen in the first operation.

In order to implement the first operation we use the data compression operation of section 3.3, using as keys the labels of the supervertices. Each PE(i,j) with edge (p,q) creates a record with edge (p,q) and label(p), label(q). Using label(p) as a key and using lemma 3 the supervertex with the minimum number (label) to which a supervertex with a particular label is connected can be computed in $O(k^{1/2})$ time, where k is the number of supervertices during the current iteration. In fact this information can be moved to a block of size $k^{1/2}\times k^{1/2}$. Within this block, relabeling of linked vertices can be performed in $O(k^{1/2})$ time [NASS 80]. The reconfigurable mesh is partitioned into N/k distinct blocks of size $k^{1/2}\times k^{1/2}$ each one. The block of size $k^{1/2}\times k^{1/2}$ containing the updated labels, can be copied to each block of size $k^{1/2}\times k^{1/2}$ in $O(k^{1/2})$ time by using the broadcast buses. The label of each PE inside a block of size $k^{1/2}\times k^{1/2}$ can be updated in $O(k^{1/2})$ time. It is easy to verify that the number of supervertices decreases at least by a factor of two in every two iterations. Thus, the time for collecting edges for merging, updating labels and distributing this information to all PEs is $O((V/2^i)^{1/2}+logN)$ during the ith iteration. Details of the algorithm are shown in the figure 4.1a. This leads to,

Theorem 2: Connected components in a V vertex graph under unordered edge input format can be computed in $O(V^{1/2})$ time on the proposed array, $N^{1/2}\leq V\leq N$.

As a comparison note that on a pyramid computer of size $N^{1/2}\times N^{1/2}$, known solution to the connected components problem requires $O(logN+V^{1/2}[1+log(N/V)]^{1/2})$ time [MILL 87]. It is easy to modify the above procedure to compute a minimum spanning forest in $O(V^{1/2})$ time in a weighted graph with V vertices and N edges. Using a spanning tree of a graph G, several properties of G can be deduced [ATAL 84]. Using these techniques and data movement operations on the proposed array it is easy to show:

Corollary: Given N weighted edges of a V vertex graph G in an unordered fashion, in $O(V^{1/2})$ time it is possible to

a. obtain a minimum spanning tree,
b. find the biconnected components of G,

c. decide if G is bipartite,
d. determine the cyclic index of G.

Several graph problems under adjacency matrix input can be solved in $O(logN)$ time [PRAS 87].

4.2 Image processing applications

Several image processing problems related to digitized pictures have been well studied on the pyramid computer (see [MILL 84a] for an excellent exposition of use of pyramid computer in image processing). Efficient solutions to some of these problems on the mesh of trees have been studied in [PRAS 86]. By using data movement techniques of section 3 and additional techniques to exploit the bus reconfigurability we can achieve parallel algorithms superior to these known solution times. In this section we will illustrate the performance of the reconfigurable mesh in several basic problems on digital images.

In the remainder of this section we will assume a $N^{1/2} \times N^{1/2}$ white/black (0/1) digitized picture as input, with PE(i,j) having pixel (i,j). Algorithms developed in this section are of the divide and conquer type, finding desired information within blocks of size $k \times k$, merging adjacent blocks to result in a block of size $2k \times 2k$. This is repeated until the desired information over the complete $N^{1/2} \times N^{1/2}$ array is extracted. For several problems the merging step can be performed efficiently on the proposed array. This leads to *polylog* algorithms for several problems.

An early step in image processing is identifying figures in the image [ROSE 83]. Figures correspond to connected 1's in the image. Informally, two 1's are said to be connected if a path exists between them through neighboring 1's.

The labeling problem is to identify the figure to which each 1 is connected. Thus, at the end of the algorithm each PE with a 1 will have a label indicating the figure to which the pixel belongs. The idea of our method is to divide the entire array into blocks of size $k \times k$, label the parts of the figures which are lying inside a block for all the blocks in parallel. Using the connectivity information along the boundary of adjacent blocks, blocks are merged to yield new labels in larger sized blocks. This is repeated for $k=1$ to $N^{1/2}/2$. Figures in adjacent blocks can be merged as follows:

Assume that the MCC is divided into blocks of size $k \times k$ and all figures in each block are labeled using connectivity information within each block. Then to relabel the figures of two neighboring blocks we use the following representation. Each label corresponds to a vertex. Let p and q be nodes of the graph with corresponding labels l_p, l_q. An edge between nodes p and q exists in the graph if and only if there exists a pair PE(i,j) and PE($i,j+1$) at the boundary such that PE(i,j) has label l_p and PE($i,j+1$) has label l_q. To detect the connectivity of figures which belong to two neighboring blocks we examine the connected components of the graph defined above. The input to our problem at each step is a set of m ($m \leq k$) edges for two blocks of size $k \times k$. This is available in a linear array of size k which is formed by the border PEs of the two blocks to be merged. The connected components algorithm takes $O(logk)$ time [PRAS 87]. This leads to,

Theorem 3: The figures in a $N^{1/2} \times N^{1/2}$ digitized image can be labeled in $O(log^2N)$ time.

Notice that the above problem requires $O(N^{1/4})$ time on a $N^{1/2} \times N^{1/2}$ pyramid computer [MILL 87].

Distance problems occur naturally in image processing. A basic problem can be formulated as follows: Given a $N^{1/2} \times N^{1/2}$ 0/1 image, compute a nearest 1 to each 1 in the image. A general problem is: after the figures have been labeled find a nearest figure to each figure in the image. In the remainder of this section we will address this problem.

Distance problems have been considered by several researchers. Computing a nearest figure to each figure can be solved in $O(N^{1/2})$ time on a 2-MCC [MILL 84b] and in $O(N^{1/4})$ on a pyramid computer [MILL 84a]. A straight forward divide and conquer strategy leads to a $O(log^2N)$ time solution on the reconfigurable array. However, by efficiently making use of the buses to simulate tree computations within segments of the bus and using buses to merge blocks in constant time, this problem can be solved in $O(logN)$ time. In the following discussion any metric d_k, where k is an integer, can be used. Also, let $dist((i,j),(r,s))$ denote the distance between pixels (i,j) and (r,s) in the plane.

The algorithm operates in two phases. In the first phase, it computes the nearest figure to each border PE of the figure, for all figures. In the second phase blocks are merged to identify a unique nearest figure to each figure. Define a PE with a 1 to be a border PE if any of its four neighboring PEs (with respect to the mesh connections) has a 0. In the first phase of the algorithm each border PE computes the label and the coordinates of a PE with a different label. If a PE is unable to find a PE with a different label, then it will store a label *undefined* in its register. This information can be gathered by using the buses as follows. Each PE computes the nearest 1 to its left, right, up and bottom. For example, to find a nearest neighbor PE with a 1 to its left each PE with a 1 isolates the segment of the row bus to its left and broadcasts its index. For a border PE(i,j) the coordinates of the nearest figure is contained in the PEs in the four segments L, R, T, B as shown in figure 4.2a. The nearest PE to each border PE can be located by performing a tree computation in a distributed fashion. The PEs

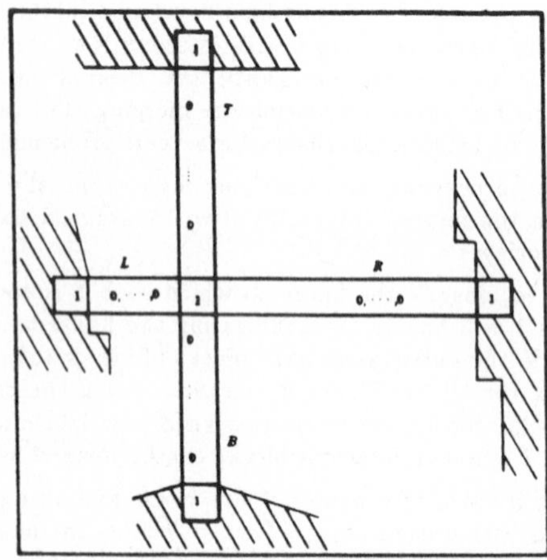

Figure 4.2a

inside each segment co-operate simulating the computations of a binary tree to find the minimum in $O(logk)$ time, where k is the length of the segment. At this time it is easy to verify: For each label l, there exists a $PE(i,j)$ with label l such that the computed distance at the end of phase 1 is the minimum distance to a figure with a different label.

The second phase of the algorithm merges blocks. A divide and conquer algorithm is followed so that each figure can obtain its closest figure. Each border PE constructs a record with its label, the label of the closest figure (found in phase I) and the distance between them. PEs at the border between two blocks know the closest label of the figure inside each block. Throughout the merging procedure, all PEs with the same label athe border between two blocks have the same information with respect to the nearest neighbor of the figure within the block. The border PEs decide which is the closest label inside the new block. This can be done in constant time. Then each PE along the border between the blocks broadcast the updated closest label. The PEs along the border of the new block can identify which row or column has updated information with respect to their label and read this information in constant time using the buses. When the bottom up procedure is completed we follow the same steps but in a top down fashion so that all PEs will be informed about the closest label to the figure they belong to. This leads to:

Theorem 4: The closest label to each figure can be computed in $O(logN)$ time simultaneously for all figures.

5. Conclusion

In this paper we presented a reconfigurable VLSI implementable array. The proposed architecture is basically a mesh connected computer augmented with reconfigurable broadcast buses, such that the area complexity of a N processor organization is $O(N)$. The ability to perform basic operations on data efficiently as well as move sparse data are used as a tool in designing fast parallel algorithms. Also, in any partition of the mesh into submeshes each submesh can operate in parallel as the original mesh. This is an attractive feature for developing and implementing divide and conquer algorithms.

6. References

[BATC 68] K. Batcher, "Sorting Networks and their Applications", Spring Joint Computer Conference 32, pp 307-314, AFIPS PRESS, Montwole NJ, 1968.

[BERM 83] F. Berman, "Parallel Computations with Limited Resources", In Proceedings of the Conf. on Information Sciences and Systems, John Hopkins University, 1983.

[BERM 84] F. Berman and L. Snyder, "Parallel Programming and the Pocket Programming Environment", Computer 17(7):27-36, July 1984.

[BOKH 84] S. H. Bokhari, "Finding Maximum on an Array Processor with a Global Bus", IEEE Transactions on Computers, Vol. C-33, No. 2, February 1984, pp 133-139.

[CARL 85] D. Carlson, "The mesh with a Global mesh: A flexible high speed organization for parallel computation", Tech. Report, Electrical & Computer Engineering dpt., University of Massachusetts, 1985.

[CUNY 84] J.E. Cuny and L. Snyder, "Testing the Coordination Predicate", Trans. on Computers, C-33(3):201-208, IEEE, March, 1984.

[DAVI 84] R. Davis and D. Thomas, "Systolic Array chip matches the pace of high speed processing", Electronic design, October 1984.

[DUFF 76] M. J. Duff, "A large scale integrated circuit image processor", Proc. IJCPR, 1976.

[DYER 81] C. R. Dyer, "A VLSI pyramid machine for hierarchical parallel image processing", Proc. IEEE conference on Pattern Recognition and Image Processing, 1981

[GANN 81] D. Gannon and L. Snyder, "Linear Recurrence Systems for VLSI: The Configurable, Highly Parallel Approach", In Proceedings of ICPP, pp. 259-260, IEEE, 1981.

[GOPA 85] P. S. Gopalakrishnan, I. V. Ramakrishnan, L. N. Kanal, "An Efficient Connected Components Algorithm on a Mesh-Connected Computer", Tech. Report, Dept of Computer Science, 1985, University of Maryland.

[HEDL 82] Kye S. Hedlund and L. Snyder, "Wafer Scale Integration of Configurable, Highly Parallel Processors", In Proceedings of ICPP, pp. 262-264, IEEE, 1982.

[HIRS 79] D. S. Hirschberg, A. K. Chandra and D. V. Sarwate, "Computing connected components on parallel computers", Communications of ACM, 1979.

[JAJA 84a] J. Ja'Ja' and V. K. Prasanna Kumar, "Information Transfer in Distributed Computing with Applications to VLSI", Journal of ACM, Jan. 1984.

[JAJA 84b] J. Ja'Ja', V. K. Prasanna Kumar and J. Simon, "Information transfer under different sets of protocols", SIAM Journal on Computing, 1984.

[KUNG 77] H. T. Kung and C. D. Thompson, "Sorting on a Mesh Connected Computer ", Comm ACM, 1977.

[LGHT 82] F. T. Leighton, "Parallel computations using Mesh of Trees", Technical Report MIT, 1982.

[MILL 84a] R. Miller and Q. F. Stout, "Convexity algorithms for pyramid computers", Proc. 1984 International Parallel Processing Conference.

[MILL 84b] R. Miller and Q. F. Stout, "Computational Geometry on a Mesh-Connected Computer", Proc. 1984 International Conference on Parallel Processing, pp. 66-74.

[MILL 87] R. Miller and Q. Stout, " Data Movement techniques for the Pyramid Computer", SIAM journal on computing, Vol. 16, No. 1, February 1987.

[NASS 81] D. Nassimi and S. Sahni, "Data Broadcasting in SIMD Computers", IEEE Transactions on Computers 1981.

[NATH 83] D. Nath, S. N. Maheshwari, P. C. Bhat, "Efficient VLSI networks for parallel processing based on orthogonal trees", IEEE, Transactions on Computers, 1983.

[OVER 80] M. H. Overmars and J. Van Leeuwen, "Dynamically maintaining configurations in the plane", Proceedings of the 12th Symposium on Theory of Computing, 1980.

[PRAS 83] V. K. Prasanna Kumar, "Communication Complexity of various VLSI Models", Ph. D. thesis, Dept. of Computer Science, Pennsylvania State Univ., 1983.

[PRAS 85] V. K. Prasanna Kumar and C. S. Raghavendra, "Array Processor with Multiple Broadcasting", Proceedings of the 1985 Annual Symposium on Computer Architecture, June 1985.

[PRAS 86] V. K. Prasanna Kumar and Mehrnoosh Eshaghian, "Parallel Geometric algorithms for Digitized pictures on the Mesh of Trees organization", International Conference on Parallel Processing, 1986.

[PRAS 87] D. Reisis and V. K. Prasanna Kumar, "VLSI Arrays with Reconfigurable Buses", Technical Report, Computer Research Institute University of Southern California, May 1987.

[PRAS 87b] V. K. Prasanna Kumar and D. Reisis, "Parallel Image Processing on Enhanced Arrays", Proceedings of the International Conference on Parallel Processing, 1987.

[ROSE 83] A. Rosenfeld, "Parallel Processors for Image Processing: 2-D arrays and extensions", IEEE Computer, Jan. 1983.

[SHIL 82] Y. Shiloach and U. Vishkin, "A $O(logN)$ Parallel Connectivity Algorithm", Journal of Algorithms 3, 1982.

[SNYD 82] L. Snyder, "Introduction to the Configurable, Highly Parallel Computer", Computer 1S(1):47-56, January, 1982.

[STOU 83] Q. F. Stout, "Mesh Connected Computers with Broadcasting", IEEE Trans. on Computers, pp. 826-830, 1983.

[TANI 83] S. L. Tanimoto, "A Pyramidal approach to Parallel Processing", Proc. 1983 International Symposium on Computer Architecture.

[UHR 84] L. Uhr, "Algorithm-Structured Computer Arrays and Networks", Academic Press, 1984.

1. Let PE(i ,j) have edge (x_i ,y_j).

2. In PE(i ,j) initialize: label(x_i):=x_i , label(y_j):=y_j .

3. REPEAT

4. Reset flag *changes* .

5. In each PE create a record with *key* :=label(x_i) and another field having data (x_i ,y_j).

6. Perform data compression using lemma 3 to move a record for each supervertex into upper left block of size $k^{1/2} \times k^{1/2}$, where k is the number of supervertices during the iteration.

7. Sorting on each record in the $k^{1/2} \times k^{1/2}$ in shuffle major order, merge the supervertices in the block. Set the flag *changes* if the label of a supervertex is modified.

8. Update label(x_i) and label (y_j) in each PE in $O(k^{1/2})$ time.

UNTIL flag *changes* is reset.

Figure 4.1a

A WAVEFRONT ARRAY PROCESSOR USING DATAFLOW PROCESSING ELEMENTS

John A. Vlontzos, S.Y. Kung
Department of Electrical Engineering
University of Southern California

ABSTRACT

In this paper, a prototype Wavefront Array Processor based on the NEC μPD7281 dataflow chip is presented. The interconnections of this array are reconfigurable and its processor addressing scheme permits construction of very large arrays. The programming methodology and high level language are presented. These, facilitate the expression and mapping of linear algebra and signal/image processing algorithms on this array. To illustrate the performance and programming of this machine some indicative applications are discussed.

1. INTRODUCTION

The processing rates required of the supercomputers of the near future range from one billion to tens of billions of operations per second . Since a uniprocessor would require a cycle time of under one nanosecond to achieve this performance, the use of multiple processors is mandatory. The supercomputer designer can choose to use either a small number of processors coupled with very fast hardware (i.e., Cray) or a very large number of slower processors (i.e., MPP, Connection Machine). In both cases however mapping the algorithm to the architecture is the real bottleneck since we see machines with theoretical performance of hundrends of MFLOPs to have average performance in the tens of MFLOPS .

In this paper we present a programmable, reconfigurable wavefront array processor capable of sustaining high computational rates of some classes of applications. The performance achieved is based on the canonical algorithm mapping methodology developed in |*1*|, |*4*|, |*5*|, on the dataflow nature of the processing element and the flexibility of communications in the proposed architecture.

Our target applications are signal and image processing and numerical analysis since they require very high computation rates both when they are real time because of high data throughput (i.e. radar, satellite imaging) and when they are off-line because of high data volume (i.e. seismic processing).

In section 2 we discuss the arthitecture, the advantages and limitations of the array, the processing element and the communications interface. In section 3 we discuss the programming issues such as the mapping methodology and the high level languages suitable for this design. Section 4 is devoted to examples of using the wavefront array for some applications.

2. HARDWARE

The wavefront array processor |*1*| is a collection of asynchronous processing elements operating on data availability and thus it can be considered as a *static dataflow machine*. For simplicity and economy reasons we chose to use a commercially available processing element that would match our architecture. Such a processor is the NEC μPD7281 Dataflow chip described in the following. This chip provides a simple and elegant mechanism for processor communications as well as relatively high processing rate. An additional advantage is that there exist a companion chip (NEC μPD9305) for host/memory interfacing thus facilitating our design. The main disadvantages of the NEC chip are its lack of floating point instruction and its linear I/O interface which makes it more difficult to design two dimensional arrays. The second disadvantage led us to the design of a processor interface that facilitates the construction of two dimensional arrays at the same time providing a degree of reconfigurability.

2.1 The Dataflow Chip

The NEC μPD7281 chip |2| is a dataflow microprocessor initially designed for image processing applications using linear arrays or rings. Its instruction set however is powerful enough to permit its use in more general signal processing applications.

From figure 1 we see that the chip consists of 10 functional blocks, the

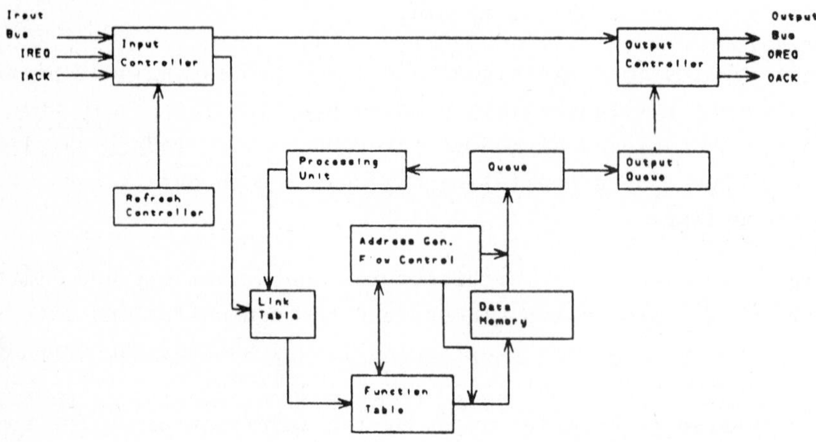

Figure 1: Architecture of the μPD7281.

input controller (IC), the refresh controller (RC), the link table (LT), the function table (FT), the data memory (DM), the execution queue (Q), the processing unit (PU), the address generator and flow controller (AG/FC), the output queue (OQ) and the output controller (OC). The LT, FT, DM, Q and PU form a circular pipeline with 200nsec cycle time under the control of the AG/FC block.

The μPD7281 chip processes data as *tokens* that have the form of figure 2. The Module Number field (MN) is the number of the processor and the

IC checks this field and if the number matches it accepts the token sending it to the LT, otherwise it sends it directly to the OC to be passed to the next processor. The LT uses the ID field (identify field) that is the label of an edge in the dataflow graph executed. The LT entries contain a function field that is used to address the FT which contains the actual instruction to be executed using the token. The AG/FC monitors the token and recognizes one operand instuctions sending them to the execution queue (Q) and two operand instructions which are either queued on the data memory (DM) if the second operand has not arrived yet or sent to the Q if both operands are ready. The DM can also be used for coefficient storage as well as temporary data storage.

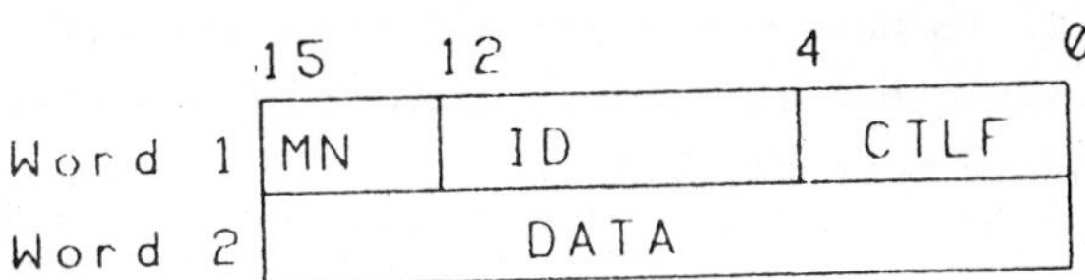

Figure 2: μPD7281 data token.

The PU is a two input/two output device which can perform arithmetic and logic operations in a single cycle (including multiplications) as well as generate instructions which produce multiple copies of a token. The output queue is a 8 slot FIFO used for temporary storage of outgoing tokens when the output controller is waiting for the acknowledge signal from the next processor.

Communications are handled by a handshaking mechanism that utilizes the LACK and OREQ lines. When a token is output, the processor sets the OREQ line to logic 1 and at the same time puts the first word of the token on the output bus until it receives the LACK signal from the receiving processor and then it outputs the second part of the token.

2.1.1 The Host/Memory Interface

The μPD7281 can be connected to a host and to memory using the μPD9305 chip |3|. Communication with a processor has the same handshaking protocol as the inter-processor communication. Memory can be up to 16M words of 18bits and is addressed using tokens with module numbers between 1 and 6. The module numbers are used to control the internal operation of the interface chip (i.e., MN=1 → Set High 8 bits of address to be read) and the data part of the token is the actual address. Direct memory access is also supported as well as independent Read/Modify/Write operations.

2.2 The Processor Interface

The μPD7281 chip was originally designed for linear array or ring systems and for this reason it has a single input bus and a single output bus. To use this chip in a two dimensional array, we must provide the means of interfacing the neighboring processor elements in an efficient and fair way. Fairness is necessary because of the dataflow nature of the chip. If a processor has always priority over the others and the processor it connects to uses one operand from it and one from another, very soon we will have queue overflows and loss of operation speed because of the unbalanced communications.

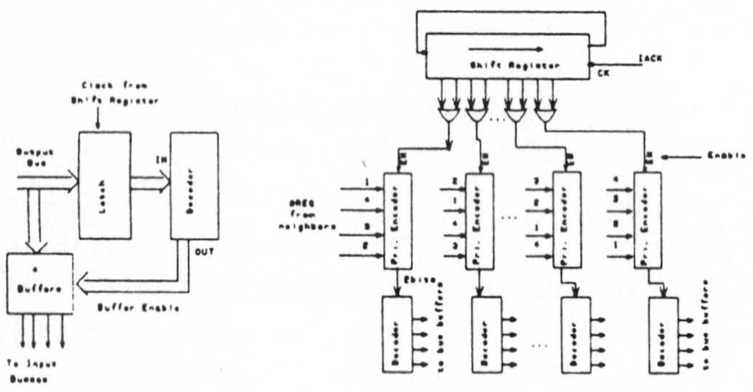

Figure 3: Processor Interface.

To meet the above demands, we designed the interface of figure 3 which uses the handshaking signals of the μPD7281 and the module number field to connect the input bus of the processor to the output busses of its neighbors.

Assuming a four neighbor mesh connected array, the operation of the interface is as follows:

1) Input: The OREQ lines of the four neighbors are connected to all priority encoders in different positions each time. The shift register is used to enable only one priority encoder for the duration of two LACK cycles. The PE's that want to send data start by setting their

OREQ lines to logic 1 and putting the first word of the data token on the output bus. The enabled priority encoder produces an output corresponding to the position of the highest priority requesting processor. This code is decoded by the bus decoders and the corresponding connection is set. The rest of the communication is handled by the built-in handshaking mechanism of the μPD7281. The LACK signals from the receiving PE are used to clock the shift register so that after two cycles the priority encoder is disabled and another enabled setting a new priority sequence thus giving the opportunity to other waiting processors to send data.

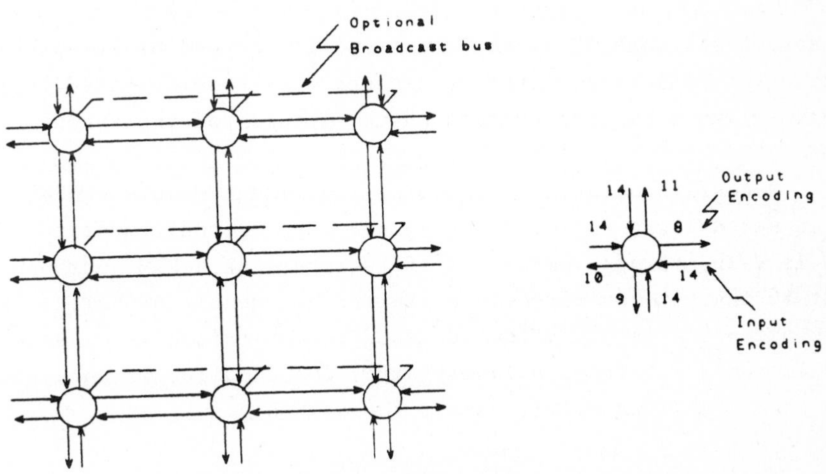

Figure 4: Wavefront Array and Module number assignment.

2) Output: In our array we make non standard use of the Module Number field of the data tokens. We assign an identical module number for each processing element of the array and associate a module number for each *direction* of communication, that is we map the directions, counter clockwise, to the numbers 8-12 (see fig. 4).

As before, a processor that wants to send data sets its OREQ line to logic 1 and puts the first word of the data token on its output bus. The interface decodes the Module number field and replaces the direction Module Number with the number used throughout the array at the same time connecting the output bus with the input section of the interface of the receiving processor. The remaining communication is handled by the input section.

3) **Broadcasting:** The interface as described thus far, assumes only near neighbor interconnection. However, some times it is necessary to provide broadcasting interconnections and the fact that we use an identical Module Number for all PE's in the array is very helpful. To provide row and column broadcasting the only we have to assign a module number to the row direction and one to the column direction and using an interface similar to the output section described above, we can decode the direction Module Number and connect the output bus to the broadcast bus. If more than one PE are trying to broadcast data, we can use the input section of the interface to connect the highest priority PE to the bus.

In some cases some PE's should not operate on the broadcosted tokens. Masking of PE's is achieved by sending the incoming token (using its ID field) to a CUT instruction which disposes of the token.

4) **Reconfiguration:** Since the individual Module number for each PE is set using a register during power-up, reconfiguration of the array is easy, using a small set of registers as a RAM section for the host so that it can directly write the new module numbers. The interface operation is not affected since communication is directed by the module numbers. Thus, a linear array for example, is obtained using the same direction module number for all PE's.

5) **Implementation:** Since the interface building blocks are simple standard functions (encoders, decoders, shift registers, latches and bus drivers) it is easy to implement using a standard cell approach or by programming VLSI PAL devices. The only limitation we may encounter is the pinout of each chip which because of the multiplicity of the busses, is very high. Partitioning the interface into three chips however, avoids the pinout problem thus providing a very compact and powerful communication and reconfiguration mechanism.

2.3 Performance of the Wavefront Array Processor

Using the μPD7281 and the interface chips described above, we can build arrays with very large size since there is no clock skew problem |*1*| and because of the chip addressing method there is no limitation on the number of chips.

Arrays of modest size can achieve processing rates of the order of billions of operations per second and the speed-up increases linearly with increasing array size, |*1*|, |*2*|. For example, a 16x16 array would use 256 four chip sets (1 processor + 3 interface chips) achieving a maximum of 1130 MIPS assuming all computations can proceed at the maximum 200 nsec rate. The performance is limited only by the communication cost which is expected to be quite low using the programming methodology described in the next section.

3. SOFTWARE

3.1 Programming Methodology

The programming methodology for Wavefront Array Processors is described in detail in |*1*|, |*4*| , |*5*|. In this paper we will give only a brief outline.

Generating programs for a Wavefront Array processor centers around the *Dependency Graph* (DG) which expresses an algorithm as a collection of asynchronous communicating processes forming a directed acyclic graph. Each node in the graph expresses the application of a function (i.e., multiply/add) on the input operands. The DG nodes have no internal state and fire (produce results) when all input operands have arrived. The edges of the DG represent dependencies between calculations, that is the result of a node in an input operand of its sons.

Direct execution of this algorithm description by a one to one mapping of nodes to processors would be extremely inefficient in terms of hardware utilization. To avoid this problem, we first choose a scheduling function defining the wavefront of computation and project the DG and the wavefront along a particular direction, in effect lumping together all nodes (computations) that lie along this direction on the DG (see fig. 5). The projection of the wavefront serves to preserve the dependencies since by projecting, some operations become sequential and the value passing between nodes must be synchronized in order to arrive to a correct result. The synchronization mechanism is implemented with FIFO queues and a handshaking protocol which ensures that a node does not send a value if its successor is not ready to accept it (e.g., its FIFO is full). The graph resulting from the projection is called *Signal Flow Graph* (SFG) and is no longer acyclic. The SFG can be *retimed* using the cut-set procedure of |*1*| to eliminate proadcasting thus forming the Wavefront Array program. From the above brief description of the programming methodology we see that there is a close correspondence of the hardware of our array and the Wavefront Array program thus per-

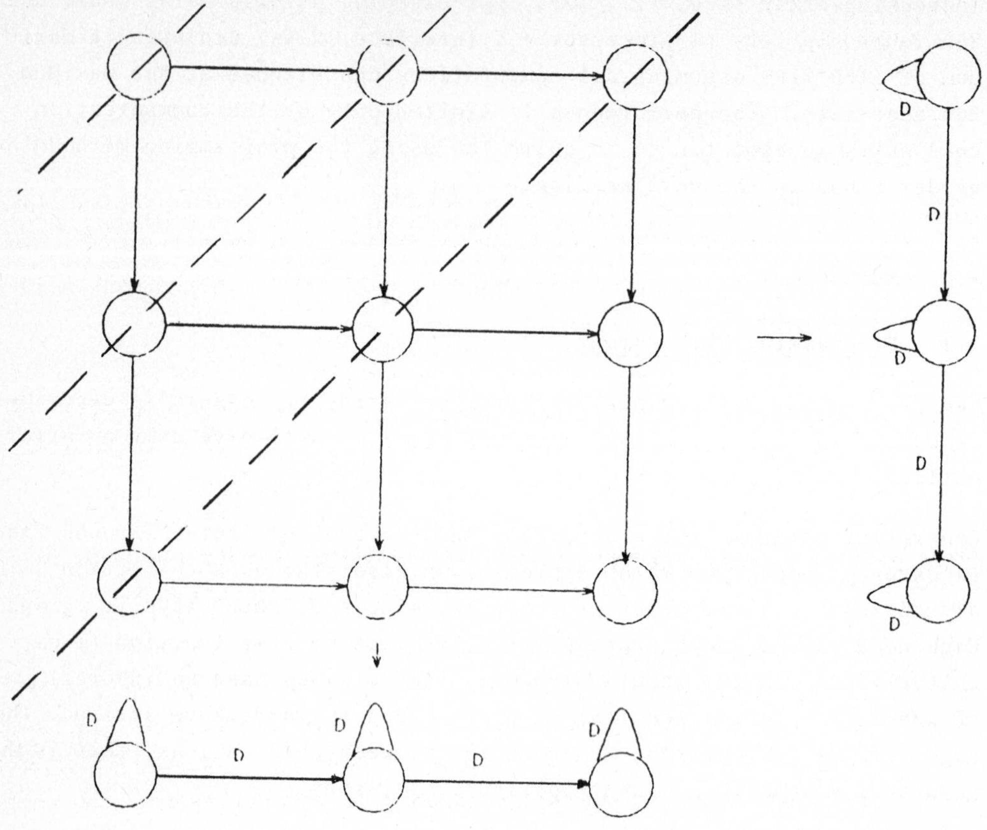

Figure 5. Dependency Graph projection.

mitting a direct mapping of the program to the array. In |*1*| additional techniques for mapping are presented in the case that the size of the physical array does not match the size of the program.

3.2 Language Issues

Application of the above methodology is easy for simple algorithms (i.e. matrix multiplication, 2-D convolution) but becomes very difficult in more complex problems thus creating the need for automatic DG generation and subsequent processing.

The language for the wavefront array processor must have the capability of expressing the computation the designer wants in a natural and concise way. To achieve this it must be sufficiently close to the mathematic expressions and at the same time to be able to describe a dependency graph. Concise representation requires the use of loops which means that the language compiler must be able to perform the loop unfolding needed to expose the available parallelism taking into account the data dependencies between iterations.

Ideally the programmer/designer should not be aware of the dependency graph structure and should only have to deal with the task of expressing the algorithm at hand in the language. However in complex problems the compiler intelligence may not be enough so the programmer should be able to specify the parallelism needed.

To be sufficiently close to the algorithm expression, the language must have the expressive power of languages like FORTRAN or Pascal which have proved to be adequate. Additionally, in order to be able to generate a dependency graph it must obey the single assignment rule and have a mechanism of identifying data dependencies.

The languages developed to this date for wavefront arrays (i.e., MDFL |*1*|) require the programmer to explicitly describe the data flow and inner workings of each functional unit. According to the above desirable features they would be more suitable as intermediate level languages, between the high level language and the code generator.

A lot of research has been done on applicative languages for data flow machine programming |*12*|, |*13*| and since the wavefront array is essentially a data flow machine, it is worthwhile to investigate these languages.

The dependency graph nodes are purely functional modules and a functional (applicative) language would provide a good mapping of conceptual functional blocks to program modules. In the case of wavefront array processors however, we do not execute the DG directly but we create the program after some processing as shown in the previous section. This leads us to the introduction of an *intermediate form* which is the output of the high level language compiler and which subsequently is manipulated to create the actual program for our array. Such intermediate forms are introduced in |*7*|, |*9*|, |*11*|. In some cases, the compiler intelligence may not be adequate to uncover the parallelism available or the programmer may already know the optimum mapping of the algorithm . To aid the programmer in these cases, the intermediate form must be accessible to the programmer so that he can either modify it or directly program in it.

For our system we chose FP |*6*| because of its simplicity and power. Our compiler will use the primitive definitions of the language as *rewriting rules* to create the DG in the intermediate form which in this case will be a simple graph data structure to facilitate subsequent processing (i.e., projections, retiming). After processing the DG, the SFG or the wavefront program can be directly translated to the μPD7231 assembly language which is essentially a graph description in textual form. The programmer can intervene at the DG stage or the assembly language translation stage to optimize the program. Examples of the above procedures are given in the applications section.

FP is not the only possible language that can run on our machine. SISAL |*7*| can also be used since it compiles to the intermediate form IF1 |*10*| which can be very easily translated to μPD7281 assembly language since its primitives are very close to the assembly language instructions. This gives us the advantage of having a quite large body of programs already programmed in SISAL as well as their timing to compare the performance of our machine with other dataflow machines, |*7*| , |*8*|. Other alternative languages are Lisp variants |*14*| and Concurrent Prolog |*15*|.

4. APPLICATIONS

The following applications help illustrate some aspects of our system. The 2-D convolution shows how an image processing algorithm can be directly mapped to our architecture and how this machine performs compared to other architectures. The matrix multiplication shows the FP to

DG translation and the perspective transformation illustrates the actions we can take when the size of the array is smaller than the size of the problem.

4.1 2-D Convolution

In this section we will present the edge detection operation implemented as a 2-D convolution between the image data and a 3x3 edge detector mask. The same analysis and implementation holds for any 2-D convolution.

To calculate the convolution of the mask with an NxN image, we can formulate the problem as the calculation of N^2 inner products of 9 element vectors consisting of the pixel values in a neighborhood and the mask data. Then in total, we would need

$$(9T_m + 8T_a)N^2$$

where T_m is the multiplication time and T_a is the addition time.

In order to speed up the computation, considering the 2-D convolution equation

$$y_{ij} = \sum_{k=i-1}^{i+1} \sum_{l=j-1}^{j+1} x_{k,l} m_{k-i,l-j}$$

we can see that for the calculation of the central pixels of a 3xN strip of image, we need only the data contained in this strip and that some partial sums at position i are useful for the computation of the computation of the sum in position i+1.

In fig. 6 the dependency graph obtained from the above observations is shown for the calculation of the *center column* of a 3xN image strip. We can use three copies of this dependency graph, each responsible for one image column (fig. 7). Since the computations for each strip are independent, N/3 copies of fig. 7 will calculate the convolution for the whole image.

4.1.1 SFG Generation and Design

From the dependency graph of fig. 7, using projections we can generate SFG's for the edge detector. We see that we have the choice of either using N processors or using only three. The advantage of using N processors in addition to faster operation, is that we can pipeline the image data to form the strips to be operated on.

From the SFG's shown in fig. 7 we chose to implement the one produced by the downward projection. In fig. 8 we show the SFG using data pipelining. This SFG operates on all three image columns. To implement this SFG, we may choose to use one processor per node, one processor per row or one processor per column as well as other combinations. The first choice leads to an implementation where the computation cost is

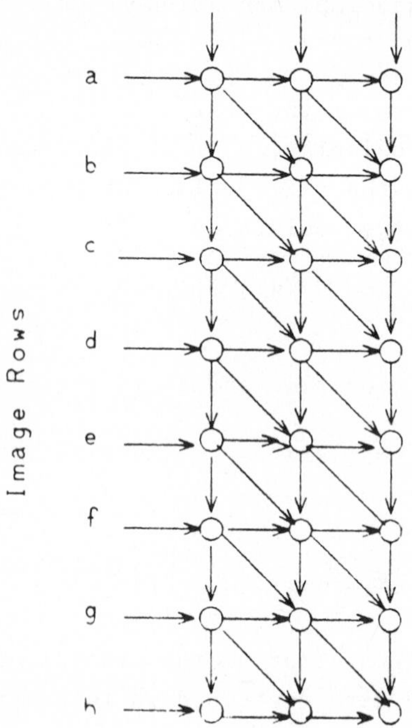

Figure 6: Data dependencies for 2-D convolution.

not balanced with the communications cost since each node needs two input values and produces one output. With communication costing twice as much as computation in the μPD7281, the total ratio of communication to computation would be 6 to one. The second choice is not feasible because of the limited node capacity of the processor (only 64 nodes).The third choice uses N processors and has the advantage that the data communication is unidirectional thus facilitating the address decoding of the processing elements. Since the number of operations per column is small we can implement more than one column in one chip. A very important advantage of this choice is that many communication paths are internal to the processing element and can proceed at full speed (200nsec).

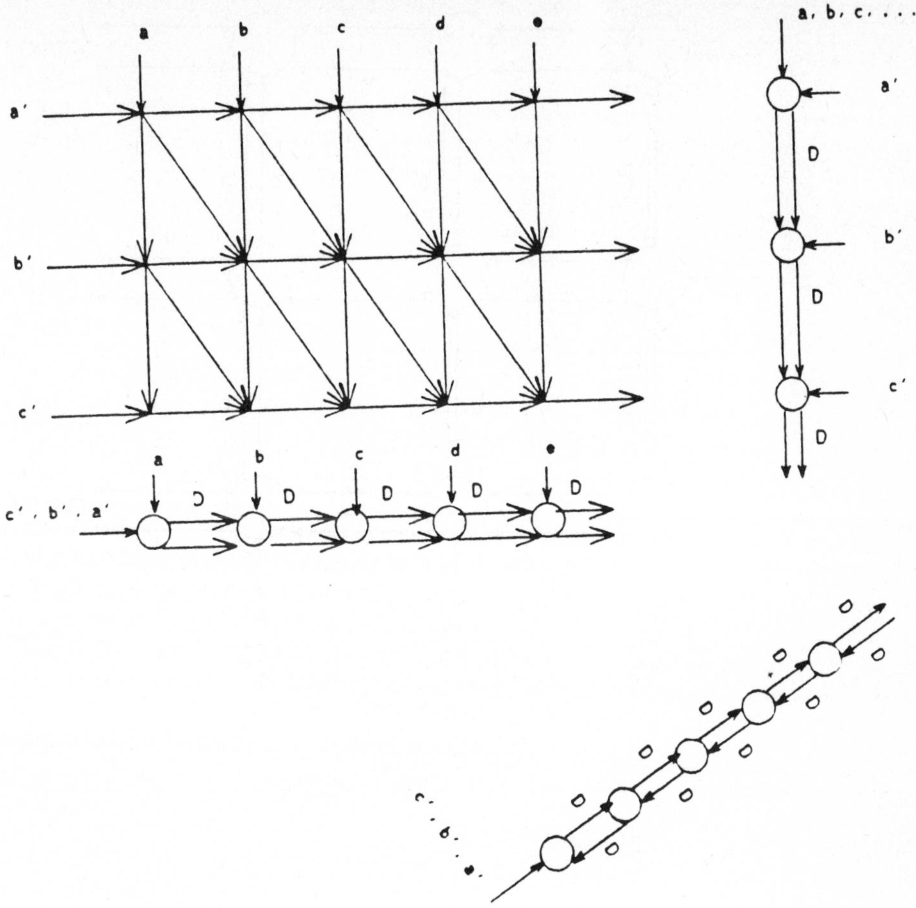

Figure 7. Dependency graph for a 3xN strip of image.

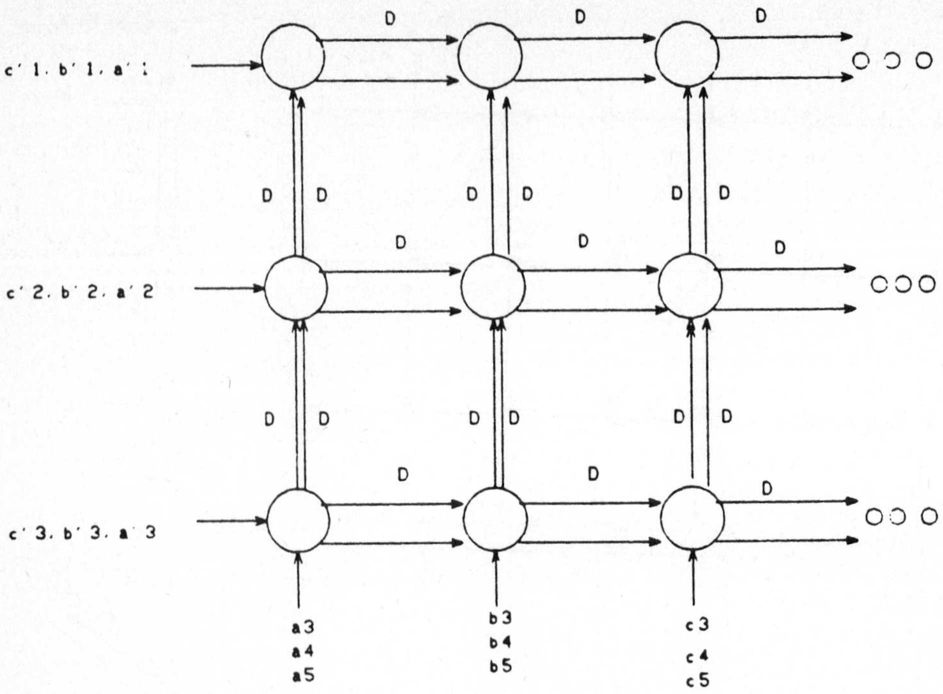

Figure 8. SFG for 2-D computation.

4.1.2 Description of the Node Program

In figure 9 we present the program that implements the SFG of fig. 8. First we observe that broadcasting the mask data is not really necessary since we can store the 9 values of the mask in the internal data memory (DM) of each processor thus avoiding retiming the SFG.

The program is in μPD7281 assembly language, presented in its graph form and implements one column per processor and the adders between columns. Thus, each chip contains three copies of the program (one for each column) but only one adder section.

The image data are reproduced three times (CPYBK 3) in order to be multiplied by the mask values which are cyclically read from the data memory (DM) using the RDCYS-MUL instruction. After multiplication, the product is added to the delayed partial sum from the stage to the left (QUEUE-ADD). The DIVCYC instruction is used to select every third adder output to be sent to the final adder stage while the first two results go to the next SFG node after a unit delay, implemented by storing an initial value in the adder queue. Since each processor implements three column computations, the last stage sends its results to the next PE.

The image data are pipelined by means of the queues in figure 9. Since each processor contains one ALU, the instructions are executed one after the other with an arbitrary order, based on data availability. For this reason the processor will execute three copies of figure 9 except for the final additions which are executed only once. Thus we have 3x26 cycles for the multiple part and 12 cycles for the single (adder) part. This means that using a linear configuration of 256/3 = 86 processors, each containing the program described, we can calculate the values for a 256 pixel column in 16.8 μsec including I/O time. For the whole image, the array would need 4.24 msec. Using a 86x86 array, we could calculate the image convolution in just 50.4 μsec. To compare the performance of our approach is difficult because various systems use different kinds of parallelism and I/O. Fig. 10 shows the relative performance of various systems executing similar but not identical operations.

4.2 Matrix Multiplication

The matrix multiplication algorithm can be very concisely and easily written in the FP language. Before we present the program, we must de-

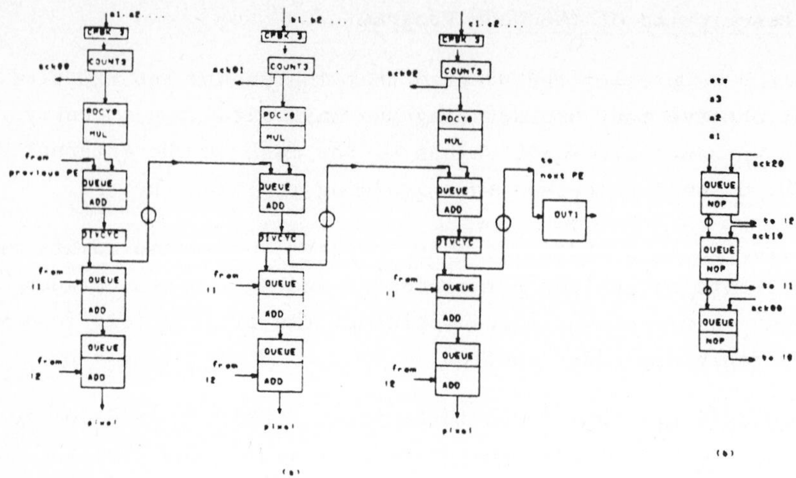

Figure 9: a) Column implementation. b) Input pipelining.

System	No.of PE's	Communicat.	Algorithm	Time	Comments
ICL DAP	32x32 (1bit)	4 nearest neighbors	3x3 Sobel	2.5msec	Frame 512x512
RSRE Transp.	(8x8)+1 (16bit)	4 nearest neighbors	3x3 conv.	18msec	Frame
UCL CLIP-7	512x4	8 neighbors	3x3 aver.	15msec	Frame 512x512
Goodyear MPP	128x128 (1bit)	4 neighbors	3x3 conv.	1msec	Frame 128x128
Hughes 3D Comp.	256x256	4 neighbors	3x3 Sobel	20msec	Frame 256x256
Linear Transp.	256	vertical neighbors	3x3 conv.	25μsec	Column 256x256
Linear Transp.	64	vertical neighbors	3x3 conv.	65.8μsec	Column 256x256
Linear μPD7281	86	vertical neighbors	3x3 conv.	16.8μsec	Column 256x256

Figure 10: Performance comparison of various systems in mask operations.

fine some of the primitives and the notation used.

In the following, f, g, h denote *functions*, < x> is an *argument* which may be a scalar or a vector denoted by $<x_1, x_2, \ldots, x_n>$ or a matrix denoted as a vector of row vectors such as for a matrix of dimension 2: $<<x_{11}, x_{12}> <x_{21}, x_{22}>>$. The symbols f: < x> mean that function f is applied to argument < x>. The following functions are some of the language primitives |6|:

$distr: <<x_1,x_2,\ldots,x_n>, y> \rightarrow <<x_1,y>, <x_2,y>,\ldots, <x_n,y>>$

$distl: <x, <y_1,y_2,\ldots,y_n>> \rightarrow <<x,y_1>,\ldots, <x,y_n>>$

$trans: <<x_1,\ldots,x_n>, <y_1,\ldots,y_n>> \rightarrow <<x_1,y_1>,\ldots, <x_n,y_n>>$

$/f: <x_1,x_2,\ldots,x_n> \rightarrow f: <x_1, f: <x_2,\ldots,f: <x_n> \ldots. >$

$af: <x_1,x_2,\ldots,x_n> \rightarrow <f: x_1,f: x_2,\ldots, f: x_n>$

$|f,g|: <x> \rightarrow <f: x,g:x>$

$f \; o \; g: <x> \rightarrow f: (g:<x>)$

$1: <x_1,x_2,\ldots,x_n> \rightarrow x_1$

$k: <x_1,x_2,\ldots,x_k,\ldots,x_n> \rightarrow x_k$

Using the above primitives we can now proceed to write the program in FP. First we define the *inner product* operation as

*def IP = (/+) o (a***x***) o trans*

which means that if IP is applied to $<<x_1,\ldots,x_n>, <y_1,\ldots,y_n>>$ will first execute the *trans* operation forming pairs of elements $<<x_1,y_1>, \ldots, <x_n,y_n>>$. Then, all pairs are multiplied forming a vector $<z_1,\ldots, z_n>$ of products and then the + operator is applied recursively, that is $+: <z_1, +: z_2,\ldots,+: <z_{n-1},z_n> \ldots>$ giving the inner product. The matrix-matrix multiplication program takes the form:

def MM = aaIP o adistr o distl o |1,trans o 2|

which is equivalent to saying that we first form the transpose of the

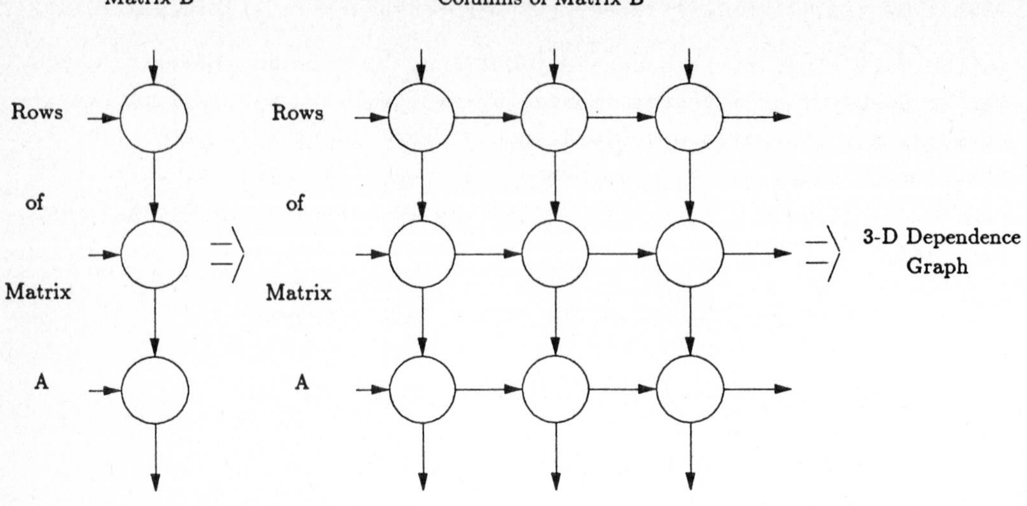

Figure 11. Matrix-matrix multiplication dependency graph.

second matrix, then form the row-column pairs and finally apply to all pairs the inner product operation.

The above program can be easily converted into a dependency graph if we interpret the *distr* and *distl* operators as *broadcast* operators. With this interpretation, the *adistr o distl* operation forms the cartesian product of the row-column vectors and the dependency graph is shown in figure 4.2.

The matrix multiplication program in our implementation of FP which is written in Lisp, can be written as

```
(de f un ip(arg)
(∴ 'pl (aa 'tl (trans arg))))
(de f un mm(arg)
(aaa 'ip(aa 'distr (distl (|'(id trans)arg))))
```

The main differences from the standard FP notation are /f → ∴' f, a → aa, $|f_1\ f_2| \to |'(f_1\ f_2)$ and aa → aaa. The operators pl and tl are the non executable versions of the plus and times operators respectively.

The program as is presented here calculates the square of a matrix and for input:

```
((X11 X12 X13)(X21 X22 X23)(X31 X32 X33))
```

it produces the following data structure:

```
(((p1(("t1"(x11 x11))(pl(("t1"(x12 x21))(p1(("t1"(x13 x31)))))))
  (p1(("t1"(x11 x12))(p1(("t1"(x12 x22))(p1(("t1"(x13 x32)))))))
  (p1(("t1"(x11 x13))(p1(("t1"(x12 x23))(p1(("t1"(x13 x33)))))))
 ((p1(("t1"(x21 x11))(p1(("t1"(x22 x21))(p1(("t1"(x23 x31)))))))
  (p1(("t1"(x21 x12))(p1(("t1"(x22 x22))(p1(("t1"(x23 x32)))))))
  (p1(("t1"(x21 x13))(p1(("t1"(x22 x23))(p1(("t1"(x23 x33)))))))
 ((p1(("t1"(x31 x11))(p1(("t1"(x32 x21))(p1(("t1"(x33 x31)))))))
  (p1(("t1"(x31 x12))(p1(("t1"(x32 x22))(p1(("t1"(x33 x32)))))))
  (p1(("t1"(x31 x13))(p1(("t1"(x32 x23))(p1(("t1"(x33 x33)))))))
```

From this data structure we can immediately see that it represents the dependency graph since each column (starting with the p1 operator) is a horizontal plane of the dependency graph and the elements in each row have dependencies in the vertical direction.

A preorder tree traversal of this data structure leads to the creation of a new representation of the dependency graph in the form of an array with elements containing both functional (operators) and structural (edges) information. The new data structure is used for projections, retiming and final code generation.

The implementation of the language primitives is done in LISP since it is itself an applicative language and its built in mechanisms (i.e., parameter passing, function evaluation) match the target language very well.

4.3 Perspective Transformation

A useful operation in computer graphics and image processing is the perspective transformation |*16*|. It is presented here to illustrate the actions we can take when we must apply a series of matrix-vector multiplications on a set of data and only one array is available.

The perspective transformation consists of a series of translation, rotation and clipping transformations in the form of 4x4 matrices |*16*|:

$$VN = T_1 T_2 T_3 T_4 T_5 N$$

where T_1 is a translation matrix from the world coordinate system to the eye coordinate system, T_2, T_3, T_4, T_5 are rotation transformations to align the axes of the coordinate systems and N is a clipping transformation that identifies the points that lie within the vieweing pyramid defined by the eye and the vieweing screen.

Assume for the purposes of our example that the matrices are continously changing so that the matrix multiplications have to be recomputed. Assume also that we have only a 4x4 array. From fig. 12 we see that we actually need five cascaded arrays to compute the new vectors defining the points on the screen. Reusing our single array would be possible if we had feedback lines connecting the output of the array to its inputs. Such lines however are not really necessary in this case since instead of using a linear scheduling funct-on (wavefront), we use a nonlinear one (dashed lines in fig. 13). Projecting this DG we obtain the

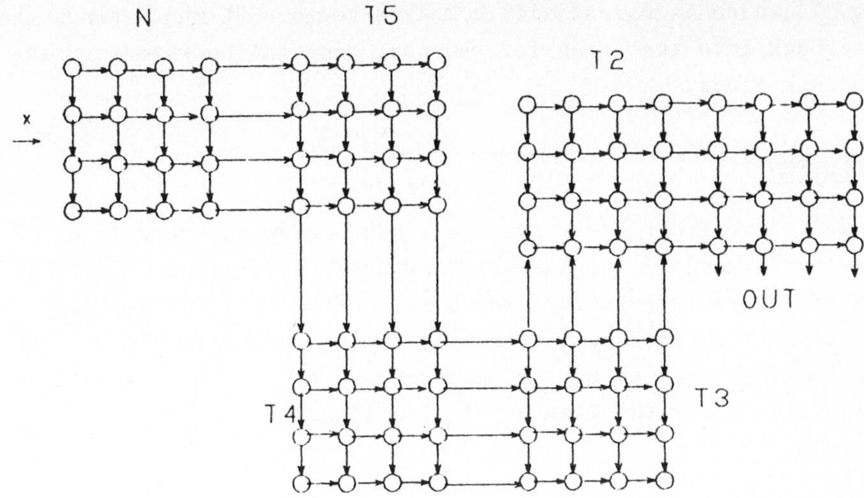

Figure 12. Cascaded DG's for Perspective Transformation.

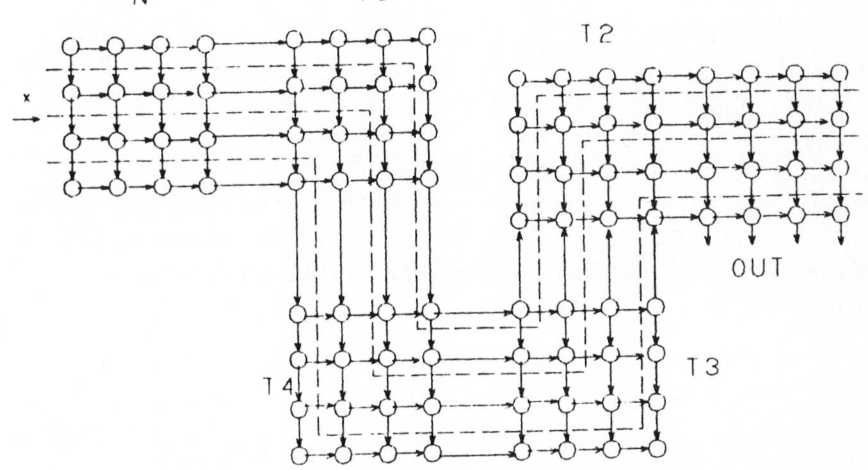

Figure 13. Non-linear scheduling of matrix-vector computations.

SFG of fig. 14 which is essentially a matrix-vector SFG which sends the output data back into the array for the next computation without using global feedback lines.

5. CONCLUSION

In this paper a Wavefront Array processor was presented, capable of supercomputer performance. The hardware is based on dataflow chips that permit building very large arrays which in addition can be reconfigurable. Central to the design is the programming methodology and the high level language that makes the machine easy to use while maintaining high efficiency for the classes of algorithms of interest.

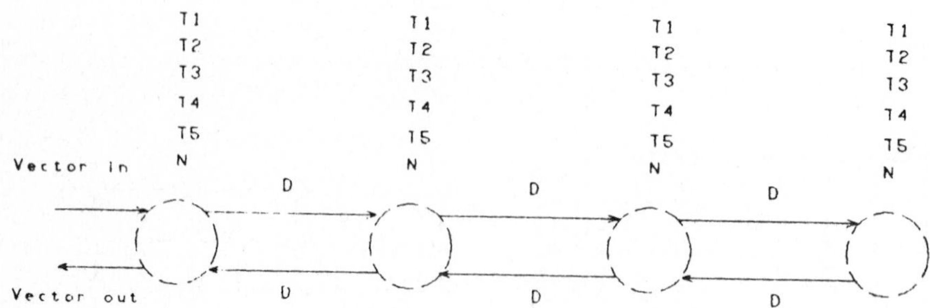

Figure 14: SFG for cascaded matrix-vector computations.

References

|1| S.Y. Kung, *"VLSI Array Processors"*, Prentice Hall 1987.

|2| *"μPD7281 User's Guide"*, NEC Electronics 1985.

|3| *"μPD9305 (Magic) User's Guide"*, NEC Electronics 1985.

|4| Karp, R.M., Miller, R.E., Winograd, S. *"The Organization of Computations for Uniform Recurrence Equations"*, Journal of ACM, vol. 14, no. 3, 1967, pp 563-590.

|5| Rao, S.K., *"Regular Iterative Algorithms and their Implementation on Processor Arrays"*, Ph.D. Thesis, Stanford University 1985.

|6| Backus, J., *"Can Programming be Liberated from the Von Neumann Style"* Communications ACM, vol. 21, No. 8, Aug. 1978.

|7| McGraw, J., Skedzielewski, S., et al., *"Sisal Reference Manual"* Lawrence Livermore Laboratory 1985.

|8| Gurd, J., Watson, I., *"Preliminary Evaluation of a Prototype Dataflow Computer"*, Proc. IFIP, 1983.

|9| Gaudiot, J.L., Dubois, M., Lee, L.T., Tohme, N., *"The TX16: A Highly Programmable Multimicroprocessor Architecture"*, IEEE Micro, Oct. 1986.

|10| Skedzielewski, et. al. *"IF1 Reference Manual"*, Lawrence Livermore Laboratory 1985.

|11| Hudak, P., Smith, L., *"Para-Functional Programming: A Paradigm for Programming Multiprocessor Systems"*, 12th ACM Symp. on Principles of Programming Languages, Jan. 1986, pp 243-254.

|12| Ackerman, W.B., Dennis, J.B., *"VAL - A value oriented algorithmic language"*, Tech. Rep. TR-218, Lab. for Computer Science,MIT, June 1979.

|13| Arvind, Gostelow, K.P., Plouffe, W., *"An Asynchronous Programming Language and Computing Machine"* TR 114a, Dept. of Info. and Comp. Sci., Univ. of California, Irvine, Dec. 1978.

|14| Dewilde, P., Annevelink, J., *"Hierarchical Design of Processor Arrays, Applied to a New Pipelined Matrix Solver"*, VLSI Signal Processing II, IEEE Press, Nov. 1986.

|15| Shapiro, E., *"Concurrent Prolog: A Progress Report"*, IEEE Computer, Vol. 19, No. 8, Aug. 1986.

|16| Newman, W.M., Sproull, R.F., *"Principles of Interactive Computer Graphics"*, McGraw Hill 1973.

FINITE ELEMENT METHODS ON PARALLEL AND VECTOR COMPUTERS APPLICATION IN FLUID DYNAMICS

J. ERHEL
INRIA - Domaine de Voluceau
Rocquencourt - BP. 105
78153 Le Chesnay Cédex, FRANCE

INTRODUCTION

Finite Element methods are efficient numerical tools in many applications, such as solid and structural mechanics or aerodynamics as well. The main interest of unstructured meshes is the flexibility to generate them around complex geometries. Another advantage is the facility to use mesh-adaptation devices, for example local self-adaptive mesh refinements or even mesh movement. This approach yields more accurate results near shocks and boundary layers in flow simulations [1].

Typically, most time-consuming parts in finite element codes are the computation of rigth-hand sides or matrix coefficients, and quite often the resolution of a linear system. These kernels must be optimized to use efficiently parallel and vector supercomputers. Examples of such machines are the Cray-XMP [2], the Cray-2 [3], the ETA^{10} [4], where each processing unit has vector capabilities and can work simultaneously with other units on the same application. In general, to construct right-hand sides, or matrices, elementary contributions, computed at each element, are accumulated at the nodes. To eliminate data dependencies, elements are grouped into blocks of disjoint elements, without common node, using graph coloring techniques [5,6]. The use of unstructured meshes require indirect addressing to define the correspondance between elements and nodes.

Iterative techniques are commonly used to solve the large sparse linear system arising in the process of solution. Many of them, such as Jacobi relaxation and conjugate gradient with polynomial preconditionning, are based on the product of the sparse matrix by a vector. A storage by edges, associated with pointers, yields a fairly good vectorized algorithm, though penalized by indirect addressing.

Two main approaches can be taken to design parallel algorithms for multiprocessors machines. The bottow-up programming, also referred as microtasking [7], exploits parallelism at a low level, such as DO loops containing independant iterations. The top-down programming, also called multitasking [8], takes into account global parallelism in the algorithm. Domain decomposition techniques allow parallelism between the different subdomains [9].

Factors affecting the performances of parallel algorithm are load balancing, granularity, and multitasking overhead. Load balancing reflects the workload in each task, which must be as equal as possible in each task to avoid idle time. Granularity measures the time of useful execution in a task between two points of communication. Finally, the multitasking overhead is the time spent to schedule the tasks and to communicate between them.

Usually, the bottom-up approach yields a small granularity, but quite well balanced tasks. Furthermore, it is relatively easy to implement either by using microtasking directives (on the Cray-XMP for example) or the multitasking library (on the Cray-2 for example). Conversely, the top-down method creates large granularity, but needs careful task partitionning to get well-balanced work-load. Also, it requires some programming effort, to design automatic domain decomposition, and to schedule synchronizations and communications between tasks [10].

The sequel presents an overview of explicit and implicit upwind schemes for compressible flow simulation governed by Euler equations. The algorithm uses a finite element spatial discretization, with P1 interpolation, based on unstructured triangulations for 2-D domains [11]. While the explicit code is representative of right-hand sides computations, the implicit algorithm includes a linear sparse system solver. [12].

Results of execution are given on vector computers, namely Cray-1, Cray-XMP, Cray-2 and also IBMVF [13].

Two multitasked versions of the explicit code were also implemented on the Cray-2, in order to compare bottom-up and top-down approaches. [14]. Preliminary results are given, but in a context of a shared, non dedicated system.

NUMERICAL ALGORITHM

equations

We solve the Euler equations for a steady compressible flow in a 2-D domain. With the usual conservative variable U, fluxes F and G, the system can be written as follows :

(1)
$$\frac{\partial U}{\partial t} + \frac{\partial F}{\partial x} + \frac{dG}{\partial y} = 0$$
boundary conditions
initial value

explicit scheme

We use an upwind spatial approximation and perform numerical integration with flux splitting, introducing linear interpolation to get second-order accuracy. To speed-up the convergence towards a stationnary solution, we use a local time-stepping.

Each time-step iterationn can be decomposed into the following computations :

(2) local time step and derivatives
(3) predictor step
(4) flux splitting
(5) boundary conditions
(6) residuals and change to new iteration.

Parts (2) and (4) are the most time-consuming.

implicit scheme

Implicit schemes combined with relaxation give rise to much faster solvers. The global scheme for one time-step can be written :

(7) explicit phase : $\delta\hat{U} = \Delta t\ E_2(U^n)$

(8) implicit phase : $(Id - \Delta t\ E'_1\ (U^n))\ \delta U^{n+1} = \delta\hat{U}$

$$U^{n+1} = U^n + \delta U^{n-1}$$

where E_2 is a second-order accurate approximation constructed as for the explicit scheme, and E'_1 is a first-order accurate linearization constructed via the linearization involved in the flux splitting. It should be noted that different flux splittings can be used in the two phases.

Each time-step iteration is now decomposed into the following computations :

(2) local time-step and derivatives
(4) flux-splitting
(5) boundary conditions
(9) (not every time-step) matrix construction
(10) resolution of linear system (8)
(6) residuals and change to new iteration.

Parts (2,4,5,6) are identical in both explicit and implicit schemes. The matrix coefficients are frozen over several time-steps, according to a tuning parameter depending on the value of the residuals.

Since the implicit phase only acts as a preconditionner of the problem, it does not require neither an exact solution nor an exactly linearized system. A 4x4 block Jacobi nodewise relaxation has proved to be very efficient, with only a few iterations. Though it converges more slowly than the Gauss-Seidel algorithm, it is finally more efficient on a vector computer.

VECTORIZATION ISSUES

Explicit scheme

Computations in parts (2) and (4) have the same structure. Elementary variables are computed at the elements in part (2) and at the edges in part (4) and then accumulated at the nodes.

This computation can be split into three steps :

- "gather" operations to copy variables from nodes to elements
- vector operations on the elements
- "scatter" operations to accumulate results from elements to nodes.

To eliminate data dependencies in the scatter operations, due to adjacent elements (having a common node), elements are grouped into blocks of disjoint elements, using a graph coloring algorithm, and then renumbered according to their color. This renumbering occurs only once in the preparation of the algorithm. The same technique applies for edges. For 2-D meshes, the numbers of colors are bounded by the following :

$$D \le NCT \le 3*D-5 \qquad D \le NCE \le 2*D-1 \tag{11}$$

where D is the maximal degree of a node, ie the maximal number of adjacent nodes to a node, NCT is the number of colors of triangles, NCE is the number of colors of edges. Computations are thus vectorized for each color. The vector operations are optimized for the target architecture, using loop distribution and loop partition techniques [15]. The vector length is chosen to get a good tradeoff between vector efficiency and memory requirements.

The boundary conditions formulation exploits the regularity of the boundary, where each node has the same degree. Thus part (5) can be performed directly at the nodes and is easily vectorized. Parts (3) and (6) are also vector computations on the nodes.

Implicit scheme

The matrix structure is chosen to design a vectorized linear solver. The matrix is a 4×4 block-matrix. The main diagonal blocks are stored in an array of length the number of nodes. The extra-diagonal blocks are computed and stored directly at the edges, so that this computation does not require node accumulation.

A Jacobi iteration can be viewed as a matrix-vector product. To perform the product by extra-diagonal blocks, consists by a vector loop on the edges, using gather and scatter operations, with preliminary renumbering of edges by color to eliminate data dependencies. The product by the diagonal blocks is simply a vector loop on the nodes.

The product by a 4×4 block is expanded to get efficient vectorization such as chaining of operations.

Results

A test case was designed to obtain performances on various computers. We compute the steady flow around a NACA0012 airfoil, both with explicit and implicit schemes. The Mach number at infinity is 0.8 and the angle of attach is null, but this is not relevant for rate considerations. We used two triangulations : the first one has 1006 nodes (figure 1), while the second one, constructed by local mesh refinement, has 2765 nodes (figure 2). The number of operations for one iteration and the memory requirements are roughly proportional to the number of nodes.

The efficiency means the ratio of the sequential time (with vectorization disabled) over the vectorial time.

Figure 3 gives detailed timings for the explicit scheme, on the Cray-1 and Cray-XMP. Execution time was roughly proportional to the number of nodes, and is given only for the first triangulation.

Figure 4 gives the same timings on the Cray-2 for both triangulations.

Figure 5 gives similar results for the implicit scheme, with the first triangulation, on the Cray-1 and the Cray-2, while figure 6 shows the same results on a IBMVF (in double precision, ie with 64 bits word length).

Figure 7 shows the convergence rates for both the explicit and implicit scheme, while figure 8 shows the cost of convergence for both schemes, on the Cray-2.

PARALLEL ALGORITHMS

microtasking approach

A self-scheduling DOPAR technique is used to execute in parallel independant vector loops on elements or edges in the same color. But parallel tasks must be synchronized between different colors to perform the scatter operation. We tried two techniques : a strong synchronization forced by a barrier after each color, and a weak formulation executing the scatter operation in a critical section. The loops on nodes are executed by only one task, because of their small granularity. Currently, the explicit algorithm has been parallelized and implemented on a Cray-2, using the multitasking library. This approach will be easily extended to the implicit algorithm.

Domain decomposition approach

The domain of simulation is split into slices so that each subdomain has at most two neighbors (figure 9). The decomposition is made automatically, taking into account the possible symmetries, trying to minimize the separator sizes, and to obtain subdomains of almost equal size. Optimization of the partitioning is currently under investigation.

Each subdomain is assigned to a task, running in parallel with others and communicating values on the separators with the two neighboring tasks. Communications are expressed by means of SEND and RECEIVE operations.

Communications for the separators occur at each iteration, to update the time-step and the derivatives, then the fluxes, finally the current variable U^n. Global synchronization is necessary at the end of each iteration to compute the global residuals and to check for convergence.

This algorithm has been implemented on the Cray-2, for the explicit case, but can be extended to the implicit version. It should be noted that this approach is also well-suited to local memories architectures such as the ETA[10].

Preliminary results

Both algorithms were executed on the Cray-2 with two, and four tasks. Unfortunately, we could not run them in a dedicated environment, so that the elapsed time was not significant. We measured the CPU time spent in each task to get an idea of the performances. The speed-up is the ratio of the sequential time (for the original sequential algorithm) over the maximum CPU time in the tasks. Figure 10 and 11 give the results for the microtasking and multitasking algorithms, where the mesh used is the NACA0012 with 2765 nodes (figure 2).

Results show that the workload is well-balanced between two tasks, but becomes unequal with four tasks. This is due to the small size of the problem, yielding a small granularity and consequently non-trivial overhead. However, results are promising and we should obtain better performances with large problems, especially for 3-D domains.

CONCLUSION

The experiences described in this paper show that finite element methods can be vectorized efficiently, though they are slightly penalized by the need of indirect addressing. The extension to 3-D problems is currently under investigation. The main question is to find a graph coloring algorithm to get a small number of colors, with enough elements in each color. A useful heuristic is to freeze in advance the maximal size of each group, thus the vector length. Implicit schemes without storage of the matrix are also examined, to get a good tradeoff between memory requirements and CPU time.

Concerning the parallel algorithms, the subdomain approach seems more efficient. But the microtasking approach should give better results on larger problems, with a larger granularity. It is easier to implement and does not require a preliminary partitionning.

However, we plan to investigate partitionning methods, with more general configurations (variable number of neighbors), using general graph separation algorithms. Simulated annealing techniques are also considered to optimize locally the separator length.

Acknowledgements

The access to CRAY-1 and CRAY-2 was provided by the C.C.V.R scientific committee. We wish to thank V. Billey, from AMD/BA, who helped us to run programs on IBM. We are indebted to A. Azar and D. Charpin, from Cray Research France, who run programs on the CRAY-XMP at EDF.

REFERENCES

[1] A. Dervieux, J.A. Desideri, F. Fezoui, B. Palmerio, J.P. Rosenblum
Euler calculations by upwind finite element methods and adaptive mesh algorithms.
GAMM Workshop, France 1986.

[2] CRAY-XMP reference manual
Cray Research, Inc.

[3] CRAY-2 reference manual
Cray Research, Inc.

[4] ETA^{10} reference manual
ETA Systems, Inc.

[5] A. Jameson, T.J. Baker
Improvements to the aircraft Euler method
AIAA 25th aerospace sciences meeting, January 1987, USA

[6] T. Hugues, R. Ferencz, J. Hallquist
Large-scale vectorized implicit calculations in solid mechanics on a Cray X-MP/48 utilizing EBE preconditioned conjugate gradients
Stanford University Report.

[7] Cray X-MP microtasking user guide
Cray Research, Inc.

[8] Cray X-MP and CRAY-2 multitasking user guides
Cray Research, Inc.

[9] Proceedings of first international symposium on domain decomposition methods for partial differential equations, January 1987, France

[10] G. Johnson, J. Swisshelm, D. Pryor, J. Ziebarth
Multitasked embedded multigrid for three-dimensional flow simulation.
10th international conference on numerical methods in fluid mechanics, June 1986, China.

[11] F. Fezoui, B. Stoufflet, J. Periaux, A. Dervieux
Implicit high-order upwind finite element schemes for the Euler equations
4th International Symposium on numerical methods in engineering, March 1986, USA

[12] F. Angrand, J. Erhel
Simulation par éléments finis d'écoulements compressibles sur calculateurs vectoriels
INRIA Research report n° 622, February 1987.

[13] IBM-VF reference manual

[14] J. Erhel
INRIA Research report, to appear

[15] D. Kuck, R. Kuhn, D. Padua, B. Leasure, M. Wolfe
Dependence graphs and compiler optimizations
Proc. 8th ACM Symp. on Principles of Programming Languages, USA, January 1981.

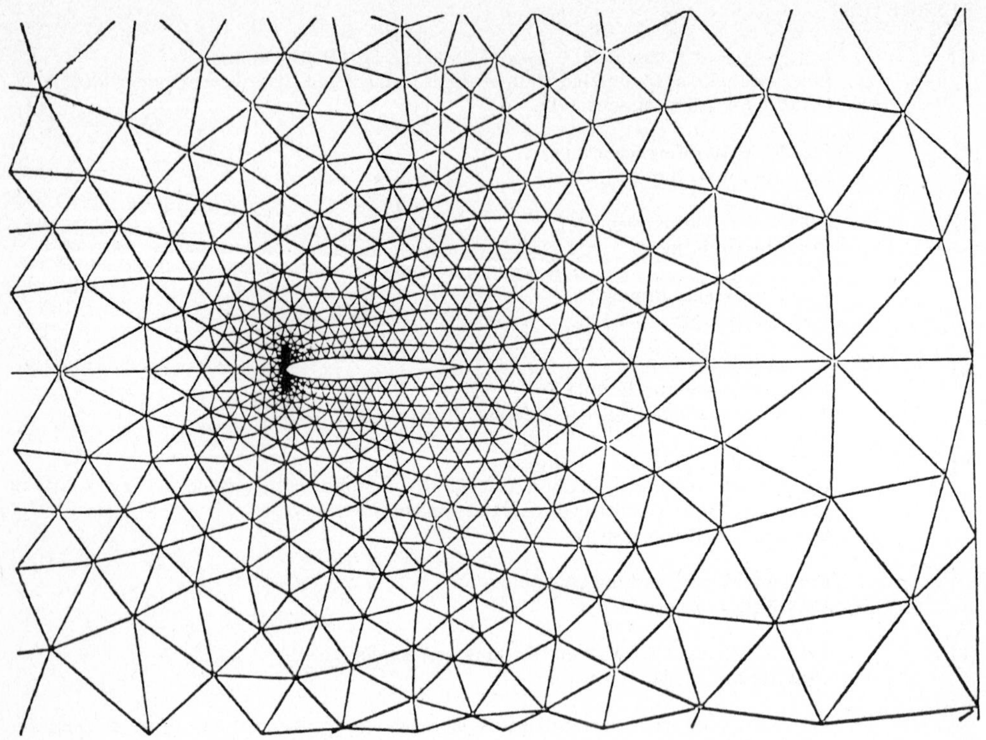

Figure 1. Initial Triangulation (Partial)

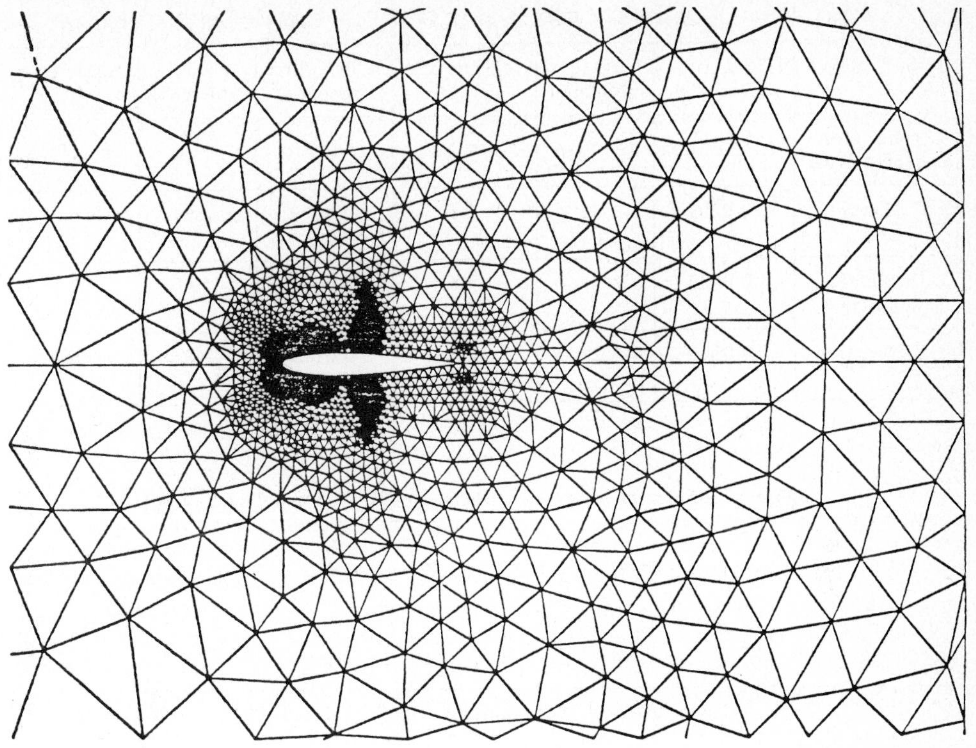

Figure 2. Local Mesh Refinement

computation 1006 nodes	CRAY-1 / CFT 1.14			CRAY-XMP / CFT 1.15		
	CPU time (seconds)	rate (Mflops)	efficiency	CPU time (seconds)	rate (Mflops)	efficiency
time step derivatives	0.0190	7	2.1	0.0038	37	5.9
fluxes	0.0203	32	3.1	0.0079	83	6.3
boundary conditions	0.0003	51	4.6	0.0001	100	7.5
1 iteration	0.0396	20	2.4	0.0119	68	6.2

Figure 3. Results for the explicit scheme on CRAY-1 and CRAY-XMP

computation CRAY-2/CFT 2	Naca 0012 - 1006 nodes			Naca 0012 - 2765 nodes		
	CPU time (seconds)	rate (Mflops)	efficiency	CPU time (seconds)	rate (Mflops)	efficiency
time step derivatives	0.0069	18	4.9	0.0171	21	5.6
fluxes	0.0081	83	9.9	0.0201	93	11.8
1 iteration	0.0158	53	7.5	0.0383	61	9.0

Figure 4. Results for the explicit scheme on CRAY-2/CFT2

computation 1006 nodes	CRAY-1 / CFT 1.14			CRAY-2 / CFT 2		
	CPU time (seconds)	rate (Mflops)	efficiency	CPU time (seconds)	rate (Mflops)	efficiency
time step derivatives	0.0190	7	2.1	0.0080	16	4.0
fluxes	0.0200	32	3.1	0.0073	88	9.9
resolution	0.0510	17	1.8	0.0171	52	4.8
1 iteration	0.1010	17	2.0	0.0376	48	5.9

Figure 5. Results for the implicit scheme on CRAY-1 and CRAY-2

computation	IBM VF		
1006 nodes	CPU time	rate	efficiency
1 iteration	0.23	10	2.2

Figure 6. Results for the implicit scheme on IBMVF

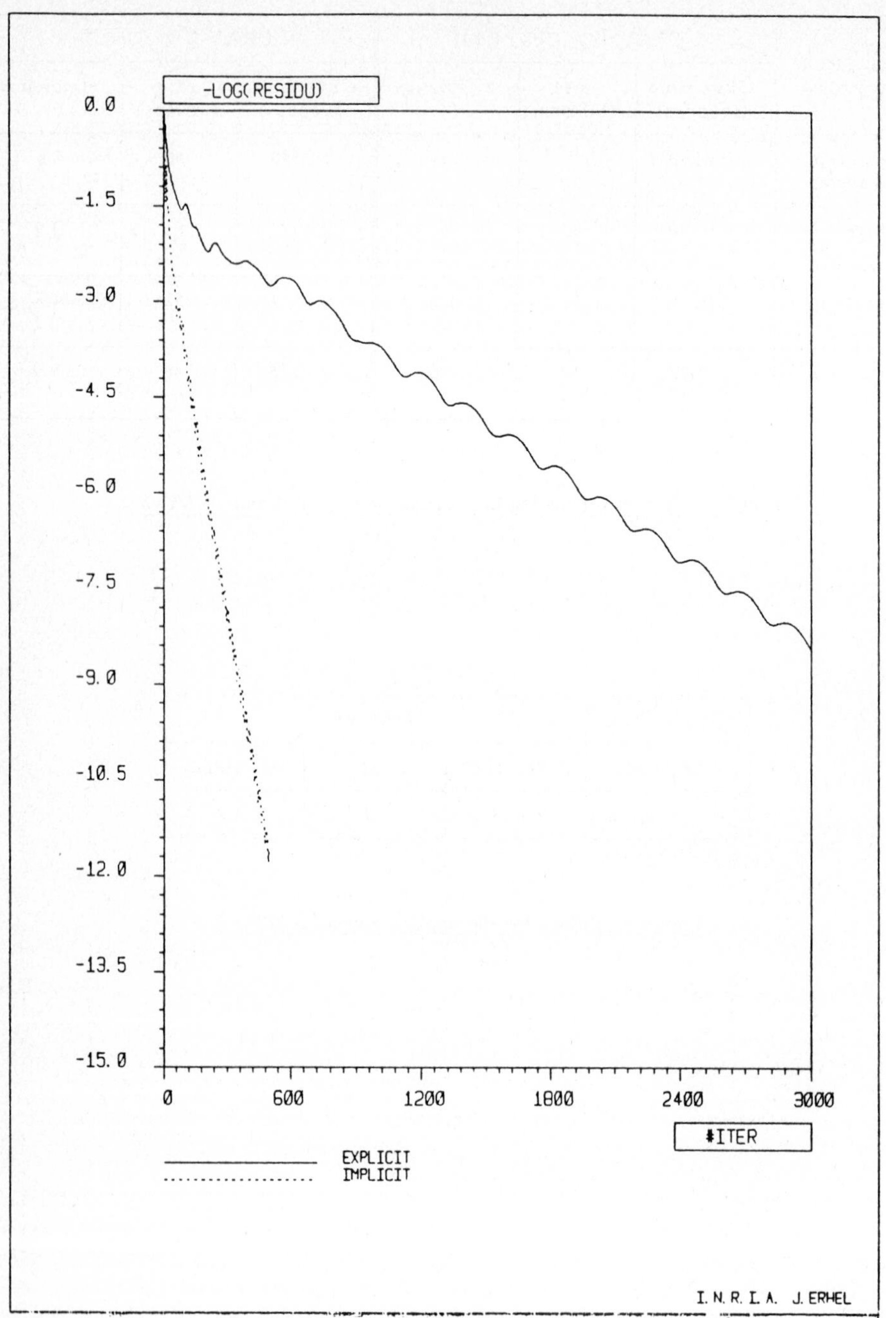

Figure 7. Convergence rates

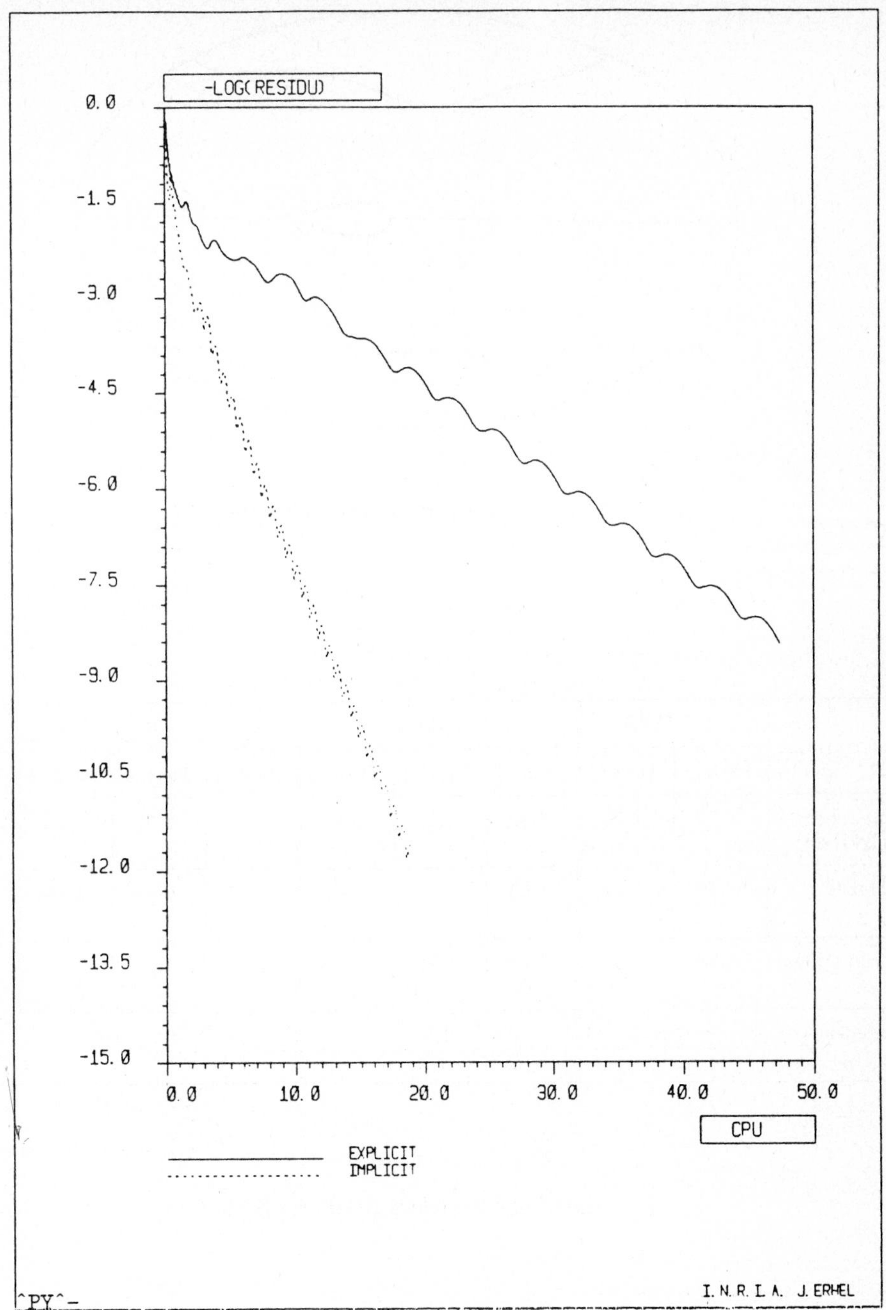

Figure 8. Cost of convergence

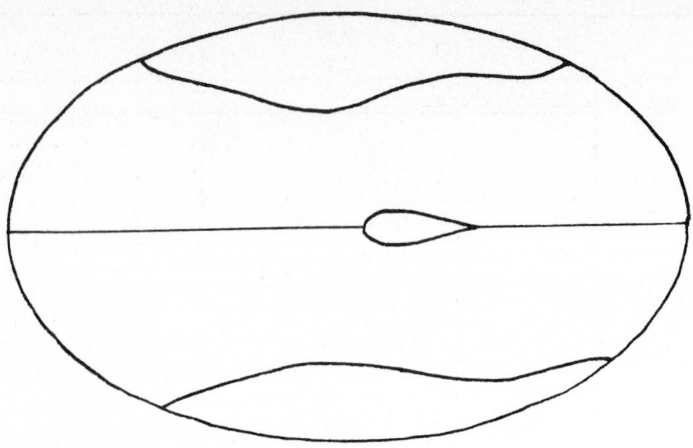

Figure 9. Domain decomposition into slices

computation	2 TASKS		3 TASKS			4 TASKS			
	Task 1	Task 2	Task 1	Task 2	Task 3	Task 1	Task 2	Task 3	Task 4
time step derivatives	1.25	1.12	1.00	1.02	0.83	0.82	0.67	0.82	1.08
fluxes	1.49	1.41	1.03	1.15	1.01	0.97	0.67	0.69	1.05
100 iterations	2.84	2.56	2.14	1.90	2.20	1.84	1.39	1.74	2.17
speed-up	1.5		1.9			1.9			

Figure 10. Microtasking results on CRAY-2

computation 100 iterations	2 TASKS		4 TASKS			
	Task 1	Task 2	Task 1	Task 2	Task 3	Task 4
# of nodes	1361	1361	565	662	662	565
time step derivatives	1.06	1.07	0.667	0.740	0.736	0.656
fluxes	1.31	1.31	0.856	0.903	0.950	0.797
100 iterations	2.49	2.49	1.69	1.78	1.81	1.59
speed-up	1.7		2.3			

Figure 11. Multitasking results on CRAY-2

LU FACTORIZATION WITH MAXIMUM PERFORMANCES ON FPS ARCHITECTURES 38/64 BIT

A. Corana, C. Martini, S. Ridella, C. Rolando
Consiglio Nazionale delle Ricerche
Istituto per i Circuiti Elettronici
Via All'Opera Pia 11 - 16145 Genova - ITALY

ABSTRACT

A technique for dense linear system solution is presented which reaches the maximum performances on attached processors like FPS-120, 5000 and X64 using the Fortran language with calls to the vector routines.

Starting from the Dongarra's LU factorization algorithm the key idea is to carry out a pseudo-transposition of the lower triangular matrix L (including the main diagonal) around the minor diagonal. The pseudo-transposition allows to carry out all the matrix vector operations involved in LU factorization with only stride 1 dot product operations which, using the TM Auxiliary Memory and the TMDOT routine, can be executed in the FPS processor obtaining the maximum speed.

Since the algorithm uses only vector instructions it is fully portable on all the FPS 38/64 bit machines and in general on all the vector computers with a similar memory structure. Furthermore the algorithm can be easily translated into the new FORTRAN 8X, which will probably become the standard for future SIMD computers for numerical applications.

The algorithm has been implemented on a FPS-100 yielding the asymptotic speed r_∞ = 8 MegaFLOPS (FPS-100 peak performances) and the half performances length $N_{1/2}$ = 235. The $N_{1/2}$ value could be lowered by using the APAL Assembly Language to code some critical parts, losing however the code portability.

INTRODUCTION

Dongarra in [1] proposed a technique to improve the performances of the LU factorization algorithm in a Fortran enviroment by using the two kernels SMXPY and SXMPY.

These two routines can be used in a wide variety of algorithms in linear algebra and belong to the LEVEL 2 BLAS routines [2] in which the basic operation is the matrix vector product.

The routine SMXPY adds a matrix times a vector to another vector

$$Y \leftarrow Y + M \cdot X \qquad (1)$$

the routine SXMPY adds a vector times a matrix to another vector

$$Y^T \leftarrow Y^T + X^T \cdot M \qquad (2)$$

The two cases are reported graphically in Fig. 1.

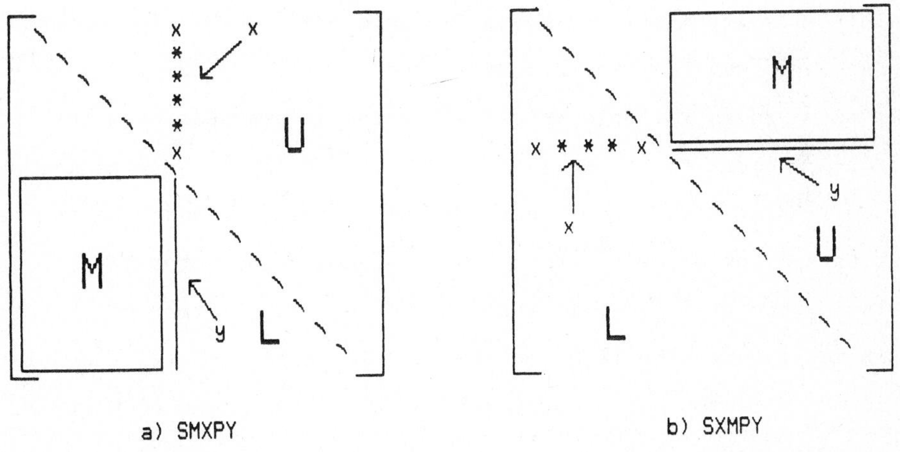

Figure 1. Graphical representation of the matrix vector products.

In [1] the goal was to obtain the best performances on the CRAY computers and so the unrolling technique was used in order to improve the use of the vector registers of the machine.

THE ALGORITHM

Our goal is to reach the maximum performances on attached processors like FPS-120, 5000, X64 with the LU factorization algorithm using the Fortran language with calls to the vector routines. The architecture of these machines is well known [3]; in particular it includes a Main Data Memory (MD) and an Auxilary Memory (TM) which allows to carry out the dot product operation with peak performance by storing a vector in MD and the other one in TM.

The algorithm, we are presenting, can be used, therefore, for all the vector processors with a similar memory structure.

To achieve the maximum performances some modifications are needed in the original algorithm proposed by Dongarra: the kernels SMXPY and SXMPY have to be implemented with the dot product routine and it is necessary to change the matrix elements organization to have always dot product with stride 1.

Initially the matrix to factorize is stored in MD. To perform in an efficient way the vector matrix products (1) and (2) the vector X has to be moved in TM; this operation causes an overhead of order N_1 if X has stride equal to 1 (Fig. 1a) and of order $3N_1$ if X has stride not equal to 1 (Fig. 1b) for each vector matrix product having an execution time of order N_1^2 (N_1=number of elements in vector X).

The main difference is that in (1) the i-th element of Y is the dot product between the i-th row of M and X while in (2) the i-th element of Y is the dot product between the i-th column of M and X . So M is addressed by row (stride $\neq$ 1) in the first case and by column (stride =1) in the second case.

In a FPS like machine the maximum performances are reached when M is addressed by column (when the stride is equal to 1) while only about half of the maximum performances can be obtained when M is addressed by row (when the stride is not equal to 1) because extra cycles are lost in the computation of the matrix addresses.

The key idea in the algorithm is to carry out a pseudo-transposition of the lower triangular matrix L(including the main diagonal) around the minor diagonal.

The transformation law is given by:

$$a_{I,J} \longleftarrow a_{N-J+1,N-I+1} \tag{3}$$

Denoting with M^*,Y^*, and X^* the pseudo-transposed, following (3), of M, Y and X the (1) and (2) become:

$$Y^{T*} \longleftarrow Y^{T*} + X \cdot M^* \tag{4}$$

$$Y^T \longleftarrow Y^T + X \cdot M^* \tag{5}$$

The arrangements after the pseudo-transposition (3) are reported graphically in Fig. 2.

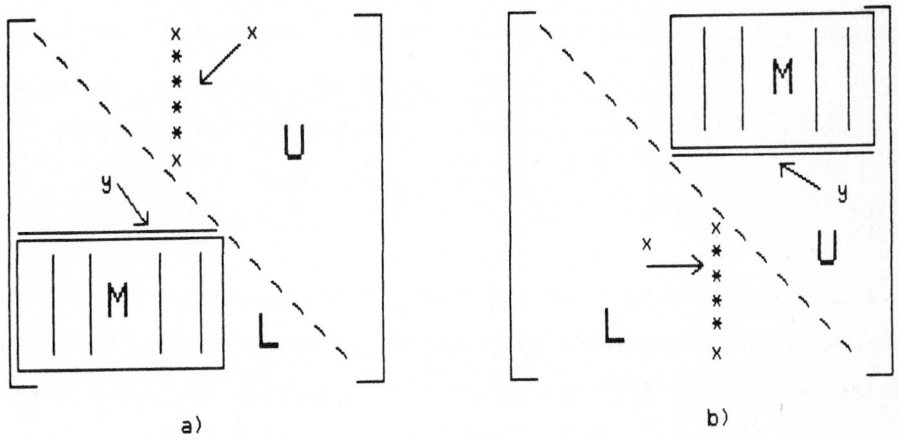

Figure 2. Graphical representation of the matrix vector products after the pseudo-transposition.

Owing to the pseudo-transposition the two kernels SMXPY and SXMPY have to be modified to obtain the previous results.

A closer inspection reveals that in Fig. 2a the matrix M is now addressed by column so the routine SXMPY can be used with stride=1 providing the maximum performances of the processor; in the case of

Fig. 2b less changes are needed because only the vector X has been transposed.

The resulting modified algorithm is the following:

```
perform the pseudo-transpositon L ---> L*
do I=1,N
  perform the (N-I+1)st vector matrix product to obtain the (N-I+1)st
  row of L
  (CALL SXMPY(N-I+1,LDA,A(N-I+1,1),I-1,LDA,A(1,I),LDA,A(N-I+2,1)))
  search for a pivot and interchange
  perform the i-th vector matrix product to obtain the i-th row of U
  (CALL SXMPY(N-I,LDA,A(I,I+1),I-1,LDA,A(N-I+2,N-I+1),LDA,A(1,I+1)))
enddo
perform the pseudo-transposition L* ---> L
```

The application of (3) allows to carry out all the matrix vector operations involved in LU factorization with only stride 1 dot product operations which, using the TM auxiliary memory and the TMDOT routine, can be executed in the FPS processor obtaining the maximum speed.

RESULTS

We implemented the algorithm on our FPS-100 (with PS=4 KW,MD=64 KW, TMROM=4.5 KW, TMRAM=8 KW) attached to a VAX-11/730 using CPFORTRAN language [4] and the following elementary routines in MATH Library FPS: MTIMOV, SVE, VADD, VMOV, VSMA, VSMUL, VSWAP, TMDOT [5].

The proposed pseudo-transposition doesn't change the number of floating point operations required to perform the LU factorization that is approximately, as reported in [6], $(2/3)N^3$.

Execution times on FPS-100 are measured with elapsed time on the VAX in single-user configuration.

The measured speeds are reported in Fig. 3 versus the dimension N of the system.

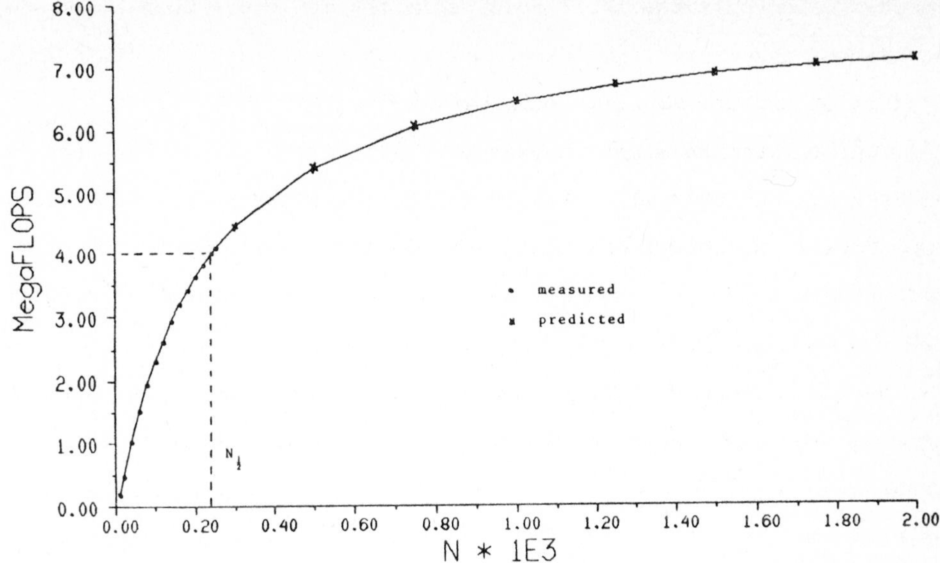

Figure 3. Measured and predicted speeds vs. the system dimension N.

We stress that for the proposed algorithm the asymptotic speed is $r_\infty = 8$ MegaFLOPS that is the FPS-100 peak performance because in all the innermost loop we use only the TMDOT routine.

From measured speeds the half performances length is:

$$N_{1/2} = 235 \quad (\text{for } N= N_{1/2} \quad r_{N_{1/2}} = r_\infty /2).$$

Since the MD memory of our FPS-100 doesn't allow to have dimension of the equation system greater than 250,in Fig. 3 are also reported some predicted speeds obtained using the Hockney law:

$$r= \frac{r_\infty}{1 + N_{1/2}/N} \tag{6}$$

CONCLUSIONS

The proposed algorithm allows to carry out the LU factorization on FPS-5000 and X64 series Attached Array Processor with efficency unitary when N increases. Such a result is possible because, with the pseudo- transposition used, both the kernels SMXPY and SXMPY can be computed using only the TMDOT routine in the innermost loop.

Since the algorithm uses only vector instructions it is fully portable on all the FPS like machines.

Furthermore the algorithm can be easily translated into the new FORTRAN 8X, which will probably become the standard for future SIMD computers for numerical applications. So the algorithm has not only a theoretical interest but it can be useful from a practical point of view.

The $N_{1/2}$ value could be lowered by using the APAL Assembly Language to code some critical parts, losing however the code portability.

The memories of our FPS-100 doesn't allow to have dimension of the equations system greater than 250.

We are waiting for a FPS M64/330 with MD=2 MW, so we will also be able to obtain performances for matrix dimension grater than 250.

REFERENCES

[1] Dongarra J.J., Eisenstat S.C.: Squeezing the Most out of an Algorithm in CRAY FORTRAN, ACM Transaction on Mathematical Software, Vol.10, No. 3, September 1984, pages 219-230.

[2] Dongarra J.J., Du Croz J. Hammarling S., Hanson R.J.: A Proposal for an Extended Set of Fortran Basic Linear Algebra Subprograms, Argonne National Laboratory, Mathematics and Computer Science Division, Technical Memorandum No. 41, December 1984.

[3] Charlesworth A.E.: An Approach to Scientific Array Processing: The Architectural Design of the AP-120B/FPS-164 Family. IEEE Computer, September 1981, Pages 18-27.

[4] 5000 FORTRAN 77 Manuals, FPS Technical Pubblication, 1986.

[5] FPS-5000 APMATH Library Manual, FPS Technical Pubblication, 1985.

[6] Dongarra J.J.: Performance of Various Computers Using Standard Linear Equations Software in a Fortran Enviroment. Argonne National Laboratory, Mathematics and Computer Science Division, Technical Memorandum No. 23, May 1985.

MSC/NASTRAN ON AMDAHL VECTOR PROCESSORS: ADAPTATION AND PERFORMANCE

C. Y. Chen
Amdahl Corporation
1250 East Arquest Avenue
Sunnyvale, California 94088
U. S. A.

ABSTRACT

Because increasingly sophisticated large-scale finite element models are being used in areas of research and application and the theories of structural dynamics and nonlinear analyses are being used more frequently in the techniques of finite element analysis, the requirement for more powerful computer is growing rapidly. Since 1980 many finite element programs have been adapted on supercomputers. This paper describes the general architecture and functional use of MSC/NASTRAN@ , provides a brief introduction to the hardware and software of the Amdahl vector processor system; describes the work of adapting MSC/NASTRAN to the Amdahl system; and provides a performance analysis of this version of MSC/NASTRAN, including a comparison with other machines.

1.1 OVERVIEW OF MSC/NASTRAN

MSC/NASTRAN is a large-scale, general-purpose application program which solves a wide variety of engineering problems by using finite element techniques. It is regarded as one of the most popular finite element programs in use today. The capabilities of the program include static and dynamic structure analysis (linear and nonlinear), heat transfer, acoustics, and electromagnetics. Applications of MSC/NASTRAN are used in a wide range of engineering fields,

---

@ NASTRAN is a trademark of the National Aeronautics and Space Administration. MSC/NASTRAN is an enhanced, proprietary version of NASTRAN, developed, marketed and supported by the MacNeal-Schwendler Corporation. MSC and MSC/ are trademarks of the MacNeal-Schwendler Corporation.

including aerospace, automotive, civil engineering, naval engineering, chemical engineering, offshore oil, biomedical research and optics.

MSC/NASTRAN source code consists of more than 480,000 statements. Ninety-eight percent are written in FORTRAN; the rest are coded in Assembler for system dependencies and performance improvements. The program is designed in modular form for ease of maintenance, ease of optimization, ease of quality assurance, and to allow easy expansion of new features. Advanced features of MSC/NASTRAN are component mode synthesis, design sensitivity, creep analysis capability, optimization of structural design, and transient analysis with geometry and material nonlinearity.

MSC/NASTRAN provides a comprehensive element library which enables the user to create mathematical models close to the real physical objects being analyzed. With more than 40 pre-formatted solution sequences built into MSC/NASTRAN, the user can solve a very complicated problem with a minimum of effort. MSC/NASTRAN has unique features which are easy to incorporate into the solution sequence, including command-driven restart, matrix singularity suppression, optimal nodal number resequencing, error analysis, and extensive graphical aids for pre- and post-processing. The sparse matrix solution algorithm, superelement analysis, cyclic symmetry, and generalized dynamic reduction capability make MSC/NASTRAN very suitable to solve large scale problems. MSC/NASTRAN also provides a high-order language, Direct Matrix Abstraction Programming (DMAP), which allows the user to create his own solution sequence by manipulating data files and functional modules. With pre- and post-processors and the early detection features, MSC/NASTRAN is extremely user friendly.(1,2,3,4,5)

1.2 AMDAHL VECTOR PROCESSORS

Amdahl announced the Vector Processor Models 1100 and 1200 in 1984. In 1985, Amdahl announced two additional supercomputer models, the entry-level Model 500 and high-end Model 1400. In 1986, Amdahl announced the software product VP/XA, which enables Amdahl Vector Processors to use the standard IBM MVS/XA operating system. Currently, there are more than 40 installations of this series worldwide, making it the second largest supercomputer group in the world.

The Amdahl vector processors are generally used as back-end systems for batch workloads. Front-end processors can be any System/370 processor running MVS/370 or MVS/XA. The Amdahl vector processor consists of a vector processing unit, a main storage unit, a channel processor, and a service processor. The vector processing unit includes a scalar unit and a vector unit. The scalar unit performs systems control and executes scalar instructions while the vector unit executes vector instructions. The 500, 1100, 1200 and 1400 all have identical scalar units. The vector units are different, with vector performance doubling between each successive model. In general, the Amdahl vector processors are regarded as one of the most powerful supercomputers, with a performance range of 143 to 1,143 millions of floating point operations per second (MFLOPS).

Table 1 shows the hardware specifications of the four models. These vector processors support System/370 architecture, enhanced with 83 unique vector instructions. Several advanced features are incorporated into these vector processors: Dynamically reconfigurable vector registers, masked operations, parallel processing, and serialization of memory access. (6,7,8,9) Because of these features, DO loops can be optimally vectorized even if there are arithmetic IF, block IF, IF statements. The Amdahl FORTRAN 77/VP compiler has been recognized as one of the most advanced automatic vectorizing compilers available. (9,10)

In addition to the compiler, the Amdahl Vector Processor/Application Development System (VP/ADS) provides several software tools: the Interactive Vectorizer, a full-screen tuning tool which allows the user to tune one's program to higher vectorization rate interactively; FORTUNE, an execution cost analyzer which can provide the execution frequency of each statement and true ratio of IF statements; and DOCK/FORT77, a full-screen interactive FORTRAN debugger. All of these tools can be executed in batch or interactive mode. In addition, a highly vectorized scientific subroutine library, SSL II, is available. These hardware and software features, coupled with large, high-speed main memory, make the Amdahl vector processor system a reliable, easy to use, and high performance supercomputer. (10,11)

Model	500	1100	1200	1400
Peak MFLOPS	143	286	571	1143
Cycle Time (ns)				
Vector Unit	7	7	7	7
Scalar Unit	14	14	14	14
Concurrent Vector Pipelines				
Arithmetic	1	2	2	2
Mask	1	1	1	1
Load/Store	1	2	2	1
Vector Registers				
Size (KB)	32	32	64	128
Number	8 to 256	8 to 256	8 to 256	8 to 256
Length (64-bit words)	16 to 512	16 to 512	32 to 1,024	64 to 2,048
Main Storage (Maximum MB)	128	128	256	256

Table 1. Hardware Specifications

2.0 ADAPTATION OF MSC/NASTRAN

Before starting the conversion of MSC/NASTRAN to the Amdahl vector processor system, several guidelines were set:

(1) Solution accuracy should not be sacrificed.

(2) Because of the superiority of the Amdahl FORTRAN compiler, FORTRAN codes would be used as much as possible for ease of future tuning, debugging and maintenance.

(3) Tuning of the source code would be suspended whenever quality assurance (QA) was started for each release. Any further enhancement after QA began would be incorporated into the next revision instead of the one under the QA process.

(4) If a major change in algorithm or data structure causes the availability of the Amdahl version of MSC/NASTRAN to slip more than six months, the change would be left to the next release.

(5) All major and minor changes should be documented and reported to the MacNeal-Schwendler Corporation (MSC) for review and approval.

(6) Two scalar load modules with optimization levels 0 and 3 (OPT(0) and OPT(3)) would be created for debugging purposes. In case an incorrect solution is detected, these two scalar load modules would be checked. By doing so, it would be easy to identify whether the wrong solution is caused by tuning or by compiler optimization.

(7) The converting of the program, tuning of the source code and QA test runs will be carried out by Amdahl with assistance from MSC. Final solution checking would be done by MSC.

2.1 CONVERSION OF VERSION 64A

Because the Amdahl vector processor is compatible with System/370, it was decided to start working with version 64A of the standard MVS system. The original MSC/NASTRAN code consists of close to half-a-million statements. The subroutines total more than 2,200; 50 of them are coded in Assembler and the rest are written in FORTRAN. The purpose of the Assembler routine is mainly to improve I/O operations, to avoid using non-standard FORTRAN intrinsic functions, and to improve the execution speed of the scalar computations.

The first step of conversion was to change the FORTRAN interface library names and to compile using FORTRAN 77/VP compiler. This compilation found some nonstandard statements that caused compiler warning messages. A quick modification eliminated the messages. To keep the executable load module from being too large, the original scalar MSC/NASTRAN version consists of 16 individual links. Each link is created by using a very complicated overlay scheme. Because the object code generated by the vectorizing compiler is larger than the scalar code, the vector version might cause one segment to destroy another, depending on the calling sequence. During the conversion, Amdahl internally developed an overlay checking tool, OVLYCHK, which automatically provides the information on the entry address of each segment, length of the control section, and a tree chart which shows the hierarchical relationship of the whole segment table. With this tool, the scalar load module was easily analyzed and compared with the newly created vector load module. It was also recognized that as the tuning went on, the vectorization ration of some key subroutine would increase, the object code will be enlarged further. In order to avoid such impact, MSC approved simplifying the overlay structure. Most of the code text was placed in one region and common blocks were placed in another. In this way the load modules would be easy to maintain no matter how the size of object code might change. The Amdahl version of MSC/NASTRAN still keeps the Open Core Method used in the original scalar load module.

The original MVS scalar version of MSC/NASTRAN uses the Open Core Method to provide a working common block area. By using the region size provided by the user and subtracting the size of the load module, the remaining area becomes the 'core size' of the working area declared in the common block. This feature is very important and useful for supercomputer. If a problem can be solved in memory, the I/O can be significantly reduced and the vector length increased, which not only reduces CPU time but also speeds up the job turnaround time. This gives the user the freedom to decide the region size of his job and allows him to use more system resources when a job is a big and urgent one, and less resources when his job is not urgent or just a small one. The Amdahl version of MSC/NASTRAN can be executed with a minimum job size of 2.5 megabytes (MB) and a maximum allowable size of 8 MB. Many tests show that a region size of 4 MB is sufficient for most jobs with degree of freedom (DOF) less than

50,000, depending on the type of the analysis. Although requesting the region size too large will not cause the job to use excessive CPU and elapsed time, the user is wasting memory and may block others from getting their jobs done promptly. Therefore, if the user feels a need to use a region size larger than 4 MB, either an MSC consultant or the MSC Application Manual (Vol.2, Chap. 7) should be consulted.

2.2 TUNING OF MSC/NASTRAN

Because of the complicated structure of MSC/NASTRAN, Amdahl internally developed a program performance analyzer. This tool, SNOWBALL, samples the target program during execution and produces the target program during execution and produces CSECT level tuning information by using a CPU sampling method. Several capabilities of SNOWBALL are: (1) Calling-sequence analysis, which provides information on whether CPU consumption is due to data crunching or excessive calling overhead. The by-product of this option is to offer user a trace of the subroutine-dynamic-calling sequence for debugging purpose; (2) vector-length analysis, which offers the ability to monitor vector lengths in certain DO loops. With vector length information, the user can determine if further tuning is needed or if certain parts are 'over-vectorized';(3) wait-time analysis, which gives the user a good idea whether the job is I/O bound or not; (4) vector-ratio analysis, which gives the global vector ratio of each job as well as the vector ratio of each individual subroutine, allowing the user to judge if a key subroutine is well vectorized or if a new algorithm should be tried; (5) source-code analysis, which provides information on the number of times that each single statement has been sampled during the execution of a job.

With these enhancements, it is found that SNOWBALL is very useful for other programs, although the original purpose was aimed for MSC/NASTRAN tuning purposes. Combining FORTUNE and SNOWBALL, Amdahl offers very unique and flexible software tools for program performance analysis which makes tuning of programs for Amdahl vector processors easier.

Generally speaking, the procedures of the finite element method consist essentially of three phases:

(1) Formulation (assembly) of the structural matrices, which includes stiffness matrix, mass matrix, displacement and load vectors.

(2) Solution of equilibrium equations.

(3) Evaluation of local quantities, e.g., local stress and strain.

For a traditional scalar computer, the stage of solving the equilibrium equations takes a large percentage of the total execution time. This applies to static, dynamic, and nonlinear analysis. Therefore, the first step of tuning focused on the equilibrium solution stage, and specifically on the linear algebra-related subroutines.

It was impractical to go through more than 2,000 subroutines for tuning purposes. With the aid of SNOWBALL, key subroutines were identified easily. For the current release of the Amdahl version, the tuning was concentrated on specific routines only. Due to the structure of MSC/NASTRAN, it is not a surprise that 25 out of 32 dominant subroutines were doing the linear algebra-related operations. Among these 32 subroutines, most of the tuning was minor except for two subroutines, SDCOM2 and SDCOM4,which deal with matrix decomposition. With suggestions from MSC, the two subroutines were tuned to satisfactory level and copied into the current Amdahl version, version 64A. Figure 3 shows the performance difference before and after tuning.

The equilibrium equation for static analysis can be expressed as:

$$\{K\}\,[U]=[R]$$

where:

{K} is the stiffness matrix of the structure.

[U] is the displacement vector of each DOF of the nodes (usually unknown).

[R] is the load vector applied to nodal points of the finite element system.

The size of these matrices depends on the total DOF of a mathematical model; it is very common to see a model consist of more than 50,000 DOF. Most of the stiffness matrix comes on the form of a banded or sparse matrix. Therefore, it is more economical to store only nonzero terms and to adapt certain efficient algorithms to solve the equations. MSC/NASTRAN uses the sparse matrix solution algorithm and optimally uses main and secondary storage as well as CPU power to solve problems efficiently. (12,13)

2.3 PROCEDURES OF QUALITY ASSURANCE

The QA procedures were mainly set up by MSC and included three steps. The first step was to run more than 600 problems at the Amdahl site. The results were written to tape and shipped to MSC for solution checking. Then, after 95 percent of the jobs were proved correct, the MSC Application Manual of the Amdahl version was updated and a beta-test tape of executable load module was created by Amdahl. MSC remotely dialed into the Amdahl site to verity the installation procedure. The last step of the QA procedures was to send the modified source code of the Amdahl version back to MSC for final checking.

In general, the entire adaptation process took around 16 man-months, which included 13 man-months of conversion and tuning and three man-months of QA runs and checking. When MSC/NASTRAN was adapted to the Cray 1S, the process took three man-years.(14) The main reasons that it took Amdahl less time to complete the adaptation effort are: the Amdahl vector processor is System/370 compatible; FORTRAN 77/VP is a powerful compiler; good tuning tools were available to aid vectorization; MSC has a good program layout; and a close relationship existed between MSC and Amdahl.

3.0 PERFORMANCE OF MSC/NASTRAN

To understand the performance of a supercomputer, there are three methods of analysis. The simplest one is based on the peak performance announced by the vendor. Such peak performance can rarely be achieved in the real computation world. However, it is a good guide to judge which category the machine belongs to.

The second method of judging the performance of a machine is to test kernels on the machine. These kernels can be created by users to represent their working environments. There are several 'standardize' packages, e.g., the Livermore Loops, the Los Alamos Benchmark Set, and LINKPACK. Dr. L. Komzsik of MSC has done a kernel-type benchmark on several supercomputers. From these results, the Amdahl vector processors are some of the best supercomputers. Figs. 1 through 3 illustrate Komzsik's results. These figures show that as the problem size increase, the advantage of the Amdahl vector Processor becomes more significant. It should be noted that the original curves of the Amdahl 1200 for the DECOMP operation is an untuned one. Figure 3 shows that the performance of the tuned DECOMP operation on the Amdahl 1200 improves rapidly as the vector length becomes longer. Kernel-type testing provides good information about the machine if these kernels are well set up to represent the real workload. (9,10,15,16)

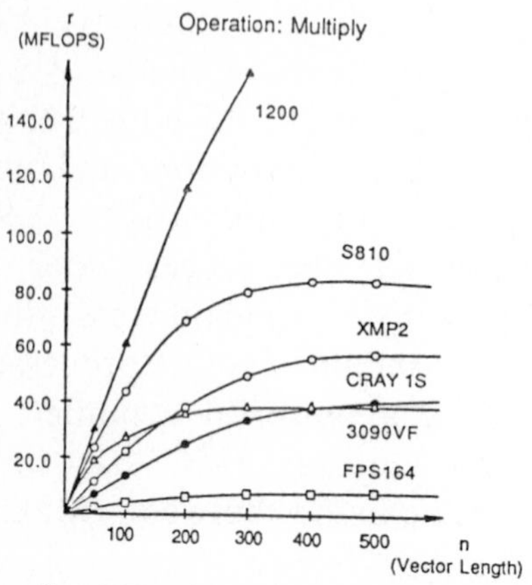

Figure 1. MSC/NASTRAN Performance Data

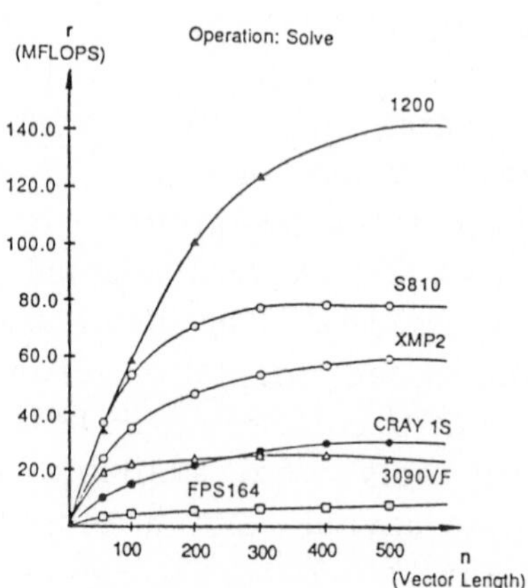

Figure 2. MSC/NASTRAN Performance Data

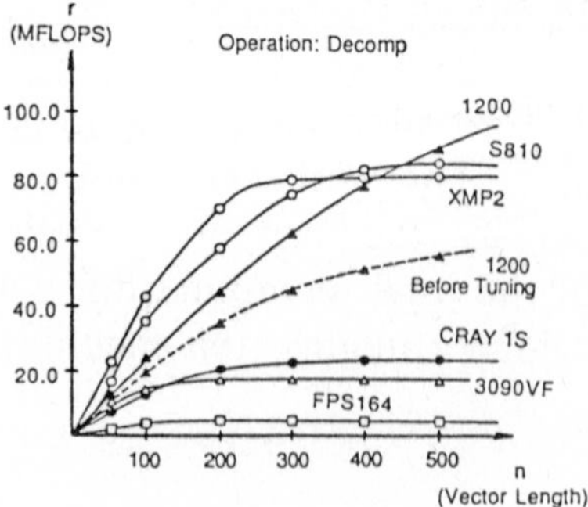

Figure 3. MSC/NASTRAN Performance Data

The third method of benchmarking is to use a set of 'real case' problems. This set of problems can cover different kinds of standard application packages and in-house programs. The size of the problems for each package ranges from small to very large to simulate the daily work situation of a data processing system. In doing this real case simulation benchmark, not only are the programs thoroughly tested, but the I/O performance, operating system, hardware reliability, compiler, etc. are all examined in detail. (17)

A rectangular plate loaded by a concentrated force, as shown in figure 4, has been used for a performance study on the Amdahl 5860 and 1200. The number of active DOF used in the mathematical model was increased from 515 to 50,000. Correspondingly, the number of nodes increased from 100 to 10,000. The number of DOF is usually used to describe the size of a finite element model. If the problems are different, then the use of DOF can be misleading because of differences in geometry and topology. However, if the same problem and the same numbering scheme are used to compare performance with respect to a different number of grids, then the number of DOF can be used as a parameter of performance analysis. The number of operations required for decomposition of the stiffness matrix {K} was approximately equal to (18)

$$\frac{1}{2} * MB * N - MB$$

where:

MB is the half-bandwidth of the matrix {K}.

N is the number of DOF.

As the DOF grows, the CPU time increases rapidly on a traditional scalar machine (like the 5860 as shown in figure 5). With parallel executable vector instructions and faster vector unit clock time, the CPU time of the Amdahl 1200 does not increase as rapidly as the 5860. Furthermore, as the number of DOF increases, the curves of the CPU times of the 1200 have a tendency to flatten, which shows the increase of CPU time between the increments of DOF reduces when the number of DOF exceeds 20,000.

Figure 6 shows the speedup ratio of the Amdahl 1200 relative to the Amdahl 5860. The ratio ranges from 1.77 to 9.44 for total job CPU time and from 1.82 to 13.39 for the DCMP stage. Figure 7 shows the percentage of total CPU time spent in the DCMP stage of the scalar and vector machines. The Amdahl 5860, with the largest difference after 20,000 DOF. All of these observation indicate that the Amdahl vector processors are suitable for medium- to large-scale finite element problems.

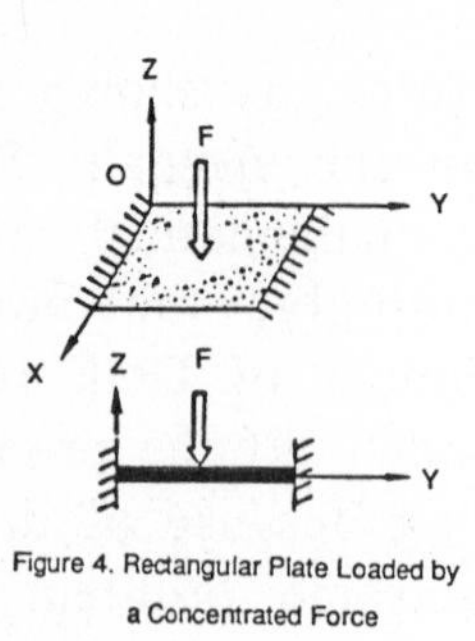

Figure 4. Rectangular Plate Loaded by a Concentrated Force

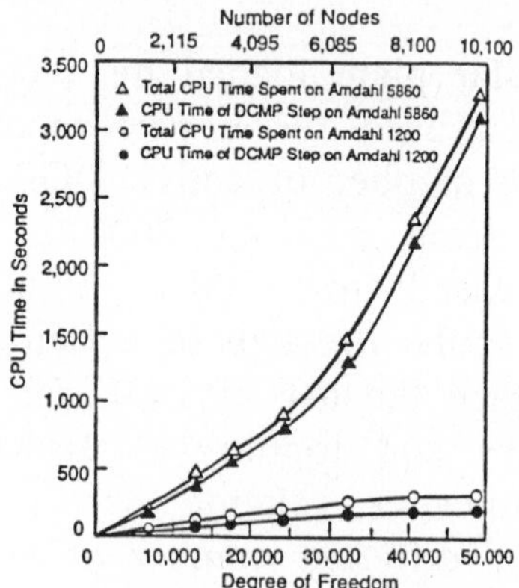

Figure 5. CPU Time of Static Analysis of a Plate Clamped on Two Edges

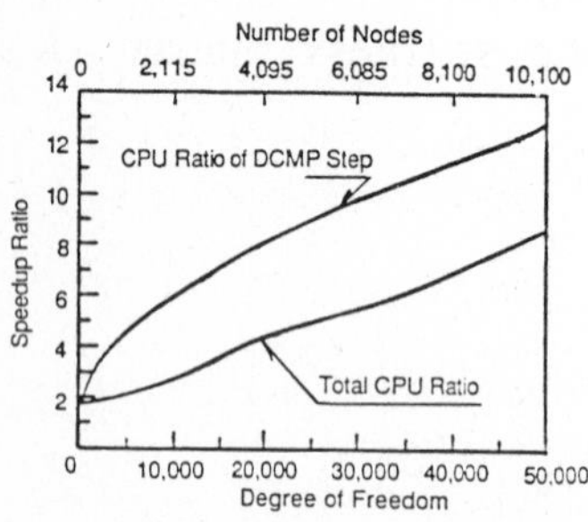
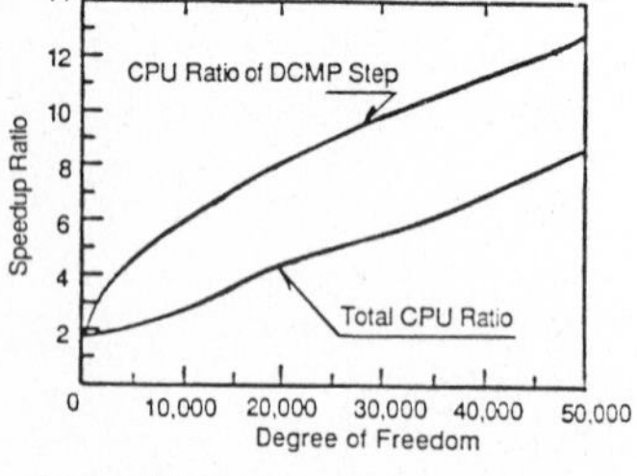

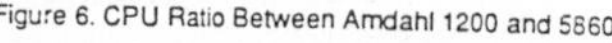
Figure 6. CPU Ratio Between Amdahl 1200 and 5860

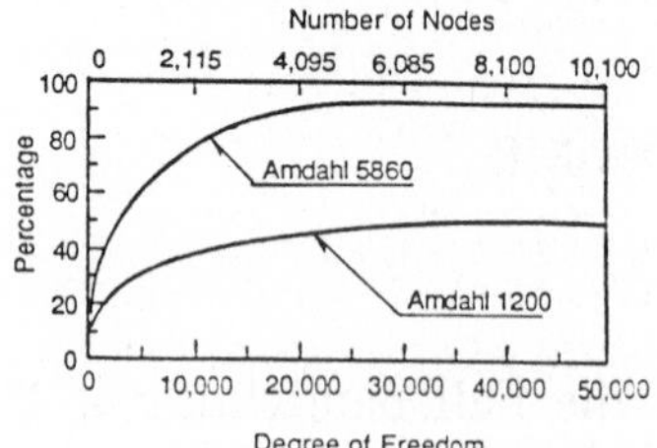

Figure 7. Percent of Total CPU Spent in DCMP Step

Tables 2 through 4 show the performance comparison of Amdahl vector processors relative to the Amdahl 5860, IBM 3084QX, and CDC Cyber 855 scalar machines with respect to different solution types. The speedup ratios range from 4 to 21, depending on machine, size of problem and the solution type. One notable item from table 3 is that the speedup of the Amdahl 1200 is only 6 to 40 percent more than the 500. For the current size of problems in industry, the 500 might offer better price/performance. If 90 percent of a workload of a data processing center is mainly for structural analysis, the 500 might be the best choice. When the CPU becomes saturated, the 500 can be field-upgraded to higher models.

Solution Type	DOF	Amdahl 5860*	Amdahl 500
Static	47,929	3,976(1.0)	650(6.1)
Static	39,841	3,060(1.0)	280(10.9)
Static	24,971	2,900(1.0)	170(17.1)
Static	12,421	515(1.0)	85(6.1)
Normal Modes	24,826	2,200(1.0)	440(5.0)

Notes: CPU time in seconds.
( ) Speedup ratio relative to Amdahl 5860.
* 5860 with High Speed Floating Point Feature.

Table 2 Comparison of CPU Time of MSC/NASTRAN on Amdahl 5860 and 500.

Solution Type	DOF	IBM 3084QX	Amdahl 500	Amdahl 1200
Static	57,118	30,520(1.0)	1,781(17.1)	1,222(25.0)
Static	25,263	10,924(1.0)	855(12.8)	654(16.7)
Static	16,390	3,871(1.0)	437(8.9)	350(11.1)
Static	7,287	573(1.0)	127(4.5)	119(4.8)
Normal Modes	23,040	13,333(1.0)	1,434(9.3)	1,089(12.2)
Normal Modes	18,847	7,724(1.0)	1,003(7.7)	843(9.2)
Normal Modes	10,235	4,596(1.0)	485(9.5)	410(11.2)

Notes: CPU time in seconds.
( ) Speedup ratio relative to IBM 3084QX.

Table 3. Comparison of CPU Times of MSC/NASTRAN on IBM 3084QX, Amdahl 500 and Amdahl 1200.

Solution Type	DOF	CDC Cyber 855	Amdahl 500
Static	55,000	13,110(1.0)	626(20.9)
Normal Modes	30,000	18,620(1.0)	1,500(12.4)
Direct Freq.	6,500	12,310(1.0)	1,122(11.0)

Notes: CPU time in seconds.
( ) Speedup ratio relative to CDC Cyber 855

Table 4 Comparison of CPU Time of MSC/NASTRAN on CDC Cyber 855 and Amdahl 500.

Figures 8,9,10 and 11 show the CPU times and elapsed times of a superelement analysis on four different vector processors: Amdahl 1200, Cray X-MP/14, IBM 3090 and NAS XL V60. The structure has number of DOF of around 15,000. The solution type is the superelement static analysis. These timings are based on the the DMAP stage output generated by MSC/NASTRAN. The timing measurements were carried out when the machines were used standalone, i.e., only one job was running on the machine during the benchmark. In the superelement generation job (first run), the Amdahl 1200 and Cray X-MP/14 are very close in both CPU and elapsed time. The IBM 3090 and NAS XL V60 are around two times slower in CPU times and 1.5 times slower in elapsed time. In the restart run, both IBM and NAS terminated prematurely at stage 10 but Amdahl and Cray ran to stage 14.

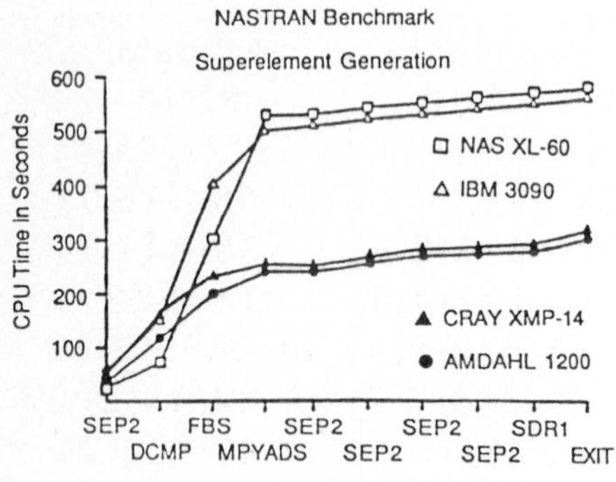

Figure 8. CPU times of DMAP Stage of NASTRAN Run

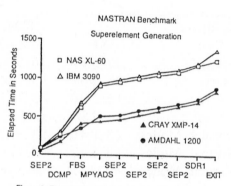

Figure 9. Elapsed Time of DMAP Stage of NASTRAN Run

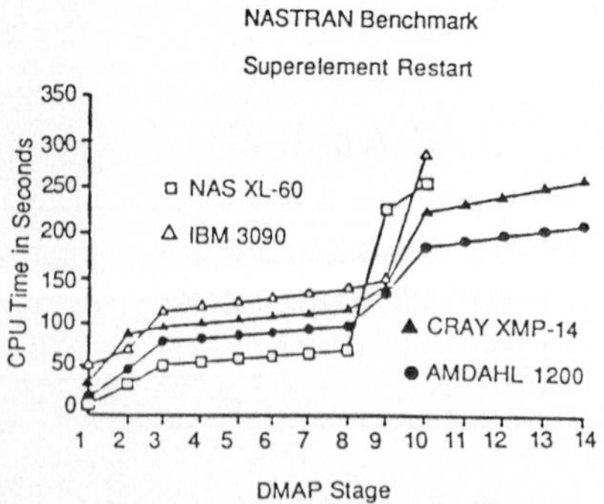

Figure 10. CPU Time of DMAP Stage of NASTRAN Run

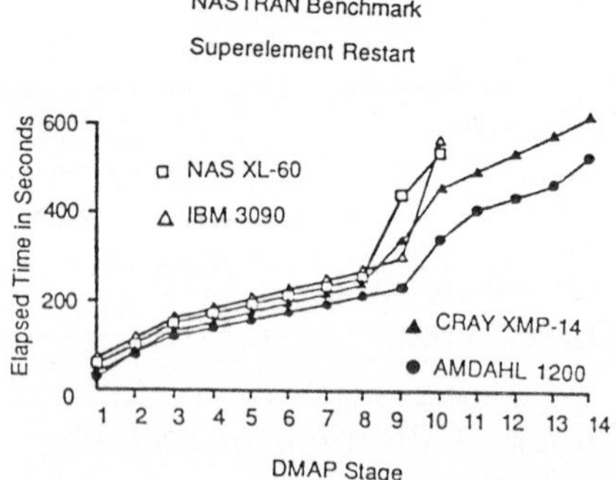

Figure 11. Elapsed Time of DMAP Stage of NASTRAN Run

4.0 CONCLUDING REMARKS

For such a large program as MSC/NASTRAN with a very detailed system interaction method and a complicated overlay structure, the overall adaptation within a short period was quite successful. The performance of MSC/NASTRAN on Amdahl vector processors is quite impressive when compared with scalar machines. Even compared with machines in the category of supercomputers, the Amdahl vector processor system provides comparable speed especially when the size of the problem becomes large.

Generally speaking , with the exception that the size the load module of the Amdahl version is larger than the scalar load module, the usage of the Amdahl version of MSC/NASTRAN is the same as the MVS version, even with the flexible Open Core Method is still available.

5.0 ACKNOWLEDGEMENTS

The author would like to thank C. Pangali, J. Roberts, R. Sivertson and H. Wada of Amdahl Corporation and Y. Tago of Fujitsu for their patience, trust, encouragement and understanding. Special thanks to W. Plappert and K. Itoh of Amdahl for their initial efforts on starting this project and the development of tools. The contribution of T. Ishigai of Fujitsu, who spent several sleepless nights and staring with red eyes at the terminal to speed up the completion of this project, should not be forgotten. Special thanks to B. Bilyeu, M. Caetta, H. Delgadillo and D. Nagy of MacNeal Schwendler Corporation for their assistance. Several valuable suggestions in tuning the DCMP portion provided by L. Komzsik of MSC are deeply appreciated.

6.0 REFERENCES

(1) R. H. MacNeal, "Some Organizational Aspects of NASTRAN," Nuclear Engineering & Design 29, 1974.

(2) J. F. Gloudeman, "The Modularity of MSC/NASTRAN," IEEE Computer Software & Applications Conference, Chicago, Illinois, Nov. 13-16, 1978.

(3) "MSC/NASTRAN Application Manual," The MacNeal-Schwendler Corporation, 1986.

(4) D. L. Herendeen, "Interactive Pre- and Postprocessors for Finite Element Computer Programs," AIAA Aircraft System & Technology Conference, August, 1981.

(5) "MSC/NASTRAN Programmers Manual," The MacNeal-Schwendler Corporation, 1985.

(6) H. Tamura, S. Kamiya and T. Ishigai, "FACOM VP-100/200: Supercomputers with ease of use," Parallel Computing 2, 1985.

(7) T. Matsuura, K. Miura and M. Makino, "Supervector Performance without Toil: Fortran Implemented Vector Algorithms on the VP-100/200," Computer Physics Communication 37, 1985.

(8) "Vector Processor Systems, Technical Overview," MM-142002-005, Amdahl Corporation, 1986.

(9) J. Dongarra and I. S. Duff, "Advance Architecture Computers," Mathematics and Computer Science Division Technical Memorandum No. 57, Argonne National Lab., Oct. 1985.

(10) I. Y. Bucher and M. L. Simmons, "Performance Assessment of Supercomputers," Vector and Parallel Processors: Architecture, Applications and Performance Evaluation, North Holland, 1985.

(11) J. Dongarra, A. Hinds, "Comparison of the Cray XMP-14, Fujitsu VP-200, and Hitachi S-810/20: An Argonne Perspective," Mathematics and Computers General (UC-32), ANL-85-19.

(12) S. C. Jasuja, M. P. Anderson, "Computational Requirements for Powertrain Analytical Simulations," SAE Technical Paper Series 850474, International Congress & Exposition, Detroit, Michigan, 1985.

(13) J. F Gloudeman, "The Anticipated Impact of Supercomputers on Finite-Element Analysis," Proceedings of the IEEE, Vol. 72, No. 1, Jan. 1984.

(14) J. F. Gloudeman, J, C. Hodge, "The Adaptation of MSC/NASTRAN to a Supercomputer," Parallel and Large-Scale Computers: Performance, Architecture, Applications, North-Holland, 1983.

(15) J. J. Dongarra, "Performance of Various Computers Using Standard Linear Equations Software in A Fortran Environment," Technical Memorandum No. 23, Argonne National Lab., Jan. 30, 1986.

(16) L. Komzsik, "Performance of MSC/NASTRAN on Vector and Parallel Processors," 2nd SIAM Conference on Parallel Processing for Science Computing, 1985.

(17) M. Ginsberg, "Some Observation on Supercomputer Computational Environments," Parallel and Large-Scale Computers: Performance, Architecture, Application, North-Holland, 1983.

(18) K. J. Bathe, E. L. Wilson, "Numerical Methods in Finite Element Analysis," Prentice Hall, 1976.

PARALLEL SYSTOLIC LU FACTORIZATION FOR SIMPLEX UPDATES

K. Margaritis & D.J. Evans
Department of Computer Studies
University of Technology
Loughborough, Leicestershire, U.K.

0. ABSTRACT

This paper presents systolic designs for modifying an LU factorization of a matrix A when a Simplex update is performed on A. It is assumed that no pivoting is required for the LU updating. Two systolic networks are proposed: one two-dimensional square array and a linear array which can be interconnected with the LU factorization hex-array in [L]. Soft-systolic simulation programs in OCCAM for both designs are given in the Appendix.

1. INTRODUCTION

In the Simplex method for linear programming a representation of a non-singular (n×n) matrix A is stored which enables inverse operations to be carried out readily, i.e. the solution of three linear systems of equations for each iteration of the method, [BRH].

Suppose that the solution of the linear systems is effected by decomposing A into the LU product, i.e. $A\underline{x}=\underline{b}$ is analysed to $LU\underline{x}=\underline{b}$ and further on we solve the triangular systems $L\underline{y}=\underline{b}$ and $U\underline{x}=\underline{y}$. Thus, the unit lower triangular matrix L and the upper triangular matrix U can be stored in some form instead of matrix A.

Now at the beginning of a cycle for the Simplex method, matrix A has the form,

$$A = [\underline{a}_1,\underline{a}_2,\ldots,\underline{a}_{m-1},\underline{a}_m,\underline{a}_{m+1},\ldots,\underline{a}_n] \tag{1}$$

and the representation of A is,

$$A = LU = \sum_{i=1}^{n} \underline{\ell}_i\underline{u}_i^T , \tag{2}$$

where $L=[\underline{\ell}_1,\underline{\ell}_2,\ldots,\underline{\ell}_n]$ and $U=[\underline{u}_1,\underline{u}_2,\ldots,\underline{u}_n]^T$ in column form.

At the end of the cycle matrix A is updated, i.e. column $\underline{a}_m$ is removed and a new column $\underline{a}_s$ is added:

$$A' = [\underline{a}_1,\underline{a}_2,\ldots,\underline{a}_{m-1},\underline{a}_{m+1},\ldots,\underline{a}_n,\underline{a}_s] \tag{3}$$

U is modified accordingly to U* as shown in Fig.(1a); notice that the column $L^{-1}\underline{a}_s$ that is added to U is produced as a by-product during the computations of the chosen Simplex cycle. Hence U* can be constructed with no significant computational effort.

The main point at issue is to return to the standard form,

$$A' = L'U' , \tag{4}$$

in which L' and U' are the updated LU factors. U* can be reduced to U' by using a Gaussian elimination procedure for the subdiagonal elements in columns m through n. Thus, U' is obtained from U* by applying a sequence of simple transformations:

$$U' = G_n G_{n-1} \cdots G_m U^* \tag{5}$$

where each G_i has the form shown in Fig.(1b). Thus we have,

$$L' = L G_m G_{m+1} \cdots G_n . \tag{6}$$

This update method is suggested, in [BJM] for a rank one update of the LU factors; also in [BRH] the same method is applied on the Simplex method. It is proposed in [BRH] and [T] that only U is explicitly updated while a file of the elementary operators G_i is created; however, this file expands after each iteration and so the computation time required per cycle of the Simplex method increases steadily. When this file becomes sufficiently large it is necessary to reinvert, i.e. to explicitly update L, so as to keep the total computation time per iteration within bounds.

Alternatively explicit updating of both L and U matrices in each cycle can be adopted and therefore no expanding file of operators is required [FM].

2. THE UPDATING METHOD

Consider the matrix U* as shown in Fig.(1a): Fig.(1c) shows the elements of L and U that are affected by the updating of matrix A, i.e., by the application of the Gauss elimination procedure on U*. As is obvious vectors $\underline{\ell}_i$ and $\underline{u}_i$, for i=1,2,..., m-1 can be produced without any computation since all their elements are already known. Therefore it is sufficient to consider the case that m=1 - thus the problem of updating the LU factors of an (n×n) matrix A is reduced to the updating of the LU factors for an (m×m) submatrix of A.

Suppose, therefore, that $\underline{a}_1$ is removed from A in (1), giving:

$$A' = [\underline{a}_2, \underline{a}_3, \ldots, \underline{a}_n, \underline{a}_s] , \tag{7}$$

which is equivalent to removing the first column from U, as shown in Fig.(1d); i.e. the first element of each vector $\underline{u}_i$ in (2) is now removed. The subdiagonal elements $u_{21}, u_{32}, \ldots$ have to be eliminated in successive steps, and it is sufficient to describe only the first step in which u_{21} is eliminated. This step is based on the identity form [FM],

$$[\underline{\ell}_1, \underline{\ell}_2] \begin{bmatrix} \underline{u}_1^T \\ \underline{u}_2^T \end{bmatrix} = [\underline{\ell}_1, \underline{\ell}_2] BB^{-1} \begin{bmatrix} \underline{u}_1^T \\ \underline{u}_2^T \end{bmatrix} = \begin{bmatrix} J & \\ & I \end{bmatrix} [\underline{\ell}'_1, \underline{\ell}'_2] \begin{bmatrix} \underline{u}'^T_1 \\ \underline{u}'^T_2 \end{bmatrix} \tag{8}$$

where B,J are (2×2) real matrices and J is the permutation matrix.

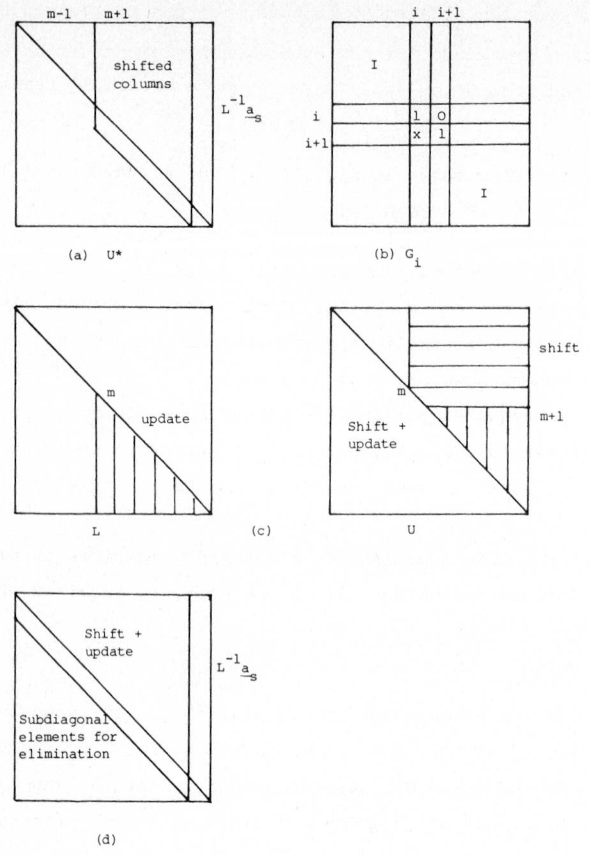

FIGURE 1

For simplicity it is assumed that no permutation is required throughout the LU updating computation, and therefore (8) is simplified to:

$$[\underline{\ell}_1, \underline{\ell}_2] \begin{bmatrix} \underline{u}_1^T \\ \underline{u}_2^T \end{bmatrix} = [\underline{\ell}_1, \underline{\ell}_2] \; BB^{-1} \begin{bmatrix} \underline{u}_1^T \\ \underline{u}_2^T \end{bmatrix} = [\underline{\ell}_1', \underline{\ell}_2'] \begin{bmatrix} \underline{u}_1'^T \\ \underline{u}_2'^T \end{bmatrix} \tag{9}$$

The coefficients of B are chosen to fix the conditions $\ell_{11}'=\ell_{22}'=1$ and $\ell_{12}'=u_{21}'=0$ (i.e. $(\underline{\ell}_2')_1=(u_2')_1=0$). The new vectors $\underline{\ell}_1'$, $\underline{u}_1'$ are the new first row and column of L', U', and $\underline{\ell}_2'$, $\underline{u}_2'$, are intermediate quantities that are changed again in the second step.

The modification is determined by the sub-matrix:

$$\begin{bmatrix} 1 & 0 \\ (\underline{\ell}_1)_2 & 1 \end{bmatrix} BB^{-1} \begin{bmatrix} (\underline{u}_1)_1 \\ (\underline{u}_2)_1 \end{bmatrix} = \begin{bmatrix} 1 & 0 \\ (\underline{\ell}_1')_2 & 1 \end{bmatrix} \begin{bmatrix} (\underline{u}_1')_1 \\ 0 \end{bmatrix} \tag{10}$$

or from Fig.(1d):

$$\begin{bmatrix} 1 & 0 \\ \ell_{21} & 1 \end{bmatrix} BB^{-1} \begin{bmatrix} u_{12} \\ u_{22} \end{bmatrix} = \begin{bmatrix} 1 & 0 \\ \ell'_{21} & 1 \end{bmatrix} \begin{bmatrix} u'_{11} \\ 0 \end{bmatrix} . \qquad (11)$$

By taking $r=(\underline{u}_2)_1/(\underline{u}_1)_1 = u_{22}/u_{12}$, it follows from (11) that:

$$B = \begin{bmatrix} 1 & 0 \\ r & 1 \end{bmatrix} \qquad B^{-1} = \begin{bmatrix} 1 & 0 \\ -r & 1 \end{bmatrix} \qquad (12)$$

and,

$$\begin{array}{llll}
(\underline{u}'_1)_1 = (\underline{u}_1)_1 & u'_{11} = u_{12} & \\
(\underline{\ell}'_1)_2 = (\underline{\ell}_1)_2+r & \ell'_{21} = \ell_{21}+r & \\
(\underline{\ell}'_1)_i = (\underline{\ell}_1)_i+r(\underline{\ell}_2)_i & \ell'_{i1} = \ell_{i1}+r\ell_{i2} & \left.\right\} 2<i\leq n \\
(\underline{\ell}'_2)_i = (\underline{\ell}_2)_i & \ell'_{i2} = \ell_{i2} & \\
(\underline{u}'_1)_j = (\underline{u}_1)_j & u'_{1j} = u_{i,j+1} & \left.\right\} 1<j<n \\
(\underline{u}'_2)_j = (\underline{u}_2)_j-r(\underline{u}_1)_j & u'_{2j} = u_{2,j+1}-ru_{1,j+1} & \\
(\underline{u}'_1)_n = u'_{1n} = (L^{-1}\underline{a}_s)_1 & & \\
(\underline{u}'_2)_n = u'_{2n} = (L^{-1}\underline{a}_s)_2-ru'_{1n} = (L^{-1}\underline{a}_s)_2-r(L^{-1}\underline{a}_s)_1 . & &
\end{array}$$

Fig.2 illustrates the modification of the LU factors based on the relations (12). The LU updating fails if $(\underline{u}_1)_1=0$ and causes a large growth in the updated factors when r is large, i.e. $(\underline{u}_2)_1>(\underline{u}_1)_1$: thus the assumption that no pivoting occurs throughout the LU modification is valid if $u_{i,i+1}\neq 0$, $i=1,2,\dots,n$ and $|r|\leq 1$. If these conditions are not valid then row parameters are necessary, [FM]: the possible systolic implementation of the modification of LU factors with pivoting will be investigated in a subsequent paper.

3. SYSTOLIC LU MODIFICATION

The LU updating procedure illustrated in Fig.2 can be performed on an $(n\times n)$ processor array as is shown in Fig.3.

At the commencement of the computation each processor of the mesh is loaded with the value of the corresponding element of the LU matrices. Also, since the diagonal elements of L are all 1, there is no need to explicitly store them.

The array computation starts in the top-left corner, where u_{11} is replaced by u_{21}; this shift-left operation happens to all the cells of row 1 with one cycle delay between adjacent cells. As soon as u_{21} takes its place as u_{11} the calculation of $r_2=u_{22}/u_{12}=u_{22}/u'_{11}$ is performed; then u_{22} is replaced by $u_{23}-r_2u_{13}= u_{23}-r_2u'_{12}$. For the second row, as well as for all the subsequent rows the shift-left operation is accompanied with the modification of u_{ij} by means of r_i and $u'_{i-1,j-1}$: the first row shift-left operation can be seen as a degenerate case, i.e. $r_1=0$ and $u'_{0,j}=0$ for all j. The right-most cell of row i receives $(L^{-1}\underline{a}_s)_i$ as a result of its shift-left computation.

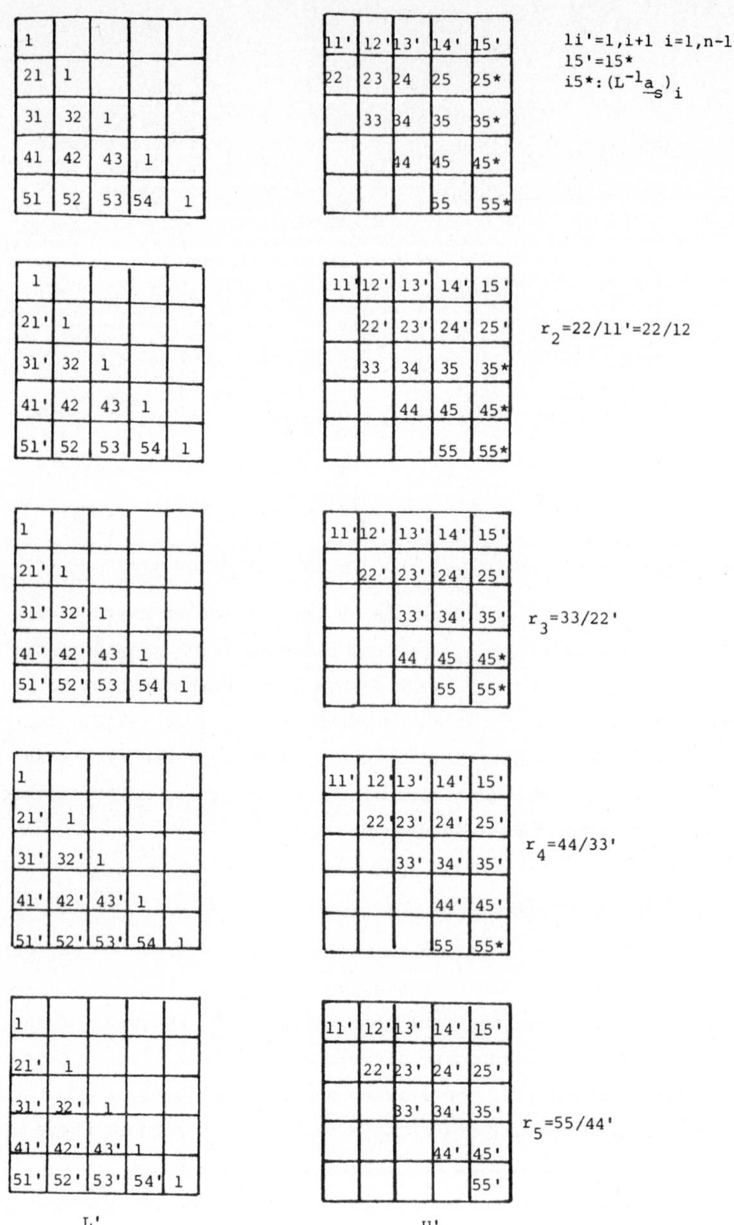
li'=1,i+1 i=1,n-1
15'=15*
i5*:(L^-1 a_s)_i
r_2=22/11'=22/12
r_3=33/22'
r_4=44/33'
r_5=55/44'
L'
U'

FIGURE 2: (n=5)

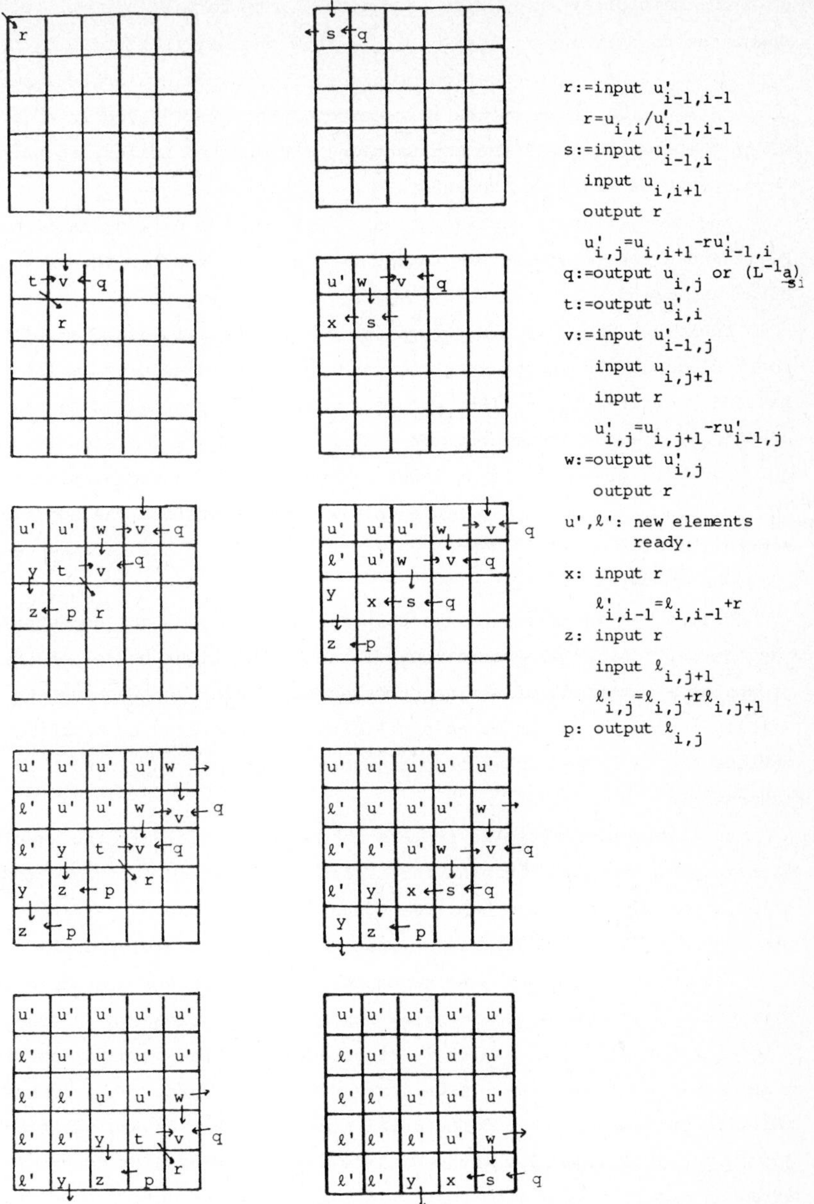
r:=input u'i-1,i-1
r=ui,i/u'i-1,i-1
s:=input u'i-1,i
input ui,i+1
output r
u'i,j=ui,i+1-ru'i-1,i
q:=output ui,j or (L-1a)si
t:=output u'i,i
v:=input u'i-1,j
input ui,j+1
input r
u'i,j=ui,j+1-ru'i-1,j
w:=output u'i,j
output r
u',ℓ': new elements ready.
x: input r
ℓ'i,i-1=ℓi,i-1+r
z: input r
input ℓi,j+1
ℓ'i,j=ℓi,j+rℓi,j+1
p: output ℓi,j

FIGURE 3: (n=5)

The multiplier r_2 is also passed to ℓ_{21} to form $\ell'_{21}=\ell_{21}+r_2$; then it moves downwards to calculate $\ell'_{31}=\ell_{31}+r_2\ell_{32}$; thus the matrix L updating procedure is performed. A new r computation occurs every two cycles and thus a total computation time of 2n cycles is required. The area needed is n^2 processors. After the completion of the computation, the updated LU factors have replaced the original LU matrices in the array.

The overall array configuration as well as the cell definitions are given in Fig.4 and a soft-systolic simulation program in OCCAM for the rectangular array is given in Appendix A.

There are four different types of cells: the main diagonal cells, the first lower diagonal, the upper diagonals and the lower diagonals cells. All are basically inner-product (IPS) processors; however the main diagonal cells have an additional diagonal communication channel and perform division in order to calculate r. Also, the first lower diagonal cells can be simple adders instead of IPS processors since they compute only $\ell'=\ell+r$: therefore the additional complexity of the main diagonal cells is balanced by the reduced complexity of the cells of the first subdiagonal.

Notice the wavefront - like computation in Fig.3: the computation starts from the top-left corner and moves towards the bottom-right corner of the array producing a wavefront of active processors. Taking into account that in the Simplex method there can be no pipelining of successive LU updatings, it is obvious that a large number of processors is idle at any instant of the computation.

An alternative systolic implementation is possible if the wavefront concept is reversed: instead of having the LU factors in fixed positions and the computation moving along them, the computation can now be performed in fixed processors and the LU factors can pass through these processors.

The input and output data sequences, as well as the overall configuration of a linearly connected systolic array for the LU modification are shown in Fig.(5a). A total number of 2(n-1) cells is required, while the computation time is (2n+1) time units; therefore the linear array reduces the area requirements from n^2 to 2n while it retains the same computation time $\cong$2n. Notice the relation of the input and output data sequences with the data and computation movements in the square array in Fig.3, notice also that each element of the column $L^{-1}\underline{a}_s$ enters the array from a different input port.

In Fig.(5b) the cell definitions are given: the middle cell of the array is a combination of the divider and adder, of the main diagonal and the first sub-diagonal processors of the rectangular array of Fig.4. The remaining cells are simple inner product processors.

In Fig.6 some snapshots of the array operation are depicted and a soft-systolic simulation program in OCCAM is given in Appendix B. Notice that the linear

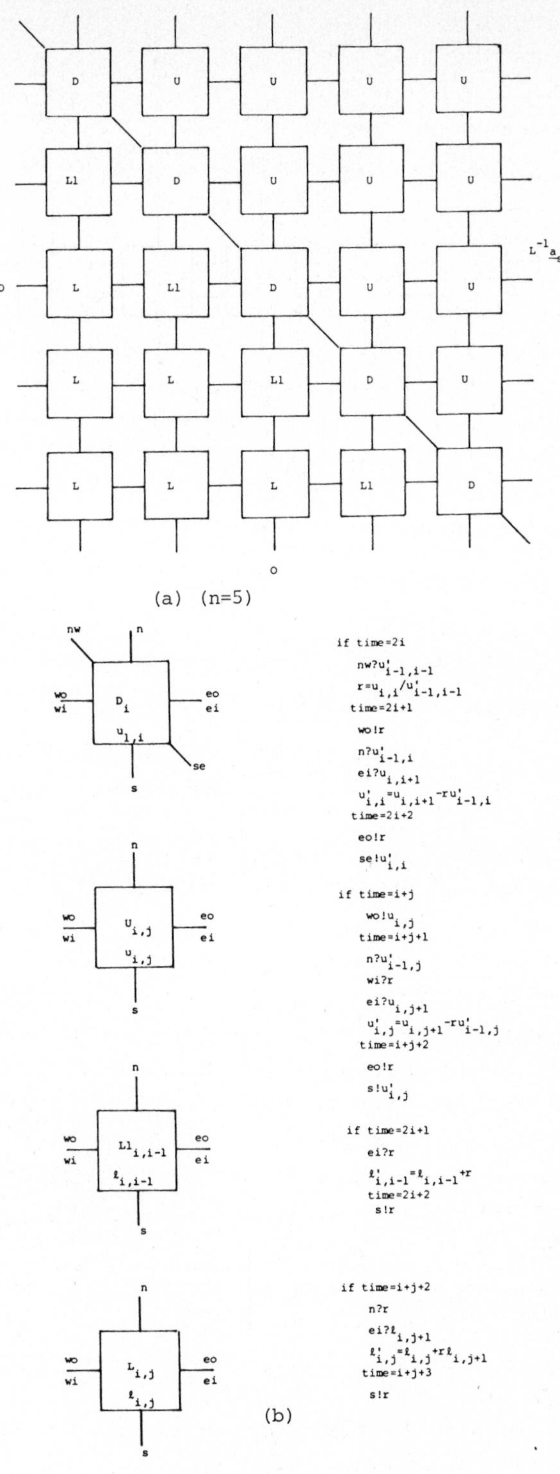

D
U
U
U
U
L1
D
U
U
U
$L^{-1}\underline{a}_s$
o
L
L1
D
U
U
L
L
L1
D
U
L
L
L
L1
D
o
(a) (n=5)
nw
n
wo
wi
D_i
$u_{1,i}$
eo
ei
se
s
if time=2i
$nw?u'_{i-1,i-1}$
$r=u_{i,i}/u'_{i-1,i-1}$
time=2i+1
wo!r
$n?u'_{i-1,i}$
$ei?u_{i,i+1}$
$u'_{i,i}=u_{i,i+1}-ru'_{i-1,i}$
time=2i+2
eo!r
$se!u'_{i,i}$
n
wo
wi
$U_{i,j}$
$u_{i,j}$
eo
ei
s
if time=i+j
$wo!u_{i,j}$
time=i+j+1
$n?u'_{i-1,j}$
wi?r
$ei?u_{i,j+1}$
$u'_{i,j}=u_{i,j+1}-ru'_{i-1,j}$
time=i+j+2
eo!r
$s!u'_{i,j}$
n
wo
wi
$L1_{i,i-1}$
$\ell_{i,i-1}$
eo
ei
s
if time=2i+1
ei?r
$\ell'_{i,i-1}=\ell_{i,i-1}+r$
time=2i+2
s!r
n
wo
wi
$L_{i,j}$
$\ell_{i,j}$
eo
ei
s
if time=i+j+2
n?r
$ei?\ell_{i,j+1}$
$\ell'_{i,j}=\ell_{i,j}+r\ell_{i,j+1}$
time=i+j+3
s!r
(b)

FIGURE 4

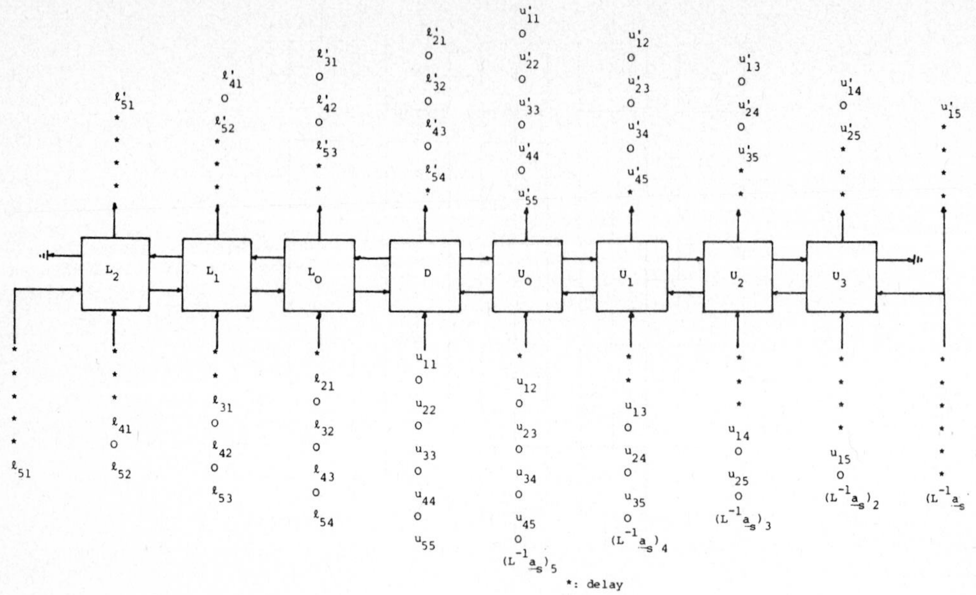

(a) (n=5)

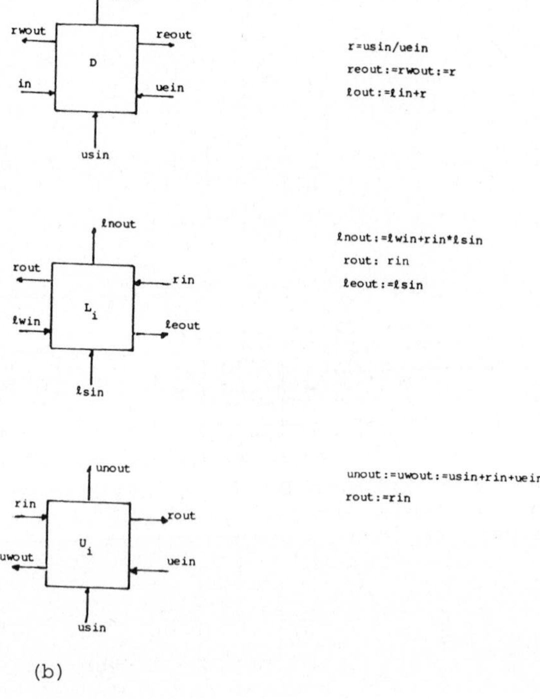

(b)

FIGURE 5

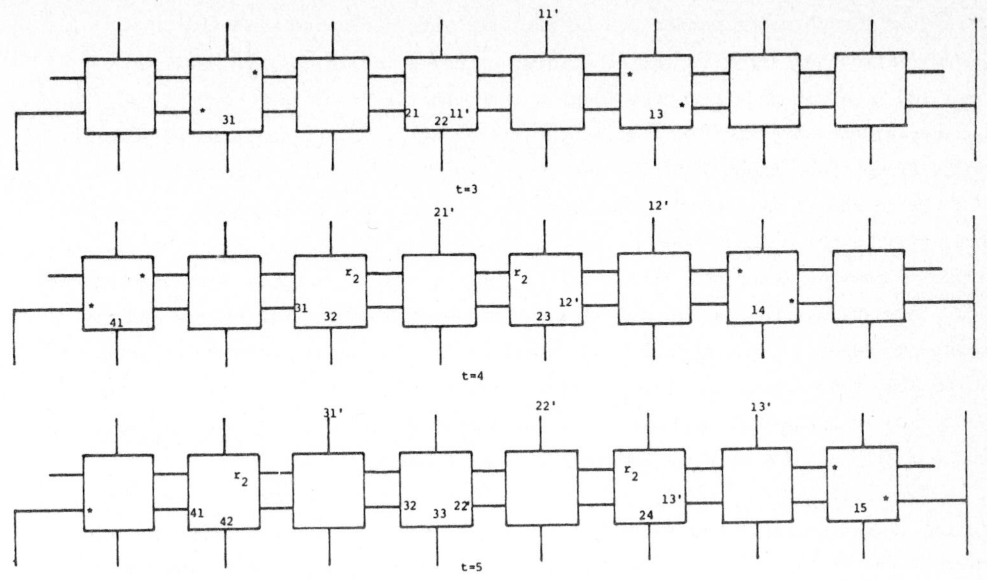

(a)

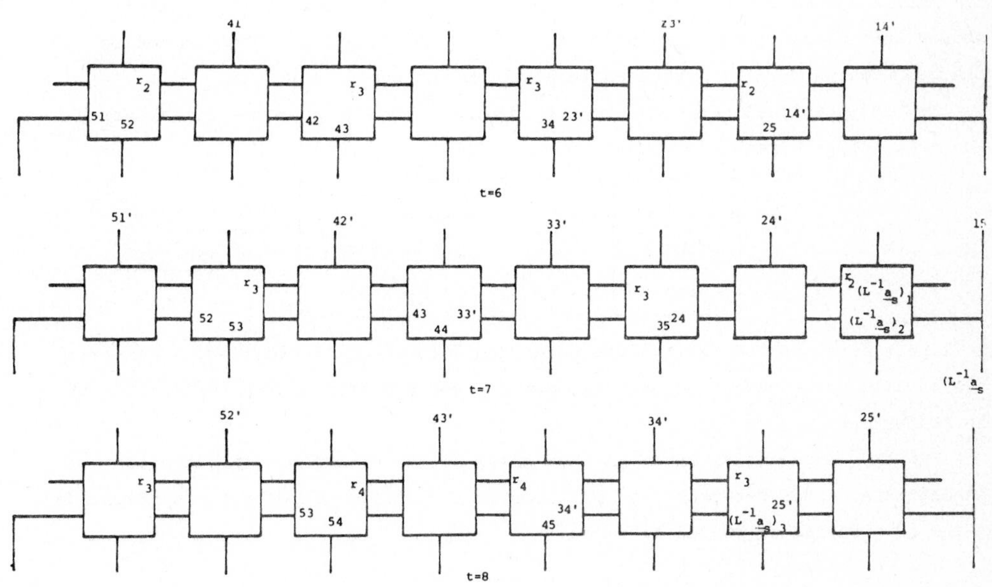

(b)

FIGURE 6

array for the LU modification can be directly interconnected with the LU factorization hex array in [L]; the input sequence in Fig.(5a) is easily modified to allow a data format identical to that of the output sequence of the hex-array; the only modification on the linear array is the addition of some delay elements as shown in Fig.7 where the array operation is also detailed.

Up to now it is supposed that the first column of A is replaced, as in (7), i.e. m=1; in the general case of (3), shown in Figures (1a,c), m≠1. The two systolic designs described can be easily modified to accommodate this general case.

The square array design can be augmented by two vectors of column and row pointers indicating the location of the first main diagonal element of matrix U to be affected, namely u_{mm}. For the subarray A_{22} (see Fig.(8a)) the modification procedure is as described. No modification is required for subarrays A_{11},A_{21}, while a simple shift-left is adequate for the subarray A_{12}.

The modification required in the input data sequence of the linear array design is shown in Fig.(8b); for the first m-1 steps r=0 and therefore the L,U factors are produced exactly as they are input; from then on the normal LU updating operation takes place. Thus there is no additional complexity in the array itself but the input data stream.

4. CONCLUSIONS

This paper describes two systolic designs for modifying an LU factorisation of a matrix A when a Simplex update is performed on A. For simplicity it is assumed that no pivoting is required for the LU updating; the LU modification with permutation will be discussed in a subsequent paper.

Two computational networks are proposed: a square array and a linear array with area and time requirements as shown in Table 1.

	Square	Linear
Time	2n	2n-1
Area	n^2	2(n-1)

TABLE 1

The linear array can be easily interconnected with the LU factorisation hex-array in [L] while both designs can accommodate the modification of the submatrices of the LU factors.

Finally, the Simplex update method makes no use of any possible sparsity of the matrix A; a further extension of the systolic design would be the application of the LU updating on banded matrices.

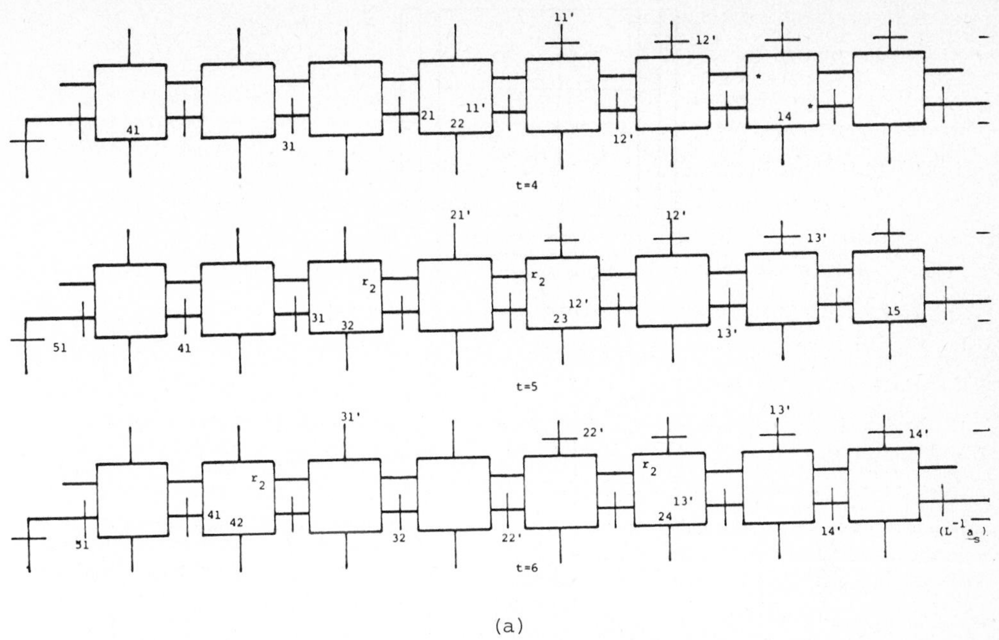

(a)

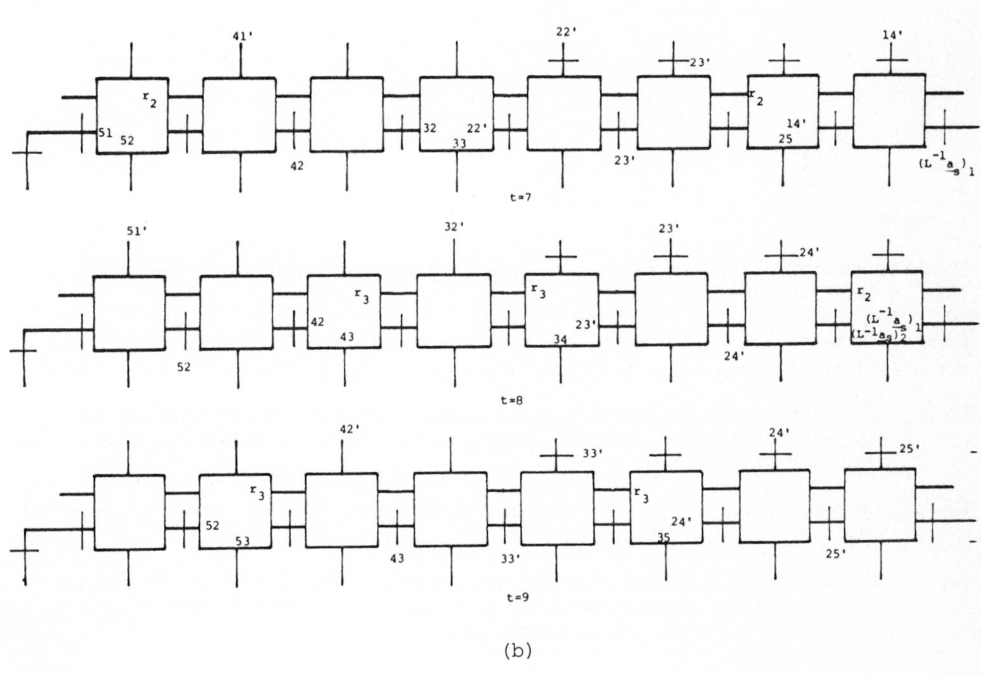

(b)

FIGURE 7

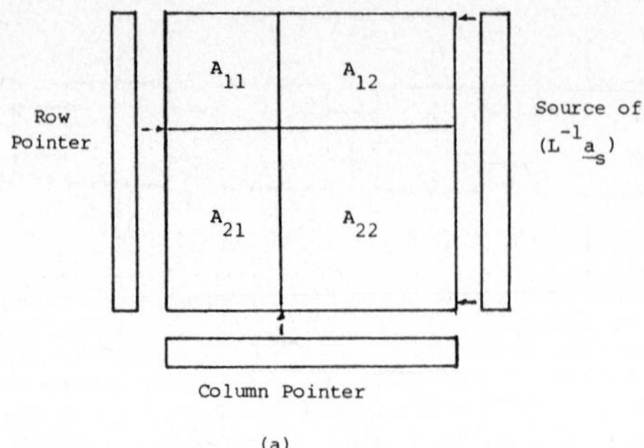

(a)

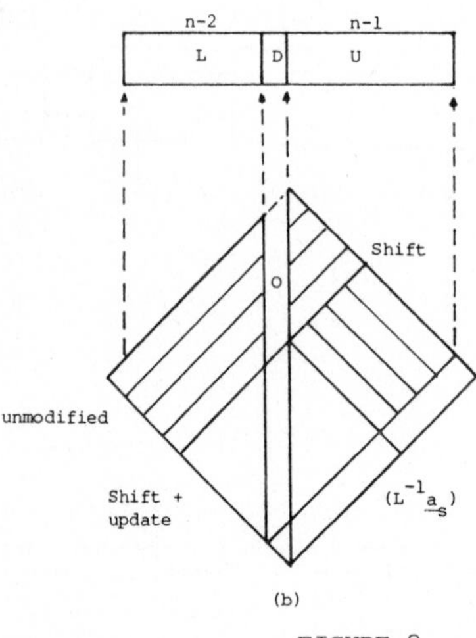

(b)

FIGURE 8

5. REFERENCES

[BJM] Bennett, J.M., "Triangular Factors of Modified Matrices", Numer.Math. 7, 217-221 (1965).

[BRH] Bartels, R.H., "A Stabilization of the Simplex Method", Numer.Math. 16, 44-434 (1971).

[FM] Fletcher R. and Matthews, S.P.J., "Stable Modification of Explicit LU Factors for Simplex Updates", Report NA/64, Dept. of Mathematical Sciences, Univ. of Dundee, June 1983.

[L] Leiserson, C.E., "Area-Efficient VLSI Computation", Ph.D. Thesis, Dept. of Computer Studies, CMU, Oct. 1981.

[T] Tomlin, J.A., "Modifying Triangular Factors of the Basis in the Simplex Method", 77-85, 'Sparse Matrices and Their Applications', edit. Rose, D.J. & Willoughby, R.A., Plenum Press, 1972.

APPENDIX A

```
-- Square array of processors for the updating of the LU
 -- factors in Simplex method.Matrix U is shifted one column
 -- to the left and a new nth column is added.

 -- Library Routines.
 external proc get ( var v, value s[] ) :
 external proc fp.get.n ( var float v[], value n, s[] ) :
 external proc fp.put.n ( value float v[], value n, s[] ) :

 -- Maximum size of problem.
 def no = 10 :

 -- Diagonal cell.
 proc diag ( var float u, eo, se, wo,
             value float nw, n, ei,
             value start, t ) =
   if
     t = start
       if
         nw = 0.0
           wo := 0.0
         true
           wo := (u / nw)
     t = (start + 1)
       seq
         par
           u := ei - (wo * n)
           eo := wo
         se := u :

 -- Upper Diagonal cell.
 proc updi ( var float u, eo, s, wo,
             value float n, ei, wi,
             value start, t ) =
   if
     t = start
       wo := u
     t = (start + 2)
       seq
         par
           eo := wi
           u := ei - (wi * n)
         s := u :

 -- First Lower Diagonal cell.
 proc ldil ( var float l, s,
             value float ei,
             value start, t ) =
   if
     t = start
       seq
         l := (l + ei)
         s := ei :

 -- Lower Diagonal cell.
 proc lodi ( var float l, s,
             value float n, ei,
             value start, t ) =
   if
     t = start
       seq
         l := l + (n * ei)
         s := n :

 -- Generic cell for main diagonal.
 proc gend ( chan nwin, nin, eout, ein, seout, sout, wout, win,
```

```
              var float x,
              value start, time ) =
  var float nw, n, eo, ei, se, s, wo, wi :
  seq t=[0 for time]
    seq
      par
        nwin ? nw
        nin ? n
        eout ! eo
        ein ? ei
        seout ! se
        sout ! s
        wout ! wo
        win ? wi
      diag(x, eo, se, wo, nw, n, ei, start, t) :

-- Generic cell for other diagonals.
proc gene ( chan nin, eout, ein, sout, wout, win,
            var float x,
            value type, start, time ) =
  var float n, eo, ei, s, wo, wi :
  seq t=[0 for time]
    seq
      par
        nin ? n
        eout ! eo
        ein ? ei
        sout ! s
        wout ! wo
        win ? wi
      if
        type = 0
          updi(x, eo, s, wo, n, ei, wi, start, t)
        type = 1
          ldil(x, s, ei, start, t)
        true
          lodi(x, s, n, ei, start, t) :

-- Dummy source.
proc soud ( chan xout,
            value time ) =
  seq t=[0 for time]
    xout ! 0.0 :

-- Dummy sink.
proc sind ( chan xin,
            value time ) =
  seq t=[0 for time]
    xin ? any :

-- Source for elements of new column a.
proc soua ( chan xout,
            value float x,
            value start, time ) =
  seq t=[0 for time]
    if
      t = start
        xout ! x
      true
        xout ! 0.0 :


-- System configuration.
proc syst ( var float lu[],
            value float a[],
            value n, time ) =
```

```
chan v.c[no*(no+1)], h1.c[no*(no+1)], h2.c[no*(no+1)], d.c[no+1] :

-- Main Array.
proc sqar ( var float lu[],
            value n, time ) =
  par i=[0 for n]
    par j=[0 for n]
      var k :
      seq
        k := (i * n) + j
        if
          i = j                       -- main diagonal cells
            gend(d.c[i], v.c[k], h1.c[(k+1)+i], h2.c[(k+1)+i], d.c[i+1
],
                 v.c[k+n], h2.c[k+i], h1.c[k+i], lu[k], (2*i), time)
          i < j                       -- upper diagonal cells
            gene(v.c[k], h1.c[(k+1)+i], h2.c[(k+1)+i],v.c[k+n],
                 h2.c[k+i], h1.c[k+i], lu[k], 0, ((i+j)-1), time)
          i = (j + 1)                 -- first lower diagonal cells
            gene(v.c[k], h1.c[(k+1)+i], h2.c[(k+1)+i],v.c[k+n],
                 h2.c[k+i], h1.c[k+i], lu[k], 1, ((2*i)+1), time)
          true                        -- rest lower diagonal cells
            gene(v.c[k], h1.c[(k+1)+i], h2.c[(k+1)+i],v.c[k+n],
                 h2.c[k+i], h1.c[k+i], lu[k], 2, ((i+j)+2), time) :

-- Sources - Sinks.
proc sosi ( value float a[],
            value n, time ) =
  par
    par i=[0 for n]
      par
        soud(v.c[i], time)
        sind(v.c[(n*n)+i], time)
        soud(h1.c[(n+1)*i], time)
        sind(h1.c[((n+1)*i)+n], time)
        soua(h2.c[((n+1)*i)+n], a[i], (n+i), time)
        sind(h2.c[(n+1)*i], time)
    soud(d.c[0], time)
    sind(d.c[n], time) :

par
  sqar(lu, n, time)
  sosi(a, n, time) :

-- Main.
var float lu[no*no], a[no] :
var n, time :
seq
  get(n, " problem size ")
  fp.get.n(lu, (n*n), " LU row-wise ")
  fp.get.n(a, n, " new column ")
  time := (2 * n)
  syst(lu, a, n, time)
  fp.put.n(lu, (n*n), " LU updated ")
```

APPENDIX B

```
-- Systolic Array for the Updating of the LU factors
 -- of a full (n*n) matrix A: the first column of A is
 -- removed and a new nth column (An) is added (Simplex).
 -- For the updating: the new nth column in the form
 -- a = ((L)**-1)An is added to U and the main diagonal is
 -- removed; L is modified accordingly.It is assumed that
 -- no permutations needed.

 external proc get ( var n, value s[] ) :
 external proc fp.get.n ( var float v[], value n, s[] ) :
 external proc fp.put.n ( value float v[], value n, s[] ) :


 def no = 10, to = (2 * no) + 1 :


 -- Divider calculating r := u[i,i] / u'[i-1,i-1];
 -- Adder calculating l'[i,i-1] := l[i,i-1] + r.
 -- Output : l'[i,i-1]; r.
 proc dva ( chan ein, win, sin, eout, wout, nout,
            value time )=
   var float r, u[2], l[2] :
   seq
     -- initialisation
     par
       par i=[0 for 2]
         par
           u[i] := 0.0
           l[i] := 0.0
       r := 0.0
     -- main operation
     seq i=[0 for time]
       seq
         -- i/o
         par
           ein ? u[1]
           win ? l[0]
           sin ? u[0]
           eout ! r
           wout ! r
           nout ! l[1]
         -- calculations
         if
           u[1] = 0.0
             r := 0.0
           true
             r := (u[0] / u[1])
         l[1] := (l[0] + r) :


 -- Inner Product calculating : u'[i,j] := u[i,j] - r * u'[i-1,j]
 -- Propagates u'[i,j] and r in opposite directions.
 proc ipu ( chan ein, win, sin, eout, wout, nout,
            value time )=
   var float r[2], u[3] :
   seq
     -- initialisation
     par
       par i=[0 for 2]
         r[i] := 0.0
       par i=[0 for 3]
         u[i] := 0.0
     -- main operation
     seq i=[0 for time]
       seq
         -- i/o
```

```
          par
            ein ? u[1]
            win ? r[0]
            sin ? u[0]
            eout ! r[1]
            wout ! u[2]
            nout ! u[2]
          -- calculation
          par
            u[2] := u[0] - (u[1] * r[0])
            r[1] := r[0] :


-- Inner Product calculating : l'[i,j] := l[i,j] + r * l[i,j+1]
-- Propagates l[i,j+1], r in opposite directions.
proc ipl ( chan ein, win, sin, eout, wout, nout,
           value time )=
  var float l[4], r[2] :
  seq
    -- initialisation
    par
      par i=[0 for 4]
        l[i] := 0.0
      par i=[0 for 2]
        r[i] := 0.0
    -- main operation
    seq i=[0 for time]
      seq
        -- i/o
        par
          ein ? r[0]
          win ? l[1]
          sin ? l[0]
          eout ! l[2]
          wout ! r[1]
          nout ! l[3]
        -- calculation
        par
          l[3] := l[1] + (r[0] * l[0])
          l[2] := l[0]
          r[1] := r[0] :


-- Delay-branching cell.
proc dba ( chan ain, u1out, u2out,
           value time ) =
  var float a[2] :
  seq
    -- initialisation
    par i=[0 for 2]
      a[i] := 0.0
    -- main operation
    seq i=[0 for time]
      seq
        -- i/o
        par
          ain ? a[0]
          u1out ! a[1]
          u2out ! a[1]
        -- calculation
        a[1] := a[0] :

-- Source for a vector x.
proc srx ( chan xout ,
           value float x[],
           value time ) =
```

```
  seq i=[0 for time]
    xout ! x[i] :

-- Sink for a vector x.
proc six ( chan xin,
           var float x[],
           value time ) =
  seq i=[0 for time]
    xin ? x[i] :

-- Dumm sink.
proc sid ( chan xin,
           value time ) =
  seq i=[0 for time]
    xin ? any :

-- Delay cell.
proc del ( chan xin, xout,
           value time ) =
  var float x[2] :
  seq
    par i=[0 for 2]
      x[i] := 0.0
    seq i=[0 for time]
      seq
        par
          xin ? x[0]
          xout ! x[1]
        x[1] := x[0] :


-- System configuration : n-1 ipu, 1 dva and n-2 ipl linearly
-- interconnected; L, U matrices enter the array diagonally,
-- together with the new column a.Output the updated matrices
-- L1, U1 .
proc system ( var float l1[], u1[],
              value float l[], u[],
              value n, time ) =
  -- data communication.
  chan ru.c[no], rl.c[no-1], ui.c[no+1], uo.c[no], li.c[no-1],
       lo.c[no-1], u.c[no], l.c[no-1] :
  par
    -- n vector sources / sinks for U-diagonals; the source
    -- vectors have last element from new column a.
    par i=[0 for n]
      var float uti[to], uto[to] :
      seq
        par j=[0 for time]
          uti[j] := u[(i*time)+j]
        par
          srx(ui.c[i], uti, time)
          six(uo.c[i], uto, time)
        par j=[0 for time]
          u1[(i*time)+j] := uto[j]
    -- 1 vector source for the first element of new column a.
    var float uti[to] :
    seq
      par j=[0 for time]
        uti[j] := u[(time*n)+j]
      srx(ui.c[n], uti, time)
    -- n-1 vector sources / sinks for L-diagonals.
    par i=[0 for (n-1)]
      var float lti[to], lto[to] :
      seq
        par j=[0 for time]
          lti[j] := l[(i*time)+j]
```

```
        par
          srx(li.c[i], lti, time)
          six(lo.c[i], lto, time)
        par j=[0 for time]
          l1[(i*time)+j] := lto[j]
    -- 2 dummy vector sinks for r.
    sid(ru.c[n-1], time)
    sid(rl.c[n-2], time)
    -- delay-branching cell for the first element of column a..
    dba(ui.c[n], u.c[n-1], uo.c[n-1], time)
    -- delay for lowest L-diagonal.
    del(li.c[n-2], l.c[n-2], time)
    -- main systolic array.
    par i=[0 for (n-1)]
      ipu(u.c[i+1], ru.c[i], ui.c[i+1], ru.c[i+1], u.c[i], uo.c[i],
          time)
    par i=[0 for (n-2)]
      ipl(rl.c[i], l.c[i+1], li.c[i], l.c[i], rl.c[i+1], lo.c[i+1],
          time)
    dva(u.c[0], l.c[0], ui.c[0], ru.c[0], rl.c[0], lo.c[0], time) :


var float l[(no-1)*to], u[(no+1)*to], l1[(no-1)*to], u1[no*to] :
var n, time :
seq
  get(n, " size of matrix ")
  time := (2 * n) + 1
  fp.get.n(u, ((n+1)*time), " U data seq ")
  fp.get.n(l, ((n-1)*time), " L data seq ")
  system(l1, u1, l, u, n, time)
  fp.put.n(u1, (n*time), " U1 data seq ")
  fp.put.n(l1, ((n-1)*time), " L1 data seq ")
```

SOLVING ELLIPTIC PROBLEMS BY THE DOMAIN DECOMPOSITION METHOD USING PRECONDITIONING MATRICES DERIVED BY MULTILEVEL SPLITTINGS OF THE FINITE ELEMENT MATRIX

R.D. Lazarov, P.S. Vassilevski
Bulgarian Academy of Sciences Institute of Mathematics with Computing Center, 1090 Sofia, P.O. Box 373, Bulgaria

S.D. Margenov
Bulgarian Academy of Sciences Center of Informatics and Computer Technology, 1113 Sofia, Acad. G. Bontchev Str. Block 8 Bulgaria

Abstract. We study some aspects of domain decomposition technique applied to a multilevel iterative method in solving second order elliptic problems by the finite element method. This iterative method makes use of a preconditioning matrix which is constructed by using a sequence of nested discretizations of the considered elliptic problem. The main computational task in solving problems with this preconditioning matrix is solution of problems, on each fixed level, with matrices which have condition number bounded on h_k (- the discretization parameter on the level k). Here we propose to use, in connection with parallel implementation of this multilevel iterative method, domain decomposition technique in order to solve these problems with constantly conditioned matrices. Numerical tests are presented and they are compared with tests in which the solution method is the preconditioned conjugate gradient method with preconditioning matrices derived by approximate (blockwise) factorizations of the constantly conditioned matrices. The last methods suffers of the fact that it is not well parallelizable but it is very fast convergent.

1. Background to the domain decomposition technique

D.D. (domain decomposition) is a well studied subject and is still in search. Here we emphasize the works of P. Bjorstad & Windlund [5], Widwund [29], Dryja [11], [12], Proskurowski & Dryja [13], Lebedev & Agoshkov [18], Kuznetsov [17], Dryja, Proskurowski & Widlund [14]; [6], [7], [8]; [20]; [21]; [15]; [13], [26], [27]. A full bibliography is given in Widlund [28].

DD may be regarded as a block Gaussian elimination with a certain pivoting strategy, in which the matrix admits 2x2 block structure, such that the first diagonal block is block diagonal, and the second one is of order of magnitude less than the others. The off-diagnal blocks are very sparse. This is due to the following facts.

Consider the bilinear form

$$a_\Omega(u,v) = \int_\Omega \Big(\sum_{i,j=1}^{2} a_{i,j}(x) \frac{\partial}{\partial x_i} u \frac{\partial}{\partial x_j} v + a_o(x)uv\Big)dx,$$

where Ω is a plane polygonal region, which is triangulated into triangles (say) and with this triangulation is associated the finite element space of piece wise linear and continuous in Ω functions which vanish on the Dirichlet part of the boundary $\Gamma_D \subset \Gamma = \partial\Omega$. Using the nodal basis functions $\{\Phi_i\}$, i.e. functions which take value zero in each node of the triangulation except of a given one, not lying on Γ_D, in which Φ_i takes value 1 we obtain the following linear algebraic problem

$$A\,\underline{x} = \underline{b},$$

where

$$A = (a_\Omega(\Phi_i,\Phi_j))$$

is the stiffness matrix associated with the bilinear form $a_\Omega(.,.)$.

Let us now partition $\Omega \cup \Gamma_N$ (Γ_N is the part of $\partial\Omega$ on which Neumann boundary conditions are imposed) into two parts Ω_1 and Ω_2 by an interface boundary γ and the same do with the unknowns $\underline{x}$, i.e. they are split up into three groups $\underline{x}_{11}$, $\underline{x}_{12}$ and $\underline{x}_2$ corresponding to the nodes lying in Ω_i, i = 1,2 and on γ, respectively. Then we obtain the following equivalent problem

$$\begin{vmatrix} A_{11} & A_{12} \\ A_{21} & A_{22} \end{vmatrix} \begin{vmatrix} \underline{x}_1 \\ \underline{x}_2 \end{vmatrix} = \begin{vmatrix} \underline{b}_1 \\ \underline{b}_2 \end{vmatrix}$$

with

$$A_{11} = \begin{vmatrix} A_1^{(11)} & 0 \\ 0 & A_2^{(11)} \end{vmatrix}, \quad \underline{x}_1 = \begin{vmatrix} \underline{x}_{11} \\ \underline{x}_{12} \end{vmatrix}$$

where $A_i^{(11)}$ are the stiffness matrices associated with the bilinear forms defined on Ω_i, i = 1,2, respectively.

Now we are able to perform the basic steps of the DD. We have

$$A = \begin{vmatrix} A_{11} & 0 \\ A_{21} & S \end{vmatrix} \begin{vmatrix} I & A_{11}^{-1}A_{12} \\ 0 & I \end{vmatrix}.$$

where $S = A_{22} - A_{21}A_{11}^{-1}A_{12}$ is the Schur complement.

The solution process is

1) Solve a system with block diagonal matrix A_{11} (i.e. solving in

subregions)

$$A_{11}\, \underline{y}_1 = \underline{b}_1$$

or

$$A_i^{(11)} \underline{y}_{1,i} = \underline{b}_{1,i}, \quad i = 1,2$$

which may be done in parallel;

2) Transfering of data, i.e. evaluating the r.h.s. part for the reduced problem

$$S\, \underline{x}_2 = \tilde{\underline{b}}_2,$$

where

$$\tilde{\underline{b}}_2 = \underline{b}_2 - A_{21}\, \underline{y}_1.$$

As A_{21} is very sparse this transfering of data is minimal (of order h^{-1});

3) Solving the reduced problem

$$S\, \underline{x}_2 = \tilde{\underline{b}}_2.$$

As in general, S is not computed explicitely, this step is done iteratively. It has to be emphasized that to form the product $S\, \underline{y}_2$ for a given vector $\underline{y}_2$ (this is one of the basic operations in the conjugate gradient method) it requires solving systems in subregions with the matrix A_{11} and r.h.s. $- A_{12}\, \underline{y}_2$.

A main dificulty here is to find good preconditioners in order to solve this problem by a finite number of iterations using the preconditioned conjugate gradient method. This means that we have to derive preconditioning matrices easily invertible, which are spectrally equivalent to the Schur complement S. In this direction we emphasize the works Dryja [11], [12], Bjorstad & Widlund [5], Neponnyashtchich [21]. A different approach may be used which leads to nearly optimal iterative methods (a factor $\log h^{-1}$ appears). For this see Dryja, Proskurowski & Widlund [14], Dryja, Proskurowski [13], Bramble, Pasciack, Schatz [6], [7], [8].

To complete the DD we have to solve the separated problems

4) Solving in subregions (parallel step)

$$A_i^{(11)} \underline{x}_{1,i} = \underline{b}_{1,i} - A_i^{(12)} \underline{x}_2, \quad i = 1,2,$$

where we again have minimal transfering of data $- A^{(12)} \underline{x}_2$.

2. Multilevel methods

Here we describe a method proposed in Vassilevski [23], which gives a nearly optimal preconditioning matrix M.M is constructed by induction and uses the following sequence of discretization spaces

$$V_1 \; V_2 \; \ldots \; V_l,$$

where V_i are spaces of piecewise linear functions on the triangulations τ_i of Ω. τ_{i+1} is a direct refinement of τ_i, which means that if "e" is a triangle in τ_i then the triangles in τ_{i+1} can be obtained as follows - either by connecting the midpoints of the sides of "e", or by connecting a vertex of "e" by the midpoint of the opposite side of "e" or "e" remains not changed in τ_{i+1}. We require that in this refining procedure the minimal angle condition to be satisfied, i.e. the minimal angle in each triangle to remain greater than a fixed positive angle independent of the level of discretization.

Let N_k be the set of the nodes on the level k, $1 \leq k \leq l$.

Thus at each level k we have a stiffness matrix $A^{(k)}$, $1 \leq k \leq l$. We partition each $A^{(k+1)}$ into 2 by 2 block structure as follows

$$A^{(k+1)} = \begin{vmatrix} A_{11}^{(k+1)} & A_{12}^{(k+1)} \\ A_{21}^{(k+1)} & A_{22}^{(k+1)} \end{vmatrix},$$

where

$$A_{22}^{(k+1)} = (a_\Omega(\Phi_i,\Phi_j)/x_i,x_j:\Phi_i(x_i) = 1,\ \Phi_j(x_j) = 1 \text{ are nodes in } N_k),$$

$$A_{11}^{(k+1)} = (a_\Omega(\Phi_i,\Phi_j)/x_i,x_j:\Phi_i(x_i) = 1,\ \Phi_j(x_j) = 1 \text{ are nodes in } N_{k+1}\setminus N_k)$$

and

$$A_{12}^{(k+1)} = (a_\Omega(\Phi_i,\Phi_j)/x_i\in N_{k+1}\setminus N_k,\ x_j\in N_k \text{ such that } \Phi_i(x_i) = 1,\ \Phi_j(x_j) = 1).$$

Now we are able to define by induction our preconditioning matrix $M = M^{(1)}$

Set $M^{(1)} = A^{(1)}$.

If $M^{(k)}$ is defined, then

$$M^{(k+1)} = \begin{vmatrix} A_{11}^{(k+1)} & 0 \\ A_{12}^{(k+1)} & M^{(k)} \end{vmatrix} \begin{vmatrix} I & A_{11}^{(k+1)^{-1}} A_{12}^{(k+1)} \\ 0 & I \end{vmatrix}$$

In [23] the following basic result is proven

<u>Theorem 1.</u> For any k, $1 \leq k \leq l$ the following estimate holds true

$$\underline{x}^t A^{(k)} \underline{x} \leq \underline{x}^t M^{(k)} \underline{x} \leq (1 + Ck^2) \underline{x}^t A^{(k)} \underline{x},$$

$C = \text{Const} > 0$ independent of k.

To solve systems with $M^{(k+1)}$ we need to solve systems with the first pivot block $A_{11}^{(k+1)}$. In related papers, concerning two-level iterative methods, e.g., Axelsson & Gustafsson [2], Bank & Dupont [4] Maitre & Mussy [19] the following simple but important result has been proven.

Theorem 2. The condition number of the first pivot block $A_{11}^{(k)}$ remains bounded on k, i.e. we have the estimate

$$\mathrm{cond}(A_{11}^{(k)}) = O(1).$$

To solve systems with first pivot blocks $A_{11}^{(k)}$ we use some iterative methods. Due to Theorem 2 it may be advisible to use the conjugate gradient method which would require finite number of iterations (see, e.g., Concus, Golub & O'Leary [10] or R. Chandra [9]). It may be speed up if some preconditioning is used. Due to its minimal communication requirements the CG method is very suitable for solving these systems with first pivot blocks $A_{11}^{(k)}$ in the parallel DD context. So we apply the technique described in the Section 1 in order to solve systems with $A_{11}^{(k)}$. The next step in solving systems with $M^{(k+1)}$ (in the forward substitution process) is the elimination of the unknowns on the level k+1 and not belonging to the level k, in order to form the r.h.s. part for the problem with the matrix $M^{(k)}$. I.e. in the forward substitution we have to solve

$$\begin{vmatrix} A_{11}^{(k+1)} & 0 \\ A_{21}^{(k+1)} & M^{(k)} \end{vmatrix} \begin{vmatrix} \underline{y}_1^{(k+1)} \\ \underline{v}_2^{(k+1)} \end{vmatrix} = \begin{vmatrix} \underline{b}_1^{(k+1)} \\ \underline{b}_2^{(k+1)} \end{vmatrix}$$

which is done in the following steps

1) solving the system

$$A_{11}^{(k+1)} \underline{y}_1^{(k+1)} = \underline{b}_1^{(k+1)}$$

by the domain decomposition technique;

2) calculating the r.h.s. part

$$\underline{b}^{(k)} = \underline{b}_2^{(k+1)} - A_{21}^{(k+1)} \underline{y}_1^{(k+1)}$$

for the problem on the next level

$$M^{(k)} \underline{y}^{(k)} = \underline{b}^{(k)},$$

where $\underline{y}^{(k)} = \underline{y}_2^{(k+1)}$.

As computation the product $A_{21}^{(k+1)} \underline{y}_1^{(k+1)}$ is a local process, i.e. it requires local communication of data, this step is also very well suited for parallel implementation.

To solve the problem

$$A\,\underline{x} = \underline{b}, \quad A = A^{(1)}$$

we use the PCG (preconditioned conjugate gradient method) (for this see, e.g., Concus, Golub, and O'Leary [10] or R. Chandra [9]) with preconditioning matrix $M = M^{(1)}$. Basing on the Theorem 1 we see that the number of iterations is proportional to $\log h^{-1}$, i.e. we have a nearly optimal iterative method. In each iteration step we perform the following substeps

1) computing the product A times a vector;
2) solving a system with the preconditioning matrix M;
3) computing inner products of two vectors, defined on the V_1.

Let Ω is partitioned into a number of subregions

$$\Omega_1, \Omega_2, \ldots, \Omega_p$$

and let the number of nodes (on the highest level 1) lying on γ be n_p.

Then the communication complexity at each iteration of the PCG method is:

1) $O(n_p)$ elements in total have to be transfered from one region to its neighbouring for computing a product A times a vector;

2) $O(n_p \nu)$ elements in total have to be transfered across the interface boundary γ in solving systems with matrix M, where ν is the number of iterations performed in order to solve systems with $A_{11}^{(k)}$, $1 \leqq k \leqq l$;

3) Communications in computing inner products depend on the architecture of the parallel computer used. In each subregion the local inner product has to be added to all other inner subproducts computed in these subregions.

A more detailed study in this direction is given in [16].

It should be pointed out that the rate of convergence is independent of the number of subregions used and the way of partitioning the original region Ω.

In Dryja, Proskurowski & Widlund [14] a DD method is proposed, which requires the same number of iterations (i.e., proportional to $\log h^{-1}$) but it is based on a different idea. In this direction we emphasize also Dryja & Proskurowski [13], Brambl, Pasciak & Schatz [8], [7], [8].

3. Numerical tests

We have performed some tests in order to compare the number of iterations in the solution of systems with the first pivot blocks $A_{11}^{(k)}$ if the following two methods are used - the CG method with and without precondinioning. For preconditioning we have used matrices derived by approximate (blockwise) factorizations of $A_{11}^{(k)}$, which is a blocktridiagonal matrix (with alternating equasized blocks) for the model problem we consider $-\Delta u=0$ with exact solution $u=1$ on $\Omega = (0,1)x(0,1)$. Then

$$A^{(k)} = \text{tridiag}(-I,\ T,\ -I) \text{ is a}$$

n by n block tridiagonal matrix, where

$$T = \text{tridiag}\ (-1,\ 4,\ -1) \text{ is a}$$

n by n tridiagonal matrix.

Using the same ordering (i.e. line blocks as in A) $A_{11}^{(k)}$ admits the following blocktridiagonal structure -(n+1)/2 by (n+1)/2 blocks

$$A_{11}^{(k)} = \begin{vmatrix} C_1 & -J_1 & & \\ -J_1^t & C_2 & -J_1^t & 0 \\ \ddots & \ddots & \ddots & \\ 0 & & -J_1 & C_1 \end{vmatrix}$$

where

$C_1 = T$, $C_2 = \text{diag}(4,4,\dots,4)$ - (n+1)/2 by (n+1)/2 diagonal matrix and

$$J_1 = \begin{vmatrix} 1 & 0 & & \\ 0 & 0 & & \\ 0 & 1 & & \\ \vdots & \vdots & \ddots & \\ 0 & 0 & \dots & 1 \end{vmatrix} \text{ - n by (n+1)/2 matrix.}$$

The following approximate factorization of $A_{11}^{(k)}$ is used (the so - called inverse - free version, for details see Axelsson & Polman 3).

Let B be a block tridiagonal matrix ($B_{i,i-1}$, B_{ii}, $B_{i,i+1}$) then

$$C = \begin{vmatrix} Y_1^{-1} & & \\ B_{21} & Y_2^{-1} & 0 \\ & \ddots & \ddots \\ 0 & B_{n,m-1} & Y_n^{-1} \end{vmatrix} \begin{vmatrix} I & Y_1B_{12} & & 0 \\ & I & \ddots & \\ & & \ddots & \\ & 0 & I & Y_{n-1}B_{n-1,n} \end{vmatrix}$$

is derived by the following algorithm

$$Y_1 = \left\| B_{11}^{-1} \right\|^{(p)}$$

$$Y_i = \left\| (B_{ii} - B_{i,i-1}Y_{i-1}B_{i-1,i})^{-1} \right\|^{(p)},\ i = 2,\dots,n,$$

where by $\|\cdot\|^{(p)}$ we mean the innermost (2p+1) banded part of the matrix. Algorithms for computing this p - banded part of the inverse of a given p-banded matrix without full inversion of the matrix exist, see, e.g., Axelsson [1], Vassilevski [24].

Below we present the numerical tests in Table 1 and Table 2.

h^{-1} \ ν	2	4	8	16	exact
32	28	14	14	13	13
64	71	17	15	15	15

Table 1

The number of iterations of the PCG method with preconditioning matrix M; Problems with $A_{11}^{(k)}$ are solved by performing ν iterations of the CG method.

p \ h^{-1}	32	64
1	16	20
2	15	19

Table 2

The number of iterations of the PCG method with a preconditioning matrix M; Problems with $A_{11}^{(k)}$ are solved by the PCG mathod; p - the haffbandwidth used.

It is seen that if we even do not solve exactly problems with $A_{11}^{(k)}$ but the number of iterations is sufficiently large ($\nu = 4$ for $h^{-1} = 32$ and $\nu \geqq 4$ for $h^{-1} = 64$) the convergence of the global method remains the same.

4. Concluding remarks

It should be pointed out that this technique is applicable in solving 3D problems. There as in Theorem 1 the factor k^2 is replaced by 2^k we have to perform some smoothing (pre- and post-) iterations on the level k before starting the solution with the matrix $M^{(k)}$. This is in direct connection with the ordinary MG method (see, e.g., Stuben & Trottenberg [22]).

REFERENCES

1. Axelsson, O.: A survey of vectorizable preconditioning methods for large scale finite element matrices. In: Colloquium Topics in Applied Numerical Analysis, J.G. Verner (Ed.), CWI syllabus 4&5, Amsterdam 1983.

2. Axelsson, O. and I. Gustafsson: Preconditioning and two-level multigrid methods of arbitrary degree of approximation. Math. Comput. 40 (1983), pp. 219-242.

3. Axelsson, O. and B. Polman: On approximate factorization methods for block-matrices suitable for vector and parallel processors Lin. Alg. Appl., 77 (1986), pp. 3-26.

4. Bank, R. and T. Dupont: Analysis of a two-level Scheme for solving finite element equations. Report CNA-159, Center for Numerical Analysis, The University of Texas at Austin, 1980.

5. Bjorstad, P.E. and O.B. Widlund: Iterative methods for the solution of elliptic problems on regions partitioned into substructures. SIAM J. Numer. Analysis.

6. Bramble, J.H., J.E. Pasciak and A.H. Schatz: An iterative method for elliptic problems on regions partitioned into substructures. Math. Compt., 46(1986), pp. 361-369.

7. Bramble, J.H., J.E. Pasciak and A.H. Schatz: The construction of preconditioners for elliptic problems by substructuring. I. Math. Comput., 47(1986), pp. 103-134.

8. Bramble, J.H., J.E. Pasciak and A.H. Schatz: The construction of preconditioners for elliptic problems by substructuring, II. Preprint, BNL - AMD - 1986, Cornell University, Ithaca, New York, 1986.

9. Chandra R.: Conjugate gradient methods for partial differential equations. Research Report #119, 1978, Dept. Comput. Sci., Yale University.

10. Concus, P., G.H. Golub and D.P. O'Leary: A generalized CG method for the numerical solution of elliptic partial differential equations. In: J.R. Bunch and D.J. Rose, Eds: Sparse Matrix Computations, pp. 309-332, New York, Academic Press, 1976.

11. Dryja, M.: A capacitance matrix method for Dirichlet problem on polygon region. Numer. Math., 39 (1982), pp. 51-64.

12. Dryja, M.: A finite element-capacitance method for elliptic problems on regions partitioned into substructures. Numer. Math., 44 (1984), pp. 153-168.

13. Dryja, M. and W. Proskurowski: Iterative methods in subspases for solving elliptic problems using domain decomposition. Technical report CRI-86-10, 1986, Department of Mathematics, DRB 306, University of Southern California, Los Angeles.

14. Dryja, M., W. Proskurowski and O.B. Widlund: A method of domain decomposition with cross points for elliptic finite element problems. In: Proceedings from an International Symposium on Optimal Algorithms held in Blagoevgrad, Bulgaria, April 1986.

15. Golub, G.H. and D. Mayers: The use of pre-conditioning over irregular regions. In: Proceedings of the Sixth International Conference on Computing Methods in Science and Engineering, Versailles, France, December 1983, pp. 3-14.

16. Keyes, D.E. and W.D. Gropp: A comparison of domain decomposition techniques for elliptic partial differential equations and their parallel implementation. Research Report YALEU/DCS/RR-448, December 1985.

17. Kuznetsov, Yu.A.: Computational methods in subspaces. In: Computational Processes and Systems, vol. 2, Nauka, Moscow, 1985, pp. 265-360. In Russian.

18. Lebedev, V.I. and V.I. Agoshkov: Poincare-Steklov operators and their applications in analysis. Department of Computational Mathematics, USSR Academy of Sciences, Moscow, 1983. In Russian.

19. Maitre, J.F. and F. Musy: The contraction number of two-level methods; An exact evaluation for some finite element subspaces and model problems. In: Multigrid Methods, W. Hackbusch and U. Trottenberg, (eds.)., Lect. Notes Math., #960, Springer-Verlag, Berlin-Heidelberg-New York, 1982, pp. 535-544.

20. Matsokin, A.M.: Methods of fictitious components and alternation in subregions. Preprint 612, 1985. Computing Center, Sibirian Branch of the USSR Academy of Sciences, Novosibirsk, In Russian.

21. Nepomnyashtchich, S.V.: On application of bordering method to mixed b.v.p. for elliptic equations and on network norms in $W_2^{1/2}(S)$. Preprint 106, 1984. Computing Center, Sibirian Branch of the USSR Academy of Sciences, Novosibirsk. In Russian.

22. Stuben, K. and U. Trottenberg: MG methods: Fundamental Algorithms, Model Problem Analysis and Applications. In: W. Hackbuch and U. Trottenberg. Eds.: Multigrid Methods. Lecture Notes Math., #960, Springer-Verlag, Berlin-Heidelberg-New York, 1982, pp. 1-172.

23. Vassilevski, P.S.: Nearly optimal iterative methods for solving f.e. equations based on multilevel splitting of the matrix. (Submitted) 1987.

24. Vassilevski, P.S.: On some ways of approximating inverses of banded matrices in connection with deriving preconditioners based on incomplete blockwise factorizations. (Submitted), 1987.

25. Vassilevski, P.S.: The role of inaccurate residuals of the Schur complement in solving f.e. elliptic problems by substructuring. (Submitted), 1987.

26. Vassilevski, P.S.: On some ways of constructing preconditioners for solving f.e. elliptic problems by substructuring. (Submitted), 1987.

27. Vassilevski, P.S. and S.I. Petrova: A note on construction of preconditioners in solving 3D elliptic problems by substructuring. (To appear), 1987.

28. Widlund, O.B.: A guide to the literature on iterative substructuring. Courant Institute, Dept. Comput. Sci., New York University, August 1986.

29. Widlund, O.B.: An extension theorem for finite element spaces with three applications. Technical Report #223, 1986, New York University, Dept. Comput. Sci., Courant Institute.

Major Research Activities in Parallel Processing in Japan

Yoichi Muraoka and Toshikazu Marushima
School of Science and Engineering
Waseda University
Tokyo, JAPAN

1. INTRODUCTION

This paper reports the recent progress in Japan of research and development efforts in parallel processing.

A recently published survey[1] reported that, in Japan, during the last 9 years, that there have been about 77 projects ranging from both small to large. Thirty five percent of the projects were conducted either by manufacturers or by research laboratories such as the ICOT and the Electrotechnical Laboratory. The rest were conducted in universities. The popularity of research work in parallel processing in universities is not surprising if one considers the current trend in VLSI technology which enables one to purchase, say, 8 microprocessors and a few hundred KB of memory chips for a few hundred dollars. This is quite affordable for even a moderate sized school. In fact, with a very few exceptions (4 or 5), most university projects utilized off-the-shelf microprocessors such as INTEL 80186 as their processing elements. Of course, connecting a few microprocessors via a simple bus alone may not constitute an interesting parallel processing research project, although it is at least a good starting point.

Borrowing the terminology of Flynn, we may classify the architecture of the above parallel processing machines as follows:-

(1) *SISD architecture*

Since there is no other proper place to put dataflow architecture, we classify it here.

(2) *SIMD architecture*

In addition to ordinary SIMD machines, we place pipeline machines in this class.

(3) *MIMD architecture*

Array processors are included in this category.

Nearly seventy percent of the 77 projects surveyed in the report concerned with MIMD architecture, and eighteen percent were on dataflow architecture. The rest are on SIMD architecture. The reason why MIMD architecture is popular may be that a machine based on MIMD architecture is easier for universities to build using microprocessors. As for the processor connection scheme, a bus is most popular (about fourty one percent) followed by a tree connection scheme.

Since the majority of projects are either still ongoing or, in case of finished ones, explicit performance eveluation data based upon real bench mark programs were rarely published, it is rather hard to assess the machines in terms of thier performance or their size (i.e. the number of processors in a machine).

About 29 percent of the 77 projects claimed explicitly that the goals of their projects were to develop machines for scientific and engineering applications, and about 20 percent of them were for, so called, artificial intelligence applications such as PROLOG machines and logic programing machines (Figure 1). The rest were special purpose machines such as a CAD machine.

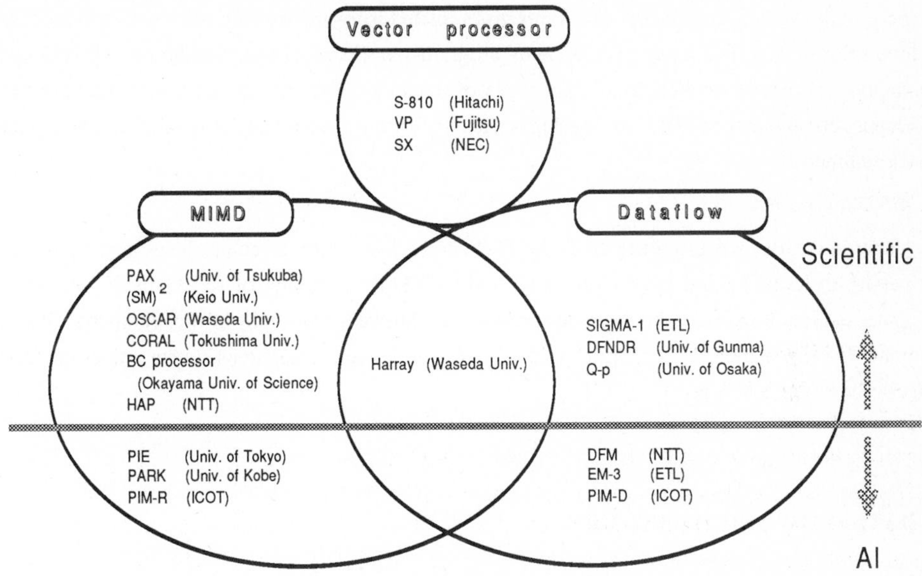

Figure 1. Classification of Japanese parallel computers

Of course, every project is interesting and deserving of some comment, but, in this short paper, it is impossible to deal with them all. Therefore, we shall focus our attention upon machines with scientific and engineering applications. There are two reasons for this: firstly, there are wider applications and markets for them at this time, and, secondly, they are more mature and therefore they cover the important aspects of the other machines in terms of their technologies.

In the rest of the paper we discuss the following topics:-

(1) *Dataflow architecture*

The SIGMA-1 computer of the Electrotechnical Laboratory, the Q-p computer of Osaka University and the Harray computer of Waseda University will be presented under this heading. The SIGMA-1 project is being conducted as a part of a government supported national project, entitled '*High-speed Computing System for Scientific and Technological Use*'. The Q-p computer is also a dataflow type machine. It adopts an original idea called a stream processing system. While the SIGMA-1 project and the Q-p project aim to construct machines based on the most advanced pure dataflow architecture, the Harray project aims to develop a hybrid of dataflow and array architecture.

(2) *SIMD architecture*

Most of the research and development efforts in this class have been conducted by manufacturers with the result being the development of commercial supercompuetrs. Here we present the NEC SX series as an example in order to show the trend in SIMD architecture development efforts in Japan. We choose this machine as an example for the reason that it is simply the most recently announced one.

Additionly we introduce recent developments in related software research work with special emphasis on loop analysis (e.g. *DO loops* of *FORTRAN* programs) and parallel task scheduling. Of course, these techniques are readily applicable to other types of machine, however, more effort have been put into developing compilers for SIMD type machines since these constitute the majority of machines available in the current market.

(3) *MIMD architecture*

Under this title, we introduce both the PAX computer which is being developed jointly by the University of Tsukuba and Keio University, and the $(SM)^2$ computer of Keio University. The PAX computer is unique in that it has been designed to simulate real world physical phenomena. The $(SM)^2$ computer is a sparse matrix solver which is at the core of scientific calculations. Other interesting machines will also be introduced here.

2. DATAFLOW ARCHITECTURE

2.1 SIGMA-1 [2]

In January, 1982, a national project for the development new generation supercomputer systems was initiated. The objective of the project was to develop necessary technologies to construct an ultra-high-speed system which runs at the speed of more than 10 GFLOPs. The project is currently being carried out as a joint effort between major Japanese manufacturers such as Hitachi, Fujitsu, NEC, and, the Electrotechnical Laboratory which is a governmental organization.

Major activities in the projects include:-

(1) *development of new high-speed devices.*

(2) *development of new architecture.*

As for device technology development, the following three devices have been selected as candidates: Josephson devices, GaAs devices and High Electron Mobility Transistor devices. The device development projects have been conducted mainly by manufactures. The initial targets for device development are as follows.

(1)	Logic devices:	Delay time	10-30 ps/gate
		Integration scale	3 Kgates/chip
(2)	Memory devices:	Access time	10 ns
		Integration scale	16 Kbits/chip

However, these values have now become rather conservative.

In addition to device development, research work on parallel architecture has been carried out. Since it was obvious that parallel processing was essential in attaining the required performance, the architectural research has been designed to pursue this goal. In terms of number-crunching development efforts, there are two streams of research. The major difference between the two lies in the granularity of parallel processing. One way to attain a high-speed processor is to design a multiprocessor system with a few very powerful processors. In this case, the granularity of parallel processing occurs at task level. This approach has been pursued by Fujitsu to construct a multiprocessor with up to 16 pipelined processors. Apart from a private memory unit in each , the sixteen processors share a common memory unit of 64 Mbytes. A common mapping unit takes care of data access synchronization from the sixteen processors.

Another approach taken in the project was to investigate the feasibility of instructon level parallelism. Dataflow architecture was selected from among the many candidates for instruction level parallelism as it was thought to be the most challenging. The development of the dataflow machine has been conducted by the Electrotechnical Laboratory, and the project was named SIGMA-1. The project started in 1982 and will last until the end of 1987. The design goal of the project is a dataflow machine with more than 128 processors to achieve 100 MFLOPs. A prototype of the processor has been in operation since 1984, and they are now working on a VLSI version using gate array technology to configure a 128 processor machine.

The special features of the SIGMA-1 computer are:-

(1) A parallel processor system with up to 128 hierarchically connected processors, in which four processors form a cluster.

(2) Each processor adopts dataflow architecture based on a dynamic model.

(3) A structured memory unit is provided for each processor to store structured data such as arrays.

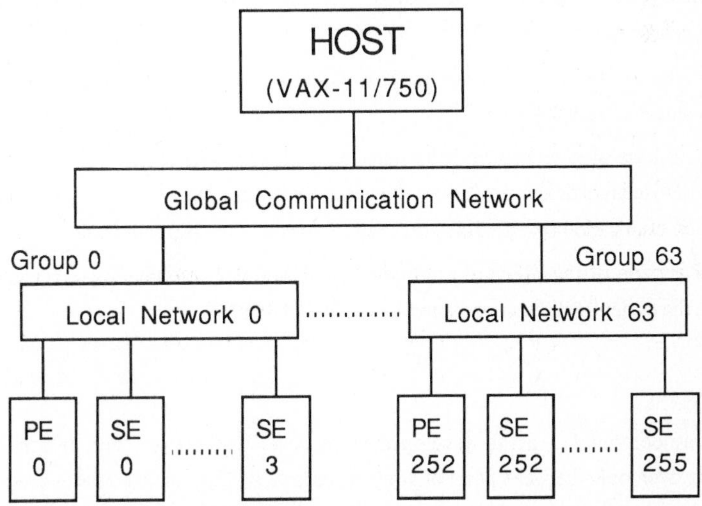

Figure 2. Global organization of the SIGMA-1

Figure 2 shows the system configuration and the organization of the processor. A cluster consists of four processors and four structured memory units. The eight units are connected by a local network. The local network is constructed as a 10 by 10 crossbar switch where the control is handled in a store-and-forward manner. The reason that a 10 by 10 crossbar switch is adopted is that 8 ports are for eight units, one port is for a global network connection while the final one is reserved for maintenance. Up to 32 clusters are connected by a global network, which is organized as a two stage omega network. A host computer, VAX 11/750, is connected to the global network and serves as an I/O controller.

A processor has an execution unit, an instruction fetch unit, an operand matching memory unit, an input buffer unit and a destination unit. The whole processor operates syncronously and every instruction is executed in, at most, three basic machine cycles. The instruction fetch unit has a 64K instruction memory to store programs. The matching unit pairs operands of each instruction, and, if an operand is not available, it keeps the instruction until one does become available. A chained hashing scheme is used in constructing the matching memory unit. The size of the matching memory unit is 64K cells. A simulation was performed to evaluate the optimal size of the matching memory unit, and it was observed that the life-time of a packet residing in the matching memory unit was rather short, i.e. in most cases, it was less than ten time units. The length of an instruction is 40 bits and the size of a cell is 80 bits. To improve the execution efficiency of a loop, a *LOOP-DO* instruction was introduced. The *LOOP-DO* instruction generates tokens corresponding to the values of a loop index automatically. It corresponds to a *FORALL* statement in a high level language. Also, an *FADD-LP* instruction is introduced which checks if the terminating condition of a loop was met. By introducing these instructions, the execution efficiency was improved by more than 54 percent in terms of execution time.

The structured memory unit is composed of an input buffer unit and a structure unit. The input buffer is a *first-come-first-served* queue and has 8K cells. The structure unit has 256K cells.

A primary version of the processor has been implemented using gate arrays and standard cell custom LSIs. It consists of six print circuit boards. According to a test run using a Livermore loop, its performance is 1.32 MIPs.

The language for the SIGMA-1 computer is called DFC,: a subset of language C being modified to conform to a single assignment rule.

Basically, a loop or a procedure is assigned to a cluster. To utilize a multiple of processors, it is necessary to devise an efficient processor allocation algorithm. Several algorithms have been studied in terms of (a) communication cost minimization and (b) execution cost minimization.

The final version of the SIGMA-1 computer is now under construction using gate aray LSIs. It is expected that the system will be in operation by the end of 1987.

2.2 Harray

The Harray computer is being developed by Waseda University. The design goal of the Harray computer is to overcome the weak point of array processors by introducing dataflow architecture within the processor. In order to attain a performance exceeding Giga FLOPs, an array processor approach utilizing a large number of processors is very attractive. This approach, however, suffers from an inevitable degradation of performance due to the delay in memory access introduced by the memory switch between processors and memory units. The Harray computer tries to overcome this difficulty by adopting dataflow architecture with multiple execution units for each processor. As dataflow control allows execution of instructions as their operands become available, and need not follow the execution order being issued by a control unit, the memory access delay will be overcome. Another architectural feature of the Harray computer is a mechanism to control the execution order of blocks. To fully utilize multiple processors, it is necessary to execute different portions (blocks) of a program concurrently by allocating a set of processors to them. To do this efficiently, the introduction of some kind of a control unit is advantageous and the Harray computer has a Global Control Unit (GCU) for this purpose. Thus, the Harray computer implements both instruction level parallelism (in each processor) and task level parallelism (between processors).

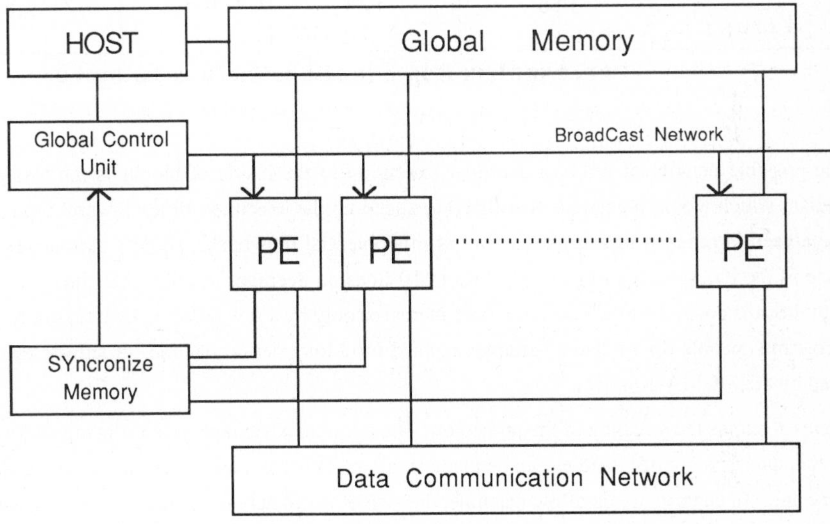

Figure3. Global organization of the Harray

The objective of the Harray project is to design a large scale parallel processing system which accepts programs written in an ordinary language such as FORTRAN. An overall structure of the Harray computer is shown in *Figure 3*. The compiler analyzes a program and divides it into blocks. An example of a block is a *DO loop* or a *jump-free block of assignment statements.* A *DO loop* is further analyzed for parallel processability. Each block or portion of a *DO loop*, if it can be processed in parallel in terms of a loop index is allocated to a processor. Hence, in the case of a parallel *DO loop*, a set of processors is allocated to a block. The execution sequence of blocks is controlled by the Global Control Unit. Thus, the block level execution control (the inter-block control) is done in a control flow fashion between processors whereas the execution control inside of each block (the intra-block control) is done in dataflow fashion within a processor. The Harray computer is therefore being named after this method of organization, that is, a Hybrid ARRAY.

Table 1 . simulation results with block division

program	time steps without block division	time steps with block division	increase rate (%)	average time steps with blosk division
Gradient Biconjugate method *	65	67	3.0	3.5
Gauss elimination method *	81	85	4.9	3.6
KENO code (begin)	698	726	4.0	3.8
KENO code (cros)	116	121	4.3	9.6

* here matrix A in equations Ax=b is 10 by 10

The possible penalty of limiting dataflow execution to the inside of blocks is the loss of potential parallelism which would otherwise be utilized to speed up the execution time. Several typical programs were analyzed in order to measure the effect of this potential drawback. *Table 1* surmarizes the results. The size of the blocks range from a few lines to 10 lines on average. As the table shows, even after the block division is done, the total execution time increases only by a few percent. One reason may be that in real programs, people do not leave variables unused for a long period of time. A similar result was also obtained by the SIGMA-1 project.

Figure 4 shows the structure of the processor. The possible advantage of introducing a block is that the extent that dataflow control handles can be made smaller. This fact is reflected in the size of the matching memory unit. In an ordinary dataflow machine, the size of the matching memory tends to be very large. If it is too small, the overflow occurs frequently thereby degrading the performance severely. To make it very large, however, is very expensive, especially when a large number of processors is to be used. In the Harray computer, the extent of dataflow control can be kept rather small due to an introduction of block division. This fact was confirmed again by analyzing real programs. Results are shown in *Figure 5* As may be seen in the figure, about 10 to 20 cells of the matching memory unit are sufficient.

As there are multiple execution units in a processor, it is important to design their allocation algorithm to maximize their utilization. The best scheme is to allocate the least used execution unit to the next instruction. This scheme, however, is expensive in terms of the hardware cost. The analysis showed that the round robin allocation scheme would do as well.

The project is now in the system design stage, and a compiler as well as a prototype processor will be constructed in this year.

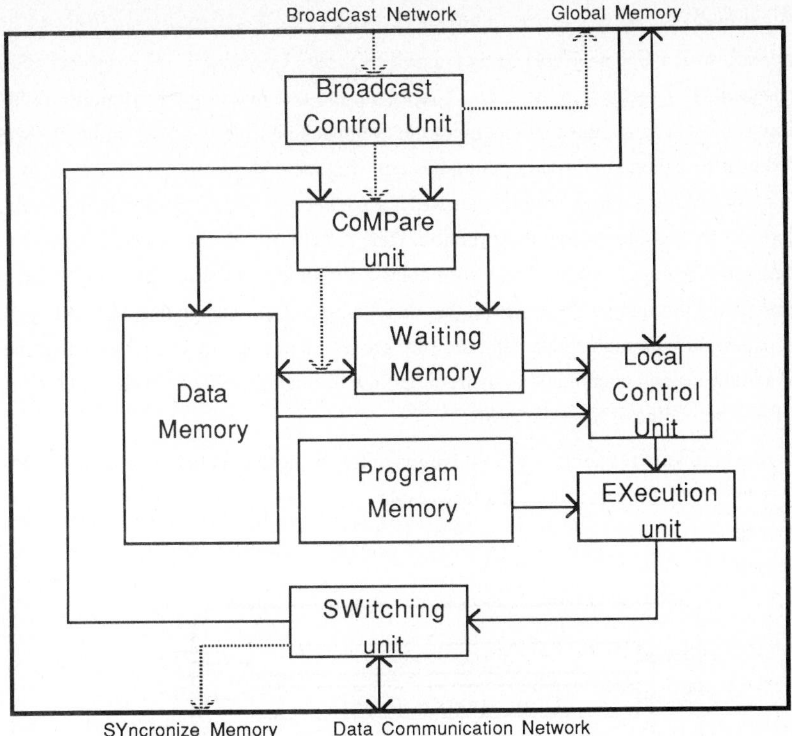

Figure 4. Organization of a PE of the Harray

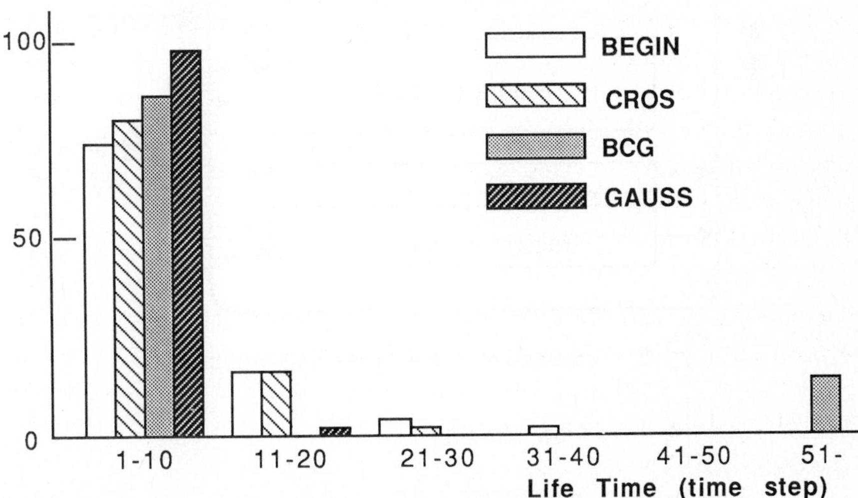

Figure 5. Distribution of the life time of packets (after block division)

2.3 Q-p [3]

Another dataflow machine project is being pursued by Osaka University. The projects name is Q-x and its prototype machine is designated the Q-p. Apart from the fact that the Q-p computer uses a dynamic mode dataflow control scheme, the architecture of the Q-p machine is very unique in that the whole system is constructed as a so-called stream processing system. *Figure 6* shows the overall structure of the Q-p machine. In addition to the above features, an ALU, a packet pair generator (PAIR) and a data path are used in the stream processing system construction. The stream processing system is implemented via a functional buffering storage scheme which resembles a pipeline control mechanism in that the control function is distributed throughout the system rather than being concentrated in one unit. As operand data or control information flow through a data path, they are processed as necessary. In the case of the PAIR, the first operand and the second operand of an instruction flow through the circular path until they are matched (*Figure 7*). They then will exit from the PAIR.

In addition to hardware research, a special language for the system is being developed. The language allows the user to specify his algorithm via a flowgraph.

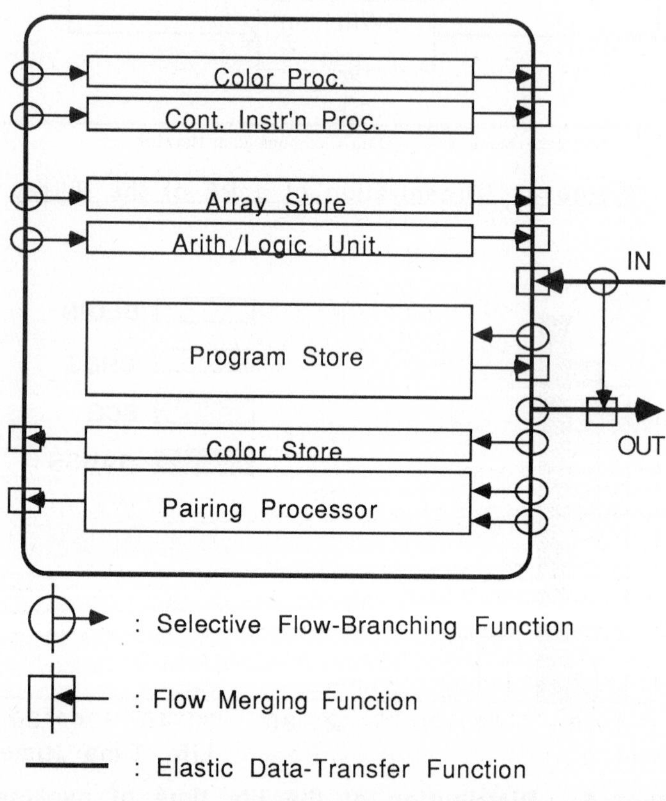

Figure 6. Organizaiton of the Q-p

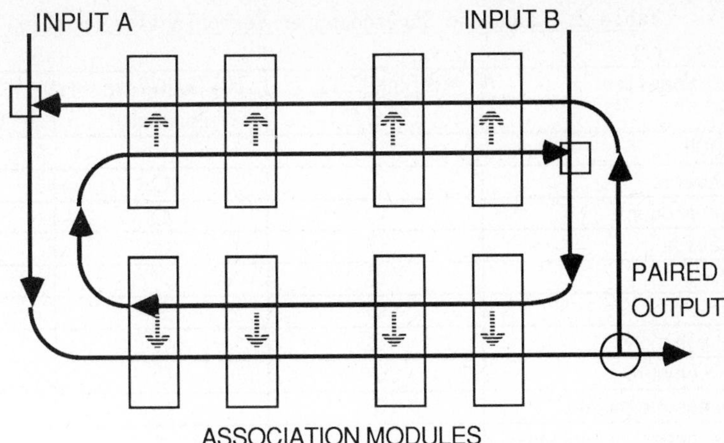

Figure 7. Structure of PAIR

3. SIMD MACHINES

3.1 Software

There are many important areas in the field of software for parallel processors. However in this paper we deal only with (a) *DO loop* analysis and (b) scheduling.

3.1.1 DO loop analysis

Table 2 shows comparison of the various compilers used in Japanese supercomputers. The main features of these compilers are:

(1) *Automatic vectorization by data dependency analysis.*

Improvement has been made on techniques first introduced by Kuck, et al.

(2) *Improvement in the execution speed of certain typical operations by the introduction of macro vector instructions.*

One way in which macro vector operations are provided for is through a summation and an inner product operation, with the compiler detecting cases where these operations are applicable.

(3) *Vectorization of IF statements by mask vectors.*

Mask vector operations have been introduced to enable certain *IF statements* inside a *DO loop* to be vectorized.

(4) *Support of indirect indexing.*

A list vector is used to index a vector indirectly.

(5) *Tools to assist users in writing good programs for supercomputers.*

Table 2. Japanese Supercomputer Vectorization Function List

Compiler	FORTRAN77/SX [4] (NEC)	FORTRAN77/VP [5] (Fujitsu)	FORT77/HAP [6] (Hitachi)
FUNCTION			
arithmetic	○	○	○
inner product	○	○	○
summation	○	○	○
product	○	/	○
power	○	/	○
max/min	○	○	○
type convert	○	○	/
compress/expand	○	○	○
first-order recurrence	○	×	○
mth-order recurrence	×	×	×
builtin function	○	○	○
user function	/	×	×
subroutine CALL	/	×	×*
exit LOOP	/	○**	×
VECTOR TYPE			
contiguous	○	○	○
constant stride	○	○	○
indirect	○	○	○
STATEMENT			
assignment	○	○	○
IF/ELSE ***	○	○	○
GOTO	○	○	○
CONTINUE	○	○	○
VARIABLE TYPE			
real	○	○	○
complex	○	○	○
integer	○	○	○
logical	○	○	○
PROGRAM TRANSFORMATION			
loop distribution	○	○	○
loop collapse	○	○	○
loop interchange	○	○	○
statement interchange	○	○	○
temporary vector	○	/	×

○ ...... vectorizable
× ...... unvectorizable
/ ...... unknown to the authors
* : inlined by another tool
** : with limitations
*** : three times nested at most

In addition to these techniques already adopted in commercial compilers, research is also continueing to improve their capability. The basic idea is to transform a program into another form which is easier to analyze. Next we will introduce a few recent results.

(1) *Transformation of a nested DO loop into a single loop.*

Existing compilers generate parallel codes either for the inner-most *DO loop* of a *nested DO loop*, or for a restricted class of *nested DO loops*. Hence, for certain classes of programs, rather poor codes are generated. To overcome this problem, an algorithm has been proposed to analyze a nested *DO loop* for parallel computation (*Figure 8*). Furthermore, to increase the length of a vector, an algorithm to transform a nested *DO loop* into a single *DO loop* has been proposed (*Figure 9*).

```
DO  i=1,10                                 DOALL  i=1,10
  DO  j=i+1,20                               DOALL  j=i+1,20
    A(i,j) = C(j)+3                            A(i,j) = C(j)+3
  END DO                     =>              END DO
  DO  k=i+1,10                               DOALL  k=i+1,10
    D(i,k) = D(i,k)+A(k,i)                     D(i,k) = D(i,k)+A(k,i)
  END DO                                     END DO
END DO                                     END DO
```

Figure 8. Nested loops analysis

```
DO i=1,10
  DO j=1,10                                DOALL ij=1,100
    A(i,j)=B(i,j)+5          =>              XA(ij)=XB(ij)+5
  END DO                                   END DO
END DO
```

Figure 9. Loop collapsing

(2) *Application of a macro instruction on a linear recurrence relation.*

The compiler generates sequential codes if it finds a recurrence relation over multiple statements in a DO loop. An algorithm has been proposed to transform such a recurrence relation into a form to which a macro instruction is applicable.

(3) *Loop unfolding.*

A portion of a *DO loop* execution corresponding to certain values of the loop index variable (e.g. the initial value of the loop index variable) is unfolded to the outside of the *DO loop* to make the *DO loop* parallel processable (*Figure 10*).

```
DO i=1,N
  IF (i .EQ. 1)  THEN                      X(1)=0.0
    X(i)=0.0                               DOALL i=2,N
  ELSE                       =>              X(i)=A(i-1)+B(i-1)
    X(i)=A(i-1)+B(i-1)                     END DO
  END IF
END DO
```

Figure 10. Loop unfolding

(4) *Induction unfolding.*

So far, a *DO loop* containing *IF statements* has been judged as a sequential loop. If the conditional part of the *IF statement* depends only upon the loop index variable, e.g.

```
      DO 100 I=1,100
      ..........
      IF (I+5 .GT. 70) ....
      .........
  100 CONTINUE
```

then it is possible to analyze at compile time what portion of the DO loop may be computed in parallel.

Recently, the development of special purpose languages for parallel processors has become popular. SPLM of the PAX computer, NCC of $(SM)^2$ and DEQSOL of the S-810 computer are examples. They. allow programs to be written on a numerical algorithm level and produce optimized codes for parallel processors.

3.1.2 Scheduling

The fact that finding an efficient algorithm for task scheduling on multiple processors is important need not be repeated here. It is almost impossible to find the optimum solution for a task-scheduling problem on a multiple machine where some dependency restriction exists among the tasks. Recently, however, a near-optimum solution has been proposed by Kasahara, et al[7]. The algorithm is called the CP/MISF and it adopts a modified-depth first search. Tasks are scheduled according to their distance from the termination point. They are further worked to include the algorithm so that the compiler can schedule tasks efficiently for the multiprocessor.

3.2 SIMD architecture

Research and developments of SIMD machines are mostly carried out by manufacturers with the result being commercial supercomputers. As an example of these efforts, we introduce, in this paper, the architecture of the NEC SX series[4]. Although details vary from machine to machine, the architectural trend is similar in all machines. Features of the SX computer are as follows:-

(1) *Multi-pipelined vector arithmetic units.*

The SX computer has 16 pipelined vector arithmetic units which can operate concurrenctly. Thus, there are two levels of parallelism: pipelining for instruction level parallel processing and; multiprocessing for task level parallel processing. The chaining of arithmetic units is controlled by hardware so that if the second arithmetic unit is in use during the time that the chaining is required, the hardware automatically chains it when the unit becomes available.

(2) *A pipelined scalar arithmetic unit.*

To increase the efficiency of a pipelined scalar arithmetic unit, the compiler re-orders the scalar operations in order to minimize interdependency between operations. A rearrangement algorithm for operations has been reported to increase the speed of execution of Livermore loops by up to 36 percent. The scalar arithmetic unit can also operate concurrently with vector arithmetic units.

(3) *Functional distribution system.*

The SX computer consists of an arithmetic processor and a control processor. The latter is used for the execution of such operating system functions as file control and job scheduling. Thanks to this configuration, the arithmetic processor can be dedicated solely to number crunching.

4. MIMD ARCHITECTURE

In this category, we introduce the PAX computer, the $(SM)^2$, and other computers.

4.1 PAX [8]

Though the architecture of the PAX computer may seem to be rather old, the idea behind the PAX computer is both fascinating and unique. While other projects use existing programs and try to find ways to execute them more efficiently, the designers of the PAX computer took another view. They started from the begining by investigating the physical phenomena of the real world. They observed that the physical quantity corresponding to a point in space is influenced only by the physical quantity of neighbouring points. In terms of numerical calculation, this amounts to the fact that a physical space may be mapped on a grid and values of each grid point are computed in terms of the values of its four neighbouring points. If we map this to parallel computer architecture, it is sufficient to arrange processors to form a grid (or an array) and connect a processor to four neighbouring processors. This fact is also quite advantageous because to execute problems of a meaningful size, tens of thousands of grid points may be required, and, if we are to map a grid point to a processor, a large number of processors would be required. In practice it is only possible to connect a processor to four neighbouring processors.

The development of the PAX computer started in 1977 with the result that the PAX-64J computer with 64 processors has been built. The PAX-64J computer runs with the clock speed of 15MHz and a claimed peak performance of 6.4MFLOPs.

The architecture of the PAX computer is shown in *Figure 11.* In the processor, in addition to a microprocessing unit (MPU), there is also a local memory unit (LM) (which is only accessible to the MPU in the processor and stores programs and local data) and a communication memory unit (CM) (for communicating with the four neighbouring processors.) Processors are connected to form an end-wrapped array. Strictly speaking, the PAX computer is not intended to behave completely in an MIMD fashion. It may be viewed as quasi-MIMD in that it executes identical tasks in parallel and occasionally (as when task syncronization is required) different tasks are executed.

According to the designers , the most important concept in using the machine is the mapping of a real-world problem space onto the PAX computer's processor array. Direct one-to-one mapping is the most suitable, but if the problem space is too large to fit on the processor array, it may be divided into subtasks and mapped on the array.

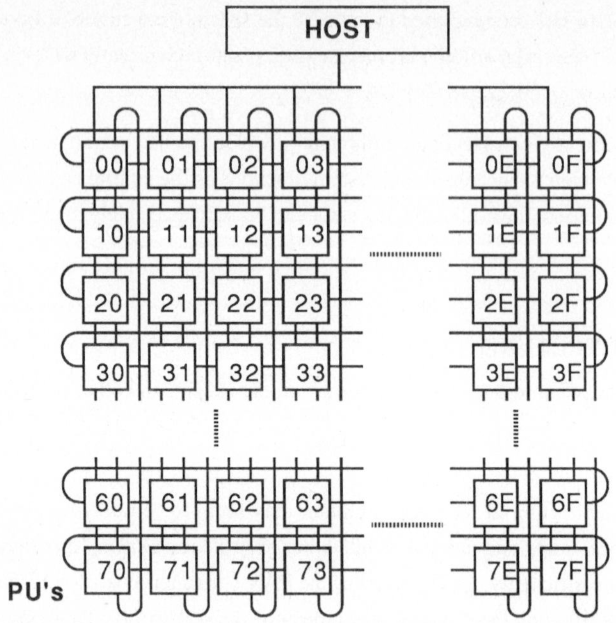

Figure 11. System configuration of the PAX-128

To program the machine, a high level language called SPLM is provided. The SPLM language is not a parallel processing language in that it does not have a mechanism to specify parallel execution explicitly as does for example the OCCAM language. This is because, on the PAX computer, it is sufficient for a user to describe a task for one processor. This implies that the identical execution is performed on all processors. In other words, it may be thought that an implicit *DOALL* statement is specified. Then, it is only necessary for the language to provide a mechanism by which the user may describe the way processors communicate. For this purpose, the SPLM language has the facility to specify the variables to be allocated in a desired memory unit such as LM and CM. Otherwise, the SPLM language looks quite like a conventional language.

Depending on how one looks at it, the PAX computer may be thought of as for example a special-purpose PDE solver. Nevertheless, the project is very interesting as the machine has already been built and many real applications have been tested upon it. Due to the nature of the project, the designers would rather classify the machine as a multi-purpose machine. The designers foresee that in 1990's it may be possible to attain a 1 TFLOPs machine with 10,000 processors.

4.2 $(SM)^2$ [9]

The $(SM)^2$ computer has been designed as a dedicated parallel machine for the solution of sparse matrix problems. In the case of solving a band matrix on an array machine by the relaxation method, usually processors are allocated to one or a few columns of the matrix and the communication pattern between processors become regular as shown in *Figure 12.* In the case of a non-band sparse matrix, however, the communication pattern between processors tends to be irregular as the figure shows. To deal with this situation, an array computer with shared memory units and common buses is an obvious solution. The major problem with this solution is the memory access conflict. In order to circumvent the problem, the $(SM)^2$ computer adopts the multi-access memory technique. A memory unit based on this idea has a configuration as shown in *Figure 13.* Identical data are copied in all memory units at the same address. A write request from a processor propagates to all memory units and writes the same item in all. Read requests to the same address from multiple processors may be processed without any access conflict since they are read from different memory units. It is clear that write requests from multiple processors will cause write access conflicts. One way to minimize the effect of this conflict is to divide memory units into several banks. Then, as long as write access from processors are to the different banks, write conflicts can be avoided. Of course, a drawback to this idea is the increase in total memory requirement. In principle, the idea increases memory capacity by n folds where n is the total number of processors. To overcome this weakpoint, the designers of the $(SM)^2$ computer used the fact that, in general, processors tend to communicate with neighbouring processors. Then it is only necessary to provide multi- access capability to memory only for those addresses which will be accessed by nearby processors, and leave other addresses non-multi-accessible. The architecture of the $(SM)^2$ computer then takes on the form shown in *Figure 14.* A prototype of the machine has been built and now several applications are being tested. A language is also being developed and tested.

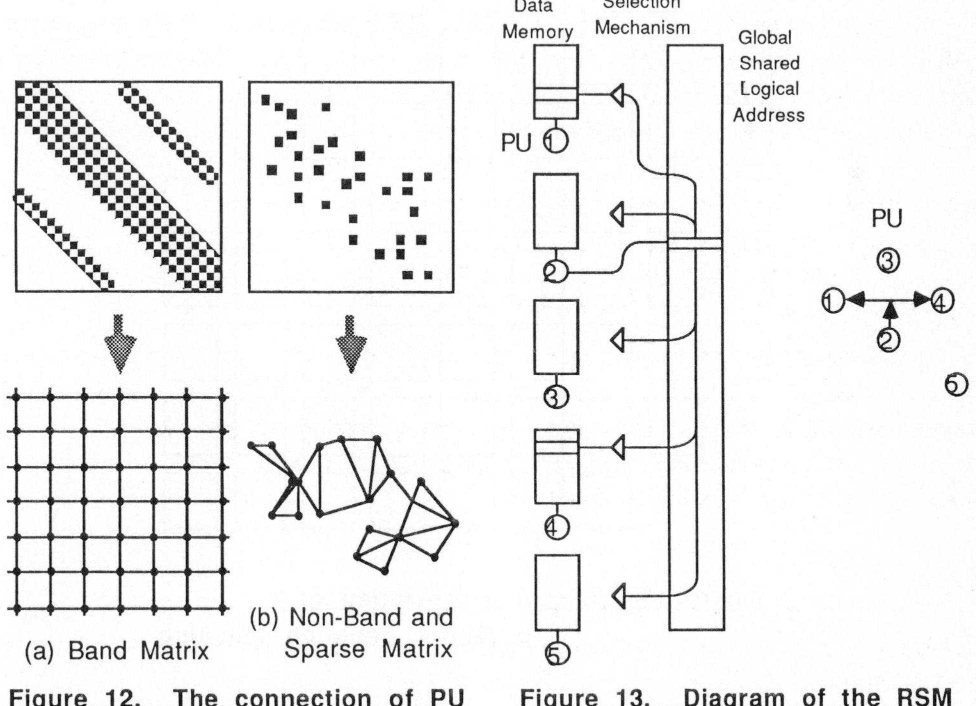

Figure 12. The connection of PU

Figure 13. Diagram of the RSM

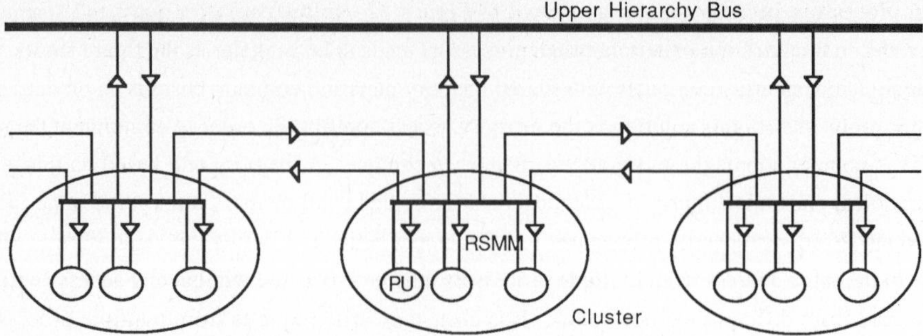

Figure 14. Structure of $(SM)^2$-II

4.3 OTHER MACHINES

The CORAL computer[10] is a multiprocessor in which processors are connected to form a binary tree. As of now, a prototype with fifteen processors is operational.

Onaga et al. are studying a special purpose machine for solving large scale band-limlted matrix equations based on systric array architecture (*Figure 15*) [11].

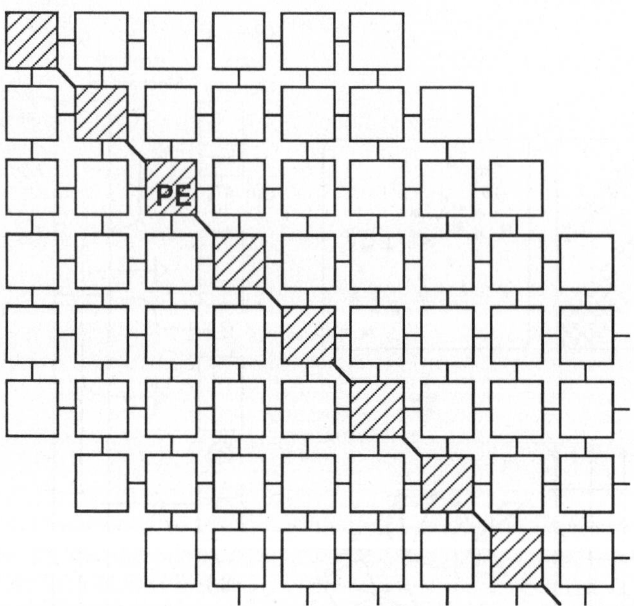

Figure 15. Global organization of a matrix equation machine

The BC processor array system[12] consists of 256 Z8 chips connected as a linear list. These processors work in one of the following three modes.

(1) *Pipeline mode.*

Each processor receives data from its left neighbouring processor and outputs data to its right neighbouring processor.

(2) *Direct mode.*

The host computer sends data to a processor.

(3) *Broadcast mode.*

The data are broadcast from by the host computer to all processors.

The BC processor array system behaves as a systric array and is suited for, for example, matrix operations and linear equation solving.

5. CONCLUSION

In this paper we presented a short survey of the current status in Japan of research and development of parallel processors for scientific and engineering applications. We would like to add that although there are many other interesting machines we did not mention, we omitted them, not because they are less interesting but because we lack sufficient information about them. Finally we must say that although the quantity of research into AI in Japan and the world is enormous, we also did not report them here as they have been adequently reported elsewhere.

References

[1] Takahashi,Y. : "Currently developed parallel computers", Journal of Information Processing Society of Japan, Vol.28, No.1, pp.10-18 (Jan. 1987) (in Japanese).

[2] Yuba,T. and Kashiwagi,H. : "The Japanese national project for new generation supercomputing systems", Parallel Computing, Vol.4, No.1, pp.1-16 (Feb. 1987).

[3] Terada,H., et al. : "A data-driven processor Q-p", IECE Data flow workshop, pp.75-78 (May 1986) (in Japanese).

[4] NEC Corp. : "FORTRAN77, 77/SX programing manual", (June 1985) (in Japanese).

[5] Fujitsu Ltd. : "FACOM VP system programing manual", (Aug. 1984) (in Japanese).

[6] Hitachi Ltd. : "Optimization FORTRAN77, HAP FORTRAN77 users manual", (Dec. 1984) (in Japanese).

[7] Kasahara,H. and Narita,S. : "Practical multiprocessor scheduling algorithms for efficient parallel processing", IEEE Trans. on Computer, Vol.C-33, No.11, pp.1023-1029 (Nov. 1984).

[8] Hoshino,T. : "An invitation to the world of PAX", COMPUTER, Vol.19, No.5, pp.68-79 (May 1986).

[9] Amano,H., Boku,T., Kudoh,T. and Aiso,H. : "$(SM)^2$-II: A new version of the Sparse Matrix Solving Machine", Proc. of the 12th Int. Symp. on Comp. Arch., pp.100-107 (June 1985).

[10] Takahashi,Y., et al. : "Efficiency of parallel computation on binary-tree machine Coral '83", Journal of Information Processing, Vol.8, No.4 (Mar. 1985).

[11] Onaga,K. and Takechi,T. : "On design of rotary array communication and wavefront-driven algorithms for solving large-scale band-limited matrix equations", Proc. of the 13th Int. Symp. on Comp. Arch., pp.308-315 (June 1986).

[12] Kaneda,Y., et al. : "BC processor array and highly parallel matrix computation", Trans. of Information Processing Society of Japan, Vol.24, No.2, pp.175-181 (Mar. 1983) (in Japanese).

A HIGH RESOLUTION PARALLEL LEGENDRE TRANSFORM ALGORITHM

D. F. Snelling

European Centre for Medium-Range Weather Forecasts
Shinfield Park,
Reading/Berkshire,
England

Abstract

The spectral weather forecasting model at ECMWF is a sophisticated parallel program which uses global memory for the large shared data structure which contains the spectral representation of the atmosphere. In this paper the structure of this model is described and the section of the program which updates and references the shared spectral data structure is isolated. This extract, the Legendre transforms, contains all the critical parallel structure in the model. These transform algorithms are described and their relative performance on the Cray X-MP and the ETA 10 is presented.

Introduction

The ECMWF (European Centre for Medium-Range Weather Forecasts) weather forecasting model performs calculations in three spaces: grid point space where physics and the dynamics of atmospheric motion are calculated, Fourier space where some east/west calculations are performed, and spectral space where some parts of the time stepping and horizontal diffusion are performed. The calculations in grid point space and Fourier space are completely independent for any north/south pair of latitude rows and can therefore be processed in parallel. In the current ECMWF operational model, the production resolution includes 320 lines of longitude and 160 lines of latitude. Since the north and south rows of latitude are paired, there is the potential of 80 parallel processes which can be easily separated from each other. The bulk of the calculation is in grid point space and, since a full line of latitude (across all points of longitude) is the typical vector, quite long vectors are used in all grid point calculations. For more details on the structure of the ECMWF model see [1,2,3]. The diagram below shows the basic structure of the model.

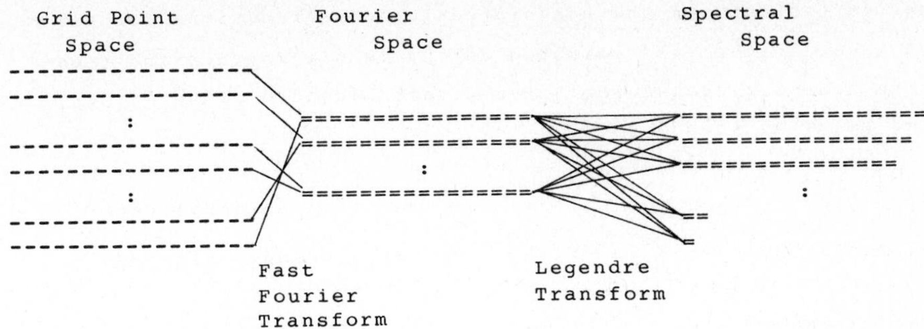

In the course of a single time step the data is cycled from grid point space, to Fourier space, to spectral space, and back through Fourier space to grid point. The difficult step in the process, from the point of view of parallel processing, is in transforming from Fourier space into spectral space. The Legendre transform requires all the elements in each Fourier row to update the entire spectral data structure at every time step. Hence it is only in the Legendre transforms that parallel processes must synchronise with each other. The Legendre transforms, direct and inverse, are the focus of the remainder of this paper.

The Legendre Transforms

The spherical harmonics defined below are used as basis functions for integration in spectral space.

$$y_n^m(\lambda,\theta) = e^{im\lambda} * P_n^m(\sin(\theta))$$

where: λ = longitude

θ = latitude

m = zonal wavenumber (from the Fourier transform)

n = total wavenumber n >= m

P = the associated Legendre function.

For the purposes of this paper we will restrict our discussion to a triangular truncation of the wave numbers such that m=1,N and n=m,N. This is the truncation used in the model at ECMWF. The value of N which corresponds to the 320 by 160 resolution in grid point space is

106. The coefficients of the associated Legendre functions for all m and n and each latitude are computed during initialisation and then used in the Legendre transforms. The direct Legendre transform is summarised below in pseudo code.

```
Spec(*,*) = 0.0                            / zero the spectral data

FOR row=1 TO 80 DO                         / north & south already
                                           / combined

   FOR m=0 TO 106 DO                       / for all zonal wave numbers

      FOR n=m TO 106 DO                    / for all total wave numbers

         Spec(n,m) = Spec(n,m) +           / add in the Fourier
                                           / contribution

            Four(m,row) * Lcof(n,m,row)    / times the Legendre
                                           / coefficients
```

The inverse Legendre transform is summarised below:

```
FOR row=1 TO 80 DO                         / compute each row
                                           / independently

   Four(*,row) = 0.0                       / zero the Fourier data

      FOR m=0 TO 106 DO                    / for all zonal wave numbers

         FOR n=m to 106 DO                 / for all total wave numbers

            Four(m,row) = Four(m,row) +    / add in the Spectral
                                           / contribution

               Spec(n,m) * InvLcof(n,m,row) / times the Inverse
                                            / Legendre coefficients
```

It should be noted that the above summaries are only intended to give an indication of the structure of the transforms and are not precise definitions. In particular the variables Spec and Four in the inner loop are really vectors and therefore in this algorithm the innermost operation is a vector equals vector plus vector times scalar. The length of this vector operation is equal to the number of atmospheric levels times the number of prognostic variables times two for real and imaginary parts. In this case we are using 19 levels and 4 variables and therefore the vector length is 152. For more information on the Legendre transform and the spectral method see [4,5,6,7].

The Parallel Algorithm Structure

There are two major issues involved in the development of parallel algorithms for the Legendre Transforms. The first is memory allocation and management, and the second is the synchronisation of the associative reduction of the spectral data structure in the direct Legendre transform. (In the inverse transform, reduction is not performed).

Memory

Since the spectral data structure requires 878256 words of memory, the allocation of memory resources cannot be ignored. In the version running on the Cray X-MP two copies of the data are kept in memory.[1] The Fourier data is then processed back into the other copy by associative reduction. In a full weather forecasting model, the Fourier data would be transformed by FFT into grid point space before being added to the new spectral data. The second copy is then copied onto the first, the second is zeroed, and a the next time step is performed.[2] During the direct Legendre transform on the Cray X-MP all parallel processes update the same data structure and are controlled as described below. On the ETA 10, the approach is quite different.

Since the shared memory on an ETA 10 is not directly addressable by parallel processes, the memory allocation must be handled differently. The local memories on the ETA 10 are quite large (four million words), hence two copies of the spectral data are kept in each

---

1 In this paper a one scan approach is used. In a two scan approach, as is used at ECMWF for the current production model, the Fouriere data is generated and written to data files in a separate scan. In this way only one copy of the spectral data is required in main memory at the cost of additional I/O. This approach requires more total memory than the one scan approach, but the Fourier data may reside on secondary memory such as the Cray SSD.

2 A less costly approach is available on a Cray X-MP if the POINTER extension is employed to perform the transfer of the spectral data. This was avoided because of the non-standard nature of this extension to FORTRAN and the fact that compared to the transforms themselves the transfer of data is a small and rapid operation.

processor's local memory.[3] Each processor then performs the necessary calculation on the rows which are assigned to it. In this case no synchronisation is required during the calculation phase since each processor has a private copy of the spectral data. After all the rows have been added to the local copies of the spectral data, all copies are combined by associative reduction as described below.

Synchronisation

In the inverse Legendre transform there is no synchronisation required. The first spectral data structure is only read by each parallel process and the Fourier and grid point data are local to the process. On the Cray this local data is kept in TASK COMMON [9]. In the direct transform each process must read, increment, and write back the entire spectral data structure for each row of latitude. There are two ways this global reduction is performed. The first is under the control of "locks" [9]. Locks are a Cray facility to implement critical regions. The spectral data structure in divided into six parts and each process in turn locks each part in succession, updates that part, and then unlocks it. In this way no two processes are allowed to update the same part of the spectral data at the same time. This approach, although easily implemented, has a draw back as a result of the non-associative nature of floating point arithmetic. The locks do not control the order in which the parts of the spectral array are updated. As a result, any two runs of the same program may produce different results.

Although it is easily argued that both results are equally correct, the fact that the results are not reproducible can cause difficulties during debugging and program behaviour analysis.

A second version of this code is therefore provided which, through the use of Cray "events" [9], forces the parallel processes to update

---

3 If an approach similar to the two scan method above is employed on the ETA, only one copy of the spectral data need be resident on each processor. In addition, algorithms have been developed by the author which require that only a small portion of the spectral data structure reside in the local memory, but these algorithms require frequent transfers to and from the shared memory like in the Cray algorithm. This would be necessary on a local memory machine with much smaller memories.

the spectral data structure in a fixed order. This has some impact on the performance, but does provide reproducible results.

In the ETA 10 version of this code, the multiple copies of the second spectral data structure are combined in a very simple way. The first process copies its version of the spectral data to the shared memory. Then each other process copies this data from shared memory into its local memory, updates it with its local copy, and then returns it to the shared memory. In this way the spectral data is always updated in the same order thus providing reproducible results. In addition the full spectral data structure is only transferred to and from the global memory once for each parallel process. Whereas in the Cray version, since there is no local memory, the full spectral data structure is transferred to and from global memory once for each pair of grid point rows. This means that there is a greater potential for memory bank conflicts.

The reduction algorithm implemented on the ETA 10 is purely sequential. This is an artificial limitation imposed because the ETA Multitasking Simulator makes no allowances for memory bank conflicts in the shared memory. Since in the above algorithm only one processor at a time is accessing the shared memory, there would be no memory conflicts at all. The algorithm could easily be altered to allow for parallel reduction, this would still provide reproducible results, and hence the present approach represents a worst case in terms of performance.

Results

The table below summarizes the results of test runs carried out at ECMWF on the Cray X-MP/48, the ETA 10 single processor at Florida State University, and the ETA Multitasking Simulator running on the 205 at the University of Minnesota. The Fortran compiler for the Cray runs was CFT 1.14, and for the ETA and simulator runs, the FORTRAN-200 compiler was used. Although the simplicity of the code is such that very little improvement is expected from later versions of these compilers, when a compiler which generates code timed for the ETA-10 instead of the 205 is available, some improvement is expected. In all cases greater performance could be achieved through the use of assembler. In all versions 64 bit floating point arithmetic was used throughout.

Program Version	Machine	Clock	1 Time	2 Time	2 Ep	3 Time	3 Ep	4 Time	4 Ep
Serial	X-MP	8.5	2.434						
Serial	205	20.0	3.706						
Serial	ETA/E	10.5	1.571						
Serial	ETA/G	7.0	1.047						
Locks	X-MP	8.5		1.329	0.916	0.950	0.854	0.778	0.782
Events	X-MP	8.5		1.330	0.915	0.946	0.858	0.791	0.770
Reduction	ETA/E	10.5		0.800	0.982	0.491	0.938	0.449	0.875
Reduction	ETA/G	7.0		0.533	0.982	0.327	0.938	0.299	0.875

These timings were measured as elapsed wall clock time in machine cycles and converted to seconds.[4] The multitasking efficiency (Ep) is equal to the serial time divided by the product of the number of parallel processes and the parallel time. All the parallel times for the ETA are projections based on runs of the ETA Multitasking Simulator. These figures are corrected for the paging which occurred on the 205 and which would be absent on the ETA. The paging degradation was measured at 3%, 5%, and 8% for 2, 3, and 4 task simulation runs.

Conclusions

There are two issues that are noteworthy in the above results. The first is that after compensating for the difference in clock speeds, the ETA is about twice as fast as the Cray. This is what would be expected from a two pipe machine on very long vectors. It should be noted that with a vector length of 152 this result is quite impressive. It is clear that some of the difficulties which required very long vectors on the 205 have been remedied on the ETA 10. This

[4] The Cray runs were made, in February 1987, on the 9.5 ns X-MP at ECMWF and took 286.35 million cycles per time step for the serial run. On February 25, 1987, when the ETA run was made, the clock on the FSU machine was set at 12.5 ns, and the serial ETA run took 149.51 million cycles per time step. The 205 took 185.3 million cycles per time step. As neither the FSU ETA nor the X-MP at ECMWF represent the most current machines offered by these manufactures, the timings have been scaled to the 8.5 ns X-MP and the G and E series ETA machines.

is particularly apparent when the timings of the 205 and ETA are adjusted for cycle time and compared (see footnote [4]).

The second issue is that of the difference in multitasking efficiency. The results here are contrary to intuition. The ETA multitasking library is much more cumbersome than the Cray multitasking library, and requires the transfer of data to and from the shared memory [8, 9]. The difference, in the author's opinion, lies in the memory bank conflicts which arise in the Cray when the number of tasks is increased. Note that the difference between the two machines increases as the number of tasks is increased to four.

Lastly, it should be noted that the Legendre transforms make-up only about 20% of the execution time of the full model. Since all the multitasking activity in the model can be isolated in the Legendre transforms, it is the author's belief that the relative multitasking behaviour of these machines would not change in an operational weather model. However, the raw performance of a full weather model would depend more on the vectorisation characteristics of the physics than on the multitasking structure of the model.

Acknowledgments

Special thanks are due to to George Mozdzynski of Control Data Limited and Dr. Clifford Arnold of ETA Systems Inc., for their help with the ETA and 205 tests.

Bibliography

[1] Louis J-F. ed., Research Manual 2, ECMWF Forecast Model, Adiabatic Part: a Meteorological Bulletin (ECMWF, Reading: 1985).

[2] Louis J-F. ed., Research Manual 3, ECMWF Forecast Model, Physical Parameterization: a Meteorological Bulletin (ECMWF, Reading: 1984).

[3] Dent, D., The Multitasking Spectral Model at ECMWF, from Proceedings of Workshop on Using Multiprocessors in Meteorological Models (ECMWF, Reading: 1984).

[4] Belousov, S.L., Tables of Normalized Associated Legendre Polynomials, (Pergamon Press, New York: 1962).

[5] Daley, R. and Bourassa, Y., Rhomboidal versus Triangular Spherical Harmonic Truncation: some Verification Statistics., Atmosphere No. 16, 1978, p.187-196.

[6] Eliasen, E., Machenhauer, B., and Rasmussen, E., On a Numerical Method for Integration of the Hydrodynamic Equations with a Spectral Representation of Horizontal Fields. Rep. No. 2 Institut for Teoretisk Meteorologi, University of Copenhagen, 1970.

[7] Machenhauer, B., and Rasmussen, E., On the Integration of the Spectral Hydrodynamic Equations by a Transform Method. Rep. No. 2 Institut for Teoretisk Meteorologi, University of Copenhagen, 1972.

[8] Arnold, C.N., "Multitasking Library: Design Summary and Specification", ETA Internal document, July 1985.

[9] Cray Research Inc., Programming Library Reference Manual, SR-0113, (Cray Research Inc., Mendota Heights, Minnesota), 1986, p. 14-1 to 14-31.

Parallelization of a reservoir simulator

by Terje Kårstad and Adolfo Henriquez, Statoil
and Knut Korsell, IBM

Abstract

Numerical reservoir simulation demands very high computing performance. Vectorization has been widely used as a performance enhancing technique. Parallel computing can also be used to satisfy the increasing requirements of more sophisticated models.

This paper presents the implementation of a novel method of parallelizing an already vectorized reservoir simulator, which has the significant advantage of reducing not only the elapsed CPU-time, but also the total CPU-time used. The method relies on the physical independence of isolated geological structures, coupled through the wells, a feature present in many of the hydrocarbon reservoirs found in the North Sea.

The vectorized and parallelized code has already been in production a period of time. Results are shown for a realistic case.

Introduction

There are strong economical incentives for reservoir simulation. Small increases of the recovery of the proven reserves in, for example, the Norwegian sector of the North Sea are worth millions of dollars at the current prices. Grid sizes for full field simulations may be several tens of thousands of cells, and large computer resources are used in pursuing optimal recovery strategies.

Statoil has vectorized the reservoir simulator currently in use in the IBM 3090-200 with vector facility [1] (later on called 3090-200/VF) with satisfying speed-up and reduction of CPU-times. However, for some of the largest fields, further reductions are required to decrease turnaround times. Most of the CPU-time used is bound to the solution of the large sparse systems of linear equations arising at each time step. Parallelization of the algorithms used in solving these equations is, at the present time, still an inmature field. Several of the techniques proposed, even at high levels of sophistications [2], actually increase the CPU-time involved, though reducing the total elapsed time. This involves, in any realistic accounting system, higher prices of execution and therefore a deterrence to more detailed simulations.

It is our feeling that in the current state of the research efforts, the focus for industrial applications has to be concentrated on the possibilities given by the natural independence of some of the physical processes involved. In our case, an opportunity is given by the fact that in the North Sea, and in several other oil producing areas, some hydrocarbon reservoirs consist of isolated geological structures which are coupled through the offshore platforms or through clusters of wells, and through the production control which has to be provided at this level for complying with sale contracts or optimal exploitation. Many of the reservoirs where Statoil has interests fall on this category.

The basic idea behind our method is to solve the set of linear equations arising at each Newton, or non-linear, iteration independently for each isolated structure, and couple the results only at the end of the successful convergence of each of the linear iterations.

This approach has several advantages.

- It may be implemented in any reservoir simulator, as only the numbering of the blocks must be modified, and the algorithm of the linear solver requires only minor modifications.

- The granularity of the tasks generated is very coarse. As the presently available mechanism from Fortran of parallelizing in the IBM 3090 family of machines by means of macrotasking has an overhead of 75 microseconds (for empty subroutines) [3] , gains can only be achieved if a large amount of machine instructions are sent to the separate central processors. Our approach meets this rather stringent requirement.

- Most linear solvers require an amount of work proportional to a power of the number of unknowns. By decomposing the matrix in smaller matrices, a significant reduction of the number of floating operations is achieved.

- In cases where some of the isolated structures have different requirements for the number of linear iterations needed in order to get convergence, the solution of the whole matrix involves iterating for regions which essentially have converged. Our method performs only the number of linear iterations needed for each structure, giving important savings of the CPU-time used.

In the following sections, we will give a short description of the algorithm as needed for the understanding of the method used. We will then give some details of the implementation in our machine and the mechanisms used for multitasking. Results and conclusions will be given in the last two sections.

Short description of the linear solver

The solution of the coupled non-linear equations arising in reservoir simulation, using Newton's method, involves the repeated solution of sets of linear equations.

A seven point discretization using finite difference methods for three dimensional systems leads to a seven-banded matrix.

Reservoir simulation also includes modelling multiblock wells. The well terms introduce extra degree of coupling between cells. In many simulation problems the flow rates of a well are directly influenced by the behavior of other wells in the field. For the well flow rate targets to be met exactly, they must be recalculated at every Newton iteration, and the derivatives of the flow rates with respect to all other wells should be included in the Jacobian matrix equation.

Including all the derivatives of the well flow rates in the Jacobian matrix of the wells, denoted as D in formula 1 below, could make it a very dense matrix. This would of course be difficult to invert. In the simulator which we have modified only the diagonal elements are included. As we will see later, this makes it easier to decouple the full matrix in one matrix for each independent structure in the reservoir [4].

When the well flow rate targets change at each iteration, the convergence rate is reduced since the solution itself becomes a moving target. In order to speed-up the simulation, the flow rates of the wells are updated only in the first few Newton iterations [5].

Figure 1.a shows an example of an idealized oil field consisting of two isolated structures being produced by one platform and a usual ordering of the grid blocks and the wells, which leads to the matrix structure shown in figure 1.b. In the following we describe briefly the solution procedure used to solve the matrix shown in figure 1.b. This is described in detail by Holmes [6].

Let Ncell be the total number of active grid cells and Nwell be the number of wells. Further let
A be a banded Ncell x Ncell matrix,
B be a sparse Ncell x Nwell matrix,
C be a sparse Nwell x Ncell matrix,
D be a diagonal Nwell x Nwell matrix,
b be a vector of lenght Ncell and

b_w, a vector of length Nwell.
Then the matrix equation can be written in the following way:.

$$\begin{vmatrix} A & B \\ C & D \end{vmatrix} \times \begin{vmatrix} x \\ x_w \end{vmatrix} = \begin{vmatrix} b \\ b_w \end{vmatrix} \qquad (1)$$

With this partitioning, the matrix equation becomes:

$$Ax + Bx_w = b \qquad (2)$$

$$Cx + Dx_w = b_w \qquad (3)$$

$$x_w = D^{-1}[b_w - Cx] \qquad (4)$$

$$[A - BD^{-1}C]x = b - BD^{-1}b_w \qquad (5)$$

The linear equations are solved using an iterative technique. The ORTHOMIN algorithm [7] is used as accelerating technique and Nested Factorization [8] is used as preconditioning method.

Description of the parallelization method

In reservoir simulation different ordering of the grid blocks have been used. These methods usually treat the reservoir as just one box of cells. Below we show an ordering scheme which uses the fact that the reservoir may consists of several isolated geological structures.

Figure 2.a shows the same reservoir as figure 1.a. Since the reservoir actually consists of two independent isolated geological structures, there can be no flow of reservoir fluid between the two structures. By ordering the grid blocks and wells as in figure 2.a, we get two sets of linear equations which can be solved independently, as shown in figure 2.b. Each independent matrix is composed of a seven-banded matrix and the well matrices. Therefore on each separate set of linear equations we can use the solution method described previously.

We have used natural ordering of the cells within each structure, but other types of ordering schemes could be used. The only information the program needs is given in the input data file, and consists of the number of independent structure (two in this example) and the first and the last cell number in the X, Y and Z directions for each structure. In fig. 1.a, this is 1-2, 1-2, 1-3 for the first structure, and 3-5, 1-2, 1-3 for the second structure in the example.

The iterative linear solver part of the simulator consists of several Fortran subroutines, including the routine with the main iteration loop controlling the convergence. The multitasking is achieved by dispatching all the linear solver routines for each of the independent reservoirs. Syncronization is done after the linear equations for all reservoirs are solved. The support for doing this on the IBM-3090/VF is through the Multitasking Facility (later on called MTF), which is part of the standard Fortran provided by IBM. The multitasking facility is supported through calls to the run time library routines that use standard operating system facilities to schedule the tasks to run on the available CPU's.

The multitasking facility is suitable for coarse grain granularity of the independent tasks and therefore to be considered as macrotasking. The overhead involved, as previously mentioned, is approx. 75 microseconds and therefore requires the parallel task to execute several thousands instructions to make it worthwhile to use the MTF. In our case the independent tasks execute several millions instructions and the overhead involved in using MTF is therefore negligible.

The parallel version of the simulator is running together with other batch programs and interactive users on the 3090-200/VF and the system is typically running at 100 percent utilization for long periods of time. However, we have no indications of any negative effect on the system and on the other users when running our parallelized code using the vector units simultaneously. The main reason for this is that the tasks which have been dispatched for parallel execution are being controlled by the operating system MVS/XA, as any other task in the system asking for CPU resources and therefore under control of the priority system in MVS/XA.

As other workers in the field of parallelization have pointed out before, we experienced that debugging a parallelized program is a non trivial exercise, as the updating of the variables and its protection is dependent on the undetermined time when they are calculated by the different processors. However, the relative coarse way in which this is done in the MTF, where all the variables are passed on to the subroutines in the call statement, make this part of the parallelization somewhat easier than in microtasking environments.

Results

Presently this parallelized code is being run for a large oil field which Statoil operates, consisting of three isolated structures. The number of cells used in the numerical simulation study is 8700 cells for structure 1, 6960 for structure 2 and 12180 for structure 3. The physical characteristics of the reservoirs, and the fact that we have only a two-way machine, are such that it is convenient to run two of the three isolated structures together, as separate tasks.

Some timing measurements for a typical run are as follows:

Tasks 1 and 2	19.60
Task 3	28.12
Linear solver	47.72
Whole simulation	104.64

The numbers are derived from using a sampling utility [9] with a 1 ms sampling rate. The sampling utility was executed for 40 minutes. The numbers are therefore only relative, and indicate how many times a certain piece of the code was sampled. Therefore, they are directly proportional to the CPU-time used.

This gives 41 percent of the CPU-time spent in the linear solver used by tasks 1 and 2 and 59 percent is used by task 3.

Since the linear solver, which has been parallelized, takes 46% of the total simulation time in this example, the savings in turnaround time are significant.

It is more difficult to measure in this realistic example the gains achieved by the decomposition of the matrices in smaller matrices and by the use of just the amount of linear iterations needed in each reservoir. It is sufficient indication that task 3, in many cases, needed up to 25 iterations, whereas tasks 1 and 2 converged after 2 or 3 iterations. One measure of the total efficiency may also be given by the fact that the total CPU-time used in one of the runs with the previous vectorized version was 1.6 times more than the present parallelized, vectorized version. The degree of overlap between the tasks and the number of tasks is very dependent on the physical model and will therefore vary between cases.

Several of the other routines in the simulator using significant amount of CPU-time can be parallelizable with the same scheme as used for the linear solver.

It has been gratifying that in several of the runs, the elapsed time has been significantly less than the total CPU-time used.

We emphasize that our approach is not limited to two or three isolated structures, but in this particular case the number of processors available, the relative size of the reservoirs and the amount of work needed to solve the numerical problem was such that this was a convenient division.

Another important issue is the memory requirement for running the parallelized version of the code. Running a simulation on a large grid is a very demanding task not only from a computational point of view but also on the memory system of the computer. Some of the larger simulations require more than 30-40 MBytes of real memory for the main working arrays that need to stay in physical memory during the whole simulation. The total size of the program is such that this is the amount of real memory which is needed in order to fully utilize the CPU (100% utilization) without being slowed down by the virtual memory system. Measurements of memory use while running the parallel version of the simulator on this field showed a working set (the amount of memory that must be available in real memory) of approximately 9000 pages (36 Mbytes). The total size of the program was much bigger, but because of the virtual memory system on the 3090 family of machines, parts of the program are moved to secondary storage as soon as they have not beed used during a system defined period, in order to release main memory. The 36 Mbytes are the minimum that is needed to let the program run efficiently, and consists mainly of the key working arrays used by the linear solver. The number of grid cells in this problem was several tens of thousands.

Conclusions

We would like to summarize our work in the following points:

- The total speedup of the linear solver is significant, the CPU-time was drastically reduced and the use of multitasking reduced the elapsed time in the linear solver significantly.
- Running large simulations using both the 3090 vector units and multitasking together gave no negative effects on the other concurrent users on the same system.
- For this particular application, parallelization and vectorization techniques have complemented each other. Since most of the vectorizing effort was concentrated in getting vectors with a length equal to the total number of active blocks, the decomposition resulted in vector lengths which still made successful use of the vector facility. It is interesting to notice that, once physical processes have been identified, inhibitors to parallelization are weaker than for vectorization.
- We have experienced no negative effects in using the macrotasking facility on our 3090-200/VF system.
- The method of independent structures can be used on other parts of the simulator to increase the parallelization and therefore reduce the elapsed time even further.
- The debugging phase of the project was more time consuming than expected, as debugging tasks that runs in parallel requires a conceptually different approach to that commonly used for serial codes.

Nomenclature

A = Matrix of coefficients for the linear equations of the cells.
B = Matrix of coefficients for the linear equations showing interactions between the wells and the cells
C = Matrix of coefficients for the linear equations showing interactions between the wells and the cells
D = Matrix of the wells interactions
x = Vector of solutions of the linear equations
x_w = Vector of solutions of the well linear equations
b = Vector of residuals of the cells
b_w = Vector of residuals of the wells

Acknowledgments.

ECL has given us its support in this work, which we acknowledge.

The authors thank Dr. T. Steihaug for his support and advice during this project, and S. Gulbrandsen for useful discussions.

The permission of Statoil to publish this work is gratefully acknowledged.

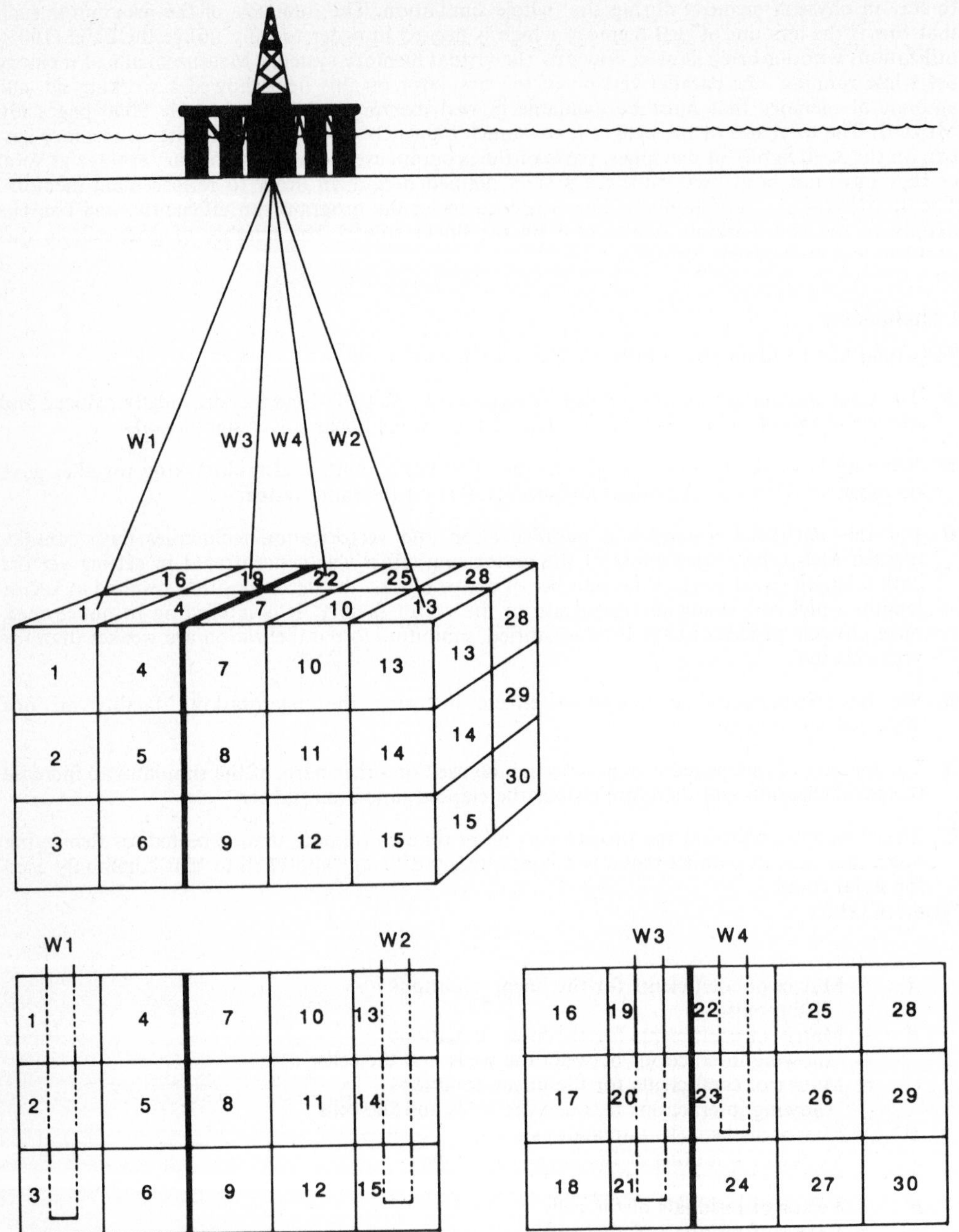

Fig. 1.a) Example of a reservoir consisting of two isolated structures coupled through the production control at the platform level and cross sections showing the well connections and a natural ordering of the cells.

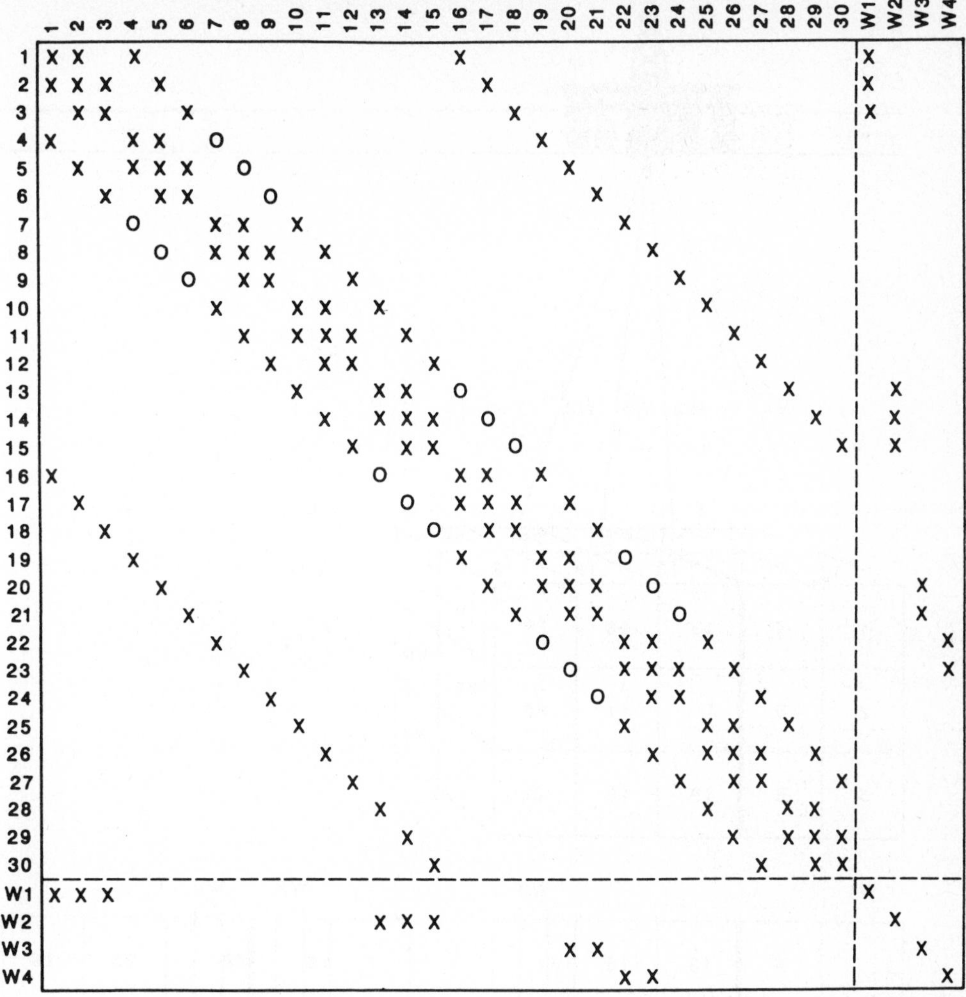

Fig. 1.b) Matrix originated from the ordering shown in fig. 1.a.

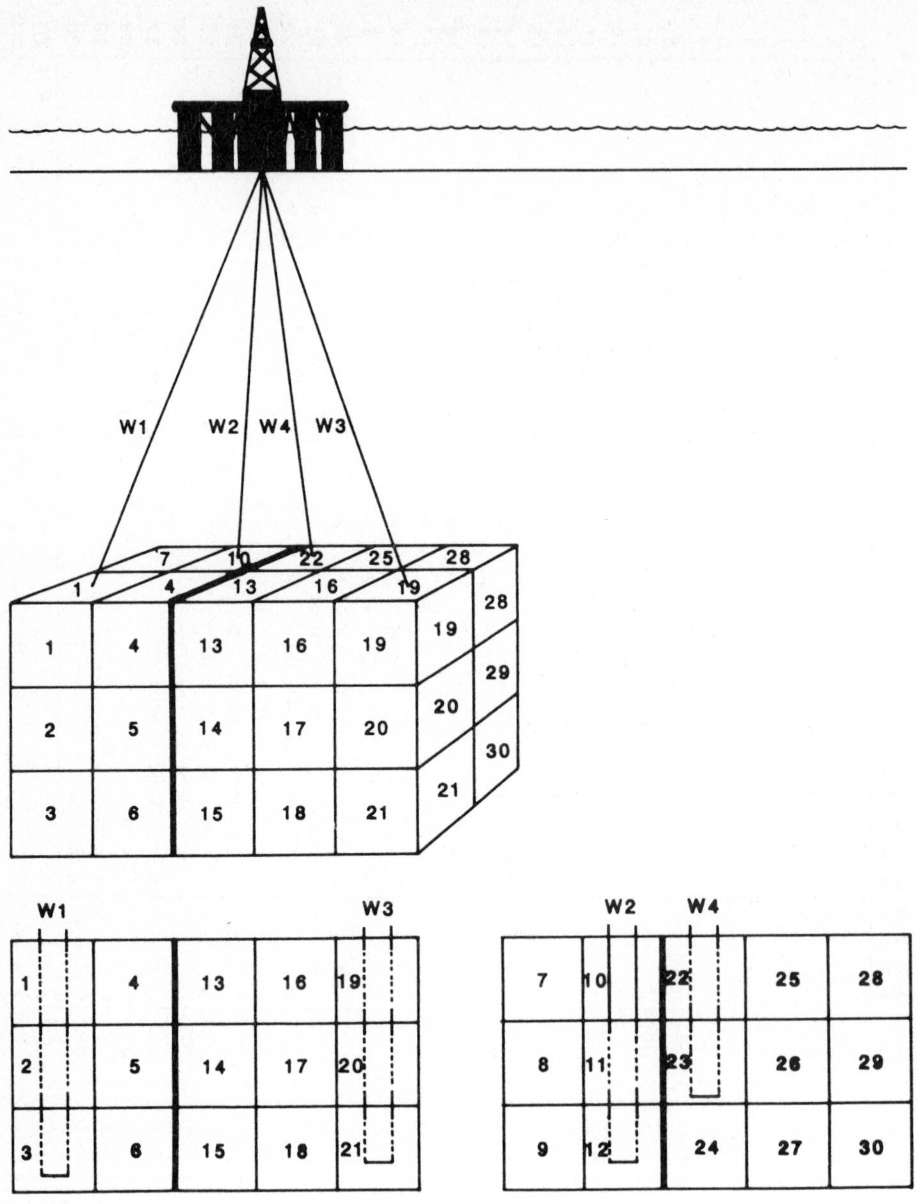

Fig. 2.a) Each structure of the reservoir shown in fig. 1.a is ordered separately. The cross sections show the well connections and the new ordering of the cells numbers.

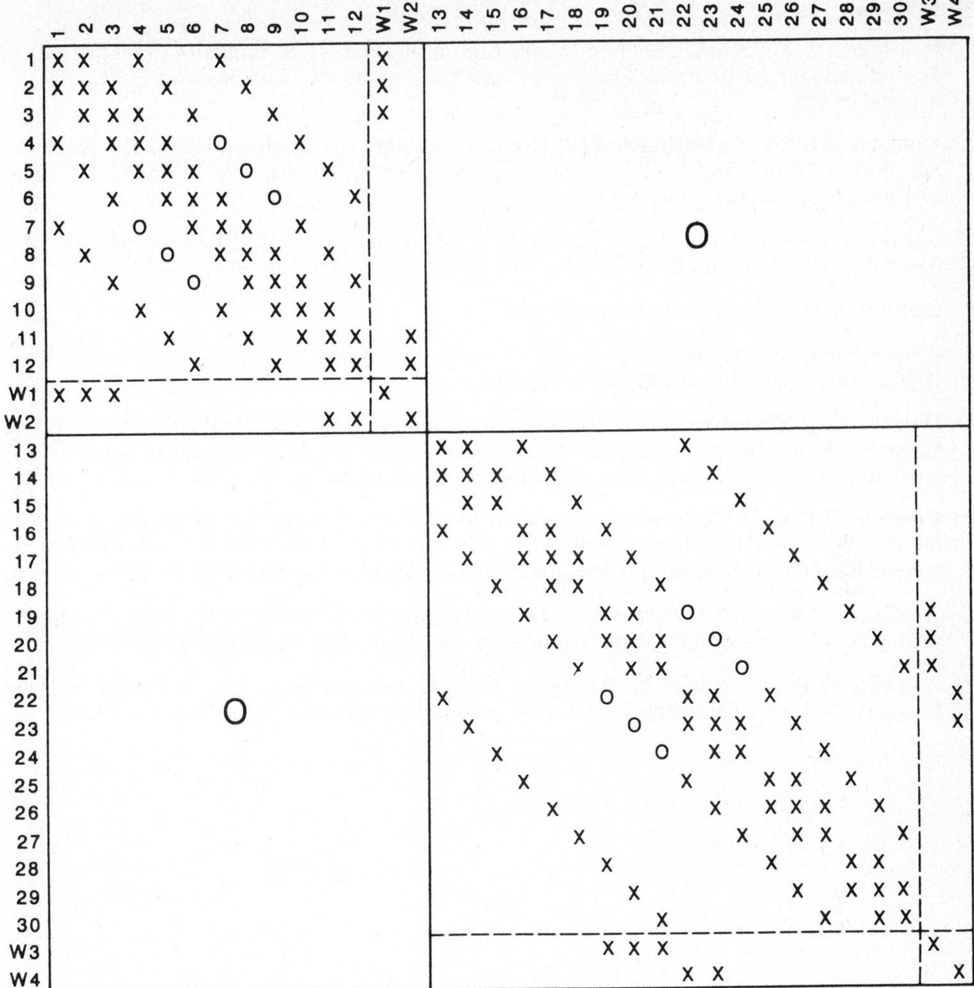

Fig. 2.b) Matrix originated from the ordering shown in fig. 2.a.

References

1. Henriquez, A. : "Vectorization and Parallelization of a Reservoir Simulator', presented at the Second Seminar on Reservoir Description and Simulation with Emphasis on EOR, Oslo, 3-5 September 1986.

2. Killough, J.E, "A Three-Dimensional Domain Decomposition Algorithm for the Numerical Solution of Elliptic and Parabollic Partial Differential Equations", Ph. D. thesis, University of Rice, Houston, Texas, March 1986.

3. Carnevali, P., Sguazzero, P. and Zecca, V. : "Microtasking on IBM multiprocessors", IBM Journal of Research and Development, Vol. 30, No. 6, November 1986, 574-582.

4. Cheshire, I.M., personal communication.

5. Eclipse Reference Manuals, Exploration Consultants Limited, Highlands Farm, Greys Road, Henley-on-Thames, Oxon RG9 4PS, England.

6. Holmes, J.A. :"Enhancements to the Strongly Coupled, Fully Implicit Well Model: Wellbore Crossflow Modelling and Collective Well Control', paper SPE 12259, presented at the Seventh Reservoir Simulation Symposium, San Francisco, November 15-18, 1983.

7. Vinsome, P.K.W. : "Orthomin, an Iterative Method for Solving Sparse Banded Sets of Simultaneous Linear Equations", paper SPE 5729 presented at the Fourth Symposium on Numerical Simulation of Reservoir Performance, Los Angeles, California, (Feb. 1976).

8. Appleyard, J.R. and Cheshire, I.M. :"Nested Factorization", paper SPE 12264, presented at the Seventh Reservoir Simulation Symposium, San Francisco, November 15-18, 1983.

9. Program Problem Evaluator, Reference Manual for MVS/370 and MVS/XA Systems, European Software Company Ltd., Unit 5, Leopardstown Office Park Foxrock, Dublin 18.

A Computer Graphics Rendering Algorithm for use on a SIMD Machine

Scott Whitman Scott Dyer

The Ohio Supercomputer Project
The Ohio State University

ABSTRACT

An algorithm to render shaded pictures is presented which takes advantage of the architecture of a vector computer for improved performance. This paper indicates the changes which need to be considered when designing and implementing a vectorized scanline rendering algorithm. This paper includes general information on the Convex C-1, a SIMD computer, and specific details on an approach taken to vectorize a scanline algorithm.

Introduction

Polygon scan conversion algorithms have always been the mainstay of computer graphics production. They afford a good compromise between speed and image quality, and continue to be the subject of significant research. Recent shading models for these algorithms have improved the "realism" in still images as well as animated sequences. As more complex image renderings have been developed, the computation time to display a single frame has increased. Hence, we needed to consider advances in computer architecture to help speed up the rendering process. Vector computers are continuing to become more affordable and this type of machine was the logical choice for a scanline algorithm due to the inherent parallelism in the rendering calculations. However, hardware alone cannot solve the problem of calculation time. Software needs to be revised to most effectively achieve a high level of performance from vector machines. This paper presents the initial effort on a scanline algorithm designed for extracting high performance from a vector computer.

Scanline algorithms are well understood, and a wealth of material has been written about them. In 1971, Schumacker et. al. [9] compared a variety of hidden surface algorithms and included the Watkins, Romney and Bouknight scanline techniques in their survey. Since then, Carpenter [12], Crocker [16], and others have further refined the scanline algorithm.

Members of the Computer Graphics Research Group (CGRG) are involved in the Ohio Supercomputer Project, which, through a statewide multi-university cooperative effort will bring a Cray XMP-2/4 to Ohio State in June of 1987. A major component of the Ohio Supercomputer Project is **apE**, the animation production Environment, which will provide sophisticated graphics tools for scientific data analysis. CGRG began design work on the apE system in late 1986. As a part of the supercomputer graphics project, CGRG has acquired a Convex C-1 computer. The Convex uses a vector architecture similar to the Cray, runs a version of UNIX, and provides one of the first commercial vectorizing C compilers. The arrival of the Convex in the summer of 1986 prompted us to examine the possibilities of a vectorized scanline algorithm. The challenge was to design and implement an algorithm that could take advantage of vectorizing hardware and still run efficiently on a broad range of workstations and computers.

None of the individuals involved in the design and implementation of this algorithm had worked on a vector computer previously. This paper will illustrate the process of code optimization, the successes (and mistakes) we experienced along the way, and some general guidelines on vectorization. The work presented here illustrates some techniques which may be employed in designing a scanline algorithm for a vector machine.

Previous Work

There have been a variety of implementations of hidden surface removal algorithms on multiprocessors (Multiple Instruction Multiple Data, or MIMD) and vector processors (Single Instruction Multiple Data, or SIMD). In the case of MIMD implementations, the main problem seems to be anti-aliasing, since the pixel coverage information is not available when each processor needs it. Weinberg [17] illustrates an algorithm which handles this problem, but it is designed for a hardware implementation. Fiume, Fournier, and Rudolph [13] describe an algorithm that handles anti-aliasing which was implemented on a general purpose ultracomputer. The ultracomputer allows connections of processing elements in such a way that programs appear to have serial semantics but parallel execution.

Several MIMD and SIMD hardware implementations exist; see [10,11] for further reference.

In regards to SIMD implementations, published accounts deal with vectorized ray tracing algorithms. Max [14] designed a program for the specific application of ray tracing water wave reflections of islands in a scene. The rays are reflected a maximum of two times from the water, insuring a simple vectorization. Several specific tasks are vectorized, including the calculation of the normal vectors for the waves, the depth buffer for hidden surface elimination, and the calculation of intersections between reflected rays and the islands. This represents a highly specific use of vectorization for ray tracing and is not generally applicable to other types of rendering.

Plunkett and Bailey [15] describe a general implementation of vectorization for ray tracing Constructive Solid Geometry (CSG) models. Their approach vectorizes both ray intersection calculations and the CSG tree traversal of primitive volumes. The ray calculations can be vectorized by placing all rays (whether incident from the eye or from a reflection) into a ray queue. When the queue is full (500 elements), all intersections are calculated in a vector mode. Since the objects are constructed from primitives, the construction tree can be traversed in a vector mode as well.

None of these published accounts deal with the vectorization of a traditional scanline algorithm. The natural parallelism of ray tracing makes it particularly appropriate for vectorization. A scanline algorithm also exhibits significant parallel operation, and, as we will show, can be vectorized.

The Convex C-1

The Convex C-1 computer is an entry-level vector supercomputer that offers, for under one million dollars, approximately twenty-five percent of the power of a Cray 1S. The Convex has a scalar processing unit which operates at 6.2 MIPS and a vector processor with a peak speed of 60 MFLOPS and a sustained speed of approximately 10 MFLOPS. The C-1 can support up to one gigabyte of real memory; our system has 16 megabytes. The system uses a variant of the UNIX operating system with Berkeley enhancements. Convex provides vectorizing FORTRAN and C compilers. The Vectorizing C Compiler is a recent Convex product, and we have worked closely with Convex in understanding both its power and its limitations. Convex provides ***csd***, an enhanced version of Berkeley's ***dbx*** symbolic debugger, as well as the normal complement of profiling and compilation tools. No tools specifically designed to debug vector code are provided.

The Vectorizing C Compiler provided a number of challenges. While C allows the programmer to build complex interlocked data structures, these data models do not always lend themselves to efficient, vectorized code. Indeed, as we will discuss below, one of our most significant optimization steps involved abandoning our interlocked hierarchical data structure for a FORTRAN style list of arrays.

Design of the Algorithm

A polygon scanline algorithm renders a scene by shading the polygons for each object based on simple lighting models. The z-buffer approach sorts all polygons which intersect a particular pixel and shades the polygon closest to the eye. A scanline z-buffer reduces the memory requirement of a traditional z-buffer by limiting the values chosen to those on the current scanline. The main problem with the z-buffer approach lies in anti-aliasing: when a polygon overwrites a pixel, it destroys any information that could be used to eliminate aliasing. Loren Carpenter has proposed a solution to this problem which he calls the A-buffer [12].

Essentially, the A-buffer maintains information about all polygon fragments (that portion of a polygon which intersects a pixel) which contribute to a pixel. A mask is stored indicating how each fragment crosses the pixel and what part of the pixel is covered. All of these fragments are sorted in Z. The fragment masks are compared and can be "summed" until they are exhausted or the pixel is completely covered. The implementation presented here uses ideas from the A-buffer in addition to Crow's anti-aliasing technique [18], area coverage of fragments is computed but the fragment location within the pixel is not computed.

Algorithm Outline

The algorithm is a scanline z-buffer which postpones all calculations of area and z-depth of pixel fragments to the final step before rendering. Although a typical scanline z-buffer algorithm would calculate these values sequentially for each pixel, that process is inherently scalar and must be modified to allow vectorization. The key to vectorization of an algorithm comes in the realization that it is necessary to construct blocks of code which perform simple computations on a large amount of data. This general idea was extended to the steps below by placing the data into arrays that could be processed by a vector instruction. In some cases, a seemingly inefficient order of processes was constructed so that some portions of the algorithm could be vectorized. For example, an array of <u>all</u> fragments is kept available until the obscured fragments are culled just prior to rendering, in order to be able to vectorize the shader module. This process ends up using extra space in favor of the significant speedup provided by vectorization. The algorithm combines traditional steps with several new steps designed for vectorization (a • indicates a step which employs vectorization).

1. Read the object and scene descriptions.

2. Reject backfacing polygons; discard any polygons which are completely off the screen.

• 3. Calculate surface normals.

4. Clip the remaining polygons to the viewing pyramid, interpolating normals and colors as necessary.

5. Decompose the remaining polygons into edges and edge pairs. Since all polygons are convex, each right edge matches one left edge (except at vertices).

• 6. Calculate interpolation values for all parameters associated with all edges (i.e. normals, position, texture coordinates).

7. Insert each edge pair into the appropriate Y bucket.

8. For each scanline ...

    a. Add any new edge pairs which become active on this scanline to the active edge pair list.

    • b. Interpolate the edge pairs from the top of the current scanline to the bottom, using the delta values computed in step 5 above.

- c. Decompose each active edge pair into a series of fragments clipped to the pixel boundaries. The fragments are loaded into an array. Calculate the z depth of each fragment.

  d. Sort the fragments for each pixel, and load those fragments which contribute to the final image into a second array.

- e. Shade all pixel fragments, interpolating the necessary values across the scanline.

  f. Anti-alias each pixel fragment with all fragments in the pixel bucket and the background.

  g. Write the scanline to the frame buffer or virtual device.

In particular, we were interested in vectorizing the Y and X interpolation steps, the area (or anti-aliasing) step, and the shading step. As will be described later, the anti-aliasing portion was not vectorized. These processes account for the bulk of the time required to render an image.

Implementation

The original design of the algorithm included complex, interlocked data structures to represent the scene. These data structures effectively linked the lowest levels of the program, such as the edge interpolation, to the higher level data structures, such as the polygon and object descriptions. For example, the declaration of the edge pair looked like:

```
struct edge_pair {
            edge          *left, *right;
            polygon             *poly;
            object        *obj;
             bounding_box *bbox;
        }
```

The edges were declared as

```
struct edge {
            point   *p1, *p2;
            terps   *terp_array;
        }
```

Note: The syntax used here is from the **C** programming language. In C, braces are used to delimit code blocks, * is used to indicate a pointer data type, -> is used to dereference a pointer within a structure, and . is used to reference a field within a structure.

The **terp_array** contains the items to be interpolated for the edge; such as the normals, colors, and other attributes.

The problem with this kind of structure is twofold. First, address calculations of the form

edge_pair->edge->terps->value

involve multiple indirect references. This is inherently more expensive than addresses such as

edge_list[edge_pair[ep]]terps.value

since only offset calculations are required in the second instance. Secondly, the first type of addressing often leads to non-constant stride, meaning that the distance between operands in a loop is not fixed. While non-constant stride operands can be vectorized, the problems involved are significantly more complex.

Performance was enhanced by replacing the first type of data structure and building a series of simple arrays to hold the underlying structures. Virtually no pointers are used, except in the sense of using array indices as "pointers" to data structures. In addition, memory is not dynamically allocated during the execution of the program. The resulting data structures are somewhat less flexible, but they allowed us to easily vectorize major sections of the program.

For example, all edge pairs are stored in a linear array. Each edge pair contains two indices into a linear array of edges. The active edge pair list is merely another array of indices into the edge pair array. Thus, a particular edge might be referenced as

edge list[edge pair list[active array[i]].left]

In the same manner, pixel fragments are stored in a linear array in the shader and are manipulated through a series of index arrays. Sorting and shading the fragments is accomplished by using these arrays.

Interpolation

After the objects to be rendered have been transformed and culled, leaving only polygons which will contribute to the scene, the objects are decomposed into edges and edge pairs. Each edge in the scene is assigned a separate data structure, and those edges which form the boundary between polygons are entered as two distinct edges. Likewise, each polygon is broken into a set of non-overlapping edge pairs in screen space. If an edge on one side of the polygon matches two edges on the other side of the polygon, the single edge is duplicated so that each edge on the second side has a corresponding edge on the first side. While a traditional algorithm might take advantage of sharing to reduce both memory and computation, any overlap in edges and edge pairs results in a recurrence which prevents vectorization.

Each edge contains a list of interpolants; these may be any floating point values such as color, position, texture coordinates, or normals. The interpolation routine need only know how many interpolants are present for each edge, not what they represent. The process of Y interpolation consists simply of adding the Y deltas to each of the interpolants, to "move" them down to the next scan line. Both an old value (the value at the top of the scan line) and a new value (the value at the bottom of the scan line) are stored. Interpolation is simply

$$V_{new} = V_{old} + V_{inc}$$

This step vectorizes easily. Since the number of interpolants for each edge pair is typically small (less than 10), this step is inverted, and the loop through the active edge pairs is done as the vectorized loop while the loop through each of the interpolants is moved to the outside and left in scalar mode. In scenes of moderate complexity, the active edge count far exceeds the interpolant count. Thus, what might have been

```
for each edge pair
    for each interpolant
    Vnew = Vold + Vinc
```

is swapped in a vector version:

```
for each interpolant
    for each edge pair
        Vnew = Vold + Vinc
```

and the inner loop is vectorized. This is a common technique which is referred to as loop interchange. The X interpolation involves determining a set of constants so that the various interpolants can be computed across the scan line. The Y interpolation step results in a series of edges pairs clipped to the current scan line. The basic problem in X interpolation is to find a set of values for the equation

$$V = V_{left} + (V_{inc} * \text{DISTANCE})$$

The **DISTANCE** variable in this case represents the distance along the scan line in X. Once V_{left} and V_{inc} are found, the interpolation of any of the values of interest (be it Z depth, texture coordinates, etc.) can be found for the entire edge pair as a vectorized step. We apply a number of compromises to determine these values. If the edge pair vertical edges are not too steep, they can be found trivially by averaging the edge pair values at the top and bottom of the scanline on each end. For long, thin, triangular edge pairs a bias is applied to minimize the shading error. These values are stored with each edge pair, and are used in the vectorized shader for each active pixel fragment.

Area Calculation

The algorithm uses a simple box filter for anti-aliasing. This reduces the problem to a matter of calculating the area of the edge pairs as they are clipped by each pixel. All possible edge pairs can be reduced to two cases as shown in Figure 1.

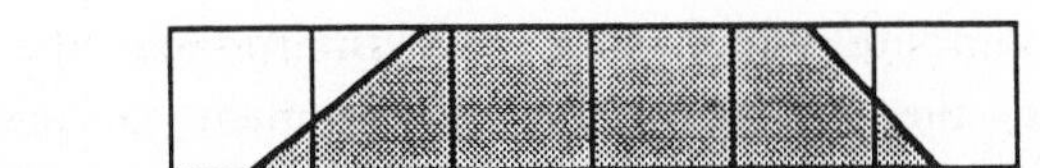

Case 1. Right and left edges of edge pair do not overlap.

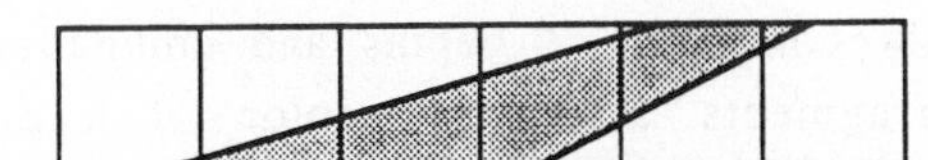

Case 2. Right and left edges of edge pair overlap.

Figure 1. Area Calculation

These cases represent the two possible ways an edge pair can cross a scanline. All edge slopes can be mirrored to produce these configurations. Cases in which the left and right edge meet in the scan line (forming a triangle) can be treated as trivial examples of these two cases. These two cases can be solved using a combination of triangles and rectangles. A typical scalar solution would effectively "clip" the edge pair polygon to the pixel, stepping along the edge pair, and summing the triangular and rectangular portions. To test this process, a scalar version of the area calculator was developed.

For vectorization, the calculation was divided into a scalar "loading" phase and a vectorized computation phase. While the vectorized section provided a significant speedup, the loading phase actually added execution time. This illustrates an example where the preparation for vectorization ended up requiring more time than could be made up by the resultant vectorized code. The total time required by the two phases exceeded the time required by the prototype scalar version. Therefore, we decided to implement this section using pure scalar code.

Shading Setup

A traditional scanline algorithm proceeds across each scanline, activating edge pairs and computing the spans they cover. Most algorithms follow the Y bucket sort by an X sort to facilitate this process. Then, as each edge pair is removed from the list, no additional sorting is required until the next edge pair becomes active. This technique does not easily vectorize. Since neither the number of active edge pairs across the scanline nor the length of a span is a constant (and both are typically small), the expected gain in vectorization is minimal.

In order to vectorize this process, all edge pairs are activated simultaneously and decomposed into a serial list of pixel fragments. These pixel fragments contain the information needed to compute their area and interpolate the appropriate parameters. In particular, the Z depth of each fragment is computed as it is created. The serial list is then sorted in Z for each pixel, and is culled to a list of only those pixel fragments which will contribute to the scene. This step does not vectorize, but involves only comparing Z depths and computing areas in order to determine which pixel fragments affect the color of a given pixel. Those fragments which are left after the cull are placed in a linear array which can then be shaded as a vector. For a typical scanline, the count of pixel fragments can be quite high (often over 1000 for a 512 pixel scanline). A diagram illustrating this is shown in Figure 2.

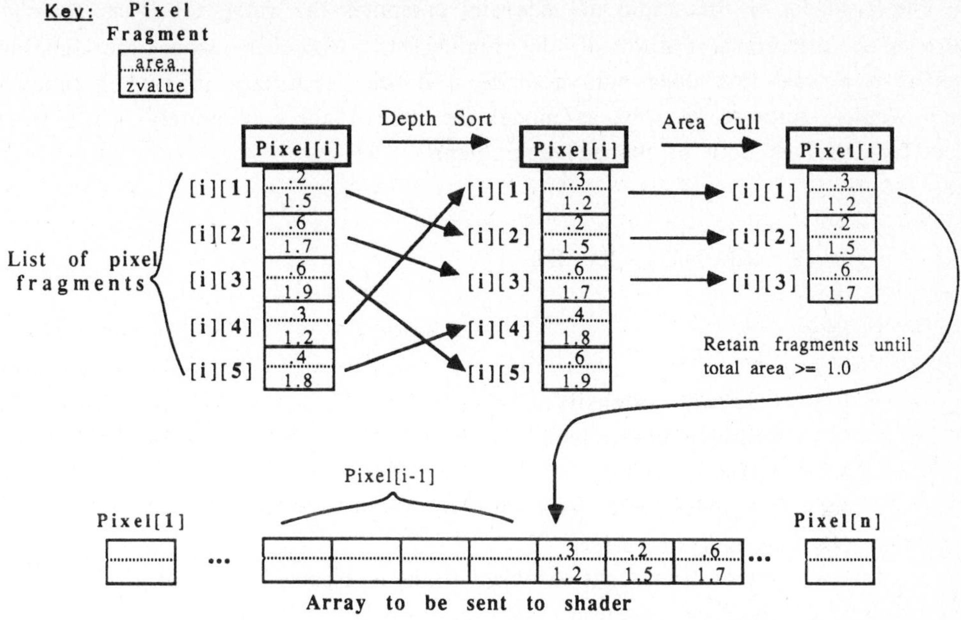

Figure 2. Shading Setup

Shading Models

There are several important features included in the shader module which are not usually found in other implementations. The shader module allows the user to select at runtime which shading model he wishes to use for a particular object. Included in this feature is the ability to change the shading parameters independently for each model chosen. Since each model is separate, new models may be added at any time making the shader very versatile. Initially, three specular models were implemented: Phong, Blinn, and Cook-Torrance. Flat and Gouraud shading are also implemented (see [3] for a discussion on shading models). Phong's basic shading equation is the method used in calculating smooth shading across a polygonal surface. In all the shading models, the specular highlight is based on a function of the cosine of α, where α is the angle between the normal and the reflection vector H ($\cos(\alpha) = (N \cdot H)$). The surface is assumed to be made up of tiny micro facets, and the specular function, D, indicates the proportion of micro facets reflecting light toward the viewer.

The Phong shader is the traditional one and computes the value for D as $\cos(\alpha)^n$, where n is the concentration of the highlight. However, since the function involves a power, this does not vectorize. It was necessary to find a function which would vectorize as well as model the micro facets accurately. The Blinn model for D solves both of the above problems.

$$I = Ia + Kd\,(N \cdot L) + Ks\,(D)$$

Key:

I = resultant intensity
Ia = ambient coefficient
Kd = diffuse coefficient
Ks = specular coefficient
N = normal to surface
L = vector from light to object (light is assumed to be at ∞)
D = specular function

Equation 1: Phong's Shading Model

Blinn uses a function determined from optics by Trowbridge and Reitz (see [6] for details). This distribution function models the micro facets as ellipsoids of revolution, where c_3 is the eccentricity of these ellipsoids. C_3 approaches zero for very shiny surfaces and one for very diffuse surfaces.

Blinn's microfacet distribution: $$\left[\frac{c_3^2}{\cos^2\alpha(c_3^2-1)+1}\right]$$

Equation 2: Blinn's Specular Function

Although Blinn calculates the value of c_3 from a formula, we let the user provide the value depending on the shininess desired. Blinn also incorporates a shadowing function and the *Fresnel* factor, which indicates the proportion of light reflected from a micro facet. These factors are not used in our shading model in order to save computations.

The Cook-Torrance specular model is similar to the Blinn model. The only difference is that the Fresnel term is used to determine the color shift in the specular component. The color shift is needed to account for the fact that, in some cases, an object may not reflect a white highlight. For instance, it turns out that for most metallic objects, the specular component tends towards the object color at values of the angle α which are not close to the grazing angle of $\Pi/2$. The equation used is:

$$\mathrm{Color}_{\alpha} = \mathrm{Color}_{0} + (\mathrm{Color}_{\pi/2} - \mathrm{Color}_{0}) \left[\frac{\mathrm{MAX}(0, F_{\alpha} - F_{0})}{F_{\pi/2} - F_{0}} \right]$$

Key:

F = Fresnel factor
Color = (R,G,B)
α = angle between N and H (varying from 0 to $\Pi/2$)

Equation 3: Cook-Torrance Color Shift

Vectorization of the Shader

Most shading modules are written to perform the appropriate calculations to determine the shade of a single pixel at a time given the normal, color, and reflectance vector. Initially, this module was written in a similar manner. However, in order to vectorize the calculations so that all pixels on a scanline would be processed in parallel, it was necessary to determine what events could occur simultaneously and what calculations needed to proceed serially. As mentioned above, the shader receives an array of pixel fragments to be shaded for the current scanline. The X interpolation values for the surface normals and colors are determined earlier. The vectorized shader algorithm is simply:

1) Send the shader an array of span pixel indices which point to structures that provide the necessary information to shade all pixels.

2) In a ***Vector*** step, load colors and normals (calculated by X-interpolation) for each pixel to be shaded, into arrays for processing.

3) In a ***Vector*** step, normalize the normals.

4) In a ***Vector*** step, calculate the diffuse and specular components of each pixel and load the resultant color back into the color array for the scanline.

To vectorize multiple light source shading, step 4 is computed for each light source contributing to a fragment and the intensities are summed in another vector step. This is illustrated below:

for each light source

  for all fragments (inner loop is step 4)

    Calculate intensity (diffuse and specular)

for all fragments

  Sum intensities for each light source

Typically, the number of lights is rather small so it is not necessary to vectorize the outer loop in the first set of statements. This method is preferred over a solution which would have the loops inter-changed. In such a circumstance, the loop running through the fragments would not vectorize since a recurrence would be present in order to sum the intensities.

Several modifications of the above steps are necessary to handle multiple shading models applied to different objects in the scene. The array which is sent to the shader as described in step 1 above is actually different arrays loaded separately for each active shading model. The pixels contain the information regarding which shading model is to be applied to a particular fragment. Based on this, the fragment is loaded into the appropriate shader model array. On return from the shader, all active fragments for the scanline are loaded from the various shading model arrays back into a single color array to be sent to the frame buffer. The number of fragments per pixel is maintained so that the each fragment is loaded into the correct color array slot. In this way, each shader model is vectorized separately. A picture illustrating different shaders applied to different objects is shown in Figure 3(three light sources are used).

Results

Four test images were used in determining times for the algorithm. No clipping is performed on the test images. Each skull contains 1910 points and 2084 polygons. The picture in Figure 3 is called **SKULL5** and uses five small skulls as different objects. The next image is **SKULL1** which is a single Cook-Torrance shaded skull (see Figure 4). **SKULLGOLD** contains five skulls combined as one object with a total of 9550 points and 10420 polygons. The image is rendered with Cook-Torrance shading with 1 light source (see Figure 5). The next image is **SKULLLINE** five different skulls each shaded the same as Figure 3 but arranged differently on the screen and illuminated with one light source.

Each image was calculated at a resolution of 640 by 480 pixels and the it was rendering to a virtual device for optimum speed. The program was run on the Convex C-1 first in scalar and then in vector mode. The program was not physically altered, the timings reflect different compilers.

TIMINGS (CPU seconds)

Test Image	Scalar	Vector	Ratio
SKULL1 (1 light)	53.3	18.9	2.8/1
SKULL1 (3 lights)	81.2	23.4	3.5/1
SKULLGOLD (1 light)	125.1	55.1	2.3/1
SKULLGOLD (3 lights)	177.2	66.0	2.7/1
SKULL5 (1 light)	103.4	47.2	2.2/1
SKULL5 (3 lights)	140.5	58.6	2.4/1
SKULLLINE (1 light)	106.8	50.1	2.1/1

It is interesting to note that due to the optimizations of vectorizing the multiple light source calculations, the increase in time for vector mode for three lights from one light is typically in the 20 percent range. However, the increase in time for scalar mode is in the 40 percent range. In this case, vectorization of a small section of code saves a considerable amount of time for an ordinarily computation intensive operation.

In addition to the above results, Cray Research, Inc. recently has provided us access to a Cray XMP-4/16 running UNICOS in Minneapolis. Preliminary results of a non-optimized version of the algorithm were determined on the image SKULL1 with one light source. Running in a scalar mode, the time was 6.2 CPU seconds.

It is also valuable to examine the difference between the scalar and vector versions of the algorithm. The following table summarizes speed information on the single skull for the vectorized sections:

Function	Scalar	Vector	Ratio
Y interpolation	6.8	2.7	2.5/1
X interpolation	18.9	7.9	2.4/1
Cook-Torrance shader	11.1	1.5	7.2/1

The vectorization of a scanline z-buffer renderer was achieved by several key changes to the interpolation and shading algorithms. We have shown that the resulting algorithm enjoys a significant speed advantage over its scalar version.

Conclusion

The algorithm presented in this paper has taken approximately 6 man-months to implement from scratch. Almost 2 man-months of this time was spent on optimizing and debugging the vector sections of the algorithm in order for these modules to run properly. Although this may seem like a large percentage of the total time, a portion of this time was spent learning the techniques of vectorization. After these techniques have been mastered, an experienced programmer would most likely not spend any additional time debugging than his scalar counterpart.

The scanline renderer is one of a number of graphical operations which are prime candidates for vectorization. Compositing, for example, is a process which is ideally suited to a vector processor, since the vectors (of pixels) are long, fixed in length, and the operations on each pixel are the same.

In reference to our goals, we have demonstrated a method for constructing an algorithm which can effectively use a vector computer for rendering scenes. Performance is exceptional and proves that a SIMD machine can provide significant better results when used up to its full potential. Since vector computers are decreasing in price, it is reasonable to assume that most graphics labs will have access to a machine of this type in the near future. The design of a scanline algorithm for a vector machine has proven to be a worthwhile undertaking.

Acknowledgements

We'd like to acknowledge the assistance of many people at CGRG in preparing this report. Chuck Csuri provided invaluable guidance and direction for this research and for the entire supercomputer graphics project. Ed Tripp aided in the initial design of the algorithm and provided several key vectorized routines vital to the shader. Bob Marshall and Jeff Faust reviewed the research and were patient while none of our other work was completed. Convex provided excellent hardware support and gave us insight (and updates) on the Vectorizing C Compiler. Finally, we appreciate the help of everyone at The Computer Graphics Research Group and The Computer and Information Science Department at Ohio State (especially Rick Parent and John Chadwick) who helped with this research and reviewed this paper.

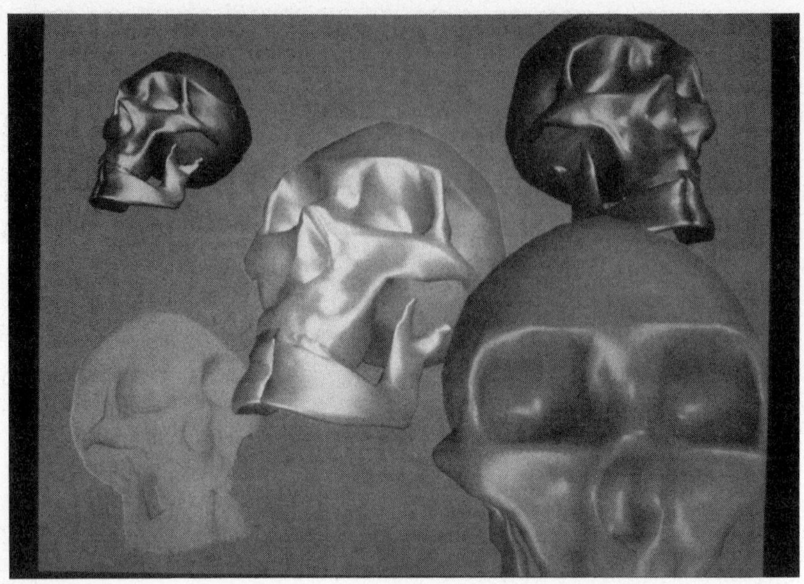

Figure 3: **SKULL5** (shown illuminated with 3 lights)
(Top Left: Modified Cook-Torrance,
Top Right: Blinn, Bottom Left: Gouraud, Bottom
Right: Cook-Torrance, Center: Phong)

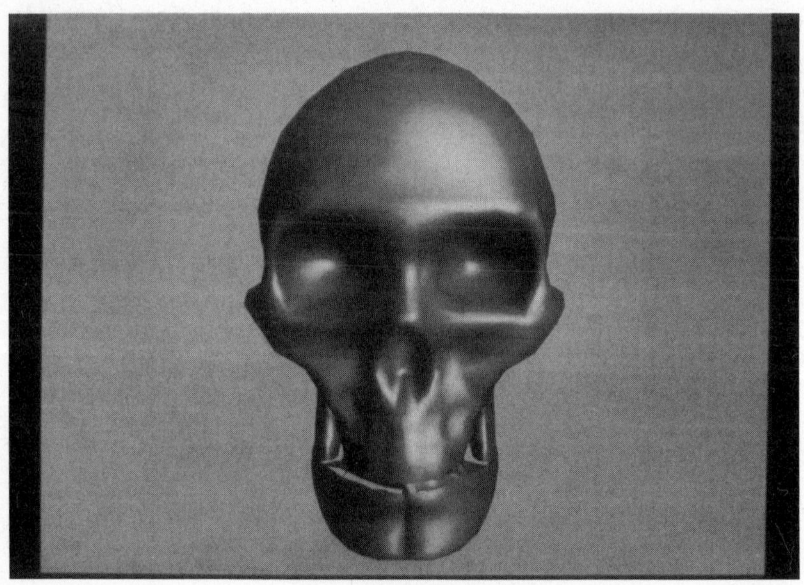

Figure 4: SKULL1

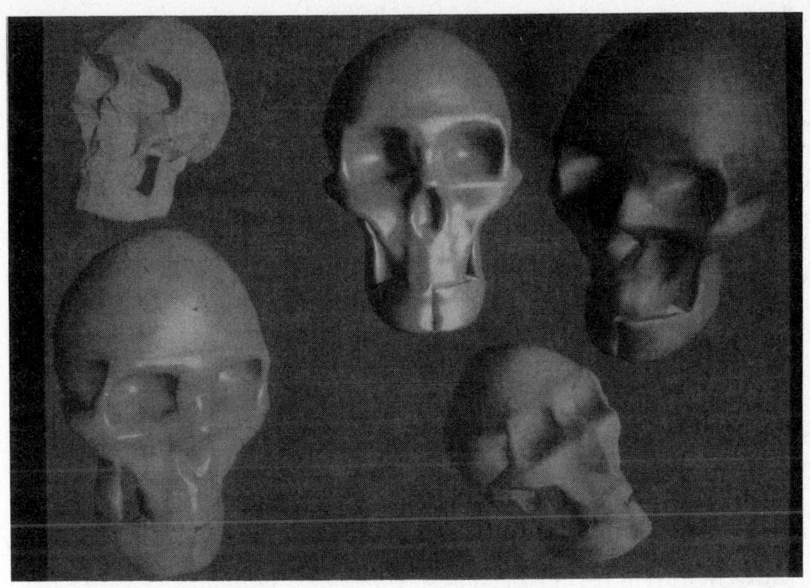

Figure 5. SKULLGOLD
(Five Skulls - combined as one object)

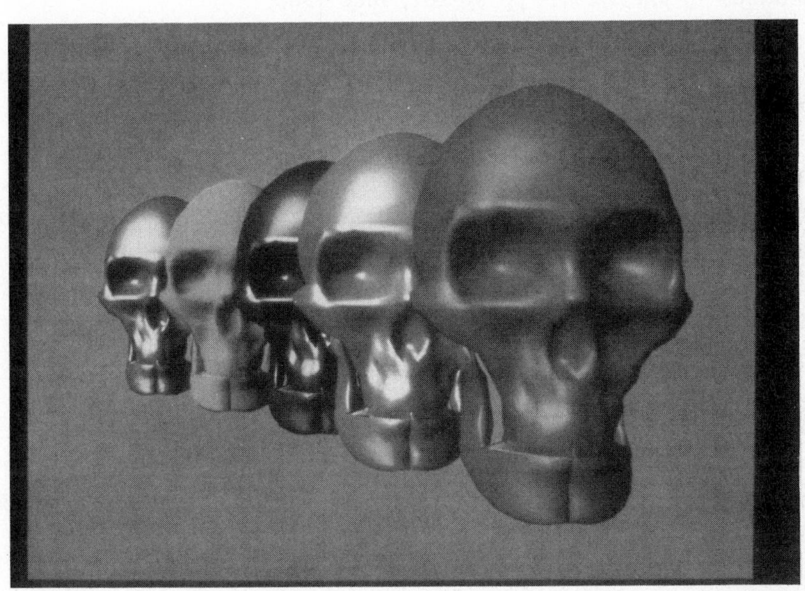

Figure 6: SKULLLINE

References

1. Padua, David A. and Michael J. Wolfe. "Advanced Compiler Optimizations for Supercomputers", *Communications of the ACM*, December, 1986, pp 1184-1201.

2. Newman, William M. and Robert F. Sproull. Principles of Interactive Computer Graphics. McGraw-Hill, 1979.

3. Rogers, David F. Procedural Elements for Computer Graphics. McGraw-Hill, 1985.

4. Convex Computer Corporation. CONVEX Vectorizing C Compiler User's Guide. Version X1.0. April 29, 1986.

5. Cook, Robert L. and Kenneth E. Torrance. "A Reflectance Model for Computer Graphics," SIGGRAPH 1981 Proceedings, *Computer Graphics*, v.15 #3 pp 307-315.

6. Blinn, James F. "Models of Light Reflection for Computer Synthesized Pictures," SIGGRAPH 1977 Proceedings, *Computer Graphics*, v.11 #2, pp 192-198.

7. Whitted, Turner. "An Improved Illumination Model for Shaded Display," *Communications of the ACM*, pp 96-102, June 1980.

8. Norrie, Chris. "Supercomputers for Superproblems : An Architectural Introduction," *Computer*, pp 62-73, March 1984.

9. Schumacker, Robert A, Robert Sproull, and Ivan E. Sutherland. "A Characterization of Ten Hidden-Surface Algorithms," *ACM Computing Surveys*, pp 1-55, March 1974.

10. Fuchs, Henry and Jack Goldfeather, Jeff P. Hultquist, Susan Spach, John D. Austin, Frederick P. Brooks, Jr., John G. Eyles, and John Poulton. "Fast Spheres, Shadows, Textures, Transparencies, and Image Enhancements in Pixel Planes," SIGGRAPH 1985 Proceedings, *Computer Graphics*, v. 19 #3, pp 111-120.

11. Levinthal, Adam and Thomas Porter. "Chap - A SIMD Graphics Processor," SIGGRAPH 1984 Proceedings, *Computer Graphics*, v.18 #3, pp 77-82.

12. Carpenter, Loren. "The A-buffer, an Antialiased Hidden Surface Method," SIGGRAPH 1984 Proceedings, *Computer Graphics*, v.18 #3, pp.103-108.

13. Fiume, Eugene and Alain Fournier and Larry Rudolph. "A Parallel Scan Conversion Algorithm with Anti-Aliasing for a General-Purpose UltraComputer," SIGGRAPH 1983 Proceedings, *Computer Graphics*, v.17 #3, pp. 141-149.

14. Max, Nelson L. "Vectorized Procedural Models for Natural Terrain: Waves and Islands in the Sunset," SIGGRAPH 1981 Proceedings, *Computer Graphics*, v.15 #3, pp. 317-323.

15. Plunkett, David J. and Michael J. Bailey. "The Vectorization of a Ray-Tracing Algorithm for Improved Execution Speed," *IEEE Computer Graphics and Applications*, pp. 52-60. August 1985.

16. Crocker, Gary A. "Invisibility Coherence for Faster Scan-Line Hidden Surface Algorithms", SIGGRAPH 1984 Proceedings, *Computer Graphics*, v.18,#3, pp.95-105.

17. Weinberg, Richard. "Parallel Processing Image Synthesis and Anti-Aliasing," SIGGRAPH 1981 Proceedings, Computer Graphics, v.15 #3, pp. 55-62.

18. Crow, Franklin C. "The Aliasing Problem in Computer-Generated Shaded Images," *Communications of the ACM*, v. 20, #11, pp. 799-805. Nov. 1977.

BENCHMARK OF THE EXTENDED BASIC LINEAR ALGEBRA SUBPROGRAMS ON THE NEC SX-2 SUPERCOMPUTER

R.M. Dubash[2], J.L. Fredin[1], O.G. Johnson[1,2]

[1]Houston Area Research Center
Computer Systems and Applications Research Center
The Woodlands, Texas 77380/USA
and
[2]Computer Science Department
University of Houston
Houston, Texas 77004/USA

ABSTRACT

The Basic Linear Algebra Subprograms (BLAS) covering most basic vector operations have been widely used in numerical applications including LINPACK. The Extended Basic Linear Algebra Subprograms (EBLAS) were developed recently as an extension to the strictly vector operations of the BLAS. The EBLAS, also known as Level-2 BLAS, are a set of subprograms that represent basic matrix-vector operations and were written to take advantage of the architecture of today's supercomputers.

The sixteen double precision EBLAS have been installed and benchmarked on the NEC SX-2 Supercomputer at the Houston Area Research Center, The Woodlands, Texas. The EBLAS code, as received, is highly vectorized. The timings and performance rates are presented. Techniques to optimize the EBLAS code on the NEC SX-2 in particular are presented. Performance increases of 10-30% are typical, but dramatic performance increases are obtained for a few routines.

I. INTRODUCTION

In the late 1970's a package of 38 low level subprograms for many of the basic operations of numerical linear algebra was presented by C.L. Lawson, R.J. Hanson, D.R. Kincaid and F.T. Krogh. The operations in the Basic Linear Algebra Subprograms (BLAS) package include the dot product, elementary vector operation, Givens transformation, vector copy and swap, vector norm, vector scaling, and the determination of the index of the vector component of the largest magnitude [1]. These routines have been very successful and have been used in a wide range of software packages including LINPACK [2] and many other algorithms published by the ACM Transactions on Mathematical Software.

In 1986, an extension to the set of BLAS designed for matrix-vector operations was developed. The new subprograms are referred to as the Extended Basic Linear Algebra Subprograms (EBLAS) [3] or the Level-2 BLAS. These routines involve O(mn), order m times n scalar operations where m and n are the dimensions of the matrix involved. The routines have been written at the Argonne National Laboratory, by J.J. Dongarra, J. Du Croz, S. Hammarling and R.J. Hanson.

In this paper we will present timings, performance rates and a few optimization strategies for the EBLAS on the NEC SX-2 Supercomputer system. This work was done at the Houston Area Research Center (HARC) in The Woodlands, Texas.

II. PREVIOUS RELATED BENCHMARKS

One measure of the performance of a supercomputer is its speed on basic numerical subprograms. Published benchmarks containing timings for the NEC SX-2, include LINPACK [4], the Livermore Loops [5], the Los Alamos Benchmark [6], and the NASA Kernels [7]. Other supercomputer benchmarks which include timings for the NEC SX-2, are SDOT and SAXPY from the BLAS [8], and the Mendez Hydrodynamics benchmarks [9]. Each of these benchmarks reflects the workload and computational needs of the environment in which they were developed.

The EBLAS were chosen for this benchmark activity due to the fact that they are written for matrix-vector operations and the NEC SX-2 is a vector machine. Thus, benchmarking the system with EBLAS would certainly present the machine more correctly.

III. SCOPE, NAMING CONVENTIONS, STORAGE CONVENTIONS OF EBLAS

The EBLAS routines are written in standard ANSI FORTRAN 77. There are 16 real routines, in single, double and extended real precision performing 43 different operations, and 17 complex routines in each precision performing 58 different operations.

The Extended BLAS cover three basic types of operations:

1) The Matrix-vector products
2) Solution of triangular equations
3) Rank-one and Rank-two updates.

The naming convention for the EBLAS includes, the precision of the routine indicated by the first character of the name, the next two letters describe the data structure and the last two letters describe the type of operation performed by the routine. For example, DGEMV is a double precision real, general, matrix-vector product routine. Each EBLAS subprogram can be used to perform several similar tasks within the constraints of data representation and format, and the operation type for that routine.

The naming convention, the purpose, and the data format and structure required by each of the routines is presented in greater detail in Appendix A.

IV. EXTENDED BLAS BENCHMARK PROCESS

The FORTRAN source code of the Extended Basic Linear Algebra Subprograms (EBLAS) and the test program were obtained from the authors at Mathematics and Computer Science Division of the Argonne National Laboratory. The program used for benchmarking and timing these subprograms was written at HARC.

Each of the subprograms was timed separately, with a call within a DO-loop in the main program. The calling program generated its own run data. The routines were timed for different values of N, the dimension of the vector or matrix used in the calculation. Values of N ranging from 16 (2**4) to 513 (2**9+1) were used. In this benchmark set the most straightforward use of the routines was chosen for timing. The arguments required by the routines are described in reference [3]. An explanation and the particular values of the arguments for all the routines used in this benchmark are presented in Table I. There were no zero elements in the run data. The routines were timed from before the first executable statement in the routine up to immediately before the return from the routine with the clock calling overhead removed.

Table I. Values of the parameters and the number of operations used in the process of benchmarking.

ROUTINE	LDA	K	KL	KU	INCX	INCY	UPLO	TRANS	DIAG	NUMBER OF OPERATIONS
DGEMV	513				1	1		N		2*(N*N+N)
DGBMV	3*KL+1		8	8	1	1		N		2*((2*K+1)*N-K*(K+1))+2*N
DSYMV	513				1	1	U			2*(N*N+2*N)
DSBMV	2*K+1	8			1	1	U			2*((2*K+1)*N-K*(K+1))+2*N
DSPMV					1	1	U			2*(N*N+2*N)
DTRMV	513				1		U	N	N	N*N
DTBMV	2*K+1	8			1		U	N	N	2*N*K-K*(K+1)+N
DTPMV					1		U	N	N	N*N
DTRSV	513				1		U	N	N	N*N
DTBSV	2*K+1	8			1	1	U	N	N	2*N*K-K*(K+1)+N
DTPSV					1		U	N	N	N*N
DGER	513				1	1				2*N*N+N
DSYR	513				1		U			N*N+2*N
DSPR					1		U			N*N+2*N
DSYR2	513				1		U			2*(N+1)*N+2*N
DSPR2					1	1	U			2*(N+1)*N+2*N

LDA : first dimension of A as declared in the calling program

K : number of super or sub-diagonals depending on whether the matrix is upper triangular or lower triangular

KL : number of sub-diagonals in case of band matrix

KU : number of super-diagonals in case of band matrix

INCX : increment on elements of X

INCY : increment on elements of Y

UPLO : specifies whether the matrix is upper triangular ('U') or lower triangular ('L')

DIAG : specifies whether the matrix is unit triangular ('U') or non unit triangular ('N')

TRANS : specifies whether the matrix or its transpose is taken for computation ('T' : Transpose, 'N' : Matrix as it is)

The number of floating point operations for the path traced in each routine, was computed and checked against the value used by the Mathematics and Computer Science Division at the Argonne National Laboratory. These values are as in Table I. The performance rate, millions of floating point operations per second (MFLOPS) calculation uses this operation count.

All the timings presented here are for the double precision EBLAS routines. The double precision (64 bits) was chosen because arithmetic processor on the NEC SX-2 is a 64 bit processor although memory may be fetched in either 32 or 64 bit words. Vectorization of complex variable routines is limited at this time, hence the complex routines were not considered for this study.

The routines were tested before and after the changes, using the test program obtained from Argonne National Laboratory and were found to pass all the tests. Also, the results from the calculations were verified as being correct.

V. EXTENDED BLAS BENCHMARK RESULTS

The results in the tables and charts have been grouped using the last two characters of the name of the routines.

In general, the speed of the routines as received varied between 10 MFLOPS and 500+ MFLOPS. Figures 1 through 5 give the speed in MFLOPS plotted against the dimension N, for each of the subprograms without any source code changes. The MFLOPS were computed using the timings presented in Table II and the number of operations in Table I. Table III gives the numerical value of MFLOPS for each of the routines.

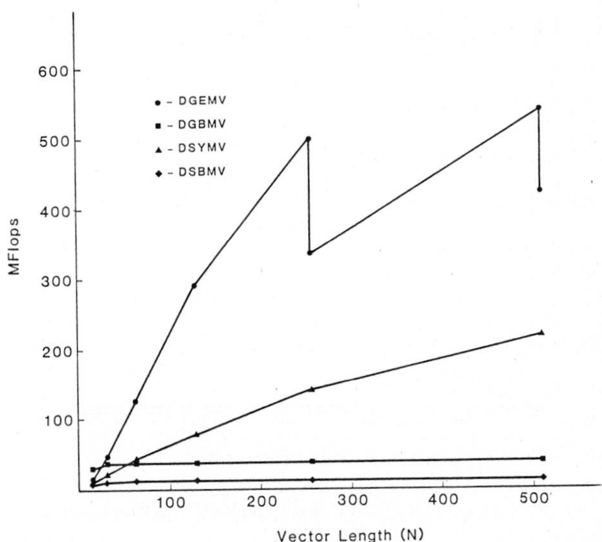

Figure 1. Plot of N versus MFLOPS for DGEMV, DGBMV, DSYMV, DSBMV routines.

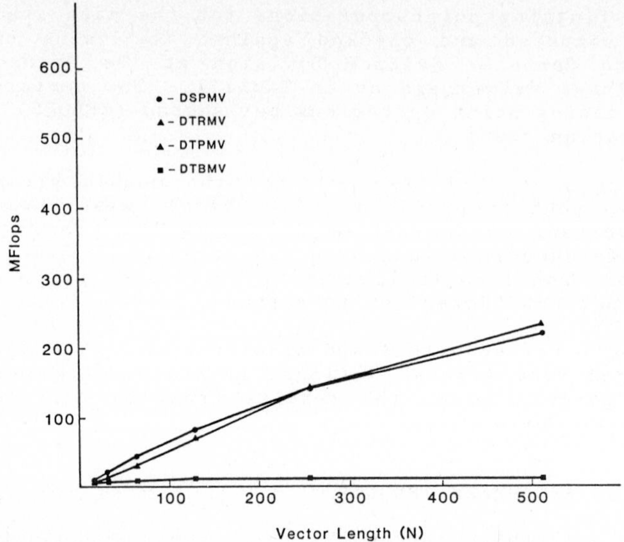

Figure 2. Plot of N versus MFLOPS for DSPMV, DTRMV, DTBMV, DTPMV routines.

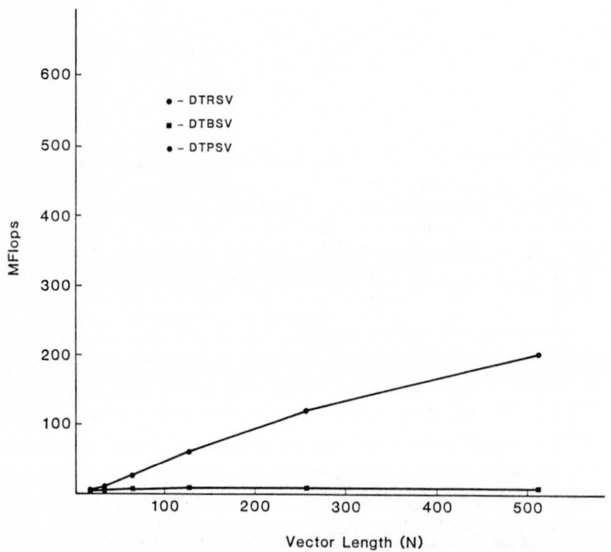

Figure 3. Plot of N versus MFLOPS for DTRSV, DTBSV, DTPSV routines.

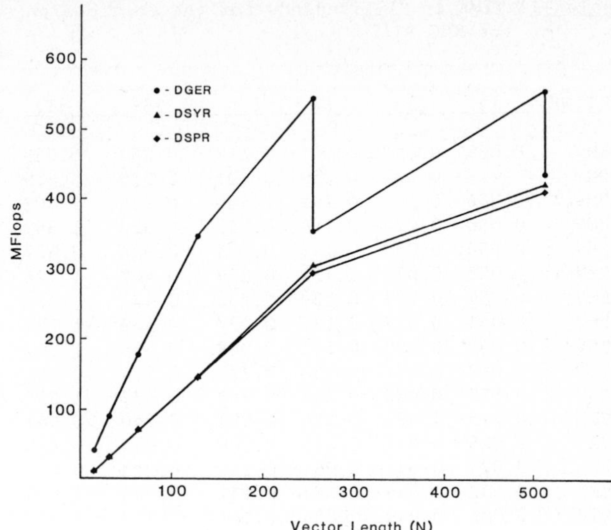

Figure 4. Plot of N versus MFLOPS for DGER, DSYR, DSPR routines.

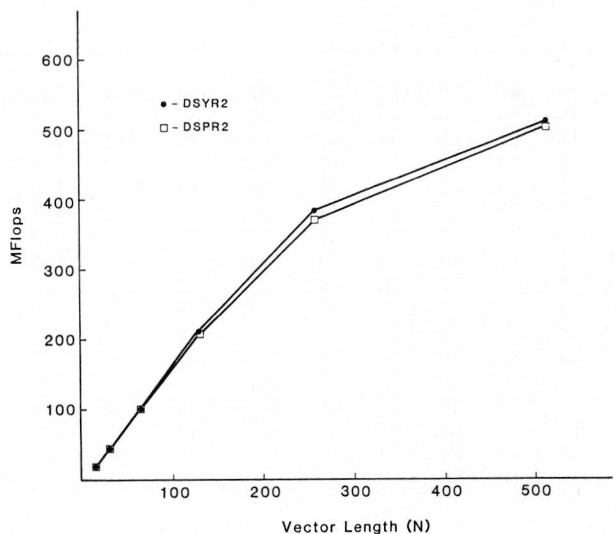

Figure 5. Plot of N versus MFLOPS for DSPR2, DSYR2 routines.

Table II. TIME in Milliseconds for the routines on the NEC SX-2

ROUTINE	16	32	64	128	256	512
DGEMV	0.034	0.044	0.065	0.113	0.262	0.969
DGBMV	---	0.029	0.059	0.121	0.239	0.479
DSYMV	0.056	0.100	0.192	0.400	0.935	2.402
DSBMV	0.050	0.099	0.184	0.353	0.692	1.369
DSPMV	0.055	0.099	0.193	0.405	0.946	2.427
DTRMV	0.055	0.079	0.127	0.229	0.462	1.126
DTBMV	0.057	0.083	0.132	0.232	0.431	0.829
DTPMV	0.053	0.077	0.125	0.227	0.459	1.124
DTRSV	0.060	0.089	0.147	0.268	0.538	1.297
DTBSV	0.062	0.093	0.153	0.273	0.514	0.995
DTPSV	0.059	0.088	0.147	0.268	0.537	1.297
DGER	0.012	0.023	0.046	0.094	0.240	0.941
DSYR	0.025	0.037	0.060	0.108	0.215	0.619
DSPR	0.025	0.037	0.062	0.112	0.223	0.636
DSYR2	0.032	0.049	0.083	0.157	0.344	1.025
DSPR2	0.032	0.049	0.084	0.161	0.353	1.044

Table III. MFLOPS for the routines with different values of N on the NEC SX-2 without any code changes.

ROUTINE	16	17	32	33	64	65	128	129	256	257	512	513
DGEMV	16	18	47	49	126	129	292	292	501	335	542	428
DGBMV		30	34	34	36	36	37	37	38	38	38	38
DSYMV	10	11	22	22	44	45	83	84	141	142	219	219
DSBMV	8	8	10	10	12	12	13	13	13	13	13	13
DSPMV	10	11	22	22	44	44	82	82	139	140	217	217
DTRMV	5	5	13	13	32	33	71	72	142	142	233	233
DTBMV	3	4	6	6	8	8	9	9	10	10	10	10
DTPMV	5	5	13	14	33	33	72	72	143	143	233	233
DTRSV	4	5	11	12	28	28	61	62	122	122	202	202
DTBSV	3	3	5	5	7	7	8	8	8	9	9	9
DTPSV	4	5	12	12	28	28	61	62	122	122	202	202
DGER	43	44	88	90	177	180	347	346	545	355	558	437
DSYR	11	12	29	30	69	70	153	153	307	306	425	425
DSPR	11	12	29	30	68	69	148	149	296	296	414	413
DSYR2	18	19	44	45	102	103	212	213	383	383	513	513
DSPR2	18	19	44	45	100	101	207	208	371	371	504	504

Table IV contains the MFLOPS for N=256 with the corresponding values for CRAY-1 [10]. It should be noted that the purpose of this study is not to compare CRAY-1 and NEC SX-2 results.

The performance characterization parameters as defined by Hockney and Jesshope [11] namely, r_∞ and $n_{1/2}$ were also computed for the routines and are presented in Table V.

Table IV. MFLOPS for some routines with N = 256 for NEC SX-2 and CRAY-1.

ROUTINE	MFLOPS	
	CRAY-1	NEC SX-2
DGEMV	39	501
DSYMV	31	141
DTRMV	33	142
DGER	39	545
DSYR	36	307
DSYR2	47	383

Table V. Values of the performance characterization parameters r_∞ and $n_{1/2}$ for the routines executed on the NEC SX-2.

ROUTINE	r_∞ (MFLOPS)	$n_{1/2}$
DGEMV	568	109
DGBMV	38	8
DSYMV	231	141
DSBMV	14	13
DSPMV	228	140
DTRMV	254	172
DTBMV	11	30
DTPMV	254	170
DTRSV	220	173
DTBSV	9	26
DTPSV	220	172
DGER	573	81
DSYR	457	150
DSPR	444	149
DSYR2	542	133
DSPR2	533	133

The routines were also run in the scalar mode. All the scalar speeds were between 8 MFLOPS and 11 MFLOPS.

The vectorization achieved by the compiler on all DO-loops in the original code for most of the routines was 100%. This reflects on the quality of the code written by the authors of the routines.

In Figures 1 and 4, a point worth discussing, is that the MFLOPS when N=257 is significantly lower than when N=256. A similar phenomenon is observed for values of N=512 and N=513. Further, this is observed only for the general matrix routines. This can be reasoned by taking a look at the NEC SX-2 architecture [12].

The NEC SX-2 is a heterogeneous multi-processor system in which the system consists of two independent processors called the Control Processor (CP) and Arithmetic Processor (AP). The AP is the one that does the high-speed vector and scalar processing. In the AP the major components contributing to the performance are the arithmetic and logical pipelines and the vector registers. There are eight vector arithmetic registers which are used for vector arithmetic operations. Each vector register can contain up to 256 words, where one word equals 64 bits. It is the loading time of these registers that causes the observed dip in the MFLOPS. When N=256 all the 256 words in the register are used but, as soon as N crosses over to 257 a single element needs to be processed activating the loading machinery all over again, throttling the flow. An immediate question that arises is 'Why is this not observed in all the routines ?'. This can be answered by a look at the code. In the routines where this dip is observed operate on all the elements of the array or the matrix, repeatedly in a loop, mandating the loading of the lone element too. In the other routines only a part of the array or the matrix is operated on. Even when all the elements are acted on, this is not done as a part of a major repetitive loop and hence does not have a very pronounced effect on the performance.

VI. OPTIMIZATION OF EBLAS FOR NEC SX-2

A few of the installed routines were picked for optimization of code with respect to the NEC SX-2 system. As noted earlier, the original code was highly vectorized although five techniques that improved performance were identified. The improvement achieved by optimization is presented in Table VI.

Table VIa. MFLOPS after optimization and the percentage improvement for some routines with different values of N.

	16		32		64		128		256		512	
ROUTINE	A	B	A	B	A	B	A	B	A	B	A	B
DGEMV	22	56.2	76	61.7	215	70.6	498	70.5	775	54.6	852	38.7
DGBMV	--	--	31	-8.8	66	83.3	129	248.6	221	481.5	310	715.7
DSBMV	10	25.0	13	30.0	15	25.0	17	30.7	17	30.7	17	30.7
DTRSV	6	50.0	15	25.0	34	21.4	72	18.3	142	16.3	225	11.3
DTPSV	6	50.0	15	25.0	34	21.4	72	18.3	142	16.3	225	11.3

Column A : MFLOPS after optimization
Column B : Percentage improvement

Table VIb. Improvement due to optimization in terms of time (in msecs).

ROUTINE	16	32	64	128	256	512
DGEMV	0.022	0.027	0.038	0.066	0.169	0.616
DGBMV	---	0.032	0.033	0.035	0.041	0.059
DSBMV	0.043	0.076	0.140	0.269	0.527	1.04
DTRSV	0.047	0.072	0.121	0.226	0.462	1.16
DTPSV	0.045	0.070	0.121	0.226	0.462	1.16

Table VIc. MFLOPS for DGEMV with different levels of unrolling and N.

	16	64	256	512
Rolled	22	151	520	552
Unrolled Level 2	24	190	618	598
Unrolled Level 4	25	215	775	852
Unrolled Level 16	20	187	772	964

The strategies used for optimization are discussed with the relevant piece of code. These strategies are well known and are with reference to the NEC SX-2 system to serve as a guiding tool to users intending to use EBLAS on this system.

In the DTRSV and DTPSV routines a significant change in the speed was observed by removal of a temporary variable in the loop. Further improvement was achieved by replacing all the calls to the logical function which is used for comparing the values of character variables by in-line code. The result presented in Table VI is after both of these changes were made. The original piece of code and the changes made are:

Routine DTRSV :

Original Code :

```
          .......
          .......

          IF ( INCX .EQ. 1 ) THEN
             DO 20, J = N, 1, -1
                IF ( X(J) .NE. ZERO ) THEN
                   IF ( NOUNIT ) X(J) = X(J) / A(J,J)
                   TEMP = X(J)
                   DO 10, I = J-1, 1, -1
                      X(I) = X(I) - TEMP * A(I,J)
10                 CONTINUE
                END IF
20           CONTINUE
          ELSE
          .......
          .......
```

```
Changed to :
   .......
   .......

   IF ( INCX .EQ. 1 ) THEN
      DO 20, J = N, 1, -1
            X(J) = X(J) / A(J,J)
            DO 10, I = J-1, 1, -1
               X(I) = X(I) - X(J) * A(I,J)
10          CONTINUE
20    CONTINUE
   ELSE
   .......
   .......
```

From the above change it can be seen that use of temporary variables like TEMP, is not a good practice. The compiler is smart enough to notice X(J) as a constant of the loop and come up with a better code. Moreover, it is not a good idea to insert logical conditions of the type 'IF (X(J) .NE. ZERO)' in the code since the saving achieved by not performing a piece of code for certain values in the data set is offset by the time spent on the logical condition evaluation. This might fail in case the data has a high concentration of zeroes.

The performance can be further improved by replacing calls to a function by in-line code. The call to the logical function LSAME was replaced by in-line code as:

```
Original code :
   .......
   .......
   IF ( .NOT. LSAME (UPLO, 'U') .AND
        .NOT. LSAME (UPLO, 'L')      ) THEN
   ......
   ......

   FUNCTION LSAME (A, B)
   LOGICAL LSAME
   CHARACTER*1 A,B
   IF ( A .EQ. B ) THEN
      LSAME = .TRUE.
   ELSE
      LSAME = .FALSE.
   ENDIF
   RETURN
   END

Changed to :
   .......
   .......
   IF ( UPLO .NE. 'U' .AND
        UPLO .NE. 'L'       ) THEN
   .......
   .......
```

A very commonly used strategy of unrolling the outer loop cannot be applied to DTRSV because of the data dependencies involved. The DTPSV routine can be optimized using all of the techniques applied to DTRSV. This routine does not lend itself to unrolling because of its data structure and format.

The DGEMV routine unlike the previous two routines has a code structure that permits the unrolling of the outer loop. A very significant improvement in speed is achieved by applying this technique. The routine was improved further by replacing a temporary variable by an array of temporary variables. This replacement allowed the splitting of the outer loop containing unvectorized statements into a vectorizable code. Also, calls to the LSAME function were replaced by in-line code as before. The original code and the changes with loops unrolled to a depth of four are:

Routine DGEMV :

Original code :

```
          .......
          .......
          DO 60, J = 1, N
             IF ( X(JX) .NE. ZERO ) THEN
                TEMP = ALPHA * X(JX)
                DO 50, I = 1, M
                   Y(I) = Y(I) + TEMP * A(I,J)
 50             CONTINUE
                JX = JX + INCX
             END IF
 60       CONTINUE
          .......
          .......
```

Changed to :

```
          .......
          .......
          DO 45, J = 1, N
             TTEMP(J) = ALPHA * X(JX)
             JX = JX + INCX
 45       CONTINUE
          NMOD = MOD (N,4)
          JJ = 1
          IF (NMOD.NE.O) THEN
             DO 47, J = 1, NMOD
                DO 471, I = 1,M
                  Y(I) = Y(I) + TTEMP (J) * A (I,J)
471             CONTINUE
 47          CONTINUE
             JJ = NMOD + 1
          END IF
          DO 60,J = JJ,N,4
             DO 50, I = 1,M
                Y(I) = Y(I) + TTEMP(J) * A(I,J)
                            + TTEMP(J + 1) * A(I,J + 1)
                            + TTEMP (J + 2) * A(I,J + 2)
                            + TTEMP (J + 3) * A(I, J + 3)
  50         CONTINUE
  60      CONTINUE
          .......
          .......
```

It should be noted that replacing TEMP by ALPHA*X(JX) in the inner loop does not amount to any improvement.

The routine was executed with several different levels of unrolling. Table VIc presents the MFLOPS for different values of vector length (N) and different levels of unrolling.

The routine DGBMV did not yield any improvement by the use of the above mentioned techniques. This routine operates on band matrices. The code written is such that it operates only on the non zero elements (Appendix A). When the dimension of the matrix becomes large, the time saved by locating the non-zero elements using the MAX and MIN functions in the DO-loop indices is offset by the large dimension. The indices of the inner loop require a change so that the operation can be performed on all the elements. Even though we indulge in a lot of useless computation on zero elements there is a very significant increase in MFLOPS and reduction in time. The change of indices also allows for unrolling of the outer loop. The DO 60 Loop was unrolled to level 4 for the timings given in Table VI although for simplicity the unrolled code is not presented here. It should be noted that in the original routine the non-band elements are not referenced and hence their value does not affect the outcome. With the change these elements will be referenced and care should be taken to see that their value is zero. The change to achieve this is:

Routine DGBMV :

Original code :

```
      .......
      .......
      DO 60, J = 1, N
         IF ( X(JX) .NE. ZERO ) THEN
            TEMP = ALPHA * X(JX)
            K = KUP1 - J
            DO 50, I = MAX(1,J-KU), MIN(M,J+KL)
               Y(I) = Y(I) + TEMP * A(K+I, J)
50          CONTINUE
         END IF
         JX = JX + INCX
60    CONTINUE
      .......
      .......
```

Changed to :

```
      .......
      .......
      DO 45, J = 1, N
         TTEMP(J) = ALPHA * X(JX)
         JX = JX + INCX
45    CONTINUE
      DO 60, I = 1, KU + KL + 1
         L = KU + 1 - I
         DO 50, J = 1, N
            Y(J-L) = Y(J-L) + TTEMP(J) * A(I,J)
50       CONTINUE
60    CONTINUE
      .......
      .......
```

To optimize the DSBMV routine all of the above strategies were employed. As in the previous example, a change of indices would lead to unrolling of loop, and although not done in this case, will certainly speed it up. The changes are:

Routine DSBMV :

Original Code :

```
       .......
       .......
       DO 60, J =1, N
          TEMP1 = ALPHA * X(J)
          TEMP2 = ZERO
          L= KPLUS1 - J
          DO 50, I = MAX(1,J-K), J-1
             Y(I)  = Y(I) + TEMP1 * A(L+I,J)
             TEMP2 = TEMP2 + A(L+I,J) * X(I)
50        CONTINUE
          Y(J) = Y(J) + TEMP1 * A(KPLUS1,J) + ALPHA * TEMP2
60     CONTINUE
       .......
       .......
```

Changed to :

```
       .......
       .......
       DO 45, J = 1, N
          TTEMP1(J) = ALPHA * X(J)
          TTEMP2(J) = ZERO
45     CONTINUE
       DO 60, J = 1, N
          L= KPLUS1 - J
          DO 50, I = MAX(1,J-K), J-1
             Y(I)      = Y(I) + TTEMP1(J) * A(L+I,J)
             TTEMP2(J) = TTEMP2(J) + A(L+I,J) * X(I)
50        CONTINUE
60     CONTINUE
       DO 65, J = 1, N
          Y(J) = Y(J) + TTEMP1(J) * A(K+1,J)
          Y(J) = Y(J) + ALPHA * TTEMP2(J)
65     CONTINUE
       .......
       .......
```

Similar strategies of replacing single temporary variables in the outer loop by an array of temporary variables and loop splitting may be used for optimizing other routines.

Although the speeds reported, MFLOPS rates, are mostly affected by the compiler, hardware etc. a fairly large amount of time is spent on the validation of parameters being passed into the routines. A run of DTRSV without the initial parameter checks resulting in the elimination of several logical IF statements contributed to a substantial increase in the MFLOPS. The change was from 142 MFLOPS for N=256 in the already optimized code to 168 MFLOPS after the removal of the initial parameter tests. In a highly vectorized code it is not just the vector instructions that cost time but also statements that are used for validation purposes.

VII. ACKNOWLEDGEMENTS

Acknowledgements are due to J. Dongarra and J. DuCroz for providing the routines, the test program and the timing for Cray-1. Thanks are also due to the NEC Corporation for allowing the usage of the NEC SX-2 system and release of timings during the period of system installation.

VIII. REFERENCES

1. C.L. Lawson, R.J. Hanson, D.R. Kincaid, F.T. Krogh, "Basic Linear Algebra Subprograms for FORTRAN Usage", ACM Transactions on Mathematical Software, (September 1979).

2. J. Dongarra, J. Bunch, C. Moler, G. Stewart, "LINPACK Users' Guide", SIAM Publications, Philadelphia, 1979.

3. J. Dongarra, S. Hammarling, J. Du Croz, R. Hanson, "An Extended Set of FORTRAN Basic Linear Algebra Subprograms", Argonne Natl. Lab., Technical Memorandum No. 41 Rev. 2, January 1986. (in press ACM Trans. on Math. Software, 1987).

4. J.J. Dongarra. "Performance of Various Computers Using Standard Linear Equations Software in a FORTRAN Environment", Argonne National Laboratory, Technical Memorandum No. 43, October, 1986.

5. K.G. Stevens, Jr., "Today's Supercomputers", Spring Compcon, pp. 2-6, March 1986.

6. O. Lubeck, J. Moore, and R. Mendez. "Benchmark Comparison of the Japanese Supercomputers", International Conference on Supercomputing, Dec. 1985. (update to be published, IEEE Computing, 1987).

7. D. H. Bailey, "NASA Kernel Benchmark Results", International Conference of Supercomputing, December 1985. and NEC SX-2 performance data.

8. R.W. Hockney. "Parameterization of Computer Performance", invited paper at an International Conference on Vector and Parallel Computing, June 1986, Loen, Norway.

9. R. Mendez, "The Performance of the NEC SX-2 Supercomputer System Compared with that of the Cray X-MP/4 and Fujitsu VP-200", Technical Report for Naval Postgraduate School (period April-August 1986), September 1986. (in press Parallel Computing 1987).

10. Private communication J. Du Croz, December 1986.

11. R.W. Hockney and C.R. Jesshope, "Parallel Computers", Adam Hilger Ltd. Bristol, 1986.

12. T. Watanabe, "Architecture and Performance of NEC Supercomputer SX System", International Conference on Vector and Parallel Computing, June 1986, Leon, Norway.

Appendix A

Naming Convention :

First Character 'D' specifies that all the variables are double precision.

Second and Third characters stand for the following :

GE : General Matrix
GB : General Band Matrix
SY : Symmetric Matrix
SB : Symmetric Band Matrix
SP : Symmetric Matrix in Packed Form
TR : Triangular Matrix
TB : Triangular Band Matrix
TP : Triangular Matrix in Packed Form

Fourth and Last (if present) characters specify the following :

MV : Matrix Vector Product
SV : Solving a system of linear equations
R : Rank One Update
R2 : Rank Two Update

Purpose and, data format and structure of each routine :

<u>DGEMV :</u>
Purpose : Performs one of
Y := Alpha * A * X + Beta * Y or
Y := Alpha * A'* X + Beta * Y
where Alpha and Beta are scalars, X and Y are vectors and A is an M by N matrix.

Matrix A is passed as an array of dimension (LDA,N). Before entry the leading M by N part of the array must contain the matrix of coefficients. On exit, the vector Y is overwritten by the updated vector.

<u>DGBMV :</u>
Purpose : Performs one of
Y := Alpha * A * X + Beta * Y or
Y := Alpha * A'* X + Beta * Y
where Alpha and Beta are scalars, X and Y are vectors and A is an M by N band matrix, with KL sub-diagonals and KU super-diagonals.

Matrix A is passed as an array of dimension (LDA,N). Before entry the leading (KL+KU+1) by N part of the array A must contain the matrix of coefficients, column by column, with the leading diagonal of matrix in the row (KU+1) of the array, the first super-diagonal starting at position 2 in row KU, the first sub-diagonal starting at position 1 in row (KU+2) and so on. The elements in the array A that do not correspond to elements in the band matrix, such as the top left KU by KU triangle are not referenced. On exit, the vector Y is overwritten by the updated vector.

<u>DSYMV :</u>
Purpose : Performs Y := Alpha * A * X + Beta * Y
where Alpha and Beta are scalars, X and Y are N element vectors and A is an N by N symmetric matrix.

Matrix A is passed as an array of dimension (LDA,N). Before entry with UPLO=U, the leading N by n part of the array must contain the upper triangular part of the symmetric matrix. The strictly lower triangular part is not referenced. Similarly with UPLO=L, the leading N by N part of the array must contain the lower triangular part of the symmetric matrix. The strictly upper triangular part is not referenced. On exit, Y is overwritten by the updated vector Y.

<u>DSBMV :</u>
Purpose : Performs Y := Alpha * A * X + Beta * Y
where Alpha and Beta are scalars, X and Y are N element vectors and A is N by N symmetric band matrix, with K super-diagonals.

Matrix A is passed as an array of dimension (LDA,N). Before entry, with UPLO=U, the leading (K+1) by N part of the array A must contain the upper triangular band part of the symmetric matrix, column by column, with the leading diagonal of the matrix in row position (K+1) of the array, the first super-diagonal starting at position 2 in row K and so on. The top left K by K triangle of the array is not referenced. Before entry with UPLO=L, the leading (K+1) by N part of the array A must contain the lower triangular band part of the symmetric matrix, column by column, with the leading diagonal of the matrix in row 1 of the array, the first sub-diagonal starting at position 1 in row 2 and so on. The bottom right K by K triangle of the array is not referenced. On exit, the vector Y is overwritten by the updated vector Y.

<u>DSPMV :</u>
Purpose : Performs Y := Alpha * A * X + Beta * Y
where Alpha and Beta are scalars, X and Y are N element vectors and A is an N by N symmetric matrix.

Matrix A is passed as a single dimension array of dimension at least ((N*(N+1))/2). Before entry with UPLO=U the array AP must contain the upper triangular part of the symmetric matrix packed sequentially, column by column, so that AP(1) contains A(1,1), AP(2) and AP(3) contain A(1,2) and A(2,2) respectively and so on. Before entry with UPLO=L the array AP must contain the lower triangular part of the symmetric matrix packed sequentially, column by column, so that AP(1) contains A(1,1), AP(2) and AP(3) contain A(1,2) and A(2,2) respectively and so on. On exit, the vector Y is overwritten by the updated vector Y.

<u>DTRMV :</u>
Purpose : Performs one of

X := A * X   or   X := A'* X

where X is an N element vector and A is an N by N unit or non-unit upper or lower triangular matrix.

Matrix A is passed as an array of dimension (LDA,N). Before entry with UPLO=U, the leading N by N upper triangular part of the array A must contain the upper triangular matrix and the strictly lower part is not referenced. Before entry with UPLO=L, the leading N by N lower triangular part of the array must contain the lower triangular matrix and the strictly upper part is not referenced. When DIAG=U, the diagonal elements of A are not referenced, but are assumed to be unity. On exit, the vector X is overwritten by the updated vector X.

<u>DTBMV :</u>
Purpose : Performs one of

X := A * X   or   X := A'* X

where X is an N element vector and A is an N by N unit or non-unit, upper or lower triangular matrix with (K+1) diagonals.
K : With UPLO=U, K specifies the number of super-diagonals of the matrix A. With UPLO=L, K specifies the number of sub-diagonals of the matrix A.

Matrix A is passed as an array of dimension (LDA,N). Before entry with UPLO=U, the leading (K+1) by N part of the array must contain the upper triangular band part of the matrix of coefficients, supplied column by column, with the leading diagonal of the matrix in row (K+1) of the array, the first super-diagonal starting at position 2 in row K, and so on. The top left K by K triangle is not referenced. With UPLO=L the leading (K+1) by N part of the array must contain the lower triangular band part of the matrix of coefficients, column by column, with the leading diagonal of the matrix in row 1, the first sub-diagonal starting at position 2 in row 2 and so on. The bottom right K by K triangle of the array A is not referenced. When DIAG=U the elements of the array corresponding to the diagonal elements of the matrixare not referenced, but are assumed to be unity. On exit, the vector X is overwritten by the transformed vector X.

<u>DTPMV :</u>
Purpose : Performs one of

X := A * X or X := A'* X

where X is an N element vector and A is an N by N unit or non-unit, upper or lower triangular matrix.

Matrix A is passed as a single dimensional array AP of dimension at least ((N*(N+1))/2). Before entry with UPLO=U, the array AP must contain the upper triangular matrix packed sequentially, column by column, so that AP(1) contains A(1,1), AP(2) and AP(3) contain A(1,2) and A(2,2) respectively, and so on. Before entry with UPLO=L, the array AP must contain the lower triangular matrix packed sequentially, column by column, so that AP(1) contains A(1,1) and AP(2) and AP(3) contain A(2,1) and A(3,1) respectively, and so on. When DIAG=U, the diagonal elements of A are not referenced, but are assumed to be unity. On exit, the vector X is overwritten by the transformed vector X.

<u>DTRSV :</u>
Purpose : Solves one of the systems of equations

A * X = B or A'* X = B

where B and X are N element vectors and A is an N by N unit, or non-unit upper or lower triangular matrix.

Matrix A is passed as an array of dimension (LDA,N). Before entry with UPLO=U, the leading N by N upper triangular part of the array A must contain the upper triangular matrix and the strictly lower triangular part of A is not referenced. Before entry with UPLO= L, the leading N by N lower triangular part of the array A must contain the lower triangular part of the matrix and the strictly upper triangular part of A is not referenced. When DIAG=U, the diagonal elements of A are not referenced either, but are assumed to be unity. On exit, the vector X is overwritten by the solution vector X.

<u>DTBSV :</u>
Purpose : Solves one of the systems of equations

A * X = B or A'* X = B

where B and X are N element vectors and A is an N by N unit or non-unit, upper or lower triangular band matrix with (K+1) diagonals.

K : On entry with UPLO=U, K specifies the number of super-diagonals of the matrix A. On entry with UPLO=L, K specifies the number of sub-diagonals of matrix A.

Matrix A is passed as an array of dimension (LDA,N). Before entry with UPLO=U, the leading (K+1) by N part of the array A must contain the upper triangular band part of the matrix of coefficients, supplied column by column, with the leading diagonal of the matrix in row (K+1) of the array, the first super-diagonal starting at position 2 in row K and so on. The top left K by K triangle of the array A is not referenced. Before entry with UPLO=L, the leading (K+1) by N part of the array A must contain the lower triangular band part of the matrix of coefficients supplied, column by column, with the leading diagonal of the matrix in row 1 of the array, the first sub-diagonal starting at position 1 in row 2 and so on. The bottom right K by K triangle of the array A is not referenced. On exit, X is overwritten by the solution vector X.

DTPSV :
Purpose : Solves one of the system of equations

A * X = B   or   A'* X = B

where B and X are N element vectors and A is an N by N unit or non-unit, upper or lower triangular matrix.

Matrix A is passed as a single dimensional array AP of dimension at least ((N*(N+1))/2). Before entry with UPLO =U, the array AP must contain the upper triangular matrix packed sequentially, column by column, so that AP(1) contains A(1,1), AP(2) and AP(3) contain A(1,2) and A(2,2) respectively and so on. Before entry with UPLO=L, the array AP must contain the lower triangular matrix packed sequentially, column by column, so that AP(1) contains A(1,1), AP(2) and AP(3) contain A(2,1) and A(3,1) respectively, and so on. When DIAG=U the diagonal elements of A are not referenced, but are assumed to be unity. On exit, the vector X is overwritten by solution vector X.

DGER :
Purpose : Performs the Rank 1 operation

A := Alpha * X * Y'+ A

where Alpha is a scalar, X is an M element vector, Y is an N element vector and A is an M by N matrix.

Matrix A is passed as an array of dimension at least (LDA,N). Before entry, the leading M by N part of the array A must contain the matrix of coefficients. On exit A is overwritten by the updated matrix.

DSYR :
Purpose : Performs the symmetric Rank 1 operation

A := Alpha * X * X'+ A

where Alpha is a scalar, X is an N element vector and A is an N by N symmetric matrix.

Matrix A is passed as an array of dimension (LDA,N). Before entry, with UPLO=U, the leading N by N upper triangular part of the array A must contain the upper triangular part of the symmetric matrix and the strictly lower triangular part of A is not referenced. On exit the upper triangular part of the matrix A is overwritten by the updated matrix. Before entry with UPLO=L, the leading N by N lower triangular part of the array A must contain the lower triangular part of the symmetric matrix and the strictly upper triangular part of A is not referenced. On exit, the lower triangular part of the array A is overwritten by the lower triangular part of the updated matrix.

DSPR :

Purpose : Performs the symmetric Rank 1 operation

A := Alpha * X * X' + A

where Alpha is a scalar, X is an N element vector and A is an N by N symmetric matrix.

Matrix A is passed as a single dimensional array AP of dimension at least ((N*(N+1))/2). Before entry, with UPLO=U, the array AP must contain the upper triangular part of the symmetric matrix packed sequentially, column by column, so that AP(1) contains A(1,1), AP(2) and AP(3) contain A(1,2) and A(2,2) respectively, and so on. On exit, the array AP is overwritten by the upper triangular part of the updated matrix. Before entry, with UPLO=L, the

array AP must contain the lower triangular part of the symmetric matrix, packed sequentially, column by column, so that AP(1) contains A(1,1), AP(2) and AP(3) contain A(2,1) and A(3,1) respectively, and so on. On exit, the array AP is overwritten by the lower triangular part of the updated matrix.

DSYR2 :

Purpose : Performs the symmetric rank 2 operation

A := Alpha * X * Y'+ Alpha * Y * X'+ A

where Alpha is a scalar, X and Y are N element vectors and A is an N by N symmetric matrix.

Matrix A is passed as an array of dimension (LDA,N). Before entry with UPLO=U, the leading N by N upper triangular part of the array A must contain the upper triangular part of the symmetric matrix and the strictly lower part of A is not referenced. On exit, the upper triangular part of the array A is overwritten by the upper triangular part of the updated matrix. Before entry with UPLO= L, the leading N by N lower triangular part of the array A must contain the lower triangular part of the symmetric matrix and the strictly upper triangular part of A is not referenced. On exit, the lower triangular part of the array A is overwritten by the lower triangular part of the updated matrix.

DSPR2 :

Purpose : Performs the symmetric Rank 2 operation

A = Alpha * X * Y'+ Alpha * Y * X'+ A

where Alpha is a scalar, X and Y are N element vectors and A is an N by n symmetric matrix.

Matrix A is passed as a single dimensional array AP of dimension ((N*(N+1))/2). Before entry with UPLO=U, the array AP must contain the upper triangular part of the symmetric matrix packed sequentially, column by column, so that AP(1) contains A(1,1), AP(2) and AP(3) contain A(1,2) and A(2,2) respectively, and so on. On exit, the array AP is overwritten by the upper triangular part of the updated matrix. Before entry with UPLO=L, the array AP must contain the lower triangular part of the symmetric matrix packed sequentially, column by column, so that AP(1) contains A(1,1), AP(2) and AP(3) contain A(2,1) and A(3,1) respectively, and so on. On exit the array AP is overwritten by the lower triangular part of the updated matrix.

For a more detailed discussion please refer to [3] and the inline documentation of the FORTRAN source code.

Least-Squares Iterative Solution on a Fixed-Size VLSI Architecture

E.P. Papadopoulou and T.S. Papatheodorou

Mathematics and Computer Science, Clarkson Univ., Potsdam, NY 13676

and

C.T.I. and Dept of Computer Eng., Univ. of Patras, Greece

ABSTRACT

The VLSI implementation of the Accelerated Overrelaxation (AOR) method, when used for the accurate computation of the least-squares solutions of overdetermined systems, is the problem addressed here. As the size of this computational task is usually very large, we use space-time domain expansion techniques to partition the computation and map it onto a fixed size VLSI architecture.

1. Introduction

In recent years, least-squares problems of very large size have arisen with increasing frequency. They are integral parts of significant scientific research programs such as geodetic surveying, PDE computation, pattern recognition, earthquake studies, molecular structures and tomography (cf. [1],[2],[9],[14],[20]). The large size of this computational task and the demand (by the applications) of fast and accurate solutions naturally led us to consider their iterative solution in parallel environments. In this work we are concerned with the problem of partitioning the computation, so that it can be carried out on fixed size VLSI architectures.

The method used here is the block AOR [10], a two parametric generalization of the SOR [22]. The theoretical motives for this have been established in [17],[18], where its behavior, when applied on large scale least squares problems, is successfully investigated revealing fast rates of convergence. In Section 2, together with a brief description of the least-squares problems and the AOR method, the iteration equations are derived and the time dependency of the computation is shown (see Figure 1).

Section 3 is devoted to the partitioning phase of the computation and the design of a fixed size VLSI architecture based on space-time domain expansion techniques (cf. [7]). The partitioning of the computation is mainly motivated by the simple fact that the size of the computational problem exceeds the size of a fixed VLSI architecture or the number of processing units on the VLSI chip or both. Therefore, the partitioning problem is a significant step in extending the computational capability of a VLSI structure (cf. [5],[6],[7],[8],[11],[12],[15],[16]). Our main concerns in designing the VLSI architecture were:

(a) increase the speed-up factor

(b) keep the overhead as low as possible.

For this, we overlapped the execution of parts of the computation. Moreover, in order to efficiently pipeline different processes, we designed a new "column-oriented" VLSI unit for matrix-vector multiplication. It is shown that this unit can be successfully pipelined with an existing matrix-vector multiplication unit (cf. [7]), so that, two such multiplications can be performed at roughly the time cost of one. All the above led to the design of a fixed size VLSI architecture capable to perform one iteration step in time proportional to (N^2/k), namely, proportional to the time required for a VLSI matrix-vector multiplication.

2. Block AOR for Least-Squares

In this section, we give a brief description of the block AOR method, as it applies to the solution of large-scale least-squares problems.

To fix notation consider the overdetermined system

$$\hat{A}\hat{x} \cong \hat{b} \tag{2.1}$$

where $\hat{A}\varepsilon\mathbf{R}^{m,n}$ ($m \geq n$), with full column rank n, $\hat{x}\varepsilon\mathbf{R}^n$ and $\hat{b}\varepsilon\mathbf{R}^m$. The least-squares solution to (2.1) is the vector $\hat{y}\varepsilon\mathbf{R}^n$ satisfying

$$||\hat{b}-\hat{A}\hat{y}||_2 = \min_{\hat{x}\varepsilon\mathbf{R}^n} ||\hat{b}-\hat{A}\hat{x}||_2,$$

which can equivalently be expressed as the set of <u>normal equations</u> described by the system

$$\hat{A}^T\hat{A}\hat{y} = \hat{A}^T\hat{b} \tag{2.2}$$

If we now let $\hat{r}\varepsilon\mathbf{R}^m$ to denote the residual vector, then the system in (2.2) can be written as

$$\begin{cases} \hat{A}\hat{y} + \hat{r} = \hat{b} \\ \hat{A}^T\hat{r} = 0 \end{cases} \tag{2.3}$$

Assuming further that the matrix $\hat{A}$ is assembled (see e.g. [9],[13], [19]) into the form

$$\hat{A} = \begin{bmatrix} A_1 \\ \\ A_2 \end{bmatrix} , \tag{2.4}$$

where $A_1 \varepsilon \mathbf{R}^{n,n}$ is nonsingular, and considering the conformal partitioning of the vectors $\hat{r}$ and $\hat{b}$ as

$$\hat{r} = \begin{bmatrix} \hat{r}_1 \\ \\ \hat{r}_2 \end{bmatrix} \quad \text{and} \quad \hat{b} = \begin{bmatrix} \hat{b}_1 \\ \\ \hat{b}_2 \end{bmatrix} , \tag{2.5}$$

the vectors $\hat{y}$ and $\hat{r}$ satisfy (2.3) if and only if

$$\begin{cases} A_1\hat{y} + \hat{r}_1 = \hat{b}_1 \\ A_2\hat{y} + \hat{r}_2 = \hat{b}_2 \\ A_2^T\hat{r}_2 + A_1^T\hat{r}_1 = 0 \end{cases} . \tag{2.6}$$

Thus, (2.3) can be expressed as (m+n)x(m+n) system (cf. [4])

$$Ax = b \tag{2.7}$$

where

$$A := \begin{bmatrix} A_1 & 0 & I \\ A_2 & I & 0 \\ 0 & A_2^T & A_1^T \end{bmatrix} , \tag{2.8}$$

$$x = \begin{bmatrix} x_1 \\ x_2 \\ x_3 \end{bmatrix} := \begin{bmatrix} \hat{y} \\ \hat{r}_2 \\ \hat{r}_1 \end{bmatrix} \quad \text{and } b = \begin{bmatrix} b_1 \\ b_2 \\ b_3 \end{bmatrix} := \begin{bmatrix} \hat{b}_1 \\ \hat{b}_2 \\ 0 \end{bmatrix} . \tag{2.9}$$

Note that, since A_1 is nonsingular, it can be easily verified (e.g. constructively) that the matrix A of (2.8) is nonsingular, hence the system (2.7) has a unique solution. A natural 3-block AOR method can be now conveniently applied for the solution of (2.7). More specifically, upon writing A as

$$A = D - C_L - C_U , \tag{2.10}$$

where

$$D = \begin{bmatrix} A_1 & 0 & 0 \\ 0 & I & 0 \\ 0 & 0 & A_1^T \end{bmatrix} C_L = \begin{bmatrix} 0 & 0 & 0 \\ -A_2 & 0 & 0 \\ 0 & -A_2^T & 0 \end{bmatrix} C_U = \begin{bmatrix} 0 & 0 & -I \\ 0 & 0 & 0 \\ 0 & 0 & 0 \end{bmatrix} , \tag{2.11}$$

The associated block AOR iterative method is defined (cf. [10]) by

$$\begin{cases} x^{(m+1)} = L_{r,\omega} x^{(m)} + c_{r,\omega} & m=0,1,\ldots \\ L_{r,\omega} \doteq (D-rC_L)^{-1}[(1-\omega)D+(\omega-r)C_L+\omega C_U]. \\ c_{r,\omega} \doteq \omega(D-rC_L)^{-1}b \end{cases} \tag{2.12}$$

The parameters r and ω are respectively referred to as acceleration and overrelaxation factors and well-known iterative schemes are recovered by their special combinations. For instance, when $(r,\omega)=(0,1)$, $(1,1)$ and (ω,ω) the AOR reduces to Jacobi, Gauss-Seidel and SOR methods respectively.

Evidently, the computation taking place in each iteration step is equivalent to

$$(D-rC_L)\tilde{x} = [(1-\omega)D+(\omega-r)C_L+\omega C_U]x+\omega b, \tag{2.13}$$

where $\tilde{x}$, x respectively denote the new and the old iterate. Recalling now the structure of D, C_L, C_U and b from (2.11) and (2.9), the above relation is equivalent to

$$\begin{bmatrix} A_1 & 0 & 0 \\ rA_2 & I & 0 \\ 0 & rA_2^T & A_1^T \end{bmatrix} \begin{bmatrix} \tilde{x}_1 \\ \tilde{x}_2 \\ \tilde{x}_3 \end{bmatrix} = \begin{bmatrix} (1-\omega)A_1 & 0 & -\omega I \\ -(\omega-r)A_2 & (1-\omega)I & 0 \\ 0 & -(\omega-r)A_2^T & (1-\omega)A_1^T \end{bmatrix} \begin{bmatrix} x_1 \\ x_2 \\ x_3 \end{bmatrix} + \begin{bmatrix} \omega b_1 \\ \omega b_2 \\ 0 \end{bmatrix},$$

whence, solving for $\tilde{x}_1$, $\tilde{x}_2$, $\tilde{x}_3$ we obtain

$$\begin{aligned} A_1\tilde{x}_1 &= (1-\omega)A_1x_1 - \omega x_3 + \omega b_1 \\ \tilde{x}_2 &= -(\omega-r)A_2x_1 + (1-\omega)x_2 - rA_2\tilde{x}_1 + \omega b_2 \\ A_1^T\tilde{x}_3 &= -(\omega-r)A_2^Tx_2 + (1-\omega)A_1^Tx_3 - rA_2^T\tilde{x}_2 \end{aligned} \quad . \tag{2.14}$$

with respect to the computation involved in (2.14) we would like to remark that:

(a) For the determination of $\tilde{x}_1$ and $\tilde{x}_3$, an nxn system of the form $A_1\tilde{x}=w$ has to be solved. Assuming a parallel environment with, say, $0(\frac{n}{k})$ processing units an L-U decomposition can be performed in $0(\frac{n^2}{k})$ time steps (cf. [12]). The L-U decomposed matrix A, can be written as $A_1=L_1U_1$, where L_1 and U_1 are triangular matrices. The inversion of a triangular matrix in the same environment can also be performed in $0(\frac{n^2}{k})$ time steps (cf. [12]). Therefore, in $0(\frac{n^2}{k})$ time units ($n>>k>>1$) the inverse of A_1 can be computed. (For inverses of banded triangular matrices see also [3],[21]).

(b) In each iteration step there is a number of invariant calculations. These are assumed to be precalculated and saved.

Taking into consideration the remarks above, (2.14) can be written as

$$\left\{\begin{array}{l}\tilde{x}_1 = (1-\omega)x_1 - \omega M_1 x_3 + c_1 \\ \tilde{x}_2 = (1-\omega)x_2 - (\omega-r)M_2 x_1 - rM_2\tilde{x}_1 + c_2 \\ \tilde{x}_3 = (1-\omega)x_3 - (\omega-r)M_3 x_2 - rM_3\tilde{x}_2\end{array}\right. \quad . \tag{2.15}$$

where $M_1 \doteq A_1^{-1}$, $M_2 \doteq A_2$, $M_3 \doteq (A_2 A_1^{-1})^T$, $c_1 \doteq \omega A_1^{-1} b_1$ and $c_2 \doteq \omega b_2$ are invariant in each iteration step, hence assumed precalculated before entering the iteration process.

By inspection now of (2.15), it is seen that, while the computation of $\tilde{x}_1$ can be performed independently, the evaluation of $\tilde{x}_j | j=2,3$ depends on the computation of $\tilde{x}_{j-1}$. However, part of the computation for the evaluation of $\tilde{x}_j | j=2,3$ can be overlapped with that of $\tilde{x}_1$. The time dependency and the overlapping of the computation in (2.15) is graphically demonstrated in Figure 1.

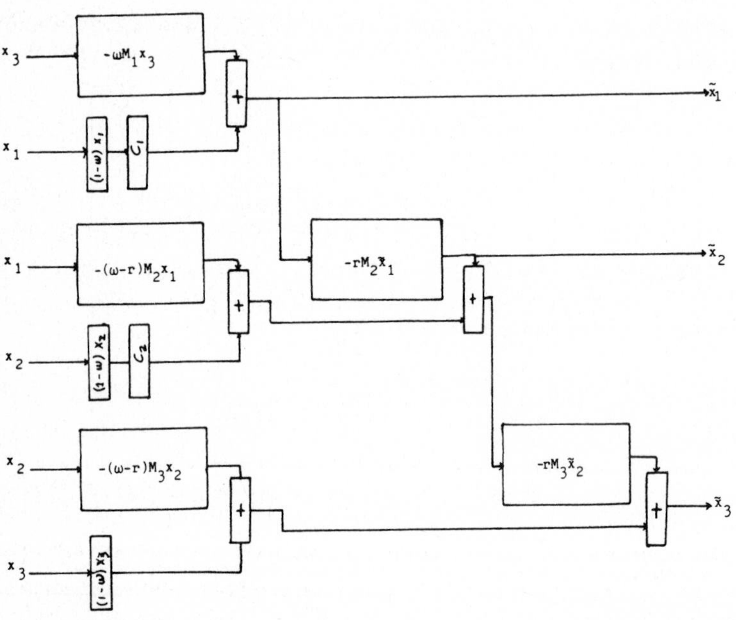

Figure 1. Time dependency of the calculation.

Finally, observe that the dominant operation in the whole calculation is that of matrix-vector multiplication.

3. Partitioned Computation on a Fixed Size VLSI Architecture

In this section, we use space-rime domain expansion techniques to partition and map the computation on a proposed VLSI architecture.

Roughly speaking a k-space expansion, in any one space direction, means the physical presence of k copies of the same processing unit in this direction. A k-time expansion basically means that J events occur sequentially and each adjacent pair of events has equal time interval (1 time unit). The following rules (cf. [7]) for space-time expansion apply in order to design a VLSI architecture for solving a recursive task.

Space-time expansion consistency rules. Maintain time consistency by requiring that the input data of the k-th processing element reach it after k time units have elapsed. Maintain space consistency by requiring that the j-th set of input reaches a processing element after j time units have elapsed. In the presence of limited hardware the data are pipelined.

The computation model of a VLSI architecture obtained by space-time expansion is described in [7] by a tupple $(k_1,k_2,k_3,Q_1,\dots,Q_\ell)$ where k_i denotes a k_i space expansion along the x_i direction and Q_j denotes the size of the j-th time expansion. The values of these parameters are set to 1 in the absence of the corresponding expansion. It is necessary that:

$$\Pi k_i \times \Pi Q_j \geq N$$

where N is the size of the computational problem. This corresponds to conservation laws described in [12] and it means that a space reduction must be compensated by analogous time expansion. For more details in all the above see [7].

The description and the dataflow of basic VLSI units, used in the design of the VLSI architecture, follow. Their design is based on the space-time expansion rules described above.

a) SV+V unit (cf. [17])
Performs computations of the type $\alpha x+c$, where $\alpha\varepsilon R$, and $x,c\varepsilon \mathbf{R}^N$.

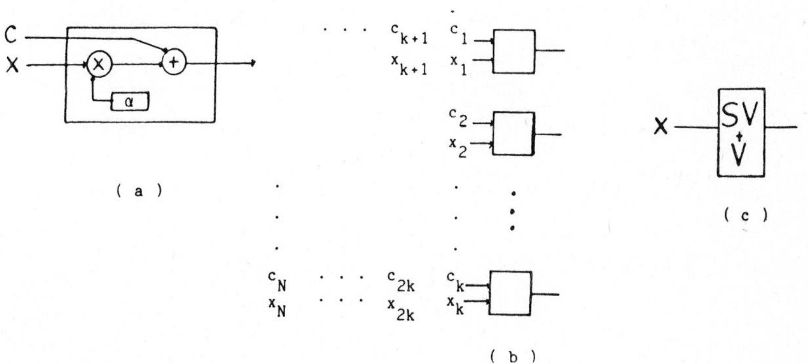

(a) The elementary unit, (b) k-space expansion, (c) Schematic representation

b) Matrix-Vector Multiplication Units

Perform Mu=v, $M \epsilon \mathbb{R}^{N,N}$ and $u,v \epsilon \mathbb{R}^{N}$

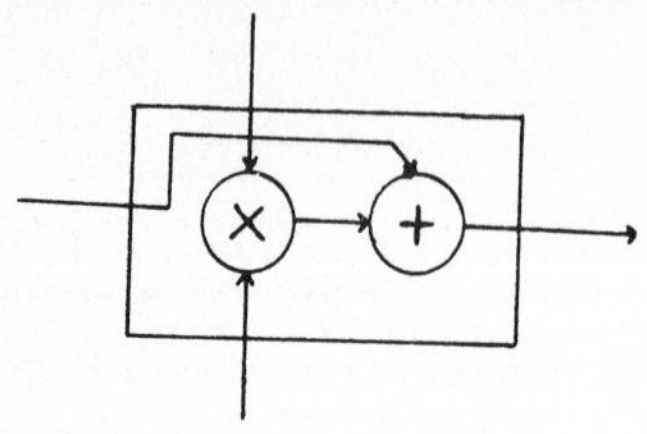

Single PE for matrix-vector multiplication (Row-Unit).

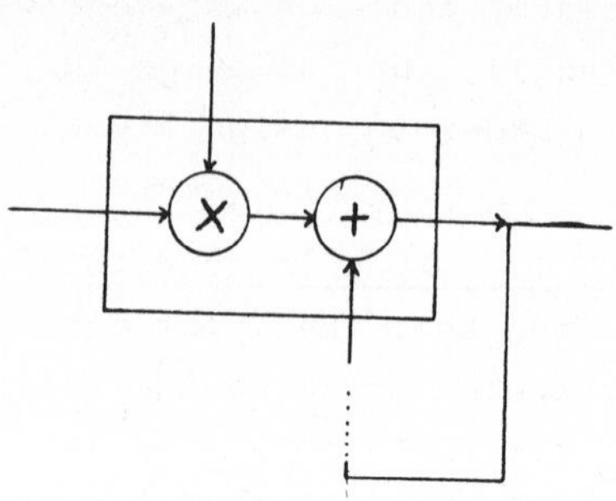

Single PE for matrix-vector multiplication (Column-Unit).

a) Row oriented [7]

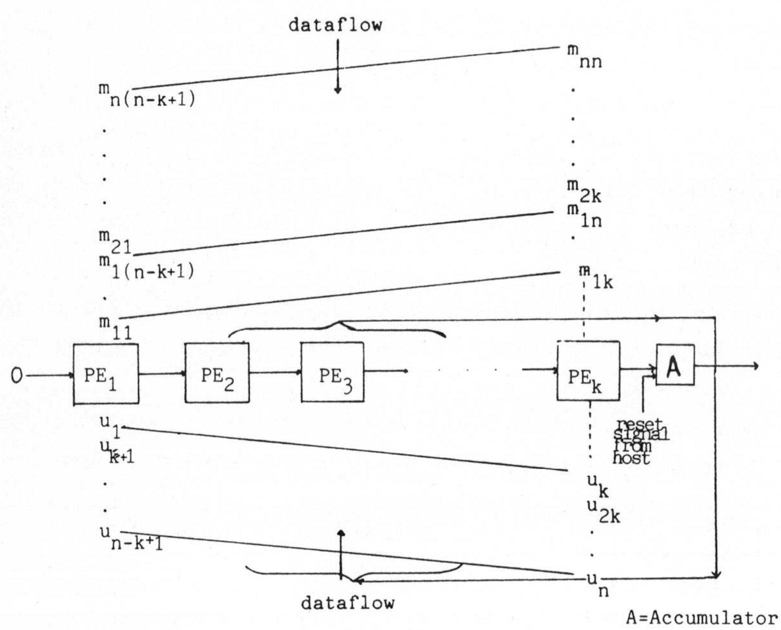

b) Column-Oriented [17]

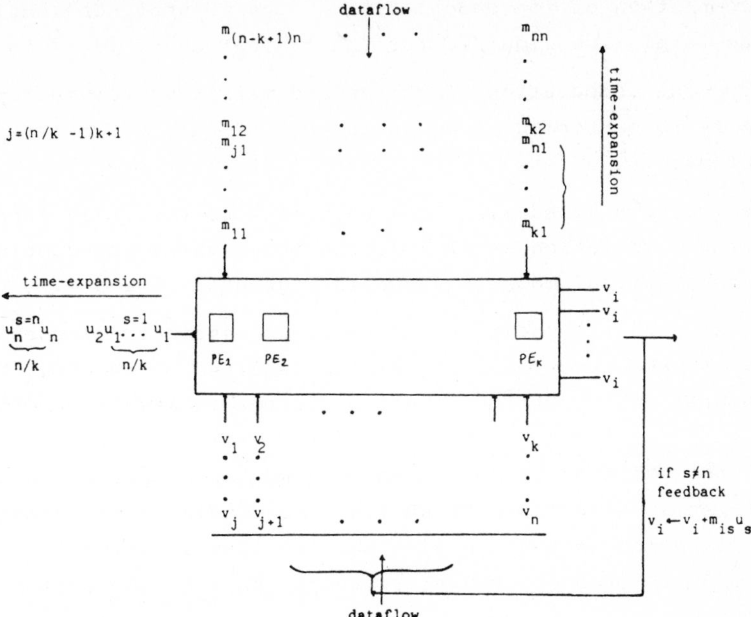

Dealing with computational problems of order N, on VLSI units designed using k-space domain expansion, one can easily show that:

(i) The first output coordinate from the RU unit is available after $\frac{N}{k}$ + k+1 time units. The rest follow one every $\frac{N}{k}$ time units (time unit = time for (addition+multiplication)). Thus the total time required to perform a matrix-vector multiplication on the RU unit is $\frac{N^2}{k}$ + k+1.

(ii) The result from the CU unit is produced in groups of k output coordinates at a time every $\frac{N}{k}$ time units. Thus the last group is available after $\frac{N^2}{k}$ time steps (for simplicity $\frac{N}{k}$ is assumed integer).

The reason for designing the CU unit is that significant time is saved by overlapping the execution of the RU and CU units. For a demonstration, consider the evaluation of

$$u = M_1 v \qquad\qquad (3.1)$$

$$z = M_2 u$$

on a system consisting of RU unit followed by a CU unit. The first output coordinate u_1 from the RU unit is available after $\frac{N}{k}$ +k+1 time units. At this instance the CU unit may begin its calculation overlapping its execution with the computation of u_2 from the RU unit. The coordinate u_2 is available after $\frac{N}{k}$ time units, namely at the same time with the completion of the calculation in the CU unit. Obviously, therefore, the total time required for the evaluation of (3.1) is $\frac{N(N+1)}{k}+$ $+k+1$. Hence, the computation of the second matrix-vector multiplication in (3.1) is performed at an extra cost of only $\frac{N}{k}$ time steps (i.e. an order of magnitude less).

For the design of a fixed size VLSI architecture (Fig. 5), capable to carry out the computation in (2.15), the above units are combined to form the computational modules shown in Figures 2, 3 and 4.

The Basic Unit (BU) is shown in Figure 2. On entrance all coordinates of x and y ($x,y \in \mathbf{R}^N$) must be available as required by the RU. Observe that the operations of SV+V unit are performed in parallel with those of RU and end faster. The time cost of SV+V unit is therefore ignored. Since the last addition is pipelined with RU the output of the BU unit follows the same pattern as the RU i.e. coordinate by coordinate every $\frac{N}{k}$ time steps. Hence accounting also for the last addition the time required by a BU to produce the entire vector z is 1 time unit more than that of RU i.e.

$$T(BU) = N*N/k + k+2. \tag{3.2}$$

The Extended Basic Unit (EBU) is shown in Figure 3. It consists of a BU and a CU where the two units are pipelined. When each coordinate is produced by the BU, it is used immediately by the CU. Thus the total of (EBU) is that of BU plus the excess time required for the calculation of terms involving only the last coordinate produced by BU i.e. plus $\frac{N}{k}$. Therefore

$$\begin{aligned} T(EBU) &= T(BU) + N/k \\ &= N*N/k + N/k + k+2. \end{aligned} \tag{3.3}$$

The extended RU (ERU) is shown in Figure 4. It consists of (i) a group of k adders which perform simultaneous addition of k coordinates of the top two input vectors. (ii) an RU and (iii) a single adder.

The appropriate combination of the units presented above form the Iteration Unit, which is illustrated in Figure 5. As all coordinates of the vector produced by BU are available before the first k coordinates produced by EBU, addition in ERU begins as soon as these k coordinates are exited by EBU i.e. the operation of the first group of adders of ERU is pipelined with EBU. The additional time cost required is that of the last k-coordinate addition i.e. 1 time unit. To this time we must add first the time required by an RU. The results of RU as produced coordinate by coordinate are added to the corre-coordinate of the results produced by a BU (vector z) which are assumed to be already calculated. Thus only one more time unit is required to account for the addition of the last coordinate. Thus the last result of ERU is produced at time

$$\begin{aligned} & T(EBU) + 1 + T(RU) + 1 = \\ & = N*N/k + N/k + k + 2 + 1 + N*N/k + 1 + 1 \\ & = 2N^2/k + N/k + k + 5. \end{aligned}$$

This is total time required by the Iteration unit. For the correct implementation of the method appropriate delays must be enforced on vectros $\tilde{x}_1$ and $\tilde{x}_2$.

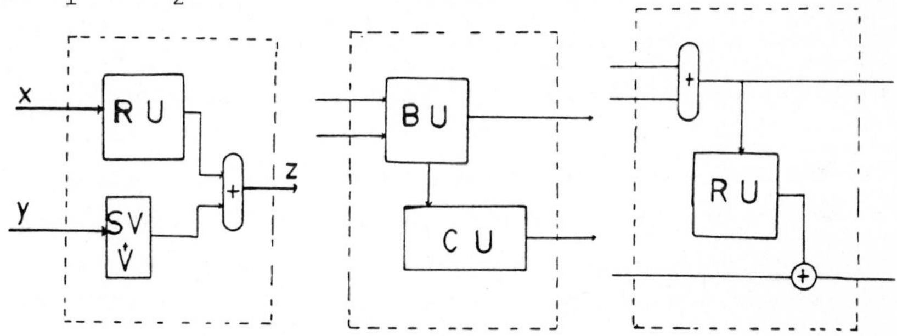

Figure 2 The Basic Unit (BU)

Figure 3 The Extended Basic Unit (EBU)

Figure 4 The Extended Unit (ERU)

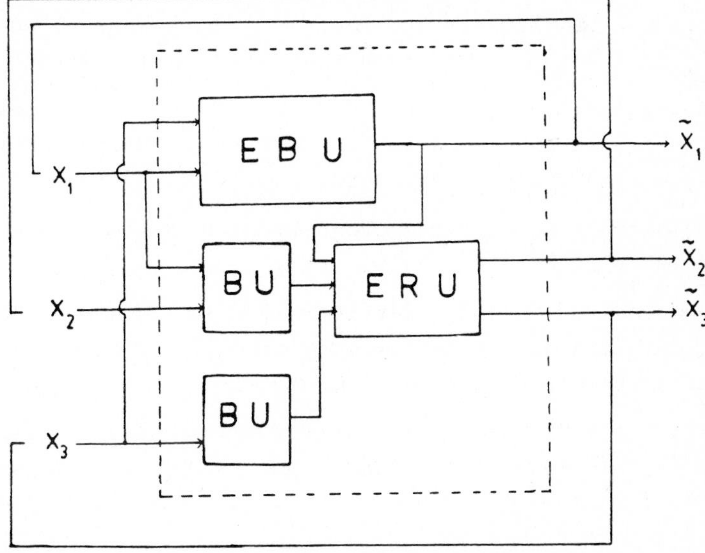

Figure 5 The Iteration Unit

REFERENCES

1. J.H. Argyris and O.E. Brönlund, "The natural factor formulation of the stiffness matrix displacement method", Comput. Meth. Appl. Mech. Engrg. 5: 97-119, 1975.

2. J.H. Argyris, T.L. Johnson and H.P. Mlejnek, "On the natural factor in nonlinear analysis", Ibib. 15: 389-406, 1978.

3. S.C. Chen, D.J. Kuck and A.H. Sameh, "Practical Parallel Band Triangular System Solvers", ACM Trans. Math. Software, Vol. 4, No. 3, pp. 270-277, Sept. 1978.

4. Y.T. Chen, "Iterative methods for linear least-squares problems", Ph.D. Dissertation, Univ. of Waterloo, Canada, 1975.

5. H.D. Cheng and K.S. Fu, "Algorithm partition and parallel recognition of general context free languages using fixed size VLSI architecture", June 1984, Purdue University.

6. H.D. Cheng and K.S. Fu, "VLSI architectures for pattern matching using space-time domain expansion approach", October 1984, Purdue University.

7. H.D. Cheng and K.S. Fu, "Algorithm partition for a fixed size VLSI architecture using space-time domain expansion", Proc. 7th Symp. Comput. Arithmetic, June 1985, pp. 126-132.

8. H.D. Cheng, W.C. Lin and K.S. Fu, "Space-time domain expansion approach to VLSI and its application to hierarchical scene matching", IEEE Trans. on Pattern Anal. Mach. Int., March 1985.

9. G.H. Golub and R.J. Plemmons, "Large scale geothetic least squares adjustments by dissection and orthogonal decomposition", Linear Algebra and Appl., 34: 3-28, 1980.

10. A. Hadjidimos, "Accelerated Overrelaxation Method", Math. Comp. 32: 149-157, 1978.

11. K. Hwang and Y.H. Cheng, "Partitioned algorithms and VLSI structures for large-scale matrix computations", Proc. 5th Symp. Comput. Arithmetic, May 1981, pp. 222-232.

12. K. Hwang and Y.H. Chen, "Partitioned Matrix Algorithms for VLSI Arithmetic Systems", IEEE Trans, Comp., C-31 (12): 1215-1224, 1982.

13. I. Kaneco, M. Lawo and Thieraut, "On computational procedures for the force method", Intern. J. Num. Meth. Eng. 18: 1469-1495, 1982

14. C.B. Kolata, "Geodecy: dealing with an enormous computer task", Science, 200: 421-422, 1978.

15. D.I. Moldovan and J.A.B. Fortes, "Partitioning and Mapping Algorithms into fixed size systolic arrays", IEEE Trans. on Comp., C-35(1): 1-12, 1986.

16. D.I. Moldovan, C.I. Wu and J.A.B. Fortes, "Mapping an arbitrarily large QR algorithm into a fixed size VLSI array", Proc. of 1984 Int. Conf. on Parallel Processing, August 1984.

17. E.P. Papadopoulou, "VLSI structures and iterative analysis for large scale computation", Ph.D. Thesis, Clarkson University, 1986

18. E.P. Papadopoulou, T.S. Papatheodorou and Y.G. Saridakis, "Block AOR Iterative Schemes for Large-Scale Least-Squares Problems", to appear.

19. R.J. Plemmons, "Adjustment by least squares in geodesy using block iterative methods for sparse matrices", ARO Rept. 79-3, Proc. 1979 Army Num. Anal. Comp. Conf., El Paso, 1974.

20. J.R. Rice, RHRVEC workshop on very large least squares problems and supercomputers, CSD-TR 464, Computer Science Dept., Purdue University, Purdue, Indiana, 1983.

21. A.H. Sameh and R.P. Brent, "Solving Triangular Systems on a Parallel Computer", SIAM J. Numer. Anal., Vol. 14, No. 6, pp. 1101-1113, Dec. 1977.

22. D.M. Young, "Iterative Solution of Large Linear Systems", Academic Press, New York, 1971.

PARALLEL MATRIX FACTORIZATIONS ON A SHARED MEMORY MIMD COMPUTER

N. M. Missirlis[1]
Department of Computer Science
Rutgers University
New Brunswick, N.J. 08903

F. Tjaferis
Department of Mathematics
University of Athens
Athens, Greece

Abstract: *This paper is concerned with the study of parallel algorithms for matrix factorization on a shared memory multiprocessor MIMD type computer. We consider the implementation of LU and WZ factorizations of general nonsymmetric matrices when the number of processors p is $\sim O(n)$, where n is the order of the matrix. We show how each of these methods can be divided into noninterfering tasks which can then be executed in parallel. By studying the precedence graph of these tasks we are able to find a schedule for each algorithm which is optimum for a certain number of processors. We also consider the use of the resulting factors to solve a linear system of equations and compare the two algorithms in terms of their speedup and efficiency. It is shown that the parallel WZ algorithm attains a better efficiency using only half the processors of Doolittle's method.*

1. Introduction

This paper is concerned with the numerical solution of linear systems of the form

$$\mathbf{A}\mathbf{u} = \mathbf{b} \tag{1}$$

where $\mathbf{A} = (a_{i,j})$ is a real nonsingular dense matrix of order n, u=(u_i) is the n dimensional vector of unknowns and b=(b_i) is a known n dimensional vector. Many numerical methods exist for the solution of such a system and efficient codes for uniprocessor machines have been developed. With the advent of parallel computers, algorithms suitable for such architectures were also designed and are surveyed in [8], [16] and [13]. Most of the research was based on the modification of the sequential form of the algorithm into its parallel version, suitable for vector and SIMD machines. It is only recently that research is carried out to develop efficient algorithms for solving (1) on an

---

[1]On leave of absence from Section of Numerical Analysis and Computer Science, Department of Mathematics, University of Athens, Panepistimiopolis 157 10, Athens, Greece.

This research is supported by the Greek Ministry of Industry, Research and Technology under grant no. 9707.

MIMD type computer (see e.g., [10], [11], [4], [5], [12]). The current research in this area follows two main streamlines according to the specific MIMD architecture. The first considers parallel algorithms suitable for various types of Distributed Memory Message Passing (DMMP) machines (see e.g., [4]). A typical machine of this type is the hypercube [14]. The second develops parallel algorithms for a shared memory multiprocessor [5], [7], [9]. Our specific purpose is to study parallel algorithms for factorizing the coefficient matrix A using the Doolittle and the Quadrant Interlocking (or the WZ factorization) [2] methods. The developed algorithms are designed for shared memory MIMD computers since it is assumed that global communication is carried out via the common memory. However, our general aim is to exhibit a mode of analysis and methodology which in our opinion is applicable to other numerical algorithms and will make possible the study of their parallelism. In section 2 we divide Doolittle's algorithm into noninterfering tasks of computational complexity O(n) arithmetic operations (medium grained parallelism). The selection of these tasks is such that at the ith step of the algorithm the elements of the: (i) ith row in the upper triangular matrix U and (ii) all operations except the last division for the computation of the ith column of the unit lower triangular matrix L can be computed in parallel. By studying the precedence graph of these tasks we find a schedule which is optimum for n-1 processors and determine the speedup S_p and the efficiency E_p of this algorithm. We close this section by developing a parallel algorithm for solving the two resulting triangular systems from the factorization process, thus completing the solution of (1). Following a similar approach we develop in section 3 a suitable parallel form of the WZ factorization. This is accomplished by solving at the kth stage n-2k linear systems of order 2 and then updating concurrently the columns of an (n-2k)x(n-2k) submatrix. It is shown that WZ factorization achieves a better efficiency than Doolittle's method with half its processors when solving a linear system. Finally, in section 4, we summarize our results and state our conclusions.

2. Parallel LU Factorization

Under certain conditions the coefficient matrix A has the unique representation

$$\mathbf{A} = \mathbf{LU} \tag{2}$$

where L is a unit lower triangular matrix and U is an upper triangular matrix. The elements of the matrices L and U are determined as follows. Assume that the first i-1 columns of L and the first i-1 rows of U have been determined. Then, we first compute the elements of the ith row of U from the formula

$$u_{ij} = a_{ij} - \sum_{k=1}^{i-1} l_{ik} u_{kj} , \qquad j=i(1)n . \tag{3}$$

Next, the elements of the ith column of L are computed by

$$l_{ji} = (a_{ji} - \sum_{k=1}^{i-1} l_{jk} u_{ki})/u_{ii} , \qquad j=i+1(1)n \tag{4}$$

The above approach is known as the Doolittle's method and a pseudo-code for this algorithm is given in figure 1. Assuming that one division or one subtraction and one multiplication constitutes one time step, the sequential time of this algorithm is

$$T_1=\frac{n^3}{3}-\frac{n}{3} \quad \text{steps} . \tag{5}$$

```
U^1_j  {for j=1 to n do          (initialization)
          u_1j=a_1j}

L^1_j  {for j=2 to n do          (computation of the first column of L )
          l_j1=a_j1/u_11 }

   for i=2 to n do               (computation of the other elements of L and U)
    begin
     U^i_i  {u_ii=a_ii-Σ_{k=1}^{i-1} l_ik u_ki }
     for j=i+1 to n do
         begin
          U^i_j   {u_ij=a_ij-Σ_{k=1}^{i-1} l_ik u_kj}
          DL^i_j  {l_ji=a_ji-Σ_{k=1}^{i-1} l_jk u_ki}
          L^i_j   {l_ji=l_ji/u_ii}
         end
    end
```

Figure 1. Definition of noninterfering tasks in the Doolittle algorithm

As stated in section 1 our aim is to use a number of processors $p \sim O(n)$. We therefore choose our tasks to be those code segments shown in figure 1. In particular, for a specific value i , task U^i_j computes the elements of the ith row of the matrix U, whereas tasks DL^i_j and L^i_j compute the elements of the ith column of L. We denote the set of these tasks by

$$\mathrm{J} = \{ U^i_j \mid 1\leq i\leq n ,\ 1\leq j\leq n ,\ DL^i_j \mid 2\leq i<n ,\ i<j\leq n ,\ L^i_j \mid 1\leq i<n ,\ i<j\leq n \}$$

The precedence constraint set $<\bullet$ imposed on J is indicated by the flow of the sequential algorithm (see figure 1). If $C_1=(J,<\bullet)$ is a task system representing the sequential algorithm of figure 1, then by examining the range and the domain of the tasks in C_1 we find that the set of tasks

$$U^i_i,\ U^i_{i+1},\ \ldots,\ U^i_n,\ DL^i_{i+1},\ DL^i_{i+2},\ \ldots,\ DL^i_n$$

are all mutually noninterfering and can be executed in parallel [1]. The maximally parallel graph of these tasks can be determined and is shown in figure 2. Considering this as a weighted graph with the weights of the nodes as their execution time, its longest path is given by

$$\mathrm{s} = (U^1_1,\ L^1_2,\ U^2_2,\ L^2_3,\ \ldots,\ L_n^{n-1},\ U^n_n).$$

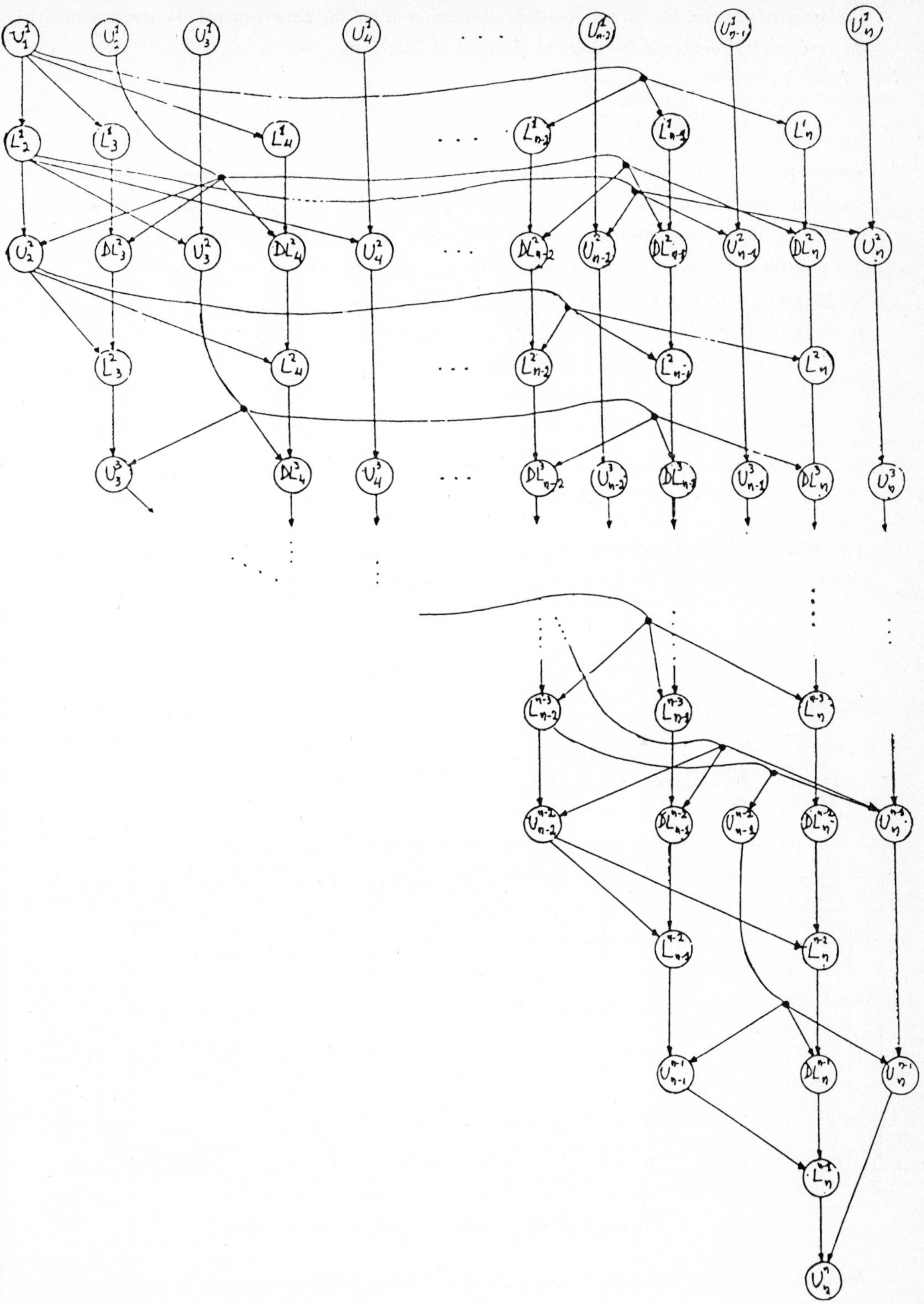

Figure 2. Maximally parallel graph of Doolittle's method

The completion time L(s) of our parallel algorithm will be the time required for the execution of the tasks which constitute the tasks of the path s. Therefore,

$$L(s)=\sum_{i=2}^{n} W(U^i_i) + \sum_{i=1}^{n-1} W(L^i_{i+1}) = n^2 - 2n + 2 \tag{6}$$

where $W(U^i_i)$, $W(L^i_{i+1})$ denote the execution time of the tasks U^i_i *and* L^i_{i+1}, respectively. Since the execution time of our tasks cannot be less than the length L(s) of their graph, we study the problem of finding schedules not exceeding this length and using $p \sim O(n)$ processors. A solution to this problem is to assign the n-1 processors $P_1, P_2, \ldots, P_{n-1}$ to the task set as follows :

$P_1 \leftarrow (L_2^{\,1}, U_2^{\,2}, U_3^{\,3}, U_4^{\,4}, \ldots, U_{n-1}^{\,n-1}, U_n^{\,n})$

$P_2 \leftarrow (L_3^{\,1}, DL_3^{\,2}, U_3^{\,2}, L_3^{\,2}, DL_4^{\,3}, U^3_{\,4}, L_4^{\,3}, \ldots, DL_n^{\,n-1}, U_n^{\,n-1}, L_n^{\,n-1})$

.

.

.

$P_j \leftarrow (L_{j+1}^{\,1}, DL_{j+1}^{\,2}, U_{j+1}^{\,2}, L_{j+1}^{\,2}, DL_{j+2}^{\,3}, U^3_{\,j+2}, L_{j+2}^{\,3}, \ldots, DL_n^{\,n-j+1}, U_n^{\,n-j+1}, L_n^{\,n-j+1})$

$P_{n-1} \leftarrow (L^1_{\,n}, DL^2_{\,n}, U^2_{\,n}, L^2_{\,n})$

This schedule is illustrated in figure 3 and since its completion time is equal to the length of the longest path, is optimal for n-1 processors. The speedup and the efficiency are given by

$$S_p = \frac{T_1}{T_p} = \frac{n^3/3 - n/3}{n^2 - 2n + 2} \simeq \frac{n}{3} \tag{7}$$

for large values of n and

$$E_p = \frac{S_p}{p} = \lim_{n \to \infty} \frac{n^3/3 - n/3}{(n^2 - 2n + 2)(n-1)} = \frac{1}{3} \approx 0.3333\,. \tag{8}$$

P_{n-1}	L^1_n	DL^2_n	U^2_n	L^2_n					....				
P_{n-2}	L^1_{n-1}	DL^2_{n-1}	U^2_{n-1}	L^2_{n-1}	DL^3_n	U^3_n	L^3_n		....				
P_{n-3}	L^1_{n-2}	DL^2_{n-2}	U^2_{n-2}	L^2_{n-2}	DL^3_{n-1}	U^3_{n-1}	L^3_{n-1}	DL^4_n	....				
⋮	⋮	⋮	⋮					⋮	⋮				
P_4	L^1_5	DL^2_5	U^2_5	L^2_5	DL^3_6	U^3_6	L^3_6	DL^4_7	....				
P_3	L^1_4	DL^2_4	U^2_4	L^2_4	DL^3_5	U^3_5	L^3_5	DL^4_6	....				
P_2	L^1_3	DL^2_3	U^2_3	L^2_3	DL^3_4	U^3_4	L^3_4	DL^4_5	....	DL^{n-1}_n	U^{n-1}_n	L^{n-1}_n	
P_1	L^1_2	U^2_2			U^3_3			U^4_4	....	U^{n-1}_{n-1}			U^n_n

Figure 3. Doolittle schedule using p=n-1 processors

Next, let us consider the case of solving system (1) using Doolittle's method. In this case we have to solve two triangular systems. Following a similar approach as previously, let us study the solution of the lower triangular system Cu=d. Its solution is given by the following code :

```
for k=1 to n do
   begin
     T^k_k { u_k = d_k/u_kk}
      for i=k+1 to n do
     T^k_i {d_i = d_i - c_ik u_k}
   end
```

Clearly, the set of tasks $T^k_{k+1}, T^k_{k+2},\ldots,T^k_n$ for each k can be executed in parallel after T^k_k is completed. Working similarly we can find the maximally parallel graph of these tasks. The completion time L(s) of the algorithm will be the time for the path that traverses the nodes

$$T^1_1, T^1_2, T^2_2, T^2_3, \ldots, T^{n-1}_{n-1}, T^{n-1}_n, T^n_n .$$

Therefore,

$$L(s)=\sum_{i=1}^{n} W(T^i_i) + \sum_{i=1}^{n-1} W(T^i_{i+1}) = 2n-1$$

A schedule for this problem can be found by assigning the tasks constituting s to processor 1 and the remaining tasks to the additional $\lceil n/2 \rceil - 1$ processors[2]. Processor 2 will execute the tasks $T^1_3, T^1_4, T^2_4, T^2_5, \ldots, T_n^{n-2}$ and more generally, processor j will execute the tasks

$$T^1_{2j-1}, T^1_{2j}, T^2_{2j}, T^2_{2j+1}, \ldots, T_n^{n-2(j-1)}$$

Letting A=LU in (1) we obtain

$$\mathbf{Lv} = \mathbf{b} \tag{9}$$

and

$$\mathbf{Uu=v} \tag{10}$$

Since L is a unit triangular matrix the completion time of the system (9) is n-1, whereas for (10) is 2n-1. For the solution of the system (1) the total completion time using Doolittle's method is

$$T^D_p = n^2 + n . \tag{11}$$

Thus the speedup and the efficiency of our algorithm is not affected for large values of n.

3. Parallel WZ Factorization

In [2] a new factorization method for the coefficient matrix A was proposed. The idea is to express the coefficient matrix as

$$\mathbf{A=WZ} \tag{12}$$

[2] $\lceil a \rceil$ denotes the largest integer not greater than the real number a

where the matrices W and Z have the following structure

$$W = \begin{bmatrix} 1 & 0 & \dots & 0 & 0 \\ w_{21} & 1 & & 0 & w_{2n} \\ w_{31} & w_{32} & & w_{3,n-1} & w_{2n} \\ & & & & \\ w_{n-2,1} & w_{n-2,2} & & w_{n-2,n-1} & w_{n-2,n} \\ w_{n-1,1} & 0 & & 1 & w_{n-1,n} \\ 0 & 0 & \dots & 0 & 1 \end{bmatrix}$$

and

$$Z = \begin{bmatrix} z_{11} & z_{12} & \dots & z_{1,n-1} & z_{1n} \\ 0 & z_{22} & \dots & z_{2,n-1} & 0 \\ & & & & \\ 0 & z_{n-1,2} & \dots & z_{n-1,n-1} & 0 \\ z_{n1} & z_{n2} & \dots & z_{n,n-1} & z_{nn} \end{bmatrix}$$

In order to compute the elements of the matrices W and Z we note that

$$A=\sum_{i=1}^{n} W_i Z^T_i \tag{13}$$

where W_i *and* Z_i^T denote the ith column of W and the ith row of Z, respectively. Next, the algorithm proceeds as follows. The elements of the first and last rows of Z are easily determined by simply matching the corresponding elements of the factorization (12). Thus, letting $A^{[1]}=A$ we have

$$z_{1j}=a_{1j}^{[1]} \qquad \text{and} \qquad z_{nj}=a^{[1]}_{nj} \qquad j=1(1)n \tag{14}$$

which means that the first and the last rows of Z are equal to the first and last rows of $A^{[1]}$. Then, the elements of the first and last columns of W are computed by solving the n-2, 2x2 systems

$$\begin{aligned} z_{11}\,w_{j1} + z_{nj}\,w_{jn} &= a_{j1} \\ z_{1n}\,w_{j1} + z_{nn}\,w_{jn} &= a_{jn}\,, \qquad j=2(1)n-1\,. \end{aligned} \tag{15}$$

Now the first and last columns of W and the first and last rows of Z have been determined and the elements of A are updated using the formula

$$A^{[2]} = A^{[1]} - W_1 Z_1^{\,T} - W_n Z_n^{\,T} \tag{16}$$

Because of (13), the elements of the first and last columns and rows of $A^{[2]}$ are zero. This means that (16) is equivalent to the following computations

$$a^{[2]}_{ij} = a^{[1]}_{ij} - w_{i1}z_{1j} - w_{in}z_{nj} , \qquad i,j = 2(1)n-1 \tag{17}$$

The first stage of the factorization is now complete and the second stage starts by determining the elements of the second and (n-1)st rows of Z, then the elements of the second and the (n-1)st columns of W are computed and finally the elements of the central (n-4)x(n-4) submatrix of A are updated e.t.c. Since at every stage, the elements of two columns of W and two rows of Z are computed, the determination of all the elements of the matrices W and Z will complete after $\lceil\frac{n+1}{2}\rceil$ stages. From the above description we can easily generalize our algorithm. Thus, by starting with $A^{[1]}$, we find at the kth stage the elements different from zero and 1 in the kth and (n-k+1)st columns of W and the corresponding rows of Z.

---

for k=1 to $\lceil\frac{n-1}{2}\rceil$ do
  begin
  1. for j=k to n-k+1 do
      begin
        $z_{kj} = a^{[k]}_{kj}$
        $z_{n-k+1,j} = a^{[k]}_{n-k+1,i}$
      end
  2. for j=k+1 to n-k do
      begin
        Find w_{jk} and $w_{j,n-k+1}$ by solving the system
          $z_{kk}\, w_{jk} + z_{n-k+1,k}\, w_{j,n-k+1} = a^{[k]}_{jk}$
          $z_{k,n-k+1}\, w_{jk} + z_{n-k+1,n-k+1}\, w_{j,n-k+1} = a^{[k]}_{j,n-k+1}$
      end
  3. for i=k+1 to n-k do
      for j=k+1 to n-k do
        $a_{ij}^{[k+1]} = a_{ij}^{[k]} - w_{ik}z_{kj} - w_{i,n-k+1}\, z_{n-k+1,j}$
  end

Figure 4 WZ Factorization algorithm

Figure 4 presents a first form of the WZ algorithm. Note that step 1 has to be executed for $k=\lceil\frac{n+1}{2}\rceil$, since when n is odd, say n=5, then the central element z_{33} is equal to $a_{33}^{[3]}$, so only the first statement of step 1 has to be executed. Also, when n is even then both statements of step 1 have to be executed. However, since these substitution statements require negligible execution time, we will not take them into account. We therefore focus our attention to steps 2 and 3 of the WZ algorithm. For the solution of the 2x2 systems we apply Gaussian Elimination, so step 2 of our algorithm has to be modified. This is shown in figure 5, where we also store z_{ij}'s in $a_{i,j}$'s. For a given value of k, the tasks T^k_k and T_k^j are defined by the code segments as shown in figure 5.

```
for k=1 to ⌈(n-1)/2⌉ do
  begin
   T^k_k  {m=a_{k,n-k+1}/a_{kk}

            m_1=a_{n-k+1,n-k+1} - m a_{n-k+1,k}

            for j=k+1 to n-k do
                begin
                    a_{j,n-k+1}=(a_{j,n-k+1} - m a_{jk})/m_1
                    a_{jk}=(a_{jk} - a_{n-k+1,k} a_{j,n-k+1})/a_{kk}}
                end
            for j=k+1 to n-k do
   T^j_k   {for i=k+1 to n-k do
                      a_{ij} = a_{ij} - a_{ik} a_{kj} - a_{i,n-k+1} a_{n-k+1,j}}
  end
```

Figure 5 Definition of noninterfering tasks in the WZ factorization

Let

$$\{J=T^j_k \mid 1\leq k\leq \lceil\frac{n-1}{2}\rceil\ ,\quad k\leq j\leq n-k\}$$

be the set of tasks. Then C_2=(J,<•) is a task system representing the sequential program of the WZ algorithm, where the precedence constraints set <• is given by

$$<\bullet \;=\; \{\ (T^j_k\,, T^l_m)\ \ j<l \quad \text{and} \quad k=m \quad \text{or} \quad k<m\}$$

By examining the range and the domain of these tasks we can easily verify that the set of tasks

$$\{T^{k+1}_k,\ T^{k+2}_k,\ \ldots\ ,\ T^{n-k}_k\}$$

are all mutually noninterfering and can be executed in parallel. In particular we note that $C'(J,<'\bullet)$, where $<'\bullet$ is the transitive closure of the relation

$$\mathrm{X} \;=\; \{(T^k_k\,, T^j_k) \mid k<j\leq n-k\}\cup\{(T^j_k\,, T^j_{k+1}) \mid k<j\leq n-k\}$$

is a maximally parallel system equivalent to C_2 as defined in [1]. The maximally parallel graph of C' when n=7, is shown in figure 6. For the execution of T^k_k, 4(n-2k)+2 time steps are required. Also, the execution of T^j_k requires 2(n-2k) time steps, thus the execution time for each of the tasks T^j_k is given by

$$W(T^j_k) \;=\; \begin{cases} 4(n-2k)+2 & k=j \\ 2(n-2k) & k\neq j \end{cases}$$

Denoting again by s the longest path in the graph of figure 6 we find

$$L(s)=\sum_{i=1}^{m} W(T^{i}_{i}) + \sum_{i=1}^{m} W(T_{i}^{i+1}) \leq 3/2\,n^2 - 2n + 1/2 \tag{18}$$

where $m = \lceil \frac{n-1}{2} \rceil$. An optimal schedule for our problem will be to assign the tasks constituting s to processor 1 and the remaining tasks to $\lceil \frac{n}{2} \rceil - 1$ additional processors. When n=7 this schedule is shown in figure 7. Using this schedule we obtain

$$S_p = \frac{T_1}{T_p} = \frac{n^3/3 + O(n^2)}{3n^2/2 - 2n + 1/2} \simeq \frac{2n}{9} \tag{19}$$

for large n and

$$E_p = \frac{S_p}{p} = \lim_{n \to \infty} \frac{n^3/3 + O(n^2)}{(3n^2/2 - 2n + 1/2)n/2} = \frac{4}{9} \approx 0.444. \tag{20}$$

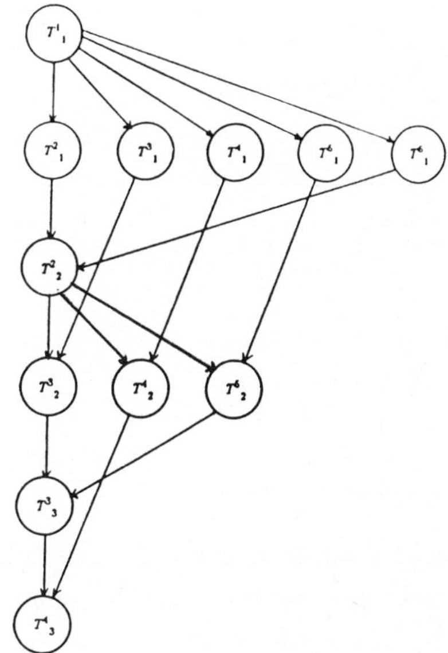

Figure 6. Maximally Parallel **graph** of **WZ factorization** for n=7.

In order to solve (1) using the WZ algorithm we modify it to yield

$$\mathbf{WZu=b} \tag{21}$$

hence the unknown vector u can be obtained by solving the following two systems

$$\mathbf{Wv=b} \tag{22}$$

and

Zu=v (23)

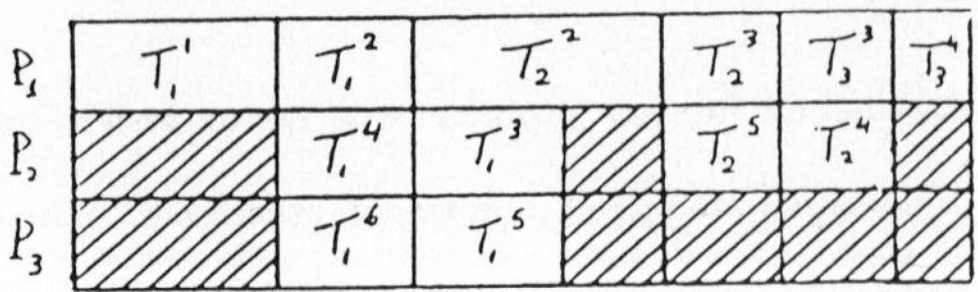

Figure 7. WZ schedule when number of processors p=7

To solve system (22) we let

$$Wv = b = b^{[1]}$$

or

$$\sum_{i=1}^{n} v_i W_i = b^{[1]}$$

So at the kth stage we compute

$$v_k = b^{[k]}{}_k$$

$$v_{n-k+1} = b^{[k]}{}_{n-k+1}$$

and

$$b^{[k+1]} = b^{[k]} - v_k W_k - v_{n-k+1} W_{n-k+1}$$

Therefore, the computation of v can be carried out concurrently with the update of the elements of the central submatrix $A^{[k]}$. On the other hand, the solution of the system (23) cannot start unless the whole factorization is complete. It can be shown that the solution of this system can be accomplished in O(n) time steps using only $\lceil n/2 \rceil$ processors. So the basic characteristics of the WZ algorithm remain the same for completing the solution of the system (1).

4. Summary and Conclusions

In this paper we developed two algorithms for factorizing a matrix on a shared memory multiprocessor. Both algorithms are based on the concept of scheduling tasks with precedence constraints. The first algorithm was based on Doolittle's method for finding the LU form of a matrix. Clearly, the approach presented applies also for the Crout's method with minor modifications. In case where the matrix is symmetric and positive definite we can easily apply the same ideas for the Cholesky method (see also [9]). By studying the precedence constraints among the tasks we were able to find the completion time of the algorithm, thus estimating its speedup (n/3) and efficiency (1/3) using n-1 processors. Following a similar approach we developed another algorithm which was based on the WZ factorization method. The attained efficiency of this algorithm was proven to be 4/9 using only $\lceil n/2 \rceil$ processors. These results indicate that the parallel factorization method based on WZ utilizes better the processors than the classical LU. Finally, for introducing pivoting techniques as well as various modified versions of WZ, the reader is referred to [3], [6], [15].

ACKNOWLEDGEMENTS

The first author would like to thank Professor Apostolos Gerasoulis for his support and many usefull discussions regarding this research. This research was supported in part by the Parallel Computer Laboratory of the Center for Computer Aids for Industrial Productivity (CAIP) and the Computer Science Department, Rutgers University. CAIP is supported by the New Jersey Commission on Science and Technology, Rutgers-The State University of New Jersey, and the CAIP Industrial Members.

References

1. E. G. Jr. Coffman and P. J. Denning, Operating systems theory, Prentice-Hall, Englewood Cliffs, N.J. (1973).
2. D. Evans and M. Hatzopoulos, A parallel linear system solver, *Inter. J. Computer Math.*, 7, 227-238, 1979.
3. D. Evans and A. Hadjidimos, A modification of the quadrant interlocking factorization parallel method, *Inter. J. Computer Math.*, 8, 149-166, 1980.
4. G. A. Geist and M. T. Heath, Matrix Factorization on a hypercube multiprocessor, *Hypercube Multiprocessors 1986*, Proceedings of the first Conference on Hypercube Multiprocessors, 161-180, 1986.
5. A. George, M. T. Heath and J. Liu, Parallel Cholesky factorization on a shared-memory multiprocessor, *Linear Algebra and Its Appl.*, 77, 165-187, 1986.
6. M. Hatzopoulos, A symmetric parallel linear system solver, *Inter. J. Computer Math.*, 13, 133-141, 1983.
7. M. Hatzopoulos and N. M. Missirlis, Advantages for solving linear systems in an asynchronous environment, *J. of Comp. and Appl. Math.*, 12 & 13, 331-340, 1985.
8. D. Heller, A survey of parallel algorithms in numerical linear algebra, *SIAM Rev.*, 20, 740-777, 1978.
9. S. P. Kumar, Parallel algorithms for solving linear systems of equations on an MIMD computer, Ph.D, Department of Computer Science, Washington State University, 1982.
10. H .T Kung, Synchronized and asynchronous parallel algorithms for multiprocessors, *Algorithms and Complexity : New Directions and recent results*, Academic Press, New York, 153-200, 1976.
11. R. E. Lord, J. S. Kowalik and S. P. Kumar, Solving linear algebraic equations on an MIMD computer, *J. Assoc. Comput. Mach.*, 30, 103-117, 1983.
12. N. M. Missirlis, Scheduling parallel iterative methods on multiprocessor systems, *Parallel Computing* (to appear).
13. A. Sameh and D. Kuck, On stable parallel linear systems solvers, *J. ACM*, 25, 81-91, 1978.
14. C. L. Seitz, The cosmic cube, *Comm. ACM*, 28, 22-33, 1986.
15. J. Shanehchi and D. Evans, New variants of the quadrant interlocking factorization (QIF) method, *CONPAR 81 Conf. Proc. Lecture Notes in Computer Science IIII*, W. Handler, Springer-Verlag, Berlin, 493-507, 1981.
16. R Voigt, The influence of vector computer architecture on numerical algorithms, *High speed computer and algorithm organization*, Academic Press, New York, 229-244, 1977.

FAST PARALLEL ALGORITHMS FOR PROCESSING OF JOINS

Dennis Shasha[+] and Paul Spirakis[+*]

\+ Courant Institute, NYU, USA

* Computer Technology Institute, Greece

Abstract

We present and analyze here some innovative techniques for processing a join (or a semi-join) in a parallel computing environment. Our algorithms employ perfect hashing and, in some cases, copying of data in a group of processors, or filtering the data as they move through the network. By using the combinatorial properties of hashing we are able to prove almost optimal speedup, with high probability, when some uniformity assumptions hold for the data. Even in the absense of these assumptions our techniques achieve sub-optimal speedup and can be used as practical heuristics.

1. Introduction

The purpose of this paper is to present and analyze some innovative techniques for computing a join or a semi-join on two relations, in a synchronous parallel environment. Our model of parallel computation is a realization of the PRAM (see [Wyllie, 79]) called a Parallel Modular Computer (see [Vishkin, 83]). This consists of n identical processing elements connected to n memory-modules via a network anto which many processors may send at the same time. For simplicity we assume each of the memory modules to be local to one processor (different processors correspond to different memory modules).

Our technique partitions each relation "horizontally" among the n processors, thru the use of a perfect hashing function applied to a key of each relation. Then, the basic stategy consists of projecting each relation on the joining and result columns (locally, each processor its own tuples) and of having each processor to send its truncated tuples to the processor which is the result of the hashing function applied to the join columns. Each receiving processor then performs a

---

This research was supported in part by the NSF grant DCR 8503497 and by the Ministry of Industry, Energy and Technology of Greece.

local join. Thus, the result of the join operation appears partitioned among the n processors.

The basic scheme described above is satisfactory when at least one of the relations (which participate in the join) has a key among the join attributes. However, when this does not hold, then the hashing alone does not manage to equidistribute work among the n processors. In that case we consider combinations of three possible remedies:

(a) We copy the tuples of each processor to several neighboring processors (for one of the two relations). The tuples of the other relation are then allowed to hash to any of those neighbours of their destination processor. We call this technique smearing.

(b) We use some intelligence on the network switches to filter out duplicate data going to the same destination. This technique is called combining (see e.g. [Schwartz, 80]).

(c) In case of a semijoin (say $\Pi_R(R \bowtie S)$) we may project locally onto the join attributes of R, send the truncated tuples to destination processors and have the recepients quicly check if the arriving values are matched by some local tuple of s. If yes, then the (matched) arrivals are sent back. This technique is called tagging and may interact with combining to speed-up the computation, in the cases where there are far fewer distinct join attribute values than join and result values.

2. Previous Work

A lot of work was done in the past on distributed query processing (see e.g. [Chu and Hurley, 82] and [Goodman, Sequin, 81]), on semijoin processing (e.g. [Bernstein, Chiu, 81]), on database machines as special purpose hardware for such operations (see [Badd, 79], [Kitsuregawa et al 84] and on parallel algorithms for database operations (see [Boral et al, 83]).

Most of the work on distributed query processing is concerned with minimizing the amount of messages (see e.g. [Epstein, Stonebraker, 80], [Hevner, Yao, 78], [Hevner, Yao, 79] and [Wang, Youssefi, 76]). [Chu, Hurley, 82] examine the case of optimizing both communication and processing costs. However, they do not exploit the idea of partitioning the data initially, and they get only insignificant speed-up. [Gavish, Segev, 82] consider relations spread out on n processors, but they compute intra-relation queries (thus, each partition piece plays the role of a relation, and partition is not really exploited).

The idea of filtering out duplicates inside the network is both old and fruitful (see e.g. [Su, 79], [Su, Lipkovsky, 75] for special purpose i/o controllers to do local selections and projections). Also the works of [Berra, Oliver, 79], [D, 79], [Menor, Hsiao, 81] propose architectures with specialized processors to perform algebraic database operations. However, filtering is only a good heuristic when used alone, since a join may need a lot of communication despite the filtering. Finally, [Kitsuregawa, 83] used the hashing idea for a pipelined ring. However, no combinatorial analysis was offered.

3. The basic algorithm

3.1 Notation and Definitions

In the general case we have to compute the (natural) join of two relations R,S on join attributes C, projected on attributes A of one or both R,S. We denote the join by $JOIN_C(R,S)$ and the projection by $\Pi_A(JOIN_C(R,S))$. Let R_i denote the tuples of R at processor i (and similarly for S). We assume that the projection operator removes duplicates. The hash functions we use are functions from combinations of values of attributes to the set $\{1,...,n\}$ where n is the number of processors. When a tuple, t, is sent through the network, we append to it a tag indicating the relation to which this tuple belongs. E.g. $<t,R_{tag}>$ denotes that tuple t belongs to relation R.

3.2 Description of the Algorithm

Preprocessing Phase Each relation is partitioned among the n processors by hashing on a key (called the partition key of that relation). The hashing is done through a perfect hashing function h_o, from the key to $\{1,...,n\}$. This has the effect that the propability that a particular tuple t will be assigned to a particular processor is 1/n.

Stage 1

At each processor i, compute the projections

$$R_i' = \Pi_{AUC}[R_i]$$

$$C_i' = \Pi_{AUC}[C_i]$$

Stage 2 (Communication). Let h be a perfect hashing function

For each processor i
For each typle $t \in R_i'$, send $<t,R_{tag}>$ to $h(\Pi_c[t])$.
For each tuple $t \in S_i'$, send $<t,S_{tag}>$ to $h(\Pi_c(t))$.

Stage 3

At each processor i, join the arriving tuples from R and S and produce a join result.
Note that, at the end, the result is partitioned among the n processors.

3.3 Our network assumptions

We assume a Parallel Modular Computer (see e.g. [Vishkin, 83]) with a packet-switched network in which a message can travel from one processor to any other in $\log_2 n$ time in case of no conflicts (no intermediate queueing). The switches of the network have buffers which queue the messages in case of conflicts. We will assume here a particular interconnection network (called a Banyan network, see [Goke, Lipovsky, 73] and [Kruskal, Snir, 83]) which has the property that for any particular pair of processors there is a unique path (thru the network switches) joining the two processors. For symmetric Banyan networks, where each switch has k inputs and k outputs, the set of memory modules reachable by any particular processor is at the leaves of a balanced k-ary tree.

3.4 Analysis of the basic Algorithm

3.4.1 Basic Results and Communication Costs

The performance of our basic algorithm depends on how perfect hashing maps m ($m \geq 0$) distinct values to $\{1,2,\ldots,n\}$. For example, the partition based on a key in the preprocessing stage and also the case where C is a key of either S or R (or both) are cases where the performance of the algorithm depends crucially on this mapping. The following results are useful:

Lemma 1 (Equidistribution)

Suppose h is a random function from the set M (of cardinality m) to $\{1,\ldots,n\}$ such that the probability that h(x) is i is 1/n for every $x \in M$ and for every $i \in \{1,\ldots,n\}$.

Let w be the maximum over all i) of the cardinalities of the sets $C_i = \{x \in M \,/ h(x)=i\}$.

(1) If $m \geq an\log n$ and $a \geq 4$ a constant, then

$$\text{Prob}\{w \leq \frac{2m}{n}\} \geq 1-n^{-(a-1/2)}$$

(2) If $n \leq m \leq n\log n$ then

$$\text{Prob}\{w \leq \log m\} \geq 1-n^{1-(\log\log n)/2}$$

(3) If $m \leq n$ then

$$\text{Prob}\{w \leq \log m+1\} \geq 1-(\frac{m}{n})^{\log m}$$

Proof: We sketch here only the proof of (1). See the full paper for proofs of (2), (3).

(1) Consider first a particular value i (e.g. a particular processor).

Each different value $x \in M$ has probability $\frac{1}{n}$ to map to i. So, the number of values mapped to i follows a Bernoulli distribution of m trials and "success" probability $p=\frac{1}{n}$. The mean number of successes is $\frac{m}{n}$ and, by the Chernoff bounds [Chernoff, 59]

$$\text{Prob}\{\#\text{ values mapped to } i \geq (1+\beta)\frac{m}{n}\} \leq \exp(-\beta^2 \frac{m}{n}\frac{1}{2})$$

where $\beta \in (0,1]$ a constant.

For $\beta=1$, we get, for $x(i)=\#$ values mapped to i:

$$\text{Prob}\{x(i) \geq \frac{2m}{n}\} \leq \exp(-\frac{m}{2n}) \leq n^{-a/2}$$

Hence, $\text{Prob}\{w \geq \frac{2m}{n}\} = \text{Prob}\{\text{at least one } x(i) \geq \frac{2m}{n}\} \leq n\, n^{-a/2}$

So, $\text{Prob}\{w < \frac{2m}{n}\} \geq 1-n^{-(a-1)/2}$

□

Lemma 2 (variety of values)

Let h be a random function from a set M of cardinality m to $\{1,2,\ldots,n\}$ such that the probability that h(x) is i is $\frac{1}{n}$, for any $x \in M$ and any $i \in \{1,\ldots,n\}$.

If $m \geq bn\log n$ with $b>2$, then

$$\text{Prob}\{\forall i\ \exists\ x \in M: h(x)=i\} \geq 1-n^{-b+1}$$

Proof sketch

Consider a particular (processor) i first. The probability that there is a $x \in M: h(x)=i$ is $1-(1-\frac{1}{n})^m = 1-(1-\frac{1}{n})^{bn\log n} \geq 1-n^{-b}$. The probability that there is not such a x is therefore $\leq n^{-b}$. So, the prob $\{\exists i$: there is not such a x$\}$ $\leq n\, n^{-b}$.

□

Corollary 1 (Proof in full paper)

For the partition based on a key and for large relations, with high probability, the relation will be equi-distributed among the n processors within a factor of 2.

Also, consider the case where C is not a key but the multiplicity of each value of $\Pi_C(R)$ is $\geq bn\log n$. In that case, all values of $\Pi_C(R)$ will appear in every processor with probability at least $1-n^{-b+2}$.

Definition

Let outmax be the maximum over all the processors of the number of tuples, out_j, that each processor j sends during the algorithm.

Let inmax be the maximum over all the processors of the number of tuples, in_j, that each processor j receives during the algorithm.

We use a sending protocol in which any processor that has to send a set of tuples will send with probability 1/2 in each cycle. This helps to avoid loading the network and to avoid long queues at the switches (see also [KS, 83]).

Lemma 3 (Uniform Network Traffic)

If C is a key of the relations to be sent then the total time needed for communication is O(logn+outmax+inmax).

Proof sketch

The situation implies a uniform load on the intermediate switches. The result follows, due to the pipelining operation of the network. □

Corollary 2

Consider the conditions of Lemma 3 for relations whose sizes exceed anlogn where $a \geq 2$. Then the total time needed for the communication step is O(alogn) with probability at least $1-2n^{(-a+1)/2}$.

Proof

By Lemma 1 (1), both outmax and inmax are less than alogn, each with probability $\geq 1-n^{-(a-1)/2}$. □

Note (*)

In [Bouras, Garofalakis, Spirakis, Triantafillou, 87] it is shown that the mean queue size at intermediate switches is bounded above by a constant, even when processors transmit for ever, with probability less than 1 in each cycle.

In the general case, C does not constitute a key, and the performance might degrade at each of the logn network levels.

Lemma 4 (Network Traffic, general case)

The total time for the communication (when C is not a key) is O(logn *(outmax+inmax)).

Proof sketch

(outmax+inmax) is the worst queue size in any switch at any cycle. □

Corollary 3

(a) Consider the conditions of Lemma 3 for relations whose sizes are between n and nlogn. If m is the maximum of |R|,|S|, then the total time for communication is O(logn+loglogn) with probability $\geq 1-n^{2-(\log\log n)/2}$.

(b) As above, but m<n. Then the total time for communications is O(logn) with probability $\geq 1-n(\frac{m}{n})^{\log n}$.

Proof sketch

Just apply Lemma 1 (2), (3) for both inmax and outmax, for all processors.

□

3.4.2 Processing Costs

Suppose R_{dest}, S_{dest} are the sets of tuples from R and S reaching some destination processor dest.

Lemma 5

The local join of the two relation subsets takes $O(|R_{dest}|+|S_{dest}|)$, in each processor dest.

Proof sketch

We preprocess the relation during the communication phases as follows: Every time a tuple from R comes to processor dest, we insert in into a B^+ tree named R. (The same for S), based on the C values. After all tuples are entered, we intersect the C-values of the two B^+-trees. Since the C-values are in sorted order at the leaves of the B^+ trees, this takes time $O(|R_{dest}|+|S_{dest}|)$.

□

Corollary 4

Note that each insertion in the B^+ trees takes O(logn) time. Hence the actual processing cost is $O(\log n.(|R_{dest}|+|S_{dest}|)$.

Theorem 1 (Optimal Speedup)

Suppose we join two relations R,S with cardinalities at least anlogn, $a \geq 2$. Suppose C is a key (or superkey) of both relations. Then, the total parallel time for processing the join is $O(\frac{|R|+|S|}{n})\cdot\log n)$ with prob $\to 1$ as $n\to\infty$, which is optimal.

Proof sketch

By corollaries 2,3 the total communication cost is $O(\frac{|R|+|S|}{n})$ with probability at least $1-2n^{(-a+1)/2}$ for large relations, with very high probability in general. The total processing cost is $O(\log n \frac{|R|+|S|}{n})$ with the same probability.

□

4. Algorithm Optimizations

We consider three optimizations of the basic algorithm: combining, tagging and smearing. These optimizations may be applied in combination, independently to the two relations. However, only tagging and smearing may apply together to a single relation.

A combining network tries to prevent more than one copy of the same tuple from going to any processor. In the ideal combining case, as soon as a tuple passes through the network, the network remembers it and eliminates every other instance of that tuple. In the non-ideal combining, each switch stores the q distinct values that passed through the switch most recently. If a value entering the switch is one of those stored, then the new value is removed. The parameter q depends on the design of the switch (especially size of switch memory).

Tagging changes the basic algorithm by projecting on the join columns only instead of the join and result columns. We will use tagging only in a semi-join case (is when A has attributes only in R and the result to compute is Π_A(R join S on C).

The destination processors receive the $\Pi_C(R)$ (if tagging is applied on R) and either $\Pi_C(S)$ (if tagging is applied to S) or $\Pi_{CUA}(S)$. They compute whether $\Pi_C(R)$ is in the join result (even if tuples from R, S hash to the same processor, this does not imply $\Pi_C(R)=\Pi_C(S)$). If this happens, they return $\Pi_C(R)$ to the sending processor, who then computes that part of the semijoin.

Smearing on S, sends the tuples, t, of S_i (projected on CUA) not only to x=h[t projected on C] but also to all of the processors

$$\{(x-k)\text{mod}n,\ (x-k+1)\text{mod}n, \ldots, (x+k)\text{mod}n\}.$$

At the same time, each $t \in R_i$ is send to some one of the above processors at random (or to each processor in turn, deterministically).

5. Analysis of the Optimizations

5.1 Notation and Assumptions

The two parameters we want to minimize are inmax and outmax, since they are the values that both the communication and the processing costs depend on.

In the following, let R[C] denote the Relation R projected on the set of attributes C.

Let $R[C]=\{rc_1,\ldots,rc_m\}$, where $|R[C]|=m$. Let $R[CUA]=\{rca_{11},\ldots,rca_{mk}\}$, where $rca_{ij}[C]=rc_i$. Finally, let v_{ij} be the number of processors containing rca_{ij}.

If all this information were available and if we knew the exact distribution of the rca values, we could arrive at exact values of inmax and outmax. However, it is infeasible to obtain this information in a real system. Therefore, we make the following simplifying assumptions called uniformity assumptions:

1) The number of distinct R[CUA] values whose projection on C is rc_i is the same for all i and is $r=|R[CUA]|/|R[C]|$.
2) Each value in R[CUA] is in v processors.

Crude as these assumptions are, they help us decide when to apply the optimizations. One assumption that would be too crude would be to assume that the R[C] tuples are distributed evenly over the destination processors. The reason is that $|R[C]|=m$ could be small. We define the parameter c to be the maximum number of distinct R[C] values that hash to a single processor. By the equidistribution lemma, with high probability, $c \leq \frac{2m}{n}$ if $m>n\log n$, otherwise $c \leq \log m$.

So, we get

<u>Lemma 6</u>

Under the uniformity assumptions and assuming that $mrv>n \cdot \log n \cdot a$ $(a \geq 2)$, we get

$$\frac{mrv}{n} \leq \text{outmax} \leq \frac{2mrv}{n} \quad \text{and}$$

$$\text{inmax}=crv$$

with probability $\geq 1-O(n^{(-a+1)/2})$ □

<u>5.2 Analysis of Combining</u>

For concreteness, let us say we are going to apply combining to R[CUA] whose cardinality is mr. This will only help if CUA is not a superkey of R. In that case, tuples with the same values on those attributes should be distributed across the processors, because the partitioning is based on a key of R. According to our uniformity assumption, each R[CUA] value is in v processors. Thus, the total number of tuples that will be sent is mrv. These tuples are approximately equi-distributed across the processors. Hence we have the following lemma.

<u>Lemma 7</u>

Under the uniformity assumptions, ideal combining causes inmax to be reduced to c r . □

To see how useful combining is, we should note first that since combining occurs in the network, combining will not reduce outmax. Combining helps significantly if crv>outmax. Since we can approximate outmax by $\frac{mrv}{n}$ provided mrv is large, combining helps significantly whenever $c>\frac{m}{n}$.

Uniformately, the network has no global oracle to eliminate duplicate values, so we now analyze a "non-ideal" implementation of combining, which approximates existing implementations. Our model is the following:

(1) Each switch stores the q distinct values that passed through the switch most recently. If a value enters the switch that is one of those stored, the new value is removed. (It is a duplicate). The value q is a design parameter of the switch.

(2) Given that a value passed through a switch at least once in the past, the probability that it is stored is equal to $\frac{q}{f_s}$ where f_s is the number of distinct values that every pass through switch s.

(3) Due to network symmetry, half the distinct values passing through a switch follow each of the 2 outputs (we assume here 2 by 2 switches).

Fact: Given these assumptions, the probability of that a value is removed at a switch of level i (measured from the destination end, see network description) is the same for all switches of level i.

According to our assumptions above, at most 2cr distinct values pass through a switch connected to a destination processor. Hence, the combining probability at the last switch is $p_1=\min(1,q/2cr)$. The compining probability at the stage i (measured from destination) is p_l equal to min $(1,q/(cr(2^{l+1})))$.

A particular value passes through the network without combining, with probability Pass equal to $(1-p_1)(1-p_2)\ldots(1-p_{\log n})$. Therefore, inmax is reduced from crv to crv+(crv-cr) Pass.

<u>Lemma 8</u> <u>(Non-ideal Combining)</u>

Let a be the ratio of the maximum number of distinct R[CUA] values arriving at one destination processor, cr, and the memory size (of the switch) q. Then, under the uniformity assumptions, the mean value of inmax is

$$E(\text{inmax})=cr+(crv-cr)(1-\frac{1}{a})$$

(Proof in full paper) □

5.3 Analysis of Tagging

Tagging reduces both outmax and inmax in its first communication step, but requires an extra communication step whose cost is no more than the cost of the first one. (We consider the semi-join case here).

<u>Lemma 9</u>

Under the uniformity assumptions, the mean values of outmax and inmax become

$$E(\text{outmax})=\min\{\frac{mrv}{n},m\}$$

and $$E(\text{inmax})=c*\min\{n,rv\}.$$

In addition, outmax and inmax are bounded by twice their expected values with high probability

(Proof in full paper)

□

5.4 Analysis of Smearing with Tagging

What follows is a mean-value analysis (exact analysis in the full paper). Let us first assume that $|R|$ is large enough so that every $\Pi_C(R)$ value is in every processor (by the lemma of variety of values) with high probability. In that case (and by assuming our smearing parameter k to be m/2), we get for the part of inmax due to R ($inmax_R$)

$$\frac{cn}{2k+1} \leq E(inmax_R) \leq \frac{mn}{2k+1} .$$

The communication cost for S however increases (because we copy the S tuples). There are 2 cases.

(a) No tuples of S would have been sent if R were not smeared (i.e. C is a key of S). In that case,

$$E(inmax_S)=E(outmax_S)= \frac{2k}{n} |\Pi_{CUA}(S)|$$

(b) Tuples from S were sent. Then the $outmax_S$, $inmax_S$ increase by a factor of 2k, over the basic algorithm.
For example, if

$|\Pi_{CUA}(S)|=an$ (for a constant a>0) and if $|\Pi_C(R)|=m$, and if C is the partition key of S, then, if $k=\frac{m}{2}$, we get (for small m)

$$E(inmax)=\frac{mn}{m+1} +ma.$$

In contrast, by tagging alone,

$$E(inmax)=n(\log m+1).$$

I.e. smearing helps only if

$$n \log n > 2ma.$$

6. Conclusions

We proposed a method for the parallel processing of joins in a PRAM implementation using a high-bandwidth network. In many cases our techniques give optimal speedup over the sequential case. It seems that hardware associative memory features such as combining can be useful.

Tagging improves the parallel processing of semi-joins. Smearing is only rarely useful, unless the copying of S's tuples has to be done only once for a lot of join computations. We are currently working on extending the techniques to a general strategy about query processing in parallel environments.

REFERENCES

[Babb, 79] E. Babb, "Implementing a Relational Database by Means of Specialized Hardware", ACM TODS 4,1 (March, 1979), 1-29.

[Bernstein, Chiu, 81] P.A. Bernstein and D.W. Chiu, "Using Semijoins to Solve Relational Queries", J.ACM 28:1, pp. 25-40, 1981.

[Boral, DeWitt, 80] H. Boral and D.J. DeWitt, "Design consideration for data-flow database mechines", in proceedings of the ACM-SIGMOD conference on management of data, 1980, pp. 94-104.

[Boral, DeWitt, Friedland, Wilkinson, 83] H. Boral, D.J. DeWitt, D. Friedland, and W.K. Wilkinson, "Parallel Algorithms for the execution of relational database operations", ACM Transactions on Database Systems vol. 8, no. 3, September 1983, pp. 324-353.

[Bouras, Garofalakis, Spirakis, Triantafillou, 87] C. Bouras, Y. Garofalakis, P. Spirakis and V. Trianatafillou "Queuing Delays in Buffered Multistage Interconnection Networks", 1987 ACM SIGMETRICS Conference, Perf. Evaluation Review, vol. 15 no. 1 pp. 111-122.

[Bernstein, Goodman, Wong, Reeve, Rothnie, 81] P.A. Bernstein, N. Goodman, E. Wong, C.L. Reeve, and J.B. Rothnie Jr. "Query Processing in a System for Distributed Databases" (SDD-1). ACM Trans. Database Syst. 6,4 pp. 602-625, 1981.

[Berra, Oliver, 79] B. Berra and E. Oliver 1979 "The role of associative array processors in database machine architectures" IEEE Computer, 12,3,53-61.

[Carter, Wegman, 77] Carter J.L. and Wegman M.N. "Universal classes of hash functions", Proc. 9th Symposium on Theory of Computing, 1977, pp. 106-112.

[Ceri, Pelagatti] S. Ceri and G. Pelagatti, "Allocation of Operations in Distributed Database Access" IEEE Trans. Comput. C-31,2, pp. 119-128.

[Chu, Hurley, 82] W.W. Chu and P. Hurley, "Optimal Query Processing for Distributed Database Systems" IEEE Trans. Computing, C-31,9, pp. 835-850, 1982.

[DeWitt, 79] D.J. DeWitt, "DIRECT-a multiprocessor organization for supporting relational database management systems", IEEE Transactions on Computers, C-28,6, 1979.

[Epstein, Stonebraker, 80] R.S. Epstein and M. Stonebraker, "Analysis of query processing stategies for distributed database systems", sixth international conference on very large databases, Mondreal, October, 1980.

[Forker] H.J. Forker, "Algebraical and operational methods for the optimization of query processing in distributed relational database management systems. In Proceedings of the 2nd International Symposium on Distributed Databases (Berlin, FRG). Elsevier North-Holland, New York, pp. 39-59.

[Gonnet, 81] Gonnet G.H., "Expected length of the longest probe sequence in hash code searching", JACM 28, 1981, 289-304.

[Goke, Lipovsky, 73] L.R. Goke and G.J. Lipovsky, "Banyan networks for partitioning multiprocessor systems", in proceedings 1st annual symposium on computer architecture, 1973, pp. 21-28.

[Goodman, Sequin, 81] J.R. Goodman and C.H. Sequin, "HYPERTREE: a multiprocessor interconnection topology", IEEE Transactions on Computing, 30,12, 1981.

[Gavish, Segev, 82] B. Gavish and A. Segev, "Query Optimization in Distributed Computer Systems" In Management of Distributed Data Processing, J. Akoks, Ed. Elsevier North-Holland, New York, pp. 233-252, 1982.

[Goodman, Shmueli, 82] N. Goodman and O. Shmueli, "Tree queries: A simple class of relational queries" ACM Transactions of Database Systems vol. 7, no. 4, December 1982, pp. 653-677.

[Henver, Yao, 79] A.R. Henver and S.B. Yao, "Query Processing in Distributed Database systems", IEEE Trans. Softw. Eng. SE-5,3 pp. 177-187, 1979.

[Henver, Yao, 78] A.R. Henver and S.B. Yao, "Query Processing on a Distributed Database" proceedings Third Workshop on Distributed Data Management and Computer Networks, August 1978, pp. 91-107.

[Hsiao, 79] D.K. Hsiao, 1979 "Database Machines are Coming, Database Machines are Coming" IEEE Computer 12,3, pp. 7-9.

[Jarke, Koch, 84] M. Jarke and J. Koch, "Query Optimization in Database Systems", ACM Computing Surveys, vol. 16, no. 2, June 1984, pp. 111-152.

[Kruskal, Snir, 83] C.P. Kruskal and M. Snir, "The Performance of multistage interconnection networks for multiprocessors", in IEEE transactions on computers, vol. C-32, no. 12, December 1983.

[Kitsuregawa, Tanaka, Moto-oka, 84] M. Kitsuregawa, H. Tanaka, and T. Moto-oka, "Architecture and Performance of Relational Algebra Machine Grace" IEEE Parallel Processing Conference 1984.

[Kitsuregawa, Tanaka, Moto-oka, 83] M. Kitsuregawa, H. Tanaka, and T. Moto-oka, "Grace: Relational Algebra Machine Based on Hash and Sort-Its Design Concepts" Journal of Information Processing, vol. 6, no. 3, 1983.

[Menon, Hsiao, 81] M.J. Menon and D.K. Hsiao, "Design and Analysis of a Relation Join Operation for VLSI", Proceedings International Conference on Very Large Database, 1981.

[Ozkarahan, 82] E.A. Ozkarahan 1982, RAP "Database Machine/Computer Based Distributed Databases", In Proceedings of the 2nd International Symposium on Distributed Databases. (Berlin, FRG). Elsevier North-Holland, New York, pp. 61-80.

[Schwartz, 80] J. Schwartz "Ultracomputers" ACM Transactions on Programming Languages and Systems, 1980.

[Su, 79] S.Y.W. Su 1979 "Cellular-logic Devices: Concepts and Applications" IEEE Computer 12,3, 11-25.

[Schkolnick, 82] M. Schkolnick, "Physical database design techniques", In Data Base Design Techniques II S.B. Yao and T.L. Kunii, Eds., Springer-Verlag, pp. 229-252, 1982.

[Schmidt, 79] J.W. Schmidt, "Parallel processing of relations: a single-assignment approach", In proceedings of the IEEE 5th international conference on very large data bases, pp. 398-408, 1979.

[Su, Lipovsky, 75] S.Y.W. Su and G. Lipovsky 1975, "CASSM: A Cellular System for Very Large Databases" In Proceedings of the 1st International Conference on Very Large Data Bases" Framingham, Mass., Sept. 22-24. ACM, New York, pp. 456-472.

[Shasha, 86] D. Shasha, "Query Processing in a Symmetric Parallel Environment" 6th Advanced Database Symposium, Proceedings.

[Shultz, Zingg, 84] R.K. Shultz and R.J. Zingg, "Response Time Analysis of Multiprocessor Computers for Database Support" ACM Transactions of Database Systems, vol.9, no.1, March, 1984, pp. 100-132.

[Ullman, 82] J.D. Ullman, Principles of Database Systems second edition. Computer Science Press, 1982.

[Valduriez, Gardarin, 84] P. Valduriez and G. Gardarin, "Join and Semijoin Algorithms for a Multiprocessor Database Machine" ACM Transactions of Database Systems, vol. 9, no. 1, March 1984, pp. 133-161.

[Vishkin, 83] U. Vishkin, "A parallel-design distributed-implementation (PDDI) general-purpose computer", Technical Report no. 96, New York University department of computer science, June, 1983.

[Wong, Youssefi, 76] E. Wong and K. Youssefi, "Decomposition a strategy for query processing" ACM TODS 1,3 Sept. 1976, pp. 223-241.

PERFORMANCE ANALYSIS FOR A JOIN PROCESSOR

Guang-sheen Liu
Department of Electrical Engineering
Tatung Institute of Technology
Taipei 10451, Taiwan, Republic of China

Huei-huang Chen
Department of Information Engineering
Tatung Institute of Technology
Taipei 10451, Taiwan, Republic of China

ABSTRACT

An architecture which not only elliminates cross referencing but also maintains ordering reservation (suitable for non-equijoin operation) is proposed. The techniques such as parallel processing and pipelining are applied to greatly enhance the system performance. Response time is derived, by comparing the speed of hardware modules, and analyzed for the efficient evaluation of the join operation on the system architecture.

1. INTRODUCTION

Almost all of the database systems developed over the past few years are relational, since relational query languages are easy to use for casual users. In the relational database system, the evaluation of a relational query can be quite time-consuming especially when binary operations are involved. Among the binary operations, join is the most frequently used one.

A lot of algorithms have been proposed to evaluate join more efficiently [Bab 79] [Dew 79] [BHK 79] [WY 80] [Hon 85] [TNM 80] [SNOS 79] [SNEL 79] [TY 82] [HM 83] [Glin 83] [KIS 85]. Among them, some are parallel algorithm. That is, we can use hardware -- parallel processor -- to speed up the evaluation of join operation.

The proposed parallel algorithms can be classified into two types:

(a) partitioning: divide the relations into uniform partitions and join each partition of one relation with each partition of the other relation (such as the nested-loop algorithm in DIRECT [Dew 79] [BDFW 82] and ring routed algorithm in DBC [BBH 78] [BHK 79]).

(b) hashing: hash the relations into buckets (also called partition in [Hon 85]) with the same hash function and join the corresponding buckets togather [WY 80] [TY 82]. The scheme elliminates the cross-referencing, but the tuples are not uniformly distributed to buckets.

Since the hash scheme cannot resolve the ordering reservation, the execution of non-equijoin is based on the cross-product method as partitioning scheme. This paper describes a new scheme which satisfies both the cross-reference ellimination and ordering reservation as follows:

(1) sort the smaller relation and divide the sorted result into segments. For each segment, we record the smallest key value and for the last segment we also record the largest key value. If there are n segments in the smaller relation, then we establish n+2 segments for the other relation, that is $S_0, S_1, S_2, \ldots, S_n, S_{n+1}$.

(2) Each tuple of the other relation is then distributed to the segments accordong to its key value, that is, the segment which cover the key value.

(3) Each segment of the second relation is then sorted (in parallel if possible) if that is necessary.

(4) The corresponding segments are joined.

The new scheme also satisfies the uniform distribution in job partition.

This paper is divided into five sections. Section 2 describes a prototype architecture. Section 3 expresses the system response time of a general join. It also illustrates how the operation is performed. Case studies of response time with particular data and machine parameter values are examined in Section 4. The summary of results and conclusions appears in Section 5.

2. SYSTEM ARCHITECTURE

The join operation hardware is constructed with many modules as shown in Figure 1. It consists of a back-end controller, one or more mass storage devices (MSD), a data filter (DF), a data module (DM), three sets of <u>buffers</u> (called BS1, BS2 and BS3), multiple <u>initial sorters</u> (ISs), a <u>merger tree</u> (MT), two <u>interconnection networks</u> (INs), and multiple <u>processing elements</u> (PEs). User queries are compiled by front-end machine into a sequence of relational algebra operations, so called <u>query packets</u>, which are sent to the back-end controller. The back-end controller interacts with the front-end machine and instructs the system modules to execute the machine instructions assigned by the backend controller.

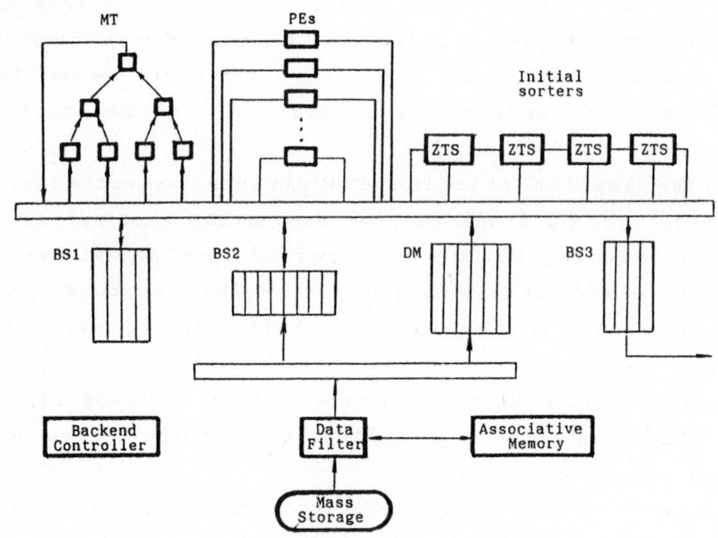

Figure 1. System Architecture.

The mass storage may be a fixed head disk with head per track, a modified moving head disk that provides parallel read/write of tracks on the same cylinders, or a number of commercial moving-head disks. The organization of the database is chosen to be bit-serial and word-parallel (i.e. multiple tuples will be available simultaneously at the read heads). Since we assume that data filter can process one tuple at a time, a buffer is added between the mass storage and the data filter so that all the parallel tuples are sequenced succeedingly.

In the data filter, a set of cell processors execute concurrent search tasks on a multiplexed data stream produced by the simultaneous reading of several disk channels. The qualified tuples are stored in DM, and the corresponding key values and tuple addresses (a pointer to data module) are stored in the BS2. Each time a buffer is full, the contained keys, called a <u>page</u>, is fed into IS and then extracted back to the same buffer. If the overall sorting of the relation's key is required, then the initial sorted pages will be sent through MT to buffers of BS1. The keys contained in each of these buffers is called a segment. An associative memory is attached to the data filter. It's function will be explained in Section 3.1.

The initial sorters are modified from the zero time sorter (ZTS) of Miranker et al.[MTW 83], which operates in a parallel and pipelined fashion with the actual sorting time absorbed by the input/output time. When a page has fed into the sorter, there may be no ready page waiting for sorting. For each page must be sorted as rapid as possible (this influent on the starting time of the page join), the page is extracted immediately. In our design, meanwhile the page is extracting, an arriving page can be input at any time. The modified sorter looks like a production line, the first page to be sorted is placed from one of the two sides. Until the page shift to the limit place of other side, the rotating direction of the belt conveyor is reversed, and the page will be extracted. Each time a page arrive to the production line, it can be place to one side only if the previous page is extracting from other side; otherwise the page must be keep waiting until the previous page is extracted.

During join, two relations are stored in BS1 and BS2. The PEs join and store the results to BS3. The buffers in BS1 and BS3 are made of serial memories (such as CCD or magnetic bubble), and the buffers in BS2 are made of random access memories. The interconnection network allows each PE to read any buffer. Since the serial memory has a smaller access rate than random memory, each PE has a small local memory as a queue of keys read from BS1. During join, the PE compares each of the keys in queue with some keys read from a buffer of BS2. It is assume that a PE can input keys from BS1 in parallel with the processing of one or more keys from BS2.

The response time analysis presented in Section 3 is based on some assumptions about the physical characteristics of the system architecture. Table 2-1 summarizes the disk parameters. Table 2-2 shows the quantitative specification of the system module and their processing time. Since initial sorter possesses higher access rate than BS2, the buffers of BS2 must be modified only if it is slower than disk. To improve the access time of BS2, each buffer must be constructed in parallel form, and the low-order interleaving is chosen for addressing scheme [HB 84]. And then, the average access time of BS2, t_{bf2}, is a fraction of the RAM access time, t_{rm}. In the same reason, DM is also required to be constructed in parallel form.

parameter	meaning	value
S_{bk}	size of block	320 bytes
N_{bkcyl}	# of block in a cylinder	690 blocks/cylinder
T_{cyl}	average cylinder access time	25 us
T_{lat}	average latency time	83 us
T_{bk}'	block transfer time	260 us/block
N_{dd}	# of disk drivers	16
T_{bk}	average block transfer time	16.4 us/block

Table 2-1. Disk Parameters and Values.

parameter	meaning	value
$N_{bf1}(=m_1)$	# of buffers in BS1	16
$N_{bf2}(=m_2)$	# of buffers in BS2	64
N_{st} (=s)	# of sorters	4
N_{mg} (=g)	# of mergers in the lowest level of MT	16
N_{pe} (=n)	# of Processing Elements	16
S_{bf1}	the size of each buffer in BS1	256K bytes
S_{bf2}	the size of each buffer in BS2	64K bytes
N_{kyst}	the maximun # of keys available in each sorter	1K
S_{st}	the size of keys in sorter (60-byte key field and 4-byte address)	64 bytes
t_{sm}	access time of a serial memory chip.	730 ns/byte
t_{rm}	access time of an RAM chip.	300 ns/byte
t_{bf1}	average access time of BS1	730 ns /byte
t_{bf2}	average access time of BS2	150 ns/byte
t_{bf3}	average access time of BS3	730 ns/byte
t_{dm}	average access time of DM	-- ns/byte
t_{st}	time taken to feed a key to sorter	3 us/key
t_{cmp}	time taken to compare two bytes.	1 us/byte

("K" means 1024)

Table 2-2. System depend Parameters and Values.

3. RESPONSE TIME ANALYSIS

Useful information on the performance of relational database algebra operations by conventional systems has been derived from the analysis of the execution of a query containing the operations selection, projection, and join [BE 77]. Part of the query has been chosen as a basis for our evaluation. For relations R1 and R2 (the cardinality of R1 is smaller than that of R2), the query is:

JOIN PROJECT(SELECT(R1)) AND PROJECT(SELECT(R2))

To execute the query, the compiled messages are generated and requested from host to the backend controller, and then attributes of the join field, attributes to be removed by projection, and the selection criteria are sent to data filter.

3.1 Implementation of Join Operation

The query to be analyzed is executed in following two steps in which the flow of keys are described in Figure 2.

(1) Select, Project, and Sort the smaller relation R1.

(2) Select, Project, and Join R2 with the qualified R1.

Not repeating these steps assumes both BS1 and BS2 can, in the worst case, store all of the smaller relation R1. The slowest rate at which data is transferred between system modules determines the response time of the system.

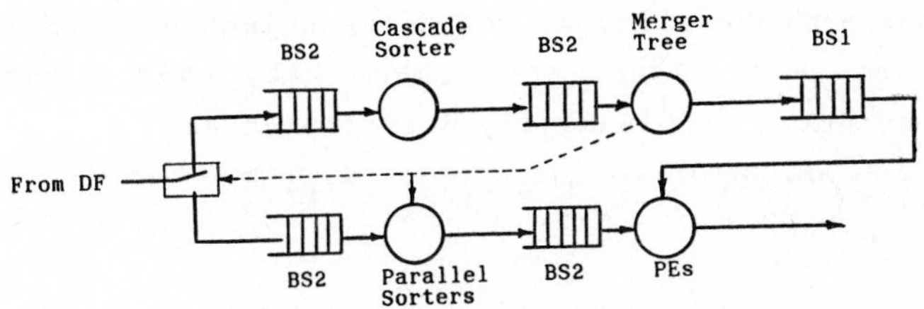

Figure 2. The Flow of keys.

During step 1, N_{st} sorters are connected in cascade. Those qualified keys sent from DF are collected into pages with K_2 keys per page. Each time a buffer is full (means a page result), the page will be fed to the cascade sorter. When N_{st} pages have been stored in the sorter, a run with N_{st} page long is extracted back to the BS2. After all qualified pages have been sorted, the MT starts to merge those initial runs to a final run in BS1 in which the run is partitioned into N_{bf1} equal-size segments. After the first step completes, the smallest key of all N_{bf1} segments and the largest key of the last segment are recorded in the associative memory. By these $N_{bf1}+1$ keys, the qualified keys of R2 will be divided into $N_{bf1}+2$ partitions in the next step.

During step 2, N_{st} sorters operate in parallel. By using the associative memory, DF classify the qualified keys on the fly. Each time a buffer is full, the stored page will be sorted, and then a PE is assigned to join the sorted page with the corresponding segment in BS1.

In order to present the response time expression in a general form, we must give the database-dependent parameters. The list of parameters and data that are used to simplify the ensuring discussion is given in Table 2-3. In the Table, we use the database given by Shultz and Zingg [SZ 84] as the parameter values which will be used in Section 4 as the <u>initial values</u> of ours case studies. N_{kybf1} and N_{kybf2} are the buffer capacity which depends only on tuple length, but K_1 and K_2 are the real number of keys in the corresponding buffers. R_{s1} (R_{s2}) are the probability of R1's (R2's) tuple which satisfies the query's constraints.

3.2 Interarrival-time of Pages

The tuples of relation R1 arrive directly at BS2 from the disk after selection and projection executed by data filter. Each of the N_{tp1} tuples has a probability R_{s1} of being selected by DF and hence of being stored into BS2. Thus, the probability that k tuples out of N_{tp1} will be selected is binomially distributed as

$$P(k) = \binom{N_{tp1}}{k} * R_{s1}{}^{k} * (1-R_{s1})^{N_{tp1}-k}$$

The time taken to read N_{tp1} tuples and select k of them is $N_{tp1}/@_{df}$, where $@_{df}=(S_{bk}/S_{tp1})/T_{bk}$ is the average arrival rate of tuples from disk to data filter. Thus, the probability of k arrivals in a time interval of $N_{tp1}/@_{df}$ is

$$P_k(N_{tp1}/@_{df}) = P(k)$$

Finally, the probability of k arrivals in time t is

$$P_k(t) = \frac{(R_{s1}@_{df}t)^k}{k\,!} * e^{-R_{s1}@_{df}t} , \qquad t > 1/@_{df}$$

Since the arrival process is Poisson, the pdf (probability density function) of the interarrival-time of qualified tuples to BS2 is given as follows:

$$a_{b2}(t) = R_{s1}@_{df}\ t\ e^{-R_{s1}@_{df}t} , \qquad t > 1/@_{df}$$

and the mean arrival rate is

$$@_{b2} = R_{s1}@_{df}$$

In order to evaluate the interarrivel time of pages to initial sorter, we can consider the arriving facility is similar to a K_2-stage

parameter	meaning	value
N_{tp1}	# of tuple in R1 (cardinality of R1)	32K
N_{tp2}	# of tuple in R2 (cardinality of R2)	128K
S_{tp1}	tuple size of R1	320 bytes
S_{tp2}	tuple size of R2	320 bytes
N_{bk1}	# of block in R1 = $\lceil N_{tp1}/\lfloor S_{bk}/S_{tp1}\rfloor\rceil$	32K
N_{bk2}	# of block in R2 = $\lceil N_{tp2}/\lfloor S_{bk}/S_{tp2}\rfloor\rceil$	128K
S_j	size of the join key (include 4-byte address)	64 bytes
N_{kybf1}	the maximun # of keys available in each buffer of BS1 (the capacity of buffer in BS1) = $\lfloor S_{bf1}/S_j\rfloor$	4K
N_{kybf2}	the maximun # of keys available in each buffer of BS2 (the capacity of buffer in BS2) = minimum of $\lfloor S_{bf2}/S_j\rfloor$ and Nkyst	1K
K_1	# of keys in each segment of R1 = $\lceil R_{s1}*N_{tp1}/N_{bf1}\rceil$ (K1 must be less than N_{kybf1})	2K
K_2	# of keys in each page of R2 = N_{kybf2} (K2 equals to N_{kybf2})	1K
N_{pg1}	# of page in which qualified tuples of R1 stored = $\lceil N_{tp1}*R_{s1}/K_2\rceil$	48
N_{pg2}	# of page in which qualified tuples of R2 stored = $\lceil N_{tp2}*R_{s2}/K_2\rceil$	190
R_{s1}	reduction ratio of R1 for selection	1
R_{s2}	reduction ratio of R2 for selection	1
R_{p1}	reduction ratio of R1 for projection	1
R_{p2}	reduction ratio of R2 for projection	1
R_j	reduction ratio of R1 for join	1
T_{dk1}	average interarrival time of R1's page from DF	16.8 ms
T_{dk2}	average interarrival time of R2's page from DF	16.8 ms
T_{st}	time taken to feed a page to sorter = $S_{bf2}*t_{bf2}$	9.8 ms
T_{mg}	average page merging time	26.2 ms
t_j	time taken to join two keys = $(1/4)*S_j*(t_{bf2}+t_{cmp})$	18.4 us
T_j	average time taken to join two pages.	42.6 ms

Table 2-3. Database Depend Parameters and Values.

Erlangian facility, and then the mean arrival rate of page to be sorted is

$$@_{st} = @_{b2}/K_2 = R_{s1}@_{df}/K_2,$$

i.e., the average interarrival time of page to be sorted is

$$T_{dk1} = 1/@_{st} = (S_{tp1}/S_{bk})*T_{bk}*K_2/R_{s1}$$

Also, large K_2 will cause the interarrival time approach to this mean value. In the case of R2, the arrival process has the same characteristic as that of the R1's, i.e., $T_{dk2} = (S_{tp2}/S_{bk})*T_{bk}*K_2/R_{s2}$.

3.3 Response Time

Useful time marks for execution of the query are defined in Table 3-1. Expression of parameters are derived to represent each of these time instants. The system timing is described in Figure 3. Since sorters is bit-parallel and word-serial, the time taken to access a key from BS2 is larger than sorting time. Thus, the average page sorting time, T_{st}, is the time to access one page from BS2, i.e. $T_{st}=K_2*S_j*t_{bf2}$. If S_j is larger than S_{st}, then pages that to be sorted must pass the sorter more times with least-significant part first, and the time taken to sort a page becomes

$$T_{st} = K_2*[S_j*t_{bf2}+(\lceil Sj/S_{st}\rceil-1)*2*Sj*tbf2],$$

where the notation $\lceil x\rceil$ means the smallest integer larger than x.

Mark	meaning
TM1	all of R1 transferred from mass storage to system.
TM2	MT begins to merge the sorted pages of R1.
TM3	all of the required keys of R1 have been sorted and merged into BS1.
TM4	all of R2 transferred from mass storege to system.
TM5	all of R2 have been sorted.
TM6	all of join has been done.

Table 3-1. Time Instants.

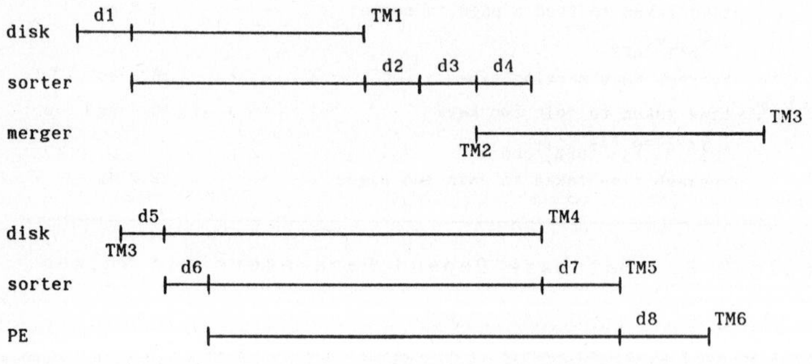

Figure 3. Timing Diagram.

(1) The calculation of TM1 and TM2:

The total time of reading R1 from mass storage to data filter is $t_{cyl}+t_{lat}+N_{bk1}*T_{bk}$ and the total time of writing the qualified keys and records to BS2 and DM are $N_{tp1}*S_j*t_{bf2}$ and $N_{tp1}*S_{tp1}*t_{dm}$, respectively. Since BS2 can, in the worst case, store all the qualified tuples of R1, so the time instant TM1, in which all of R1 is transferred from mass storage to BS2, depends upon the disk access rate (the number of pages produced in BS2 per second --- $1/T_{dk1}$) and sorting rate (the number of pages sorted per second).

(a) If the disk access rate is smaller than the sorting rate, i.e. $T_{dk1}>T_{st}$, then the time instant TM1 is given by

$$TM1 = t_{cyl}+t_{lat}+N_{bk1}*T_{bk} .$$

At the time TM1, $N_{tp1}*R_{s1}$ qualified keys of R1 are stored in BS2 and the last K_2 (or less) keys are ready to be fed into the sorter. After d_2 time later, the number of pages stored in cascade sorter is ($N_{tp1}*R_{s1}/K_2$ mod N_{st}) and further time -- d_3+d_4= ($N_{tp1}*R_{s1}$ mod $N_{st}*K_2)*S_j*t_{bf2}$ -- is required to extract them back (here notation "mod" stands for modular operation). Just after time d_3, some keys are extracted and the MT can starts to merge the sorted pages. Thus the time instant TM2 is given by

$$TM2 = TM1+d_2+d_3,$$

Where $d_2<K_2*S_j*t_{bf2}$, $d_3=(N_{tp1}*R_{s1} \bmod K_2)*S_j*t_{bf2}<K_2*S_j*t_{bf2}$.

(b) If the disk access rate is larger than sorting rate, i.e. $T_{dk1}<T_{st}$, then the time instant TM2 becomes:

$$TM2 = t_{cyl}+t_{lat}+d_1+N_{tp1}*R_{s1}*S_j*t_{bf2}+d_3,$$

where d_1 is the time required to produce first page to be sorted in BS2. If $N_{tp1}*R_{s1}<K_2$ then $d_1=N_{bk1}*T_{bk}$ else $d_1=T_{dk1}$.

(2) The Calculation of TM3:

During the merge process, MT reads BS2 and write them to BS1. The average page merging time, T_{mg}, is the time to access and merge K_2 keys read from one or more buffers of BS2. Here the time taken to merge two keys was selected as an approximation of one-fourth of S_j bytes compared at speed t_{cmp} per byte, i.e. $T_{mg} = K_2*(S_j*t_{bf2}+(1/4)*S_j*t_{cmp})$. Thus the time instant TM3 is given by

$$TM3 = TM2+N_{tp1}*R_{s1}*(T_{mg}/K_2)$$

(3) The calculation of TM4, TM5 and TM6:

After time TM3, the system starts to access relation R2 from disk. By refering the associative memory, DF sends each qualified key to one of the $N_{bf1}+2$ buffers. The time required to fill a buffer with an entile page, called d_5, is not predictable. If $N_{tp2}*R_{s2}>(N_{bf1}+2)*K_2$, then in the best case, $d_5=T_{dk2}$ means the previous keys are centralized to one region. In the worst case, $d_5=(N_{bf1}+2)*T_{dk2}$ means the previous keys are uniformly distributed to all $N_{bf1}+2$ regions. Otherwise, $d_5=N_{bk2}*T_{bk}$. The time required to fed the first page into sorter depends on the actual number of keys in the page. If $N_{tp2}*R_{s2}<K_2$ then d_6 is less than or equal to $N_{tp2}*R_{s2}*S_j*t_{bf2}$, otherwise d_6 is less than or equal to T_{st}.

When the first page is already fed into the sorter, a PE begins to load the corresponding segment from BS1. The time to join a key in PE with a key read from BS2, t_j, was selected as an approximation of one-fourth of S_j bytes compared at one micro-second per byte, i.e. $t_j = (1/4)*S_j*(t_{bf2}+t_{cmp})$. Thus, the page joining time, T_j, must be the sum of segment loading time, $K_1*S_j*t_{bf1}$, page comparing time, $(K_1+K_2)*t_j$, and result sending time. Here the result sending time is the time to read the required tuple from DM, $K_2*R_j*(R_{p1}*S_{tp1}+R_{p2}*S_{tp2})*t_{bf2}$, and the time to write the join tuple to BS3, $K_2*R_j*(R_{p1}*S_{tp1}+R_{p2}*S_{tp}-S_j)*t_{bf1}$. At time instant TM4, the number of left key to be sorted is less than $N_{tp2}*R_{s2} \bmod (N_{bf1}+2)*K_2$. By overlaping in/out the left pages to N_{st} sorters, the sorting time, d_7, approximates to $(N_{tp2}*R_{s2} \bmod (N_{bf1}+2)*K_2)*S_j*t_{bf2}/N_{st}$, and the time required to join these left pages is $d_8=(N_{tp2}*R_{s2} \bmod (N_{bf1}+2)*K_2)*T_j/K_2$. As shown in Figure 3(b), the following three cases are considered:

(a) If T_{dk2} is larger than T_{st} and T_j, then

$$TM4 = TM3+N_{bk2}*T_{bk} \text{ and}$$
$$TM6 = TM4+d_7+d_8 .$$

(b) If T_{st} is larger than T_{dk2} and T_j, then

$$TM5 = TM3+d_5+2*N_{tp2}*R_{s2}*S_j*t_{bf2}/N_{st}, \text{ and}$$
$$TM6 = TM5+d_8 .$$

(c) If Tj is larger than T_{dk2} and T_{st}, then

$$TM6 = TM3+d_5+d_6+N_{tp2}*R_{s2}*T_j/K_2$$

4. CASE STUDY

In this section we present case studies of the system by setting parameter values and examing calculated query response times. Controlled variation of parameter values within an expression derived from the system architecture and the query implemented on the system predicts the effect of the parameters on response time. The comparing time and shifting time are calculated as an approximation of one microsecond per byte. Since the initial sorter is designed to be bit-parallel and word-serial fashion, three non-overlapping clocks are used to compare and shift keys, thus the maximum key sorting (excluded the restriction of data access from BS2) is set at 3 microsecond.

The secondary store parameter values are listed in Table 2-1 which is taken from specifications of the Digital Equipment Corporation's RM80 disk driver. The avereage block transfer time is

$$T_{bk} = (T_{cyl} + T_{lat})/N_{bkcyl} + T_{bk}'$$

Table 2-2 shows the quantitative specification of the system module and their processing time.

During the quantitative design, we take some assumption about the system modules and relation to be joined as follow:

(1) The sorter is designed to be bit-parallel and word-serial fashion.

(2) The smaller relation is not larger than X=64K tuples.

(3) The key length is not larger than Y=64 bytes which includes 4-byte address.

Then the system parameters will be set by the following <u>design rule</u>:

Given N_{st}, N_{kyst}

Then $S_{bf2} := N_{kyst} * Y$

$N_{bf2} := X * Y / S_{bf2}$

$N_{mg} := N_{bf2} / N_{st}$

$S_{bf1} := N_{st} * S_{bf2}$

$N_{bf1} := X * Y / S_{bf1}$

$N_{pe} := N_{bf1}$

Here the parameters N_{st} and N_{kyst} are set at 4 and 1024 respectively. In fact, N_{pe} may be smaller than N_{bf1} to increase the PEs utility. This require further evaluation or simulation and not included here.

At the design time, tuple size is assumed to be equal to block size and the reduction ratios are set at 1, then the interarrival time of tuples from disk is Tbk=16.4 us and the key sorting time is $S_{st}*t_{rm}$ =19.2 us. To increase the access rate of sorter, each buffer of BS2 must be contructed in parallel form. For example, if each buffer is composed of $\lceil 19.2/16.4 \rceil$=2 chips with Sbf2/2=32K byte chip size, and the low-order interleaving is chosen for addressing scheme, then the average tuple access time of BS2 (Sj*tbf2=64*300ns/2=9.6us) is less than average block transfer time.

Database-dependent parameter values are listed in Table 2-3. The blocking factor has been chosen to give one tuple per block of secondary store. The size of join key is set to 64 bytes which is equal to the key size of initial sorter, and other parameter values are derived from all previous parameter values.

The effect on response time of the selectivity factor, projection factor, join factor and sorter capacity are respectively plotted in Figure 4 to Figure 7. Each Figure shows the response time ranging from 0 second to 10 second, and the value of the corresponding parameters.

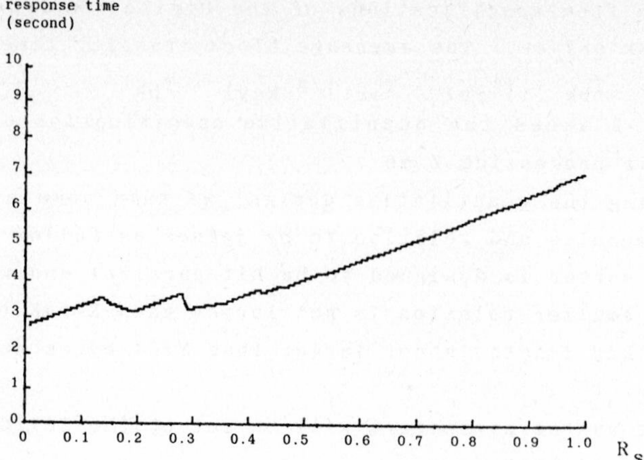

Figure 4. Response time with variant ratios of selection.

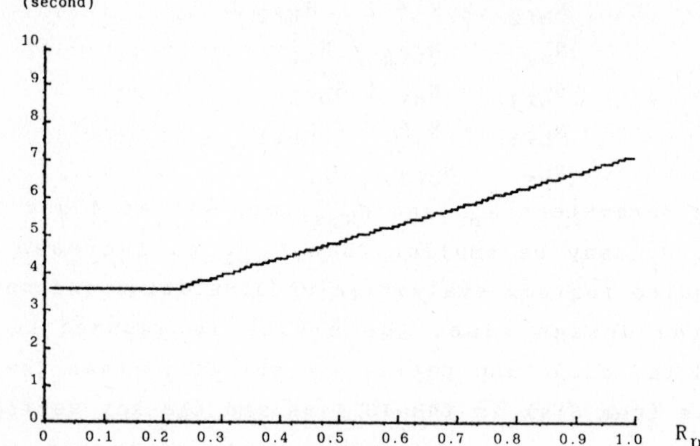

Figure 5. Response time with variant ratios of projection.

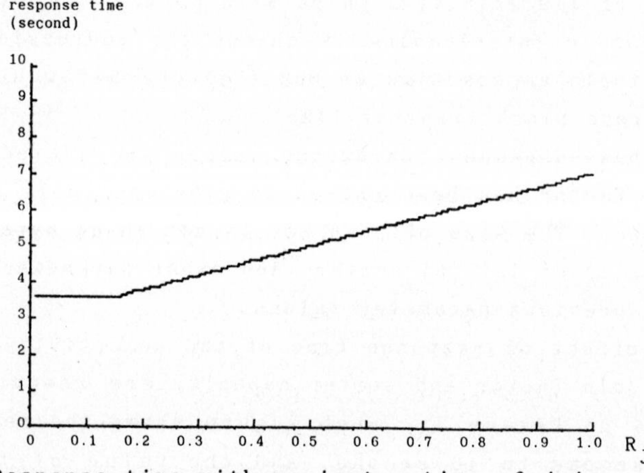

Figure 6. Response time with variant ratios of join.

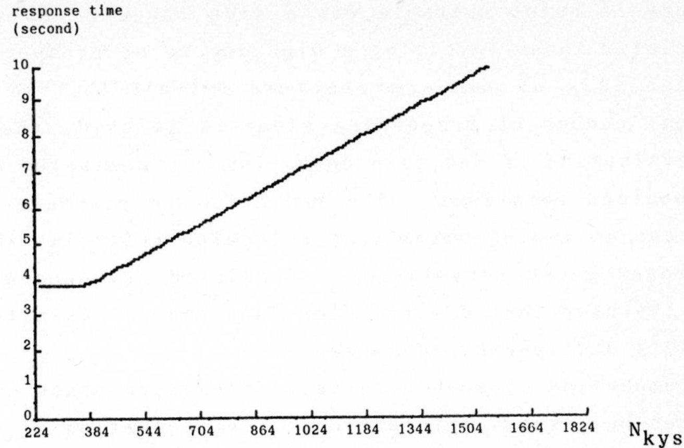

Figure 7. Response time with variant sorter capacity.

Since the time intervals d5, d7 and d8 are decrease as Rs1 and Rs2 increase, and the time intervals are dominant factor of response time when Rs1 and Rs2 are small. This is the reason why the drop phenomenon is appeared as shown in Figure 4. As the ratio further increase, response time is dominant by page join time T_j. In Figure 5 and Figure 6, the dominant factor is changed from T_{dk2} to T_j as the reduction ratio is larger than 0.2. Thus for reducing the system response, the PE processing time must be reduced.

Figure 7 show that the system response time will be further reduced by reducing the buffer size of BS2. But the decrease of buffer size cause more loading to backend controller, thus the system trade-off must be solved by further investigation of the details about how to control the system modules.

5. DISCUSSION AND SUMMARY

We have described and analyzed a join processor. The join processor reported here is an intrgral part of a database machine which also contains a hardware data filter that performs selection functions and a database operating system. Since one of the operand relations can be stored in the system buffer, cross-referencing is resolved by sorting, merging and duplicate removing the smaller relation, and the non-equijoin can be implemented easily but with larger join time.

Further performance improvements are achieved by using parallelism in key-sorting, tuple comparison and tuple concatenation. This architecture is quiet suitable for a wide range of database applications, especially those involving a high degree of cross-referencing.

Analysis of the architecture reveals that in the case where the optimal number of processing elements is used, the time required for the evaluation of the join operations is dominated by the time to load the operand relations. The reduction in response time, owing to the decrease in tuples satisfying selection criteria, shows the importance of proper query formulation. Predicted response time can be used to warn the user that a particular join has potentially large result cardinality and lengthy response.

Comparison of module rates to derive response expressions provides limited but useful information. The evaluation of the response should be considered in the context of more complex queries.

ACKNOWLEDGEMENTS

The work reported herein is supported in part by Tatung Company grant 75-08-14.

REFERENCES

[Bab 79] E. Babb, "Implementing a relational database by means of specialized hardware," ACM Trans. on Database Syst. vol.4, no.1, pp. 1-29, 1979.

[Bab 82] E. Babb,"Joined Normal Form: A storage encoding for relational databases," ACM Trans. on Database Syst. vol.7, no.4, pp. 588-614, 1982.

[BBDW83] D.Bitton, H.Boral, D.J.DeWitt and W.K.Wilkison, "Parallel Algorithms for the Execution of Relational Database Operations," ACM Tarns. Database Syst., vol.3, pp. 324-353, Sept. 1983.

[BBH 78] J. Banerjee, R. I. Baum, and D. K. Hsiao, "Concepts and capabilities of a database computer," ACM Trans. on Database Syst., vol.3, no.4, pp. 347-384, 1978.

[BDFW82] H.Boral,D.J.Dewitt, D.Friedland, and W.K.Wilkinson, "Implementation of the database machine DIRECT," IEEE trans. Software Engineering, vol.SE-8, no.6, pp. 533-543, 1982.

[BE 77] M. W. Blasgen andK. P. Eswaren, "Storage and access in relational database," IBM System Journal, vol.16, no.4, pp. 363-378, 1977.

[BHK 79] J.Banerjee, D.K.Hsiao and K.Kannan, "DBC --- A database computer for very large database," IEEE trans. Comput., vol.C28, no.6, pp. 414-429, June 1979.

[DeW 79] D.J.Dewitt, "DIRECT --- A multiprocessor organization for supporting relational database managements system," IEEE trans. Comput., vol.C-28, no.6, pp. 395-406, June 1979.

[Glin83] Martin Glinz, "A Dataflow Retrieval Unit for Relational Database Machine," in Database Machines, H.-O.Leilich and M.Missikoff, Editor, Springer-Verlag Berlin Heidelberg, 1983, pp.20-40.

[HB 84] K.Hwang and F.Briggs, "Computer Architectures and Parallel Processing," McGraw Hill, 1984, pp. 58-60.

[HM 83] M.J.Menon and D.K.Hsiao, "Design and Analysis of Join Operation," in Advanced Database Mavchine Architecdture, D.K. Hsiao, Editor, Prentice Hall, 1983, pp.203-255.

[Hon 85] Y.C.Hong, "Efficient Computing of Relational Algebraic Promitives in a Database Machine Architecture," IEEE Trans. Comput., vol. C-34, no.7, pp. 588-595, July 1985.

[KIS 85] Shigeo Kamiya, Kazuhide Iwata, and Hiroshi Sakai, "A Hardware Pipeline Algorithm for Relational Database Operation and It's Implementation Using Dedicated Hardware," in Proc. Annu. IEEE Symp. Comp. Arch., June 1985, pp.250-257.

[MTW 83] G. Miranker, L. Tang, and C. K. Wong, "A Zero-Time Sorter," IBM J. Res. Develop, vol.27, no.2, pp. 140-148, March 1983.

[SNEL79] S.Y.W.Su, L.H.Nguyen, A.Eman and G.J.Lipovski, "The architectural features and implementation techniques of the multicell CASSM," IEEE trans. Comput., vol.C-28, no.6, pp. 430-445, June 1979

[SNOS79] S.A.Schuster, H.B.Nguyen, E.A.Ozkarahan and K.C.Smith, "RAP.2 --- An associative processor for database and Its applications," IEEE trans. Comput., pp. 446-458, June 1979.

[SZ 84] R. K. Shultz and R. J. Zingg, "Response time analysis of multiproce- ssor computer for database support," ACM Trans. on Database Syst., vol.9, no.1, pp. 100-132, 1984.

[TNM 80] Y. Tanaka, Y. Nozaka, and A. Masuyama, "Pipelined Searching and Sorting Modules as Components of a Data Flow Database Computer," in Proc. of IFIP'80, Oct.1980, pp. 427-432.

[TY 82] Fu Tong and S.B.Yao, "Performance Analysis of Database Join Processor," in Proc. AFIPS Nat. Comp., vol.51, 1982, pp.627-638.

[WY 80] B.W.Wah and S.B.Yao, "DIALOG -- A Distributed Processor Organization," in Proc. AFIPS Nat. Comp., vol.49, 1980, pp. 243-253.

PARALLEL ALGORITHMS FOR PARENTHESIS MATCHING AND GENERATION OF RANDOM BALANCED SEQUENCES OF PARENTHESES*

Dilip Sarkar

Narsingh Deo

Department of Computer Science

University of Central Florida

Orlando, FL 32816

ABSTRACT: Parallel parenthesis-matching algorithm has in the past been used to design parallel algorithms for generation of computation tree forms and parsing. In this paper we present a parallel parenthesis-matching algorithm. A variant of binary search tree is constructed in parallel. The search tree is used to find the matching of each parenthesis. The algorithm takes $O(\log n)$ time on a $(n / \log n)$-processor CREW-PRAM. We also present an $O(\log n)$-time parallel algorithm for generation of random sequences of parentheses. These two algorithms can be used to design an $O(\log n)$-time parallel algorithm for generation of a class of random permutations.

I. INTRODUCTION

The computation model used in this paper is concurrent-read, exclusive-write, parallel random-access machine (CREW-PRAM), where the processors may read simultaneously from a common memory, but cannot write simultaneously into the same memory cell.

In this paper, we consider the parenthesis-matching problem. The problem is to find the matching parenthesis for each parenthesis in a given "legal" sequence of n parentheses. By "legal" it is meant that every parenthesis has its matching parenthesis in the sequence. It is easy to construct an $O(n)$-time sequential algorithm for the problem. Bar-On and Vishkin [2] have proposed an $O(\log n)$-time parallel parenthesis-matching algorithm and used it to design an optimal parallel algorithm for generation of computation tree forms. To design the algorithm for parallel generation

* This work was supported by the Washington Technology Center grant, subcontract number 384709

algorithm for generation of computation tree forms. To design the algorithm for parallel generation of computation tree form they have adopted the parenthesis-insertion technique of Knuth [6]. Their $O(\log n)$-time parallel algorithm on a $(n/\log n)$-processor CREW-PRAM is an improvement over Dekel and Sahni's [5] algorithm for construction of computation tree forms of arithmetic expressions on an EREW-PRAM. The motivation behind their construction of computation tree forms in logarithmic time is logarithmic-time arithmetic expression evaluation algorithms of Brent [3] and Miller and Reif [7]. They have shown that if the computation tree of an arithmetic expression is given, the expression can be evaluated in $O(\log n)$-time using n processors, even if the height of the computation tree is greater than $\log n$. Sarkar and Deo [8] have shown that a class of Pascal-like block-structured languages can be parsed in $O(\log n)$-time using an $O(\log n)$-time parenthesis-matching algorithm.

To construct an $O(\log n)$-time parallel parenthesis-matching algorithm, Bar-On and Vishkin observed that: (1) each of the $(n / \log n)$ processors assigned to a substring of length $\log n$, can find the pairs of matching parentheses in its subsequence in $O(\log n)$ time; (2) after this local parenthesis matching, each processor is left with an unmatched sequence of parentheses of the form)) . . .)((. . .(; finally, (3) from the remaining sequence of parentheses, if matching for the leftmost left and rightmost right parentheses can be found in $O(\log n)$ time, the matchings for all other parentheses can also be found in $O(\log n)$ time. Then, they proposed an algorithm to find the matching of a parenthesis in $O(\log n)$ time. They used a binary tree to compute the nesting level of each parenthesis and used these nesting levels to construct a variant of balanced binary search tree. Finally, they proposed a search procedure to find the matching of a given parenthesis in $O(\log n)$ time.

In this paper, we propose a simple and elegant optimal algorithm to find the matching of a parenthesis in $O(\log n)$ time. We also use a variant of binary search tree. However, we do not compute the nesting level of each parenthesis. We observe that if the number of unmatched left parentheses and the number of unmatched right parentheses in each of the two adjacent substrings are known, we can compute the number of unmatched left parentheses and unmatched right parentheses in the string obtained by concatenating these two strings. Using the technique of concatenating two strings recursively, we build a binary tree. This binary tree is used as the search tree to find the match for each parenthesis. With some more observations and moving top-down, we can construct a random legal sequence of parentheses. But the string obtained is not uniformly distributed, as given by sequential algorithm of Arnold and Sleep [1].

In Section II, we present a procedure to construct the search tree and a procedure to find the matching of a parenthesis. In Section III, we present a procedure for generating legal sequences of balanced parentheses. Section IV concludes the paper with a brief discussion on possible extensions of this work.

II. PARENTHESIS-MATCHING ALGORITHM

Let S be a legal sequence of balanced parentheses stored in a linear array. Let s_1 and s_2 be two arbitrary consecutive subsequences in S (see Fig. 1). A right parenthesis in s_2 without a matching parenthesis in s_2 must have its matching parenthesis in the substring to the left of the substring s_2. Similarly, a left parenthesis in s_1 without a matching parenthesis in s_1 must have its matching parenthesis in the substring to the right of substring s_1. Let r_1 (respectively r_2) be the number of right parentheses in s_1 (respectively in s_2) that do not have their matching parentheses in s_1 (respectively in s_2) and l_1 (respectively l_2) be the number of left parentheses in s_1 (respectively in s_2) that do not have their matching parentheses in s_1 (respectively in s_2). In the concatenated string $s = s_1 s_2$, the number of right parentheses r is given by

$$\begin{aligned} r &= r_1 && \text{if} \quad r_2 \le l_1 \\ &= r_1 + (r_2 - l_2) && \text{if} \quad r_2 > l_1 \end{aligned}$$

Thus, concatenated string s must have $r_1 + r_2$ - $\min(l_1, r_2)$ right parentheses whose matching parentheses are in the substring to the left of s. Similarly, s must have $l_1 + l_2$ - $\min(l_1, r_2)$ left parentheses whose matching parentheses are in the substring to the right of s.

We utilize this observation to construct ith level of a balanced binary search tree in a bottom-up fashion using values r_x and l_x at every node x at (i - 1)th level of the tree (the leaf nodes are at the zeroth level of the tree). To find the match of a parenthesis, we search on this binary search tree. Each parenthesis in the sequence S is a leaf-node in the tree. We label a node of the binary tree by an ordered pair $<i, j>$ of nonnegative integers, where the first integer represents the level of the node (from the bottom) and the second represents its position from the left in that level. Nodes $<i-1, 2j-1>$ and $<i-1, 2j>$ are then the left and the right children of the node $<i, j>$. We also use two arrays, $r[i, j]$ and $l[i, j]$, to store the values at nodes

$<i, j>$, $0 \le i < \lceil \log_2 n \rceil$ and $1 \le j \le 2^i$. If the parenthesis at position j (in string S) is a right (respectively left) parenthesis then $l[0, j] = 0$ (respectively $l[0, j] = 1$) and $r[0, j] = 1$ (respectively $r[0, j] = 0$). The search tree for a given balanced sequence of parentheses is shown in Fig. 2. The algorithm for construction of the binary search tree is as follows.

CONSTRUCTION OF THE BINARY TREE:

Input: A legal sequence of n parentheses stored in a linear array.

Output: A binary search tree of height $\lceil \log_2 n \rceil$ stored in two arrays.

Step 1: {Initialization -- for all j **do in parallel** }

    if there is a right parenthesis at position j **then**

        $r[0, j] := 1$

    else

        $r[0, j] := 0$;

    if there is a left parenthesis at position j **then**

        $l[0, j] := 1$

    else

        $l[0, j] := 0$;

Step 2:

    for $i := 1$ **to** $\lceil \log_2 n \rceil$ **do**

        for $j := 1$ **to** $2^{\lceil \log_2 n \rceil - i}$ **do** {in parallel}

        begin

            $r[i, j] := r[i-1, 2j-1] + r[i-1, 2j] - \min(l[i-1, 2j-1], r[i-1, 2j])$;

            $l[i, j] := l[i-1, 2j-1] + l[i-1, 2j] - \min(l[i-1, 2j-1], r[i-1, 2j])$;

        end ;

In the following discussion, two descendants of a node in the search tree are identified as its left child and right child; left (respectively right) child is called left (respectively right) brother of the right (respectively left) child. Let us consider the search procedure to find the matching right parenthesis of a left parenthesis at position x of the input string (for convenience we shall call parenthesis at position x as parenthesis x or simply x). We search on the search tree constructed by the previous procedure. Obviously, the matching right parenthesis of a left parenthesis x is in the substring to the right of the x. Suppose in the searching process we have arrived at a node of the search tree such that there are c_1 unmatched left parentheses to right of x in the substring corresponding to this node. If the present node is a right child, its string concatenates with a substring on the left side of the its substring, and hence, no left parenthesis comes to the right of x in the concatenated string, and value of c_1 does not change. If the present node is a left child, we determine how many right parentheses in the substring corresponding to its right brother do not have a match i.e., find the value of r corresponding to its right brother. If $r \leq c_1$ then the match for x is not in the string corresponding to the right brother and we climb up to the father of the present node. The number of left parentheses to the right of x in the concatenated string is given by $c_1 - r + l$. Thus, c_1 is assigned $c_1 - r + l$ (l is the number of unmatched left parentheses of its right brother). We continue to climb towards the root of the search tree by these rules until we reach a node whose right brother has r unbalanced right parentheses such that $r > c_1$. At this point we know that the matching parenthesis for x is in the substring corresponding to the right brother, and we move to the right brother and continue to climb down towards the leaves until we reach a leaf-node which has the match for x. While we are climbing down towards the leaf-nodes, we test the number of unbalanced right parentheses in the string corresponding to the left child. If its r-value is greater than c_1 then move to the left subtree, otherwise $c_1 := c_1 - r$ and move to the right child. We continue this process until a leaf-node is reached. The formal description of the procedure is as follows.

SEARCHING FOR THE RIGHT MATCHING PARENTHESIS;

Input: Search tree and the position of a left parenthesis in the sequence of the parentheses.
Output: Position of the matching right parenthesis is j.

{for the matching of a left parenthesis at position x}
begin

count := 0; i := 0; j := x;
{present node is <i, j>}
if j is odd {i.e., present node is a left-child} **then**

```
begin
  if (count - r[i, j]) < 0 then {end of climbing towards the root}
    begin
      j := j + 1; {move to the right brother}
      while i ≠ 0 do
        begin
          if count - r[i − 1, 2j − 1] ≥ 0 then
            {move down to the right child} begin
              count := count - r[i − 1,2j − 1];
              i := i - 1;    j := 2j;
            end
          else {move down to the left child}
            begin
              i := i - 1;    j := 2j -1;
            end
        end {right parenthesis at location j is the match for left parenthesis
             at location x }
    end
  else {update count and climb towards the root}
    begin
      count := count + l[i, j + 1] − r[i, j + 1];
      i := i + 1;    j := (j + 1) / 2 ;
    end
end
else { present node is a right child  -  climb towards the root}
  begin
    i := i + 1;    j := j / 2;
  end
end ;
```

A similar procedure for searching the match of a right parenthesis can be constructed. It is not difficult to implement these two procedures in $O(\log n)$ time using $(n / \log n)$ processors along the line shown in Chin and Chen [4], Vishkin [9] and Wyllie [10].

AN EXAMPLE

A legal sequence of parentheses and its search tree are shown in Fig. 2. Construction of the search tree using the given procedure is easy. Let us illustrate the searching procedure by searching the matching right parenthesis of the left parenthesis at position five of the input sequence. Initially, we start at node <0, 5> with the count value $c_1 = 0$. The node <0, 5> is a left node, and hence, we compare the r-value of its right brother with c_1 and find that c_1 is not smaller than the r-value. Therefore, c_1 is assigned $c_1 - r + l$ (= 1) and climb to the node <1, 3>. Repeat similar steps and climb to the node <2, 2> with c_1-value one. Node <2, 2> is a right child, hence move to its father, the node <3, 1>, without changing the value of c_1. From the left child node <3, 1>, we compare the c_1 value with the r-value of its right brother, node <3, 2>, and find that c_1 is smaller. Therefore, we move to right brother <3, 2>. The left child of the node <3, 2> has r-value greater than c_1. Hence, we move to left child node <2, 3> and then, for similar reason, to node <1, 5>. At this point c_1 value is one and comparing this value with r-value of its left child we find that c_1 is not smaller than r-value of its left child. Therefore, we move to the right child node <0, 10> assigning c_1 to $c_1 - r + l$ (= 0) where r and l are the r-value and l-value of the left child of the node <1, 5>. The node <0, 10> is a leaf node, and hence, parenthesis at position ten is the matching parenthesis for the left parenthesis at position five.

III. GENERATION OF RANDOM BALANCED PARENTHESIS STRINGS

In this section, we investigate some properties of search trees and use these properties to design a parallel algorithm for generation of random balanced-parenthesis sequences. We investigate properties of fully-balanced search trees only. However, it is easy to extend the method for any balanced search trees. Let us consider a nonleaf node and its two children. Let s be the string corresponding to the node and $n = 2^i$ be its length. The length of the string corresponding to each of its children is $\frac{n}{2} = 2^{i-1}$. Let s_1 be the string corresponding to the left child and s_2 be that for the right child (see Fig. 3).

We know that,

$$l = l_1 + l_2 - \min(l_1, r_2)$$

and

$$r = r_1 + r_2 - \min(l_1, r_2)$$

where l and r (with and without subscripts) represent the number of unmatched left and right parentheses. There are three cases,

Case I: $l_1 < r_2$

All unmatched l_1 left parentheses of s_1 are matched by l_1 unmatched right parentheses of s_2 and there are $(r_2 - l_1)$ extra unmatched right parentheses. Thus, $l = l_2$ and $r = r_1 + r_2 - l_1$.

Case II: $l_1 = r_2$

All unmatched l_1 left parentheses of s_1 are matched by l_1 unmatched right parentheses of s_2. Thus, we have $r = r_1$ and $l = l_2$.

Case III: $l_1 > r_2$

All unmatched r_2 right parentheses of s_2 are matched by r_2 left parentheses of s_1 and there are extra $l_1 - r_2$ unmatched left parentheses. Therefore, we have $r = r_1$ and $l = l_1 + l_2 - r_2$.

Lengths of the strings s, s_1, and s_2 satisfy the following properties,

Property 1: $l + r \leq n$, $l_1 + r_1 \leq \frac{n}{2}$, and $l_2 + r_2 \leq \frac{n}{2}$

Property 2: If $l > \frac{n}{2}$ (respectively $r > \frac{n}{2}$) then $r_2 < l_1$ (respectively $l_1 < r_2$)

Property 3: If $l \leq \frac{n}{2}$ and $r \leq \frac{n}{2}$ then either $l_1 \leq r_2$ or $l_1 > r_2$

Property 4: $l_2 \leq l$, and $r_1 \leq r$

Property 5: $\min(l_1, r_2) \leq \frac{n - (l + r)}{2}$

Property 6: Except at leaf-nodes, the sum of number of unmatched left parentheses and number of unmatched right parentheses are even number.

Now we consider the generation of random sequences of balanced parentheses. To simplify the presentation we consider sequences of length 2^i, $i \geq 1$. The root of any search tree has zero unmatched left and right parenthesis and each leaf has a left or a right parenthesis. But any node other than the leaves and the nodes at level just above the leaf-nodes must satisfy two conditions,

$$\max(l, r) > \frac{n}{2}$$

and,

$$\max(l, r) \leq \frac{n}{2}$$

Case 1: $\max(l, r) > \frac{n}{2}$

Say $r > l$. In this case we have to split r into two parts r_2 and $r - (r_2 - l_1)$ such that the following conditions are satisfied.

$$n \geq r > \frac{n}{2} > l \geq 0 \tag{1}$$

$$l_2 = l \geq 0 \tag{2}$$

$$r_2 > l_1 \geq 0 \tag{3}$$

$$r_1 = r - (r_2 - l_1) \geq 0 \tag{4}$$

$$r + l \leq n \tag{5}$$

$$\frac{n}{2} \geq r_1 + l_1 \geq 0 \tag{6}$$

$$\frac{n}{2} \geq r_2 + l_2 \geq 0$$

$$\text{or,} \quad \frac{n}{2} \geq l + r_2 \geq 0 \tag{7}$$

From Conditions 4 and 6 we get ,

$$r_2 \geq r - \frac{n}{2} + 2l_1$$

From Condition 3 lower bound of l_1 is zero. Thus,

$$r_2 \geq r - \frac{n}{2}$$

Using Condition 7 we can write,

$$\frac{n}{2} - l \geq r_2 \geq 0$$

Thus,

$$\frac{n}{2} - l \geq r_2 \geq r - \frac{n}{2} \tag{8}$$

From Conditions 3, 4 and 6 we get,

$$\frac{1}{2}(\frac{n}{2} - r + r_2) \geq l_1 \geq 0 \tag{9}$$

Now r_1 can be obtained by Condition 4.

Similarly, when $l > \frac{n}{2}$ we split l such that,

$$\frac{n}{2} - r \geq l_1 \geq l - \frac{n}{2} \tag{10}$$

$$\frac{1}{2}(\frac{n}{2} - l + l_1) \geq r_2 \geq 0 \tag{11}$$

From Conditions 8, 9, 10 and 11 we can compute the values of l_1, r_1, l_2, and r_2 in the subtree shown in Fig. 3.

Case 2: $\max(l, r) \leq \frac{n}{2}$

To generate the subtree, we can split either l or r. We have to select one randomly. Let r is selected for splitting. Then Conditions 2 - 7 hold as in earlier Case 1 and also,

$$\frac{n}{2} \geq r, l \geq 0 \tag{12}$$

Using these conditions it is easy to determine the following two ranges for the values r_2 and l_1.

$$\frac{n}{2} - l \geq r_2 \geq 0 \tag{13}$$

$$\frac{1}{2}(\frac{n}{2} + r - r_2)) \geq r_1 \geq \max(0, r - r_2) \tag{14}$$

Similarly, we can determine the ranges of values for r_1, l_1, r_2, and l_2 in other cases. These ranges of values can be used to generate two children of a node when the values r and l at the node are known. The procedure for it is as follows.

SUBTREE GENERATION

Input: Number of unmatched left and right parentheses at a node of the tree.

Output: Number of unmatched left and right parentheses at the two children of the node.

if max $(l, r) > \frac{n}{2}$ **then**

  if $r > \frac{n}{2}$ **then**

```
begin
    l_2 := l;
    if l_2 is an odd number then
        randomly generate an odd number r_2 such that
        n/2 - l >= r_2 >= r - n/2
    else {l_2 is an even number }
        randomly generate an even number r_2 such that
        n/2 - l >= r_2 >= r - n/2;
    randomly generate l_1 such that 1/2(n/2 - r + r_2) >= l_1 >= 0;
    r_1 := r - (r_2 - l_1)
end
else { l > n/2 }
begin
    r_1 := r;
    if r_1 is an odd number then
        randomly generate an odd number l_1 such that
        n/2 - r >= l_1 >= l - n/2;
    else {r_1 is an even number}
        randomly generate an even number l_1 such that
        n/2 - r >= l_1 >= l - n/2;
    randomly generate r_2 such that 1/2(n/2 - l + l_1) >= r_2 >= 0;
    l_2 := l - (l_1 - r_2)
end
else { max(r, l) <= n/2}
    select l or r randomly;
    if r is selected then
    begin
        l_2 := l;
        if l_2 is an odd number then
            randomly generate an odd number r_2 such that
```

$$\frac{n}{2} - l \geq r_2 \geq 0$$

else {l_2 is an even number }

randomly generate an even number r_2 such that

$$\frac{n}{2} - l \geq r_2 \geq 0$$

randomly generate l_1 such that

$$\frac{1}{2}(\frac{n}{2} + r - r_2)) \geq l_1 \geq \max(0, r - r_2);$$

$l_1 := r_1 + r_2 - r$

end

else

begin

$r_1 := r;$

if r_1 is an odd number **then**

randomly generate an odd number l_1 such that

$$\frac{n}{2} - r \geq l_1 \geq 0$$

else {r_1 is an even number }

randomly generate an even number l_1 such that

$$\frac{n}{2} - r \geq l_1 \geq 0$$

randomly generate r_2 such that

$$\frac{1}{2}(\frac{n}{2} + l - l_1)) \geq r_2 \geq \max(0, l - l_1);$$

$r_2 := l_1 + l_2 - l$

end

Starting at the root with zeroes for r and l values, and using the subtree generation procedure a search tree can be generated. From this search tree we can get the corresponding string of parentheses.

The algorithms for generation of random balanced sequences of parenthesis and the one for parenthesis matching can be combined to design a parallel algorithm for generating a class of random permutations. More specifically, permutations that can be generated with a stack can also be generated by the two algorithm presented here. To generate a permutation of n elements the steps will be: (1) generate a random sequence of balanced parentheses of length $2n$; (2) find the matching of each left parenthesis; (3) assign one element to every left parenthesis and move the element to its matching right parenthesis. These three steps can be implemented in $O(\log n)$ time using $(n / \log n)$ processors.

IV. CONCLUSION

We have presented an $O(\log n)$-time cost-optimal parallel algorithm to find the match of a given parenthesis in a balanced sequence of parentheses. Our algorithm is neither a simulation nor adaptation of any existing sequential algorithm. The algorithm has been designed from a simple observation. Further extension of the observation has allowed us to design an algorithm for parallel generation of random sequences of balanced parentheses. However, the algorithm does not generate every possible sequence of parentheses with equal probability. It would be useful to extend the algorithm for generating legal parentheses-sequences with uniform distribution.

REFERENCES

[1] D. B. Arnold and M. R. Sleep, "Uniform Random Generation of Balanced Parenthesis Strings," *ACM Trans. Program. Lang. Syst.,* Vol. 2, No. 1, Jan. 1980, pp. 122 - 128.

[2] I. Bar-On and U. Vishkin, "Optimal Parallel Generation of a Computation Tree Form," *ACM Trans. Program. Lang. Syst.,* Vol. 7, No. 2, April 1985, pp. 348 - 357.

[3] P. R. Brent, "The Parallel Evaluation of General Arithmetic Expressions," *J. ACM,* Vol. 21, No. 2, April 1974, pp. 201 - 206.

[4] Y. F. Chin and I. Chen, "Efficient Parallel Algorithms for Some Graph Problems," *Commun. ACM,* Vol. 25, No. 3, March 1982, pp. 659 - 665.

[5] E. Dekel and S. Sahni, "Parallel Generation of Postfix and Tree Forms," *ACM Trans. Program. Lang. Syst.,* Vol. 5, No. 3, July 1983, pp. 300 - 317.

[6] D. E. Knuth, "A History of Writing Compilers," *Comput. Autom.,* 1962, pp. 6 - 19.

[7] G. L. Miller and J. H. Reif, "Parallel Tree Contraction and Its Application," in *Proc. Symposium on Foundations of Computer Science, IEEE,* 1985, pp. 478 - 489.

[8] D. Sarkar and N. Deo, "An Optimal Parallel Parsing Algorithm for a Class of Block-Structured Languages," TR-CS-87-01, Department of Computer Science, University of Central Florida, Orlando, Florida, Jan. 1987.

[9] U. Vishkin, "An Optimal Parallel Connectivity Algorithm," *Discrete Appl. Math.,* Vol. 9, 1984, pp. 197 - 207.

[10] J. C. Wyllie, "The Complexity of Parallel Computation," TR 79-387, Department of Computer Science, Cornell University, Ithaca, N.Y., 1979.

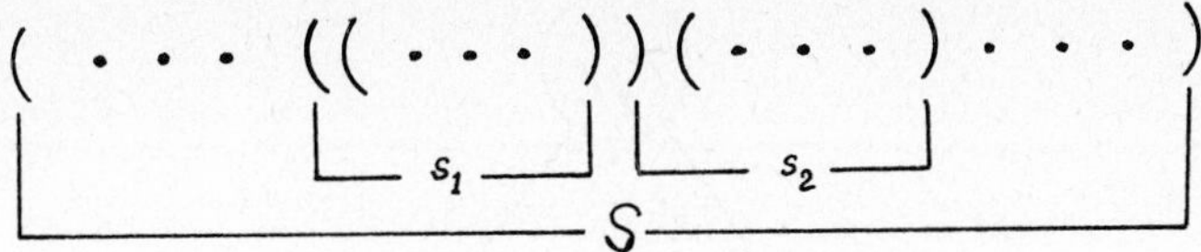

Fig. 1 A legal sequence of parentheses.

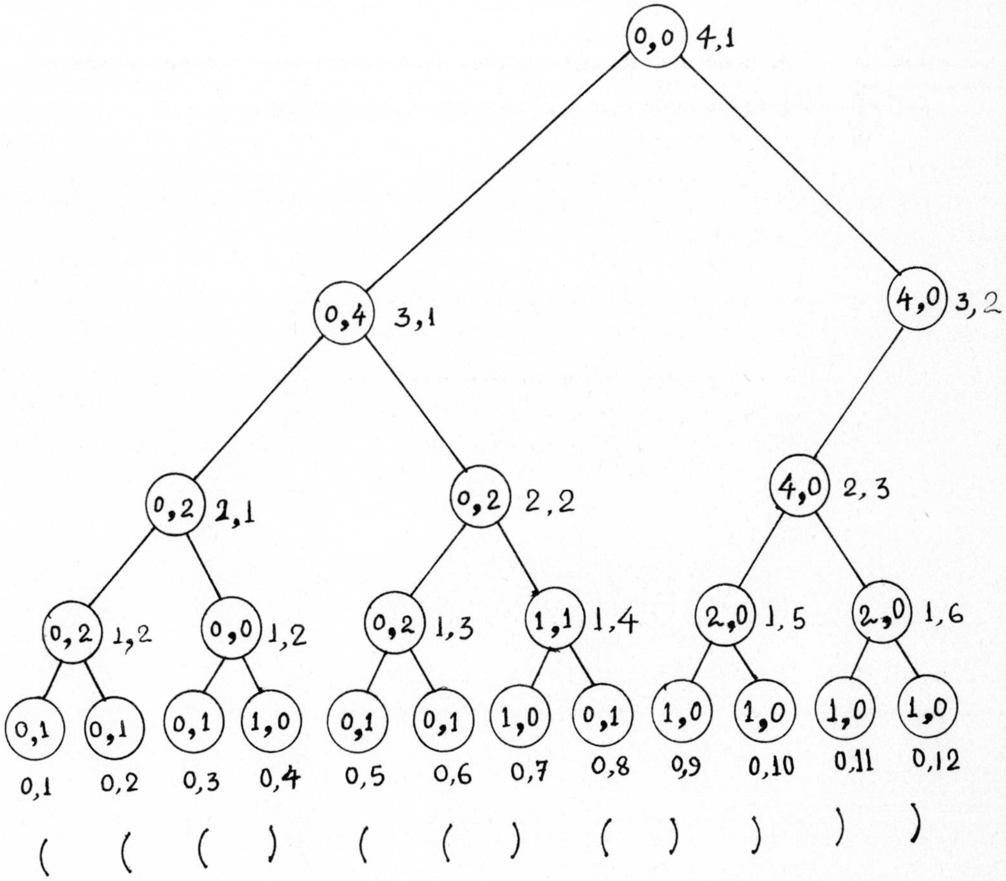

Fig. 2 A sequence of parentheses and its search tree. Node labels are shown next to the nodes, and the (r, l) values are shown within the circles.

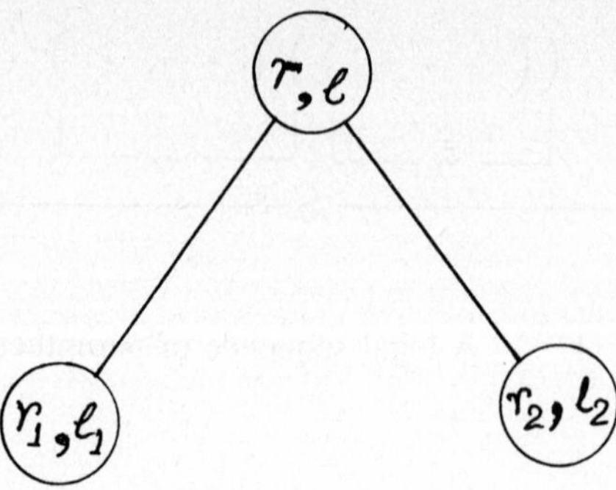

Fig. 3 A node and its two children in a search tree. Length of string corresponding to the node is $n = 2^i$ and that at the children is $\frac{n}{2} = 2^{i-1}$.

SUPERLINEAR SPEEDUP FOR PARALLEL BACKTRACKING

Ewald Speckenmeyer
Burkhard Monien
Oliver Vornberger

Universität-GH Paderborn
D-4790 Paderborn
West Germany

ABSTRACT

We have implemented a backtracking strategy for the satisfiability problem on a ring of processors and we observed a superlinear speedup in the average. In this paper we describe a model from which this superlinear speedup can be deduced. The model is based on the fact that in the average the solutions are distributed nonuniformly in the case of the satisfiability problem. To our knowledge this phenomenon was not used before in the analysis of algorithms.

1. INTRODUCTION

In recent years the design and analysis of algorithms for parallel computer architectures have become a central research area in theoretical and applied computer science. Different types of algorithms have been designed and implemented on different types of architectures. In this paper we are interested in explaining experimental results found in Paderborn by implementing a backtracking strategy for the satisfiability problem on a ring of processors [6]. It is not surprising, and was observed by many authors that for a single problem instance by using k processors a speedup greater than k (or smaller than 1) can occur. We found a wellknown natural problem such that the parallel implementation of the backtracking strategy usually used for solving this problem leads to a superlinear speedup in the average. To our knowledge this is the first time that such a behaviour has been observed.

For formulas from the class $K_3(25,100)$, where $K_s(n,r)$ denotes the class of Boolean formulas in conjunctive normal form over n variables with r clauses, each of length s, we found the following speedup in the average.

number of processors	2	4	8
speedup	2.46	4.68	9.59

We get different speedup values for different values of s, n, and r, the reason will become clear in section 4.

We want to stress the point that we did not design a new heuristic which is poor in the 1-processor case, just in order to get this superlinear speedup, but that we considered (on the contrary) a strategy which is known to behave well in the case of one processor. In our parallel version each processor performs the same strategy, an idle processor getting new work form its predecessor in the ring. For more details about the implementation the reader is referred to [6]. Related work about parallel implementations of algorithms for solving combinatorial problems can be found in [2, 4, 7].

In section 4 we describe a model from which the superlinear speedup can be deduced. This model is based on the fact that the solutions are distributed nonuniformly in the average. I.e., if p is the average solution density of the formulas from $K_s(n,r)$ (average solution density = average number of solutions divided by average number of truth assignements) then for example in the case of splitting F into two subformulas F_x and $F_{\bar{x}}$ by setting some varible x to true or false, resp., one of the two subformulas has an average solution density of p_1 and the other of p_2 with $p_1 > p > p_2$. For the class $K_3(25,100)$ we obtained $p \approx 0.002003$, $p_1 \approx 1.6036 \cdot p$, $p_2 \approx 0.3345 \cdot p$. In section 5 we derive a formula estimating the average degree of unbalanced distribution of the solutions on the subformulas F_x and $F_{\bar{x}}$ of $F \in K_s(n,r)$. We were not able to give a total analytical proof for the superlinear speedup, but we think that our model describes the essential reasons for it. To our knowledge the nonuniform distribution of the solution density was not used before to explain the behaviour of an algorithm.

Therefore a superlinear speedup is to be expected if a problem has a similar nonuniform distribution of the average solution densities Note that our parallel algorithm essentially consists of a strategy following down k paths, $k > 1$, simultaneously in the backtracking tree expanded by a strategy for distributing work to processors which have finished their subproblems. Of course such an algorithm could be simulated also on a sequential computer but this does not lead necessarily to a better sequential algorithm since such an implementation would need (as the algorithm is parallel in nature) an organisation overhead. More information about the underlying satisfiability problem can be found in [1, 3, 5].

2. DEFINITIONS

Let $L = \{x_1, \bar{x}_1, \ldots, x_n, \bar{x}_n\}$ be the set of literals over the set $V = \{x_1, \ldots, x_n\}$ of Boolean variables, and let $cl(n, s) := \{(\xi_{i_1} \vee \ldots \vee \xi_{i_s}) \mid 1 \leq i_1 < \ldots < i_s \leq n,$ $\xi_{i_j} \in \{x_{i_j}, \bar{x}_{i_j}\}\}$ be the set of clauses of length s over V. $c = (\xi_{i_1} \vee \ldots \vee \xi_{i_s})$ is represented by $\{\xi_{i_1}, \ldots, \xi_{i_s}\}$. By $K_s(n, r) := cl(n, s)^r$ we denote the set of formulas in CNF with r clauses from $cl(n, s)$. Let $F \in K_s(n, r)$ be a formula represented by an ordered multiset of clauses $F = \{\{\xi_{11}, \ldots, \xi_{1s}\}, \ldots, \{\xi_{r1}, \ldots, \xi_{rs}\}\}$ and let $\xi \in L$ then $F_\xi := \{c - \{\bar{\xi}\} \mid c \in F, \xi \notin c\}$.

F is called satisfiable iff there are a subset $\{i_1, \dots, i_\ell\} \subseteq \{1, \dots, n\}$ and literals $\xi_{i_j} \in \{x_{i_j}, \bar{x}_{i_j}\}$, $1 \le j \le \ell$, s.t. $F_{\xi_{i_1} \dots \xi_{i_\ell}} = \emptyset$. By [] we denote the empty clause, which is unsatisfiable by definition.

The following simple backtracking procedure decides whether a formula $F \in K_s(n, r)$ is satisfiable.

```
push input formula F on the stack;
repeat
   pop top formula F from the stack;
   if F = Ø then report "satisfiable"
      else begin
         choose the largest indexed new variable x, w.r.t. F;
         split F into F_x and F_x̄;
         for ξ ε {x, x̄} do
           if [] ∉ F_ξ then push F_ξ
   end
until stack is empty or satisfiable has been reported;
```

To each formula $F \in K_s(n, r)$ corresponds in a natural way a binary tree $T = T(F)$, where the root of T is assigned by F and if an inner node v of T at depth i, $0 \le i < n$, is assigned by F', where $F' \ne \emptyset$ and $[] \notin F'$, then the left son of v in T is assigned by $F'_{\bar{x}_{n-i}}$ and the right son by $F'_{x_{n-i}}$. The leaves of T are assigned either by $\emptyset$ indicating satisfying truth assignements (solutions) or by formulas containing [] (non-solutions). This node-labeled tree T is called the state space tree (SST) of F.

Then the computation of the algorithm above applied to $F \in K_s(n, r)$ corresponds to a depth first search in T(F) until the first solution leaf of T(F) is found or T(F) has been visited without sucess. Using k identical processors $P_0, P_1, \dots, P_{k-1}$ connected as a ring, i.e., P_i is connected to $P_{i-1 \bmod k}$ and $P_{i+1 \bmod k}$, $0 \le i < k$, the problem "is $F \in K_s(n, r)$ satisfiable" can be solved using this architecture as follows. W.l.o.g. let $k = 2^\ell$. All processors start with the above backtracking algorithm, where at the beginning the stack of P_0 is initialized with $F_{\bar{x}_n \dots \bar{x}_{n-\ell+1}}$, P_1 with $F_{\bar{x}_n \dots \bar{x}_{n-\ell+2} x_{n-\ell+1}}$, ..., and P_{k-1} with $F_{x_n \dots x_{n-\ell+1}}$. All processors stop computing, if a fist solution is found by some processor or if the whole SST of F has been visited without success.

In order to hold all processors busy as long as possible during the computation the implemented version of this parallel k processor algorithm also allows the following action. If processor P_i, $0 \le i < k$, has computed its subformula without finding a

solution, it asks processor $P_{i+1 \bmod k}$ to send a formula F' from its stack. The exchange of formulas between processors will be ignored in our analysis. This restriction is not severe, if the class of formulas solved by the above parallel algorithm is dominated by far by formulas with the property that each of the subformulas F is split into during the initial phase contains a solution.
Note that each processor P_i searches in exactly one state space subtree $T(F_{\xi_n \ldots \xi_{n-\ell+1}})$ of T(F).

For $F \in K_s(n, r)$ we denote by $t_k(F)$ the time needed by the parallel k-processor algorithm to test whether F is satisfiable and by $su_{k,\ell}(F) := \frac{t_\ell(F)}{t_k(F)}$ the speedup achieved by using k instead of ℓ processors, $1 \le \ell \le k$, to solve F. The <u>average speedup of k versus ℓ processors</u> is defined by $\overline{su}_{k,\ell} := \frac{E(t_\ell)}{E(t_k)}$, where $E(t_j) := \frac{1}{|K_s(n,r)|} \cdot \sum_{F \in K_s(n, r)} t_j(F)$, $j \in \{k,\ell\}$.

Throughout the paper we assume that each processor of the parallel k-processor algorithm evaluates exactly one leaf of its SST during every time unit. Under this assumption $t_k(F)$ denotes the number of time units needed during each of which k new leaves of the SST are visited, if no solution exists.

Even under this assumption it is not known how to determine $E(t_k)$ efficiently even in the case of k = 1. So we will construct a simpler, mathematical tractable problem, which incorporates important parameters of the original problem, and it is our hope that properties of this simpler problem allow some conclusions concerning the original problem. The two parameters we will adopt from the original problem, and which certainly strongly influence the result of the original problem, are 1.) the average number λ of solution leaves, and 2.) the average number N of leaves of the SST's of the formulas $F \in K_s(n, r)$. Then the number $p = \frac{\lambda}{N}$ is a measure for the average solution density of the problem. I.e., p lies in the interval [0,1] and the smaller p is, the greater the expected value of $E(t_k)$ will be and vice versa.

<u>3. THE AVERAGE SOLUTION DENSITY AND A FIRST MODEL</u>

Using a counting technique developed by Brown and Purdom [1] the average number M of nodes of the SST's of $K_s(n, r)$ is determined by

$$M = 1 + \sum_{i=1}^{n} 2^i \left[\left[1 - \binom{i-1}{s} / \left[2^s \binom{n}{s}\right]\right]^r - \left[\binom{i-1}{s} / \left[2^s \binom{n}{s}\right]\right]^r \right].$$ Because all nodes in SST's have 0 or 2 successors and such trees are known to have t inner nodes and t+1 leaves, for some t, the average number N of leaves of SST's is $N := \frac{M+1}{2}$.
In [1] the average number of full satisfying truth assignments of formulas from $K_s(n, r)$ is shown to be $2^n \left(\frac{2^s-1}{2^s}\right)^r$. This number overestimates the average number λ of solution leaves in the SST's of $K_s(n, r)$. Again using the counting technique from [1] we obtain

$$\lambda := \sum_{i=1}^{n} 2^i \frac{\left[2^s\binom{n}{s} - \sum_{j=0}^{s} 2^j\binom{n-i}{j}\binom{i}{s-j}\right]^r - \left[2^s\binom{n}{s} - \sum_{j=0}^{s} 2^j\binom{n-i+1}{j}\binom{i-1}{s-j}\right]^r}{\left[2^s\binom{n}{s}\right]^r} .$$

Then $p = \frac{\lambda}{N}$ is the average solution density of the class $K_s(n, r)$.
These formulas applied to the class $K_3(25,100)$ e.g. yield $N = 25171.26$, $\lambda = 48.17$, and $p = 0.001914$, compared with the values of 23670.02, 47.42, and 0.002003, resp., supplied by the randomly chosen 50 formulas from $K_3(25,100)$ of our experiment, the sample of formulas used throughout the paper.
The following simplifying assumption allows the determination of $E(t_k)$ for each $k \geq 1$.

<u>M_1</u>: Suppose all SST's of $K_s(n, r)$ to have exactly N leaves and each leaf to be a solution leaf independently with probability p, where p and N are as defined above.

Then the random variable $t_k = i$ denoting the event that a formula F is tested for which it takes the parallel k-processor backtracking algorithm exactly i time units to solve F, is distributed geometrically with probability

$$Pr\ (t_k = i) = (q^k)^{i-1} \cdot (1-q^k) \quad , q = 1-p,$$

in case of finding a solution. Let k divide N and $p > 0$. Then

$$E(t_k) = \sum_{i=1}^{\frac{N}{k}} i \cdot Pr\ (t_k = i) + \frac{N}{k}\ (q^k)^{\frac{N}{k}} = \frac{1-q^N}{1-q^k} .$$

<u>Theorem 1:</u>

Under assumption M_1 the speedup of k versus ℓ processors is $\overline{su}_{k,\ell} = \frac{1-(1-p)^k}{1-(1-p)^\ell}$

Because $\overline{su}_{k,\ell}$ depends on the solution density p we write $\overline{su}_{k,\ell}(p)$.
The speedup function $\overline{su}_{k,\ell}(p)$ has the following properties:

- If the number of processors k is growing arbitrarily, then the average speedup of k processors versus one is bounded by $\frac{1}{p}$, i.e., $\lim_{k\to\infty} \overline{su}_{k,1}(p) = \frac{1}{p}$.
- If the average solution density p is arbitrarily close to zero, then the average speedup of k processors versus ℓ is going to $\frac{k}{\ell}$ from values smaller than $\frac{k}{\ell}$, i.e., $\lim_{p\to 0} \overline{su}_{k,\ell}(p) = \frac{k}{\ell}-$.

The superlinear average speedup observed in the experiment with 2, 4 and 8 processors supplies strong evidence that the assumption M_1, which does not allow for superlinear average speedup values unsufficiently characterizes our problem.

4. THE MODEL

We will change the assumption from M_1 that each leaf of the SST's of $K_s(n, r)$ is a solution leaf independently with probability p, and we will see that after splitting the formulas $F \in K_s(n, r)$ into the k subformulas, which are given to the k processors of the parallel algorithm the average solution densities of the k subformulas will differ significantly. To make this more precise we define the notion of average solution density of the k subformulas of formulas of $K_s(n, r)$.

Let

$F \in K_s(n,r)$, $k = 2^{\ell}$, and $S(F,\ell) = \{F_{\xi_n \xi_{n-1} \dots \xi_{n-\ell+1}} \mid \xi_{n-i} \in \{x_{n-i}, \bar{x}_{n-i}\}, 0 \le i < \ell\}$ be the (multi-)set of the k subformulas originating from F by assigning all possible truth values to the variables $x_n, \dots x_{n-\ell+1}$. Let $N(F_{\xi_n \dots \xi_{n-\ell+1}})$, $\lambda(F_{\xi_n \dots \xi_{n-\ell+1}})$ be the number of leaves, solution leaves, resp. of $T(F_{\xi_n \dots \xi_{n-\ell+1}})$. Order the k subformulas from $S(F,\ell)$ according to the values of $\frac{\lambda(F_{\xi_n \dots \xi_{n-\ell+1}})}{N(F_{\xi_n \dots \xi_{n-\ell+1}})}$ (= solution density of $F_{\xi_n \dots \xi_{n-\ell+1}}$) s.t. $N_i(F)$, $\lambda_i(F)$ denote the number of leaves, solution leaves, resp., of the SST of that subformula

$F_{\xi_n \dots \xi_{n-\ell+1}} \in S(F,\ell)$ for which $\frac{\lambda(F_{\xi_n \dots \xi_{n-\ell+1}})}{N(F_{\xi_n \dots \xi_{n-\ell+1}})}$ is i-th largest, $1 \le i \le k$.

Then $p_i = \frac{E(\lambda_i)}{E(N_i)} = \frac{\sum_{F \in K_s(n,r)} \lambda_i(F)}{\sum_{F \in K_s(n,r)} N_i(F)}$, $1 \le i \le k$, denotes the average solution density taken over the subformula from $S(F,\ell)$ with i-th largest solution density for all $F \in K_s(n,r)$.

A computer experiment with our sample of 50 formulas from $K_3(25,100)$ in the case of $k = 2$ supplied the following estimations $E(\lambda_1) = 39.88$, $E(\lambda_2) \approx 7.54$, $E(N_1) \approx 12\,416.24$, $E(N_2) = 11\,253.78$ implying $p_1 \approx 0.00321$ and $p_2 \approx 0.00067$. I.e., splitting formuals $F \in K_3(25,100)$ into $F_{\bar{x}_n}$ and F_{x_n} the average solution density of one of the two subformulas (nothing is said, which of them) is $p_1 \approx 1.6036 \cdot p$ and that of the other $p_2 \approx 0.3345 \cdot p$, where the average solution density p of $K_3(25,100)$ here is taken from the experiment with our sample. We have observed a similar behaviour also with tests with other values of k and with other classes $K_s(n,r)$. We have no "simple" formula to compute p_i, as we have for p, but we develop in the next chapter a formula indicating that the outcome of the above experiment depends on properties of the class $K_3(25,100)$ itself and not on the poor choice of our sample. This formula applied to $K_3(25,100)$ and to $k = 2$ says that the average numbers of full satisfying truth assignments of the two subformuals differ at least by a factor of 2.21.
The discussion above indicates that there are strong dependencies between the probabilities of the leaves of the SST's of the formulas from $K_s(n,r)$ to be solution leaves. The assumption of our second model reflects these dependencies between the leaves in SST's of different subformulas but not between the leaves within the SST of the same subformula.

The following simplifying assumption allows the determination of $E(t_1)$ and $E(t_k)$, for a fixed k.

$\underline{M_2}$: Let N and p_i, $1 \leq i \leq k$, for $K_s(n,r)$ as defined above. Suppose all SST's of $K_s(n,r)$ to have exactly N leaves and each leaf belonging to the SST of the subformula evaluated by processor j, $1 \leq j \leq k$, to be a solution leaf independently with probability $p_{\P(j)}$, for some randomly chosen permutation $\P \in S_k$.

Note that under M_2 the SST's of all subformulas must have $\frac{N}{k}$ leaves.

The introduction of a random permutation ¶, which assigns the average solution desities $p_1,\dots,p_k$ to the k processor reflects the fact that any order of the solution desities of the k subformulas is possible and equally likely. This part of assumption M_2 has no influence on the calculation of $E(t_k)$, but it is important when calculating $E(t_1)$. We will estimate here only $\overline{su}_{k,1} = \frac{E(t_1)}{E(t_k)}$.

The estimation of $E(t_k)$ under M_2 is nearly identical to that under M_1. The random variable $t_k = i$ again is distributed geometrically with

$Pr\ (t_k = i) = (q_1 \cdot \ldots \cdot q_k)^{i-1} \cdot (1 - q_1 \cdot \ldots \cdot q_k)$, $q_j = 1-p_j$, $1 \leq j \leq k$, in case of finding a solution. Let k divide N and assume there is some $p_i > 0$. Then

$$E(t_k) = \sum_{i=1}^{N/k} i \cdot Pr(t_k = i) + \frac{N}{k}(q_1 \cdot \ldots \cdot q_k)^{N/k}$$

$$= \frac{1-(q_1 \cdot \ldots \cdot q_k)^{N/k}}{1-q_1 \cdot \ldots \cdot q_k} .$$

We now estimate $E(t_1)$ under M_2. Note that the sequential backtracking algorithm searches T(F) by first searching $T(F_{\bar{x}_n \ldots \bar{x}_{n-\ell+1}})$. If this search ends unsuccessfully then $T(F_{\bar{x}_n \ldots \bar{x}_{n-\ell+2}\, x_{n-\ell+1}})$ is searched etc. Under M_2 for a fixed permutation $\P \in S_k$ it means that the algorithm starts searching among the first $\frac{N}{k}$ leaves for a solution where each of the leaves is a solution leaf independently with probability $p_{\P(1)}$. In case of an unsuccessful search among the first $\frac{N}{k}$ leaves the algorithm starts searching among another $\frac{N}{k}$ leaves where each of these leaves is a solution leaf independently with probability $p_{\P(2)}$ etc.

Thus under M_2 for a fixed $\P \in S_k$ we define $E(t_1|\P)$ to be the average number of leaves which have to be visited until a first solution is found under the condition that each of the first $\frac{N}{k}$ leaves of the SST is a solution leaf independently with probability $p_{\P(1)}$, each of the second $\frac{N}{k}$ leaves is a solution independently with probability $p_{\P(2)}$, etc.

Let $f(N,P) := \sum_{i=1}^{N} i(1-p)^{i-1} \cdot p$, for $N \in \mathbb{N}$ and $p \in [0,1]$.

Then (again suppose k divides N)

$$E(t_1|\P) = f\left(\frac{N}{k},p_{\P(1)}\right) + (1-p_{\P(1)})^{N/k} \cdot \Big[\frac{N}{k} + f\left(\frac{N}{k}, p_{\P(2)}\right)$$

$$+ (1-p_{\P(2)})^{N/k} \cdot \Big[2\,\frac{N}{k} + f\left(\frac{N}{k}, p_{\P(3)}\right)$$

$$\vdots$$

$$+ (1-p_{\P(k-1)})^{N/k} \cdot \Big[(k-1)\,\frac{N}{k} + f\left(\frac{N}{k}, p_{\P(k)}\right) + (1-p_{\P(k)})^{N/k} \cdot N\Big]\ldots\Big]\Big],$$

and finally $E(t_1) = \frac{1}{k!} \cdot \sum_{\P\in S_k} E(t_1|\P)$.

If all $p_i > 0$ and N/k is sufficiently large, then a good approximation of $E(t_1)$ is supplied by $E(t_1) \approx \frac{1}{k} \cdot \sum_{i=1}^{k} \frac{1}{p_i}$.

Because $\overline{su}_{k,1}$ under M_2 depends on $p_1,\ldots,p_k$, and N, we write $su_{k,1}(p_1,\ldots,p_k,N)$.

Theorem 2:

The speedup function $\overline{su}_{k,1}\ (p_1,\ldots,p_k,N)$ under M_2 has the following properties:

- There are values $p_1,\ldots,p_k \in (0,1)$, $N \in \mathbb{N}$ s.t. $\overline{su}_{k,1}\ (p_1,\ldots,p_k,N) > k$,
- $\overline{su}_{k,1}\ (p_1,\ldots,p_k,N)$ is decreasing in p_i, for $1 \le i \le k$ and $p_i \in [0,1]$.

Our experiments with the sample from $K_3(25,100)$ and $k = 2$ yielded $p_1 \approx 0.00321$, $p_2 \approx 0.00067$, $N \approx 23670.02$. Then $E(t_1) \approx 902.0319$, $E(t_2) \approx 257.8749$ implying a predicted average speedup achieved by 2 processors of 3.4979 for this class compared with the experimental value of 2.46.

5. UNBALANCED DISTRIBUTION OF SOLUTIONS

As mentioned above we will show here, that splitting $F \in K_s(n,r)$ into F_x and $F_{\bar{x}}$ yields two subformulas with significantly differing average numbers of solutions. Denote here by $\lambda(F)$ the number of solution of F among all 2^n full truth assignments of F. W.l.o.g. set $x = x_n$. Define by $\mu_i(n,r,s)$ the average number of solutions taken over the shorter, if $i = 1$ (longer, if $i = 0$) subformula of F_x and $F_{\bar{x}}$, for $F \in K_s(n,r)$.

Theorem 3:

$$\mu_i(n,r,s) = 2^{n-1} \sum_{\ell=0}^{r} \binom{r}{\ell} \left(\frac{s}{n}\right)^{\ell} \left(\frac{n-s}{n}\right)^{r-\ell} \cdot 2^{-\ell} \left(\frac{2^s-1}{2^s}\right)^{r-\ell} \cdot \sum_{j=0}^{\ell} \binom{\ell}{j} \left(\frac{2^{s-1}-1}{2^{s-1}}\right)^{m_i\{j,\ell-j\}},$$

where $m_i = \min$ (max) for $i = 1$ (0).

Proof: The probability that x occurs in ℓ clauses of $F \in K_s(n,r) = cl(n,s)^r$, j times negated, and $\ell-j$ times unnegated, is $\binom{r}{\ell}\cdot\left(\frac{s}{n}\right)^{\ell}\cdot\left(\frac{n-s}{n}\right)^{r-\ell}\cdot\binom{\ell}{j}\,2^{-\ell}$ and F satisfies $F_x \in cl(n-1,s)^{r-\ell} \times cl(n-1,s-1)^j$ and $F_{\bar{x}} \in cl(n-1,s)^{r-\ell} \times cl(n-1,s-1)^{\ell-j}$. For each $F \in cl(n-1,s)^{r-\ell} \times cl(n-1,s-1)^j$ the sets $\{F \in cl(n,s)^r \mid F_x = \hat{F}\}$ have the same cardinality. The expectation of the random variable λ applied to $cl(n-1,s)^{r-\ell} \times cl(n-1,s-1)^j$ is $E(\lambda) = 2^{n-1} \left(\frac{2^s-1}{2^s}\right)^{r-\ell} \times \left(\frac{2^{s-1}-1}{2^{s-1}}\right)^j$. From these facts the theorem follows. □

By Theorem 3 we obtain, e.g., for

$K_3(25,100)$: $\mu_0 = 16.6, \mu_1 = 36.7, \mu_1/\mu_0 = 2.21$, and

$K_3(50,200)$: $\mu_0 = 884.59$, $\mu_1 = 1954.05, \mu_1/\mu_0 = 2.209$.

6. REFERENCES

[1] Brown, C.A./Purdom, P.W.: An average time analysis of backtracking. SIAM J. Comput., Vol 10,No.3, August 1981, 583-593

[2] Finkel, R./Manber, U.: DIB - a Distributed Implementation of Backtracking. Computer Science Technical Report 588, University of Wisconsin, Madison, March 1985

[3] Garey, M.R./Johnson, D.S.: Computers and Intractability: A Guide to the Theory of NP-Completeness. Freeman, San Francisco, Calif., 1979

[4] Mohan, J.: A study on Parallel Computation: the Travelling Salesman Problem. Technical Report CMU-CS-82-136(R), Dept. of Computer Science, Carnegie Mellon University, 1983

[5] Monien, B./Speckenmeyer,E.: Solving satisfiability in less than 2^n steps. Discrete Appl. Math., Vol. 10, 1985, 287-295

[6] Monien, B./Speckenmeyer,E./Vornberger,O.: Superlinear Speedup for Parallel Backtracking. Technical Report No.30, Reihe Theoretische Informatik, Universität-GH Paderborn, 1986

[7] Quinn,M./Deo,N.: Parallel Graph Algorithms. Computing survey, Vol. 16, No. 3, September 1984, 319-348

ON THE PROCESSING TIME OF A PARALLEL LINEAR SYSTEM SOLVER

A.Stafylopatis and A.Drigas
National Technical University of Athens
Department of Electrical Engineering
Computer Science Division
157 73 Zographos, Athens, Greece

Abstract

The speed-up obtained by the use of multiprocessor systems is of major importance for numerical applications involving the solution of large dense systems of linear equations. We are interested here in the performance evaluation of an algorithm for the parallel solution of linear systems. The structure of the algorithm's task graph is representative of a class of recently proposed parallel linear system solvers. We develop a probabilistic model for two different parallel execution schemes depending on the synchronization policy adopted. The analytical solution of the model provides the mean algorithm execution time and therefore the speed-up and efficiency obtained with respect to the single processor environment.

1. Introduction

The growing development of modern multiprocessor technology provides an interesting alternative to the need of high computation speeds for the solution of large numerical applications. In the last decade a considerable number of parallel algorithms have been proposed, which should exploit the advantages of multiprocessor architectures. Some of these algorithms are parallel versions of existing sequential ones, other are completely new algorithms [1], [2], [9]. In all cases, the job is divided into a number of tasks, each executing concurrently with

This work was supported by the General Secretariat of Research and Technology of Greece, Grant No.9707.

other tasks. This decomposition of a job into a set of tasks with well-defined interdependencies is governed by the logical structure of the parallel algorithm, which is usually represented by a computation graph, or task graph. The precedence relations among tasks imply the existence of synchronization points within the computation, which are the main factor limiting the effective parallelism of programs. An important performance measure concerning the execution of parallel algorithms is the processing time of a job described by a computation graph, which is used to derive the speed-up and the efficiency obtained with respect to the single processor case.

Several models have been proposed so far for the performance evaluation of parallel algorithms. Let us quote, for instance, models concerning numerical computations [3], [5], [7], tree-structured algorithms [6], [8], or general program structures [4]. In most cases, probabilistic models seem best adapted for the description of the issues involved in parallel computation.

In this paper, we consider a probabilistic model for the execution of a parallel algorithm for solving linear systems. This algorithm is a parallel implementation of the Gauss-Jordan method with partial pivoting [9], described by a task graph of triangular structure with distinct computation levels and particular precedence constraints. The interest of this graph is that its general structure is the same for several direct or iterative linear system solvers involving various triangularisation techniques [9], so that the model can be used for the comparative evaluation of a class of parallel algorithms. We consider two different synchronization policies resulting to two parallel computation schemes. For the first one we obtain the exact solution assuming an arbitrary number of available processors. For the second policy, considering an infinite number of processors, we develop an approximate solution, whose accuracy is validated by simulation results.

In the next Section we describe the numerical algorithm and its parallel implementation. Section 3 concerns the general framework for our modeling approach, whereas in Sections 4 and 5 we present the model for the two synchronization policies considered.

2. The parallel algorithm

Let us consider the solution of linear algebraic equations of the form

$$Au = b \tag{1}$$

where A is a real nonsingular dense matrix of order n, u is the n-dimensional vector of unknowns and b is a given n-dimensional vector. We consider the parallel implementation of the Gauss-Jordan method with partial pivoting for solving (1). The Gauss-Jordan algorithm is a variation of the classical Gauss-elimination method in that it reduces A into a diagonal matrix instead of an upper triangular, so that the solution vector u is obtained immediately. In order to illustrate the decomposition of the algorithm into a set of tasks, we quote the sequential program for the diagonalisation of the matrix A using the Gauss-Jordan method [9]:

```
Program GAUSSJORDAN(A(n,n))
for k:=1 to n do
    Find ℓ such that                                  ┐
    |A(ℓ,k)|=max(|A(k,k)|,...,|A(n,k)|)               │
    PIV(k):=ℓ {pivot row}                             │
    A(PIV(k),k)<--->A(k,k)                            │
    c:=1/A(k,k)                                       │  T_k^k            (2)
    for i:=1 to n do                                  │
    Skip the value i=k                                │
    A(i,k):=A(i,k)xc                                  ┘

    for j:=k+1 to n do
    A(PIV(k),j)<--->A(k,j)                            ┐
    for i:=1 to n do                                  │
      Skip the value i=k                              │  T_k^j,  j>k
      A(i,j):=A(i,j)-A(i,k)xA(k,j)                    ┘
```

As shown in the program, we consider a task to be the code segment which works on a particular column j for a particular value of k. We denote a task by T_k^j, $1 \leq k \leq j \leq n$. Taking into account the precedence constraints imposed by the sequential program, one can verify that the set

$$\{T_k^{k+1},\ T_k^{k+2},\ldots,T_k^n\} \quad , \quad 1 \leq k < n$$

is composed of mutually noninterfering tasks, which could be executed in parallel. This decomposition results to the maximally parallel computation graph of Fig.1, where vertices represent tasks and directed edges represent precedence relations. The computation graph is characterized by the processing times of the tasks; as a first approach, we can consider a deterministic evaluation for the processing times. The execution of T_k^k requires n-k comparisons, 1 division and n-1 multiplications; assum-

Level
1
T_1^1
2
T_1^2
T_1^3
T_1^4
T_1^n
T_2^2
3
T_2^3
T_2^4
T_2^n
n-1
T_{n-2}^{n-1}
T_{n-2}^n
T_{n-1}^{n-1}
n
T_{n-1}^n
T_n^n

Figure 1

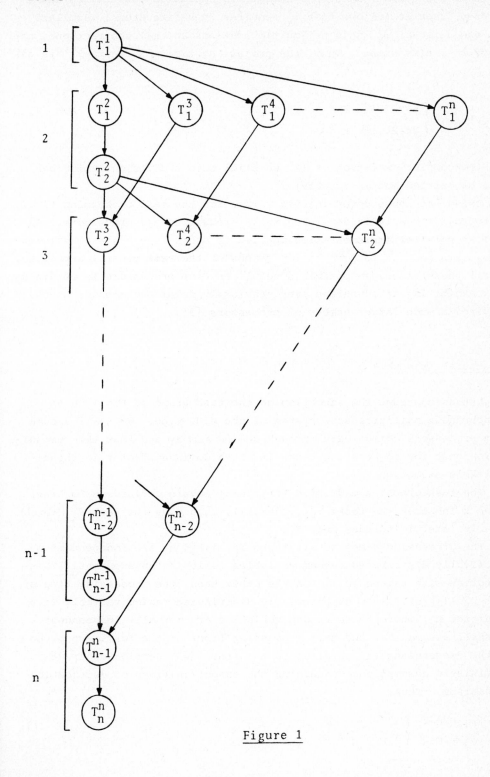

ing that one comparison or one arithmetic operation constitutes one time step, then it follows that T_k^k requires 2n-k time steps. Similarly the execution of T_k^j needs n-1 multiplications and n-1 subtractions, namely, 2n-2 time steps. Thus, the processing times of the tasks are given by:

$$w(T_k^j) = \begin{cases} 2n-k & \text{if} \quad k=j \\ 2n-2 & \text{if} \quad k<j \end{cases}$$

For the complete solution of (1) we still need n divisions which can also be carried out in parallel.

Using the above deterministic values for the task processing times, an optimal schedule is developed in [9] requiring n/2 processors. A similar parallel implementation applied to other linear system solving algorithms results to computation graphs of the same general structure. In all these cases, an optimal schedule on O(n) processors is obtained, thus exhibiting an advantage over previously developed methods which required a much larger number of processors [9].

3. General framework

Let us consider the execution of the task graph of Fig.1 on an asynchronous multiprocessor system of the MIMD type. We shall assume that processors communicate through shared memory and that the communication cost for cooperating tasks is not a dominant factor in the algorithm's execution

The task graph is made of n horizontal levels defined as follows: level k includes the tasks T_{k-1}^j, j=k,k+1,...,n plus the task T_k^k (Fig.1). Clearly level 1 includes only T_1^1.

The processing times of all tasks T_k^j, $1 \leq k \leq j \leq n$, are independent identically distributed random variables following an exponential distribution with parameter λ. On the other hand, the processing time of task T_k^k $(1 \leq k \leq n)$, is an exponentially distributed random variable with parameter μ_k, where these random variables are mutually independent. We shall assume that the mean processing times of the tasks are given by the expressions (3) obtained in the previous Section under deterministic assumptions concerning the execution times of arithmetic operations. Thus:

$$\left.\begin{array}{l} 1/\mu = 2n-k \\ 1/\lambda = 2n-2 \end{array}\right\} \qquad (4)$$

The above probabilistic assumptions express the fact that, although a task requires in general a constant amount of service, its processing time depends upon the current state of the system due to overhead associated with resource sharing.

We are given a set of m processors, with $m<n$. Since the maximal parallelism of the computation graph is n-1 (Fig.1) we will refer to the case $m=n-1$ as the case of infinite available processors. Tasks are executed following the precedence relations represented by the structure of the computation graph. We shall consider two different parallel execution schemes depending on the synchronization policy adopted:

1. Level-by-level policy. The tasks of a given level k are executed in parallel by the available processors. If some processor terminates the processing of a task and there still exists a task of the same level with no processor assigned to it, then the free processor is reassigned to one such task. At the begining of the processing of level k there is always a processor assigned to task T^k_{k-1}; also, since the tasks T^k_{k-1} and T^k_k must be executed sequentially, we assume that the some processor is assigned to both of them. Processors are synchronized at the end of execution of each level, that is, no task of level k+1 may be executed if there are non-executed tasks of level k, even if there exist free processors.
2. Anticipatory policy. At any instant of the algorithm processing no processor remains unassigned as long as there exists a task ready for execution with no processor assigned to it. A task is ready when all precedence constraints regarding it are satisfied. The assumptions introduced for the first policy concerning the tasks T^k_{k-1} and T^k_k hold for this policy too. When a processor terminates the processing of a task and there exist more than one ready tasks, then a task is chosen among those of minimum level (lowest-level-first policy).

The above synchronization policies are introduced in [8], where tree-structured programs are studied, and are referred to as non-anticipatory and anticipatory respectively.

4. Modeling of the level-by-level policy

We are interested in evaluating the mean processing time of the computation graph under the assumptions of the previous section. We suppose that the m parallel processors are executing an infinity of such graphs, in the sense that as soon as the processing of task T^n_n of a graph is terminated, then the processing ot task T^1_1 of another graph is immediately assumed (we will consider here that the time required to perform the n divisions at the end of the graph's execution is negligible). The system's behaviour can be described by a finite state-space Markov process whose states are defined as follows:

- The system is in state $(1',0)$ when the task T_1^1 is being executed.
- The system is in state (k,ℓ) $2\le k\le n$, $0\le \ell\le n-k$, when the task T_{k-1}^k is being executed and there are ℓ non-executed tasks (including the ones being executed) among T_{k-1}^j, $k+1\le j\le n$.
- The system is in state (k',ℓ) $2\le k\le n$, $0\le \ell\le n-k$, when the task T_k^k is being executed and there are ℓ non-executed tasks (including the ones being executed) among T_{k-1}^j, $k+1\le j\le n$.
- The system is in state (k'',ℓ) $2\le k\le n-1$, $1\le \ell\le n-k$, when the execution of task T_k^k is terminated and there are ℓ non-executed tasks (including the ones being executed) among T_{k-1}^j, $k+1\le j\le n$.

Synchronization at the end of execution of level k corresponds to exit from one of the states $(k',0)$ or $(k'',1)$.

The process is a finite state-space irreducible Markov process, so there exists a steady-state distribution that we will denote by π.

Let us define the following parameters for each level k:

$$\left.\begin{array}{l} a_k = \min(m-1, n-k) \\ b_k = \min(m, n-k) \end{array}\right\}$$

which correspond to the number of available processors for the execution of tasks T_{k-1}^j, $k+1\le j\le n$, depending on the fact that one of the tasks T_{k-1}^k and T_k^k is being executed or not respectively.

The steady-state probabilities must satisfy the following system of linear equations:

$$\mu_1\pi_{(1',0)} = \mu_n\pi_{(n',0)}$$

$$\left.\begin{array}{ll} (a_k+1)\lambda\pi_{(k,n-k)} = \mu_{k-1}\pi_{((k-1)',0)} + \lambda\pi_{((k-1)'',1)} & \\ (a_k+1)\lambda\pi_{(k,\ell)} = a_k\lambda\pi_{(k,\ell+1)} & , a_k\le \ell\le n-k-1 \\ (\ell+1)\lambda\pi_{(k,\ell)} = (\ell+1)\lambda\pi_{(k,\ell+1)} & , 0\le \ell\le a_{k-1} \end{array}\right\} \quad 2\le k\le n \qquad (7)$$

$$\left.\begin{array}{ll} (\mu_k+a_k\lambda)\pi_{(k',n-k)} = \lambda\pi_{(k,n-k)} & \\ (\mu_k+a_k\lambda)\pi_{(k',\ell)} = \lambda\pi_{(k,\ell)} + a_k\lambda\pi_{(k',\ell+1)} & , a_k\le \ell\le n-k-1 \\ (\mu_k+\ell\lambda)\pi_{(k',\ell)} = \lambda\pi_{(k,\ell)} + (\ell+1)\lambda\pi_{(k',\ell+1)} & , 0\le \ell\le a_k-1 \end{array}\right\} \quad 2\le k\le n \qquad (8)$$

$$\left.\begin{array}{ll} b_k\lambda\pi_{(k'',n-k)}=\mu_k\pi_{(k',n-k)} & \\ b_k\lambda\pi_{(k'',\ell)}=\mu_k\pi_{(k',\ell)}+b_k\lambda\pi_{(k'',\ell+1)} \quad , & b_k\leq\ell\leq n-k-1 \\ \ell\lambda\pi_{(k'',\ell)}=\mu_k\pi_{(k',\ell)}+(\ell+1)\lambda\pi_{(k'',\ell+1)} \quad , & 1\leq\ell\leq b_k-1 \end{array}\right\} \quad 2\leq k\leq n-1 \tag{9}$$

as well as the normalizing condition that steady-state probabilities for all states must sum to 1.

From the solution of the above linear system we can readily obtain the mean parallel processing time of the graph T_p. In fact, T_p is given by the mean recurrence time of state (1',0), since the process visits this state once for every graph execution. Hence:

$$T_p = [\mu_1\pi_{(1',0)}]^{-1} \tag{10}$$

In order to derive the speed-up due to the parallel processing we need the mean sequential processing time T_s of the algorithm, which can be obtained by summing the mean processing times of all tasks:

$$T_s = \frac{1}{\mu_1} + \sum_{k=2}^{n}\left[(n-k+1)\frac{1}{\lambda} + \frac{1}{\mu_k}\right] \tag{11}$$

So the speed-up and the efficiency of the parallel scheme can be expressed as:

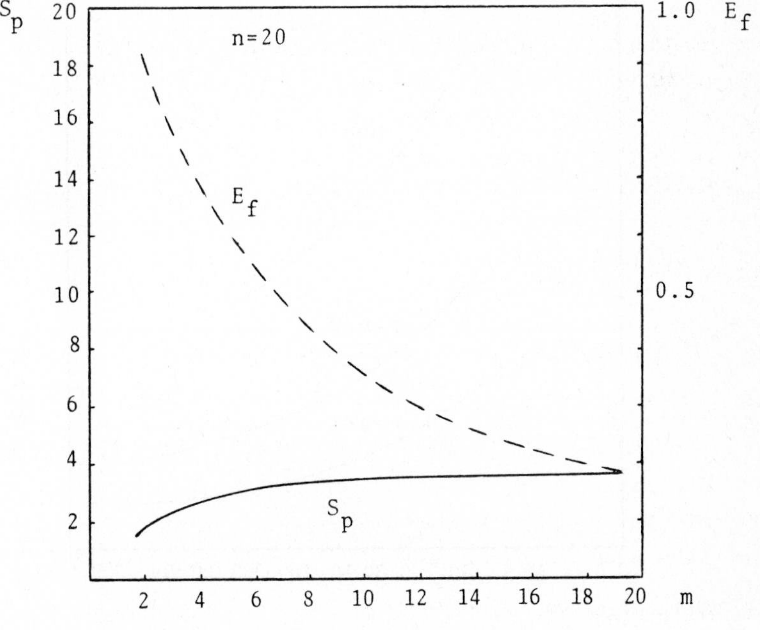

Figure 2

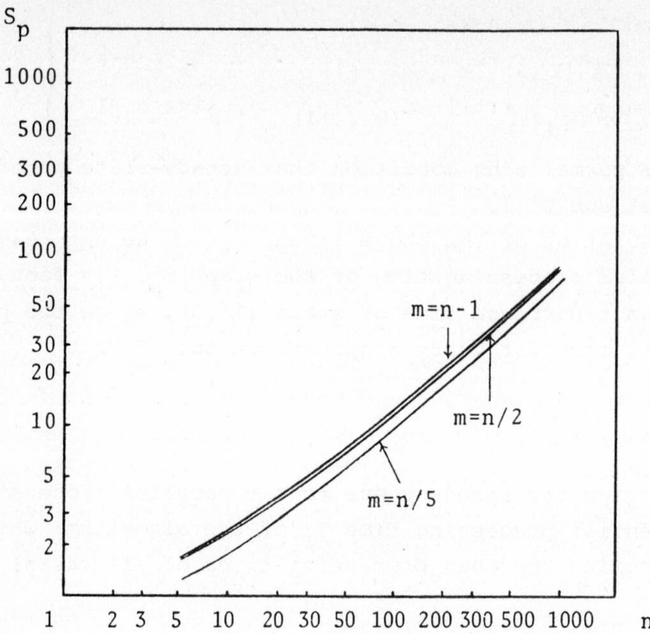

S_p
1000
500
300
200
100
50
30
20
10
5
3
2
1
2 3 5 10 20 30 50 100 200 300 500 1000
n
m=n-1
m=n/2
m=n/5

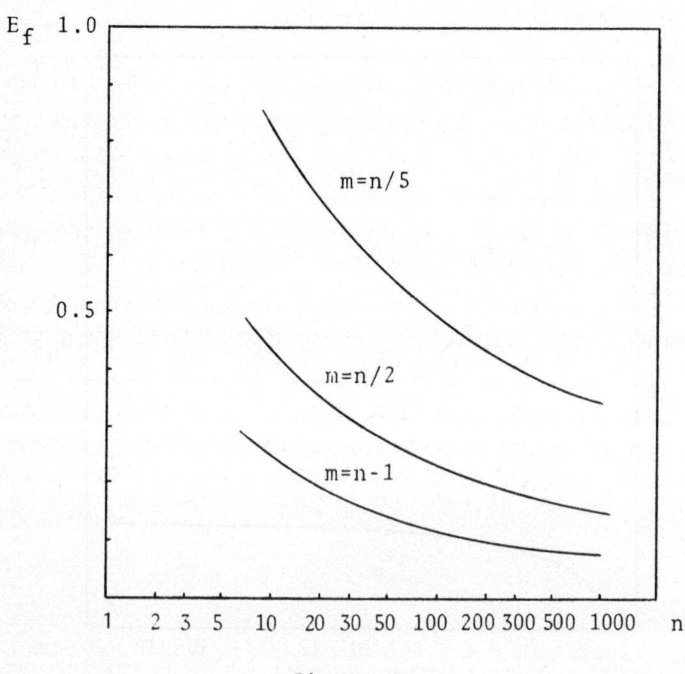

E_f
1.0
0.5
m=n/5
m=n/2
m=n-1
1 2 3 5 10 20 30 50 100 200 300 500 1000
n

Figure 3

$$S_p = T_s/T_p \tag{12}$$

$$E_f = S_p/m \tag{13}$$

We have plotted in Figure 2 and 3 some numerical results illustrating the behaviour of the parallel system. The curves of Fig.2 represent the speed-up and the efficiency obtained for a problem of fixed size as a function of the number of available processors. The same quantities are shown in Fig.3 as a function of the problem size for selected values of the number of available processors. We first notice that the speed gain grows almost linearly as the size of the problem increases but is limited with respect to the number of processors used. This is due, on one hand, to the fact that the maximal parallelism of the algorithm is inherently limited and, on the other hand to synchronization delays which are particularly effective under the level-by-level synchronization policy. Another important remark is that the speed-up is almost stabilized for $m>n/2$, which validates the optimal scheduling developed in [9] using $n/2$ processors.

5. Modeling of the anticipatory policy

As in the previous Section we want to evaluate the mean processing time of the computation graph under the assumptions of Section 3. Unfortunately, in the case of the anticipatory policy, a complete state description is impossible to handle due to the size of the state-space. Even in the limiting cases of two or infinitely many processors the model does not have an analytically tractable solution. So, we are going to develop a heuristic approach for the infinite number of processors case, based upon the principle of process decoupling by using a "markovian approximation" [3]. According to this method we express the interaction between concurrent processes through coupling parameters. These parameters are evaluated by separately solving parts of the whole problem and taking into account only the first order effects of coupling between processes. The results obtained using this approach will be validated by simulation results.

Our heuristic method is based upon the following considerations:

- The parallel execution of the computation graph (Fig.1) using an infinite number of processors can be viewed as the execution of n-1 concurrent processes. The first of these processes, which will be referred to as the "main" process, concerns the execution of the tasks $T_1^1, T_1^2, T_2^2, T_2^3, \ldots, T_{n-1}^n, T_n^n$. In fact, these tasks constitute the longest path of the graph and the time required for the execution of this path determines the processing time of the algorithm. Besides the main process, we consider the n-2 processes concerning the diagonal paths of the graph $\{T_i^j, 1 \leq i \leq j-2\}$ for $3 \leq j \leq n$. These processes will be called "secondary" processes, and will be numbered from 2 to n-1.

- The secondary processes do not directly interact with each other, but each one of them interacts with the main process. In fact, a secondary process k can be blocked at level i ($2 \leq i < k$) due to waiting for completion of the task T_i^i. On the other hand the main process can proceed to level k+1, only if the execution of secondary process k has terminated.
- In order to obtain the mean processing time of the graph, we are going to consider the behaviour of the main process taking into account its interaction with each one of the secondary processes studied separately. A secondary process k can produce delay to the main process at the end of execution of level k. This delay will be expressed by means of a branching probability f_k towards a waiting state with mean residence time $1/\gamma_k$ (Fig.4). The coupling parameters f_k, γ_k can be obtained by solving a markovian model describing the evolution of these two processes independently of the remaining secondary processes. Since this model concerns the behaviour of the main process up to level k, it can be successively solved for $2 \leq k \leq n-1$, each time yielding the corresponding coupling parameters. It should be noticed, that the solution of the model for a particular value k takes into account the effect of the secondary processes i, $2 \leq i \leq k-1$ through the coupling parameters f_i, γ_i that have already been determined.

We proceed now to the description of the model concerning the interaction of the main process with secondary process k ($2 \leq k \leq n-1$). For each value k the model represents the execution of a part of the main process, namely from level 2 to level k. After succesively solving the model for all values of k we can obtain the mean processing time for the part of the graph composed of levels 2 to n-1. The contribution of levels 1 and n to the total mean processing time can be added straightforwardly, since the execution of these levels concerns only the main process.

We consider that the part of the graph corresponding to the secondary process k is executed infinitely many times. Our main simplifying assumption is that the waiting states of the main process at levels i, $2 \leq i \leq k-1$ are markovian. Their behaviour is characterized by the parameters f_i, γ_i, which are known since they have already been computed

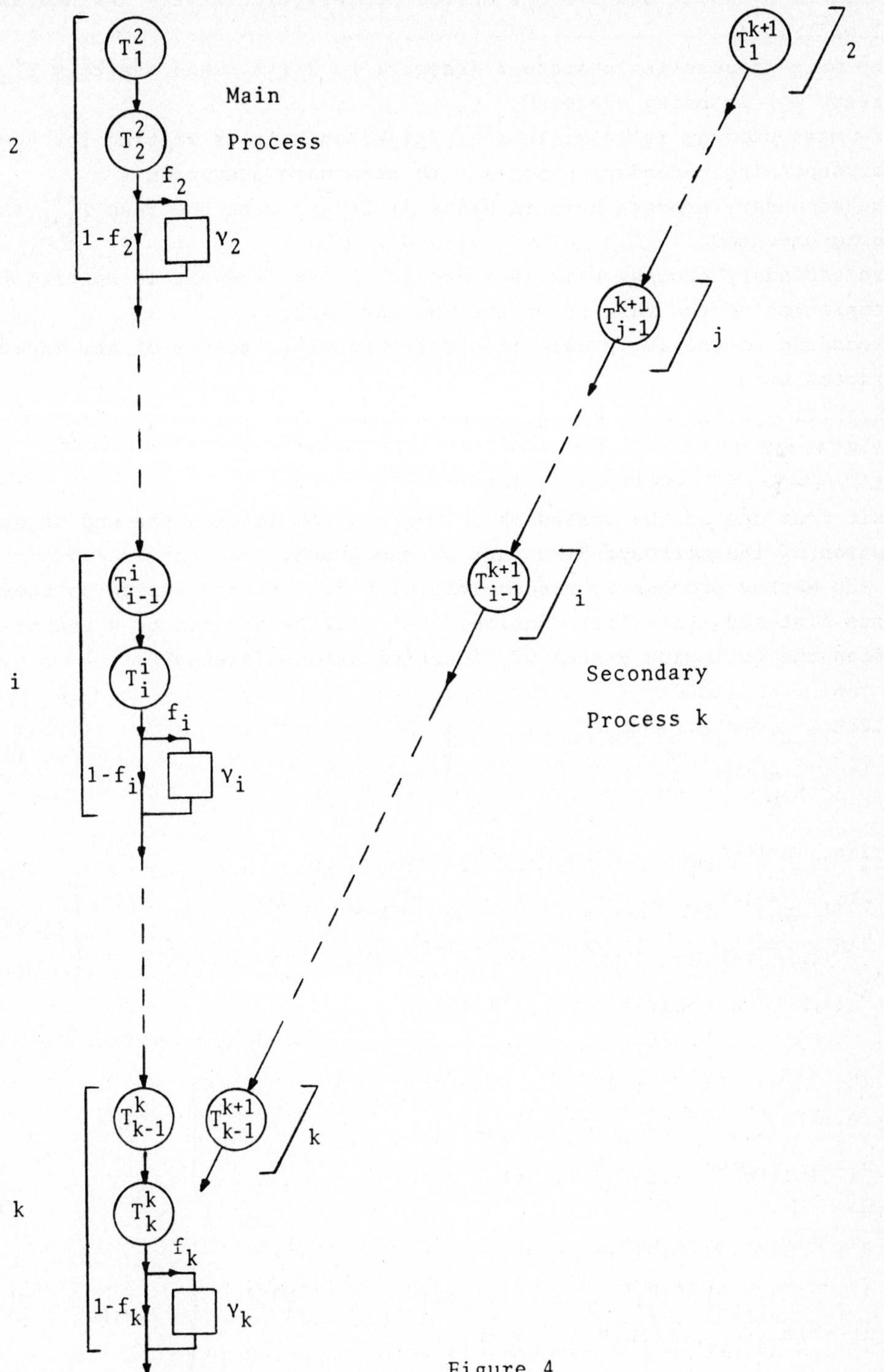

Level
Level
T^2_1
Main
T^2_2
Process
2
f_2
$1-f_2$
γ_2
T^{k+1}_1
2
T^{k+1}_{j-1}
j
T^i_{i-1}
T^{k+1}_{i-1}
i
T^i_i
i
Secondary
Process k
f_i
$1-f_i$
γ_i
T^k_{k-1}
T^{k+1}_{k-1}
k
k
T^k_k
f_k
$1-f_k$
γ_k

Figure 4

while solving the model for the corresponding secondary process i. We are led to a finite state-space Markov process with states defined as follows (Fig.4).

- The main process is in state i (resp. i'), $2\leq i\leq k$, when the task T^{i}_{i-1} (resp. T^{i}_{i}) is being executed.
- The main process is in state i'', $2\leq i\leq k$, when it is waiting for the corresponding secondary process i to terminate execution.
- The secondary process k is in State j, $2\leq j\leq k$, when the task T^{k+1}_{j-1} is being executed.
- The secondary process k is in state j'', $2\leq j\leq k$, when it is waiting for completion of the task T^{j}_{j} of the main process.
- According to the above definitions the possible states of the Markov process are:

  $\left.\begin{array}{l}(i,j),(i',j),(i'',j),\\(i,i''),(i',i'')\end{array}\right\}\quad 2\leq i\leq k$

  $(i'',i+1),(i'',(i+1)''),\quad 2\leq i\leq k-1$
- Exit from one of the states (k',k'') or (k'',k) implies the end of execution of the corresponding part of the graph.

The Markov process is irreducible with finite state-space so there exists a steady-state distribution, that will be denoted by π and satisfies the following system of linear equations ($2\leq k\leq n-1$):

$$\left.\begin{array}{l}2\lambda\pi_{(2,2)}=\lambda\pi_{(k'',k)}+\mu_k\pi_{(k',k'')}\\ \lambda\pi_{(2,2'')}=\lambda\pi_{(2,2)}\end{array}\right\}\qquad(14)$$

$$\left.\begin{array}{l}2\lambda\pi_{(i,2)}=(1-f_{i-1})\mu_{i-1}\pi_{((i-1)',2)}+\gamma_{i-1}\pi_{((i-1)'',2)}\\ 2\lambda\pi_{(i,j)}=(1-f_{i-1})\mu_{i-1}\pi_{((i-1)',j)}+\gamma_{i-1}\pi_{((i-1)'',j)}+\lambda\pi_{(i,j-1)},\ 2<j<i\\ 2\lambda\pi_{(i,i)}=\gamma_{i-1}\pi_{((i-1)'',i)}+\lambda\pi_{(i,i-1)}+(1-f_{i-1})\mu_{i-1}\pi_{((i-1)',(i-1)'')}\\ \lambda\pi_{(i,i'')}=\gamma_{i-1}\pi_{((i-1)'',i'')}+\lambda\pi_{(i,i)}\end{array}\right\}\ 2\leq i\leq k\qquad(15)$$

$$\left.\begin{array}{l}(\mu_i+\lambda)\pi_{(i',2)}=\lambda\pi_{(i,2)}\\ (\mu_i+\lambda)\pi_{(i',j)}=\lambda\pi_{(i,j)}+\lambda\pi_{(i',j-1)}\quad,\ 2<j\leq i\\ \mu_i\pi_{(i',i'')}=\lambda\pi_{(i,i'')}+\lambda\pi_{(i',i)}\end{array}\right\}\ 2\leq i\leq k\qquad(16)$$

$$\left.\begin{array}{l}(\gamma_i+\lambda)\pi_{(i'',2)}=f_i\mu_i\pi_{(i',2)}\\ (\gamma_i+\lambda)\pi_{(i'',j)}=f_i\mu_i\pi_{(i',j)}+\lambda\pi_{(i'',j-1)}\quad,\ 2\leq j\leq i\\ (\gamma_i+\lambda)\pi_{(i'',i+1)}=f_i\mu_i\pi_{(i',i'')}+\lambda\pi_{(i'',i)}\\ \gamma_i\pi_{(i'',(i+1)'')}=\lambda\pi_{(i'',i+1)}\end{array}\right\}\ 2\leq i<k\qquad(17)$$

$$\left.\begin{aligned}&\lambda\pi_{(k'',2)}=\mu_k\pi_{(k',2)}\\&\lambda\pi_{(k'',j)}=\mu_k\pi_{(k',j)}+\lambda\pi_{(k'',j-1)}\quad ,\end{aligned}\right\}\ 2<j\leq k \tag{18}$$

plus the normalizing condition that the steady-state probabilities must sum to 1.

From the solution of the above linear system we obtain the coupling parameters f_k, γ_k as follows:

- The branching probability f_k can be derived as the asymptotic relative fequency with which the main process visits the waiting state k″ during an execution of the corresponding part of the job.
  The mean departure rate from state k″ (and hence the rate of visiting this state) is $\lambda\pi_{(k'',k)}$ since the main process leaves the waiting state only through state (k″,k).
  On the other hand, the mean rate at which execution is completed is equal to the departure rate from state (2,2), which is $2\lambda\pi_{(2,2)}$, since each execution includes exactly one visit to this state. Hence, the desired quantity is:

$$f_k = \frac{\pi_{(k'',k)}}{2\pi_{(2,2)}} \tag{19}$$

- The exit rate γ_k from the waiting state k″ can be derived as the departure rate from state k″ given that the main process has entered this state. The probability of the latter event is $\sum_{j=2}^{k} \pi_{(k'',j)}$.
  Hence we obtain:

$$\gamma_k = \frac{\lambda\pi_{(k'',k)}}{\sum_{j=2}^{k} \pi_{(k'',j)}} \tag{20}$$

Summarizing, our heuristic approach can be described as follows:

- For the values of k from 2 to n-1 we successively solve the linear system (14)-(18) and compute the corresponding parameters f_k, γ_k from (19), (20) respectively.
- At each step the solution of the linear system makes use of the values of the parameters computed at the previous steps.
- At the end of this procedure the mean parallel processing time of the graph can be obtained as the mean processing time of the main process:

$$T_p = (n-1)\frac{1}{\lambda} + \sum_{k=1}^{n} \frac{1}{\mu_k} + \sum_{k=2}^{n-1} \frac{f_k}{\gamma_k} \tag{21}$$

By using the value T_s of the mean sequential processing time from (1) we obtain for the speed-up and the efficiency of the parallel scheme:

$$S_p = T_s/T_p \tag{22}$$

$$E_f = S_p/(n-1) \tag{23}$$

It can be easily verified that the method provides for an easily implemented, efficient computation requiring $O(n^2)$ time and $O(n)$ space.

The accuracy of our markovian approximation was validated by simulation results obtained using the method of independent replications. More precisely, for each value of the problem size n considered, after a minimum of 30 replications, the replication process was carried on until a 5 percent relative precision was obtained considering a 95 percent confidence interval or until a maximum of 1000 replications had been performed. In all cases examined, the values of the mean parallel processing time obtained from the model exceeded the corresponding simulation estimates by less than 5 percent.

Numerical results for the anticipatory policy are represented by the bold line curves of Fig.5, which illustrate the variation of the speed-up and the efficiency as a function of the problem size n. The corresponding curves for the level-by-level policy are plotted in dashed line for comparison and single points represent simulation results. Again the speed-up varies almost linearly with respect to n, whereas, as expected, the anticipatory policy is clearly superior to the level-by-level policy.

6. Conclusion

We have studied in this paper the performance of a particular parallel processing case, which is representative of a class of parallel linear system solvers. A markovian model of the system was introduced considering two different synchronization policies for the parallel execution of the algorithm. The model was solved exactly in the first case for an arbitrary number of processors, whereas a heuristic method was developed providing the solution in the other case for an infinite number of processors. The efficiency of our heuristic method was validated by simulation results. Numerical results obtained from the model illustrate the speed-up and the efficiency of the parallel computation scheme. The speed-up is important but is far from beeing ideal, because of the limited intrinsic parallel of the algorithm and the effects of synchronization.

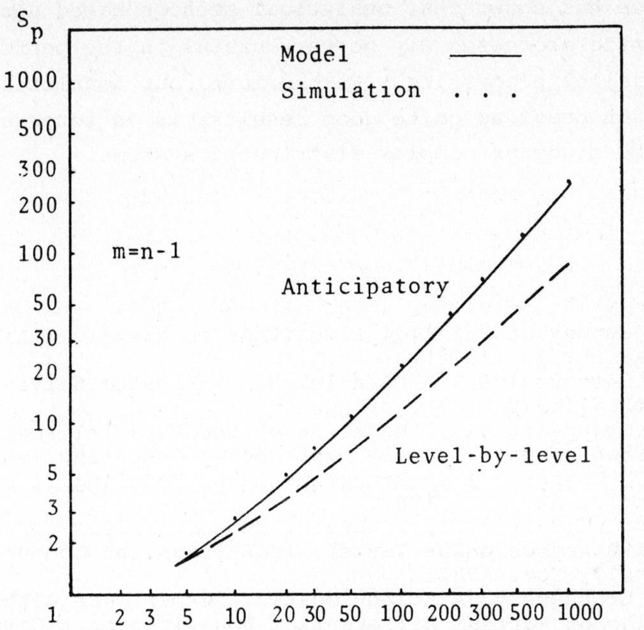
Sp
Model
Simulation . . .
1000
500
300
200
100
50
30
20
10
5
3
2
m=n-1
Anticipatory
Level-by-level
1 2 3 5 10 20 30 50 100 200 300 500 1000
n

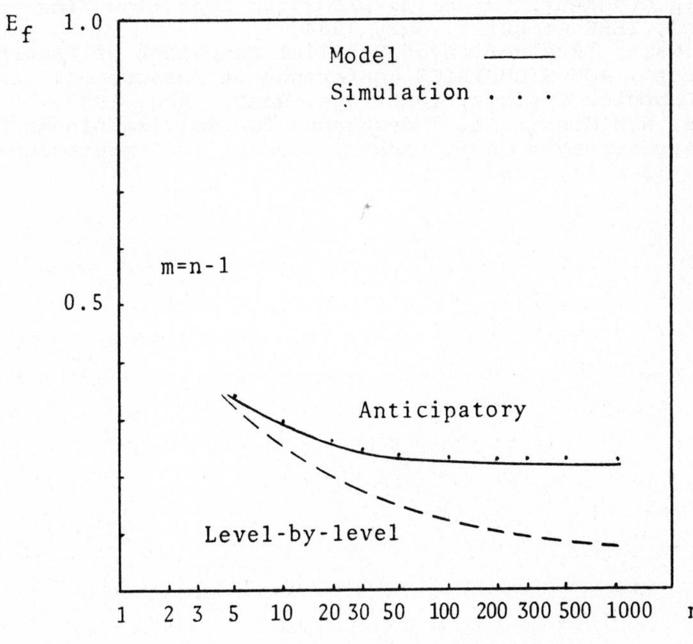
Ef
1.0
Model
Simulation . . .
m=n-1
0.5
Anticipatory
Level-by-level
1 2 3 5 10 20 30 50 100 200 300 500 1000
n

Figure 5

Our experience has shown that analytical methods based upon the theory of stochastic processes may be very useful in the performance evaluation of parallel processing. Furthermore, our heuristic decoupling approach, which provided quite good results, is an interesting alternative in the study of complex distributed systems.

References

[1] D.Heller, "A Survey of Parallel Algorithms in Numerical Linear Algebra", SIAM Rev.20 (1978).

[2] D.J.Evans, M.Hatzopoulos, "A Parallel Linear System Solver", Intern. J. Comput. Math.7 (1979).

[3] B.Plateau, A.Staphylopatis, "Modeling of the Parallel Resolution of a Numerical Problem on a Locally Distributed Computing System", ACM SIGMETRICS Conference on Measurement and Modeling of Computer Systems, Seattle, WA, Aug. 1982.

[4] P.Heidelberger, K.S.Trivedi, "Queueing Network Models for Parallel Processing with Asynchronous Tasks", IEEE Trans. on Computers, Vol. C-31, No.11, Nov. 1982.

[5] E.Gelenbe, A.Lichnewsky, A.Staphylopatis, "Experience with the Parallel Solution of Partial Differential Equations on a Distributed Computing System", IEEE Trans. on Computers, Vol. C-31, No.12, Dec. 1982.

[6] G.Fayolle, P.J.B.King, I.Mitrani, "On the Execution of Programs by Many Processors", PERFORMANCE '83, A.K.Agrawala and S.K.Tripathi (editors), North-Holland, 1983.

[7] L.M.Adams, T.W.Crockett, "Modeling Algorithm Execution Time on Processor Arrays", IEEE Computer, July 1984.

[8] Ph.Mussi, Ph.Nain, "Evaluation of Parallel Execution of Program Tree Structures", ACM SIGMETRICS Conference on Measurement and Modeling of Computer Systems, Cambridge, Mass., Aug. 1984

[9] M.Hatzopoulos, N.M.Missirlis, "Advantages for Solving Linear Systems in an Asynchronous Environment", Journal of Computational and Applied Math. 12 & 13, 1985.

A RISC-TYPE STRUCTURAL DESIGN OF THE HERMES MULTIPROCESSOR KERNEL

Dimitris Fotakis and Nikolaos Bourbakis
Dept. of Electrical and Computer Engineering
George Mason University, Fairfax, VA 22030
and
Computer Technology Institute, Patras, Greece

ABSTRACT

HERMES is a heterogeneous, real-time, reconfigurable, mulitprocessor vision machine, consisted of $[N^2/4]$ microprocessor-nodes in a 2-D array structure. It receives the image data directly from the environment, using a 2-D photoarray of NxN cells, and processes them in a parallel-hierarchical (bottom-up and top-down) manner without using a host computer for its function.

This paper deals with the RISC-type structural organization of the HERMES multi-processor kernel and with some ideas for its VLSI geometric configuration. The kernel of the HERMES vision system consists of four Z-adjacent microprocessor-nodes which occupy a square type area.

1. INTRODUCTION

In the recent years, a great number of computer vision system architectures claims the top of the computer vision area [1-8,10-15,17,18]. These mulitprocessor vision architectures such as, pyramids, arrays, trees, cubes can be separated into two categories [2,3]. The first category, homogeneous, includes vision systems with 2-D array configurations. These arrays consist of a big number of identical processing elements (PE) which operate on a one-bit basis, and they are called Bit-Serial Array Processors [5]. Although their computational power is huge, operating in an SIMD manner, these systems can not by themselves deal with high level image analysis and recognition tasks [6,7]. There is a need for a powerful host computer not only to do the miscellaneous operations (like the I/O routines), but also to combine the data generated by the array-processor [6]. The second category, heterogeneous, includes visions machines in various multiprocessor configurations. These machines consist of a number of microprocessor-nodes with non-identical internal structure. Their main characteristic is the big number of bus-lines throughout the system, thus one could call them bus-oriented [3,6]. Note that, there are bus-oriented homogeneous multi-microprocessor vision machines [10,11]. The heterogeneous vision system architectures operate in SIMD and MIMD manners. Some of them, such GOP,PIPE,PICAP,FLIP, use a host computer for their function [1,2,5,6,7], while some other, such as HERMES,DIAS, they do not [2,18].

The HERMES vision system, which belongs to the heterogeneous category, has been designed at GMU [2,12]. It has a 2-D array topology of $[N^2/4]$ microprocessors. These microprocessor-nodes varying from simple ones to high-level sophisticated processors [21,23]. This has the impact that both primitive operations and high level vision tasks can be performed by HERMES [6,12]. Another factor that reinforces the HERMES performance over the previously discussed systems is the neighboring connectivity of 3k+1 microprocessor neighbors, where k is the highest level at which the processor is able to operate [3,5,6]. In addition, it is important to note that none of the systems mentioned previously has the parallel input capability of the image pixels directly from the environment. In contrast, HERMES is able to have direct access to the visual environment via a 2-D photoarray [2,3,12,19]. Moreover, the pseudo-quad-tree structure of the HERMES machine adds a number of features that the pyramids and the tree structures have [1,3].

The first prototype design and construction of the HERMES multiprocessor kernel was based on commercial microprocessor chips [16,17]. However, that design did not explore the capabilities of the HERMES machine. For this purpose a new RISC-type structural configuration of the HERMES kernel is presented in this paper. The new RISC-type design reinforces the kernel's performance in speed and reduces the size of the occupied chip area. The VLSI geometric topology of the HERMES kernel is also discussed based on VLSI ideas discribed in [9,14,15,19,20].

This paper is organized into five sections. Section II provides a brief description of the HERMES vision machine. Section III presents the structural design, the operation, the hardware complexity and the performance of the HERMES multiprocessor kernel. In the fourth section, the kernel VLSI geometric topology is discussed. Section V summarizes the overall presentation and proposes extensions for future research.

2. HERMES VISION MACHINE

A brief introduction of the HERMES vision architecture will accomodate the reader to understand the purpose of the following analysis of the multiprocessor kernel.

The overall structure of the HERMES vision machine is illustrated in figure 1. The horizontal busing and switching organization of the HERMES architecture, for 64 microprocessor-nodes, N=16, is shown in figure 2.

This vision machine receives image data in parallel from the environment, by using a two-dimensional photoarray of NxN cells, and processes them in a parallel-hierarchical (bottom-up and top-down) manner, by opening and/or closing of its $5x4^i$,$i=\log_2 N-2$ switches [2,3]. The microprocessor-nodes undertake the opening and closing of these switches [2,3], which allow the information flow through the HERMES buses. Table 1 presents the algorithmic opening and closing of those switches for the bottom-up and top-down operations of the HERMES structure. In particular, during a bottom-up procedure "abstracted-coded" picture information goes up along the HERMES hierarchy, while during a top-down procedure "orders" go down from the father-nodes to their own son-nodes [2]. Specifically, all the microprocessor-nodes process the available picture information in parallel, at the L0 level of the HERMES hierarchy. At each of the rest levels of processing along the HERMES hierarchy, a designated node ("the upper left" in each quartet of Z-adjacent nodes) accumulates, correlates, syntesizes and attempts to recognize the available picture information, feeding the results upwards, as shown in figure 1 and 2. The full master designated node of the HERMES architecture receives various commands from its users. It then makes decisions based on its decision making algorithms and built up experience, and if necessary, it sends "orders" down to its successors, thus determining the processing tasks that they have to be executed.

3. HERMES MULTIPROCESSOR KERNEL

Definition : The HERMES multiprocessor kernel consists of 4 z-adjacent microprocessor-nodes which occupy a square-type area. A designated microprocessor (the "upper left" of this quartet of processors) is considered to be the master-node, while the rest three nodes are the slave-ones associated to their master. The master-node is the most powerful node in this quartet, which communicates with its slave-nodes through a common bus configuration (Figure 3).

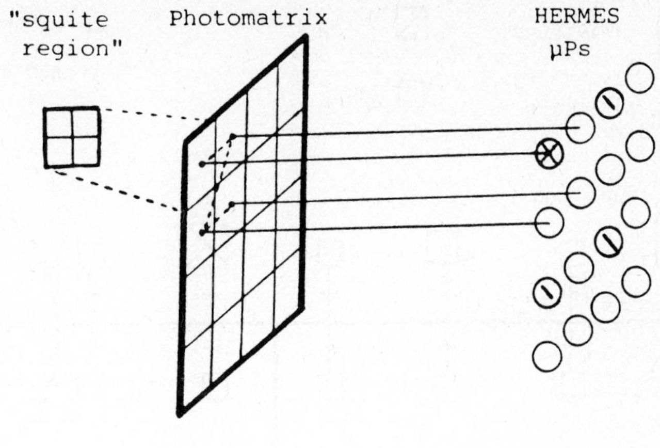

(a)

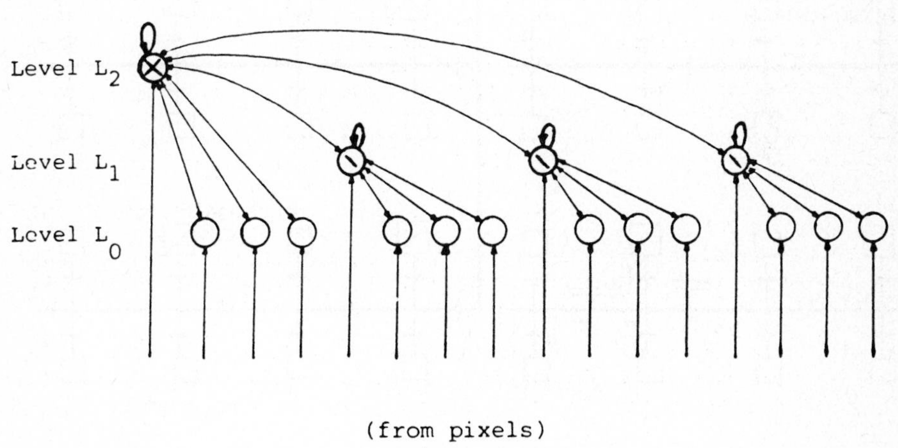

(b)

Figure 1: a) HERMES 2-D array structure of 16 nodes

b) Hierarchical operation of the HERMES nodes.

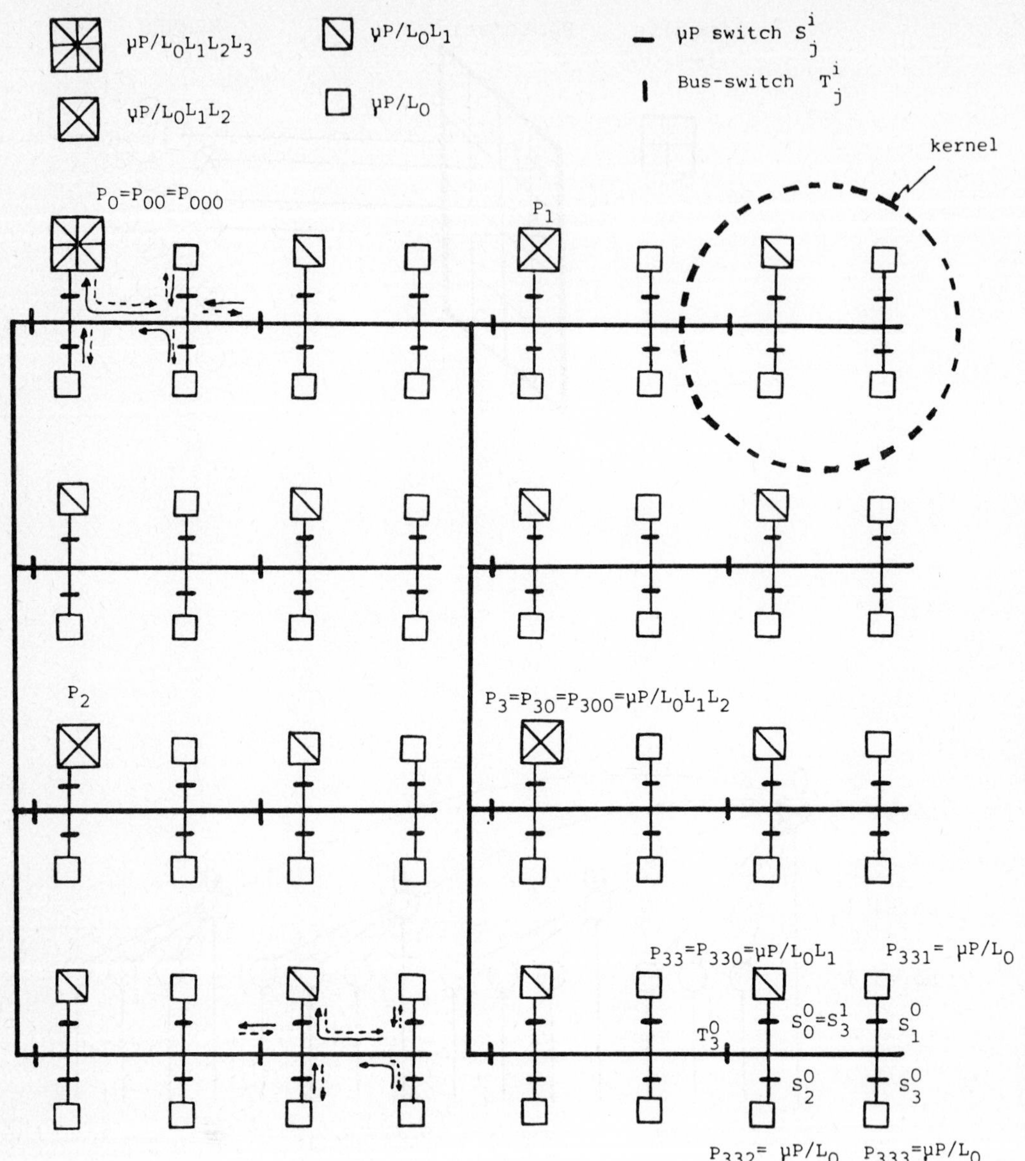

Figure 2: Busing and switching horizontal organization of the HERMES architecture of 64 microprocessor-nodes. The dashed lines indicate "orders" that go down and the solid arrows indicate "abstracted-coded" picture information which goes up along the HERMES hierarchy.

TABLE 1

FORMULATION OF SWITCH STATES FOR THE $\lceil N/2\rceil \times \lceil N/2\rceil$ MICROPROCESSORS OF THE HERMES STRUCTURE

---

a) Bottom-up mode of operation at the k level

$$S_j^i = 0, \quad i = k-1, k-2, \ldots, 0$$

$$S_j^i = 1, \quad i = k, k+1, \ldots, \log_2 N$$

$$T_j^i = 1, \quad i = k, k+1, \ldots, \log_2 N-1$$

$$T_j^i = 0, \quad i = k-1, k-2, \ldots, 0$$

and $j = 0,1,2$

b) Top-down mode of operation at the k level

$$S_j^i = 1, \quad i = k+1, k+2, \ldots, \log_2 N$$

$$S_j^i = 0, \quad i = k, k-1, \ldots, 0$$

$$T_j^i = 0, \quad i = k, k+1, \ldots, \log_2 N-1$$

$$T_j^i = 1, \quad i = k-1, k-2, \ldots, 0$$

and $j = 0,1,2$

---

where $S_j^i = 0$, or $T_j^i = 0$ means that the corresponding switch is closed,

while $S_j^i = 1$, or $T_j^i = 1$ means that the corresponding switch is open.

3.1 STRUCTURAL DESIGN OF THE KERNEL

In this section, the structural design of the HERMES kernel will be described. Firstly, the topology of the four processors in the square area of the kernel will be presented along with the appropriate communication buses. Secondly, the internal architectural and organizational design of the slave processor-node is presented in detail.

3.1.1 Kernel Intercommunication Scheme

A common bus configuration was chosen to realize the communication requirements of both the processors in the kernel and the kernel with the rest of the HERMES machine [2]. In this subsection, the design as well as the operation of this scheme will be presented.

The basic idea of this scheme (figure 3) is the 8-line data bus which is coming out of each processor. In addition, these buses are connected together and also to the main bus of the HERMES system as described in [2].
The selective transmission/reception of the master of a kernel is occured using the individual switches of the processors. The direction of the flow of the information on the data bus is selected by the enable signals of the tri-state individuals switches which could be resided on the input/output registers of the nodes. The manner in which the "opening" and the "closing" of switches work, is described in the architectural design of HERMES [2].

The data-bus is 8-lines wide because not only it represents one byte of information but also improves the communication procedure between the processors in the best case of the HERMES operation (i.e., when a region of a picture is of one gray level only). The data that are going to be tansmitted or received in each processor (four processors per kernel) are latched on an 8-bit register (IN-OUT). The communication packages are packets of 8 bits. Once a communication session is initialized between two processors (master-slave), has to be terminated before another session occurs.

Note that, the 8-line bus carries pure data without including control bits. Thus, the opening and the closing of a communication session is supervised by two control lines namely : "one-way interrupt" line from the slave processor to the master and an "one-way acknowledgement-interrupt" line in the opposite direction. When the master wants to transmit to the slaves, there is the capability to transmit in parallel to all of the processors by opening the individual switches and at the same time interrupting them through the int.-achnowledgement line. This interrupt has the highest priority in the internal structure of the processors. As what the design of the overall HERMES architecture concerns, the master sends the same information to each processor, at the same time. However, there is the possibility for the master not to send information to a number of processors so they remain idle (wait-state). When a slave-processor wants to transmit information to the master, it enables its interrupt line and lets it be enabled until the last packet of information is sent to the master. Moreover, the processor does not send the first packet until the master enables the int.-acknowledgement line. After the first packet is sent, the rest of the packets are transmitted in a synchronous manner.

On the other hand, the master has a service policy for the interrupts : the first interrupt reached the master is going to be serviced, and there is a fixed priority on the processors (i.e., z-manner), in the case of the simultaneous occurence of two or three interrupts. It is important to note, that any interrupt form a procesor, higher in the hierarchy of the HERMES than the master, is of a higher priority than the three processors. The individual switch of the master is controlled by itself and by its master in a wider operational kernel (processor of higher priority).
It goes without saying that the kernel structure described is compatible with the global structure of the HERMES machine [16].

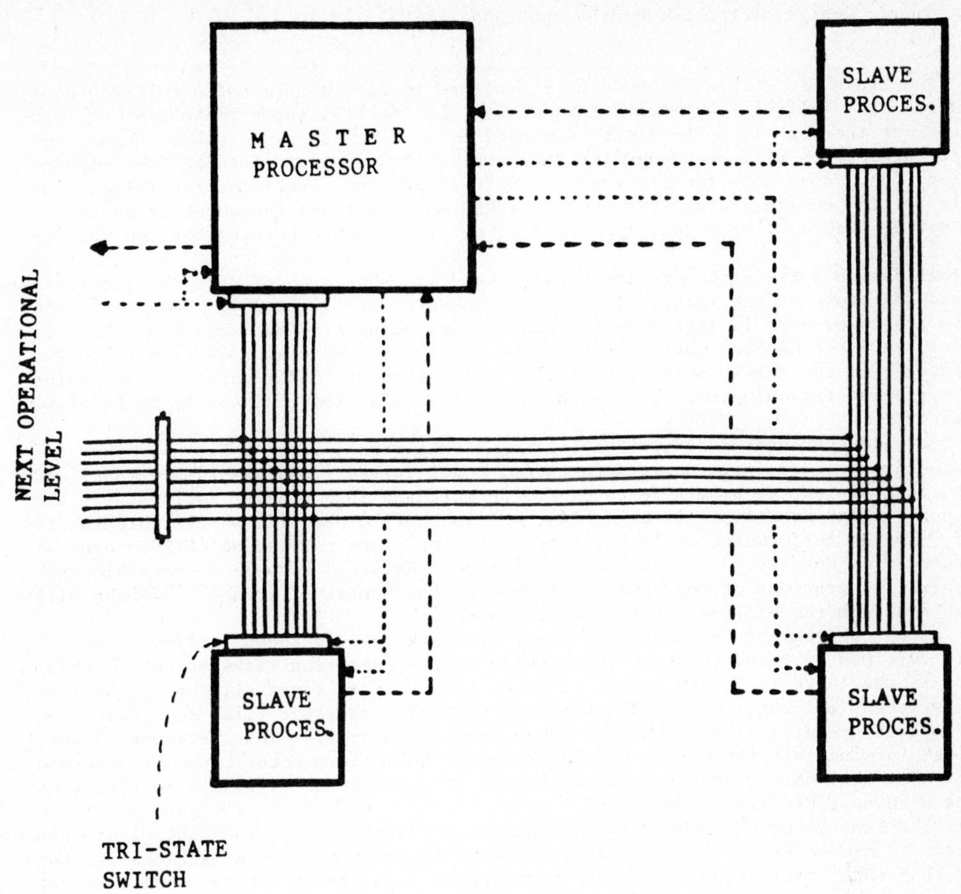

------- : Interrupt Line

.... : Interrupt-Acknowledgement Line

_______ : Data Line

FIGURE 3 : A common bus configuration is used to implement the intercommunication scheme of the HERMES kernel.

3.1.2 Design of the Slave Processor-Node (SPN)

The slave microprocessor-node is considered to be a simple and a fast piece of hardware to fulfill the requirements of low cost and the quick responses to the master of the kernel. The first requirement is essential since a big number of these processors will be needed for the complete fabrication of the HERMES machine vision [3], even more for its future VLSI realization. The later requirement is basic for the entire design idea of the HERMES machine since the quick responses to the master orders allow a real-time processing of the picture taken through photoarray [19].
In this design a RISC-type architectural scheme was shosen to provide the simplicity and the speed of the kernel slave microprocesor-node [21,22,23]. However, the slave processor-node is less powerful than the existing RISC machines [23] since it is only an 8-bit machine mostly appropriate for the HERMES vision machine [2]. Two prototypes of the design presented in this subsection are under construction using two different technologies, TTL and bipolar at George Mason University in Fairfax, Virginia.

The Slave Processor-Node (SPN) of the HERMES kernel is an 8-bit machine (as mentioned earlier) with 8-bit data paths. All instructions are 16-bit long and each instruction is primitive enough to be executed in a single cycle. If the current bipolar technology is used [24], a clock of 10 MHz will be evitable to be used, so a performance of 10 millions of instructions per second (MIPS) can be guaranteed. However, a slower clock will be considered because of possible synchronization problems of the communication with the master of kernel, (which will be chosen from the off-the-shelf microprocessors).
The block diagram of the slave processor of the kernel is shown in figure 4. A 4Kx16 bit ROM is used to store the program of the operation tasks on the pixels. That is why there is no RAM memory to store any programs since all the algorithms are written in ROM. Instead there is a 64x8 bits register file to store the intermidiate results along with any orders from the master. This is enough space, having in mind that the slaves are not supposed to perform complicated tasks and that they deal only with a very special area of the picture (4 pixels for the time being with possible extension to 16).
While the control unit of the RISC machines is hardwired [24], the control of this design is microcoded. The only difference with microprogammable machines is the fact that each instruction of the SPN corresponds to a 32-bit control word, and not to a microsubroutine. All the control words are stored in 16x32 bit control store PROM (Look-up Table). The four least significant bits of each machine instruction is the opcode and at the same time a 4 direct address to the 16x32-bit Look up table.
No decoding is needed. The short access control store produces practically immediately (within even 30ns) a 32-bit, horizontal word, capable of activating up to 32 control lines simultaneously. In this way a streamlined microcoded-based instruction execution is achieved. The control lines are connected directly to all parts of the SPN ,so the appropriate combination of 0's and 1's will guarrantee the execution of a certain instruction. Among the control lines, there is the interrupt line to the master which is used to set up communication with the master of the kernel. Besides the streamlined execution, the design benefits from the usual microcode advantages of greater flexibility for modification and error recovery, while maintaining a high speed of instruction handling (no decoding, control lines activated within 30ns).
The Look up Table is very similar to the Nanomemory in the MC68000 used also in [21,22]. A two-stage instruction pipeline would be recognized. In fact, while a instruction i-1 is being executed by the ALU, instruction i is being fetched and decoded. The only data format recognized in the slave processor is the 8-bit byte. The instruction set (Table-2) includes 16 standard instructions according to the 4-bit opcode field of the instruction. However, there is an extra field in the SHF instruction for the different types of shift operations. That increases the instruction set to 21 without increasing the size of the Look up Table. The shifting operations were taken in consideration because they are necessary for any possible

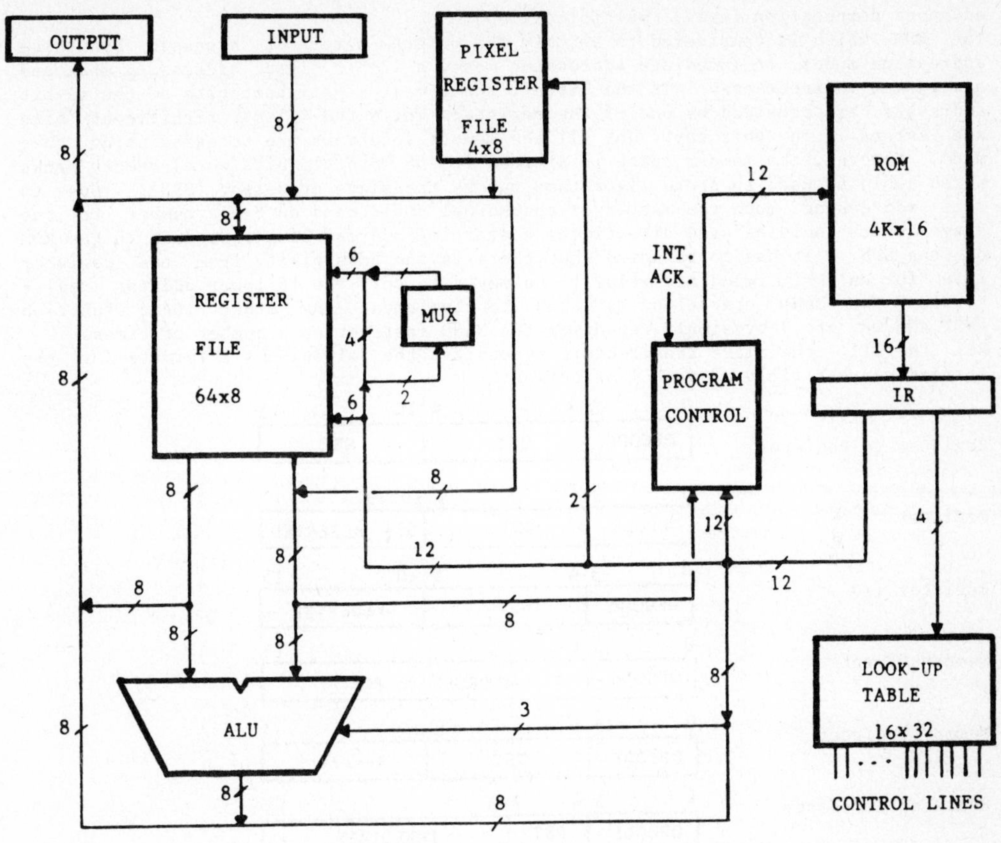

FIGURE 4 : Slave Microprocessor Node (SPN).

advanced computation (i.e., multiplication).
The ROM which is considered to be only the program memory is accessed by three addressing modes. An immediate addressing mode, a 12-bit direct addressing mode and a register indirect one. In the latter, the 8 most significant bits of the 12-bit addresses are provided by one of the registers while the 4 least significant bits are zeroes. In this way, not all the memory locations are accessed using this mode. However, the memory space is divided in 256 word (16 bits/word) memory banks which could be used to store algorithms run by the slave processor (SPN). Due to this addressing mode the master of the kernel could send an 8-bit number to the slave which could be used directly as a starting address of a procedure in the ROM of the SPN. It has to be noted that there is the possibility from the register file for an 8-bit immediate value to be moved to only the 16 lower address registers. The NAND operation is used to implement any other logic function (NOT,AND,OR, etc.) by simply repeating the NAND instruction a number of times.
All in all, the slave architecture recognizes the following six formats for the operand address field of each instruction:

Register to Register

0–3	4–9	10–15
OPCODE	DST	SRC

Register

0–3	4–9	10–13	13–15
OPCODE	DST	SS	RESERVED

Register I/O

0–3	4–9	10–15
OPCODE	DST	RESERVED

Memory Direct

0–3	4–15
OPCODE	ADDRESS in ROM

Memory Indirect

0–3	4–9	10–15
OPCODE	DST	Reserved

Register Immediate

0–3	4–7	8–15
OPCODE	DST	IMMEDIATE

The register fields are 6 bits wide. That means that 64 registers can be accessed each time. The register file is implemented as a dual memory in which the DST and the SRC can be accessed simultaneously and the result can be stored back into the DST register. Using the current technology [24] the above execution procedure can be done within one CPU cycle(100ns). The slave processor-node is composed of the following main units (Fig. 4):

a) <u>Program Control Unit (PCU)</u>

Provides the address of the next instruction to be executed. It contains a 12-bit program counter (PC) register. The address is in a 12-bit direct format. Only, in the case of the register indirect mode, the 4 MSBs of the address are multiplexed with zeroes.

b) <u>Instruction Register (IR)</u>

Stores the 16-bit instruction, fetched from the ROM memory (Program Memory). It is loaded with an instruction every clock cycle.

TABLE-2

INSTRUCTION SET

Assembly	Notation	Operation	Description
1. ADD	Rd, Rs	Rd ←- Rd+Rs	Integer Add
2. SUB	Rd, Rs	Rd ←- Rd-Rs	Integer Subtraction
3. NAND	Rd, Rs	Rd ←- Rd•Rs	Logical NAND
4. ADDP	Rd, Ps	Rd ←- Rd+Ps	Integer Add with Pixel value
5. SUBP	Rd, Ps	Rd ←- Rd-Ps	Integer Subtract with Pixel value
6. NADP	Rd, Ps	Rd ←- Rd • Ps	Logical NAND with Pixel value
7. MOV	Rd, Rs	Rd ←- Rs	Move from register
8. MOVP	Rd, Ps	Rd ←- Ps	Move from a pixel register
9. MOVI	Ri, #A	Ri ←- A	Move immediate
10. IN	Rd	Rd ←- (INPUT)	Move from the input register
11. OUT	Rs	(OUTPUT) ←- Rs	Move to the output register
12. JMZ	M	Address ←- M	Jump on zero result
13. JMN	M	Address ←- M	Jump on negative result
14. JMP	(Rm)	Address ←- (Rm)	Jump indirect unconditionally using the contents of Rm with 4 zeroes in the LSB position
15. NOP			No operation
16. SHF	Rd, #S	Rd ←-Rd shifted	Shift operations according to S where,

S	shift operation
000	shift left
001	shift left through carry
010	shift right
011	shift right through carry
100	Rotate left
101	Rotate right
110	Reserved
111	Reserved

Comments

Rd, Rs, Rm - Registers from the Register File
Ps - Register from the Pixel Register File
Ri - Register from the 16 lower-address registers of the Register File
A - Immediate 8-bit constant
S - 3-bit constant

c) ROM

Stores the programs (functional and pixel algorithm) to be run by SPN. The starting address of some procedures in ROM could be sent directly by the master as orders to be executed. The memory space is enough for the node to perform different processing tasks. A PROM memory could be used instead, to have the possibility of updating the pixel processing algorithms.

d) Look-up Table

A 16x32 ROM Control Store. Each 32-bit Control Word constitutes a horizontal microcode entry equivalent to a specific instruction from the instruction set [Table-2]. The 4-bit address to access it, resides in the 4 LSB of the instruction register.

e) Register File

The size of the dual port register file is 64x8 bits. The address for each port is stored in the instruction register. The 2 MSBs of the DST-address register are multiplexed with zeroes, the MUX unit (Figure 4). That is necessary for the Immediate addressing mode.

f) ALU

Performs all the necessary arithmetic and logic operation on 8-bit operands. Moreover,it has also the appropriate logic to do different shifting operations, as well as the logic NAND hardware. The shifting selection code comes directly from the instruction register, enabled by a control line coming from the Look-up Table. A set of flags are also resident in the ALU.

g) DST-Address MUX

It Multiplexes the two LSB of the DST-field in the instruction register with zeroes in the case of register indirect node. It is enabled by a control line directly from the Look-up Table.

h) Pixel Register File

Each microprocessor-node processes 4 pixels (8-bit) which are stored in the Pixel Register file. Some Arithmetic and Logic Operations can take an operand directly from this file, so pixel operations are speeded-up . For the time being, its size is four but the current design permits an expansion up to 64.

i) Input Register

It is an 8-bit Register which stores data coming from the master. It can be loaded only by the master of the kernel. It is enabled by a control line from the look-up Table, when the IN instruction is executed.

j) Output Register

It is an 8-bit Register which stores data forwarding to the master. It can be loaded only by the microprocessor-node with the OUT instructions. It can be enabled by the master of the kernel when a transfer to the master is desired.

To summarize, the expected throughput and the significance of the slave configuration is due to the following:

1. Streamlined handling of simple instructions.
2. Avoidance of instruction decoding.
3. Possible direct processing of Pixels.
4. Existence of a Register File instead of RAM.
5. Simple architectural scheme.
6. Fast, horizontally microcoded Look-up Table.
7. Fast memory (ROM) access.
8. Powerful 8-bit ALU, including the appropriate logic to perform any advanced computation (Multiplication) as well as any logic function.
9. Easy implementation of the design.

Concludingly, the inclusion of all basic arithmetic and the universal logic operation (NAND) in the instruction set, as well as the availability of three addressing modes, give the programmer the flexibility to design powerful and fast pixel processing algorithms.

3.2. OPERATION OF THE MULTIPROCESSOR KERNEL

The vertical operation of the HERMES multiprocessor kernel is shown in figure 5. In particular, the four microprocessor-nodes of the kernel receive, in parallel, the pixel average intensities from their "squite" regions through the corresponding A/D converters. In addition, the master-node has the hardware flexibility, by using AGC (Automatic Gain Control) and AMUX (Analog Multiplexer) devices, to receive the average intensities of four Z-adjacent subregions, immediately. This feature, when it is required, provides a quick decision making parameter related to the information included in a picture region [25]. Note that, the selection of those average intensities, from the corresponding μP-node, is realized by issuing the appropriate control signals (A,B).

Each kernel node attempts to recognize the existing patterns into its own picture region (squite), at the L0 level of the functional hierarchy, and transfers it in a coded form (see figure 6) to its own master-node through the common system bus. The master-node accumulates, correlates, synthesizes, normalizes the information received from its own slave-nodes (including itself) and attempts to recognize it, preparing an abstracted-coded package to the next higher level of the HERMES operational hierarchy in accordance with the opening and closing of the bus-switches (T).

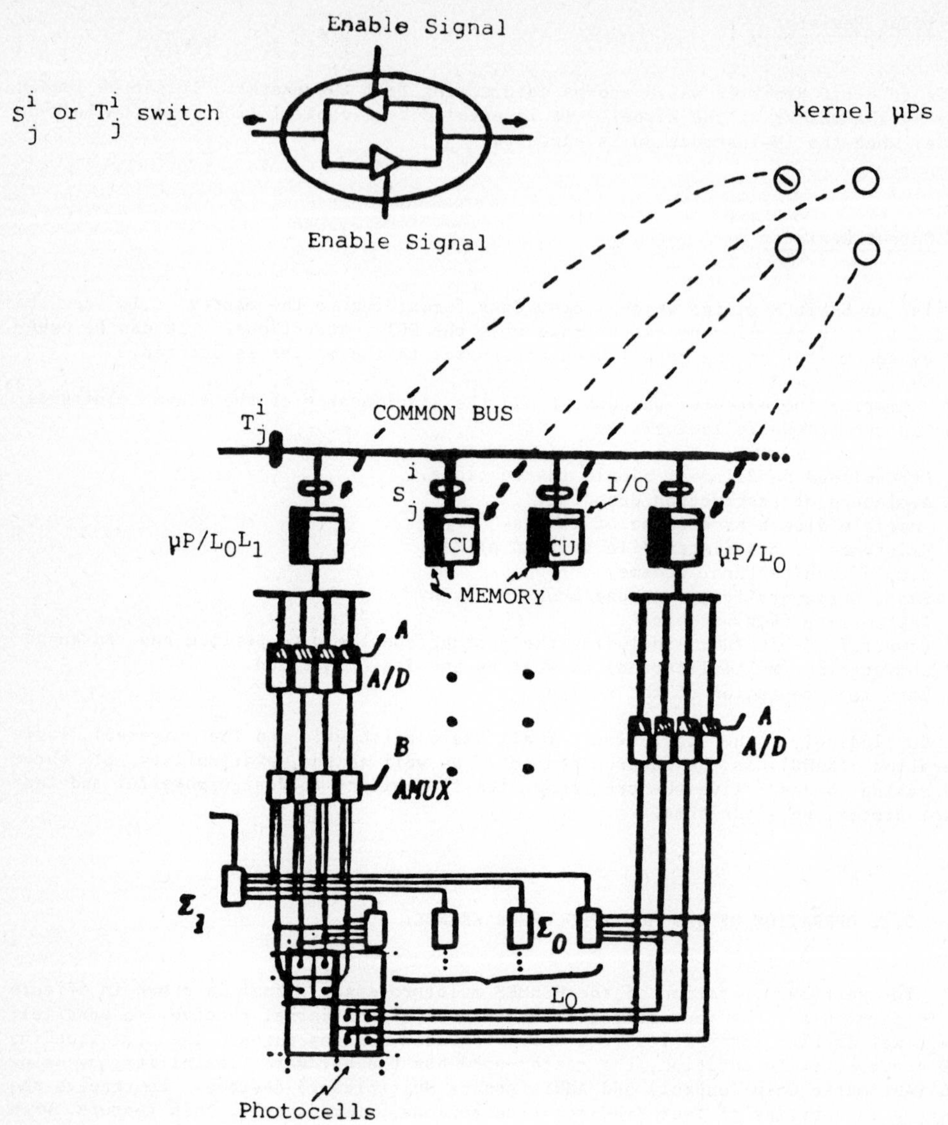

Figure 5: The vertical hardware organization of the multi-processor kernel.

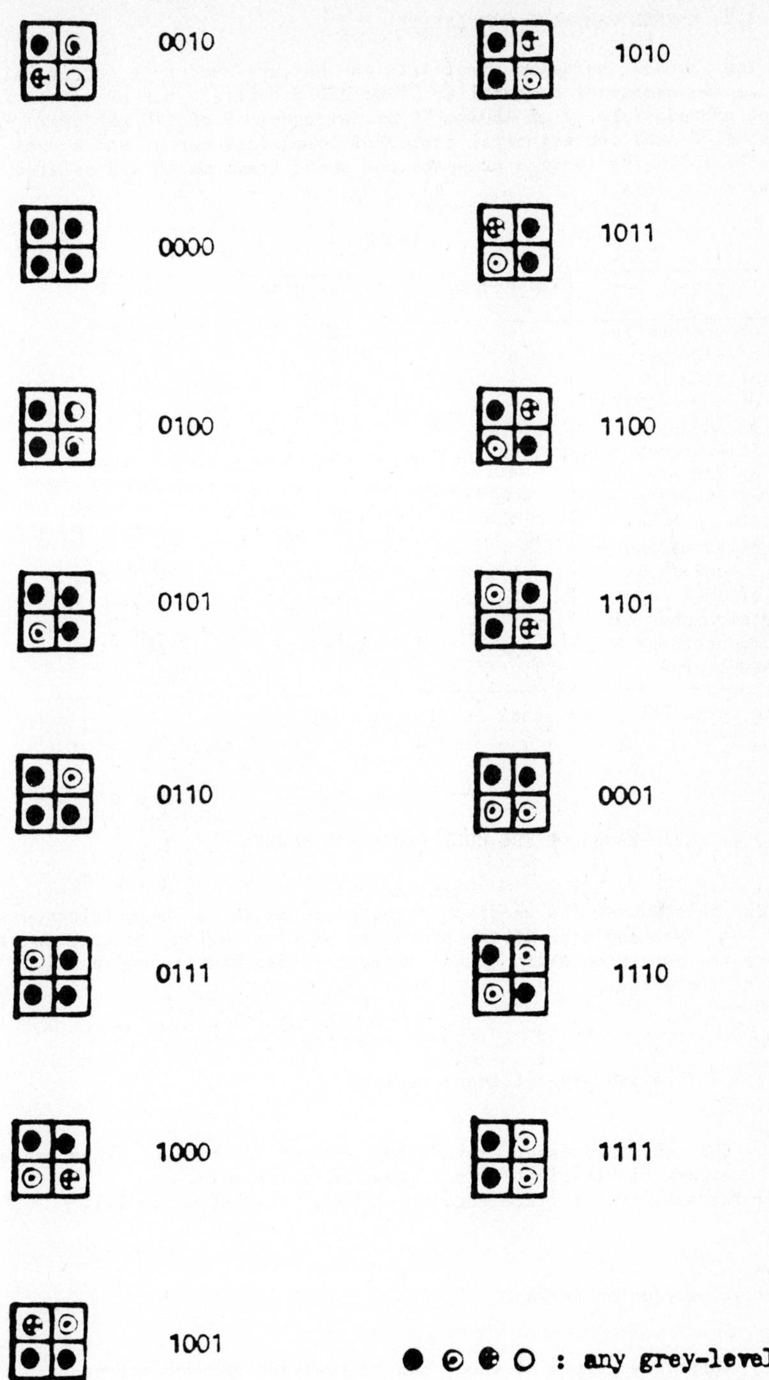

FIGURE (6) : Coding sceme for the four pixels treated at level-0.

3.3. KERNEL HARDWARE COMPLEXITY

The kernel hardware complexity can be expressed by a set of simpler items, such as the number of photocells; # of A/D converters per μP-node; # of AGSs or (Σ); of μP-nodes/μP; # of AMUXs; # of switches; # of I/O per μPs; # of lines per buses; # of AMUX inputs; total number of components per μP and kernel area.

The following table 3 presents the above items which are related to the kernel hardware complexity.

TABLE 3

Items	Slave-node	Master-node	Kernel
# of photocells	4^i	4^i	4^{i+1}
# of A/Ds per μP	4^i	4^i	4^{i+1}
# of AGCs	-	4	5
# of slave-μPs/μP	-	3	4
# of AMUXs	-	4	4
# of switches	1	2	5
# of I/O per μPs	2	2	8
# of lines/common bus	8	8	8
# of lines/photo-cells-bus	$4^i \times 8$	$4^i \times 8$	$4^{i+1} \times 8$
# of AMUX inputs	-	j+1	j+1
Total number of components/μP & kernel area	$10 \times 4^i + 11$	$10 \times 4^i + 24 + j$	$10 \times 4^{i+1} + 35 + j$

Note that, $i \in Z$, $i \geq 1$, and $1 \leq j \leq \log_2 n$, $n \geq 4$.

3.4. PERFORMANCE OF THE MULTIPROCESSOR KERNEL

In this subsection we discuss the performance of the multiprocessor kernel in terms of type and size of the processed picture region; execution tasks on the picture region; processing speed; memory requirements; and possible operational modes of the kernel.

3.4.1 Type and size of image regions

- The multiprocessor kernel can process any type of image region, such as binary (1-bit/pixel), grey level (8-bit/pixel).
- The size of the image region can be 4^{i+1} pixels, where $i \geq 1$.

3.4.2 Execution tasks

- **Input:** Two types of input can be realized at each processor-node. The first one is the input of the average intensities provided by the photoarray. The second type of input is "orders" or "abstracted-coded" picture information through the common bus [2].

- **Segmentation:** Each processor-node, at the L0 level of the HERMES hierarchy can implement segmentation on the pixels of its own picture region. A form of the segments provided can be the coded scheme of the figure 6, by separating in groups the pixel values.

- **Texture Coding:** The coding scheme of the figure 6 can also be used for texture image processing (in particular, texture synthesis and recognition), by using 4^{2m} different patterns as texture primitives of a texture hierarchical language [26]. The m parameter depends on the number of grey levels, where for a binary image m=1.

- **Freeman coding** [27]: Each processor-node can code its own pixels using the known Freeman code, by providing upwards to its master-node a string of 4 coded elements:
  (i,j)abc
  where (i,j) are the coordinates of the starting point (pixel) in the picture region, and $a,b,c \in [1,2,3,4,5,6,7,8]$.

- **Decoding:** A μP-node is able to realize decoding on the "orders" received from its master-node in order to "understand" which are the tasks required for the current process.

- **Synthesis :** Each processor-node of a kernel, at the j level, $1 \leq j \leq \log_2 N-1$, can apply synthesis functions on the information received from the previous level (j-1) of the hierarchical operation. In particular, at the L0 level, each node synthesizes the pixels received from its own picture region, while, at the rest levels of the HERMES hierarchy each node attempts to synthesize "abstracted-coded" picture information [2].

- **Normalization:** This is a "filtering" function which each processor-node, at the j level, $j>0$, executes in order to reduce the unevenness introduced during the synthesis function [28].

- **Recognition:** The goal of each processor-node is to recognize the picture information of its own region by using patterns matching, or syntactic, or decision theoretic recognition processes.

- **Abstraction:** This is a procedure which gives a coded "name" or form to the recognizable picture information, based on its specific features, if it is possible for further processing such as, transmission, synthesis, etc.

- **Output:** Each processor has only one output port, through the common system bus, in order to communicate with the other processor-nodes sending "orders" or "abstracted-coded" information.

3.4.3 Processing speed

Each uP slave node has a RISC-type architectural structure, which provides 10 MIPS for a clock of 10 MHz (see details in the 3.1.2 section). The processing speed of the multiprocessor kernel depends on the communication delay D(t) of the information transfered through the common bus.
The structure of the master node will be a RISC-type one (not available in this paper) with processing capacity of (10+b) MIPS of a clock of (10+b) MHz. The total processing capacity of the kernel could be expressed as 40 MIPS approximately.

3.4.4 Memory requirements

Each processor-node has 64 registers in order to store immediately a maximum number of 64 pixels values or pixels and intermediate results. However, each node, at the j level of the HERMES hierarchy, $1 \leq j \leq \log_2 N$, includes an extra RAM memory to service the information received from the common bus. The size of the ROM memory for every node of the kernel is 8K bytes. The size of the ROM memory for the most powerful processors, at the highest levels of the HERMES hierarchy, is greater than 8K bytes and depends on the user requests.

3.4.5 Operational modes [3]

The functionality of the multiprocessor kernel can be characterized by a variety of modes depended on the type of the processed image and the user requirements. In particular, the kernel can function as:

Serial: The master-node can service its own slave nodes with a predefined priority, such as FRFS (First Request First Service), or a fixed one (P0,P1,P2,P3) where P0 node is served first.
Parallel: All the processor-nodes of the kernel, at the L0 level, receive in parallel the pixel average intensities from their squites and process them in a parallel manner too [17]. Note that, the HERMES machine functions in parallel [3].

Pipelined (one image): The functionality of the kernel has pipelined mode for only one image at a time. This means that, some processing tasks are implemented at the i level, while additional processing tasks are executed at the i+1 level. (i.e., if the four kernel nodes, at the i level, can not recognize their own picture information, this could be able to happen at the i+1 level, if the accumulated information is an "integrated" one [12,28]).

Concurrent: The kernel presents concurrency if the priority mode allows it (FRFS). In particualr, if some nodes continue their process, while at the same time some other has already transfered its picture package to its master-node. This could be possible during a synthesis process.

Systolic: The multiprocessor kernel presents a specific systolism, when at the i level 4 processors work, while at the i+1 level only one designated processor-node continues to work. The systolic feature is more clear on the HERMES structure, where 4^{K} processors work at the j level, while 4^{K-1} nodes are active at the j+1 functional level [2,3,12].

Reconfigurability: The kernel structure described in this paper does not support reconfigurability. However, the development of a multilevel operating system (MYLOS) could provide that feature to the HERMES machine [29]. In particular, the MYLOS operating system will provide the capability to the HERMES processors, at the j functional level, $1 \leq j \leq \log_2 N$, to replace each other during the operation.

Hierarchical (bottom-up and top-down): The kernel nodes participate in a hierarchical bottom-up mode, when the slave-nodes feed upwards "abstracted-coded" picture information to their master-node. During a top-down procedure the master-node sends "orders" to its slave nodes determining the processing tasks that they have to be executed. The hierarchical mode of the kernel and generally of HERMES is similar to the pseudo-quadtree structure.

4. KERNEL'S VLSI GEOMETRIC TOPOLOGY

In this section we discuss two possible geometric topological schemes for the

VLSI design of the HERMES multiprocessor kernel.

The first scheme follows the traditional VLSI chip design methods as illustrated in figure 7a. The second one is close to the physical geometric configuration of the HERMES system and follows the current VLSI systems design [20] (see figure 7b). In particular, the first chip layout includes the photoarray of nxn cells, n=2, in the middle of the integration area. The surround areas are dedicated to the A/Ds, AGCs, AMUXs, bus-switches and the external area includes the microprocessor-nodes. Thsi chip configuration occupies a square area Ea.

The second chip-layout , figure 7b, presents a different geometric configuration, which accumulates all the μP components in the same chip subarea. Specifically the RAM memory, required for the 4 processors, is accumulated at the same area. The same policy is followed for the ROMs, Registers, ALUs, and Control Units. However, the multiprocessor kernel is associated with a number of analog devices, bility of the VLSI design a 3D version is proposed [3].

A general comparison between these two chip-layouts provides the following: The first layout seems to be more realistic with the existing 2D VLSI capabilities. However, the disadvantage of this configuration, for a future VLSI or ULSI chip design of the HERMES machine, is the high complexity of the hardware interconnections among the system subparts, such as μPs to μPs at the various levels, μPs to analog components. On the other hand, the second chip layout occupies less square area Eb<Ea, in the 2D point of view, but requires a 3D expensive design in order to be compatible with a future system chip design. The advantage of the second layout is the fair hardware complexity for the interconnection of the systems components. The VLSI design of the multiprocessor kernel is in progress and open for future research.

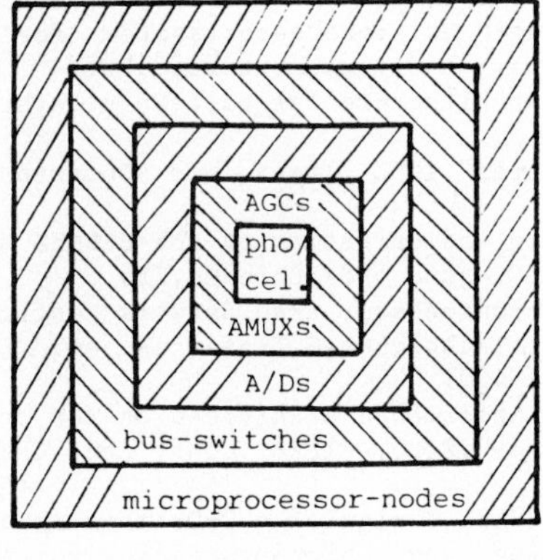

(a)

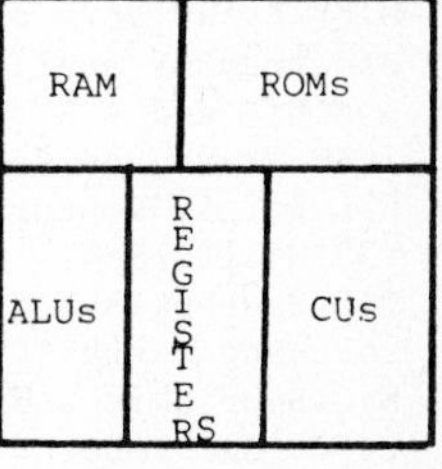

Photocells

(b)

Figure 7: Practical chip-layout configurations for the HERMES multiprocessor kernel (not under scale).

5. CONCLUSIONS

The detailed structural design of the HERMES multiprocessor kernel, based on a RISC-type architecture, has been described in this paper. Moreover, the performance of the kernel in terms of picture type and size, processing tasks, speed, memory requirements, and operational modes has also been discussed. Ideas for the kernel's VLSI design have been proposed. Future extensions could be the RISC-type design of the master-node, the completion of the kernel VSLI design and fabrication. Note that the simulation of the HERMES operation using Petri-nets formal models has been already done [2].

REFERENCES

[1] S.Tanimoto and A.Klinger,"Structured Computer Vision", Academic Press, N.Y., 1980.

[2] N.G.Bourbakis and D.K.Fotakis,"HERMES - A hierarchical, multiprocessor machine vision system architecture", submitted

[3] N.G.Bourbakis,"Design of real-time supercomputing vision architectures", Proc. of IEEE Conf. on SUPERCOMPUTING, May 1987, Santa Clara, CA.

[4] S.Tanimoto,"A pyramidal approach to parallel processing", Proc. Int. Symp. on Comp. Archit.,Stockholm,Sweden,June 1983, pp. 372-378.

[5] M.Duff,"Computing Structures for Image Processing", Academic Press,N.Y. 1983.

[6] E.P.Danielson and S.Levialdi,"Computers architectures for pictorial information systems",IEEE Computer, Nov.1981,pp.53-67.

[7] G.H.Granland,"GOP image Processor",Picture Processing Lab, Linkoeping University, Sweden.

[8] G.J.Li and B.W.Wah,"The design of optimal systolic arrays",IEEE Trans. on Computers, Vol.34,No.1,pp.66-77,1985.

[9] J.L.Hennessy,"VLSI Processor architecture",IEEE Trans. on Computers,vol-.33,No.12,1221-1246,1984.

[10] N.Dimopoulos,"On the structure of the HOMOGENEOUS multiprocessor, IEEE Trans. on Computers,vol.34,pp.141-150,1985.

[11] N.G.Bourbakis and H.Nguyen,"TALOS - A distributed image analysis/synthesis multiprocessor system", submitted to IEEE Conf.,1987.

[12] N.G.Bourbakis and P.Ligomenides,"A real-time,hierarchical multimicroprocessor vision system",Proc.IEEE Conf.on CVPR 86,June 1986,Miami,Florida, pp.381-387.

[13] G.Fritsch et. al.,"EMS-85- The Erlangen Multiprocessor system for board spectrum of applications",Proc.IEEE Conf. on Supercomputers, 1985.

[14] L.M.Ni and A.K.Jain,"A VLSI systolic architecture for pattern clustering", IEEE Trans. on PAMI,vol.7,No.1,1986.

[15] C.L.Seitz,"Concurrent VLSI architectures",IEEE Trans. on Computers,vol-.33,No.12,1984.

[16] N.G.Bourbakis and D.K.Fotakis,"Structure and operation of the HERMES Multiprocessor kernel",Proc. IEEE Conf. on NCC, June 1987,Chicago,IL.

[17] N.G.Bourbakis and C.Vaitsos,"A multimicroprocessor tree network configuration used on robot vision systems",Digital Techniques,S.Tzafestas ed. Elsevier Sc.Pub.,North Holland,IMACS 1985,pp.483-490.

[18] N.G.Bourbakis and P.Ligomenides,"High performance architectures for realtime multilevel picture information systems",Proc. IEEE Conf. on LFA, June 1985,Mallorca, Spain,pp.271-276.

[19] D.Panagiotopoulos and N.Bourbakis,"The VLSI design of a 2-D image processing array",Int.Journal on Microprogramming and Microprocessing,vol.14,No.3-4,pp.125-132,1984.

[20] "Clipper 33 MHz performance",FAIRCHILD CO., CA.,1987.

[21] D.K.DuBose,D.K.Fotakis and D.Tabak,"A microcoded RISC", Computer Architecture News,vol.14,No.3,pp.5-16,1986, (Also,19th Microprogramming Workshop N.Y.Oct. 1986).

[22] D.Tabak,"Reduced Instruction Set Computer RISC-Architecture", Research Studies Press,1987.

[23] D.A.Patterson and C.H.Sequin,"A VLSI RISC",IEEE Computer,vol .15,No.9, 1982, pp.8-21.

[24] "AMD 2900 Family 1985 Databook", Bipolar microprocessor logic and interface.

[25] A.Klinger,"Regular decomposition and picture structure", Proc.IEEE Conf. on SMC, Dallas,Texas,pp.307-310.

[26] N.G.Bourbakis and D.K.Fotakis,"KALYPSO-A picture recognition and knowledge creation language", GMU-ECE-TR-1987, to be submitted.

[27] H.Freeman,"On the encoding of arbitrary geometric configuration", IRE Trans. Eletron Computing, EC-10,260-268,1961.

[28] N.G.Bourbakis and D.K.Fotakis,"A heuristic scheme for recognition of progressive digital straight lines with unevenness",Proc. IEEE Workshop on LFA, Aug.1988,

[29] N.G.Bourbakis,"MYLOS-A multilevel operating system for the HERMES machine", to be submitted.

Supercomputing in Europe — 1987

Iain S. Duff
Computer Science and Systems Division
Harwell Laboratory
Didcot, Oxon
England, OX11 0RA

Abstract

In recent years there has been a large increase in the number of supercomputers in Europe. We examine their distribution both by country and by manufacturer and also by the major application of the supercomputer sites. We discuss reasons for their acquisition and the main advantages of supercomputing as perceived by the installations themselves. Throughout, we compare our findings with a survey which we conducted in 1984 and highlight the major differences in the European supercomputing scene since that time.

1 Introduction

In 1984 we conducted a survey for EURATOM on supercomputing in Europe (Duff 1984) and naively thought that it would be a simple matter to update that report for this present study. In the event, we found the number of supercomputers had more than doubled since that time and our updating task was thus greater than for the original survey. We consider the growth in supercomputing in Section 2 and discuss the number and distribution of supercomputers in the various countries in Europe. We study the current situation more fully on a country by country basis in Section 3. In Section 4, we divide the installations into their primary application area and consider the main uses of supercomputers in Europe. We then examine the principal reasons for acquiring supercomputer power in Section 5 and finally comment on the observed deficiencies and possible future trends in Section 6.

Before we continue, it is very important to define what we mean by a supercomputer.

There are many definitions which of course change, at least quantitatively, with time. For our present purposes we use the industry standard of the CRAY-1 and define a supercomputer as a machine which performs as well or better than the CRAY-1 on a range of applications. This means that we include all the machines of Cray Research, the CYBER 205, and the Fujitsu FACOM VP series (marketed in Europe by Amdahl and Siemens). The ETA-10 and NEC SX series are not included since there are presently no such machines in Europe, although there are orders for both. We know of no European orders for the Hitachi supercomputers. In many of our calculations, we also include the IBM 3090 with vector facility. Although this machine rarely equals CRAY-1 performance, the multiprocessor versions pass our test and we feel the impact of this machine on European supercomputing promises to be very significant. There are, of course, other vector or array processors than the IBM 3090/VF, for example the National Advanced Systems AS/91X0 or the Sperry ISP, but their numbers are low and their effect quite marginal compared to the IBM product, so we do not consider these.

We are thus excluding from our survey the powerful new range of so-called mini-supercomputers which include machines like the Alliant, Convex, SCS, and FPS machines. We also exclude the recent machines exhibiting MIMD parallelism like the shared memory machines from Sequent, Encore, Elxsi, and Flex or the local memory machines based on a hypercube interconnect. Although these machines might provide an architectural base for future supercomputers they are generally much lower in power than current supercomputers. There are four European machines verging on the supercomputing market, namely the BULL Isis, the AMT DAP, Suprenum, and a range of transputer-based products, although the latter two projects are not yet providing supercomputing power. We do not discuss these in the main body of the report but consider their possible future influence in Section 6.

Before continuing with the report, we should define the other main term in the title, namely the geographical region called Europe. We include all countries in Western Europe, not only those in the European community, but we exclude states in the Middle East which are often included in the European marketing area for operational reasons. For example, Cray Research UK (Ltd) have sold machines to Abu Dhabi and Saudi Arabia.

A major problem with conducting such a survey is that some manufacturers are unwilling to provide information on their sites and most will naturally only give information once the order is confirmed and any necessary export licences have been obtained. The time lag from initial decision, to order, to delivery, to acceptance is often about a year. Clearly, one often knows from scientific colleagues of forthcoming machines, but it would be improper to include comments on these here. Thus my figures pertain to systems delivered by June 1987 although not all have passed their acceptance test at that time.

2 Growth and distribution of supercomputers

In recent years there has been a great increase in the number of supercomputer installations in Europe. We show the year-end figures in Table 2.1, excluding the IBM 3090/VF largely because it would only appear in the 1986 figures. These figures show a steady linear growth but they mask the fact that many configurations are much more powerful than in previous years, for example there are now several X-MP/4 and three CRAY-2 installations. If we count the number of installed processors and also include the 23 IBM 3090/VFs then our current total rises to 90 which could be considered indicative of a more exponential growth in supercomputing power. The IBM 3090/VF figures reflect the number of installations and not the total number of vector boxes (the IBM 3090-600 can have up to 6 VFs). Indeed, most of the IBM 3090/VF installations in Europe have only one vector facility.

Table 2.1 Growth of supercomputing in Europe

Year	Number of installations at year end
1981	9
1982	12
1983	27
1984	36
1985	45
1986	53

The current number of installations, including the IBM 3090/VFs, is 78 with the geographical distribution shown in Table 2.2. Although the number of machines in the three most heavily populated countries is nearly the same, their distribution within each country is quite different. In both Britain and France, there is a great centralization of supercomputer installations around London and Paris respectively while in Germany the distribution is much more uniform. This is due to the federal nature of Germany and to the fact that many of their supercomputers have been purchased with funds from both State and Federal Government. Thus there is at least one supercomputer in most of the states in that country. A fuller discussion of the situation in each country is given in Section 3.

When these figures are compared with the current world figures of around 263 supercomputers and just over 100 IBM 3090/VFs, then it is clear that Europe still has a significant supercomputer base. Indeed, the number of supercomputers is similar to Japan although, of course, the distribution by manufacturer is considerably different.

Table 2.2 Distribution of supercomputers in Europe

Country	Number of installations in June 1987
Britain	20
Germany	20
France	18
Norway	6
Italy	4
Netherlands	3
Sweden	4
Belgium	1
Denmark	1
Switzerland	1

The pattern of supercomputing has indeed changed little since 1984. The numbers have risen fairly uniformally and several countries have acquired supercomputers which did not have them in our previous survey. Perhaps the greatest growth has been in Scandanavia which had only one supercomputer in our previous survey but now has 11.

If we look at the distribution by manufacturer, as shown in Table 2.3, we see that the main change since our earlier survey is in the increase of Fujitsu machines (none in 1984) and the rapid increase in the IBM 3090/VF installations, a machine only announced about one year ago. It is interesting to note that the percentage of each machine (IBM 3090/VF excluded) reflects the world distribution fairly closely with perhaps a slightly greater advantage for CRAY and Fujitsu over the world figures. We reflect on these figures further in Section 6.

Table 2.3 Distribution of European supercomputers by manufacturer

Manufacturer		Number of installations	
Cray..			
	CRAY-2	3	38
	CRAY-XMP	22	
	CRAY-1	13	
CDC..			
	CYBER 205		7
Fujitsu..			
	Amdahl	5	10
	Siemens	5	
IBM..			
	3090 + VF		23

3 Country by country overview

We now discuss the current situation in each country in more detail and try to forecast future developments within the country and their impact on supercomputing in Europe. The importance of supercomputing in the political world is witnessed by the fact that virtually every country from Britain to Finland has one or more national committees reporting on trends in supercomputing and their implications for supercomputing in the country in question.

In Britain, the supercomputer installations are divided fairly evenly between research laboratories, universities/regional centres, and the petroleum industry, the most recent growth being in the latter area, particularly seismic data processing. A major influence in the research councils area was the publication, in June 1985, of the report of a working party chaired by Professor A J Forty which led directly to the installation of a CRAY X-MP/48 at the Rutherford Appleton Laboratory. Other recommendations of the "Forty Committee" included major improvements to JANET (an academic network), fellowships in computational science, and funding for special architecture machines. It also proposed that a second supercomputer be purchased in 1990. The overall funding requested for all the projects was £47.5M over the period 1986-1991. Another committee has been formed to continue the work of the Forty Committee and to report both on requirements for supercomputers and advanced parallel computing facilities. The only CRAY-2 in Britain is located at the Harwell Laboratory. Although it was purchased for use by the Atomic Energy Authority, surplus time on this facility is being marketed by Harwell and Cray Research (UK) Ltd.

In the Federal Republic of Germany, most of the supercomputers are in regional centres, although the car industry may soon have three machines. Most of the centres obtain a large part of their funding from the local state government which accounts for the well-distributed location of supercomputers in that country. The most recent centre to be established is HLRZ at Jülich which houses a Cray X-MP/48 primarily servicing High Energy and Particle Physics at DESY, GMD, and KFA. The Suprenum project is centred at GMD near Bonn and has elements of a national project. Indeed, there is some possibility that the second phase of the project may involve significant collaboration with partners in other European countries. The only CRAY-2 in Germany is at the University of Stuttgart and was the first to be installed in Europe. Germany is notable for its high number of CYBER 205s (4) and indeed an ETA-10 machine has been ordered for the weather forecasting centre Wetter AMT at Offenbach and another is likely to be installed at Karlsruhe. Although the Denelcor company has gone into liquidation, it is interesting to observe that two of it's HEP computers are still being used as flight simulators by MBB in Munich. Using our yardstick, this machine is not of course a supercomputer but we did include it in our earlier report (Duff 1984).

In contrast to Britain and Germany, France has relatively few supercomputers in the public sector, the main machine for university access being the CRAY-2 at the Ecole Polytechnique near Paris. There are presently no CYBER 205s in France, with CYBERNET users of the machine at the CDC data centre near Paris now being serviced by machines in the USA and the 205 at Karlsruhe. A Piper (a single processor air-cooled version of the ETA-10) has been ordered for use by CERFACS, the European Centre at Toulouse. This centre presently receives all of its funding from French sources (Central and local governments and local industry) but has been established very much as a European centre rather than a regional or national centre. A separate European proposal for a computational fluid dynamics centre originated largely from a French initiative although this proposal is still in the discussion stage. A national committee has been set up to report on future supercomputing needs, particularly with respect to the main public bodies. France appears more concerned than most European countries about the dependence on non-European equipment and have their own supercomputer development plans currently centred on the Isis machine from Bull.

In the Netherlands, all academic supercomputing is coordinated by the Woerkgroup Gebruik Supercomputers which currently supply 205 time from the machine at SARA (Amsterdam) and CRAY time from the Cray Research Centre at Bracknell. The purchase of this time is actually conducted by the ENR service bureau at Petten. Shell have a CRAY at their centre in Rijswijk which was formally used by ENR but now is used exclusively by Shell. The first NEC SX-2 in Europe has been ordered by the aerospace laboratory NLR, with delivery expected late this year.

In Sweden there was much discussion about the siting of another supercomputer centre to supplement that at Saab in Linkoping. It now seems that that machine will be upgraded to an X-MP from the present CRAY 1, with some other time being made available on the 4 processor IBM 3090/VF installation at Skelleftea. There is much current interest in Sweden in building up research in parallelism using some of the new super-minis which we discussed in the introduction.

Denmark has recently concentrated much of its academic computing resources at Lyngby, near Copenhagen. The first major supercomputer, an Amdahl 1100 was installed there this May and is easily accessible by most researchers in universities and laboratories throughout the country.

There has been considerable growth in supercomputing in Norway largely supported by the oil industry and oil revenues. The main supercomputer for university access is the CRAY X-MP at Trondheim although the bureau at Nortodden offers a service on its Amdahl 1100. There are a number of IBM 3090/VFs in the country, with a major facility at the IBM Scientific Centre at Bergen. This Centre runs an active visitors' programme and has many joint projects with researchers in other European countries and the USA.

Although the only supercomputer currently in use in Switzerland is at EPFL in Lausanne, there are plans to install another supercomputer at ETH Zurich and a CRAY X-MP will shortly be delivered to the CERN laboratory in Geneva, assuming export approval is obtained.

The major centres for supercomputing in Italy are CINECA at Bologna and the IBM Scientific Centre in Rome which has a two-processor 3090/VF facility. As with the Bergen Centre, there is an active visitors' programme and many collaborative projects.

4 Use of supercomputers

We show, in Table 4.1, the distribution of supercomputers by the principal application of the site at which they are installed. We have included some autonomous or partially autonomous laboratories under the heading "government laboratory" and recognize that many of the users of the regional centres (normally located at universities) are industrial and non-university users. These figures are not too dissimilar to the overall world pattern given that much depends on how one classifies certain sites with characteristics of more than one class. Generally it would appear that Europe has a greater preponderance of supercomputers in the regional centres than in the world as a whole and a correspondingly lower number in "government" laboratories.

In 1984 we attempted to assess the volume of supercomputing for each major application area by asking each site for a list of applications which consumed at least 10% of its resources. We then summed that on the assumption that all supercomputers were equal. The validity of such a calculation was marginal then and would be even more in doubt were we to attempt such an exercise again. Not only is our equal power assumption much less valid but the growth in the number of centres without direct control of their users, means that such statistics are often impossible to obtain. Additionally, as in 1984, the sites euphemistically labelled "defence" are not very free with information on their usage, and we have nowhere attempted to report on the level of supercomputing used in SIGINT applications. One thing that does remain true from our earlier survey is that except for the "defence" applications, seismic processing is still easily the biggest application area of supercomputing power in Europe. Although we have coupled reservoir modelling with seismic processing in the table, less than 20% of these machines are used on the reservoir modelling side.

An interesting feature of research council machines is that, in most countries, use is determined by peer review of prospective projects so that their usage is likely to reflect current trends in research and thus might change more quickly than in other installations.

Table 4.1 Distribution of installations by applications

Application	Number	Percentage
Univ/Regional Centre	24	31
Petroleum/Seismic	13	17
Government Laboratories	11	14
Defence	7	9
Aerospace	6	8
Manufacturer/Bureaux	5	6
Power	5	6
Automotive	4	5
Meteorology	3	4

Although several of the supercomputers are now multiprocessors, very little use is made of multitasking at present. Such use as there is, is principally in algorithm research and development and, with the singular exception of the European Centre for Medium Range Weather Forecasts (ECMWF), multitasking is not used in production mode. Much more emphasis is now placed on vectorization which was merely considered an added bonus three years ago.

There is very little interactive use made of supercomputers although the advent of the UNICOS system on the CRAY machines, in particular the CRAY-2, may soon change this situation.

Other significant differences from 1984 include a much greater variety of front-end machines, including often a wide selection on a single supercomputer, facilitated by the move towards standardization of local area network protocols and the development of interconnect facilities from many mainframe and minicomputer manufacturers. Additionally, there is greater use of wide area networks, both standard PTT systems, "European" networks like EARN, and private company networks.

5 Reasons for supercomputing

Many of the reasons for supercomputing remain unchanged from three years ago although the market is now much more mature and, if anything, computational scientists are playing a more prominent role in the selection of machines. The essential nature of the machine as an instrument of large-scale scientific computing is now widely recognized and indeed many large simulations, including any realistic 3-D simulation, would be impractical without such equipment. Although some manufacturers can make a convincing case that supercomputing is "cost effective", the strongest argument is in the effectiveness, an argument so powerful that an excellent case can be made for the high level of funding required. Indeed, although supercomputers may at first seem expensive, their real cost is comparable to the fastest machines of yesteryear and their cost is often considerably less than the experiment they are used to simulate, oil reservoir modelling and computational wind tunnels being two outstanding examples. Perhaps the true yardstick should be to compare the cost of a supercomputer with the cost of not doing the calculation for which it is intended. The prestige aspect is still important, not just in a simple "macho" sense but in the important sense of establishing that a centre is serious about large-scale scientific computing, thus attracting and retaining high quality staff, research contracts, and customers, as appropriate. The unique resource aspect was an important factor in the siting of three CRAY-2s in Europe; at Harwell in Britain, Ecole Polytechnique in Paris, and Stuttgart in Germany.

The role of benchmarks in selecting supercomputers is now more recognized than it was in 1984. It is clearly important to indicate that one's prospective machine will perform satisfactorily on at least some of the problems from the intended site, but benchmarking is rarely used as an impartial way of selecting a particular machine. The choice of supercomputer is more normally determined by rather mundane market forces and is influenced by such marketing strategies as reduced prices, free software, inclusion of additional hardware, or some type of sharing of the machine or its resources with the manufacturer.

Clearly, if particular applications are envisaged to run on the prospective machine, then the availability of a good software base in that application area on the machine is a very important factor in determining the choice.

The brand loyalty of supercomputer owners is very strong. There have been no installations which have changed their major supercomputer supplier although some have both an IBM 3090/VF and another supercomputer. It is interesting to note that over 80% of the sites surveyed in 1984 have undertaken a significant upgrade to their installation, where significant is measured in millions of dollars.

6 Future trends

The pattern is clearly that, once a site installs a supercomputer, it is very likely to upgrade its installation perhaps as often as once every three years. There is no reason to suppose that this trend will not continue. An obvious direction is in the quest for more memory since about 75% of the sites considered their present situation at least partially inadequate ... notably none of the CRAY-2 sites have yet complained about this!! Other major current problems include I/O capability, not just in transfer speeds but also in the capacity of secondary storage devices. Apart from the obvious upgrade remedies, more effort and funds are being expended in ways of reducing the amount of data which must be transferred, for example by using graphical devices more closely coupled to the supercomputer. Most people are very happy with the reliability of their supercomputer with many of the problems occurring not with the machine itself but in the interface mechanism, either in the front-end connections or in the capacity and reliability of networks through which the supercomputer is accessed. Unquestionably great strides have been made over the last few years, but clearly further development in this area is necessary.

It is interesting that a major complaint in 1984 was the standard of Fortran compilers. While few people explicitly commented on them in a very positive sense, there was clearly much greater satisfaction in this area than formerly.

It is interesting to reflect that vectorization is now of much greater concern than in 1984. Indeed, the level of interest in MIMD parallelism is not dissimilar to that for vectorization at that time. This, coupled with the trend of supercomputer manufacturers towards multiple processor machines, leads us to believe that indeed such parallelism will become of much greater concern to computational scientists over the next three to five years. Most probably at a low level of parallelism at first although the general trend to higher levels later seems likely. Also one might expect higher interactive use of supercomputers, driven partly by the pervasiveness of UNIX and partly by the need to intelligently post-process data before output.

IBM watchers have been quoted as suggesting a 10000 unit market for the 3090 with around 1000 coupled to a vector facility. If this is so, then the IBM factor will become very important ... introducing supercomputing for the masses and indeed helping to increase the growth of other larger systems as well. The increase in 3090/VF installations from zero to 23 in one year indicates that this influence will indeed be strong.

Other developments include attempts to coordinate training and research on supercomputing on a European level, the most noticeable attempt being the recent creation in Toulouse of CERFACS which will begin a program in September centred on the themes of parallel algorithms, turbulence, and computational aerodynamics. A proposal for a European Computational Fluid Dynamics Centre is also being discussed.

Some European governments have been concerned about the reliance on imported machines, particular in the light of increasing problems in obtaining export licences. Thus it is highly likely that further growth will include a European element. Obvious contenders are the Suprenum machine from Germany or the Isis from BULL although there are several projects designing potential future supercomputers using the INMOS transputer, many of them supported by European funding. The AMT DAP line also has many plans for further development.

There is of course many resources in Europe devoted to fifth generation computer projects, for example substantial funding from the ESPRIT programme, and significant national funding as in the Alvey project in Britain. Although there is some overlap with our present area of concern, notably in the use of parallelism, we have not considered this here because such enterprises are not primarily concerned with large scale scientific computing.

Certainly there is a great awareness of the importance of supercomputing within the worldwide and European scientific community. Evidence of this can be found in the rapid growth in new journal titles in this area and the seemingly endless succession of conferences with supercomputing as a major theme. There are now three series of major conferences running in Europe; the VAPP series (VAPPIII in Liverpool in August 1987), the Norway series (Loen II in Tromso in June 1988), and the ICS series (the first at Athens in June 1987 and more planned). In addition, many centres run fairly regular conferences of a more workshop oriented format, for example, Bochum, Amsterdam, Antwerp, GMD, and Rome.

References

Duff, I. S. (1984). *The use of advanced large computers in Europe.* AERE-R 11432, HMSO, London.

C^3P-392

Domain Decomposition in Distributed and Shared Memory Environments

I: A Uniform Decomposition and Performance Analysis for the NCUBE and JPL Mark IIIfp Hypercubes

Geoffrey C. Fox †
Caltech Concurrent Computation Program
Mail Code 158-79
California Institute of Technology
Pasadena, CA 91125
June 8, 1987

Invited Paper at ICS 87, International Conference on Supercomputing, June 8-12, 87, Athens, Greece. To be published as a *Lecture Note in Computer Science* by Springer-Verlag, and edited by Constantine Polychronopoulos.

Abstract:

We describe how explicit domain decomposition can lead to implementations of large scale scientific applications which run with near optimal performance on concurrent supercomputers with a variety of architectures. In particular, we show how one can discuss from a uniform point of view two architectural characteristics; distributed memory and hierarchical memory where a large relatively slow memory is buffered by a faster cache or local memory. We consider two hypercubes in particular; the commercial NCUBE and JPL's Mark IIIfp with hierarchical memory at each node of a hypercube. We remark on the application of these ideas to other architectures and other concurrent computers. We present a performance analysis in terms of basic parameters describing the hardware and the applications.

I: Introduction

This paper is the first of a series from Caltech that will discuss some of the issues in developing decomposition and software tools for concurrent supercomputers. In particular we need to develop implementations of major scientific problems that run well on concurrent supercomputers with a variety of different architectures. At Caltech, there is widespread support among many of the computational scientists and engineers for the use of concurrent supercomputers [1]. However, there is clearly no agreement among either research groups or commercial vendors as to the "right" architectures either at the present or in the future. It is important that we can find techniques that will allow (Caltech) users to develop code which will be useable not only on today's prototypes but will not need major revision for future machines.

Presently available concurrent supercomputers suitable for scientific computations can be divided into three classes [2-4]

- Small grain size, SIMD, Distributed Memory: Such as the ICL DAP, Goodyear MPP, and Connection Machine.
- Large grain size, MIMD Distributed Memory: Such as the various hypercubes and the transputer based systems like the MEIKO Computing Surface.

† Work supported in part by DOE grant DE-FG03-85ER25009 and DE-AC03-85ER40050, the Program Manager of the Joint Tactical Fusion Office, and the ESD division of the USAF. Also, grants from IBM, SANDIA and the Parsons and the System Development Foundations.

- Large grain size, MIMD Shared Memory: Such as the CRAY, ETA, ELXSI, ALLIANT, ENCORE, SEQUENT, CEDAR, BUTTERFLY, and RP3.

Here we will concentrate on a version of domain decomposition that is appropriate for the large grain size machines and not consider the SIMD architectures. This is not due to lack of interest - the SIMD machines have been very successful in many scientific problems - rather I am largely constrained by ignorance. Further, we will not consider dataflow which could in the future be an interesting approach to supercomputers. In order to focus the paper further, we will not discuss shared memory machines in general but rather concentrate on one aspect of some of these machines - namely a hierarchical memory where good performance requires data to lie in a cache or local memory and not fetched from a relatively slow shared memory each time. We note that a memory hierarchy is difficult to avoid in high performance machines with pipelined floating point units. We will not discuss important issues such as the contention in a shared memory access network nor will we consider alternative programming methodologies such as automatic (user or computer generated) parallelization of *do* and *for* loops even though these techniques have had important successes [28, 29, 32].

I have chosen domain decomposition because it is the natural and at present required method for programming the hypercube. Further, we understand it reasonably well and shared memory machines typically support it elegantly [5] whereas the favored shared memory methodologies are not easy to port to the simpler hardware of the distributed memory machines. I will sharpen the hypercube discussion further by considering two particular machines.

- The commercial NCUBE hypercube with 1/2 megabyte of memory on each node and up to 1024 nodes. Our initial 512 node machine has 0.25 gigabytes of memory and 0.05 gigaflops peak performance.
- The so-called Mark IIIfp hypercube under construction at Caltech's Jet Propulsion Laboratory (JPL). This will have 128 nodes each with 4 megabytes of slow memory and a high performance WEITEK XL chip based floating point unit buffered by a 64 - 128K bytes data cache i.e., each node has a hierarchical memory. The total machine has 0.5 gigabytes of memory and up to 1 gigaflop performance.

We expect these two machines to be the initial hardware facility around which we will build our new "Concurrent Supercomputing Initiative at Caltech" or CSIC [4,6].

In Sec. II, we describe the target machines in greater detail and introduce and quantify the necessary hardware parameters to measure performance. In the third section, we describe domain decomposition, its application to distributed and hierarchical memories and relation to the theory of complex systems [2, 7].

The heart of the paper lies in Sec. IV where we analyze several specific scientific algorithms including particle dynamics, iterative methods for partial different equations (PDE), fast fourier transform (FFT), matrix inversion and multiplication and finally neural network simulation. We conclude in Sec. V.

II: Characterization of Concurrent Machines

The hardware architectures considered here are shown in Fig. 1. In 1(a) we show a generic sequential machine with a cache as a buffer to a main memory. It should be noted that this conventional machine is not the focus of this article; however, the techniques described here could allow coding such machines in a way that makes excellent use of the cache. In Figs. 1(b) and (c), we generalize this architecture in two ways. Firstly in 1(b), we show a hierarchical shared memory machine with a group of C.P.U.'s connected by an unspecified network to a large global shared memory. This model is a reasonably accurate description of such machines as the CRAY-2, ETA-10, ELXSI, BUTTERFLY, and RP3 among others. This design, or variants of it, is more or less required if one either has a large number of nodes (as in the BUTTERFLY or RP3) or very fast C.P.U.'s (as in the other cases). We note that the memory denoted as "cache" in Fig. 1 should often be more properly called local memory. The functions of cache and local memory are similar; both provide faster access to variables than is possible from the main memory. Our discussion will apply to both memory constructs but is perhaps more natural for local memory which is user (software) controlled rather than the hardware controlled cache. We will hereafter use the term "cache" to describe the dual concept. The necessity of a multistage network connecting nodes to the global memory implies the importance of the "cache" for machines like the RP3 and BUTTERFLY with very many nodes. The use of a fast C.P.U., even with a small number of processors, also typically needs a "cache" to get good performance. Presumably the future will see shared memory machines with many very high-performance nodes; these may depend on the "cache" to an even greater extent. We note that there is no reason for the memory hierarchy to only have two levels; many machines have more. For instance, the RP3 has global memory, local memory, and a true cache. The analysis presented here can be extended to a multilevel hierarchy or just applied to one part of it. For instance on the RP3, the high-speed network gives good access to the shared memory and it would probably be most natural to apply the analysis here with the "cache" being the hardware cache on each node and the local and global memory being lumped together at a single level.

In Fig. 1(c), we show a distributed memory architecture. The initial hypercubes had rather simple nodes but newer machines have gone to hierarchical node designs to obtain high performance. Examples of the latter include the INTEL iPSC-VX and the new JPL Mark IIIfp design. We will concentrate on the latter here as we understand it better and INTEL's current tools do not, we believe, allow the VX hypercube to be programmed in the fashion we will suggest. The Mark IIIfp uses complex nodes with large memory and potentially high performance on each node. These NCUBE and Mark IIIfp nodes are contrasted in Fig. 2 and pictured in Figs. 3 and 4.

The NCUBE does actually have a small on chip cache but for our purposes it should be viewed as a simple uni-level memory at each node. We need a reasonably large "cache" - at a minimum the 64 - 128K bytes of the Mark IIIfp - for our considerations to be relevant. This will become clearer later when in Secs. III and IV we quantify the role of the "cache" size. Similarly, in the transputer based system, the on chip memory of 2K bytes is probably usually too small to be used as a "cache" in the sense advocated in this paper.

In Fig. 5 and Table 1, we introduce three basic parameters t_{calc}, t_{mem} and t_{comm} which we use for our performance analysis. We will restrict ourselves to considering 32-bit arithmetic as this is sufficient for many calculations and the WEITEK XL chip set used on the Mark IIIfp currently only supports 32-bit arithmetic. t_{calc} represents the typical time to perform a floating point application including any overheads such as memory ("cache") access and indexing. t_{mem} and t_{comm} are effectively communication parameters. t_{comm} is the time taken to transmit a 32-bit word between nodes of a hypercube and t_{mem} the time taken to send a word back and forth between "cache" and main memory. We now need to make several comments and caveats on these parameters.

Firstly, we note that these three parameters are a very incomplete description of the hardware. For this paper, we will need the "cache" and node memory sizes as well. We will describe these in application dependent fashion as n_{cache}, n_{node}, and n_{total} for the number of basic entities (e.g., matrix elements in a matrix problem or particles in a dynamics problem) that can be held in the "cache", node of hypercube or total memory respectively. The performance of a system will also depend crucially on whether communication (either node to node or "cache" to memory) is concurrent or sequential with other operations. For the Mark IIIfp, node to node communication (governed by t_{comm}) is concurrent with calculation while "cache" to node memory transfers can *not* be overlapped with calculation. For the NCUBE, communication is presently not concurrent with calculation.

The NCUBE has a scalar processor and the speed t_{calc} of typical floating-point operations will not depend drastically on circumstances although, even here, factors of two variations can be expected. Pipelined or vector machines like the Mark IIIfp, ETA-10, and CRAY-2 can expect very different values of t_{calc} on different applications. We have listed the approximately smallest possible value of t_{calc} as this will be the pacing value for the performance analysis. The techniques described here are in some sense designed to improve t_{calc} by ensuring minimal "cache" misses.

All three parameters t_{calc}, t_{comm}, and t_{mem} depend on the size of the operation performed i.e., on the size of the vector (t_{calc}) or size of the "message" (t_{comm}, t_{mem}). We will ignore the startup time for small vectors and messages even though these are usually important. The techniques needed to minimize startup effects are interesting but are outside the scope of this paper.

The parameter t_{mem} has been defined in a somewhat unnatural fashion in Fig. 5 as the time to read *and* write a word between "cache" and main memory. This makes the definition symmetric with t_{comm} and indeed if one uses a shared memory machine to emulate a distributed memory environment, then with our definition t_{mem} is the appropriate value of t_{comm} to use to describe node to node communication in the emulation. This assumes that in the emulation, a hypercube node process is fully contained in the "cache". We will describe in Sec. III how one takes care of the case when the problem is too large for all the processes to fit into "cache". In Sec. IV, we will use $1/2\ t_{mem}$ as the transfer time when we are just reading or writing. We again emphasize that the shared memory value and indeed our later discussion of t_{mem} completely ignores any contention when accessing the global memory.

The Mark IIIfp can be seen to have interesting multi-level hierarchy with "cache" $\rightarrow$ node memory $\rightarrow$ other nodes' memories. The relevant communication speeds t_{comm}, t_{mem} between the three levels have comparable values although as we will see they do enter the performance analysis in related but rather different ways. The Mark IIIfp illustrates another tactically important issue controlling performance. Namely, in the default node, variables written to "cache" are also stored in main memory. As we will find that this can degrade performance, the Mark IIIfp has the capability to temporarily disable the "write through" nature of the cache and so allows the communication between "cache" and main memory to be under user control. This control structure is implied for machines where the "cache" is designed as a local memory. Referring back to our previous discussion of concurrency, we note that on the Mark IIIfp direct loads of either the cache or local memory cannot be overlapped with calculation. The storing of variables into main memory is similarly non overlapped with one exception; automatic write through from cache is transparently overlapped with other operations as long as a small "pending write" buffer of three requests is not filled i.e., if the writes are sparse, they are overlapped. We will not use this overlap feature in our discussion although it would be possible to improve performance in many cases if full overlap had been allowed in the Mark IIIfp design.

In discussing the hypercubes, we have listed t_{comm} as the node to node transmission time; messages between nodes that are not directly connected in the hypercube topology will be characterized by a larger value of t_{comm}. We will accommodate this by reflecting this as an application dependent effect which will be seen in Sec. IV as a $1/2 \log N_{proc}$ factor in the communication overhead for the FFT. We will use N_{proc} as the number of physical processors throughout this paper.

We will use the term *hypercube* broadly in this paper to include simple nodes like the NCUBE or more complex designs such as the Mark IIIfp. When we wish to single out machines like the NCUBE, we will use the term *homogeneous hypercube* while terming machines like the Mark IIIfp as a *hierarchical hypercube*.

Finally, we summarize many of the caveats by noting that a performance analysis in terms of simple parameters such as t_{comm}, t_{mem}, t_{calc} is usually accurate but the simplifications imply that the parameters are not universal but need to be adjusted by different, but usually modest and understandable factors for each application [9].

III: Domain Decomposition and Complex Systems

One can formulate concurrent computation as a mapping of a problem onto a computer [2, 7, 8]. We consider both the problem and the computer as *complex systems*; for our purposes, these can be considered as a set of, in general, dynamically interconnected entities. The performance of a particular implementation can be related to the structure of the systems describing the problem and computer [2, 3, 9]. In this paper, we are only considering large grain size concurrent computers i.e., each node has substantial memory. In this case, it is natural to consider the problem, or more precisely its underlying complex system, as being divided up into subdomains which we will call *grains*. At any one time, each node of the concurrent computer is responsible for a single grain. In this context, *domain decomposition* is the division of the problem, or typically its defining data domain, into appropriate grains. We can make this clearer by considering the map of the problem onto the computer in more detail. We can isolate four stages. The use of a vectoring or parallelizing computer corresponds to the map:

$$\textit{Problem} \rightarrow \textit{Algorithm} \rightarrow \textit{Code} \rightarrow \textit{Compiler Generated Decomposition} \rightarrow \textit{Concurrent Computer} \quad (1)$$

i.e., performing the map onto the concurrent computer between the last two stages.

We will consider domain decomposition corresponding to the map being generated by:

$$\textit{Problem} \rightarrow \textit{Algorithm} \rightarrow \textit{Domain Decomposition} \rightarrow \textit{Code} \rightarrow \textit{Concurrent Computer} \quad (2)$$

where one forms the basic grains not from the code as in (1) but from the basic algorithm or problem in (2). The advantage of (1) is that one directly uses existing software on concurrent machines whereas in (2) it is implied that one must generate code that describes individual grains. (1) is presently only practical on shared memory machines and indeed the ability to use this programming methodology is a key advantage of this architecture over distributed memory systems.

The hypercube and other distributed memory machines are traditionally programmed by domain decomposition as described above. This methodology has advantages of generality (it is potentially useable over a broad range of architectures) but it does require significantly more user involvement in the concurrency and software. In particular, there is no easy way to make use of existing sequential software and at Caltech, we have typically recoded our hypercube applications from scratch. As will become clear, we are interested in domain decomposition for the shared memory architecture, not only because it allows the porting of hypercube targeted programs but also because it may give near optimal performance for some problems on shared memory machines.

In a series of papers, we have developed a set of optimization methods, in particular, neural networks and simulated annealing, for choosing the optimal definition of the grains for a particular problem [7, 8, 10, 11, 12]. This work was in the context of a simple hypercube as the target machine. We will not discuss this research here but note that the discussion of the current paper lays the groundwork for extending the earlier work to give optimal domain decompositions for complicated hypercubes like the Mark IIIfp and some shared memory machines.

The optimal decomposition for a simple hypercube divides the problem into grains satisfying two criteria:

- The amount of communication between grains is minimized.
- Each node of the hypercube does the same amount of work; measured in terms of calculational complexity, each grain is the same "size".

We can now see qualitatively the possible importance of domain decomposition for hierarchical memory systems. The latter perform well as long as references to memory are largely local to the "cache" and do not require access to the slower main memory. This is clearly analogous to minimizing communication in a distributed memory machine. We will see that there are important quantitative differences in the "locality" constraints for hierarchical and distributed memories. However, the purpose of the current paper is to explore and explain their similarities and derive the ground rules for a uniform user interface which can be implemented well on either architecture.

The second constraint of the hypercube decomposition given above corresponds to load balancing the work of the nodes. We will not stress this here as it is not central to our discussion. We will choose as our examples *regular* problems for which load balancing is not a difficulty [2, 7]. In the future explicit realizations of the ideas presented here the constraints of load balancing may, in fact, be very important. In particular, an elegant dynamic load balancer for the hypercube appears to require a full multitasking environment with each node responsible for several (~ 10) processes or grains [13-15]. We will adopt a simpler point of view here with, in the case of the NCUBE and other hypercubes with simple nodes, only one process per node. This is sufficient for the problems discussed here and will be pedagogically clearer. In fact, the multitasking environment already introduces hierarchy into a simple hypercube environment as now one has different process to process communication speeds depending on whether or not the communicating processes lie in the same or different nodes. Thus the multitasking environment will tend to unify the ideas across architectures and we will include it in future discussions. In this paper, we are not attempting to discuss the detailed user environment and explicit software implementation but rather the functional structure of the software environment as "seen" by the machine. We will address the (very important) implementation issues elsewhere.

Let us focus our ideas by considering a specific problem of particle dynamics with a short-range interaction. An example is shown as a complex system in Fig. 6. Typically, the computation involves particles linked by a force and the number of such links measures the calculational complexity. Consider the underlying complex system as a graph whose nodes are the particles and nodes are linked if and only if the corresponding particles interact with each other. Then the calculation complexity is measured by the number of edges in the graph. Domain decomposition will divide the graph into grains (subgraphs) such that each grain has approximately equal numbers of edges and we minimize the number of edges that cross grain boundaries. When implemented on a homogeneous hypercube, the ratio f_C of communication to calculation is measured by the ratio of the number of edges crossing grain boundaries to the total inside a given grain. In many previous papers, we have shown that this leads to the result [2,3,7,9]

$$f_C = \frac{constant}{n_{grain}^{1/d}} \frac{t_{comm}}{t_{calc}} \tag{3}$$

Where n_{grain} is the number of entities (number of nodes of graph i.e., particles in our example) in each grain and the parameters t_{comm} and t_{calc} were introduced in Sec. II.

The application dependent *constant* in Eq. (3) is typically of order unity. The *connection dimension d* has been defined generally in Refs. [2] and [7] and coincides with the geometric dimension for short-range or nearest-neighbor problems.

In architectures where communication is serial with calculation such as all the initial (Caltech's Cosmic Cube and Mark II, INTEL iPSC, NCUBE) hypercubes, one aims for $f_C \leq 0.25$ which was obtained for the initial Caltech applications as long as

$$\frac{t_{comm}}{t_{calc}} \leq 3 \text{ ; } non\ overlapped \tag{4}$$

The goal $f_C \leq 0.25$, corresponds to a *speed-up* $S = \epsilon N_{proc}$ with efficiency ϵ given as

$$\epsilon = \frac{1}{1+f_C} \text{ ; } non\ overlapped \tag{5}$$

$$\geq 0.8 \text{ for } f_C \leq 0.25$$

This is a phenomenological result averaged over the values of n_{grain}, d, and *constant* seen in typical applications. In table 2, we give a current list of Caltech hypercube applications to indicate the problem areas from which our results have been obtained. We do not wish to discuss here the many issues underlying the validity of (3) but rather refer the reader to the detailed discussions in Refs. [2, 3, 7, 9]

In the case where communication is overlapped with calculation, one can afford an order of magnitude more message traffic with a typical goal of $f_C \leq 1.25$ or the less stringent constraint:

$$\frac{t_{comm}}{t_{calc}} \leq 15 \text{ ; } overlapped \tag{6}$$

with efficiency

$$\epsilon = \min(1, 1/f_C) \; ; \textit{overlapped} \tag{7}$$
$$\geq 0.8 \;\; \text{for} \; f_C \leq 1.25$$

We see that the difference between (6) and (4) partly explains why the Mark IIIfp and NCUBE can both give good performance even though the former has an order of magnitude larger value for t_{comm}/t_{calc}. As we see from (3) and is explored in detail in Ref. [16], the Mark IIIfp will also have the value of f_C lowered by the larger value of n_{grain} allowed by the larger memory of the Mark IIIfp. Explicitly for systems of dimension d=3, we see that $1/n_{grain}^{1/d}$ is decreased by a factor $(4/0.5)^{1/3} = 2$ in comparing the Mark IIIfp to the NCUBE.

Now return to the original particle dynamics example and consider its implementation on a variety of architectures. In the case of a *homogeneous hypercube* we have already described how we divide the particles into groupings and assign each grouping to an individual hypercube node. We have a number N_{grain} of grains equal to the number of processors N_{proc} in the concurrent machine. Using the notation of Sect. II, we also have the number of particles in each grain, $n_{grain} = n_{node}$ and a total number n_{total} of particles given by

$$n_{total} = N_{proc} \, n_{grain} \tag{8}$$

Now consider a hierarchical shared memory machine such as that pictured in Fig. 1(b). As explained earlier, we would naturally expect best performance if memory references were largely local to each "cache" and this will be achieved if one can assume that each "cache" contains a complete grain. However, there is a crucial complication that in general, one can not expect that the full problem can be held in the "caches". Some fraction of it can be in "cache" with the remainder "waiting" in the large shared memory. In contrast, it is reasonable to assume that the homogeneous hypercube will be able to contain the full problem in the aggregate of it's nodes' memories. In general, we will define a *grain* so that it can be contained in the "cache" or lowest level of the memory hierarchy under consideration; this *grain* can contain n_{grain} members (nodes of graph). We can now **define** an effective or virtual number N_{grain} of processors so that the total system can be contained in N_{grain} nodes. Thus

$$n_{total} = N_{grain} n_{grain} \tag{9}$$

In general, N_{grain} is larger than the real number N_{proc} of nodes and we can assume that the grains have been defined so that the ratio $r_{virtual} = N_{grain}/N_{proc}$ is an integer.

We can now summarize three relevant circumstances:

Homogeneous Hypercube

$$n_{node} = n_{grain} \; \text{entities fit in a single node} \tag{10a}$$
$$N_{grain} = N_{proc}$$
$$r_{virtual} = 1$$

Hierarchical Shared Memory Machine

$$n_{grain} \; \text{entities fit in a single "cache"} \tag{10b}$$
$$N_{grain} = n_{total}/n_{grain}$$
$$r_{virtual} \geq 1$$
$$(r_{virtual}-1)N_{grain} \quad \textit{processes "waiting" for loading into "cache"}$$

Hierarchical Hypercube

$$n_{grain} \; \text{entities fit in a single "cache"} \tag{10c}$$
$$N_{grain} = n_{total}/n_{grain}$$
$$r_{virtual} \geq 1 \; \text{grains in each node}$$
$$n_{node} = r_{virtual} \, n_{grain} \; \text{entities fit in a single node}$$

The computer system is to be viewed as having N_{grain} virtual nodes which, except in the case of the homogeneous hypercube, is typically larger than the number of physical processors N_{proc}. For small problems, one could find that $r_{virtual}$ was unity even for the hierarchical designs. In this case, hierarchical shared memory or distributed memory architectures can be considered by the same performance analysis given earlier in Eqs. (3 to 7) for homogeneous hypercubes. In this case, one can substitute t_{mem} for t_{comm} on these equations when considering the shared memory case. However, it is the purpose of this paper to consider the more general and interesting case $r_{virtual} > 1$.

Consider an example of the consequence of these ideas comparing the 1024 node NCUBE, each node having 0.5 megabytes of memory with the 128 node Mark IIIfp, each node having 4 megabytes of memory. Normally one considers the latter machine as having larger grain size but consider the use of these machines to solve a problem requiring the full 512 megabytes available on each machine. The NCUBE has 1024 grains each of 0.5 megabyte size but the Mark IIIfp with $r_{virtual} = 32$ has 4096 grains each of 0.125 megabytes! The addition of the floating point unit has, in fact, given the Mark IIIfp a smaller grain size and required one to decompose the problem into more and not less (than for the NCUBE) grains. Note that if the total problem size had been 128 megabytes, then both machines would be used with 1024 grains, each of 128 kilobytes.

Let us consider some of the issues from a more fundamental, or perhaps philosophical, point of view. In the particle dynamics example, we have a spatially distributed system which nature evolves simultaneously in time. On a homogeneous hypercube, the spatial complex system corresponding to the problem is directly mapped onto a spatially distributed memory of the hypercube. Then as in nature, each node evolves different parts of the spatial system simultaneously. In this case, we have a rather clean association.

$$\begin{gathered}\textit{Space in Problem} \rightarrow \textit{Space in Homogeneous Hypercube} \\ \textit{Time in Problem} \rightarrow \textit{Elapsed Time in Computer Execution}\end{gathered} \tag{11a}$$

This association is particularly precise in the case when each node of the computer holds a single particle. In the normal case, where each grain has several particles, then we have an intermediate situation when the spatial system within each node is evolved sequentially in time by the node; i.e., we have partially mapped the spatial extent of the system into a temporal extent in the computer implementation.

To extend the above picture, we generalize the concept of a complex system to include both the spatial and temporal aspects of a problem. This is illustrated in Figs. 7 and 8, and in the particle dynamics case, we would consider the extended complex system as the physical system or a graph generated by, for instance, a space-time region defined by some condition such as:

$$|\underline{x} - \underline{x}_0| \leq r \tag{11b}$$

In Fig. 7, we show this for one spatial dimension and a regular lattice. In our previous work [2,7], we have only needed to consider the spatial aspects of complex systems because of the rather clean correspondence of space and time, expressed in Eq. (11a), between the computer and problem present for the homogeneous hypercube.

Returning to Fig. 1, we now see that the sequential computer shown in Fig. 1(a) corresponds to:

$$\begin{matrix}\textit{Space} \text{ and } \textit{Time} \\ \textit{in Problem}\end{matrix} \rightarrow \begin{matrix}\textit{Elapsed Time in} \\ \textit{Sequential Computer}\end{matrix} \tag{11c}$$

Typically one cycles through individual particles and processes them sequentially. If we now consider the hierarchical memory systems 1(b) and 1(c), we find the intermediate situation:

$$\begin{gathered}\textit{Space in Problem} \rightarrow \begin{matrix}\textit{Space} \text{ and } \textit{Time} \\ \textit{in Heirarchical Memory Machine}\end{matrix} \\ \textit{Time in Problem} \rightarrow \textit{Time in Computer}\end{gathered} \tag{11d}$$

(11d) would reduce to (11a) in the degenerate case where the problem can be contained in the "caches" - summed over nodes.

Above we have pointed out that varying degrees of parallelism correspond to mapping spatial aspects of the problem into different mixes of space and time on the computer system. Fig. 8 illustrates an important technical reason to introduce a complex system extended in space and time. For a homogeneous hypercube, communication costs are related to graph edges crossing spatial boundaries of the system. For the "cache" based architectures in Fig. 1(b) and 1(c) we will need to load the initial value of the system at the time t_0 and store back in main memory after evolution to time t_1. We see that this load and store correspond to the temporal boundaries of the system. t_{mem} and t_{comm} correspond respectively to the costs associated with temporal and spatial limitation of the system.

Figure 8 makes it clear why we may need to disable "write through" on the Mark IIIfp and machines with comparable architectures. We will find cases where we need significant (t_1 many time steps larger than t_0) time extent to minimize "edge" effects corresponding to the boundaries formed by cache load and store. "Write through" typically implies that the system is stored to main memory after every time step.

We will now quantify this general picture with several examples in the next section. We will find similarities and differences between the temporal (t_{mem}) and spatial (t_{comm}) aspects of the problems. We will only summarize the results with the intention of providing a detailed analysis elsewhere.

IV: Examples

IVA: The Long Range Force or Complete Interconnect

This case is interesting because we will find low overheads from both the spatial and temporal boundaries in Fig. 8 with these two overheads having the same dependence on grain size n_{grain}. The generic problem, that we will consider, is the time evolution of a set of particles interacting with a long-range force; we use the brute force algorithm and not the faster FFT [2] or clustering method [17]. We calculate the force on each particle by summing the contribution of all others [2]. We now consider first homogeneous hypercubes and then hierarchical memory computers.

a) Homogeneous Hypercube

One decomposes the problem with an equal number n_{grain} of particles in each node [2]. Another set (identical copy) of the particles travels completely around the cube (which can be mapped into a ring) updating the mutual interaction as the travelers pass through the node containing the fixed particles. There is some care needed to ensure Newton's law of action and reaction is exploited and each interaction is only calculated once [2]. However, the performance analysis is straightforward and if at each step one transports M particles

$$\textit{Calculation Time } T_{calc} \sim \frac{M\, n_{grain}}{2}\, t_{calc} \tag{12a}$$

$$\textit{Communication Time } T_{comm} \sim M\, t_{comm} \tag{12b}$$

and the overhead f_C introduced in Sec. III, Eq. (3), is given by:

$$f_C \sim \frac{1}{n_{grain}} \frac{t_{comm}}{t_{calc}} \tag{12c}$$

independent of M.

b) Hierarchical Machines

Now M is the total number of particles cycled from main memory through the "cache". Each grain takes time

$$T^{(1)}_{cache} = n_{grain}\, t_{mem} \tag{13a}$$

to load and store. The travelling particles must be read from main memory and stored back with their force updated. This takes time:

$$T^{(2)}_{cache} = M\, t_{mem} \tag{13b}$$

These numbers should be compared with the identical values (12a) and (12b) for calculation and communication in the case of the hierarchical hypercube. We see that good performance requires that M be chosen large ($\geq n_{grain}$) but this is algorithmically possible and natural. Hence for this case, the calculation time (12a) is much larger than the "cache" overhead and one finds for $M \geq n_{grain}$ that:

$$f_H \sim \frac{1}{n_{grain}} \frac{t_{mem}}{t_{calc}} \tag{13c}$$

is the hierarchical memory access overhead to be compared with the communication overhead f_C in (12c). The latter needs to be added to f_H for the hierarchical hypercube which has both forms of overhead.

For the hierarchical shared memory machine, the natural value of M is n_{total} and for the hierarchical hypercube the smaller value $M = n_{node} = r_{virtual}\, n_{grain}$; in each case Eq. (13c) is valid.

We do find that care is needed to reduce f_H. One must cycle all particles through the "cache", i.e., choose a large value of M, in between reloading the "cache". Further, one needs to update each particle in the cache in a fashion that one only writes out the results after all M particles are considered. In the case of the Mark IIIfp, this implies that one disables the cache "write-through" feature until all M particles have travelled through.

Comparing Eqs. (12c) and (13c) with Eq. (3), we see that both exhibit our standard form with *connection dimension* $d = 1$ independent of the underlying topological structure of the space.

IVB: Two Dimensional Finite Difference

We will consider a finite difference solution to Poisson's equation, $\nabla^2 \phi = 4\pi\rho$, solved by an iterative (relaxation) method on a regular two dimensional mesh. This problem is simple but the discussion generalizes to other short-range problems including wave equations, image processing, particle dynamics, and Monte Carlo. The choice of two dimensions is not essential and at the end we will generalize to higher dimensions. We will use the simplest stencil where the value at the next iteration only depends on the original value and its four neighbors at the current step. This is shown in Fig. 9(a); as discussed in Ref. [2] and later in this paper, more complicated stencils such as that in 9(b), do **not** alter one's conclusions. We are not underestimating the difficult implementation issues in realistic problems, but we believe that our simple case embodies the essential issues for the performance estimate.

(a) Homogeneous Hypercube

One performs a simple two dimensional decomposition with each node containing a $\sqrt{n_{grain}} \times \sqrt{n_{grain}}$ submesh. A typical iteration takes a calculation time for each iteration of

$$T_{calc} = 5\, n_{grain}\, t_{calc} \tag{14a}$$

and the communication is associated with the edges of the region in each processor and takes time:

$$T_{comm} = 4\sqrt{n_{grain}}\, t_{comm} \tag{14b}$$

and one finds a communication overhead

$$f_C \sim \frac{1}{n_{grain}^{1/2}} \frac{t_{comm}}{t_{calc}} \tag{14c}$$

with the form of Eq. (3) and the connection dimension d equal to the topological dimension.

(b) Hierarchical Machines

As in the previous example, Eq. (13a), one takes time for load and store of:

$$T_{cache} = n_{grain}\, t_{mem} \tag{14d}$$

The grain is stored in the "cache" and one also needs to load the neighboring points and in analogy to (14b), one finds a communication cost.

$$T_{comm} = 4\sqrt{n_{grain}}\, (1/2\, t_{mem} \text{ or } t_{comm}) \tag{14e}$$

where the communication may be from a process in the same or neighboring node; the corresponding communication time is either $1/2\, t_{mem}$ or t_{comm}. In fact, in terms of the ratio $r_{virtual}$ introduced in Sec. III, one can rewrite Eq. (14e) as

$$T_{comm} = 4\sqrt{n_{grain}}\, \frac{(1/2 t_{mem}\, (\sqrt{r_{virtual}} - 1) + t_{comm})}{\sqrt{r_{virtual}}} \tag{14e^I}$$

$$\sim 2\sqrt{n_{grain}}\, t_{mem} \tag{14e^{II}}$$

in the interesting case with large values of $r_{virtual}$.

If we compare (14a) with the overheads (14d) and (14e^{II}), we see that cache loading dominates (for large n_{grain}) and

$$f_H \sim \frac{1}{5} \frac{t_{mem}}{t_{calc}} \tag{14f}$$

and unlike our previous results summarized in Eq. (3), f_H does not decrease as one increases n_{grain}. The reason for this is clear from Fig. 8 and the discussion at the end of Sec. IV. We have a space-time complex system stored in our cache, with as shown in Fig. 10(a), a single iteration (time) count as its temporal extent. We need to reduce the edge/area ratio in the temporal direction. This can be achieved by updating the region stored in "cache" by more than one time step. This is a nontrivial issue because it now implies a different decomposition than that usually used for the homogeneous hypercube. In Sec. IVA, we saw a somewhat similar situation where the hierarchical implementation required M large whereas $M \simeq 1$ was sufficient for the homogeneous case. Now the hierarchical case has required that each grain update for several, say M, iterations or time cycles.

Two possibilities are shown in Figs. (10b) and (10c) for the case of one spatial dimension. If the wave equation was the underlying problem, Fig. (10b) separates regions by the characteristics of the equation. We see that Fig. (10b) still corresponds to short range (spatial) communication. T_{cache} is unchanged. T_{calc} and T_{comm} in Eqs. (14a, $14e^{II}$) are increased by a factor equal to the number M, of iterations. Optimal is the choice of equal extents in the space and time dimensions, $M = n_{grain}{}^{1/d}$, when we get back the result

$$f_{C,H} \sim \frac{1}{n_{grain}^{1/d}} (t_{mem} \text{ or } t_{comm})/t_{calc} \tag{14g}$$

for a system of dimension d.

A simpler alternative, shown in Fig. (10c), is easier to implement. We chose cylinders with sides parallel to the time axis for our space-time complex systems. These have an interesting property illustrated precisely in Fig. 7 of cutting more edges with the temporal planes. In fact the number of edges cut is proportional to M^2 where M is the number of temporal steps. This leads to communication costs, appearing as additional calculations, proportional to M^2. We find in with the dimension $d = 2$,

$$\begin{aligned} T_{calc} &\propto n_{grain}\, M \\ T_{comm} &\propto n_{grain}{}^{1-1/d}\, M^2 \\ T_{cache} &\propto n_{grain} \end{aligned} \tag{14h}$$

The ration $f_C + f_H$ is proportional to $(\frac{1}{M} + \frac{M}{n_{grain}^{1/d}})$ and is minimized for $M \sim n_{grain}^{1/2d}$

and we find the amusing total overhead

$$f_C + f_H \sim \frac{1}{n_{grain}^{1/2d}} \frac{(t_{mem} \text{ or } t_{comm})}{t_{calc}} \tag{14i}$$

Although the dependence on the grain size is slower than for Eq. (14g), this overhead does decrease as the grain size increases.

IVC: Matrix Multiplication

We now consider a simple matrix algorithm which is not the most important but exhibits interesting contrasts with the previous two cases. Take the multiplication of large full matrices

$$C = A \cdot B \tag{15}$$

where each matrix is $\sqrt{n_{total}} \times \sqrt{n_{total}}$. The basic ideas in this section are the same as in Refs. [2, 18, 23, 31].

(a) Homogeneous Hypercube

Here one considers a simple decomposition dividing each matrix into N_{proc} square subblocks each of size $\sqrt{n_{grain}} \times \sqrt{n_{grain}}$ where the dimensions are given by $\sqrt{n_{grain}} = \sqrt{n_{total}} \,/\, \sqrt{N_{proc}}$. As discussed in Ref. [18], there is an efficient algorithm in which the subblocks of A and B are respectively broadcast (along a subcube) and shifted along nearest neighbor links of the hypercube. The basic calculation at each stage involves subblock multiplication with

$$T_{calc} \propto n_{grain}^{3/2}\, t_{calc} \tag{16a}$$

and overhead

$$T_{comm} \propto n_{grain}\, t_{comm} \tag{16b}$$

One obtains a conventional overhead formula

$$f_C \sim \frac{1}{n_{grain}^{1/2}} \frac{t_{comm}}{t_{calc}} \tag{16c}$$

corresponding to connection dimension $d = 2$.

(b) Hierarchical Machines

The interesting feature now is that one does not need to modify the algorithm at all because the cache loading time is

$$T_{cache} \propto n_{grain}\, t_{mem} \tag{16d}$$

and so we obtain, with an unchanged algorithm

$$f_H \sim \frac{1}{n_{grain}^{1/2}} \frac{t_{mem}}{t_{calc}} \tag{16e}$$

The constant in (16e) can be affected by the exact algorithm used as it depends on the number of blocks read in between cache stores; this is analogous to the M dependence in Sec. IVA.

Let us compare this case with that of the finite difference algorithm in Sec. IVB. As shown in Eqs. (14c) and (16c), both have similar overheads in the case of the hypercube. However, the matrix multiplication naturally retains this result for hierarchical machines while for IVB, we needed to change the algorithm to reduce the memory overhead f_H. We can understand the issue by comparing Eqs. (14a) and (16a). In the finite difference case, we have a small communication overhead because we are transmitting a few ($\propto n_{grain}^{1/2}$) variables but doing little (0(1) per variable) work with them. In matrix multiplication, we communicate more variables ($\propto n_{grain}$) but do a lot of work ($\propto n_{grain}^{1/2}$) for each transmitted variable. The algorithms obtain the same result for f_C but for different reasons. In fact the matrix multiplication algorithm "succeeds" on the hierarchical memory machines for the same reason as the long range problem. Both do a lot of work per fundamental entity; in IVA, the work is proportional to n_{grain} and in IVC, proportional to $n_{grain}^{1/2}$. This is the origin of the different connection dimensions shown in Eqs. (12c) and (16c).

IVD: LU Decomposition

Now let us consider, a more important matrix algorithm; namely LU decomposition of full matrices or the related problem of matrix inversion. This has been studied in detail on the hypercube in Refs. [2, 19, 20-24] and we will find that the issues are more similar to those of Sec. IVB than those of IVC. We will not consider pivoting here; this is an interesting and tricky complication which leaves the results below qualitatively unchanged [2, 23]. We note that the issues discussed here and in Sec. IVC are closely related to the important work on the "Level-3 BLAS" discussed by Dongarra at this conference [25].

(a) Homogeneous Hypercube

We use the same square subblock decomposition introduced in IVC. At a typical stage of LU decomposition, one is subtracting the row containing the eliminated variable from all other rows. There is a separate multiplier for each row calculated from the column containing the eliminated variable. This is illustrated in Fig. 11 and one sees a situation rather similar to that of Sec. IVB.

Namely in a typical stage, one has a calculation

$$a_{ij} \rightarrow a_{ij} - c_i\, r_j \tag{17}$$

taking time

$$T_{calc} = 2n_{grain}\, t_{calc} \tag{18a}$$

and a communication

$$T_{comm} = 2\sqrt{n_{grain}}\, t_{comm} \tag{18b}$$

with our standard form

$$f_C \sim \frac{1}{\sqrt{n_{grain}}} \frac{t_{comm}}{t_{calc}} \tag{18c}$$

Actually Eqs. (18a, b) ignore certain overheads connected with the calculation of the c_i and r_j as well as load imbalance overhead and the effect of the reduction in value of n_{grain} as one eliminates rows and columns. These effects alter the *constant* in Eq. (3) but leave the form (18c) unchanged.

(b) Hierarchical Memory

We are faced with the same problem as in Sec. IVB, with a "cache" load and store time which has the same n_{grain} dependence as the calculation in Eq. (18a). The solution is similar to that of IVB and involves eliminating several, say M, rows (and columns) at the same time. One can show that the M values of r_i and c_j can be calculated in a separate concurrent step which itself can be efficiently implemented. Given this, one will find a simple block algorithm in which the times in Eqs. (18a, b) are both increased by a factor M whereas the "cache" loading is still given by a time $t_{mem}\, n_{grain}$. Choosing $M \propto n_{grain}^{1/2}$, one will find overheads f_H of comparable form to f_C and a total overhead that is proportional to $n_{grain}^{-1/2}$ as in the original homogeneous hypercube case.

IVE: Fast Fourier Transform (FFT)

Originally we implemented the FFT in a natural fashion on the hypercube [2] using local communication in the hypercube topology where necessary. It is well known that the hypercube architecture exactly matches the pattern of the binary FFT. However, the discussion here will be easier using a formulation due to Furmanski [2, 33] which ingeniously lumps all the communication into a single stage and avoids any communication during the calculation steps.

(a) Homogeneous Hypercube

We will consider a one dimensional FFT and we can label the variables by a binary digit B illustrated in Fig. 12. This example shows the case $n_{total} = 2^{14}$ and $N_{proc} = 2^5$. Five digits g_{0-4} of B are used to label processor number and the remaining nine digits l_{0-8} the position within the local memory of the node. The FFT algorithms systematically alters the variable starting at the highest digit of B (l_0 in Fig. 12(a)) and ending at the lowest (g_4 in Fig. 12a). There are log n_{total} steps each of which takes calculation time n_{total}.

Furmanski's algorithm does the first nine steps, each altering one digit, as labelled in Fig. 12(a); then it transforms the data to the situation of Fig. 12(b) where the lower order bits are now stored locally. This is performed by a communication primitive called *index* in Ref. [33]. After the transformation the remaining five digits are processed locally in each node. The calculation is load balanced at each stage and takes total time

$$T_{calc} \sim \frac{1}{N_{proc}} n_{total} \log(n_{total})\, t_{calc} \tag{19a}$$

$$= n_{node} \log(n_{total})\, t_{calc}$$

while the communication primitive *index* takes time

$$T_{comm} \sim n_{node} \log(N_{proc})\, t_{comm} \tag{19b}$$

In this formula the log N_{proc} dependence just represents the typical distance (1/2 log N_{proc}) between points in a hypercube topology. This communication time could be reduced on machines with automatic routing. One finds an overhead

$$f_C \sim \frac{\log(N_{proc})}{\log(n_{total})} \frac{t_{comm}}{t_{calc}} \tag{19c}$$

which corresponds to infinite connection dimension in Eq.(3).

(b) Hierarchical Memory

The discussion of hierarchical memory machines is now straightforward. We will use the same idea of calculating a certain number of bits in B at a time. Clearly we can perform a number of steps corresponding to at most log (n_{grain}) bits at any one time and we find a set of calculations each taking time

$$T_{calc}^{elementary} \sim n_{grain} \log(n_{grain})\, t_{calc} \tag{19d}$$

and a cache load and store time of

$$T_{cache} \sim n_{grain}\, t_{mem} \tag{19e}$$

Thus, we perform log (n_{grain}) steps for each cache loading and obtain an overhead

$$f_H \propto \frac{1}{\log(n_{grain})} \frac{t_{mem}}{t_{calc}} \tag{19f}$$

We have found a slightly different overhead formula from the original case, Eq. (19c), but fortunately we have been able to use the same decomposition to deal with distributed and hierarchical memories. This equivalence would not have been direct if one had used the traditional hypercube FFT approach.

IVF: Neural Networks

We have a growing interest at Caltech in using the hypercube to model both biological and applied (theoretical) neural networks. In general, distributed memory machines are well suited to modelling nature's own distributed memory "computers". It turns out that the optimal decomposition of the neural network is sensitive to the structure of the interconnection between the neurons [26]. Some cases have a rather full interconnect and the hypercube decomposition resembles the long range force algorithm described in Sec. IVA; other cases have a dominant short range structure and the analysis is then similar to that in Sec. IVB. The issues in neural network simulation are of course related to those in other circuit simulations.

We can discuss a recent explicit implementation on the hypercube of a model of the piriform cortex [27]. This corresponds to a nearly full interconnect but an interesting subtlety that changes the analysis from that in IVA. One is calculating the effect $G_{i \to j}$ of neuron i on j. A symmetry of the propagation Green's function ($G_{i \to j}$) means that it is optimal to associate the calculation of $G_{i \to j}$ with i and not the target neuron j. In the particle dynamics case in IVA we made the opposite choice of shipping the information to the target particle and then doing the calculation. The calculation of all the Green's functions ($G_{i \to j}$) is local to each grain and involves no communication. The latter is needed as one forms the global sums

$$\sum_i G_{i \to j} \text{ for each } j \tag{20}$$

Thus, the problem is reduced to the calculation of a large number of sums. The components of the sum (i) and the storage of the final result (j) are both uniformly distributed throughout the hypercube. This problem was solved in Ref. [33] in terms of a hypercube communication primitive called *fold*. It is straightforward to implement *fold* on a hierarchical memory; the issues are similar to those in Sec. IVA.

We see that the neural network decomposition can be unified over the various architectures as long as it is implemented in terms of the basic primitives *fold* which is then separately implemented in an optimal fashion on each architecture.

V: Conclusions

We have considered the issues involved in a unified approach to distributed and hierarchical memory machines. Our techniques also allow optimal implementations of message passing on shared memory parallel processors. We have discussed the general approach in Sec. III and the prettiest result is inclusion of both space and time in the description of complex systems. In Sec. IV, we worked through six problem classes and were able to show decompositions that effected our desired unifications. In all cases, the overheads were small as long as the "cache" size n_{grain} was big enough and that the communication performance of the computer, measured by t_{mem}/t_{calc}, t_{comm}/t_{calc} was good enough. Another way of summarizing our results is to say that problems are associated with data domains. Homogeneous machines just need the decomposition of this domain; this is often a spatial decomposition. Hierarchical computers also need one to consider the label (e.g., DO loop index) of the processing of elements in the domain. These machines require both spatial (data domain) decomposition and that associated with this new label; this label often corresponds to time i.e., hierarchical machines need "space-time" and not just "spatial" decompositions. Our results contain the essential information to make the necessary tradeoffs between memory/communication bandwidth and "cache" size. We note that technology improvements should permit "cache" sizes to increase in the future. This will increase the applicability of our techniques.

In future papers, we will present details of the ideas sketched in IV and describe the implementation issues in providing the desired portable high performance environments.

We would also point out that the basic ideas presented here are the message passing version of principles that have been used for some time in the field of vectorizing and decomposing compilers [28, 29, 30]. The manipulation of DO loops described by Gannon at this conference are similar in spirit to the physical transformations suggested here.

Acknowledgements

I would like to thank the many members of the Caltech Concurrent Computation Program (C^3P) on whose work many of the results discussed here are based. I hope they are content with implied reference in Table 2. The ideas presented here were first developed during a study of the use of the RP3 and the porting of hypercube applications to it. I would like to thank IBM for their support of this work and in particular, A. Frey, S. Harvey and A. Norton. The support of the Electronic Systems Division of the U. S. Air Force has allowed us to extend our basic hypercube research to a variety of different architectures. Our ELXSI implementations were funded by SANDIA. I would thank the organizers of ICS '87 for an excellent conference and the honor of the invitation to talk.

References

1. C^3P-394: "Caltech Supercomputer Initiative: A Commitment to Leadership and Excellence," A. H. Barr, R. W. Clayton, A. Kuppermann, L. G. Leal, A. Leonard, T. A. Prince, December 29, 1986.

2. G. Fox, M. Johnson, G. Lyzenga, S. Otto, J. Salmon, D. Walker, "Solving Problems on Concurrent Processors," April 1986. To be published by Prentice Hall, 1987.

3 C^3P-391: "The Hypercube as a Supercomputer," G. C. Fox, January 7, 1987. Published by the International Supercomputing Institute, Inc., St. Petersburg, Florida, May 1987.

4. C^3P-409: "Concurrent Supercomputer Initiative at Caltech," G. C. Fox, January 31, 1987. Published by the International Supercomputing Institute, Inc., St. Petersburg, Florida, May 1987.

5. "Portable Programs for Parallel Processors," J. Boyle, R. Butler, T. Disz, B. Glickfield, E. Lusk, R. Overbeek, J. Patterson, R. Stevens, published by Holt, Rinehart, and Winston, Inc., N. Y. 1987.

6. C^3P-435: "The Concurrent Supercomputing Initiative at Caltech," G. Fox and co-authors.

7. C^3P-255: "Concurrent Computation and the Theory of Complex Systems," G. C. Fox, S. W. Otto, March 3, 1986. Published in proceedings of 1985 Hypercube Conference at Knoxville, August 1985, edited by M. Heath and published by SIAM.

8. C^3P-214: "Monte Carlo Physics on a Concurrent Processor," G. C. Fox, S. W. Otto, E. A. Umland, Nov 6, 1985, invited talk by G. Fox at the "Frontiers of Quantum Monte Carlo" Conference at Los Alamos, September 6, 1985, and published in special issue of Journal of Statistical Physics, Vol. 43,1209, Plenum Press, 1986.

9 C^3P-161: "The Performance of the Caltech Hypercube in Scientific Calculations: A Preliminary Analysis:" G. Fox, April 1985, Invited Talk at Symposium in Austin, Texas, March 18-20, 1985, and published in "Supercomputers-Algorithms, Architectures and Scientific Computation," edited by F. A. Matsen and T. Tajima, University of Texas Press, Austin, 1985.

10. C^3P-292: "A Preprocessor for Irregular Finite Element Problems," CALT-68-1405, J. W. Flower, S. W. Otto, M. C. Salama, June 1986.

11. C^3P-363: "Load Balancing by a Neural Network," CALT-68-1408, G. C. Fox, W. Furmanski, September 1986.

12. C^3P-327B: "A Graphical Approach to Load Balancing and Sparse Matrix Vector Multiplication on the Hypercube," G. C. Fox, December 5, 1986. To be published in proceedings of IMA Workshop, Minnesota, November 1986.

13. C^3P-385: "A Review of Automatic Load Balancing and Decomposition Methods for the Hypercube," G. C. Fox, November 1986. To be published in proceedings of IMA Workshop, Minnesota, November 1986.

14. C^3P-328: "The Implementation of a Dynamic Load Balancer," G. Fox, A. Kolawa, R. Williams, November 1986, published in proceedings of 1986 Knoxville Hypercube Conference, edited by M. Heath and published by SIAM as "Hypercube Multiprocessors 1987."

15. C^3P-427: "A MOOSE Status Report," J. Salmon, S. Callahan, J. Flower, A. Kolawa, May 6, 1987.

16. C^3P-390: "An Evaluation of Mark III and NCUBE Supercomputers," G. C. Fox, December 9, 1986.

17. J. Barnes, P. Hut, "A Hierarchical O(NlogN) Force-Calculation Algorithm," Nature 324,446 (1986).

18. C^3P-206: "Matrix Algorithms on the Hypercube I: Matrix Multiplication," G. Fox, A. J. G. Hey, S. Otto, October 1985, published in Parallel Computing, 4, 17 (1987).

19. C^3P-97: "Square Matrix Decompositions: Symmetric , Local, Scattered," G. Fox, August 15, 1984, unpublished.

20. C^3P-99: "LU Decomposition for Banded Matrices," G. C. Fox, August 15, 1984, unpublished.

21. C^3P-347: "Gauss Jordan Matrix Inversion with Pivoting on the Hypercube," P. Hipes, A. Kuppermann, August 8, 1986.

22. C^3P-348: "A Banded Matrix LU Decomposition on the Hypercube," T. Aldcroft, A. Cisneros, G. Fox, W. Furmanski, D. Walker, paper in preparation.

23. C^3P-386: "Matrix," G. C. Fox and W. Furmanski, paper in preparation.

24. G. A. Geist, M. T. Heath "Matrix Factorization on a Hypercube Multiprocessor;" C. Moler "Matrix Computation on Distributed Memory Multiprocessor." Both these articles are contained in "Hypercube Multiprocessors, 1986", edited by M. T. Heath, SIAM, 1986.

25. J. Dongarra, Invited talk at 1987 International Conference on Supercomputing, Athens, June 8-12, 1987.

26. C^3P-405: "Hypercube Communication for Neural Network Algorithms," G. C. Fox, W. Furmanski, paper in preparation.

27. C^3P-404: "Piriform (Olfactory) Cortex Model on the Hypercube," J. M. Bower, M. E. Nelson, M. A. Wilson, G. C. Fox, W. Furmanski, February 1987.

28. D. Gannon, Invited talk at 1987 International Conference on Supercomputing, Athens, June 8-12, 1987.

29. K. Kennedy, Invited talk at 1987 International Conference on Supercomputing, Athens, June 8-12, 1987.

30. A. Sameh, "Numerical Algorithms on the Cedar System," Second SIAM Conference on Parallel Processing, Norfolk, Virginia, November 1985.

31. W. Jalby and U. Meier, "Optimizing Matrix Operations on a Parallel Multiprocessor with a Hierarchical Memory System," CSRD-555, University of Illinois report, 1986.

32. D. J. Kuck, E. S. Davidson, D. H. Lawrie, A. H. Sameh, "Parallel Supercomputing Today and the Cedar

Approach," *Science* **231**, 967 (1986).

33. C^3P-314: "Optimal Communication Algorithms on the Hypercube," G. C. Fox, W. Furmanski, July 8, 1986; "Communication Algorithms for Regular Convolutions on the Hypercube," G. C. Fox, W. Furmanski, September 1, 1986, published in proceedings of 1986 Knoxville Hypercube Conference, edited by M. Heath and published by SIAM as "Hypercube Multiprocessors, 1987."

Table 1: Hardware Parameters of Some Concurrent Supercomputers

	~ optimal t_{calc}	t_{comm}	$\frac{t_{comm}}{t_{calc}}$	Main Memory Size M Byte	t_{mem}	$\frac{t_{mem}}{t_{calc}}$	"Cache" Size M Byte
NCUBE Hypercube	10 μs	13 μs	1.3	0.5	-	-	-
Mark IIIfp	0.1 μs	2.5 μs *	25	4	1.5	16	0.13

*Operation concurrent with calculation

Table 2: Some Hypercube Implementations at Caltech

General Field	Associated Scientists	Topic
Applied Math & Computer Science	A. Barr J. Goldsmith (JPL)	Computer Graphics
	B. Beckman (JPL) D. Jefferson (UCLA)	Time Warp Event Driven Simulation
	M. Buehler (JPL)	Computer Aided Design
	G. Fox	Matrix Algorithms Load Balancing Algorithms Optimization Computer Chess
	H. Keller P. Saffman	Parallel Shooting Multigrid Adaptive Meshes
	C. Seitz	Mathematics and Logic Computer Aided Design
Biology	J. Bower J. Hopfield C. Koch	Modelling of Cortex and Applied Neural Networks
Chemistry and Chemical Engineering	J. Brady	Flow of Porous Media
	W. Goddard	Protein Dynamics
	A. Kuppermann	Chemical Reaction Dynamics
Engineering	N. Corngold	Turbulence (strange attractors)
	R. Gould P. Liewer (JPL)	Plasma Physics (PIC)
	J. Hall	Finite Element Analysis of Earthquake Engineering
	W. Johnson	Condensed Matter Simulations for Material Science

	A. Leonard B. Sturtevant	Fluid Turbulence in Computational Aerodynamics
	R. McEliece E. Posner F. Pollara (JPL)	Convolution Decoding
	J. Solomon (JPL)	Image Processing
Geophysics	R. Clayton	Seismic Waves Tomography
	B. Hager	Geodynamics
	T. Tanimoto	Normal Modes of Earth
Physics	R. Blandford D. Meier (JPL)	Fluid Jets in Astrophysics
	M. Cross	Condensed Matter Two Dimensional Melting
	G. Fox	High Energy Physics Lattice Gauge Theory
	S. Koonin	Nuclear Matter
	A. Readhead T. Prince	Astronomical Data Analysis
	T. Tombrello	Granular Physics Molecular Dynamics

Figure Captions

Fig. 1. Block diagram of the three machine architectures considered in this paper. We allow either a hardware controlled cache or user local memory to be the lowest level of the memory hierarchy. We ignore the important issues concerning the network connecting the global memory in (b) to the local "cache" and CPU's of the shared memory architecture.

Fig. 2. Block Diagrams of the NCUBE and Mark IIIfp hypercube nodes. We do not show a 68020/68882 based applications controller in (b) as it is irrelevant for this paper. The WEITEK XL unit is a complete computer.

Fig. 3. 64 node NCUBE board and packaging into a 1024 node system

Fig. 4. The two printed circuit boards making up the Mark IIIfp node. The WEITEK board is functional but will be cleaned up for the production unit.

(a) Main board with 4 megabytes of memory and two 68020's.

Fig. 4. The two printed circuit boards making up the Mark IIIfp node. The WEITEK board is functional but will be cleaned up for the production unit.

(b) Floating Point coprocessor built around WEITEK XL chip set.

Fig. 5. Definitions of the three hardware parameters t_{calc}, t_{mem}, and t_{calc} discussed in Sec. II.

Fig 6. The complex system corresponding to a short range force particle dynamics problem with its decomposition into four grains.

Fig. 7. A complex system in space and time that corresponds to a regular nearest neighbor problem in one spatial dimension; the finite difference solution of $\frac{\partial^2\psi}{\partial x^2} = c\frac{\partial^2\psi}{\partial t^2}$ would lead to such a complex system.

Fig. 8. The boundaries of a space-time complex system of the type illustrated in Fig. 7. Edges of the graph crossed by spatial boundaries correspond to messages with neighboring systems. Those crossed by temporal boundaries corresponding to the loading and ejection of the grain to and from cache and main memory.

Fig. 9. Two stencils for the solution of Poisson's equation in two dimensions.

Fig. 10. Three decompositions in space and time of the one dimensional wave equation discussed in the text of Sec. IVB.

Fig. 11. A typical step in LU decomposition discussed in Sec. IVD.

Fig. 12. The *index* transformation used in the FFT discussion of Sec. IVE.

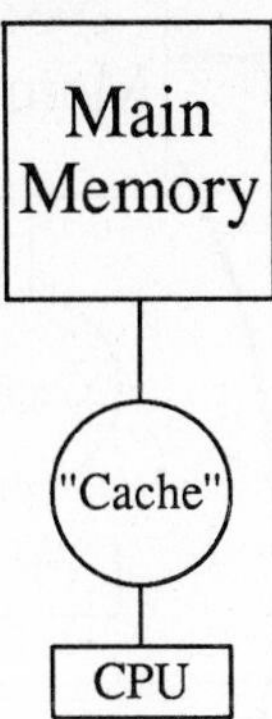

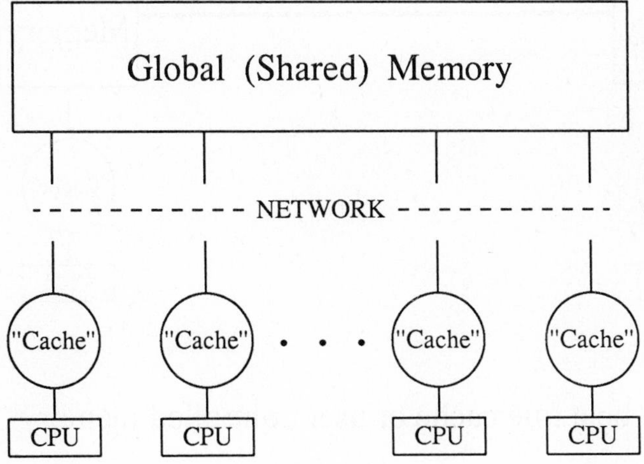

Fig. 1. Block diagram of the three machine architectures considered in this paper. We allow either a hardware controlled cache or user local memory to be the lowest level of the memory hierarchy. We ignore the important issues concerning the network connecting the global memory in (b) to the local "cache" and CPU's of the shared memory architecture.

(c) Hierarchical Memory Hypercube (d=2)

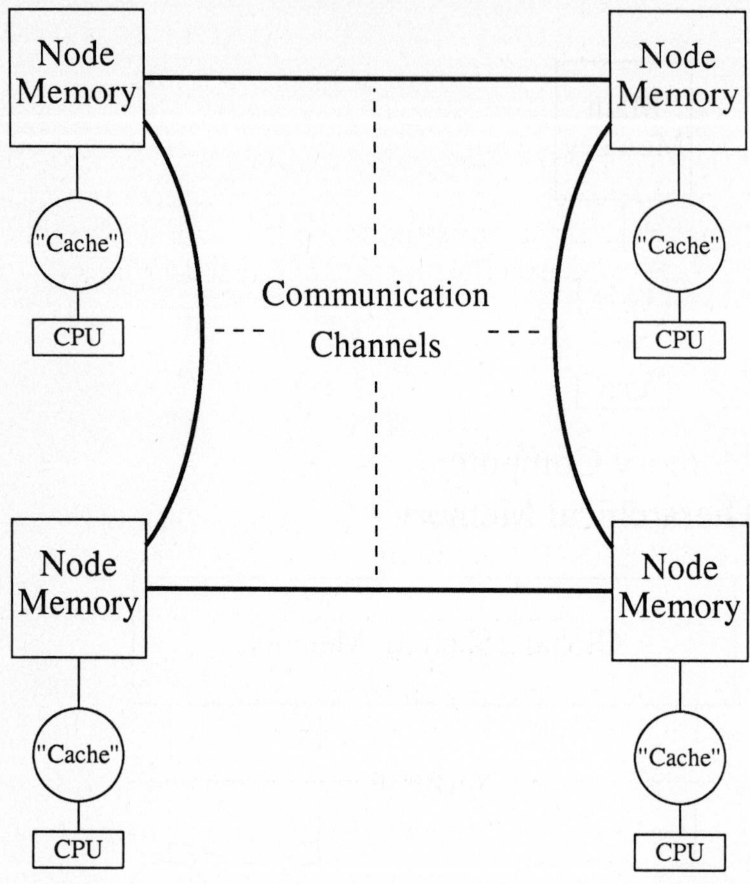

"Cache" may be a true cache or user controlled memory

Fig. 1. Block diagram of the three machine architectures considered in this paper. We allow either a hardware controlled cache or user local memory to be the lowest level of the memory hierarchy. We ignore the important issues concerning the network connecting the global memory in (b) to the local "cache" and CPU's of the shared memory architecture.

Contrasting Hypercube Nodes

(a) Commercial NCUBE

Each Node is 7 Chips

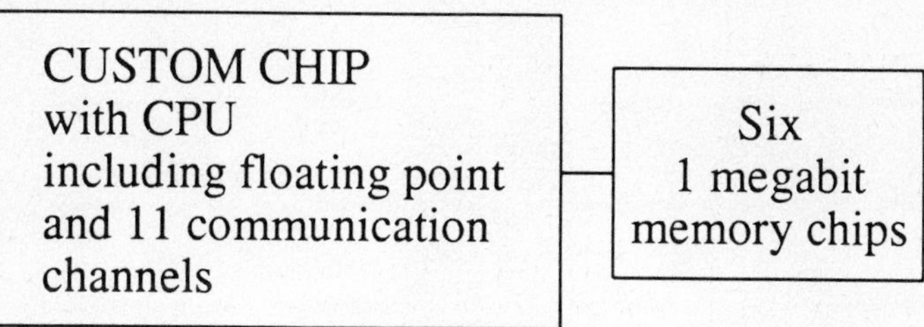

(b) Mark IIIfp Constructed at JPL

Each Node is 2 Printed Circuit Boards and a Total of 440 Chips

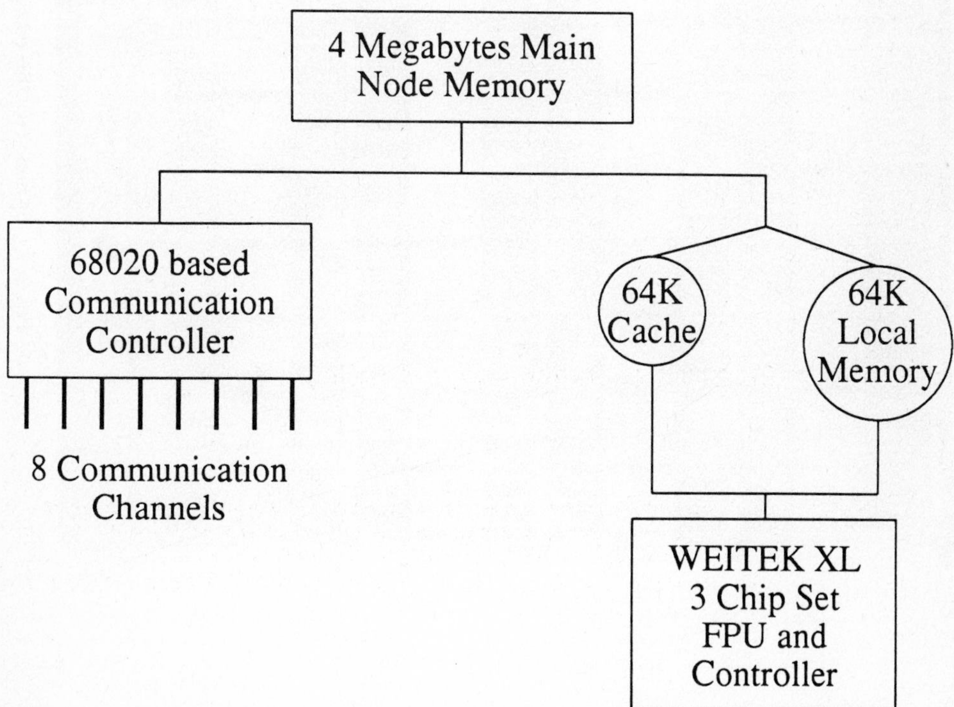

Fig. 2. Block Diagrams of the NCUBE and Mark IIIfp hypercube nodes. We do not show a 68020/68882 based applications controller in (b) as it is irrelevant for this paper. The WEITEK XL unit is a complete computer.

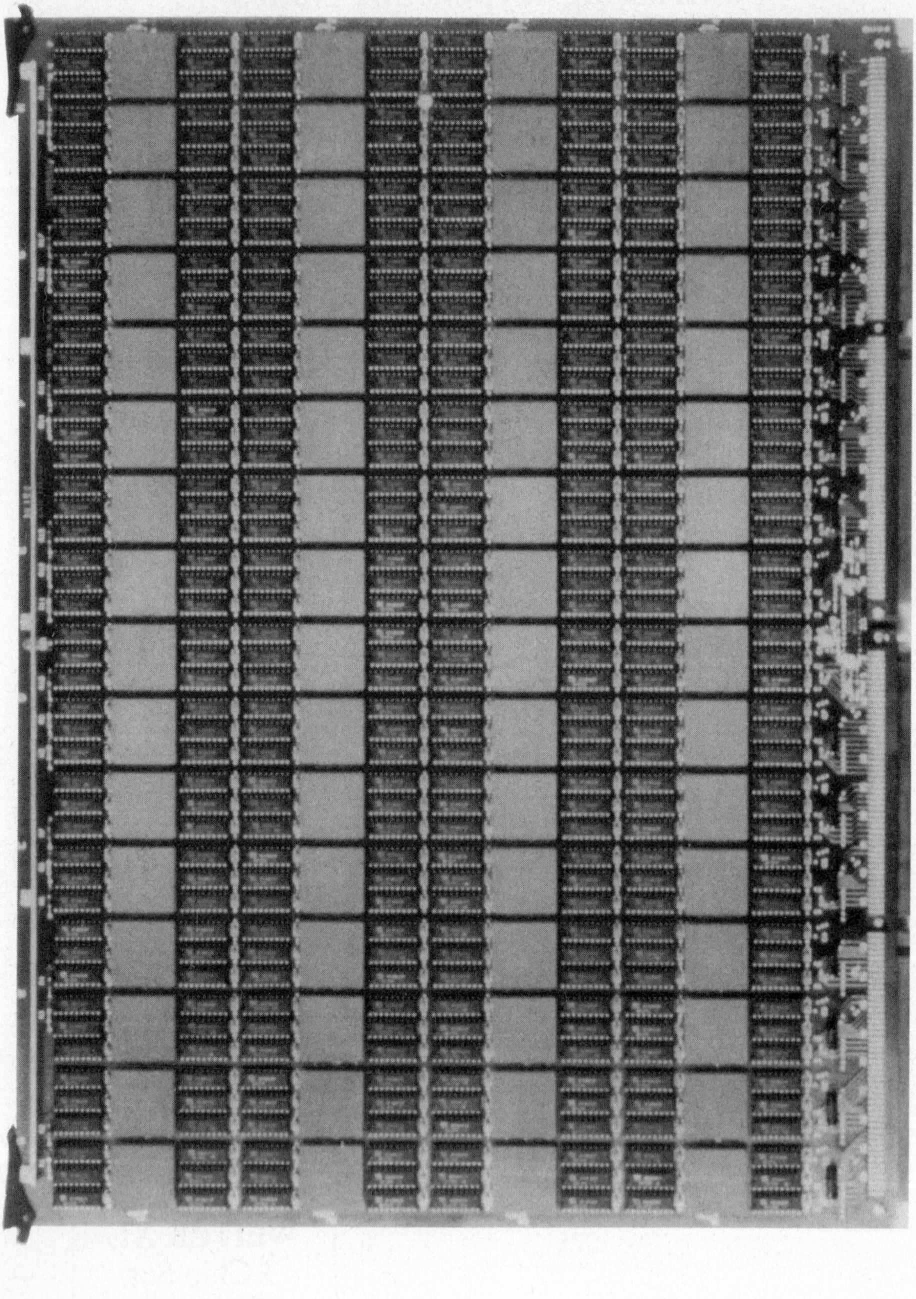

Fig. 3. 64 node NCUBE board and packaging into a 1024 node system

Fig. 3. 64 node NCUBE board and packaging into a 1024 node system

Fig. 4. The two printed circuit boards making up the Mark IIIfp node. The WEITEK board is functional but will be cleaned up for the production unit.

(a) Main board with 4 megabytes of memory and two 68020's.

CALTECH/JPL CONCURRENT
SUPERCOMPUTER NODE

Fig. 4. The two printed circuit boards making up the Mark IIIfp node. The WEITEK board is functional but will be cleaned up for the production unit.

(b) Floating Point coprocessor built around WEITEK XL chip set.

Basic Hardware Parameters

Calculation Time

CPU t_{calc} = Time for basic floating point operation.

"Cache" - Main (Global) Memory Transfer Time

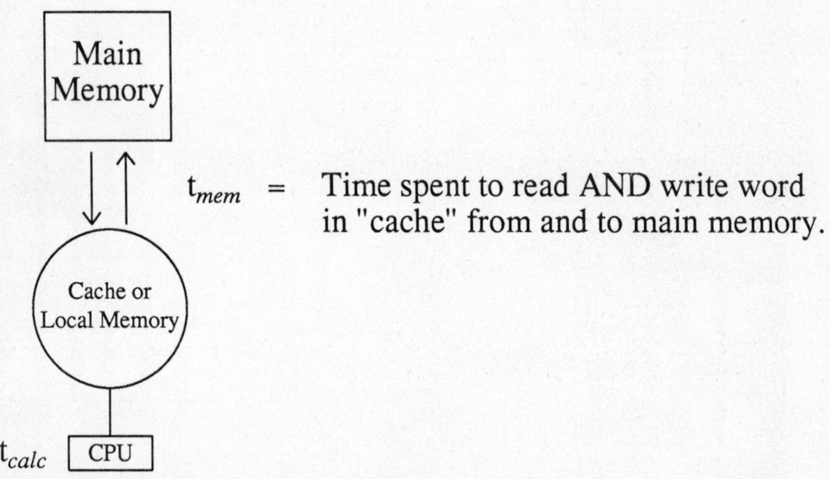

Node to Node Communication Time

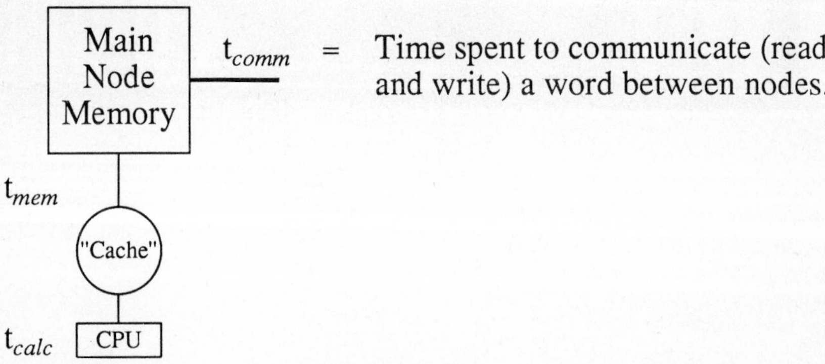

Fig. 5. Definitions of the three hardware parameters t_{calc}, t_{mem}, and t_{calc} discussed in Sec. II.

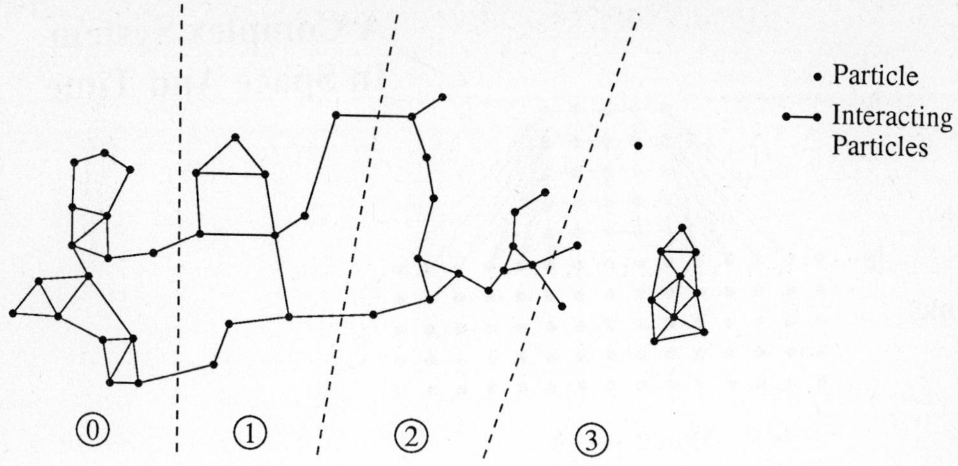

Domain Decomposition Into 4 Grains

Fig 6. The complex system corresponding to a short range force particle dynamics problem with its decomposition into four grains.

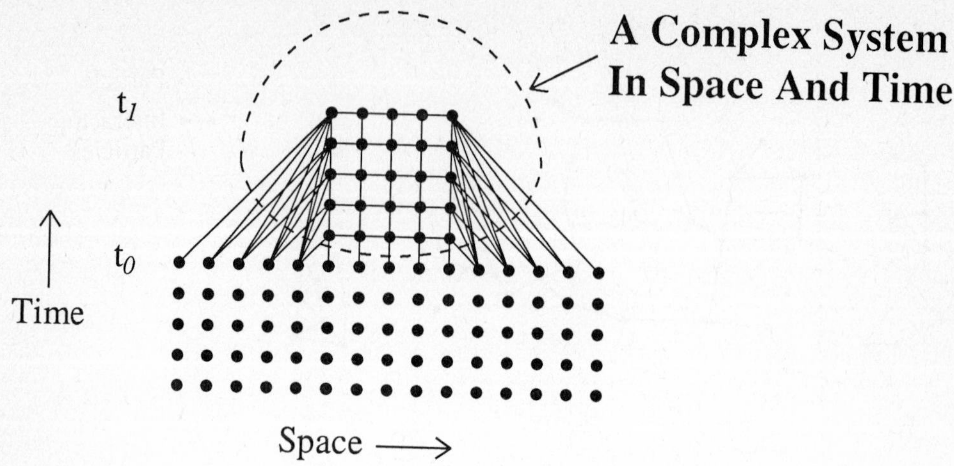

Fig. 7. A complex system in space and time that corresponds to a regular nearest neighbor problem in one spatial dimension; the finite difference solution of $\frac{\partial^2\psi}{\partial x^2} = c\frac{\partial^2\psi}{\partial t^2}$ would lead to such a complex system.

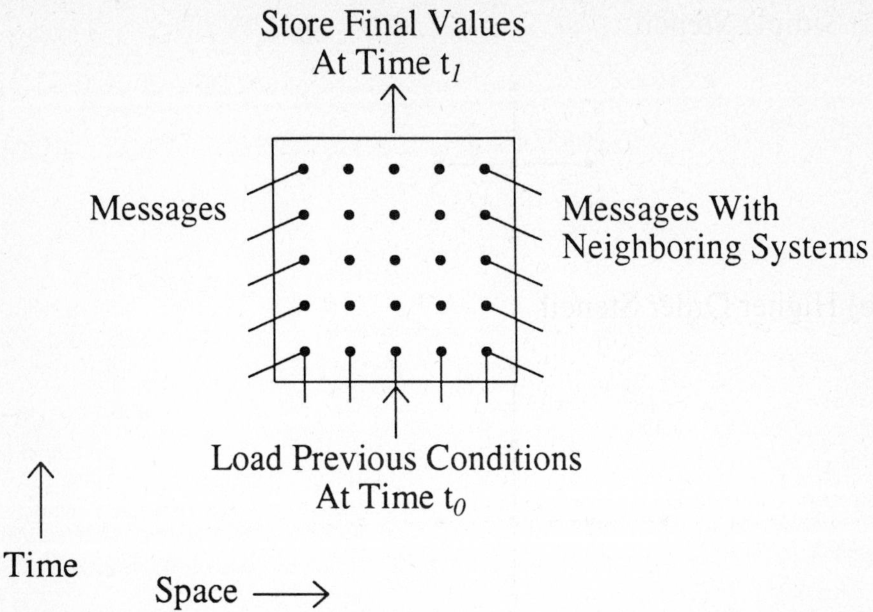

Fig. 8. The boundaries of a space-time complex system of the type illustrated in Fig. 7. Edges of the graph crossed by spatial boundaries correspond to messages with neighboring systems. Those crossed by temporal boundaries corresponding to the loading and ejection of the grain to and from cache and main memory.

(a) Simple Stencil

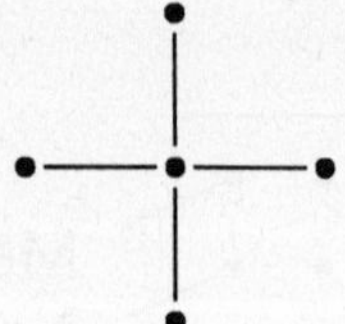

(b) Higher Order Stencil

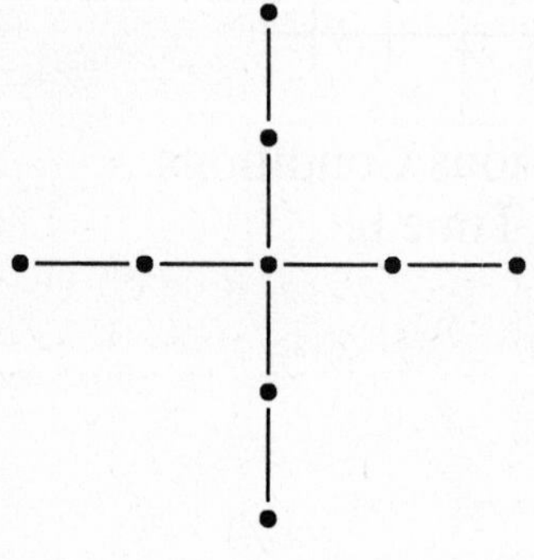

Fig. 9. Two stencils for the solution of Poisson's equation in two dimensions.

(a) A High Edge/Area Ratio In The Time Direction

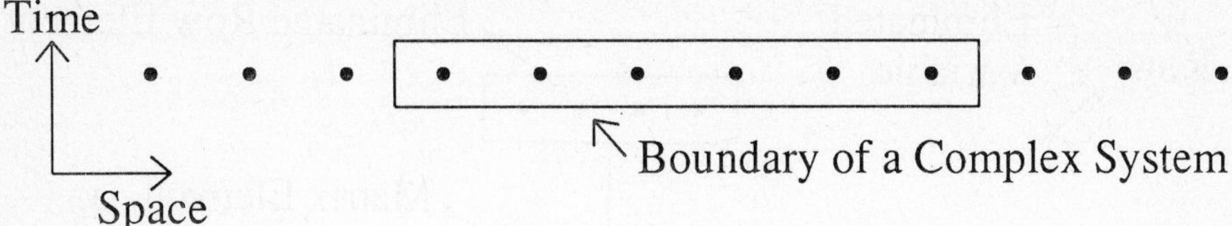

(b) A Better Edge/Area Ratio With Modest Communication

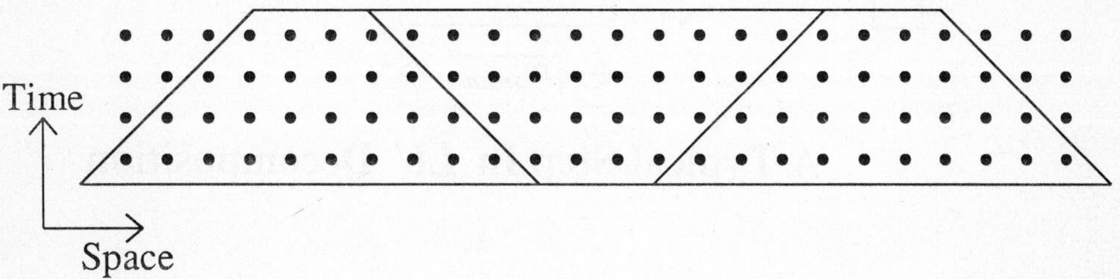

(c) A More Practical Decomposition With More Communication

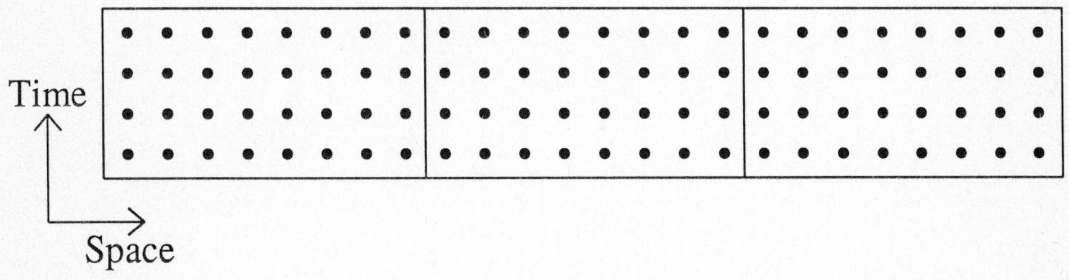

Fig. 10. Three decompositions in space and time of the one dimensional wave equation discussed in the text of Sec. IVB.

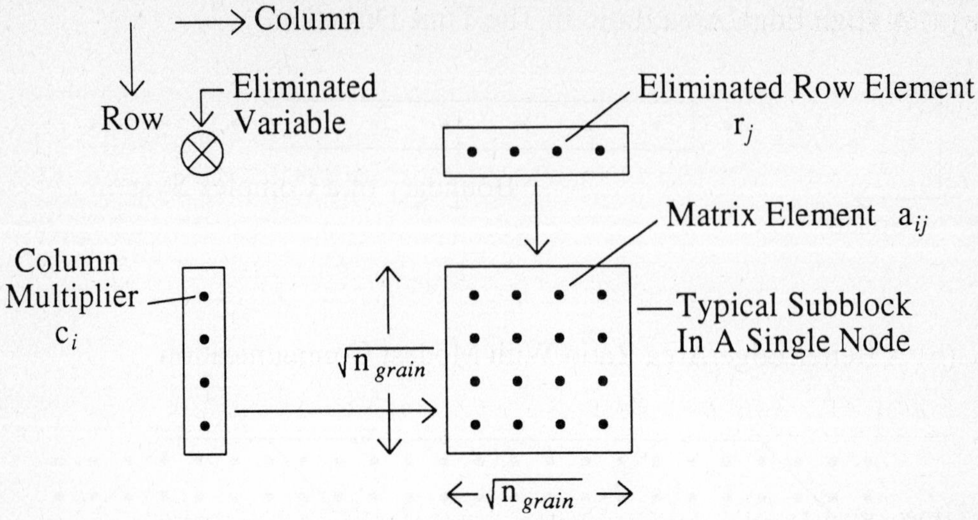

Fig. 11. A typical step in LU decomposition discussed in Sec. IVD.

(a) Initial Storage

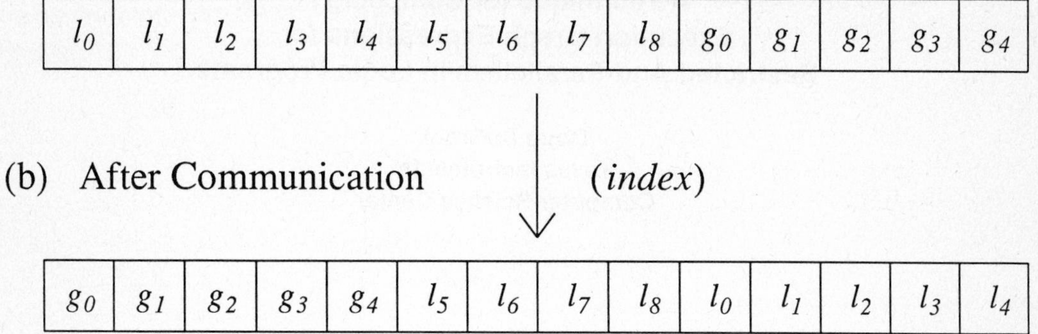

The digits of a binary index B labelling variables to be further transformed

Fig. 12. The *index* transformation used in the FFT discussion of Sec. IVE.

A Technique for Compiling Execution Graph Expressions for Restricted And-Parallelism in Logic Programs

Doug DeGroot
Texas Instruments
Computer Science Center

1. Introduction

Several novel approaches have been developed recently for executing logic programming languages, such as Prolog, in parallel. Although several approaches are being pursued, the majority involve variations of two basic mechanisms: *and-parallelism* and *or-parallelism* [Conery 81]. In Conery's *And/Or Process* model, a compile-time data dependence analysis coupled with a set of run-time tests and algorithms are executed in order to derive a run-time ordering of goals within a Prolog clause and to produce a possibly-parallel execution graph based on this ordering. Although Conery's approach does retain the original Prolog syntax and semantics, it does so at a fairly considerable expense. A simpler and cheaper model, the *Restricted And-Parallelism (RAP)* model, was presented in [DeGroot 84]. It also retains the original syntax and semantics of Prolog, but with significantly less run-time expense. The run-time expense is reduced through a set of approximation techniques which make certain assumptions on the possible execution traces of a clause. Because the techniques used are approximation techniques, they may in fact occassionally result in less parallelism than possible. Conery's model does not suffer from this fault; his approach remains the standard by which maximal parallelism can be achieved.

The RAP model trades maximal detection of parallelism for more efficient execution. As explained in [DeGroot 84], it is believed that the RAP model will detect more than enough parallelism to keep a moderately-sized parallel processor system busy. Recent empirical evidence certainly lends support to this thesis [Carlton 88]. It has long been recognized that data dependence analysis can be used to detect at compile-time locations and types of possible parallel execution in logic programs. The RAP model requires such analysis to generate the parallel execution graph expressions. While extensive work has been performed in the area of analysis of data dependencies in traditional, imperative computing languages such as Fortran for use in providing parallel execution and vector processing, work is really just beginning in this area for logic programming languages. This paper presents a new technique based on limited data dependence analysis for compiling Prolog clauses into parallel execution graph expressions and discusses ways in which more complex data dependence analysis can improve it.

2. An Overview of Prolog

This section presents a simple overview of Prolog [Shapiro 86]. Readers familiar with Prolog and unification may skip this section.

Prolog and other logic prgramming languages based on Horn-clause logic [Lloyd 84] define only three types of statements: facts, rules, and queries. All three statement types are called **clauses**. The formats of these three statement types are:

facts:	p.	
rules:	g :- s1, s2, . . . , sn.	where n≥ 1
queries:	?- s1, s2, . . . , sk.	where k ≥ 1

Facts are simple assertions; they constitute the fundamental "truths" of a logic program. Examples of facts include:

```
isa(fido,dog).
father(john,mary).
part(partno(p2),pname(bolt),color(green),weight(17)).
```

Each fact asserts that a specific relation holds between its arguments; the meaning of the relation is implicit and is uninterpreted, except for certain predefined system relations. In the above, constants begin with lowercase letters; they refer to specific individual elements of the name space. Variables can be used to refer to unspecified elements, as in:

```
likes(X,money).
```

This fact states that everyone (actually, everything) likes money. Variable identifiers begin with uppercase letters and are universally quantified [Lloyd 84]. Variables may assume any value whatsoever, including the value of another variable. As discussed below, when this occurs, aliases may arise.

Rules express conditional conclusions. As shown above, the format of a rule is:

```
g :- s1, s2, . . . , sn.
```

where n ≥ 1. Each rule specifies a*conclusion*, say g, to the left of the arrow (" :- ") and one or more *preconditions* to the right of the arrow, here, s1 through sn. When considered from the imperative or operational point of view, the conclusion is also called the *goal* (or *head*) of the clause, and the preconditions are called the *subgoals* (or *body*) of the clause. Examples of rules include:

```
grandparent(X,Y) :- parent(X,Z), parent(Z,Y).
happy(D) :- isa(D,dog), has_a(D,X), isa(X,bone).
```

To determine the truth of the conclusion of a rule, a Prolog proof procedure system must recursively establish the truth of each of the preconditions in the rule. This proof procedure is described below.

Queries are the language mechanism used to activate the proof procedure on rules. Typical queries include:

```
?- grandparent(sue,C).
?- country(C), borders(C,mediterranean), country(C1),
      asian(C1), borders(C,C1).
```

The last query can be interpreted as asking, "Is there a Mediterranean country that borders an Asian country?" As can be seen in the above examples and from the general query format, queries also contain one or more subgoals. Every subgoal in a query must be solved for the query to to be solved (or, proven).

The data structures appearing as arguments in goals, subgoals, and facts are called **terms**. Terms can be arbitrarily structured; they are defined inductively as follows:

1. All atomic elements are terms (e.g., constants, integers, characters).
2. All variables are terms.
3. If f is an alphanumeric symbol (or more precisely, a *functor* [Lloyd 84]), and t1 through tn are terms, then f(t1,t2,...,tn) is also a term.

For the remainder of this paper, the important points to notice are that a term can contain any number of variables, and variables can be arbitrarily-deeply nested within a term. Additionally, the same variable identifier may appear in more than one term and more than once within a single term, thereby giving rise to more than one access path to that variable. It is also important to note that in Prolog clauses, the scopes of all variable identifiers appearing within a clause are strictly local; there are no such things as global variable identifiers. Thus a variable identifier X in one clause is entirely different from all other variable identifiers named X in all other clauses or even from the X identifiers in a recursive call to that clause. When no confusion can arise, the variable referred to by a variable identifier X is also called simply X. The lack of global variable identifiers greatly simplifies the task of data dependence analysis.

Normal Prolog execution involves the sequential, left-to-right, recursive execution of the subgoals in a clause or query. Given a simple query consisting of a single subgoal, Prolog tries to solve (prove) the subgoal. If it can find a fact that "matches" the subgoal exactly, Prolog considers that it has solved the query. If it can find no fact that matches the subgoal but it can find a rule whose head matches the subgoal, then the subgoal is replaced by the subgoals in the body of the rule. Each of these subgoals must then be solved in a recursive manner, from left to right. If this is done, then the original query is solved.

Although many forms of "matching" are possible in logic programming [Jaffar 87], the matching process used in Prolog is **unification** [Lloyd 84]. It is a recursive process in which each term of a subgoal is matched with the corresponding term in the same position of the fact or rule head with which the match is to be attempted. Unification operates on two terms. The two terms unify if they are identical atomic symbols, if either or both is a variable, or if the terms have the same functor name and same number of arguments and if these arguments are themselves recursively unifiable. During unification, assignment occurs if one or both of the terms to be unified is a variable. In such cases, (one of) the variable(s) is assigned the value of the other term. The variable assigned the value of the other term can be either in the subgoal, in which case it is considered an **output variable**, or in the fact or rule head, in which case it is considered an **input variable**. There is thus two-way assignment through unification [Reddy 86]. The assignment is by reference and not by value, and thus aliases can easily arise.

3. And-Parallel Execution of Logic Programs

As mentioned above, normal Prolog execution involves the sequential, left-to-right, recursive execution of the subgoals in a clause or query. In logic programming, **and-parallelism** occurs when two or more subgoals in a single clause execute in parallel rather than sequentially. The main problem with and-parallelism is that the subgoals in a clause may easily (and ususally do) share one or more terms. Because these shared terms may contain one or more variables, the variables themselves are shared, thereby giving rise to possible data dependencies; care must therefore be taken to ensure that either 1) only one subgoal is allowed to assign a value to the variable, and in proper order, or 2) if multiple subgoals do assign values to a shared variable, then they all assign the same value to the variable.

For example, consider the following simple program and query:

```
parent(bob,sally).
parent(jim,sue).
grandparent(X,Y) :- parent(X,Z), parent(Z,Y).
?- grandparent(bob,sue).
```

When the *grandparent(bob,sue)* query is executed, it unifies with the head of the *grandparent* rule, giving the value of *bob* to the variable *X* and the value *sue* to the variable *Y*. To solve the grandparent rule then, the two subgoals must be solved with the assigned variable values. The two modified subgoals are *parent(bob,Z)* and *parent(Z,sue)*. An and-parallel execution model may attempt to execute the two subgoals in parallel. The first subgoal may succeed by matching the fact *parent(bob,sally)*, thereby assigning the value *sally* to the variable *Z*; the second subgoal may succeed by matching the fact *parent(jim,sue)*, thereby assigning the value *sue* to the variable *Z*.

But even though both subgoals succeeded, they succeeded only by assigning two different values to the shared variable *Z*. No single value of *Z* has been found such that bob is the parent of *Z* and sue is the child of *Z*. Consequently, the clause has not been successfully executed, and it has not been proven if bob is a grandparent of sue. When two different values are assigned to a single value, a **binding conflict** is said to have occurred.

In this example, it is easy to see that the two subgoals will share a variable; compiler analysis can detect this. Consider this clause however:

f(X,Y) :- g(X), h(Y).

Here it is not generally possible to determine at compile time whether the two subgoals will share a variable; it depends entirely on the run-time values passed to the clause head. For example, if a call is made of the form f(h(W),k(W)) then the two subgoals will share the variable W, and binding conflicts may arise if the two subgoals are executed with and-parallelism. If however a call is made of the form f(dog,h(W)) then the two subgoals cannot possibly share a variable, and thus in this case no binding conflicts can arise. Clearly, determination of whether the two subgoals can execute in parallel is a data-dependent determination and is thus frequently possible only at run-time. Additional complications arise as a result of the relational nature of logic languages; a given variable in a clause head may be an input variable in one call, an output variable in another, and both input and output in yet another [Kowalski 74]. This significantly complicates the data dependence analysis of logic programs.

Several and-parallel execution techniques have been proposed to prevent binding conflicts; each exhibits significantly different performance characteristics, and no single model has yet emerged as "best". Pollard has investigated techniques that allow multiple subgoals to assign values to a variable; these multiple values are then "reconciled" at run-time, and common assignments are sought [Pollard 81]. Conery has developed a technique that instead prevents two subgoals from executing in parallel if they share a variable; to accomplish this, a partial ordering of execution is determined at both compile-time and run-time which is dynamically imposed on the subgoals as the terms undergo modification [Conery 87]. Several other approaches utilize variable annotations to inform the compiler which subgoals are allowed to assign values to a variable and which are allowed to only read the value of a variable [Clark 86, Shapiro 83, Wise 86]. Quite a few other approaches have been studied as well. In Section 5, a model called Restricted And-Parallelism is described [DeGroot 84].

4. Types of Data Dependencies

When two terms share one or more unbound variables, the two terms are said to be **data dependent**; otherwise, they are said to be **independent**. Two terms which are at first data dependent can later become independent, and two independent terms can again later become data dependent. To understand this, it is useful to examine the different ways two terms can be data dependent. Tung and Moldovan classified data dependencies in logic programs into four types: functional dependencies, internal dependencies, coupling dependencies, and run-time dependencies [Tung 84, Tung 86]. Each of these is described below. But first, some notation. As stated before, the format of a rule is considered to be:

g :- s1, s2, . . . , sn. (where $n \geq 1$).

The head, *g*, is the goal, and the *s*'s in the body are the subgoals. Below, the format of a clause is also considered to be:

C+ :- C-.

Here, C+ represents the clause head, and C- represents the clause body. Given the previous representation, it can be seen that:

C+ = g

and

C- = s1, s2, . . . , sk.

The variable identifiers of a goal or subgoal *p*are denoted as v(p). Note that these variables are those appearing in the source code and are not the set of variables that occur in the run-time values bound to these variables.

The types of data dependencies identified by Tung and Moldovan can now be described. First, there is a **functional dependency** between two subgoals si and sj, $i \leq j$, if there is a variable X such that X is an output variable of si and an input variable of sj. We call si the **producer** of X and sj the **consumer** of X.

The most common example of a functional dependency can be seen in the following example clause and query:

```
grandfather(X,Y) :- father(X,Z), parent(Z,Y).
?- grandfather(tom,C).
```

Here, the first subgoal will derive a child of tom and pass that value on to the parent subgoal. The father subgoal will produce values for Z which are consumed by the parent subgoal. This type of data dependence is called **data** or **flow dependence** in data dependency analysis schemes of imperative languages such as Fortran [Banerjee76, Kuck78].

An **internal dependency** exists between two subgoals si and sj if there is a variable $X \in v(si) \cap v(sj)$ such that X is an output variable in both si and sj. A **coupling dependency** exists between two subgoals si and sj if there are two output variables X and Y such that $X \in v(si)$ and $Y \in v(sj)$ and the values of X and Y share one or more unbound variables. And finally, a **run-time dependency** is introduced between two subgoals si and sj if there are two variables X and Y such that $X \in v(si) \cap v(C+)$, $Y \in v(sj) \cap v(C+)$, and X and Y are both input variables that receive as values terms that are themselves data dependent (share one or more variables). The example above in which the clause

f(X,Y) :- g(X), h(Y).

is called at run-time with the query

?- f(h(W),k(W)).

is an example in which a run-time dependency arises.

These data dependence definitions are representative of the types of definitions that are required for a complete description of data dependence analysis of parallel logic programming schemes and are presented here only as example definitions, but they are not believed to be complete. An alternative way of reasoning about data dependence is presented in [Chang85] and [DeGroot85].

5. Restricted And-Parallelism

An approach to and-parallel execution of logic programs called **Restricted And-Parallelism (RAP)** is described in [DeGroot 84]. The RAP model provides an efficient means of executing traditional, unannotated Prolog programs in parallel while retaining the complete semantics of sequential Prolog. Thus Prolog code written for sequential systems will perform correctly when compiled for RAP execution. This is an important advantage, as many approaches to and-parallel execution of Prolog abandon the traditional syntax and semantics of Prolog. The approach of the RAP model is to perform a partial, compile-time data-dependence analysis of program clauses in an attempt to determine the potential occurrences of parallelism. Each clause is then compiled into a single parallel execution-graph expression which at run-time can result in more than one actual execution graph. Simple tests on the data values provided at run-time determine which of the different possible execution graphs is to be used.

Determination of whether or not two subgoals can execute in parallel depends on whether the two subgoals are **independent**, that is whether there are no data dependeces between them. In the RAP model, two terms are independent if neither shares a variable with the other; in such cases, there can be only a single access path to any variable contained in the two terms. If the terms of one subgoal are all independent of the terms in another subgoal, the subgoals themselves are said to be independent. Independent subgoals can execute in parallel, as no binding conflicts or flow dependences can occur due to the single access paths to all variables.

There are three main components to the RAP model: 1) the typing algorithm, 2) the independence algorithm, and 3) the execution graph expressions. Each of these is described below.

The role of the **typing algorithm** is to monitor terms during run-time in an attempt to keep track of whether a term still contains any unbound variables within it. Several possible typing algorithms are possible. A run-time checking algorithm was described in [DeGroot 84]. In this scheme, each term is assigned a type code to indicate its current type. If the term is ground, i.e., contains no variables, then its type is set to G. If the term is an unbound variable, its type is V. And if the term is not a variable but contains at least one variable within it, its type is set to N (non-ground, non-variable). During run-time, terms of type V and N may be altered by having values assigned to the variables within them. Terms of type V may be changed to terms of type N or G; terms of type N may be changed to terms of type G. Terms of type G remain type G. This particular typing algorithm attempts to lower the run-time overhead by making only a partial check of a term's contents. As a result of this partial check, a term may occassionally be typed too strongly, that is, it may be typed as non-variable, non-ground when in fact, it may be ground. To make an asbolute determination of the type of a term in run-time typing schemes, it may frequently be necessary to perform a run-time scan of the entire term to see if it contains any variables. This is the approach used by Conery. Because a term may be arbitrarily large, run-time scans are prohibitively expensive, especially when it is considered that in the worst case, these scans may occur following every successful subgoal invocation. The approximation to the typing is a compromise between run-time overhead and the need to make accurate type determinations.

Another typing algorithm based on a static data-dependency analysis is possible which incurs even less run-time overhead but which may occasionally have poorer performance [Chang 85, DeGroot 88b]. In certain cases, this algorithm may make an accurate assessment of a term's type throughout the entire program execution; in others, it may consistently underestimate the term's type. Underestimation may result in significantly less parallelism being detected at run-time.

Other typing algorithms are clearly possible, and several are currently being investigated. The RAP model is defined independently of any particular typing algorithm.

The role of the **independence algorithm** is to determine whether two terms are independent, that is, whether they share an unbound variable, and thus whether a possible data dependence exists between them. One way to do this is to perform a run-time scan of the two terms and note all their variables. Then the variables of one are compared to the variables of the other; if none of the variables are identical, the two terms are independent. But, again, because terms can be arbitrarily large, run-time scanning of terms is impractical. A simpler, approximate independence algorithm can be used; it is shown in Figure 1. Other indpendence algorithms are possible as well.

The **execution graph expressions** are responsible for encoding at compile-time all the possible parallel run-time execution graphs that might be possible for a given clause. Because the independence of two subgoals cannot be determined until the actual run-time values of their arguments are provided, it is

```
function  INDEPENDENCE(arg1,arg2):boolean;
begin
 if  ground(arg1)  or  ground(arg2)  then
   INDEPENDENCE  :=  true
 else  if  (type(arg1)  =  type(arg2)  =  V)  and
  address(arg1)  ≠  address(arg2)  then
   INDEPENDENCE  :=  true
 else  {assume}  INDEPENDENCE  :=  false;
end;  {INDEPENDENCE}
```

Figure 1. The Independence Algorithm

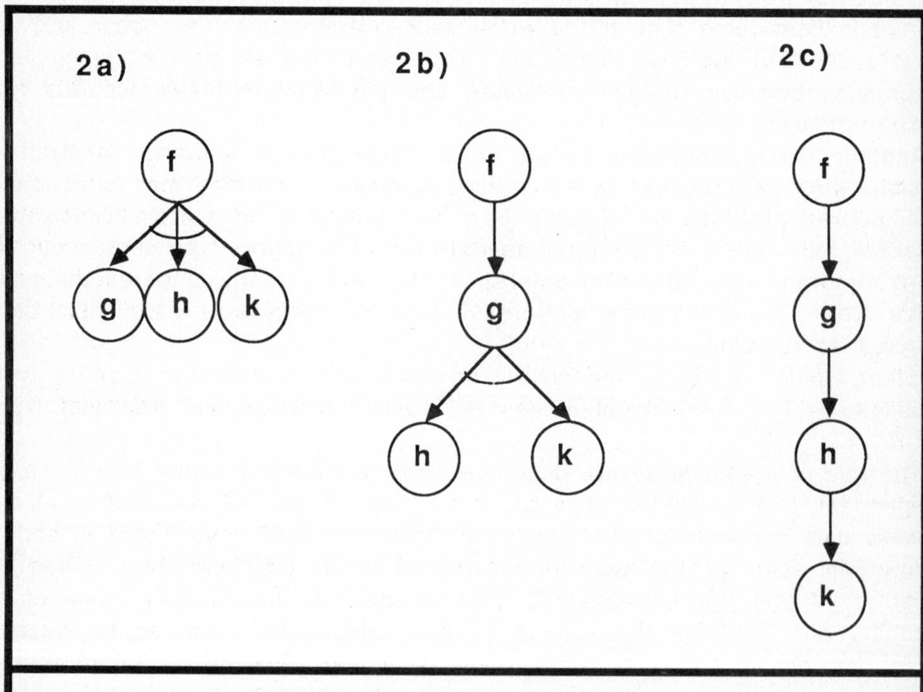

Figure 2. Execution Graphs for f(X) :- g(X), h(X), k(X).

impossible, in general, to compile a single execution graph that embodies all possible parallel execution graphs.

The execution graph expressions are defined recursively with six expression types:

1. G
   a simple goal (or subgoal); this is the simplest expression type
2. (SEQ E1 . . . En)
   execute expressions E1 through En sequentially
3. (PAR E1 . . . En)
   execute expressions E1 through En in parallel
4. (GPAR(V1...Vk) E1. . . En)
   if all the variables V1 through Vk are ground (have type G), then execute expressions E1 through En in parallel; otherwise, execute E1 through En sequentially
5. (IPAR({V1...Vk}{Vm ... Vp}) E1 . . . En)
   if each variable V1 through Vk is independent from every variable Vm through Vp , then execute expressions E1 through En in parallel; otherwise, execute E1 through En sequentially.
6. (IF B E1 E2)
   if expression B evaluates to true, execute expression E1; otherwise, execute expression E2

The GPAR test simply examines the type fields of the specified terms to see if they are ground (type G). The IPAR test simply invokes the independence algorithm on all required pairs of variables in the IPAR expression; generally, the number of tests required is very small.

As an example of the type of execution graph expressions generated for a Prolog clause, consider the following:

```
f(X) :- g(X), h(X), k(X).
```

This clause may be compiled into the following execution graph expression:

```
f(X) :- (GPAR(X) g(X)
                 (GPAR(X) h(X) k(X)) ).
```

This execution graph expression can result in any of the three run-time execution graphs of Figure 2. For example, if f is invoked with a ground value of X, the first GPAR test succeeds, thereby activating the two subexpressions in parallel. The first subexpression activates the subgoal g(X). Because X is ground, the second subexpression can simultaneously begin execution since now it is guaranteed that no binding conflicts can occur. This second subexpression also contains a GPAR test; X is tested again, found to be ground, and the two additional subexpressions are then activated in parallel. Thus h(X) and k(X) begin parallel execution with g(X). The resulting execution graph is that shown in Figure 2.a.

Suppose now that the first GPAR test fails. Then clearly X is not ground and so contains an unbound variable somewhere within it. Consequently, no two of the subgoals can be allowed to execute in parallel, as otherwise a binding conflict might occur. Since the GPAR test failed, the two subexpressions must execute sequentially. So the first subgoal, g(X), begins execution alone. When and if it successfully completes, the second subexpression can begin execution. Because the execution of g(X) may have resulted in X's becoming ground, the second subexpression retests X. If X is now ground, the GPAR test succeeds, and the two subgoals h(X) and k(X) can execute in parallel; the resulting run-time execution graph is shown in Figure 2.b. If the GPAR test fails again, X is still non-ground, and so h(X) and k(X) must execute sequentially, resulting in the run-time execution graph of Figure 2.c.

Note that three different run-time execution graphs are possible for the example Prolog clause but that only one RAP execution graph expression is needed to express all three execution graphs. Only simple run-time tests are used to dynamically select one of a number of possible execution graphs. This is a significant advantage of the RAP model.

For another example, consider the clause:

```
f(X,Y) :- p(X), q(Y), s(X,Y), t(Y).
```

This clause may be compiled into the execution graph expression:

```
f(X,Y) :- (GPAR(X,Y)
             (IPAR(X,Y) p(X) q(Y))
             (GPAR(Y) s(X,Y) t(Y)) )
```

or even into:

```
f(X,Y) :- (GPAR(X) p(X)
             (GPAR(Y) q(Y)
                 (GPAR(Y) s(X,Y) t(Y)))).
```

The set of possible execution graphs which can be derived from these two expressions is shown in Figure 3. Not all graphs are achievable by either of the two expressions. The first execution graph expression can result in a slightly different set of run-time execution graphs than the second. It is interesting to compare the two.

The execution graph expression tests can be combined when necessary. For example, consider the clause:

```
f(X,Y,Z) :- g(X,Y), h(Y,Z).
```

This clause can be compiled as:

```
f(X,Y,Z) :- (GPAR(Y) IPAR(X,Z)  g(X,Y)  h(Y,Z)).
```

Here, both the GPAR and IPAR tests must succeed for the two subgoals to execute in parallel.

It should be noted that the run-time tests are very simple and efficient. They can easily be implemented in hardware or firmware. Manuel Hermenegildo has in fact produced an extened Warren Abstract Machine for Prolog (the WAM [Warren 83]) that incorporates direct architectural support for the RAP model. The RAP graph expressions are easily compiled into this extended WAM model, and a sophisticated run-time kernel supports efficient, parallel execution of the compiled RAP expressions [Hermenegildo 87].

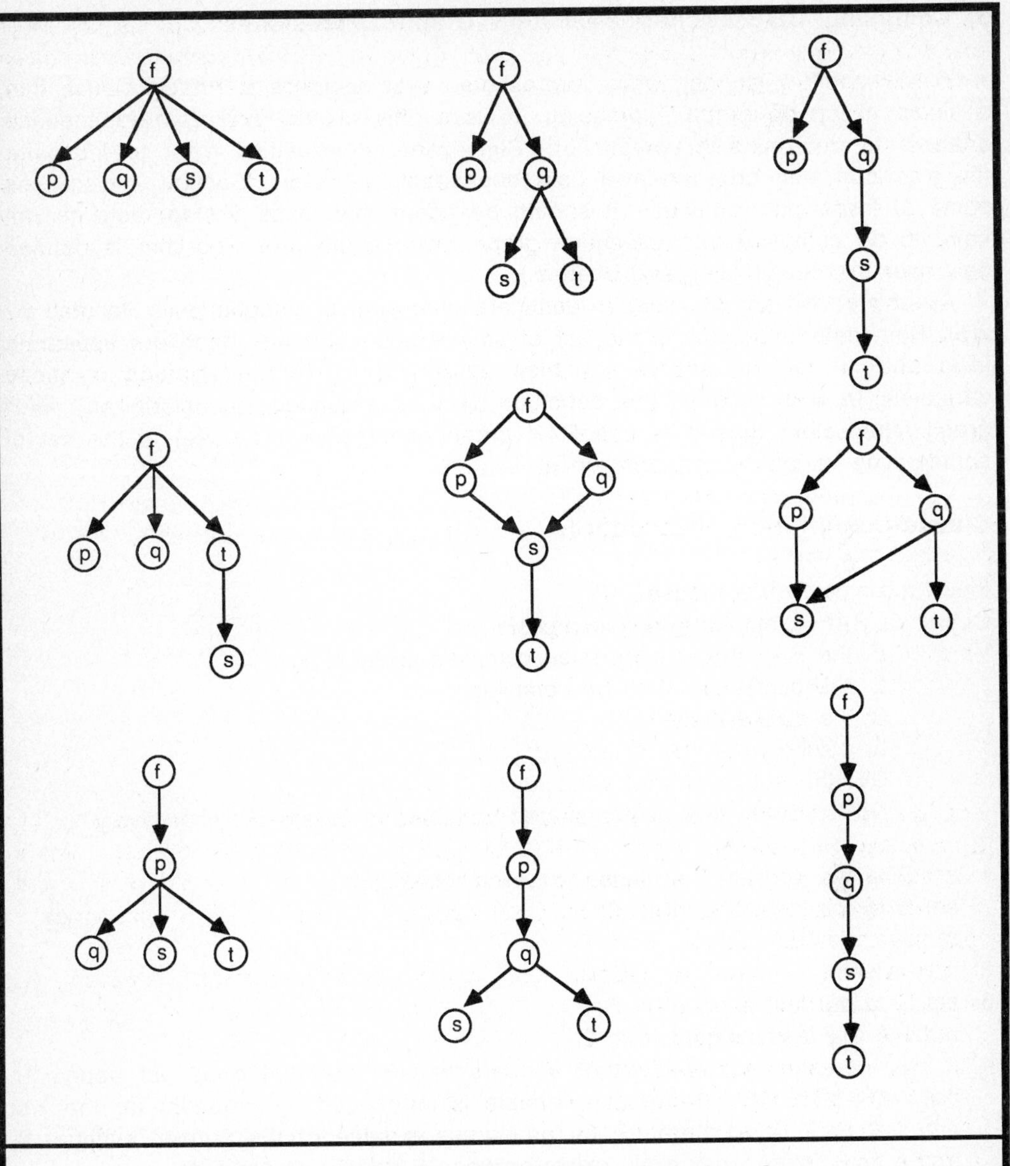

Figure 3. Multiple Execution Graphs for f(X,Y) :- p(X), q(Y), s(X,Y), t(Y).

6. Compiling Clauses into Execution Graph Expressions

In this section, an algorithm is presented that compiles a Prolog clause into a single execution graph expression. It uses only clause-level data-dependence analysis to determine a compilation. Significant opportunities exist to improvbe the algorithm with program-level data dependence analysis; Section 7 discusses some of these opportunities. (It should be noted that since Prolog facts do not have to be compiled into execution graph expressions, the algorithm is defined only over the set of rules and queries.)

As above, the set of variable identifiers of a goal or subgoal p is denoted by v(p). Remember that v(p) is the set of source code variable identifiers appearing in p and is not the set of variables appearing in the term-values of these variables. In this section, the definition of v is extended to include any RAP graph expression; thus if e is a RAP graph expression, then v(e) is the set of source-code variables appearing in e.

Clause-Compilation Procedure:

Input: a single Prolog clause
Output: a RAP execution-graph expression
Vars: E: the RAP graph expression compiled so far
C: the clause (rule) to be compiled
B: the clause body
S: a subgoal
SV: the set of shared variables
NSVs,NSVe: sets of non-shared variables in S and E, respectively

1. set B to the body of the clause to be compiled
   set E to the last subgoal in B
   remove the last subgoal from B
2. if B is empty, return (C+ :- E).
3. set S to the last subgoal in B;
   remove the last subgoal from B
4. if v(S) contains a variable that appears in v(E) but that does not appear in both v(B) and v(C+), then this variable is introduced by (appears for the first time in) S; it must therefore be an output variable of the current subgoal S, and a flow dependency likely exists between S and E; so set E to
   (SEQ S E)
   go to 2
5. set SV to v(S)$\cap$v(E); {this is the set of variables shared by S and E}
   set NSVs to v(S) - SV; {these are the non-shared variables of S}
   set NSVe to v(E) - SV; {these are the non-shared variables of E}
6. if either NSVs or NSVe is empty, then

a. if SV is empty, then either S or E or possibly both contain no variables, so set E to
(PAR S E)
b. else set E to
(GPAR(SV) S E)
else neither NSVs nor NSVe is empty, so
a. if SV is empty, set E to
(IPAR(NSVs,NSVe) S E)
b. else set E to
(IPAR(NSVs,NSVe) GPAR(SV) S E)
7. go to 2

Example 1:

For a simple example, consider the grandfatherclause:
grandfather(X,Y) :- father(X,Z), parent(Z,Y).
The behavior of the algorithm is as follows:

On entry: C = grandfather(X,Y) :- father(X,Z), parent(Z,Y).
v(C+) = {X,Y}

Iteration 1:

1. E = parent(Z,Y).
B = father(X,Z).
2. fails
3. S = father(X,Z).
B = nil.
v(S) = {X,Z}
v(B) = {}
v(E) = {Z,Y}
4. succeeds; so
E = (SEQ father(X,Z) parent(Z,Y)).
2. succeeds; so return
grandfather(X,Y) :- (SEQ father(X,Z) parent(Z,Y)).

Example 2:

Now reconsider the clause:
f(X,Y,Z) :- g(X,Y), h(Y,Z).
The algorithm's behavior is as follows:

On Entry: C = f(X,Y,Z) :- g(X,Y), h(Y,Z).
v(C+) = {X,Y,Z}

Iteration 1:

1. E = h(Y,Z)
   B = g(X,Y).
2. fails
3. S = g(X,Y)
   B = nil
   v(S) = {X,Y}
   v(B) = {}
   v(E) ={Y,Z}
4. fails
5. SV = {Y}
   NSVs = {X}
   NSVe = {Z}
6. E = (IPAR({X},{Z}) GPAR(Y) g(X,Y) h(Y,Z))
2. succeeds, so return
   f(X,Y,Z) :- (IPAR({X},{Z}) GPAR(Y) g(X,Y) h(Y,Z)).

Example 3:

Finally, reconsider the following clause:
f(X,Y) :- p(X), q(Y), s(X,Y), t(Y).
Four iterations through the algorithm are required:

On entry: C = f(X,Y) :- p(X), q(Y), s(X,Y), t(Y).
v(C+) = {X,Y}

Iteration 1:

1. E = t(Y)
   B = p(X), q(Y), s(X,Y).
2. fails
3. S = s(X,Y)
   B = p(X), q(Y).
   v(S) = {X,Y}
   v(B) = {X,Y}
   v(E) = {Y}
4. fails
5. SV = {Y}
   NSVs = {X}
   NSVe = {}
6. E = (GPAR(Y) s(X,Y) t(Y))

Iteration 2:

```
on entry:        B = p(X), q(Y).
                 E = (GPAR(Y)  s(X,Y)  t(Y) ).
2. fails
3. S = q(Y)
   B = p(X)
   v(S) = {Y}
   v(B) = {X}
   v(E) = {X,Y}
4. fails
5. SV = {Y}
   NSVs = {}
   NSVe = {Y}
6. E = (GPAR(Y)q(Y)
                 (GPAR(Y) s(X,Y)  t(Y) )
```

Iteration 3:

```
on entry:        B = p(X)
                 E = (GPAR(Y) q(Y)
                          (GPAR(Y) s(X,Y)  t(Y) )
2. fails
3. S = p(X)
   B = nil
   v(S) = {X}
   v(B) = nil
   v(E) = {X,Y}
4. fails
5. SV = {X}
   NSVs = {}
   NSVe = {Y}
6. E = (GPAR(X) p(X)
          (GPAR(Y) q(Y)
                 (GPAR(Y) s(X,Y)  t(Y) )
```

Iteration 4:

```
on entry:        B = nil
                 E = (GPAR(X) p(X)
                          (GPAR(Y) q(Y)
                                 (GPAR(Y) s(X,Y)  t(Y) )
2. succeeds, so return
          f(X,Y) :- (GPAR(X)p(X)
                          (GPAR(Y) q(Y)
                                 (GPAR(Y) s(X,Y)  t(Y) )
```

7. Using Program-Level Data-Dependence Analysis

As described above, the compilation algorithm presented requires only a clause-level data-dependence analysis. However, with a complete program-level data-dependence analysis, it may frequently be possible to generate more efficient or more potentially-parallel graph expressions.

For example, in Section 5, the clause

```
f(X) :- g(X), h(X), k(X).
```

was compiled into the following execution graph expression:

```
f(X) :- (GPAR(X) g(X)
                 (GPAR(X) h(X) k(X)) ).
```

In some sense, this expression is "optimal" in that it can achieve any of the three possible execution graphs for this clause. It is of course possible to compile the above clause into more than one execution graph expression, however. Examples of other expressions include:

1. f(X) :- (SEQ g(X) h(X) k(X)).
2. f(X) :- (PAR g(X) h(X) k(X)).
3. f(X) :- (GPAR g(X) h(X) k(X)).

The first graph expression forces all three subgoals to execute sequentially, as in normal Prolog. No parallelism will be exhibited, and the execution graph of Figure 2.c will result. This expressions is always correct, however. The second expressions always executes the three subgoals in parallel; this behavior can be guaranteed correct only if X is ground upon entry; if it is not, binding conflicts might easily occur. However, if program-level data dependence analysis (not simply clause-level data-dependency analysis) determines that f is called only with X ground, then generating this graph expression is indeed correct and slightly more efficient.

The third execution graph expression lets all three subgoals execute in parallel if X is ground upon entry; the resulting execution graph is shown in Figure 2.a. If however X is not ground upon entry, the GPAR test fails, and the three subgoals are forced to execute sequentially, as in Figure 2.c. If program-level data-dependence analysis determines that f is only sometimes called with a ground argument and that further, g does not alter its argument, then the SEQ expression might indeed be the preferred expression to generate, as it will generate less overhead.

Other improvements can be gained by analyzing the implications of the built-in predicates appearing in the program. For example, in the clause

```
f(X,N,M) :- g(X), plus(N,1,M), h(M), k(M).
```

the predicate plus requires its first two arguments to be ground, and it will produce a ground third argument. It can be guaranteed then that the last two subgoals can execute in parallel. But additionally, it is now known that both h and k are called, at least here, with ground arguments. If it can similarly be determined that h and k are always called with ground arguments, then the execution graph expressions for the clauses in the h and k procedures can perhaps be optimized.

Suppose the above clause for f is called by the following clause:

p(J,A) :- m(J,A), f(J,A,B), w(A), v(B).

Because it has been determined that f requires a ground value for A and will return a ground value for B, we might be able to compile the clause for p as:

```
p(J,A) :- (GPAR(J,A) m(J,A)
                     (SEQ (PAR f(J,A,B) w(A) )
                          v(B))).
```

Of course, a full program-level data-dependency analysis is required to determine if this is indeed the case.

Clearly, significant opportunities exist for improving the graph compilation procedure presented above. Several of the requirements of such compile-time analysis are examined in [Chang 85] , [Mellish 81], [Tung 84], and [Tung 86]. The impact of side-effect analysis on RAP execution graph expressions is discussed in [DeGroot 87] and [DeGroot 88a].

Summary

An efficient model of and-parallel execution of logic programs has been described; this model is called the *Restricted And-Parallelism* model. It uses a compile-time data-dependence analysis to generate single execution graph expressions for the clauses in a Prolog program. These execution graph expressions use simple run-time tests to determine the possibilities of parallelism. An algorithm has been presented which automatically produces these execution graphs. The algorithm can be significantly improved by using the results of program-level data-dependence analysis; these improvements are currently the focus of additional research in this area.

Bibliography

[Banerjee 76] Utpal Banerjee, *Data Dependence in Ordinary Programs,* MS Thesis, University of Illinois at Urbana-Champaign, DCS Report No, UIUCDCS-R-76-837, November, 1976.

[Carlton 88] Mike Carlton and Peter Van Roy, "A Distributed Prolog System with And-Parallelism," Dept. of EECS, Univ. of California at Berkeley, submitted to the 1988 Hawaii International Conference on System Sciences, 1988.

[Chang 85] Jung-Herng Chang, Alvin Despain, and Doug DeGroot, "AND-Parallelism of Logic Programs Bases on a Static Data-Dependency Analysis," *Procs of the Spring Compcon 85.* IEEE Computer Society Press, 1985, pp. 281-225.

[Clark 86] Keith Clark and Steve Gregory, "PARLOG: Parallel programming in logic," *ACM Transactions on Programming Languages and*

Systems, January, 1986, pp. 1-49.

[Conery 81] John Conery and Dennis Kibler, "Parallel Interpretation of Logic Programs," *Procs. of the Conf. on Functional Programming Languages and Computer Architecture*, ACM, 1981, pp. 163-170.

[Conery 87] John Conery, *Parallel Execution of Logic Programs*, Kluwer Academic Publishers, 1987.

[DeGroot 84] Doug DeGroot, "Restricted And-Parallelism," *Proceedings of the International Conference on Fifth Generation Computer Systems 1984,* North Holland, 1984, pp. 471-478.

[DeGroot 85] Doug DeGroot and Jung-Herng Chang, "A Comparison of Two And-Parallel Execution Models," *Hardware and Software Components and Architectures for the 5th Generation, AFCET Informatique*, March 1985, Paris, pp. 271-280.

[DeGroot 87] Doug DeGroot, "Restricted And-Parallelism and Side-Effects," *Procs. of the Symposium on Logic Programming*, IEEE Computer Society, San Francisco, 1987.

[DeGroot 88a] Doug DeGroot, "Restricted And-Parallelism and Side-Effects in Logic Programming," in *Supercomputers and AI Machines,* Kai Hwwang and Doug DeGroot, Editors, McGraw-Hill, to be published, 1988.

[DeGroot 88b] Doug DeGroot, "And-Parallelism in Logic Programs," in *Advanced Semiconductor Technology and Computer Systems,* Guy Rabbat, Ed., Van Nostrand Reinhold, New York, 1988.

[Hermenegildo 87] Manuel Hermenegildo, *A Restricted And-Parallel Execution Model and Abstract Machine for Prolog Programs*, Kluwer Academic Press, 1987.

[Jaffar 87] Joxan Jaffar and Jean-Louis Lassez, "Constraint Logic Programming," Technical Report, Dept. of Computer Science, Monash University, Australia, June, 1986.

[Kowalski 74] Bob Kowalski, "Predicate Logic as a Programming Language," *Procs. of the IFIP Congress,* North-Holland, 1974, pp. 569-574.

[Kuck 78] Dave Kuck, *The Structure of Computers and Computations,* Vol. 1, John Wiley and Sons, New York, 1978.

[Lloyd 84] John Lloyd, *Foundations of Logic Programming,* Springer-Verlag, 1984.

[Mellish 81] Chris Mellish, "The Automatic Generation of Mode Declarations for Prolog Programs," DAI Research Paper 163, Dept. of Artificial Intelligence, Univ. of Edinburgh, August 1981.

[Pollard 81] G. H. Pollard, *Parallel Execution of Horn Clause Programs,* Ph.D. dissertation, University of London, Imperial College of Science & Technology, United Kingdom, 1981.

[Reddy 86] Uday S. Reddy, "On the relationship between logic and functional languages," in *Logic Programming: Functions,*

Relations, and Equations, Doug DeGroot and Gary Lindstrom, Editors, Prentice-Hall, 1986, pp. 3-36.

[Shapiro 83] Ehud Shapiro, "A Subset of Concurrent Prolog and Its Interpreter," ICOT Tech. Report TR-003, ICOT, Tokyo, February, 1983.

[Shapiro 86] Ehud Shapiro, *The Art of Prolog,*MIT Press,1986.

[Tung 84] Yu-Wen Tung and Dan I. Moldovan, "Detection of And-Parallelism in Logic Programming," *Procs. of the 1986 Int'l Conf. on Parallel Processing,* IEEE, 1986, pp. 984-991.

[Tung 86] Yu-Wen Tung, *Parallel Processing Model for Logic Programming,* Ph.D. Dissertation, Dept. of EE, Univ. of Southern California, 1986.

[Warren 83] David H.D. Warren, "An Abstract Prolog Instruction Set," Tech. Note 309, SRI International, Oct. 1983.

[Wise 86] Michael Wise, *Prolog Multiprocessors,* Prentice/Hall International editions, 1986.

Lecture Notes in Computer Science

Edited by G. Goos and J. Hartmanis

297

E. N. Houstis T. S. Papatheodorou
C. D. Polychronopoulos (Eds.)

Supe

1st Intern
Athens, G
Proceedir

Springer-V

Berlin Heidelberg

Editors

Elias N. Houstis
Department of Computer Science, Purdue University
West Lafayette, IN 47907, USA

Theodore S. Papatheodorou
Computer Technology Institute
P.O. Box 1122, 26110 Patras, Greece

Constantine D. Polychronopoulos
305 Talbot Laboratory
Center for Supercomputing Research and Development
University of Illinois at Urbana-Champaign
104 South Wright Street, Urbana, IL 61801, USA

CR Subject Classification (1987): C.1.2–3, C.4, C.5.1, D.1.2–3, D.2.6, D.3.4, F.1.2, F.2.1, G.4, J.2

ISBN 3-540-18991-2 Springer-Verlag Berlin Heidelberg New York
ISBN 0-387-18991-2 Springer-VlaNew 05ork Berlin Heidelberg

Library of Congress Cataloging-in-Publication Data. Supercomputing: 1st International Conference, Athens, Greece, June 8–12, 1987: proceedings. (Lecture notes in computer science; 297) "The conference was organized and sponsored by the Computer Technology Institute (C.T.I.) of Greece"–Pref. Includes bibliographies. 1. Supercomputers–Congresses. I. Houstis, E.N. (Elias N.) II. Papatheodorou, T.S. (Theodore S.) III. Polychronopoulos, C.D. (Constantine D.) IV. International Conference on Supercomputing (1st: 1987: Athens, Greece) V. Computer Technology Institute (Patrai, Greece) VI. Series.
QA76.5.S8979 1988 004.1'1 88-4374
ISBN 0-387-18991-2 (U.S.)

Printing and binding: Druckhaus Beltz, Hemsbach/Bergstr.
2145/3140-543210